THE

CONSTITUTIONAL HISTORY
AND LAW
OF SOUTHERN RHODESIA
1888–1965
WITH SPECIAL REFERENCE
TO IMPERIAL CONTROL

CLAIRE PALLEY

CLARENDON PRESS · OXFORD
1966

Made and printed in Great Britain by
William Clowes and Sons, Limited, London and Beccles

TO AHRN

PREFACE

SOUTHERN RHODESIA occupies a unique constitutional position as a self-governing dependency subject to attenuated but overriding British authority. The aim of the first part of this book is to describe the evolution of the Southern Rhodesian Constitution in the context of the legal techniques of British Imperialism and to illustrate Britain's role in Southern Rhodesian constitutional development. Particular attention has been directed not merely to the theoretical provisions permitting Imperial control but also to the practical operation of such controls. This revealed that the generally accepted view that Southern Rhodesia has enjoyed full internal self-government for over forty years is quite misleading.

In the second part the present institutions of government have been examined in detail. Since a misleading impression might be obtained from superficial study of Southern Rhodesian legislation, which largely avoids reference to race, mention has been made of the racial realities underlying the legal structure. Political issues cannot entirely be avoided when dealing with constitutional questions, but so far as was possible political analysis and accounts of pressures and reactions either European or African were eschewed. Similarly, informal mechanisms employed to effect policy decisions have not been examined. Only where constitutional development would otherwise have been inexplicable was reference made to such factors.

The text reflects the legal position as at 30 October 1965. The subsequent illegal declaration of independence on 11 November 1965, necessitated a short addendum outlining the purported changes introduced by the regime in Southern Rhodesia and legal counter measures taken by the United Kingdom. Despite these changes Part II still approximately reflects the legal position in Southern Rhodesia.

In substance this book is the dissertation for which I was awarded the Ph.D. in Laws of the University of London. It is difficult to acknowledge adequately the assistance given me by colleagues and by my supervisor, Professor S. A. de Smith, who read the manuscript and gave me much advice. My special thanks go to Dr. David Murray for his penetrating criticisms of the draft; to Dr. Ronald Robinson for illuminating many of the basic issues; and to Professor F. M. G. Willson and Mr. Richard Brown who commented on the earlier chapters. Many of their suggestions I accepted, but for any opinions expressed the responsibility is entirely mine.

I should also like to thank the Hon. Mr. Justice Davies, Mr. J. Gaunt, Lord Howick, Sir John Kennedy, the Rt. Hon. Lord Malvern, the Hon. R. S. Garfield Todd, the Rt. Hon. Sir Robert Tredgold, the Hon. Sir Edgar Whitehead, and the Hon. W. A. E. Winterton, who answered my numerous questions patiently and courteously. I received invaluable help in gathering material from the Librarians and their staffs of the Public Records Office, the Foreign Office Library, the National Archives of Southern Rhodesia, and the Library of the University College of Rhodesia and Nyasaland.

Finally I gratefully acknowledge the help afforded me by the staff of the Clarendon Press.

University College of Rhodesia and Nyasaland   CLAIRE PALLEY
Salisbury
Southern Rhodesia
December 1965

LIST OF ABBREVIATIONS

A 2/4/1	High Commissioner for South Africa and Administrator. Correspondence.
A 2/5/1	Administrator and Resident Commissioner. Correspondence.
A 3/18/1	Administrator and High Commissioner for South Africa. Correspondence.
A.C.	Appeal Cases (House of Lords and Privy Council).
A.D.	Appellate Division (Union of South Africa).
African	Further correspondence respecting the affairs of Bechuanaland and adjacent territories. Confidential Print series. Colonial Office.
African (South)	C.O. 417/series. Colonial Office. South Africa. British South Africa Company. Correspondence.
A.J.I.L.	American Journal of International Law.
All E.R.	All England Law Reports.
All N.R.	All Nigeria Law Reports.
App. Cas.	House of Lords and Privy Council.
B. & C.	Barnewall and Cresswell.
Buch.	Buchanan's Law Reports (Cape Supreme Court).
Burr.	Burrow.
B.Y.I.L.	British Yearbook of International Law.
C. Fed. 1	Command Paper. Federation of Rhodesia and Nyasaland.
Ch. D.	Chancery Division
Cl. & F.	Clark and Finelly.
C.L.J.	Cambridge Law Journal.
C.L.R.	Commonwealth Law Reports (High Court of Australia).
C.O.	Colonial Office.
CO 8/1/2	Coghlan Papers.
Co. Rep.	Coke's Reports.
Cowp.	Cowper.
Cox C.C.	Cox's Criminal Cases.
Cranch.	Cranch, Supreme Court of United States of America.
CT 1/3/1	Administrator and Cape Town Office, British South Africa Company. Correspondence.
CT 1/10/30	Cape Town Office, British South Africa Company. Correspondence on proposed legislation.
C.T.R.	Cape Times Reports (Cape Supreme Court).
DO 1/1/6	Downie Papers.
E.A.L.R.	East Africa Law Reports.
Ecc. & Adm.	Spink's Ecclesiastical and Admiralty Reports.

E.R.	English Reports.
Ex. D.	Exchequer.
F.C.	Federal Supreme Court.
Fed. A. 1	Federal Assembly Select Committee Report.
Fed. Parlty. Deb.	Federal Assembly Parliamentary Debates.
F.G.N.	Federal Government Notice.
F.J.	Federal Judge.
F.O. Conf.	Foreign Office Confidential Print.
G.N.	Government Notice (British South Africa Company).
H.C. Deb.	House of Commons Debates.
H.L. Deb.	House of Lords Debates.
I.C.L.Q.	International and Comparative Law Quarterly.
I.R.	Irish Reports.
J.A.	Judge of Appeal (Appellate Divisions of South Africa and of Southern Rhodesia).
JA 1/1/1	Jameson Papers.
J.A.L.	Journal of African Law.
J.P.	Judge President (Appellate Division of Southern Rhodesia and Provincial Divisions in South Africa).
Judgement A.D.	Judgement Appellate Division, Southern Rhodesia.
Judgement G.D.	Judgement General Division, Southern Rhodesia.
Judgement F.S.C.	Judgement Federal Supreme Court, Rhodesia and Nyasaland.
Juta	Juta's Reports (Cape Supreme Court).
K.B.	King's Bench Division.
Knapp P.C.	Knapp.
L.A.S.C.	Legislative Assembly Select Committee Report, Southern Rhodesia.
LE 3/2/1	Leggate Papers.
L. Ed.	Lawyer's Edition (United States).
L.J.C.P.	Law Journal Reports, Common Pleas.
L.O.R. Conf.	Law Officers' Reports. Confidential Print.
L.Q.R.	Law Quarterly Review.
L.R. Ex.	Law Reports, Exchequer.
L.R.I.A.	Law Reports, Indian Appeals (Privy Council).
L.R.Q.B.	Law Reports, Queen's Bench.
M.L.R.	Modern Law Review.
MO 13/1/1	Moffat Papers.
Moo. P.C. (N.S.)	Moore, Privy Council Cases, New Series.
N.A.D.A.	Native Affairs Department Annual (Southern Rhodesia).
NE 1/1/7	Newton Papers.

N.O.	*Nomine officio.*
P. P.D.	Probate Divorce and Admiralty Division.
P.L.R.	Pakistan Law Reports.
O.P.D.	Orange Free State Provincial Division (South Africa) Law Reports.
Q.B. Q.B.D.	Queen's Bench Division.
R. & N.	Rhodesia and Nyasaland Law Reports.
RC 3/7/1	Resident Commissioner's files. Southern Rhodesia.
R.G.N.	Rhodesia Government Notice.
R. & N.L.J.	Rhodesia and Nyasaland Law Journal.
RO 7/1/1	Rodwell Papers.
S 138/1	Native Affairs Department files, Southern Rhodesia.
S.A.	South African Law Reports.
S.A.L.J.	South African Law Journal
S.A.R.	South African Republic Law Reports.
S.C.	Supreme Court (Cape) Law Reports.
S.C.R.	Supreme Court Reporter (India).
SM 4/1/1	Smit Papers
S.R. S.R.R.	Southern Rhodesian Law Reports.
S.R.A.D.	Southern Rhodesia, Appellate Division.
S.R.L.A.D.	Southern Rhodesia Legislative Assembly Debates.
S.R.G.N.	Southern Rhodesia Government Notice.
S.R. Legco. Deb.	Southern Legislative Council Debates.
S.R.N.	Southern Rhodesia Notice.
St. Tr.	State Trials.
S.W.A.	South West Africa Law Reports.
T.H.R.—H.R.	Tydskrif vir Hedendaagse Romeinse–Hollandse Reg.
T.L.R.	Times Law Reports.
T.S.	Transvaal Supreme Court Law Reports.
U.S.	United States (Supreme Court).
Wheat.	Wheaton (Supreme Court of United States).
W.L.R.	Weekly Law Reports.

N.O.   Nomine officio.

P.J.
P.D.J.   Probate Divorce and Admiralty Division

P.L.R.   Pakistan Law Reports

O.P.D.   Orange Free State Provincial Division, Union African Law Reports

Q.B.
Q.B.D.   Queen's Bench Division.

R. & N.   Rhodesia and Nyasaland Law Reports.

R.C.S.Rh.   Resident Commissioner's files, Southern Rhodesia.

R.G.N.   Rhodesia Government Notice.

S. & N.L.J.   Rhodesia and Nyasaland Law Journal.

R.O.D.P.   Rodwell Papers.

N.A.D.   Native Affairs Department files, Southern Rhodesia.

S.A.   South African Law Reports.

S.A.L.J.   South African Law Journal.

S.L.R.   South African Republic Law Reports.

S.C.   Supreme Court Law Reports.

S.C.R.   Supreme Court Reports (India).

S.M.D.J.   Sun Papers.

S.R.
S.R.R.   Southern Rhodesia Law Reports.

S.R.A.D.   Southern Rhodesia, Appellate Division.

S.R.L.A.D.   Southern Rhodesia Legislative Assembly Debates.

S.R.G.N.   Southern Rhodesia Government Notices.

S.R. Leg.co Deb.   Southern Rhodesia Legislative Council Debates.

S.P.N.   Southern Rhodesia Statutes.

St. Tr.   State Trials.

S.W.A.   South West Africa Law Reports.

T.H.R.   Tijdskrif vir Hedendaagse Romeins-Hollandse Reg.

T.L.R.   Times Law Reports.

T.S.   Transvaal Supreme Court Law Reports.

U.S.   United States Court.

W.on S.   Wessels on Sale, Union of South Africa.

W.L.R.   Weekly Law Reports.

CONTENTS

PART I

THE CONSTITUTIONAL HISTORY OF SOUTHERN RHODESIA

PART II

THE CONSTITUTIONAL LAW OF SOUTHERN RHODESIA

APPENDIXES

Table

INTRODUCTION

> The general law of the commonwealth is not ordinary law. It lies rather on the periphery of municipal law, where it marches with politics, with constitutional convention, and with international law. Questions on the margin of a subject necessarily stir more extraneous issues than do points which lie comfortably in the centre of established doctrine; in such frontier regions to require self-sufficiency of legal scholarship is to ensure not its chastity but its sterility.[1]

LATHAM'S oft-quoted statement epitomizes the many-sided character of commonwealth constitutional law. Doubtless the bare bones of constitutional rules can be adumbrated, but such learning becomes an abstract catalogue of constitutional devices and prescriptions and does not convey an understanding of reality unless it is encased in its historical context of relevant Imperial policy, and unless also various constitutions are seen as stages in an evolutionary process of the development and later abandonment of Imperial power. This book is therefore concerned not merely to elaborate the formal rules setting out the structure of government during various constitutional phases but also to examine such provisions in their historical context of the development of British power both in International and in Municipal Law, and the subsequent exercise of that power in the light of general Imperial policy as applied to the particular relations between Britain and Southern Rhodesia.

As a particular case-study of a small part of the Commonwealth and its historical development, Southern Rhodesia is exceptionally interesting. Whereas in most other dependent African territories developments, particularly in the stages approaching independence, have been telescoped, in Southern Rhodesia evolution has proceeded through many constitutional phases over a relatively long period of time. But the most significant feature in the Southern Rhodesian situation is that Southern Rhodesia had and has a considerable proportion of immigrant races[2] which created problems calling for additional constitutional mechanisms—problems which today have become pressing.[3] The difficulties in Southern Rhodesia with its mixed

---

[1] R. T. E. Latham 'The Law and the Commonwealth', in *Survey of British Commonwealth Affairs* by W. K. Hancock, Vol. I, *Problems of Nationality 1918–1936*, Oxford, 1937, p. 521.

[2] At 30 June 1965 the estimated *de facto* population of Europeans was 219,500. In addition there were an estimated 8,000 Asians and 12,700 Coloureds, whereas there were 4,070,000 Africans. See *Monthly Digest of Statistics*, July 1965, Central Statistical Office, Salisbury, p. 1.

[3] With the rise of African Nationalism, which is determined to destroy European political power, has come the problem of containing this new force in Southern Rhodesia in parliamentary and constitutional channels and of giving its protagonists a proper say in the government of the country.

population were exacerbated by decisions taken when the Imperial authorities first decided on involvement in the area that was eventually to become Southern Rhodesia. On the assumption that Southern Rhodesia would ultimately become part of a South African federation and would therefore follow the pattern of 'the white Dominions', the area was thrown open to white settlement, and the settlers soon had considerable powers devolved on them by the Imperial authorities. Indeed the major institutions, the instruments of administration, and legislative policies, most of which were to endure until the present day, were at an early stage established on this view of Southern Rhodesia's future, and the structure of Southern Rhodesian institutions is even today almost entirely a reflection of European politics. As a result, although Southern Rhodesia is geographically a tropical dependency, the ultimate aims and application of British policy in Southern Rhodesia have been different from those in other tropical dependencies. Britain's early delegation of power to the settlers under an overtly non-racial constitution, but with a franchise effectively ensuring a predominantly European electorate, in fact operated to preclude Great Britain from modifying her policy in Southern Rhodesia and subsequently treating it as a territory inhabited mainly by Africans whose interests should be paramount and to whom British power should be transferred. However, the reservation must be made that despite this delegation the Imperial Government never entirely classified Southern Rhodesia as a 'white colony' and, until very recently, retained a considerable degree of control in order to protect the African population. Within the limitations which Britain imposed on herself by her early decisions to devolve power, she has exercised as fully as possible those restraints she possessed in the interests of the African people.

At the same time the constitutional history of Southern Rhodesia is illuminative of general Imperial policy in Africa, since British intervention in the area eventually to become Southern Rhodesia [1] occurred in the period of European acquisition of territory in Africa generally described as 'the scramble'. [2] Late Victorian acquisition of new dependencies in Africa contrasts with earlier

[1] Southern Rhodesia lies between the Limpopo and Zambezi Rivers between 15° to 22° south latitude and 26° to 34° east longitude. It comprises the former Matabele Kingdom, Mashonaland, and Manicaland. It is within the area usually described as South Central Africa.

[2] The motives underlying this Imperial intrusion during the last two decades of the nineteenth century have been subjected to refined analysis. See R. Robinson, J. Gallagher, and A. Denny, *Africa and the Victorians*, Macmillan, 1961; *The Cambridge History of the British Empire*, Vol. III, 1959 (in particular Chapters IV and VIII by F. H. Hinsley and Chapter V by R. Robinson); W. L. Langer, *The Diplomacy of Imperialism*, A. A. Knopf, 2nd ed., 1956; R. Koebner and H. D. Schmidt, *The Story and Significance of Imperialism*, Cambridge, 1964 (Chapter VIII deals with 'The Incorporation of Africa into the Imperial Scheme'); A. P. Thornton, *The Imperial Idea and its Enemies*, Macmillan, 1959; J. D. Hargreaves, *Prelude to the Partition of West Africa*, Macmillan, 1963 (a valuable factual survey); P. T. Moon, *Imperialism and World Politics*, Macmillan, 1928; and K. E. Knorr, *British Colonial Theories 1570–1850*, Frank Cass, 1963, Chapter XII.

Victorian policy opposing formal expansion in that continent.[1] Before 1880 Africa had been considered by the Colonial Office as 'but a worthless possession'[2] and the 1865 Parliamentary Select Committee on the West Coast of Africa considered that 'all future extension of territory or assumption of government in West Africa or any new treaty implying protection of native tribes should be peremptorily prohibited and carefully prevented'.[3] Imperial policy had before 1880 been characterized by informal influence,[4] a policy of self-denial in respect of new territorial acquisitions, diplomatic negotiations to dispose of French challenges to British influence, and even a willingness to permit other nations formal control if British trade was left unhindered. As late as 1882 the Colonial Secretary, Lord Kimberley, rejected negotiations for the declaration of a protectorate possibly administered by a chartered company in the Cameroons and Old Calabar on the West Coast of Africa, on the ground that this 'would probably lead to war with the interior native tribes and heavy demands upon the British taxpayer'.[5]

Many theories have been formulated to explain Britain's sudden change in attitude. Emphasis has been placed on the international rivalry which led to the partition of tropical Africa. Britain's traditional concepts of world strategy, designed to secure her national safety by maintaining the balance of power and keeping control of the routes to the East, have been singled out. Economic imperialism and capitalism's needs for new markets have been elaborated.[6] Emotional factors urging a national mission and national

[1] Although it is quite consistent with the period from 1787 to 1826, the slaving period, a short period of expansion between 1850 and 1863, and that of the encouragement of early African chartered companies. See *C.H.B.E.*, Vol. I, *The Old Empire* (1929), Introduction, Chapters VII, X and XV; and Vol. II, *The New Empire*, Chapter XVIII.

[2] Minute of Sir James Stephen in 1840 cited in Robinson, Gallagher, and Denny, op cit., p. 16. See also C. W. Newbury, *British Policy Towards West Africa*, Oxford, 1965, p. 419, quoting Lord Stanley's prohibition in 1841 of treaties assuming sovereignty or protection over any portion of Africa.

[3] Report from the Select Committee on Africa (Western Coast) No. 412 *H.C. Sessional Papers 1865*, Vol. V, p. xv, Draft Report. Motives of self interest and not of altruism occasioned the Committee (at p. iii) to state that the object of British policy should be 'ultimate withdrawal' from all settlements, and encouragement 'in the natives of those qualities which may render it possible for us more and more to transfer to them the administration of all the governments'.

[4] Formal influence often entailed inconvenient responsibilities, as did the creation of protectorates. See Report from the Select Committee on the West Coast of Africa, *H.C. Sessional Papers, Reports from Committees, 1842*, Vol. XI, pp. v–vi.

[5] He considered the country pestilential, and that, in any event, it was undesirable for Britain to add to her already heavy responsibilities on the West African Coast. See F.O. Conf. 4824, Wingfield to Pauncefote, 15 April 1882. For the Cabinet's adverse reaction see Robinson and Gallagher, op cit., p. 165. A request by Goldie for a Royal Charter for his trading concerns in the Lower Niger was also rejected in 1881; see J. Flint, *Sir George Goldie and the Making of Nigeria*, Oxford, 1960.

[6] The economic theory is best stated by its pioneer J. A. Hobson, *Imperialism—A Study* (1902), Macmillan, 3rd ed., 1933. Hobson quotes Rhodes as saying that Her Majesty's flag is 'the greatest commercial asset in the world'. See also V. I. Lenin, *Imperialism: The Highest Stage of Capitalism*, Vanguard, 1926 edition. Although strategic motives were uppermost in the minds of Imperial policy makers—and in the last analysis it is only Governments that

expansion degenerating into 'jingoism' have been described.[1] Humanitarian-ism, seeking to end the slave trade by occupation of the areas in which it was conducted, and missionary enthusiasm for spreading the gospel and the benefits of civilization played some part. Finally, the emergence of nationalism in territories formerly subject to informal British influence, and internal events in Africa might force direct action on the United Kingdom Government in order to maintain its power. This latter thesis has been advanced to explain British intervention in Egypt which, as a secondary consequence, triggered the international rivalries of the European powers in Africa by breaking down their previous policy of co-operation and mutual self-denial. It has also been advanced to explain British action in South Africa to counter the influence of the anti-British but wealthy South African Republic.[2] Whatever the parti-cular reasons, the last quarter of the nineteenth century saw the African con-tinent finally divided between the European powers.

The constitutional history of Southern Rhodesia also illustrates the methods by which Britain obtained governmental rights in Africa and the legal mechanisms she evolved for employment in her new African acquisitions. Positive intervention in Africa during the nineteenth century posed new legal problems for British policy makers, who, having once decided to take action, sought to restrict their involvement to a minimum and to achieve their aims without establishing a costly administrative structure or burdening Britain with the responsibilities that would follow from annexation. It was in these circumstances that the concept of spheres of influence, radical changes in the doctrine of protectorates, and the resuscitation of chartered companies en-joying executive and even legislative powers as instruments for indirect Imperial expansion occurred. Such involvement led to developments in International Law, an increasing strictness in the conditions required for acquisition of sovereignty by occupation, and new concepts recognizing interests and authority falling short of territorial dominion, while the distinc-tion between annexation and lesser forms of intervention led ultimately to a recognition in International Law of the rights of indigenous peoples in terms of the mandate and trusteeship systems first of the League of Nations and subsequently of the United Nations Organization.[3]

can take decisive action—economic motives predominated in the minds of financiers and traders who exercised pressure on Government to involve itself in areas they sought to exploit. The B.S.A. Company was particularly adept at using British political machinery and in drawing in the Imperial influence to assist it in its schemes: Hobson, *The Evolution of Modern Capitalism*, Allen & Unwin, 1949, pp. 250, 266. For a reasoned criticism of Hob-son's views see D. K. Fieldhouse,'"Imperialism": An Historiographical Revision', *Econo-mic History Review*, Vol. XIV, No. 2, 1961, p. 187.

   [1] Langer, op. cit., pp. 69–96; Koebner and Schmidt, op. cit., pp. 202–4.

   [2] Robinson and Gallagher, op. cit., pp. 162 et seq., 467 et seq. See also Hargreaves, op. cit., pp. 282 et seq. The former book argues that late Victorian British governments con-quered and peopled half the world not indeed 'in a fit of absence of mind' (J. R. Seeley, *Expansion of England*, Macmillan, 1883, p. 8), but nevertheless somewhat reluctantly.

   [3] See *C.H.B.E.*, Vol. III, Chapter XVIII, pp. 679–84, by H. Lauterpacht and R. Y.

In acquiring governmental rights and determining their extent, legality was a fundamental British principle which played an important part in shaping policy.[1] Indeed British insistence on the observance of legal forms[2] influenced the subsequent history of her African gains, since particular legal mechanisms employed to establish any administration often affected the future structure of government.[3] On the other hand, legal doctrines were adapted to accord with practice and the scope of legal powers was considerably extended.[4] Compliance with such legalities might also be a two-edged weapon, as this enabled Africans to point to the limits of British power.[5] Another consequence was that British obligations could be invoked and this might occasion unwelcome military involvement.[6] Similar involvement might result from the 'forward' activities of a chartered company in an area subject to protection.[7]

Once Britain had decided upon intervention in an area, the mechanisms she employed were determined by attempts to attain balance between various

Jennings. See also M. F. Lindley, *The Acquisition and Government of Backward Territory in International Law*, Longmans, 1926.

[1] Because it was considered that unless a protectorate was first declared in the area of the Lower Niger a chartered company could not be established, a Protectorate over the Niger Districts was declared: Robinson and Gallagher, op. cit., p. 181, and Flint, op. cit., pp. 72 et seq. Similarly the future Southern Rhodesia was declared a protectorate in 1891, despite Colonial Office reluctance to pursue this course, since the Law Officers advised that unless the area were formally declared to be a British protectorate no jurisdiction would be acquired over the subjects of other European powers: F.O. Conf. 6207, pp. 18*–18,† Law Offices to Knutsford, 30 April 1891.

[2] Her agents and those of her chartered companies went through Africa with packets of treaty forms in their kit: Thornton, op. cit., p. 65. Such treaties were contemptuously described by a German Chancellor as 'scraps of paper'.

[3] The grant of a charter to Cape Colonial interests and the throwing open of Southern Rhodesia to white settlement led to the early establishment of representative government in 1898 and made further devolution an almost automatic consequence.

[4] Powers conferred on the Crown under the Foreign Jurisdiction Act and the jurisdiction of Protecting Powers were extensively interpreted by the Law Officers to justify the development of colonial protectorates.

[5] Thus 'King' Aggery, Town Chief of Cape Coast on the Gold Coast, pointed out that Gold Coasters were not British subjects and challenged British jurisdiction: D. Kimble *A Political History of Ghana*, Oxford, 1963, pp. 203–5. These difficulties continued in the Gold Coast until 1901: C.O. 96/371, Memorandum advocating proclamation of former protected territories on (the) Gold Coast to be part of the Gold Coast Colony, Brandford Griffith C.J., 22 March 1900. In Sierra Leone the Government was embarrassed in 1898 by a ruling by the Law Officers that a protected person could not commit treason: C. Fyfe, *A History of Sierra Leone*, Oxford, 1962, p. 590. Although the question was raised in *R. v. Joyce*, [1946] A.C. 347 the issue was not decided.

[6] Report from the Select Committee on Africa (Western Coast) No. 412, *H.C. Sessional Papers 1865*, Vol. V, p. xiv: 'The protectorate of tribes about our forts in the Gold Coast assumes an indefinite and unintelligible responsibility on our part. It excites vague expectations among the chiefs and practically engages the English Government in maintaining weak tribes against their former sovereigns, and to keeping peace among them all . . .' In Uganda chiefs also argued that they were entitled to British protection: H. M. Thomas, 'More Early Treaties in Uganda', *Uganda Journal*, Vol. 13, No. 1, March 1949, p. 173.

[7] e.g., the Matabele War of 1893, and Sir George Goldie's Royal Niger Company expedition against the Emir of Nupe in 1897—even though in both cases the outcome was successful.

principles. Paramount in that age of Gladstonian financiers—and even later— was the principle that the British taxpayer should not be asked to contribute in any large measure to the establishment and maintenance of administrations in Africa. Expenses of empire were to be kept to the minimum and no increases in estimates could be permitted.[1] Even when Britain intervened in an area such as the Lower Niger, the aim was rather to prevent other powers from interfering with British interests in the area than positively to administer or develop the country. Thus either a minimum form of administration run on 'treasury principles' with a tiny consular staff or devolution of power to chartered companies willing to undertake the expenses of government was favoured. Later, in Southern Rhodesia, the devolution was made to the European settlers who had opened up the territory. This step was inherent in the decision to throw open the country to white settlement from the Cape Colony. It reflected another aspect of British policy—that of devolution. Since the loss of her first Empire, Britain had realized that delegation of power and ultimate emancipation was inevitable in areas occupied by settlers. This occasioned the introduction of representative government progressing through the stages of a minority of elected members, equality, and eventual majority. It then led to responsible government subject to certain limitations, and finally to the present position of internal self-government and certain powers in the external field subject to attenuated British authority.

At the same time some Imperial control had to be retained, as too great a devolution of power might involve the British Government in military expenditure in wars against African chiefs or might conflict with the other major strand of Imperial policy—that of trusteeship. This was first explicitly formulated by Burke when speaking on Fox's India Bill of 1783. Burke considered that political powers over men 'are all in the strictest sense a trust; and it is of the very essence of every trust to be rendered accountable; and even totally to cease, when it substantially varies from the purpose for which alone it could have a lawful existence'.[2] After the Report of the Parliamentary Select Committee on Aborigines in 1837 Imperial policy makers became increasingly conscious of their duties of safeguarding the indigenous races in areas where white settlement had been permitted. The Report had suggested that 'the protection of the Aborigines should be considered a duty peculiarly belonging and appropriate to the executive government, as administered either in this

---

[1] See *C.H.B.E.*, Vol. III, p. 17, citing Lord Carnarvon's letter to Shepstone that 'Parliament does not like to be made to pay even for what it approves . . . your object therefore must be to bear in mind these two opposite considerations—effective government and economy—and as far as possible to reconcile them'. See also p. 187 for some of the expenses of Empire from 1870 to 1880 which emphasized this attitude, which was adopted both by Conservative and Liberal statesmen. For the opinions of Viscount Goschen and Sir Michael Hicks-Beach see Robinson, Gallagher, and Denny, op. cit., pp. 233 and 249, and for the similar attitude of Sir William Harcourt see A. G. Gardiner, *The Life of Sir William Harcourt*, Constable, 1923, Vol. II, p. 199.

[2] Hansard's *Parliamentary History of England*, 23, cols. 1316–17.

country or by the government of the respective colonies'.[1] This trust successive British governments in greater or lesser degree attempted to observe, insofar as it could be executed within the limitations imposed by their treasury principles. By the beginning of the twentieth century emphasis on the negative facet of the concept—protection against excesses—began to shift to its positive aspect—development of the peoples and resources of the Empire.[2]

The most striking declaration of the British mission 'to work continuously for the training and education of the African' and to advance his interests came in 1923 when the United Kingdom Government announced in respect of Kenya that they thought 'it necessary definitely to record their considered opinion that the interests of the African natives must be paramount, and that if, and when, those interests and the interests of the immigrant races should conflict, the former should prevail'.[3]

The Devonshire Declaration with its emphasis on African advancement and the paramountcy of African interests came too late to affect the situation in Southern Rhodesia. There the settlers had just obtained responsible government subject to certain limitations. Nonetheless the negative concept of Imperial trusteeship, which had previously been employed in relation to Southern Rhodesia, was still applied through devices intended for use and indeed extensively used to protect the African population against possible action by a government controlled by immigrants. Still later, a major motive from the Imperial point of view in engaging in the multi-racial experiment of the now defunct Federation of Rhodesia and Nyasaland was the hope that this might eventually restore the balance in favour of the African peoples through influence from the Northern Territories. Even when Southern Rhodesia was granted a new constitution which gave her virtually complete internal self-government in 1961, the basis of agreement by the United Kingdom Government was that Africans would be brought into the Southern Rhodesian legislature for the first time, and that there would be more effective control of discriminatory legislation by a combination of a declaration of rights, constitutional council, and judicial review including a right of appeal to the

[1] See Report of the Parliamentary Select Committee on Aborigines (British Settlements), *H.C. Parliamentary Papers, Reports from Committees, 1837*, Vol. VII. See also p. 76, 'He who has made Great Britain what she is will enquire at our hands how we employed the influence He has lent us in our dealings with the untutored and defenceless savage.'

[2] This change in emphasis was largely occasioned by the policy of Joseph Chamberlain. See *C.H.B.E.*, Vol. III, pp. 382–4. The philosophy of the changed concept, is outlined in *The Dual Mandate in British Tropical Africa*, Blackwood, 3rd ed., 1926, by Lord Lugard.

[3] Cmd. 1922, Indians in Kenya, p. 10. See also *H.C. Deb.*, Vol. 167, col. 508, 25 July 1923. Under-Secretary of State for the Colonies: 'We are the trustees of many great African dependencies ... and our duty is to do justice and right between the various races and interests, remembering above all, that we are the trustees before the world for the African population. Our administration of this trust must stand eventually before the judgement seat of history, and on it we shall be judged as an Empire.' Cynics however have accused the British Government of expediency and insincerity in this declaration, suggesting that the prime object was to prevent Asians from attaining any political power in East Africa.

Judicial Committee of the Privy Council. Recent Commonwealth and world pressure on Britain, as the power internationally responsible for Southern Rhodesia, has made her even more conscious of her professed aims both of trusteeship for the indigenous inhabitants of her overseas territories and of rapid advancement of such colonial peoples and countries to independence.

The constitutional history of Southern Rhodesia and her relationship with Great Britain is a reflection of the interplay between these various principles of Imperial policy: informal expansion to avoid expense to the British tax-payer; devolution to settler groups who would develop and finance[1] the government; conciliation of interests whose disaffection would endanger wider principles of Imperial strategy; and creation of constitutional mechanisms designed to fulfil Imperial duties of protection of the African inhabitants.

Finally, the particular reasons for Britain's original involvement in the future Southern Rhodesia must be examined. British intervention in the territories that were eventually to become Bechuanaland Colony and Protectorate, Southern Rhodesia, Northern Rhodesia, and Nyasaland was occasioned by a concatenation of the factors which led to her general late Victorian expansionism. Britain sought to retain her influence in South Africa and thus to create an Imperial federation which would be pro-British and not dominated by the South African Republic. For these reasons she required to conciliate the Cape colonists,[2] who were urging Cape colonial expansion by Cape financial interests and reservation of the Cape hinterland leading into Central Africa for their future exploitation. At the same time, she desired to prevent penetration from German South West Africa and a possible linkage between Germany and the anti-British South African Republic. Similarly, Portuguese pretensions in South Central Africa were also to be thwarted lest Portugal should join with the Republic in attempting to diminish British influence. This consideration was reinforced by the demand of her Cape colonists that Portugal should be kept out of the area which they aimed to take for themselves. In addition, humanitarian and religious interests pressed for extension of British rule in the Nyasa Districts, in order to eliminate the slave trade and keep out the Catholic Portuguese.[3]

Already in 1884, in order to protect the 'Road to the North' against South African Republic expansionism, Britain had been drawn into intervention. As

[1] The significance of the financial contribution of Southern Rhodesian Africans by virtue of their cheap labour was not understood. In any event, Africans only came into the Southern Rhodesian labour market in any numbers from the beginning of the twentieth century. Indirect taxation was only subsequently imposed, and direct taxation although heavy in relation to the means of Africans did not bring in large revenues. Later this position was altered.

[2] The Cape Town Naval Base was considered vital for Imperial defence and maintenance of the southern route to the East. See Robinson and Gallagher, op. cit., p. 461, quoting Goschen, Hicks-Beach, and Chamberlain.

[3] See Robinson and Gallagher, op. cit., pp. 219–27. Religious and humanitarian considerations did not determine British policy but were a factor in justifying British involvement and might well be in accord with the personal inclinations of Ministers.

a result both the Colony of British Bechuanaland and Bechuanaland Protectorate were proclaimed in September 1885. Such involvement proved expensive and caused friction with the Cape Colony which favoured a policy of
white settlement that conflicted with British notions of trusteeship for the
indigenous inhabitants.[1]

To retain Imperial supremacy in South Africa the then High Commissioner
for South Africa, Sir Hercules Robinson, believed it essential that the Cape
Colony's influence be extended rather than that of the South African Republic. He urged the British Cabinet that in any future extension through
Bechuanaland north to the Zambezi River, loyalists from the Cape should be
encouraged to settle and be given control of the government of the region, as
this would give added weight to the pro-British elements in any future South
African federation.[2] Robinson, the prime advocate of 'Colonial expansion
with Imperial aid',[3] favoured Cape Colony expansion as opposed to direct
involvement of 'the Imperial factor', which would occasion Cape hostility.

By 1887 in the area to the north-east of Bechuanaland an influx of concession hunters and speculators of German, Transvaal, and Cape origin began
to press claims for mineral and land rights on the African tribes of Matabeleland and Mashonaland, and at the same time Portuguese claims were supported by expeditions along the Zambezi. This and other information that an
agent of the South African Republic had, in July 1887, entered into a treaty
with Lobengula, King of the Matabele,[4] reached the High Commissioner,
through the medium of Rhodes, the Cape politician and financial magnate.
Rhodes urged Robinson to instruct Moffat, the Assistant Commissioner in
Bechuanaland, to obtain a treaty from Lobengula on the model of a treaty
made by the Governor of Natal with the Queen of Amatongaland—a negative type of Colonial Office treaty, undertaking that the other contracting
party would refrain from entering into any correspondence or treaty with any
foreign state or from ceding territory without sanction of Her Majesty's High
Commissioner for South Africa.[5] Capitulating to these pressures, Robinson
decided to intervene, and instructed Moffat to obtain a similar treaty with
Lobengula which would turn the area into a British sphere of influence.

[1] See *C.H.B.E.*, Vol. III, pp. 139–41.
[2] C.O. 806/268, 1–4, Sir H. Robinson, Cabinet Memo., 'Proposed Extension of Bechuanaland Protectorate to the northwards as far as the Zambezi River', 23 May 1886.
[3] C.O. 806/319, p. 4, Speech at Cape Town, 27 April 1889.
[4] The Grobler Treaty of 30 July 1887, entered into between Lobengula and the South
African Republic, acknowledged Lobengula as an 'independent chief', made him an 'ally
of the South African Republic', and provided for a consul having jurisdiction over South
African Republic subjects: see C. 5918, No. 4, Encl. 1, pp. 3–6.
[5] Rhodes was in close contact with the Administrator of Bechuanaland, Sir Sidney
Shippard, who had been informed of these events by J. S. Moffat, the Assistant Commissioner. Both Rhodes and Shippard persuaded Robinson to adopt this policy. See J. G.
Lockhart and C. M. Woodhouse: *Rhodes*, Hodder & Stoughton, 1963, pp. 136 et seq.;
Cecil Rhodes, by Imperialist, Chapman & Hall, 1897, p. 43 (written with Rhodes's approval);
and Howard Hensman, *Cecil Rhodes*, William Blackwood, 1901, pp. 103–4.

PART I

THE CONSTITUTIONAL HISTORY
OF SOUTHERN RHODESIA

1

THE MATABELE KINGDOM AS A
SPHERE OF INFLUENCE IN THE
LATE NINETEENTH CENTURY

ONCE having embarked on the partition of Africa and having decided that areas in Africa were not worth fighting over, the European Powers evolved techniques which enabled them, despite their rivalry, to carry on their mutual competition for colonies peacefully. Extension of their possessions in areas adjacent to each other was made possible without resorting to force.

This the Powers did in two ways: they employed a new diplomatic concept —that of mutual demarcation by treaty arrangements of territories exclusively reserved for the future occupation of the states in question; and they recognized that where any Power was the first to conclude an agreement with the local chiefs, she acquired exclusive control over that area and an eventual right of annexation. Realizing the inevitability of African partition, the European chancelleries had decided on the rules of the game: if these were observed, the successful Power's claims were internationally recognized— thence the races between Powers to obtain agreements with African chiefs.[1] In such circumstances Bismarck's 'scraps of paper' determined whether international recognition would be afforded.[2]

Once one Power had successfully obtained the requisite agreement from the chiefs to buttress its claims to any area, the other Powers concerned would enter into reciprocal stipulations that they should not intervene in the area in question. Such treaties prevented subsequent clashes between the Powers, although there could still be serious misunderstandings on ultimate delimitation of boundaries. The normal stipulation contained in such a treaty was that 'neither power will make treaties, accept Protectorates, or exercise any

---

[1] France and England competed on the Niger, England and Germany in the Cameroons, Great Britain and Germany in East Africa. It was essential to get the treaty from the right chief—not a sub-chief. See F. Shaw, *A Tropical Dependency*, Nisbet, 1905, p. 359, retailing the race by Captain Lugard to Nikka. For Captain Lugard's method of treaty-making see *Early Treaties in Uganda* by Sir J. Gray, *Uganda Journal*, Vol. 12, 1948. See also *Rise of Our East African Empire* by F. D. Lugard, Blackwood, 1893. The European powers were not willing to countenance any possibility of treaties once acquired being impugned or to allow any investigation of the 'reality' of African consent. A United States proposal to allow such investigation was dismissed at the Berlin Conference as raising 'delicate questions': C. 4361, p. 209. Westlake, who acknowledged that many of the treaties did not rest on genuine consent, nevertheless justified this attitude as otherwise civilized governments would be led into disputes. Indeed, he thought, they should be freed from 'insecurity and vexation': *International Law*, Cambridge, 1894, p. 140.
[2] Lindley, op. cit., pp. 34, 186–7.

act of sovereignty within the spheres of influence assigned to the other party'.[1] Such a provision accorded the powers 'the moral right to exclude other states from interference in the territory in question',[2] the real object being to prevent other powers from stepping in and annexing 'the sphere of influence'.

This rule 'in the great game of colonial aggrandisement'[3] was employed after the Berlin West Africa Conference of 1884 to 1885. As a United States Secretary of State subsequently said in 1896: 'spheres of influence ... are new departures which certain Great European Powers have found necessary and convenient in the course of their division among themselves of great tracts of the Continent of Africa, and which find their sanction solely in their reciprocal stipulations'.[4] Although this terminology was new in the late nineteenth century, the concept was an old one. Analogies can be seen in the earlier Papal Bulls dividing the new world between Spain and Portugal, in the Portuguese–Spanish Treaties of 1479 and 1494, in the Treaty of Paris (1763) between England and France, recognizing that the area west of the Mississippi was exclusively to be acquired by France, and in the Anglo–Netherlands Treaty of 1824, agreeing that no British establishments would be made in Malacca, Sumatra, and other islands south of the Straits of Singapore.

Sphere of influence by agreement between colonizing Powers

The modern concept of 'a sphere of influence' was first formally recognized in Articles 6 and 9 of the Berlin Act, which indicated that countries might be under influence as opposed to protection, and laid upon 'the powers exercising sovereign rights or influence' in the Congo Basin an obligation 'to watch over the preservation of the native tribes ... and so to help in suppressing slavery'.[5] The term was first officially used in a treaty between Britain and Germany in May 1885 agreeing to separate and define their 'spheres of action' in portions of Africa.[6]

[1] Article IV of Agreement of 14 November 1890, between the Portuguese and British Governments: Hertslet, *The Map of Africa by Treaty*, Vol. II, p. 729. Anson, *Law and Custom of the Constitution*, 4th ed. (Keith), 1935, Vol. II, Part II, p. 106, describes spheres of influence in this sense.

[2] Ridge's *Constitutional Law*, 7th ed. (Keith), Stevens, 1939, p. 561.

[3] J. Scott Keltie, *The Partition of Africa*, Stanford, 1895, p. 179.

[4] Olney to Lord Salisbury, U.S. No. 2, 1896, p. 27, cited in *Encyclopaedia Britannica*, 14th ed., 1932.

[5] Hertslet, op. cit., Vol. I, p. 27–29.

[6] Hertslet, op. cit., Vol. II, p. 596. The treaty was preceded by an Exchange of Notes in April 1885: ibid., Vol. I, p. 394. The term had apparently been used about ten years earlier in Anglo–Russian negotiations on Central Asia: Lindley, op. cit., p. 210. But the concept had been recognized in 1869 by the Colonial Office which envisaged that Britain should 'come to an arrangement with the French that they should not attempt to acquire political influence in territories within a certain distance from Sierra Leone ... and that Great Britain on her part would not interfere with their acquiring political influence beyond that territory to the north': C.O. 267/299, Sir F. R. Sandford to F.O., 9 March 1869. Proposals were made and accepted (but fell through owing to the Franco–Prussian War) 'that England should cede

In respect of the area that was eventually to become Southern Rhodesia, Great Britain proceeded to enter into treaties with Germany, the South African Republic, and Portugal in order to obtain the recognition of each state that the Matabele Kingdom was within the sphere of British influence. Thus in July 1890 the British and German Governments signed an Agreement relating to Africa and Heligoland, which recognized the Matabele Kingdom as being within the British sphere.[1] Article X of a similar Convention with the South African Republic, entered into in the same month, provided that the Republic would withdraw all claims to extend its territory or to enter into treaties with the tribes to the north and north-west. The Republic undertook 'to aid and support by its favouring influence the establishment of order and government in those territories by the British South Africa Company within the limits of power and territory set forth in the Charter granted by Her Majesty to the said Company'.[2]

Similarly, although the Portuguese Government failed to obtain ratification of a Convention arranged in August 1890 defining British and Portuguese spheres of influence, an Agreement of 14 November 1890[3] acknowledged that neither Government would interfere with the spheres of influence assigned by the August Convention. Ultimately in June 1891 a final treaty delimiting British and Portuguese spheres was agreed upon.[4]

Legal consequences of such treaties

The effects in International Law of treaties creating spheres of influence were limited. They conferred but shadowy privileges. *Inter partes* the treaties were fully binding and breach by a high contracting party would have led to the normal sanctions afforded by International Law. Such agreement also prevented companies chartered by one of the parties to the treaty from exercising sovereign rights within the sphere of the other party unless consent were given,[5] but this would not prevent the exercise of normal commercial rights.

On the other hand, as far as third parties were concerned, such treaties were not binding: states which were not party to the treaty were neither

the settlement of the Gambia and all sovereignty or political influence over tribes to the north of the River Dembia and that France should cede all sovereignty or political influence in respect to natives dwelling between the R. Dembia and the R. Shebar': C.O. 267/327 Minute by A. W. L. Hemming, 8 October 1874. See also Newbury, op. cit. at pp. 130 and 458.

[1] Hertslet, op. cit., Vol. II, p. 642 at p. 646, Treaty 1 July 1890.
[2] Hertslet, op. cit., Vol. II, p. 871, Treaty 24 July 1890.
[3] Hertslet, op. cit., Vol. II, p. 727.
[4] Ibid., Vol. II, p. 731, Treaty 11 June 1891, Articles IV and VI laying down the lines and Article VIII agreeing to non-interference.
[5] Such a clause was expressly incorporated in the Anglo–Portuguese Treaty of 11 June 1891 in Article VIII: Hertslet, op. cit., Vol. II, p. 735.

limited nor affected by it. The treaty only had political not legal consequences in so far as they were concerned. Clearly such a treaty was a virtual announcement of an intention to appropriate territory, and other states might be restrained by political reasons: interference would have amounted to an unfriendly act, but although such an 'understanding that a territory is within a sphere of influence warns off friendly powers; it constitutes no barrier to covert hostility'.[1] Only if a state effectively exercised rights in the area did the rules of International Law insist that other members of the International Family should not dispute the validity of the acquisition (provided however that no other state had a valid prior claim). A mere claim to a sphere of influence (even though it might have been recognized by treaties with other states), unless followed by signs of jurisdiction and authority or a real occupation, permitted other nations to dispute the assertion. No territorial rights of a legal nature were vested in a state that merely laid claim to 'influence'.[2]

This was evident when Portugal alleged exclusive right to the territories in Central Africa 'which lie between the Portuguese possessions of Angola and Mozambique'.[3] Britain disputed and refused to acknowledge this claim to legal title, which Portugal supported both by arguments that she had occupied the area for centuries and on the strength of her agreements with France and Germany.[4] Indeed, while Portugal was still asserting these pretensions, the British Government ratified the treaty entered into by J. S. Moffat and Lobengula, King of the Matabele, which gave Britain exclusive control over the external relations of Matabeleland and Mashonaland—an area covered by the French and German treaties with Portugal. Ultimately, the Anglo–Portuguese Treaty of June 1891 involved Portuguese renunciation of much of

---

[1] W. E. Hall, *The Foreign Powers and Jurisdiction of the British Crown*, Oxford, 1894, p. 229. See also G. W. Rutherford, 'Spheres of Influence: An Aspect of Semi-Suzerainty', 20 *A.J.I.L.*, 1926, p. 304.

[2] Oppenheim, *International Law*, ed. Lauterpacht, Vol. I, 7th ed., Longmans, 1948, § 228, p. 514. An opinion of the Law Officers of 8 June 1893 stated that the British Government could not as of right claim to represent natives of British spheres of influence in the event of a question arising with any power which had not by treaty recognized the sphere of influence: A. D. McNair, *International Law Opinions*, Cambridge, 1956, Vol. I, p. 57. Somewhat earlier, although Sir Henry Bergue in a Foreign Office Memorandum on Nationality and Protection had suggested that natives of spheres of influence were British Protected Persons (F.O. Conf. 6256, October 1892, p. 34), W. R. Davidson refused to accept that natives of spheres were Protected Persons.

[3] This claim was recognized in treaties between France and Portugal, 12 May 1886, and Germany and Portugal, 30 December 1886: Hertslet, op. cit., Vol. I, pp. 300 and 324.

[4] See C. 5904, Correspondence respecting action of Portugal in Mashonaland 1887–90. Lord Salisbury rejected this 'paper annexation' (81 S.P. 1031–2). He also paid little heed to Portugal's 'archaeological arguments': *Salisbury 1830–1903* by A. L. Kennedy, John Murray, 1953, pp. 231–5. Though Portuguese explorers and colonizers had reached the interior of the future Southern Rhodesia as early as the sixteenth century and built occasional settlements and forts, Portugal in fact had entered into many recent treaties in the area, particularly in Manicaland and Mashonaland. For a lengthy period official Portuguese policy had, however, frowned on political involvement. Economic rather than political penetration was from the eighteenth century onwards the Portuguese aim.

the territory previously recognized by France and Germany as being within her sphere of influence.

Nor were native sovereigns affected by such treaties: they did not give the parties any right to interfere with the autonomy of such sovereigns or jurisdiction over the people of the territory in question.[1]

Alternative meanings of sphere of influence

Agreement with the sovereign

The term 'sphere of influence' was used in yet another sense to describe the result of an agreement with the sovereign of a territory that he would not alienate it save to the other contracting party.[2] A variant of such agreement would be one where the sovereign agreed that no alienation could be made by him without the consent of the other contracting party. Such an agreement was entered into by Lobengula at Bulawayo on 11 February 1888, with J. S. Moffat, Britain's Resident Commissioner in Bechuanaland. Lobengula agreed 'that peace and amity shall continue forever between Her Britannic Majesty, Her subjects, and the Amandebele people', that he would 'refrain from entering into any correspondence or treaty with any foreign state', and that he would not permit any cession of Amandebele territory 'without the previous knowledge and sanction of Her Majesty's Commissioner for South Africa'.[3]

Lobengula also repudiated the alleged Grobler Treaty entered into in July 1887 with the South African Republic.

A new British 'sphere of influence' had therefore been acquired and other powers were warned off since Lobengula's territories were now earmarked for future British acquisition should further events render this desirable.

Sphere of influence by unilateral declaration

Finally, the term 'sphere of influence' was given yet another meaning: a declaration by a single state that she considered certain territory open to acquisition by her alone. Such declaration amounted to notice that the particular state would not allow any other Power to take possession of the territory

[1] Lindley, op. cit., p. 211, citing Germany's reply to the Sultan of Zanzibar in 1887.

[2] Lindley, op. cit., p. 225. Such an 'exclusive' agreement does not amount to a protectorate in International Law: J. E. S. Fawcett, *The British Commonwealth in International Law*, Stevens, 1963, p. 116. Cp. the view adopted by Sir Edward Hertslet that a nonalienation agreement implied a British protectorate: F.O. Conf. 5562, Memo. 12 January 1888.

[3] Full text in C. 5524, No. 5, Encl., p. 13. An earlier treaty with Lobengula's father, Mzilikazi, had been arranged in 1836. See treaty between Sir Benjamin D'Urban, Governor of the Cape Colony, and Umsiligaas of 3 March 1836, providing that the Matabele people (Abaqua Zooloos) would be the subjects and friends of the Governor of the Cape and that a British Resident might be appointed: *House of Lords Papers 1884* (42), p. 13. Mzilikazi and his people were then in the Transvaal and only moved into the territory eventually to become Southern Rhodesia in 1838. For fifty years the Treaty was not implemented.

in question. Such a declaration relative to the Matabele Kingdom was made by the High Commissioner for South Africa, Sir Hercules Robinson, in April 1888 subsequent to conclusion of the Moffat Treaty with Lobengula.[1] Again on 1 August 1888, the South African Republic was informed by telegram that 'the Lobengula country was regarded as being within the sphere of exclusively British interest'.[2] Eventually in April 1891, the High Commissioner issued a Proclamation declaring that any attempt to occupy the British sphere of influence would be deemed an unfriendly act.[3]

It is in this sense that Oppenheim defines a sphere of influence as being 'the description of territory exclusively reserved for future occupation by a power which has effectively occupied adjoining territories'.[4] Such claim to a sphere of influence was, however, merely a political claim to exclusive control which other states might or might not recognize. Thus Count Hatzfeld was not prepared to recognize Lord Granville's British Monroe Doctrine for Africa, laying claim to areas contiguous to the Cape Colony but actually unappropriated, and Germany declared a protectorate over South West Africa.[5]

In like fashion the South African Republic was indisposed to recognize British claims to a sphere in the Matabele Kingdom. Although a copy of the Moffat Treaty was handed to the Transvaal State President on 16 May, the High Commissioner was obliged in July to invoke the Treaty against the Transvaal when Kruger attempted to appoint a consul to Lobengula. This, the High Commissioner urged, 'would be in contravention of the treaty with Her Majesty's Government recently communicated officially to your Honour, in which Lobengula engages not to enter into correspondence with any foreign power without the consent of Her Majesty's Government'.[6] Although this dispute continued throughout 1888 and early 1889 with the Transvaal objecting 'to acknowledge the existence and validity' of the Treaty, Kruger

[1] African 358, No. 38, Telegraph Knutsford to Robinson, 24 April 1888. Only three weeks earlier Knutsford had doubted 'whether it may be expedient to accept responsibility with regard to Lobengula and his territory': African 358, No. 5, Telegraph Knutsford to Robinson 29 March 1888.

[2] C. W. Dilke, *Problems of Greater Britain*, Macmillan, 1890, p. 309. Dilke commented on the 'curious fact that the telegram was wilfully omitted from the Blue-book which came up to 27 August of that year'.

[3] Proclamation of 13 April 1891: see also African 403, No. 217, Telegraph Loch to Knutsford, 18 April 1891.

[4] Oppenheim, op. cit., Vol. I, § 227, p. 513: see also Hall, *Foreign Powers*, p. 228.

[5] Fitzmaurice, *Life of Granville*, Longmans, 1906, Vol. II, pp. 349 et seq.; and Flint, op. cit., p. 64. See *Life of Robert, Marquis of Salisbury*, Vol. IV, Lady G. Cecil, Hodder & Stoughton, 1932, at pp. 225–6, for the contemporary British attitude and realization that such claims had no legal foundation: 'We left enormous stretches of coast to the native rulers in the full confidence that they would gradually acquire their own proper civilization without any interference on our part. Then suddenly we found out that that position, however convenient, had no foundation whatever in International Law. We had no rights over all these vast stretches of coast . . . .. We had no power of preventing any other nation from coming in and seizing a portion of them' (Lord Salisbury speaking on 10 July 1890).

[6] C. 5524, No. 33, Encl. 3, Telegraph High Commissioner to State President, 22 July 1888.

eventually capitulated as Britain insisted that the Treaty was not open to discussion and also relied on Article 2 of the Convention of London as restraining northward extension of the Transvaal.[1] Furthermore, Britain put diplomatic pressure on the Transvaal by refusing to come to an arrangement on Swaziland unless affairs in Mashonaland were satisfactorily settled.[2] Similarly considerable correspondence ensued with Portugal which had protested against the ratification of the Moffat Treaty.[3]

Eventually all the powers concerned recognized the new sphere of influence in treaties with Britain. Thus the Matabele Kingdom became a sphere of influence in all the senses of its meaning as at that time, viz. non-alienation agreement with the local sovereign, Lobengula, British declaration that she considered the area her preserve, and Anglo–German, Portuguese, and South African Republic treaties acknowledging this.

Confusion of Spheres and Protectorates

Nevertheless since the concept of spheres of influence was new, its scope was confused.[4] Indeed, most contemporary English politicians were unable to distinguish between a sphere of influence and a protectorate—yet another concept that was being rapidly developed and adapted to meet the needs of the African partition and to justify the exercise of jurisdiction in Indian Native States.

The essential feature of a protectorate is that one power assumes control of the foreign relations of the other power, part of the sovereignty of the protected power being handed over to the protector. In the words of Hall 'the mark of a protected state or people, whether civilized or uncivilized, is that it cannot maintain political intercourse with foreign powers except through or by permission of the protecting state'.[5] Similarly, Sir Henry Jenkyns, earlier the Senior Parliamentary Counsel, described a British Protectorate as 'a country which is under the exclusive control of the King so that its government cannot hold direct communication with any other foreign power, nor a foreign power with that government'.[6] These views were later approved by

[1] C. 5918, No. 79, Encl. 2, High Commissioner to President, 23 March 1889.
[2] African 392, Nos. 72 and 95.
[3] C. 5904, No. 130, pp. 93, 126. Portugal also protested against the granting of the Charter at a later stage since it denied that Lobengula had effectively occupied Mashonaland (the north-eastern portion of Southern Rhodesia). For a detailed study see P. R. Warhurst, 'Anglo–Portuguese Relations in South Central Africa 1890–1900', The Royal Commonwealth Society, *Imperial Studies No. XXIII*, Longmans, 1962.
[4] English writers on International Law did not mention it in their editions of that period: see Hall, *International Law*, 3rd ed., 1889; Woolsey, *Introduction to the Study of International Law*, 1888 edition; Halleck's *International Law*, 1893 edition; and Piggott, *Exterritoriality*, Clowes, 1892 edition.
[5] Hall, *Foreign Powers*, p. 218.
[6] *British Rule and Jurisdiction beyond the Seas*, Oxford, 1902, p. 165, adopted in *Sobhuza II v. Miller*, [1926] A.C. 518 at 523. When he drafted the Foreign Jurisdiction (Consolidation) Bill 1888 Jenkyns already recognized and described protectorates in the sense of

Kennedy L.J. in *R*. v. *Crewe*[1] who held that 'the one common element in protectorates is the prohibition of all foreign relations except those permitted by the protecting state'.

By 1888 these concepts had however not crystallized,[2] and it was not generally recognized that a sphere of influence, effected by agreement with an African chief that he would not enter into arrangements with foreign powers or cede land to foreign governments without the consent of the other contracting party, was 'a very rudimentary form of Protectorate'.[3] Some writers then generally considered that, unless there was not only the right of excluding rival influence but also a duty of defence, there was no protectorate.[4]

Precise differentiations between spheres and protectorates were not made. Writing in 1894 Hall commented on the indefiniteness of the meaning of a 'sphere of influence', and that spheres were merely temporary phases 'destined to be merged in some unorganized form of protectorate'.[5] This was borne out by practice, as in Africa spheres of influence were converted into protectorates in the fullest sense by gradual assertion of control and

debarring the government of an uncivilized country from having direct relations with any European Power: F.O. Conf. 6264*, Notes on Clause for British Protectorates in Foreign Jurisdiction Bill, p. 3.

[1] [1910] 2 K.B. 576 (C.A.) at 619.

[2] Just as they did not recognize the concept of spheres the writers on International Law failed in their editions of that period to describe the development of African protectorates. Hall made only a bare mention of the new protectorates, and it was left to Sir Henry Maine to be the first to recognize the protectorate system on the coasts of Africa 'where the local tribes are forbidden all foreign relations except those permitted by the protecting state': *International Law*, London, 1888, p. 58. Indeed Maine's writings decisively influenced the thinking of the Crown's legal advisers as it was his view that sovereignty was divisible that provided Sir Henry Jenkyns and C. P. Ilbert with legal justification for the new developments: see F.O. Conf. 5624*, Memo. 859 by Sir H. Jenkyns, 26 October 1888 at p. 8; and F.O. Conf. 5750, Indian and African Protectorates, Memo by C. P. Ilbert, 24 January 1889 at p. 2.

[3] Sir C. P. Lucas, a former Assistant Under-Secretary to the Colonial Office, in *The Partition and Colonisation of Africa*, Oxford, 1922, Appendix II, p. 212.

[4] In such circumstances a protectorate might have been pending but had not yet been completely formed: Sir A. Lyall, 'Imperial Frontiers and Protectorates', *Nineteenth Century*, XXX, August 1891, pp. 312 et seq. See also F.O. Conf. 4824. Memorandum by Sir E. Hertslet on the Protectorate of States, 24 April 1883, in which Hertslet considered the essential element in a protectorate was the duty of defence and not any engagement that there would be no foreign relations except through the intermediacy of the protecting power. See also F.O. Conf. 4825, Foreign Office to Colonial Office, Lister to Herbert, 22 May 1883, in which this attitude was adopted by the Foreign Office to a series of treaties made in 1863 with African chiefs. By 1888 Hertslet however recognized that a prohibition of relations with foreign powers or a non-alienation agreement implied a protectorate: F.O. Conf. 5562, 12 January 1888.

[5] *Foreign Powers*, pp. 4–10, and 228–30. Hall (at p. 213) found difficulty in explaining the position in 1894 of the territories of the British East Africa Company and of the Nyasa Districts: 'so far as I am aware there is nothing to show whether these last are to be considered a protectorate, or a possession, or simply a barbarous country over which an unclassed jurisdiction has been assumed.'

assumption of the duties of a protecting power,[1] within a reasonable time of the announcement of its claims to exclusive power by the state concerned.

By 1899 Sir Henry Jenkyns, who had been intimately concerned with the legal developments, was able to write with more definition that 'a sphere of influence is a portion of a non-Christian or uncivilized country which is the subject of diplomatic arrangement between European states, but has not yet developed into a protectorate'.[2] Hall, in 1904, concluded that in a sphere of influence 'no jurisdiction is assumed, no internal or external sovereign power is taken out of the hands of the tribal chief'.[3] Once external sovereignty was assumed—as for instance by the Moffat Treaty with Lobengula—the territory in question would be a protectorate. This followed as a result of the control of the chief's external relations and the prohibition on any intercourse with other powers. In such circumstances other powers were forced to look to the power enjoying paramountcy, which, as a corollary of the right to control external relations, was subject to correlative duties of protection.[4] Thus in International Law, as it had developed by the beginning of the twentieth century, such an area would be regarded as a protectorate despite the fact that the relevant treaty contained no direct reference to protection, to duties of defence, or to the transfer of sovereignty.

However, when the partition of Africa commenced, it was not realized that such treaties created a protectorate. This was shown when Britain decided to intervene in the Niger and Oil Rivers areas on the West Coast of Africa to preclude French advance. The Foreign and Colonial Offices pointed to the existence of treaties made in 1863 stipulating that no Treaty or Agreement should be made by the Chiefs of the Niger without the consent of Her Majesty's Government but considered that these could not prevent French intervention in the area or the declaration of a French Protectorate. Nor would the treaties afford grounds for calling on the French to cancel subsequent engagements in the area.[5]

Indeed the confusion between spheres and protectorates and imprecision as to the powers and duties therein prevailed until 1894. British statesmen shared in the general unenlightenment. The first Colonial Secretary to pronounce on the new developments, Lord Knutsford, is quoted as having said in January 1889 'sphere of influence is a term which I do not want to define

---

[1] i.e. the establishment of an administration sufficient for the protection of life and property of subjects of Members of the Family of Nations, viz. Europeans.

[2] op. cit., p. 1.

[3] Hall, *International Law*, 5th ed., Oxford, 1904, at p. 129. The Germans realized the distinction between territories under influence and protectorates in 1886. Only in the former would they permit British officials to exercise civil and criminal jurisdiction over British subjects: McNair, *Opinions*, Vol. I, p. 44.

[4] Lindley, op. cit., p. 185.

[5] F.O. Conf. 4825, Lister to Herbert, 22 May 1883, and F.O. Conf. 4824, Memorandum by Sir E. Hertslet on the Protectorate of States, 24 April 1883, *supra*.

now, but it amounts to this, we should not allow the Portuguese, Germans or any foreign nation or republic to settle down and annex that territory'.[1]

In March 1889 Baron de Worms was little more precise in answer to questions about events in Matabeleland. When asked in the Commons about the meaning of a sphere of influence, he replied that it was 'rather a vague term',[2] and that within a British sphere of influence Britain was 'able to advise, but we cannot do more in a country which is not under our protection, and we cannot prevent the Ruler of that country from making a concession'.[3]

The first full definition was given by Sir John Ferguson, Under-Secretary of State for Foreign Affairs, in June 1891.[4] A sphere of influence, he stated, means what 'the instrument declares, and does not restrict the parties ... from exercising their influence or control within their respective spheres, according to their individual discretion. Her Majesty's Government have repeatedly stated that within the spheres assumed by them they do not assume sovereignty or administration except with the concurrence of the Native rulers'. Other powers, he said, bound themselves to abstain from attempting to set up their own authority within such a district. Subsequently, Sir John explained that: 'A sphere of influence defined the area within which this country may enter into treaties with the tribes; and until the tribes have entered into agreements with us we exercise no power or act of sovereignty.' When asked if after the treaty the area became British territory, for which the British Government was responsible, he evaded the question and replied: 'That depends on the terms of the Treaty.'[5]

Even in 1892 when the British sphere in East Africa was under discussion, the confusion was remarkable. The Chancellor of the Exchequer considered that 'our obligations under the Brussels Conference ... are such that we are compelled to take some step', while Mr. Gladstone replied that the obligations of progressive organization of administration in African territories applied only to countries under the sovereignty or protectorate of civilized nations.[6] Sir William Harcourt considered that 'A sphere of influence confers no right, no authority over the people; a sphere of influence confers no right

---

[1] 'The British South Africa Company. General Information of the Company and Press Notices, 1889.' Extracts from the *Fortnightly Review*, March 1889, by Sir Charles Metcalfe and Major F. J. Ricarde-Seaver. National Archives. At the same time H. H. Johnston urged the Foreign Office to expand in Nyasaland: 'Let us keep open a belt of free British ... territory, sphere of influence or whatever you like to call it, so that it be coloured pink': R. Oliver, *Sir Harry Johnston and the Scramble for Africa*, Chatto & Windus, 1957, pp. 149–50. Lugard showed the same attitude in *The Times* of 28 November 1893: 'It matters not whether we call East Africa a "sphere" or a "protectorate" or whether some diplomatic genius shall invent a brand new phrase which shall defy definition.' The attainment of legal power was all he considered necessary.

[2] *H.C. Deb.*, 3rd ser., Vol. 334, col. 838, 23 March 1889.

[3] *H.C. Deb.*, 3rd ser., Vol. 334, col. 1386, 2 April 1889.

[4] *H.C. Deb.*, 3rd ser., Vol. 354, cols. 404–5, 15 June 1891.

[5] *H.C. Deb.*, 3rd ser., Vol. 355, col. 1761, 20 July 1891.

[6] *H.C. Deb.*, 4th ser., Vol. 1, cols. 1868–71, 3 March 1892, Goschen and Gladstone.

or authority over the land of any kind . . . Every act of force you commit against a native within a sphere of influence is an unlawful assault; every acre of land you take is a robbery; every native you kill is a murder, because you have no right and authority against these men.'[1] These views were understandable since as late as 1891 even the Law Officers had been uncertain of the scope of the powers exercisable by British officials in spheres of influence and whether they were competent to order the execution of native criminals.[2]

Similar confusion prevailed as to the status of the Matabele Kingdom, the future Southern Rhodesia. When the Moffat Treaty had been concluded the High Commissioner had urged Lord Knutsford, the Colonial Secretary, to ratify the Treaty unless he was willing to let the country 'fall under influences adverse to British interests', since the South African Republic was pressing Lobengula to accept its protection and also a Resident. Accordingly ratification was authorized and so was a declaration by the High Commissioner that the Matabele Kingdom was 'within the sphere of British influence'.[3] In March and April 1889 when questioned in Parliament about concessions granted by Lobengula, Baron de Worms replied that Her Majesty's Government had 'refrained from interfering with any concession granted by Lobengula as that chief is not under their protection, is independent, and has not till lately, asked for advice'.[4] But in May 1889 Lord Salisbury was speaking of the area as 'under the protectorate of England'.[5] Later in the year, when a company was chartered to administer the area, *The Spectator* commented that Britain was already 'committed to a formal protectorate over the greater part of the area concerned. Even if the company had not been formed we should have been bound in some form or other to have assumed a position of sovereignty.'[6]

That Matabeleland was a protectorate was recognized by C. P. Ilbert in a memorandum written for the Foreign and India Offices in January 1889.

[1] ibid., Vol. 2, col. 71, 4 March 1892. Cp. Margery Perham, *Lugard: The Years of Adventure*, Collins, 1956: 'Lugard was pointing out the difficulties for a Commissioner in exercising justice legally in a sphere of influence so as to satisfy "Labby & Co.", who might say that he was liable to trial for hanging a man. Yet he added . . . in Africa *practically* there would be no difficulty, there were lots of ways of doing things.'

[2] *Law Officers' Reports 1891*, F.O. Conf. 6207, pp. 90–91, Webster and Clarke to Knutsford, 20 August 1891. The Law Officers, referring to a case in the New Hebridean sphere, considered that there was 'great difficulty', and that 'it would be well if definite instructions could be laid down for the guidance of officers in such cases'.

[3] African 358, No. 38, Telegram Knutsford to Robinson, 24 April 1888.

[4] *H.C. Deb.*, Vol. 333, col. 1401, 11 March 1889. See also Vol. 334, cols. 1401–2, 2 April 1889. Chamberlain had referred to the area as 'a sphere' and enquired whether if at any future time 'a protectorate' were to be extended over the area the Rudd Concession providing for arms for Lobengula would be recognized.

[5] *The Times*, 18 May 1889. Salisbury to deputation from Scottish Missions and Nyasaland Trading Company. Writing in April to the Foreign Office, Johnston urged action in Nyasaland similar to 'the recent assumption of protectorates over Matabeleland and Mashonaland': Oliver, op. cit., p. 149.

[6] *The Spectator*, 19 October 1889.

He was one of the first to acknowledge that where the conduct of external affairs was removed from a ruler by another power there was a protectorate. Giving a general outline of the development of African and Indian protectorates he referred on several occasions to the British protectorate in South Central Africa as including Matabeleland—and to the likely diplomatic difficulties with Portugal on this score.[1]

On the other hand the Colonial Office consistently described the area merely as a sphere. When issuing Sir Hercules Robinson his commission as High Commissioner in August 1889, a preamble was inserted declaring that 'We do exercise influence in Bechuanaland, Matabeleland, and other countries adjoining thereto.'[2] Subsequently when the British South Africa Company was chartered, Article 34 of the Charter specifically safeguarded the right of the Crown to declare protectorates: a clear indication that the area of the Company's operations was not then considered as forming a protectorate. When the Colonial Secretary despatched this Charter, he drew attention to the Company's security of tenure 'in the absence of any paramount necessity for . . . annexation or protectorate' and 'to the Queen's right at any time to declare a protectorate'.[3] Parliamentary questions of the period also invariably referred to the area as a 'sphere of influence',[4] while Sir Charles Dilke writing in 1890 throughout his book described 'the Lobengula country' as 'a sphere of influence'.[5]

It is not surprising that even the High Commissioner remained confused. In a Proclamation issued in April 1891, he declared that the area fell 'within the sphere of British influence' and warned persons against entering 'the British sphere of influence' in Mashonaland as this would be an 'aggressive act against a country under British protection'.[6]

Similar lack of precision occurred in the Judicial Committee of the Privy Council in 1919 when it gave an analysis in legal terms of the major events in Southern Rhodesia until 1914. The assumption is implicit in the judgement that until 1891 the territory eventually to comprise Southern Rhodesia was merely within a sphere of British influence, and that a protectorate was only established in 1891.[7] Statements by the British Government that Lobengula's territory 'was under British influence'[8] were merely recounted, while it was accepted that Bechuanaland was already a protectorate.

[1] F.O. Conf. 5750, Memo. on Indian and African Protectorates, pp. 16–17 and 21.

[2] See Jenkyns, op. cit., p. 234 where Robinson's Commission appears. This shows remarkable confusion since a protectorate had already been declared over Bechuanaland.

[3] Despatch of 14 November 1889 to the Company. Quoted in H. Wilson-Fox, *Memorandum on Constitutional, Political, Financial, and Other Questions Concerning Rhodesia*, printed for information of the Board, London, 1912.

[4] *H.C. Deb.*, 3rd ser., col. 345 (1890); cols. 845, 1006.   [5] Dilke, op. cit., pp. 341–2.

[6] African 403, No. 217, Sections 1 and 5 of High Commissioner's Proclamation of 13 April 1891.

[7] *In re Southern Rhodesia*, [1919] A.C. 211 at 217.

[8] *In re Southern Rhodesia*, [1919] A.C. 211 at 214.

Although the Matabele Kingdom may have been a protectorate both in International Law and in British constitutional law as it had developed by the beginning of the twentieth century, at the time of Britain's first involvement in Matabeleland this was not the general attitude of the British Government.

In dealing with the actions of statesmen, it is often more important to consider the light in which they considered their own actions and thus the powers which they assumed unto themselves, rather than to analyse the theoretical legal position and consequences not applied in practice, even though the failure to do this may have been the result of a misconception.

Since the British Government and most statesmen considered that the territories merely fell within a British sphere of influence between 1888 and 1891 and that British power within the area was therefore limited, from the historical point of view it is better to treat the area as a sphere of influence even though it would have been permissible for Britain to have considered herself a Protecting Power entitled to exercise fuller authority and to set up an administration to maintain peace, order, and good government.[1]

[1] By 1893 the Law Officers considered that the British spheres of influence recently constituted in Africa 'although being neither British territory nor British Protectorates properly so called were still under the exclusive control of Great Britain, their foreign relations being moreover entirely conducted by Her Majesty's Government': Law Officers to Roseberry, 8 January 1893, quoted in McNair, *Opinions*, Vol. I, p. 56.

2

FUTURE ADMINISTRATION OF THE NEW SPHERE OF INFLUENCE

HAVING secured the Matabele Kingdom as a sphere of influence Britain's next problem was to assert her title by effective occupation.

Although the Berlin Act in Article 35 only laid down the obligation on signatory powers in all new occupations 'to insure the establishment of authority in the regions occupied by them on the coasts of the African continent sufficient to protect existing rights',[1] the European states were already tending to accept a rule of International Law (which Britain had herself invoked against Portugal in respect of Matabeleland and Mashonaland) that effective occupation supported by substantial and continuous acts of jurisdiction was necessary in any sphere or protectorate whether coastal or internal in order to preclude other powers from claiming the area.[2]

The general arguments for Chartered Company government

The expedients which Britain could employ were limited. Late Victorian politicians had too much regard for the British tax-payer's pocket to permit of any considerable expenditure in establishing an administration in any new African acquisition. It was in these circumstances that British statesmen resuscitated the concept of the Chartered Company enjoying governmental powers as an instrument for inexpensive and unostentatious colonial expansion.[3] A Chartered Company could 'to some considerable extent, relieve Her Majesty's Government from diplomatic difficulties and heavy expenditure'.[4] Continuous appeals for funds to a reluctant Treasury and Commons could be avoided, while the Empire could be expanded at the expense of the private shareholders of the Company.[5]

---

[1] Hertslet, op. cit., Vol. I, p. 43. See generally S. E. Crowe, *The Berlin West Africa Conference 1884–1885*, London, 1942; and A. B. Keith, *The Belgian Congo and the Berlin Act*, Oxford, 1919.

[2] Hall, *International Law*, 5th ed., 1904, pp. 113–15. See *Great Britain and the Law of Nations*, ed. H. A. Smith, Vol. II, King, 1935, p. 7, for comment on the British view and on Portugal's view that the rule applied only to coastal occupations. See also C. 5904.

[3] Cf. the British North Borneo Company chartered in 1881, the Royal Niger Company in 1886, the British East Africa Company in 1888, and the British South Africa Company in 1889.

[4] C. 5918, No. 88.

[5] For the advantages of Chartered Companies, see *Cambridge History of the British Empire*, Vol. III, 1959, p. 172 and 227. For general Imperial policy evading formal expansion see 'The Imperialism of Free Trade' by J. Gallagher and R. Robinson, *The Economic*

The views of an Assistant Under-Secretary for the Foreign Office on the proposed Royal Niger Company are a perfect illustration of these considerations. The Company he considered 'is perfectly able and willing to discharge the duties of administration for which Her Majesty's Government have become responsible, and unless it should be considered necessary that this country should go to the great expense of setting up the machinery of government up on the two rivers where the Company now rules supreme, there seems to be no other course open, and certainly no better one, than that of legalizing and affirming the position of the Company and placing the business of administration into its hands.'[1]

It would be incorrect to regard the late Victorian Charters as being obtained as a result of pressure exercised by parasitic capitalistic elements on British Governments.[2] The motives of their promoters might possibly have been thus categorized (and even these were mixed, with humanitarian motives dominant in the formation of the British East Africa Company and motives of British Imperial expansion in Rhodes' British South Africa Company), but governmental attitudes were determined by broader issues involving questions of Imperial defence, financial policy, and international obligations. A Charter would only be granted if the state creating the Chartered Company was not at the time prepared to administer territory directly, but either felt that its influence must be secured in the area or it had acquired international obligations. Thus on the first basis a Charter was granted to the British North Borneo Company in order to secure that the territories in which the Company sought governmental powers 'should not fall into the possession of any other nation, and especially of Spain'.[3] The second basis occasioned the Crown to charter the Royal Niger Company as the cheapest and most effective way to fulfil British obligations on the Niger undertaken as a result of the Niger Navigation Act agreed upon at the 1884–5 Berlin Conference.[4]

Indeed all three African Chartered Companies were intended to avoid any necessity for direct British action and occupation of the areas within their spheres. As Hall says: 'Obviously the acts of a mercantile company acting

History Review, Vol. VI, No. 2, 1953, at p. 12. *Africa and the Victorians*, by R. Robinson, J. Gallagher, and A. Denny, Macmillan, 1961, pp. 221–53, gives full details of the British attitude and negotiations leading to the chartering of the British South Africa Company. For a sympathetic account see H. E. Egerton, *A Short History of British Colonial Policy*, Methuen, 12th ed., 1950, pp. 400–2.

[1] F.O. 84/1879, Memo. by T. V. Lister, 30 January 1885.

[2] As suggested by J. A. Hobson in *Imperialism*, op. cit.

[3] *Law Officers' Reports 1880*, F.O. Conf. 4539, p. 7, James, Herschell, and Deane to Granville, 17 September 1880. According to the information given the Law Officers, 'although advantages might result from the opening up of new outlets for British trade', the decisive factor was that H.M.G. wished to prevent the territories in question from 'falling into foreign hands'. However, 'they were unwilling to increase their responsibilities in the East by the annexation or protectorate of new territories which, moreover in the case of North Borneo, could hardly fail to excite political jealousies'.

[4] See Flint, op. cit., pp. 68 et seq.

under a charter enabling it to form establishments and exercise jurisdiction in an uncivilized country are to be classed in point of competence with those of commissioned agents of the State.'[1] Thus, the chartering of a British company in West Africa, to perform acts of jurisdiction on behalf of Britain, would preclude Germany and France from objecting to lack of effective occupation. Similarly since in East Africa the British East Africa Company operated, Germany, Italy, and France could not point to non-compliance with International Law, and Britain's strategic interests were thereby secured. Again, by the chartering of a company in South Central Africa, Portuguese, German, and South African Republican pretensions to the area were thwarted.

Legal limitations on the grant of a charter

It has been suggested that when the question arose in 1884 of chartering the Royal Niger Company, the Law Officers advised that the Crown must enjoy jurisdiction in an area before it was competent to charter a company exercising governmental powers and operating within such area.[2]

This was not the attitude adopted when the first of the late Victorian Companies, the British North Borneo Company, was chartered. The British Government was then concerned to make it clear that by chartering a company there had been no implied assumption of sovereign rights in the area since an assumption might have conflicted with the Anglo–Netherlands Treaty of 1824.[3] They informed the Dutch Government in 1879 that by chartering the Company they had no 'present intention' of assuming dominion or protectorate.[4] Indeed, to emphasize that there was no assumption of sovereignty the Law Officers suggested modifications to the draft clauses in the Charter dealing with the powers of the Secretary of State in relation to the Company. Consequently, instead of the Company being 'bound to obey the directions of the Secretary of State in all matters concerning relations with foreign states' the Secretary of State was merely given power to dissent from and object to Company activities and to make suggestions.[5] The Foreign Secretary, Lord Granville, reiterated that the British Government had

[1] *International Law*, 5th ed., 1904, p. 103, n. 1.

[2] Robinson, Gallagher, and Denny, op. cit., p. 181. The authors suggest that a formal protectorate was at that period a prerequisite to the grant of a charter.

[3] C. 3109, Papers relating to the Affairs of Sulu and Borneo and the Grant of a Charter of Incorporation to the British North Borneo Company.

[4] F.O. Conf. 5552, p. 6, Memo. by Sir J. Pauncefote, 30 December 1887. British rights to do so in future were nonetheless reserved.

[5] *Law Officers' Reports 1880*, F.O. Conf. 4539, p. 7, James, Herschell, and Deane to Granville, 17 September 1880. In 1885 the Law Officers still considered that the Charter merely conferred incorporation on the Company, and that since Britain had assumed no dominion or sovereignty over North Borneo she could confer no powers of sovereignty over it: F.O. 84/1879, Law Officers to Salisbury, 8 August 1885.

assumed 'no sovereign rights whatever in Borneo' and that the territories would 'be administered by the Company under the suzerainty of the Sultans of Brunei and Sulu'.[1] It was in reliance on cessions made by the Sultans of Brunei and Sulu in 1877 and 1888 to Baron Overbeck and Sir Alfred Dent and without reliance on any British sovereignty in the area that the North Borneo Company was chartered on 1 November 1881. The attitude of the British Government was clearly intended to avoid international responsibility in the area. Indeed the official attitude was inconsistent with the doctrine that where a subject acquires by cession he does so for the Crown. This inconsistency was even more apparent when in 1888 Britain abandoned her view that sovereignty was vested in the Sultans and entered into an agreement of protectorate with the Company as an independent state, treating it as being vested with sovereignty.[2]

However, prior to the chartering of the Royal Niger Company doubts were expressed in 1884 by the Foreign Office as to whether a company enjoying governmental powers might be chartered unless the Crown had jurisdiction within the area of its operations, and the area had been declared a protectorate. Furthermore the Law Officers queried whether the declaration of a protectorate would *ipso facto* confer jurisdiction.[3] As a consequence of these doubts and of arguments advanced by Sir John Pauncefote of the Foreign Office[4] it was arranged that a delimitation between the German Cameroons and the Niger Districts should first be agreed. Thereafter a protectorate should be declared over the banks of the Niger and Oil Rivers. Finally a company should be chartered to operate in the area. German and English spheres were then agreed upon[5] and a protectorate was declared,[6] but even then the Foreign Office doubted whether a charter could be granted without parliamentary intervention.[7] However, the Law Officers considered that since the Foreign Jurisdiction had 'conferred upon Her Majesty the most ample discretion as to the mode of exercising any power and jurisdiction' which Her Majesty had acquired by treaty, usage or sufferance it 'would not be beyond the power of the Crown to vest such powers and jurisdiction in a Chartered Company, which should be authorized to exercise there all such power and jurisdiction as Her Majesty may possess'. Nonetheless they felt that the

[1] Lindley, op. cit., p. 106. See also *B.F.S.P.*, lxxiii, 1906, Granville, 7 January 1882. 'The grant of a charter does not in any way imply the assumption of sovereign rights in Borneo.'

[2] 79 S.P. 237.

[3] F.O. Conf. 5246, No. 106, James and Herschell to Derby, 7 March 1885.

[4] Flint, op. cit., pp. 72 et seq.

[5] Hertslet, op. cit., Vol. II, p. 596. The May 1885 Treaty was preceded in April by an Exchange of Notes: Vol. I, p. 394.

[6] Hertslet, op. cit., Vol. I, p. 445. Notified in the *London Gazette* of 5 June 1885.

[7] F.O. 84/1879, L.O. to Salisbury, 8 August 1883, for instructions. The F.O. thought that the Hudson Bay Company could only exercise jurisdiction by reason of two statutes—43 Geo. III, c. 138 and 1 & 2 Geo. IV, c. 66.

grant of a charter with governmental powers was not in accordance with precedent in an area where the Crown had not assumed sovereignty.[1]

A further obstacle was the questionable legality of assuming jurisdiction over foreigners and of then delegating this sovereignty to a Chartered Company. The Law Officers considered that neither existing treaties nor the accession of foreign powers to the Berlin Act were sufficient to have given Britain such jurisdiction.[2]

Eventually on 10 July 1886 a Charter was issued authorizing and empowering the Royal Niger Company to hold and retain the full benefit of all cessions it had obtained from the chiefs of the territories in the Niger Basin in return for a degree of Crown control.[3] The Company's powers in terms of the Charter rested on Crown recognition of the cessions it had received and not on any delegation of Royal authority—except in respect of powers under the Foreign Jurisdiction Acts.[4] That authority did not rest on Crown delegation was apparent as some of the Company's operations were beyond the protectorate in a mere sphere recognized by Germany. Only in October 1887 did the whole area of the Company's operations come under British protection when a protectorate over the Basin of the Niger and 'over the territories subject to the Royal Niger Company' was declared.[5]

The development soon thereafter of the concept of spheres of influence in Africa occasioned changes in the former Foreign Office view that declaration of a protectorate was a pre-condition to the creation of a Chartered Company operating in the area in question. Indeed the Foreign Office now considered that the purpose of formal declaration of protectorates was to prevent doubts arising of Great Britain's claims to exclusive influence, and to secure that no parts of the areas in question should fall under the dominion of any foreign power.[6] This view was also adopted by the Law Officers in 1891 in respect of

[1] F.O. 84/1879, Law Officers to Salisbury, 8 August 1885, and Addendum 20 August 1885. They considered jurisdiction should properly 'be exercised under the authority of Orders in Council and by Officers directly responsible to the Crown'. The Law Officers ignored the fact that the powers at the Berlin Conference had in respect of the Niger Districts 'recognized the preponderance of British influence', when discussing whether the grant of a charter was competent.

[2] *Law Officers' Reports 1885*, F.O. Conf. 5246, pp. 17–18, Webster, Gorst, and Deane. See also Pauncefote to L.O., 7 September 1885, on the difficulties.

[3] The decision to charter the Company was dictated by expediency owing to the international responsibility Britain had incurred of making suitable provision for ensuring the free navigation of the Niger and by the need for maintenance of peace and good order in her Niger Districts Protectorate. See F.O. 84/1880, Memorandum by the Lord Chancellor, Lord Herschell, 20 May 1886: 'The situation is an awkward one but having regard to the position of the Company and to our position under the Berlin arrangements this is probably the best thing that can be done.'

[4] R. S. Wright, the Treasury expert on Orders in Council, had advised that it was not possible to delegate Royal authority to a Chartered Company by means of a charter and Orders in Council without parliamentary intervention: Flint, op. cit., p. 81.

[5] Hertslet, op. cit., Vol. I, p. 449, for declaration of protectorate.

[6] F.O. Conf. 5449, No. 3, Pauncefote to Herbert, 13 January 1887.

an Order in Council relative to the future Southern Rhodesia, when they advised that to make the Order in Council valid in so far as it affected the subjects of foreign powers the declaration of a protectorate was necessary.[1]

Since the Foreign Office no longer considered it necessary formally to declare protectorates in areas where companies were to be chartered,[2] the British East Africa Company was chartered on 3 September 1888, to operate in territories which were merely within the sphere of British influence acknowledged by an Anglo–German Treaty of October 1886.[3] Similarly the Colonial Office agreed in 1889 to the chartering of the British South Africa Company since the conclusion of the Moffat Treaty with Lobengula and other treaties with Bechuana chiefs created a sphere of British influence in South Central Africa in which a company could be chartered.[4]

Needless to say the Crown took the view that annexation of territory would be incompatible with the exercise of administrative functions by a Chartered Company. The Colonial Office made it clear to the British South Africa Company that there was 'no precedent for the administration by a Chartered Company of territory actually forming part of the British Dominions'.[5]

Consequences in International Law of the grant of charters

Although the British Government sought, when granting charters, to avoid international responsibility for the acts of British Chartered Companies, it was forced in 1882 to consider its responsibilities in this respect when Spain and Holland objected to the creation of the British North Borneo Company. The problem was fully discussed in 1892 when questions arose as to Her Majesty's Government's liability to French citizens for injuries occasioned by activities of the British East Africa Company in Buganda.[6]

---

[1] F.O. Conf. 6207, pp. 18*–18†, L.O. to Knutsford, 30 April 1891.

[2] Cp. the views of F. D. Lugard, *The Dual Mandate in British Tropical Africa*, Blackwood, 1926, at p. 18, who considered that technicalities became irrelevant once Britain determined to extend her influence. Earlier (at p. 14) Lugard described the Foreign Office decision to grant charters in areas where it was hesitant to declare protectorates as being based on 'a subterfuge' and he considered that treaties of cession by native chieftains were salves to the 'sensitive official conscience'.

[3] For text of treaty see Hertslet, op. cit., Vol. II, p. 615. For Charter see *S.P.*, Vol. 79, p. 641.

[4] Technically, there was also an implied protectorate although this was not recognized at the time. See *supra*.

[5] See African 461, No. 52, Rhodes to Ripon, 28 November 1894, recording the Colonial Secretary's views on Bechuanaland. See also H. Wilson-Fox, *Memorandum on the Position, Policy, and Prospects of the Company*, printed for information of the Board, London, 1907, at pp. 18–19, where the author records an 1899 interview with Mr. Graham of the Colonial Office to this effect.

[6] See F.O. 84/2275, Memo. by the Lord Chancellor, Lord Herschell, on the Liability of Her Majesty's Government for Acts of a Chartered Company in British Protectorates and Spheres of Influence, 5 November 1892. Such memoranda and opinions by the Law Officers are of vital significance, since, as McNair has pointed out, they 'govern the practice of the state': 'Aspects of State Sovereignty', 1949, *B.Y.B.I.L.*, pp. 6–7.

The Lord Chancellor considered that, since clauses in the British East Africa Company's Charter reserved power to the Secretary of State to dissent from or object to the dealings of the Company with any foreign power and conferred similar powers in regard to the proceedings of the Company in its internal administration,

it is obvious that circumstances might arise which would enable a foreign Government to insist that the British Government by not exercising the powers reserved to it, had rendered itself liable for acts which would not have occurred if it had exercised those powers. It is not necessary at the present moment to attempt to define the limits of such liability . . . . It does not extend to all the acts, and not even to all the wrongful acts, of the Company's officials.

The Lord Chancellor considered that there was no principle whereby the British Government became liable for the acts of British subjects by the mere formation of a Company under English law. The position might be different where powers of intervention were reserved to the Crown, or if Britain had assumed a protectorate over the area in question, or if the dispute were 'with a Power as between whom and ourselves it had been agreed that the territory should be within our sphere of influence'. In any event the Lord Chancellor considered it would be politic to assume some liability for the acts of the East Africa Company as not only had the Company's enterprise received British sanction, but Britain would not

permit France to make good such claim as she may have against the Company by force of arms . . . If we interpose to prevent her adopting it [this remedy] I think we necessarily take on ourselves at least the obligation, if the claim be a just one, of pressing it upon the Company, and that France may properly insist that we should do so.[1]

Both because the Imperial authorities retained the right to dictate to the various Companies and because Britain would not permit military intervention, foreign powers would turn to the British Government in any disputed matter.

Furthermore, since in the case of all the Chartered Companies (except the British South Africa Company) the cession of sovereign powers obtained from the local authorities was in remarkably complete form, and since any acquisition of territory by British subjects is made for the benefit of the Crown,[2] it seems that the British Government in these circumstances became vested with external sovereignty. For international purposes the territories of the Chartered Companies were in the same position as protectorates, the

---

[1] Cp. the claims pressed on Britain by the South African Republic as a result of the Jameson Raid. These were eventually disposed of by the Second Boer War.

[2] *In re Southern Rhodesia, supra,* at p. 221 (Conquest); *Campbell* v. *Hall,* 20 St. Tr., p. 287 (Settlement) and also at pp. 322, 323 (Conquest).

companies themselves not enjoying sovereignty and merely acting as agents for the state under whose charter they existed.[1]

Thus, despite the attempts of the Law Officers to limit British liability when charters were granted, as these invariably reserved power to the Secretary of State to dissent from the proceedings of the Company, international responsibility of the British Government followed. That the Crown could control the Companies was unquestionable since, even though it might limit its power to modify the provisions of any charter (as it did by Article 33 of the British South Africa Company's Charter), such a provision would not in law fetter the Crown, which enjoyed plenary authority under the Foreign Jurisdiction Acts quite apart from powers of revocation reserved to it by the various charters themselves.

Comparison of powers granted to earlier and later Chartered Companies

Charters granted during this late Victorian revival of the Chartered Company as an instrument for unostentatious colonial expansion were considerably different from the charters granted during the sixteenth and seventeenth centuries. The later charters were full from first to last in express statements of control by the Government granting the charter.[2] Furthermore, numerous duties were imposed upon the Companies both in the interests of good government and for the benefit of the natives: the Imperial Government retained rights of supervision over their native policy.[3] Chartered Companies were obliged to promote civilization as well as commercial development. Again, Britain had exclusive control over Chartered Companies' external relations. In some charters there was also supervision of the Company's financial affairs through the rendering of accounts to the Colonial Secretary. Most significantly the Crown retained the right to withdraw the charters if

[1] This view was adopted by the Law Officers in an opinion of 21 December 1897, in considering whether the Royal Niger Company could assign treaties of cession in its favour. In entering into such treaties, the Company's acts had been 'those of the commissioned agents of the state'—quoted by A. D. McNair, 'Aspects of State Sovereignty', 1949, *B.Y.B.I.L.*, 6 at p. 43. This was later the attitude of the arbitrator in the Island of Palmas Case (1928), 2 R.I.A.A. 829, when he considered that the acts of a Chartered Company 'must be assimilated to acts of the state itself'.

[2] David Hannay, *The Great Chartered Companies*, Williams & Norgate Ltd., 1926, p. 250. This control the Government demanded in return for the advantages conferred in the way of recognition by the grant of a charter. In the case of the Royal Niger Company, the Charter was not even the instrument of incorporation as the Company had already been incorporated under the Joint Stock Companies Acts as the National Africa Company Limited.

[3] Since the word 'native' has unfortunate connotations the word 'African' is generally used today. However in this work it would be unhistorical to antedate the change, and therefore for the most part the usage of the time, particularly where it was official terminology, has been employed. See M. Perham, *The Lugard Diaries*, Faber, 1959, Vol. I, p. 40. The word 'settler' has similarly become considered a word of abuse. It has nonetheless been employed to avoid unnecessary circumlocution.

4—C.H.L.S.R.

the objects for which they had been granted were not achieved to its satisfaction, or the Companies failed to observe their provisions.[1] In yet another
respect they differed from the earlier Companies in that they were given no
trade monopolies.[2]

The ultimate fate of the new Chartered Companies and degree of Crown
intervention differed in each particular case. The British North Borneo
Company governed for a lengthy period in an area which the Crown declared
in 1888 to be a protectorate, but which it recognized as the independent
State of North Borneo, the Company being left internal independence. On
the other hand, in the case of the African Chartered Companies, whereas they
were originally allowed a very free hand, the Crown relatively early claimed
full sovereignty. By 1895 the British East Africa Company had surrendered
its Charter, while in 1900 governmental powers were removed from the Niger
Company, the Crown taking over the internal government of the Company's
territories. In the case of the British South Africa Company a far greater
degree of British control was exercised from 1896, but Company rule continued until 1923.

The case for a Chartered Company in South Central Africa

The general arguments as to the need for effective occupation which had,
at the same time, to be reconciled with minimum financial involvement, played
a part in Britain's decision to create a Chartered Company with governmental
powers in her new Matabele sphere of influence. A final and decisive factor
was Britain's desire to perpetuate her influence in South Africa and ultimately to create a predominantly pro-British dominion. If Mashonaland
could be developed and controlled by Cape influence this would strengthen
pro-British elements in any future South African federation.

Already in 1888, soon after the ratification of the Moffat Treaty, correspondence had occurred between the Colonial Office, prospective concessionaires and the High Commissioner. The High Commissioner pressed the Colonial
Secretary to permit the extension of British interests in the interior of South
Africa by a Chartered Company. Not only would this save the British taxpayer
money and stop excessive concession hunting such as had occurred in Swaziland, but government 'by a chartered company with Cape associations would

---

[1] G. Cecil, op. cit., Vol. IV, p. 231. Cp. the difficulties with earlier charters: see W.
Forsyth, *Cases and Opinions on Constitutional Law*, Stevens, 1869, p. 381.

[2] However in the case of the British South Africa Company, Article 20 permitted concessions for banks, railways, tramways, telegraphs, or other similar undertakings which
were not to be deemed monopolies. Article 16 of the British East Africa Company Charter
contained a similar provision. The Charter of the Royal Niger Company (Article 14) contained special provisions by means of the imposition of customs duties for repayment of
expenses incurred in the acquisition of Treaty rights. This was in lieu of claims for a monopoly which could not be given in view of the Berlin Act and the Anglo–German Agreement
of 1885. See Flint, op. cit., pp. 79–85. Cp. the German Chartered Companies: see W. O.
Henderson, *Studies in German Colonial History*, Cass, 1962, pp. 11 et seq.

be more in unison with the Africander sentiment than if the same result were attempted by the establishment of another inland Crown Colony'.[1] Later, when a Concession had been obtained that would justify the grant of a charter to financial interests headed by Rhodes, the High Commissioner urged the Colonial Secretary against annexation suggesting instead a Chartered Company. If a Crown Colony were to be established, there would, he considered, be a 'perpetual wrangle with the Treasury for the means of maintaining a decent administration', while disastrous effects would follow from 'attempting to administer a Crown Colony—if I may be permitted to use the expression— "on the cheap"'.[2] Counter views expressed by a prominent missionary, the Rev. John Mackenzie, did not prevail. With remarkable foresight he had urged that

it would be a mistake of the gravest character for Her Majesty's Government, in view of certain difficulties in Matabeleland, to divest itself of duties specially devolving upon it as the supreme power in South Africa and to impose those duties on a mercantile company. In taking such a step Her Majesty's Government would have all the disadvantages and unpopularity of shirking responsibilities, while of course in the end, when serious difficulties arose, it would find that the responsibility really and truly had never ceased to rest on its shoulders, and that the British Government could only escape the responsibility by abdicating its position and leaving South Africa . . .. Quite an opposite course is loudly demanded of Her Majesty's Government . . . by our solemn engagements with native races.[3]

In reply the Colonial Office informed Mackenzie that 'Her Majesty's Government do not feel that they would be justified in inviting Parliament to provide the very large annual sums which would be required in order to extend the boundaries of the present Crown Colony as you suggest.'[4]

Similar financial arguments were being advanced by the Colonial Secretary to the Prime Minister at first in private correspondence,[5] and later officially. Lord Knutsford considered, in view of the Government's experience with the British East Africa Company, a similar body might 'to some considerable extent, relieve Her Majesty's Government from diplomatic difficulties and heavy expenditure'.[6] He marshalled the High Commissioner's arguments that the Company would provide proper administration[7] as opposed to Crown

---

[1] African 372, No. 1, High Commissioner to Knutsford, 21 July 1888.

[2] African 372, No. 44, Robinson to Knutsford, 18 March 1889. See also *H.C. Deb.*, 5th ser., Vol. 59, col. 1807, 16 March 1914, for Robinson's extensive British South Africa Company shareholdings. Robinson subsequently became a director of De Beers, which had large holdings in the British South Africa Company.

[3] African 372, No. 48, Rev. J. Mackenzie to the Colonial Office, 10 April 1889.

[4] African 372, No. 118, Colonial Office to Rev. J. Mackenzie, 13 August 1889.

[5] Quoted in Robinson, Gallagher and Denny, op. cit., p. 237.   [6] C. 5918, No. 88.

[7] The financiers seeking a charter would give 'a contribution to Her Majesty's Government which would be sufficient to cover all the expenses of the supervision of Matabeleland': African 372, No. 86, Rhodes to Colonial Office, 1 June 1889. In addition, Rhodes was prepared to build a railway in Bechuanaland which would develop the area, to take over that territory, and to relieve the financial drain on the British Treasury. Rhodes was also prepared to pay for the administration and policing of the Nyasa area, which changed the

Colony administration 'on the cheap', and emphasized the inconvenient fact of the large Parliamentary grants which had been required in Bechuanaland. The grant of a charter could also be justified on the ground that otherwise a company would be incorporated under the Joint Stock Acts. In such an event the British Government could not prevent the company from taking its own line of policy, which might result in complications with native chiefs and thence military expenditure and operations.[1]

The High Commissioner even went so far as to suggest that the charter would secure the continuous development of the country with a proper consideration for the feelings and prejudices of the natives and that 'any objection which might otherwise be made that the grant of a charter locks up indefinitely a large portion of South Africa in the hands of a commercial association' was precluded by the 'novel principle' of permitting revision of the charter twenty-five years after the grant.[2]

In view of these arguments and British policy at that time it would have been surprising had the British Government not agreed to establish a Chartered Company.

The local sovereign—Lobengula

Before further steps to consolidate British influence could be taken in the area, it was necessary to obtain some agreement from the local sovereign, Lobengula, who ruled Matabeleland, and who held the Mashona and the Makalaka tributary.[3]

The Judicial Committee of the Privy Council has described Lobengula's Kingdom in legal terms as follows:

After a fashion Lobengula's was a regular government in which the actual rule was his. He assigned to individuals 'gardens' for their personal cultivation. Under a system of short tillage and long fallows no occupation lasted long except perhaps that of the kraals themselves, which he apparently respected. The community was tribally organized. It had passed beyond the purely nomad stage, though still

whole policy of Britain in that part of Africa: see F.O. 2/53, Johnston to Rhodes, 8 October 1893.

[1] C. 5918, No. 88, Colonial Office to Foreign Office, 16 May 1889. Lord Granville originally employed this argument in 1881, justifying the grant of a Charter to the British North Borneo Company: see Lindley, op. cit., p. 106. The Royal Niger Company was originally incorporated as the National African Company Limited in June 1882 and was only chartered in 1886, in order to obtain the special benefits of a Charter which entitled it to levy customs duties, exercise governmental powers, and obtain a higher status in the eyes of investors. Since it had obtained, before the grant of its Charter, wide treaties of cession from African chiefs giving the National African Company Limited 'the whole of our territories to their administrators for ever' the Lord Chancellor (Lord Halsbury) felt that the corporation would still exist if its Charter were revoked, and would possess substantially all its property and rights'—quoted in Flint, op. cit., p. 87.

[2] In re Southern Rhodesia, [1919] A.C. 211 at 214 et seq., quoting Robinson.

[3] In re Southern Rhodesia, [1919] A.C. 211 at p. 214. Lord Sumner commented that the latter were held in subjugation by Lobengula by sufferance.

remaining fluid. It practised a rude agriculture, chiefly mealies. Its wealth was mainly cattle, and of that wealth the greatest bulk belonged to the King. What individual rights his subjects had is very doubtful . . . . He had under him a kind of senate and a kind of popular assembly. He was expected to consult the council of indunas or chiefs in matters of moment. The assent of the assembled people added authority to his public acts. . . . It cannot be said of the Matabele and Mashona in Lobengula's day that they had progressed towards a settled policy (polity) further than this, that they acknowledged a sovereign in the person of a tyrant.[1]

The Court also briefly considered the nature of Lobengula's subjects' rights to land and concluded that the notion of separate ownership in land or of the alienation of land by a chief or anyone else was foreign to their ideas.[2] They continued:

The estimation of the rights of aboriginal tribes is always inherently difficult. Some tribes are so low in the scale of social organization that their usages and conceptions of rights and duties are not to be reconciled with the institutions or the legal ideas of civilized society. Such a gulf cannot be bridged. It would be idle to impute to such people some shadow of the rights known to our law, and then to transmute it into the substance of transferable rights of property as we know them. In the present case it would make each and every person by a fictional inheritance a landed proprietor 'richer than all his tribe'. On the other hand, there are indigenous peoples whose legal conceptions though differently developed are hardly less precise than our own. When once they have been studied and understood, they are no less enforceable than rights arising under English law. Between the two there is a wide tract of much ethnological interest, but the position of the natives of Southern Rhodesia within it is very uncertain; clearly they approximate rather to the lower than to the higher limit.[3]

The Court's view of African land tenure in Southern Rhodesia has been disproved by modern sociological research. This has established that in

---

[1] ibid., at pp. 214–15. For a more balanced analysis both of tribal administration and land tenure see 'The African Peoples', Chapter 5, by J. C. Mitchell in *Handbook to the Federation of Rhodesia and Nyasaland*, ed. W. F. Brelsford, Cassell, 1960.

[2] See also *Hermansberg Mission Society* v. *Commissioner for Native Affairs*, 1906, T.S. 135 at 142 per Innes C.J.

[3] *In re Southern Rhodesia* at pp. 233–4. This passage was recently approved by Davies J. in *Zihumbga* v. *Harper, Robertson, and Dodd*, NN.O. Judgement No. GD/CIV/20/65. The Judicial Committee's attitude was in strange contrast to the meticulous examination of native land rights which occurred in the case of *Amodu Tijani* v. *Secretary, Southern Nigeria*, [1921] 2 A.C. 399 at 403 et seq. Rights were examined both in terms of English legal concepts and historically. Native title was 'a usufructuary right, which is a mere qualification of or burden on the radical or final title of the Sovereign where that exists. In such cases the title of the Sovereign is a pure legal estate, to which beneficial rights may or may not be attached. But this estate is qualified by a right of beneficial user . . . .. The title . . . may not be that of the individual . . . but may be that of a community. Such a community may have the possessory title to the common enjoyment of a usufruct, with customs under which its individual members are admitted to enjoyment, and even to a right of transmitting the individual enjoyment as members by assignment *inter vivos* or by succession.' A valuable analysis of community land rights by Ryder C.J. in the Report on Land Tenure in West Africa 1898 was also included. The Court considered that, in general, the holder of native land held as trustee for the use of the community or family.

respect of Shona land tenure the traditional tribal ward (dunhu) functions primarily as a land unit: 'The ward community as a component part of the chiefdom holds the communal right over all the territory within its boundaries. It is as an accepted and eligible member of this community that a person has a right to make use of the land for building and cultivation purposes. Land used as such was invariably held by the village community as a collective unit, but eligible villagers could vest subsidiary rights in individual portions of the village allotment'.[1]

At all events, despite the British Government's low estimation of the scale of social organization of the indigenous peoples of Southern Rhodesia and notwithstanding the fact that 'there was in all juridicial conceptions a great gulf fixed, which it would, perhaps, be only fanciful to try to span'[2] Queen Victoria in 1888, through her Ministers, recognized Lobengula as the Sovereign of both Matabele and Mashona: 'The British Government stated to the Portuguese Government that he was an independent King, undisputed ruler over Matabeleland and Mashonaland, who had not parted with his sovereignty, though his territory was under British influence,'[3] and that 'he would tolerate no doubt of his rule over both territories. His authority over Mashonaland is so complete that no person of any nationality can enter it without his permission.'[4] Indeed, in 1889 the Colonial Secretary wrote to Lobengula himself saying that he, Lobengula, 'is King of the country' (i.e. of Matabeleland) 'and no one can exercise jurisdiction in it without his permission'.[5] Even after the decision to charter a Company the Colonial Secretary merely suggested that Lobengula should entrust to the Company's chief representative the duty of deciding disputes among Europeans, but continued that 'of course, this must be as Lobengula likes as he is King of the country'.[6] As the Judicial Committee concluded in its 1919 analysis: 'Lobengula's sovereignty over what is now Southern Rhodesia is therefore the starting point . . .. After a fashion Lobengula's was a regular Government in which the actual rule was his,'[7] and this Queen Victoria acknowledged. Should, however, the British Government have disregarded Lobengula's

---

[1] Report of the Mangwende Reserve Commission of Enquiry 1961. Southern Rhodesia Government, Salisbury, 1961, pp. 18–19.

[2] *In re Southern Rhodesia, supra,* at p. 216.

[3] *In re Southern Rhodesia, supra,* at p. 214.   [4] African 358, No. 5.

[5] C. 5918, 26 March 1889: 'Lo Bengula is the ruler of his country, and the Queen does not interfere in the Government of his country'—a letter suggesting the desirability of appointing a British Resident. Appointment of a consul would amount to acknowledgement of Lobengula's sovereignty: see Law Officers' Opinion, 6 May 1873, re Fiji quoted by H. A. Smith, *Great Britain and the Law of Nations,* King, 1932, Vol. I. The Law Officers even as late as 1894 informed the Colonial Secretary that Lobengula was sovereign of the country: F.O. Conf. 6641, Russell and Rigby to Ripon, 18 December 1894.

[6] C. 5918, No. 129, Encl., Knutsford to Lobengula, 15 November 1889.

[7] *In re Southern Rhodesia* at p. 214; C. 5918, Nos. 129 and 136; and *B.S.A. Co.* v. *Williams,* 1936, S.R. 247 at 242 where it was held that in 1891 Lobengula was 'the governing sovereign of this country'.

acknowledged sovereignty there was little he could have done—other than to have embarked on war. International Law of the period did not acknowledge the rights of such chiefs beyond recognizing that their territories could not be acquired by occupation or settlement but only by cession, prescription or conquest, and that their territories were not *territoria nullius*.[1] There was however some vague and undefined obligation on Britain to observe natural law in her dealings with Lobengula but no tribunal or sanctions to enforce this.[2]

First actions in the new sphere

The first step taken by the Imperial authorities after the ratification of the Moffat Treaty was the despatch of the Deputy Commissioner in charge of Bechuanaland Protectorate to establish friendly relations with Lobengula. Before the arrival of Sir Sidney Shippard a host of concession hunters had established themselves at Lobengula's kraal. Among them were Rhodes' agents, Messrs. Rudd, Maguire, and Thompson, who had come armed with an introduction to Moffat from the High Commissioner's Private Secretary stating how desirable it would be if they were to obtain a concession and others were to be kept out.[3] When the Deputy Commissioner arrived he assured Lobengula as to the standing and influence of Rhodes' group and that he 'could treat with them with security and faith'.[4] Soon after this advice Rhodes' agents obtained from Lobengula and his Council of Indunas the Rudd Concession, which gave the concessionaires and their assigns 'the exclusive charge over all metals and minerals situated and contained in my Kingdoms, principalities and dominions together with full power to do all things they may deem necessary to win and procure the same'.[5] In return the concessionaires promised Lobengula £100 per lunar month, a thousand breech-loading rifles, 100,000 suitable ball cartridges,[6] and an armed steamboat for use on the Zambezi.

[1] In an earlier period of International Law the opposite attitude was adopted. See *C.H.B.E.*, Vol. I (1929), Chapter VI, 'International Law and the Outer World', by A. P. Higgins, pp. 191–4. Cp. the case of Australia which was considered a *res nullius* and acquired by occupation: *Cooper* v. *Stuart* (1889), 14 App. Cas. at 291. On the other hand Britain, between 1831 and 1840, treated the Maori tribes of New Zealand as if they were governed by International Law: Smith, op. cit., Vol. I, pp. 31–33.

[2] Lindley, op. cit., Chapter xxxvi. See *C.H.B.E.*, Vol. III, Chapter xviii, 'International Law and Colonial Questions 1870–1914', by Sir H. Lauterpacht and R. Y. Jennings, p. 675, for subsequent developments. According to Westlake, writing in 1894, the natives were left to 'the conscience' of the state to which sovereignty had been awarded, op. cit., p. 143.

[3] National Archives MO 1/1/4, Newton to Moffat.

[4] H. M. Hole, *The Making of Rhodesia*, Macmillan, 1926, at p. 73. Hole, a later director of the British South Africa Company, was acquainted with the persons involved. Sir Sidney did not mention this advice in his Report: see C. 5918, No. 32, p. 116, report by Sir Sidney Shippard.

[5] For text see C. 5918, No. 38, Encl., p. 139.

[6] The High Commissioner attempted to justify this on humanitarian grounds. The

As soon as the Concession had been obtained Rhodes bought out other concessionaires and brought his main rival, Lord Gifford of the Bechuanaland Exploration Company, into his own Central Search Association which held the Rudd Concession.[1]

By March 1889 it became clear that the British Government would not oppose the Concession despite humanitarian objections by the South African Committee headed by Mackenzie and Joseph Chamberlain.[2] In that month pressure began to get Lobengula to accept a Resident. The Colonial Secretary required the High Commissioner to discover Lobengula's views and to inform him of British willingness to appoint a representative.[3]

A visit to England by Rhodes, and the exercise of discreet influence through his contacts in high positions[4] assisted him in his plans for a Chartered Company. Eventually at the end of April 1889 formal proposals for a charter were sent to the Colonial Office.[5] Rhodes' proposals would solve all the problems the British Government was facing in respect of Matabeleland: there would be effective occupation by British interests; the British taxpayer would not be involved—he would even be relieved of liability in Bechuanaland;[6] and, since the area would be developed by Cape Colonial influences rather than by direct Imperial intervention, which would have antagonized all elements in South Africa, the Cape element, which was pro-British, would be strengthened in any future federation in Southern Africa. Soon afterwards the grant of a charter was accepted in principle on the strength of Rhodes' Rudd Concession.

Strangely, the British Government did not enquire whether the Concession would become the property of the Chartered Company when it agreed to a charter. Apparently, it assumed that this would be the position. Only later in 1891 did the Colonial Office discover that the Concession was held by the United Concessions Company which, by agreement, was entitled to one-half of the net profits of the British South Africa Company in return for permission

Matabele would aim too high and do less harm than by the use of their spears. The Colonial Office acquiesced. This was scarcely reconcilable with the negotiations which were in progress for the Brussels Act which, as finalized in Articles 8–14, prohibited the importation of fire-arms into large areas of Africa. See also Report of the Select Committee on Aborigines in 1837, *Parliamentary Papers 1837*, Vol. VII (425) which condemned further familiarization of indigenous peoples 'with the use of our most potent instruments for . . . violent destruction of human life, viz. . . . gun powder'.

[1] In Rhodes' phrase all competing interests were 'squared': see J. G. Lockhart and C. M. Woodhouse, *Rhodes*, Hodder & Stoughton, 1963, p. 150.

[2] See W. D. Mackenzie, *John Mackenzie, South African Missionary and Statesman*, Hodder & Stoughton, 1902, p. 432.

[3] C. 5918, No. 69, pp. 163–4, Knutsford to Robinson, 19 March 1889.

[4] For a lively but polemical account see F. Gross, *Rhodes of Africa*, Cassell, 1956, pp. 160 et seq.

[5] African 372, p. 65, Gifford and Consolidated Goldfields to Colonial Office, 30 April 1889.

[6] It was also a condition of the grant of the Charter that Rhodes pay monies annually for the maintenance of peace and order in the Nyasa Districts: see F.O. Conf. 6537, No. 41, Memo. on Considerations re Nyasaland by Sir P. Anderson, 26 February 1894.

to exploit the Concession.[1] Eventually, in July 1893, it was agreed that the Concession should be sold to the Chartered Company in return for one millon paid-up shares of £1 each.[2]

This was not the only misconception on which the Charter was granted—unless it be that the British Government was so anxious to shift the burden of Matabeleland on to a Chartered Company that all other considerations were irrelevant. Although Lord Knutsford, in enthusiastically commending Rhodes' proposals to Lord Salisbury, referred to 'the large concession from Lobengula',[3] the Rudd Concession did not give the concessionaires any governmental powers since there was no delegation in it by Lobengula of legislative or administrative functions.[4] This was realized by the Colonial Office when the Charter was despatched, as it pointed out to the Company that before powers of government and administration mentioned in Articles 3 and 4 of the Charter could be exercised, these would have to be obtained 'whenever a proper and favourable time for approach to Lobengula on the subject arrives'.[5] Indeed later difficulties arose because the Colonial Office became concerned with the legality of Company land grants, which again the Concession failed to permit,[6] and because there was no agreement by Lobengula to the Company exercising jurisdiction over Europeans in his territory.[7]

Probably it was realized that the Concession was far from permanent or secure. Such a concession was subject to cancellation by Lobengula at any time, since an independent chief has the right to cancel any grants within his territory.[8] This must clearly have been so since there was no court to which Lobengula could have been made amenable.[9] It was no wonder that Rhodes sought Imperial recognition of the Concession and 'an assurance that such rights and interests as have been legally acquired in these territories . . . shall

[1] African 426, No. 272, p. 306, Colonial Office to British South Africa Co., 10 October 1892; African 439, p. 11, Knutsford to Herbert; see also *H.C. Deb.*, 4th ser., Vol. 18, col. 587, 9 November 1893, Mr. Buxton, Under-Secretary of State for the Colonies: 'I believe if the Colonial Office possessed the information at that time, while it would not have prevented the Charter being granted, it would have considerably modified the terms on which the Charter was given.'

[2] African 459, No. 38, pp. 42–54. The actual profit to the sellers was approximately £4 million—that being the market value of the shares: see Maguire's remarks in *H.C. Deb.*, 3rd ser., Vol. 355, cols. 940–2, 10 July 1891. (Maguire was one of the group who obtained the Concession.)

[3] Quoted in Robinson, Gallagher, and Denny, op. cit., p. 237.

[4] *In re Southern Rhodesia, supra*, at p. 218.

[5] C. 5918, No. 127, p. 224, Colonial Office to British South Africa Company, 6 November 1889.

[6] See C. 7171, p. 7.

[7] African 414, No. 1, Loch to Knutsford, 20 November 1890.

[8] *Estate of Doms* v. *Leyds*, N.O. 3 S.A.R. at 210 per Kotze C.J. referring to land grants.

[9] See *Cook Brothers* v. *The Colonial Government* (1895), 12 S.C. 86 at 97 where de Villiers C.J. in discussing concessions by Sigcau, the Pondo chief, held that such concessions 'created no legal obligation because their execution depended solely upon the will of the chief, and there existed no possible means of enforcing it'. When the Privy Council decided the case on appeal they refused to rule on this point: *Cook* v. *Sprigg*, [1899] A.C. 572.

be recognized by and receive the sanction and moral support of Her Majesty's Government'.[1] He needed a Charter as Lobengula would be less likely to revoke the Concession once the British Crown was involved. Lobengula in fact repudiated the Concession on a number of occasions. In January 1889 a newspaper notice to this effect was published through the instrumentality of rival concessionaires.[2] On 23 April 1889, by a letter addressed to Queen Victoria, Lobengula stated that his indunas would not recognize the Concession,[3] and he again repudiated it and any suggestion that he had asked for a Resident in a letter actually dictated to Moffat, which arrived three weeks after the grant of a Charter and three days after Lord Knutsford had despatched a letter to him.[4] Lord Knutsford's message informed Lobengula that Queen Victoria had approved of the Rudd Concession, had granted the Royal Charter so that the whites could settle their own disputes and keep peace among themselves, and that Mr. Moffat, then Assistant Commissioner in British Bechuanaland, had been appointed as Resident.[5] Lobengula's objections were diplomatically dismissed.[6]

[1] African 372, p. 65, Gifford to Colonial Office, 30 April 1889.

[2] See P. Mason, *Birth of a Dilemma*, Oxford, 1958, pp. 129–30.

[3] In Correspondence relating to the Question of the Ownership of the Mineral Rights in Southern Rhodesia, Government Printer, Salisbury, 1933 (CSR 18–1933), Counsel took the view that the Rudd Concession was a revocable licence revoked in 1889 by Lobengula's letter of 23 April 1889. It was later revoked by Lobengula on a number of other occasions but he continued to receive and accept payments of £100 per month until 30 June 1893, when payments were suspended by the Company on account of the impending Matabele War. The Concession provided that if payments were in arrears for three months the concessionaires' rights were to be extinguished. Lobengula accepted the 1,000 rifles, but he was never given the armed steam-boat. He also alleged that the effect of the Concession and its extent was misrepresented to him but, as indicated, he accepted payments long after he discovered the truth.

[4] C. 5918, No. 130, Encl., p. 235, Lobengula to Sir Sidney Shippard, 10 August 1889. It is interesting to note the dates of despatch and arrival of this letter on its intermediate stages. The usual time taken for delivery of letters from Bulawayo to London was at that time forty-seven days. On 10 August 1889 it was despatched to Sir S. Shippard, Administrator of Bechuanaland, a 'Rhodes man' who had been responsible for putting pressure on Lobengula to grant the Rudd Concession. On 14 October 1889 Shippard sent it on to the High Commissioner, who remitted it to the Colonial Secretary on 25 October 1889. It arrived at the Colonial Office on 18 November 1889. The Colonial Office were doubtless not displeased at the letter's late arrival, while Shippard's sympathies were all in favour of the granting of a Charter. On retirement he became a director of the Chartered Company.

[5] C. 5918, No. 129, Encl., p. 233, Knutsford to Lobengula, 15 November 1889. African 392, No. 77, Encl., p. 100, Moffat to Shippard, shows how the Resident dared not give the full text to Lobengula and modified it to omit the statement that Lobengula had requested a Resident. He also 'touched lightly' on the proposal to delegate jurisdiction to a body of white men. Dr. Jameson, Rhodes' personal delegate to Lobengula, was in fact responsible for 'improvements' on Knutsford's letter to Lobengula: Hole, op. cit. It has even been stated that Jameson tore up the letter from Knutsford to Lobengula. Lockhart and Woodhouse, op. cit., p. 156.

[6] C. 5918, No. 136, p. 239, Knutsford to Loch, 5 December 1889.

3

THE CHARTER, THE ESTABLISHMENT OF COMPANY GOVERNMENT, AND IMPERIAL CONTROL 1890–91

O N 29 October 1889, the British South Africa Company was chartered.[1] The various strands of Imperial policy that had led to its grant were reflected in the provisions of the Charter as were the avowedly commercial aims of the Company's promoters. The Charter attempted to reconcile the Treasury desire to avoid calls for Imperial funds with the need to control the Company so as to protect British foreign relations and to preclude disputes with native chiefs that might lead to military involvement. At the same time regard to humanitarian views and duties of trusteeship towards the indigenous inhabitants required the insertion of provisions to prevent possible excesses and to preserve native rights. The Charter made it obvious that humanitarian principles, although lip service was paid to them, were not really intended to be enforced, as it contained no provision for the appointment of Imperial officers on the spot who could either report on or intervene with the Company. There was not even provision for Imperial judicial officers.[2]

That the Charter was intended as a semi-permanent instrument of government until such time as any settlers[3] could take over the administration was also indicated by the provision that the Company was to enjoy at least a twenty-five-year period of administration and that its Charter was only to be revocable in circumstances amounting to misconduct.[4] As a governmental instrument the Charter of course dealt with administrative, legislative, and judicial powers,[5] while its imperially expansive purpose was shown in the extensive sphere of territorial operations permitted to the Company.[6] Finally,

---

[1] For text of Charter see C. 5918, No. 128, Encl., pp. 227–32.

[2] Cp. the Charter of the British North Borneo Company, Article XI, which provided for Crown power to appoint consuls exercising jurisdiction in the Company's territories. In the area of operations of the Niger Company and the East Africa Company consular courts had been established in terms of the Africa Order in Council 1889, whereas the British South Africa Company Charter (Article 22) merely provided that the Company should, if required, appoint officers to administer justice under the Foreign Jurisdiction Act.

[3] Article 24 authorized the Company to make land grants, and the Imperial authorities knew it was Rhodes' intention that the country be occupied by settlers from the Cape Colony. See also the preamble which avowed European immigration as an object.

[4] In the case of the Royal Niger Company the Charter could be revoked at any time if it appeared 'expedient'.

[5] Articles 3, 4, 10, 14, and 22. The Company was empowered to establish and maintain a force of police.

[6] Article 1 permitted expansion as no northward limit was placed on the large area

prevailing free trade notions demanded a prohibition against monopolies, but this was not to prevent the grant of concessions for banks, railways, tramways, telegraphs, and similar undertakings.[1]

The new Company differed from the other two late Victorian African Chartered Companies in that the provisions of its Charter permitted more control should the Imperial authorities decide to assert their views[2]: in its treaty-making power with African chiefs, the Company was more limited than the Royal Niger Company; unlike any of the other Chartered Companies it was to be subject to supervision by the High Commissioner for South Africa; and its officers were to pay due regard to his and the requirements of any other Imperial officers who might be stationed in its territories. Although the Company was conditionally given capacity to legislate, its Ordinances were subject to approval by a Secretary of State. It was bound to furnish not only accounts of its expenditure for administrative purposes and its receipts by way of public revenue, but also a report on its public proceedings, the condition of its territories and an estimate of its expenditure and revenue for the ensuing year.[3] In addition, the Crown reserved the right to purchase public works belonging to the Company and expressly provided that it reserved its right to annex the Company's territories or declare a protectorate.

The powers conferred by the Charter

The Charter gave the Company capacity to administer and govern in the region of South Africa lying immediately to the north of British Bechuanaland, to the north and west of the South African Republic, and to the west of the Portuguese Dominions.[4] But, while the Charter gave the Company legal capacity and conditional permission from the Crown to exercise governing powers which it might in the future acquire, the Company could only seek the

described. The article also envisaged the acquisition of administrative powers in Bechuanaland: see African 439, p. 40, Knutsford to Loch, 14 November 1889.

[1] Article 20.

[2] Such controls were not in fact utilized until 1896: see *infra*.

[3] The provisions were probably stricter because of the many complaints about the Royal Niger Company. See H. Wilson-Fox, *Memoranda on Constitutional, Political, Financial and Other Questions Concerning Rhodesia*, printed for information of the Board, London, 1912, pp. 551–65, for a comparison of the detailed provisions of all the Chartered Companies. Wilson-Fox's emphasis is on the financial provisions and the unfair difference that the Niger Company was permitted to establish a public debt and reimburse itself therefrom for deficits incurred by it as the National Africa Company Limited: see p. 556.

[4] Article 1. There was no northward limit so the Company could expand its operations north of the Zambesi. Furthermore, 'the field of the Company's operations was so defined that while the existing protectorate south of 22° south latitude remained unaffected, beyond that boundary the Company was empowered to acquire from the lawful rulers (subject to the approval of the Secretary of State) certain powers of government or administration': *In re Southern Rhodesia, supra*, at p. 217. In February 1891 the British Government recognized that the Company's sphere extended north of the Zambesi: see C. 7637.

source of its actual administration in the grant of governing powers by the sovereign of the country, King Lobengula.[1]

The Privy Council subsequently made it quite clear that 'Queen Victoria recognized Lobengula as sovereign of both peoples (Matabele and Mashona)', and that Lobengula's sovereignty was 'the starting point'.[2]

Analysis of the Charter shows this to be the case. Article 2 of the Charter merely authorized the Company to hold any concessions 'so far as they are valid'; Article 3 authorized the Company to exercise such rights, interests, authorities, jurisdictions, and powers as might be conferred by concession subject to the approval of a Secretary of State; while Article 4 provided that such powers should not be exercised without approval by the Secretary of State, who might add conditions for their exercise.[3]

Although Article 10 provided that—

The Company shall to the best of its ability preserve peace and order in such ways and manners as it shall consider necessary and may with that object make Ordinances to be approved by our Secretary of State, and may establish and maintain a force of police

it seems clear that except for its recognition of concessions already obtained in terms of Article 2, the Charter created a conditional authority recognizing potential powers which the Company might in the future acquire by concession, agreement, grant, or treaty, subject to the approval of a Secretary of State. Since neither the Charter nor the Rudd Concession, which had been approved, gave powers of government or administration to the Company, it did not at this time enjoy any such powers. As the Colonial Office pointed out, these had to be obtained on a 'proper and favourable' occasion from Lobengula and his consent was a prerequisite to Company governmental activities.[4]

This view is not affected by Article 10 imposing the duty of preserving peace and order on the Company,[5] and empowering it, with that object, to pass Ordinances. Article 10 must be construed subject to Articles 3 and 4, fulfilment of the terms of which was a condition precedent to the exercise of

[1] *In re Southern Rhodesia, supra*, at p. 222.

[2] ibid., p. 214.

[3] The Imperial authorities did not consider that the approval of the Secretary of State was necessary for exploitation of commercial concessions: see F.O. Conf. 6613, No. 71, 13 August 1894.

[4] This attitude was maintained by the Colonial Office until 1891 when it changed its ground. In fact Company powers depended not only on the Rudd Concession from Lobengula but also on concessions later obtained and recognized from Umtassa and Gungunghana on the Portuguese East African border which were wider in scope. Westlake, op. cit., pp. 151 et seq., castigates those who obtained a treaty from Umtassa which he could not possibly have understood, particularly as he suffered from *delirium tremens*.

[5] In *B.S.A. Co.* v. *Salisbury Reef Gold Mining Co.*, 8 C.T.R. 447 at 449 de Villiers C.J. doubted whether this clause imposed 'on the Company any definite duty for the non-performance of which it would be legally liable'. The lower Court had held that the Charter imposed on the Company a statutory duty to maintain some sort of civilized government.

governmental powers by the Company.[1] On this construction the Charter conferred capacity rather than power, and the Company enjoyed no legislative powers other than those derived from Lobengula. Whereas the Rudd Concession might by extensive interpretation have permitted legislation in respect of mining and its control, it could not be construed as delegating any other powers. Any exercise of governmental or legislative powers by the Company was, if it relied on the Charter and Rudd Concession, therefore *ultra vires*.[2] Nor could such power be conferred on the Company by the Crown as the Matabeleland Kingdom was at that time a foreign country in which the Crown exercised no power or jurisdiction.[3]

Limitations on the Company

Britain's power to control Company activities was secured by several provisions. Thus the Secretary of State had to approve the acquisition of concessions[4] while governmental powers could not be exercised before such approval.[5] Such legislative power as the Company enjoyed could only be exercised by means of Ordinances made by the Board of the Company in London with the assent of a Secretary of State.[6] Furthermore, subject to the directions of a Secretary of State, the Company was obliged to provide courts and other requisites necessary for the administration of justice.[7] The Secretary of State was also entitled to information on the Company's administrative expenditure so that he would be in a position to assess the financial state of affairs of the Company.[8]

Britain's foreign relations were safeguarded by providing that in any dealings with foreign powers the Company was bound to act on the suggestions made to it by a Secretary of State,[9] while the Company was to be bound by all treaties and arrangements entered into by Britain at any time with

---

[1] In *R.* v. *McChlery*, 1912, A.D. 199 at 220 Innes J.A., discussing the amplitude of legislative power conferred when powers to preserve 'peace and order' were given said that such powers were plenary 'always assuming that the restrictive limits of the empowering documents are observed'.

[2] Although it has been held that the doctrine of *ultra vires* is inapplicable to Chartered corporations—*Baroness Wenlock* v. *River Dee Co.* (1887), 36 Ch. D. 675 at 685n, and *British South Africa Co.* v. *De Beers Consolidated Mines Ltd.*, [1910] 1 Ch. 354—that the remedy for breach of its Charter is revocation by the Crown, and that a Chartered Corporation has full powers, this must mean the powers of an ordinary person, i.e. it can deal freely with its property, enter into contracts, and do all acts within the competence of an ordinary person. Acts beyond the capacity conferred by Common Law on persons must also be beyond the power of chartered corporations unless expressly conferred. It will be seen that the Company promulgated and enforced 'Mining Regulations' (which amounted to a general code of civil and criminal law) without any authority therefor.

[3] *In re Southern Rhodesia, supra,* at p. 239, where the Court held that the Charter 'did not amount to an anticipatory grant by the Crown of land which in 1889 was not the Crown's to bestow'. It seems that legislative power in 1889 was equally 'not the Crown's to bestow'.

[4] Article 3.   [5] Article 4.   [6] Article 10.   [7] Article 22.   [8] Article 17.   [9] Article 8.

other powers.[1] Where there was any claim adverse to the Company's authority to exercise power within any part of the territory, the Company was bound to defer to any objections by a Secretary of State until he had settled such claim.[2] The Company furthermore had always to remain British in character and domicile and so must its directors, unless specially approved by a Secretary of State,[3] while certain respectable life directors were also appointed.[4] In addition, the Company's flag was to indicate its British Character.[5]

The first signs of concern for the indigenous peoples of the future Southern Rhodesia and the origin of devices to protect them were also to be found in the Charter. Where any dispute with a chief or tribe arose a Secretary of State was to decide the matter and the Company was to be bound by his decision.[6] The Charter also laid down that the Company was bound to fulfil all the terms of any agreement it might have made when obtaining a concession.[7] It was to abolish any system of slave trading or domestic servitude[8] and to prevent the sale of spirits to natives.[9] It was not to interfere with the religion of the inhabitants[10] and due regard had to be paid to native customary law.[11] The most significant provision, however, was that, if at any time a Secretary of State objected to the conduct or administration of the Company relative to the inhabitants in respect of any matter, the Company was bound to act in accordance with any directions given by such Secretary.[12] Yet another clause subjected the officials of the Company to a duty to communicate freely with the High Commissioner in South Africa and other Imperial officials stationed in the territories, and a further duty to pay due regard to their requests and suggestions.[13]

The Crown was careful to safeguard its rights to declare protectorates or to annex any territory in the future.[14] The Charter also provided that at the end of the first twenty-five years of Company rule and at the end of every subsequent period of ten years, the Crown should have the right of repealing or varying any of its provisions relating to administrative or public matters, with the additional right to take over Company property on payment of reasonable compensation.[15] At any time, too, the Crown might revoke the

---

[1] Article 22.   [2] Article 9.
[3] Article 6. Under the common nationality code of the time Cape Colonists were British subjects.
[4] Article 29. Duke of Abercorn, Duke of Fife, and Mr. Albert Grey (later Earl Grey). Lord Salisbury had indicated that if a Charter were to be granted certain socially acceptable directors should be appointed.
[5] Article 19.   [6] Article 7.
[7] Article 5.
[8] Article 11. See R. v. Gutayi, 1915, S.R. 49 at 61 where, relying on Article 11, it was held that an African woman no longer has to submit herself to the power of her guardian after widowhood or divorce. Previously she might be sold as a wife or retained as a servant.
[9] Article 12.   [10] Article 13.   [11] Article 14.   [12] Article 15.   [13] Article 18.
[14] Article 34.   [15] Article 33.

Charter if the Company failed to observe its provisions or to advance the interests and objects which its promoters had professed to have in view.[1]

In a despatch to the Company soon after the issue of the Charter, Lord Knutsford drew particular attention to the provisions dealing with the revocation and amendment of the Charter and indicated to the Company that it had been granted security of tenure for twenty-five years in the absence of any paramount necessity for annexation, or failure, or misconduct on its part. At the end of that time and periodically thereafter the continuation of Company administrative powers would have to be reconsidered in the light of Imperial and South African interests.[2]

The Charter was supplemented by a Deed of Settlement which further defined the objects of the Company, making it clear that the Company was intended to have both commercial purposes and governmental powers.[3]

Abdication of the Imperial authorities

Thus did the Imperial authorities recognize the possibility of a commercial company exercising legislative and executive power throughout a vast area of Africa within the sphere of British influence, subject only to remote controls exercisable by the Secretary of State for the Colonies and the High Commissioner in South Africa. Once the principle that the Colonial Office would not itself administer these territories was accepted, then it necessarily followed that Imperial control could not be fully effective. This the Colonial Office knew, as from experience in South Africa it had long ago recognized that 'in dealing with natives legislation has little importance compared with administration'.[4] Negative controls there were. Criticism of and objection in retrospect to administrative action was possible, as was scrutiny and vetting of legislation, but power to supervise the daily application and administration of laws, the true touchstone of control, was not assumed by the Imperial authorities. Britain abandoned the possibility of exercising really effective power in 1889 when she decided against direct administration and conceded this power to a Cape-controlled Chartered Company. Even those controls

[1] Article 35. See the preamble to the Charter: the promotion of trade, commerce, civilization, and good government, the suppression of the slave trade, material improvement in the conditions of the natives and their civilization, and the opening up of territories to European immigration and trade. A government spokesman justifying the intention to grant a Charter said: 'We wish to spread the influence of civilization to the barbarous districts of Africa.' *H.C. Deb.*, 3rd ser., Vol. 340, col. 486, 26 August 1889.

[2] Despatch of 14 November 1889 to the Company. Quoted in H. Wilson-Fox, *Memoranda on Constitutional, Political, Financial, and Other Questions concerning Rhodesia*, printed for the information of the Board, London, 1912.

[3] For text see *The Charter of Incorporation, Deed of Settlement, Supplemental Charters, and Deeds of Settlement*, The British South Africa Co., London, 1937. Articles 25 to 27 of the Charter required the Deed of Settlement to be executed within one year and to be approved by the Privy Council.

[4] African 304, p. 4, para. 2.

that Britain possessed were reluctantly and seldom exercised for the same reasons that she had initially granted the Charter: fear, lest action might antagonize South African opinion and financial concern lest she be forced through intervention to take over administration of the territories.

The establishment of Company government

Company occupation of Mashonaland

Britain, although she was not herself 'prepared to exercise jurisdiction',[1] was satisfied to allow the Company to occupy Mashonaland. Discussions between the High Commissioner and the Company proceeded early in 1890, with the Colonial Office and High Commissioner at first insisting that Lobengula should specifically consent to any movement in force.[2] They were then informed by Rhodes that 'Lobengula has sanctioned our occupation in Mashonaland'[3] and, although doubtful whether this was true, they felt that in view of a probable Boer occupation of the territory it was dangerous to delay action by the Company any longer.[4] Although the British authorities paid lip service to Articles 3 and 4 of the Charter, demanding continuously that these be fulfilled before the Company could legally exercise any jurisdiction, they knew perfectly well that the Company intended 'to take over the civil administration of the country'[5] and to 'occupy' Mashonaland and ultimately Matabeleland.[6] Indeed the Imperial Secretary, in authorizing the British South Africa Company's forces to set out, explicitly stated that 'the object to be attained is the peaceable occupation of Mashonaland',[7] but safeguarded the British position by keeping up the pretence that this was done 'in accordance with the permission' granted by Lobengula to the Chartered Company.

[1] African 392, No. 328, Knutsford to Loch, 27 October 1890.

[2] The Colonial Office told the British South Africa Company that if any police force were to be sent into his country it would be necessary 'to ascertain clearly that its presence there will be acceptable to Lobengula, as otherwise serious complications might ensue': C. 5918, No. 127, Colonial Office to B.S.A. Co., 6 November 1889. At this time the Crown was treating him as an independent king exercising sovereignty over the whole area.

[3] African 392, No. 40, Telegraph Loch to Knutsford, 20 February 1890, quoting Rhodes. See Mason, op. cit., pp. 139–42 for an account of the real position.

[4] African 392, No. 58, Foreign Office to Colonial Office, 7 March 1890, and also No. 64. On 12 March 1890 Loch, President Kruger, and Rhodes met at Blignaut's Point to discuss the proposed Boer Trek into Southern Rhodesia.

[5] African 392, No. 12, Encl., p. 29, Rhodes to High Commissioner, 11 January 1890; also No. 162, pp. 194–5, Encl. 1.

[6] African 392, No. 141A, p. 171, B.S.A. Co. to Colonial Office enclosing copy of letter from Rhodes to Abercorn. In 1889 Rhodes entered into an agreement with Frank Johnson for the occupation of both Matabeleland and Mashonaland: see *Rhodesia Herald*, 12 September 1930, by F. Johnson. A copy of the Agreement is in the National Archives. A final agreement for the occupation of Mashonaland only was signed on 1 January 1890. See F. Johnson, *Great Days*, Bell, 1940, Appendix E, p. 326.

[7] African 392, No. 221, Encl. 1, Telegraph Imperial Secretary to B.S.A. Co., 6 June 1890.

That Lobengula in reality strongly objected, the British Government knew.[1]

Nonetheless with Imperial consent[2] the Company forces set off on their incursion on 27 June 1890, and reached their objective, Fort Salisbury, on 12 September where they raised the flag and took possession of Mashonaland avowedly for the Queen.

Despite pioneer avowals that the country was a British possession, the pioneers were unauthorized agents to acquire territorial sovereignty for Britain. Nor did Britain subsequently ratify this unauthorized annexation. In fact the British Crown remained reluctant to extend its jurisdiction, holding until 1891 that Lobengula was the sovereign and that the area occupied by the Company was merely part of the sphere of British influence in Central Africa. Since Lobengula ruled a definite community there could be 'no question of white settlement among aborigines destitute of any recognizable form of sovereignty'. Nor was there any 'question of the rights attached to civilized nations who claim title by original discovery or in virtue of their occupation of coastal regions backed by an unexplored interior'.[3] Title at that time was neither obtained by settlement, discovery, occupation,[4] or conquest, and the country was recognized, despite the great gulf 'in all juridical conceptions', as belonging to an independent (if backward and tyrannical) sovereign.[5]

The administration established by the Company

The Company had appointed A. R. Colquhoun, an ex-Indian civil servant, to act as 'Administrator' of Mashonaland. He and Dr. Jameson, a close associate of Rhodes, were in *de facto* control of the country as the Company's delegates although they had no official status vis-à-vis the British Government. In truth, Jameson was authorized by Rhodes to exercise control and Colquhoun's province was 'limited to the administration of Mashonaland' under his supervision.[6]

On arrival in Salisbury the Administrator set up a headquarters there,[7] laid out a township, dealt with mining laws and regulations which were in draft, initiated surveys and the opening of roads to the various mining centres, established postal communications and despatched missions to native chiefs.[8]

[1] African 392, No. 281, Encl., Pennefather to Imperial Secretary, 23 July 1890.
[2] African 392, No. 221, Encl. 1, Imperial Secretary to B.S.A. Co. 6 June 1890.
[3] *In re Southern Rhodesia, supra* at pp. 215–16.
[4] The Company subsequently contended that it had occupied empty country, but this was not upheld by the Privy Council.
[5] *In re Southern Rhodesia, supra* at p. 216.
[6] National Archives JA 1 1 1, L. S. Jameson to S. Jameson, 27 December 1890.
[7] The Administrator divided the 'colony' into three districts—North, Central, and Southern with headquarters at Forts Salisbury, Charter, and Victoria respectively on 28 September 1890: Johnson, op. cit., p. 155.
[8] A. R. Colquhoun, *From Dan to Beersheba*, Heinemann, 1908, p. 288.

Eventually, by the end of 1890, there was a three-fold division of authority—Colquhoun dealing with administrative details, Dr. Jameson dealing with all political and important matters, and Colonel Pennefather with police questions.[1]

The administration set up by the Company was at first of the most rudimentary nature. There were then only 1,000 whites in the country, the bulk of whom dispersed everywhere seeking for gold. Colquhoun reported in 1890 on the work of the administration in a somewhat inflated fashion: 'Applications for licences and mining rights had to be dealt with; disputes had to be settled; mining commissioners appointed; regulations for the proper control of the settlers prepared; roads constructed to the different parts of the country where mining operations were taken in hand; a postal system inaugurated; townships laid out (Fort Victoria, Salisbury, Umtali); sanitary and municipal regulations framed; and measures taken generally for the settlement of the country and for raising revenue required to meet the expense of government.'[2]

In fact the Report of the Administrator in 1892 shows the smallness of the administrative apparatus established by the Company. Even at that time, when the Administration had expanded, the personnel consisted of a Chief Magistrate (also Administrator), four other magistrates, a public prosecutor, five justices of the peace and seven field cornets (both these latter categories consisting of private individuals), five marriage officers, a Master to administer estates of minors, lunatics, deceased or absent persons, and insolvents, five mining commissioners, five district surgeons, a Surveyor-General, and an acting postmaster.[3]

By December 1895 services had however expanded as there were some 130 European members of the Company staff, exclusive of the police, organized in various departments. In 1897 there was a fixed establishment of over 200 Europeans.[4]

Imperial control in practice 1890 to June 1891

It is instructive at this stage to enquire how much control Britain exercised over Company administration and legislation during this period in which Mashonaland was considered to be merely a British sphere of influence.

[1] National Archives CT 2/1/10, Harris to Colquhoun. The Company Police were, when in the area of Bechuanaland, governed by High Commissioner's Proclamation of 11 September 1890, which provided for their discipline in terms of the Cape Mounted Rifles Act. This only extended to the areas under protection to the north of Bechuanaland because the enabling Order in Council of 30 June 1890, conferring proclaiming powers on the Governor of British Bechuanaland had limited the applicability of these powers to that area. However the Proclamation was in practice applied for disciplining the police in Mashonaland.

[2] B.S.A. Co. *Report on Administration 1889–92*, report by A. R. Colquhoun.

[3] B.S.A. Co. *Report on Administration 1889–92*, report by L. S. Jameson.

[4] B.S.A. Co. *Report on Administration 1896–7*.

Legislative supervision

In the legislative sphere the Company did not employ the Ordinance-making power conferred by the Charter upon the Board of Directors as the opinion prevailed that consent by Lobengula was necessary to the assumption by the Company of legislative powers within his territories. However the Company still purported to indulge in legislative activity. Within Mashonaland it declared that its 'Mining Laws' were in force.[1] These went far beyond regulations for mining or for the grant of licences to persons to mine: they purported to set up courts with civil and criminal jurisdiction and laid down penalties for offenders. Although Lord Knutsford warned the Company that it had 'not received from Lobengula any authority to exercise such sovereign rights as are implied by setting up courts of justice', that it did not 'appear that the Company yet possessed such a delegation of authority as would warrant them in appointing Magistrates, or an "Administrator" holding a court of appeal', and that such regulations 'could easily be represented as an attempt to govern his (Lobengula's) country without his permission',[2] he merely suggested that the laws should be re-styled 'regulations' and the provision as to courts and sanctions omitted. The stratagem was suggested that the regulations should remain as a matter of contract, and that the Company could warn the miners that, if the regulations were disobeyed, the offender would lose his rights to a licence and would be subject to removal from the country.[3]

Administrative supervision

Although the Charter gave the Secretary of State power to dissent from the Company's proceedings and authorized the High Commissioner to give instructions to the Company's officials, the Colonial Office apparently decided to restrict its intervention to the minimum. Only if Imperial issues arose as a result of Company action was it prepared to act. Disapproval would be voiced if Company action was likely either to result in diplomatic difficulties,[4]

[1] This was done by Proclamation No. 1 of 1890 issued on 28 September 1890 by Colquhoun. Johnson, who had brought in the pioneers, states that 'in order to save time the Administrator instituted most of the Cape laws in their entirety': op. cit., p. 160.

[2] African 392, No. 303, Colonial Office to B.S.A. Co., 11 August 1890. Earlier the Colonial Office suggested that Lobengula's authority should be obtained and an Ordinance passed: African 392, No. 274, Colonial Office to B.S.A. Co., 11 August 1890.

[3] In terms of the laws leave was granted to peg out and occupy farms of 3,000 acres in Mashonaland and also to obtain fifteen gold claims.

[4] In December 1890 the High Commissioner directed the withdrawal of Company forces from places outside the lines agreed by the Anglo-Portuguese Convention of August 1890. Observance of the *modus vivendi* by the Company was insisted on (African 403, Nos. 32, 43; F.O. Conf. 6227, No. 67). Again in 1891, when Company action in Gazaland endangered Anglo–Portuguese accord, firm action was taken (African 403, No. 143).

to involve Britain with powerful chiefs,[1] to involve exploitation of the British name,[2] or to occasion adverse parliamentary or press comment.[3]

In the year of Company occupation of Mashonaland prior to the formal declaration of a protectorate, the period of the first influx of pioneers, rough and not too scrupulous as all pioneers must be, the Colonial Office saw fit to exert its influence and control on Company action on a negligible number of occasions.[4] Clearly the attitude of Her Majesty's Government was to turn the Imperial blind eye.

[1] Mining in territory disputed between Khama and Lobengula was prohibited (African 403, No. 110) and allegations that pioneers had destroyed the gardens of some of Lobengula's subjects were investigated (African 403, No. 34).

[2] Rhodes was warned against using the Queen's name in concessions of a commercial character, while if political objects were involved the High Commissioner should be consulted (African 403, No. 295). Nor would any reference to the British name be permitted as a basis for Company authority: all references to the High Commissioner were cut out of the Company proclamation announcing the appointment of Colquhoun as the Company's chief executive officer in Mashonaland lest this indicate approval of such appointment (African 414, No. 22).

[3] After a question in the House about the flogging of an African wagon driver who had deserted, the Colonial Office reminded the Directors of the Company that they were 'doubtless duly sensible of the importance of repressing anything like harshness or violence on the part of comparatively irresponsible persons attaching themselves to an African expedition' (African 403, No. 113). Another question, and publicity in Labouchere's Truth, caused the Colonial Office to inquire whether the Company was infringing the provisions of the Charter (Article 20) prohibiting the granting of monopolies (African 403, No. 307).

[4] The Imperial records reveal seven cases in all.

THE EVOLUTION OF THE POWERS OF THE CROWN IN PROTECTORATES

Protectorates

THE notion of protectorates is extremely ancient. One writer has described it as existing in Greece in the sixth century B.C.[1] So too in Rome the client status of subject cities and states under the protection of Rome, their *patronus*, was well recognized.

From its inception International Law acknowledged this type of relationship in which a comparatively powerful state took over the duty of protecting a weaker state and conducting its external affairs. The relationship involved a division of sovereignty with the protector controlling external affairs, the protected state remaining, however, a person in International Law. This was the type of protectorate exercised in the early nineteenth century by European powers over small civilized states, which retained their internal sovereignty, e.g. the Ionian Islands and Monaco.[2]

During the course of the nineteenth century a new type of protectorate came into existence. European states began to exercise powers of protection over countries in Asia and Africa regarded by International Law as imperfectly civilized and barbarous, such powers arising either as a consequence of treaties or as a result of the gradual assumption of control. These protectorates were considered as debarring other civilized states from maintaining relations with the protected state, since external relations of the protected state were under the exclusive control of the protector who bore international responsibility.[3] Foreign states, being precluded from asserting by force against the protected state any claims for redress that they might have, had the right to expect from the protecting state such supervision as would secure that due regard was paid to the rights of the subjects of foreign

---

[1] See E. Engelhardt, *Les Protectorats Anciens et Moderns*, Paris, 1896. Athens in the fifth century B.C. enjoyed hegemony over certain Greek states in a relationship similar to protection. See also G. Glotz, *The Greek City and its Institutions*, Routledge & Kegan Paul, 1929, pp. 272–94.

[2] For a short account of the development of protectorates in Europe see A. M. Kamanda, *A Study of the Legal Status of Protectorates in Public International Law*, University of Geneva, 1961, pp. 17–21. The evolution of the doctrine in International Law is described at pp. 33–45.

[3] See Hall, *The Foreign Powers and Jurisdiction of the British Crown*, p. 218; Jenkyns, op. cit., p. 165, adopted by Lord Haldane in *Sobhuza II* v. *Miller*, *supra* at 523 and also *R.* v. *Crewe, supra* at p. 619.

states and that compensation would be paid for the violation of any such rights.[1]

In International Law the majority of these new protectorates were not recognized as persons,[2] and treaties conferring jurisdiction were not considered as binding on the protecting power. Indeed, such treaties were merely regarded as statements of limitations which the protecting power would place on its own action. In practice, however, such treaties often had considerable political consequences, as the local inhabitants might invoke the treaty,[3] while the protecting power would in normal circumstances attempt to act within its limits.

In English municipal law protectorates were nowhere defined, but it has been recognized that, for the purposes of the Foreign Jurisdiction Acts, a protectorate 'means territory outside the dominions of the Crown, but over which the Crown exercises some jurisdiction'.[4]

A similar distinction to that in International Law was drawn between protected states and colonial protectorates, the basis of classification being the degree of assumption of administrative authority by the protecting power. In protected states (mainly in the East, which were brought under British protection from 1874 onwards), 'a longer tradition of governmental forms . . . presented the possibility of preserving the existing State form, while the British Government was most anxious not to extend its responsibilities'.[5] In these states, where a treaty originated British jurisdiction, there was relatively little interference by the protecting power with internal affairs, control remaining with the local ruler, although external powers were assumed. Protected states are, as already indicated, recognized in International Law.[6]

On the other hand, colonial protectorates resulted 'in Africa, where (a similar) policy would have been willingly followed (but) it proved impracticable of maintenance in the long run owing to the inferiority of political

[1] Wheaton, *International Law* (ed. Keith), Vol. I, p. 80; and Jenkyns, op. cit., pp. 175–6. See F.O. to L.O., 27 February 1895, quoted in McNair, *Opinions*, Vol. I, pp. 58–9.

[2] Both the internal and the external sovereignty of the protected state were absorbed within the personality of the protecting state. It has been suggested that such a protectorate is merely a concept of constitutional or municipal law and is not recognized by International Law which is only concerned with protected states: see G. Fitzmaurice, 'The Law and Practice of the International Court of Justice' (1953) *B.Y.B.I.L.* XXX at 3. Westlake commented that the term protectorate was used in respect of such states to give 'a flavour of international law': *International Law*, Vol. I, Cambridge, 1904 edition. That the personality of the protected state was absorbed was impliedly recognized as early as 1893, when the Law Officers held that the flag of Zanzibar protectorate was not a 'foreign' flag in terms of Article XLVII of the Brussels Act: F.O. Conf. 6508, No. 50, Russell and Rigby to Roseberry, 28 February 1893, p. 96.

[3] The Bond of 1844, whereby jurisdiction in the Gold Coast Protectorate was partially regularized, was constantly invoked by Gold Coasters in their relationship with Britain.

[4] Farwell L.J. in *R. v. Crewe*, *supra* at p. 611.

[5] Keith, *The Governments of the British Empire*, Macmillan, 1935, p. 508.

[6] G. Fitzmaurice, op. cit.; and M. Wight, *British Colonial Constitutions, 1947*, Oxford, 1952, p. 10.

organization and capacity of those concerned'.[1] Here there were numerous
tribes and chiefs, some of whom entered into treaties of protection or of
cession, or alternatively acquiesced in or suffered jurisdiction to be assumed.
Of such treaties International Law took no account. The colonial protectorates eventually differed from Crown colonies in little more than name, apart
from the fact that they were not formally annexed, were administered by
Orders under the Foreign Jurisdiction Act, and did not form a portion of
British territory.[2] Both internally and externally, the Crown eventually came
to exercise full sovereignty, although the assertion of power was a gradual
process accompanied by doubts as to the competence of the Crown to act.

Outline of the historical development of the Crown's power

The legal machinery which Britain employed in exercising power and
eventually governing her protectorates was the Foreign Jurisdiction Act. The
Act was originally passed for an entirely different purpose as a consequence of
doubts which had arisen in 1843 as to how far jurisdiction enjoyed by the
Crown in foreign countries was controlled by and dependent on the law and
custom of the realm.[3] Foreign jurisdiction had first become important in 1579
when by the first of a series of Capitulations, the Sultan of Turkey agreed that
the British Crown was entitled to adjudicate on crimes committed by British
subjects and in civil disputes in which they were involved, although these had
arisen within the Ottoman Dominions. Later the Crown's right under various
treaties with the Porte were delegated to the Levant Company (chartered in
1581). When the Levant Company was extinguished by an Act of Parliament
in 1825 all such jurisdiction over British subjects in the ports of the Levant
was transferred to Consuls and other officials appointed by the British Crown

[1] Keith, op. cit., p. 508.

[2] Cp. Oppenheim, op. cit., § 94, p. 178 on the position in International Law: 'Colonial
protectorates are protectorates over African tribes which European states acquire through
a treaty with the chiefs of these tribes and by which the territory in question is usually preserved for future occupation on the part of so-called protector.'

[3] Report on British Jurisdiction in Foreign States by Mr. Hope Scott, 18 January 1843,
printed in Jenkyns, op. cit., pp. 242–66; *Papayanni* v. *The Russian Steam Ship Navigation and
Trading Co.* (1863), 2 Moo. P.C. (N.S.) 161; W. Forsyth, *Cases and Opinions on Constitutional
Law*, Stevens & Haynes, 1869, p. 233; and Hall, *Foreign Powers*, pp. 9–10, pp. 149–150.
Hall suggests that doubt as to the power of the Crown to exercise criminal jurisdiction and
to punish British subjects was a major reason for the first Act. The Law Officers in an opinion
of 29 June 1887 considered it doubtful whether, but for the authority conferred by the Acts,
the Crown could exercise jurisdiction over British subjects in foreign countries: McNair,
Opinions, Vol. I, p. 44. R. S. Wright, co-draftsman of the 1890 Foreign Jurisdiction Act,
thought that the 'principal object of the 1843 Act was to remove doubts whether English
Law must not be applied without modification in substance to British subjects' and 'to
remove doubts as to the mode of exercise of jurisdiction already existing': F.O. Conf. 5719,
Memo. on Foreign Jurisdiction by R. S. Wright, 15 November 1888. It has also been suggested that the purpose of the Act was 'formally to subject the exercise Her Majesty's
foreign jurisdiction to Parliamentary control' since otherwise the Crown would enjoy
'despotic powers and autocratic authority': F.O. 412/28, F.O. Conf. 5736, Correspondence
respecting Foreign Jurisdiction 1887–8, No. 4, Memo. by James Scoble 16 August 1887.

and was thus brought directly under the supervision of the British Government. The position was further regulated by an Act of 1836.[1] Need for proper regulation of extraterritorial jurisdiction was exacerbated by the Treaty of Nanking (August 1842) entered into at the close of the Opium War with China. This was expected to result in an increase of traffic by British subjects, as, in terms of the Treaty, Shanghai and other ports were opened while British subjects in China secured something of the capitulary privileges long enjoyed in the Ottoman Empire.[2] A further factor was that a Select Committee appointed in March 1842 'to enquire into the state of the British possessions on the West Coast of Africa more especially with reference to their relations with the neighbouring native tribes' had reported that criminal jurisdiction exercised by George Maclean, President of the Council of Merchants of Cape Coast (the Gold Coast), over the neighbouring tribes should be regularized.[3] Similar problems had arisen in respect of the Colony of Sierra Leone where an attempt had been made in 1841 to pass an Act (declared *ultra vires* by the Colonial Office) providing for extraterritorial jurisdiction over British subjects for offences committed beyond the frontier.[4]

As a consequence of the various extensions in foreign jurisdiction, the first Foreign Jurisdiction Act was passed in August 1843.[5] Its major purpose was to regulate Crown jurisdiction over British subjects who lived outside the British dominions and yet were not, in whole or part, subject to the jurisdiction of the country in which they were living. In order to leave the Crown unfettered the Act was deliberately widely drafted and permitted the Crown to exercise jurisdiction wherever 'by treaty, capitulation, grant, usage, sufferance, and other lawful means' it had come to enjoy such power.[6] This was the measure which, both by extensive interpretation and amendment, eventually provided the machinery of government in protectorates.

The Act was immediately interpreted on the Gold Coast as providing not only for the exercise by the Queen of jurisdiction over her own subjects in a

[1] Foreign Jurisdiction in Ottoman Dominions Act, 6 & 7 Will. IV, c. 78.

[2] *C.H.B.E.*, Vol. II, 'The New Empire', Cambridge, 1940, p. 575; Keith, *Governments*, op. cit., p. 491; C. P. Lucas, op. cit., pp. 213–15; Jenkyns, op. cit., pp. 242–66. Although in 1833 the Foreign Jurisdiction in China Act (3 & 4 Will. IV, c. 93) had been passed, the Law Officers had reported in December 1838 that Regulations controlling the conduct of the crews of British ships trading with China would, unless justified by positive treaty or implied permission from usage, be an infringement of China's sovereignty: McNair, *Opinions*, Vol. I, p. 70.

[3] *H.C. British Sessional Papers 1842*, Vol. XI, 'Report from the Select Committee on the West Coast of Africa', pp. v–vi. See G. E. Metcalfe, *Maclean of the Gold Coast*, Oxford, 1962, pp. 282–93; and *C.H.B.E.*, Vol. II, op. cit., pp. 666–7.

[4] *C.H.B.E.*, op. cit., pp. 666–7; and Newbury, op. cit., p. 547 quoting a Minute by James Stephen of 22 September 1841 on Extraterritorial Jurisdiction, Sierra Leone.

[5] 6 & 7 Vict. c. 94. There was little debate in either House when the Act went through.

[6] See Mr. Hope Scott's Memorandum where he advocated 'that great latitude should be allowed by the Act in its description of the means by which the jurisdiction has been, or may hereafter be, acquired, and of its extent and nature': Jenkyns, op. cit., p. 260.

foreign country, but also for jurisdiction over the subjects of a foreign power within the dominions of that foreign power itself. This extension was first made by an Order in Council of September 1844[1] appointing Cape Coast Castle a place for the trial of offenders under the Foreign Jurisdiction Act after the local chiefs had signed a treaty of 6 March 1844, known as the 'Bond', by which the signatories acknowledged that power and jurisdiction had been exercised on behalf of the Crown 'within divers places adjacent to H.M. forts and settlements on the Gold Coast' and that they, the 'chiefs of countries and places so referred to, . . . do hereby acknowledge that power and jurisdiction'.[2]

At this time the Imperial authorities made it clear that such jurisdiction 'must be founded on the assent and concurrence of the sovereign power of the state within which it is exercised, either express as in the case of the . . . [Bond], or implied from long usage as in the case of the long and general acquiescence which can be shown in many districts, in the authority hitherto exercised by Mr. McLean'.[3]

Subsequently in 1850 the Colonial Secretary, Earl Grey, laid it down that such extraterritorial jurisdiction could only be exercised in territories where a treaty had been concluded with the African chiefs.[4] Following this injunction the requisite treaties were concluded and an Order in Council extended jurisdiction over British subjects residing in countries under the dominion of native princes adjacent to Sierra Leone.[5]

Jurisdiction at this stage was purely judicial and, except for the fact that in areas adjacent to the Gold Coast forts it made 'foreigners', who were subjects of African chiefs, liable to both criminal and civil jurisdiction, was similar to that exercised in centres where capitulations had been entered into. Gradually the jurisdiction exercised in the Gold Coast came to be sharply distinguishable from the extraterritorial or consular jurisdiction that was exercised in Mahometan and other non-Christian states and states in the East.[6] Consular jurisdiction was limited to judicial matters and punishment of British subjects and

---

[1] Gold Coast Jurisdiction Order in Council of 3 September 1844, *Parl. Pap.*, 1855, xxxvii (383), p. 81.

[2] See G. E. Metcalfe, op. cit., pp. 292. For text of the Bond see *H.C. Sessional Papers 1865*, Vol. V, p. 419.

[3] Lord Stanley to Lt. Governor Hill 22 November 1844 quoted in *H.C. Sessional Papers 1865*, Vol. V, at p. 437. Indeed, where capital punishment was necessary, 'the execution must be carried into effect by the native authorities and take place in the country in which the offender is tried'.

[4] Newbury, op. cit., pp. 558–9, quoting Grey to Macdonald 24 July 1850.

[5] Order in Council of 13 July 1850, *S.P.*, Vol. xlviii, p. 1292. A similar Order in Council was issued on 25 November 1853 after the passage of an Act to provide that liberated Africans domiciled or resident in Sierra Leone should be deemed British subjects (16 & 17 Vict. c. 86). The position was later governed by the Sierra Leone Offences Act 1861 (24 & 25 Vict. c. 31) which dealt with crimes committed by British subjects in areas adjacent to the Colony and provided for their arrest and surrender to the Colonial Courts. Similar provision was made in 1863 to cover offences committed adjacent to the Cape Colony: 26 & 27 Vict. c. 35.

[6] Jenkyns, op. cit., p. 148.

certain classes of person who had been given British protection. Although the consuls administering the jurisdiction were also given power to make regulations subject to approval by a Secretary of State, in order to enforce the treaties whereby the jurisdiction had been obtained, or to secure the observance of native custom, or the peace, order and good government of British subjects,[1] the purpose of this exterritorial jurisdiction was, in fact, to secure personal protection to British subjects, satisfactory judicial tribunals, and protection of property such as was afforded British property by English law.[2] Orders in Council providing for the exercise of such jurisdiction could not confer on the consular court a jurisdiction wider than that agreed by the original treaty.[3] This position was entirely different from that which evolved in protectorates, where jurisdiction was exclusive and where eventually 'protection' extended not merely to persons resident in the protected territory but to the area itself, protection thus acquiring a territorial character.

Development of British protectorates in Africa

Britain's criminal and civil jurisdiction exercised under the Foreign Jurisdiction Act in the areas adjacent to the Gold Coast and Lagos gradually involved the Crown in duties of protection.[4] In 1856 an Order in Council referred to the 'protected Territories' and gave to the Supreme Court of the Gold Coast jurisdiction outside the forts in all matters in which Her Majesty might exercise jurisdiction without the co-operation of any native chief or authority.[5] By 1865, as a result partly of numerous treaties with the tribes

[1] Such power being given by Order in Council in 1865 in respect of China and Japan. See Piggott, *Exterritoriality*, Clowes, 1892, p. 111.

[2] *Secretary of State for Foreign Affairs* v. *Charlesworth Pilling & Co.*, [1901] A.C. 373 at 384.

[3] *Imperial Japanese Government* v. *P. & O. Company*, [1895] A.C. 644 at 658. The judgement is rather ambiguously worded as to the consequences of any conflict. It states that in such event the Court must conform (to the Order or to the treaty?) and the party must seek redress through diplomatic intervention (which party?). Jenkyns, op. cit., at p. 144 suggests that the Court may have to conform to the Order leaving the dissatisfied party to seek a diplomatic remedy. *Contra* Piggott, op. cit., (1907, ed. Butterworths) at p. 188 and at pp. 29 *et seq.* Piggott's views are wrong in the light of *Inland Revenue Commissioners* v. *Collco Dealings Ltd.*, [1961] 1 All E. R. 762 (H.L.).

[4] In the Report of the 1865 Select Committee at p. 2 the Assistant Under-Secretary of State for the Colonies, T. F. Elliot, denied that there was any protectorate over the tribes adjacent to Sierra Leone as there had been no mention of any protection. At p. 5 he considered that Britain 'exercised a protection but not a protectorate before annexation' of Lagos. At pp. 3 and 8 he denied any protectorate existed adjacent to the Gambia and stated that an earlier Governor of the Gambia in his zeal to obtain treaties had held out promises of protection to the chiefs but that these had been repudiated by Lord Stanley, the Secretary of State, who informed the Governor that no pledge of protection should ever be given. See also Newbury, op. cit., p. 227.

[5] Order in Council of 4 April 1865, quoted in *A Note on the History of the British Courts in the Gold Coast Colony with a brief account of Changes in the Constitution of the Colony*, by W. Brandford Griffith, Gold Coast Government Printer, 1936, at p. 16.

(some giving cession of territory, others agreeing to protection, and yet others agreeing to amity) and also because of the levying of a Poll Tax by resolution of the chiefs who were constituted into a 'Legislative Assembly' for this purpose in 1852, it was considered that Britain had assumed a protectorate over the tribes adjacent to the Gold Coast Forts.[1] This, the 1865 Parliamentary Select Committee on the West Coast of Africa considered, involved the Crown in 'an indefinite and unintelligible responsibility on our part, uncompensated by any adequate advantages to the tribes'.[2] The powers of the Crown in the area were at that time undefined and a 'Protectorate amounts in fact to whatever any Governor chooses to make of it'.[3] Indeed, when the Assistant Under-Secretary of State for the Colonies was asked how such jurisdiction of the Crown was used he could but reply: 'The whole thing is very new, it has but just sprung up.'[4] The most significant feature of the Report and the evidence was the emphasis placed on British responsibility and its concomitant disadvantages rather than on British power in the area in question.

Statements as to British powers were however scattered through the evidence and these revealed the opinion that the Crown had no power to tax without the consent of the chiefs as it was then considered that only British subjects could be taxed.[5] On the other hand, customs duties had been levied from 1823 but this was possible because they were levied in the port of entry, which was part of the Gold Coast Colony, and only indirectly affected the inhabitants of the protected area.[6] It was also suggested that the judicial powers exercisable under the Foreign Jurisdiction Act applied only to British

[1] See Kimble, op. cit., pp. 172 et seq. The Agreement—subsequently called the Poll Tax Ordinance—stated that 'having taken into consideration the advantages which the natives and chiefs derived from the protection afforded by Her Majesty's Government they considered it reasonable and necessary that the natives generally should contribute to the support of the Government by paying a tax and thereupon they agree to pay a tax': see Report of the 1865 Select Committee at p. 420: The Agreement called the Poll Tax Ordinance, 19 April 1852, whereby it was agreed that 1s. per head would be paid for 'every person residing in districts under British protection'.

[2] Draft Report of the 1865 Select Committee, p. xiv.

[3] Report (Evidence), p. 315 and at p. 319, Ross, Colonial Secretary of the Gold Coast. Governor Sir Benjamin Pine at p. 127 described 'the exceeding difficulty of exercising the jurisdiction and the undefined nature of it'.

[4] Report (Evidence), p. 6.

[5] ibid., pp. 47, 52, Colonial Ord.; p. 294, Governor Pine; p. 318, Colonial Secretary Ross. At p. 330 it was disclosed that the Secretary of State refrained from disallowing the Spirit Ordinance 1864, which required traders in spirits to take out a £2 annual licence, lest this damage the Governor's authority. But he had considered it 'beyond the letter of the law in imposing a tax on territory over which we did not claim to exercise any sovereignty'. The Governor maintained that he had consulted the chiefs in imposing this tax (at p. 304). See also H.C. Deb., 3rd ser., Vol. 177, col. 536, 21 February 1865 debating Adderley's motion for a Select Committee to consider the state of the British Establishments on the Western Coast of Africa in which the Governor was quoted as saying that he could not 'call on the inhabitants to supply either their labour or their money'. See later doubts regarding the Niger Districts Protectorate: Flint, op. cit., p. 56.

[6] For a short history of the application of the Navigation Acts and those regulating Trade with British Possessions see Newbury, op. cit., pp. 80 et seq.

subjects and should be amended to cover Africans.[1] Yet the same witness, who had earlier that year been commissioned to enquire into the condition of the West African settlements, considered that British rights should not be defined as it would only tend to the natives 'being led away by mischievous advisers who would make them aware of what they were told would be their rights; and would involve us in difficulties'. On the other hand, although there was doubt as to the extent of executive powers, the Governor considered he was empowered to issue orders and to see that these would be obeyed throughout the Protectorate: he might interfere in internal quarrels of the chiefs to maintain peace and could supervise the policy and defences of the Protectorate.[2] Indeed, the chiefs did 'not stop to question whether it was law or not' and the same position as in a colony obtained.[3] In practice, large powers over the native chiefs were assumed: the Gold Coast Colonial Secretary informed the Committee that 'we fine the native chiefs and we imprison them and treat them as if they were subjects of the Crown'.[4] Nonetheless, it was quite clear from the beginning that Britain did not claim any territorial sovereignty. Earlier, in 1841, Lord John Russell had said:

> Whatever influence Great Britain may exercise beyond those precincts, my supposition is that beyond the very walls of the forts there is no sovereignty, properly speaking, vested in the Crown; but that the whole adjacent country is subject to the dominance of the native powers.[5]

Again, in 1853, Lord Newcastle instructed the Governor to 'abstain from creating any supposition that these people by paying poll tax, place themselves on the footing of British subjects inhabiting the dominions of the Crown'.[6]

In view of British policy of that period which looked with disfavour on expensive intervention in West Africa, the Committee recommended that 'all further extension of territory or assumption of Government, or new treaties offering any protection to native tribes would be inexpedient'.[7] Despite this

[1] ibid., p. 329, Colonial Ord. *contra* Elliot at p. 2: any 'persons' could be charged with offences and he considered that this term included natives.

[2] ibid., Governor R. Pine at p. 287. Later the 'Fantee Confederation' was suppressed on the grounds that so long as tribes lived 'under the protection of Great Britain, the protecting Government must be consulted as to any new institutions which may be proposed': Newbury, op. cit., pp. 325–6 quoting Kimberley to Kennedy, 16 January 1872.

[3] ibid., at p. 298.

[4] ibid. at p. 315, Ross.   In 1848, 1858, and 1866 Fanti chiefs were punished and deposed: see Newbury, op. cit., pp. 300–1, 309–10, and 316–19. On the first occasion the Governor was censored for interfering beyond the British settlements. In 1861 the Acting Consul for the Niger Districts was reprimanded for deposing a chief, as British Consuls possessed no such authority. Newbury, op. cit., p. 395. In 1878 and 1883 further powers of control over the Gold Coast Chiefs and administration were taken by the Native Jurisdiction Ordinances: Kimble, op. cit., pp. 460–3.

[5] Appendix to the Report from the Select Committee on West Coast of Africa. *H.C. Sessional Papers 1842*, Vol. XII, p. 139, Russell to Maclean, 14 July 1841.

[6] 1865 Report, p. 440, Newcastle to Hill, 18 March 1853.   [7] ibid., p. iii.

recommendation British power continued to develop on the Gold Coast. In 1867 a Smuggling Ordinance and in 1868 a Spirit Licence Ordinance were passed, applied practically to the whole coastline, and enforced—although there was no authority for this.[1] Yet the extent of the jurisdiction was still confused. Lord Derby was quoted as having said in 1874 that: 'I greatly doubt whether any man in or out of the Colonial Office exactly knows or could define the limits of our activity and of our responsibility in regard to the tribes included within the protected territory.'[2]

By 1874 the Imperial Government decided to assert legislative authority in the Gold Coast by a device that was subsequently adopted in other cases: an Order in Council authorized the Legislative Council of the Gold Coast Colony (which had been constituted by Charter of 24 July 1874) to make Ordinances for the Protected Territories to the extent of Her Majesty's jurisdiction in such territories.[3] From that time on the Gold Coast legislative powers in both Colony and Protected Territory were regarded in practice as co-extensive.[4] Nonetheless direct taxes were not imposed.[5] The Gold Coast Protectorate was ultimately annexed under the Royal Prerogative and the British Settlements Act on 2nd September, 1901, after it had been pointed out by the Law Officers that there was still a distinction between Colony and Protectorate despite a Statute Law Revision Ordinance in 1895 which had purported to provide that the Protected Territories were part of the Gold Coast Colony.[6]

[1] W. Brandford Griffith, op. cit., p. 17.

[2] H.C. Deb., 3rd ser., Vol. 218, col. 1598, 4 May 1874, Sir W. Lawson. See also Lord Carnarvon, Vol. 219, c. 166, 12 May 1874.

[3] Order in Council of 6 August 1874. This was preceded by numerous treaties. See Hertslet, op. cit., Vol. I, pp. 390–2. Although a Draft Proclamation Defining the Nature and Extent of the Queen's Jurisdiction on the Gold Coast was prepared it was considered inexpedient to issue this. The Proclamation had asserted power to preserve the public peace, to protect individuals and property, to administer civil and criminal justice, to enact laws relative to crimes and property rights, to protect trade, to encourage public works, to maintain an armed police force, to settle chiefly disputes, to impose rates in villages, and to raise 'revenue by licences and customs and by such direct imposts as the native Chiefs or Rulers or a major part of them may agree to': Parl. Pap., 1875 [C. 1139], pp. 3–6.

[4] W. Brandford Griffith, op. cit., p. 19. A similar Order in Council was issued in 1887. The same expedient was adopted in respect of Lagos Colony and the adjacent Protectorate in 1887, in respect of the Gambia Colony and Protectorate in 1893, and in respect of Sierra Leone Colony and Protectorate in 1896.

[5] It was doubted whether the imposition of Hut Tax in 1897 in Sierra Leone was competent: C. Fyfe, A History of Sierra Leone, Oxford, 1962, p. 559.

[6] The Law Officers denied the power of the local legislature to change Protectorate into Colony: C.O. 96/347, L.O. to Chamberlain 21 September 1899. The Chief Justice, Brandford Griffith, advised that the protected territories be annexed to avoid the difficulties which had previously arisen from this distinction: 'when natives desired to embarrass the Government they would endeavour to draw a distinction between the powers of the Governor of the Colony and his powers in the Protected Territories and would ask for the treaties under which we exercised jurisdiction and the general absence of such treaties bred disaffection of a sort'. Difficulties also arose as to whether a place was in the Colony or Protected Territories, whether natives of the Territories were British subjects (R. W. Antrobus minuted

The development of British jurisdiction on the Gold Coast illuminates the progression from judicial powers to ultimate assumption of full power ending, in fact, in annexation.[1] In other areas there was from 1885 a similar faltering progression to the assumption of full powers—the doubts being more marked when the Foreign Office was in control of any area.

The Foreign Office had become involved in the development of protectorates when it decided, after research by Hertslet, the Foreign Office librarian, as to the nature of the protectorates,[2] to employ the protectorate system to prevent French and German expansion in the Niger and Oil Rivers and Cameroons areas of West Africa.[3] By 1885 the British Consul for the Oil Rivers area had, on Foreign Office instructions, entered into numerous treaties of protection with African chiefs while, at the same time, the National Africa Company (Ltd.) had secured treaties of cession from many chiefs in the Niger Basin.[4] Eventually on 5 January 1885 the first Foreign Office protectorate, the Niger Districts Protectorate, was established. The Foreign Office envisaged such a protectorate as amounting to a minimum form of control which would have the effect of excluding foreign interference. In this new Protectorate judicial powers would be exercised by a small local consular staff, while Britain would be saved the responsibility and expense of administration by the willingness of Mr. Goldie's National Africa Company to undertake the administration of the area in return for the grant of a charter. This would relieve Britain of her responsibilities occasioned by the Berlin West Africa Conference and the resulting Act of Navigation for the Niger[5] while the expense of and duty of executing these could conveniently be delegated to the future chartered company (ultimately the Royal Niger Company).[6]

By 1887 the Foreign Office recognized the value of the protectorate system as it considered that if formal protectorates were declared in areas where the authority of the Crown had not been precisely defined such declaration would prevent doubts in respect of Great Britain's claims to exclusive

on this memorandum that he thought they were), and whether they were subject to the West Africa Offences Act 1871: C.O. 96/37, Memorandum advocating Proclamation of Former Protected Territories on Gold Coast to be part of the Gold Coast Colony by W. Brandford Griffith C.J., 22 March 1900.

[1] The Gold Coast Protectorate was annexed by the Gold Coast Order in Council of 26 September 1901. It was 'making *de jure* what has for the last five years been *de facto*': C.O. 96/371, Memorandum by Brandford Griffith C.J., *supra*.

[2] Although he made no mention of the powers that had evolved on the Gold Coast: F.O. Conf. 4824, Memorandum by Sir E. Hertslet on the Protectorate of States, 24 April 1883. Hertslet defined a protectorate as implying 'an obligation on the part of a powerful state to protect and defend a weaker state against its enemies, in all, or in certain specified eventualities'.

[3] See Flint, op. cit., pp. 52 et seq.; Hargreaves, op. cit., at pp. 313–15 and 328–9.

[4] See Hertslet, op. cit., p. 457 et seq. By well settled constitutional practice a British subject who acquires territory does so on behalf of the Crown: *In re Southern Rhodesia*, *supra*, at p. 221.

[5] Hertslet, op. cit., pp. 39–43.

[6] See Flint, op. cit., p. 70 et seq.

influence. Indeed her rights 'would be fully secured without involving any interference with the internal administration of those countries by their present Rulers'.[1]

The legal basis of Crown power

The 1843 Foreign Jurisdiction Act, which had envisaged only the regularization of consular jurisdiction and the extra-territorial jurisdiction originally exercised on the Gold Coast, had been the legal instrument for this expansion. The Act had given the Crown power

to hold, exercise and enjoy any power or jurisdiction which Her Majesty now hath or may at any time hereafter have within any country or place out of Her Majesty's dominions, in the same and as ample a manner as if Her Majesty had acquired such power or jurisdiction by the cession or conquest of territory.[2]

It was clear from this formulation that the Crown might legislate in terms of the Foreign Jurisdiction Act.[3]

In a protectorate, since the Crown is authorized to exercise its power in as ample a manner as in a conquered or ceded territory, it has 'unfettered powers of every kind'[4]; it 'has a power to fix such terms and conditions as (it) thinks proper'[5]; and it 'may change and alter the laws of that Kingdom'.[6] The Crown, therefore, possesses 'absolute power subject to the provisions of any Act of Parliament to say from time to time what law should be applied'.[7] As Lord Halsbury said: 'There is no doubt that under such circumstances as these the Queen may make such laws as she pleases.'[8] The Crown may in practice interfere with the administration to such an extent that it is 'difficult to draw the line between a protectorate and a possession'.[9] Even where there is little internal intervention foreign relations are in all cases under the exclusive control of the Crown.

The sole limitation on the Crown's power was imposed by section 12 of the Foreign Jurisdiction Act which was in virtually identical terms to section 2

[1] F.O. 572/16, F.O. Conf. 5449, No. 3, Proposed British Protectorate, Pauncefote to Herbert, 13 January 1887. For other advantages see *infra*.

[2] Sec. 1.

[3] This was emphasized by R. S. Wright who relied on *Campbell* v. *Hall* in a Memorandum on the Nature and Limits of the Power of the Crown to legislate by Order in Council under the Foreign Jurisdiction Act, F.O. Conf. 5165*, 3 December 1884.

[4] *Calvin's Case* (1608), 7 Co. Rep. 1 at 176.

[5] *Campbell* v. *Hall*, 1 Cowp. 204 at 209.

[6] *Abeyesekera* v. *Jayatilake*, [1932] A.C. 260 at 264.

[7] *R.* v. *Crewe*, *supra* at 607.

[8] *R.* v. *Staples* cited in *R.* v. *Crewe* at p. 607. Lord Mansfield however suggested in *Campbell* v. *Hall* at 209 that the Crown 'cannot make any change contrary to fundamental principles'.

[9] *Sobhuza II* v. *Miller*, [1926] A.C. 518 at 523 per Viscount Haldane.

of the Colonial Laws Validity Act.[1] Thus an Order in Council in conflict with an Act of Parliament extending to Her Majesty's subjects in a country subject to that Order or any regulations thereunder, was to be read subject to such Act of Parliament, and was, to the extent of any repugnancy only, void. But the Crown was not bound by legislation prior to any Order in Council. In Staples' Case the appellant had been convicted by a judge and four assessors in Bulawayo for theft, and had appealed to the Privy Council submitting that Magna Carta entitled him to a jury trial. The appeal was dismissed on the basis that there would be an 'unreasonable limit on the Crown's powers of introducing laws fitting to the circumstances of its subjects in a foreign country, if it were made impossible to modify an Act of Parliament which, prior to the Order in Council, might be invoked as applicable to a British subject'.[2] Furthermore, the Crown could not, excepting by statute, deprive itself of freedom to make Orders in Council while later Orders might be inconsistent with previous Orders.[3] Finally the Crown was by virtue of its plenary power competent to legislate retrospectively by Order in Council.[4] In fact its legislative power was 'wholly unfettered' except as provided in the Foreign Jurisdiction Act.[5] Thus the Crown was able to exercise effective sovereignty in protectorates thereby obviating the necessity of annexation.

This extensive interpretation of the Crown's powers was not initially adopted. Gradually, however, powers were assumed in practice and were then formally regulated by Order in Council or by further parliamentary intervention. Thus power to legislate and to govern was assumed on the Gold Coast and was eventually regulated by Order in Council in 1874. Similarly in the areas adjacent to the other West African settlements consular jurisdiction was assumed by informal Equity Courts which decided disputes between British subjects and others. The West Africa Order in Council 1872 then regularized this jurisdiction in areas other than those which were under

---

[1] 28 and 29 Vict. c. 63.

[2] Heard in the Privy Council on 27 January 1899. Unreported, but reference is made to it in *R.* v. *Crewe* at pp. 607 et seq. See also dicta by Farwell L.J. at pp. 614–15. In *Salisbury Reef Gold Mining Co.* v. *B.S.A. Co.* (1898), 15 S.C. 375, de Villiers C.J. at 381 said that, although the law of the Cape Colony 'as nearly as the circumstances of the country permit' was to be applied, 'the law relating to trial by jury in civil cases never was in force in Rhodesia. The fact that there has never been a trial by jury either in civil or criminal cases, although not sufficient to abrogate the law if once introduced, goes far to prove that the circumstances of the country were considered not to admit of its introduction.' Jury trial in criminal cases only was introduced by the Juries Ordinance No. 4 of 1899 providing for a jury of nine men, or five or more men if nine were not available.

[3] *Sobhuza II* v. *Miller, supra* at 528–9 and *North Charterland Exploration Co (1910) Ltd.* v. *The King,* [1931] 1 Ch. 169 at 187. Thus the Crown could not irrevocably grant a constitution. Nor would any reservation of Crown power be necessary as the rule in *Campbell* v. *Hall* applies only to dominions of the Crown. In *Ol le Njogo* v. *Attorney-General* (1913), 5 E.A.L.R. 70 at 80 the Court misinterpreted dicta in *R.* v. *Crewe, supra* at pp. 606–7, and stated that had an irrevocable constitution been granted the East Africa Protectorate it would have become part of the dominions.

[4] *Sabally and N'Jie* v. *H.M. Attorney-General,* [1964] 3 W.L.R. 732.

[5] *North Charterland Exploration Co. (1910) Ltd.* v. *The King, supra* at 185.

6—C.H.L.S.R.

protection.[1] The Order however stipulated that voluntary submission to the jurisdiction was required of natives and of foreigners. Parliament was even prepared to extend jurisdiction over persons who were not British subjects. This it did by the West Africa Offences Act 1871 which gave the courts of the settlements jurisdiction over crimes committed either by British subjects or by those of uncivilized powers (natives) against British subjects or residents of the settlements if such crimes were committed within 20 miles of the settlement boundaries or those of adjacent protectorates.[2]

While Crown power had gradually been increasing through its practical application, there had been minor amendments of the Act to bring the legal position into line with developing practice. Thus in 1865 the Foreign Jurisdiction Amendment Act authorized the sending of offenders to particular possessions for trial.[3] A further Foreign Jurisdiction Amendment Act in 1866 provided for conferring on courts in British dominions jurisdiction in respect of acts committed outside such dominions.[4] Yet a further extension occurred in 1875 when preventive deportation, which over a course of years had been permitted in practice, was authorized after its legality had been challenged.[5] The first changes of great moment however occurred in 1878 as a result of the need to control British subjects who were penetrating into countries 'without regular government'. Jurisdiction was then conferred on Her Majesty over British subjects who were for the time being resident in or resorting to such a country.[6] The Crown was also given power to extend and adapt certain

[1] Areas under protection were excepted from the operation of the Order 'so as clearly to preserve intact any British jurisdiction of a non-consular character already existing': F.O. Conf. 4973, West Africa Draft Order in Council, Memo. by Sir F. S. Reilly, 27 Nov. 1882.

[2] 34 & 35 Vict. c. 8. The Act was occasioned by colonial decisions in 1870 that persons who were not British subjects could not be tried for offences committed beyond the colonial boundaries: Newbury, op. cit., pp. 572–5.

[3] 28 & 29 Vict. c. 116. It also made provisions as to the subjects of Indian princes in Indian protectorates where analogous developments were occurring.

[4] 29 & 30 Vict. c. 87. This also related to India: see W. Forsyth, *Cases and Opinions on Constitutional Law*, p. 232. Developments in India have not been discussed at length because India Office practice apparently did not affect Colonial Office or Foreign Office notions about protectorates until 1887. The standard work is C. P. Ilbert, *The Government of India*, 3rd ed., Oxford, 1915. The sections dealing with protectorates are virtually a reproduction of F.O. Conf. 5750, Indian and African Protectorates, Memo. by Ilbert, 24 January 1889.

[5] 38 & 39 Vict. c. 85. F.O. Conf. 5679, Memo. 873 by F. S. Reilly, 6 July 1874, discussed the illegality of transporting British subjects by ship once they were out of the extraterritorial jurisdiction. Despite these amendments the Law Officers considered in 1892 that the Foreign Jurisdiction Act did not confer powers of administrative but only of punitive deportation and advised that further legislation was necessary to allow the expulsion of persons dangerous to public peace and good order: F.O. Conf. 6347, No. 1*, Webster and Clarke to Salisbury, 15 June 1892, p. 4A. In practice such powers had previously been exercised in respect of Mashonaland in terms of a High Commissioner's Proclamation of 30 June 1891 authorizing the expulsion of persons endangering the peace.

[6] 41 & 42 Vict. c. 67, sec. 5. The precedent for this was the Pacific Islanders Protection Act 1875, 38 & 39 Vict. c. 51. Wight, op. cit., suggests that this section of the Foreign Jurisdiction Act was not in practice employed because it was expressly limited to 'subjects' and because by extensive interpretation and assumption of power under Section 1, its invocation proved unnecessary. However the section was relied upon as conferring jurisdic-

Imperial Acts dealing with extraterritorial matters in areas subject to its jurisdiction.

At the same time gradual changes were occurring in the scope of the Orders issued under the Foreign Jurisdiction Act. The West Africa Order in Council 1885, providing for consular jurisdiction and Regulations, brought within its provisions British subjects, British protected persons, natives of Africa whose chief had consented to the jurisdiction, and any person who submitted thereto, whereas the West Africa Order in Council 1872 had only conferred power to make Regulations for British subjects. An even greater jurisdiction was assumed by the South Africa Order in Council 1885.[1] This was wider in its scope as not only did it apply to British subjects and British protected persons, but to all persons within the limits of the areas covered by treaties entered into with Montsioa and Mankoroane, chiefs of the Baralongs and Batlapings respectively.[2]

Thereafter in 1888 the Foreign Office decided to rationalize its foreign jurisdiction by consolidating the Foreign Jurisdiction Act and by issuing a comprehensive Order in Council for Africa. The task of consolidation of the Act was delayed by disputes as to the compatibility of the exercise of foreign jurisdiction with rules of International Law, but the Africa Order in Council was prepared and brought into force on 15 October 1889. This laid down the basis for consular jurisdiction throughout the continent, except where other provisions were made. In practice, four local jurisdictions were established: one in the Oil Rivers Protectorate, another for the Congo Free State, one in the British sphere on the East Coast exclusive of the Dominions of the Sultan of Zanzibar, and one for the British sphere north of the Zambesi.[3] The consuls' judicial powers were properly regulated and defined and it was made clear by Article 99 that consuls were authorized to make Queen's Regulations for the peace, order, and good government of subjects with the approval of a Secretary of State, who was also given powers to apply to such areas laws of any of the African possessions with modifications and adaptations.[4]

tion when the West Africa Order in Council 1885 was under consideration: F.O. Conf. 4973, West Africa Draft Order in Council 1883, Memo. by Sir F. S. Reilly 27 November 1882. The Law Officers also relied on the section to justify action taken in New Guinea: L.O.R. 1884, F.O. Conf. 5121, p. 56A. James and Herschell to Derby, 11 December 1884.

[1] This was prepared at the behest of the Colonial Office, which, from the first exercise of its power in Bechuanaland Protectorate, took a broader view of its power than that taken by the Foreign Office which was apparently unaware of Gold Coast precedents until the eighteen nineties.

[2] The Law Officers, concerned with the International Law aspects of this Order, advised that although as against the Chiefs the Crown could lawfully acquire jurisdiction over foreigners, this jurisdiction, whatever its 'theoretical limits', should be exercised with care and could not 'safely be exercised without the assent of the powers concerned': F.O. Conf. 5440, pp. 47–48, Russell and Davey to Granville, 21 April 1886. They had earlier advised that Britain had no jurisdiction over the subjects of other civilized nations without the consent of their governments: McNair, op. cit., Vol. I, p. 45, citing opinion of August 1885.

[3] See F. E. Hodges, *Consular Jurisdiction in Her Majesty's Protectorate of the Niger Coast*, Stevens, 1895, p. 189.

[4] On this basis certain Gold Coast Ordinances were applied to the Niger Coast Protectorate.

The delay in preparing the consolidation Act was occasioned by fundamental differences of opinion between Jenkyns, the Senior Parliamentary
Counsel, and Ilbert of the India Office on the one hand, and Wright of the
Treasury on the other. Jenkyns and Ilbert considered that, although the Act
was not expressly limited in its application to British subjects,[1] it should be
made clear that, so far as English municipal law was concerned, the courts
established by the Crown in protectorates could exercise jurisdiction not only
over British subjects but over others. Whether used or not they felt such
powers should exist as a reserve. In addition they suggested powers of extradition should be taken in protectorates.[2] They argued that duties of protection
and the right to punish were correlative, that the corollary of responsibility
was control over persons, and that 'power to legislate for and punish persons
resorting there who are not natives of that state' was consistent with International Law.[3] Indeed, so far as International Law was concerned,

the act of state in excluding European powers from the protected state throws upon
the Queen the duty of rendering justice there to subjects of European powers and
therefore confers on the Queen the right to exercise legislative and judicial powers
over those within the protected state.[4]

Both Jenkyns and Ilbert in any event contended that 'the African protectorates constitute a new set of facts to which both municipal law and International Law will have to adapt themselves',[5] and that if municipal law asserted
a jurisdiction against foreigners International Law would grow out of such
assertion.[6] Jenkyns in particular urged that the question was not merely one
of law to be decided by lawyers, but that it was a major issue of 'policy of

[1] Hall in his *Foreign Jurisdiction* (1894), at p. 221 questioned whether sec. 1 of the Foreign
Jurisdiction Act applied to other than British subjects and Jenkyns in his *Foreign Powers*
(written in 1899) at p. 194 still doubted whether in municipal law the Crown had been given
statutory jurisdiction over foreigners. Eventually in *R.* v. *Crewe, supra* at pp. 596 and 625
Vaughan Williams and Kennedy L.JJ. held that although foreigners would not, on a strict
interpretation of the Act, be within the jurisdiction, contrary practice had brought them
within its scope.

[2] The Law Officers had ruled that the Extradition Act 1870 applied only to dominions
and possessions and that a foreign criminal could not be extradited from the extraterritorial
jurisdiction: *L.O.R. 1873*, F.O. Conf. 4259, p. 166A.

[3] F.O. Conf. 5736, Correspondence respecting Foreign Jurisdiction 1887–8. Memo on
Draft Foreign Jurisdiction Bill by Jenkyns and Ilbert, 18 June 1888; F.O. Conf. 5624*,
Memo. 859, Application of Principles of International Law to Foreign Subjects in British
Protectorates, Jenkyns, 26 October 1888, pp. 1, 5; F.O. Conf. 5750, Indian and African
Protectorates, Memo. by Ilbert, 24 January 1888, pp. 3 and 21.

[4] F.O. Conf. 6264*, Foreign Jurisdiction Bill, Notes on Clause for British Protectorates,
Jenkyns, 16 November 1888, p. 4. Such an opinion was contrary to the view of the Law
Officers that the mere declaration of a protectorate (over the Malay Peninsula) conferred
no sovereignty or jurisdiction upon the Crown in those states: F.O. Conf. 5246, James and
Herschell to Derby, 7 March 1885 at p. 103.

[5] F.O. Conf. 5750, Ilbert at p. 22.

[6] F.O. Conf. 5624*, Jenkyns, p. 1; F.O. Conf. 5750, Ilbert, p. 21; and F.O. Conf. 6264*
Jenkyns, Note B, 22 November 1888.

adopting a particular view of protectorates with reference to foreign policy and British world interests'.[1] Uppermost in the minds of both Jenkyns and Ilbert was the question of British jurisdiction in India: Britain should not lay down or assent 'to any general proposition of International Law which does not square with the Indian facts'.[2]

The adoption of these views was urged on the Prime Minister by Sir John Pauncefote who suggested that the Bill 'should be declaratory and to remove doubts and not framed as if importing any new power'.[3] However such opinions were heretical to Wright. The Law Officers had in a series of opinions from 1879 onwards ruled that Crown jurisdiction outside the British domin-ions depended in regard to natives upon the express terms of the treaty with the native sovereign and in regard to civilized foreigners on the consent of their own sovereign.[4] The opinions were politically motivated as Govern-ments of the time did not wish to take upon themselves the obligation of establishing and maintaining a jurisdiction sufficient to redress all wrongs of which foreigners might complain.[5]

Wright outspokenly opposed Jenkyns' and Ilbert's proposals:

Mr. Jenkyns proposes to 'declare' and enact that the Queen has 'jurisdiction' within the Protectorate over all natives and over all foreigners residing therein or resorting thereto: and this as a mere consequence of, or incident to, the Protectorate, and without reference to the assent or dissent of the native power in the one case or of the sovereign or the foreigner on the other.

Wright assumed such jurisdiction was confined to judicial matters

for if it were to be taken to include all the power and jurisdiction which could be exercised under the Foreign Jurisdiction Acts, the proposed Enactment would by a stroke of the legislative pen convert a 'Protectorate' into an arrangement under

---

[1] F.O. Conf. 5624*, Jenkyns, p. 12.

[2] F.O. Conf. 5750, Indian and African Protectorates. Memo. by Ilbert, 24 January 1889, p. 9; F.O. 412/28, Memo. on 1888 Draft Foreign Jurisdiction Bill by H. Jenkyns and C. P. Ilbert, 18 June 1888; and F.O. Conf. 5624*, Memo. 859, Memo. by Ilbert, 16 May 1888, p. 13 pointing out with reference to India that it was not politic to take the view that juris-diction was limited. This problem had long been concerning the India Office advisers: F.O. 412/28, F.O. Conf. 5736, No. 3, Fitzpatrick to James, 9 May 1887, pp. 2–3, stating that although their action had never been challenged 'our only course so long as Parliament will not help us is to keep the point as much as possible out of sight'. Ilbert considered that 'many questions arising out of jurisdiction over foreigners are discreetly shirked': F.O. Conf. 5750, p. 7.

[3] F.O. 412/28, F.O. Conf. 5736. Correspondence respecting Foreign Jurisdiction 1887–8, No. 35, Sir John Pauncefote to Lord Salisbury, 29 June 1888. Pauncefote argued that since the Crown had the same 'rights of legislation as in a Crown Colony (ergo over all persons therein)' it enjoyed power over foreigners.

[4] F.O. Conf. 4539, p. 55A. James and Herschell to Colonial Office, 3 August 1880; F.O. Conf. 5121, p. 56A. James and Herschell to Derby, 11 December 1884; F.O. Conf. 5246, p. 9, Lord Selborne L.C. to Pauncefote, 21 January 1885; ibid. at pp. 14B and C, Webster and Gorst to Col. Stanley, 10 August 1885; and F.O. Conf. 5440, pp. 47–48, Russell and Davey to Granville, 21 April 1886.

[5] F.O. Conf. 5246, No. 1, Note by Lord Selborne L.C., 3 January 1885 at p. 5 and Further Note, 11 January 1885, at pp. 6–7.

which the Queen in Council would have (although not free to exercise) every legislative, executive, and judicial power, including some power of taxation and power of deportation over the natives and foreigners. . . . It cannot be truly 'declared' that jurisdiction in this sense is involved in Protectorate nor can it properly be so 'enacted' without consideration by Parliament of the vast consequences which might ensue.[1]

All that should be done, in Wright's view, was to make minor verbal changes in the Act to bring it into line with the practice whereby jurisdiction was exercised over natives and foreigners submitting to the consular courts with the consent of their own governments. Wright's views prevailed and the clauses proposed by Jenkyns and Ilbert, declaring that in British protectorates the courts had jurisdiction over foreigners and that the Crown might provide for extradition, were eliminated.

Eventually the various Foreign Jurisdiction Acts were consolidated in 1890.[2] The 1890 Act was described as a consolidation and it did not make major changes in the law. However it is odd that the measure passed through the Commons without debate and that neither House was informed of the changes that had been occurring in practice through extensive interpretation of the Act viz. that it was employed not merely to regulate consular jurisdiction but for governmental and legislative purposes in areas where there had been 'delegations' of authority from the local Rulers. One important change occurred as a consequence of re-wording of section 4 of the Act. Previously, when questions as to the existence or extent of the Crown's jurisdiction in a foreign country arose, conclusive evidence on the question would be put before the Court by a Secretary of State, but the Court could nonetheless examine the instruments and means whereby the Crown acquired jurisdiction, and interpret its scope.[3] The new section provided that, if in any proceedings any question arose as to the existence or extent of the jurisdiction of the Crown in a foreign country, 'a Secretary of State shall, on the application of the Court (which must raise the question),[4] send to the Court within a reasonable time his decision of the question, and his decision shall for the purposes of the proceedings be final'. It has been held that: 'It is the duty of the Court to accept the statement . . . as conclusive upon the point.'[5] Such a section

---

[1] F.O. Conf. 5719, Foreign Jurisdiction, Memo. by R. S. Wright on the Foreign Jurisdiction Bill, 15 November 1888, pp. 1–2.

[2] 53 & 54 Vict. c. 37.

[3] See Piggott (1892 edition), pp. 58–59.

[4] *Contra* K. Polack, 'The Defence of Act of State in Relation to Protectorates', (1963) 26 *M.L.R.* 138 at 147 n. 64.

[5] *Duff Development Co.* v. *Kelantan Government*, [1924] A.C. 797 at p. 808. See also *The Fagernes*, [1927] P. 311 (C.A.) at 324 per Atkinson L.J. and at 330 per Lawrence L.J.; and *Sayce* v. *Ameer Ruler Sadig Mohammed Abbasi Bahawalpur State*, [1952] 2 Q.B. 390 (C.A.) at 393–5 per Somervell L.J. See also Denning L.J.'s remarks in *Nyali Ltd.* v. *Attorney-General*, [1956] Q.B. 1 at 14. Hall, *Foreign Jurisdiction* at pp. 150–1 adopted this view. *Contra* Piggott (1892 edition) at p. 58 who argued that such a significant change could not be intended in a consolidating Act.

made it impossible in English, colonial or protectorate courts to query the extent of the Crown's jurisdiction.[1]

Ironically, although Jenkyns' and Ilbert's opinions were rejected when the 1890 Foreign Jurisdiction Act was drafted, the Law Officers soon thereafter modified their views on International Law. The first step was taken in 1891 when they agreed that consent of a foreign power could confer jurisdiction over its subjects and that accession to the Acts of the Berlin and Brussels Conferences amounted to such consent.[2] Finally in 1895 the Law Officers held that 'the exercise of a protectorate in an uncivilized country imported the right to assume whatever jurisdiction over all persons may be needed for its effectual exercise' and that it was in each case a question of fact which powers or authority it was proper for the protecting power to assume.[3] Thus, without any amendment to the Foreign Jurisdiction Act, owing to the new view of International Law adopted by the Law Officers (by a stroke of the Law Officers' pens *pace* Wright), it was recognized that the Crown had absolute power (subject to Parliament) to provide for all aspects of the government of British protectorates.

Alternative basis of Crown power

Not only did the Crown possess powers under the Foreign Jurisdiction Acts but it is submitted that it enjoyed further powers by virtue of the Royal Prerogative. Hall has suggested that the Crown, in addition to powers under the Act, possesses prerogative powers.[4] Anson also makes a similar suggestion,[5] as does Hood Phillips.[6] There is also a dictum by Lord Haldane

[1] See Hall, *Foreign Jurisdiction*, p. 151, n. 1, who suggests that power in the Secretary of State authoritatively to determine the existence and extent of jurisdiction might afford the opportunity of avoiding inconvenient jurisdictional claims. However the extent of jurisdiction is examinable in order to determine whether habeas corpus can be issued in respect of a person detailed in such a territory: see *ex parte* Mwenya, [1960] 1 Q.B. 241 at 302 per Lord Evershed M.R. and at 306 per Romer L.J. Cp. dicta by Lord Denning M.R. in *Sabally and N'Jie* v. *H.M. Attorney-General*, [1964] 3 W.L.R. 732 at 741 that Crown jurisdiction in a Protectorate 'is in the eye of the law complete, because it cannot be challenged in any court of law. It is an act of state.' Indeed at p. 743 he considered that the *vires* of an Order in Council relative to a protectorate could not be challenged.

[2] F.O. Conf. 6207, pp. 10–11, confirming a Memo. at p. 11 written by J. Bramston in February 1891 on the draft South Africa Order in Council which was to govern the future Southern Rhodesia. See also F.O. Conf. 6347, pp. 96–98, 30 June 1892, confirming this view.

[3] F.O. Conf. 6796, Reid and Lockwood to Ripon, 14 February 1895, approving a draft despatch to Sir Brandford Griffith, Governor of the Gold Coast Colony.

[4] *Foreign Jurisdiction*, op. cit., at p. 10 and at pp. 223–5. See also Jenkyns, op. cit., p. 195 who suggests that the Crown at Common Law has power to legislate in respect of any portion of sovereignty it may acquire. This was Mr. Hope Scott's view in his Memorandum which led to the Act. Lord Stanley writing in 1844 to the Governor of Cape Coast on the granting of jurisdiction under the Act over tribes in the neighbourhood of the forts said: 'I am not to be understood as affirming that the exercise of that jurisdiction is not capable of being justified and maintained independently of any such sanction of the legislature': quoted in Report from the Select Committee on Africa (Western Coast), pp. 437 et seq.

[5] Anson, op. cit., p. 109.

[6] Hood Phillips, *Constitutional Law*, 3rd ed., Sweet & Maxwell, 1962, p. 752.

that the Crown possesses power under the Act 'or otherwise', and that Crown action can in any event be justified as an 'act of state',[1] while there are similar dicta in *R.* v. *Crewe.*[2] Kennedy L.J. also felt that the Crown was entitled to legislate 'independently of any statutory powers'.[3] The answer would seem to be that the authority exercised in terms of the Foreign Jurisdiction Act springs from the prerogative. The Act did not create a power but merely 'removed doubts regarding the operation of one branch of the already existing Prerogative rights of the Crown. If that is a correct appreciation of the effect of the section, then, when an instrument is made by virtue of section 1, it is not made simply *under* the Act, it is made under the Prerogative as explained by the Act.'[4] Thus 'orders made by virtue of section 1 are Prerogative Orders and not statutory orders'.[5] The wording of the Act seems to bear out this since the section declares that 'It is and shall be lawful for Her Majesty the Queen to hold, exercise and enjoy any jurisdiction which Her Majesty now has or may at any time hereafter have within a foreign country.'[6] Since the section refers to jurisdiction which the Queen 'now has' this could only be by virtue of the Prerogative before the enactment of the statute.[7]

The point seems to have been decided by Denning L.J. (as he then was) in *Nyali Ltd.* v. *Attorney-General,*[8] when he held that the Foreign Jurisdiction Act

does not extend the jurisdiction of the Crown at all. It only provides for the manner of exercising it. It says that the Crown can exercise its jurisdiction in the protectorate 'in the same and as ample a manner' as it exercises its jurisdiction in a country which has been conquered or ceded. This means that the Crown can exercise its jurisdiction by means of an Order in Council or otherwise, just as it can in a conquered or ceded country, but it does not enlarge the area of its jurisdiction.

Parker L.J. in the same case thought that 'Her Majesty governs by virtue of the prerogative.'[9] It would seem therefore that dicta by Farwell L.J. in *R.* v. *Crewe* are misleading. He had suggested that at common law the Crown had

---

[1] *Sobhuza II* v. *Miller,* [1926] A.C. 518 at 524, 525, and 528.

[2] *Supra* at pp. 606, 624, and 628. There had been suggestions to this effect on a number of occasions by the Crown's legal advisers: F.O. 412/28, Conf. 5736, Correspondence Respecting Foreign Jurisdiction 1887–8, No. 3, Fitzherbert to James, 9 May 1887 at p. 3; F.O. Conf. 5719, Memo. on Foreign Jurisdiction Bill by R. S. Wright, 15 November 1888 at p. 2; F.O. Conf. 6264*, Foreign Jurisdiction Bill, Notes on Clause for British Protectorates, H. Jenkyns, 16 November 1888 at p. 4.

[3] ibid. at p. 626.

[4] 'The Authority of the United Kingdom in Dependent Territories' at p. 20. Essay by Sir Kenneth Roberts-Wray in *Changing Law in Developing Countries,* ed. J. N. D. Anderson, Allen & Unwin, 1963. See Jenkyns, op. cit., p. 194, who states that the Act 'does not confer jurisdiction on the Crown, but merely enables the Crown to exercise jurisdiction obtained *ab extra*'.

[5] Roberts-Wray, op. cit., at p. 25.   [6] 53 & 54 Vict. c. 37, sec. 1.

[7] See also Ridge's *Constitutional Law,* op. cit., p. 554, which suggests that the Act placed on a statutory basis the Crown's prerogative powers based on allegiance and the power to accept cession of jurisdiction, or to take it by force of arms, or to exercise it without challenge.

[8] *Supra* at p. 14.

[9] *Nyali Ltd.* v. *Attorney-General, supra* at p. 33. See Jenkyns, op. cit., p. 153, who states

no power of legislation outside its dominions, that except as obtained by treaty, capitulation, grant, usage, sufferance, and other lawful means, it had no jurisdiction outside its dominions, and that the authority for the Crown's powers rested therefore on an Act of the Imperial Parliament.[1]

Even though it be conceded that the Crown governs by virtue of the Prerogative, when a statute either confers on the Crown similar powers or regulates their use, then the Prerogative is superseded to the extent that the Crown can only act in accordance with the statutory provisions and 'its prerogative power is in abeyance'.[2] In any event, the powers enjoyed by the Crown in terms of the Act are so extensive that the question of invoking alternative powers could scarcely arise.

The confused state of opinion on Crown powers in protectorates in the late nineteenth century

Despite the passage of the consolidated Foreign Jurisdiction Act 1890 many problems relative to both the International Law and municipal constitutional law aspects of protectorates were unsolved. Although some of these were subsequently determined either by Colonial or Foreign Office practice or by later judicial interpretation, even today certain aspects of the scope of Crown power are controverted.

Method of acquisition of jurisdiction

The Foreign Jurisdiction Act enumerated 'treaty, capitulation, grant, usage, sufferance and other lawful means' as being the methods whereby the Crown acquired jurisdiction in foreign countries. Although the Act envisaged

that the Act does not confer jurisdiction on the Crown 'but facilitates the exercise by the Crown and its officers of the jurisdiction acquired *ab extra*'; and *Secretary of State for India* v. *Sardar Rustam Khan*, [1941] A.C. 356 at 369 per Lord Atkin who states that 'the statute does not increase the powers given to His Majesty in a foreign country'. There is also a dictum in *Papayanni* v. *The Russian Steam Navigation and Trading Co.*, *supra* at p. 185 that 'the effect of section 1 is that the jurisdiction of the British Consul . . . became, with the limits within which it existed by usage or sufferance, liable to be regulated by Order in Council'. See Roberts-Wray, op. cit. at p. 25 who suggests jurisdiction may also be lawfully exercised by Letters Patent. In *Jephson* v. *Riera* (1835), 3 Knapp 152 charters were used as instruments. *Cameron* v. *Kyte* (1835), 3 Knapp 332 envisages the use of Instructions under the Royal Sign Manual and Signet.

[1] *Supra* at p. 611–12. Fawcett, op. cit., p. 125 submits—on the analogy of common law power to legislate for territories acquired by settlement or occupation—that the Crown had no prerogative powers. Fawcett also emphasizes that at common law the English courts had no extraterritorial jurisdiction and that it was found necessary to enact the Foreign Jurisdiction Acts. Cp. Jenkyns, op. cit. at p. 195 who suggested the analogy should be Crown power to legislate in conquered or ceded territory and that similar rules should apply to any portion of sovereignty acquired.

[2] *Attorney-General* v. *de Keyser's Royal Hotel Ltd.*, [1920] A.C. 508 at 539 per Lord Atkinson, at 554 per Lord Moulton, and at 561 per Lord Sumner. See also dicta by Russell L.J. in *Sabally and N'Jie* v. *H.M. Attorney-General* at 749.

jurisdiction based on acquiescence the Colonial Office originally held that an express grant of jurisdiction was necessary before powers could be exercised.[1] The Foreign Office also adopted this attitude stating, in a circular of 2 July 1844 quoting the Earl of Aberdeen, that the right to exercise jurisdiction 'depends originally on the extent to which that right has been conceded by the Sultans of Turkey to the British Crown and, therefore, the right is strictly limited to the terms in which the concession is made'.[2] However, by 1867 the Law Officers advised in respect of certain Indian principalities that formal treaties were unnecessary and that consent might be 'evidenced by acquiescence, usage and sufferance'.[3] In practice political jurisdiction outside the Crown's dominions was assumed and exercised by British officials—particularly by those stationed in British India. When an official queried the validity of such action the Secretary of State for India in 1875 replied: 'Go on as best you can, and do not trouble yourself about nice points of that sort.'[4]

Although the India Office thought that the exercise of jurisdiction could not, owing to the doctrine of act of state, be challenged in the courts,[4] the Law Officers and legal advisers to the Treasury and the Colonial Office still concerned themselves with International Law aspects of the assumption of jurisdiction. In 1884 and again in 1893 the Law Officers considered that the question whether jurisdiction had been acquired was dependent on the terms of the particular treaty on which the Crown relied.[5] It was thought by English lawyers of the time that the exercise of jurisdiction could only be reconciled with International Law on the hypothesis that jurisdiction had either been acquired by settlement, cession, or delegation, and that it was otherwise merely consular jurisdiction.[6] In fact, when justifying in 1893 the jurisdiction exercised in various protectorates, the Foreign Office adopted the view that the assumption of internal sovereignty had occurred with the consent of the rulers of these territories.[7]

[1] Cf. Lord Stanley's and Earl Grey's rulings in 1844 and 1850 respectively.

[2] *Papayanni* v. *The Russian Steam Navigation and Trading Co.* at p. 167.

[3] Forsyth, op. cit., p. 232. See also *Papayanni* v. *The Russian Steamship Navigation Co.* (*The Laconia*), 2 Moo. P.C. (N.S.) 161 at 181: 'Consent may be expressed in various ways by constant usage permitted and acquiesced in by the authorities of the State, active assent, or silent acquiescence, where there must be full knowledge.' *The Laconia* was in fact relied on by Jenkyns as the basis for the acquisition of Crown jurisdiction in uncivilized states: F.O. Conf. 5624*, Memo. 859, Applications of Principles of International Law to Foreign Subjects in British Protectorates, H. Jenkyns, 26 October 1888, at p. 10.

[4] F.O. 412/28, Correspondence respecting Foreign Jurisdiction 1887–8, No. 3, Fitzpatrick (Secretary, Legal Department, Government of India) to James, 9 May 1887 at p. 2.

[5] F.O. Conf. 5121, p. 2A, James and Herschell to Colonial Office, 15 November 1884; and F.O. Conf. 6508, pp. 100–1, Russell and Rigby to Rosebery, 8 May 1893, where the Law Officers considered whether the Sultan of Zanzibar's concession to the British East Africa Company conferred criminal jurisdiction over natives.

[6] F.O. 412/28, Correspondence respecting Foreign Jurisdiction 1887–8, No. 18, Memo. by Davidson and Wright, 19 December 1887, pp. 16–20.

[7] *L.O.R. 1893*, F.O. Conf. 6508, p. 2, Memo. by A. Gray in consultation with the Foreign Office, 9 June 1893.

By the mid-eighteen nineties legal views were, however, expediently adapted to justify the factual assumption of power by Britain and it was considered that mere sufferance—at best an implied grant—was sufficient to found jurisdiction.[1]

Eventually in 1899 Jenkyns wrote that:

jurisdiction will depend on the existence in fact of the assumption of the protectorate, and not on the question whether some naked chief living in the country is or is not sufficiently civilized to cede jurisdiction, or has or has not by some informal agreement in fact ceded it. It really seems absurd that the question of the jurisdiction of a British court should depend upon such points.[2]

Thus in practice Britain conveniently changed her views of the legal requirements, frequently fictitiously satisfied these, and exercised power over large tracts of Africa on the 'assumption that every act done by Her Majesty's Government ... is in the name of, and by and with the consent of the natives'.[3]

Limitations on the Crown

Originally the attitude was adopted that the Crown could only act within the scope of the powers acquired by it.[4] Although International Law did not recognize the rulers of uncivilized communities, the British Government 'much regarded' the 'due observance of these treaties' and attempted to observe any agreements concluded with such rulers 'as in the case of treaties with civilized powers. They are concluded by the British sovereign as with an equal Sovereign Prince.'[5] In practice many of the provisions of such treaties

[1] *H.C. Deb.*, 4th ser., Vol. 19, col. 1039, 11 December 1893. Mr. Buxton informed the House with reference to the exercise of jurisdiction over Lobengula's subjects that 'The Foreign Jurisdiction Act authorizes the exercise of jurisdiction over other than British subjects and it contemplates the acquisition of jurisdiction not only by Treaty and Grant but by usage and sufferance.'

[2] Jenkyns, op. cit., pp. 179–80. See also Westlake, op. cit., p. 144: 'jurisdiction is not based on the consent of those who are ignorant of the meaning of civilized government'. Cp. the position in countries in which consular foreign jurisdiction was exercised where the treaty conferring the jurisdiction was the foundation of power and made the Queen an authority of that country: *Secretary of State for Foreign Affairs* v. *Charlesworth Pilling & Co.*, supra at 385.

[3] For this fiction see the Gold Coast Protectorate documents quoted in Newbury, op. cit., pp. 447–8.

[4] A. B. Keith, *The Constitution, Administration and Laws of the Empire*, Collins, 1924, p. 269.

[5] Piggott, op. cit. (1892 edition), pp. 4–8. Cp. C.O. 87/25, Minute by J. Stephen on the Implications of the Kataba Treaty, 6 September 1841, where the writer emphasized Lord Palmerston's prohibition against the use of 'Diplomatic language' in such circumstances: 'Compacts ... made with African chiefs should be described as "Arrangements or Agreements". .... The distinction is not verbal or trivial. It means to reserve to the Secretary of State for Foreign Affairs his own exclusive power of negotiating Treaties, and it is also meant to mark the distinction between Agreements with barbarous Chiefs and the international Compacts of Civilized States. For example, a Treaty must be ratified under the

were incorporated in Orders in Council or statutes dealing with the particular territory,[1] and in all normal cases the Crown would attempt to act in terms of the provisions of the treaty in question.[2]

It was at first considered that there was a division of sovereignty between the Crown and the chiefs,[3] but by 1900 there was, in practice, no longer any idea on the part of the Colonial Office that sovereignty was divided between the Crown and chiefs where cession occurred by treaty. Chamberlain ruled in respect of Lewanika's Concession of 1899 that 'the Queen's authority has already taken the place of that of Lewanika and the grants made by him will be only operative so far as they are ratified by Her Majesty or are not inconsistent with the Order in Council'.[4] On the other hand the Foreign Office and subsequently the Colonial Office adopted the view that the Uganda Agreement of 1900 left residual sovereign powers with the Kabaka of Buganda, and decisions in the courts of the Protectorate upheld this view in 1907 and 1908.[5] Subsequent cases have stated that in a protectorate there is a 'division of sovereignty in the hands of protector and protected',[6] and that 'it would be idle to contend that sovereignty is destroyed by the fact that a protecting power has charge of foreign relations'.[7] However, although some national sovereignty in theory remained in such rulers there was no mechanism for vindicating their rights as International Law of the period took no cognisance of these. Indeed disregard of their rights would not even incur international disapprobation.[8]

Great Seal, and with the advice of the Privy Council—form which would be totally misplaced in these cases.'

[1] e.g. The Northern Rhodesia Order in Council 1911. Similar action was taken in Nigeria and in Buganda (*Mukwaba and Others* v. *Mukabira and Others*, 7 Uganda L.R. 74 at 120), and parts of the Treaty of Waitangi 1840 were incorporated in New Zealand statute law (*Hoani Te Heuheu Tukino* v. *Aotea District Maori Land Board*, [1941] A.C. 308).

[2] In Buganda Britain consistently sought to act within the scope of the Uganda Agreement 1900 and, in fact, purported to rely on Article 6 of the Agreement in withdrawing recognition from Kabaka Mutesa II in 1953. See Cmd. 9320, p. 4, and *Mukwaba* v. *Mukabira*, *supra*. Buganda was in practice treated as if it were a protected state: Cmd. 9028, p. 34; S. A. de Smith, 'Constitutional Monarchy in Buganda', *Political Quarterly*, Vol. XXVI, January–March 1955, pp. 4 et seq.; and D. A. Low and R. C. Pratt, *Buganda and British Overrule*, Oxford, 1960.

[3] See Hall, *Foreign Powers*, pp. 223 et seq.

[4] African 656, No. 65, Colonial Office to British South Africa Company, 8 May 1900.

[5] *Katozi* v. *Kabizi*, 1907, Uganda L.R., Vol. I, p. 22; and *Nasanairi Kibuka* v. *A. E. Bertie Smith*, 1908, Uganda L.R., Vol. I, p. 41.

[6] *Sobhuza II* v. *Miller*, [1926] A.C. 518 at 523 per Lord Haldane. See also *Ol le Njogo and Others* v. *The Attorney-General and Others* (1913), E.A.L.R. 70 at 91, per Morris Carter C.J. who held that a protectorate 'presupposes the existence of both a protecting and protected state and the continuance in the latter of some elements of sovereignty'. At p. 92 the learned Chief Justice continued: 'Until annexation takes place the territorial sovereignty must be taken to be in suspense or it, or some part of it, must be taken to remain in the native authorities.'

[7] *Duff Development Co.* v. *Kelantan Government*, [1924] A.C. 797 at 815 per Viscount Finlay.

[8] This was so in the earlier period of Western European expansionism. From the beginning of the twentieth century there were, however, changes in international attitudes.

From the viewpoint of English municipal law the Crown, later cases declared, was not bound by any treaties by which it originally acquired its jurisdiction[1]: 'Rights purporting to be conferred by such a treaty of cession cannot be enforced in the municipal law.'[2] This view has recently been confirmed by Denning L.J.:

Although the jurisdiction of the Crown in a protectorate is in law a limited jurisdiction, nevertheless the limits may IN FACT be extended indefinitely so as to embrace almost the whole field of government. . . . The courts themselves will not mark out the limits. They will not examine the treaty or grant under which the Crown acquired jurisdiction nor will they enquire into the usage and sufferance or other lawful means by which the Crown may have extended its jurisdiction. . . . Once jurisdiction is exercised by the Crown the Courts will not permit it to be challenged.[3]

It seems therefore that the courts will look at any instruments issued by the Crown to see what jurisdiction the Crown has in fact exercised and that these 'are conclusive as to the extent of the Crown's jurisdiction'.[4]

Furthermore, it is generally accepted that the doctrine of 'Act of State' precludes any British court from challenging acts performed by the Crown or its authorized agents acting under the Royal Prerogative against foreign subjects in foreign territory. The courts are not permitted jurisdiction over claims arising out of the assumption of sovereignty or 'to enquire into the consequence of acts of the British Government which are inseparable from the extension of its sovereignty'.[5] Perhaps the doctrine has best been defined by Professor Wade: 'Act of State means an act of the Executive as a matter of policy performed in the course of its relations with another State, including

[1] *Sobhuza II* v. *Miller*, [1926] A.C. 518 at 528; Jennings' *Constitutional Law of the Commonwealth*, Vol. 1, 'The Monarchies', at p. 17; *Tshekedi Khama and Bathoen Siepapitso Gaseitsiwa* v. *The High Commissioner* reported in Colonial Reports, Bechuanaland Protectorate, 1936, No. 1809, p. 35, where Watermeyer J. (later Chief Justice of the Union of South Africa) ruled that an answer by the Secretary of State that the Crown's power was not limited by treaty or agreement is conclusive; *Mukwaba* v. *Mukabira*, *supra*—litigation involving the Uganda Agreement of 1900 where it was held that the Crown was not bound by the terms of the Agreement. Cp. Piggott, op. cit. (1892 edition), p. 119, and Hall, op. cit., writing in 1894, who considered that the Crown was bound by the treaties by which it obtained jurisdiction. However, Jenkyns writing in 1899 (op. cit. at p. 194) already considered it doubtful 'whether a convention with a half-savage tribe or its chief can be considered to be a treaty conferring jurisdiction'.

[2] *Hoani Te Heuheu Tukino* v. *Aotea District Maori Land Board*, [1941] A.C. 308, where the Judicial Committee refused to enforce the New Zealand Treaty of Waitangi, 1840. See also *Cook* v. *Sprigg*, [1899] A.C. 572.

[3] *Nyali Ltd.* v. *Attorney-General*, [1956] Q.B. 1 at 14 per Denning L.J. (as he then was). Lord Denning M.R. in *Sabally and N'Jie* v. *H.M. Attorney-General*, *supra* at 741 reiterated these views and at 743 stated that the exercise of Crown jurisdiction in a protectorate by means of an Order in Council was unchallengeable.

[4] *Nyali Ltd.* v. *Attorney-General*, *supra* at p. 14.

[5] D. P. O'Connell, *The Law of State Succession*, Cambridge, 1956, p. 88 and pp. 85–90 on Act of State.

its relations with the subjects of that State unless they are temporarily within the allegiance of the Crown.'[1] The Courts have held that 'In the event of such an act of state occurring, it may be just or unjust, politic or impolitic, beneficial or injurious. . . . These are considerations into which this Court cannot enter. It is sufficient to say that even if a wrong has been done it is a wrong for which no municipal court of justice can afford a remedy.'[2]

In practice, the doctrine has been interpreted to mean that native inhabitants of protectorates cannot challenge the right of the Crown to act by virtue of the Prerogative. Such 'despotic power' was not originally claimed by the Crown and only after the decision in *R.* v. *Crewe* in 1911 did it become generally accepted that the Crown had such far-reaching powers.[3] This view is based on judicial dicta that, despite the declaration of a protectorate, the territory in question remains not British but foreign.[4] In a protectorate the Crown has power and jurisdiction but not territorial dominion, as it does not possess 'that absolute ownership which was signified by the word *dominium* in Roman Law, and which, though not quite satisfactorily, is sometimes described as "territorial sovereignty"'. Since, in spite of the Crown's unfettered powers and the declaration of a protectorate, 'the protected country remains in regard to the protecting state, a foreign country; . . . the inhabitants of the protectorate, whether native-born or immigrant settlers, do not by virtue of the relationship between the protecting and the protected state become subjects of the protecting state'.[5] As a result the inhabitants do not owe allegiance to the Crown, which is only owed by British subjects properly so called. They would, however, as British-protected persons, owe a limited obedience as an equivalent in return for Crown protection.[6] Such obedience

---

[1] 'Act of State in English Law' by E. C. S. Wade, *B.Y.B.I.L.*, 1934, p. 98 at 103. This definition covers distinct situations: the rule that no action can be brought in British Courts on a treaty; the rule that when the Crown annexes territory it does not succeed to the obligations of the former government; and the rule that Crown action against a foreigner in a foreign country is not justiciable. See also the definition of Fletcher Moulton L.J.: an Act of State is 'essentially an exercise of sovereign power and hence cannot be challenged, controled or interfered with by municipal courts. Its sanction is . . . that of sovereign power': *Salaman* v. *Secretary of State for India*, [1906] 1 K. B. 613 at 639.

[2] *Secretary of State for India* v. *Kamachee Boye Sahaba* (1859), 13 Moo. P.C. 22. See also *Vajesingji Joravarsingji* v. *Secretary of State for India*, [1924] L.R. 51 I.A. 357 at 360 per Lord Dunedin who considered the right to enforce a treaty remained 'only with the high contracting parties'—fanciful language to describe Crown dealings with an African tribe as was shown by the Masai Land Case—*Ol le Njogo* v. *Attorney-General, supra*.

[3] In *R.* v. *Crewe* the Crown was held entitled to detail a chief; in Sobhuza's Case, and the North Charterland Case, the Crown was entitled to expropriate land, and in the 'Kabaka Case', withdrawal of recognition of the Kabaka of Buganda was permitted.

[4] *Staples* v. *The Queen*, 1899, an unreported Privy Council decision cited in *R.* v. *Crewe, supra* at 586. See *dicta* by Kennedy L.J. in *R.* v. *Crewe, supra*, at 620, by Vaughan Williams L.J. at 603, by Farwell L.J. at 611 and also by Lord Haldane in *Sobhuza II* v. *Miller, supra* at 523.

[5] *R.* v. *Crewe, supra* per Kennedy L.J. at 619.

[6] ibid. at p. 620 confirming *The Ionian Ships* (1855), 2 Sp. Ecc. and Adm. 212 at 226 per Mr. Lushington. This was followed in *Ol le Njogo* v. *Attorney-General, supra* at 77. In many

might, in fact, be demanded to a practically unlimited extent. Nevertheless there were considerable doubts in practice on this point in 1898, when the Law Officers doubted whether a British-protected person could be charged with treason.[1]

These however are still vexed questions. It has been argued [2] that this ortho-dox view as to the rights and liabilities of British-protected persons is incorrect. The counter-argument is based on the premise that the exclusion of the defence of act of state and the incidence of the law of treason are both correlative and geographically co-extensive. The learned writers suggest that *R. v. Joyce, supra*, has laid down that persons enjoying protection are subject to the law of treason, and that therefore inhabitants of protectorates may owe allegiance and may not have the defence of act of state successfully raised against them. This argument though weighty can be questioned since the mere fact that there is in practice a striking correlation between allegiance and protection in relation to the law of treason and the occasions on which the defence of act of state is incompetent does not necessarily mean that those persons who can commit treason are those who cannot have an act of state pleaded against them. Indeed, if the authorities on act of state are examined, the expressed reasons for which the defence has failed have been, not because the court has found that allegiance was owed, but because the plaintiff has been a British subject even if only 'for the time being in virtue of local allegiance' or has occupied the 'position of an ordinary subject'.[3] Nonetheless it must be admitted that, if the arguments adduced by Glanville-Williams and Polack are placed before a court, and if the court wishes to adopt a construction favouring liberty, it will be possible to distinguish the earlier decisions.

It will however be more difficult to distinguish the *dicta* in relation to act

protectorates Africans, who were merely British-protected persons and not British subjects, were on the basis of this distinction until recently denied franchise rights, e.g. in Northern Rhodesia. In Southern Rhodesia Africans were not at any time disqualified on this basis since from the first franchise legislation in 1898 they could qualify, provided they met the other requirements, by taking an oath of allegiance.

[1] Fyfe, op. cit., p. 590, referring to the 1898 Sierra Leone Hut Tax Rebellion. For an earlier opinion to the same effect given in 1855 see McNair, *Opinions*, Vol. I, p. 40. *Dicta* in *The Ionian Ships, supra*, confirmed this view. The point can at most be said to have been set-tled by implication in *R. v. Joyce*, [1946] A.C. 347. See also H. Lauterpacht 'Allegiance, Diplomatic Protection and Criminal Jurisdiction over Aliens' (1947) 9 C.L.J. 330 at 341.

[2] See Glanville Williams in 'The Correlation of Allegiance and Protection' (1948) 10 C.L.J. at 63 et seq. and Kenneth Polack in 'The Defence of Act of State in Relation to Protectorates' (1963) 26 M.L.R. 138.

[3] See *Walker v. Baird*, [1892] A.C. 491 at 494; *Johnstone v. Pedlar*, [1921] 2 A.C. 262 per Viscount Finlay at 272, per Viscount Cave at 276, per Lord Atkinson at 282, Lord Sumner at 292, and Lord Phillimore at 295 and 297. See also Sir J. Salmond in 'Citizenship and Allegiance' (1902) 18 L.Q.R. pp. 49–50, who states that a resident alien becomes for the time being a British subject. It is submitted that the real reason why an act of state is not possible within the realm against a subject is because the Crown may not change the law or legal rights by its own act. Exclusion of the defence of act of state therefore depends not on questions of allegiance *per se*, but on the absence of Crown power by prerogative to seek to interfere with legal rights.

of state in protectorates in *R.* v. *Crewe* and *Sobhuza II* v. *Miller* as being merely *obiter*[1]: they were alternative *rationes decidendi*, and are therefore binding.[2] Another difficulty is that there is a clear conflict between the authorities that British-protected persons are not British subjects and do not owe allegiance, and any extensive interpretation of the *ratio* in the Joyce Case. A factor favouring a narrow interpretation of that decision is that a great extension in the incidence of the law of treason would otherwise follow.[3]

The second line of attack on the validity of the defence of act of state in protectorates, viz. that protectorates may in reality be part of Her Majesty's dominions, is less persuasive than the first argument advanced by Williams and Polack. There are numerous dicta that protectorates are foreign countries.[4] Furthermore, despite the ambiguous *dicta* in *In re Southern Rhodesia*[5] as to whether territory could not factually be annexed without a proclamation, the point that the Crown cannot be forced to take territory unto itself has been decided by the Privy Council in *R.* v. *Staples* cited at length in *R.* v. *Crewe*, *supra*. The Lord Chancellor's judgement in Staples' Case is quite explicit:

I do not know at present—perhaps you will show me if I am wrong—any mode in which a territory which the Sovereign Herself declines to accept as a part of Her Dominions, can be made part of Her Dominions. I never heard of such a thing being done. It is unknown in International Law that you can force any country to take territory they have never assumed the sovereignty of.

Their Lordships then went on to recognize that the Crown could 'acquire large powers of administration: in some so large that the native ruler has a very limited range of sovereign power left to him'. The country would remain 'still a foreign state'.[6]

Perhaps the differing views can be reconciled on the basis that in International Law colonial protectorates are treated as having been annexed, but

---

[1] Polack, op. cit., pp. 139, 155.

[2] Incidentally, although the point was not taken in *R.* v. *Salaman*, *supra*, the Indian state in question was clearly a protectorate. Thus the plaintiff was a British protected person injured by acts of the East India Company and the Crown in a protectorate but was unable to obtain redress. A possible ground of factual distinction in Sobhuza's case would be that land rights were involved and not *habeas corpus* but this does not apply to *R.* v. *Crewe*.

[3] Lauterpacht: 'Allegiance', op. cit., at 341 suggests that it may be that Joyce's Case merely establishes that an alien already subject to the duty of allegiance, because of his residence in the realm, continues to owe allegiance if, on leaving the realm, he applies for and obtains the continued protection of the Crown.

[4] The most recent *dicta* appear in *Sabally and N'Jie* v. *H.M. Attorney-General*, [1964] 3 W.L.R. 732 at 741 where Lord Denning M.R. stated that a protectorate is not a possession of the Crown.

[5] *Supra* at 239–40. There are also *dicta* to this effect in a direction to a criminal jury; see *R.* v. *Jameson* (1896), 12 T.L.R. 551, and *infra*, p. 112, n. 1.

[6] Extracts from Staples' Case quoted in *Notes Concerning the Cases submitted to the Judicial Committee of the Privy Council in relation to the Unalienated Land of Southern Rhodesia* by H. Wilson-Fox, printed for the information of the Board of the British South Africa Company, London, 1915, at pp. 101, 94. 'Their Lordships were clear that Matabeleland was in such a position.'

that in English municipal law there has been no annexation since the Crown has not accepted them as part of the dominions. Thus the test of whether annexation has occurred might from the point of International Law be objective, e.g. whether there had been effective occupation, appointment of an officer to administer and govern the particular territory,[1] or the giving of facilities for arresting foreigners.[2] Apparently there would be no need to notify foreign powers or to go through any recognized formalities.[3] However in municipal law the courts in deciding whether the Crown had annexed territory or not would be bound to accept Crown statements as to its conduct —annexation or refusal to annex being exercises of sovereign power, i.e. acts of state which could not be challenged, controlled or interfered with by municipal courts.

A further suggestion that, by analogy with *Ex parte Mwenya*,[4] the courts may decide that the applicability of the defence of act of state depends on the extent of Crown power in the particular protectorate, is not in accordance with authority. There has never been any question that the defence depends on whether the act has been committed in a foreign country, and not on whether the action was taken in a territory in which the Crown has power.

The arguments advanced by the learned authors have yet to be pronounced upon in any court, and it may well be that the orthodox view in so far as it recognizes the defence of act of state in respect of Crown action against British protected persons will be rejected. Unless this occurs, the law will not be consistent with the factual assumption of sovereign powers in protectorates.

Until very recently it was suggested that, since a protectorate was a foreign territory, *habeas corpus* would not issue.[5] This question was only settled in 1960 when it was held that in such a territory, provided its internal governance is in legal effect indistinguishable from a British colony, *habeas corpus* runs to a British subject as the territory is under the subjection of the Crown.[6]

---

[1] F.O. Conf. 5121, James and Herschell to Derby, 11 December 1884 at 56B.

[2] F.O. Conf. 6508, Russell and Rigby, 21 November 1893 at p. 5.

[3] F.O. Conf. 5032, Memo. by Sir E. Hertslet on the Formalities Necessary for the Effective Annexation of Territory, 18 October 1884, relying on an opinion of the Law Officers relative to the Guano Islands on 21 February 1877. Cp. F.O. Conf. 5246, No. 1, Note by the Lord Chancellor, Lord Selborne, 3 January 1885 at p. 1 on the inexpediency of any attempt to settle the subject of annexation and protectorates or to lay down new rules and positive definitions of International Law. Lord Selborne thought that 'Annexation is the direct assumption of territorial sovereignty. Protectorate is the recognition of the right of the aboriginal or other actual inhabitants to their own country, with no further assumption of territorial rights than is necessary to maintain the paramount authority and discharge the duties of the protecting Power.'

[4] [1960] 1 Q.B. 241.

[5] See *R.* v. *Crewe, supra* per Kennedy L.J. at 624. *Contra* Vaughan Williams and Farwell L.JJ. at pp. 605 and 618. See also *In re Ning'Yi Ching* (1939), 56 T.L.R. 3 in which Cassels J. adopted the views of Kennedy L.J.

[6] *Ex parte* Mwenya, [1960] 1 Q.B. 241 (C.A.) at p. 302. Lord Evershed M.R. declined to state a general proposition that *habeas corpus* runs in all protectorates: in each case an

Other difficulties have arisen as to whether a protectorate is comprised within the words 'possessions' or 'dominions' contained in particular statutes—the Habeas Corpus Act 1862,[1] the Naturalization Act 1870,[2] the Foreign Enlistment Act 1870,[3] and the Extradition Act 1870.[4]

Although all protectorates are foreign territory, apparently only the rulers

enquiry would have to be made as to the extent of the jurisdiction exercised by the Crown. In any event it only ran to British subjects—this point was not, however, argued. The Law Officers in 1891 thought that *habeas corpus* ran generally in a protectorate and for this reason objected to the conclusion of extradition treaties without further statutory provision: F.O. Conf. 6207, Webster and Clarke to Salisbury, 31 August 1891, pp. 80–81.

[1] For purposes of the Habeas Corpus Act 1862 (25 & 26 Vict. c. 20) a protectorate is not a 'foreign dominion' of the Crown: *Ex parte* Mwenya, *supra* per Lord Evershed M.R. at 289. One of the Law Officers was doubtful in 1891 whether a protectorate was a dependency: F.O. Conf. 6207, pp. 80–81.

[2] In 1898 the question whether Southern Rhodesia was a British possession for purposes of Sections 16 and 17 of the Naturalization Act 1870 arose since, when representative government was to be established and voting qualifications determined, it was desired that alien settlers should be allowed to exercise the vote. The Law Officers thought that Southern Rhodesia was a possession so that the Crown could exercise powers under the Act. Even if this was not so, they considered that the Crown's power to provide for naturalization outside its dominions was not negatived by the Act: *L.O.R. 1898*, F.O. Conf. 7199, No. 4A, 29 October 1898. The 1899 Southern Rhodesia Naturalization Order in Council was then issued but the preamble was amended to read 'Whereas Her Majesty the Queen has power and jurisdiction in the territories known as Southern Rhodesia' with no enunciation of reasons, African 599, No. 450, Encl., p. 466, 7 March 1899. In any event a recital of such reasons would not be conclusive: see Polack, op. cit., p. 148, n. 66.

[3] The point whether Bechuanaland was within the 'dominions' for purposes of the Foreign Enlistment Act 1870 was taken in *The Queen* v. *Jameson and Others*, [1896] 2 Q.B. 425 (the trial of the Jameson Raiders) but in this judgement on objections to the indictment the Court did not decide the matter. However in (1896), 12 T.L.R. 551 at 594 Lord Russell of Killowen in directing the jury, treated this as a question of fact. He gave a very strong direction that the Crown in fact exercised dominion and sovereignty in the area, pointed to the fact that otherwise there would be a ridiculous distinction in the operation of the Act, and finally stated: 'The question is whether the Crown exercised and assumed by its representatives sovereignty and authority.' Indeed in F.O. Conf. 6948, Memo. 1079, the Foreign Office considered that the Lord Chief Justice had given a direction of law that the Act applied at Pitsani Pothlugo in Bechuanaland. Subsequently the Law Officers suggested that for purposes of International Law the Crown might, in dealing with other powers, treat protectorates as being within the dominions since the protected territories were in fact under Crown control: Law Officers' Report of 6 June 1901 quoted in McNair, *Opinions*, Vol. I, p. 61. See also 6 B.D.I.L., pp. 752–3. Read in conjunction with earlier opinions this allowed the Crown the best of both worlds as the Law Officers advised that German protectorates were not part of the German dominions for purposes of Section 11 of the Act while such protectorates might themselves be 'foreign states' within the meaning of sections 11 and 30 of the Act: F.O. Conf. 5956, p. 13, Webster and Clarke to Salisbury, 7 June 1889, and Opinion of 8 March 1895 quoted in McNair, op. cit. at pp. 60–61.

[4] In 1873 the Law Officers advised that the Extradition Act applied only to dominions and possessions: F.O. Conf. 4259, p. 166A. Again in 1893 they held that the Act did not recognize the surrender of a criminal to be dealt with under the extraterritorial jurisdiction: F.O. Conf. 6508, No. 44, p. 84, Russell and Rigby to Rosebery, 1 January 1893. Earlier they had advised against legislation to legalize the mutual surrender of fugitive criminals as this could not be done without admitting that protectorates conferred rights and duties of territorial sovereignty, a view which would conflict with the attitude publicly maintained at that time by British Governments as to the nature of protectorates in International Law: F.O Conf. 5785, Webster and Clarke to Salisbury, 3 March 1888.

of protected states and certain former heads of Indian and Malay states enjoyed jurisdictional immunity.[1] The Crown apparently does not consider that the African chief of a colonial protectorate retains any elements of sovereignty as the Crown does not accord him similar immunity.[2]

Persons comprised within the jurisdiction

Considerable doubt was felt even after the passage of the Foreign Jurisdiction Act 1890 as to whether the Crown had power in a protectorate to deal with foreigners and natives. The view adopted until 1895 was that 'in regard to natives the jurisdiction of the Protecting Power depended upon the express terms of the Treaty with the native Sovereign, and in regard to civilized foreigners on the consent of their own Sovereign'.[3]

Jurisdiction over foreigners

Except on the Gold Coast Crown intervention was originally confined to the appointment of consuls and vice-consuls exercising jurisdiction over British subjects and over foreigners, who had consented to the exercise of jurisdiction or whose governments had agreed to this. The British attitude was based on current views of International Law and *dicta* that, although subjects of foreign countries might resort to British consular tribunals 'with the consent of their own sovereigns and that of the sovereigns to whose tribunals they resort, ... there is no compulsory power ... over any but English subjects'.[4]

As already indicated, a succession of Law Officers considered that the Crown could not validly exercise jurisdiction over foreigners unless their governments had consented to this.[5] Although Germany and France adopted

[1] *Mighell* v. *Sultan of Johore*, [1894] 1 Q.B. 149; *Duff Development Co.* v. *Kelantan Government, supra*; *Sayce* v. *Ameer Sadig Abbasi Bahawalpur State*, [1952] A.C. 318 (P.C.); and Fawcett, op. cit., pp. 128 et seq. where he suggests that the British Government by convention treated certain rulers as retaining elements of sovereignty.

[2] *Tshekedi Khama* v. *Ratshosa*, [1931] A.C. 784 at 785–6. In *Ol le Njogo* v. *Attorney-General* (1913), E.A.L.R. 70 at 96 it was left open whether a sovereign ruler of the Masai could claim jurisdictional immunity.

[3] *L.O.R. 1895*, F.O. Conf. 6796, Reid and Lockwood to Ripon, 14 February 1895.

[4] *Papayanni* v. *The Russian Steam Navigation and Trading Co.* at p. 183–4 per Dr. Lushington. Hall, *Foreign Jurisdiction*, op. cit. at p. 206 suggests that the British attitude was a result of the Austinian theory of the indivisibility of sovereignty under which it was considered that protected states remained independent and that the Crown only possessed power over British subjects in such states. Hall must have had sight of either Jenkyns' Memorandum on the Application of Principles of International Law to Foreign Subjects in British Protectorates, 26 October 1888 (F.O. Conf. 5624*) or Ilbert's Memo. on Indian and African Protectorates, 24 January 1889 (F.O. Conf. 5750) as they took the same view that it was the Austinian theory of sovereignty that was bedevilling the Law Officers. Indeed Hall's arguments closely follow those of Jenkyns and Ilbert.

[5] The basis of the opinions was that only where there was territorial sovereignty could jurisdiction be exercised over all inhabitants. Other jurisdiction depended on allegiance (as

a different attitude and maintained that in a protectorate the protecting power was entitled to exercise jurisdiction over all inhabitants Britain persisted in her attitude.[1] The British stand was occasioned by political factors—unwillingness to assumed the responsibility of effective occupation and 'the burden of establishing in all parts of protected territories courts and magistrates with jurisdiction and authority capable of redressing all wrongs of which foreigners may complain'.[2] At the Berlin West Africa Conference Britain contended that her jurisdiction was limited in order to resist demands for effective occupation in the territories she had penetrated.[3] Indeed she put her views into practice by annexing part of New Guinea, where there had formerly been a protectorate, in order to be able, with the assumption of direct sovereignty, to exercise jurisdiction over foreigners.[4] Britain consistently followed this line throughout the eighteen eighties, despite counter arguments put forward by some of her legal advisers.[5]

Thus the Africa Order in Council of 1889, regularizing the exercise of foreign jurisdiction in Africa, was limited so that only British subjects, consenting foreigners, and foreigners (including natives) whose governments had consented to the exercise of power or authority by the Crown, came within its scope.[6]

Although the arguments propounded by Jenkyns and Ilbert that at least

in the case of subjects) or on consent or delegation by foreign powers: see Holker and Giffard to Hicks Beach, 20 March 1879 quoted in F.O. Conf. 6113; Conf. 4539, p. 55A, James and Herschell to C.O., 3 August 1880; Conf. 5121, p. 56A, James and Herschell to Derby, 11 December 1884; Conf. 5246, p. 9, Lord Selborne to Pauncefote, 23 January 1885; Conf. 5246, pp. 14B, C, Webster and Gorst to Stanley, 10 August 1885; Conf. 5440, pp. 47–48, Russell and Davey to Granville, 21 April 1886; Conf. 5736, No. 18, Memo. by Davidson and Wright, 19 December 1887, pp. 16–20; Conf. 5785, Webster and Clarke to Salisbury, 3 March 1888; Conf. 5719, Memo. on Foreign Jurisdiction by Wright, 15 November 1888; Conf. 6113, Webster and Clarke to Knutsford, 11 July 1890; Conf. 6508, Russell and Rigby, 21 November 1893; and Conf. 6641, Russell and Rigby to Ripon, 18 April 1894.

[1] Germany and France meant by protection 'annexation under another name': F.O. Conf. 5246, Selborne L.C. to Pauncefote, 23 January 1885 at p. 9. The Germans took the attitude that all persons irrespective of their nationality were subject to German jurisdiction: Conf. 5597, Webster and Clarke to Salisbury, 29 June 1887. Indeed in German protectorates the Emperor enjoyed unrestricted sovereignty: F.O. 412/28, F.O. Conf. 5736, Correspondence respecting Foreign Jurisdiction 1887–8 No. 7, Memo. by C. S. Scott on the Legal Position of German Protectorates both Crown and Company, 13 September 1887 at pp. 9–12 and No. 25, pp. 22–24.

[2] F.O. Conf. 5246, pp. 6–7, Further Note by Lord Selborne L.C., 11 January 1885.

[3] F.O. See Crowe, op. cit., pp. 179 et seq.

[4] F.O. Conf. 5246, Lord Selborne L.C. to Pauncefote, 21 January 1885.

[5] F.O. Conf. 5736, Memo. on 1888 Draft Foreign Jurisdiction Bill, Jenkyns and Ilbert, 18 June 1888; F.O. Conf. 5626*, Memo. on Foreign Jurisdiction (Consolidation) Bill, Jenkyns and Ilbert, 30 June 1888; F.O. Conf. 5624*, Application of Principles of International Law to Foreign Subjects in British Protectorates, Jenkyns, 26 October 1888; F.O. Conf. 6264*, Foreign Jurisdiction Bill, Notes on Clause for British Protectorates, Jenkyns, 16 November 1888; and F.O. Conf. 5750, Indian and African Protectorates, Memo. by Ilbert, 24 January 1889.

[6] Sections 3 and 10. Section 3 stated that 'British subject includes a person enjoying Her Majesty's Protection'.

those foreigners whose governments had acceded to the Berlin Act were amenable to the jurisdiction, had been rejected,[1] a change in the attitude of the Law Officers was occasioned by the Brussels Conference of 1890, which imposed heavier obligations on protecting powers of 'progressive organization of the administrative, judicial, religious and military services in the African territories' and a duty 'to make their protective or repressive acts effectively felt' in the suppression of the slave trade.[2] In April 1891 the Law Officers approved a Colonial Office Memorandum urging that signatories to the Berlin and Brussels Acts had implicitly consented to 'the exercise of coercive jurisdiction and administrative powers over their nationals in British Protectorates'.[3] They subsequently confirmed that by signature of the Berlin Act the Powers 'admitted that a Protectorate in Africa included the right of administering justice over the subjects of other civilized Powers within its limits'.[4] To acquire such jurisdiction as against the subjects of signatory powers they considered however that is was necessary formally to declare territories to be under the protection of the Crown.[5] Having changed their views to this extent the Law Officers then sanctioned changes in the Africa Order in Council to permit the exercise of jurisdiction over foreigners who were subjects of the signatories to the Brussels Act. Accordingly, by a further Order in Council of 28 June 1892, the Africa Order was amended.[6]

However they considered that accession to the Brussels Act did not mean that subjects of signatories could be extradited in all cases. Indeed they felt that extradition was only confirmed in respect of slave trade offences.[7] Furthermore, so far as foreigners, who were not subjects of signatories, were concerned, they did not concede that there was yet 'an established doctrine of International Law that such a jurisdiction (over foreign subjects) can be founded on the assumption of a Protectorate without a grant from the Protected Power whose right depends upon territorial sovereignty'.[8] They rejected the view put forward in the 1891 Colonial Office Memorandum that correlative to the duty of protecting subjects of foreign powers the protector had a right to exercise jurisdiction over all persons who resorted to the protected state and that this was so even where a protected Ruler had not expressly given jurisdiction over all white persons within his territory. (The

[1] Similar arguments had been rejected by the Law Officers in 1885: F.O. Conf. 5246, Webster, Gorst, and Deane, pp. 17–18.

[2] Art. 1, Brussels Act, Hertslet, op. cit., p. 51.

[3] F.O. Conf. 6207, pp. 10–11, 17 April 1891 on Memo. by J. Bramston, February 1891, at pp. 11–15.

[4] F.O. Conf. 6347, pp. 96–98, 30 June 1892.

[5] F.O. Conf. 6207, pp. 18*–18†, Law Officers to Knutsford, 30 April 1891. It was for this reason that a protectorate was formally declared over the territories of Lobengula by the South Africa Order in Council 1891.

[6] F.O. Conf. 6256, Memo. by Sir H. Bergue respecting Nationality and Protection at p. 49.

[7] F.O. Conf. 6641, Russell and Rigby to Ripon, 18 April 1894, at pp. 1–4.

[8] F.O. Conf. 6347, No. 19, Law Officers' Report, 16 November 1892.

Colonial Office argued that by acceptance of a Protectorate the Ruler had surrendered so much sovereignty as was necessary for giving effect to the protection granted.)

The Colonial Office view ultimately prevailed in 1895.[1] The Law Officers then acknowledged that 'the existence of a protectorate in an uncivilized country imports the right to assume whatever jurisdiction over all persons may be needed for its effectual exercise'.[2] This decision was reached when they examined Crown jurisdiction in the protected territories adjacent to the Gold Coast and approved a draft despatch to the Governor. They agreed that

the existence of a Protectorate in an uncivilized country carries with it a right on the part of the Protecting Power to exercise within that country such authority and jurisdiction, in short, such of the attributes of sovereignty as are required for the due discharge of the duties of a Protector both for the purposes not only of protecting the natives from the subjects of civilized Powers, and such subjects from the natives and from each other, but also for protecting the natives from the grosser forms of ill-treatment and oppression by their Rulers . . . It then becomes a question of fact, what are the powers which in any particular case it is proper for the protector to assert.[3]

It is interesting to note that once the view that the declaration of a Protectorate would in itself confer jurisdiction was adopted in practice—even though the Law Officers had not yet formally recognized this—the advisers to the Crown became less concerned to elicit treaties conferring jurisdiction from African chiefs in areas which they envisaged would ultimately become protectorates. Although the Law Officers had earlier ruled that as against native chiefs the Crown might by treaty acquire jurisdiction over subjects of foreign powers,[4] the Foreign Office laid it down that jurisdiction could not genuinely be obtained 'by devolution of powers from native chiefs . . . in a country split up into tribes ruled by savages of a low type'.[5]

Natives of protectorates

When the Imperial authorities first exercised extra-territorial jurisdiction they insisted that it be based on the consent of the sovereign power of the

[1] It was possibly the publication of Hall's *Foreign Jurisdiction* in 1894 that wrought the change in attitude of the Law Officers. They relied on Hall, Part III, Chapter 3 in reaching their new conclusions. Hall had shown how over the last ten years Great Britain had been assimilating her practice to that of Germany and France. As already suggested, Hall's arguments so closely followed those of Jenkyns and Ilbert that it is an irresistible inference that he had seen their memoranda.

[2] F.O. Conf. 6796, p. 1, Reid and Lockwood to Ripon, 14 February 1895.

[3] F.O. Conf. 6796, Draft Despatch to Governor, Sir B. Griffith, approved by the Law Officers at p. 2. The Law Officers also held that 'a protectorate . . . involves a right in the Protecting Power to exercise whatever military or naval authority may be needed for preventing foreign intrusion'.

[4] F.O. Conf. 5440, pp. 47–48, Russell and Davey to Granville, 21 April 1886.

[5] F.O. Conf. 6613, No. 213, Memo. by Sir P. Anderson, 20 November 1894.

state within which it was exercised. However as already indicated the original requirement of express consent was replaced by implied consent manifested by sufferance.[1] On this basis the Colonial Office had since 1872[2] in West Africa permitted consuls to make regulations for the peace, order, and good government of British subjects, who were defined as including 'natives or others properly enjoying Her Majesty's Protection', and since 1874 had allowed the Gold Coast Colony Legislative Assembly to legislate for the Gold Coast Protectorate. Nonetheless doubts as to the scope of Crown legislative and taxing powers continued. In practice the Crown did not impose direct taxation on the West Coast of Africa and was even doubtful as to whether the imposition of indirect taxation was permissible.[3] In fact the first area in which direct taxation was imposed was the British Central Africa Protectorate (Nyasaland) where a Hut Tax was imposed in 1894 on the assumption that, as the Foreign Office noted, 'nearly the entire internal sovereignty has in the South African and Gold Coast Protectorates been transferred to Her Majesty and a similar condition is rapidly developing in the Niger Coasts Protectorate'.[4]

The powers had largely been assumed in Colonial Office administered areas as the Colonial Office had from the first adopted a bolder line than the Foreign Office and a more liberal construction of the Foreign Jurisdiction Act. This was evident from the Order in Council of 9 May 1891 governing Bechuanaland and Lobengula's territories. The Order made it clear that the fullest powers were exercisable by the Crown.[5] Legislative powers were assumed, and there was no limitation on the persons subject to the jurisdiction. The Order (and all subsequent Colonial Office Orders in Council followed the pattern set by it)[6] delegated the Crown's power to the High Commissioner for South

[1] Where there was no consent to the exercise of jurisdiction Britain would nonetheless protect her nationals and their property and would not hesitate to use force for this purpose: see Newbury, op. cit., pp. 126–7. The Law Officers in fact advised that where savage tribes inflicted violence or injury Britain should not legislate to assume jurisdiction over them but should treat their conduct as acts of war and vindicate justice accordingly: Report of 20 March 1879 approved in Report of 11 July 1890, the former being quoted in McNair, *Opinions*, Vol. II, p. 154.

[2] Order in Council of 21 July 1872.

[3] From 1892 onwards, owing to a ratification of an amendment to the Berlin Act, it was accepted that *ad valorem* duties might be imposed on imports. See Declaration annexed to the General Act of the Brussels Conference, Appendix in *The Belgian Congo and the Berlin Act* by A. B. Keith, Oxford 1919. See also F.O. Conf. 6347, No. 1. Webster and Clarke to Salisbury, 13 April 1892.

[4] *L.O.R. 1893*, F.O. Conf. 6508, Memo. by A. Gray in consultation with the F.O., 9 June 1893. See also F.O. Conf. Print 7537, Gray to F.O., 11 May 1894 commenting on 'the fiction' of British law and administration being enforced in the guise of native law.

[5] Anson, *Law and Custom of the Constitution*, Oxford, 1908 edition, Vol. II at p. 94 commented that 'The Order goes a long way beyond any powers conferred by the Foreign Jurisdiction Act.' The Order had nonetheless been approved by the Law Officers: F.O. Conf. 6207, pp. 10–11, 18*–18†.

[6] Hailey, *Native Administration in the British African Territories*, Part V, London, 1953, pp. 202–4.

Africa who was empowered to provide by Proclamation 'for the administration of justice, the raising of revenue, and generally for the peace, order and good government of all persons within the limits of the Order'.[1] However, the High Commissioner was at first instructed to refrain from exercising jurisdiction over natives since the extent of jurisdiction by the Crown had 'not yet accurately been defined'.[2] Nonetheless authority over natives was soon to be exercised and in 1893 Buxton, the Under-Secretary for the Colonies, explained that in Mashonaland Lobengula 'acquiesced in the exercise by the white authorities of jurisdiction over the whites in Mashonaland and over the natives immediately connected with them'.[3] Although there were doubts in Municipal Law as to the Crown's power to legislate for natives (sections 2, 5, and 12 of the Act indicated that extraterritorial jurisdiction was limited to British subjects)[4] these were ignored by the Colonial Office on the assumption that Crown powers applied also to natives of foreign countries. This assumption of power was justified by the Colonial Office on the basis that a ruling had been given by the Law Officers that the grant of a Protectorate carried with it 'an acknowledgement of the right of Her Majesty to make such regulations as may be necessary for the maintenance of order and good government within the territories affected'.[5] Eventually in 1895 the Law Officers fully acknowledged that 'the existence of a protectorate in an uncivilized country imports the right to assume whatever jurisdiction over all persons may be needed for its effectual exercise'.[6]

The Foreign Office had however adopted a more conservative attitude. It considered that jurisdiction over natives depended on consent. In any event it thought that it had not taken power to legislate for natives under the Africa Order in Council 1889.[7] Unless the ruler of a protectorate had consented to the exercise of jurisdiction over his subjects, or unless they were British protected persons, the Foreign Office argued that they were not liable to the jurisdiction regulated by the Africa Order. That they were British protected persons was considered doubtful because it had been found necessary expressly to state in section 15 of the Foreign Jurisdiction Act that

[1] Order in Council, 9 May 1891, section 4.

[2] African 414, No. 2, Knutsford to Loch, 15 May 1891.

[3] *H.C. Deb.*, 4th ser., Vol. 19, col. 373, 4 December 1893.

[4] See *supra*.

[5] F.O. Conf. Print 6613, No. 71, C.O. to F.O., 13 August 1894, quoting Law Officers. This was a somewhat generous interpretation of the Law Officers' opinion on the Draft South Africa Order in Council.

[6] F.O. Conf. 6796, Reid and Lockwood to Ripon, 14 February 1895. See *supra*.

[7] F.O. Conf. Print 7143, No. 70, querying whether Queen's Regulations and Ordinances in British Central Africa were *ultra vires* as they purported to legislate for natives. See also A. J. Hanna, *The Beginnings of Nyasaland and North Eastern Rhodesia*, Oxford, 1956, at p. 202, where the Foreign Office laid down that 'natives of the Protectorates are not justiciable under the Africa Order in Council and cannot be deported under its provisions . . . they should be dealt with according to native laws as the maintenance of peace and good order require'.

the inhabitants of Indian Protectorates enjoyed such a status.[1] Indeed as late as 1897 there were ambiguous *dicta* by the Law Officers indicating limits on Crown power: the Crown 'in substance and in fact exercises dominion in these territories (the British Central Africa Protectorate) subject to the rights of the Chiefs over their own followers, and the tribal usages observed by them'.[2]

As late as 1898 the Foreign Office maintained that, in terms of the Africa Order in Council 1889, it had not 'jurisdiction over the subjects of chiefs whose territories lie within the limits of any jurisdiction constituted under the Order; neither do they give power to make legislative regulations binding on such natives',[3] although it acknowledged that in practice the difficulty had been met by allowing British officers 'to exercise all these powers on the assumption that they were acting on behalf of the chief'.[4]

However the realities of power in African and Indian protectorates eventually changed the Foreign Office attitude. In 1899 the Foreign Office informed the Law Officers that an important change had

of recent years come over the juridical conception of a Protectorate. The original conception precluded the supercession of the Protected by the Protecting Power as regards the government of the subjects of the Protecting Power; jurisdiction within the Protectorate over the subjects of the Protecting Power and over other persons was strictly limited to such cases as were directly provided for in the Treaty creating the Protectorate. The Colonial Department appears . . . to assume that even in the absence of a Treaty between the Protecting Power and the local Sovereign granting jurisdiction over the subjects of that Sovereign, the existence of a Protectorate in an uncivilized country implies the right to assume whatever jurisdiction, over all persons, may be needed for the effectual exercise of the Protectorate.[5]

These views were accepted by the Law Officers. Ultimately in 1910 the legal position was clarified by a Court of Appeal decision that the Crown had the right 'to subject to its administration all persons upon the protected soil . . . The Crown can legislate for all inhabitants.'[6]

Crown land rights

Yet another point that caused difficulty was the right of the Crown to land

[1] F.O. Conf. 6508, Memo. by A. Gray in consultation with the Foreign Office, 9 June 1893. This view is reflected by the Africa Order in Council of 17 June 1893 which extended the application of the Order to the natives of any protectorate outside the local jurisdiction when in that jurisdiction.

[2] F.O. Conf. 7058, Webster and Finlay to F.O., 28 September 1897.

[3] F.O. Print 7143, No. 70, Memorandum by Mr. Farnall on Colonial Office letter of 23 September 1898.

[4] Section 10 of the Order extended jurisdiction to persons whose chief or government had by treaty agreed to the exercise of authority by the Crown.

[5] F.O. 834/19, Foreign Office to Law Officers, 18 November 1899.

[6] *R.* v. *Crewe*, *supra* at 596 (discussing Hall's views in *Foreign Jurisdiction*, op. cit. at p. 221), and at p. 626 per Kennedy L.J. who gave the ruling quoted above.

within a protectorate. Initially the Colonial Office declared that in protectorates it made

no claim to the ownership of the land which is regarded as being still vested in the chiefs and tribes except in so far as it has been duly alienated to grantees or concessionaires. All that the Crown claims as the Protecting Power is to investigate and recognize or disallow the grant by the chiefs and tribes of 'concessions' and probably minor grants.[1]

In Colonies, on the other hand, the Crown considered itself supreme owner of the land.

This view was reiterated in 1894 when the Colonial Office informed the Foreign Office that

Whilst Her Majesty the Queen acquires powers of control and rule, more or less complete, the property in the soil and minerals does not necessarily pass to her by the act of extending Her protection. So far as the natives had the enjoyment of the land they continue to enjoy it, subject to any laws which Her Majesty may subsequently make for the public good, and subject of course to any transfer of their title in the land to Her Majesty which they make as a distinct act.[2]

Where the natives had exercised the right to alienate land or minerals to Europeans, these rights were admitted in principle, but any claims were subject to scrutiny. The Crown, therefore, recognized

a right in the natives to the occupancy and reasonable use of the country, and a power to grant reasonable rights to white men over lands and minerals, the Protecting Power contenting itself, under the circumstances of the case, with claiming a right to such land as may be required for public purposes . . .[3]

The recognition of concessions depended on whether they were likely to interfere with the working of the Protecting Power's present or future administration.[4] The method of enquiry prior to recognition might differ from Protectorate to Protectorate: thus in the case of Bechuanaland Protectorate, a

[1] F.O. Conf. Print 6482, No. 77, Colonial Office to Foreign Office, 29 April 1893, referring to the land in Mashonaland and in Bechuanaland Protectorate. See also R. Oliver, op. cit., p. 220, quoting Johnston to Rosebery and the attitude in Nyasaland that Crown land rights depended on cession by the chiefs. This view was probably based on an early opinion given in 1833 long before the establishment of African Protectorates that a protector has not necessarily power to alienate land: see McNair, *Opinions*, op. cit., Vol. I, p. 39.
[2] F.O. Conf. Print 6613, No. 31, Colonial Office to Foreign Office, 19 July 1894.
[3] ibid.
[4] Concessions exempting the grantees from taxation, giving them a monopoly of postal, railway, and telegraph services, of trade, manufacture, and banking, exempting them from the general laws applicable to whites, empowering them to hold courts and make regulations, or alienating unduly large quantities of land or areas with mineral rights, concessions by the chief acting alone, or obtained fraudulently, or without the understanding of the chief and his people, or without fair pecuniary consideration, or where the conditions were not fulfilled, would not be acknowledged. It is questionable whether measured by these standards the Rudd Concession should have been recognized.

Concessions Commission was appointed to report upon alleged land grants;[1] in Nyasaland the Commissioner of the British Central Africa Protectorate made an individual assessment[2]; and in the Matabele Kingdom all concessions had to be recognized as valid by the High Commissioner and approved by the Secretary of State.[3] But in general the same principles of recognition were followed.

The Colonial Office explained that the reason why it did not

assert a wider and more immediate right on the part of its Representatives to make grants of land in protected territories is that it is not usually desired that such territories should be regarded as open to extensive agricultural occupation by whites, such protectorates being regarded rather as places where, subject to the establishment of mining camps and towns, the natives may find homes protected against the ever-spreading flood of colonial advance.

If an influx of white farmers seemed inevitable and desirable, the Crown would then annex the area, administer it as a Crown Colony, treat the land as Crown land, and eventually grant 'responsible government'.[4]

Again in 1895 the Colonial Secretary informed the High Commissioner that the Crown laid no claim to mineral rights or land in Protectorates and that any quit rent payable or reservations of minerals should therefore be made in favour of the chiefs.[5] Soon thereafter the Colonial Office declined to grant the British South Africa Company ownership of lands in the Bechuanaland Protectorate since, if as administering authority it did not itself claim ownership, it could not make such a grant to another.[6]

At this time, therefore, the Crown confined itself to fixing the boundaries of protectorates: to fixing boundaries of any Reserves it might create[7]; to examining the validity of claims to land and mineral rights arising from con-

---

[1] For its instructions see F.O. Conf. 6383, Memo. on Land Claims in the British Central Africa Protectorate, pp. 10–12, Loch to Surmon, 20 January 1893. See also *Vilander Concessions Syndicate* v. *Cape of Good Hope Government*, [1907] A.C. 186.

[2] Apparently the Commissioner, H. H. Johnston, was not clear as to whether his area was a protectorate or merely a sphere as his certificates of claims related to the territories under 'British influence North of the Zambezi': Wilson-Fox, *Memorandum 1912*, op. cit., p. 117.

[3] High Commissioner's Proclamation of 10 April 1891, sections 43 and 45.

[4] F.O. Conf. Print 6613 No. 31. Cp. H. Wilson-Fox, *Memorandum on the Position, Policy, and Prospects of the Company*, printed for the information of the Board, London, 1907. Wilson-Fox considered that, in the light of discussions Company officials had had with the Colonial Office, the Crown was reluctant to take up ownership of land in protectorates, as it was thought that such action would involve annexation.

[5] Ripon to Loch, 15 January 1895, quoted in Wilson-Fox, *Memorandum 1907*, op. cit. In 1896 the Colonial Office advised the Foreign Office not to make grants in protectorates since land in such areas was not vested in the Crown. See Colonial Office to Foreign Office, 4 September 1896. Annexure F to Foreign Office to Colonial Office of 18 November 1899 in F.O. 834/19.

[6] African 498, No. 182, Colonial Office to B.S.A. Co., 10 December 1895. See Wilson Fox, *Memorandum 1907*, op. cit., p. 18. This attitude was reaffirmed in 1899.

[7] This was done in Matabeleland in 1894 and in Bechuanaland in 1895.

cessions, occupation or otherwise; to adding conditions[1]; to limiting the scope of or recognizing such claims; and to giving certificates which recognized a right of occupation.

Nonetheless the extent of Crown rights remained in doubt. When in 1897 problems arose respecting the succession to real property in the British Central Africa Protectorate, the Foreign Office thought that devolution must be governed by native law as the Crown had not technically acquired power to legislate on such matters. The Law Officers then reported that the Crown had in fact authority to regulate such questions.[2] The issue was only finally settled in 1899 when the Foreign Office enquired from the Law Officers whether 'in regions where Her Majesty exercises rights of protectorate under treaties . . . which do not specifically grant to Her Majesty the right of dealing with waste or unoccupied land' rights accrued to Her Majesty 'by virtue of the rights of Protectorate'.[3] Having been informed by the Foreign Office that the natives of certain regions were 'practically savages without any proper conception of ownership of land',[4] the Law Officers replied that the right of dealing with all waste and unoccupied land accrued to the Crown by virtue of its protectorate, since protectorates over territories occupied by savage tribes 'really involve the assumption of control over all lands unappropriated. Her Majesty might if she pleased, declare them to be Crown lands, or make grants of them to individuals in fee, or for any term'. The Law Officers advised that any system which might be utilized was really one of policy and that, while the term 'public lands' might be employed, 'lands which are "public" must under the circumstances of such a Protectorate be Crown lands, or under the control of the Crown'.[5]

The Law Officers also relied on the doctrine of act of state in such circumstances.[6] Appropriation of land for public purposes (the Mombasa Railway), although not within the terms of any Order in Council, since 'it was issued by Order of the Secretary of State for Foreign Affairs . . . was therefore, the act of the Crown and cannot be questioned'.

Despite this opinion the Foreign Office was reluctant publicly to acknowledge the scope of Crown power over the lands in protectorates. Indeed new

---

[1] These might include stipulations that concession-holders should be liable to tax in return for protection afforded. In Nyasaland, Commissioners derogated from grants by reserving mining royalties, water rights, and the right to take land for public purposes without compensation. See African 1085, No. 178, Encl. 5. Despatch from the Governor of Nyasaland, 27 February 1922.

[2] F.O. Conf. 7058, Webster and Finlay to F.O., 28 September 1897.

[3] F.O. 834/19, Foreign Office to Law Officers, 18 November 1899.

[4] Except perhaps in the Kingdom of Uganda. The Foreign Office was remarkably ignorant of the nature and extent of native land rights as it denied that even the idea of tribal ownership of land was known in East Africa. Cp. the Colonial Office's more enlightened attitude to land tenure in West Africa.

[5] F.O. 834/19. Law Officers to Foreign Office, 13 December 1899.

[6] Earlier India Office advisers (F.O. 412/28, No. 3) and Jenkyns (F.O. Conf. 6264, p. 4) had rationalized the exercise of jurisdiction on this basis.

Orders in Council although they referred to 'Crown lands' did not assert ownership and euphemistically referred to 'rights of Her Majesty in or in relation to any Crown land'.[1] Nonetheless in practice the Crown assumed full control of such lands and purported to give title by grants.

The decision in *R. v. Crewe* in 1911, however, made the extent of Crown power obvious. The Law Officers' view that an 'act of the Crown' cannot be questioned was dramatically upheld when the Court indicated its surprise at the extent of the powers possessed by the Crown which, despite the fact that it did not have absolute ownership or territorial sovereignty,[2] had 'powers identical with those which it could have in a conquered country'.[3] These views were thereafter applied in the Masai Case when it was held that a treaty entered into by the Masai and the East Africa Protectorate Authorities regarding Masai land rights could not be enforced by the courts as the acts of the Crown in carrying out the treaty were acts of state.[4]

Whether the Crown chose to respect land rights of native peoples became, in each instance, therefore, a policy decision. In Nigeria land rights were respected.[5] In East Africa, in Southern Rhodesia, and Swaziland, all areas of white settlement, the Crown decided to exercise its powers and to override native land rights. Although there is a presumption that private rights should continue,[6] Crown action inconsistent with such rights would serve either to extinguish or to modify them.[7]

In 1921, presumably on the basis of Amodu Tijani's Case, the Crown was given legal opinion that the extent of Crown rights in Northern Rhodesia was uncertain, it being suggested that the land belonged to the natives.[8] However,

[1] Bechuanaland Protectorate (Lands) Order in Council 1904, section 2. See also British Central Africa Order in Council of 11 August 1902 which defines Crown lands as 'all public lands in the Protectorate which are subject to the control of His Majesty by virtue of any Treaty, Convention, or Agreement, of His Majesty's Protectorate, and all lands which shall have been acquired by His Majesty for the public service or otherwise howsoever'. There is no allegation of vesting of ownership of such land in the Crown except such as is 'acquired'.

[2] *R. v. Crewe, supra* per Kennedy L.J. at 620.

[3] *R. v. Crewe, supra* per Kennedy L.J. at 626. This had been recognized much earlier by the Crown's legal advisers—by some as early as 1888.

[4] *Ol le Njogo and Others* v. *The Attorney-General and Others, supra.* See also *Hoani Te Heuheu Tukino* v. *Aotea District Maori Land Board, supra.*

[5] *Amodu Tijani* v. *Secretary, Southern Nigeria,* [1921] 2 A.C. 399. In New Zealand, which was not of course a protectorate, a similar policy was followed: see *Nireha Tanaki* v. *Baker,* [1901] A.C. 961.

[6] *Amodu Tijani* v. *Secretary, Southern Nigeria, supra* at p. 407. Throughout Africa native land rights are in the nature of private rights whether of the community or of the individual.

[7] In *Ol le Njogo* v. *Attorney-General, supra,* in *In re Southern Rhodesia, supra,* and in *Sobhuza II* v. *Miller, supra,* Crown disposal of the land inconsistent with such rights— amounting in Southern Rhodesia to the termination of native land rights other than in Reserves—was upheld. In *Gathomo* v. *Indangara,* 1921, E.A.L.R. 102 it was held that when land was vested in the Crown (under the Crown Lands Ordinance 1915) as a native Reserve, individual African rights under the Gethaka system of tenure similarly disappeared: 'Natives in occupation of such Crown land became tenants at will of the Crown.' Cp. *Kabato* v. *Nago,* 1920, E.A.L.R. 129.

[8] See Cmd. 1471, § 12. Since there had been no conquest of Northern Rhodesia the

shortly thereafter it was conclusively established that any Crown action in relation to land in protectorates was unchallengeable as an act of state and that the Crown could vary previous Orders in Council.[1]

Although International Law respects private rights it is clear that the un-fettered powers of the Crown in protectorates (as eventually interpreted) left native land rights at the mercy of the protecting power since no municipal tribunal would enforce these rights against the Crown.

Conclusions

It is apparent from this outline of the evolution of Crown powers in pro-tectorates that, even after the passage of the consolidated Foreign Jurisdiction Act 1890, the scope of these powers was uncertain. In fact, the extensions of power made after 1890 were originally to come into operation in South Central Africa: it was in that area that all inhabitants, including foreigners and natives, were first subjected to Crown power; in the Bechuanaland and British Central Africa Protectorates the practice governing Crown dealings with unoccupied land developed; in Nyasaland the first direct taxation without chiefly authority was imposed[2]; in Bechuanaland the implications of the doctrine of act of state in protectorates were first exposed; and in Southern Rhodesia Crown freedom to override native land rights was illustrated.

What was certain however was that the concept of protectorates had been invaluable to Britain in the extension of her Empire. Before the powers had hit upon the expedient of agreeing to spheres of influence, protectorates had served the same purpose of securing exclusive British influence in any area. Indeed they had been more effective because formal declaration of protector-ates had the consequence in International Law of effectively excluding intervention by other powers.[3]

Until the Law Officers changed their view of the nature and extent of Crown powers in protectorates the Crown could assume protectorates and yet avoid the responsibility of exercising jurisdiction over natives and foreign-ers and of maintaining a satisfactory authority for this purpose.[4] Nor need

Buxton Commission considered that the land might belong to the natives and recommended a special reference to the Judicial Committee. See also African 1085, No. 165, Colonial Office to Treasury, 18 January 1921. Churchill agreed to arrange for a special reference on this point, but this fell away as a result of agreement between Crown and Company to determine Company administration, to make certain payments to the Company and to recognize Company mineral rights.

[1] *Sobhuza II* v. *Miller, supra* at p. 523, and *The North Charterland Exploration Co.* (*1910*) *Ltd.* v. *The King,* [1931] 1 Ch. 169. Both cases related to Crown interference with land rights —in the latter case in order to create adequate native Reserves in Northern Rhodesia.

[2] The 1894 Hut Tax was modelled on that imposed in the Colony of Zululand.

[3] F.O. Conf. 5449, No. 3, Proposed British Protectorate, Pauncefote to Herbert, 13 January 1887.

[4] F.O. Conf. 5719, Memo. on Foreign Jurisdiction by Wright, 15 November 1888; and

it interfere with the internal administration of protected territories by their native rulers, or assume sovereignty in any way.[1]

Even when it was accepted that a protectorate carried with it full executive, legislative, and judicial power the doctrine allowed the protecting power to exercise as much or as little jurisdiction as it saw fit.[2]

A major consideration in using the combination of spheres followed soon thereafter by protectorates was that since normally minimal powers were assumed and skeleton consular staffs appointed (these only later being drawn into fuller administration), expansion could occur without calls on the Treasury. This reason was described at the beginning of the phase of protectorate-making by Harry H. Johnston, who had been Consul in the Oil Rivers Protectorate and was to be instrumental in establishing Nyasaland Protectorate. Writing in 1888, Johnston urged that by the declaration of a protectorate 'we are thereby enabled to obviate the jealous interference of a rival European power with our commercial and propagandist enterprise, without at the same time charging ourselves with the internal administration of the country and being compelled on that account to incur considerable initial expense and greatly increased responsibility'.[3] Naturally if a Chartered Company could be interposed to bear even the small costs involved in a protectorate so much the better.[4]

A further advantage was that the mere declaration of a protectorate did not import either English common or statute law. In particular, the Slave Trade Act 1824, the Slavery Abolition Act 1833, and the Slave Trade Act 1843 were inapplicable.[5] Had they been operative, domestic slavery would have been a

Conf. 5246, Note by the Lord Chancellor, Lord Selborne, 3 January 1885 at p. 5, and Further Note, 11 January 1885 at pp. 6–7.

[1] F.O. Conf. 6264*, Notes on Clause for British Protectorates, H. Jenkyns, 16 November 1888, p. 3.

[2] F.O. Conf. 6796, Reid and Lockwood to Ripon, 14 February 1895.

[3] *The Times*, 22 August 1888, by an African Explorer. The letter was written at the instance of Lord Salisbury, then Prime Minister: see Oliver, op. cit., p. 140.

[4] e.g. in Mashonaland and Matabeleland, in the Niger Districts, and in parts of East Africa. See also F.O. Conf. 6613, No. 213, Memorandum by Sir P. Anderson, 20 November 1894, on the advantages of a protectorate in the area North of the Zambesi with the B.S.A. Co. exercising authority: 'it would entail no Imperial expenditure and the responsibility would fall on the administering company. It only requires a Gazette Notice.'

[5] 5 Geo. 4, c. 113; 3 & 4 Will. 4, c. 73; and 6 & 7 Vict. c. 98. This was early realized by the British Government. The Earl of Kimberley insisted in 1873 that expansion of sovereignty beyond Lagos should be limited and that further acquisitions should only be 'protected' territory because of the slave question: C.O. 147/24, Minute on No. 53 by the Earl of Kimberley, 25 February 1873. It was for the same reason that Lord Selborne, the Lord Chancellor, pointed out that Britain would not annex territories and treat protectorates as being annexed since 'the immediate consequence must be that, in that territory, slavery must at once cease to exist': *L.O.R. 1885*, F.O. Conf. 5246, p. 9, Lord Chancellor to Pauncefote, 23 January 1885. The same attitude was adopted by the Law Officers when drafting the 1892 Africa Order in Council, it having been suggested that the areas governed by the Order should be placed under the direct sovereignty of the Queen: F.O. Conf. 6347, No. 1*, Webster and Clarke to Salisbury, 15 June 1892, at p. 4A.

serious crime and expensive machinery would have been necessary to stop the trade.[1]

In addition, treaties of protection were more easily procurable than treaties of cession or acquiescence in annexation by native chiefs. As Keith says: 'The native chief, ignorant as he was, was much more likely to sign an agreement promising him protection than to agree to an annexation out and out.'[2]

Finally, protectorates could be used as counters in the diplomatic game: when foreign claims came into competition, it was infinitely easier to relinquish a right of protection of a chief than to abandon territory which had been made part of the dominions, and which probably required Parliamentary approval for its cession.[3]

[1] Many of the difficulties of early governors in the Gold Coast and Sierra Leone were occasioned by their attempts to prevent domestic slavery. Slavery was only finally abolished in Sierra Leone in 1927; see Keith, *Governments*, op. cit., p. 464. See also F.O. Conf. 6851, No. 97, 18 February 1896, Johnston to Salisbury. Johnston had been told in 1894 that he was exceeding his instructions in the Nyasaland Protectorate by declaring that slavery was abolished.

[2] Keith, op. cit., p. 464.

[3] The Law Officers advised in 1884 that the Crown could cede non-colonial possessions (e.g. in India) without parliamentary consent: F.O. Conf. 5121, James and Herschell, 3 June 1884. *Contra* Deane. However they advised that British territory could not be ceded without parliamentary intervention: F.O. Conf. 5440, Webster and Clarke to Iddesleigh, 13 December 1886. See the debates on Heligoland in 1890: *H.C. Deb.*, 3rd ser., Vol. 347, where it was regarded as a moot constitutional point whether Parliamentary assent was required for the cession of British territory. A. D. McNair, *Law of Treaties*, Oxford, 1961, pp. 94–97, 107–10, suggests that there is probably a binding convention that all cessions be submitted for parliamentary approval in the form of a statute. Cp. the position in Germany at the end of the nineteenth century where the second article of the Imperial Constitution enumerated German colonies. This could only be varied with the consent of the Imperial Legislature, so that there was considerable convenience in creating protectorates as opposed to amending the Constitution on the formation of each successive colony.

5

THE ATTAINMENT OF PROTECTORATE STATUS, THE ADMINISTRATION THERE ESTABLISHED, AND IMPERIAL CONTROL IN PRACTICE 1891–1894

Protectorate status for the future Southern Rhodesia

ALTHOUGH the Matabele Kingdom had been declared a sphere of British influence and the British South Africa Company had been chartered in order that the territory would effectively and economically be occupied, these steps were insufficient to secure Britain's rights in the area. Despite its unwillingness to undertake further commitments in the Company's territories events forced action upon the Crown. A proposed trek from the South African Republic into the Banyai territory north of the Limpopo, with a view to forming a Republic as far as the Zambezi, stirred the Imperial authorities into suggesting that a protectorate should be declared, otherwise there would be difficulty in supporting the British South Africa Company in repelling the advance of the trekkers.[1] Somewhat earlier the High Commissioner had been urging the Crown to assume jurisdiction in Mashonaland and to delegate this to the Company. He had pointed out that there were 400 miners in the country not subject to any discipline and, if they learnt that 'they are not subject to any lawful authority, the place would become an Alsatia and a disgrace to civilization'.[2] In fact, officers of the Company had been 'administering a sort of lynch law', which position could not continue if peace were to be kept with the natives and anarchy prevented among the Europeans.[3]

These reasons impelled the Colonial Office to acknowledge that some more formal extension of British authority in Lobengula's territories was imperative and should be secured. To that end an Order in Council was drafted and approved by the Law Officers. In the meanwhile the High Commissioner had on the 13 April 1891 issued a 'Proclamation warning all persons that any unauthorized attempt to enter or occupy the British sphere of influence for the purpose of setting up an independent form of Government would be deemed an unfriendly and aggressive act against a country under British protection.'[4] Not only was the area in question formally declared as being

[1] African 403, No. 177, Colonial Office to Foreign Office, 9 April 1891.
[2] African 414, No. 1, Loch to Knutsford, 20 November 1890.
[3] African 414, No. 125, Loch to Knutsford, 24 June 1891.
[4] African 403, No. 217, Telegraph Loch to Knutsford, 18 April 1891. Approved by Knutsford in No. 219 (Tel.) 18 April 1891, stating that 'any attempt to set up any form of government in that country . . . will be deemed an act of hostility against Her Majesty the Queen'.

8—C.H.L.S.R.

within the British sphere of influence but the Proclamation ordered persons who entered the territory to observe the rules and regulations of the Company, which was 'charged with the establishment of a form of rule and administration' there.[1]

Nonetheless the Colonial Office urged that 'Lobengula's consent should, if possible, be obtained to such measures as we may deem necessary for the government of the whites':[2] such consent would give grounds for assuming 'sufferance' which would then permit of the creation of a protectorate under the Foreign Jurisdiction Act.

Already the High Commissioner had informed the Colonial Office that there was 'no probability of Lobengula granting any concession of jurisdiction',[3] while in January 1891 Lobengula informed the High Commissioner that he was unwilling 'to give Mr. Rhodes power to punish those who do wrong in Mashonaland'.[4] In practice, however, Lobengula acquiesced by remaining passive when the Company exercised jurisdiction in Mashonaland, but this acquiescence could not be interpreted as extending to Matabeleland, where no jurisdiction was at that time exercised.

Owing to the probability of the trekkers from the Transvaal taking the law into their own hands, and to the fact that 'the term "sphere of British influence" has not been understood to preclude the establishment in the country within that area of other governments than those sanctioned under Royal Charter',[5] the scruples of the Colonial Office regarding Lobengula's consent were nonetheless swallowed.

The Foreign Office was informed that 'it now appears that Sir Henry Loch has communicated to Lobengula his intention to govern and punish the whites in his (Lobengula's) country, and Lord Knutsford therefore considers that there is ground for assuming the existence of the "sufferance" on the part of Lobengula so as to give Her Majesty jurisdiction in his country within the meaning of the Foreign Jurisdiction Act 1890'.[6]

Despite its desire to keep other territories and subjects of the South African Republic out of the area, the Colonial Office was nonetheless undesirous of going so far as to declare a British protectorate and warned the High

[1] Article 5 of High Commissioner's Proclamation of 13 April 1891. The Proclamation did not purport to confer governmental power on the Company and was intended merely to be declaratory. It was incidentally a perfect example of the prevailing confusion between spheres of influence and countries under protection, since in the same sentence both terms were used interchangeably.
[2] African 403, No. 220, Telegraph Knutsford to Loch, 18 April 1891. The Moffat Treaty did not confer such powers, nor did the Rudd Concession.
[3] African 414, No. 1, 20 November 1890.
[4] African 403, No. 272, Encl. 1, Lobengula to Loch, 1 January 1891, communicated to Knutsford by Loch, 4 April 1891. The Resident, J. S. Moffat, had attempted to obtain from Lobengula signature of a document that would have given the Company such power.
[5] African 403, No. 299, Loch to Knutsford, 15 April 1891.
[6] African 403, No. 248, Colonial Office to Foreign Office, 23 April 1891.

Commissioner not to take such action.[1] It even asked the Law Officers to consider whether an Order in Council under the Foreign Jurisdiction Act might be issued without declaring the territories comprised therein to be under the Queen's protection. When the answer was given that unless such territories were declared to be under British protection the Order would have no validity as against the subjects of foreign powers,[2] in view of the emergency created by the imminent South African Republic Trek, an Order in Council was issued on the 9 May 1891, alleging that 'by treaty, grant, usage, sufferance, and other lawful means' Her Majesty possessed power and jurisdiction in 'the parts of South Africa bounded by British Bechuanaland, the German Protectorate, the rivers Chobe and Zambezi, the Portuguese possessions, and the South African Republic' (i.e. the present Southern Rhodesia), and declaring the area to be a protectorate.

The administration established by the Crown in the new Protectorate

Although a protectorate had now been declared there was no intention on the part of the Imperial authorities to involve themselves in the administration of the area. The Company was to continue as the instrument of administration under the protection of the Crown and powers conferred on the Company by the Charter were not to be abridged.[3]

Formally Crown power was delegated to the High Commissioner for South Africa subject to any instructions from the Secretary of State.[4] The High Commissioner was empowered to legislate by Proclamation for 'the administration of justice, the raising of revenue, peace, order, and good government' but, in so doing, he was enjoined to respect native laws and customs,[5] and such Proclamations were subject to disallowance either in whole or in part by the Secretary of State.[6] Furthermore, the High Commissioner was empowered to appoint and remove such Deputy Commissioners, Resident Commissioners, Acting Commissioners, judges, magistrates and other officers as might be required. He could define their duties and they were to act in accordance with his instructions, but any such delegation was in no way to be regarded as derogating from his own powers.[7] However, as the Colonial Office explained to the Company, the real reason for the issue of the Order had been the decision to support Company powers only if this proved necessary.

[1] African 403, No. 251, Knutsford to Loch (Tel.).
[2] F.O. Conf. 6207, pp. 18*–18†, Law Officers to Knutsford, 30 April 1891.
[3] South Africa Order in Council of 9 May 1891, section 8.
[4] ibid., section 2.
[5] South Africa Order in Council of 9 May 1891, section 4.
[6] Section 6. Sections 5 and 6 of the Order in Council relating to the time of coming into operation of Proclamations and the effect of disallowances were amended by an Order in Council of 30 July 1891 providing that any Proclamation should take effect until such time as it had been disallowed.
[7] Section 3.

The Company was, therefore, to continue to appoint and remove all executive and administrative officers within its field of operation. Although judicial officers would be appointed and removed by the High Commissioner even here the Colonial Office did not 'desire to interfere with the patronage of the Company in regard to such appointments, as the salaries attached to them will be provided by the Company; and, subject to any objection as to the character or ability of any particular candidate' indicated that the High Commissioner would doubtless act on any Company recommendation.[1]

In so far as legislation was concerned it was 'contemplated that for all ordinary matters the Company should provide by Ordinance under the Charter' and, only if necessary or expedient to validate any Ordinance, would the High Commissioner legislate by Proclamation.[2]

High Commissioner's Proclamation of 10 June 1891

When the High Commissioner received the authorization under the Order in Council, he issued a Proclamation dated 10 June 1891, providing for the administration of the whole of the territory south of the Zambezi which fell within the sphere of the British South Africa Company. Obviously ignorant of the attitude of the Colonial Office, the High Commissioner set up a system of government under his control. He was to enjoy full executive control through a Resident Commissioner, who would exercise administration and control subject to his instructions,[3] and who would also be Treasurer and would thus control finance.[4] Other officials in the administration would be appointed by the High Commissioner and act under the Resident Commissioner.[5] Inspectors of Police were to be similarly appointed and to act in terms of rules made by the Resident Commissioner under a rule-making power given him for the government and guidance of the police forces in the territory.[6] All appointees were to hold office during the High Commissioner's pleasure.[7]

The High Commissioner was also to control the judicial system. The Proclamation set up a system of courts staffed by magistrates appointed by the High Commissioner, who were to exercise civil and criminal jurisdiction, except over natives, and who were to apply the law of the Cape Colony as at that date.[8] The Resident Commissioner was to have both civil and criminal jurisdiction, to hold an appellate court, and to enjoy powers of review.[9]

[1] C. 7171, No. 1, p. 1, 12 May 1891, Colonial Office to British South Africa Company.
[2] C. 7171, No. 1, p. 1, 12 May 1891, Colonial Office to British South Africa Company.
[3] High Commissioner's Proclamation of 10 June 1891, section 1. For full text see African 414, No. 98, Encl. 1, pp. 84–90.
[4] Section 2.   [5] Section 6.   [6] Section 5.   [7] Section 7.
[8] This did not introduce Cape revenue laws: Stevenson v. B.S.A. Co. (1899), S.R.R. 1 (by R. Burns Begg).
[9] Sections 3 and 8 to 21. Natives were excluded from the jurisdiction of the courts unless the assumption of jurisdiction was necessary to maintain peace, or prevent violence to

Subsequently, by Proclamation of the 27 June 1891, the High Commissioner set up magisterial districts and thereafter appointed magistrates.[1]

Besides legislating for the provision of a civil service, police, a system of courts, and judicial officers, the Proclamation went on to provide for marriage officers,[2] the regulation of trading and the necessity for obtaining licences subject to fees and penalties,[3] the prohibition of the supply of liquor to natives,[4] control of immigration by means of forbidding wagons to enter the country without a permit from an official appointed by the High Commissioner,[5] control of the supply of arms and ammunition subject to regulations by the High Commissioner and prohibition of its supply to natives,[6] the introduction of Cape coinage, weights and measures,[7] control by the High Commissioner of land rights, occupation and ownership,[8] the non-recognition of concessions by native chiefs unless approved by the Secretary of State,[9] and finally a prohibition against the levying of any rate or tax, or imposition of any licence without the High Commissioner's sanction.[10] It was apparent from this Proclamation that the High Commissioner proposed virtually to take over the government of the country. Indeed the Assistant Commissioner charged with the duty of informing Lobengula about the Order in Council and the Proclamation refrained from giving him full details lest Lobengula should be alarmed by 'a sinister report of the Proclamation'.[11] But it was not from Lobengula that the High Commissioner was to have difficulty, as Lobengula recognized the realities of the situation and Moffat eventually reported that he was agreeable to allowing the High Commissioner to deal with Europeans in his country.[12]

High Commissioner's views of future Imperial policy

Before issuing the Proclamation, Sir Henry Loch had written to Lord Knutsford pressing upon him the analogy of the East India Company with an Imperial Commander-in-Chief and Administrator, responsible both to the Company and the Imperial Government, officers appointed and removable by the High Commissioner, and a Board of Control to discuss policy with directors of the Company. He requested that a senior Imperial officer 'clothed

person and property: Section 8. Natives might, however, consent to jurisdiction, in which case native law and custom should be applied unless it was incompatible with peace, order, or good government: Section 9. For a later example under the Proclamation, see *Khama* v. *Ratshosa*, [1931] A.C. 784 at 797. Native chiefs, subject to consent by both Resident Commissioner and High Commissioner, could hold courts for natives only: Section 10.

[1] This Proclamation gave magistrates the same criminal and civil jurisdiction as Resident Magistrates of the Cape Colony: African 414, No. 138, p. 123, Encl.
[2] Section 22.   [3] Sections 23–28, 30–34, 36, and 42.
[4] Section 29.   [5] Section 35.   [6] Sections 37–40.
[7] Section 41.   [8] Section 43.   [9] Section 45.   [10] Section 46.
[11] African 414, No. 192, Encl., p. 198, Moffat to Shippard, 4 July 1891.
[12] African 414, No. 250, p. 269, Moffat to Loch, 11 September 1891.

with all necessary authority over the administrative service of the Colony' be appointed.[1] After issuing the Proclamation, Loch began to urge that the High Commissioner should be the sole legislative authority for the area and managed to secure Rhodes's approval of this suggestion.[2] The British South Africa Company's legislative powers should, Loch wrote, be very rarely, if ever, exercised. Not only would there be inconvenience in the existence of two concurrent legislative authorities but a danger that the High Commissioner might not be informed of proposed Company Ordinances and that they might not reflect his views. Furthermore, he denied the existence of legislative powers to the Company since the Order in Council conferred no additional powers on the Company, and neither the Rudd Concession nor the Charter permitted the exercise of legislative powers without the permission of Lobengula. Litigation about the validity of Ordinances must inevitably follow.[3] Indeed, High Commissioners' Proclamations were essential to supplement the Company's deficient legislative powers.[4] There was also the danger that 'the interests of the B.S.A. Chartered Company and those of the natives may not always be in common, and that any legislation in connection with natives should, in the interests of peace and good government, be similar throughout the Protectorate (i.e. Bechuanaland and the future Southern Rhodesia) and directly under the High Commissioner's control'.[5]

Loch pointed out that 'whilst Her Majesty's Government have accepted responsibility for the protection of the Company's territories, there is at present no security to prevent the officers of the Company from committing Her Majesty's Government to a course of policy the Government may not be desirous of adopting'.[6] With strange prescience he commented: 'Mr. Rhodes has always shown himself desirous of complying with my wishes and of giving effect to the views of Her Majesty's Government. Still I think it is evident that the control of the High Commissioner should be so regulated that Her Majesty's Government could not by any possibility be committed to a line of policy of which they disapproved, or find their hands forced by the excessive zeal of an officer entirely independent of the High Commissioner and dependent only upon a politically irresponsible Company for his appointment and position.'[7]

He felt that it was the duty of the High Commissioner to exercise political control and enquired from the Colonial Office 'if the policy of the Company towards the native, the Portuguese, or towards the South African Republic is, in the opinion of the High Commissioner, impolitic, provocative, or unjust,

[1] African 414, No. 30, p. 25, Loch to Knutsford, 25 May 1891.
[2] African 414, No. 43, p. 40, Telegraph Loch to Knutsford, 25 June 1891.
[3] African 414, No. 136, p. 118, Loch to Knutsford, 29 June 1891.
[4] African 414, No. 115, p. 97, Loch to Knutsford, 13 July 1891.
[5] African 414, No. 125, p. 109, Loch to Knutsford, 24 June 1891.
[6] African 414, No. 136, p. 118, Loch to Knutsford, 29 June 1891.
[7] African 414, No. 136, p. 118, Loch to Knutsford, 29 June 1891.

to what extent is the High Commissioner responsible and how is he to exercise control if any?'[1]

Imperial withdrawal

Colonial Office reaction to the High Commissioner's views was revealing of its negative attitude towards direct Imperial expansion, and indeed to any further involvement and expense in the area. The proposals met with a blank refusal. The Colonial Secretary pointed out the suggestions 'involved the assumption of a direct responsibility on the part of the Imperial Government for the administration of the territories'. There were strong reasons of policy for the control of the territories through a Company: the British Government was not prepared to assume fresh responsibilities of a financial and political character, whereas if Loch's proposals were carried out the Company would cease supplying funds. Nor could such proposals be justified to a reluctant Parliament.[2] Knutsford telegraphed that Her Majesty's Government 'cannot entertain suggestion of annexation nor approve of High Commissioner becoming sole legislating authority or controlling details of administration. Her Majesty's Government feel strongly no step should be taken practically superseding the Company's Charter and relieving it of its principal obligations.'[3] It was in fact 'the cardinal principle' of the Company's existence that, since it was to enjoy the profits of successful administration, it should 'also discharge the duties and bear all the responsibilities of government'.[4]

In view of this attitude it is not surprising that when Lord Knutsford received the despatches containing the Proclamation of 10 June, he was horrified. A series of critical cables was then sent to the High Commissioner. The Proclamation was 'contrary to what was intended by Her Majesty's Government', which had merely envisaged 'temporary arrangements for the administration of legal jurisdiction rendered of urgent necessity to provide for pressing cases'. No steps were to be taken under the Proclamation except the bringing of the courts of law into operation and the appointment of legal officers, and then only if necessary. Nor was a Resident Commissioner to be appointed.[5] The Colonial Secretary felt that by the Proclamation the High Commissioner had 'practically undertaken duties of civil administration', particularly by conferring the Treasurership on the Resident Commissioner (Section 2) and by providing for appointment of the police (Section 5).[6]

So violently had Colonial Office reaction been manifested that Sir Henry

[1] African 414, No. 136, p. 118, Loch to Knutsford, 29 June 1891.
[2] African 414, No. 51, p. 43, Knutsford to Loch, 26 June 1891.
[3] African 414, No. 55, p. 45, Telegraph Knutsford to Loch, 28 June 1891, and also No. 58, p. 46, Telegraph Knutsford to Loch, 29 June 1891.
[4] African 414, No. 51, p. 43, Knutsford to Loch, 26 June 1891.
[5] African 414, No. 104, p. 91, Telegraph Knutsford to Loch, 8 July 1891.
[6] African 414, No. 114, p. 97, Telegraph Knutsford to Loch, 11 July 1891.

Loch felt constrained to threaten his resignation as High Commissioner if his Proclamation were cancelled or withdrawn, though he was prepared to see it amended.[1] Unfortunately, unaware of the impending storm, he had innocently put its provisions into effect by appointing A. R. Colquhoun as Acting Resident Commissioner.[2] He enquired sarcastically whether Her Majesty's Government objected to the inclusion in his Proclamation of the Articles of the Brussels Convention of 1890 dealing with the prohibition of the supply of arms and ammunition to natives. He also pointed out that the provisions as to police (Section 5) and the entry of wagons (Section 35) were a necessity in view of the projected Boer trek, while Sections 43 and 45 were designed to stop concession hunters who stirred up strife among the natives.[3]

Faced with this attitude, Lord Knutsford, 'in order to avoid weakening the position of the High Commissioner', decided that the High Commissioner 'should not be at once required to take steps for cancellation or withdrawal', but that Colquhoun was to be redesignated as Chief Magistrate,[4] and that no steps should be taken other than the establishment of courts, the appointment of magistrates, and the application of the judicial provisions of the Proclamation.[5] The Company was, therefore, to be requested to make Ordinances to replace the provisions of the Proclamation dealing with the regulation of trade (Sections 23–36), the supply of arms and ammunition (Sections 37–40) and coinage (Section 41)[6] and, as soon as this was done, provisions of the Proclamation dealing with these topics were to be withdrawn insofar as they applied to the Company's territories.

Legislative powers of the Company

The Colonial Office made its refusal to admit the principle of Loch's Proclamation clear beyond doubt by ordering him in future to exercise his 'legislative and administrative authority only in exceptional cases'. Legislation in all 'ordinary matters' including changes in the system of courts was to be the prerogative of the Company,[7] and 'wherever and insofar as may be practicable the Company should legislate and administer'.[8]

[1] African 414, No. 110, p. 94, Loch to Knutsford, 9 July 1891.
[2] High Commissioner's Notice, 29 June 1891. See Encl. in African 414, No. 138, p. 124. Four magistrates were also appointed for Fort Victoria, Fort Salisbury, Hartley, and Umtali.
[3] African 414, No. 115, p. 97, Loch to Knutsford, 13 July 1891.
[4] 'Some other title denoting exclusive magisterial authority' must be adopted.
[5] African 414, No. 128, p. 111, Telegraph Knutsford to Loch, 16 July 1891.
[6] African 414, No. 128, p. 111, Telegraph Knutsford to Loch, 16 July 1891. On the same day the Colonial Office requested the Company to pass Ordinances on these subjects. African 414, No. 129, p. 111, Colonial Office to British South Africa Company, 16 July 1891.
[7] The High Commissioner might 'in some cases' acquire knowledge of draft Ordinances through communication to him by the Company's Managing Director: African 414, No. 145, Knutsford to Loch, 24 July 1891.
[8] African 414, No. 229, Telegraph Knutsford to Loch, 18 September 1891.

The Colonial Office in fact adopted a most inconsistent attitude to the powers of the Company. During the period until 1891, while it suited British policy, the Office maintained that Lobengula's consent was a prerequisite to Company governmental activities on the basis that the original source of its power, the Rudd Concession, gave no legislative power to the Company, while the Charter gave no additional powers, but merely recognized those granted to the Company by virtue of approved concessions.[1] Disturbed, however, by the possibility of being involved in responsibility in the new Protectorate, the Office did a *volte face*. Lord Knutsford now argued that, despite Articles 3 and 4 of the Charter, Article 10 gave the Company power to legislate generally by making Ordinances for the maintenance of peace and order. In any event, he considered that if such an assumption had originally been unjustified, the declaration of a protectorate had confirmed full powers to the Company. Article 10 of the Charter, he now maintained, much to the surprise of the High Commissioner who resented this sudden change of attitude, had been inserted lest the contingency should arise that native rulers would not give consent to the Company exercising power.[2] Company legislative powers were not, Knutsford held, limited by the Rudd Concession.[3]

Despite this attitude, on a true construction of the Charter, which conferred capacity rather than power,[4] read with Section 8 of the South African Order in Council 1891, which did not augment but merely preserved Company powers,[5] the Company had even at this time no legislative powers other than those derived from Lobengula. Nor had the Company powers of taxation (which it purported to exercise) since the Rudd Concession did not delegate Lobengula's royal prerogative of taxation.[6] Subsequently, when questioned in the Commons, as to the method by which the Company acquired jurisdiction in Mashonaland, the Under-Secretary for the Colonies acknowledged that 'the Order in Council of 9 May 1891 does not purport to confer jurisdiction but, as authorized by the Foreign Jurisdiction Act 1890, provides the machinery for exercising jurisdiction which had already been, or might thereafter be, acquired by Her Majesty'. He explained that the attitude of the British Government was that the Company was entitled to exercise power in

---

[1] See *supra*, Chapter 3.

[2] African 414, No. 229, p. 238, Knutsford to Loch, 18 September 1891; No. 145, pp. 134–5, Knutsford to Loch, 24 July 1891; and No. 173, p. 171, Loch to Knutsford, 21 July 1891.

[3] African 414, No. 128, Telegraph Knutsford to Loch, 16 July 1891; and No. 229, Telegraph Knutsford to Loch, 18 September 1891.

[4] See *In re Southern Rhodesia, supra* at p. 222: 'In 1891, the Company deriving from its charter capacity to administer and govern and from the Crown permission to do so subject to the Crown's direction could only seek the source of its actual administration in the governing sovereign of the country, King Lobengula.'

[5] See African 414, No. 136, p. 118 et seq., Encl., 29 June 1891. Opinion by W. P. Schreiner, Attorney General of the Cape Colony.

[6] African 414, No. 38, Encl. 3, p. 32, 30 May 1891. Opinion by W. P. Schreiner, Attorney-General of the Cape Colony.

Mashonaland since 'Lobengula acquiesced in the exercise by the white authorities of jurisdiction over the whites in Mashonaland and over the Natives immediately connected with them'.[1]

Even if Lobengula had by acquiescence delegated powers in regard to the administration of justice among Europeans, he had made no such delegation in respect of natives, nor had he delegated legislative, taxing or administrative powers to the Company, all of which it purported to exercise. That doubt as to the validity of such action existed was shown in a Memorandum for the directors in 1912 that, although 'in regard to the administration of justice among Europeans, it may, I think, be assumed that Lobengula delegated his powers', there was doubt 'to what extent administrative powers could legally have been exercised by the Company within the limits of Lobengula's dominions until the period of the occupation of Matabeleland in 1894, having regard to his sovereignty which had been officially recognized'.[2] This view was subsequently borne out by judicial *dicta* that from 1891 to 1893 the administration established by the Company 'rested on the assumption by the Crown within the territorial sovereignty of a native ruler and (was) yet subject to the recognition of his rights as such'.[3]

Nor can it be argued that the Crown had delegated authority to govern and legislate to the Company. Except for the delegation for the time being of judicial authority over British subjects and foreigners under the Foreign Jurisdiction Acts, the Company being bound to set up courts and appoint officers for this purpose,[4] there was no delegation of British authority to the Company. Furthermore, the Crown had not recognized any delegation of this nature from Lobengula, while by its constitution the Company could not exercise such powers, unless they were recognized by the Crown, since Article 4 of the Charter provided that no powers of government or administration might be exercised by the Company, unless a copy of such concession had been transmitted to the Secretary of State and he had signified his approval thereof. Mere deemed acquiescence by Lobengula in the exercise of jurisdiction by the Company over whites could not constitute a 'concession, agreement, grant, or treaty', which could be transmitted to the Secretary of State. In any event a copy of such grant was never sent to any Secretary of State.

Nor is there any evidence of a subsequent delegation of Britain's authority

---

[1] *H.C. Deb.*, 4th ser., Vol. 19, col. 373, Mr. Buxton, 4 December 1893. Cp. the opinion of the Law Officers (given at the same time) in relation to whether the power of extradition had been acquired. They held that the evidence did not show 'that Her Majesty had acquired from Lobengula such powers as would form the basis of an effective system of extradition': *L.O.R. 1893*, F.O. Conf. 6508, No. 2, Russell and Rigby to Ripon, 21 November 1893.

[2] H. Wilson-Fox, *Memorandum on Constitutional, Political, Financial, and other Questions concerning Rhodesia*, printed for the information of the Board, London, 1912.

[3] *In re Southern Rhodesia, supra* at p. 220.

[4] Article 22 of the Charter.

to the Company after the formal declaration of a Protectorate in 1891. It could scarcely be argued that mere consent by the Secretary of State to Company Ordinances amounted to a delegation of legislative power, which could only have taken place by virtue of an Order in Council, Letters Patent, Proclamation, Supplementary Charter, or a sub-delegation by the High Commissioner. It seems therefore that, until there was a proper delegation of authority to the Company by the Matabeleland Order in Council 1894, the Company exercised administrative and governmental powers *ultra vires* its Charter and without delegation of such power from either Britain, the protecting state, or Lobengula, the protected sovereign. Nevertheless the Colonial Office acquiesced in this position. Indeed the Secretary of State assented to a number of Company Ordinances, while 'regulations' by the Administrator were permitted, although for these latter there was no statutory basis whatsoever.

Administrative powers of the Company

A similar attitude was adopted by the Colonial Office to the exercise of administrative powers by the Company. Again the High Commissioner was not to intervene in such matters. The Administrator (chief Company official in the territory) was neither to be appointed nor removable by the Crown, nor was the High Commissioner to correspond directly with any officer of the Company on matters of importance, but only with and through the Managing Director and Company staff in Cape Town.[1] This last injunction was in breach of Article 18 of the Charter, which enjoined Company servants to communicate freely with the High Commissioner. Furthermore, the High Commissioner was informed, in answer to his 'hypothetical' questions about possible abuse of the natives and disputes with Portugal and the South African Republic, that in such an event he should 'address to the representatives of the Company in South Africa, under Section 18 of the Charter, a requirement, suggestion or request, according to the circumstances of the case, that their objectionable proceedings should be discontinued or reversed; and then, if further action is required, to advise the Secretary of State, in order that he may be in a position to exercise those powers of restraint which are given to him by the Charter'.[2]

It soon became apparent that, in addition to this negative attitude of Imperial withdrawal in Matabeleland and Mashonaland, the Crown was hoping that the Company would soon take over the administration of Northern Bechuanaland as well as its present territories and that this would save Britain the costs incurred in maintaining police forces in Bechuanaland.

That fear of incurring expense was the major motivating factor in the

---

[1] African 414, No. 145, Knutsford to Loch, 24 July 1891.
[2] African 414 No. 145, p. 133, Knutsford to Loch, 24 July 1891.

attitude of the Imperial authorities was shown early in 1892 by a Government refusal to appoint Residents in the territories of each African chartered company, since this would involve 'heavy expenditure' and 'a large demand upon Imperial funds'.[1]

Company action

As a result of these events the rudimentary Company administration which had been established in September 1890 continued controlling the area of the new protectorate. At the same time Company legislative activity began in earnest.

As a result of a Colonial Office request to the Company to replace the provisions of the High Commissioner's Proclamation by its own legislation, on the 30 July the British South Africa Company submitted Ordinances 2 and 3 of 1891 Regulating Trading and the Delivery of Fire Arms, and Coinage and Weights and Measures, which had previously been 'approved by Lord Knutsford'.[2]

After the enactment of these Ordinances, the High Commissioner, on Colonial Office instructions, issued another Proclamation removing the Company's sphere of operations from the provisions of the Proclamation of 10 June, except for Sections 3, 4, 8 to 22, 43, and 45, i.e. the judicial provisions, and the provisions that land grants must be approved by the High Commissioner and concessions by the Secretary of State.[3] The judicial provisions were amended to the effect that, where no Resident Commissioner was appointed, the Chief Magistrate should enjoy equivalent judicial powers. On 18 September, Dr. Leander Starr Jameson was appointed Chief Magistrate by the High Commissioner and designated as 'Administrator' by the British South Africa Company.

The only topic on which the Colonial Office still had doubts was the question of ownership of the land. At the end of June 1891 Company requests that the High Commissioner should proclaim a land settlement were refused. The High Commissioner was instructed not to 'take any step purporting to be an assumption of jurisdiction over the land: . . . some further understanding' with Lobengula was to be arrived at.[4] Although the High Commissioner had suggested a land settlement in favour of the Crown, since 'by this means a control could be exercised over questions in connection with native

[1] *H.C. Deb.*, 4th ser., cols. 1525–6, 23 May 1892, and Vol. 5, cols. 46–47.

[2] C.O. African (South) 417/No. 15356, folio 180 et seq., British South Africa Company to Sir R. G. W. Herbert, 30 July 1891.

[3] High Commissioner's Proclamation, 4 September 1891. *Statute Law of Southern Rhodesia from the Charter to December 1898*, M.O. Evans, Argus Printing and Publishing Company, Salisbury, 1899.

[4] African 414, No. 56, Colonial Office to Messrs. Hollams Sons, Coward and Hawksley (the Company's Solicitors), 29 June 1891.

reservations, &c., and the Crown could better provide in their land grants for the protection of native rights than it might be in the power of a commercial company to do under pressure of commercial and probably divergent interests',[1] Lord Knutsford, again fearing new responsibilities, rejected the proposal. He considered that 'any actual vesting of land in the Crown would, I apprehend, involve at no distant date the question of annexation',[2] and suggested instead that the right of land occupation and dealing with land should be granted directly by Lobengula to the Company.

The High Commissioner, however, again urged the necessity of placing the land question on a legal basis as the Rudd Concession gave the Company no rights in respect of land, and it was becoming increasingly embarrassed by this.[3] The problem was eventually solved for the interim by the Company's purchase of the Lippert Concession. In this concession Lobengula had granted E. A. Lippert, a German financier, and his assigns the sole right to lay out, grant, and lease farms and townships and to appropriate land in his name. Earlier the High Commissioner and the Colonial Office had looked askance at the concession, but when it was perceived that the concession would end the legal difficulties attending Company land grants, the High Commissioner instructed J. S. Moffat to assist in the ratification by Lobengula and proper witnessing of the concession.[4] Lobengula duly ratified the concession on 17 November 1891 and in March 1892 the Colonial Office recognized it as valid.

Company paramountcy

The net result of this voluntary abdication of power by the Imperial authorities was that a 'politically irresponsible' Company was put in control of a huge area in South Central Africa. The senior Imperial official, the High Commissioner for South Africa, was enjoined neither to interfere administratively nor to legislate within the Company's sphere.[5] Indeed, for the next

[1] African 414, No. 152, Loch to Knutsford, 8 July 1891.

[2] African 414, No. 188, p. 195, Knutsford to Loch, 25 August 1891.

[3] C. 7171, No. 7, p. 7, High Commissioner to Secretary of State, 16 December 1891; see also Colonial Office to Foreign Office, 4 December 1891.

[4] Moffat considered his instructions despicable as he was required to leave the King under the impression that he was strengthening a corporation hostile to the B.S.A. Co., whereas he was in reality dealing with them: Moffat to Loch, 9 October 1891, quoted in *J. S. Moffat* by R. U. Moffat, London, 1921.

[5] The only other Proclamations issued by the High Commissioner in 1891 relating to the Company's territories were both expressly authorized by the Colonial Office. One related to peace preservation and the expulsion of persons endangering the peace, stirring up strife and creating military difficulties with chiefs: High Commissioner's Proclamation, 30 June 1891, African 414, No. 148, Encl. (authorized by No. 58). The second Proclamation conferred on the High Commissioner powers to commute any sentence imposed by the courts and laid down that no death sentence should be carried into effect until a special warrant had been issued by the High Commissioner after receipt of the record and a report on the case from the Chief Magistrate: High Commissioner's Proclamation, 18 November 1891, African 414, No. 281.

three years the High Commissioner was hesitant to make any enquiries as to Company administration, while the Secretary of State was similarly averse to controlling the Company.

Furthermore, the only Imperial official in the territory was soon to be moved out. Early in 1892 the Imperial Government's Resident with Lobengula, the Rev. J. S. Moffat, was moved down to Palapye in Bechuanaland where he became Assistant Commissioner.[1] He was no longer to reside at Bulawayo, although he was to make periodical journeys to see Lobengula on important questions. The Company then appointed its own agent, Mr. J. W. Colenbrander, to reside at Bulawayo and to represent it in relations with Lobengula.[2]

Officially all the controls imposed by the Charter still stood, but, in practice, the Company was virtually unfettered in its administration and enjoyed powers analogous to those of the Crown in a Crown Colony. In the legislative sphere supervision by the Secretary of State was to remain, but even this was largely evaded by extensive promulgation of *ultra vires* 'Regulations' by the Administrator.[3]

Imperial control in practice, 1891–1894

Although the territory eventually to become Southern Rhodesia had now become a protectorate and was no longer merely within the sphere of British influence, there was little interference by the Crown in the executive sphere of the Company's operations and little more in the legislative field, except in respect of formal Ordinances.

Imperial legislative supervision

In the legislative sphere Company activities took two forms: either they took the shape of a formal Ordinance passed by the Board and approved by the Secretary of State under the purported authority of Article 10 of the Charter, or they took the shape of 'Regulations' promulgated by the Administrator.

The possibilities of control inherent in the Secretary of State's power to approve or disapprove of Ordinances were illustrated when the Company's first legislative proposals were received. Shortly before the High Commissioner's Proclamation of 10 June 1891, the Company submitted for Colonial Office vetting a draft code of laws based on the laws of British Bechuanaland. Although no such code was passed, as the Office advised that certain of the proposed laws were more suitable for enactment by High

---

[1] Although styled Resident, Moffat was merely representative of the High Commissioner and a 'medium of communicating the views of Her Majesty's Government'.

[2] African 426, No. 107, Encl., Loch to Shippard, 25 March 1892.

[3] *Infra.*

Commissioner's Proclamation[1] and that others should be delayed until legislation became necessary,[2] the incident illustrated the procedure that would be employed and principles on which the Colonial Office would exercise its control: the first indications of the development of a regular practice whereby draft Ordinances were submitted in advance for informal approval, discussions and amendment were seen; it became clear that the Colonial Office would not permit provisions in legislation that would arouse public criticism;[3] in view of doubts as to the extent of its powers the Company was at this time prohibited from dealing legislatively with Africans;[4] and technical advice on suitable provisions might be given.

Supervision of Ordinances

The first Ordinance actually passed by the Company was an Ordinance Providing for the Maintenance of Discipline and Good Order in the British South Africa Company's Police Force. It applied the provisions of the Cape Mounted Riflemen's Act of 1878 to the Force and gave the right of review of Boards of Officers' proceedings to the Administrator of Mashonaland.[5] The procedure followed in the passage of this Ordinance set the precedent that was followed in respect of all Ordinances passed by the Board of the Company. In advance of the Board of Directors passing the Ordinance, it was sent in draft to the Colonial Office where it was revised and returned to the Company in a form which the Secretary of State would be prepared to approve.[6]

[1] e.g. Peace Preservation.

[2] e.g. Marriage, minors, deceased estates.

[3] A provision for the imposition of sentences of whipping by Company Courts was not to be permitted.

[4] African 414, No. 20, Colonial Office to B.S.A. Co., 29 May 1891. 'The Company had better leave the natives and their law suits alone, for the present.' Provisions giving magistrates jurisdiction over natives were not to be inserted as 'the company has no jurisdiction over natives'. No provision for Chiefs' courts or appeals therefrom was permitted and a proposed pass law was also to be omitted as 'the hold of the Company on the country will not justify such an enactment for some time to come'. Indeed the High Commissioner himself was instructed by the Colonial Secretary to confine, in any Proclamation he might issue, the jurisdiction of the Courts as far as possible to Europeans, as the 'extent of jurisdiction exercisable by Her Majesty over the natives has not yet accurately been defined'. (African 414, No. 2, Knutsford to Loch, 15 May 1891.) The High Commissioner passed on to the Company the instruction that 'the natives and chiefs should be left to follow their own laws and customs without interference from the officers of the administration'. (African 414, p. 55, Encl. 3, Imperial Secretary to B.S.A. Co.)

[5] It was based on the provisions of the Order in Council of June 1890 governing the Company's forces when in Bechuanaland Protectorate.

[6] An interesting sidelight on the conduct of Company affairs at that time is shown by the fact that the Colonial Office found it necessary to point out (in view of the frequency of delegation of Company functions to Rhodes) 'that the Ordinance must be made by the Company itself acting through the London Board and not by the Managing Director in South Africa or the Administrator representing the Company in Mashonaland': African 414, No. 24, Colonial Office to B.S.A. Co.

The second and third Ordinances, the only other exercises by the Company of its Ordinance-making power during 1891, were in fact enacted at the express request of the Colonial Office to replace those portions of the High Commissioner's Proclamation of 10 June 1891, to which Lord Knutsford had objected. They were in reality, Colonial Office drafts approved by the Colonial Office legal advisers.[1]

In 1892 no Ordinances were passed, but 1893 was to produce a spate of legislation by the Board, all of which was cleared in draft by the Colonial Office. Most of the Ordinances were local adaptations of Cape Law and a majority dealt with topics necessarily arising in a rural community.[2] Others dealt with Trade Marks, Oaths and Declarations, Vagrancy,[3] and Convict Stations and Prisons. Again, the Colonial Office used its revisory powers over the draft Ordinances. Thus the Convict Stations and Prison Management Act 1888 Amendment Ordinance 1893 was changed on its suggestion so that the maximum corporal punishment which could be inflicted was thirty six instead of fifty lashes. Other Ordinances were amended on points of draftsmanship rather than principle.[4]

A significant stand, however, was taken on a draft Ordinance imposing a hut tax, although informal negotiations with Edward Fairfield of the Colonial Office led the Company to believe that the United Kingdom Government would agree to such tax.[5] However, the matter was referred to the High Commissioner for his views,[6] who replied that Colonial Hut Taxes were not comparable since they only applied to natives living on Crown land or private property alienated by the Crown, whereas in the Company's territories there was no such land and to impose a Hut Tax would be to impose on the natives

---

[1] Both the Ordinance Regulating Trading and the Delivery of Fire Arms and that Regulating Coinage, Weights and Measures were virtual copies of the High Commissioner's Proclamation, the only changes being those rendered necessary by the different media of enactment. They were requested by the Colonial Office on 16 July 1891 and approved by Knutsford on 31 July 1891. See African 414, No. 129.

[2] Cattle Removal, Stock and Produce Thefts, Game Law, Pounds and Trespasses, and Brands Registration.

[3] Despite its earlier attitude that the Company should not legislate in respect of natives, the Colonial Office took no action against the Vagrancy Ordinance which was an amendment of the Cape Village Management Act of 1881 and which provided for the appointment of inspectors of native locations, who were to have the sole right to grant permission to settle in such locations.

[4] A proposed Ordinance to provide for the office of Master (to deal with deceased and insolvent estates) was delayed until 1894 so that the High Commissioner could be consulted. The Colonial Office 'explained the regulations we would lay down' and as 'the Company stated its intention of providing for his (the Master's) fidelity on the same lines' agreement was given: Africa (South) C.O. 417/231, 23 February 1897.

[5] The Company's solicitor, Hawksley, was intimate with Fairfield. When Rhodes pressed for the Ordinance 'as we are losing large revenue', Hawksley was able to reassure Rhodes that 'the form has been unofficially approved by Mr. Fairfield' and that the United Kingdom Government would even agree to a poll tax. See National Archives CT 1/3/1, Hawksley to Harris, 22 April 1893.

[6] Hawksley was somewhat displeased at this. Ibid., Hawksley to Rhodes, 27 May 1893.

'a charge for the occupation of their own lands'.[1] The Colonial Office then suggested to the Company that they should not press for the Ordinance, particularly since it 'would involve the serious responsibility of possibly rousing grave antagonism on the part of the natives or of Lobengula or of both'.[2]

The matter was not pushed to a conclusion as the Matabele War intervened.[3] However, after the successful war against the Matabele, Hut Tax was eventually imposed at the end of 1894, the Ordinance having been 'drafted by Mr. Fairfield'.[4] At this stage, when Lobengula's views no longer required consideration, the Colonial Office merely delayed the enactment of the measure, the senior officials neither objecting to the principle of such legislation, nor altering the incidence and details of the tax. They only insisted that it was not to be imposed in Matabeleland until a Lands Commission established by Order in Council had made a settlement providing for native Reserves, approved by the Secretary of State.[5]

Ultra vires *legislation permitted*

By far the greater part of the Company's legislative activity, however, was to be found in the promulgation by the Administrator of 'Regulations'. This activity was *ultra vires*. The Administrator made laws many of which contained penal provisions without shadow of authority for his action. Dr. Jameson was wont even to declare 'Ordinances' to be in force and to take action under them, when he well knew that such laws were merely in the initial stages of drafting. Although the Colonial Office must have been aware of this activity either through publication of such 'Regulations' in the local weekly newspaper *The Mashonaland Herald and Zambezi Times*, or because the Company had on several occasions proposed legislation on particular topics

[1] African 441, No. 117, Encl. 1, Loch to Ripon. The High Commissioner was fortified in his views by an opinion from the Attorney General of the Cape Colony that there had as against the natives been no grant or concession by which the land had been vested in the Company and that the proposal savoured 'of taxing the real owners of the soil for the support of a Government which is in the country only by permission from the native sovereign'.

[2] African 441, No. 122, Colonial Office to B.S.A. Co., 29 June 1893. A Colonial Office Minute of 7 July by Mr. Olivier on the draft Ordinance shows that some members of the Colonial Office were well aware of the implications: 'The usual inclination is of course to kill two birds with one stone, and to appropriate the land with a view to starving the natives into working for the white expropriator on their own former property.' (It is not surprising that the forthright writer of this Minute, later Lord Olivier, became disliked by settlers in British African territories.)

[3] The sympathetic Fairfield informed Hawksley in a private letter 'not closing the door of hope or damning the tax eternally but pointing out that . . . this is hardly the moment to proceed with the consideration of the subject. Rhodes' argument that the necessity of paying the tax will compel the Mashonas to work for the Mining Companies is all well enough in a Stock Exchange luncheon room, but is hardly a *Parliamentary* argument.' National Archives CT 1/3/1, Fairfield to Hawksley, 29 July 1893.

[4] Africa (South) C.O. 417/231, 23 February 1897.   [5] African 461, No. 270.

9—C.H.L.S.R.

and informed the Office that 'Regulations' were already in force. Colonial Office reaction was normally a lackadaisical one of 'turn it into an Ordinance'. In the case of 'Regulations', the Colonial Office did not even take steps to prevent the assumption by the Company of jurisdiction over the African population.

The Company's mining 'Regulations', or 'Mining Laws' as they were called, were flagrant examples of *ultra vires* legislative activity. When originally put into force in 1890 they contained provisions dealing with criminal law and the establishment of courts, and although they were put to the Colonial Office in January 1891[1] and revised on its suggestion, later that year they were still subject to discussion and amendment.[2] 'Amendments' were notified to the 'Laws' from time to time during this period and it was only in 1895 after the Matabeleland Order in Council 1894 that the position was regularized by legislation.[3] The Colonial Office was, in practice, satisfied to see these irregular mining 'laws' continue for five years without insisting on any action to regularize the position.

Legislative activity was not, however, confined to Mining Laws. A series of 'Regulations', many of which contained penal provisions, on the questions of Licence Fees,[4] Lungsickness, Deaths, Liquor Licences, Pounds, Storage of Explosives, Forestry, Game, Sanitary Boards in Townships, and Natives, were promulgated during the period 1891 to 1893.[5] In respect of the two latter topics it is strange that the Colonial Office remained entirely passive. Even when 'Regulations' were officially submitted to the Colonial Office[6] its only reaction was to safeguard its official position by stating that Ordinances would have to be made before these 'Regulations' would enjoy the force of law. Even then, the Secretary of State would concern himself only to approve the principle of measures but not the details.[7]

[1] African 403, pp. 457–62, Colonial Office to B.S.A. Co., 17 January 1891.

[2] African 426, No. 88, Colonial Office to Company Solicitors, 6 July 1891: the Company's rights in respect of the flotation of companies. As indicated earlier the Colonial Office attitude throughout this period was that the Company should proceed on a contractual basis towards those persons mining under their auspices and should obtain from them a declaration that, in the event of breach of the Company's 'Regulations', they could be removed from the Company's territory.

[3] General Mining Regulations Amendment Regulations, No. 1 of 1895.

[4] Advocates and Attorneys were to pay £20 p.a. while Dentists and Doctors were to pay £5 p.a., a not surprising differentiation since an intelligent lawyer with African sympathies could have wrought havoc with the Administration.

[5] 'Rhodesian High Commissioners' and Administrators' Proclamations, B.S.A. Company's and Government Notices 1891–4', reprinted from *Mashonaland Herald and Zambezi Times*, pp. 4–14; Government Notices 12 August 1891, 16 November 1891, 17 May 1892, 17 June 1892, 17 December 1891, 23 February 1892, 22 February 1892, 16 April 1892, 13 June 1892, 23 December 1891, 31 December 1891, 6 October 1892, 23 December 1892, 28 December 1893. Copy in National Archives.

[6] The 'Regulations' as to pounds, forests, storage of explosives, and sanitation of townships were forwarded by the Company to the Colonial Office, with the information that they were already in force.

[7] African 426, No. 95, p. 130, Colonial Office to B.S.A. Co., 8 April 1892.

The 'Regulations' providing for the creation of Sanitary Boards,[1] the first organs of local government, had in fact been sent to the High Commissioner in October 1891. He approved the proposed 'Regulations' and told the Company that, in order to have the force of law, they should be enacted in the form of an Ordinance approved by the Secretary of State.[2] However, on 1 August 1891, Dr. Jameson had already appointed a Sanitary Board which had, during that month, passed 'Regulations' including penal provisions. At the end of October, after hearing the High Commissioner's reaction, Dr. Jameson purported to set up a Board of Management for Salisbury with four members elected in public meeting by adult male inhabitants and a further three nominated by the British South Africa Company. This Board immediately set about providing for sanitary inspection and a pound, and proposed native 'Regulations' for the control of Africans in its area.

Subsequently in October 1892, the Administrator purported to amend the so-called 'Sanitation and Management of Towns and Villages Ordinance' by repealing Section 24 and giving permission to Boards to levy rates,[3] knowing full well that such 'Ordinance' was really in draft form.

That the Colonial Office took no action in respect of this illegal activity shows its remarkable passivity towards Company action. This was the more emphasized because Mr. H. Labouchere, M.P., forwarded the Colonial Secretary a petition from the inhabitants of Fort Salisbury complaining about the British South Africa Company's charges and taxes, and the representation on sanitary boards, and asking for the introduction of the jury system. Lord Knutsford's reaction was merely to reply that 'Her Majesty's Government do not propose to interfere with the administrative and fiscal arrangements of the Company'.[4]

The B.S.A. Company Native Rules and Regulations were an even more significant case calling for intervention as they involved major decisions on legislative policy towards Africans.[5] Provision was made for a Registrar of Natives to whom all Africans who came into Salisbury were required to report for registration in order to obtain a pass from him.[6] Any African found in any township without such a pass or without having registered was rendered liable to criminal penalties.[7] Nor was any African to be in the European part of Salisbury between 9 p.m. and daylight unless he was on his employer's premises or possessed a written pass from such employer.[8]

---

[1] Created without authority in July 1891 in Salisbury by Government Notice 6 of 1891—rates were even levied by the Board—and in October 1892, in Fort Victoria.
[2] National Archives, LO 5/2/14. Letters from the Cape Office of the B.S.A. Co. Imperial Secretary to B.S.A. Co., 28 October 1891.
[3] G.N., 6 October 1892. Rates of 10s. per stand were in fact levied.
[4] African 426, No. 153, p. 199, 7 June 1892.
[5] G.N., 22 February 1892. Reprinted at pp. 12–13 of the B.S.A. Company's Notices. These laws and adaptations of them were the basis of control of Africans in urban areas for many years. Similar laws existed until 1960 and certain analogous provisions still remain.
[6] Section 1.   [7] Section 2.   [8] Section 6.

Furthermore, the employers of Africans had to have their 'contracts of service' registered with the Registrar otherwise the contract of employment was not to be in force.[1]

Thus at this early stage in the history of the country a pass system, a curfew, and the registration of African labour contracts were enforced. The Colonial Office did not attempt to intervene.[2]

Imperial unconcern with administration unless Imperial interests involved

The Colonial Office was even less concerned with the administrative activities than it was with legislative activities of the Company. The only spurs to action were the possibility of Imperial expenditure being incurred,[3] the possibility of disputes with Lobengula (which would lead to Imperial military involvement), pressure by influential rival concessionaires in England, the possibility of conflict with Portugal over Company activities, and difficulties with Khama in Bechuanaland. In view of his earlier correspondence with Lord Knutsford, the High Commissioner, Sir Henry Loch, refrained from intervention or identification with the Company.[4]

Even when an African chief, Moghabi, was killed in a collision with B.S.A. Company forces the High Commissioner took no action other than to consult Lord Knutsford whether he should 'take notice of such acts when committed within the territories under the direct administration of the Company'.[5] He was told not to intervene, since he was to take no action tending 'to relieve the Company's Representatives at the Cape from a full sense of their primary responsibility for the policy of the Company in Mashonaland'. All he was permitted to do was to deliver a message to Lobengula on the

[1] Section 3.

[2] When the position was regularized in 1895 by the Registration of Natives Regulations under an entirely new constitution virtually identical provisions were permitted by the Colonial Office.

[3] African 414, No. 194, Encl. 1, 30 July 1891, Imperial Secretary to the B.S.A. Co. querying the reduction of the Company's Police Force and suggesting an organized system of military service for citizens. The sequel to this enquiry as described by Marshall Hole, an official at the time and subsequently a director of the Company, was the enrolment of men in the Mashonaland Horse to save expenditure on Company police. He says in his memoirs *Old Rhodesian Days*, Macmillan, 1928, at p. 33: 'The authorities at the Colonial Office were consulted only when the arrangements had been completed. They were rather taken aback, but were loth to object too strongly for fear of furnishing the Company with a pretext for claiming Imperial protection at the expense of the British Exchequer. It was another case of successful bluff on the part of the Doctor.' (Jameson.)

[4] The High Commissioner refused a Company request to act in any way in respect of the appointment of field cornets and informed the Company that it must make its own appointments and draw up an Ordinance for this purpose: African 426, No. 62, Encl. 2, Imperial Secretary to B.S.A. Co., 1 March 1892.

[5] African 441, No. 171, Loch to Knutsford, 31 May 1892.

situation if an impartial statement would counteract 'the evil effects of malicious and exaggerated reports'.[1]

But the Colonial Office could not maintain such an attitude when difficulties with Lobengula might result. Thus, when native kraals in the Mazoe district were burnt by Company officers after the murder of a European, the High Commissioner deprecated the unnecessary burning of native kraals.[2] Subsequently, when a chief suspected of the murder was detained without trial, he felt constrained to point out that Mashonaland was now under a regular system of law 'binding not only on citizens but also on the Administration'.[3]

Nonetheless, even when a serious incident, the killing of a chief and twenty-two natives occurred,[4] the High Commissioner was hesitant to admonish the Company, since he understood that 'Her Majesty's Government desire I should not interfere in any way in the Administration of the B.S.A. Company's territories'.[5] For once, however, the Colonial Office asserted itself, commenting on this recklessness and undue harshness, and telling the Company that 'stringent instructions' must be addressed to its Administrator 'as to the steps to be taken for the prosecution and arrest of natives charged with offences in respect of which magistrates have jurisdiction'.[6] Such admonition, so rarely given, was effective: Dr. Jameson, the Administrator, immediately issued a circular instructing the field cornets not to interfere with natives and their disputes and to communicate with the magistrate of any district before taking action in the event of danger.[7]

When danger of dispute with Lobengula and resultant British involvement was evident, the High Commissioner could take a firmer line. Thus, when it was rumoured that a Matabele impi was on the warpath, the High Commissioner ordered that 'every precaution' was to be taken to avoid any dispute or collision between the impi and prospectors.[8] Similarly, when telegraph wire was cut by natives and the Company confiscated cattle but subsequently restored them when Lobengula informed Jameson that the cattle were his property, a report was demanded.[9] So too, when a misleading map describing the Bechuanaland Protectorate as being within the 'Chartered Company's territories' was issued, which was 'apt to mislead both the European and

[1] African 441, No. 209, Knutsford to Loch, 18 July 1892.
[2] African 426, No. 101, Encl. 2, 25 March 1892.
[3] African 426, No. 128, Encl. 3, 22 April 1892.
[4] A Maxim gun was used by Captain Lendy at Ngomo's kraal, after the theft of some goods and an assault on a farmer.
[5] African 426, No. 131, Loch to Knutsford, 27 April 1892.
[6] African 426, No. 143, Colonial Office to B.S.A. Co., 31 May 1892. Lord Knutsford confirmed Loch's attitude in respect of the Mazoe incident and that at Ngomo's kraal.
[7] African 441, No. 218, Encl., 1 June 1892.
[8] African 441, No. 40, Encl. 3, Imperial Secretary to B.S.A. Co., 30 November 1892.
[9] African 414, No. 42, 22 May 1893; African 441, No. 166, Encl. 4, 9 May 1893, Imperial Secretary to B.S.A. Co.

native publics and ... cause a very uneasy feeling in the minds of the chiefs in the Protectorate if the Company claimed territorial rights over their country without any previous agreement', the Colonial Office was willing to demand that the Company correct the map.[1]

The Company was also restrained in its activities when Britain's diplomatic interests were likely to be affected. Thus it was that the Company had great difficulty in 1892 in obtaining recognition of its land concession from Gungunhana, a chief whose territories lay both sides of the border between the Company's territories and Mocambique.[2] Only in 1893, when it was clear that the Company was not breaking the Anglo–Portuguese Treaty of 1891, and in view of the Portuguese attitude of freely granting concessions in Gungunhana's territory, was the Foreign Office prepared to recognize the Company's concession.[3]

Rival concessionaires with influence in England could also brake Company action and cause enquiry into it. This was the case in disputes with the Bechuanaland Exploration Company during 1892 and 1893.[4] Another instance occurred when the African–Portuguese Syndicate, who claimed a concession in Manicaland, alleged that the Company was ill-treating chief Umtassa and his people. This caused the Colonial Office, although disbelieving the allegation, to procure the British Vice-Consul at Beira to make enquiries.[5] But so reluctant was the Colonial Office to become involved in a dispute with the Company that, when the Foreign Office suggested informing the Company that such enquiries were being made, it replied that it would 'deprecate' any such communication.[6] Nothing was found by Major Leverson,[7] the Vice-Consul, and the Imperial authorities were only stirred to ask the Company to enquire into the situation, when they became aware of a possible mission to England by Umtassa's son to complain against the British South Africa Company.[8]

Imperial action to avoid war

Other than these few incidents there were no enquiries made about Company administration or occasions on which the Crown intervened until the outbreak of the Matabele War of 1893. At this stage Britain suddenly became vitally concerned with events in the Company's territories and began to exert control over the Company.

[1] African 441, No. 61, Loch to Ripon, 3 January 1893; No. 69, Colonial Office to B.S.A. Co., 31 March 1893.

[2] African 426, No. 269, Colonial Office to Foreign Office, 7 October 1892.

[3] African 441, No. 57, Foreign Office to Colonial Office, 17 January 1893.

[4] African 414, voluminous correspondence scattered throughout the volume.

[5] African 426, No. 219; No. 226, Colonial Office to Foreign Office, 30 July 1892.

[6] African 426, No. 251, Colonial Office to Foreign Office, 24 August 1892.

[7] African 441, No. 46, Encl., 10 November 1892.

[8] African 441, No. 101, Encl. 4, Imperial Secretary to B.S.A. Co., 15 March 1893.

As soon as it was obvious that war between Lobengula and the Company was likely, the High Commissioner, with the backing of the Colonial Secretary, the Marquess of Ripon, began to restrain the Company. At Fort Victoria Company forces had collided with a raiding Matabele impi which had slaughtered servants and cattle of the European settlers but, on Lobengula's express instructions, had not interfered with the settlers themselves. In dispersing the impi the settlers, led by Captain Lendy, had fired on the retreating Matabele and rendered war likely. The High Commissioner then deprecated extravagant demands by the Company for compensation and the commission of any act that might exacerbate the situation:[1] the Company was ordered to take no hasty steps which 'might involve the prestige and safety of the European race in other parts of South Africa';[2] no aggressive movement was to be made without the previous knowledge and consent of the High Commissioner;[3] and Dr. Jameson, the Administrator, was not to correspond with Lobengula on political matters.[4]

But, in view of the dangerous situation, the High Commissioner felt that unless Her Majesty's Government was prepared to assist the Company with money and men and to accept all the responsibilities, it could not interfere with the Company's freedom of action.[5] By this time, however, the Imperial authorities had realized that war between the Company and the Matabele would sooner or later ensue and were willing to support the Company. Their worry at this stage was whether the Company was sufficiently prepared to be successful. Eventually, satisfied that the Company forces were ready, Sir Henry Loch authorized Dr. Jameson to advance,[6] although the actual beginning of hostilities occurred when a Matabele impi attacked members of the Bechuanaland Border Police on the Bechuanaland side of the Shashi River near Macloutsie.[7] This was the opening of the Matabele War 1893, which was to result in conquest of the country and consequent fundamental legal changes.

[1] African 454, No. 22, Loch to Ripon, 5 August 1892.
[2] African 454, No. 42, Encl. 8, Imperial Secretary to B.S.A. Co., 4 August 1893.
[3] African 454, No. 48, Telegraph Loch to Ripon, 27 August 1893.
[4] African 454, No. 61, Encl. 6, 18 August 1893.
[5] African 454, No. 67, Loch to Ripon, 21 September 1893.
[6] African 454, Encl. 27, in No. 137, 2 October 1893; and African 459, Encl. 9 in No. 25, 5 November 1893. Jameson's forces had extracted from him the Victoria Agreement of 14 August 1893, before they would agree to participate. They were promised gold claims and 'loot'. See S. G. Millin, *Rhodes*, Chatto & Windus, 1952, p. 191.
[7] E. A. Walker: *A History of Southern Africa* (Third Edition), Longmans, 1957, at p. 428, casts some doubt on the genuineness of the attack which made Imperial intervention inevitable. Suggestions have also been made that the war was deliberately provoked by the Company both as a means of seizing Matabeleland and of causing a rise in the stock market prices of its shares, which at that time had considerably declined. See Robinson, Gallagher, and Denny, op. cit., p. 252.

6

THE CONQUEST OF SOUTHERN RHODESIA, THE MATABELELAND ORDER IN COUNCIL 1894, AND IMPERIAL CONTROL IN PRACTICE 1894–96

THE outcome of the war was a complete defeat of the Matabele at the joint hands of the Chartered Company and the Imperial force, the Bechuanaland Border Police.[1] As a result the Matabele Kingdom became a conquered territory at the disposal of the British Crown. Even if Imperial forces had played no part the same result would have ensued since a subject acquires territory not for himself but for the Crown.[2]

Prior to 1894 there had not been any acquisition of the territory by Britain. Since Lobengula's was 'after a fashion . . . a regular government in which the actual rule was his',[3] no question of settlement or occupation could have arisen despite the fact that prior to 1894 there had been considerable white settlement in Mashonaland.[4]

Britain's powers in the area therefore depended on conquest. As a result the Crown was endowed with the powers of a conqueror: it might fix such terms and conditions as it thought proper; it might yield up or retain the conquest; and it might change part or the whole of the law of the conquered territory.[5]

[1] Although the Company proclaimed the conquest of the country as being solely its achievement, the British forces played a very important part: African 461, No. 25, Loch to Ripon, 26 December 1893.

[2] In later analysing these events, the Privy Council said: 'If there was a conquest by the Company's arms, then, by well settled constitutional practice, that conquest was on behalf of the Crown': In re Southern Rhodesia, supra at p. 221. See also 'Aspects of State Sovereignty', by Sir Arnold McNair, B.Y.B.I.L., 1949, p. 6 at p. 30 quoting an opinion by the Law Officers in 1854 that British subjects acquiring by conquest or cession acquire solely for the Crown. See also McNair, Opinions, Vol. I, pp. 15–22, 295–8, and F.O. Conf. 7058, pp. 35–36, Webster and Finlay to F.O., 28 December 1897, advising that the rule that a subject acquiring territory acquires for the Crown applies also to territory ceded or acquired by treaty.

[3] In re Southern Rhodesia, supra at pp. 214–15.

[4] In International Law it is clear that 'the territory of any state, even though it is entirely outside the Family of Nations, is not a possible object of occupation, and it can only be acquired by cession or subjugation': Oppenheim, op. cit., § 221, pp. 507–8; In re Southern Rhodesia, supra at pp. 215–16; and R. v. Crewe, supra at p. 603, where Vaughan Williams L.J. ruled that the territories covered by the 1891 Order in Council had not been acquired by settlement or cession. Thus certain consequences such as the automatic introduction of English law, and a representative Legislature did not follow: Campbell v. Hall, 20 St. Tr., pp. 239, 292, 323, 330. Nor would the British Settlements Act 1887 (50 and 51 Vict. c. 54) be of application as it is inapplicable to conquered colonies (Section VI).

[5] Campbell v. Hall, 1 Cowp. 204 at 209–10. See also Calvin's Case, 1608, 7 Co. Rep. 1; Abeyesekera v. Jayatilake, [1932] A.C. 260 at 264; West Rand Central Gold Mining Co. Ltd.

Such powers would continue so long as the territory was not constituted a colony but remained simply a conquest.[1]

The Crown, therefore, had full powers to make provision for the government of the conquered territory, previously Lobengula's domain.[2] Any administration there established would be based on authorization by the Crown and would no longer depend on a purported delegation from Lobengula. There would therefore be a fundamental change in the legal basis of any authority exercised within the area.

In addition, neither the Company nor any of the inhabitants of the area were entitled in constitutional law[3] to any rights which they had enjoyed under Lobengula except insofar as these were recognized by the new sovereign. If rights were of a public nature they lay at the disposal of the Crown on the conquest, while, if they were of a private nature, in order to be enforceable they required recognition either by agreement express or implied, or by legislation.[4] On this basis rights possessed by the Company under the Rudd and Lippert Concessions were unenforceable until they were recognized by the Crown.[5] In any event, the Lippert Concession, which conferred personal rights on Lippert, lapsed with Lobengula's death[6] and by analogy the fate of the Rudd Concession must have been similar.[7]

v. *Rex*, [1905] 2 K.B. 391 at 403–4. There are *dicta* in *Campbell* v. *Hall* at 209 that the Crown 'cannot make any change contrary to fundamental principles', e.g. so as to exclude the power of parliament.

[1] *Abeyesekera* v. *Jayatilake, supra* at p. 264. Once it became a colony, prerogative powers would be suspended if representative institutions were granted and were in operation, unless a reservation as to the Crown's right to legislate concurrently were made: *Sammut* v. *Strickland*, [1938] A.C. 678 at 704 and 706 interpreting *Campbell* v. *Hall*.

[2] It 'rested with Her Majesty's advisers to say what should be done with it': *In re Southern Rhodesia, supra* at p. 221.

[3] Although in International Law a change in sovereignty ought not to affect private property no municipal court has authority to enforce such an obligation: *Cook* v. *Sprigg*, [1899] A.C. 572 at 578.

[4] *Vajesingji Joravarsingji* v. *Secretary of State for India*, [1924] L.R. 51 I.A. 357 at 360; *Secretary of State for India* v. *Bai Rajbai*, [1915] L.R. 42 I.A. 229 at 337; and see *In re Southern Rhodesia, supra* at 234 where the Privy Council applied these principles to native land rights. Cp. *Amodu Tijani* v. *Secretary Southern Nigeria, supra* at 407 where it was held that there is a presumption that a change in sovereignty does not affect private rights. See also O'Connell, op. cit.

[5] The Crown did not recognize the Lippert Concession (except for its earlier recognition in 1892) although it only indicated for the first time in March 1915, when it lodged its case for the special reference in regard to the ownership of unalienated land in Southern Rhodesia, that it laid claim itself to these lands. Lobengula's Tati Concession was recognized by the Colonial Office on 13 June 1894, while the B.S.A. Company's mineral rights under the Rudd Concession were recognized only in 1923 as part of the final settlement with the Company: see Cmd. 1984, Clause 2D. However, it may be that the Company had no rights under the Concession as payments made by the Company under the Concession ceased on 30 June 1893, prior to the outbreak of the Matabele War. The Concession had provided that, if payments were in arrear for three months, the grant was to cease to be of effect as from the date of the last payment.

[6] *In re Southern Rhodesia, supra* at p. 237.

[7] See *The Mineral Rights*, by H. H. Phear, Salisbury, 1929, pp. 8–10; and *Correspondence relating to the Question of the Ownership of the Mineral Rights in Southern Rhodesia*,

In the event the same reasons of Imperial policy that had occasioned the Crown to charter the Company, to insist on its remaining responsible for administration in 1891, and that had dictated Imperial abdication of responsibility in the area, were decisive in the decisions taken in 1894.

The British Government decided against annexation at that time of Matabeleland and Mashonaland since they felt that 'under the existing system there were serious objections to the creation of a Crown colony in that region, or to placing Matabeleland under the direct administration of the High Commissioner.[1] They determined, therefore, to extend the existing system with such modifications as might be considered necessary to that part of the country known as Matabeleland.'[2] By virtue of the prerogative to deal with conquered territory and to assign territories for administration and control, it was decided that the area should continue as a protectorate and power was

Government Printer, Salisbury, 1933 (CSR18—1933) containing opinions by counsel to similar effect.

[1] By not annexing there was no renunciation of the right to annex in the future: *In re Southern Rhodesia, supra* at 240. Some of the *dicta* in this case are ambiguous as it appears at pp. 230–40 that a formal proclamation is only declaratory of a state of fact. If, as the Crown did in Southern Rhodesia, it makes itself the owner of the land the forms of annexation do not affect the substance of such an act of state. The Court considered that the monarch took steps making the Crown complete owner of the lands 'by public acts of state which indicate the same election and confer the same supreme rights of disposition over his conquered realm as annexation would have done'. On this view Matabeleland was informally annexed in 1894 while Mashonaland was annexed in 1898 when Reserves were established. In 1898 the Law Advisers gave an opinion that Southern Rhodesia had become a British possession: F.O. Conf. 7199, No. 4A, Webster and Finlay to Colonial Office, 29 October 1898. This was given on the basis of *dicta* in *The Queen* v. *Jameson* (1896), 12 T.L.R. 551, that although no formal annexation had occurred a protectorate might, by a necessary inference from acts of sovereignty by the Crown, have become part of Her Majesty's dominions. Indeed the Attorney-General had argued in that case that, even though passages in documents might be open to the construction that Bechuanaland was a protectorate, in fact sovereignty was exercised in the area. He even suggested that occupation and possession would be enough in itself to show such sovereignty: F.O. Conf. 6948, Memo. 1079. Argument in *R.* v. *Jameson*, p. 22. Polack, op cit., pp. 148–9, takes the view that formal annexation is unnecessary. However, despite argument that the territory had been annexed, the Privy Council held in a case in 1899, that no annexation had occurred. As Lord Halsbury said: 'I never heard that you can force a sovereign to take territory': see *Staples* v. *The Queen*, cited in *R.* v. *Crewe, supra*. See also *Wong Man On* v. *The Commonwealth* (1952), 86 C.L.R. 125 per Fullagar J. at 130 where annexation and cession on the one hand are contrasted with mere military conquest and occupation on the other. In the latter case there is no change of sovereignty. See also R. Y. Jennings, *The Acquisition of Territory in International Law*, Manchester University Press, 1963. *Contra Campbell* v. *Hall* (1774), 1 Cowp. 204 at 208: 'A country conquered by the British arms becomes a dominion of the King in the right of his crown', while conquered inhabitants 'become subjects, and are to be universally considered in that light, not as enemies or aliens'. The Law Officers themselves were not consistent in their attitudes, as they had in 1895 approved a draft despatch that stated that the administration of Matabeleland was being provided for by Order in Council but that sovereignty was not being assumed: F.O. Conf. 6796, Reid and Lockwood to Ripon, 14 February 1895.

[2] *In re Southern Rhodesia, supra* 224–5, quoting a dispatch from Ripon to the Acting High Commissioner, 24 May 1894.

delegated by an Order in Council to the Company. The Crown had therefore 'set up by its own authority its own appointee as administrator'.[1]

This settlement which the Crown made in 1894 was described by the Privy Council in 1918 as being 'of capital importance because the rights and the system under which Southern Rhodesia had since been administered were in all essentials settled then'.[2]

The 1894 settlement

In this new settlement Britain had completely unfettered legal power to establish any administration of her choice. Alternatively, in deciding to continue Company rule, she equally had the opportunity to reassert control over Company activity.

Although at the beginning of the Matabele War it had seemed as if British authority would be asserted in the future settlement[3] the Colonial Office agreed, after Company representations, that Company views would 'receive the most attentive consideration' and the High Commissioner was ordered to keep on 'good terms with Rhodes, learning his wishes and giving them every just consideration'.[4] In practice the future settlement was to be put into the hands of Rhodes, who would obtain all he wanted, subject to minor restraints inserted in the constitutional instruments by the Colonial Office.[5]

The reason for this was that all the economic arguments in favour of Company rule still applied. Indeed early in November, in answer to a question in the House, the Government publicly committed itself to handing over power in the whole of Southern Rhodesia to the Company.[6] It justified this decision on the basis of the terms of the Charter, the applicability of the Company's concessions to both Matabeleland and Mashonaland, the fact that the war had been conducted largely at the cost of the Company, and the general feeling in South Africa against direct Imperial intervention. Both for financial reasons and out of fear of antagonizing pro-British elements in South Africa,

[1] *In re Southern Rhodesia, supra* at p. 240.

[2] ibid. at 225.

[3] Initially it was ordered that all negotiations about the future status of the country were to be under the sole superintendence of the High Commissioner subject to revision by the Colonial Secretary: African 454, Nos. 95 and 128.

[4] African 459, Nos. 8, 10, and 39. The Company had alleged that it had the right to settle affairs subject only to the control of the Colonial Secretary—African 459, No. 1, B.S.A. Co. to Colonial Office, 24 October 1893—and the Colonial Office capitulated, particularly in view of pressure by the Cape Cabinet (Rhodes was Prime Minister) that the British South Africa Company should be entitled to exercise a free hand: African 459, No. 30, Telegraph Loch to Ripon. The High Commissioner, who was also Governor of the Cape, surrendered to Ministerial pressure and forwarded this cable although he felt that Ministers had no right to give him advice on matters outside the Colony: Lockhart and Woodhouse, op. cit., p. 268.

[5] J. Scott Keltie, op. cit., at p. 436, made the generalization (in 1895) that the Company was dealt with as an independent power by Downing Street.

[6] *H.C. Deb.*, 4th ser., Vol. 18, col. 586, 9 November 1893.

the Crown was not prepared to take over the responsibility of direct administration. The only reservation was that Her Majesty's Government 'would
wish with a view to securities for good government that the powers of
guidance and control given by the provisions of the Charter and Order in
Council should be exercised somewhat more fully than heretofore over the
actions of the Company, especially in regard to the rights and protection of the
natives'.[1]

Annexation of the country, direct administration by the Crown, and
appointment by and control of the Administrator by the Crown were all
rejected.[2] Even a proposal by the Colonial Secretary that 'an officer independent of the Company should, in the future, reside in Matabeleland or visit
the country from time to time as a representative of the High Commissioner,
and report as to the government of the native' was dropped when Rhodes
opposed this.[3] Only where Rhodes's wishes would cut across Imperial policy
was the British Government firm.[4]

The 1894 'Agreement between Her Majesty's Government and the British South Africa Company relative to Matabeleland and Mashonaland'

On 24 May 1894, an 'Agreement between Her Majesty's Government and
the British South Africa Company relative to Matabeleland and Mashonaland' was signed in London.[5] This provided that the government of the said
territories was to be conducted by the Company in accordance with its Charter
and a scheme of administration set out in the Agreement.

These arrangements without any significant changes were formally enacted
in the Matabeleland Order in Council of 18 July 1894,[6] which, despite its
misleading title, applied to all the territories which were to comprise the future
Southern Rhodesia, viz. Matabeleland, Mashonaland, and Manicaland.

[1] African 459, No. 50, Telegraph Ripon to Loch, 13 November 1893.
[2] This course was advocated by the High Commissioner who pointed to the analogy of the
East India Company. He also argued that not only had the Imperial authorities been involved in war with Lobengula, but that Britain 'might be at any time committed to a policy
brought about by the independent action of the B.S.A. Company and of which Her Majesty's
Government had no previous knowledge or control': African 459, Nos. 35 and 38A.
[3] African 459, No. 105, Telegraph Ripon to Loch, 2 December 1893; No. 160A, Encl.,
Memo. by Rhodes, 2 April 1894. Rhodes argued such a dual administration would 'lead to
friction and render Government by the Company impossible to carry on'.
[4] It refused to permit the insertion of the 'Rhodes Customs Clause' whereby the territory would be debarred from imposing higher duties on British goods than those then in
force in the Cape Colony. Lord Ripon wrote to Lord Roseberry that such a major question
of fiscal policy should be considered both by Government and Parliament and should not
be introduced by 'a side wind'. On these grounds he deprecated 'giving way to King Rhodes
in this case': Lucien Wolf, *Life of Lord Ripon*, John Murray, 1921, Vol. II, pp. 216–17.
See also African 461, No. 221, Colonial Office to B.S.A. Co., 11 June 1895.
[5] For text see African 461, No. 195, Encl., 23 May 1895.
[6] For text see African 461, No. 265, Encl., pp. 376–82, 18 July 1894.

The Colonial Secretary accurately described the new scheme as being merely 'a development and reform of the existing scheme of administration'.[1] The main change as between old and new administrative arrangements was that the Company was to enjoy real legislative power based on authorization by the Crown after British conquest of the country. Not only was its legislative power now firmly based, but it was augmented by a grant to the Administrator and an advisory Council of power to pass Regulations. The Company thereby acquired local legislative machinery in addition to the Ordinance-making powers of the Board of Directors in the United Kingdom, which was always more amenable to Colonial Office views.[2] Another change was that on executive matters the Administrator was now to be assisted by an advisory Council composed largely of Company officials. Furthermore, executive and judicial functions were to some degree separated as a High Court with one judge was constituted to replace the Chief Magistrate's (Administrator's) Court, where appeals had until then been heard. Finally, certain clauses protecting the indigenous population were inserted in the Order in Council, while control over important judicial and executive appointments was vested in the hands of the High Commissioner and the Colonial Secretary.

The Crown's legislative controls

Analysis of the 1894 settlement shows that legislative power was divided between Crown and Company. The Secretary of State retained control over legislative matters in that his consent was necessary in the case of Ordinances, and also in respect of Regulations discriminating against the natives. His nominee, the High Commissioner, was responsible for consenting to other Regulations, while the members of the Regulation-making body, the Administrator and members of Council, were to be appointed only with the approval of the Secretary of State.[3] Even after approval by the High Commissioner, Regulations were subject, within a year of their promulgation, to disallowance by the Secretary of State[4] while, in the event of repugnancy to any Order in Council or Proclamation (unless the High Commissioner had in the latter case given his prior consent), an Ordinance or Regulation was to be void.[5] In addition, the Order in Council preserved the powers of the High Commissioner to legislate by Proclamation[6] while no Proclamation could be amended or repealed either by Regulation or Ordinance, unless consent from the

[1] African 461, No. 195, Ripon to Cameron, 24 May 1895.
[2] Early in 1893 Rhodes had been negotiating with the Colonial Office for power either for himself or the Administrator to make laws 'without reference to the Home Board', but the Colonial Office had refused. Rhodes continued to press for increased power but in August 1893 he was told that it was inexpedient at that stage to ask for a Supplemental Charter giving the Managing Director power to pass Ordinances: see National Archives CT 1/3/1, Hawksley to Rhodes, 11 March 1893 and 12 August 1893.
[3] Sections 8 and 12.   [4] Section 18.   [5] Section 20.   [6] Section 6.

High Commissioner had previously been obtained.[1] Finally, the Crown's right to revoke, alter, add to, or amend the Order was preserved.[2]

Company legislative power

The Company on the other hand enjoyed legislative power, subject to the Imperial control outlined above, by virtue of the power of the Board of Directors to pass Ordinances and the power of the Administrator with the consent of at least two members of his Council to pass Regulations.[3] Such Regulations might suspend Ordinances in part or whole, but were themselves subject to repeal or amendment by Ordinances passed by the Board,[4] which could also, within a year of promulgation of any Regulation, disallow it.[5] Although taxation and customs duty might only be imposed by Ordinance,[6] both Ordinances and Regulations could empower municipalities to levy rates and pass bye-laws imposing fines up to £10.[7]

Colonial Office controls on executive action

Power of the Colonial Office ultimately to control executive action was preserved by the retention of the provisions of the Charter allowing the High Commissioner to give directions to the Company.[8] Furthermore, the Colonial Secretary's consent was necessary both for appointment and removal of the Administrator[9] and for appointment (but not removal) of the ordinary Council members. The judge's tenure of office—he was an *ex officio* member of the Council—was also at the pleasure of the Colonial Secretary. In addition it was intended that certain control over military matters should be secured by a provision in the Agreement between Her Majesty's Government and the Company that the Company's armed forces were not to act outside its territories without the permission of the British Government.[10]

Executive power in the Company

In reality full executive powers were vested in the Administrator and his

[1] Section 19.   [2] Section 57.

[3] Section 17: the Colonial Office had suggested that regulating power should only be accorded 'in cases of emergency' (African 461, No. 160A, Encl., p. 248) but these restrictive words were removed from the draft so that Rhodes obtained the power to legislate locally in nearly all circumstances through the Administrator and Council with the concurrence of the High Commissioner.

[4] Section 19.   [5] Section 18.   [6] Section 22.

[7] Section 21. From 1891 such rates and fines had been enforced in practice but such action was *ultra vires. Supra.*

[8] Rhodes had wanted to terminate the High Commissioner's supervisory functions and had suggested that the High Commissioner should only be permitted to correspond with the Company through the Managing Director in South Africa (himself) and not with the Administrator: African 461, No. 40, Loch to Ripon, 10 January 1894.

[9] Section 8.   [10] Clause 35 of the Agreement: African 461, No. 195, Encl.

advisory Council of Company officials meeting at his instance.[1] Although in all matters of importance the Administrator was to consult the Council, in matters too urgent to admit of advice being taken he might act immediately, in which case the Council was to be summoned as soon as possible and acquainted with any action taken and the reasons therefor.[2] The Administrator, however, was free to disregard Council advice, although if he did so he was obliged to report to the Board his actions and reasons,[3] which might reverse any action taken by him irrespective of whether such action had been taken with, without, or against the advice of the Council.[4]

An important addition to the machinery of government, not contained within the Order in Council, was the appointment by the Company at this time of the first native commissioners. Their establishment was, however, merely an internal Company arrangement and it was not until 1896 that such appointments became subject to control by the Secretary of State.

Reorganization of the judicial system

For the first time an attempt was made to establish a proper judicial system. Accordingly a High Court enjoying both civil and criminal original and appellate jurisdiction and applying Cape substantive and procedural law as at the commencement of the Order,[5] except in native civil cases, was established. Appellate jurisdiction of the Chief Magistrate's Court was abolished, while an appeal from the High Court was to lie to the Cape Supreme Court in civil cases where the disputed amount was in excess of £100.[6] Existing Magistrates' Courts were, however, to continue until the Company determined the number of magistrates' courts necessary for the territory.[7]

Imperial control of the judiciary

Colonial Office supervision over the personnel of the judicial system was now to be enforced. Not only was the appointment, salary, and removal of the judge subject to approval by the Colonial Secretary,[8] but magisterial

---

[1] A quorum was to be formed by two members and the Administrator, who was to possess a casting vote: Section 14.

[2] Section 15.

[3] Where Council members dissented from any action they might require their dissent and reasons to be recorded.

[4] Section 16.

[5] Section 26. Cape Law was to be applied 'as nearly as the circumstances of the country permit'. In *Salisbury Reef Gold Mining Company* v. *B.S.A. Co.* (1898), 8 C.T.R. 443 at 446, de Villiers C.J. held that the circumstances did not permit of jury trial in civil cases. Cape revenue laws were not applicable either: see *Stevenson* v. *B.S.A. Co.* (1899), S.R.R. 1.

[6] Section 35.

[7] Sections 36 and 37 and High Commissioner's Proclamation, 10 September 1894.

[8] Section 29.

appointments were to be made only with the approval of the High Commissioner subject to confirmation by the Secretary of State.[1] Similarly, suspension for misconduct of both the judge and magistrates was in the hands of the High Commissioner subject to confirmation by the Colonial Secretary, who might in lieu of removal reduce the salary of the judicial officer concerned.[2] In addition, sentences by the courts were subject to remission by the High Commissioner while death sentences required his confirmation.[3]

Safeguards for Africans

African interests were intended to be protected by the establishment of a Land Commission (for Matabeleland only) which was to assign sufficient agricultural and pastoral land and cattle for their needs.[4] The Commission was composed of the judge and two other members appointed by the High Commissioner, one on the nomination of the Secretary of State and the other of the Company.[5] Decisions made by this Commission might be reviewed, reversed or altered by the Colonial Secretary, provided he gave notice of his intention so to do within a year.[6] Except after full enquiry and an order by the Commission, any dispossession of Africans from their land and kraals was now to become a criminal offence,[7] while in cases where land was required for purposes of mineral development, townships, railways, and public works, Africans were to be liberally compensated and given equally suitable land.[8] They were also permitted to acquire, hold, and dispose of land on the same conditions as non-natives, but were specially protected from overreaching by the requirement that, in any land transaction in which a native was involved, a certificate by a magistrate must be issued to the effect that the African understood the matter and was receiving a fair and reasonable consideration.[9] Finally, Africans might not be subject to discriminatory

[1] Sections 37 and 38.   [2] Sections 41 and 42.

[3] Sections 33 and 32. Fines imposed on native chiefs or tribes, in the event of their misconduct, by the Administrator and Council were also subject to remission by the High Commissioner—Section 25. Here Rhodes secured a change from the Colonial Office proposal that prior approval of the High Commissioner should be a requirement.

[4] Section 49. The only important matter regarding the rights of the native people on which Rhodes did not get his way was the obligation of the Company's Administrator to deliver to the natives cattle sufficient for their needs. He had urged the insertion of a proviso to the effect that distribution should only occur 'after proof that the cattle were the private property of the people' as opposed to the property of King Lobengula, maintaining that the Company as conqueror was entitled to take as its own private property all the cattle that had belonged to the King. This issue had, however, provoked a number of questions in the House and since it was so important to the future peaceful settlement of the country, the Colonial Office rejected Rhodes's proviso.

[5] Section 46.   [6] Section 54.   [7] Section 52.   [8] Section 51.

[9] Section 24. This safeguard was insisted upon by the Colonial Office despite Rhodes's opposition. On the other hand Rhodes succeeded in obtaining a provision that natives who held land should be liable in the usual manner for their debts and that their property could be executed upon. This was based on the argument that, as natives had the ordinary rights, they should be subject to the normal liabilities of citizens.

laws except in respect of the supply of arms, ammunition and liquor unless the Secretary of State, upon the recommendation of the High Commissioner authorized such laws.[1]

Company paramountcy to continue

Despite the elements of Imperial control enumerated, the Colonial Office's intention was to permit the Company to exercise its powers freely. The High Commissioner was informed that it was 'not intended' that his supervisory powers should be used in ordinary course, so as to oust or interfere with the management by the Company of the internal affairs of the territory. 'The latter has been given very full powers of legislation, and it would be well as a rule to leave the Company to exercise these powers, except where, as in the latter part of Article 31 (sittings of the High Court to be determined by High Commissioner's Proclamation), the intervention of the High Commissioner is required by the Order in Council, or unless in particular cases there is some special reason for desiring to proceed by High Commissioner's Proclamation.'[2] The High Commissioner faithfully observed these injunctions.[3]

Despite the professions of the Colonial Office that it intended to exercise its supervisory powers 'more fully than heretofore' Rhodes obtained greater freedom from the Colonial Office and less control was exercised by it than in the period prior to the conquest of Matabeleland. Rhodes even obtained appointment of his nominee to the post of High Commissioner: Sir Henry Loch, who had clashed with Rhodes on the degree of control which should be exercised by the Crown, was not reappointed while in his place the compliant Sir Hercules Robinson, formerly High Commissioner until 1890, was, after pressure by Rhodes, sent out on a further tour as High Commissioner.[4]

Imperial control over legislation in practice, 1894–96

Since legislation could now be enacted locally without the strict scrutiny of officials in Whitehall by means of Regulations passed by the Administrator

[1] Section 23. Although a Colonial Office draft Agreement had placed an absolute prohibition on discriminatory legislation other than on specified matters (viz. the supply of arms, ammunition and liquor) at Rhodes's insistence and with the High Commissioner's support, the Colonial Office agreed to allow discriminatory legislation on the basis of argument by Rhodes that the need for consent to such legislation was sufficient safeguard: African 461, No. 160A, Encl., pp. 248–51, 2 April 1894.

[2] African 461, No. 309, Ripon to Cameron, 7 September 1894. The High Commissioner might consolidate the Proclamations already in force 'should such a course appear desirable to you and the Managing Director of the Company (Rhodes)'.

[3] The only uses of his proclaiming power after the Order in Council in 1894 and 1895 were in respect of sittings of the High Court, an extradition agreement with the Orange Free State and a delegation of his jurisdiction over the territories of the Baralong and the Balamiti to the Company.

[4] See Robinson, Gallagher, and Denny, op. cit., at p. 253; Lockhart and Woodhouse, op. cit., p. 285. At p. 235 the authors state that Rhodes 'manipulated the Colonial Office by means of the High Commissioner'.

10—C.H.L.S.R.

and Council, the Company was to utilize this alternative method of legislation extensively.

Although the passage of Regulations became the normal method of legislation, several Ordinances were passed during 1894 and 1895. These were necessary since Ordinances alone were permitted to impose taxation and to repeal or amend earlier Ordinances: otherwise, the Home Board's Ordinance-making powers were virtually allowed to fall into abeyance. This is illustrated by the following table:

TABLE 1

	Ordinances	Regulations
1894 (after 1894 Order in Council)	1	0
1895	4	25
1896	0	9
1897	1	7
1898	3	33
1899 (before establishment of the Legislative Council)	1	Regulating power ceased after 1898 Order in Council.

Note: Amendments to Ordinances, hut tax, and taxation could only be effected by Ordinance. Most of the Ordinances passed during the period necessarily took this form, in order to legislate on topics which could not have been dealt with by Regulations.

Colonial Office scrutiny of Ordinances

Colonial Office control at this time is illustrated by a reply to a question on the procedure followed in passing Ordinances and whether conditions had been imposed or suggestions made as to the spirit in which such Ordinances should be administered. The Colonial Secretary replied that 'the practice has been for the Company to submit them informally and to ascertain whether the Secretary of State was prepared to approve them or desired any alteration to be made. In some cases alterations have been made but this has practically always taken place before the Ordinance was submitted for formal approval, and in no case has the Secretary of State in approving laid down conditions or limitations or enjoined the spirit in which Ordinances should be carried out'.[1] In fact, Ordinances were carefully scrutinized by the Legal Advisers, while an Office Memorandum in 1898 on the future government of

[1] Africa (South) C.O. 417/231, 23 February 1897. The Colonial Office draft answer had originally also added that 'it was never regarded as the province of the Secretary of State to look closely into the details of Ordinances submitted to him, the Company's territories not being in the position of a Crown Colony and the Secretary of State not being in the same way responsible for legislation'. So frank an avowal in the Commons of a lack of supervision would have been impolitic at the time of the Raid Enquiry.

Southern Rhodesia stated that Ordinances 'have always been duly submitted to him (the Secretary of State) and frequently modified by him'.[1]

Controversial Ordinances were thoroughly vetted and the Colonial Office might insist on insertion of particular provisions.[2] In one case in 1895 an Ordinance was even refused. This was a Consolidated Stock and Produce Theft Repression Ordinance providing for flogging. When Dr. Jameson urged that the measure should be pushed through, citing the Cape Act which provided for flogging, the Colonial Office remained adamant, and informed the Company that only if the provision for flogging were omitted would the Ordinance be approved.[3]

On the other hand, the Colonial Office permitted a Towns Management Ordinance, providing for local government authorities who would have power to pass regulations subject to approval, alteration, or amendment by the Administrator, there being no Imperial control over such legislation.[4]

Regulations as the main vehicle of legislation and Imperial control thereof

The main vehicle of Company legislation was the issue of Regulations by the Administrator and Council. No Regulations were passed by the Council

[1] African 559, No. 14, Encl., p. 37, Memo. by Colonial Office.

[2] The Hut Tax Ordinance 1894 had been the subject of negotiations for two years and was drafted by Fairfield; the Office of Master, Ordinance 1894, had been revised by the High Commissioner; the Towns Management Ordinance was amended in draft: African (South) C.O. 417/136, Vol. XXVI. The Mining Ordinance 1895 was also amended by the Colonial Office, while the Companies Ordinance was required to contain provisions for the liability of directors for prospectus statements that were more stringent than corresponding United Kingdom provisions: African (South) C.O. 417/160, Vol. XXIII, 189—perhaps the Colonial Office remembered the Rudd Concession. Rhodes's idiosyncrasies were illustrated in respect of the latter Ordinance. The Company solicitor was forced to reassure him that 'of course I shall not include the objectionable clause necessitating an issue of any increased capital among existing shareholders': National Archives CT 1/3/1, Hawksley to Rhodes. Nor would he permit the enactment of a Patents Ordinance prepared in 1893 and urged on him by the Legal Advisers from 1894 to 1895: there should be no Patent Laws in the Company's territories. As Managing Director, Rhodes could veto action on any topic.

[3] A long internal debate had preceded this decision. See African (South) C.O. 417/160, Vol. XXIII, 1895, 2 May 1895. The measure only came before the Colonial Office because the judge advised the Administrator that Regulations on this matter were not competent, an Ordinance having been passed in 1893: National Archives CT 1/10/30–39, Vincent to Acting Administrator, 22 January 1895.

[4] Towns Management Ordinance No. 2 of 1895, Section 23. This was intended to legalize the activities of the irregular Sanitary Boards composed of three members elected in public meeting by adult males owning or occupying immovable property of the value of £75, and three members nominated by the Company with the local magistrate as chairman. The Ordinance permitted Sanitary Boards 'to provide for, establish, regulate, and control native locations'; to impose fines and penalties, and to pass regulations with the Administrator's consent. The Bulawayo and Salisbury Boards then passed segregatory regulations providing for locations reserved for the huts and dwellings of native races. No person might be present in a location without a permit in the absence of which penalties were to be inflicted. Furthermore permits for residence while seeking employment were required and, in addition, whites and coloured, were excluded from locations during the hours of night.

in 1894, but Dr. Jameson still followed his old course even after the issue of the Matabeleland Order in Council and, acting alone, issued patently *ultra vires* 'Regulations Amending the Brands Registration Ordinance No. 9 of 1893'.

Regulations dealing with a wide range of legislative topics started in 1895. The procedure here was less strict than where there was direct Colonial Office scrutiny. The Regulations were normally passed by the Administrator in Council and then forwarded through the Company's Cape Town Office to the High Commissioner who, in most cases, would take opinion from his legal adviser and, if there were no adverse comments, assent.[1] As long as there was technically no discrimination the High Commissioner would agree.[2]

There was not even difficulty in obtaining assent to discriminatory Regulations as the High Commissioner would recommend that the Colonial Secretary should assent.[3] A major decision was taken when the Colonial Secretary agreed to the Registration of Natives Regulations 1895—although *ultra vires* 'regulations' to this effect had been in force from 1893.[4] This legislation discriminated in three respects: Africans could only seek employment in towns if they obtained passes from a Registrar of Natives (Section 1); Africans could not remain in towns unless they either had a pass to seek work or a registered contract of employment, and were subjected to criminal penalties in the event of default (Section 6); and Africans found outside the native location at night, unless they were on their registered employer's property, or had been given a special pass by their employers, were guilty of a criminal offence (Section 7). On Sir Hercules Robinson's recommendation that such Regulations had 'a beneficial effect' Mr. Chamberlain assented.[5]

Only in one case did the Company not proceed with a proposed Regulation. This would have amounted to an amendment to the 1894 Order in

[1] See National Archives CT 1/10/30–39, Correspondence on Regulations. See also African 484, No. 136, 26 January 1895.

[2] The High Commissioner assented without demur to the Matabeleland Cattle Proprietary Regulations No. 49 of 1895 vesting all cattle present in Matabeleland before the end of 1893 and their offspring in the Company. The cattle were assumed to have been Lobengula's personal property vesting therefore in his conqueror. An onus lay on any person disputing this to prove his individual ownership of the cattle in question.

[3] e.g. The Sale and Disposal of Stock Regulations 1895 effectively prevented Africans from disposing of cattle, as it provided that a European not possessing a written permit from a magistrate for such purchase was liable to imprisonment and a fine. The reason given was that Europeans should be prevented from buying up the King's cattle and running them out of the country. See African 484, No. 139, Loch to Ripon, 29 January 1895.

[4] National Archives CT 1/10/30–39, Memo. of Law Department, 13 November 1895. Jameson had promulgated pass 'regulations' in Salisbury and Umtali, with which compliance could no longer be compelled. 'The proposed regulations embodied two principles—passes, for identification purposes, and registration of contracts, in order to determine employers' liabilities.'

[5] African 517, No. 1A, Robinson to Chamberlain, 9 December 1895, and No. 10, Chamberlain to Robinson, 24 January 1896.

Council and, although the Imperial representatives in South Africa sympathized, they were not empowered to give such approval.[1]

Colonial Office control of administration formally effective

In the administrative sphere Colonial Office control did not make itself noticeably felt. Insofar as the formal provisions of the Order in Council were concerned, these were ostensibly observed. Thus the appointments of the Administrator, judge, magistrates, Council members, and Land Commissioners were all formally submitted for approval to the Colonial Secretary.[2] In practice, however, Colonial Office approval was at this stage merely a rubber stamping of Company patronage since no investigation was made by the Colonial Office as to the qualifications of the Company's nominees, who were accepted by the Colonial Office without question.

In terms of the Order in Council the Land Commission also forwarded its Report. This recommended the creation of two reserves for Matabeleland, the Guay (Gwaai) and Shangani Reserves, totalling 6,500 square miles, while in respect of the cattle question, it suggested that the leading indunas should be permitted to keep some, and that the balance should be left in the possession of the natives as the property of the Company, which could draw

[1] National Archives, CT 1/10/30–39, Harris to Jameson. The Imperial Secretary was prepared to assist in obtaining legislation which would have restored to the Administrator as Chief Magistrate the right to hear appeals from Magistrates' Courts. Jameson wished this power returned to him as 'after six months of the Judge it is . . . necessary. Both here and in Matabeleland the natives boast that the magistrates can't whip them any longer and they don't mind prison' (Telegraph Jameson to B.S.A. Co., 6 May 1895). Jameson then disregarded Section 40 of the Order in Council and heard appeals and reviews from magistrates in cases involving Africans, despite objections by the judge. He instructed the magistrates to administer whippings and continued to press for a change as attorneys might give him trouble: he could not 'rely upon all of them nor blackmailing'. Rhodes then told Jameson to wait until January 1896 because at that stage the Company would get all it wanted (a reference to the projected Jameson Raid and Uitlander uprising). The incident is illustrative of the fact that Jameson was contemptuous of law and the restraints it inflicted on his action (Marshall Hole, op. cit., at pp. 30–31, described the Doctor's 'contempt for formality' and his preference for 'novel methods of his own'); that the appointment of an independent judge had resulted in the cessation of whippings previously meted out to Africans; that magistrates without judicial supervision would have inflicted floggings; that the Imperial Secretary was acting in collusion with the Company ('The Commander (The Imperial Secretary—Bower) wants to help but must know the depth of the ditch before he breaks his neck'); and that, in spite of Jameson's illegal activity, the Colonial Office took no action. It is difficult to imagine that with judge complaining, invalid Regulations introduced in Council and knowledge on the part of the Imperial Secretary, the Colonial Office was unaware of the situation.

[2] In the case of the judge, however, the Colonial Secretary found it necessary to object to a press statement before the issue of the Order in Council stating that the judge had been appointed. Ripon insisted that there was to be no appointment until such time as the Order in Council had been passed, and that his consent was required, to which the Company replied that the appointment had merely been 'provisionally offered': African 461, No. 130, 3 April 1894.

on them as and when it found it necessary. The Commission considered that this was perfectly just, since the natives would in the interim be entitled to milk the cattle, having held them for Lobengula on the same conditions. Both Secretary of State and High Commissioner approved this Report, and it was accordingly implemented.[1]

Only for a short time during the Matabele War and the period of settlement thereafter was the Colonial Office prepared to give instructions.[2] It soon reverted to its previous attitude of permitting the Company licence unless issues affecting general Imperial policy arose. Thus possible diplomatic difficulties with Portugal would cause British intervention in order to safe-guard Anglo–Portuguese relations.[3] Even then, when possible difficulties with Portugal over Barotseland arose, the Colonial Office, having denied itself the appointment of any British official in Matabeleland, could only rely on Company assurances that no expedition to Barotseland was planned.[4]

The possibility of adverse publicity in the press might also stimulate enquiries[5] particularly if the Company was accused of atrocities.[6] Similarly, questions or the possibility of questions[7] in Parliament induced the Colonial

[1] African 484, No. 68, Loch to Ripon, 19 November 1894, and No. 112, Ripon to Loch, 25 January 1895. The decision on the cattle question subsequently played a part in causing the Matabele Rebellion of 1896. See *infra*, Chapter 7.

[2] This was particularly so if any action might lead to prolongation of the war. For this reason search for Lobengula was prohibited: African 459, No. 37, 26 January 1894.

[3] A Company official, Moodie, tore down the Portuguese flag in Gazaland; Foreign Office protests stirred the Colonial Office to instruct that Company officials should respect Portuguese territory: African 484, No. 39, Colonial Office to Foreign Office, 8 November 1894; No. 134, 16 February 1895; and No. 162, 6 March 1895.

[4] African 484, No. 212, Colonial Office to Foreign Office, 5 June 1895. The Foreign Office action was partly dictated by concern lest there be diplomatic problems, but also by the fact that Sir Charles Dilke intended asking questions in the Commons.

[5] Continual press publicity in *The Times*, *Truth*, and the *Daily Chronicle* as to the true version of incidents at Fort Victoria which had led to the Matabele War, caused Ripon to demand an enquiry. After the war had been won, and Captain Lendy, the man responsible for issuing the orders to fire on Lobengula's retreating impi, had been killed, this sat under F. J. Newton, Resident Commissioner for Bechuanaland. C. 7555 contains Newton's report. See also African 459, No. 31 and No. 67.

[6] Allegations in *Truth* and another newspaper that wounded Matabele were shot in cold blood caused the Colonial Secretary to make enquiries (African 461, No. 203, Ripon to Loch, 1 June 1894). Later, when a Reuter's telegram drew attention to the summary trial and shooting by a police officer of a headman, an enquiry was ordered and Jameson was instructed to direct all officers of the Company 'that proper legal process be observed in each case' (African 461, No. 271 and Encl. 3, Imperial Secretary to B.S.A. Co., 10 July 1894). Where its own agents committed such offences the Colonial Office would sometimes take stronger action. Thus certain European troopers, who had stolen gold from peace emissaries sent by Lobengula, were prosecuted and sentenced to 14-year periods of im-prisonment which, despite the fact that such sentence was in excess of magisterial jurisdic-tion, the Imperial authorities at first refused to quash (African 461, No. 240, Cameron to Ripon, 5 June 1894).

[7] Perhaps Colonial Office concern for proper maintenance of Lobengula's family was occasioned by fear of a question on this topic (see African 461, No. 126, 31 March 1894; African 484, No. 146). Indeed Colonial Office minutes show that the Colonial Office was concerned on this topic until at least 1910.

Office to make enquiries.[1] If Company action caused difficulties with rival and influential concessionaires, the Colonial Office was prepared to act,[2] while letters by influential societies, which might occasion unfavourable publicity, also stirred enquiry.[3]

In fact, reaction by the Imperial authorities on the spot was all in favour of the Company's administration. When the High Commissioner sent his military secretary to report on conditions in Matabeleland, he was struck at 'the kind and considerate treatment of the natives' on the part of those in authority.[4] Another favourable report came from the Commanding Officer of the Bechuanaland Border Police, Colonel Goold Adams, on the state of affairs in Matabeleland.[5]

Bechuanaland

Relations with Chief Khama of Bechuanaland were the only other limiting factor in the Colonial Office attitude towards Company activity and expansionism. Thus in November 1894 in reply to Rhodes's contention that the Company was entitled 'by right of conquest' to an extension of the borders of Matabeleland to cover territory, which had been disputed between Khama and Lobengula, the Colonial Secretary refused arbitration on this claim. The 'result might be unjust in itself and most inexpedient politically' resulting in the loss of Khama's friendship.[6]

However, this attitude was not to persist as the Colonial Secretary moved towards a handover of the administration of Bechuanaland Protectorate to the Company. Notice of complaints against Company action was still taken but this was lest such action prejudice the handover of administration.[7]

[1] Labouchere's question as to the treatment of Matabele by Mashona caused exchanges of cables (see African 459, Nos. 97 and 98). Parliamentary pressure and press publicity that Jameson was marking out townships, seizing cattle from the Matabele, who were starving, and prohibiting them from sowing their lands until all arms had been surrendered resulted in the Colonial Office insisting on the appointment of the Land Commission and that sufficient cattle be kept in trust to secure Matabele requirements (African 459, No. 113, 123A, Ripon to Loch, 10 December 1893, 13 December 1893). In another case the Colonial Secretary forbade the Company to employ an official, who had killed an African, as a magistrate again (African 484, No. 83, Ripon to Loch, 19 March 1894). The Colonial Secretary considered the official's 'proceedings to have been most reprehensible'.

[2] When the B.S.A. Police drove off cattle from the Tati Company's Concession the Colonial Office ordered an enquiry and Company officials were ordered to exercise greater discretion: African 484, Nos. 104, 116, and 124; African 517, No. 22.

[3] When it was alleged that Rhodes was introducing liquor to Bechuanaland, enquiries were made.

[4] African 461, No. 53, Encl., 16 January 1894.

[5] African 461, No. 143, Encl., 22 February 1894.

[6] African 484, Nos. 44 and 45, Ripon to Loch, 13 November 1894.

[7] When allegations of flogging by the B.S.A. Police of Khama's subjects were made, the High Commission ordered enquiry into the conduct of the Police (African 484, No. 223, Encl., 26 June 1895). Similarly in February 1895, when the B.S.A. Police collected hut tax and cut grass and firewood outside the Company's territory and within the jurisdiction of

At the end of 1894 it was agreed between Ripon and Rhodes that, subject to effective guarantees for the provision of Reserves, the protection of natives and the withholding of liquor from them, the Company should be entitled to take over the Protectorate.[1] In preparation for this handover Police forces in the northern portion of the Protectorate were to be removed.

Despite objections by the High Commissioner,[2] in line with the Imperial policy of safeguarding the British taxpayer's interests, the Colonial Office proposed to go forward with this transfer of administration. Eventually a compromise was reached whereby the Company was to get a railway strip and the areas to the north, south, and west of three large Reserves created for Chiefs Bathoen, Sebele, and Khama.[3] Steps for the transfer of administration were soon implemented and on 18 October 1895, Sir Hercules Robinson, the new High Commissioner, by Proclamation transferred the territories of the Balamiti and the Baralong to the Company's administration as Chiefs Montsioa and Ikaning in that area had, after pressure by Sir Sidney Shippard, ceded their jurisdiction to the Company[4] whose Administrator, Dr. Jameson, was appointed as Resident Commissioner. Chamberlain described these territorial transfers 'as instalments of a general settlement with the B.S.A. Company with regard to Bechuanaland Protectorate, one feature of which, the Colonial Office was informed, was the indemnification of the Government against the railway subsidy'.[5] Financial considerations had determined these decisions.

Khama, lest trouble should ensue, the High Commissioner ordered that any hut tax collected should be refunded, and the Company complied with this order (African 484, No. 164).

[1] African 484, No. 55, 30 November 1894. Sir William Harcourt also approved the handover of Bechuanaland to Rhodes as it would save the Crown money: see A. G. Gardiner, *The Life of Sir William Harcourt*, Vol. II, Constable, 1923, p. 199. By that time the Company had succeeded in persuading the Colonial Office to delegate the High Commissioner's powers in the disputed territory to the Company: African 484, No. 73, 11 December 1894.

[2] 'To hand over that chief (Khama), his people, and his territory to be administered by a commercial company, dependent for their prosperity upon what they may get out of the country would be a breach of faith.' The High Commissioner was not prepared to explain to Khama and other chiefs in the Protectorate 'the change in the policy of Her Majesty's Government which they will consider as foreshadowed by the practical withdrawal of the Bechuanaland Border Police from the northern portion of the Protectorate'. See African 484, Nos. 170 and 171, Loch to Ripon, 26 February 1895, 27 February 1895.

[3] Visits to England late in 1895 by Chiefs Khama, Sebele, and Bathoen, and humanitarian pressure placed on the new Colonial Secretary, Joseph Chamberlain, caused this modification. The Chiefs asked Chamberlain whether, when the Company assumed the administration, he would appoint an Imperial officer to become 'your eyes and ears'. The origin of this phrase is particularly interesting since it was subsequently to be adopted by Chamberlain in his dealings with the Company in Southern Rhodesia: see African 498, Nos. 88 and 131, 24 September 1895, 7 November 1895.

[4] African 498, No. 121, Encl. 2, Shippard to Robinson, 2 October 1895. In addition this territory was intended to afford the Company a jumping-off ground for military assistance to possible Uitlander rebels in the Transvaal. See *The Jameson Raid*, J. van der Poel, Oxford, 1951.

[5] African 498, No. 152, p. 155, Chamberlain to Robinson, 19 November 1895. The British taxpayer would save £200,000 in Railway subsidy previously promised to the Company

There is no doubt that during this period the Imperial authorities left the Company to its own devices unless considerations of Imperial policy or external pressures forced enquiries or action on the Colonial Office. The same reasons that had impelled the grant of the Charter and delegation of power to the Company in 1894 operated to make the Colonial Office reluctant to use those powers of control which it retained. That the Colonial Office had neglected to supervise the Company's affairs in the period of Jameson's administration is clear from a Colonial Office minute of 23 June 1897 which described Dr. Jameson as 'a beneficent despot doing what was right in his own eyes, and subordinate officers must have been left to their own devices in very much the same way'.[1]

The Colonial Office subsequently admitted that, although it had previously enjoyed theoretical control, such control had 'in the past proved ineffective'. This failure it ascribed as due 'to the absence, until 1896, of any officials on the spot to represent the Crown' and also to 'the great latitude given at first by the Board of Directors to their officers in South Africa'.[2]

quite apart from the sums that would be saved on the administration of Bechuanaland Protectorate when the transfer to the Company was implemented. The Colony was transferred to the Cape Colony in 1895.

[1] Africa (South) C.O. 417/231, No. 13061.

[2] African 559, No. 14, Encl., at p. 38, Memorandum by Colonial Office. The memorandum did not comment on the voluntary abdication and non-exercise of power by successive Colonial Secretaries.

7

REASSERTION OF IMPERIAL CONTROL: CONSTITUTIONAL RECONSTRUCTION 1896–98

FUNDAMENTAL changes in the form of government in Southern Rhodesia now occurred. In the period from 1896 to 1898, the Imperial authorities abandoned their previous attitude of allowing the Company licence and intervened in its territories to establish proper governmental forms which would secure the objects of Imperial policy.

The occasion for this change in attitude was the Jameson Raid into the Transvaal during the last days of 1895.[1] This unsuccessful expedition under the command of the Administrator consisting of virtually the entire body of the B.S.A. Company's police [2] not only had serious international repercussions for Britain but was in Southern Africa to change the course of future developments: it permanently seared Britain's relationship with the Transvaal and all Afrikaner elements in South Africa; the Company's claims to take over the administration of Bechuanaland were at first postponed and then dismissed;[3] extension of the power of the Administrator and Council over Nor-

---

[1] See *The Jameson Raid*, J. van der Poel, Oxford, 1951, and also E. Pakenham, *Jameson's Raid*, Weidenfeld & Nicholson, 1960.

[2] Five European policemen were left in all Southern Rhodesia—two with broken legs: African 517, No. 423, Encl., p. 461.

[3] African 498, No. 225, Colonial Office to B.S.A. Co., 18 January 1896. Frequent Company requests for undertakings to hand over Bechuanaland in the future met with replies that it would at present be 'injudicious' (African 517, No. 67, 14 March 1896) and that the Colonial Secretary could not commit himself to any expression of opinion (No. 250, Colonial Office to B.S.A. Co., 16 September 1896). By August 1898, Chamberlain was quite definite that the Company should not obtain the administration of Bechuanaland as previously agreed. In reply to objections to the boundaries defined in the 1898 Southern Rhodesia Order in Council he said: 'The Company evidently fail to recognize that it is entirely owing to their own officers that the . . . advantages . . . have not accrued to them . . . . The whole of the arrangements for the transfer of administration must be treated as lapsed': African 559, No. 294, Colonial Office to B.S.A. Co., 10 August 1898. This decision was taken on the advice of Sir Alfred Milner, High Commissioner in South Africa from 1897, that if Rhodes were given 'the Protectorate . . . you will at once have difficulties about the settlement of Rhodesia. He will begin to kick at our control of the police and at every other reserved power of the Crown. Yet these are MOST NECESSARY for the proper development of Rhodesia itself. Rhodes is a great developer, but he is not a good administrator, and it is most necessary that in his administrative arrangement AND IN HIS CHOICE OF MEN, he should listen to good advice, as he will readily if he sees something to gain by it': *Milner Papers*, ed. C. K. Headlam, 2 vols., Cassell, 1931, Vol. I, p. 107, Milner to Selborne, 2 June 1897. The High Commissioner's Proclamation transferring Montsioa's and Ikaning's lands to the Company was also revoked (see High Commissioner's Proclamation, 3 February 1896). Only in 1905, the delay being partly occasioned by the Boer War, was the Company given title to the Lobatsi, Gaberones and Tuli blocks—'the railway strip'—Bechuanaland Protectorate (Lands) Order in Council of 16 May 1904, and High Commissioner's Proclama-

thern Rhodesia, for which a draft Order in Council had been prepared, was not carried into effect;[1] the Africans of Southern Rhodesia were to seize their chance to start the Matabele Rebellion of 1896;[2] and as a final result, direct Imperial influence reasserted itself in Southern Rhodesia through a constitutional reconstruction, while at the same time active scrutiny by the Imperial authorities of both Company administrative and legislative action began.

Why Company administration continued

The Raid could even have resulted in the revocation of the Charter and an end of Company rule.[3] However, the financial arguments in favour of Company rule were as strong as ever and, in addition, Chamberlain was 'anxious to avoid injuring commercial interests of shareholders'.[4] If the Charter were to remain, development of the Country would be more rapid,[5] and the risk involved would fall on capitalists and investors rather than on the British taxpayer at large.[6] In the deliberations, which were to continue for nearly three years before a changed scheme of government for the Company's territories was evolved, the Imperial authorities consistently emphasized their

tions of 7 February 1905, 7 June 1905, and 30 June 1905. Ultimately the South Africa Act 1909 contained provisions for the transfer of Bechuanaland to South Africa and the Company was informed that Bechuanaland could not be handed over to Southern Rhodesia: African 1003, No. 7, 28 April 1913.

[1] F.O. Conf. 6851, Colonial Office to Foreign Office, 4 April 1896, and also African 517, Nos. 1, 92, and 117A show how the Matabeleland Order in Council was merely to have been extended. See also No. 356, Encl. 1, p. 362 at 366, Colonial Office to Foreign Office, 16 January 1897: 'In consequence of the Jameson Raid and of the decision of Her Majesty's Government to suspend the assumption by the B.S.A. Company of further administrative responsibilities for the present the Company cannot now be invited to send up a British Resident with a view to negotiating a treaty with Lewanika for administrative purposes'. African 574, No. 114, Milner to Chamberlain, 5 April 1899, explains why it was undesirable that the Legislative Council of Southern Rhodesia should have power to legislate for Northern Rhodesia. The decision had been taken to treat the latter as a tropical dependency and follow lines of development similar to those in Uganda and the Niger Protectorate, leaving the way open when the Company disappeared as an administrative factor to government by Imperial officers. The Zambezi was to be the northern boundary of what would some day be self-governing British South Africa.

[2] 'The withdrawal of the police by Dr. Jameson, though not actually a cause, afforded the opportunity for the rising': African 417, No. 416, Rosmead to Chamberlain, 9 February 1897.

[3] See C. 7933, No. 13, Colonial Office to B.S.A. Co., 31 December 1895: 'If the Company were privy to Jameson's marauding behaviour . . . .. Her Majesty's Government would at once have to face a demand for the revocation of the Charter and the dissolution of the corporation.'

[4] African 517, No. 13, Telegraph Chamberlain to Robinson, 1 February 1896.

[5] The High Commissioner, Milner, agreed that 'Treasury principles would starve Rhodesia—that is one great reason for keeping the Company up': Headlam, op. cit., pp. 139–46, Milner to Chamberlain, 1 December 1897.

[6] African (South) C.O. 417/197, Vol. XXXV, 1896, Colonial Office to B.S.A. Co., 7 February 1896. See also African 498, No. 224, Telegraph Chamberlain to Robinson, 17 January 1896.

reluctance to assume financial responsibilities.[1] The Treasury was even to jib at relatively small sums required for the maintenance of two Imperial officers in Southern Rhodesia, a Resident Commissioner and Commandant General, and in any case refused to pay for them after the lapse of a period of five years.[2] The British Government's attitude and the degree of control it was prepared to exercise clearly depended on financial considerations. Lord Selborne, Under-Secretary of State for the Colonies, insisted that in any arrangements 'we must at all costs steer clear of saddling on Her Majesty's Government any responsibility in the public mind, direct or indirect, for the finances of the B.S.A. Company'.[3]

The same attitude was adopted by Chamberlain: proposals for a Board of Control, as in the case of the India Act 1784, were turned down since this 'would amount to the creation of a separate public office with full responsibility for the finances of the Company'.[4] In fact, when a fresh settlement was eventually reached the Colonial Secretary insisted on the insertion of a clause in the Supplemental Charter to the effect that

Nothing herein or in the Principal Charter contained shall be deemed to impose upon our Secretary of State or upon the Lords Commissioners of Our Treasury any liability with respect to any matter relating to the financial concerns or commercial undertakings of the Company.[5]

Nonetheless the British attitude was that it would now exercise the maximum control compatible with the limitations it had imposed on itself by refusing to take over the financial responsibility of government.[6]

An additional factor was that the Colonial Secretary, although he 'knew of nothing so mad as Jameson's Raid',[7] had unofficial knowledge of assistance intended to be given by B.S.A. Company forces under Jameson in the event

[1] This was not surprising as the expenditure was large (and was made even larger by the Matabele and Mashona Rebellions of 1896). The Company informed the Colonial Office that in the year ending March 1897, two and a half million pounds had been remitted to meet expenses while it was estimated that £700,000 would be needed the next year: African 517, No. 42, B.S.A. Co. to Colonial Office.

[2] African 559, No. 69, Treasury to Colonial Office, 19 February 1898, and No. 297, 11 August 1898, in which Chamberlain refused to reclaim such salaries from the Company as such action would mean that the officers would be less independent. The Company also repudiated any liability on its part to pay for such officers: No. 380, B.S.A. Co. to Colonial Office, 12 October 1898.

[3] Headlam, op. cit., p. 122, Selborne to Milner, 11 November 1897.

[4] African 559, No. 14, Encl., at p. 38: no great changes in the constitution of the Company or the form of local administration should be made as these would result in an 'erroneous idea as to financial responsibility'.

[5] Supplemental Charter, Article 8.

[6] See Headlam, op. cit., pp. 139-46, Milner to Chamberlain, 1 December 1897. His proposals (which were accepted) gave the 'Imperial Government very great powers of control, the maximum of power indeed, which it can possibly have without taking over the whole government, and facing the enormous cost of it'.

[7] J. A. S. Grenville, Lord Salisbury and Foreign Policy, London, 1964, pp. 98-99, quoting a letter from Chamberlain.

of an Uitlander rising in Johannesburg.[1] Aware that the transfer of territory in Bechuanaland was desired for this purpose, he had agreed 'with misgivings'[2] and, despite the fact that he took decisive action against the Company when the Raid began,[3] his knowledge of events was politically embarrassing.[4] Disclosure by the Company, which would have nothing to lose after revocation of its Charter, of his participation would have been catastrophic.[5] Similar considerations applied to the Parliamentary Opposition, as Ripon, when Colonial Secretary, had known of a similar scheme proposed by Loch as High Commissioner in 1894.[6] Indeed, the Parliamentary Select Committee appointed to enquire into the Raid and into the future administration of its territories by the Company entirely failed to carry out the latter term of reference,[7] and successfully concealed the complicity of politicians and Colonial Office in the Raid.

[1] Chamberlain sympathized with the Uitlander cause demanding immediate redress of their grievances even immediately after the Raid: C. 7933, No. 140, 13 January 1896, and No. 220, 4 February 1896, Chamberlain to Robinson.

[2] J. A. S. Grenville, op. cit., p. 101.

[3] See J. L. Garvin, *The Life of Joseph Chamberlain*, Vol. III, 1934, p. 82.

[4] See Garvin, op. cit., p. 63, and van der Poel, op. cit., pp. 255–6. In addition Lord Selborne, the Under-Secretary, Edward Fairfield, of the Office, the High Commissioner, Sir Hercules Robinson, the Imperial Secretary, Sir Graham Bower, and the Resident Commissioner in Bechuanaland, F. J. Newton, all knew that large forces were being collected near the Transvaal–Bechuanaland border by the Company with Colonial Office assistance (this was done by encouraging enrolment of members of the Bechuanaland Border Police in Company forces and by the sale of Imperial stores: see Lockhart and Woodhouse, op. cit., pp. 300–4). Cp. The Second Report of the Select Committee on British South Africa, C. 311, p. xvi, blaming Jameson and Rhodes, but finding that 'There is not the slightest evidence that the late High Commissioner in South Africa, Lord Rosmead, was made acquainted with Mr. Rhodes's plans . . .. Neither the Secretary of State for the Colonies, nor any of the officials of the Colonial Office received any information which made them, or should have made them, aware of the plot during its development.' Bower and Newton were however condemned by the Committee.

[5] See van der Poel, op. cit., and Pakenham, op. cit., for comments on the eight missing cables—correspondence mainly between Rhodes and the Company Secretary on preparations for the Raid—which apparently implicated Chamberlain. These were not produced to the Select Committee appointed to enquire into the Raid. On 6 February 1896, after the ground had been well prepared by intermediaries (M. V. Brett, *Journals and Letters of Reginald, Viscount Esher*, Vol. I, 1870–1913, Nicholson & Watson, 1934, pp. 193–6), Chamberlain and Rhodes met to discuss the future of the Company. From that meeting when they were 'closetted together . . . the Charter so far as depended upon the Colonial Secretary would be saved': Garvin, op. cit., p. 104.

[6] Garvin, op. cit., pp. 58, 63; Pakenham, op. cit., pp. 140–2; and Lucien Wolf, *Life of Lord Ripon*, Vol. II, John Murray, 1921, pp. 222, 227. Ripon vetoed Loch's plan. Van der Poel, op. cit., p. 283, on Bower's authority suggests that Lord Roseberry was aware of such plans. *Contra* J. R. James, *Rosebery*, Weidenfeld & Nicholson, 1963, Appendix, and Lockhart and Woodhouse, op. cit., p. 300.

[7] The Colonial Office had in any event decided to continue Company administration. In suggesting that the Company's directors should give evidence to the Committee, Chamberlain wrote that, although he could not 'anticipate' the Committee's final recommendations, he suggested the Company's proposals should be based 'on the assumption that the administration of these territories continues in the hands of the B.S.A. Company': African 517, No. 503, Colonial Office to B.S.A. Co., 14 May 1897.

Finally public feeling sympathized with the Raiders and Company not only because of anti-Transvaal feeling but also because of an undiplomatic telegram from the German Kaiser, which suggested the possibility of German assistance to the South African Republic.[1]

Aims of the Colonial Office in the new settlement

The purpose of the Imperial authorities in changing the constitutional arrangements, legislative position, administration and judicial system was 'to lay the foundations of future self-government' although it was realized that for some years to come the responsibility for government would continue to rest mainly on the officers of the Company and the Imperial representatives.[2] It was envisaged that Southern Rhodesia would become a self-governing colony like the Cape or Natal and would ultimately enter a South African federation.[3] On this assumption it was decided that Southern Rhodesia should in her legislative and administrative policies follow the general pattern set by the South African Colonies, and would eventually become a white self-governing state.

The other purpose, which had to be reconciled with the former aim, was to set up a proper administration to deal with the native peoples so that grievances which had led to the Matabeleland and Mashonaland Rebellions of 1896 should not recur.[4] Chamberlain made it clear that 'although Her Majesty's Government have no wish to hamper the Company in the internal administration of their territories . . . they are necessarily deeply interested

[1] See W. C. Langer, The Diplomacy of Imperialism, pp. 240 et seq.

[2] African 559, No. 6, Milner to Chamberlain, 15 December 1897.

[3] African 552, No. 78, Milner to Chamberlain, 28 July 1897. See also African 559, No. 34, in which the Cape Ministry stated that they regarded the proposals 'as an indication of preparation for the time when self-government will be accorded to the territory, probably in the form of federal union with Cape Colony'.

[4] The Rebellion was caused by the Company's appropriation of all the King's cattle, subsequent widespread slaughtering of cattle owing to a rinderpest outbreak, compulsory labour practices by the Company, the use of a native police force (formed from 'the flower of the late King Lobengula's best regiments: B.S.A. Co. Report of the Directors, 1894–5, p. 77) collecting cattle and enforcing labour for two to three months each year, the appointment of young inexperienced native commissioners, and the fact that the Matabele had never been thoroughly subdued: see C. 8547. See also Headlam, op. cit., p. 140, Milner to Chamberlain, 1 December 1897: 'a lot of unfit people were allowed to exercise power, or at any rate did exercise it, especially with regard to the natives in a manner which cannot be defended . . . the rebellion was largely due to it'. F. C. Selous, Sunshine and Storm in Rhodesia 1896, at p. xi, condemns Company handling of the cattle question and labour enforcement. See also 'The Organization of the Rebellions of 1896 and 1897', an unpublished paper by T. O. Ranger, delivered at the History of Central Africa People's Conference, Lusaka, 1963, which shows that the power ambitions of the M'limo cult and priesthood played a considerable part as did dissatisfaction of the Matabele aristocracy with loss of their former power. In Mashonaland religious authorities (M'limo–Mwari and Mondoro cults) and paramount chiefs also organized rebellion. Agricultural disaster in the form of drought from 1894 to 1897 and locust plague in 1896 combined with other dissatisfactions to trigger the Rebellion.

in the success of the native policy of the Company, which may have far-reaching results in South Africa, and may thus involve Her Majesty's Government in grave responsibilities'.[1]

At the same time the Colonial Office wished to be in a position to assert proper control if this should prove necessary, without unnecessarily interfering with the Company. The new settlement therefore aimed 'not so much at setting up new machinery for the control of the Company's administration by the Crown, as at rendering that which is already provided for the purpose more effective in its action'.[2]

The changes were intended to 'render practically effective the safeguards already provided in theory . . .. It is through effective local control . . . that this end can best be attained.'[3]

The 1896–8 settlement

The introduction of representative government—the Legislative Council

In addition to the advisory Council to the Administrator provided for by the Matabeleland Order in Council 1894, there was now to be a Legislative Council containing a minority representative element. There were to be four elected members, five nominated by the Company, the Administrator as Chairman, with both a casting and a deliberative vote, and a non-voting Imperial representative, the Resident Commissioner. The settlers were for the first time thereby given some say in legislative questions though no say in executive matters, as these were the prerogative of the Administrator normally acting on the advice of the Executive Council. This was the former advisory Council which continued in existence and which consisted of the Administrator as President, any other Administrator, the Resident Commissioner, and not less than four members appointed for three years and removable by the Company with the consent of the Secretary of State.[4]

The Legislative Council was empowered to make laws 'for the peace, order and good government of Southern Rhodesia', thus, within the limitations of the Order, enjoying plenary powers of legislation including the power to raise taxes by Ordinance.[5] The sole restrictions on the legislative competence of the Council were that no Ordinance repugnant to the Order in Council might be passed,[6] the scale of customs duties that might be imposed

---

[1] African 517, No. 334, Telegraph Chamberlain to Rosmead, 10 December 1896.
[2] African 559, No. 14, Chamberlain to Milner, 13 January 1898.
[3] African 559, No. 14, Encl., at p. 38, Memorandum by Colonial Office.
[4] The Southern Rhodesia Order in Council 1898, Section 13(1).
[5] *R.* v. *McChlery*, 1912, A.D. 199 at p. 220, per Innes J.A.: 'The words are very wide and confer the amplest powers of legislation, for they cover the entire conceivable area of political action.'
[6] S.R. Order in Council 1898, Section 49.

was limited,[1] and no conditions or disabilities not equally applicable to Europeans could be imposed on natives without the previous consent of a Secretary of State.[2] An Ordinance, however, might repeal or amend a Proclamation by the High Commissioner.[3]

The Administrator's Council was now divested of its legislative powers[4] and the Administrator was warned not to issue legislative 'Proclamations' but to act within the limits of any empowering laws by Gazette Notice.[5]

The Board itself could no longer exercise powers of legislation as its Ordinance-making power was withdrawn,[6] but it might request the Secretary of State to disallow an Ordinance passed by the Legislative Council on the ground that such legislation might affect the financial responsibilities of the Board.[7] The Company was further protected by a provision that no fiscal vote or resolution might be proposed in the Legislative Council except by the Administrator acting on the instructions of the Company or by his written authority.[8] On the other hand, the Board controlled the Legislative Council as constituted in 1898 by means of the Company's majority of nominated members and the Administrator. Despite comments in *R. v. McChlery*[9] that the nominated members 'had an untrammelled right to vote as they saw fit' it appears that nominated members must take instructions from the Crown (in this case the Company), who appoints them, or resign.[10]

[1] ibid., Section 47. This was the Rhodes Customs Clause which Milner supported (African 559, No. 13, Milner to Chamberlain, 22 September 1897). Chamberlain later became an ardent advocate of Imperial preference. No customs duties on goods produced or manufactured in Her Majesty's Dominions or protectorates were to exceed the duties in the South African Customs Union or the Customs Union between the Cape, Orange Free State, and Natal in May 1898, whichever might be the higher. This was amended by the Southern Rhodesia (Customs) Amendment Order in Council of 10 August 1914 (as a result of the Cigarette Excise and Surtax Ordinance 1914 which was in conflict with it) in order to allow duties on tobacco and intoxicating liquor higher than those in the South African Customs Union. The elected members objected to their not being consulted but the Secretary of State said consultation with them was not necessary and went ahead: African 1016, No. 219.

[2] Section 81: see *R. v. McChlery, supra* at p. 221.

[3] Section 38: see *R. v. Bere*, 1921, S.R. 12.

[4] Other than as the executive body responsible for advising the introduction of legislation and advising the Administrator to consent to subordinate legislation.

[5] African 517, No. 40, Telegraph Chamberlain to Rosmead, 16 February 1897. This was said particularly with reference to Jameson's Proclamation of 1 May 1895, dividing Southern Rhodesia into districts and provinces and defining the jurisdiction of magistrates and mining commissioners. The Proclamation was in conflict with the High Commissioner's Proclamation of 10 June 1891.

[6] Supplemental Charter drafted in October 1899 but in force in June 1900.

[7] Southern Rhodesia Order in Council 1898, Section 37; African 559, No. 65, Colonial Office to B.S.A. Co., 15 February 1898.

[8] S.R. Order in Council 1898, Section 40. This was inserted at the special request of the Company: African 559, No. 88, B.S.A. Co. to Colonial Office, 4 March 1898. See also No. 166 asking that the practice in Crown colonies be followed.

[9] Per Vincent J. in *R. v. McChlery*, 1912, S.R. 79.

[10] See Alpheus Todd, *Parliamentary Government in the British Colonies*, 2nd ed., 1894, p. 39; and M. Wight, *Development of the Legislative Council*, Faber, 1946, pp. 100–1.

The Company was also instructed to establish a system of financial administration which would enable it to comply with Article 17 of the Charter by which it was bound to furnish before the commencement of each financial year an estimate of its expenditure for administrative purposes and of its public revenue for the ensuing year, as well as at the close of each financial year. It was suggested that the Company 'should follow the accounting practices of Crown Colonies, and copies of Model Financial Instructions' and 'instructions for the preparation of Colonial Estimates' were forwarded.[1] Chamberlain then insisted that the Company 'should lose no time in initiating a system of estimates and accounts that will satisfy public requirements'.[2]

The financial provisions of the Southern Rhodesia Order in Council 1898 imposed the necessity on the Company of dealing with its finance in a manner analogous to that employed by a country possessing parliamentary institutions,[3] and from 1896 to 1903 the Colonial Office rigorously insisted on compliance with these provisions.[4] However, when the Company sought an assurance that 'all future administrative expenditure not met by revenue, as also a fair proportion of past expenditure of the same nature should in justice to the shareholders, be regarded as a first charge upon the country and eventually be constituted a national debt',[5] Chamberlain saw the future implications of this request and that it would tie the hands of the British Government in arranging any future scheme of government. He replied that 'he must decline to pledge Her Majesty's Government in advance to acknowledging anything in the nature of a public debt, or of a charge on the administration as distinguished from the Company itself, which has been placed in possession of all the assets of the country'.[6]

The electoral system

In order to provide for the election of the four representative members of the Legislative Council a High Commissioner's Proclamation created two

---

[1] African 517, No. 220, Colonial Office to B.S.A. Co., 14 August 1896.

[2] African 559, No. 78, Colonial Office to B.S.A. Co., 26 February 1898.

[3] Sections 40 to 46 contain the financial provisions of the Order. In *Burrowes* v. *B.S.A. Co.*, 16 Juta 482, it was held that Sections 41 and 44 were merely directory, not imperative. See also *R.* v. *McChlery, supra* at 218 and 222, where it was unsuccessfully argued that the financial provisions for a budget, estimates, &c., prevented tax being imposed by mere Ordinance and that the Labour Tax Ordinance 1911 was invalid by virtue of non-presentation of estimates and non-passing of an Appropriation Ordinance as required by Sections 41, 44, 45, and 46 of the Order in Council.

[4] Wilson-Fox, *1912 Memorandum*, op. cit., pp. 126–8.

[5] African 559, No. 68, B.S.A. Co. to Colonial Office, 18 February 1898.

[6] African 559, No. 249, Colonial Office to B.S.A. Co., 18 July 1898. Despite this farsightedness by Chamberlain, the Land Case, *In re Southern Rhodesia*, was to upset British calculations, as the Privy Council decided the Company was to be compensated for past administrative deficits. The negotiations for responsible government depended largely on a satisfactory settlement of this debt between the local settler representatives, the British

11—C.H.L.S.R.

electoral districts, each returning two members, and made provisions for elections, franchise qualifications and the registration of voters. Male persons over the age of twenty-one, who were either British subjects by birth or by naturalization, or had taken an oath of allegiance, and had for six months preceding the registration of voters either occupied a building in the electoral district to the value of £75, or owned a mining claim, or received wages at the rate of not less than £50 per annum, were entitled to register, provided they could write their name, address and occupation (i.e. literacy was in effect a requirement). Although property communally or tribally held was excluded for purposes of the property qualifications, a house to the value of £75 excluding the value of communal land would be sufficient.[1] This franchise was couched in non-discriminatory language and Africans who met the qualifications were entitled to register.[2] The Company was concerned to see that all settlers could vote and that aliens were not excluded. It therefore negotiated the issue of the Southern Rhodesia Naturalization Order in Council of 7 March 1899, to enable easy naturalization by an alien after a period of twelve months' residence. Subsequent registration of such settler as a voter was then permitted.

Local government

The representative principle was also to be effective through the creation of elective municipalities.[3] These replaced the earlier Sanitary Boards whose regulations were however preserved.[4] Such municipalities might be constituted by the Administrator after petition by not less than three-quarters of the members of any existing Sanitary Board or, in cases where no Sanitary Board existed, on the petition of twenty-five or more persons being owners or occupiers of stands and being resident within the proposed municipality.[5] The Administrator might determine the number of councillors, who (except in the case of the Mayor) might not hold any office under the Company, and were to be elected for three-year terms, one-third retiring annually by rotation.

Government and the Company. A detailed account appears in J. D. Fage, 'The Achievement of Self-government in Southern Rhodesia, 1898–1923'. Unpublished Ph.D. thesis, Cambridge, 1949, copy in Southern Rhodesia Legislative Assembly Library. See also *infra* Chapter 10.

[1] High Commissioner's Proclamation 17 of 25 November 1898, Sections 3, 4, and 5. Other land might be taken into account in valuing a building.

[2] The Chief Secretary informed the Imperial Secretary on 26 February 1908 that on examination of the lists in 1904 it was calculated that about 50 voters were 'natives', the names being the only guide. These qualifications remained in force until 1912 when they were raised by Ordinance to a salary of £100 p.a. or occupation of property to the value of £150.

[3] By Regulations Providing for the Constitution of Municipalities, No. 101 of 1897. These were based on the Cape Municipal Act 1896, and were cleared with and amended by the High Commissioner and Colonial Secretary: see African 517, No. 469, Rosmead to Chamberlain, 24 March 1897.

[4] Section 3(2).   [5] Sections 7, 8, and 9.

The Mayor was to be appointed by the Administrator.[1] The franchise was given to owners or occupiers of immovable property, multiple votes being given depending on the value of the property.[2]

The Municipal Councils were given a considerable by-law making power. By-laws for regulating markets and public sales, for prohibiting the over-crowding of buildings, control of their erection, regulation of offensive trades, regulation of water supplies, drainage, lighting, preserving public decency, and many other powers normally given to local councils in the Cape were permitted with the approval of the Administrator.[3] Such by-laws could stipulate penalties not in excess of £10 for their breach.[4] The municipalities also had power to appoint and employ a municipal police force, and to provide members with arms and to regulate their duties. Such police had the same powers of arrest and immunities as ordinary police.[5]

Thereafter Salisbury was declared a Municipality with nine councillors and Bulawayo a Municipality subdivided into three wards, each returning three councillors.[6]

Administrative structure

Considerable reforms in the administrative structure were also undertaken. The structure of the civil service was largely planned by Mr. W. H. Milton, a Cape civil servant who subsequently became Administrator. After agreement with the High Commissioner, proper civil service regulations were drawn up and put into force in 1898[7] while in 1897 the Civil Service was departmentally organized and a comprehensive system established.[8] Thus

[1] Section 76.

[2] Section 27: property of £10 to £40 p.a.—one vote; of £50–£99—two votes; and £100 or more—three votes. Where a municipality was subdivided into wards persons might vote in every ward in which they owned or occupied immovable property.

[3] Sections 108 and 110. The Administrator might also repeal any by-law: Section 111. Model by-laws on many aspects such as Council proceedings, the regulation of streets, buildings, obstructions, waterworks, drains, fire prevention, nuisances, animals, and markets were set out in the Second Schedule to the Act and might be adopted by any Council: Section 108(2).

[4] Section 112.   [5] Section 156.   [6] See G.N. 191 and G.N. 193 of 26 October 1897.

[7] See G.N. 6 of 1898: Civil Service of Rhodesia Regulations of 11 January 1898. Rules and Regulations of the Civil Service of Rhodesia (G.N. 10 of 1898) were subsequently drawn up to provide for terms of service, appointments and discipline.

[8] The High Commissioner, Milner, had a high opinion of the general administration of the country. He described it as 'a liberal and considerate administration' which recognized the mistakes of the past. A 'complete system of administration departmentally organized' had been created. He considered that 'the fact that the Chartered Company spends this enormous sum upon the machinery of government seems to me to dispose absolutely of the charge that it is running Rhodesia as a mere commercial concern and without realizing its responsibilities as the delegate of the Imperial authority in the administration of the country. On the contrary, it seems to me to recognize its administrative responsibilities to the fullest extent.' Furthermore, 'public order is perfectly maintained, and the administration of justice is as regular as in a European country': see African 552, No. 78, Milner to Chamberlain, 28 July 1897, and African 559, No. 6, Milner to Chamberlain, 15 December 1897.

within a short period the various departments of administration were grouped into administrative divisions, some under the Administrator, others under the Chief Secretary and others under the Legal Adviser. Although there were subsequent reorganizations (e.g. the office of the Chief Secretary being abolished in 1908 and that of the Treasurer being established in 1903) the basic administrative structure was laid down at that time.[1]

The most important change, however, was the setting up of what eventually became almost a separate administration in charge of the African population. This was done by a High Commissioner's Proclamation[2] which set out the powers of the administration when dealing with Africans, provided for the establishment of officials of government who would eventually become the Native Department, defined the powers of native commissioners, giving certain of them judicial powers, and defined the duties of Messengers, Chiefs, and Headmen. The Regulations vested all political power in respect of Africans in the hands of the Administrator and Council.[3]

The Administrator in Council was responsible for the appointment of Chiefs and for the amalgamation and subdivision of tribes.[4] With the consent of the High Commissioner the Administrator in Council might remove a Chief from a chieftainship and remove him and his family to other land.[5] Similarly Chiefs might be called on to supply men for military service.[6]

The Southern Rhodesia Native Department was set up by the Regulations. The principal executive officer of the Department was to be the Secretary for Native Affairs,[7] who had power to make enquiries into all tribal dissatisfaction and to act as a protector of native interests. Southern Rhodesia was divided into two provinces—Matabeleland and Mashonaland—in each of which was a Chief Native Commissioner responsible to the Secretary for Native Affairs, who was in turn responsible to the Administrator.[8] Each province was divided into districts in charge of which were Native Commissioners, who might be aided by Assistant Native Commissioners.

The Native Commissioner was the main instrument of governmental relations with the African population, whom he was to control through their

[1] By 1910 there were four divisions—that of the Administrator, of the Treasurer, of Mines and Works and of the Attorney General. Comprised within each division were several separate and distinct departments, e.g. the Treasurer was responsible for Agriculture, Customs and Excise, Posts and Telegraphs, and Veterinary Services, while the Administrator's Division comprised Courts, Police, Defence, Education, Native Affairs, Public Health, and Settlers (Immigration). For a full account see *A Guide to the Public Records of Southern Rhodesia, 1890–1923*, Central African Archives, 1956, pp. 129 et seq.

[2] High Commissioner's Proclamation of 29 November 1898—The Southern Rhodesia Native Regulations.

[3] Clause 1, Section 1.

[4] Clause 1, Section 2.   [5] Clause 1, Section 3.   [6] Clause 1, Section 3.

[7] Clause 2, Section 1. At first no Secretary for Native Affairs was appointed but later the Administrator was appointed Secretary for Native Affairs and continued as such until 1914 when Sir W. H. Milton retired.

[8] Clause 2, Section 2.

Chiefs and Headmen. Native Commissioners were given considerable discretionary powers to regulate the daily life of Africans.[1] Considerable judicial powers were also given to Native Commissioners. It was provided that certain senior Native Commissioners might be appointed special Justices of the Peace and be given the powers of resident magistrates.[2] In practice, nine of the twenty-four Native Commissioners were appointed special Justices of the Peace in terms of the 1898 Order in Council by High Commissioner's Proclamation of 12 January 1899, thus enjoying the same powers as a resident magistrate in the Cape Colony (viz. petty criminal jurisdiction) and the right to hear minor civil disputes.[3]

Under the Native Commissioners were Native Messengers responsible for conveying messages to Chiefs and Headmen, for calling natives to court, warning them of their liability to hut tax, and reporting irregularities and crimes to the Native Commissioner.[4] The Regulations made a sharp distinction between such Messengers and the police. They had no powers of arrest, and might not enforce payments of tax or carry weapons, other than assegaais or sticks.[5]

The Chiefs now became government officials appointed by the Administrator in Council. They held office during pleasure contingent upon their 'good behaviour and general fitness', receiving such pay and allowances as might be determined.[6] The Chiefs were responsible to the Administrator for the general good conduct of the Africans under their charge, notification of crimes, deaths, disappearances, diseases, the publication of government orders, the prevention of crimes, the notification of newcomers to a district, the supply of men for military service when called upon to provide such men by the Administrator in Council, the discharge of any duties required by the Administrator in Council with consent of the High Commissioner, assisting in apprehending and securing all offenders, and the collection of hut

[1] Native Commissioners were empowered to assign land for huts, gardens and grazing ground and no new huts might be built or gardens cultivated without their consent. The Native Commissioner also fixed the number of huts which might compose a kraal and allocated water supplies. Native Commissioners were responsible for the collection of hut tax: Clause 2, Sections 10–13. Further discretion was given by special legislation such as the Settlement of Colonial Natives in Kaffir Kraals Prohibition Regulations which made it a criminal offence for 'Cape boys' and non-indigenous Africans to be found in an African kraal unless such African had a written permit from the Native Commissioner or his master. This latter law was only repealed by Act 35 of 1961.

[2] S.R. Order in Council 1898, Section 79.

[3] The official reason for the grant of such powers was that otherwise 'the white settlers will take the law into their own hands'. Furthermore, Africans would not be able to travel long distances to magistrates for redress: African 552, No. 165, Milner to Chamberlain.

[4] Clause 3, Sections 1–3.

[5] Clause 3, Section 4. Chamberlain insisted on this: African 559, No. 20, Chamberlain to Milner. The Imperial authorities were adamant that armed Africans might not be employed to restore order. See also African 517, Nos. 302, 377, and 496.

[6] It has been the general practice of the Department to appoint Chiefs who were in the natural line of succession to the chieftainship. See *infra* Part II, Chapter 2.

tax.[1] The Chiefs might only communicate with the Administrator through their local Native Commissioners.[2]

Under the Chiefs were the district Headmen appointed by the Secretary for Native Affairs, usually on the nomination of the Chiefs. Such Headmen were in turn responsible to the Chiefs for the good conduct of the people in their tribal district and the notification of any unusual occurrence. Such Headmen ranked as constables with powers of arrest of Africans. They were also required to assist any Native Messengers whenever called upon. Furthermore, they were to prevent the establishment of fresh kraals in their areas or removal of existing ones unless this had been authorized by the Native Commissioner. Finally they were responsible for collecting hut tax.

These provisions have from time to time been modified[3] but the basic structure has remained the same. Although the Department has been re-styled the Department of Internal Affairs[4] the legislative pattern and concepts sustaining this form of administration, particularly in rural areas, are still applied in 1965.

Philosophy behind the establishment of the Native Affairs Department

The High Commissioner and the Administrator were responsible for drawing up these 'Regulations' which were subject to protracted negotiation and amendment. The philosophy which inspired the High Commissioner was that:

Nothing is more certain than that if the Imperial Government were to be seen taking a strong line against the Company for the protection of the blacks, the whole of Dutch opinion in South Africa would swing round to the side of the Company and the bulk of—not the whole of—British Colonial opinion would go with it. You might indeed unite Dutch and English by protecting the black man, but you would unite them against yourself and your policy of protection. [The "great thing" was] to secure the appointment of honourable and capable men as magistrates and native commissioners. If that can be done, I think the lot of the natives may be a very tolerable one and that even a system of compulsory labour indeed, under fair conditions and proper safeguards, may be turned to their advantage.[5]

[1] Clause 4, Sections 2, 3, and 5.

[2] Clause 4, Section 4. Under this clause in 1898 Milner confirmed the removal of a Chief and fines on others who had consulted an attorney to represent them at an *indaba* (meeting of the Matabele Chiefs with the Administrator): see African 514, No. 40.

[3] Notably by the S.R. Native Regulations Proclamation of 3 October 1910, High Commissioner's Proclamation No. 32 of 1913, and by the Native Affairs Act 1927.

[4] Native Affairs Amendment Act No. 22 of 1963.

[5] Headlam, op. cit., p. 178, Milner to Asquith, 18 November 1897. For similar sentiments on the importance of the improvement of personnel of Native Commissioners, who must necessarily be given 'a great deal of power' and 'a great discretion', ibid. p. 140, Milner to Chamberlain, 1 December 1897.

Milner recognized that 'of all the administrative questions affecting Rhodesia the most difficult, as well as the one with regard to which there is most chance of a conflict between local opinion (whether under the autocratic government of the Company or a representative system) and the views of the Imperial Government is the native question . . .. The successful government of natives, even under the most settled conditions is rather a question of men than of regulations, but where administration is still in an embryonic stage as it is in Rhodesia, the character of the administration is of yet more predominant influence.'[1] In a country so extensive, with districts remote and inaccessible, it was 'necessary to put large powers into the hands of the local officials responsible for the government of the natives. The only form of government which the natives understand is personal government. They are accustomed to look to a chief.' It was essential to have 'in every district a single European officer to whom the natives shall be accustomed to look as the supreme authority in all matters in which they are concerned'. He was not however inspired with confidence by the present Native Commissioners and felt that the selection of personnel required 'the closest attention'.[2]

Imperial control of native administration

For these reasons the Colonial Office now insisted on proper control of appointments of all members of the native administration. The Southern Rhodesia Order in Council 1898 provided that the Secretary of State should exercise control over appointments, salaries, and removal of the Secretary for Native Affairs, Native Commissioners, Assistant Native Commissioners and all officials employed in the administration of native affairs. These were to be subject to approval by the High Commissioner and confirmation by the Secretary of State. The High Commissioner was also to confirm the powers, duties, and districts assigned to such officials.[3]

Indeed in all questions of native administration full controls were to be exercised. In cases of settlement of Africans on land, of removal of Africans from one area to another, and in cases of fines imposed for misconduct by the Administrator in Executive Council on native Chiefs or tribes, the High Commissioner's assent was necessary.[4] The High Commissioner might, in

[1] African 552, No. 78, Milner to Chamberlain, 28 July 1897. Milner's views have been quoted at length because the 1898 arrangements were determined by him.

[2] African 559, No. 6, Milner to Chamberlain, 15 December 1897.

[3] Section 79. The Colonial Office insisted on strict compliance with this section. When Regulations provided for the appointment of inspectors of native locations and the Company proceeded to appoint inspectors without consulting the Imperial authorities, Chamberlain pointed out that 'such inspectors are clearly persons employed in the administration of native affairs' and were to be confirmed in office by him. He was only prepared to confirm such appointments after the Company had forwarded reports on each individual and after the Resident Commissioner had also sent a private report: African 559, No. 443, 4 November 1898, and African 574, No. 62, 9 February 1899.

[4] Sections 82, 84, 85, and 88. Africans were in effect guaranteed security of tenure. In

addition, refer for investigation any questions regarding natives either to a Judge of the High Court or to a magisterial tribunal, and where any report was made he was free to deal with it as he thought fit.[1] Furthermore, in every case relating to natives dealt with by him the High Commissioner was to remit all documents to the Secretary of State who might review, reverse or modify any decision taken by the High Commissioner provided that, within twelve months of receiving the report, he gave notice of his intention to review such case.[2]

The provisions of the Charter also remained in force so that the Secretary of State might, in cases where disputes ensued with native tribes, require the matter to be submitted to him, while in any case where he objected to any proceeding of the Company in regard to the natives, the Company was bound to act in accordance with his directions.[3]

Legislation providing the framework for future native policy

The Imperial authorities next proceeded to legislate for a framework that would support their native policy. They considered that 'a sound native policy would dictate that the natives must be offered an assured prospect of being able to maintain themselves by their own labour and security'.[4] The approach adopted was two-pronged. Chamberlain insisted on an investigation of the suitability or otherwise of the lands allocated to Africans by the Lands Commission of 1894. The investigation revealed the unsatisfactory nature of the Reserves.[5] Chamberlain insisted that 'additional reserves should be arranged without delay' and that this assignment 'should not be treated as final'.[6]

addition the Native Regulations provided that, if removed, Chiefs and tribes were to be placed in another Reserve or on vacant land and not merely removed to another part of the territory. (A Company Draft providing for the removal of tribes when it was 'expedient in the public interest' was struck out: African 552, No. 165.)

[1] Sections 86 and 87. These and the preceding provisions replaced the provisions in the 1894 Order in Council, which had left their determination to the Land Commission.

[2] Section 89.   [3] Charter, Articles 7 and 15.   [4] African 520, Nos. 257 and 270.

[5] The Shangani and Gwaai Reserves for the Matabele were remote, unexplored, and unsuitable for native locations, the Shangani being fever-ridden and having little permanent water, while the Gwaai Reserve was badly watered, sandy, and unfit for settlement: African 517, No. 513, Encl. 1, Martin to High Commissioner, 12 April 1897. As Sir Alfred Milner said: 'By the original scheme of the Land Commission, . . . two huge and very little known blocks of land in the Guay and Shangani Reserve were marked out on the map, and the natives were apparently expected to tumble into them as best they might'. Difficulties in allocating more suitable land were now being encountered 'owing to the fact that so large an amount of the best land in the country was, in the first days of the occupation, alienated to syndicates and private individuals': African 559, No. 32, 31 December 1897. Only 5,395,000 acres were reserved for Africans in Matabeleland and there were no Reserves in Mashonaland. In a letter to Chamberlain he described the 'reckless alienation of land to syndicates': Headlam, op. cit., p. 140, 1 December 1897.

[6] African 559, No. 20, 14 January 1898; No. 80, 26 February 1898; and No. 89, 4 March 1898.

Ultimately further Reserves were created along these lines, and the 1898 Order in Council laid down that the Company was 'from time to time' to assign to the natives inhabiting Southern Rhodesia land sufficient for their occupation'.[1] This was a great change from the 1894 settlement in which Rhodes had been successful in excluding from a somewhat similar provision the words 'from time to time'. He had realized that this was a commitment that future additional allocations of land would have to be made.

The second approach to the land question was to place Africans on private land where they were permitted to settle in small numbers, and to raise crops, paying for this right of occupation either by way of a share in the crop produced or by rent. This policy was put into force by High Commissioner's Proclamation of 14 October 1896,[2] which contained numerous safeguards inserted at the instance of the Imperial authorities.[3]

At the same time the Imperial authorities were insistent that nothing in the nature of forced labour could be countenanced. Proposals by the Company for the grant of powers to African indunas as intermediaries between the Government and African population and that they should be responsible for supplying native labour and collecting hut tax were rejected. Even Milner as High Commissioner was overruled when he prepared a draft Proclamation providing that the Administrator might, with the High Commissioner's concurrence, annually demand a male contingent to work for three months each year for fair wages on public works or private property.[4] Chamberlain would not countenance such a clause.[5] He was, however,

[1] S.R. Order in Council 1898, Section 81.

[2] The Preamble to the High Commissioner's Proclamation stated that the law was being introduced so that Africans could 'maintain themselves by their own labour and in security under suitable supervision and upon fair and reasonable conditions of employment'. Whereas the intention of the Imperial authorities was to provide a basis for the future settlement of Africans, and whereas the Company said it appreciated the 'moral aspect of the case', it is also clear that the Company was motivated by the desire to facilitate labour coming forward and entering the employment of the settlers. This Proclamation was re-enacted as an Ordinance in 1908 and later became the Private Locations Act, Cap. 83 of the Revised Edition of the Southern Rhodesia Statutes. It was repealed in 1941 since it was inconsistent with the Land Apportionment Act.

[3] The Chief Native Commissioner was to supervise the removal of Africans from such land, their employment, their hire by persons other than the owner, the allocation of arable land, and the levying of rentals or contributions; labourers were not permitted to tie themselves for more than a year; no rent or labour might be levied for the first year of occupation; a minimum period of two years' occupation before removal was laid down; and the Chief Native Commissioner was to assess repayment of the value of any seed supplied by owners to such Africans, while in all cases Africans were to be left with sufficient for the support of their families. (The Company had suggested half the value of the crop should be given.) See African 520, Nos. 258, 270, and 273; African 517, Nos. 243, 246, and 262.

[4] Milner argued that there were advantages to the Africans in 'regular employment and regular remuneration' and since the Company had 'sought to provide against harsh and arbitrary treatment of the natives, and was providing large reserves', it was not unreasonable 'to demand something in return': African 552, No. 165, Milner to Chamberlain, 13 October 1897.

[5] African 559, No. 20, Chamberlain to Milner, 14 January 1898.

prepared to allow any suitable adaptation of the Cape Glen Gray Act or other 'scheme of indirect inducement' to labour.[1]

Control of Africans in urban areas was also provided for. This was done by the Town Location Regulations 1898.[2] Under these Regulations inspectors of municipal native locations were to grant Africans residence permits. Such inspectors were also given wide powers of search and arrest as it was a crime to be idle, disorderly, drunk, loitering, or present in a location without a permit. In addition, the law also contained curfew provisions for Africans outside locations. No objection was taken by the Colonial Office to this Regulation as such laws were standard in the South African colonies.[3] Furthermore, the Registration of Natives Regulations of 1895 (put into force in 1896) provided for an urban pass system controlling Africans who were seeking work. Such control was maintained by the requirement of registering contracts of employment. Any African not in employment or in possession of a pass to seek work was committing a criminal offence by being present in a town. Africans without passes were thus excluded from the urban areas.[4]

Furthermore, by virtue of the adoption of Cape Law as it was at the 10 June 1891, many Cape statutes remained in force. Among these were the Cape Masters and Servants Acts, 1856 to 1889, which made desertion from service a criminal offence,[5] and also laws such as the Police Offences Act 27 of 1882,[6] which, for example, by section 12 gave the police power to stop and search

---

[1] African 559, No. 285, Chamberlain to Milner, 6 August 1898. The Glen Gray Act taxation provisions cannot correctly be described as 'an indirect inducement'. By section 33 of Cape Act 25 of 1894 a direct Labour Tax of 10s. per annum was imposed on every male African fit to labour. Africans who had worked outside the district for three months each year were exempt, while permanent exemption was granted to Africans who had worked a total period of three years.

[2] These embodied the provisions of the Sanitary Board Regulations made under the Towns Management Ordinance 1894 and duplicated provisions in the Vagrancy Act Amendment Ordinance 1893 for the appointment of inspectors of native locations.

[3] This legislation eventually became Chapter 85 (1939) of the Southern Rhodesia Statutes and was only repealed in 1960.

[4] The Registration of Natives Regulations were repealed and re-enacted by the Natives Registration Ordinance 1901. This was later consolidated as the Natives Registration Act 1936 (Chapter 76 of 1939) and eventually repealed by Act 50 of 1960. The Town Location Regulations were repealed by Act 54 of 1960. The Vagrancy Act making vagrancy a criminal offence was repealed and replaced by another Vagrancy Act in 1960 which, although it laid down that vagrancy was no longer a criminal offence, permits the police to arrest any person unable to show he has employment or adequate means of support. Such persons are often thereafter prosecuted for other offences such as non-payment of tax or failure to possess the registration certificate required by the Natives (Registration and Identification) Act 1957. Although the Pass Laws (Repeal) Act 1960 has made it unnecessary for Africans to carry the multiplicity of documents formerly needed, in effect passes are still required as it is necessary for all Africans either to carry a registration certificate or a certificate of exemption in terms of the Natives (Registration and Identification) Act.

[5] Still in force, although considerably amended, as Chapter 247 (Revised Edition of S.R. Statutes, 1963).

[6] Re-enacted in 1937 as Cap. 40 of the Laws of Southern Rhodesia it was again re-enacted in 1964 as the Miscellaneous Offences Act No. 18 of 1964.

any person carrying a bundle between sunset and sunrise and the right to arrest such person unless he could satisfactorily account for his possession of any property. In addition, local legislation subjected Africans and Asians to discriminatory legislation in respect of the supply of liquor,[1] arms and ammunition.[2]

Reassertion of Imperial control

The basic feature of the new settlement was that Imperial control was to be reasserted. The key to this control was to be the High Commissioner, who would enjoy considerable powers in the legislative and administrative spheres, and would also participate in approving judicial appointments. At the same time, the Colonial Secretary would continue to enjoy his 'tremendous reserve power', which was not intended to be invoked in normal circumstances, although one class of legislation was always to be reserved for his consideration—legislation affecting native rights.[3] However it was not only 'native' legislation that was to be controlled, but it was intended that Crown control over all legislation should be 'real and effective ... not that, in all but the very rare cases, purely formal assent, which is given, for instance, by the governor of a self-governing Colony to the Bills of its legislature. On general enactments involving questions of principle and policy the Crown should retain a more than nominal control.'[4]

The new mechanism whereby Imperial control was to be asserted was the creation of two posts to be filled by Imperial officers, who would be present in Southern Rhodesia, the one exercising control over military and police forces, and the other reporting to the Imperial Government on events in the country.

The Deputy Commissioner and Commandant-General

The Imperial authorities realized that real control could only be exercised if they had an Imperial official present in the country to 'act as the eyes and ears of the High Commissioner and Imperial Government, having power, however, to veto proceedings of the B.S.A. Company in case of emergency'.[5]

Such an appointment was made immediately after the Jameson Raid when Chamberlain appointed Sir Richard Martin to take office in April 1896 as Commandant-General of all police forces in the Company's employ, and also as Deputy Commissioner solely responsible to Her Majesty's Government

[1] Only repealed as far as Asians were concerned by Act 15 of 1961, and in relation to Africans by Act 63 of 1961.

[2] Still in force as Chapter 250 (Revised Edition, 1963). A High Commissioner's Proclamation of 5 November 1896 prohibiting the Supply of Assegaais to Natives was repealed by Act 35 of 1961.

[3] Headlam, op. cit., p. 120, Milner to Chamberlain, 5 October 1897; also at p. 141 on the question of reserving 'native legislation'.

[4] African 552, No. 78, Milner to Chamberlain, 28 June 1897.

[5] African 498, No. 224, Telegraph Chamberlain to Robinson 17 January 1896.

through the High Commissioner. Martin was to have a seat, but no vote, on the Administrator's Council, and was to enjoy superior authority over all the Company's armed forces, i.e. volunteers, white force, municipal police, and unmounted police. He was given the rank of Deputy Commissioner since he had, in addition, political duties.[1] As a result of the outbreak of the Matabele and subsequent Mashona Rebellions early in 1896, Martin's military and police functions as Commandant-General were however temporarily transferred to Major General Sir Frederick Carrington, who was placed in command of all forces including a large Imperial contingent.

Dualism and disputes

Within a short period friction ensued on various important issues between the Imperial representatives and the Administrator, largely because there was no clear definition of their respective spheres of authority. Major causes of friction were disputes as to the continued presence of British forces in the country, the expense of a large standing army to maintain order,[2] the terms of peace,[3] the conduct of the war,[4] and the investigation of its causes.[5] On appeal to the Imperial authorities the tendency was to support the Company unless the question involved control of the armed forces[6] or would destroy the value of having such officials present.[7]

[1] African 517, No. 63, Telegraph Chamberlain to Robinson, 14 March 1896. Chamberlain informed Martin that 'the chief reason for the assumption by the Imperial Government of the control of the police is to secure that there will be no renewal of that untoward event which led to the recent change and that no use will be made of the force which is unjust in itself or contrary to law and international obligations': African 517, No. 119, Chamberlain to Martin, 25 April 1896. Chamberlain had already informed the Company that 'the High Commissioner and the Officer Commanding and other officers of police may correspond with one another on ordinary civil and political matters, so that Her Majesty's Government may be kept adequately informed of the state of the country, and may be thus enabled to fulfil their duties towards the States and Colonies of South Africa and Foreign Governments': African 517, No. 19, Colonial Office to B.S.A. Co., 7 February 1896.
[2] African 520, No. 352, Rosmead to Chamberlain, 4 October 1896; and African 517, No. 312A, Encl., pp. 300-4, Grey to B.S.A. Co., 16 October 1896.
[3] African 520, Nos. 284, 292, 296, and 297.
[4] The Imperial Commander-in-Chief was in full control of the conduct of the war. The Colonial Office also insisted that rebels be humanely treated, proper courts be set up for their trial, that death sentences for rebellion alone were not to be executed, and that military personnel who failed to follow legal procedures be court-martialled: African 517, Nos. 118 and 401; and African 520, Nos. 140, 143A, 309, 314, 331, 386, and 399.
[5] The Administrator insisted on being associated with Martin for the purpose of taking evidence and that all enquiries from officials should be transmitted through him. This was done but Martin's Report deprecated the fact that this restriction had prevented much evidence being obtained: C. 8547, also African 517, Nos. 241 and 288. Grey not unexpectedly repudiated the Report which placed much blame on the Company.
[6] The Administrator contended that the Deputy Commissioner was to have no say in recruitment of policemen and to interfere with the force as little as possible. Chamberlain repudiated this: African 517, No. 282.
[7] Grey considered that Martin was bound to show all correspondence with the High

Nonetheless an effective brake was placed on Company action. Rhodes's Private Secretary stated that 'the Administration could do absolutely nothing without the consent and concurrence of the Imperial Government through the High Commissioner'[1] while a later director wrote that from the time of the Raid 'the policy of the Colonial Office towards those who were doing its work in Rhodesia (the Company) was ever afterwards one of restriction and interference'.[2]

The Resident Commissionership

Eventually it was decided that the offices of Commandant-General and Deputy Commissioner should be separated and that a second Imperial officer should be appointed as Resident Commissioner, with a seat in both Legislative and Executive Councils. The Resident Commissioner was to give confidential reports to the High Commissioner on any important questions and the progress of affairs generally, while he would also report on all Ordinances and appointments submitted to the High Commissioner for assent. This was done so that 'the Imperial Government should have a man of its own on the spot who will keep it informed of what is really going on in the country'.[3] However, in view of the previous disputes and Company complaints about dualism it was laid down that 'it would be no part of the duty of the Imperial representative to interfere with the machinery of administration or with the Budget'.[4]

Accordingly a Resident Commissioner was appointed by the Secretary of State to inform the Imperial authorities as to the course of events in Southern Rhodesia and to sit as a member of both Executive and Legislative Councils.[5] Apart from his valuable reporting functions, his very presence was a restraint on irresponsible action by the Company.

Commissioner to him and the High Commissioner agreed. Chamberlain countermanded this instruction: confidential communications were not to be shown to the Administrator. As he said to Rosmead: 'There must be many matters on which it would be desirable that you should be able to communicate with the Deputy Commissioner without reserve': African 517, No. 289, and also No. 270, Encl. 4.

[1] G. le Sueur, *Cecil Rhodes*, London, 1914, p. 187.

[2] H. M. Hole, *The Making of Rhodesia*, op. cit., pp. 344-5.

[3] African 552, No. 78, Milner to Chamberlain, 28 July 1897. 'Such an officer . . . would be distinctly OUR man, not the Company's tool, and . . . while getting on with them, will be the "eyes and ears" of the High Commissioner and of Her Majesty's Government.' Headlam, op. cit., Milner to Selborne, 15 June 1897.

[4] Headlam, op. cit., at p. 144, Milner to Chamberlain, 1 December 1897. Tact and conciliatoriness on the part of the Imperial officer concerned would be essential in order 'to prevent his presence from giving rise to unnecessary friction, friction which might give reasonable colour to attacks upon the system of dualism. That officer should in my judgement, interfere as little as possible with the administration of the Company': African 552, No. 78, Milner to Chamberlain, 25 July 1897.

[5] Section 12. His salary was paid by the Imperial authorities.

United Kingdom executive control over military and police forces

As mentioned above, soon after the Raid an Imperial officer, the Commandant-General, had been placed in control of the Company's police forces. Although this transfer of authority took effect early in March 1896 when the Company was informed of the change, it was not formalized until the issue of a High Commissioner's Proclamation on 31 October 1896, placing all military and police forces under the direct control and authority of the High Commissioner.

The purpose of this transfer had been to give the High Commissioner ultimate control over such forces, but it was not intended to deprive the Company of the use of the police forces for which it continued to pay. The Commandant-General was therefore ordered by the High Commissioner ordinarily to be guided in the exercise of his discretion by the wishes and requirements of the Administrator. He was to have control over border questions and the organization and discipline of the police while, in case of disagreement with the Administrator, he was to consult the High Commissioner.[1]

Eventually final provisions were made under the Southern Rhodesia Order in Council 1898 whereby the High Commissioner was placed in control of all military police forces,[2] which were to be under the Commandant-General appointed by the Secretary of State.[3] The Commandant-General was subject to orders from the High Commissioner.[4]

No military operations might be undertaken without the High Commissioner's consent or, in emergencies where this was unobtainable, without that of the Resident Commissioner,[5] while the Company was prohibited from establishing or maintaining any force of military police.[6] However, civil police forces might be exempted from the terms of the Order if the High Commissioner by Proclamation excluded them from its operation. Accordingly Municipal police enrolled for civil duty and acting within the municipal boundaries were exempted from his control in 1898.[7] Owing to Company pressure for centralized control of the police through two commandants directly responsible to the Law Department, this Proclamation was suspended in March 1899. However, the High Commissioner refused to accede to any centralization of forces, except under his own control, and insisted that each local force be under local control.[8] Subsequently, the Secretary of State in

[1] African 552, No. 78, Milner to Chamberlain, 28 July 1897, and Headlam, op. cit., p. 111, Milner to Selborne, 15 June 1897.
[2] Section 48(i).   [3] Section 48(ii).   [4] Section 48(iv).
[5] Section 48(vi).
[6] Supplemental Charter Article 4.
[7] High Commissioner's Proclamation, 31 December 1898. In cases of emergency, or when they carried arms, or operated outside municipal boundaries, they were to come under the Commandant General's control.
[8] African 574, No. 93, Encl. 7, 2 March 1899.

1901 emphasized that police forces should not be put under the Company's control.[1]

Similar control was intended to be exercised over all Volunteer forces. Although the position was only regularized by Ordinances passed after the Boer War, the Imperial authorities insisted that powers conferred by the Volunteer Regulations 1898 (which were based on the principle of local management) should be exercised only with the consent of the Commandant General and that when on active service such Volunteers were to be under his exclusive control.[2] Ultimately the Ordinance of 1902 (as amended in 1904 at the Secretary of State's insistence), provided that the Colonial Secretary's consent was necessary for appointment of officers and the making of regulations, while the High Commissioner's consent was needed for the calling out of such Volunteers on active service.

The Administrator

Since the Company was to continue administering the country the office of Administrator in charge of the administration was also to continue. It was now provided that there might be one or more Administrators, each possessing powers of appointment within his own province. Such Administrators or Acting Administrators were to be appointed and removed[3] only with the consent of the Colonial Secretary, who would also have to agree to the assignment of provinces to any Administrator.[4] The senior Administrator was to preside over both the Executive and Legislative Councils enjoying in the Legislative Council both a deliberative and a casting vote. In his absence another Administrator might act.[5]

The Administrator, however, did not in any way represent the Crown. He

[1] African 659, No. 77, Chamberlain to Milner, 12 March 1901. Chamberlain also insisted that no native police force be raised: African 659, No. 105, 21 March 1901.

[2] African 574, No. 222, Encl., Milner to Administrator, 11 July 1898. For Chamberlain's attitude instructing the High Commissioner to legislate by Proclamation on this matter, see African 559, No. 393, 21 October 1898.

[3] S.R. Order in Council 1898, Sections 9 and 11. Chamberlain did not hesitate to threaten the use of similar powers under the Matabeleland Order in Council 1894 after the Raid. He presumed that the Company would 'at once remove from office under Article 8 of the Order in Council their present Administrator [who is lodged in Pretoria Gaol] and will appoint a properly qualified and prudent person in his place . . . .. The early assurance that this will be done will relieve Mr. Chamberlain of the necessity of exercising his concurrent powers under that section.' The words in brackets appeared in the Colonial Office draft but were apparently cut out by Chamberlain: African (South), C.O. 417/160, XXIII, 1895, folio 683, No. 23265, Minute, 4 January 1896. This letter was not published in C. 7933, but No. 67, B.S.A. Co. to Colonial Office, 4 January 1896, is printed requesting the Secretary of State's permission for Jameson's removal.

[4] S.R. Order in Council 1898, Section 8.

[5] Mr. W. H. Milton was Senior Administrator and Captain A. Lawley the Administrator for Matabeleland.

was merely 'head of the administration of a British territory'[1] and the chief Company official in that area.

Imperial legislative controls

Since the Imperial authorities were now freed from policy considerations which had formerly occasioned them to accede to virtually all the Company's wishes, they now insisted on the establishment of proper legislative controls. Aware of previous illegalities and *ultra vires* legislation, a High Commissioner's Proclamation laid down that, in cases where certain laws permitted the Administrator to act by 'Proclamation', he was now only to do so by proper notice in the B.S.A. Company's Gazette.[2] The Administrator was also instructed to observe the limits of any enabling acts or to introduce proper amending legislation.[3]

There is little doubt that the Imperial authorities fully recognized the unsatisfactory nature of previous legislation. Milner's blunt comment on Regulations is apposite: 'The legislation of the Council ... is apt to be rather harum-scarum and exceedingly drastic. I have amended a good deal of it since I came here, and with the more perfect information I now have I should have amended it still more.'[4] It was therefore decided that powers of control over all legislation should be given to the High Commissioner. Accordingly the Board's Ordinance-making power and the Administrator in Council's Regulation-making power were abolished, while in their place was substituted an Ordinance-making power possessed by the Legislative Council subject to approval by the High Commissioner.[5] At the same time the High Commissioner's proclaiming power was preserved,[6] and he was given power to determine the franchise for the Legislative Council and the qualifications of members.[7]

The High Commissioner was to be kept informed of events in the Legisla-

[1] African (South) C.O. 417/420, Colonial Office to B.S.A. Co., 15 December 1905.

[2] High Commissioner's Proclamation No. 3 of 1897, 18 March 1897.

[3] African 517, No. 465, Encl. 3, High Commissioner to Earl Grey, 20 March 1897.

[4] Headlam, op. cit., p. 140, Milner to Chamberlain, 1 December 1897.

[5] Milner had advocated that the control should be a local control exercised by agents of the Crown in South Africa and that one method of making laws should be substituted 'for the present multiplicity of regulations, ordinances, and proclamations': Headlam, op. cit., p. 118 et seq., 5 October 1897.

[6] Section 6, S.R.O.C. 1898. These powers were intended to be used only in exceptional instances: the High Commissioner would be 'left with his power of proclamation which, if things are properly managed, he ought not to want to exercise once in ten years': Headlam, op. cit., p. 120, Milner to Chamberlain, 5 October 1897. However, Proclamations were extensively employed for laying down important aspects of administration and future policy between 1896 and 1898. By the Bechuanaland Protectorate and Southern Rhodesia Amending Order in Council 1909 (18 October 1909), High Commissioner's Proclamations were to be of full force and effect until such time as they were disallowed.

[7] S.R.O.C. 1898, Section 18.

tive Council by the Resident Commissioner who was a non-voting member of the Council.[1]

In addition the Secretary of State retained considerable control as the appointments of those members of the Legislative Council nominated by the Company (i.e. the majority, including the Administrator and five officials) were to be approved by him.[2] He could within a year disallow legislation,[3] while if this was repugnant to an Order in Council it would to the extent of any repugnancy be void.[4] Finally, legislation imposing disabilities on Africans had, before its introduction, to obtain the previous consent of the Colonial Secretary.[5]

That such powers were intended to be, and were, fully utilized was apparent from the active supervision of legislation, even before the implementation of the 1898 Constitution, by the Colonial Office and the High Commissioner between 1896 and 1898.[6] Ordinances passed by the Board were only permitted in exceptional or urgent cases because of an early decision to remove the Board's Ordinance-making power. Indeed the cases where they were permitted arose because Regulations could not be employed to amend earlier Ordinances or to impose taxation,[7] and because the power of Regulation-making had been withdrawn but, pending the meeting of the new Legislative Council, certain legislation was urgently required.[8] Regulations were, until this method of legislation fell away, extensively used but in all cases they were

[1] Section 12(ii). Full and exact minutes of its proceedings were to be sent to both the High Commissioner and the Colonial Secretary: Section 34.

[2] Section 17.

[3] Section 37.

[4] Section 39. Sections 17 to 47 set out the constitution and powers of the Legislative Council.

[5] Section 80. The Colonial Office took the view that this consent should be obtained before any discriminatory measure was introduced into the Legislative Council but on occasions waived this procedure. See African (South) C.O. 417/408, Lyttelton to Selborne, 21 July 1905. In *R. v. McChlery*, 1912, A.D. at 204 Vincent J. held that consent by the Secretary of State under Section 80 must 'in the absence of proof to the contrary be assumed'. On appeal the same view was taken by the Appellate Division: *R. v. McChlery* at 217.

[6] The working of the controls under the 1898 settlement from 1898 to 1923 will be examined in Chapters 8 and 9 *infra*.

[7] e.g. The Licence and Stamp Ordinance 1898, which retrospectively validated all such taxes levied by the Company from 1891. Legal doubts had arisen, since the Matabeleland Order in Council 1894, Section 22, had provided that taxation should be levied by Ordinance while Section 26 had stated that the law that should be administered was to be the same as the law in force at the Cape Colony on 10 June 1891. The Company had purported to act in terms of the Cape Stamp Acts. Soon after the passage of the new Ordinance, the High Court ruled that prior to its enactment no taxes had been leviable by the Company: *Stevenson* v. *B.S.A. Co.*, *supra*.

[8] The Apprenticeship (Native Children) Ordinance No. 1 of 1899 was passed to secure that contracts of apprenticeship be entered into by parents in the presence of a magistrate or Native Commissioner and to apply the Cape Acts relating to technical schools and agricultural colleges, &c., so that such children could be controlled when in mission schools which were to be established for training children.

carefully scrutinized and subjected to amendments in draft by the High Commissioner and his legal adviser. Even the Colonial Secretary concerned himself with such Regulations and any effect they might have on the African population.[1]

Establishment of a judicial system

Provision was also made for a complete judicial system of Magistrates' Courts, a High Court, appeals to and reservation of points of law for the Cape Supreme Court, and ultimately a right of appeal to the Judicial Committee of the Privy Council.[2] Prior to this period High Court trials had been conducted by the Judge sitting with three advisory assessors,[3] but soon after the 1898 Order in Council the jury system was introduced for the trial of criminal cases in the High Court.[4]

All courts were to apply the law of the Cape Colony as at the 10 June 1891,[5] but a special provision preserved native customary law in civil cases between Africans.[6] The latter was to be applied in the courts of the Native Commissioners who had been appointed Special Justices of the Peace,[7] and also in such cases in the High and Magistrates' Courts.

The Imperial authorities insisted here too on powers of control. Appointment, salaries and removal of judges of the High Court required the approval of the Secretary of State,[8] while magisterial appointments, salaries and removals, and those of Native Commissioners required the special approval of

[1] e.g. Chamberlain would not permit Game Regulations until it was agreed that if a closed season were to be introduced for game this would 'be fully explained beforehand to the native population and their acquiescence ensured': African 517, No. 40, Chamberlain to Rosmead, 20 February 1897.

[2] S.R.O.C. 1898, Sections 49 to 78. Section 58 provided for appeal as of right to the Judicial Committee. High Court sentences were subject to remission by the High Commissioner and the execution of death sentences required his confirmation (Sections 56 and 55). Criminal appeals were for the first time permitted to lie on matters of law and in cases where there had been a procedural irregularity to the Cape Supreme Court (Sections 60 to 68). The Cape Court later investigated the right of the High Court of Southern Rhodesia 'to test' duly promulgated Ordinances and concluded that the High Court could not investigate whether the proper machinery had been adopted in the passage of an Ordinance through the Legislative Council: it could merely see whether an Ordinance was 'correct in form, i.e. whether it on the face of it is repugnant or not to an Order in Council': R. v. McChlery, supra at 211 per Maasdorp J. See also Burrowes Case, supra at 488. Cp. Harris v. Minister of the Interior, 1952 (2), S.A. 428 (A.D.) at 470 per Centlivres C.J. and R. v. Ndobe, 1930, A.D. 297 per de Villiers C.J.

[3] S.R. Legco Deb. 1912, col. 61, 9 May 1912, the Attorney General.

[4] Ordinance No. 4 of 1899. It departed from the English model in that a jury of nine only was required. Jurors might be African but in practice no African juror was ever summoned.

[5] Section 49.   [6] Section 50. See also Part II, Chapter 3.   [7] Section 79. See also supra.

[8] Section 52. Chamberlain insisted that the appointment of the judge remained in his hands even though he might be nominated by the Company. Chamberlain regarded this 'additional guarantee of the independence and impartiality of the Bench' with 'special satisfaction in consideration of the large native population of Southern Rhodesia': African 559, No. 246, Colonial Office to B.S.A. Co., 15 July 1898.

the High Commissioner and confirmation of the Secretary of State.[1] Chamberlain early made it clear that he intended exercising such powers when he informed the Company that he would 'feel bound in all ordinary cases to refuse his approval to the appointment of anyone not having magisterial and colonial experience'.[2] Ultimately, after the Colonial Secretary had insisted that all appointees should possess suitable experience, that the High Commissioner must satisfy himself as to qualifications before expressing any approval, and that all appointments were to be confirmed by the Colonial Secretary, the Civil Service Regulations laid down that only experienced persons or those with legal training might be appointed to the offices of Magistrate or Assistant Magistrate.[3]

Increased supervision of the Company's affairs

The final change, which was embodied in a Supplementary Charter,[4] was that the powers of supervision of the Colonial Secretary over the Board were more explicitly defined and strengthened, and ampler information concerning the transactions and general financial situation of the Company demanded.[5]

[1] Sections 71, 72, 75, and 79.

[2] African 517, No. 19, Colonial Office to B.S.A. Co., 7 February 1896. Marshall Hole wrote in his memoirs of the magistrates originally appointed by the Company: 'half a dozen young officers, with no more experience of judicial practice than they had acquired in the orderly room, suddenly found themselves appointed Resident Magistrates': *Old Rhodesian Days*, op. cit., p. 66. That such approval was not a mere formality was proved when Major Forbes, a senior Company official, was nominated to fill the post of Acting Resident Magistrate at Salisbury. When Milner expressed doubts as to Forbes' suitability, Chamberlain informed the Company that another arrangement should be made: African 559, No. 79, B.S.A. Co. to Colonial Office, 26 February 1898; No. 99, Colonial Office to B.S.A. Co., 9 March 1898. Forbes had in 1891 been Resident Magistrate at Salisbury and later Administrator in Northern Zambezia but the Imperial authorities must have remembered his *coup de main* in November 1890 when, in attempting to take Portuguese territory for the Company, he had arrested Colonel Paivia d'Andrade and Gouveia, Governor of Gorongoza Province in Mozambique.

[3] African 517, No. 358, 21 January 1897, Chamberlain to Rosmead. The Civil Service of Rhodesia Regulations 1898 provided that: 'From after 1 July 1898 it shall not be lawful to appoint to any office of Magistrate or Assistant Magistrate any person who on that date had not served five years or upwards in the service of the Company, unless he shall have passed the Civil Service Law Examination of the Cape Colony, or some other law examination approved by the Administrator.' G.N. 6 of 1898, Section 16.

[4] The grant of the Supplementary Charter was delayed as the Colonial Office agreed that the proper procedure prior to its issue was that the Company should call an Extraordinary General Meeting to consent to it and also to consequential changes in the Deed of Settlement. Delay in calling this meeting occurred, but the Colonial Office condoned this, provided the Board agreed to act in the interim as if the Supplemental Charter were already in force. It was only issued on 8 June 1900: African 574, No. 220, Colonial Office to B.S.A. Co., 3 August 1899.

[5] The Company's accounts were to give fuller financial data thus enabling the Colonial Office to differentiate between administrative and commercial revenues, and to make a proper assessment of the Company's financial state. In addition Section 43 of the Order in Council had provided that the High Commissioner must be given full information as to

The Supplemental Charter provided that within eight days copies of all resolutions, minutes, orders or proceedings of the Board, which related to the administration of the Company's territories, were to be sent to the Secretary of State, who would have the right to cancel, suspend or amend any decision.[1] In addition, it was ordered that the Colonial Secretary should have access to all records, documents, reports, and accounts of the Company, particularly copies of correspondence with the Administrator and officials in South Africa. Such right of inspection would be exercisable by Colonial Office officials appointed for the purpose.[2]

The Supplemental Charter also terminated the life-time appointments of certain directors, and provided that for the future all directors were to be elected. Furthermore, the Secretary of State was entitled to demand that directors keep him fully informed, and to remove them from office if in his opinion they failed to comply with the provisions of the Charter or his requirements.[3]

Earlier it had been provided that Rhodes should no longer enjoy formal authority as Chamberlain insisted during June 1897 on his and Alfred Beit's resignation as directors.[4] Rhodes's resignation involved the surrender of an absolute power of attorney granted to him on 14 May 1890, entitling him to manage all the affairs of the Company and to exercise all its powers, the directors agreeing in advance to ratify any action he might take.[5] In practice, however, Rhodes still exercised control behind the scenes.[6]

That Rhodes was not really out of favour, despite the tarnishing of his name owing to his part in the Raid, was shown by the fact that his membership of the Privy Council was never withdrawn[7] and that early in 1897

estimates and supplementary estimates, so as to be enabled to judge the propriety of any proposed expenditure.

[1] Supplemental Charter, Article 6.

[2] Supplemental Charter, Article 5. Extensive use was made of documents forwarded to the Colonial Office by the Company. Colonial Office files show detailed analysis of policies and frequent requests for further explanations either from the Company or the Resident Commissioner. However, it has been suggested that the Company to some extent avoided this scrutiny by making use of private correspondence between officials and members of the Board: see L. H. Gann, *A History of Northern Rhodesia*, Chatto & Windus, 1964.

[3] Supplemental Charter, Articles 3 and 7.

[4] Chamberlain had been given advance warning by Sir William Harcourt of his intention to ask questions in the Commons as to why Rhodes had remained a director: see A. G. Gardiner, op. cit., p. 393.

[5] African 517, Nos. 146, 176, and 194.

[6] This sometimes occurred from the forefront of the stage as when he unofficially took command of settler volunteer troops during the Rebellion and when he made peace with the Matabele Chiefs in the Matopo Mountains. Lockhart and Woodhouse, op. cit., p. 368, state that Rhodes still retained full control through Company officials even though he had no official *locus standi*. His private secretary, Gordon le Sueur, op. cit., at p. 118, says that Rhodes's resignation made little material difference as he retained the Company's general power of attorney. In 1898 he was reappointed Chairman.

[7] On 27 July 1897 Chamberlain refused to deprive Rhodes of this honour when demands to this effect were made.

Chamberlain approved the use of the name 'Rhodesia' in official communications.[1] Chamberlain later agreed to its use in the Southern Rhodesia Boundary Regulations of 1898 which divided the country into administrative provinces, and finally ordered that the new administrative scheme for the country should be known as the 'Rhodesia Order in Council 1898'.[2]

That Rhodes still exercised power was recognized by Milner who warned the Imperial authorities that it would be unwise to grant any powers to the Legislative Council 'which for reasons of Imperial policy it is not safe to put absolutely in the hands of one strong-willed and hasty man', since the Council would 'simply be Rhodes', who was saying of the Colonial Office: 'They may bully the Company ... but they won't dare to bully a representative Council'.[3]

Structure of future administration and basic policy laid down

By the end of 1898 therefore the future structure of government had been laid down. The major institutions, instruments of administration, and legislative policies, most of which were to endure until the present day, were already in existence. The representative principle had been introduced by the creation of a Legislative Council with a minority of elected members and, although the Legislative Council had no executive responsibilities, it was acknowledged that this was but the first step towards responsible government. A franchise couched in non-discriminatory language, but with property and monetary qualifications and the additional requirement of literacy that would, in effect, exclude the majority of Africans, was laid down. A Native Affairs Department responsible for governmental relations with Africans was established. In urban areas municipalities had been created and legislation providing for the control of Africans in such areas had been enacted. Insofar as land was concerned, the Reserve system had been introduced. All this was done at a time when Britain had complete control of legislation: indeed the major legislative measures providing the framework for future administration and policy had been enacted by Order in Council and High Commissioner's Proclamation. These provisions had been made since Britain had decided that Southern Rhodesia should follow the general pattern set by the South African colonies and would eventually become part of a white self-governing South African federation.

---

[1] It had unofficially been used by the Company from 1895 and in May 1895 Jameson actually named the country as Rhodesia in an Administrator's Proclamation.

[2] African 517, No. 411, 23 February 1897: African 559, No. 154, 21 April 1898.

[3] Headlam, op. cit., p. 111, Milner to Selborne, 15 June 1897. In an earlier letter to Selborne, p. 105, 2 June 1897, Milner thought that the separate colony envisaged by Rhodes 'though nominally self-governed, will be virtually an absolute monarchy with Rhodes as monarch'. This was, however, a temporary phase as after Rhodes's death in 1902 settlers and Company rapidly became hostile to each other.

8

IMPERIAL LEGISLATIVE CONTROL IN PRACTICE
1898–1923

THE Southern Rhodesia Order in Council 1898 had established an extensive series of Imperial controls over legislative and administrative action by the Company. These were now utilized by successive Colonial Secretaries—Joseph Chamberlain in particular asserting his authority to prevent or correct Company action of which he disapproved. Such Imperial action over a lengthy period in which the institutions of the country took shape was also significant for the future, since, when eventually Southern Rhodesia was granted responsible government in 1923, the controls retained were based on the methods of supervision in respect of matters affecting the African population, which Britain had continuously employed for the preceding twenty-five years.

Imperial Control of Southern Rhodesia legislation from 1899 to 1923

Despite the introduction of a representative element in the Legislative Council, Imperial control of legislative measures was strictly enforced. Although control in the form of disallowance and non-assent occurred in the main from 1899 to 1909, even after this period, when less overt action was taken, supervision was maintained. This was enforced in questions concerning the African and Asian populations, in cases where financial measures might affect the future of the country, and in respect of laws where uniformity throughout the Empire was required.

The change from about 1909 onwards to more subtle methods of influencing Southern Rhodesian legislation can probably be ascribed to several factors. Firstly, the Colonial Office had enjoyed unfettered control of legislation for a decade in which legislative provision had already been made for the main institutions of the country. Thus new legislation introduced for the most part took the form of amendments to provide for anomalies. Secondly it was accepted as one of the rules of the legislative game that the High Commissioner should have complete control over the initiation or modification of legislation affecting Africans—and this no one, including the elected members, questioned. Finally, since in practice the elected members enjoyed a majority in the Legislative Council (this informal majority was in the course of being regularized by negotiations for a new Order in Council eventually issued in 1911), the Colonial Office was anxious not to provoke conflict by drawing attention to its vast powers which in any event could as effectively be exercised in a more discreet fashion.

Positive controls

Positive control by Imperial legislation was not at any time invoked, although such legislation was employed for measures beyond the competence of the Legislative Council or in matters of general Imperial concern.

The first method of positive action employed might be an enactment of the Imperial Parliament covering all British possessions (such as the Extradition Act, the Fugitive Offenders Act, the Patents and Designs Act 1907, the Copyright Act 1911, &c.).

A second method was the use of Orders in Council applicable to Southern Rhodesia.[1] These in the main dealt with constitutional change in the territory, applied Imperial legislation designed for all possessions of the Empire, or dealt with war and peace measures and treaties.

Finally, the High Commissioner for South Africa could legislate by Proclamation on questions affecting Southern Rhodesia. However, except for the year 1899 in which his activities were truly legislative, the use of Proclamations was confined to occasions requiring constitutional change, change in the laws affecting administration of the Native Department, the application of Imperial laws, international, and wartime matters.[2]

However, a High Commissioner's Proclamation could be, and on one occasion at least was, used to impose legislative provisions which neither the Company nor the Legislative Council wished. Thus the Southern Rhodesia Native Regulations 1910,[3] which set the pattern for the Native Affairs Act of 1927, contained provisions inserted at the insistence of the High Commissioner and against the wishes of the Administration. In fact this Proclamation was preceded by two years of negotiations in the course of which the majority of Administration requests were rejected.[4]

Threat to abolish jury system by Proclamation

On one notorious occasion in 1910 the threat of legislation to abolish the jury system in criminal trials in Southern Rhodesia by High Commissioner's

[1] See *The Statute Law of Southern Rhodesia, From the Charter to December 31st, 1898*, ed. M. O. Evans, Argus Printing Co., Salisbury, 1899; *From the Charter to 31st December, 1910*, ed. by A. Speight, Government Printer; and *From 1st January, 1911 to 31st December, 1922*, ed. by A. Speight, Government Printer, Salisbury, 1923. Including the year 1923, sixty-eight Orders in Council affecting Southern Rhodesia were issued.

[2] ibid. From 1899 to 1923 there were 110 High Commissioners' Proclamations, approximately half of these being issued as a result of the First World War.

[3] High Commissioner's Proclamation No. 55 of 1910.

[4] National Archives A 2/4/6, Administrator to High Commissioner, 12 August 1908. See also A 3/18/31/3 which reveals that the Imperial authorities would not allow Native Commissioners' powers to be strengthened as requested by the Chief Native Commissioner and Administration. The Secretary of State insisted that no Native Commissioner was to be

Proclamation led to reform being undertaken, albeit unwillingly, at the instance of the elected members of the Legislative Council.

In *R. v. Laidlaw*[1] and *R. v. Macauley* (the Battlefields Case)[2] gross miscarriages of justice had occurred. Europeans who had flogged Africans to death were in the one case found guilty of common assault and in the other acquitted. The High Commissioner, Lord Selborne, felt so strongly after the first case that he sent remonstrances to the Administration through the Resident Commissioner urging that 'it was essential to persuade that small minority whose moral standard had become depraved and deformed on questions affecting natives that any attempt to build up any part of the British Empire on any other foundation than that of justice can only end in its utter destruction'.[3] Within a short period the trial of *R. v. Macauley*, where there was an even greater miscarriage of justice, occasioned the High Commissioner to write to the Administrator suggesting that the only remedy was 'to abolish trial by jury in cases where whites are accused of crimes on blacks'.[4] Eventually the High Commissioner officially warned the Council through the Administrator that, unless it amended the law, he would himself take action with the concurrence of the Secretary of State.[5] Having first been given the opportunity to legislate, the Legislative Council appointed a Select Committee and ultimately in 1912 the Special Juries Ordinance was passed.[6] However, limitations on Colonial Office influence were already emerging as the Imperial authorities thought the new provisions insufficient safeguard, but felt that with 'an elective majority not long conceded' they should get a better case before themselves intervening with positive legislation.[7]

judge in his own cause and was to be prohibited from trying cases of insolence to himself: see Crewe to Gladstone, 8 July 1910.

[1] Reported in the *Rhodesia Herald* of 8 May 1908. The accused was found guilty of common assault and sentenced to six months' imprisonment with hard labour for flogging Africans, two of whom died, while a third survived.

[2] Reported in the *Rhodesia Herald* of 4 November 1908. See also R. G. Howman, 'Trial by Jury in Southern Rhodesia' in (1949) *Rhodes Livingstone Journal*, p. 41.

[3] African 899, No. 120, Encl. 2, High Commissioner to Resident Commissioner. Lord Crewe, Secretary of State, confirmed these views.

[4] National Archives RC 3/7/16. Correspondence between the High Commissioner, Resident Commissioner and Administrator on the Jury System. Selborne to Milton, 27 November 1908.

[5] *Southern Rhodesia Legislative Council. Minutes, Bills, Ordinances, Reports, etc. Vol. XII. Papers laid.* Selborne to Resident Commissioner, 14 April 1909.

[6] Ordinance 13 of 1912. Special juries were to try Europeans accused of serious offences against Africans. The jury was to consist only of five European males selected from a small panel of educated and wealthy people appointed by the Administrator and approved by the Legislative Council. A further departure from the principle of trial by jury was that the verdict need not be unanimous, four jurors being adequate for either conviction or acquittal. In 1922 the High Commissioner was still watching the operation of the system and requiring to be satisfied as to its efficiency: see National Archives A 2/4/13. Records sent to High Commissioner, 26 March 1922.

[7] C.O. Minute on High Commissioner's despatch No. 402, African (South) C.O. 417/512, Vol. 3, 1912. Philip Mason's account of this incident in *Birth of a Dilemma*, Oxford University Press, 1958, at p. 307 does not take sufficient note of this Imperial interference, sug-

There were no other such dramatic instances to illustrate the effect of threats to use the reserve power of legislation by Proclamation. As early as 1902 Milner recognized that Proclamation was an 'exceptional method', which should not be used 'without first consulting the Administration and explaining the circumstances which seem to me to make it desirable'.[1]

Legislation introduced at Imperial request

The Imperial authorities were also responsible for the introduction of much legislation as a result of direct requests made to the Administration. Where such requests were made the Company would comply by introducing into the Legislative Council an Ordinance along the lines of the Imperial precedent usually accompanying the request.[2] Such legislation was largely designed to secure uniformity throughout the Empire, or to make provision for matters as a result of wartime or international obligations.[3] However, one particularly large group of Ordinances concerning Africans was enacted in 1912 as a result of the Native Affairs Commission Report.[4] The appointment of this Commission had been urged by the British Government, which also prodded the Administration into introducing legislation implementing many of its recommendations.[5] Indeed in 1913, after an elected majority in the Legislative Council had been conceded, the Imperial authorities still demanded that the Administration explain why no action had been taken in respect of certain Native Affairs Commission recommendations.[6] Even immediately before the implementation of the responsible government Constitution, the High Commissioner insisted on review of the Native Regulations Ordinance Labour Regulations and Pass Laws, and after the new Constitution came into operation revised laws on these topics were enacted by the Legislative Assembly.[7]

Negative controls

Britain's consistent policy throughout the Empire was to prefer the use of negative controls. These, although employed in Southern Rhodesia

gesting that the reforms occurred as a result of change of local conscience after another serious injustice—R. v. Lewis, heard in Bulawayo in 1911. See also 'Trial by Jury in Southern Rhodesia' by M. A. Adam, Rhodesia and Nyasaland Law Journal, Vol. 2, January 1962, p. 38.

[1] African 702, No. 327, Encl. 3, 28 June 1902.

[2] This was done in at least 7·6 per cent of Ordinances introduced between 1899 and 1923: see Appendix, Tables A, B, and H.

[3] Table B in the Appendix gives a full list of such Ordinances as disclosed by the official records. Unfortunately not all records seem to have survived.

[4] Southern Rhodesia Native Affairs Commission of Enquiry, Report A 12—1911.

[5] National Archives, Resident Commissioner to Administrator, 29 August 1911.

[6] African 1003, No. 135, Encl. 2 and 175, in which the Administrator undertook to introduce legislation on the majority of these topics.

[7] See African (South) 1085, No. 55, Encl., High Commissioner's Despatch No. 381 of 23 February 1922.

particularly during the regimes of Mr. Chamberlain and Mr. Lyttelton as Colonial Secretaries, remained in use long after the principle of responsible government had been conceded. Nonetheless such methods could not be as fully effective as positive action or administrative control. As Lord Ripon said in 1905, commenting on Transvaal native policy: 'You can veto their Bills, but you cannot control their executive action. The moment you attempt to do anything of the kind you would be involved in infinite difficulty.'[1]

The development of negative controls

In the first year of representative government (1899) it became apparent that the Administration was out of touch with the attitude of the Imperial authorities and their requirements. Apparently only one Ordinance was deliberately cleared in advance with the High Commissioner—and then only because a speedy assent was required.[2] In fact, the High Commissioner was so dissatisfied with the year's legislation that he refused assent in three cases[3] and insisted on curing the defects in other Ordinances either by delegated legislation under the Ordinance or by administrative practice.[4] He informed the Resident Commissioner that 'in dealing with the Ordinances recently submitted to me, I have, in several instances, found myself compelled to choose between assenting to a measure some clause of which seemed to me very objectionable and disallowing it[5] altogether, while yet approving of its general object'.[6] In all cases of serious objection he had 'called the attention of the Administration to the provision objected to with a view to its amendment hereafter'.[7] Nevertheless he felt that he 'ought not to interfere with the legislative work of the Council except for exceedingly grave reasons as it was intended to be a semi-representative body similar to that in a Crown Colony with representative institutions'. However, if 'an Ordinance was submitted injurious to the interests of the natives . . . or manifestly inequitable to the white settlers . . . or conflicting with the interests of the Empire or the general objects of Imperial policy in South Africa' he would interfere.[8]

Draft Ordinances to be vetted by High Commissioner

It was this generally unsatisfactory situation in regard to Ordinances enacted by the Council that led to the introduction of a procedure for the

[1] Quoted by R. Hyam in 'The Frontiers of Imperial Control in Self-governing Colonies and Liberal Experience in South Africa, 1905–1908', an Institute of Commonwealth Studies Seminar Paper (unpublished).
  [2] National Archives A 2/4/1, The Legislative Rules and Procedure Ordinance 1899.
  [3] See Appendix, Table H.   [4] See Appendix, Tables D and E.
  [5] Used in a non-technical sense: as meaning refusing assent to the measure.
  [6] African 574, No. 238, Encl. 4, 8 August 1899.
  [7] African 574, No. 241, Milner to Clarke, 9 August 1899.
  [8] African 574, No. 245, 16 August 1899.

vetting of draft Ordinances by the High Commissioner and his legal advisers before they were published or introduced into the Legislative Council.[1] An additional safeguard was that draft Ordinances were transmitted via the Resident Commissioner, who was required to report on their possible effects and whether he favoured the introduction of such legislation.

Estimates, on the other hand, were always submitted in advance to the High Commissioner in terms of Sections 41 to 43 of the Order in Council.[2] Here Milner insisted that these clearly distinguished administrative expenditure in respect of Southern Rhodesia from the rest of the Company's administrative expenditure owing to 'the desirability of maintaining the constitutional distinctness of Southern Rhodesia and Northern Rhodesia'.[3] The Colonial Office was also informed of proposed expenditure and pressed the Company to balance its expenditure and revenue.[4]

Amendments to drafts suggested

When any legislation was sent to the High Commissioner it was carefully scrutinized by him and his legal adviser and in many cases amendments were suggested.[5] These usually secured equal protection under the laws for Africans and Europeans, the prevention of obvious discrimination against Asians, or the retention of the High Commissioner's control over military matters. A significant example was afforded by Ordinance 3 of 1903 amending the Criminal Law, which introduced hanging as a penalty for attempted rape.[6] The Imperial authorities insisted that all persons should be liable to such a penalty and not merely black men raping white women as the draft Ordinance had proposed[7]: as far as the Imperial authorities were concerned it was clear that the minimum of racialism was to appear on the statute book.

[1] The suggestion was originally made by his legal adviser, later one of South Africa's distinguished judges—Sir Malcolm Searle, Judge President of the Cape Provincial Division of the Supreme Court. Southern Rhodesian legislation in the early days must by any standards be considered unsatisfactory. Of the seventy-five Ordinances passed between 1899 and 1902, quite apart from six refused assent, eleven had been amended by 1906 and eight repealed. (These figures exclude numerous amendments to the Railways Ordinance.) Fage, op. cit., p. 51, is incorrect in stating that seven out of seventy-three required amendment.

[2] Section 43 provided that estimates were to be transmitted to the High Commissioner with 'such full and sufficient information as to every expense of an unusual nature therein comprised as may be necessary to enable the High Commissioner . . . to judge of the propriety of the proposed expenditure together with a table exhibiting the variations from the preceding year'. See National Archives A 2/4/1.

[3] African 574, No. 12, Encl. 2, 10 April 1899. Milner insisted that Southern Rhodesian and Northern Rhodesian administrative expenditure should be separated in order to make it clear that they were not one entity.

[4] African (South) C.O. 417/392. C.O. Minute, 28 August 1904.

[5] See Appendix, Tables A and C.

[6] African (South) C.O. 417/371, January to April 1903. The Colonial Office minutes disclose that this was agreed to otherwise 'the habit of lynching may be formed'.

[7] National Archives A 2/4/3, 17 February 1902, 11 April 1903.

Once the High Commissioner had scrutinized the draft the Administrator would be informed that the High Commissioner was agreeable to the introduction of the Ordinance in the Legislative Council. This did not, however, mean that he bound himself in advance to assent to the Ordinance when passed. Milner emphasized this in 1905.[1] He told the Resident Commissioner to continue the procedure followed previously in regard to the forwarding of draft Ordinances to be introduced into the Council 'and to comment upon any parts in which the Ordinance, if passed as drafted, will be liable to objection. I would observe, however, that the submission of draft Ordinances to me beforehand is a matter chiefly for the convenience of the Administration, and that I do not desire to insist upon the submission of all or any draft Ordinance. Neither should any suggestions that may be made in regard to the draft be taken as implying that the Ordinance will necessarily be assented to if they are adopted.'[2]

The Colonial Secretary was, however, firmer than the High Commissioner and Mr. Lyttelton admonished the Company that same year for not consulting His Majesty's Government in advance before introducing a Loan Ordinance aimed at providing loans for farmers but incidentally creating a public debt. He demanded full explanations of the measure's intended effect.[3]

In practice, most Ordinances, certainly all major Ordinances and any affecting the African population, after passing through the Resident Commissioner's hands for comment and transmission to the High Commissioner, would be scrutinized by him and subjected to amendment. When these proposals as amended in draft were introduced into the Council and passed, the process was repeated in that the Administrator would submit a report (again via the Resident Commissioner), stating that the Ordinance had not been amended in its passage through the Legislative Council, or alternatively what the purport of such amendments was. Thereafter the High Commissioner was free to consider the matter, although, in the large majority of cases, he gave his consent without further change being required.

By 1907 the attitude of the Imperial authorities towards Southern Rhodesian legislation had become less strict. The High Commissioner was instructed by the Secretary of State not to concern himself with minor questions of mere drafting, but to accept memoranda by the local legal department and for practical purposes to give final decisions. However the Secretary of State should still be in a position to decide whether or not to exercise the power of

---

[1] Probably as a result of difficulties made by Secretaries of State in respect of legislation which he had himself favoured, notably the Hut Tax Ordinance of 1903 quadrupling the hut tax payable by Africans.

[2] African 763, No. 77, Encl. 4, 4 April 1905.

[3] See Papers laid on the Table of the Legislative Council on 23 May 1906, relative to the Loan Ordinance. As late as 1921 it was laid down that the Board of Inland Revenue in the United Kingdom must be kept informed of all projected tax legislation: National Archives A 2/4/12, 30 March 1921.

disallowance.[1] Despite this instruction to rely on local legal memoranda, the High Commissioner informed the Colonial Office that he still intended, in addition, to consult his own legal adviser, which he did frequently. This procedure continued throughout the period. In 1911 Lord Gladstone, then High Commissioner, euphemistically explained it as being followed 'in order that draft Ordinances could be presented to the Legislative Council in a form acceptable to His Majesty's Government'.

Assent conditional on amendments being made

Although in most cases, since Ordinances had already been through this preliminary scrutinizing procedure, the High Commissioner would give his assent, in a number of cases he was only prepared to assent subject to the condition that the legislation be amended at the first opportunity. This was done on at least twenty-one occasions.[2] Consequently many amending Ordinances resulted, the majority of which were either designed to protect Africans, to secure equal rights and liabilities for all races,[3] to protect the Asian community against restrictive legislation and excessively stringent immigration laws, or to amend Ordinances adversely affecting Britain's control of military forces.[4]

As late as 1915 the Attorney-General informed the Legislative Council that it was 'well established in practice' that very often after an Ordinance had been passed 'a considerable amount of correspondence took place with His Excellency the High Commissioner before the formal assent to promulgation was obtained and Members knew that they had occasionally introduced amending laws'.[5]

Assent subject to administrative safeguards

Yet another method was to give assent subject to an undertaking to introduce an administrative safeguard. This occurred in ten instances, the majority of which were again concerned with securing protection for Africans.[6] The High Commissioner might also demand assurances that the administration would be satisfactory before assenting to an Ordinance.[7] Even after legislation

[1] African (South) C.O. 417/436, High Commissioner's Despatches No. 434 Annex. Elgin to Selborne, 30 August 1907. Selborne was not prepared to interfere with details of legislation or direct the details of administration, particularly where there were elected representatives, and declined to interfere when requested to do so on a visit to Southern Rhodesia: African 932, No. 235, 15 November 1909.

[2] See Appendix, Table A.

[3] e.g. Europeans' property should also be liable to search in the case of stock theft. It was not only Africans who were guilty of such crimes.

[4] See Appendix, Table C.   [5] S.R. Legco. Deb. 1914, col. 13.   [6] See Appendix, Table E.

[7] See African 763, No. 261, re the Natives Employment Ordinance Amendment Ordinance No. 1 of 1907, where the High Commissioner obtained assurances that labour touts were under the control of the Administration.

had been assented to the High Commissioner might demand assurances in regard to the administration of the Ordinance. A striking example related to the Native Passes Ordinance of 1902 where, after such requests, the Administration accepted the condition that Africans be freely granted passes to seek work and that no pressure be placed on them to go through the Native Labour Bureaux as part of government policy.[1]

A refinement of these procedures was not to insist on amendment or an administrative safeguard in respect of the actual legislation, but to require an undertaking that future legislation would not contain similar provisions or would contain some limitation.[2] The Colonial Office early recognized that Company undertakings in respect of amendments or administrative safeguards were not legally enforceable, but took the realistic attitude that 'the Company was always needing His Majesty's Government's good offices, and this of course makes a gentleman's agreement enforceable'.[3]

Assent conditional on satisfactory regulations under the Ordinance

On the other hand, the High Commissioner might insist that some points be clarified by regulations. This was done in 1899, 1900, and subsequently in 1919, on all of which occasions African interests were protected.[4] In practice in many cases proposed regulations under Ordinances were submitted to the High Commissioner at the same time as the Ordinance itself, so that he could judge how the Ordinance would be administered.[5]

Approval of High Commissioner necessary for regulations under Ordinances

Yet another safeguard which, although not part of the Ordinance-making procedure, greatly affected Southern Rhodesian legislation, was that many Ordinances provided that regulations issued thereunder required approval by the High Commissioner.[6] Even where it was not required in terms of the Ordinance, this approval was often obtained.[7] In the main, it was Regulations

[1] African 746, No. 96. Resident Commissioner to High Commissioner, 18 February 1904.

[2] Thus it was laid down in 1905 that no future legislation could impose corporal punishment in excess of twenty-four lashes: African (South) C.O. 417/408, High Commissioner's Despatch 497 of 1905.

[3] Colonial Office Minute on the Immigration Ordinance No. 18 of 1901.

[4] See Appendix, Table D.

[5] e.g. Ordinance 21 of 1904 Amending the Law Relating to Native Taxation: see African 746, No. 223, and also Ordinance 12 of 1904 Amending the Natives' Pass Ordinance (African 746 No. 228 and African 763, No. 25).

[6] African (South) C.O. 417/437, Vol. III, High Commissioner's Despatches 1907, No. 1029, 25 November 1907.

[7] See e.g. African 763, No. 249: the High Commissioner insisted that instructions to Native Commissioners under the Native Passes Ordinance be submitted for his consideration and approval.

affecting Africans that were scrutinized and amended at the hands of the High Commissioner.[1] This procedure continued until the implementation of the responsible government Constitution.[2] The Administrator also anticipated the High Commissioner's attitude as it was 'the frequent practice of the Administrator to disallow by-laws passed by the municipalities'—the most prolific source of discriminatory legislation.[3]

In practice the High Commissioner was able to achieve a great deal through the judicious use of Regulations. Thus by insisting on new Regulations under Section 28 of the Mines and Minerals Amendment Ordinance of 1910 he was able to cut African mortality in Southern Rhodesia mines by half.[4] Again he insisted by Regulation that tax could not be imposed on fourteen-year-old Africans, but only on Africans 'physically capable of earning a livelihood' and he also arranged that all prosecutions should be reported to the Resident Commissioner.[5]

Refusal of assent

Negative control might however be openly applied if the matter was serious enough. On thirteen occasions Bills passed by the Legislative Council were refused assent by the High Commissioner, six of these refusals occurring

[1] e.g. Regulations under the Native Pass Ordinances of 1902 and 1904 (African (South) C.O. 417/407, Milner to Resident Commissioner, 23 January 1905); Regulations rejected in 1906 under the Immigration Restriction Ordinance 1903 (see Annexure 3 to B.S.A. Co. Minutes of 17 January 1907); Regulations amended in 1919 dealing with the control of native locations under Native Urban Locations Ordinance 1908 (National Archives A 3/18/31/3); and Regulations amended in 1915 under Native Pass Consolidation Ordinance 1913 (National Archives A 3/18/31/3).

[2] See National Archives A 2/4/12, Administrator to Buxton, 8 April 1920—Native Pass Regulations. See also 27/10/20—Proclamations and draft Government Notices amended in accordance with the High Commissioner's request. See also A 3/18/31/7 showing the careful scrutiny given by High Commissioner and Secretary of State (Winston Churchill) from 1921 to 1923 of Regulations dealing with the occupation of Native Reserves by non-Africans.

[3] See *S.R. Legco. Deb.* 1915, col. 228.

[4] This was done by demanding new dietary scales, sanitary measures, and safety rules (African (South) C.O. 417/510). Mortality fell in 1908 from 64·96 per 1,000 per quarter to 32·31 per quarter as a result of the High Commissioner's intervention. See also National Archives A 2/15/4. Previously the Southern Rhodesian mortality rate was twice that of the Transvaal mines. See Cd. 3993, *Correspondence relating to the Recruitment of Labour in the Nyasaland Protectorate for the Transvaal and Southern Rhodesian Mines, 1908*, pp. 35 and 68, which reveal intervention by the High Commissioner and the Secretary of State in 1907, while p. 114 reveals that as a result of their intervention a proper government scheme for recruiting Africans outside Southern Rhodesia was evolved. Fage, op. cit., p. 31 gives the following figures for mortality of African mineworkers per 1,000: 66·9 (1906), 45·3 (1908), 28·6 (1911), 21·9 (1915).

[5] African 802, No. 121. The Administration had enforced tax on all fourteen-year-olds, whereupon the High Commissioner insisted on twenty-one years as the taxable age, although he subsequently came to the compromise outlined above. The Colonial Office thought this gave the Administration 'a well deserved lesson': African (South) C.O. 417/422 of 23 February 1906; and C.O. 417/423, Despatch 509 of 11 June 1906.

at the instance of the Colonial Secretary.[1] Of these refusals approximately half were the result of legislation against African interests,[2] while the others were dictated in most instances by reasons of general Imperial policy.[3]

The Secretary of State

Although the High Commissioner was the main Imperial instrument for controlling Southern Rhodesian legislation, the Secretary of State was also active in this direction, on several occasions seeking to be informed of proposed legislation.[4] In fact on his instructions the High Commissioner in 1900 requested that all 'native legislation' for that year be postponed,[5] while the Colonial Secretary himself minuted in 1901 that 'It will be necessary to keep a very tight hand on Rhodesian legislation.'[6] Many of the cases in which the High Commissioner amended draft Ordinances, gave conditional assents, or refused assent, were in practice occasioned by instructions that this be done by the Secretary of State.

Although it was not compulsory for Ordinances falling within the purview of Section 80 of the Southern Rhodesia Order in Council 1898 to be submitted in advance, the Secretary of State advocated the desirability of forwarding drafts of 'class legislation' for advance clearance by the Colonial Office, particularly when any new policy was to be adopted.[7] Even after such

---

[1] As late as 1922 the Colonial Secretary considered instructing the High Commissioner to refuse his assent to the Referendum Ordinance introduced by the leader of the elected members, but decided against this as it would prejudice future relationships between the Colonial Office and the new Southern Rhodesian Government.

[2] See in particular the Ordinance Amending the Law Relating to the Taxation of Natives, No. 20 of 1903, which sought to impose a £2 per annum hut tax instead of the previous 10s. tax.

[3] See Appendix, Table F. The possibility of prejudicing future settlement with the Company led in 1906 to the refusal to assent to the Loan Ordinance of 1905 which created a public debt 'placing a charge . . . on the revenues of the territory as distinguished from those of the B.S.A. Co . . .'. In this case 'His Majesty's Government would not be a party to allowing the local administration to incur distinct and separate obligations without any corresponding surrender by the Company of its rights to the resources of the territory': National Archives RC 3/3/11, Elgin to Selborne, 14 March 1906.

[4] In 1900 Chamberlain demanded that proposed draft Labour Recruitment and Labour Tax Ordinances be sent to him: African 656, Nos. 91 and 177, Colonial Office to B.S.A. Co. 12 July 1900, 23 November 1900. The Colonial Office was aware of proposed legislation under the system introduced in 1898 of requiring the Company to send it copies of all Board minutes and annexures.

[5] African 656, No. 49A, Encl. 2. Legislation on this topic was so long delayed that the Administrator wrote requesting that it would 'at no very distant date . . . be found possible to allow the Legislative Council as representing the people of the country the opportunity of considering and dealing with questions of such vital importance to the interests of the European population as those relating to native administration'.

[6] Minute by Chamberlain on the Masters and Servants Ordinance No. 5 of 1901, in which case he insisted on amendment by the Masters and Servants Amendment Ordinance No. 2 of 1902.

[7] African (South) C.O. 417/320, Colonial Office to Milner, 17 October 1901, re proposed

clearance the Secretary of State did 'not pledge himself on details of class legislation' and instructed the High Commissioner not to assent until the Secretary of State had again scrutinized such legislation as passed.[1] Eventually, in order to assert the necessity of obtaining the Secretary of State's advance assent to such legislation and to secure compliance with Section 80, the High Commissioner was in 1905 instructed to refuse assent to certain Southern Rhodesian legislation.[2]

Disallowance

The Secretary of State also enjoyed the reserve power of disallowance under Section 37 of the Southern Rhodesia Order in Council 1898 which enabled him to invalidate legislation already assented to by the High Commissioner. This power was exercised on three occasions between 1898 and 1923.[3]

The major instance where this power was used occurred at a time when the elected members were already in a majority in the Legislative Council.[4] The disallowance involved the fundamental question of Imperial policy towards Asian immigration into British possessions. The Southern Rhodesia Asiatic Ordinance No. 4 of 1908 made provision for restricting the immigration of Asians and for the registration of those already present in Southern Rhodesia. This legislation, which was based on Transvaal legislation, was favoured by the High Commissioner, Lord Selborne,[5] but Lord Crewe, the Colonial Secretary, disallowed the Southern Rhodesian Ordinance (to which the High Commissioner had in the meantime assented). When the Transvaal precedent was invoked the Colonial Secretary rejected the analogy, since Southern Rhodesia was not 'in possession of responsible government'. He informed the Council that both the Secretary of State and the High Commissioner retained considerable powers of control over the administration and that their

Labour Tax Ordinance. The Colonial Office euphemistically referred to discriminatory measures as 'class legislation'.

[1] African (South) C.O. 417/372, Vol. II, 1903, Chamberlain to Milner, 4 June 1903.

[2] African 763, No. 197, 21 July 1905. See also African (South) C.O. 417/408. Minutes disclose that vindication of the Secretary of State's authority was the major consideration for refusing assent to Ordinance No. 6 of 1905 providing for the Establishment of Native Reserve Locations in or near Urban Areas, and not the fact that new disabilities were imposed on Africans.

[3] See Appendix, Table G. Although the term 'disallowance' was used on a number of other occasions the correspondence reveals that what really occurred in these cases was a refusal of assent by the High Commissioner.

[4] By the acquiescence of the Company. See *infra*, Chapter 10.

[5] This Transvaal legislation had eventually been passed in 1907 after a refusal in the previous year by the Secretary of State to permit such legislation. When the responsible government constitution of 1906 came into operation a virtually identical Ordinance was passed, but the British Government did not at that stage feel able to disallow legislation by a responsible self-governing legislature. See 'The Frontiers of Imperial Control in Self-governing Colonies—Liberal Experience in South Africa, 1905–1908', an unpublished paper delivered at the Institute of Commonwealth Studies by R. Hyam. See also Cd. 3308.

13—C.H.L.S.R.

responsibility was correspondingly increased. In view of this responsibility he had refused to authorize an Ordinance which was 'open to grave objection in principle, which is likely to lead to serious complications, and which so far as I can judge is not imperatively required by the position in Southern Rhodesia'.[1] Despite earlier Colonial Office hesitancy to overrule the decision of a Council with a majority of members elected by the people of Southern Rhodesia, the Colonial Secretary was prepared to take a firm stand on such a question.[2]

Earlier the Secretary of State had exercised the power of disallowance to veto the Post Office Savings Banks Ordinance Amendment Ordinance No. 3 of 1906. This had, in the Colonial Secretary's view, made inadequate provision for safeguarding the interests of investors as it permitted the deposit of such funds with banks, and, in the event of a bank crisis, the savings bank would have been deprived of a considerable portion of its funds.[3]

The final occasion on which the power was used arose from a request by the Administrator and the elected members who wished to retrieve themselves from an unfortunate situation which had resulted from the imposition of a tax on employers of 'coloured labour' resisted by the farming community.[4] The Colonial Office had on its own initiative earlier considered disallowing this Ordinance, but was not prepared to do so as it felt it could not disallow 'an Ordinance on a matter of local interest passed by a majority consisting of six elected members with only one dissentient'.[5] Such considerations had not, however, been decisive when a fundamental policy question, such as treatment of the Asian community, had arisen.

The abandonment of projected legislation

In addition to the aforegoing controls exercised by the Imperial authorities legislation was on a number of occasions abandoned, sometimes merely in the proposal stage and sometimes even in the draft stage, when the Administration discovered the attitude of the Colonial Office towards such proposals.[6] In some cases this occurred as a result of direct Imperial refusal to permit of such legislation: thus an Ordinance providing for the introduction of indentured Asiatic labour was rejected by the Colonial Office[7]; a Labour Tax

[1] Correspondence relating to the Disallowance of the Asiatics Ordinance 1908. National Archives RC 3/3/18, Crewe to Selborne, 12 December 1908.

[2] See Colonial Office Minutes of 16 June 1908 in Africa (South) C.O. 417/452.

[3] National Archives RC 3/3/6 MS.

[4] African 989, No. 44, B.S.A. Co. to Colonial Office, 24 May 1912, re Ordinance 13 of 1913.

[5] African (South) C.O. 417/510, Minute by Lambert, 19 March 1912.

[6] See Appendix, Table A.

[7] African 656, No. 109, 18 August 1900. In 1900 legislation permitting opening of telegrams by the authorities was also refused by Chamberlain: National Archives A 2/4/1.

Ordinance imposing a universal direct labour tax on all Africans on the lines of the Glen Gray Act was refused in 1901 [1]; the Company was not permitted to introduce an Ordinance amending the Native Regulations which could only be amended by the High Commissioner [2]; a Banking Ordinance was never proceeded with as the Colonial Office insisted that in such legislation the Company must be excluded from banking operations [3]; and as late as 1920 legislation was abandoned because of Imperial requirements in connection therewith. [4]

In addition psychological factors were at work: in several cases legislation was not even drafted as the Administrator was aware of the probable response of the Imperial authorities. Thus in 1909, although the elected members requested legislation prohibiting South African recruitment of Southern Rhodesian natives, the Administrator refused to initiate such a measure as 'the Imperial Government set themselves against all legislation whereby the native was prevented from disposing of his labour in the most advantageous market'. [5] In the same year increased African taxation demanded by the leaders of the elected members was rejected by the Administration. [6] That this refusal was caused by awareness of the Imperial attitude was obvious as in that year the High Commissioner, Lord Selborne, on a visit to Southern Rhodesia, when requested that hut tax be doubled, made it clear that 'of any such policy' he was 'a determined opponent'. [7] Again in 1912 the Directors were informed by the local Administration that there was no point in asking for amendments to the Native Regulations requiring Africans to maintain roads in Reserves and to labour on public works, as the High Commissioner was unlikely to approve such a proposal. [8]

The most dramatic case of withdrawal of a projected Ordinance occurred in 1906 when a draft Ordinance to Amend the Law Relating to the Franchise of Natives was prepared. [9] The draft permitted those Africans at that time on the roll to remain on (about 51) [10] but prohibited further Africans from becoming

---

[1] African 659, No. 32, 120, 122, and 246—even though the proceeds were to be utilized exclusively for the benefit of Africans.

[2] African 659, No. 72, 80, 107, 110, 159, and 206. Only a few of the Company's requests were embodied in the High Commissioner's Proclamation and even these were considerably modified.

[3] African 659, No. 87.

[4] Thus a draft Registration of Pledges Ordinance was abandoned owing to the High Commissioner's requirement that Africans should not be omitted and that their interests should be protected by invalidating pledges not approved of and registered by the local Native Commissioner or magistrate: National Archives A 2/4/12.

[5] S.R. Legco. Deb. 1909, col. 25. In 1907 elected members had requested an Ordinance prohibiting the sale of land to Africans: 1908, cols. 151–3. The Administration likewise took no action.

[6] S.R. Legco. Deb. 1909, cols. 105, 109.

[7] African 932, No. 238, 15 November 1909. Report on visit to Southern Rhodesia.

[8] National Archives A 3/18/8, Hole to B.S.A. Co., London, 2 March 1912.

[9] Requested by the elected members in 1905. See S.R. Legco. Deb. 1905, col. 34.

[10] Cd. 2399, Report of the S.A. Native Affairs Commission, 1903–1905, p. 67. Section 434

voters. Before proceeding with the Ordinance the Administrator decided that 'it would be advisable to sound out the High Commissioner, confidentially, with a view to ascertaining whether he would be prepared to support the suspension of the right to claim the franchise'.[1] The High Commissioner replied privately to the Administrator that he was 'pretty confident the Secretary of State would veto the Ordinance under existing circumstances'.[2] The original draft Ordinance was therefore not proceeded with, but informal discussions continued in order to reach agreement on raised qualifications that would effectively exclude Africans. A private letter from the High Commissioner to the Administrator then showed how legislation couched in non-discriminatory language but discriminatory in effect could be introduced with the assistance of a sympathetic High Commissioner. Lord Selborne considered that were he to propose such legislation to the Secretary of State, it might be turned down. He therefore suggested that no reference should be made to the Secretary of State at this stage. Instead the Ordinance should be drafted, checked privately by himself, and only thereafter officially forwarded to him. As High Commissioner he would then forward it to the Colonial Office. Lord Selborne advised: 'So much for the procedure. Now about the purpose of the measure. If its real object is to check the growth of the native franchise, this cannot very well be stated. The ostensible object, therefore, must be something quite different but at the same time plausible. What do you propose to put forward? There must not be, either in the official correspondence or in the Council debates, any threat of a disability on natives if you want to avoid bringing Exeter Hall on your backs. I think you had better, in sending me privately a draft of the Ordinance, send me also a draft of the dispatch with which you propose to cover it when forwarding it officially.'[3] With Selborne's approval a draft Ordinance more than doubling the salary and property qualifications and also requiring reading tests for the franchise was prepared.[4] When this draft was forwarded to the Colonial Office, it resigned itself to accepting the Ordinance, as it felt that 'the best way of preserving the native vote in South Africa is to raise the monetary qualifications'.[5] In any event such a policy was in accordance with the then accepted view that Southern Rhodesia would form part of a large South African federation as set out in the Selborne Memorandum of 1907.[6] However, the London Board, fearing that adverse publicity would be occasioned, instructed the Administrator not to

---

described the fact that certain Africans were entitled to the vote as 'a situation not only immediately unsatisfactory but pregnant with future danger'. Southern Rhodesia was represented on the Commission by Sir Thomas Scanlen.

[1] African 802, No. 28, Encl.
[2] National Archives A 11/2/12/3, Selborne to Milton, 3 May 1906.
[3] National Archives A 11/2/12/3, Selborne to Milton, 22 January 1907.
[4] See African 872, No. 46, Encl. 1.
[5] C.O. Minutes of 29 May 1907 on H.C. Telegraph of 1907, African (South) C.O. 417/435.
[6] See Cd. 3564.

proceed with the measure. At the same time, the British Government entered a *caveat* to protect themselves, and informed the Administration through the High Commissioner that such a measure required 'a full consideration of its bearing upon the ultimate solution of the problem of the uniform franchise to be adopted for South Africa as a whole, on the assumption that Southern Rhodesia will form part of the Federation which may be established at a not remote date'.[1]

Legislation on similar lines, but not raising the qualifications so radically as the 1907 proposals, was ultimately introduced and agreed to in 1912, subject to the introduction of an amending Ordinance inserting the safeguard that appeals be allowed from the decisions of registering officials. The 1912 qualifications allowed British-born or naturalized males of twenty-one years of age, who for the preceding six months had occupied property to the value of £150 (excluding communal property unless a building to that value was on the property), or who had held a mining claim, or had earned £100 per annum as salary or wages, to claim the vote. Applicants had to fill up the registration form themselves or submit to an English dictation test of fifty words.[2] Although the leader of the elected members complained that 'if they had the power they would have got rid of the native franchise altogether',[3] these qualifications (except that women married other than by a system permitting of polygamy were subsequently permitted the vote)[4] remained the basic Southern Rhodesian voters' qualifications until amended in 1951.

Conclusions

Study of the legislative process between 1899 and 1923 shows the extensive control, particularly over matters affecting the African population, exerted by the Imperial authorities during this period of representative government. Approximately one-third of all legislation was directly, and in many cases materially, influenced by the High Commissioner and the Secretary of State,[5] while at the same time consciousness by the legislative body of these powers was a brake on the introduction of legislation which might cause their

[1] C.O. Minute of 14 June 1907. African (South) C.O. 417/435.

[2] Ordinance 14 of 1912. See African 989 No. 67. Cleared in advance and approved by the Colonial Office: African 989, Nos. 59, 67. The Resident Commissioner disapproved of the new dictation test in English since it would disqualify many Dutch inhabitants.

[3] *S.R. Legco. Deb.* 1912, Col. 53. See also *S.R. Legco. Deb.* 1917, col. 409: 'The first act of responsible government in this country would be to take away the franchise from the natives.' The Buxton Report (Cmd. 1273) § 64(2) urged that after the grant of responsible government the right of Africans to the franchise must be protected, and for this purpose advocated adoption of the reservation procedure in the Natal Constitution of 1906. This was eventually copied and embodied in Clause 28(a) of the S.R. Constitution Letters Patent, 1923.

[4] Ordinance No. 9 of 1919. Wives were deemed to possess the same occupation and salary qualifications as their husbands.

[5] See Appendix, Table H.

invocation. The most significant consequence for the future government of Southern Rhodesia was that, during this period, a method of advance clearance of possible controversial legislation had been evolved so as to obviate overt action by the Imperial authorities, and that this procedure was to be adopted in the next period of Southern Rhodesia's constitutional history.

9

IMPERIAL ADMINISTRATIVE SUPERVISION
1898–1923

The Resident Commissioner, 1899–1923

THE most significant addition made by the Southern Rhodesia Order in Council 1898 to the machinery of government had been the provision for a British Resident Commissioner stationed in Southern Rhodesia as the 'eyes and ears' of Her Majesty's Government. This gave the British Government an authoritative representative on the spot who was able to watch the Administration and its policy, convey representations to it, and warn the Administrator when any policy was likely to meet with Colonial Office disapproval. The Resident Commissioner was, in fact, the key to British supervision from the period 1899 to 1923.

Although in the period immediately after the Rebellion there had been charges of 'dualism', there were none after 1898 because the various Administrators and Resident Commissioners maintained amicable relations, reaching an understanding that Resident Commissioner and Administrator should consult each other.[1] From the beginning the problem of submitting appointments requiring the High Commissioner's consent was eased by instructions to the Resident Commissioner to 'arrive at some definite understanding' with the Administrator.[2] Nonetheless on isolated occasions the Administrator resented recommendations on policy matters made by the Resident Commissioner to the High Commissioner.[3] However, as Lord Selborne informed the Colonial Office in 1907, 'the system has on the whole worked excellently and without friction. It only required two sensible men to enable the system to work.'[4]

Despite occasional suggestions that it was no longer necessary, the Resident

---

[1] See J. D. Fage, op. cit., p. 24. See also *S.R. Legco. Deb.* 1907, 13 May 1907, p. 64, Newton (Treasurer): 'careful and valuable representations are made by the Resident Commissioner which have always been accepted in the best spirit by the Administration'. National Archives A 2/5/1–12 contains the correspondence 1898–1923 between the Administrator and the Resident Commissioner.

[2] African 483 Encl. 2, p. 457. All communications on proposed appointments passed through the Resident Commissioner's hands under flying seal when he added reports on the proposed candidates.

[3] As in the case of the Native Tax Ordinance of 1903. He also objected when the Resident Commissioner heard representations without informing him. See H. Wilson-Fox, *Memorandum on the Position, Policy and Prospects of the Company*, printed for the information of the Board, London, 1907, p. 216, quoting Administrator to High Commissioner, 20 March 1907.

[4] African 872, No. 196, High Commissioner to Secretary of State, 2 December 1907.

Commissionership remained effective until the grant of responsible government. Although in 1904 Lord Milner suggested that the post should not be filled after Sir Marshall Clarke's retirement,[1] the Colonial Secretary cabled that this was not an opportune time to dispense with an Imperial officer at Salisbury.[2] However, Treasury pressure to save the British taxpayer the expense of both Resident Commissioner and Commandant General led to a reorganization whereby the same individual was appointed to both offices from 1905 to 1909.[3]

Subsequently, Lord Selborne[4] in 1907 informed the Colonial Office that the High Commissioner could not fulfil his duties properly unless he had a delegate on the spot, and that removal of the Resident Commissioner would have left the Crown unrepresented in Southern Rhodesia.[5] Selborne felt 'that the time has not come (and never can come so long as Southern Rhodesia is governed by the B.S.A. Company) when the post of Resident Commissioner can be abolished. . . . As your Lordship will have noticed from more than one recent case, it is still necessary to exercise great vigilance in the matter of native administration.'[6] These views were reiterated by Lord Gladstone, the succeeding High Commissioner,[7] who stated how valuable he found the Resident Commissioner and how necessary he was to keep close watch on the native question.[8] This attitude persisted throughout the period, and, even after the grant of responsible government, a Rhodesian parliamentarian and a leader of the movement towards responsible government commented on the great influence exercised until 1924 by the Resident Commissioner without whose approval no 'native legislation' could be passed.[9]

The Resident Commissioner was so important because he enjoyed several

[1] African 746, No. 234, Milner to Lyttleton, 12 August 1904. Sir Marshall Clarke was Resident Commissioner from 1898 to 1905 and was active in securing proper supervision of the Company's labour recruiting practices.

[2] African 746, No. 275, Lyttleton to Milner, 25 October 1904. Colonial Office Minutes made it clear that the Resident Commissioner was necessary to watch for the possibility of any native rising, to observe native affairs, to see that functions were properly exercised in respect of Northern Rhodesia, and to watch lest His Majesty's Government might be involved in difficulties within Southern Rhodesia.

[3] See Southern Rhodesia Order in Council 1905 of 20 March 1905. In 1909 it was provided that the Resident Commissioner for the time being was to be the Commandant General of the police and volunteer forces: Southern Rhodesia Order in Council of 10 August 1909.

[4] High Commissioner for South Africa from 1905 to 1910.

[5] African (South) C.O. 417/437, Vol. III, H.C. 1907, Selborne to Hopwood, 18 November 1907.

[6] African 872, No. 196, 2 December 1907.

[7] High Commissioner for South Africa and first Governor-General of the Union of South Africa from 1910 to 1914.

[8] African (South) C.O. 417/484, High Commissioner to Secretary of State, 23 October 1910. In 1917 the Company Treasurer commented on 'their very alive Resident Commissioner' and that it would be impossible to slip in 'taxation or oppression furtively': S.R. Legco. Deb. 1917, col. 483, 30 April 1917.

[9] E. T. Jollie, *The Real Rhodesia*, Hutchinson, 1924, p. 247.

capacities: he was 'diplomatic representative' of the United Kingdom, performing the dual functions of acting as local representative and reporter of the local scene; he was the instrument for communicating Imperial directives to the Administration and enforcing them; he was a member of the Executive Council of the territory; and he was a non-voting member of the Legislative Council.

In his capacity as a member of the Legislative Council, the Resident Commissioner was in close touch with the feeling of the elected members. However, he took little active part in Legislative Council proceedings,[1] and his real legislative role was to be seen in his comments on all legislation forwarded to the High Commissioner. Much heed was paid by the Imperial authorities to his opinion and in at least one significant instance his views led to refusal of assent,[2] while in other cases either amendments resulted, or the Colonial Office left the final decision to him as to whether legislation was satisfactory and could be approved.[3]

Similarly when legislation by High Commissioner's Proclamation was under consideration, the Resident Commissioner's views were usually decisive, particularly when changes in the Native Department were urged by the Administration. In such cases the Administration would meet his objections by modified proposals.[4]

The Resident Commissioner was also a watchdog of the general administration of the country and the execution of policy, being enabled to scrutinize the administration with the insight of a member of the Executive Council since he was aware of all Executive Council decisions and all minutes and documents passed through his hands.[5] Initially, however, the Council merely registered the acts of the Administrator which made 'for a more complete autocracy than was contemplated by the Order in Council'.[6] Matters requiring to be considered were circulated to the members, but sometimes the Administrator took action before confirmation. Nonetheless, all representations made by the Resident Commissioner were duly considered, and he did

---

[1] In the thirteen years from 1911 to 1923 he spoke on twenty-five occasions, mainly on points of fact for the guidance of members. Indeed, in 1917 he was criticized since 'he never opened his mouth': *S.R. Legco. Deb.* 1917, cols. 291/2. Thereafter, in answer to a direct question as to the United Kingdom's attitude to Native Labour Bureaux, he informed the House that the Imperial Government would not allow recruitment by Native Commissioners. The Resident Commissioner's silence was very marked from 1918 to 1923, when only congratulatory statements or factual assertions were made.

[2] Native Tax Ordinance No. 20 of 1903. By this Ordinance native tax would have been quadrupled.

[3] e.g. the Native Marriage Ordinance No. 2 of 1901.

[4] See African 1003, No. 80.

[5] These the Colonial Office also received. They could and did ask the Resident Commissioner for elucidation of points discussed by the Executive Council.

[6] African 782, No. 153, Resident Commissioner to Grindle, 24 April 1902. No Executive Council meetings were held from 5 February 1901 to 18 February 1902, but this was exceptional.

not find it necessary to insist on the Council meeting. When the Council did meet, his voice was effective.[1]

The real significance of his membership was, however, that throughout his period of office the Resident Commissioner was in close contact with all decisions of the Administration taken at the highest level and was kept informed of the details of native administration.[2]

Imperial surveillance and supervision

As the main instrument for Imperial surveillance of affairs in Southern Rhodesia, the Resident Commissioner reported continuously on matters affecting the African population. He frequently initiated special enquiries or investigated questions at the request of the High Commissioner or of the Secretary of State, and he would also engage in enquiries if complaints were brought to him by the inhabitants while, despite his close contact with the Administration, he refused to send people as a matter of course to the Company's officials first.[3]

Although the Resident Commissioner's correspondence shows that he was concerned with administration generally and the African people in particular, two topics specially concerned the Imperial authorities. These were the problems associated with the regulation and conditions of African labour and the necessity of securing adequate Reserves for the African people.

Labour problems

Legislation governing labour was subjected to special scrutiny by the Imperial authorities. Whether the legislation related to importation of labourers, registration of contracts, a pass system, relations between master and servant, to inducements towards increasing the labour supply such as native taxation or compulsory payment of lobola, the Colonial Office (acting in most cases on the Resident Commissioner's advice) was prepared to mitigate those features which bore harshly on Africans. In the administrative sphere labour conditions were similarly closely scrutinized and the application of legislation watched. Pressures forcing Africans into the labour market, the enforcement of native tax, the administration of labour bureaux and boards, labour recruitment policies, the treatment of imported labour, the administration of master and servant legislation, employment conditions, accommodation for labourers on the mines, mining mortality,[4] and the operation of the pass laws

[1] Thus in 1905 he caused the Administration to drop a proposed charge for compulsory vaccination of Africans: African 763, No. 82.

[2] African 1015, No. 164 shows the Resident Commissioner received monthly reports made by all Native Commissioners.

[3] National Archives A 3/18/5 MSS, Resident Commissioner to Administrator, 10 May 1912.

[4] See National Archives A 2/4/2–14. This still concerned the High Commissioner in 1922.

all engaged the Resident Commissioner's attention and were reported on to the Colonial Office. The activities of native messengers, Native Commissioners, labour touts, and their employees were closely watched,[1] and any suspected abuses were actively followed up by the High Commissioner and the Secretary of State—particular care being given to those problems while Chamberlain was Colonial Secretary. Indeed in 1901 the Imperial authorities laid down the future labour recruitment policy of the country, which persisted until the nineteen thirties, was subsequently resuscitated after the Second World War, and is still in force.

This arose out of the events at the turn of the century when in 1899 a Matabeleland Native Labour Bureau consisting of representatives of the Company and the mines had been established in order to recruit labour. This body grew in 1900 into the Labour Bureau of Southern Rhodesia and in 1902 split into two Boards, one situated in Salisbury and the other in Bulawayo. Thereafter the Administration, which had been contributing towards finance, suggested dissolution of the Boards and future recruitment through Native Commissioners. However, in the interim the Colonial Office had instructed the Resident Commissioner to make a full report on whether the Company was engaging in forced labour practices, as it had seen from correspondence attached to Company Board minutes (now sent to it in terms of the Supplemental Charter) that the Chief Native Commissioner for Mashonaland had indicated to African Chiefs that they were expected to provide labour.[2] On receiving the Resident Commissioner's report, Chamberlain admonished Milner for not being more active in the matter,[3] and then prohibited the Administration from participating in the direct or indirect recruitment of labour,[4] instructing it to confine itself to the supervision of the activities of labour touts.[5] As a result, in 1903 an independent Rhodesian Native Labour Bureau, under supervision of and with financial assistance from the Administration, was established by Ordinance. Reconstructed in 1911 the Rhodesian

---

[1] e.g. objections to the use of the native police force to recruit labour (African 574, No. 262), and misconduct of labour agents' messengers (African 656, No. 121A), native messengers' misconduct (African 656, No. 16), and arrests by messengers (African 656, No. 166).

[2] See Cd. 1200, Correspondence relating to the Regulations and Supply of Labour in Southern Rhodesia. The Company became so sensitive on this issue that the Board itself investigated any case where there was a suggestion of forced labour 'in view of the unfounded suggestions which have so frequently been made': African 656, No. 146.

[3] See African (South) 1901, C.O. 417/319, Vol. 1, Letter to Milner, 19 March 1901. The Blue Book omitted the High Commissioner's view that he personally favoured 'a well-regulated system of state compulsion under proper securities for good treatment and for adequate remuneration'. Cp. African 694, No. 127, and Cd. 1200, No. 34.

[4] The Commandant-General also prohibited the police from taking any part in native labour recruitment: African 656, No. 6.

[5] The B.S.A. Company's paraphrase of the Imperial attitude was: 'either they appoint Imperial officers as Native Commissioners or that we must instruct Native Commissioners not to interfere in labour questions directly or indirectly': African 694, No. 110.

Native Labour Bureau continued to function in this way until it was ultimately closed in 1933 owing to a surfeit of labour.[1]

Indeed as long as it enjoyed power in Southern Rhodesia the Colonial Office made it clear that it would not countenance the Administration participating in labour recruitment in Southern Rhodesia through officials and employees of the Native Department,[2] and, whenever there were departures from this policy, it reprimanded the Administration and caused departmental enquiries to be instituted. Thus, in 1911, when there was already an elected majority in the Legislative Council, the Resident Commissioner insisted that Native Commissioners cease using their native messengers to recruit labour and urged a departmental enquiry, which resulted in the Secretary of State again prohibiting the Administration from using its employees to recruit labour.[3] Even in 1922, when responsible government had been agreed upon, the Secretary of State insisted on the Administration investigating the working of Native Regulations and Pass Laws.

The importation of foreign labour was also of great concern to the Imperial authorities, who refused requests or obstructed attempts by the Company to import West Indian,[4] Arab, Abyssinian, Indian, and Chinese labourers over the period 1900 to 1904. Quite apart from the repercussions on South African labour policy generally (and these were used as a dilatory excuse), the Secretary of State informed the High Commissioner 'that the attitude of the natives will have to be taken into account if and when the introduction of Chinese labourers into Southern Rhodesia is finally decided on'.[5] Eventually Colonial Office delay and the change in government in the United Kingdom in 1905 saved Southern Rhodesia from the complications of further racial minorities as large-scale importation of indentured labourers never occurred.[6]

Reserves

The second major question of concern to the Imperial authorities was the adequacy of Reserves for the African population. From the time of the

[1] Report of the Chief Native Commissioner for the year 1933, Government Printer, C.S.R. 9, 1934, p. 7.

[2] The same argument did not apply to recruitment outside the Territory: see Cd. 3993, p. 114.

[3] See African (South) C.O. 417/500, High Commissioner's Despatch Conf. 13 November 1911. Apparently, 827 Africans were recruited in this way: C.O. 417/510. High Commissioner's Despatch Conf. 3 of 8 January 1912. See also National Archives A 3/18/33/1, MSS.

[4] African 656, No. 7.

[5] African (South) C.O. 417/391, Lyttleton to Milner, 8 June 1904. In contrast, the further excuse was subsequently used by Lyttelton that, since there had been a Legislative Council recently elected, Chinese labourers could not be imported until such Legislative Council had been consulted.

[6] Wilson-Fox, op. cit., pp. 247–52 gives a full account of the history of attempts to import indentured labour. See also Cd. 1200, Correspondence relating to the Regulation and Supply of Labour in Southern Rhodesia, and Cd. 2028, Correspondence relating to the Proposed Introduction of Indentured Asiatic (Chinese) Labour into Southern Rhodesia.

Matabele and Mashona Rebellions there was consistent Imperial pressure for the allocation of Reserves adequate both in quality and quantity. Although before the implementation of the 1898 Constitution Milner succeeded in obtaining a proper settlement in Matabeleland, it required constant pressure from the Secretary of State [1] through the High Commissioner and the Resident Commissioner for the assignment of proper Reserves in Mashonaland. Only at the end of 1902 were proper Reserves proposed, these eventually being allocated in 1904. [2] These new Reserves had in fact been reported on by the Resident Commissioner, who had generally supervised their allocation, had also insisted on fair land exchanges, and had objected to private farms being pegged in reserved areas. [3]

Thereafter the Resident Commissioner constantly surveyed the Reserve position, commenting on the overall position and whether or not allocations were satisfactory. [4] Great care was taken when the boundaries of any native district were to be changed, and in the majority of cases the Resident Commissioner visited the areas in question, while in all cases he required to be satisfied that any proposed exchange was fair and equitable before forwarding any recommandations to the Secretary of State who was responsible for approving such changes. [5] The Resident Commissioner also investigated the condition of Africans on unalienated lands, interfering in 1914 in order to protect the interests of Africans moved from tsetse fly areas. [6]

A suggestion made by the Resident Commissioner in 1912 and taken up at the insistence of the Secretary of State against Company opposition led to the Southern Rhodesia Native Reserves Commission of 1915, which was appointed to make a final allocation of land in Southern Rhodesia. [7] In appointing the Commission, the Secretary of State rejected suggestions by the High Commissioner and the Company that the Commission should investigate

[1] African 656, No. 130, Chamberlain to Milner, 26 September 1900, requiring Reserves to be proclaimed in Mashonaland; African 694, No. 204, 11 June 1902, requesting a settlement at an early date; and African 717, No. 130, 24 April 1903.

[2] See Cd. 8674, Papers relating to the Southern Rhodesia Native Reserves Commisson, 1915, p. 9. In 1904 Reserves throughout the country constituted 38,871 sq. miles. Estimated population was 264,618, i.e. 6·8 to the square mile: African 763, No. 116.

[3] African 694, No. 10, Encl. 6, and African 717, No. 113.

[4] African 899, No. 55, High Commissioner to Secretary of State, 30 March 1908, and No. 103, Secretary of State to High Commissioner. Allocations were approved 'on the distinct understanding that such approval is not to preclude further consideration'.

[5] African 989, No. 74, see also National Archives A 2/4/6, A 2/4/7, 20 December 1910. The Resident Commissioner, as a result of visiting a proposed area, made changes which were accepted by the authorities.

[6] African 1015, Nos. 40, 55, 65, and 224.

[7] The Company had objected to additional Reserves, stating that in future less land would be needed, but the Colonial Office made it clear that it could not countenance an increasing body of Africans 'divorced from the land ... The policy of His Majesty's Government has consistently been to endeavour to develop and improve native organization rather than to break it down': African 1003, No. 107, 30 July 1913, and No. 122, 6 September 1913.

whether Africans should be precluded from holding land in territory under white occupation and *vice versa*, on the basis that this would disenfranchise any African voters and that even the Union Government had not done this in the Cape.[1]

The recommendations of the Southern Rhodesia Native Reserves Commission[2] were the basis for the final allocation of Reserves for Africans. In its Interim Report the Commission rejected the notion that every African enjoyed 'an indefeasible right to live on the soil under tribal conditions' although Section 81 of the 1898 Order in Council specified that 'the Company shall from time to time assign to the natives inhabiting Southern Rhodesia land sufficient for their occupation whether as tribes or portions of tribes . . .'.[3] The Commission then recommended a final re-assignment of Reserves. Other than for a few minor modifications to the boundaries of Reserves recommended by the Commission[4] and a small concession permitting delay in compulsory removal of Africans, the Commission's report was adopted and implemented by the Southern Rhodesia Order in Council 1920.[5] This repealed Section 81 of the Southern Rhodesia Order in Council 1898 and made the Reserve settlement final, subject to minor boundary alterations to be agreed upon by the High Commissioner and the Administration. The result of the Order was to secure for the sole and exclusive use of the African population approximately $21\frac{1}{2}$ out of the total 96 million acres of land in the country, at the same time diminishing the existing Reserve area by approximately one million acres.[6] The Reserves as defined by the Order were then vested in the High Commissioner for South Africa for the use and occupation of Africans.[7]

[1] African 1003, Nos. 154 and 168.

[2] Cd. 8674, Interim and Final Reports of the Southern Rhodesia Native Reserves Commission 1915.

[3] This question is still a political issue and the Commission's remarks were quoted at length in the Second Report of the Select Committee on Resettlement of Natives, Government Printer, Salisbury, *L.A.S.C.* 3, 1960.

[4] See Cmd. 1042, Despatch to the High Commissioner for South Africa transmitting the Order of His Majesty in Council of the 9th November, 1920. See also Cmd. 547, Southern Rhodesia: Correspondence with the Anti-Slavery and Aborigines Protection Society relating to the Native Reserves in Southern Rhodesia.

[5] Southern Rhodesia Order in Council 1920 of 9 November 1920.

[6] C. Leys, *European Politics in Southern Rhodesia*, Oxford, 1959, at p. 9, refers to a reduction of over six million acres. Cp. Cd. 8674, p. 67.

[7] The assigned areas were described in detail in the first schedule to the Order in Council of 9 November 1920. In fact they had already been assigned under a series of Government Notices issued in 1918 and 1920. The Southern Rhodesia Order in Council 1920 was continued in force by Section 42 of the Southern Rhodesia Constitution Letters Patent 1923. In 1937 by Letters Patent of 25 May 1937, the 1920 Order in Council was repealed and new provisions inserted giving control of the Reserves to a Board of Trustees and to the Secretary of State (the High Commissioner's supervisory powers disappearing). In 1961 by Sections 92–104 of the Southern Rhodesia (Constitution) Order in Council 1961 (S.I. 1961, No. 2314) these Reserves (there had only been minor boundary adjustments from time to time) and the Special Native Area, established by an amendment in 1950 to the Land

Although the Imperial authorities were scrupulous about Reserves they did not concern themselves about Africans occupying land outside the Reserves. Indeed, where Africans were moved under the Native Regulations from land outside the Reserves, the Colonial Office condoned non-observance of Article 85 (1) of the 1898 Order in Council which required full enquiry by the Administrator in Executive Council with the concurrence of the High Commissioner.[1]

General surveillance of the Administration

The Resident Commissioner, and through him the High Commissioner and the Secretary of State, kept in close touch with all events in the territory and with the general conduct of the Administration. Although the Resident Commissioner's major concerns were questions affecting the African population and possible causes of unrest[2] he was also concerned with policy in general. Thus he scrutinized the administration of justice, the accommodation in prisons, the types of sentence imposed, the severity of sentences,[3] the infliction of corporal punishment in particular,[4] and also watched the working of legislation in practice.[5]

Apportionment Act 1940 (approximately thirteen million acres in 1959) were constituted Tribal Trust Land and vested in a Board of Trustees of Tribal Trust Land 'for the use and occupation of tribesmen'.

[1] African 1016, No. 255; African 1034 No. 5, 20 January 1915.

[2] e.g. the implementation of native tax, the removal of Chiefs, unscrupulous traders (African 574, No. 101; African 702, No. 16, insisting that they be prosecuted), or the movement of Africans into and out of the territory (National Archives A 3/18/8 of 28 February 1914; African 574, No. 89; African 657, No. 5). Thus in 1913 he urged leniency in the application of the Dog Tax Ordinance of 1912 (African 1003, No. 57). In 1913 when queries were raised as to the treatment of Africans on Liebig's vast ranches and Company charges for permitting Africans to graze cattle, the Imperial Government intervened with the Administration, who arranged that Native Commissioners would give all natives land in the Reserves and assist them in moving there: see H.C. Deb., Vol. 64, col. 1225 and Vol. 65, col. 2027.

[3] This was done as late as 1923. See National Archives A 3/18/8 of 7 February 1922 and A 2/4/14 of 10 August 1923. The Secretary of State called the attention of the Administrator to the excessive nature of the punishments imposed on Africans who had committed petty offences. In addition, the High Commissioner in commuting death sentences must have taken account of the Resident Commissioner's recommendations. In 1908 and 1910 there was agitation as the result of two commutations of death sentences passed on Africans found guilty on rather scanty evidence of rape on European women.

[4] The Colonial Office insisted on annual returns of the occasions when this was inflicted. Enquiries were made if it was inflicted when it was not prescribed: African (South) C.O. 417/407 and 409; and National Archives A 2/4/2.

[5] In 1898 there was long unofficial correspondence about the discrimination against Asians. In contrast in 1922 there was no objection that, although the Civil Service regulations did not disable Africans from appointment to clerical posts 'in practice natives are not appointed to such posts': National Archives A 2/4/13 of 20 September 1922. The Public Services Act of 1931, Section 8, legalized this discriminatory practice. The Southern Rhodesia Civil Service was only opened to Africans by Act No. 42 of 1960.

Quite apart from surveillance positive pressure might at times be applied by the Imperial Authorities on the Administration to follow a particular policy. Thus from 1905 to 1907, Imperial policy urging a federation in Southern Africa led to joint meetings with the other South African territories to secure common administrative practice and uniformity in legislation.[1] Lord Selborne, the High Commissioner, was instrumental in this, as he was in favour of 'the political organization of the Northern territories' by 'the community already established in the South'.[2]

Surveillance of the Native Department

The effect of Imperial supervision was, however, most felt in the close watch kept over the officers of the Company engaged in African administration. This scrutiny was effected by the Resident Commissioner, who was the chief source of information on which the Imperial authorities could act in respect of appointments, suspensions, and removals of members of the Native Department.

From the outset of the 1898 constitutional arrangements, the Secretary of State insisted on the observance of the new provisions giving supervisory powers over those engaged in native administration. All Native Commissioners holding office at the time were only confirmed in their appointments after a report by the Resident Commissioner had been submitted and a general rule of practice evolved for the future.[3] Indeed, exact compliance with the terms of the Order in Council was required: thus the Secretary of State objected when appointments were made by the Junior Administrator, Sir Arthur Lawley, and not by Mr. W. H. Milton, the Senior Administrator.[4] Similarly, the High Commissioner refused to permit even temporary transfer of Native Commissioners without his permission. Furthermore, there was to be no general assignment of Native Commissioners: they were to go to prescribed districts.[5] Nonetheless in 1899 the Imperial authorities felt that there was 'considerable irregularity in the conduct of native administration', and the Secretary of State therefore ordered the Resident Commissioner to keep close watch on events and also pressed for the appointment of a Secretary of Native Affairs under Section 79(1) of the Order in Council.[6] Eventually it was agreed that the Senior Administrator, Mr. W. H. Milton, might be

[1] See National Archives A 2/4/2 and 3.
[2] See *The Selborne Memorandum*, ed. Basil Williams, Oxford, 1925, pp. 141–5.
[3] See African 574, Encls., reporting fully on the background of each Native Commissioner. Those appointed special Justices of the Peace with judicial powers were required to write the Cape Law examinations: African 483, p. 457.
[4] African 559, No. 453.
[5] African 574, No. 253.
[6] African 574, No. 297.

appointed, provided an efficient chief staff officer delegated with the duty of visiting the districts was also appointed.[1]

The Administration could no longer (as before 1896) rely on automatic acceptance of proposed appointments by the Secretary of State and, in several cases, the Secretary of State rejected proposed candidates: in 1902 the Secretary of State rejected Mr. Herbert Taylor as Under Secretary for Native Affairs,[2] and another leading Rhodesian for the post of Protector of Immigrants.[3] In questions of dismissals the Imperial authorities were also firm. Thus from 1899, when Lord Milner told the Resident Commissioner that 'the details of native administration will require the most careful watching for some time to come', until the end of the period, the Imperial authorities insisted on the highest standards being maintained. In 1899 the High Commissioner laid down that a proper procedure should be established and that resignations should not be permitted where serious misdemeanours had occurred,[4] while in 1903 it was laid down that dismissed Native Commissioners were not to be re-employed in any office whatever under the Company's administration.[5] Even as late as 1923 the High Commissioner insisted that a Native Commissioner found not guilty by a departmental enquiry must retire.[6] Furthermore, the High Commissioner insisted on criminal prosecution of Native Commissioners in 1907 and 1919.[7]

The Imperial Authorities made it clear that they would 'never allow Native Commissioners to be a law unto themselves'[8] and that it was 'impossible to teach natives to obey the law by breaking the law'.[9] Indeed in the case which gave rise to these remarks, the High Commissioner, finding that the Administration had not been sufficiently firm, ordered an enquiry by the judge under Section 86 of the Order in Council, which resulted in severe condemnation of the Native Commissioner at Belingwe.[10] On other occasions also the High Commissioner insisted on departmental enquiries.[11] Conversely,

---

[1] African 656, No. 172A.

[2] The Resident Commissioner reported that as member of the Labour Board and Chief Native Commissioner, Taylor had subordinated the duties of the latter office to those of the former. Furthermore, Taylor's name had figured prominently in Cd. 1200. See also African 782, No. 174 and C.O. 417/345, Imperial Secretary to Administrator, 27 October 1902. Taylor (afterwards Sir Herbert Taylor) later became Chief Native Commissioner for Southern Rhodesia and enjoyed complete Imperial confidence.

[3] African 782, No. 113.

[4] African 574, No. 279. This was again insisted upon in 1902 after a Native Commissioner, who had defalcated hut tax funds, had been allowed to resign: African 702, No. 302; African 717, No. 10; and African 717, No. 50, in which the Colonial Office reprimanded the Company.

[5] African 717, No. 345.   [6] National Archives A 2/4/13, 10 March 1923.

[7] See National Archives A 2/4/2 and Administrator's Files, National Archives.

[8] African 899, No. 20.

[9] African 872, No. 193, Encl. 4, referring to the case of a Native Commissioner who had flogged Africans.

[10] African 872, No. 115.

[11] e.g. African 899, No. 25 referring to cattle trading and dealing by Native Commissioners.

14—C.H.L.S.R.

the Imperial authorities were equally firm when the Company dismissed a Native Commissioner on grounds of redundancy without consulting the Secretary of State: Chamberlain insisted that he be given another Native Commissionership.[1]

In 1907 a leading elected member could validly say that 'The Native Commissioner found himself absolutely powerless to do anything. His Department was more strictly watched by the Imperial Government than any other.'[2] Even at the end of the period under examination this comment was still apt as the Imperial authorities retained their control over the staff of the Native Department.[3]

United Kingdom executive control over military and police forces

Under the Southern Rhodesia Order in Council 1898 the High Commissioner had been placed in control of all military police forces, which were to be directly under the control of the Commandant General, who in turn was subject to High Commissioner's Orders. All forces including civil police had been comprised within this control.[4]

Changes occurred in 1904 when civil police forces were reorganized, and the Southern Rhodesian Constabulary and forces working in municipal and town management areas, in villages and adjoining areas, on railway property and areas adjoining the railway, were exempted from the High Commissioner's control.[5] Such forces were now governed by the Police Ordinance No. 21 of 1903, which gave the Administrator powers of appointment and removal of a Superintendent of Police and all other officers. The Superintendent, subject to the direction of the Attorney-General, was to control the Southern Rhodesia Constabulary which was permitted to be armed and mounted, and was to preserve the peace, to prevent crime, and to carry out all duties laid down under the Ordinance. In case of war or emergency, however, it was liable to be employed for military purposes under the control of the High Commissioner. The British South Africa Police, on the other hand, were governed by the High Commissioner's Proclamation and remained under the control of the Commandant General.

The Company had, in fact, sought the elimination of Imperial control over all forces but Milner had refused. However, little friction occurred owing to

[1] African 659, No. 242; African 694, Nos. 11 and 107; African (South) 1901, Vol. 2, 417/320.

[2] *S.R. Legco. Deb.* 1907, p. 18, 18 December 1907.

[3] It did not often prove necessary to use their powers since, from 1912, a standing committee had been set up by the Administrator to advise on promotions and appointments (G.N. 380 of 1912), which resulted in the Southern Rhodesian Civil Service generally maintaining reasonable standards.

[4] See *supra*, Chapter 7.

[5] High Commissioner's Proclamation 11 of 19 May 1904: African 702, Nos. 31 and 85. This change had been preceded by lengthy negotiations starting in 1898.

the good sense of those who had to work the system. As Milner pointed out: 'The control of the High Commissioner, though an ultimate reserve power of great political importance, is not intended, as it is in fact never used, to keep the Commandant General from placing himself and his force in the fullest sense at the disposal of the local Administration, and not only doing the work which the local Administration requires, but doing it, wherever possible, in the way in which that Administration desires it should be done. As a matter of fact it is only in the case of appointments and matters of high policy that the High Commissioner is referred to at all.'[1] Similarly, the Commandant General did not take an active part in the detailed administration or command of the police and did not interfere with officers exercising their legitimate functions. His power as Lord Selborne said 'has been simply held in reserve',[2] while insofar as the Volunteer military forces were concerned the Commandant General did not take an active part, as if he did, 'it was not very well received'.[3]

Nonetheless, both the Resident Commissioner and the High Commissioner kept close watch on police activities.[4] The High Commissioner also insisted that all changes in the establishment of the force be approved by him[5] and that the Company keep the force up to its proper strength.[6] As indicated above, in 1905, at Treasury insistence in order to effect economies, the offices of Resident Commissioner and Commandant General were, when Sir Marshall Clarke retired, to be held by the same incumbent. Colonel Chester-Master from April 1905 held both posts.[7] As a result of this change it was

---

[1] African 702, No. 3, High Commissioner to Administrator, 28 February 1903. Milner might occasionally intervene, as he did when he insisted on proper pension provisions for police forces and refused to allow the Company 'to put the screw on His Majesty's Government to place police under Company control sooner than they thought fit': ibid. No. 308, Encl. 5, 4 August 1903. As Lord Selborne disclosed later, Milner felt it would be an advantage when the question of a South African federation came up for as many as possible of the Colonial defence forces to be under the High Commissioner's control.

[2] African 872, No. 196, High Commissioner to Secretary of State, 2 December 1907.

[3] African 948, No. 88, High Commissioner to Secretary of State, 9 November 1911— Gladstone reporting on a visit to Southern Rhodesia.

[4] Thus the Imperial authorities complained when the B.S.A. Police were used for cattle stations among natives, remonstrated on receipt of reports of hut burning, crop destruction, arrests of women and children by a police patrol in the Mtoko district, and when a recalcitrant Chief's head (M'pondera's) was brought in for identification. They also reacted strongly when police patrols in North-Eastern Mashonaland captured women and children and gave instructions to work. Even as late as 1912 they insisted on an investigation into police methods of inducing Africans to give Crown evidence. See African 659, No. 258, Encl. 2, Acting Imperial Secretary to Resident Commissioner, 7 June 1901; African 702, No. 338, Milner to Clarke, 29 September 1902 (in this case Chamberlain himself insisted on a further explanation of these arbitrary proceedings where kraals had been destroyed for non-payment of hut tax); African (South) C.O. 417/345, Chamberlain to Milner, 20 November 1902; African 763, No. 89, Encl., Resident Commissioner to Administrator, 11 January 1905; and African (South) C.O. 417/512, Vol. 3, Despatch 493 of 1912, Resident Commissioner to Administrator.

[5] African 763, No. 101.

[6] African 746, No. 266, Encl. 4, High Commissioner to Milton, 5 September 1904.

[7] African 763, No. 50, Treasury to Colonial Office, 3 March 1905. The Treasury effected

provided that the High Commissioner's consent should always be necessary for military operations.[1]

The Company, during this period, continued to press for complete control over the B.S.A. Police forces and by 1907 Lord Selborne, the High Commissioner, felt that the request was a reasonable one. A similar attitude was adopted by the Secretary of State on condition that provisions for bringing the force under the Commandant General and the Resident Commissioner in the event of any military operation remained, that the Commandant General was given powers of inspection, and that police pensions were secured.[2] Ultimately, after considerable revision by the High Commissioner of a draft Ordinance incorporating these provisions, transfer was made of the B.S.A. Police to the Company.[3] An attempt by the Colonial Office to withhold an Order in Council transferring the police to the Company 'as a means of expediting a general settlement' with the Company was made, but this failed as the High Commissioner had for some months been treating the transfer as an accomplished fact save for the completion of the necessary legislative arrangements.[4] The High Commissioner then exempted by Proclamation[5] the B.S.A. Police from the provisions of the Southern Rhodesia Order in Council 1898 and declared them to be a civil police force. Thereafter the Southern Rhodesia Order in Council 1909 came into force and declared that military police forces should only consist of those police and Volunteer forces declared by the High Commissioner to be on active service.[6]

The Southern Rhodesia Order in Council 1909 also revoked Sections 48(ii) to (vi) of the Southern Rhodesia Order in Council 1898 and the Southern Rhodesia Order in Council 1905. Military police forces, however, remained under the direct control of the High Commissioner, and the Order prohibited anything in the nature of a military operation unless the forces were declared by the High Commissioner to be on active service, when they would be subject to his control. Such police forces were to be liable for service anywhere in South Africa. The Order also provided that the Resident Commissioner for the time being should be the Commandant General for the

---

an economy of £1,705 per annum thereby. See also African 702, No. 293, which reveals that in 1902 the Treasury were objecting to paying for both these Imperial officers and suggested that the Company should do so. The Secretary of State declined to ask the Company for funds for this purpose as he would thereby lose his control over what should, he considered, be an Imperial officer.

[1] S.R. Order in Council 1905 of 20 March 1905, Section 3.

[2] See African 899, Nos. 2, 17, 51, and 90.

[3] African 899, No. 104, High Commissioner to Secretary of State, 14 July 1908. See Ordinance 7 of 1908.

[4] African 932, No. 132, Secretary of State to High Commissioner, 29 May 1909, and No. 134, High Commissioner to Secretary of State, 4 June 1909.

[5] High Commissioner's Proclamation No. 30 of 24 November 1909.

[6] Amending Article 3 of the S.R. Order in Council 1898. See Section 2 of the S.R. Order in Council of 10 August 1909 in force on 3 December 1909, and High Commissioner's Proclamation of 29 November 1909.

police and Volunteer forces and should exercise command when the force was on active service. Otherwise the Commandant General enjoyed the right of inspecting such forces at all times.

In the case of the Volunteers it was still provided that the appointment of officers had to be approved by the Secretary of State and that no regulations could be made without the Secretary of State's consent.[1] Control over volunteers was, however, maintained as they could not be called out either for active service or to aid the civil power without the concurrence of the High Commissioner or in emergency that of the Resident Commissioner.[2]

As a result of the 1909 changes the B.S.A. Police were now governed by Ordinance[3] and the Resident Commissioner-cum-Commandant General retained only nominal powers unless the forces were declared to be on active service. By 1909, therefore, the Company had regained virtual control of the internal police forces except for the Commandant General's right to inspect.

In 1913 this process was completed when the Southern Rhodesia Order in Council 1913 provided that the Commandant General should be appointed and paid by the Company subject only to approval of his appointment by the Secretary of State.[4] Thus this office would no longer be held by the Resident Commissioner and the Commandant General would no longer be an Imperial official. Thereafter an Ordinance provided that the Commandant General should direct the Superintendent in controlling the force, while the Administrator replaced the Attorney-General as the rule-making authority in respect of the police.[5] In practice, the Attorney-General was appointed Commandant-General.[6]

The High Commissioner's power to control military and police forces when on active service remained, however, until the grant of responsible government when it was transferred to the Governor in Council.[7]

Conclusions and implications for the future

From a study of British intervention in Southern Rhodesia from 1899 to 1923 several conclusions can be drawn. Firstly, since the Imperial authorities

[1] Volunteer Ordinance 1902, Sections 10 and 15 as amended by the Volunteer Amendment Ordinance 1905.

[2] Volunteer Ordinance 1902, Section 6.

[3] Police Ordinance 21 of 1903, as amended by the Police Ordinance Amendment Ordinance 1908.

[4] S.R. Order in Council of 11 February 1913, Section 2.

[5] See Ordinance No. 11 of 1913.

[6] Eventually, the S.R. Order in Council of 12 March 1923, Section 4, abolished the office of Commandant General, providing that the Commissioner of Police should exercise control of all police and Volunteer forces, whether employed on active service or not, while the powers previously exercised by the Commandant General under any Ordinance were to be exercised by the Administrator who could delegate these to the Commissioner of Police.

[7] Section 58(1) of the Southern Rhodesia Letters Patent 1923.

had effective control of both legislation and administration affecting the African population,[1] they became considerably implicated in Southern Rhodesian policy towards Africans. Indeed, Imperial officials not only commended the running of the Administration,[2] but also supported its native policy. That Southern Rhodesian native policy had Imperial approval was indicated by Bonar Law in 1919.[3] As Colonial Secretary he felt that there was 'no part of the Empire where the natives had received better treatment'. Similarly, the Buxton Commission enquiring into the constitutional future of Southern Rhodesia reported that 'the general attitude of the white population towards the natives . . . and the administration of native affairs . . . so far as we can ascertain is quite satisfactory'.[4] In fact the Imperial Government itself took part of the responsibility as in respect of native policy the Chartered Company had 'been acting as the agent, and the closely supervised agent, of the Imperial Government'.[5] Thus Southern Rhodesian native policy was praised in 1920 by Amery, the Under Secretary, as being 'a model not only in Africa, but for any part of the world where you have the very difficult problem of the white settlers living side by side with the native'.[6]

Not only the politicians but also the Imperial civil servants, particularly those in close contact with events in Southern Rhodesia approved her native policy. Thus the Resident Commissioner in 1923 commended the attempts to arrive at a proper policy,[7] while the Administrator revealed that 'on more than one occasion the High Commissioner for the time being has expressed his approval in general terms of the Administration and of the manner, in particular, in which the natives have been treated'.[8]

Secondly, since it was British policy that Southern Rhodesia should ultimately enter the Union of South Africa[9] policies towards Africans were permitted to follow the South African pattern.

Finally, and in this lay the significance for the future, it is in the context of this historical background of continuous legislative and administrative supervision by the Imperial authorities that the reservations and powers of

[1] In 1914 the Colonial Secretary admitted that the provisions of the Order in Council concerned with Africans had been 'consistently and continuously enforced by the High Commissioner': *H.C. Deb.*, 5th ser., Vol. 59, col. 1810, 16 March 1914, Harcourt.

[2] In 1906 on his first visit to Southern Rhodesia Lord Selborne, the High Commissioner, reported on the 'highly efficient administration with an administrator and a civil service reproducing the best traditions of the British Empire': African 802, No. 222, 5 November 1906.

[3] *H.C. Deb.*, Vol. 122, col. 1621, 11 December 1919; Ormsby-Gore, the Under Secretary, thought Southern Rhodesia policy 'creditable': *H.C. Deb.*, Vol. 118, col. 2200, 30 July 1919.

[4] Cmd. 1273, § 98.   [5] *H.C. Deb.*, Vol. 118, col. 2234, 30 July 1919, Amery.

[6] *H.C. Deb.*, Vol. 128, col. 953, 26 April 1920.

[7] *S.R. Legco. Deb.* 1923, cols. 584–5, 24 July 1923—referring to Southern Rhodesia as being the first country in South Africa to grapple with the problem of establishing a sound and progressive native administration.

[8] *S.R. Legco. Deb.* 1923, col. 812, 27 July 1923. Lord Buxton was High Commissioner for South Africa from 1914 to 1920.

[9] See *infra*, Chapter 10.

supervision included in the responsible government Constitution of 1923 must be construed. In requesting responsible government the leader of the elected members in the Legislative Council undertook that 'we would be quite content with the authority over the natives given to the B.S.A. Company today',[1] while the Buxton Report, which was charged with recommending a new constitution for Southern Rhodesia, specifically acknowledged this statement and advised that the present powers of control over the Administration so far as they affected Africans 'should be altered and disturbed as little as possible'.[2] The Report in fact recommended the continuance of most of the existing provisions for Imperial supervision of native administration. Thus it advised that the appointments, salaries, suspensions, and removals of Native Department officials although now to be controlled by the Governor-in-Council, should nonetheless require the High Commissioner's assent; that the Native Reserves vested in the High Commissioner by the Southern Rhodesia Order in Council 1920 should remain inalienable; that the High Commissioner should have the right to call for reports on questions relating to Africans and to remit fines on Chiefs; and that no disabilities not equally applicable to Europeans should without the previous consent of the Imperial Government be imposed on Africans.[3] As the Report concluded:

The High Commissioner's control of Rhodesian affairs will be less direct and comprehensive than it is at present . . . nevertheless, the High Commissioner will remain for certain purposes an integral portion of the constitution. He would continue to exercise on behalf of the Crown his present function of control over Native Affairs. He would deal as heretofore with appointments, salaries and disciplinary procedures in the Native Department. The Native Reserves and any statutory powers in respect thereof would remain vested in him. He would be independent of Ministerial advice; and would stand towards the Government in much the same position as he now occupies towards the Company's Administration. Recommendations affecting the Native Affairs Department would be submitted to him by the Governor as they are now submitted by the Administrator.[4]

Debating this Report the elected members' leader in the Legislative Council acknowledged again that the previous Imperial safeguards for Africans

---

[1] Sir Charles Coghlan, later first Prime Minister of Southern Rhodesia: *S.R. Legco. Deb.* 1920, col. 60, 12 May 1920. See also other statements: col. 112, 122–5. 'They knew that native policy in all essentials, was dictated by the Imperial Government, and with that state of affairs, he, for one, was very well content. (Hear, Hear.)' The Resident Commissioner described the elected members as 'all expressing willingness to submit to safeguards similar to those which His Majesty's Government had thought fit to impose on the B.S.A. Company. . . . Such safeguards . . . are absolutely necessary and this alone would I think make the exercise of self-government a matter of considerable difficulty': African 1085, No. 1, Encl. 2, 9 June 1920.

[2] Cmd. 1273, §§ 62, 63.

[3] Cmd. 1273, § 64. All these proposals were incorporated in the 1923 Constitution.

[4] ibid., § 80.

should remain and agreed that the existing procedure would be 'altered and disturbed as little as possible', under any new constitution.[1]

In the event the 1923 Southern Rhodesia Constitution Letters Patent reflected these attitudes and the Despatch transmitting the draft letters Patent stated: 'the clauses relating to Native Administration (Sections 39–47) are designed to preserve the essential features of the existing system of native administration which has worked satisfactorily in the past'.[2]

[1] *S.R. Legco. Deb.* 1921, col. 791, 19 May 1921. There were no 'serious difficulties . . . where a case for legislation could be made out'. See also E. T. Jollie, op. cit., p. 247, where the author, a leading figure in the campaign for responsible government and a member of the legislature both before and after responsible government, recognized that the system of protecting African interests was to be continued under the new constitution. She considered that the Governor would take the place of the Resident Commissioner in holding a watching brief for Africans.

[2] Cmd. 1573. Despatch to the High Commissioner for South Africa transmitting Draft Letters Patent providing for the Constitution of Responsible Government in the Colony of Southern Rhodesia.

10

CONSTITUTIONAL CHANGES FROM 1899 TO 1923

Steps leading to responsible government

THE period from 1899 to 1923 covers two stages of constitutional development. The first phase lasted until 1911 when the elected members formally
obtained a majority over the nominated members in the Legislative Council.
They thereby achieved a degree of legislative independence, but still remained
financially dependent on a commercial company, which enjoyed virtually
unfettered executive power. During the second phase from 1911 to 1923 the
elected members sought the termination of Company power and the substitution of a locally based administration under a responsible government
constitution. Both phases were characterized by a struggle, often acrimonious,
between the settlers and the Company, with the Imperial Government as a
somewhat passive referee.

The settler attitude

In this triangle of attitudes as between the Company, settlers and Imperial
Government, the settlers resented the Company's legislative and administrative policies.[1] Originally settler feeling was amorphously anti-Charter:
there were merely vague suggestions for change and, although proposals for
responsible government were made, others for representative government
under the Crown predominated.[2] There was also a general acknowledgement
that the ultimate destiny of Southern Rhodesia would be some form of closer
union with South Africa after the attainment of responsible government.
However, anti-Union feeling lest Rhodesia be submerged became predominant from 1911, when a Legislative Council containing a large majority of
anti-Union elected members was returned.

There was also antagonism to the idea of closer union with Northern
Rhodesia. As early as 1909 and again in 1911 suggestions were made of a

---

[1] They considered Company policies on railway and agricultural development, and on
legislation governing land and rights to mines, minerals, and precious stones as being detrimental to development. They questioned whether they should be liable for past administrative deficits when they gained control of the country. They objected that the Company was
not liable to tax and that the commercial branch was subsidized by the administrative
side. They also rejected the notion that the unalienated land of Southern Rhodesia was
vested in the Company for its benefit.

[2] Direct rule was rejected even in the early days: African 707, No. 322, 6 September 1902,
reporting on a public meeting in Bulawayo. See also *S.R. Legco Deb.* 1907, pp. 26 and 31.

northern state consisting of Northern Rhodesia, Southern Rhodesia, Nyasaland, and Bechuanaland.[1] In 1913, the President of the Company, Sir Starr Jameson, put forward a suggestion for a greater Rhodesia stretching from Mafeking to the Congo,[2] and in 1915 the Directors issued a statement seeking the amalgamation of Southern Rhodesia and Northern Rhodesia in order to achieve economies of administration.[3] However, the suggestion was not well received, and when amalgamation was formally proposed in 1917, after the preparation of a draft Order in Council, it was opposed by a majority of the elected members within the Legislative Council even though a favourable resolution was passed, as all the nominated members and some of the elected members voted in favour.[4] In fact by 1914 it had become clear that responsible government was the sole objective of the settler population, although it was prepared to defer its implementation.

The Imperial attitude

As in the earlier period, the Colonial Office was concerned to protect the interests of the British taxpayer. For this reason it was 'scrupulously non-committal',[5] refusing in the main to take either Company or settler side.[6] Its attitude was to delay any decisions and to avoid taking steps which might commit Britain for the future.[7] In particular, nothing which might increase

[1] See African 948, No. 68, Encl., 19 May 1911, relative to 'a great British community in the heart of Africa under its own government'.

[2] See *Rhodesia Herald*, 24 December 1913—suggestion made by Sir Starr Jameson then Chairman of the Company.

[3] Directors' Statement of 31 December 1915, printed in *The B.S.A. Co.'s Report of the Directors for the year ending 31 March 1915*, at p. 71. The Company would seek a further Order in Council if the people of Rhodesia favoured such a scheme.

[4] *S.R. Legco Deb.* 1917, col. 309 et seq. The elected members feared taking in 'that black country full of black men on terms of equality with white people': col. 380, Sir Charles Coghlan.

[5] Wilson-Fox, op. cit., p. 125. Thus in 1904 it refused to intervene requiring Company and settlers first to agree: African 746, No. 219, Encl. 5, 21 June 1904. Again in 1909 the settlers were told that His Majesty's Government's policy was a 'steady adherence to the attitude of non-interference': African 932, No. 238, 15 November 1909.

[6] The Colonial Office, however, made it clear that it would not allow 'the dispossession of the Chartered Company without reasonable compensations': African 746, No. 321, 9 December 1914.

[7] In 1906 the High Commissioner visited Rhodesia and the Colonial Office commented that 'it is desirable to put off the day when the Crown must interpose or take over Rhodesia. It is improbable that it could be done at any time without a substantial addition to the Estimates, and the later the day can be deferred the less that addition is likely to be': African (South) C.O. 417/425, C.O. Minute, 13 December 1906, on Selborne's despatch. The High Commissioner was warned to use 'no definite language on behalf of His Majesty's Government' (African 872, No. 136, 8 August 1907) although he was told that Southern Rhodesia would possibly in the early future enter a South African Federation. Again in 1909 Imperial non-committal on the question of the allocation of administrative and commercial revenue was dictated by reluctance to raise 'the whole question of the position of the Company which His Majesty's Government would prefer to avoid': African 932, No. 38, 25 February 1909.

possible British financial commitments was permitted until the future of the country had been decided. Nor could any decisions be taken which would possibly result in the future of the country being mortgaged.[1] Thus the Imperial authorities strongly opposed the creation of a public debt and only conceded this right in 1914.[2] For the same reason it insisted on the strict separation of administrative and commercial revenue and expenditure and the keeping of proper accounts and their submission under article 17 of the Charter.[3] Furthermore the Colonial Office carefully refrained from committing itself on the ownership of the unalienated land, stating in 1914 before it referred the whole question to the Privy Council that the assumption that the unoccupied lands of Southern Rhodesia were private property 'has never been, nor is . . . now accepted by His Majesty's Government'.[4]

Indeed when the first requests were made in 1902 for steps in the direction of an elected majority the Colonial Office was reluctant to accede to any changes. Officials felt that 'so long as the B.S.A. Company are responsible for finance there should be no risk of official members of the Legislative Council being outvoted'.[5] However, Chamberlain ruled that the United Kingdom could not refuse the proposal, 'supported as it is by High Commissioner, Company, and local opinion. The responsibility is theirs and if finances

[1] In 1909–1910 during disputes with the Company the Colonial Office considered issuing a new Order in Council to secure British control over the Railway Companies, which were not governed by the Charter, lest the Company sell out to foreign interests, but the matter was left in abeyance as there was no sign of such action.

[2] In 1898, and again in 1905 and 1906, the principle was rejected. (See *supra*, Chapter 8.) In 1914 this power was only conceded after a long struggle between Colonial Office and Treasury, the Colonial Office taking the attitude that the 'creation of a large elective majority is the determining element': African 1003, No. 116, Colonial Office to Treasury, 5 August 1913. Eventually the Imperial authorities agreed not to interpose an absolute veto (see Cd. 7645, §10) but, owing to the war and the delay occasioned by the reference to the Privy Council of Land Ownership in Southern Rhodesia, little use was made of the right to create a public debt except for a small loan of £17,000 for public works, for which provision was made in the Appropriation Ordinance of 1914.

[3] See e.g. African 702, No. 22, 1 July 1902. When the accounts for 1899 to 1900 were received in 1904, His Majesty's Government reserved 'the right of examining in detail the apportionment between administrative and commercial revenue and expenditure . . . and must not be taken to have expressed any opinion as to the correctness of the apportionment shown in the Balance Sheet': African 717, No. 120, 17 April 1903. There was also Colonial Office pressure for the administration to balance its expenditure and revenue: see Colonial Office minutes, 24 August 1904. From 1909 the Appropriation Ordinance was balanced except during the war years.

[4] See African 1015, No. 26, 1 January 1914.

[5] African 702, No. 384, 2 December 1912. The creation of virtual equality left the Colonial Office 'no margin especially as we cannot depend on the nominated section of the persons appointed by the Company': No. 389. The Colonial Office minutes show how concerned the officials were since 'the proposed changes . . . decrease the security for our getting any legislation we want passed': African (South) C.O. 417/345, Vol. III, 1902. Furthermore, if supplies were refused this could 'cause a deadlock and paralyse the Company's administration. His Majesty's Government might be involved in a very awkward situation for we cannot divest ourselves of the ultimate responsibility for the peace and good government of the country': African (South) C.O. 417/365, folios 357–66.

suffer the ultimate transfer would be effected on terms less favourable to them.'[1]

Again in 1907, the Colonial Office was concerned about settler claims for increased representation as this would put the administration and police at the mercy of an adverse vote in the Council and Britain might be financially involved.[2] From experience in other Colonies the Imperial authorities knew that the change would cause difficulties and throw upon His Majesty's Government 'on occasions the invidious duty of declining to accept the decisions and legislation of an elective majority'.

Once this request for increased representation was conceded the Colonial Office however tended to support the settlers in their claims for greater representation in the Legislative Council, as there was no longer any purpose in opposing it. Indeed, in 1911 the Colonial Secretary, Mr. Harcourt, forced the Company to agree to promises made by the Directors in 1907 being incorporated in a further Order in Council.[3]

When the Colonial Office took this action and forced the formalizing of a majority of elected members in the Legislative Council, it envisaged that the Union of South Africa would ultimately absorb Southern Rhodesia. As early as 1907 the Secretary of State had instructed the High Commissioner to look on Southern Rhodesia 'as a constituent part of a Federal South Africa'.[4] Indeed, Section 150 of the South Africa Act 1909 made provision for the admission into the Union of South Africa of the B.S.A. Company's territories on the advice of the Privy Council after addresses from both Houses of the Union Parliament.[5] That Southern Rhodesia should ultimately be admitted to the Union was re-affirmed in 1912 and 1913 by the Colonial Office and the High Commissioner, the basis of the decision being that this would be the cheapest course for Britain.[6] Representative government under the Crown the Colonial Office rejected as being too costly to Britain.[7] On the other hand,

[1] African 702, No. 395, Chamberlain to Onslow, 7 December 1902.
[2] African (South) C.O. 417/437, Minutes of 31 July 1907, on High Commissioner's despatch No. 544.
[3] See Cd. 7264, No. 4, 9 February 1911.
[4] African 872, No. 181, Secretary of State to High Commissioner, 8 August 1907.
[5] 9 Ed. VII, c. 9. Sir Charles Coghlan had attended the National Convention that preceded the creation of the Union of South Africa. For the events leading to Union see L. M. Thompson, *The Unification of South Africa*, Oxford, 1960. Although the views of the people of Southern Rhodesia were not mentioned the High Commissioner assured the elected members that Southern Rhodesia would be consulted if action under Section 150 were ever contemplated: African 932, No. 238, 15 November 1909.
[6] African 989, No. 72, Encl., C.O. Confidential Memorandum on the Position in Southern Rhodesia and possible changes in 1914. The Company's financial claims were so strong that it could only be got rid of by a third party—either the Union or British Governments. If Southern Rhodesia entered the Union '... it would be for the Union to settle with the Company, an arrangement which would be very convenient to His Majesty's Government'.
[7] See African 989, No. 72, Encl., C.O. Confidential Memorandum on the Position in Southern Rhodesia and possible changes in 1914, 8 November 1912. Representative government under the Crown was rejected as 'His Majesty's Government ... would probably

responsible government was not at that time economically feasible, and would again involve Britain in expenditure.

The Imperial authorities persisted until 1923 in their attitude of hoping that Southern Rhodesia would enter the Union of South Africa. Indeed from 1920 to 1923 considerable pressure was exerted and delays occasioned in the grant of responsible government in order to induce the Southern Rhodesian settlers to agree to Southern Rhodesia entering the Union.[1]

This attitude was not, however, adopted towards Northern Rhodesia: General Botha's proposals in 1913 to bring Northern Rhodesia into the Union of South Africa,[2] and those of General Smuts in June 1922, were equally coolly received.[3] Nor was the Colonial Office prepared to allow a merger of Southern Rhodesia and Northern Rhodesia in 1917 when the Legislative Council passed a resolution requesting a common administration. Conveniently, since a majority of the elected members in the Legislative Council had opposed the motion, it could on these grounds be rejected. Again in 1921 the Colonial Office rejected a Company suggestion that the central portion of Northern Rhodesia be linked with Southern Rhodesia.

Nonetheless in Southern Rhodesia, as in Northern Rhodesia, but not to the same extent, the Imperial Government was aware of the rights of the indigenous African population and was, within the framework dictated by its regard for financial considerations, prepared to secure their interests so far as was possible. This was clearly proved by its full use of those powers it possessed in respect of native legislation and administration.

The Company attitude

The Company in this situation was mainly concerned to protect the interests of its shareholders (who only received their first dividend in 1924, thirty-five

not wish to take the responsibility, with the risk of having to call on the British taxpayer for a deficit'. The same attitude was evident in 1919 when the Colonial Secretary, Lord Milner, informed the settlers that the United Kingdom was 'certainly not desirous of assuming fresh responsibilities in Southern Rhodesia': Cable from Secretary of State to High Commissioner, 15 August 1919, quoted in the *Bulawayo Chronicle*, 19 August 1919. This was also apparent in 1923 when lengthy negotiations for paying out the Company delayed the implementation of responsible government. See National Archives NE 1/1/1. Newton (the Southern Rhodesian delegate in London, previously Treasurer to the Company, later a Cabinet Minister and first Southern Rhodesia High Commissioner in London) to Coghlan, 14 June 1923: 'My suggestion of a possibility of Southern Rhodesia being bundled into the Colonial Office as a Crown Colony had given a considerable stimulus to the proceedings'.

[1] See *S.R. Legco Deb.* 1922, col. 266, 11 May 1922, Coghlan: 'The Secretary of State ... made no secret of the fact that he would have liked to see Rhodesia go into the Union'. See also *H.C. Deb.*, col. 1329, 3 May 1922; Buxton Report, Cmd. 1273, §12; and see *infra*.

[2] He made a public speech at Nylstroom on 1 November 1913, requesting His Majesty's Government to consider the incorporation of Northern Rhodesia and Southern Rhodesia in South Africa before October 1914.

[3] Personal communication from a confidential source. *Contra* R. Welensky, *Welensky's 4,000 Days*, Collins, 1964, p. 56, where Welensky states that Smuts had been told by

years after the Company's incorporation). It was concerned to retrieve its capital and to cut down expenditure to the minimum consonant with good government, hoping that, as the country developed, the appreciation of its assets, particularly land, would recompense it for past losses. This expectation was defeated when in 1918 the Privy Council pronounced that the unalienated lands of Southern Rhodesia were vested in the Crown. However, at the same time, the Privy Council held the Crown liable to recompense the Company for past administrative deficits, although the Charter was silent on this point: liability was imposed on the analogy of indemnification in the law of agency.[1] This decision having been given the Company no longer had any inducement to spend further monies in Southern Rhodesia and understandably became anxious to end its governmental duties.[2]

The Company, like the Imperial Government, favoured Southern Rhodesian entry into the Union of South Africa as the Directors hoped for more generous compensation from that country than from the British Treasury, which proved reluctant to pay the Company the sums due in terms of the Privy Council judgement, even after a Royal Commission had determined the amounts outstanding.

Ultimately when a settlement was arrived at in 1923 it was a compromise dictated by the attitudes of settlers, Company and Imperial Government, and the culmination of the constitutional changes which had gradually been made between 1899 and 1923.

Moves towards a majority of elected members in the Legislative Council[3]

The Southern Rhodesia Order in Council 1898 had introduced a Legislative Council containing a minority of elective representatives. The Council was originally composed of four elected members,[4] five members nominated by the Company,[5] the Administrators, the senior of whom had both a

Churchill that, should Southern Rhodesia choose to enter South Africa, Northern Rhodesia 'would be thrown in as a gift'.

[1] *In re Southern Rhodesia*, [1919] A.C. 211 at pp. 245 et seq. Although the Judicial Committee held that the Company had administered the country gratuitously there was no 'gratuitous endowment of that administration at the expense of the shareholders': ibid. p. 246. There was to be indemnification but no remuneration. The Court was somewhat scathing about the Imperial attitude stating at p. 248 that 'In matters of business reserves and reticences sooner or later come home to roost'.

[2] See the Buxton Report, Cmd. 1273, §34.

[3] For a detailed study from 1898 to 1923 see J. D. Fage, op. cit. See also H. Wilson-Fox, *Memorandum 1912*, op. cit., pp. 24–79, for an account from 1899 to 1912.

[4] Elected by two two-member electoral districts.

[5] For the first two sessions of the Council the senior judge was one of the nominated members despite objections by the local Bar: African 574, No. 144, 9 May 1899; and African 656, No. 18, 8 March 1900.

deliberative and a casting vote[1] and the Resident Commissioner, who could speak but not vote.

From the first meeting of the Legislative Council clashes occurred between elected members and the Company.[2] Eventually, after representations by the elected members,[3] the Company proposed an increase in the number of both nominated and elected members, which was unanimously passed by the Council. As a result an amending Order in Council was issued in 1903, giving each side an equality of members (seven nominated, seven elected), and taking away the Administrator's deliberative vote but retaining the casting vote.[4]

In addition, as a result of a suggestion by the High Commissioner that there was a need to introduce flexibility and possibility of constitutional amendment other than by Order in Council, it was provided that the High Commissioner with the consent of the Secretary of State, after resolution by the Legislative Council, might by Proclamation alter the composition of the Legislative Council, provided that he might not vary the proportions of nominated and elected members so as to make them unequal unless this was requested by a three-quarters majority of the total membership of the Legislative Council.[5]

Since the Company could not now be sure of a majority in order to secure the financial stability of the country, Section 40 of the 1898 Order in Council was amended to provide that no amendment, alteration or variation of a financial measure was to be permitted without the Administrator's consent.[6] This amendment, however, left the elected members 'without the power of questioning the financial administration of the country' and, in the following year with Company agreement, the original Section 40 was reinstated.[7]

Nonetheless dissatisfaction persisted and in 1903 Sir George Goldie

[1] Mr. (later Sir W. H.) Milton was Senior Administrator and Administrator of Mashonaand, while Sir A. Lawley was Administrator of Matabeleland. When in 1902 Sir Arthur Lawley's appointment ended, the Company continued with only the Senior Administrator. Section 23 of the Order in Council was amended in 1903 to make provision for any Council member to preside in the absence of the Administrator, as there was no longer a junior Administrator to take his place when away.

[2] The Company used its majority to pass the Appropriation, the Customs and the Land Titles Ordinances: *S.R. Legco Deb.*, 1899, cols. 40, 36, and 40, respectively.

[3] *S.R. Legco Deb.*, 1902, p. 142, 20 November 1902.

[4] Southern Rhodesia Order in Council, 16 February 1903, amending Section 32(i) and (ii). By High Commissioner's Proclamation No. 4 of 1903, Southern Rhodesia was divided into four Electoral Districts. The Northern returned two, the Western three, and the Eastern and Midlands District one member each.

[5] African 717, No. 15, 19 January 1903. Implicit in 17A(ii) of 1898 Order in Council as amended.

[6] Section 40 as amended. The High Commissioner inserted the words 'or reduction of a vote': see African 717, No. 19, 15 January 1903. In addition, as a result of *Burrowes's Case*, which had held that the provisions of Section 41 were merely directory and not imperative, this was amended to provide that an Appropriation Ordinance must each year be passed at the earliest opportunity.

[7] Southern Rhodesia Order in Council, 1904, 10 August 1904. See African 717, No. 388. The Colonial Office had in 1903 been concerned lest the official members be outvoted while

(previously Chairman of the Royal Niger Company) was appointed a director of the B.S.A. Company in order to make proposals for a settlement.[1] These, however, were unacceptable to the settler population,[2] and a deputation of residents elected by a conference to discuss Goldie's proposals then proceeded to England in 1904 to meet the Company's Board, but failed to reach agreement with the Company.[3]

Permissive elected majority conceded

By 1906 dissatisfaction was so widespread that when Lord Selborne, the High Commissioner, visited Southern Rhodesia he was requested to intervene. Lord Selborne suggested the appointment of a Royal Commission[4] but, after consultation with the Directors of the Company who promised to send out a special committee to deal with the Southern Rhodesian dissatisfaction, Lord Elgin, the Colonial Secretary, refused.[5] In the interim a motion was introduced in the Council requesting responsible government.[6]

In 1907, the Directors visited Southern Rhodesia, and made a statement of policy which took the constitutional issue out of the arena for a period. They agreed that the settlers should eventually be granted self-government and, as a step in this process, promised to allow them a majority in the Legislative Council by reducing the number of nominated members to five, undertaking that a new Order in Council to this effect would be procured. They promised that 'pending the issue of the new Order in Council, the Administrator will be required to limit the votes of the nominated members so that on divisions the elected members will have a majority of seats'.[7] In practice from 1908

the Company remained responsible for the finances of the country: African 702, No. 38. Should this have occurred the responsibility would have fallen on Britain and the Colonial Office had therefore insisted on the safeguard being inserted in 1903: Colonial Office to B.S.A. Co., 3 December 1902.

[1] For Goldie's proposals of April 1904 see Wilson-Fox, op. cit., *Memorandum 1912*, Appendix II (H), pp. 344–6.

[2] African 746, No. 190, Milner to Lyttelton, 30 May 1904. The proposals would have imposed too heavy a financial burden on any future government as there would have been a liability to repay £8,000,000 at 5 per cent. There were then 12,000 settlers.

[3] For Company proposals, see Wilson-Fox, op. cit., pp. 347–9.

[4] African 802, No. 222, Selborne to Elgin, 5 November 1906. Lord Selborne, in discussing representative government under the control of the Colonial Office, pointed out that the difficulty of this was the necessity for a division of the liabilities and assets between the B.S.A. Company and the people of Southern Rhodesia.

[5] African 872, No. 52, Secretary of State to High Commissioner, 25 March 1907.

[6] *S.R. Legco Deb.*, 1907, col. 21.

[7] *The B.S.A. Company Directors' Report and Accounts for the year ended 31 March 1907*, pp. 27 et seq. Declaration of Policy issued at Bulawayo by the Visiting Commission on 19 October 1907. See also African 872, No. 170, Encl., 19 October 1907. The Statement of Policy also attempted to placate settler opinion by defining what constituted administrative revenue and expenditure, by announcing a change in the mining royalty system and by promising a new land law and land settlement policy, promising an enquiry into education, the appointment of a commercial representative, and rationalization of the Civil Service.

onwards the Company withdrew two nominated members from the Legislative Council elected early in that year. As the Colonial Office commented, this was a very 'bold act' by the Directors since they had given a clear legislative majority to the elected representatives on all questions except financial ones.[1] It would, of course, have been possible but politically unwise for the Directors, at any time, to have nominated two further members of the Council.

The 1911 Order in Council

Although this permissive elective majority had been granted, disputes between Company and settlers nevertheless continued. The elected representatives in the new Legislative Council of 1908 questioned the Company's ownership of the unalienated land, the description of certain items as administrative expenditure or revenues and, at the same time, requested the Imperial Government to give a ruling.[2] This the Secretary of State in February 1909 and again in October of that year, after a further motion in the Legislative Council, refused to do, as it would have involved a full settlement of all outstanding questions.[3] In the meanwhile, the Company, having repented of its earlier generosity, was delaying the implementation of its promises in an Order in Council. When it forwarded the draft, the Colonial Office found that it had reneged on its undertakings proposing a majority of one only and that amendments of financial measures should not be permitted.[4] A second Draft Order suggested that, should the Administrator consider the Appropriation Ordinance unsatisfactory, he would be empowered to expend the public revenue as he considered essential, provided he obtained Company approval, notified the High Commissioner, and reported in the next session to the Legislative Council.[5] The Colonial Secretary, however, held the Company to its promises and in 1911 a further Order in Council was issued.[6]

[1] African 872, No. 181.   [2] S.R. Legco Deb., 1908, pp. 85 and 116.
[3] See Wilson-Fox, op. cit., Memorandum 1912, pp. 50–60.
[4] As a further alternative, it suggested that the High Commissioner be brought in as arbitrator in the event of any financial dispute, provided an objection was recorded by the majority of the Council. This suggestion was rejected by the Imperial authorities who did not want the High Commissioner or his proclaiming power involved since it might 'force a settlement of the very complicated question of the general rights and position of the Company in Southern Rhodesia': African 932, No. 103, 10 April 1909, No. 176, 6 August 1909, and African 948, No. 43, 28 March 1911. See also Cd. 7264. Correspondence relating to the Constitution of Southern Rhodesia.
[5] Cd. 7264, p. 5.
[6] H.C. Deb., 5th ser., Vol. 59, col. 1810, 16 March 1914, explanation by Harcourt. See also Cd. 7264, pp. 56 and 58. Cd. 7264, at p. 9, reveals the dilemma of the Company. Either it was, at the Secretary of State's insistence, necessary to obtain the concurrence of the elected members to their draft Order in Council (which in practice it would be impossible to obtain) or it had to accept the Secretary of State's proposals which the Company considered did 'not provide for the fulfilment in all circumstances of the obligations for the good government of the country imposed upon the Company by the Royal Charter'. The Company chose the latter alternative.

15—C.H.L.S.R.

The Order in Council provided that the Legislative Council membership be reduced from fourteen to twelve, of whom seven were to be elected[1] and five to be nominated, while the Resident Commissioner and Administrator remained members, the Administrator retaining his casting vote, which would be ineffective unless elected members either defected or were absent.

The Company in return was secured by being given additional financial safeguards. Provisions that had previously been in the Standing Orders and Rules of Procedure [2] of the Legislative Council were now incorporated in the Order in Council. The Legislative Council was not to consider any vote, resolution or order for the appropriation of any part of the public revenue or for any tax or impost that had not first been recommended to the Council by the Administrator during the same session, while Ordinances interfering with the land and other rights of the Company could not be proceeded with except by the consent of the Administrator.[3] The Colonial Office also indicated to the Company that there were further safeguards against financial prejudice: the Administrator could exercise his powers to dissolve a recalcitrant Council; the High Commissioner could in the last resort exercise his proclaiming power; and the Secretary of State could instruct disallowance.[4] The final sanction was, as the Colonial Secretary Mr. Harcourt pointed out, a political one:

The fact that any serious differences of opinion between the elected members and the Company must inevitably bring to the front the question of the entrance of Southern Rhodesia into the Union should in practice be a moderating influence of great value.[5]

Simultaneously the Executive Council was reconstituted. Its membership was reduced from four to three nominated members (appointed for terms of two instead of three years) with the Administrator and Resident Commissioner remaining as members.[6] Although suggestions had been made in the

[1] Section 3. Southern Rhodesia Order in Council of 4 May 1911. The increased status of the elected members was also recognized, by an amendment to Section 17(3) of the Order, leaving them free to decide who should rank first among themselves. (The 1903 Order in Council had provided that they were to rank according to their date of election.) In terms of High Commissioner's Proclamation No. 5 of 1910 determining electoral districts, there were four districts returning seven members in all: Northern and Western Districts two each, Eastern and Midlands one each.

[2] Clauses 36 and 48 of the Rules of Order adopted by the Legislative Council on 15 May 1899.

[3] Sections 6 and 7 of Southern Rhodesia Order in Council, 1911. The latter safeguard was difficult to use in practice. In 1914 the elected members amended a Mining Law Amendment Ordinance and the Administrator ruled that the Ordinance could not be proceeded with. However, after acrimonious debate and adjournments, the Administrator withdrew and permitted its enactment: S.R. Legco Deb., 1914, cols. 650 and 656–7.

[4] Cd. 7264, No. 4, Colonial Office to B.S.A. Co., 9 February 1911.

[5] Sir Starr Jameson's unauthorized quotation of this passage at a public meeting in 1913 led to the publication of most of the correspondence dealing with the 1911 Order in Council in Cd. 7264 (1914).

[6] S.R. Order in Council 1911, Section 2.

Legislative Council in 1910 and 1912 for elected members to be put on to the Executive Council, this was not accepted.

By 1911 there was therefore a clear division of sovereignty between Company and elected members in Southern Rhodesia (excluding consideration of British power in the country). The Executive Council was wholly independent of the Legislative Council, and there were no methods whereby the elected members could secure removal of the members of the Executive Council.[1] On the other hand, the elected members of Legislative Council had general legislative power and could refuse financial measures and amend them. They thus enjoyed legislative functions without executive responsibility. Perhaps the nearest analogy was that Southern Rhodesia was the equivalent of a colony with representative government except that the B.S.A. Company stood in the position of the Crown and that special powers were reserved to the High Commissioner and Secretary of State. Lord Gladstone's comment in 1911 is perhaps the most apt:

> As a permanent arrangement the system is impossible. In London there are shareholders and directors, at Salisbury the Administrator and the Legislative Council, with an elective majority that can control legislation. That power of control is at present more apparent than real, seeing that the Administrator is an absolute Executive, in full financial command. Above, or perhaps behind, these authorities stands the High Commissioner, acting for the Imperial Government. Apart from him, the various and varied authorities are usually in conflict among themselves. But unless the High Commissioner acts with circumspection he may at any moment find himself *contra mundum*.[2]

The British attitude towards pressure for responsible government

In 1911 the High Commissioner indicated on a visit to Southern Rhodesia that responsible government would be granted in 1914.[3] Shortly after this statement the basic decision as to Southern Rhodesia's future was taken. Later decisions were merely ones of timing, as the Imperial authorities had by this time finally committed themselves to the policy that Southern Rhodesia should follow the pattern of South Africa and not that of protectorates in tropical Africa.

[1] For an analysis of the Executive Council and its working see Fage, op. cit., pp. 387–95. Fage considered that in the main the meetings of the Executive Council were routine and formal in nature. From a study of the Executive Council minutes the work of the Executive Council consisted mainly of legislative business (including legislative policy, draft Ordinances, and delegated legislation), the supervision of local government, the conduct of native affairs, the conduct of external relations with the High Commissioner and the other South African Colonies, administration of the civil service, the issue of special large land grants, and the naturalization of aliens. See the Executive Council Minutes, National Archives, EC 2/1/1 and 2 and also EC 3/1/1, 2, and 3.

[2] African 948, No. 88, 9 November 1911.

[3] See African 989, No. 72, Encl., referring to Lord Gladstone's public prophecy that Southern Rhodesia would in 1914 take a long step forward in its political development.

The Colonial Office considered that Company rule should continue until a complete settlement was in view.[1] Of the alternatives available, representative government under the Crown was undesirable in that it would eventually lead to clashes on native policy between the Crown and elected members. On the other hand, Crown Colony status was undesirable since, in such circumstances, the Crown could not 'avoid financial responsibility'. Again, the Colonial Office on financial grounds rejected responsible government fortified by the additional reason that the relative sizes of African and European populations[2] would have led to criticism had so small a European group been given control of a large African population. The last alternative, absorption within the Union, was preferred by the Colonial Office, both because the Company's large financial claims could be settled by the Union Government (failing which the British Government would have to bear this heavy liability), and because it was 'impossible to doubt that ultimately it (Southern Rhodesia) must be admitted to the Union'.

The Imperial policy decision could not, however, be implemented at that time as Rhodesian public opinion was anti-Union. Accordingly the Imperial authorities decided to follow 'the only practicable course . . . continuance of the present regime for a certain period' recognizing that 'Southern Rhodesia will ultimately be admitted to the Union'.[3]

Further increase in elected representatives' majority

Soon after its election in April 1911 the new Legislative Council resolved that there should be an increase in the number of elected members.[4] After negotiation with the Company during 1912 and 1913[5] a resolution was passed by the requisite three-quarters majority of the total membership of the Legislative Council[6] and the High Commissioner exercised his power under Section 17A(ii) of the Southern Rhodesia Order in Council 1898 to alter the composition of the Legislative Council in favour of the elected members. The Administrator and Resident Commissioner continued as members, but there

---

[1] African 989, No. 72, Encl., Secretary of State to High Commissioner, 8 November 1912. 'Confidential Memorandum on the position in Southern Rhodesia and possible changes in 1914.'

[2] 24,000 Europeans, 750,000 Africans at that time.

[3] African 1003, No. 156, High Commissioner to Secretary of State, 13 November 1913. Memorandum on Political Affairs in Southern Rhodesia.

[4] S.R. Legco Deb., 1911, 18–24, 10 May 1911.

[5] S.R. Legco Deb., 1912, col. 28 et seq., 8 May 1912; S.R. Legco Deb., 1913, col. 294–5, 22 April 1913. See also Statement of Policy by the Directors on 22 March 1913, Annexure II to The British South Africa Company Directors' Reports and Accounts for the year ending 31 March 1913. This statement recognized that further increases in the number and ratio of elected members would occur. The Company also agreed that it would not claim compensation for public works constructed out of administrative funds after 29 October 1914, and made certain concessions in respect of the items constituting administrative revenue.

[6] S.R. Legco Deb., 1913, cols. 437–41, 25 April 1913.

were now to be twelve elected representatives as against six nominated members.[1]

In 1914 the High Commissioner provided for further increases in the membership of the Council up to a total of fifteen elected members by providing that voters' lists must be prepared triennially and that, wherever there was an increase of 792 voters, or any multiple thereof, an additional electoral district was to be added.[2] The effect of these changes was to consolidate and to increase the elected representatives' majority and, as a result of these provisions for automatic increase in the number of seats, the High Commissioner directed in 1917 that there was to be a new electoral district.[3] This meant that in the next election (which took place in April 1920) there would be thirteen electoral districts each returning a single member on the franchise qualifications laid down in 1912.[4]

The Supplementary Charter

In 1914 a new Council,[5] elected in terms of the 1913 High Commissioner's Proclamation, continued the agitation for further change. However, unless the rights and liabilities of the Company were first clarified—particularly in respect of the question of ownership of all unalienated land in Southern Rhodesia—any final settlement, which would necessarily involve

[1] High Commissioner's Proclamation 17 of 23 August 1913. The twelve members were elected by twelve single-member districts: High Commissioner's Proclamation No. 1 of 13 January 1914. By this Proclamation the principle of single-member electoral districts was introduced. At the same time a delimitation board was instructed to divide the territory into districts on normal principles such as physical features, means of communication, sparsity and density of population, and community or diversity of interests. In dividing the territory the board might depart from an equality of voters in all districts to an extent of not more than 20 per cent more or less than equality if it considered such a departure necessary.

[2] High Commissioner's Proclamation 47 of 31 July 1914.

[3] High Commissioner's Proclamation 20 of 21 June 1917.

[4] By the Voters' Qualification and Registration Amendment Ordinance No. 14 of 1912 the franchise qualifications had been raised by increasing the annual salary required to £100 and the value of property occupied to £150. In addition, ability to write from dictation 50 words in the English language was required. This last requirement was particularly aimed at Afrikaner immigrants from South Africa, whereas all the requirements were intended to decrease the number of prospective African applicants for the vote. In 1919 by the Women's Enfranchisement Ordinance single women possessing these qualifications and married women (other than those married under any system permitting of polygamy), who were deemed to possess the same qualifications as to salary or property occupation as their husbands, were given the vote. This doubled the potential European electorate and 3,467 women voters came onto the list. See G. Passmore and M. Mitchell, *Source Book of Parliamentary Elections in Southern Rhodesia,* University College of Rhodesia and Nyasaland, 1963, p. 14.

[5] For an analysis of the attitude of the newly elected members towards the continuance of Company rule see Fage, op. cit., pp. 156–9. The basic attitude was that Company administration should continue until population was sufficient and finance adequate to make practicable the grant of responsible government. See also Cd. 7645, pp. 1–3, where the Resident Commissioner reported on the views of each candidate in the election.

considerable financial adjustments, would have been difficult of attainment.[1] For this reason it was agreed, at the suggestion of the Imperial authorities thereafter embodied in a motion in the Legislative Council, that the ownership of the unalienated lands should be determined by means of a special reference to the Judicial Committee of the Privy Council.[2]

The outbreak of the First World War and the delay occasioned by this special reference[3] abated the pressure for change. Consequently the elected members agreed to continue under Chartered Company administration, moving a motion to this effect in the Legislative Council with the proviso that this should not prejudice their claim to seek responsible government.[4] Triangular negotiations between the Imperial authorities, Company, and settlers followed in which all parties were reluctant to see sweeping changes introduced during the War,[5] so that a compromise was reached.

Among the less important, but nonetheless significant, changes was concession of the right, subject to the High Commissioner's consent, to raise 'loans'.[6] In addition, an Auditor-General, nominated and paid by the Company but appointed and removable by the Secretary of State, to scrutinize Company administrative expenditure was to be appointed.[7]

---

[1] See Cd. 7509, Harcourt to High Commissioner, 14 January 1914, pp. 1–2.

[2] Cd. 7509. Papers Relating to a Reference to the Judicial Committee of the Privy Council of the Question of the Ownership of Land in Southern Rhodesia. The Reference was also precipitated by proposals of the Company to encourage land settlement. It then became essential to determine who owned the unalienated lands of Southern Rhodesia. Lest it prejudice the reference the draft Land Settlement Ordinance introduced into the Legislative Council was withdrawn: S.R. Legco Deb., col. 644, 6 May 1914, and 787 of 8 October 1914.

[3] The decision was only given in July 1918.

[4] See S.R. Legco Deb., 1914, col. 311 et seq. The latter stipulation was made in view of the provision in the Charter that the provisions relative to administrative or public matters were reviewable by the Crown at the end of twenty-five years from the date of the Charter and at the end of every succeeding ten years. Since twenty-five years elapsed on 21 October 1914, it was considered that the Crown could not amend the Charter until 1924 if it took no action in 1914. It is submitted that the Crown could amend the Charter at any time under Article 34 if it wished to bring the territory under the Crown as part of its dominions. See also In re Southern Rhodesia, supra at 247.

[5] Suggestions by the High Commissioner for a representative of the Native Department in the Council were coolly received by the Colonial Secretary (the Resident Commissioner and the Administrator opposed them) and it was decided that the Imperial authorities should not press for any changes in the system of native administration during the War. In the interim the Resident Commissioner was to report on how the system worked with a new Administrator (Sir F. D. Chaplin was appointed as successor to Sir W. H. Milton in 1914): see African 1034, No. 26, 16 September 1915.

[6] Technically these could not be 'loans' as the Company could not in its commercial capacity lend to itself in its administrative capacity. What was envisaged was that the Company would advance capital sums which would be replaced subsequently by appropriations from administrative revenue.

[7] Sections 4 and 5 of Southern Rhodesia Order in Council of 16 February 1915. The Auditor-General's salary could only be increased with the Secretary of State's approval. See also Cd. 7645, Correspondence Relating to the Continuance of the Administrative Provisions of the Charter of the B.S.A. Company, No. 8. The Secretary of State and the Company rejected a proposal by the elected members that they should be free, once provi-

There was however a vital decision taken. Although it was agreed that Chartered Company administration should continue, the Imperial Government now committed themselves for the future; they agreed to issue a Supplementary Charter providing that:

if at any time after the 29th day of October 1914 the Legislative Council of Southern Rhodesia shall, by an absolute majority of the whole number of the Members of the Council as then constituted, pass a Resolution praying the Crown to establish in Southern Rhodesia the form of Government known as Responsible Government and shall support such Resolution with evidence showing that the condition of the Territory financially and in other respects is such as to justify the establishment of the form of Government aforesaid, it shall be lawful for Us . . . if We . . . at any time think fit to accede to the prayer of such Resolution, to add to, alter or repeal any of the provisions of the said Charter relating to Administrative and Public Matters, or to insert other provisions in substitution therefor or in addition thereto for the purpose of establishing Responsible Government.[1]

By this Supplemental Charter the Imperial authorities had therefore conceded the right to obtain responsible government on majority resolution of the Legislative Council supported by evidence of financial fitness,[2] and fitness in other respects (viz. satisfactory native policy). Reversal of the progress to responsible government now became virtually impossible. All that the Colonial Office could do was to delay the grant, or attempt to drive Southern Rhodesia into the Union of South Africa. Representative Government under the Crown, which would have been the best protection for the indigenous inhabitants had been rejected. Little possibility of Britain insisting on Southern Rhodesia following a pattern of paramountcy or even parity of African in relation to European interests remained. This was made explicit by Mr. Harcourt, the Secretary of State, who stated that His Majesty's Government had 'felt throughout that their decision must be largely influenced by the opinion of the electors of Southern Rhodesia, who are the persons primarily interested in the form of administration insofar as that part of the Company's territories is concerned'.[3] Indeed in 1919 Amery, the

sion for the civil service, police, law and order had been made, to allocate all public monies. Only those responsible for the administration should have the right to propose the expenditure of public revenue.

[1] Cd. 7970 Supplemental Charter to the B.S.A. Company dated 13 March 1915, Article 2. Article 3 modified the provisions for compensation in the event of an end to Chartered Government and a Crown take-over of public buildings so that the Company would not be able to claim compensation for public buildings wholly provided for out of administrative revenue after 29 October 1914 or for any proportionate part so paid.

[2] Since the financial year ending 31 March 1908 Southern Rhodesia had paid its way in that current services were paid for out of current revenue. See Wilson-Fox, op. cit., p. 267. As a result of the First World War, however, there were again administrative deficits: see Fage, op. cit., pp. 201 et seq. In normal times Southern Rhodesia could balance her budget unless she had to service large loans for the repayment of monies expended for administrative purposes and public works.

[3] Cd. 7645, No. 8, Secretary of State to High Commissioner, 3 October 1914. See also

Under-Secretary of State for the Colonies, made it clear that it was to the views of the 'white people' in Southern Rhodesia that the Imperial authorities would have regard in deciding the future form of government.[1]

The achievement of responsible government

The War necessitated yet a further Order in Council to extend the life of the Legislative Council to a date not later than six months after the end of hostilities.[2]

In the interim the decision as to the ownership of unalienated land in Southern Rhodesia, eventually given in July 1918, completely altered the basis on which the Company had been prepared to govern. Although the Privy Council had found that the Company did not own the unalienated lands of Southern Rhodesia, but was merely administering them for the Crown, the Company was, the Judicial Committee considered, entitled to repayment of a considerable sum when its administration was determined. It was entitled 'to look to the Crown to secure it (either out of the proceeds of further sales of land ... or, if the Crown should grant away these lands or proceeds to others, from public funds), the due reimbursement of any outstanding balance of aggregate advances made by it for necessary and proper expenditure upon the administration of Southern Rhodesia'.[3] Although the judgement did not attempt to determine the amount outstanding, it was obvious that for the twenty-eight years of Company administration and expenditure a large sum would be claimable from the Imperial Government.[4] The Company as a result became anxious to terminate its administrative duties. As the Buxton Report commented: 'So long as the Company believed themselves to be owners of the land they were willing to spend their money liberally in carrying on the administration. But, clearly, under present circumstances, the Company would be neither willing nor able to spend their shareholders' money on any object from which they could not be sure of reimbursement with interest or profit.'[5] Since the Company could not be expected to provide further funds for development this gave an impetus to the elected

No. 1, Enclosure 1, Resident Commissioner to High Commissioner, 7 April 1914, which stated that the number of African electors at the most recent registration was estimated not to exceed 60.

[1] *H.C. Deb.*, Vol. 118, col. 2336, 30 July 1919, Amery. The Imperial authorities consistently ignored representations by Members of the House of Commons such as Col. Wedgwood who pointed out the consequences that would ensue from the low number of enfranchised Africans and who suggested that a Crown colony would have been a more appropriate form of government: *H.C. Deb.*, Vol. 144, col. 1581, 14 July 1921, Wedgwood.

[2] Southern Rhodesia (Legislative Council Extension) Order in Council of 22 September 1916. The Council had been elected in 1914 and was due to expire in April 1917.

[3] *In re Southern Rhodesia*, [1919] A.C. 211 at 248.

[4] The Company estimated £8 million was payable.

[5] Cmd. 1273, First Report of a Committee appointed by the Secretary of State for the Colonies to consider certain questions relating to Rhodesia, p. 5.

members' demands for responsible government as only a new government would raise funds for necessary development.

As a result of this situation the Legislative Council in April 1919 requested the Secretary of State to state 'what proof "financially and in other respects" will be considered sufficient to justify the grant to Southern Rhodesia of Responsible Government as provided for under Section 2 of His Majesty's Supplementary Charter, 1915'.[1] However, Lord Milner, now Colonial Secretary, declined to commit the United Kingdom, mainly on financial grounds, and also because of the relative disproportion of the small European population to the large African population. He advised the continuance of the Company's administration since settler opinion did not favour entry into South Africa. In any event, since the sum outstanding to the Company in terms of the land case judgement was at that time subject to determination by the Cave Commission appointed in July 1919, he felt no decisions could be taken as until this amount was known a settlement was impossible.[2]

When the election of April 1920 was held it was fought on this issue of responsible government, twelve of the thirteen elected members being returned on this platform. The new Legislative Council immediately moved a resolution praying for the establishment of responsible government and stating that the country was 'financially and in other respects' fitted for this.[3] However, Lord Milner again refused to give any decision until the Cave Commission had reported on the sums outstanding to the Company.[4] In reply to this statement the elected members then held a special meeting at which they repudiated the notion that responsible government depended on the findings on the Commission. This induced the Colonial Secretary to concede that Southern Rhodesia was in principle entitled to responsible government,[5] but he sought to delay its implementation until the voters of Southern Rhodesia in the next general election (to be held in 1923) had approved the grant oi responsible government. He also attempted to forestall opposition by a definite promise that responsible government would be granted not later than 30 October 1924, while, in the interim, His Majesty's Government would lend the Administration £150,000 per annum for three successive years beginning on 1 April 1921, for the purpose of erecting public works.[6] However, the elected members would not accept this delay in granting responsible government, rejecting the suggestion that there be another election on the issue, pointing to their mandate, and suggesting instead a referendum.[7]

[1] *S.R. Legco Deb.*, cols. 386–7, 14 April 1919.

[2] *Bulawayo Chronicle*, 19 August 1919, quoting cable from Secretary of State to High Commissioner, 15 August 1919.

[3] *S.R. Legco Deb.*, 1920, cols. 206 and 222, 17 May 1920. Appendix I in Cmd. 1273. Numerous statements were made as to the willingness of the elected members to retain Imperial control over legislative and administrative questions affecting Africans.

[4] African 1085, No. 2, Secretary of State to High Commissioner, 6 August 1920.

[5] The principle was in fact conceded by the Supplemental Charter of 1915.

[6] Cmd. 1273, Appendix II, 22 December 1920, Memorandum by Lord Milner.

[7] Cmd. 1273, Appendix III, Reply of Elected Members of Legislative Council to Lord

In January 1921 the Cave Award was made public.[1] The Commission awarded to the Company £4,435,225 subject to deductions for lands appropriated by the Company for commercial purposes, but a Company claim for interest on the sums expended was rejected. The Company was, however, entitled to further compensation for public works under Article 33 of the Charter (estimated at about £830,000). On the other hand, the Crown still claimed approximately £2 million from the Company for extraordinary war expenditure, rejected the Company's demand that it pay cash for sums outstanding on the termination of the Company's administration, claimed the right to take lands needed for administrative purposes and also to take movable assets without payment in cash, and a similar right to take over the Company's debtor balance. The Company contested the Crown's assertions and ultimately it initiated proceedings against the Crown by way of Petition of Right to settle whether it was entitled to the capital sum in cash immediately on termination of its administration[2] and to interest thereon from 31 March 1918.[3]

A long bargaining process between the Company and the Colonial Office now commenced, the aim of the United Kingdom Government being to avoid any burden on the British Treasury.[4] It was this desire that made Rhodesian entry into the Union of South Africa the favoured solution of the Imperial authorities. Indeed, despite the fact that, if this object were secured, neither the Secretary of State nor the High Commissioner would be able to remain in control of native affairs and that Imperial safeguards would disappear, they were nonetheless prepared to accept such a situation.[5]

The local pressure for responsible government, however, caused Mr. Winston Churchill, who had recently become Colonial Secretary, to appoint in March 1921 a Royal Commission chaired by Lord Buxton[6] to advise 'when and with what limitations (if any) responsible government should be granted to Southern Rhodesia' and 'pending the coming into effect of responsible government what measures will be required to enable the B.S.A.

Milner's Memorandum, 23 January 1921. They also disagreed with the Secretary of State's proposals for compensating the Company for public buildings.

[1] Cmd. 1129. Papers relating to the Commission appointed to take account of what would have been due to the B.S.A. Company if the administration of Southern Rhodesia by the Company had been determined on 31 March 1918. Correspondence and Report. See also Cmd. 1129B, Evidence.

[2] The Crown proposed that the unalienated land should be held by a Crown land agent who would pay out the Company from the proceeds of land sales over the years: Fage, op. cit., pp. 288–9.

[3] See The B.S.A. Company's Reports of the Directors for the years 1920 to 1923.

[4] It must be remembered that these decisions were being taken at a time when Britain was suffering the financial aftermath of the First World War and when she was deeply involved with Ireland.

[5] African 1085, No. 67, High Commissioner to Secretary of State, 9 May 1922.

[6] Governor-General of the Union and High Commissioner until 1920.

Company to carry on the administration'.[1] The terms of reference precluded any finding other than the grant of responsible government.

The Colonial Office attitude to the new constitution

While these negotiations and enquiries were being conducted, the Colonial Office had been considering what character it wished the new constitution to assume. The Imperial Secretary in South Africa, H. J. Stanley,[2] wrote a lengthy memorandum with which the High Commissioner (who was soon to be appointed to the Royal Commission enquiring into the grant of Responsible Government) declared himself to be in agreement, and which was forwarded to the Colonial Office.[3]

Stanley felt that the High Commissioner should remain 'an integral portion of the Constitution', should still exercise his functions of control over native affairs, and should continue to deal with appointments, salaries (which should not be subject to a vote of the Legislature), and disciplinary proceedings in the Native Department. The Reserves should remain vested in him, while removals of natives and regulations affecting them should have his approval. The High Commissioner should be independent of Ministerial advice and stand towards the local government in much the same position as he had occupied towards the Company's Administration, which would submit recommendations to him through the Governor, just as the Administrator had done. In addition, the Governor, as an Imperial officer, would be available for consultation by the High Commissioner and the Secretary of State in regard to the acts and proposals of his Government. Stanley also proposed control over legislation affecting the Reserves, railways, Africans, Asians, and Coloureds. Finally, he felt that though entry to the Union was not then practical politics, the door to eventual entry should be left open.

That incorporation in the Union was the best solution from the Imperial Government's point of view was also the High Commissioner's opinion but, since Southern Rhodesia would not accede to this, and since responsible government was financially feasible with a 'tight squeeze', responsible government should be granted. Representative government under the Crown was again rejected by the High Commissioner as 'the Imperial Government would not be prepared to undertake any financial liability in connection with the administration of the country under representative government'.[4]

---

[1] Terms of reference: Cmd. 1273.

[2] Private Secretary to the Governor-General, Union of South Africa, 1910-13. Secretary to the Governor-General, 1913-15. Resident Commissioner, Southern and Northern Rhodesia, 1915-18, Imperial Secretary, South Africa, 1918-24, Governor of Northern Rhodesia, 1924-7, Governor of Ceylon, 1927-31, High Commissioner for South Africa, 1931-5, Governor of Southern Rhodesia, 1935-42.

[3] African 1085, No. 3, High Commissioner to Secretary of State, 6 August 1920, and Enclosure, The Constitutional Question in Southern Rhodesia, 21 July 1920.

[4] African 1085, No. 3. Milner had, in any event, definitely rejected representative govern-

Negotiations leading to responsible government

In May 1921 the Buxton Report was published.[1] Stanley's proposed limitations on the powers of the new Government and those suggested by the Report coincided to a remarkable degree. The Report also proposed a conference between the elected members and the Colonial Office to devise the details of the new Constitution, which should then be put before the Southern Rhodesian electorate by means of a referendum. If these proposals were approved Southern Rhodesia should then be annexed and this annexation should be followed by Letters Patent granting the new Constitution.

Mr. Churchill then invited the elected members to a conference to be held in October and November 1921 in London. He insisted, however, that they have discussions on their way to England with General Smuts on the terms on which the Union of South Africa would take in Southern Rhodesia.[2] The meetings with Smuts were, however, indecisive as the elected members did not desire to negotiate, while Smuts, although welcoming the possible accession of Southern Rhodesia to the Union, insisted that proper negotiations take place at a conference.[3]

At the London discussions a Constitution based on the precedents of the Natal Constitution 1893, the Transvaal Constitution Letters Patent 1906, the Malta Constitution Letters Patent 1921 and the Southern Rhodesia Order in Council 1898, was drawn up.[4] This and draft Letters Patent constituting the Office of Governor as well as draft Royal Instructions were thereafter published in January 1922.[5] However, the Despatch transmitting them ended

ment under the Crown in his cable of 19 August 1919. The grant of responsible government became easier as the proposals for this were not even opposed by such an influential pressure group as the Aborigines Protection Society. This favoured the introduction of responsible government although it must have recognized that since the franchise was in European hands, there would for many years be an all-white Legislature. (The first non-European was elected to the Southern Rhodesian Legislative Assembly in December 1962 under the Southern Rhodesia Constitution 1961.) The Society 'looked forward with hope to an early grant of responsible government to the people of Southern Rhodesia': National Archives LE 3/1/2, Aborigines Protection Society to Milner, July 1920. See also National Archives CO 8/1/2, Secretary of Society to Newton, 7 June 1923; A 3/18/12, Secretary of Society to Churchill, 29 August 1921; and MA 15/1/1, § 96–99. See also J. H. Harris, *The Chartered Millions*, Swarthmore Press, 1920, p. 286.

[1] Cmd. 1273.

[2] See *S.R. Legco Deb.*, 1922, col. 513; and Fage, op. cit., p. 282. See also Fage, op. cit., pp. 279–80, for Smuts's intervention with Churchill in 1921 and request that Southern Rhodesia should join the Union.

[3] See Smuts's statement, *The Times*, 5 September 1922.

[4] Apparently thirty-two clauses were based on the Natal provisions, forty-nine on the Transvaal, thirty-four on the Maltese, and nine on the Southern Rhodesia Order in Council 1898, while thirteen new clauses were introduced: *S.R. Legco Deb.*, Vol. 13, col. 229. The 1923 Constitution was an early 'Westminster export model'.

[5] The draft Letters Patent constituting the Office of Governor and the Royal Instructions were both adapted from those in the Transvaal in 1906: Cmd. 1573. Despatch from the High Commissioner for South Africa transmitting draft Letters Patent providing for the constitution of Responsible Government in Southern Rhodesia, p. 1.

with an injunction that the people of Southern Rhodesia must consider the alternative policy of entry into the Union of South Africa[1]: a delegation to confer with General Smuts should be appointed, and, when the terms on which Southern Rhodesia could enter the Union became available, both policies should be placed before the electorate by means of a referendum.

As a consequence of this injunction the elected members again conferred with Smuts in April 1922[2] but, owing to protracted South African negotiations with the Company, long delay occurred in the announcement of the Union's terms for Southern Rhodesia's entry. The elected members thereupon forced the issue by introducing the Referendum Ordinance of 1922. This embarrassed the Secretary of State and the High Commissioner, who considered either refusing assent to the Ordinance, conditionally assenting and subsequently disallowing if the conditions were not fulfilled, or amending the Ordinance by High Commissioner's Proclamation.[3] However, Smuts's terms were produced in time to avoid the necessity of making such a decision. His terms were extremely favourable both to the Company and to the electorate of Southern Rhodesia.[4] Nonetheless, disregarding these advantages and British reluctance to give Southern Rhodesia financial assistance,[5] the electorate rejected the Union terms, voting in a Referendum held in October 1922 for responsible government.[6]

[1] Cmd. 1573, p. 6.

[2] Mr. Churchill also appointed two Northern Rhodesian representatives as there had been requests for this by Northern Rhodesian settlers. The majority of Northern Rhodesian settlers were, however, opposed to entry into South Africa.

[3] African 1085, No. 70, of 9 June 1922. High Commissioner to Secretary of State.

[4] The Union offered financial advantages to the Europeans, development loans for public works, development of the railway system, Crown lands freed from charges, a Land Settlement Board, free transfer of commonages to the municipalities, and subsidization in return for abolition of the Rhodes Customs Clause. Southern Rhodesia would have been entitled to elect ten members to the Union House of Assembly, this number subsequently increasing to seventeen. There would also have been four elected senators and one nominated, later increasing to eight elected and two nominated senators. In addition, there would have been a Provincial Council on the South African model. For an analysis of the Union terms and reasons for anti-Union feeling by Europeans see Fage, op. cit., pp. 298–302.

[5] Coghlan considered that the terms on which Southern Rhodesia was given self-government were parsimonious: National Archives NE 1/1/1, Coghlan to Newton, 5 June 1923. See also the High Commissioner's comments, African 1085, No. 3, 6 August 1920: 'I do not myself think that it would be either just or expedient to saddle the country with the deficits. If Southern Rhodesia had, in the ordinary sense of the term, been a Crown Colony working up to representative or responsible government, the deficits which were not met by taxation would have been met, as they arose, by grants in aid from the Imperial Treasury, and when the moment had come to confer representative or responsible government, the country would have started on its new career substantially without debt (except for public works, &c.).' In 1925 the Colonial Office was unhelpful to Southern Rhodesia and antagonistic because of its 'refusal to cave in to Smuts': Coghlan to Newton, 19 March 1925, National Archives, CO 8/1/2.

[6] The result was 8,774 in favour of responsible government and 5,989 in favour of Union with a 78·5 per cent poll. It is unlikely that the number of African voters had increased from 1914 when it was estimated that the number did not exceed sixty: Cd. 7645, No. 1, Encl. 1.

Final financial negotiations

Another year had yet to pass before Southern Rhodesia gained her new Constitution. It even became necessary to issue an Order in Council extending the life of the Legislative Council.[1] The period was marked by acrimonious dispute between the Company and the Imperial Government who were evading their obligations under the Cave Award. In fact, the Secretary of State informed the House of Commons that the 'draft Letters Patent were prepared on the basis that should they come into operation, no liability of a financial kind would fall on His Majesty's Government'.[2] The settlement was also complicated by the necessity of considering the future position of Northern Rhodesia which, since the extent of its copper deposits had not at that time been realized or exploited, was a financial liability.[3]

The elected members were in these circumstances forced to send Sir F. J. Newton[4] to London to represent their interests in the protracted negotiations which were going on between the Colonial Office and the Company. The difficulties were caused not by the Colonial Office but by the reluctance of the United Kingdom Treasury to reimburse the Company for past financial deficits.[5] Eventually, after the elected members had threatened to refuse to vote supplies[6] and had then made a generous offer of payment towards the administrative deficits, the Company, the elected members and the Colonial Offices reached agreement.[7] The Company agreed to abandon its right to

[1] Southern Rhodesia (Legislative Council Extension) Order in Council of 16 April 1923, extending the life of the Council for six months. The Council would otherwise have expired in May 1923.

[2] Except in terms of Article 33 of the Charter in respect of the acquisition of public buildings: *H.C. Deb.*, Vol. 153, col. 1329, 3 May 1922.

[3] Cmd. 1471. Second Report of the Committee appointed by the Secretary of State for Colonies to consider certain questions relating to Rhodesia. The Second Buxton Report, in attempting to solve these difficulties, advised a further special reference to the Judicial Committee to decide land ownership and liability for administrative deficits in Northern Rhodesia.

[4] Formerly Treasurer to the Company, 1907 to 1919. Resident Commissioner in Bechuanaland at the time of the Jameson Raid. Later first Southern Rhodesian High Commissioner in London.

[5] National Archives CO 8/1/2. Coghlan to Newton, 16 July 1923; and also NE 1/1/1, Newton to Coghlan, 23 March 1923, revealing that the Chancellor of the Exchequer was making difficulties. See also J. P. R. Wallis, *One Man's Hand: The Story of Sir Charles Coghlan and the Liberation of Southern Rhodesia*, Longmans, 1950, pp. 183–94.

[6] National Archives NE 1/1/1, Memorandum of a Meeting between Newton and the B.S.A. Company Directors. Newton to Coghlan, 3 May 1923.

[7] See Cmd. 1914, Rhodesia: Correspondence regarding a proposed settlement of various outstanding questions relating to the B.S.A. Company's position in Southern and Northern Rhodesia. No. 1 contains the United Kingdom terms and No. 3 sets out the settlers' offer. After approval by an Extraordinary General Meeting of the Company on 24 July 1923, a supplementary Estimate was introduced into the Commons on 25 July. On 29 September the Devonshire Agreement was signed: see Cmd. 1984 Rhodesia: Agreement between the Secretary of State for the Colonies and the B.S.A. Company for the Settlement of the Outstanding Questions relating to Southern and Northern Rhodesia dated 29 September 1923.

compensation for the administrative deficits, its claim to interest from 1918, and to withdraw the Petition of Right. It relinquished all claims to land, except that which it had appropriated for commercial purposes, and it agreed to hand over public works. On the other hand, it would retain its mineral rights in the two Rhodesias, considerable land rights in North Western Rhodesia, and all its commercial assets. It would also gain safeguards for its Railway investments, while the Crown would drop its war claim of approximately £2 million. The Crown would, in addition, pay it £3,750,000 of which the new Southern Rhodesian Government would find £2,000,000. The Southern Rhodesian Government secured in return an undertaking that the Crown would vest the unalienated lands of Southern Rhodesia in the Governor.

This agreement was incorporated in last-minute changes to the draft Letters Patent. Section 48 now provided that the Governor in Council was to pay £2,000,000 to the United Kingdom Treasury and also to repay a further £300,000 which had been advanced for public works in terms of Lord Milner's promise.[1] Southern Rhodesia also assumed liability for all creditor balances due by the Administration and any liability arising out of the administration of the country other than the United Kingdom's liability for the administrative deficits of the Company.[2]

In return for these undertakings Section 49 vested the unalienated land in the Governor for the purpose of the public service of the Colony (other than the Native Reserves which were vested in the High Commissioner). All Company land rights, other than mineral rights reserved by the Company over land alienated by it, also vested in the Governor, as did all public works and buildings, movable assets, debtor balances of the Company acquired by the United Kingdom Government, and assets of the Land Settlement Department. However, the Company was deemed to have paid the price of all lands appropriated by it for commercial purposes and was to be given title in respect of such lands, any disagreement thereanent to be settled by the Secretary of State.[3]

Annexation of Southern Rhodesia

Since agreement had been reached the long-awaited Constitution could now be put into operation. The Southern Rhodesia (Annexation) Order in

---

[1] In order to repay these liabilities Southern Rhodesia floated her first loan issue with Imperial assistance in 1923.

[2] Section 49(3) proviso. The settlers were made to pay for self-government. The Imperial Government was prepared to give them only a slender dowry.

[3] Section 49(2) proviso. In practice the Secretary of State decided such disputes without taking account of the views of the Company or the Southern Rhodesia Government, acting purely on the views of the legal advisers to the Crown: S.R.L.A.D., Vol. 4, col. 1408, 9 December 1926.

Council 1923[1] annexed the territories within the limits of the Southern Rhodesia Order in Council 1898 known as Southern Rhodesia.[2] They were in future to be known as the Colony of Southern Rhodesia.

[1] 30 July 1923. Brought into operation by High Commissioner's Proclamation No. 41 of 1923 as from 12 September 1923, thirty-three years after the unauthorized raising of the British flag by the pioneers at Fort Salisbury.

[2] Cmd. 1573, p. 5, disclosed that besides the railway strip in Northern Rhodesia, the possibility of including the Tati district of the Bechuanaland Protectorate in Southern Rhodesia had been canvassed but left open for subsequent action. See also National Archives A 2/4/12, 25 February 1921. The Annexation Order in Council expressly excluded the Tati district. Numerous requests for the incorporation of Tati have been made by successive Southern Rhodesian Governments but rejected. In 1925 a request for Tati and North Bechuanaland was rejected (National Archives CO 8/1/2, Newton to Coghlan, 26 February 1925). In 1927 after deputations from Tati and the Southern Rhodesian Government had requested the incorporation of the Tati area, Mr. Amery refused to commit the Dominions Office on this issue (National Archives LE 3/3/1/1, Cabinet Resolution 641 of 6 October 1927). In 1930 the Southern Rhodesian Government was informed that such request should not be made as it might lead to demands from the Union for the rest of the Protectorate (National Archives NE 1/1/7, Moffat to Newton, 25 April 1930). Similarly a request was refused in 1931 (see National Archives DO 1/1/6, Downie to Moffat, 15 July 1931). Again in 1933 Moffat was told such request was 'not opportune' (*S.R.L.A.D.*, Vol. 13, col. 365, 12 April 1933). In 1949 the Southern Rhodesia Minister of Justice stated, with the approval of the Secretary of State for Commonwealth Relations, that Southern Rhodesia's attitude would also be considered in determining the fate of Bechuanaland Protectorate (see *Bulawayo Chronicle*, 22 December 1949). In 1951 the Prime Minister indicated that the Imperial authorities would refuse any request for amalgamation with Bechuanaland (*S.R.L.A.D.*, Vol. 32, (1), col. 1954). In 1963 the European inhabitants of Tati petitioned for incorporation in Southern Rhodesia: see *Rhodesia Herald*, 24 March 1964. Bechuanaland has now been given a Constitution providing for internal self-government.

11

THE SOUTHERN RHODESIA CONSTITUTION
LETTERS PATENT 1923

BY Letters Patent of the 1 September 1923, Southern Rhodesia was provided with a responsible government constitution, which came into force on 1 October 1923.[1] The Constitution, however, did not allow Southern Rhodesia full self-government, and the preamble to the Letters Patent specifically provided 'for the establishment of responsible government subject to certain limitations'.[2] Indeed, the retiring Administrator, Sir Drummond Chaplin, commenting on the new Constitution, stated that the Colonial Office had 'limited the power of the proposed new government to a considerable extent',[3] while one of the leaders of the responsible government movement merely described it as 'the next step towards complete self-government'.[4] Only in recent years has the myth that 'Southern Rhodesia . . . has for over forty years enjoyed complete internal self-government',[5] been propagated. At the time of granting the 1923 Constitution it was generally recognized that the Constitution conferred partial self-government, or self-government subject to supervision: it was a responsible government type Constitution which did not confer complete self-government. Even in 1953 Southern Rhodesia was described as a self-governing territory except for Native Affairs,[6] while as late as 15 April 1959, the then Prime Minister, Sir Edgar Whitehead, stated 'neither the Federation nor Southern Rhodesia are fully self-governing'.[7]

General characteristics of the Constitution

The Letters Patent provided for a typical 'Westminster export model' of that period.[8] The Constitution was written and was subject to judicial review

[1] S.R. and O. Revised, xxi, p. 371.

[2] Cp. Mr. Churchill's despatch transmitting the draft Constitution, which stated that satisfactory control of the government and administration was being given 'subject only to the reservations which the peculiar history of the country imposed': Cmd. 1573.

[3] B. K. Long, *Drummond Chaplin*, Oxford, 1941, at p. 265. See also *B.S.A. Company. Extraordinary General Meeting of 28 July 1922*, p. 5.

[4] *S.R. Legco Deb.*, 1922, col. 771.

[5] *H.C. Deb.*, Vol. 684, col. 584, 15 November 1963. Mr. Duncan Sandys: and *H.C. Deb.*, Vol. 713, col. 1558, 1 June 1965, Mr. Bottomley referring to 'full internal self-government for a period of forty-two years'.

[6] *Halsbury's Laws of England*, 3rd ed., Vol. 5, p. 437. See also the remarks of the present Chief Justice, then Minister of Justice in *S.R.L.A.D.*, Vol. 30(1), col. 54, 28 April 1949: 'We are what may be termed a constitutional hybrid, we are neither a Colony nor a Dominion'.

[7] *S.R.L.A.D.*, Vol. 42, col. 3043.

[8] Using the phrase in its narrower sense as described by de Smith in *The New Commonwealth and its Constitutions*, Stevens, 1964, pp. 77–78. See also 'Westminster's Export

16—C.H.L.S.R.

if the procedural safeguards set out therein were not observed, or if the law enacted was beyond the competence of the Legislature.[1] Rigidity was marked in that many sections of the Constitution could not be amended by the Legislature, while others required the procedural safeguard of a two-thirds majority with the additional external control of reservation and assent by the Crown on United Kingdom Government advice.

At that time colonial constitutions did not contain Bills of Rights, but the Southern Rhodesian Constitution of 1923 safeguarded the interests of indigenous peoples (and certain United Kingdom financial interests) by the external control of reservation, required in the case of Bills, and by the requirement of prior approval by the Secretary of State of subordinate legislation discriminating against Africans. Special constitutional land provisions were also inserted preserving the right of Africans to own and hold land on the same terms as Europeans and retaining Native Reserves for the sole and exclusive use of the African people.

External controls were extensive. These included United Kingdom power to legislate by Act, Crown power to legislate by Order in Council, power by Act to revoke the Constitution, power in the Crown to amend or revoke many sections and to suspend the Constitution, the rule of repugnancy, disallowance, reservation of discriminatory and other Bills, the need for obtaining the Secretary of State's approval of delegated legislation discriminating against Africans, appointment by the Crown of the Governor, the right to give the Governor Royal Instructions, the Governor's power to dissent from Cabinet advice, his power of discretionary reservation of all Bills, and appeal by special leave to the Judicial Committee of the Privy Council.

The Legislature was unicameral, consisting of a Legislative Assembly modelled on the House of Commons, following its procedure, and giving the same parliamentary privileges to members. There was a Ministry of cabinet type selected from the Legislative Assembly and headed by a Premier. Although the Letters Patent did not mention a cabinet or conventions of cabinet government the Governor, under the Letters Patent constituting his office and the Royal Instructions was bound to select an Executive Council composed of Ministers and others and to follow their advice in all normal cases.

Models', *Journal of Commonwealth Political Studies*, Vol. I, 1961, p. 1. The Constitution was similar to the responsible government constitutions granted to the South African Colonies prior to Union. It also resembled the Malta Constitution Letters Patent 1921 except that reservation was the main instrument of Imperial control in Southern Rhodesia, whereas in Malta a dyarchical system was created permitting executive action and legislation by the Governor acting as the Maltese Imperial Government in its defined sphere.

[1] The right of review follows by implication. It was not set out in the Constitution as was the case in Malta. See Cmd. 3993, Malta Royal Commission 1931, Report, pp. 66–72. During the existence of the 1923 Constitution there were no attempts to have Southern Rhodesian statutes declared *ultra vires*. However, administrative provisions were struck down as being in conflict with the Constitution: see *City of Salisbury* v. *Mehta*, 1962 (1) S.A. 675 (S.R.) and *Mabelreign T.M.B.* v. *Chamboko*, 1962, R. and N. 493 (F.C.).

In practice, however, only cabinet ministers were appointed as members of the Executive Council, which met to confirm decisions which had earlier been taken at cabinet meetings. Although the Governor for the most part represented the Queen as constitutional monarch, he was still an Imperial officer vested with considerable power and certain duties to the United Kingdom Government. Finally, the judiciary was independent and given safeguards against removal similar to those in the United Kingdom.

Composition of the Legislature

The Letters Patent provided for a Legislature that was initially to consist of a Legislative Assembly composed of thirty members representing electoral districts. The pre-existing electoral laws relating to the old Legislative Council as adapted by the Governor were retained,[1] and although re-enacted in 1928 and 1937 with minor changes the basic qualifications for the franchise remained unaltered until 1951, when the qualifications were considerably raised.[2] In addition to the thirty elected members of the Legislative Assembly,

[1] Sections 1, 3–6, 11(2) and Section 62. Thus various High Commissioner's Proclamations and Legislative Council Ordinances were applicable. High Commissioner's Proclamation No. 28 of 1923 provided for fifteen electoral districts. By Proclamation 3 of 1924 the Governor declared that two members should be elected for each district while the Ballot Regulations were amended to enable each voter to exercise two votes. There was a transitional provision for the existing Legislative Council to function as the new Legislature until the nomination of members for election to the new Legislative Assembly (Section 1). The old Legislative Council continued until the nomination of new members and met in October 1923. However, the Governor was substituted for the Administrator and was to enjoy the B.S.A. Company's power to suspend members (Section 1 proviso). In place of certain B.S.A. Company officials, Sir Francis Newton and Mr. R. J. Hudson were nominated as members and entered the first Cabinet.

[2] The Electoral Act of 1928 made several changes. It restricted the vote to British subjects by birth or naturalization so that an alien by taking the oath of allegiance could no longer register. Unemployed persons of independent means were now permitted to register as 'income' was included as satisfying the means qualification. At the same time the dictation test for literacy was eliminated, while board, lodging and clothing could be considered in computing the total salary. Further changes were made by the Electoral Act of 1937: this allowed non-British subjects who had been on active war-time service with His Majesty's Forces to enrol provided they met the other qualifications. On the other hand, persons who had drawn Government rations or allowances in lieu thereof for a period of one year were disqualified, while the possibility of further African enrolment was decreased by provision that the property occupation qualification could no longer be satisfied by buildings to that value so long as they stood on communally-held land, which for this purpose was deemed also to include a private location (property hired from a European). The Electoral Act was consolidated in 1938 as Chapter 2 of the Revised Edition of the Laws 1939, but it exempted old age pensioners from the means qualification. Minor modifications were made by the Electoral Amendment Act 1941 to exclude members of His Majesty's Forces temporarily in the Colony during wartime and British subjects who were unwilling to declare their readiness to serve in the Colony's Defence Force. Disqualifications for disloyal conduct were also introduced by the Civil Disabilities Act of 1942. For a full account, see Passmore and Mitchell, op. cit., pp. 2–4. For the 1951 changes see *infra*, Chapter 14.

the Assembly might elect a Speaker who could be a non-member,[1] and who was entitled to exercise a casting vote.[2]

The Legislative Assembly was empowered at any time after the commencement of the Letters Patent to pass a law constituting a Legislative Council, or Upper House, and thus create a bicameral Legislature.[3] However, this provision was never utilized,[4] and the Legislative Assembly has always been 'for all purposes the Legislature'.[5]

The Legislature was to have at least one session a year without more than twelve months intervening,[6] and the life of each Legislative Assembly was to be five years from the date of its first meeting.[7] Normal provisions as to the annual meeting of the Legislature and the maximum period of its life were also made. In respect of the conduct of its proceedings the Legislative Assembly was authorized to adopt its own Standing Rules and Orders.[8]

[1] Provision for non-membership was inserted at Southern Rhodesia's wish. The Provision was utilized from 1924 to 1935, from 1939 to 1952, from 1958 to 1959. Under a similar provision in the 1961 Constitution it was utilized from 1962 to 1964 and is at present in use. In all cases, Speakers elected under this provision have been ex-members of the House (the first Speaker had been a member of the Legislative Council) and have, in all cases (except that of the first Speaker) been elected while still a member. However, a motion urging that this be accepted as a principle met with an unfavourable reception: see *S.R.L.A.D.*, Vol. 41, cols. 407–26.

[2] The casting vote is used in such a way as to allow further consideration to be given to any matter: *S.R.L.A.D.*, Vol. 25(1), col. 1102; Vol. 26(1), col. 1420; Vol. 27(1), col. 961.

[3] Section 2. Section 26(2) provided that the Legislative Assembly might not repeal or alter any of the provisions of the Letters Patent relating to the Legislative Council which could only be altered by a law passed by both Houses after its establishment. All laws and financial measures would require the consent of both the proposed Legislative Council and the Legislative Assembly (Section 26(1)). The Legislative Council was not entitled to originate (Section 52) or alter money bills but merely to transmit them with suggested amendments, and then after further consideration by the Legislative Assembly to accept or reject the Bill without alteration.

[4] Although from time to time suggestions were made that an Upper House with a racial composition be constituted, in order to induce the British Government to give up its reserve powers over the Constitution, e.g. *S.R.L.A.D.*, Vol. 12, col. 870, 21 April 1932, H. U. Moffat, the Prime Minister. In 1951, a Select Committee made recommendations that an Upper House should be established. See Final Report of a Select Committee on Amendment of the Constitution, Southern Rhodesia Votes and Proceedings of the Legislative Assembly, 12 April 1951, pp. 17–33. The recommendations were not implemented because of a decision to create the Federation of Rhodesia and Nyasaland, and to preserve the other features of the Southern Rhodesia Constitution: see *S.R.L.A.D.*, Vol. 31(1), col. 602, 3 May 1950, Sir Godfrey Huggins, and 32(2), col. 3515, J. M. Greenfield, Minister of Internal Affairs. In 1960 Sir Edgar Whitehead again suggested an Upper House for similar reasons to the Secretary of State: see *S.R.L.A.D.*, Vol. 45, col. 1669.

[5] Section 2.   [6] Section 16(1).   [7] Section 18(2).

[8] Section 23(1). These were normally framed by the Standing Rules and Orders Committee (a standing committee which, under the Chairmanship of the Speaker, governs the running of Parliament) and then approved by resolution of the whole House. There were five editions of the Southern Rhodesia Legislative Assembly Standing Rules and Orders during the existence of the 1923 Constitution and numerous small changes from time to time. In the event of any matter not being covered by the Standing Rules and Orders the practice of the House of Commons was to be followed: Clause 254 Standing Rules and Orders, 5th edition, Government Printer, Salisbury, 1956.

Legislative power and its limitations

The Legislature was given full legislative power to pass laws 'to be entitled "Acts" which shall be required for the peace, order and good government of the Colony',[1] while the High Commissioner's power of legislating by Proclamation was withdrawn.[2] Thus the new Legislature was given full powers of legislation,[3] subject to limitations which were, however, considerable.

Indeed, certain provisions of the Letters Patent were unalterable by the Legislative Assembly. These provisions were those relating to the reservation of Bills (Section 28), those relating to Native Administration—which secured the High Commissioner's control—(Sections 39 to 47), that securing the salary of the Governor (Section 55), and the section defining legislative power, providing for a special procedure for constitutional amendment, and prohibiting the alteration of certain sections of the Constitution (Section 26(2)). In the event the Legislature came into conflict with these provisions on at least two occasions. After incorrect legal advice by the Dominions Office the original Land Apportionment Bill of 1929 was passed. This was in conflict with Section 43 of the Letters Patent, which preserved the right of Africans to occupy all land on the same terms as Europeans. The Legislative Assembly was then advised by the Secretary of State that he would secure the issue of amending Letters Patent, that the Bill should thereafter be re-passed and that the Imperial Government would give its consent at that stage.[4] On another occasion a Bill to establish Native Councils was prepared and published, but the Secretary of State warned the Government not to proceed as it would be void, being in conflict with Section 47 of the Letters Patent.[5]

Again, the Legislative Assembly acting alone, either before or after the constitution of the proposed Legislative Council (Upper House), was debarred from repealing or altering any of the provisions relating to the Legislative Council which were contained in the Letters Patent.[6]

Furthermore there were procedural limitations even in respect of those constitutional amendments which were permissible: the Legislature could not repeal or alter such provisions unless the proposed law was affirmed by not less than two-thirds of the total number of members of each House of the Legislature. In practice, this was interpreted to mean that constitutional

---

[1] Section 26(1).

[2] This occurred as a result of Section 58(1), since such power was not reserved to the High Commissioner by the Letters Patent, and was inconsistent with the powers granted to the Legislature.

[3] See *R. v. McChlery*, 1912 A.D. 199 (S.R.) per Innes J.A. at 220 interpreting similar words in the Southern Rhodesia Order in Council 1898. See also *R. v. Burah*, 3 App. Cas. 889; *Hodge v. The Queen* (1883), 9 A.C. 117 at 132; and *Powell v. Apollo Candle Company* (1885), 10 A.C. 282 at 289.

[4] See *S.R.L.A.*, Votes and Proceedings, Vol. XVI, Second Session, Second Parliament, p. 12, 18 March 1930.

[5] National Archives S 235/444 MSS, Minute 253 of 5 June 1929.

[6] See Section 26(2), first proviso.

amending Bills required to be passed at the third reading by at least twenty of the thirty members.[1] Any law not passed in accordance with this procedure, or in disregard of the two earlier prohibitions imposed, was to the extent of such contravention 'absolutely void and inoperative'.[2]

There were also other minor limitations on the power of the Legislature to pass laws which involved special protections to existing and retired Civil Servants. Thus public officers in the service of the Company in its administration of Southern Rhodesia were to become public officers of the Colony, but the new Legislature could not provide for their removal from office or reduce their emoluments as these were to be determined by the laws governing their services as at the date of the new Constitution.[3] Similarly the pensions and gratuities of retired Company servants were to be governed by the laws under which they were granted,[4] while those servants already in office were entitled to claim pensions or gratuities under laws regulating the position at the time of the grant of the Letters Patent, unless such servants opted to have their claims governed by a new law passed by the Legislature.[5]

Nor could the Legislature pass a law conferring greater powers, privileges, and immunities on the Legislature and its members than those enjoyed and exercised by the House of Commons or its members.[6]

Furthermore, unless the Governor by message to the Assembly recommended any law, vote or resolution which would have the effect of imposing or repealing any rate, tax or duty the Legislative Assembly was debarred from passing such law, vote or resolution.[7]

At that time too Southern Rhodesia had no powers of extraterritorial legislation. Such powers were only given to her under the Southern Rhodesia Constitution of 1961.[8]

[1] Section 26(2), second proviso. Successive Speakers developed this practice. On such occasions Speakers who were members utilized their votes: *S.R.L.A.D.*, Vol. 45, cols. 1722–3, 24 August 1960. See also Vol. 17, cols. 1578–9, 11 October 1937. It is understood that on the last occasion the Speaker was reprimanded by the Secretary of State for using his vote as it was considered that such action was not consonant with the office of Speaker. Personal communication.

[2] Section 26(3). In any event it submitted that the Courts would enquire whether an Act had been properly passed by the Legislative Assembly: *Harris* v. *Minister of the Interior*, 1952 (2) S.A. 428 and *Bribery Commissioner* v. *Ranasinghe*, [1964] 2 W.L.R. 1301. In Malta the Courts held that they had the right to determine the validity of laws enacted by the Legislature under similar circumstances: Cmd. 3993, pp. 66–72, and *Strickland* v. *Grima*, [1930] A.C. 283.

[3] Section 56.   [4] Section 57(1).   [5] Section 57(2).

[6] Section 25(1) proviso. This limitation was removed from the Southern Rhodesia Constitution 1961 by Section 26.

[7] Section 54(1). This limitation was removed in 1937 by the substitution of a new subsection 54(1) in terms of the Constitution Amendment Act No. 22 of 1937, which laid down that the Assembly should not originate or pass any vote, resolution, address or Bill for the appropriation of any part of the Consolidated Revenue Fund or of any tax or impost unless the Governor by message recommended this. As a result the Legislative Assembly could now make proposals to reduce or repeal taxes.

[8] S.I. 1961/2314 Annex, Section 20(2). See D. P. O'Connell, 'Doctrine of Colonial

Since at this time the conduct of external affairs was not entrusted to the Southern Rhodesian Government, Southern Rhodesia had no power to legislate on this topic either. By a process of gradual evolution from 1923 onwards, Southern Rhodesia was, however, delegated authority in relation to the negotiation and conclusion of trade agreements with foreign government so far as these agreements related to the treatment of goods. In practice, it became accepted that Southern Rhodesia might enter into local agreements with neighbouring territories including representational agreements with such territories.[1] She was also permitted to join international technical organizations which contemplated Southern Rhodesian membership.[2] This entrustment was formally agreed upon between the United Kingdom and Southern Rhodesia Governments in a despatch by the Secretary of State for Commonwealth Relations dated the 17 February 1949.[3]

The United Kingdom Government always insisted that there must be prior

Extraterritorial Legislative Incompetence' (1959) 75 *L.Q.R.* 318 for views on the legal consequences of the position prior to 1962. It may be that the issue in each case is not one of extraterritorial legislative competence but whether the constitutional instruments authorize the particular legislation, i.e. whether powers for peace, order and good government of Southern Rhodesia are involved. See *Croft* v. *Dunphy*, [1933] A.C. 156 at 163. This view of *Croft* v. *Dunphy* was taken in *R.* v. *Offen*, 1934 S.W.A. 73 per van den Heever J. (as he then was). See also *Rhodesia Railways* v. *Commissioner of Taxes*, 1925 A.D. 438 at 467–8 where the Appellate Division in discussing the Southern Rhodesia Order in Council 1898 held that the Court could not investigate whether powers had been exercised for peace, order and good government and upheld legislation taxing income earned outside Southern Rhodesia by a company resident in Southern Rhodesia. Laws will be valid so long as they appertain to the country or there is a relevant territorial connection: *Johnson* v. *Commissioner for Taxes*, [1956] A.C. 331 (P.C.) at 350 and 353 per Lord Keith. The mere fact that in order to determine whether or not an act committed within Southern Rhodesia was lawful the courts had to look at something outside the country, or the fact that what was done outside the territory was an essential ingredient of the offence did not mean that the offence was an extraterritorial one: *R.* v. *Zvobgo*, 1965 (1) S.A. 653 (*S.R.A.D.*) at 655 per Beadle C.J. Thus the court held itself entitled to take into account the fact that an organization unlawful in Southern Rhodesia had continued to exist in Tanganyika in a charge under Section 9 (1) (a) of the Unlawful Organizations Act 1959, i.e. that an appellant had acted as an office-bearer of the Zimbabwe African People's Union, an organization proclaimed by the Governor to be unlawful. The court also held that, even though an unlawful organization ceased to exist within Southern Rhodesia, it remained unlawful wherever it decided to go. Quènet J.P. left open the point whether it would be permissible to declare unlawful an organization which carried on no activities in Southern Rhodesia: *R.* v. *Zvobgo*, supra at 657. The Unlawful Organizations Act, Section 3 read with Part II of the Schedule to the Act does not declare organizations such as the World Federation of Trade Unions and the International Union of Students unlawful, but provides that the Governor may declare organizations controlled by, affiliated to, promoting the objects of, or propagating the opinions of such organizations to be unlawful.

[1] Southern Rhodesia started communicating through the Prime Minister's Office with the Union of South Africa only in 1931. Previously all such correspondence had been conducted through the Governor. This change was suggested by the Governor: National Archives LE 3/2/1/4, Cabinet Resolution 1767 of 8 January 1931.

[2] She signed an International Convention which contemplated her as a signatory—The Red Locust Convention.

[3] *S.R.L.A.D.*, Vol. 58, cols. 1369–70, 7 October 1964.

consultation between the Government of Southern Rhodesia and Her Majesty's Government in the United Kingdom before the Southern Rhodesian Government might enter into any such commitment and at that period all international negotiations, even those relating to neighbouring territories were conducted by the United Kingdom Government, although Southern Rhodesian representatives might have been present[1] or the Southern Rhodesian Government might have been consulted in the preparation of notes to be exchanged.[2] Although Britain had delegated certain authority to Southern Rhodesia this did not involve any change in the constitutional position, so that Her Majesty's Government in the United Kingdom remained generally responsible for the external relations of the Colony.[3] Naturally Southern Rhodesia would have automatically been at war had the United Kingdom Government declared a state of belligerency.[4]

In accordance with British practice in respect of the treaty relations of self-governing territories, Southern Rhodesia was formally consulted as to whether she wished to accede to international treaties entered into by Britain on behalf of her overseas territories. Britain normally adhered to treaties only when they contained a negative colonial application clause permitting her to declare that her adhesion did not include any overseas possession, for which she was internationally responsible.[5] Despite the practice of consultation, when a Select Committee on the Constitution sat in 1951, the senior official dealing with external relations realistically informed the Committee that, in fact, Southern Rhodesia was bound by treaties she had never been free to consider.[6] Although Southern Rhodesia may have been formally consulted, in most cases she automatically acceded to treaties and was then informed by the United Kingdom that she must fulfil the obligations imposed by the

---

[1] e.g. in the case of the Beira Convention, Southern Rhodesia took an active part in the negotiations and was cited as a separate entity in the Convention. Nonetheless the Convention was signed by His Majesty's Ambassador in Lisbon on behalf of Southern Rhodesia.

[2] See e.g. National Archives S11, MSS. When the Southern Rhodesia–Portuguese East Africa boundary was adjusted in 1939, the United Kingdom did this by an exchange of notes which the Southern Rhodesian Government had approved: S.R. 360 of 20 October 1939.

[3] Cmd. 8574. The Federal Scheme, footnote 20. See also Survey of Developments since 1953, Cmd. 1149, Appendix VI, p. 22.

[4] See A. B. Keith, *Imperial Unity and the Dominions*, Oxford, 1916, pp. 52–53, which would be applicable to Southern Rhodesia despite changes in respect of Members of the Commonwealth.

[5] See generally J. E. S. Fawcett, 'Treaty Relations of British Overseas Territories', 1949. *B.Y.I.L.*, p. 86 at pp. 93–100.

[6] Cf. *S.R.L.A.D.*, Vol. 30(1), col. 2210, where it was stated 'Any agreement or treaty they make is binding on this country only after obtaining our assent'. Sir Edgar Whitehead also took this view in an interview. Lord Malvern, however, stated that cases might arise where Southern Rhodesia was not strong enough to stand out. He had taken this view in respect of the Bretton–Woods Agreement. Furthermore it cannot be contended that Southern Rhodesia's views could have affected the Lend Lease and War Claims Settlement between the United Kingdom and the United States of America, which settled Anglo–American

treaty.[1] However, in some cases Southern Rhodesia was permitted to decline to accede to international conventions entered into by Britain, as long as these did not cover Southern Rhodesia.[2] Britain would then, sometimes forcibly, point out the consequences of non-accession.[3]

In respect of Commonwealth relations Southern Rhodesia was not initially permitted separate representation at Conferences, although in 1923 she refused an invitation to send observers to the Imperial Economic Conference. Subsequently the Southern Rhodesian High Commissioner objected in 1925 that Southern Rhodesia was not represented on the Imperial Economic Committee and was informed that she was represented by the Under Secretary of State concerned with Crown colonies. After protest by the Southern Rhodesian Prime Minister, the Colonial Office eventually invited the Southern Rhodesian High Commissioner to become a member.[4]

When the Imperial Conference of 1926 was held, Southern Rhodesia was again not a member and her High Commissioner announced that this was because the country had not sought Dominion status. After representations the High Commissioner was, however, invited to assist in matters where Southern Rhodesian interests were concerned and was put on two of the more important Conference sub-committees.[5] Again in 1930, Southern Rhodesia was represented on sub-committees by the High Commissioner and Fynn, a Cabinet Minister.

Southern Rhodesia's status was enhanced when, after representations to this effect had been made, Southern Rhodesia was invited to send representatives as observers with liberty, by permission, to speak at full meetings and with the right of participation in committees of the 1932 Imperial Economic

war debts and related to all British colonial dependencies including Southern Rhodesia. As a result of this Agreement, Southern Rhodesia passed the Lend Lease and War Claims Settlement Act No. 27 of 1947, adjusting United Kingdom–Southern Rhodesia debts. See *S.R.L.A.D.*, Vol. 27(1), col. 2305.

[1] e.g. The Treaties of 1927 and 1930 with Turkey. In 1939 the United Kingdom issued two Orders in Council and informed Southern Rhodesia that she should take similar action to fulfil her obligations. See National Archives S11, S.R. No. 395, 22 November 1939.

[2] e.g. Southern Rhodesia has not acceded to all the International Labour Organization Conventions.

[3] After the establishment of the Federation of Rhodesia and Nyasaland and entrustment of these and other powers to the Federal Government, the Federal Government was allowed freedom to accede to or to decline to accede to treaties. Apparently only informal pressure applied by advice proffered through the High Commission in Salisbury was used to persuade the Federal Government to accede to any treaties. Personal communication from confidential source.

[4] See National Archives CO 8/1/2, Newton to Coghlan, 19 March 1925. Coghlan to Newton, 19 March 1925. The High Commissioner was telephoned to join the Committee on 22 April 1925.

[5] National Archives CO 8/1/2, Newton to Coghlan, 28 October 1926; Southern Rhodesia Legislative Assembly Votes and Proceedings, Vol. XII, p. 159; and see Cmd. 2786 (1926), p. 10, where the Secretary of State informed the Conference that he had requested the High Commissioner for Southern Rhodesia to assist particularly on the economic side where the interests of Southern Rhodesia were concerned.

Conference at Ottawa.[1] Her Prime Minister then attended the Conference and concluded separate trade agreements with Canada.[2] From this period Southern Rhodesia was permitted freedom in trade matters. Eventually a further advance occurred when her Prime Minister was invited as an observer to the Conference of Commonwealth Prime Ministers in 1935.

The next change in Southern Rhodesia's status occurred in 1948 when, as a result of a request by Southern Rhodesia, the Governor announced that whereas 'on past occasions Prime Ministers of Southern Rhodesia have attended in the capacity of observers only' at the October 1948 Conference 'my Prime Minister took a full part in the proceedings; a clear indication of recognition of this country's increased status in Commonwealth affairs'.[3] The Prime Minister himself considered that 'this Colony . . . is treated by His Majesty's Government as if it were a Dominion in regard to trade and financial matters'.[4] However, since Southern Rhodesia was not a Dominion, she was not invited to Conferences dealing with Foreign Affairs, South East Asia, the inter-relationships of the Dominions, or the constitutional position of any particular Dominion. In such cases she was represented by Great Britain. It was for this reason that she was not invited in 1949 to the Prime Ministers' Conference dealing with the Indian constitutional position. Only in 1951 was the Southern Rhodesian Prime Minister invited to a Conference entirely devoted to Foreign Affairs and the inter-relationships of the Dominions.[5]

The Southern Rhodesia Legislature would not have been permitted to pass its own nationality laws when the 1923 Constitution came into force. Indeed until 1949 Southern Rhodesia was treated as an ordinary Colony in this respect and its partial self-government was ignored. From 1923[6] until 1949 the Southern Rhodesian Government acted as an agent for the British Government merely receiving applications for nationality, collecting necessary information, making recommendations, and transmitting the papers to England, the decision whether the alien should be nationalized resting with

---

[1] *Southern Rhodesia Legislative Assembly Votes and Proceedings*, Vol. XVIII, Fifth Session, 2nd Parliament, p. 3.

[2] *S.R.L.A.D.*, Vol. 12, col. 375.

[3] *S.R.L.A.D.*, Vol. 29, cols. 5 and 6.

[4] *S.R.L.A.D.*, Vol. 28, col. 1485, 28 June 1948. The Southern Rhodesian Minister of Finance also attended the Commonwealth Finance Ministers' Conference in London from 13–18 July 1949 and took an active part in arguing the case for devaluation of sterling. Southern Rhodesia was at that time one of the only two Commonwealth countries that was on balance a dollar-earner. Subsequently a proposal was made by the Ceylon delegate that Sir Edgar Whitehead should become a member of the Commonwealth Consultative Committee on South East Asia (the Columbo Plan Committee). Sir Edgar Whitehead, to the relief of the British Government, declined to accept. Personal communication.

[5] The further development of external relations will be dealt with in Chapter 16, and Part II, Chapter 7.

[6] Prior to 1923 Southern Rhodesia was a Protectorate and persons born in Southern Rhodesia before that time, unless descended from a British father, were only British Protected Persons.

the Secretary of State.[1] As a result of the 1947 Commonwealth Conference on Citizenship which Southern Rhodesia attended, it was then accepted that Southern Rhodesia should introduce the Southern Rhodesian Citizenship and British Nationality Act of 1949[2] creating Southern Rhodesian citizenship. All details of the measure were agreed upon between the Southern Rhodesian and British Governments.[3]

The final and most effective restrictions on the Legislature's powers were however imposed by Section 28 of the Letters Patent and by the Royal Instructions to the Governor whereby legislation dealing with certain specified matters was required to be reserved by the Governor unless prior instructions had been given by a Secretary of State or unless such law contained a clause suspending its operation until notice of non-disallowance had been given. These provisions have come to be referred to over the course of time in Southern Rhodesia as the 'reserved clauses', and, as a restraining factor, they considerably affected the nature and details of legislation passed by the Legislative Assembly.[4]

Southern Rhodesian legislation at United Kingdom request

Although the Southern Rhodesian Government was not obliged to comply, from time to time the United Kingdom Government made requests for the introduction of legislation on particular topics and such requests were usually followed by Southern Rhodesian legislation. Indeed in the first year of operation of the responsible government Constitution the Legislative Assembly amended the Native Labour Regulations and the Pass Laws as a direct result of a request by the Secretary of State and the High Commissioner's intervention requiring that the operation of the pre-existing law be investigated and abuses eliminated.[5]

---

[1] *S.R.L.A.D.*, Vol. 30(1), col. 55. In most cases Southern Rhodesia's recommendations were accepted, but they were sometimes rejected. See correspondence in National Archives S11.

[2] Act No. 13 of 1949.

[3] *S.R.L.A.D.*, Vol. 30(1), col. 62. The Minister in charge informed members that all amendments must be timeous in order that the Secretary of State might be cabled for his views and that snap amendments could not be accepted. The Citizenship Act was subsequently amended by Acts No. 42 of 1951 and 63 of 1953. It was repealed by Act 1 of 1958 after the Citizenship of Rhodesia and Nyasaland and British Nationality Act No. 12 of 1957 had been enacted by the Federal Legislature. The latter Act was amended by Federal Acts 13 of 1959, 16 of 1960 and 23 of 1962. In 1963 the Southern Rhodesian Legislature enacted a new Citizenship Act No. 63 of 1963. By virtue of the Federal Laws (Cesser) Order S.R.G.N. No. 786 of 1963 issued in terms of sub-section (2) of Section 2 of the Federation of Rhodesia and Nyasaland (Dissolution) Order in Council 1963 (S.I. 1963/2085) the Federal Act was made no longer applicable to Southern Rhodesia.

[4] See Chapter 12 *infra* for analysis and comment on their operation.

[5] See African 1085, No. 55, referring to High Commissioner's Despatch 381 of 23 February 1922. Reforms had been recommended by the Report of the Native Labour Commission of Enquiry (A 16—1921).

On matters where uniformity of legislation throughout the Empire was required, requests were also made.[1] In other cases Southern Rhodesian legislation might be requested to bring the Southern Rhodesian legislative position into line with international conventions.[2] Alternatively, amendments might be suggested if proposed legislation would conflict with United Kingdom legislation.[3] Legislation might also be requested on currency matters arising out of Southern Rhodesia's membership of the sterling area.[4]

Imperial legislative controls

Quite apart from the considerable powers exercisable by the Imperial Government in respect of legislation that was reserved, there were other methods of exercising control both positive and negative.

Disallowance

A negative power which has been minimized was the Crown's right to disallow any legislation within one year from the date of the Governor's assent thereto[5] which, although it was never invoked, remained part of the

[1] Fugitive Offenders Transit Act 1925 (*S.R.L.A.D.*, Vol. 3, col. 66), Fugitive Offenders Act 1926 (*S.R.L.A.D.*, Vol. 7, col. 25–26), Protection of U.K. Designs Act 1940 (*S.R.L.A.D.*, Vol. 20, col. 199), Coinage and Currency Amendment Act 1942 (*S.R.L.A.D.*, Vol. 22, col. 2061), Southern Rhodesian Citizenship and British Nationality Act 1949 (*S.R.L.A.D.*, Vol. 30(1), col. 62), and Amendment Act 1951 (*S.R.L.A.D.*, Vol. 32(1), col. 2909), Diplomatic Privileges Extension Act 1950 (*S.R.L.A.D.*, Vol. 30(1), col. 2209), General Loans Act 1951 (*S.R.L.A.D.*, Vol. 31(2), col. 2903).

[2] e.g. Native Labour Supply Commission Act 1951 to comply with the Recruiting of Indigenous Workers Convention of 1936, Article 9: public officers were not to be associated with recruiting organizations.

[3] e.g. The Interpretation Act 1930. Section 3 was changed in its passage through the House as a result of United Kingdom objections: *S.R.L.A.D.*, Vol. 9, col. 213. Lord Malvern has indicated privately that when the Legislative Assembly was at the Committee stage of a Bill, cabled requests for amendments would frequently arrive from His Majesty's Government.

[4] If Southern Rhodesia for special reasons wished to depart from British proposals long discussions were necessary: eg. the British Treasury wished Southern Rhodesia to enact an Exchange Control Law prohibiting the taking out of the country of more than £5 currency, any amount in excess to be confiscated. This was resisted by the Southern Rhodesian authorities because of the injustice it would inflict on Africans from Nyasaland or Portuguese territory leaving Southern Rhodesia after working in the country. The limit was then raised to £20. Private communication from Sir Edgar Whitehead. It is convenient to note at this point that United Kingdom legislation, particularly subsidiary legislation on financial matters, affected Southern Rhodesia not in a legal sense but as an economic consequence. United Kingdom changes in Bank Rate, exchange control measures, &c, inevitably had and have repercussions in Southern Rhodesia as a part of the sterling area. Prior to the establishment of the Bank of Rhodesia and Nyasaland (the Central Bank of the Federation), Southern Rhodesia was more directly affected when changes were made. See *S.R.L.A.D.*, Vol. 33 (2) col. 3898, 9 February 1953, Whitehead.

[5] Disallowance was to take effect from the date of its being announced by Governor's message to the Legislature or by Proclamation in the Gazette: Section 31. Such disallowance

Constitution until 1962. In fact, despite attempts by the Southern Rhodesian Government to remove the reserved clauses from 1934 to 1937 Mr. Huggins, then Prime Minister, suggested that disallowance should remain as a safeguard,[1] and, while other 'dead wood' was removed from the Constitution the provisions relating to disallowance were preserved.[2]

On one occasion in 1958 the major opposition party even attempted to persuade the United Kingdom Government to utilize these provisions, by petitioning the Queen to utilize her powers to disallow the Electoral Amendment Act of 1957 which had created a transferable vote system.[3] However, as late as 1960, Sir Edgar Whitehead, then Prime Minister, recognized the legality of disallowance but felt that 'by convention it is not done'. Nonetheless he 'would not feel at all safe for the independence of Southern Rhodesia as long as these restrictions are there'.[4]

Subsequently, when commenting in retrospect on the 1923 Constitution, Sir Edgar Whitehead stated that he had always considered disallowance a reserved power 'for a completely irresponsible act of the Southern Rhodesian Parliament if such a thing had ever been passed and was technically legal', and that he did not feel that there was any convention that disallowance would not be used. In his view disallowance might be threatened if a measure had been obviously discriminatory in its practical effect and was intended so to be, but the wording was non-discriminatory in the legal sense. In addition, in his understanding the British Government had insisted on these provisions remaining after 1937 because legislation might possibly affect British relations with other countries and it might then be necessary to disallow such legislation.[5]

In practice, the power of disallowance was used in conjunction with Section 28 of the Letters Patent to evolve a mechanism of working the reserved

was to be published in the Gazette and enrolled in the office of the Registrar of the High Court: Section 36.

[1] L. H. Gann and M. Gelfand, *Huggins of Rhodesia*, Allen & Unwin, 1964, p. 101. This is an authorized biography, the writers having had access to Lord Malvern's private papers. The former author, as official historian of the three former Federal Territories, was also allowed access to confidential British documents in the Colonial and Commonwealth Relations Offices and Public Records Office, and to confidential documents in the Central African Archives (now National Archives of Southern Rhodesia). The book is an authoritative source for the period in which documents are closed to ordinary researchers.

[2] See Cmd. 5218. Despatch from the Governor of Southern Rhodesia, relating to the Proposed Amendments of the Southern Rhodesia Constitution.

[3] *Rhodesia Herald*, 19 May 1958. Requests for disallowance have also been made from time to time by United Kingdom Members of Parliament. According to Sir Godfrey Huggins such requests were merely directed to the Southern Rhodesian Government for advice. He considered that ever since Southern Rhodesia had been granted a parliamentary form of government, deputations to the Imperial Government 'cut no ice at all. They look to the government of this country for the time being for this sort of advice': *S.R.L.A.D.*, Vol. 31(1), col. 603, 3 May 1950.

[4] *S.R.L.A.D.*, Vol. 44, col. 3050, 1 March 1960.

[5] Personal communication in March 1963.

clauses. The method normally employed when dealing with Bills which came within the ambit of Section 28 of the Letters Patent was to permit the Governor to assent to the legislation which contained a clause that the law should not come into operation pending the signification of the Crown's pleasure not to disallow. In fact, therefore, possible disallowance was used as a substitute for reservation. There is no question, at least in the first decade after the grant of responsible government, of this procedure being considered a mere formality, because legislation assented to and containing such a clause, e.g. the Native Juveniles Act of 1926 and the Native Affairs Act of 1927, was studied carefully by the Imperial Government and lengthy correspondence resulting in administrative undertakings and safeguards ensued before a decision was taken not to disallow the legislation.[1] After any such decision, the Secretary of State would notify the Governor and thereafter the Governor would announce this decision by Proclamation and bring the law into operation.

Indeed, compliance with the procedure was rigorously insisted upon. Thus on two occasions in 1949 difficulties arose. The Constitution Amendment Act of 1948 and the Native Status Determination Act of 1948 provided that the Act should not come into operation until the Governor had declared by Proclamation in the Gazette that it was not His Majesty's pleasure to disallow them, and also that they should come into operation on a date declared by the Governor. The Governor however put these Acts into operation before he received notification of non-disallowance.[2] It was considered essential to correct the error and Proclamations 16 and 17 of 1949 revoked the earlier Proclamation and made the laws come into operation only after His Majesty had declared his pleasure not to disallow the said laws.

This procedure of notifying the Governor that the Crown would not exercise its power of disallowance was extensively used, whether or not the measure was reserved or contained as a suspending clause. Indeed the power of disallowance was actively preserved by virtue of the evolution of this extensive practice of notifying the Southern Rhodesian Government through the Governor that any particular Act would not be disallowed. Thus, for example, in the case of Acts for the Service of the Year, Acts providing for loan funds, Acts providing pensions and gratuities, Acts amending the Income Tax Act, amending the Defence Act, amending the Emergency Powers Act, amending the Electoral Act and the Insurance Act, there were notifications that the Crown would not exercise its powers of disallowance.[3]

In Southern Rhodesia it was generally recognized that a situation justifiably provoking disallowance could have arisen if legislation would have resulted in injury to the rights and remedies of the holders of existing Southern

[1] See *infra*, Chapter 12.
[2] See Proclamations No. 4 and 5 of 1949.
[3] See National Archives S11: S.R. 234 to 238 of 1940; S.R. 4 and 5 of 1940; S.R. 182 and 207 of 1941.

Rhodesian securities.[1] Indeed the Southern Rhodesia General Loans Act, Chapter 123 of 1939, Section 29, specifically provided that amendments to the Act having such effect might be disallowed by the Crown. In 1948 the Minister of Finance, introducing a new Bill, detailed these provisions and stated that in their light he had deemed it 'desirable to submit the draft Bill to the Secretary of State for Commonwealth Relations and ascertain whether any objection would be forthcoming from either the Treasury or the Bank of England'.[2] That disallowance could be used in such circumstances was the opinion of the Select Committee on the Constitution which reported in 1951.[3]

On the other hand, immediately before Federation Sir Godfrey Huggins described disallowance as 'one of these dead letters, a thing that is repeated from constitution to constitution and it would be very difficult to exercise'.[4]

The Secretary of State for Commonwealth Relations, however, recognized the existence of this power in February 1961, when at the Southern Rhodesian Constitutional Conference he informed the Conference 'that he would be prepared to recommend the elimination of the powers retained by the United Kingdom Government, to advise the Sovereign . . . to annul acts already passed' by the Southern Rhodesian Parliament.[5]

From the United Kingdom point of view, although from time to time requests were made for disallowance of specific Southern Rhodesian Acts by Members of the House of Commons, no suggestion was ever made that there was not such a power, nor was mention ever made by any Minister, in refusing such requests, of a convention that the power of disallowance could not be exercised.[6]

---

[1] Cp. Lord Milner's refusal to disallow confiscatory Queensland legislation in 1920: Keith, *Responsible Government in the Dominions*, Vol. II, Oxford, 1928, p. 768.

[2] *S.R.L.A.D.*, Vol. 29, col. 54.

[3] *S.R.L.A.D.*, Vol. 32(1), col. 301. The Committee therefore suggested that the United Kingdom be asked to extend the provisions of the Colonial Stock Act 1934 to Southern Rhodesia and at the same time to remove the section providing for disallowance from the Constitution.

[4] *S.R.L.A.D.*, Vol. 33(2), col. 2645, 23 June 1952. It must be remembered that at this time Sir Godfrey had decided to leave limitations in the Southern Rhodesian Constitution which the Opposition was seeking to remove and to achieve a federation of the British Central African territories instead.

[5] Cmnd. 1291. Report of the Southern Rhodesian Constitutional Conference, Salisbury, Southern Rhodesia, February 1961, § 32.

[6] *H.C. Deb.*, Vol. 631, col. 560, 1 December 1960. Mr. Sandys in refusing disallowance of the Vagrancy Act 1960 said he was 'not satisfied that the circumstances would justify the use of this exceptional constitutional power'. He continued (at col. 561): 'We have certain reserve powers provided for in the Constitution. Clearly however these reserve powers are only intended to be used, and it would be proper only to use them, in the most exceptional circumstances. It would be highly dangerous and highly improper if the British Government were expected to look at every Act passed by the Southern Rhodesian Legislative Assembly and to decide whether in all respects we approved of that legislation. It is only in the most exceptional case that we should use these exceptional powers.' See also Vol. 631, col. 75. 1 December 1960; Vol. 634, col. 166, 10 February 1961, where disallowance of the Law and Order (Maintenance) Act was refused by Mr. Sandys; and Vol. 637, col. 53, 27 April 1961,

Similar powers also existed in respect of legislation of the Federal Legislative Assembly and were considered by the Monckton Commission to be still operative, the Commission however suggesting other safeguards which, if adopted, would make it no longer necessary to retain the power of disallowance.[1] By analogy, the same position must have obtained in respect of Southern Rhodesia.

There is no doubt that the power of disallowance could legally have been used in Southern Rhodesia until 1962 and that it was not excluded by convention. Indeed, although no case of disallowance occurred the provision for this power, particularly as used in conjunction with the reserved clauses, was of great significance in the working of the Constitution. Nonetheless, the use of disallowance could have provoked a political crisis and its enforcement in such circumstances would have been extremely difficult. Applying Keith's description of the power in the Dominions prior to 1926 the power was 'obsolescent' though not 'obsolete'.[2]

Power of the United Kingdom Parliament to legislate for Southern Rhodesia

From the positive aspect the supreme power of the Imperial Parliament to legislate for any part of the Queen's dominions could also be invoked, to make provision, constitutional or otherwise, for Southern Rhodesia. This power was buttressed by the Colonial Laws Validity Act, providing that any colonial law repugnant to an act of the Imperial Parliament extending to the Colony should to the extent of such repugnancy be void and inoperative.[3] In practice, Southern Rhodesian Governments were on several occasions reminded of the existence and effect of the Colonial Laws Validity Act by the United Kingdom Government.[4]

Convention before 1961

Since negative control rather than positive enactment was the usual method of British control over colonies, direct legislation for any colony was unusual

where a similar refusal occurred in respect of the Inter-Territorial Movement of Persons (Control) (Amendment) Act.

[1] Cmnd. 1148. Report of the Advisory Commission on the Review of the Constitution of Rhodesia and Nyasaland, §§ 332-3. The Report clearly envisaged the possibility of this power being used as it refers to 'a twelve months period of uncertainty as to whether or not it (a law) is going to be disallowed'.

[2] Keith, *Responsible Government*, op. cit., Vol. II, p. 758.

[3] 28 & 29 Vict. c. 63, Sections 2 and 3. The Act did not enhance Imperial power: it merely declared which laws of colonial legislatures were to be void for repugnancy and which were not.

[4] Evidence of senior official in the Prime Minister's Office to the 1951 Select Committee on the Constitution.

and only occurred in special constitutional circumstances, e.g. for federating territories,[1] or separating them,[2] or for giving effect to a new constitution,[3] or for matters of general Imperial concern.[4] Indeed the cumbersome method of a United Kingdom Act of Parliament was seldom employed to enact law for colonies—even for those of a more subordinate status than Southern Rhodesia.

Eventually where colonies were self-governing the practice of Imperial consultation with such a colony before the enactment of legislation, which would be applicable there, evolved into a convention that Imperial legislation would not be applied to any Dominion without the request and consent of the Government. On this analogy of the fully self-governing states of its Empire before the Imperial Conference of 1926, the attitude was subsequently[5] adopted that a similar convention applied to the power of the Imperial Parliament to legislate for Southern Rhodesia.[6] It is however doubtful whether the analogy is correct as Southern Rhodesia was prior to 1961 not fully but only partially self-governing.

In fact on one occasion at least legislative provisions were made for Southern Rhodesia without prior agreement of her Government. In 1946 the British Government bound Southern Rhodesia to the Bretton–Woods Agreement without any previous consultation. Although the British Government apologized for this incident and requested the Southern Rhodesian Government to secure the passage of a Bill acceding Southern Rhodesia to the Agreement, and the Bretton–Woods Agreement Bill was introduced, it was subsequently withdrawn as Sir Godfrey Huggins refused to proceed with the measure. As a consequence of these events differences arose between Southern Rhodesia and Great Britain in 1949, when the Southern Rhodesia Gold Subsidy Act of 1948, giving a general subsidy on gold of 27s. 6d. per oz. was objected to by the International Monetary Fund. Southern Rhodesia maintained that she was not bound by the Agreement, but eventually her Government conceded that 'Great Britain has stated that she signed the Agreement on our behalf and therefore we are tied to it'.[7] Thereafter Southern Rhodesian representatives went to Washington to discuss the provisions of the Gold Subsidy Act 1948, and with Canadian co-operation a new basis of

---

[1] The Rhodesia and Nyasaland (Federation) Act 1953, 1 & 2 Eliz. II, c. 30.

[2] The Rhodesia and Nyasaland Act 1963, 11 & 12 Eliz. II, c. 34.

[3] The Southern Rhodesia (Constitution) Act 1961, 10 Eliz. II, c. 2.

[4] Examples of Acts extending to all dependent British possessions are the Official Secrets Acts, the Extradition Acts 1932 and 1935, the Geneva Convention Act 1937. It is doubtful whether the Southern Rhodesian Government was consulted before their enactment.

[5] There was no hint of such an attitude from 1923 to 1932 when two successive Southern Rhodesian Prime Ministers had positively declared that they wished no higher status for Southern Rhodesia. See also Keith, *Responsible Government*, op. cit., Vol. II, p. 1229, where he states that none of the discussions relating to constitutional questions at the 1926 Imperial Conference referred to the position of Southern Rhodesia.

[6] See *Halsbury*, 3rd ed., Vol. 5, p. 549. See also Hood Philips, *Constitutional Law*, 2nd ed., 1957, Sweet & Maxwell, p. 611.

[7] *S.R.L.A.D.*, Vol. 30(1), col. 1593.

17—C.H.L.S.R.

subsidy acceptable to the Fund, to Southern Rhodesia and to Canada was evolved.[1] The Gold Subsidy Act was then amended.

Furthermore, Ministers introducing legislation have from time to time indicated that the fact that the United Kingdom has permitted Southern Rhodesian legislation on topics which should have been governed by United Kingdom Orders in Council is a 'privilege' or a 'courtesy'.[2] In addition Southern Rhodesian Ministers, as well as members of the Opposition, have from time to time acknowledged that Britain had the right to legislate for Southern Rhodesia without consulting the Southern Rhodesian Government. Thus Sir Edgar Whitehead, retailing the Bretton–Woods incident, stated that he considered that there was a convention that would restrain the United Kingdom Government then in office, but that a future United Kingdom Government might legislate for Southern Rhodesia, even though this would, in his view, be a breach of convention.[3] That such a prediction could be made supports the view that there was no convention.

Finally, until the time of the Constitutional Conference in Salisbury in January 1961, no responsible United Kingdom statesman had stated that such a convention existed.[4] It was only some time subsequent to the Conference that Mr. Sandys announced the existence of such a convention. Indeed at the end of the Conference, a report was issued which stated that 'the Southern Rhodesian Government asked that the United Kingdom Government should initiate legislation to provide that, in future, Parliament at Westminster would not legislate for Southern Rhodesia, except at the

[1] *S.R.L.A.D.*, Vol. 29, col. 6. Personal communication from Sir Edgar Whitehead, then Minister of Finance.

[2] e.g. The Minister of Justice in introducing the United Nations Bill 1946. This Act implements the agreement to give effect to Security Council resolutions in terms of Article 41 of the Charter. See *S.R.L.A.D.*, Vol. 26(1), col. 35: 'We are still a colony and in the view of our law officers it would have been possible for the United Kingdom in its Orders in Council dealing with these matters simply to have included the Colony of Southern Rhodesia.' The United Kingdom 'expressly excluded us from the scope of its own Order in Council. It therefore had to request us to pass our own legislation.'

[3] *S.R.L.A.D.*, Vol. 44, col. 3050, 1 March 1960. See also *S.R.L.A.D.*, Vol. 42, col. 3043, 15 April 1959: 'Some future Government of the United Kingdom might be so completely misguided as to legislate in the sense of providing this country with a completely new Electoral Act.'

[4] Jennings, *The Law and the Constitution*, 5th ed., University of London, 1959, pp. 134–5, states how difficult it is to decide whether a convention exists 'since they arise by the gradual crystallization of practice into binding rules . . .. Mere *practice* is insufficient. The fact that an authority has always behaved in a certain way is no warrant for saying that it ought to behave in that way. But if the authority itself and those connected with it believe that they ought to do so, then the convention does exist.' Had circumstances calling for British legislation arisen and the British Government then refrained from enacting legislation on the basis that it was not entitled to do so without the consent of the Southern Rhodesian Government, it would have been clear that such a convention existed. This statement was only extorted from the British Government immediately before the finalization of the White Papers by a threat from Sir Edgar Whitehead that unless the convention was recognized he would abandon all proposed constitutional changes and would continue to work the 1923 Constitution: Personal communication from a confidential source.

request of the Government of Southern Rhodesia, in regard to any matter within the competence of the Legislative Assembly. The Secretary of State for Commonwealth Relations took note of this request without commitment.'[1]

The subsequent White Paper detailing the proposed changes, however, stated that since the conferment of responsible government on Southern Rhodesia 'it has become an established convention for Parliament at Westminster not to legislate for Southern Rhodesia in matters within the competence of the Legislative Assembly of Southern Rhodesia, except with the agreement of the Southern Rhodesian Government'.[2] This declaration was ambiguously worded[3] and did not indicate when the practice coalesced or 'congealed' into the form of a convention. The Attorney-General of the United Kingdom in fact recently declared that the existence of such a convention was 'a situation which was first recognized in 1961'.[4] Until that time, despite statements by learned writers, it cannot therefore be accepted that such a convention had crystallized. Even after the recognition of such a convention, since a number of matters were beyond the competence of the Southern Rhodesian Legislative Assembly, the Imperial Parliament could have legislated on such questions without breach of convention.[5]

It has been suggested that such a convention is directed only to normal legislative acts, viz. the power of legislating for internal matters, and not to constitutional amendments.[6] Even if this view is correct, another convention has evolved to the effect that the Imperial Parliament should not legislate to impose constitutional amendments on self-governing territories if such amendments are within the competence of the Legislature of that territory.[7]

[1] Cmnd. 1148, § 34.

[2] Cmnd. 1399. Southern Rhodesia Constitution, Part I, Summary of Proposed Changes, p. 3.

[3] See *infra*, Part II, Chapter 7.

[4] *H.C. Deb.*, Vol. 681, col. 414–5, 16 July 1963. The Attorney-General intervened to correct the First Secretary, Mr. Butler, who had stated that the convention had existed for forty years. The Attorney-General declared that the First Secretary 'was not quite accurate in saying that the convention had existed for forty years. It arises out of forty years' history and it has coalesced into the formality of a convention much more recently . . .. As from 1961 we in this Parliament have recognized that convention has put us in a situation in which it would not be right for this Parliament to legislate for matters which are within the competence of the Legislature of Southern Rhodesia without the consent of the Southern Rhodesian Parliament.'

[5] e.g. matters specified in Section 26(2) of the Letters Patent, the dissolution of the Federation of Rhodesia and Nyasaland (which affected Southern Rhodesia and which was not desired by the Southern Rhodesian Government). For full discussion see *infra*, Part II, Chapter 7.

[6] This was the argument advanced in respect of the Federal convention entered into in April 1957 and its alleged breach by the Rhodesia and Nyasaland Act 1963 (11 & 12 Eliz. II, c. 34). See the Lord Chancellor's (Lord Dilhorne's) speech in *H.L. Deb.*, Vol. 250, col. 1221, 30 May 1963; see also remarks by the previous Lord Chancellor (Lord Kilmuir), *H.L. Deb.*, Vol. 238, col. 957, 27 March 1962. The Monckton Commission had a similar opinion: Cmnd. 1148, § 335.

[7] See *Halsbury*, 3rd ed., Vol. 5, p. 443, where it is stated that a convention exists that the

Even though Southern Rhodesia was not fully self-governing prior to 1962, she was partially self-governing, and to this extent the convention must have applied to her. On this view, even prior to 1961, the British Parliament could not, without breach of this latter convention, have amended sections of the Southern Rhodesia Constitution which were within the competence of the Southern Rhodesia Legislature. It is, however, difficult to determine precisely, particularly in view of the United Kingdom Attorney-General's remarks, when this convention was considered to have become applicable to Southern Rhodesia.[1]

Power of prerogative legislation by the Crown

Apart from the power of the Imperial Parliament to legislate, since Southern Rhodesia was a conquered colony, the Crown retained the right to legislate insofar as this had not been suspended during their existence by an unreserved grant of representative institutions.[2] The Southern Rhodesia Constitution Letters Patent 1923 in fact specifically reserved[3] to the Crown full power 'from time to time to revoke, alter or amend Sections 26, 28, 39–47, and 55' of the Letters Patent.[4]

Thus the Crown retained power to make such changes as it deemed fit in respect of those matters within the scope of the aforementioned sections. This could be done by prerogative, without any necessity for the passage of an Act of the Imperial Parliament to authorize constitutional amendment by Order in Council. In fact, on eight occasions between 1927 and 1955 amendments were made to the Constitution by further Letters Patent.[5] The Crown therefore enjoyed considerable power to amend the Southern Rhodesian Constitution. Since it had reserved the right to revoke, alter, or amend the grant of legislative power, this provision could have been utilized to withdraw

constitution of self-governing territories will not be amended without their request and consent. This statement should be qualified by reference to the question of competence. See *infra*, Part II, Chapter 7, for full discussion.

[1] *H.C. Deb.*, Vol. 681, cols. 414–15, 16 July 1963. Somewhat earlier the Attorney-General stated that the application of the convention had 'always depended upon the stage of development of self-government which that Colony had reached'. Its application to Southern Rhodesia was recognized in June 1961 and in recent correspondence with the Southern Rhodesian Government: *H.C. Deb.*, Vol. 680, col. 1547, 11 July 1963.

[2] *Sammut* v. *Strickland*, [1932] A.C. 260.

[3] Section 61: inserted in view of *Campbell* v. *Hall*, *supra*. A similar section was involved in *Sammut* v. *Strickland*, *supra*. See also *Abeyesekera* v. *Jayatilake*, *supra*. Cp. *North Charterland Exploration Company* v. *The King*, *supra*, where it was suggested that the rule in *Campbell* v. *Hall* had been abrogated by the Foreign Jurisdiction Acts 1890–1913.

[4] Section 26 related to power to make laws, Section 28 to Bills requiring reservation, Section 39 to 47 to securing the High Commissioner's control over Native Administration, and Section 55 to the Governor's salary.

[5] Letters Patent of the 28 May 1927, 26 March 1930, 27 July 1931, 6 April 1934, 25 March 1937, 14 July 1949, 31 December 1953, and 7 March 1955. These amendments were all made after inter-governmental negotiations at the request of the Southern Rhodesian Government.

all power from the Legislative Assembly.[1] However the Crown could not revoke the entire Constitution[2] and, except insofar as it had reserved such rights, the Crown enjoyed no power of constitutional amendment.[3] For a short period prior to the coming into force of the Southern Rhodesia Constitution on 1 November 1962, the Crown enjoyed even greater powers of amendment as full power and authority was reserved to Her Majesty by Order in Council to amend, add to, or revoke the provisions of the new Constitution at any time prior to its coming into operation.[4]

[1] See Keith, *Responsible Government*, op. cit., p. 359, and also *Sammut v. Strickland*, *supra* at 689, where Keith, as counsel, argued this point. A similar reservation was invoked when the Maltese Constitution was suspended in 1930 by the issue of Letters Patent amending Section 14 of the Maltese Constitution dealing with the power to make laws and conferring powers on the Governor to legislate to preserve peace, order and good government in the island, 'by reason of any grave emergency which the Secretary of State shall be satisfied has arisen therein': Letters Patent of 26 June 1930.

[2] For this parliamentary intervention similar to that in Malta in 1936 would have been required. See the Malta Letters Patent Act (26 Geo. V and 1 Edw. VIII, c. 29).

[3] Unless the legislative institutions established by the Crown either ceased to exist or became incapable of functioning, *Sabally and N'Jie v. H.M. Attorney-General*, [1964] 3 W.L.R. 732 at 743; Wade and Phillips, *Constitutional Law*, 6th ed., Longmans, p. 391. Cp. Sir Kenneth Roberts-Wray's view (op. cit., pp. 17–20) that *Campbell v. Hall* merely laid down, with reference to Letters Patent imposing taxation, that where 'the King had immediately and irrecoverably granted . . . that the subordinate legislation over the island should be exercised by an assembly with the consent of the Governor and Council', then the power of making such subordinate laws could not be withdrawn as long as the institutions continued to function. However, except as so limited, the prerogative power of the Crown would continue and its constituent power would remain.

[4] Southern Rhodesia (Constitution) Order in Council 1961, Section 22.

12

THE RESERVED CLAUSES AND THEIR OPERATION

THE most effective, although negative, method by which the Imperial authorities were enabled to control the details of legislative measures enacted by the Southern Rhodesian Legislative Assembly was the procedure of reservation.

Under Section 28 of the Letters Patent the Governor was commanded to reserve any Bill in dealing with certain matters unless he had either previously obtained instructions from the Secretary of State, or unless such law contained a clause suspending its operation until such time as the King had declared that it was his pleasure not to disallow the legislation in terms of Section 31 of the Letters Patent. A law that was so reserved would lapse after one year from the date of presentment unless the Governor made known either by Message to the Legislative Assembly or by Proclamation that it had received the Royal Assent.[1]

It is apparent, though this was never tested in the Courts, that should the Governor have disregarded this mandate[2] and assented forthwith to any Bill when he should have reserved his assent, such assent would have been a nullity since he was only permitted to assent 'subject to this Constitution and any instructions in that behalf given to him'.[3]

Those Bills which the Governor was, under Section 28, duty bound either to reserve, or to assent to only after advance consent or if the Bill contained a suspending clause, were

(a) any law 'whereby natives may be subject or made liable to any conditions, disabilities, or restrictions, to which persons of European descent are not also

[1] Section 32. On several occasions prior to 1930, e.g. the Land Apportionment Bill of 1929, Southern Rhodesian Governments became concerned about the possible lapse of reserved Bills subjected to long delays before a final decision by the British Government.

[2] Both Sections 28 and 27 provide that 'the Governor shall reserve' and that he 'shall declare ... subject to this Constitution ... that he reserves the law for the signification of our pleasure'.

[3] Section 27. See Keith, *Responsible Government*, op. cit., Vol. II, p. 783, who takes this view. The matter was raised in the pre-Federation debates when the then Minister of Internal Affairs gave it as his view that such legislation would be null and void although English legal opinion to the contrary had been taken: *S.R.L.A.D.*, Vol. 33(2), col. 4107. One of the arguments advanced in favour of the African Affairs Board proposed under the Federal Constitution in comparison with the reserved clauses was that the Courts would have no testing power in respect of Federal legislation whereas they had such power in respect of Southern Rhodesian legislation. However, when such legislation was tested the onus of proving that an Act should have been reserved would have rested on any applicant seeking to upset the law: *City of Salisbury* v. *Mehta*, 1962 (1) S.A. 675 (S.R.) per Beadle C.J. at 678.

subjected or made liable' other than laws regulating the supply of arms, ammunition or liquor[1];

(b) any law amending those provisions of the Constitution which the Legislature was competent to enact;

(c) any law establishing the proposed Legislative Council;

(d) any law altering or amending the arrangements in force at the time of granting the new Constitution relating to mining revenue or imposing any special taxation on minerals in or under land in the Colony;

(e) any law dealing with railways within the Colony until legislation had been passed adopting with necessary modifications the United Kingdom law dealing with Railway and Canal Commissioners and the Rates Tribunal provided for in the Railways Act, 1921.

The purpose of reservation (d) was to protect the considerable financial interests of the British South Africa Company in respect of mineral rights, which the United Kingdom Government always considered as being the reward to the Company for the great risks undertaken by it in running Southern Rhodesia for so many years. Reservation (e) was similarly intended to protect the Railway Companies (subsidiaries of the British South Africa Company) from confiscatory and oppressive legislation and to secure the fair regulation of their charges having regard both to the need for development of the country and a just return on the capital employed by shareholders.[2]

Reservations (b) and (c) secured that all constitutional amendments should be scrutinized by the Imperial authorities.[3] But the most significant provision from the point of view of the largely unenfranchised African population was that the Imperial Government retained a power of veto through reservation (a) over discriminatory legislation.

Further reservations were imposed by the Governor's Instructions[4]: the Governor was not to assent, unless he had previously obtained instructions, or the law contained a clause suspending its operation, to any law

[1] This section applied only insofar as laws discriminated against Africans, but not against Asians or Coloureds. It had been suggested by Stanley, the India Office and the local Asian community that they be similarly protected, but such provision was not made in the Letters Patent. The leader of the Responsible Government Movement, who subsequently became the first Prime Minister, was, however, prepared to accept 'two authorities' in the case of Native Affairs: *S.R.L.A.D.*, Vol. 2, cols. 5 and 8.

[2] The Secretary of State insisted on this after representations by the Company. See *B.S.A. Co. Report of Extraordinary General Meeting*, 28 July 1922, p. 6. See also Cmd. 1573, § 7, which suggests that the Mineral Reservation was granted because the Privy Council had stated that the mineral rights were connected with the absence of provision for remuneration to the Company for administrative services, and also because the Cave Commission had proposed that they be allocated the mining royalties. § 8 states that the Railway Reservation was inserted because of the heavy financial obligations undertaken by the Companies, and the absence of a code of railway legislation. See also *S.R.L.A.D.*, Vol. 3 (1925), col. 546.

[3] Cf. Sir Edgar Whitehead's remarks in 1961: 'There is one power that we never had in the past, and that is the power to amend our own Constitution without getting the approval of London': *S.R.L.A.D.*, Vol. 47, col. 5905, 20 June 1961.

[4] Royal Instructions of 25 August 1923, given on 1 September.

dealing with divorce, making any grant of land, money or other donation to himself, affecting the currency of the Colony, imposing differential duties, appearing to His Majesty's Government inconsistent with United Kingdom treaty obligations, or of an extraordinary nature or importance whereby the Royal Prerogative or the rights of British subjects non-resident in the Colony, or British trade or shipping might be prejudiced, or containing provisions which had previously been refused or disallowed.[1] However, disregard of these instructions would not have resulted in invalidity as in the case of the instructions to reserve incorporated in the Letters Patent.[2]

Attitudes towards the reserved clauses

Estimates of the value of the reserved clauses have varied considerably depending largely on the political objectives of the speaker in making the particular speech. Thus, the first Prime Minister of Southern Rhodesia, Sir Charles Coghlan, referred to them as 'shackles'.[3] From the opposite extreme, Sir Godfrey Huggins in 1951 described them as 'not being worth the paper they were written on'.[4] On the other hand, Sir Edgar Whitehead in 1960 considered their removal a 'top priority'[5] and that he 'would not feel at all safe for the independence of Southern Rhodesia as long as these restrictions are there'.[6]

Wider world awareness of events in Southern Rhodesia in the last decade also altered the attitude adopted towards the reservations. Thus, Sir Edgar Whitehead in 1960 pointed to the very great changes which had come over Africa since 1952 and to the fact that the United Kingdom Government had begun to attach 'great importance' to the reservations.[7] Although the Prime Minister considered that such reservations in the days preceding the Second World War were not troublesome when there were no 'delegations flying home and trying to complain about their own government to another government', he felt in 1960 that misunderstandings which could 'lead to very serious trouble' were possible unless the reservations were removed.[8]

Many factors influenced the significance of the reservations at any point of

---

[1] Clause 7 of the Royal Instructions.   [2] Colonial Laws Validity Act, Section 4.
   [3] *S.R.L.A.D.*, Vol. 5, col. 1744—a speech made when the Southern Rhodesian Government was having difficulty in negotiating the Railway Act of 1926.
   [4] Speech to the Matabeleland Executive of the United Party, 16 July 1951—made at a time when in order to achieve closer union with Northern Rhodesia it was essential to leave the reservations in the Constitution.
   [5] *S.R.L.A.D.*, Vol. 45, col. 239, 6 July 1960—made when he was negotiating with the British Government for the elimination of its reserve powers in Southern Rhodesia.
   [6] *S.R.L.A.D.*, Vol. 44, col. 3050, 1 March 1960.
   [7] *S.R.L.A.D.*, Vol. 44, col. 3050, 1 March 1960.
   [8] *S.R.L.A.D.*, Vol. 45, cols. 239–41, 6 July 1960. How quickly attitudes changed between 1958 and 1960 is shown by Sir Edgar's confident statement in 1958 that he could 'not imagine that any concession will be required in exchange for removal of the reservations': *S.R.L.A.D.*, Vol. 41, col. 404, 23 July 1958.

time. Initially in the first years of responsible government Bills affecting the Railways' financial interests or mining royalties were subject to greater scrutiny and consultation with affected British interests than legislation with other purposes in view. This was the case partly because British Governments were concerned to protect British investors but more because the degree of co-ordination and similarity between general Imperial policy towards African dependent territories and local Southern Rhodesian policy towards Africans was at that time significant: in the nineteen-twenties Southern Rhodesian African policy was considered to be enlightened by the senior permanent officials of the Dominions office.[1] What in the nineteen-sixties appears highly discriminatory legislation was not in the conditions obtaining at that time considered objectionable.[2] Even in the nineteen-thirties although divergence in policy between Southern Rhodesia and the Colonial Office territories to the north was becoming more apparent, Southern Rhodesian Africans had larger sums of Government money spent on their education, health services, and agricultural development than those in the Northern Territories.[3] Labour policy rather than land policy was the major differentiating factor.[4] Thereafter the intervention of the war years obscured concern with the affairs of dependent territories. In any event at such a time there was no desire to make extensive changes.

[1] National Archives NE 1/1/7, Newton (High Commissioner) to Moffat, 7 December 1929, relative to the Native Affairs Act and the Native Juveniles Employment Act: 'I cannot understand why Olivier and those who are with him should be holding us up as a horrid example when really our native legislation and administration is worthy of all praise. And that is the opinion of the Dominions Office.' The Secretary of State in defending this Southern Rhodesian legislation has made out 'almost a better case than we did': National Archives NE 1/1/7, 8 May 1928.

[2] Thus although the Land Apportionment Act was intended in large measure to protect European land ownership it could nonetheless be described as an 'essay in trusteeship' in respect of the African people. See L. H. Gann, 'The Southern Rhodesia Land Apportionment Act 1930: an essay in trusteeship'. The National Archives, Occasional Papers, No. 1, June 1963, Government Printer, Salisbury.

[3] See Cmd. 5949. See also National Archives S 235/482, Confidential Report by Lord Hailey on Southern Rhodesia, 1941. The latter is more critical, but it acknowledges (at p. 28) the growing recognition by the white population of the natives' integral part in the life of the Colony and the increasing attention to measures for the betterment of the material and health conditions of the Reserves and other native areas. In 1950 the Southern Rhodesian Minister of Native Affairs had a comparative survey of Southern and Northern Rhodesian legislation prepared. This showed that Northern Rhodesian legislation was more stringent than Southern Rhodesian legislation (e.g. no Africans enjoyed the franchise in Northern Rhodesia at that time). The Colonial Office policy of that period was to delegate extensive powers to Governors and other officials on the spot. It was prepared to permit such delegations if it was itself in control, but was critical if Southern Rhodesian officials exercised similar powers.

[4] The Industrial Conciliation Act 1934 in the conditions obtaining at that time when there were few African artisans and little African trade union activity was not seriously discriminatory. Had the Africans been brought under the provisions of the Act throughout Southern Rhodesia and minimum wage agreements applied to them, the African artisan class could not have developed as rapidly as it has done. Even in 1965 European contractors and artisans complain that Africans escape the provisions of the now non-racial Act by doing work

Yet another very considerable factor was the personality of the Prime Minister in office. Sir Godfrey Huggins, from 1941 onwards, enjoyed the confidence of the Imperial authorities. Indeed it was obvious from 1944 that he had changed his views on the desirability of segregation between the races and had begun by stages to implement a policy designed to lead to stabilization of the African population in urban areas, at the same time adjusting those in rural areas to an agricultural revolution.[1]

His legislation and that of his successors was clearly tending in the direction of easing discrimination and aiming towards an integrated society.[2] The Imperial authorities were not in these circumstances prepared to cause difficulties, which might result in the electorate of Southern Rhodesia selecting a Prime Minister with different aims.[3] In fact Sir Edgar Whitehead claims that he had no trouble with the Imperial authorities on his land legislation since all his amendments were in the direction of relaxing the Land Apportionment Act.[4]

Also important was the relationship between the Governor and the local Prime Minister,[5] as early Governors' views on proposed legislation were virtually automatically accepted by the Imperial authorities.[6]

at cut-rates on contract terms thus not being 'employees' and therefore not subject to the Act. From other points of view, however—ability to organize trade unions, &c.—the Act became progressively more discriminatory in effect until its re-enactment in 1959. Even as re-enacted Sections 47 and 48 provide that control of unions should be in the hands of the skilled workers, i.e. in practice the European members. Northern Rhodesian labour legislation has never discriminated in this way.

[1] See R. Gray, *Two Nations*, Oxford, 1960, pp. 279 et seq. Although Sir Godfrey had originally believed in a policy of segregation he modified his views when in office: thus he ultimately promised there would be integration of African and European workers in a mixed society: see *Statement on Native Policy in Southern Rhodesia* by the Hon. Sir G. M. Huggins, Salisbury, Government Printer, 1941. Huggins frequently visited England to discuss reserved matters with the Secretary of State. He revealed in a personal communication in November 1962 that: 'I regarded the Constitution as a gentleman's agreement and we both had to try to be gentlemen.' Huggins' co-operativeness during the war years also modified the Imperial attitude. In Sir Edgar Whitehead's estimation (personal communication) the United Kingdom Government permitted the Southern Rhodesian Government to act freely during most of the period when Huggins was in office and this continued until 1953 when he was translated to the Federal sphere. The same situation obtained during the latter part of Sir Edgar's own premiership from 1959 to 1962.

[2] Sir Godfrey was succeeded by Mr. R. S. Garfield Todd (1953–58) and Sir Edgar Whitehead (1958–62). This trend was reversed on 14 December 1962, when the Rhodesian Front won the General Election of that date, but British powers under the reserved clauses had by then disappeared.

[3] A Commonwealth Relations Office official commented in a personal communication: 'Half a loaf was better than no bread'.

[4] Personal communication.

[5] Sir Edgar considers that Sir Herbert Stanley asked 'for more on behalf of the Southern Rhodesian Prime Minister than he ever did on behalf of the British Government'. Personal communication. Two distinguished ex-Governors in personal communications have indicated how essential it was to maintain close relations with the Prime Minister and that they would have considered that they had failed in their duties had they not been able to maintain such a relationship.

[6] Sir John Chancellor (1924–28), Sir Cecil Rodwell (1928–32), and Sir Herbert Stanley

Another factor affecting the British attitude was the establishment in 1951 of the United Kingdom High Commission in Salisbury when the Governor lost his functions as political representative of the Secretary of State. From this time the Commission meticulously scrutinized proposed measures, discussed them with responsible Ministers and wrote voluminous reports on them, particularly on their legal aspects.[1]

Another factor from 1953 onwards was that Britain became concerned that Federation should be successfully implemented.[2] Care was therefore taken not to antagonize the Southern Rhodesian Government by adopting an intransigent attitude to measures which required British approval.

It is also clear that the political complexion of the Government in power in Britain played some part in the policies adopted towards Southern Rhodesia.[3] In addition, world attention was not at this time focused on Southern Rhodesia. Indeed until 1961 her name was merely raised on odd occasions at the United Nations Organization.[4] This lack of publicity encouraged Britain to allow the Southern Rhodesian Government to have its head.

Effectiveness of the reservations

The effectiveness of the reservations can be analysed on a series of levels. They operated as a psychological barrier to the introduction of legislation which might be refused by the Imperial authorities as the reservations had to be taken into account by any Government when it attempted to formulate its policies.[5] Thus Southern Rhodesian Governments might tentatively

(1933–41) played a great part in smoothing the way for local legislation. Before the introduction of air communications this was even more noticeable. In Sir Edgar's view the United Kingdom Government greatly relied on the Governor's opinion, and if he considered a measure was acceptable they would agree to it despite the fact that it might contain provisions of which they did not really approve.

[1] Personal communication from Sir Edgar Whitehead.

[2] One day, the permanent officials thought, liberalizing influences from the north would affect Southern Rhodesia through the Federal Legislative Assembly.

[3] Both Lord Malvern and Sir Edgar Whitehead state that their relations with the Labour Government, 1945–51, were excellent. Contra S.R.L.A.D., Vol. 17, 11 October 1937, for fears of events when a Labour Government might be in office and S.R.L.A.D., Vol. 43, col. 863, 29 July 1959, Sir Edgar Whitehead referring to the possibility of difficulties 'if our bitter enemies' become the Government of the United Kingdom.

[4] In 1953 the United Nations Economic and Social Council and the International Labour Office appointed an Ad Hoc Committee on Forced Labour which at pp. 109–10 and 578–80 commented on the Southern Rhodesia Native Land Husbandry Act, Section 51, but did not report on the measure as it did 'not at present constitute an important element in the economy of the territory'. See Report of the Ad Hoc Committee on Forced Labour, Geneva 1953.

[5] See S.R.L.A.D., Vol. 17, col. 1593, where the Leader of the Opposition quoted Mr. Huggins' desire 'that it would be infinitely better for us, with our experience of dealing with the native, that instead of having to fine him or place him in gaol we should be allowed to administer corporal punishment'. He then concluded by stating that the Prime Minister well knew such legislation would not obtain Imperial consent.

enquire from the Imperial Government whether legislation to implement a particular policy would be permissible. A refusal at this stage would preclude even the production of a draft.[1] Even if a draft Bill were prepared its contents were subject to scrutiny by the Imperial authorities, often involving considerable delay,[2] while the final Bill as presented to Parliament had frequently been considerably modified at the suggestion of the Commonwealth Relations Office.[3] Indeed, the Bill as presented to the Legislative Assembly was virtually sacrosanct and the Legislature was competent only to make minor amendments which did not affect the principle. Finally, the Bill as passed was subject to further scrutiny, and its coming into operation was delayed by the Commonwealth Relations Office until eventual notice was given that it was not the Crown's pleasure that the law be disallowed.

The reservations as a barrier to legislation

As a psychological barrier the reservations were undoubtedly effective.[4] Numerous statements were made from 1923 to 1962 indicating that the reservations were a discouragement to the introduction of legislation which might possibly cause a clash between the Southern Rhodesian and United Kingdom Governments. Thus 'all native policy had to be considered in its impact on the United Kingdom Government'.[5]

Even ordinary members of the Legislature felt that the reservations barred the type of proposal they would otherwise have made.[6] Indeed the governing party might well reject a proposed measure on the basis that it would not receive Imperial assent.[7] Alternatively Government might be hesitant and

[1] Mr. Creech Jones, former Labour Colonial Secretary, considered the reservations 'invaluable' and that after negotiations with Lord Malvern 'certain things which Lord Malvern had proposed were not carried out simply because those powers existed': *H.C. Deb.*, Vol. 642, col. 1811, 22 June 1961.

[2] e.g. The Natives Registration Bill 1936. See *S.R.L.A.D.*, Vol. 16, col. 583. This was 'in the making for two years'. The Native Land Husbandry Act 1951 was in preparation from 1948. The Minister responsible regretted in 1950 that it could not be introduced that year 'for reasons over which I have no control': *S.R.L.A.D.*, Vol. 31(2).

[3] *H.C. Deb.*, Vol. 681, col. 415–16, 16 July 1963, Mr. Griffiths, former Secretary of State for the Colonies. The laws were usually made less discriminatory: *H.C. Deb.*, Vol. 648, col. 1288, 10 November 1961, Creech Jones.

[4] *S.R.L.A.D.*, Vol. 17, col. 1580, 11 October 1937, Huggins: 'While the reservations are there naturally there are certain people who will have to think a little harder before they wish to introduce differential legislation.'

[5] Lord Malvern in a personal communication in November 1962. For Mr. Creech Jones' view that the reservations were 'a check and restraint' see *H.C. Deb.*, Vol. 648, col. 1288, 10 November 1961.

[6] See *S.R.L.A.D.*, Vol. 7, col. 1601, 11 October 1937: 'They act on the minds of every single honourable member before any single Bill is introduced'; and also *S.R.L.A.D.*, Vol. 28, col. 1350, referring to the 'artificial atmosphere' in a House where there was 'responsibility without full authority and . . . full authority without responsibility' in the Imperial Government.

[7] In 1940 the Minister of Agriculture proposed an amendment to the Maize Control Act that Africans be limited to 10 per cent of the pool but this was rejected by his party.

delay the introduction of the measure for several years.[1] When introduced measures were usually of a temperate character.[2] As the Select Committee on the Constitution said in its 1951 Report[3] 'the reservations have been a restraining influence during the period when the people of the Colony were learning to conduct their own affairs'.

Southern Rhodesian Governments also kept watch on the course of events in Northern Rhodesia and Nyasaland and from study of events in these territories were able to gauge what the British Government would permit in Southern Rhodesia.[4] There is no doubt that the reservations 'made the Government very much more careful what they introduced'.[5]

Indeed on several occasions the British Government actively indicated that it would not permit particular legislation. These occasions in the main related to preservation of African franchise rights. Early in 1928 Mr. H. U. Moffat, the Southern Rhodesian Prime Minister, suggested the creation of special African representation in the Legislative Assembly to the Governor, who warned him of the reception he would receive.[6] When the Electoral Bill of 1928 was introduced the property qualification was therefore instead raised to property worth £500 (in view of the impending acquisition by Africans of ownership of individual native purchase area farms).[7] However,

[1] The Native Preachers' Bill was first proposed in 1924. It was then discussed at Cabinet in 1926 (see National Archives LE 3/2/1/1 and 2, Cabinet Resolutions). It was reconsidered in 1927 and again in 1929 and 1930 (National Archives S 138/226 Minute by Prime Minister of 2 May 1929) but it was only printed for introduction in 1936. In respect of this Bill the Southern Rhodesian Government was very conscious of Britain's power. When originally proposed the Attorney-General suggested that since the Bill would be reserved it should be placed before the Southern Rhodesian Missionary Conference for endorsement 'as a precautionary measure': National Archives S 138/106, Attorney-General to the Secretary for the Prime Minister, 16 April 1924. When the Conference rejected the measure it was decided not to proceed with it at that stage.

[2] National Archives DO 1/1/6, Moffat to Downie, 9 February 1933, re Native Passes Consolidation Ordinance Amendment Act: 'The legislation is really very harmless. We have purposely made it so with the desire to avoid embarrassing the Dominions Office.'

[3] S.R.L.A. Votes and Proceedings, Vol. XXXVI, p. 28.

[4] Lord Malvern in a personal communication.

[5] Sir Edgar Whitehead in a personal communication in March 1963. See also National Archives, Leggate Papers, Cabinet Minute No. 718, 5 January 1928, in which the Cabinet refused a request from the Bulawayo Town Council for 'powers to enable the Town Council to prohibit Native Taxi Drivers'.

[6] Personal communication from a confidential source. The Governor stated that these proposals would introduce a racial element in politics, and attract the attention of negrophiles to Southern Rhodesia. The Chief Native Commissioner also warned him that it would be 'bad faith' to abrogate the native franchise in the first parliament: National Archives S 138/10, Chief Native Commissioner to Minister of Native Affairs, 2 June 1928. Nonetheless Moffat wrote in 1929 that he wished to follow Hertzog's policy in South Africa but could not raise the question at present as it would 'put the Secretary of State in a difficulty' and make removal of the reservations more difficult. In any event there were then under fifty Africans on the rolls: National Archives NE 1/1/7 MSS, 6 May 1929, Moffat to Newton. In 1928 there were sixty-two African voters, and 22,000 European voters: S.R.L.A.D., Vol. 7, col. 224.

[7] A.B. 10 of 1928. See S.R.L.A.D., Vol. 7, col. 221, 22 May 1928, for this explanation of

after United Kingdom expressions of opinion, the Prime Minister moved an amendment in the House restoring the qualifications to the original value of £150.[1] Subsequently in 1932 after considerable Legislative Assembly pressure for legislation closing the voters' rolls to further African registration,[2] the Prime Minister, Mr. Moffat, asked the British Government whether they would assent to such legislation.[3] His proposals were rejected,[4] but in 1933 he accepted a motion in the Legislative Assembly for special representation for Africans in place of the franchise.

Similar proposals were put forward by Mr. Huggins (as he then was), Southern Rhodesia's next Prime Minister, when he visited the Dominions Office with the Chief Native Commissioner, Colonel Carbutt, on 23 July 1934.[5] These proposals were likewise rejected.[6] Again in 1936 Mr. Huggins

the motive by the Southern Rhodesian Prime Minister. The Land Apportionment Act was then being negotiated and one of its consequences would be to make such farms available to Africans.

[1] See Electoral Act No. 23 of 1928. For United Kingdom comments see *H.C. Deb.*, Vol. 219, col. 2730–3, 30 July 1928, where Mr. Amery said this had been done and that raising of the franchise qualifications would be a matter for discussion between the Governments if such proposals were made.

[2] In the ensuing debate the Prime Minister had declined to take action: *S.R.L.A.D.*, Vol. 10, col. 1976, 13 May 1931. There were then about 40 African voters and 27,000 European voters and the Prime Minister felt that this request would embarrass the Imperial Government 'as they might have very strong pressure brought to bear on them to refuse to agree to our legislation'. See also Vol. 12, col. 1018, 26 April 1932, where suggestions that the South African pattern as advocated by Hertzog of two representatives and the creation of a Senate with special representatives should be followed were made. See also National Archives LE 3/2/1/1–4 Cabinet Resolutions Nos. 356, 365, 517, 760, 2150, and 2410.

[3] See National Archives DO 1/1/6, Moffat to Downie, 25 April 1932, asking for an interview with the Secretary of State on this point. See also National Archives LE 3/1/1, Moffat to Leggate, 16 August 1932. The Cabinet resolved that the Prime Minister should discuss the franchise in respect of native women 'with a view to ascertaining the probable attitude of the Dominions Office': National Archives LE 3/2/1/5 Cabinet Resolution 2504 of 1 June 1932.

[4] *S.R.L.A.D.*, Vol. 13, cols. 523–4, 20 April 1933: 'I got no definite undertaking or promise.' The Prime Minister did not reply to accusations that his request had been refused. See cols. 741–2.

[5] *Huggins of Rhodesia*, by L. H. Gann and M. Gelfand, Allen & Unwin, 1964, pp. 100–1. For Huggins' views see *S.R.L.A.D.*, Vol. 14, cols. 530–6, 24 April 1934, and also *S.R.L.A.D.* Vol. 13, col. 508 et seq., 26 April 1933, where he moved a motion that there should be no further enrolment of African voters. In 1931 he had also suggested that Africans be debarred from voting: *S.R.L.A.D.*, Vol. 10, cols. 379–80, 8 April 1931—in a motion that there should be territorial segregation of the races. Huggins' views on separate areas and the native franchise and that he was putting them to the Imperial Government appear from 'Southern Rhodesia, Recent Progress and Development', Address by G. M. Huggins, 18 July 1934, Empire Parliamentary Association, London, pp. 12–13 and 18.

[6] Colonel Carbutt, the Chief Native Commissioner, supported by Huggins, had ideas for the creation of a large white dominion in Central Africa, the area south of the Zambezi to be exclusively white and the Northern Rhodesia copper belt to be added to this area. These proposals and others for the restriction of African opportunities in trade and cash crop farming and the movement of African populations were all proposed at the same time to the Dominions Office and rejected. Some of Colonel Carbutt's ideas are printed in an article, 'The Racial Problem in Southern Rhodesia', C. L. Carbutt, *NADA*, No. 12, 1934, p. 6.

suggested in London that the franchise be closed for the purposes of further African enrolment. This was again rejected.[1]

Nonetheless, closure of the franchise to Africans remained government policy.[2] Even in 1947 proposals were made by Sir Godfrey Huggins that Africans should be debarred from the common roll and be compensated by the appointment of two Europeans representing African interests in the Legislative Assembly.[3] According to his biographers the need for this induced Sir Godfrey to hold the 1948 Southern Rhodesian election.[4] Ultimately, although Huggins' party won the 1948 election on this plank, the policy was not implemented as, in 1949, Imperial officials discouraged him, while in 1950 as a concession to gain Federation, he dropped these proposals, writing to the Minister of Justice, Mr. Beadle, in London to request instead the raising of property and wage qualifications.[5]

When still Superintendent of Natives, Carbutt had suggested that abolition of the native franchise be dealt with at the same time as the Land Commission but was warned that this might prejudice reception of the Commission's recommendations. See National Archives S 138/10, 14 August 1926, Superintendent of Natives, Victoria, to Chief Native Commissioner. See also Gann and Gelfand, op. cit., pp. 99 and 116.

[1] Personal communication from a confidential source. Lord Malvern in 1962 did not recollect this, but did not deny the possibility. By 1939 there were 24,626 Southern Rhodesian electors of whom thirty-nine only were African: Cmd. 5949, p. 15.

[2] In 1944 Huggins suggested special representation by two Europeans: *S.R.L.A.D.*, Vol. 24, col. 2807, 30 November 1944.

[3] See *S.R.L.A.D.*, Vol. 27(1), col. 1163, 27 May 1947, where Sir Godfrey Huggins moved an amendment to a motion for enlargement of the Legislative Assembly to 40 members suggesting that 'two of the additional members shall be chosen to represent native interests and that in order to prevent exploitation of immature African voters, legislation be introduced to prevent the further enrolment of Africans on the Common Voters' Roll, but without removing those who are already registered'. According to a Cabinet Minister the Prime Minister had that year discussed the matter with the British Government: *S.R.L.A.D.*, Vol. 27(1), col. 1187. With foresight Sir Godfrey noted how important it was to do this 'without creating a further uproar in UNO in regard to the way the British Empire treats its dependent peoples': col. 1165. A similar suggestion, but putting a twenty-year time period for non-registration of Africans was made in February 1947: see report of a meeting between Huggins and the Fabian Colonial Bureau attended by Lord Addison, Labour Secretary of State for the Dominions, *Rhodesia Herald*, 8 February 1947. In June 1947 a question was asked in the Commons as a result of Huggins' motion quoted above urging the United Kingdom to disallow any change in the electoral law which would deprive Africans of their present right to be admitted under certain conditions to the Voters' Roll: *H.C. Deb.*, Vol. 439, col. 28–29, 23 June 1947. Earlier in 1941 Sir Godfrey Huggins had asked Mr. Tredgold to sound out African opinion on the introduction of special representatives and the closure of the voting rolls. This proposal was unacceptable to Africans and no further action was then taken: personal communication from Sir Robert Tredgold. Subsequently Sir Godfrey suggested special African representatives and the present Chief Justice, Sir Hugh Beadle, then a Parliamentary Secretary, suggested closing the roll to Africans: *S.R.L.A.D.*, Vol. 24, col. 2611, 27 November 1944.

[4] Gann and Gelfand, op. cit., pp. 203–4. He wanted a clear majority in favour of his proposals to close the roll to further African enrolment, and to increase the membership of the House to forty, two of the members being selected to look after African interests. According to Huggins, there were then only 136 Africans on the roll, but 6,000 were eligible should they have chosen to register.

[5] Gann and Gelfand, op. cit., p. 217.

As a result, after approval of this policy change by his Party Congress, the Electoral Amendment Act 1951 was passed. This was intended to 'raise both the means and educational qualifications' and to restrict the native from coming on to the roll, but not to exclude him 'entirely'.[1] Indeed there was during the passage of the legislation a back-bench revolt in which seven members stated that the Government had succumbed to world and UNO pressures.[2] There is no doubt that these attitudes had been strongly conveyed to the Government by the Imperial authorities and that it is because of the reserved clauses that the African franchise survives in Southern Rhodesia today.[3]

Draft legislation rejected

In other cases specific draft Bills were put before the Imperial authorities and even these were occasionally withdrawn. Thus a Bill entitled The Prevention of Unrest Among Natives Bill was discussed at Cabinet in 1927 and 1928.[4] Thereafter when the Secretary of State objected to certain of its provisions the Bill was allowed to lapse as it had already been introduced into the Assembly.[5] In 1931 the Bill was brought to Cabinet again and printed for publication.[6] Thereafter the Governor, the High Commissioner, and the Secretary of State took exception to its provisions.[7] When the Governor informed the Cabinet that the Imperial authorities were dissatisfied, and that he would, when the Bill was reserved, give an unfavourable report on it[8] the Bill was withdrawn.[9] Subsequently the Governor discussed and suggested

---

[1] *S.R.L.A.D.*, Vol. 31(2), cols. 3161 and 3295, Minister of Internal Affairs. The income qualifications were raised from £100 p.a. to £240 p.a., the property qualifications from £150 to £500, and ability to speak and write the English language became necessary.

[2] *S.R.L.A.D.*, Vol. 31(2), cols. 3169 et seq. Both the Prime Minister and the Minister of Internal Affairs said that they were not prepared to embarrass Britain at the United Nations Organization.

[3] It is somewhat ironical to read Cmd. 8235, § 9. Central Territories: Comparative Survey of Native Policy. This survey, because of its favourable comments on Southern Rhodesia's native policy, made Federation possible. In it commendatory references are made to the Prime Minister of Southern Rhodesia's 'determination . . . to maintain the Legislative Assembly's Common Voters' Roll on which today there are some 420 Africans registered on equal terms with Europeans as voters'. The survey referred to the fact that there must be some thousands of Africans with full qualifications who have not registered as voters. They were subsequently prevented from doing so by the Electoral Amendment Act 1951 soon after the survey was written.

[4] National Archives LE 3/2/1/2, Cabinet Resolutions Nos. 517 and 545.

[5] It was printed as The Prevention of Unrest Bill 1928. A.B. 7A of 1928. See National Archives RO 7/1/1. This was revealed in 1932 in correspondence between the Governor and the Secretary of State.

[6] National Archives LE 3/2/1/4 MSS, 6 November 1931.

[7] National Archives RO 7/1/1 MSS, High Commissioner to Rodwell, 21 January 1932, and Rodwell to Stanley, 26 January 1932, describing the Bill as 'unduly and unnecessarily drastic'.

[8] National Archives RO 7/1/1 MSS, Rodwell to Attorney-General, 1 February 1932.

[9] National Archives RO 7/1/1 MSS, Rodwell to Stanley, 19 February 1932.

amendments to the draft succeeding, with the assistance of the Chief Native Commissioner, in making the Bill penalize Europeans who inflamed feelings against Africans as well as *vice versa* and making it no longer an offence merely to possess prohibited literature. Penalties were also reduced.[1] On the Governor's suggestion the Bill was re-named The Prevention of Racial Discord Bill. Despite these modifications the measure was ultimately abandoned.

Similarly the Native Preachers' Bill of 1936 encountered considerable opposition from the Imperial authorities. This Bill which would have drastically interfered with religious freedom of Africans was printed but not introduced into the Legislative Assembly. It provided 'for the control of fanatical and ostensibly religious movements among natives by the issue of certificates to native preachers and teachers'. All African preachers had to register as such with the Chief Native Commissioner subject to the approval of the Governor. If any African who did not hold a certificate, in the presence of an assembly of three or more Africans, conducted any service or gave any instruction purporting to be or resembling a religious service or instruction, he was to be guilty of an offence and liable to three months' imprisonment or a fine of £25.[2] The Secretary of State objected to the measure,[3] as did some members of the governing party caucus[4] and the measure was therefore not proceeded with. Soon afterwards the Sedition Act 1936 was enacted. Mr. Huggins informed the Legislative Assembly that most of the objects aimed at in the Preachers' Bill would be attained under Clause 9 of this Act (which was couched in non-discriminatory language). That it had been substituted for the Native Preachers' Bill was made obvious by the Labour Party Opposition, which declared that the Sedition Bill replaced the Preachers' Bill 'that he was forced to withdraw' and was merely 'a native Bill with a little camouflage'.[5]

Although Lord Malvern has stated that he has never prepared a Bill which the Imperial Government has vetoed,[6] he acknowledges that his legislative proposals were subject to modification, amendment, and compromise.

---

[1] National Archives RO 7/1/1 MSS, Rodwell to Harding, 1 March 1932. In this letter the Governor commented to Sir Edward Harding how much more easily the Imperial authorities were satisfied in 1928. Had he informed his Ministers what the Secretary of State would then have permitted he would not now have obtained such concessions. L. S. Amery was Secretary of State in 1928.

[2] A.B. 7 of 1936. Available only in the S.R. Legislative Assembly Archives.

[3] Personal communication from Mr. J. A. Edwards, Official Historian of Southern Rhodesia from 1933 to 1953.

[4] Personal communication from Sir Robert Tredgold.

[5] *S.R.L.A.D.*, Vol. 16(1), col. 3065. The Labour Party was at that time a white artisans' party and was not pro-African: see Leys, op. cit., p. 181. Lord Malvern cannot now remember but does not deny that the Preachers' Bill may have been dropped because of United Kingdom opposition.

[6] This takes no account of the Native Preachers' Bill 1936. In addition Sir Edgar Whitehead has stated that prior to his Prime Ministership a Bill was 'withdrawn and never introduced into this House on account of the Secretary of State's objections': *S.R.L.A.D.*, Vol. 47, col. 6007, 21 June 1961.

However, Lord Malvern covered himself by saying that he may have been convinced by the Imperial authorities that he was wrong and that they were right, although he never withdrew a Bill which he considered necessary.[1] Indeed in the pre-Federation debates Lord Malvern stated that the 'procedure allows the Government to decide to withdraw the offending measure, if they consider it advisable, and no more is heard of it'.[2] More recently he stated that he would discuss matters 'with the Secretary of State and try and find out what the attitude of the British Government was likely to be and then having heard that I made up my mind what was the best thing to do'.[3]

Advance consultation and modifications

None of the occasions on which Britain exercised her powers of control are generally known. In fact it is often inaccurately stated that the reserved clauses were of little value since no Bill which was reserved was ever refused assent.[4] This is a most misleading statement because, although no Bill was refused assent, the reserved clauses were extensively used in conjunction with 'a gentleman's agreement'[5] between the Imperial and Southern Rhodesian Governments.

The agreement was to the effect that all Bills which it was proposed to introduce into the Legislative Assembly should be submitted in draft through the Governor to the Secretary of State for his approval. The suggestion originated from Sir Francis Newton[6] who proposed to the Prime Minister, Sir Charles Coghlan, that this procedure should be adopted and that it would be found that reservation was 'no barrier to legislation merely a safeguard'.[7] On this basis all details were thrashed out privately between the Governments

[1] Personal communication. My understanding of Lord Malvern's statement was that on occasions he changed his mind and withdrew proposals in the light of United Kingdom advice. If the Secretary of State put up a good case against the measure Lord Malvern might be convinced that the objections were correct.

[2] *S.R.L.A.D.*, Vol. 33(2), col. 2645.

[3] Personal communication, October 1962.

[4] e.g. *H.C. Deb.*, Vol. 668, col. 1066, 3 December 1962, Butler: 'The British reserve powers have never been used since they were introduced in 1923.' Such a bare statement although technically correct is entirely misleading. See also col. 969. In 1950 a relatively senior official at the Commonwealth Relations Office, the late G. H. Baxter, indicated to the Acting-Governor that a particular measure would not receive assent if it were proceeded with. This angered the S.R. cabinet which had, before the arrival of this letter, decided to drop the measure. Personal communication from a confidential source.

[5] Lord Malvern's phrase in a personal communication in October 1962.

[6] Sir Francis was the Southern Rhodesian Government representative in London and had formerly been Treasurer to the British South African Company and leader of the Company's nominees in the Legislative Assembly. He was also a member of the Executive Council during Company rule. He was familiar with the procedure whereby draft Ordinances were submitted for prior scrutiny to the High Commissioner during the period of Company rule.

[7] National Archives CO 8/1/2, Newton to Coghlan, 25 October 1923.

and Bills as introduced in the Legislature were agreed measures.[1] Even if a Bill was not within the ambit of the reserved clauses there was consultation between the Governments and suggestions by Her Majesty's Government to minimize any discriminatory effects.[2] Lord Malvern always consulted the Imperial authorities on any matter 'likely to cause a stir among the races'.[3]

The procedure of advance consultation was that Bills would first be drafted by the Southern Rhodesian draftsman, thereafter such Bills would be approved by the Southern Rhodesian Cabinet.[4] After Cabinet approval the draft Bill would be discussed with the Governor and agreement reached. Modifications might well be made at this stage as a result of the Governor's views. Indeed the Governor might even be consulted at an earlier stage and on at least one occasion during the late nineteen-forties suggestions made by the Governor, Sir John Kennedy, and the Chief Justice, Sir Robert Tredgold, in his capacity as a member of the Board of Trustees for the Native Reserves, resulted in the withdrawal of a provision which would have prevented Africans from remaining in Southern Rhodesia's urban areas by forcing them to return to the Reserves if after six months they had not obtained employment.[5] Invariably Governor and Cabinet would reach agreement as a spirit of compromise prevailed.

Thereafter, the Cabinet would resolve to forward the measure and explanatory memoranda[6] through the Governor's office to the Secretary of State.[7] At the same time copies were sent to the High Commissioner for South Africa when the United Kingdom Government would consult him for his views.[8] Alternatively, the Southern Rhodesian Prime Minister or Cabinet Ministers

[1] Lord Malvern Commented in 1962: 'no Bill that had not been agreed ever saw the light of day in Southern Rhodesia'.

[2] Personal communication by United Kingdom official.

[3] Personal communication from Lord Malvern.

[4] See National Archives LE 3/2/1/4, Cabinet Resolutions 1835 and 2045.

[5] Personal communication from Sir John Kennedy, Sir Robert Tredgold, and Mr. W. A. E. Winterton, then Minister of Native Affairs. In Sir Robert's view the Bill would have introduced a form of apartheid and resulted in a breakdown in the carrying capacity of the Reserves which would have been overloaded with Africans repatriated from the urban areas.

[6] These were often very lengthy. See e.g. the memoranda on the Native Juveniles Employment Bill 1926, National Archives S 138/255.

[7] After 1951 it was forwarded through the High Commissioner. The 1951 Select Committee on the Constitution reported at this time that the Governor would raise any queries or make such suggestions as he saw fit: *S.R.L.A.D.*, Vol. 31(2), col. 300, 19 April 1951. See also *S.R.L.A.D.*, Vol. 17, col. 1623, 12 October 1937, and *S.R.L.A.D.*, Vol. 33(2), col. 2640, 23 June 1952.

[8] See National Archives S 138/55, J. H. Thomas to Governor, 31 July 1931, informing the Southern Rhodesian Government that after consultation with the High Commissioner, Her Majesty's Government would assent to Section 47 of the Letters Patent dealing with Native Councils. See also National Archives S 235/382, High Commissioner to Governor, 2 November 1935, acknowledging draft Native Pass Consolidation Bill and copies of despatches to the Secretary of State.

would have to pay visits to London to explain to the United Kingdom authorities the purport and effect of the proposed legislation.[1] As Lord Malvern commented on this process shortly before Federation: 'We had to start off arguing with London.'[2]

During this two-way process of consultation Southern Rhodesia would attempt to influence United Kingdom attitudes and *vice versa*.[3] In examining Southern Rhodesian legislation permanent officials were, in the early years, more important than the Secretaries of State.[4] Nonetheless Civil Servants had to consider the views of the House of Commons in making arrangements with Southern Rhodesia.[5] They also took into consideration the views of various organizations that took particular interest in Southern Rhodesian affairs and were prepared to pass legislation if such organizations did not object.[6] According to Lord Malvern and Sir Edgar Whitehead the Imperial authorities were always anxious to reach a compromise and this was possible owing to the private nature of the negotiations.

[1] This happened frequently in Lord Malvern's regime, e.g. 1934, 1935, 1936, and 1937 visits secured the passage of much reserved legislation. A 1944 visit to attend the Commonwealth Prime Ministers' Conference also secured further reserved legislation. Sir Edgar Whitehead had to do the same thing. Similarly in 1932, Mr. H. U. Moffat discussed railway legislation, mineral rights, the closure of the rolls to further African voters, and consolidated Pass Laws. In 1926 Sir Charles Coghlan had discussed the proposed Land Apportionment Act and the Railways Act 1927.

[2] *S.R.L.A.D.*, Vol. 33(2), col. 2646. It was always a good argument that there was similar legislation in another British dependent territory. National Archives MO 13/1/1 Hudson, the Attorney-General, to Moffat, 18 August 1932 and 31 August 1932, with reference to the Native Passes Consolidation Ordinances Amendment Act of 1933—Kenya also permitted the endorsement of registration certificates with particulars of sex crimes.

[3] The influence of Whitehall and Westminster must have been considerable. As a senior British Civil Servant privately commented: 'No one can emerge from Westminster unscathed.'

[4] National Archives MO 13/1/1, Moffat to Leggate, 15 August 1932, which states that J. H. Thomas knew little about the subject: 'Harding is the man who counts.' Lord Malvern confirmed that Sir Edward Harding was 'the arbiter rather than the Secretary of State' in a recent personal communication.

[5] One of Lord Malvern's racy anecdotes best illustrates this: 'One of the things that had intrigued me in my negotiations in the early days with the United Kingdom Government was that after having had a session with the permanent head of the Department in the morning he took me to lunch at the Club and during conversation there he said: "I hope, Mr. Huggins, you do not think that any of our decisions are made on the political implications in this country." "I would like to believe that", I told him, "but twice this morning you particularly told me you would never get it past the House of Commons."'

[6] Again Lord Malvern's own words best illustrate the Imperial attitude and the informal method of negotiations: 'When I wished to amend the Industrial Conciliation Act so as to have a workable system in the event of a strike by Europeans and to make provision for African workers, I informed the Secretary of State of course. I told him they must be paid the same as a European otherwise they would become strike-breakers. My reason for wanting this amendment was to make the Bill practicable and I said "after all you can say it is equal pay for equal work—who can object to that?" But of course the Secretary of State's obvious come-back was that this would exclude the African from getting a job at all! So I said: "Well, it will hold them up I quite agree, but I can tell you what: I am going to have tea with the Aborigines Protection Society tomorrow afternoon, and I will put it up to them and see what they have got to say." So he said: "Oh, well, if they have no objection I will

There is no doubt that in this process of consultation draft Bills were subject to considerable modifications.[1] Thus, Lord Malvern could say in respect of the Native Registration Act 1936: 'It has been watered down during the last twelve months almost to vanishing point.'[2] Similarly, the Maize Control Amendment Act 1934 was a compromise between allowing African maize producers a free market and complete exclusion from the European pool.[3]

Sometimes conditions were imposed. Thus, after a long correspondence, the Municipal Amendment Act 1940 allowing segregation on municipal buses was permitted on condition that equal facilities were provided for all races.[4] On other occasions it was also necessary to agree with the Secretary of State on the proposed regulations that would be issued when the Bill was enacted.[5] Before 1937 the High Commissioner for South Africa would also submit proposals for amendment which were sometimes accepted.[6]

In any event all proposed legislation that came within the scope of the reserved clauses was subjected to considerable delays before it could even be introduced into the Legislative Assembly. A notable instance was the Land Apportionment Act 1930, which was first discussed in 1926. More recently, the Native Land Husbandry Act 1951 started as a Native Reserves

withdraw my objections." So I had my tea party with them and they thought it was marvellous. Equal rights for all civilized men in Rhodes's dictum—they thought it was a splendid suggestion! I went back the next day and saw the Secretary of State and said: "The idiots fell for it." "Oh", he said, "All right, get on with it."' Personal communication, November 1962.

[1] In 1934 the Minister responsible for the Industrial Conciliation Act 1934 said that the decision to exclude Africans from the conciliation process had necessitated the following of 'a hard road': *S.R.L.A.D.*, Vol. 14, col. 1282, 9 May 1934. Bills were 'quite substantially amended': *S.R.L.A.D.*, Vol. 47, col. 6007, 21 June 1961, Whitehead. Sir John Kennedy has stated that during his period as Governor many Bills were amended at the suggestion of the Commonwealth Relations Office. Personal communication, 17 February 1965.

[2] *S.R.L.A.D.*, Vol. 16, col. 588, 2 April 1936.

[3] *S.R.L.A.D.*, Vol. 14, col. 1438, 11 May 1934, Mr. Huggins: 'If Honourable Members insist that the Board shall not be allowed to receive maize direct from the native, I regret to say that I am quite satisfied that this Bill will not receive the assent of the Secretary of State. That is putting it plainly.'

[4] Personal communication from Lord Malvern.

[5] Native Urban Areas Accommodation and Registration Act, No. 6 of 1946. See *S.R.L.A.D.*, Vol. 25(2), col. 3078, 16 January 1946. This Act has been described as highly discriminatory and was recently indicated as an example of legislation which the reserved clauses as utilized by the Labour Government in the United Kingdom were unable to affect. In fact, in the conditions prevailing at that time the Act was a step forward: it provided for the first institutions of urban African local government—the Native Advisory Boards; it forced employers to provide free accommodation for their employees and one wife; and it was an implied acknowledgement of the permanency of African residence in urban areas.

[6] Section 16 of the Native Reserves Forest Produce Act (Chapter 93 of 1939) was amended on the High Commissioner's suggestion while it was a Bill receiving Cabinet consideration: National Archives LE 3/2/1/3, Cabinet Resolution 1140, 30 May 1929. The High Commissioner's views were taken into account and changes made in 1932 to the Prevention of Racial Discord Bill: National Archives RO 7/1/1.

Land Utilization and Good Husbandry Bill in 1948.[1] Even during the last phases of the 1923 Constitution, the average delay before Bills could be introduced was four months.[2]

This procedure fully explains the fact that there was no need to refuse consent to any reserved Bill from 1923 to 1962. As the Chairman of the Select Committee on the Constitution said in 1951: 'In this manner any awkward points are either removed or explained away long before the Bill goes before the House.'[3]

Passage of reserved measures through the Legislature

Since all Bills within the scope of the reserved clauses were agreed measures, such Bills could not be amended in the course of their passage through the Legislative Assembly: any modifications could only be minor and even these required approval by the Secretary of State. Indeed on numerous occasions the House was warned by Ministers responsible for reserved measures that, if they persisted with amendments, the Bill would not receive assent.[4] Such threats to pass legislation unamended were, quite apart from Imperial promptings, also employed by Sir Godfrey Huggins to secure the passage of legislation he desired.[5] On the other hand the Government would refuse to accept amendments which would turn a Bill into a reserved measure.[6] Should

[1] See *S.R.L.A.D.*, Vol. 31(2), col. 50, and *S.R.L.A.D.*, Vol. 32(1), col. 51, where the responsible Minister announced what 'a lot of comment in circles overseas' had been occasioned by the Bill. Mr. Winterton, in a personal communication in August 1964, has stated that lengthy negotiations occurred with the Commonwealth Relations Office and that modifications in the Bill were made as a result.

[2] Personal communication from Sir Edgar Whitehead relative to the period from 1958 to 1962.

[3] *S.R.L.A.D.*, Vol. 31(2), col. 300, 19 April 1951.

[4] The Railways Act 1926 (*S.R.L.A.D.*, Vol. 4, col. 1351); The Land Apportionment Act 1930 (*S.R.L.A.D.*, Vol. 8, col. 92); The Industrial Conciliation Act 1934 (*S.R.L.A.D.*, Vol. 14, col. 1309–10); The Maize Control Act 1934 (*S.R.L.A.D.*, Vol. 14, col. 1436—the effect of the proposed amendments wanted by members of the governing party would have been to exclude Africans from any share in the Maize Pool); The Industrial Conciliation Amendment Act 1937 (*S.R.L.A.D.*, Vol. 17, col. 241—the effect of the amendment would have been to permit the exclusion of African artisans from all peri-urban areas and not merely the small municipal areas); The Native Law and Courts Act 1937 (*S.R.L.A.D.*, Vol. 17, col. 2498); the Railways Amendment Act 1941 (*S.R.L.A.D.*, Vol. 21(2), cols. 2324 and 2498); the Land Apportionment Amendment Act 1949 (*S.R.L.A.D.*, Vol. 30(1), col. 2408—the effect would have been to have denied Africans permanency of tenure in urban African areas).

[5] Personal communications from Lord Malvern and Sir Edgar Whitehead. Lord Malvern used this device frequently to dissuade his Party from introducing legislation he disapproved: 'I loved the reservations in the Constitution because I could always use them when necessary and if I had made up my own mind a thing was right and I was having trouble, I could always say the Imperial Government would not have it.'

[6] e.g. The State Lotteries Act 1935; see *S.R.L.A.D.*, Vol. 15, cols. 720, 725 et seq. In fact the United Kingdom Government were then cabled and agreed that Africans could be excluded from State Lotteries in order to prevent them from the dangers of extensive gambling. This disability was only removed by the State Lotteries Amendment Act No. 30 of 1959. This was also illustrated by the passage of the Southern Rhodesia Citizenship

amendments be made the Prime Minister would adjourn the debate before the Report stage as this would be 'courteous to the Secretary of State'.[1]   In fact the procedure utilized by both Sir Godfrey Huggins and Sir Edgar Whitehead has been described by Sir Edgar:

We always carried on the system of the agreed measure. We used in the caucus meetings to tell our own caucus exactly what had been agreed and the points that couldn't be altered because of the agreement, and the reasons for it. We would make sure of our majority before we took even a first reading, so that although Parliament still had the right to amend the Bill we would always know that we had a majority if we didn't want it altered. If an amendment was introduced by one of the other members, we would assess pretty accurately whether the amendment would be acceptable to the United Kingdom Government. We used usually then to put a thing all the way down the Order Paper so it wouldn't be reached for a day or two and discuss it with the United Kingdom High Commissioner.[2] Then he would get clearance by telegram so that an amendment could be accepted, unless it was something we knew the United Kingdom Government would not accept.[3]

Further delays

Once a Bill that was a reserved measure had passed through the Legislative Assembly there were still further considerable delays before such Bill received assent, or alternatively, if it had received assent but with a clause suspending its operation, before the Crown's pleasure not to disallow was signified. Each Bill as passed was accompanied by a memorandum by the Law Officers and even sometimes by the Governor [4] explaining any amendments made to the Bill during its passage through the Legislative Assembly.[5] Delay might

and British Nationality Act No. 13 of 1949. Sections 9(2)(e) and 19(2)(c) provided that an applicant for naturalization or registration must 'have become assimilated with the community of the colony'. A request to insert in place the requirement that the applicant be European was refused as this would make it a reserved measure. 'In any event', said the Minister of Justice, Mr. Beadle, this was 'an extremely useful provision' as 'we have people of the coloured races applying for citizenship who might be able to comply with most of the other requirements but who might not have identified themselves with and adjusted themselves to the life of the country and we are able to turn them down on these grounds': *S.R.L.A.D.* Vol. 30(1), col. 68, 1856. (The present Southern Rhodesia Citizenship and British Nationality Act No. 63 of 1963 does not contain such a restriction but immigration of non-Europeans other than as recruited labourers is almost impossible because under Section 5(1)(a) of the Federal Immigration Act No. 37 of 1954, still in force in Southern Rhodesia, the Minister of Internal Affairs may deem persons to be prohibited immigrants on economic grounds or on account of their standard or habits of life as unsuited for the requirements of the country. A general deeming order was issued by the Federal Minister responsible in respect of all non-Europeans and has not yet been revoked by the Southern Rhodesian Minister.)

[1] *S.R.L.A.D.*, Vol. 26(2), col. 1726–7, 25 July 1946.

[2] Prior to 1951 the procedure was to go through the Governor.

[3] Personal communication from Sir Edgar Whitehead.

[4] See National Archives S 138/55, Rodwell to Passfield, 26 April 1930, on the Native Tax Act 1930.

[5] See e.g. Memorandum on the Native Marriages Ordinance 1917 Amendment Bill 1927: National Archives S 138/10.

also be occasioned by representations then made to the Secretary of State[1] who would seek explanations from the Southern Rhodesian Government. After long memoranda by the Chief Native Commissioner or the Cabinet, final agreement would then be given.

Assurances sought by the Imperial Government

In at least one notable instance the Secretary of State agreed to signify that the Crown did not intend to disallow the measure—there was a clause suspending its operation until such notification—but extracted considerable concessions from the Southern Rhodesian Government before so doing, despite the fact that before objections to the Bill had been made he had expressed no disagreement with the measure. In 1926 the Native Juveniles Employment Act regulating the employment of African juveniles was passed. Exception was taken in the House of Commons,[2] in the United Kingdom press, and by influential societies to the provisions for whipping juveniles and power of Native Commissioners to enter into labour contracts on their behalf. Considerable correspondence passed between the United Kingdom and Southern Rhodesian Governments, the United Kingdom Government enquiring what the Southern Rhodesian Government intended to do in the matter.[3] After consultations between the Premier and the Governor, the Southern Rhodesian Government made it clear that it would not permit juveniles under the age of ten years to be employed and gave administrative instructions to all Native Commissioners to this effect.[4] Furthermore, the Southern Rhodesian Government gave an undertaking that no whipping should take place except in the presence of a Native Commissioner[5] and that a report on each case would be sent forthwith to the Attorney-General. Native Commissioners were also required to report on working conditions of children in their annual reports. Only after these assurances and administrative steps implementing them had been taken was the Secretary of State prepared to notify the Crown's pleasure not to disallow the Act.

Similar difficulties occurred with the Native Affairs Act of 1927 but in this case the Imperial Government was satisfied that the safeguards were adequate,

[1] e.g. in respect of the Native Marriages Ordinance Amendment Bill made by the Archbishop of Canterbury.
[2] See H.C. Deb., Vol. 64, col. 562, 23 June 1926.
[3] National Archives S 138/255, Secretary of State to Governor, 20 December 1927.
[4] Under the Act there was no age limit. The Governor also assured the Secretary of State that there were no abuses: National Archives S 138/255 MSS for full correspondence and Cabinet minutes. The Secretary of State required to be assured that there was no 'slave' child labour on the Southern Rhodesian mica fields. See also Cmd. 3076. Papers relative to the Southern Rhodesia Native Juveniles Employment Act 1926, and the Southern Rhodesia Native Affairs Act 1927 which publishes part of this correspondence.
[5] To ensure moderation in its administration: Section 2(4) of the Act did not require this safeguard whereas Section 10 in certain circumstances did.

both at the time of the original clearance and when later agitation against the Act occurred.[1] Nonetheless, 'very careful consideration'[2] was given whether to disallow the measure and long correspondence ensued. The consequence was that the Southern Rhodesian Government was meticulous in enforcing all the safeguards to which it had pointed in obtaining eventual Imperial agreement.[3]

This procedure was still in effect in 1959 when Sir Edgar Whitehead complained to Parliament that it was apparent 'from recent unfortunate experience that a matter being a reserved measure quite often has delayed legislation up to six months. It is extremely annoying for Parliament.'[4]

It is impossible to produce accurate comparisons of the relative delay in assent as between reserved and unreserved legislation because, in many instances, assent to unreserved legislation was also delayed either for the purpose of preparing regulations[5] to be published simultaneously with promulgation, or for political reasons such as the desire to delay the implementation of legislation.[6] Certain significant features do however emerge, as the average delay between third reading and gazetting of a non-reserved measure was four weeks, although it was considerably longer in the case of reserved measures despite the vetting process to which they had already been subject.

Certain conclusions can tentatively be drawn from Table A. Firstly, delays in excess of the period needed for transmission of the measure as finally passed, retransmission of an assent by the Commonwealth Relations Office and subsequent gazetting occurred. The Table also shows that, after the War when the Labour Government was in office in the United Kingdom, the period of delay considerably increased,[7] whereas in the period immediately

[1] In any event the Act did not make far-reaching changes in existing laws as the Premier was doubtful whether such changes would have been approved: National Archives S 138/260, Coghlan to Attorney-General, Minute 1013/1927, 5 February 1927. Already in draft the Bill was amended to preserve the right of appeal to the High Court so that the Secretary of State would assent: Attorney-General to Prime Minister, 2 April 1927.

[2] Cmd. 3076, pp. 73–74.

[3] National Archives S 138/260, Circular Letter from Chief Native Commissioner to all Native Department Stations, 7 May 1928. This instructed Native Commissioners that all cases under Section 17 of the Act (sentences by a Native Commissioner of an African for contempt to himself) were to be reviewed by the Chief Native Commissioner and that every accused was to be informed of his rights of appeal to the High Court and a certificate to be given that this had been done. In addition the hope was expressed that Native Commissioners would give suspended sentences (this had been the burden of the Secretary of State's reply to the Aborigines Protection Society: Cmd. 3076).

[4] S.R.L.A.D., Vol. 44, col. 2221, 21 October 1959.

[5] e.g. The Firearms Amendment Act No. 14 of 1961.

[6] e.g. Employers' Levy Act No. 19 of 1958. This legislation was eventually repealed without ever having been put into operation: see Act 47 of 1960. The Public Services Act 1944 was assented to but only put into operation in 1950. This is a practice open to considerable abuse.

[7] In personal communications Sir Edgar Whitehead and Lord Malvern maintain that they had no difficulty in obtaining assent to their legislation from the Labour Government

TABLE A

Delays in gazetting of reserved legislation

Year	Interval from third reading to gazetting [1]	
	Reserved measures Average period	Non-reserved measures Approximate average period
1924	110 days (excluding Railway Enquiry Act delayed 6½ months)	4 weeks
1937	49 days	
1941	72 days	
1944	80 days	4 weeks
1948	106 days	4 weeks
1949	138 days	4 weeks
1950	147 days	4 weeks
1953	71 days	4 weeks
1954	75 days	4 weeks
1955	72 days	4 weeks
1956	49 days (one measure only involved)	4 weeks
1958	150 days	1 month
1959	98 days	1 month
1961	54 days	1 month

[1] This Table was prepared from information in the Southern Rhodesian Legislative Assembly Votes and Proceedings which do not consistently show dates of assent. Date of gazetting has therefore been used instead. The years relate to volumes of the Southern Rhodesian Statutes and therefore in some cases do not always represent legislation initiated in a particular year, legislation sometimes being included which had its third reading in the preceding year.

after the establishment of Federation when a Conservative Government was in office, the delays diminished. Finally, in the year in which a 'palace revolution' occurred in the governing party, causing the resignation of Mr. Todd and his replacement as Prime Minister by Sir Edgar Whitehead, there were very lengthy delays before reserved measures were put into operation.[1]

and did not notice any delay. Sir Edgar's view is that it was the establishment of the United Kingdom's High Commissioner Office in Salisbury in 1951, which made exhaustive enquiries and reports bringing up legal points, that caused delays. He considered measures were held up by lawyers not by Ministers. His hypothesis is not however brought out by the figures, see 1954–6, where there were relatively short delays. That the Labour Party did have considerable effect on Southern Rhodesia is clear from remarks made by Mr. Drysdale on the authority of Mr. Creech Jones: see H.C. Deb., Vol. 642, col. 1811, 22 June 1961. Mr. Creech Jones considered that 'his negotiations with Lord Malvern were indeed very helpful' and that as a result certain things which Lord Malvern had proposed were not carried out.

[1] The Native Councils Act 1957 and the Natives (Registration and Identification) Act 1957, both making considerable changes in the law, were delayed for seven and ten months respectively, the latter only being assented to after Sir Edgar had been Prime Minister for four months. There might also be a delay if the measure was not originally reserved as seems to have been the case in respect of the Natural Resources Amendment Act 1950, which was delayed six months. Only at the third reading was it pointed out to Government that the measure should have been reserved.

Advance assent in place of reservation

It is apparent from the nature of much Southern Rhodesian legislation that, although Bills did not recite that the necessary assent had been received, advantage was taken of the constitutional provision under which it was possible to obtain the instructions of His Majesty's Government upon a Bill before it was introduced in the Legislative Assembly. This was done in respect of the Constitution Letters Patent Amendment Act 1925[1] and the Public Services Economy Act 1931.[2] Indeed from 1927 to 1932 this seems to have frequently been done, while on at least three occasions in the years immediately preceding the 1961 Constitution, the Imperial Government instructed the Governor in advance to assent to legislation, as there were differences between the Southern Rhodesian and United Kingdom Governments as to whether such legislation came within the ambit of the reserved clauses.[3] The justification for this was that in the event of a disagreement of the Governments, the validity of the legislation could only be decided by the Courts, and ultimately the Privy Council, which would have involved long delay, and that therefore the Governor should be instructed to assent in advance when the Southern Rhodesian Government urgently required such a measure. In fact, the genesis of the arrangements in the new Constitution of 1961 occurred when the United Kingdom Attorney-General and the Southern Rhodesian Attorney-General disagreed as to whether a certain trivial measure was discriminatory or not.[4] As a compromise the Governor was ordered to give his immediate assent. Had an attempt been made to declare such a law invalid on the ground that the proper procedure had not been observed, the

[1] See *S.R.L.A.D.*, Vol. 3, col. 38. This Act deleted Section 22(2) of the Letters Patent which provided that Members of Parliament who entered into contracts with the Crown must vacate their seats.

[2] Sections 38 and 56 of the Constitution were temporarily suspended. Judges and Civil Servants had their salaries reduced by ten per cent: *S.R.L.A.D.*, Vol. 11, col. 99–100.

[3] Personal communication from Sir Edgar Whitehead. I am also informed by a confidential source that the Preventive Detention Act No. 39 of 1959 was assented to on this basis, there being a dispute between the Governments as to whether it should be reserved or not. Such method of agreement would be convenient to any British Government which could then reject pleas to intervene by Members of Parliament of the United Kingdom on the grounds that such matters were not within the competence of the Secretary of State. Official correspondence for this period is not available. From *S.R.L.A.D.*, Vol. 42, col. 2974, 3 April 1959, it is clear that the Prime Minister, Sir Edgar Whitehead, discussed with the Secretary of State for Commonwealth Relations the problem whether the 1959 'Emergency Legislation' should be reserved or not. *H.C. Deb.*, Vol. 607, col. 1361, 25 June 1959 (and also Vol. 602, col. 165, 26 March 1959) confirms that there were consultations between the Governments which could not be disclosed on the Unlawful Organizations Act and the Preventive Detention Act. When earlier requested to exercise British reserve powers in respect of the Preventive Detention Act, the Secretary of State was able to inform the House that the Preventive Detention Bill as first introduced had been withdrawn: *H.C. Deb.*, Vol. 602, col. 111, 24 March 1959. Subsequently another Bill, which ultimately became the Act, was introduced. This provided for a review tribunal, whereas in the former Bill the Legislative Assembly had been the reviewing body.

[4] Personal communication from Sir Edgar Whitehead.

presumption of regularity would have applied and the onus would have rested on the person challenging the law to show that the Governor had not received prior Royal Instructions.[1] Furthermore, the onus of proving that the measure was discriminatory and thus *ultra vires* would rest on the applicant seeking to set it aside.[2]

The scope of Section 28(a)

It could also be argued that legislation which would in its practical application have a discriminatory effect, and not merely overt discriminatory legislation came within the ambit of Section 28(a).[3] This was maintained from time to time by various Imperial Governments and equally disputed by Southern Rhodesian Governments.[4] As a consequence when the Federal Constitution was drafted, this point was made clear in dealing with the African Affairs Board which had the duty of reporting on legislative measures which differentiated against Africans, or which would in their 'practical application have such an effect'.[5]

In any event the degree of disability, which would have brought legislation within the ambit of Section 28(a) was relatively slight as 'tangible discrimination' was not necessary and 'intangible discrimination' was sufficient.[6] In practice, however, since the working of the reserved clauses and Section 28(a) in particular had become the subject of this 'gentleman's agreement', such disputes never assumed great importance. As Sir Godfrey Huggins pointed out in 1952 'the exact form of the reservations in the Constitution is of no

[1] Keith, *Responsible Government*, op. cit., Vol. II, p. 758.

[2] *R. v. Campbell (Pvt.) Ltd.*, 1956 (1) S.A. 256 (S.R.) per Murray C.J. at 259.

[3] Since the criterion was whether 'persons of European descent are ... *subjected* or *made liable*'. From the use of the passive form and the past tense, viz. the use of the words 'subjected' and 'made', actual application is indicated, whereas the use of the words 'subject' and 'liable' alone would not have indicated actual enforcement. From this language it can be inferred that laws which in effect would be applied against Africans and not against Europeans would come within the scope of Section 28(a).

[4] In interviewing Sir Edgar Whitehead on this point, he maintained that the British Government only adopted this attitude after Federation. When he became Prime Minister in 1958, the United Kingdom Government conceded after many precedents were quoted that there must be 'actual legal discrimination' before any Bill had to be reserved. See Sir Godfrey Huggins' similar attitude: *S.R.L.A.D.*, Vol. 33(2), col. 264, 23 June 1953. But Lord Malvern has privately informed me that there would be advance consultation on any measure which would 'cause a stir among the races'. See also Mr. Amery's attitude that raising of the franchise qualification which would in effect exclude Africans was a matter for discussion between the Governments: *H.C. Deb.*, Vol. 219, col. 2733, 30 July 1928. Sir Edgar Whitehead was forced to argue this point in respect of the 1959 Emergency legislation with the Secretary of State who was on a visit to Southern Rhodesia: see *S.R.L.A.D.*, Vol. 42, cols. 2974 and 3032, also mentioning liquor legislation.

[5] S.I. 1199/1952 Annex, Article 71(2).

[6] Per Beadle C.J. in *Mehta* v. *City of Salisbury*, *supra* at p. 678. In discussing this problem and the meaning of discrimination, tangible, and intangible, Beadle C.J. relied on *Brown* v. *Board of Education, Topeka*, 1953, 98 L.Ed. 873, and other American decisions.

great importance . . . what does matter is the way in which they are used by the two Governments concerned'.[1] If in fact the procedure was invoked and Imperial consent obtained, the Legislature was fully entitled to enact laws bringing about discrimination and to enable subordinate bodies to legislate or to act in a manner involving racial discrimination.[2] Various Southern Rhodesian Governments took little chance that legislation would be invalidated for lack of consent: 'the Southern Rhodesian Legislature has always been particularly sensitive to this type of legislation, and where there has been any doubt as to whether or not an enactment does so differentiate the enactment has been reserved'.[3]

Despite the fact that the exact number of reserved measures cannot at this stage be precisely determined, the printed sources disclose that up till the end of 1961[4] at least 162 measures were cleared with the Imperial authorities.[5] Of these measures seventy were cleared in the period after 1950. This procedure, so extensively used, and in which all the niceties were observed, considerably affected Southern Rhodesian legislation. That 'native legislation' was scrutinized, amended, and permitted only if the Imperial authorities were satisfied has already emerged. Similar supervision occurred in respect of other matters which came within the scope of the reserved clauses.

Mineral rights

The 'mineral rights reservation' (Section 28(d)) was also fully effective during its existence. The reservation provided that

any law altering or amending arrangements relating to the collection and allocation of mining revenue in force at the commencement of these our Letters Patent under any existing law of the Colony or otherwise or any law imposing any special rate, tax or duty on minerals in or under land within the Colony is reserved for the approval of the Secretary of State.

[1] *S.R.L.A.D.*, Vol. 33(2), cols. 2632–3, 23 June 1952.

[2] *City of Salisbury* v. *Mehta* at 692 (F.C.) per Clayden F.C.J.

[3] *City of Salisbury* v. *Mehta* per Beadle C.J. at 681 (S.R.), referring to the Old Age Pensions Act 34 of 1936 (Chap. 287 of 1939) and the Education Act 35 of 1938, both approved by the Secretary of State before submission to Parliament. Beadle C.J. was taking 'judicial notice' of this procedure. He was Parliamentary Secretary to the Prime Minister from 1941 to 1946 and Minister of Justice and Internal Affairs until 1950.

[4] The Southern Rhodesian Constitution 1961, was published on 6 December 1961; but the 1923 Constitution continued in operation until the 1 November 1962, so that during 1962 there were further reserved measures.

[5] The Colonial Office till July 1925; the Dominions Office till 1947; the Commonwealth Relations Office till 19 March 1962, and for the rest of 1962, the Central African Office. For history of the Commonwealth Relations Office see the *Commonwealth Relations Office Handbook 1964*, London, H.M.S.O., 1964, pp. 1–6. For the work of the Commonwealth Relations Office, see the Commonwealth Relations Office: Memoranda submitted on behalf of the Secretary of State for Commonwealth Relations to the Select Committee on Estimates (Sub-Committee E), 1959, quoted in N. Mansergh, *Documents and Speeches on Commonwealth Affairs 1952–1962*, Oxford, 1963.

From 1923 to 1933 the Imperial Government was insistent that no legislation affecting the British South Africa Company's rights could be permitted unless there had been prior consultation and agreement between the Southern Rhodesian Government and the Company. Thus the Mining Bill of 1926 was 'drawn up by the Secretary of Mines in the office of the Chartered Company'.[1] Similar difficulties had occurred in 1931, when there were lengthy negotiations in order that new mining legislation might be passed.[2] Subsequently the Secretary of State refused to allow the Southern Rhodesian Gold Premium Tax Bill of 1932 unless the Company agreed to such legislation.[3] Understandably, although the British South Africa Company agreed to the legislation, the Prime Minister inveighed against the indignity of a free government being unable to impose taxation without the matter being referred to a private financial concern.[4] This situation was so irksome to the Southern Rhodesian Government, particularly since the Opposition suggested that, on the analogy of the Land Case, the Company had no mineral rights either, that the Prime Minister made representations in London in 1932 on the whole question of the Company's rights.[5] Earlier the Imperial Government had made it clear to the Prime Minister[6] and to the Southern Rhodesian High Commissioner in London that they would not countenance expropriatory legislation[7] as they regarded the mineral rights (quite apart from the legal niceties) as having been conferred on the Company to compensate it for the absence of any remuneration for the administrative services it had rendered to Southern Rhodesia.[8] Indeed the Imperial Government considered that Clause 2D of the Devonshire Agreement of 29 September 1923,[9] was both a recognition by the Crown of the Company's ownership of the mineral rights and a promise not to call into question the rights recognized. This Clause constituted part of the consideration for the Company's agreement to the settlement of outstanding questions before the implementation of responsible government.

[1] *S.R.L.A.D.*, Vol. 7, col. 377.

[2] National Archives DO 1/5/5, Mitchell to Sir Edward Harding, 31 December 1931.

[3] This legislation was intended to absorb part of the fortuitous windfall producers in gold obtained as the result of Southern Rhodesia's departure from the gold standard. See also National Archives DO 1/1/6, Moffat to Downie, 23 March 1932, which reveals the Secretary of State's attitude.

[4] *S.R.L.A.D.*, Vol. 13, col. 2270, 1 June 1933.

[5] National Archives LE 3/1/1, 16 August 1932, Moffat to Leggate. LE 3/2/1/5, Cabinet Resolution 2464 shows that the Prime Minister was to discuss the matter with the Dominions Office to attempt to get its consent to a special reference to the Judicial Committee as to the ownership of the mineral rights.

[6] The Prime Minister refused in the Legislative Assembly to challenge the Imperial Government by passing expropriatory legislation: *S.R.L.A.D.*, Vol. 13, col. 2283.

[7] Nor would a Labour Cabinet approve this: National Archives MO 13/1/1, Passfield to Rodwell, 9 January 1930, refusing to allow the Company's mineral rights to be questioned and pointing to the reservations in Section 28.

[8] These were mentioned in the Land Case. The Company did not even obtain interest on the monies it expended for Southern Rhodesian administration: Cmd. 1129, p. 10.

[9] Cmd. 1984.

Furthermore, Section 49(1) and (2) of the Letters Patent expressly exempted the Company's rights to minerals, so that they should not vest in the Governor. The Imperial Government in fact considered that recognition of the Company's claims was an integral part of the terms on which self-government had been granted.[1]

Despite public agitation in Southern Rhodesia and a formal request by the Government that the question of ownership of the mineral rights be referred to the Judicial Committee of the Privy Council, the Imperial Government consistently refused[2] to permit a special reference under the Judicial Committee Act 1833.[3] The difficulties were only solved by the purchase of the rights in 1934 for two million pounds, the Imperial Government then agreeing to remove the mineral reservation from the Constitution.

Railway reservation

Yet another reservation which was fully effective was the 'railway reservation' reserving any law dealing with railways in the Colony

until legislation shall have come into force, adopting so far as may be applicable provisions for the law in force in our United Kingdom relating to the Railway and Canal Commissioners and to the Rates Tribunal provided for in the Railways Act 1921.

This was originally contained in Section 28(e) of the Southern Rhodesian Constitution Letters Patent, 1923.

From 1924 to 1927 Section 28(e) was a major barrier to legislation on railway matters, satisfactory settlement of which was essential for the development of the country. Even the Railway Inquiry Act of 1925 setting up a Commission to establish the facts of railway operation in Southern Rhodesia, was considerably delayed[4] by representations of the British South Africa Company, which was the major shareholder in the Railway Companies through the Rhodesia Railways Trust, which it controlled[5] and also by the Secretary of State, who maintained that Southern Rhodesia could only pass legislation subject to the approval of the Railways.[6] The Bill was eventually

[1] See National Archives RO 7/1/1 MSS, Harding to Downie, 2 November 1932.

[2] See Correspondence Relating to the Question of the Ownership of the Mineral Rights in Southern Rhodesia, C.S.R. 18–1933. In 1919 Lord Milner rejected a similar request for a special reference made by a resolution of the then Legislative Council: National Archives MO 13/1/1, High Commissioner to Administrator, 12 August 1919, stating that Lord Milner would not invite the Company to concur in a reference.

[3] 3 & 4 Wm. IV, c. 41, sec. 4.

[4] S.R.L.A. Votes and Proceedings, Vol. XI, 3rd Session, 1st Parliament, shows that the Bill was read a third time on 13 July 1924, presented for assent on 28 July 1924 and that the Order in Council assenting thereto was only issued on 6 February 1925.

[5] S.R.L.A.D., Vol. 3, col. 1516.

[6] National Archives CO 8/1/2, Memorandum from Moffat, 9 December 1924. Moffat was then Minister of Mines and reported on his interview to this effect with the Secretary of State.

only assented to when an undertaking had been given by the Southern Rhodesian Government that they would repeal the Act as soon as the enquiry was completed.[1]

However, the Southern Rhodesian Government was determined to remove 'that impediment in our Constitution'[2] and after lengthy negotiations in London in 1926 with the Company and with the Imperial authorities, the Railways Bill was drafted. Even after agreement, further amendments were cabled to the Southern Rhodesian Government by the Secretary of State. These had been suggested by the Company and many of them were accepted. The Secretary of State also required to be informed of any amendments made by the Southern Rhodesian Government.[3] The British Government agreed as part of the settlement that, conditionally on the Railways Bill being passed unamended, the bar in the Constitution would be removed,[4] but not, however, entirely.[5] Furthermore, the Attorney-General announced that any

legislation providing for the compulsory expropriation of property of the Railways ... would however fall within the provisions of paragraph VII(b) of His Majesty's Instructions to the Governor whereby it is provided that the Governor shall not assent in His Majesty's name to any law of an extraordinary nature and importance whereby the rights and property of His Majesty's subjects not residing in the colony may be prejudiced unless he shall have previously obtained His Majesty's instructions on such law ... or unless such law shall contain a clause suspending the operation thereof.[6]

As a consequence of these negotiations the Railway Act 1927 provided in Section 33 that 'any Act repealing this Act or amending any of its financial provisions shall not take effect until His Majesty's pleasure thereupon has been signified'. This somewhat narrowed the situations in which railway legislation could be reserved since only a repeal of the whole Act or an amendment to the financial provisions was to be reserved while the balance of the Act could be amended.[7] Thereafter, the original Section 28(e) was deleted by Letters Patent.[8]

---

[1] See National Archives CO 8/1/2, Letter of 8 November 1924, making this suggestion from the Colonial Office, and Governor's note of 2 December 1924, proposing this to Ministers. See also Cable from Coghlan to the Secretary of State, 11 December 1924, undertaking to repeal the Act if it were assented to.

[2] S.R.L.A.D., Vol. 4, col. 1116, Sir Charles Coghlan.

[3] National Archives LE 3/2/1/1, Cabinet Resolution 401, 22 October 1926, and attached correspondence. The Legislative Assembly was informed that 'these amendments had been put forward by the representative of the High Commissioner': S.R.L.A.D., Vol. 5, col. 1755.

[4] S.R.L.A.D., Vol. 5, col. 1619, 13 December 1926.

[5] S.R.L.A.D., Vol. 5, col. 1744.

[6] S.R.L.A.D., Vol. 7, col. 52, answer by the Attorney-General to a question in the Legislative Assembly.

[7] In fact the Act gave the Secretary of State even greater powers as Section 7 gave him the power to appoint a referee to decide any disputes under the Act. This was based on

Footnote 8 on opposite page.

Nonetheless it remained necessary, whenever changes in railway legislation or operation were required, to obtain the consent of all 'those interests which would be taken into consideration whether the legislation should be assented to'.[1] Thus Mr. Moffat discussed the possibility of railway legislation on his London visit in 1932[2] and, when a new Railway Agreement was negotiated in 1934, the Company's assent was first obtained and the Imperial Government kept informed throughout the negotiations.[3] Finally, when the Southern Rhodesian Government bought out the railway companies in 1947, obtained a large British loan to facilitate further development, and requested that the reservation be removed from Section 33 of the Railways Act, Sir Godfrey Huggins visited London in connection with this constitutional problem.[4] The Colonial Office[5] insisted, as a condition of Southern Rhodesia being permitted to purchase the railways and being given a British loan, that the Southern Rhodesian Government undertake 'to promote the welfare and advancement of African employees of Rhodesia Railways' and to provide 'facilities and encouragement for any steps which the African employees may take towards the formation of a Trade Union or Unions'.[6] Ultimately, the Rhodesia Railways Act 1948 repealed the reservation. From 1923 to 1947 the provisions had however been fully effective in protecting the interests of the railway companies and had eventually provided the occasion for African advancement on the Railways.

The land reservation

In the years preceding the grant of responsible government there had been pressure for the repeal of Section 83 of the Southern Rhodesia Order in Council 1898, which provided that natives might hold land on the same terms

Section 49(2) of the Letters Patent and gave the Secretary of State an absolute discretion in his choice. Furthermore the Railways Board set up to control the railways was to be dominated by Imperial nominees. Section 2 provided that the Governments of Southern Rhodesia, Northern Rhodesia and Bechuanaland Protectorate were each to nominate a member and a Chairman was to be appointed after consultations between the Governments with the approval of the Secretary of State.

[8] See Letters Patent of the 26 March 1930, and Southern Rhodesia's Governor's Proclamation No. 11 of 1927.

[1] *S.R.L.A.D.*, Vol. 21(2), col. 2318, on the 1941 Railways Amendment Act.
[2] National Archives LE 3/1/1, Moffat to Leggate, 16 August 1932.
[3] *S.R.L.A.D.*, Vol. 17, col. 1122, 8 April 1937.   [4] *S.R.L.A.D.*, Vol. 26(2), col. 2880.
[5] Through Mr. Creech Jones. Although Southern Rhodesian matters were normally dealt with by the Dominions Office and later the Commonwealth Relations Office, Lord Malvern has stated in a private communication that 'the Colonial Office could always be relied on to butt in if any of our affairs impinged on their business and sometimes when they didn't'.
[6] *S.R.L.A.D.*, Vol. 27(1), col. 81. See also Gann and Gelfand, op. cit., p. 198. An agreed memorandum was then drawn up. It is for this reason that the African Railway Workers' Union has been the strongest and best organized African Trade Union and the first to receive official recognition.

as Europeans.[1] A proposal to this effect was put forward by the Southern Rhodesian delegates at the London constitutional talks in 1921. The Imperial Government at that stage refused to accede to this proposal and secured native land rights by Section 43 of the Southern Rhodesia Constitution Letters Patent 1923. However, Mr. Churchill, Secretary of State for the Colonies, undertook that 'if full and impartial enquiry should show, after responsible government has come into force, that some amendment of the law is necessary, His Majesty's Government would be prepared to consider an amendment'.[2]

When this request was renewed after the implementation of responsible government, a Land Commission, chaired by Sir Morris Carter, who was nominated by the Secretary of State, was appointed in 1925 to investigate whether separate areas should be set aside for exclusive African and European occupation and whether special native purchase areas, in which individual Africans could own land, should be permitted. The appointment of the Commission met with general approval.[3] So also did its Report.[4] However it was recognized that, unless full approval of the United Kingdom Government was obtained, nothing could be done.[5]

The Report was therefore discussed in 1926 with the Dominions Office when Sir Charles Coghlan visited England.[6] There it met with 'approbation'[7] and, provided legislation did not depart from the principles of the Report,[8] the British Government was prepared to revoke the 'incubus contained in Section 83 of the 1898 Order in Council, and our present Constitution'.

---

[1] The Southern Rhodesia Native Affairs Committee of Enquiry 1910 (Report p. 10: A 12, 1911) had recommended that no further land should be alienated to individual Africans. The suggestion was repeated in the Report of the Secretary for Native Affairs and Chief Native Commissioner for the year 1920: Salisbury, Government Printer, p. 1.

[2] Cmd. 1573.

[3] National Archives NE 1/1/1, Newton to Coghlan, 12 February 1925; Harris to Newton, 10 February 1925, which disclosed that the Aborigines Protection Society favoured the appointment of such a Commission.

[4] *Report of the Land Commission 1925*, Salisbury, Government Printer, 1926, C.S.R. 3. The Southern Rhodesian Missionary Conference and leading missionaries such as A. S. Cripps approved the Report: see T. O. Ranger, 'State and Church in Southern Rhodesia 1919–39', *Historical Association of Rhodesia and Nyasaland Local Series No. 4*. They felt its implementation would protect Africans from further encroachment by European purchasers. In 1925 Europeans had bought 31 million acres of land, whereas Africans had only bought 45,000 acres. However, Native Department files show that Africans were gradually beginning to buy land and approaching the Department for assistance: see National Archives S 138/21: letters from various Native Commissioners from 1926 to 1929. The Department at this stage attempted to block these requests.

[5] *S.R.L.A.D.*, Vol. 4, col. 280, 26 May 1926. Section 43 of the Letters Patent could not be amended by the Southern Rhodesian Legislative Assembly. See also *S.R.L.A.D.*, Vol. 8, col. 77, Moffat.

[6] *S.R.L.A.D.*, Vol. 4, col. 427.

[7] *S.R.L.A.D.*, Vol. 6, col. 96, 5 May 1927, Coghlan.

[8] The minority Report cutting out a neutral area was incorporated in the Bill. This was approved by Amery: *S.R.L.A.D.*, Vol. 8, col. 77, 25 April 1929.

Detailed agreement was still necessary. For this constitutional change and in order to obtain a final land settlement, the Southern Rhodesian Government proposed to give an additional seven and a half million acres to the African population as native purchase area. Sir Charles also promised that before he introduced legislation, a final draft would be submitted to the Secretary of State.[1] The proposed legislation was again discussed when Mr. Amery, the Secretary of State, visited Southern Rhodesia in August 1927. Later that year, the British Government was still enquiring as to the method of dealing with unallocated areas.[2] Indeed, in 1928, consultations were still continuing and legislation could not at that stage be introduced.[3]

Eventually after these lengthy negotiations, a Land Apportionment Bill was introduced in 1929. The Bill provided for the division of the Colony into European and African areas, a native purchase area where Africans could have individual tenure, and an unassigned area.[4] In urban areas Africans would retain their rights until such time as the municipalities created African urban areas. The Minutes of a Cabinet meeting in January 1929 show some of the considerable modifications suggested even at that late stage by the Secretary of State, which the Government accepted.[5] The Bill was then passed by the Legislative Assembly but there was a change of government in the United Kingdom, which considerably delayed assent. Almost simultaneously the *Manchester Guardian* attacked the Bill, while it was then discovered that the procedure advised by the Dominions Office was incorrect, that the Bill was *ultra vires* Section 43 of the Constitution, that it was necessary that the

[1] *S.R.L.A.D.*, Vol. 7, 5 June 1928, Moffat (the Prime Minister).

[2] National Archives LE 3/2/1/2, Cabinet Resolution No. 673 of 21 November 1927.

[3] *S.R.L.A.D.*, Vol. 7, 5 June 1928, Moffat.

[4] The effect of the Act is given in the Second Report of the Select Committee on Resettlement of Natives. Government Printer, Salisbury, L.A.S.C. 3, 1960. In 1930 the European area was approximately 49 million acres and the African 29 million acres out of a total area in Southern Rhodesia of 96 million acres. At the end of 1964 the land distribution was as follows: European Area 35,710,400 acres, African Purchase Area and Tribal Trust Land 44,407,200 acres, National Land 10,524,800 acres, Unreserved Land open to all races 5,876,900 acres, the total area of Southern Rhodesia being 96,519,500 acres: Report of the Secretary for Internal Affairs for the Year 1964, C.S.R. 39, 1965, p. 9.

[5] National Archives LE 3/2/1/3. Minutes of a special meeting of the Cabinet held on Tuesday, 8 January 1929. The cable of 12 May 1928 from the Secretary of State was fully discussed and the proposals put forward by Mr. Amery were considered *seriatim*: (1) That legislation be passed instead of an Order in Council was accepted. (This later led to the first Bill being *ultra vires*.) (2) 'It was agreed that one of the members of the Native Land Board be nominated by the High Commissioner in lieu of a missionary appointment. It was also agreed that no member of the Legislative Assembly be appointed to the Board.' (3) Ministers were agreeable to the insertion of a clause safeguarding the right of Africans to reside in certain areas. (4) Clause 18 would be 'altered to provide that no land from the unassigned areas should be assigned either to the European or to the Native Areas without the previous consent of the High Commissioner'. (5) It was agreed that provisions for natives be made in town areas. (6) It was impossible to lay down in an Act every detail as to how it was to be executed and the Government must be trusted to act fairly 'but the Minister of Native Affairs would prepare a memorandum giving the general lines on which all native land policy would be worked'.

Constitution be amended to permit the enactment of the legislation, and that a new Bill should be introduced and passed by the Legislative Assembly.

Lord Passfield (Sidney Webb), the new Labour Colonial Secretary, recognized that this measure had been agreed upon by the previous Conservative Government, but insisted that the new Government required 'to familiarize ourselves with the facts of the situation and the issues involved'.[1] Passfield assured the Southern Rhodesian Government (the Prime Minister had considered resigning) that 'he fully recognizes the sincerity of your aim, namely to improve the condition of the native under the Bill'.[2]

However, the obstacles were removed when the chief permanent official responsible for Southern Rhodesia in the Dominions Office, Sir Charles Davis, returned from leave and persuaded Passfield of the merits of the measure.[3] A Southern Rhodesian Cabinet Minister, W. M. Leggate, also went to England and persuaded the Aborigines Protection Society to cease opposing the Bill.[4] Similarly he persuaded the Editor of the *Manchester Guardian* to withdraw his objections to the measure.[5] In the meanwhile the Secretary of State sought and obtained an assurance that no natives would for the present be removed from Crown land and unoccupied farms.[6] It was also agreed that to meet the wishes of the High Commissioner a missionary would be appointed to the proposed Board to be set up under the Act when passed.[7] Ultimately, after further amendment of the draft at the Secretary of State's suggestion and after the issue of new Letters Patent amending the Southern Rhodesian Constitution, which now permitted the enactment of a law that Africans alone might hold certain land and Europeans alone might hold and acquire land in other parts of the Colony, provided such law was reserved,[8] the Land Apportionment Act 1930 was passed. The measure was assented to and was the joint responsibility of both the Imperial Government and the Southern Rhodesian Government.[9]

[1] National Archives MO 13/1/1, Cable Passfield to the Governor, 11 September 1929.
[2] National Archives NE 1/1/7, Newton to Moffat, 24 July 1929.
[3] See National Archives NE 1/1/7, Newton to Moffat, 31 October 1929.
[4] National Archives MO 13/1/1 MSS, Leggate to Moffat, 22 November 1929. Leggate in describing his meeting with C. R. Buxton said: 'His Society was not opposed to the principle of the Land Apportionment Act. This information I am conveying to Mr. Ponsonby this morning.' See also 19 November 1929, Notes of meeting with Buxton and Harris: 'He took no exception to the principles of the Bill but confined himself to hoping that a better arrangement could be got about the undetermined area.'
[5] National Archives NE 1/1/7 MSS, Newton to Moffat, 21 November 1929.
[6] National Archives S 138/21, Chief Native Commissioner to Minister of Native Affairs, 25 November 1929.
[7] National Archives S 138/21, Chief Native Commissioner to Minister of Native Affairs, 18 November 1929.
[8] Sections 43(2)(a) and (b) as amended and Section 43(3) as amended by Letters Patent of 26 March 1930. See Governor's Proclamation, 1 May 1930. 'Europeans' here refers to all non-Africans, viz. Europeans, Asians, and Coloureds.
[9] It only later became controversial. Since the mid-nineteen-fifties it has been regarded as highly discriminatory. See Report of the Constitutional Council, No. 29 of 5 February 1964.

When the Imperial Government amended the Letters Patent to permit the enactment of the Land Apportionment Act 1930, it provided that any amendment or alteration to that Act was to be reserved in the same way as any other reserved measure. From this time all amendments to the Act—and they were frequent—underwent the process of advance consultation and amendment.[1] Thus in 1936 a Land Apportionment Amendment Act was negotiated as part of the constitutional changes which were implemented in 1937. In fact the Act limited the powers of the Crown to remove Africans from alienated land rented by them in the European area, as they could not now be moved unless the Minister was satisfied that suitable land elsewhere was available for their occupation.

Not only amendments to the Act but all regulations thereunder had to receive the High Commissioner's consent. These regulations were similarly negotiated, cleared,[2] and delayed.[3] The Governor might also suggest amendments to the Regulations.[4] Later, when the Secretary of State was substituted as the authority in place of the High Commissioner[5] similar approval had to be obtained.[6] In addition any exchange of land from one area to another had to receive the Secretary of State's assent. Indeed Southern Rhodesian Governments sometimes encountered difficulties: as Lord Malvern said: 'we still have to get the consent of the Secretary of State to any of these exchanges and if they can dot an "i" and cross a "t" they will always do so'.[7] This was shown during the Todd regime in the mid-nineteen-fifties when considerable difficulty was experienced in effecting land exchanges in the Essexvale area of Southern Rhodesia,[8] while Sir Edgar Whitehead had to visit London in 1959 to iron out difficulties as a result of the creation of Lake Kariba, as originally none of the land abutting the Lake could be occupied by Europeans.[9]

Gann's article, cited earlier, makes it clear that the measure was more liberal than corresponding legislation in the Northern Territories. Members of the Parliamentary Opposition stated: 'This Bill is in effect an Imperial measure ... indeed we regard it as part of the native policy of the Imperial Government': S.R.L.A.D., Vol. 8, col. 1202. Lord Malvern, who was then a back-bencher, confirms that this was his attitude at that time. Personal communication.

[1] Sir Godfrey Huggins had Imperial co-operation for many of these amendments as he was attempting to adapt the Act to find a solution to the problem of increasing African urbanization and had decided not to enforce the Act entirely owing to the fact that the land set aside for Africans was not sufficient. See Gann and Gelfand, op. cit., p. 173 et seq., and also at p. 127 referring to the decision to delay African population transfers.

[2] S.R.L.A.D., Vol. 30(1), col. 2408.   [3] S.R.L.A.D., Vol. 28, col. 1487, 28 June 1948.

[4] National Archives MO 13/1/1, folio 243, Rodwell to Moffat, 11 February 1931.

[5] By changes made in 1937.

[6] These provisions were observed in practice and no regulations came into force until the Secretary of State had agreed. This was no mere formality. Thus in 1937 and 1939 amending regulations were consented to by the Secretary of State: National Archives S 11, S.R. 400 and 423, Eden to Stanley.

[7] S.R.L.A.D., Vol. 24, col. 2365, 20 November 1944.

[8] Personal communication from Mr. Todd.

[9] Personal communication from Sir Edgar Whitehead.

When amendments were passed to the Act conditions were frequently exacted. Thus when African rights in urban areas generally were abrogated a bargain was made, that they must be given grants in perpetuity in specially created native urban areas.[1] Regulations for these areas were also approved by the Secretary of State before enactment.[2]

That Mr. Huggins was extremely concerned about the operation of the Act was shown in the early days by the fact that the Southern Rhodesian Government went so far as to refrain from taking action under the Act until any doubts as to its ambit had been clarified with the Imperial Government.[3] Indeed from certain points of view the Act was regarded as a protection similar to the constitutional provisions for Reserves to prevent Europeans from purchasing all African-owned land.[4] Eventually in 1960 a Southern Rhodesian Parliamentary Select Committee reported that the Act should eventually be repealed at the same time as the constitutional provisions setting aside Native Reserves.[5] Eventually the 1961 Constitution permitted amendment of the Act and its repeal, providing that no Bill imposing any racial limitation on the ownership or occupation of any land in Southern Rhodesia, which was more restrictive than the Act at the time of coming into force of the Constitution, could be enacted unless it was subjected to the same procedure as a constitutional Bill amending a specially entrenched provision of the Constitution.[6]

Constitutional amendments

Constitutional amendments within the competence of the Legislative Assembly were subject to the same procedure of scrutiny. The Constitution was amended on nine occasions[7] by the Legislative Assembly between 1925

[1] *S.R.L.A.D.*, Vol. 30(1), col. 2408.   [2] *S.R.L.A.D.*, Vol. 25(2), col. 1945.
[3] *S.R.L.A.D.*, Vol. 14, col. 631, 26 March 1934. Mr. Huggins cleared up these points on a visit to London.
[4] The Act prevented further decreases in the quantity of African-held land. In practice European-held areas have greatly diminished while considerable additions have been made to the African areas, particularly as a result of the creation of the Special Native Area by the Land Apportionment Amendment Act 1950. Sir Edgar Whitehead, in a personal communication, claimed that the British Government was horrified when he first suggested the repeal of the Act and that they only became convinced of the necessity for its repeal over a period of years.
[5] See Second Report of the Select Committee on Resettlement of Natives, *L.A.S.C.* 3, 1960, pp. 58–62. The Committee recognized that the Act's 'protective aspect has some value even today'. For a summary of the history of Land Apportionment in Southern Rhodesia see M. Yudelman, *Africans on the Land*, Oxford, 1964, pp. 57–84.
[6] Southern Rhodesia Constitution, Section 102(2)(g) and Section 103(c). The rigid amendment procedure will be discussed *infra* in Part II, Chapter 1.
[7] The Constitution Letters Patent Amendment Act 1925, the Ministerial Titles Act 1933, the Constitution Amendment Act 1937, the Constitution Amendment Act 1938, the Constitution Amendment Act 1948, the Constitution Further Amendment Act 1948, the Constitution Amendment Act 1951, the Constitution Amendment Act 1953 and Constitution Amendment Act No. 37 of 1960.

and 1960. In all these cases there was prior consultation and advance approval by the British Government, while in the majority of cases there was a visit by the Prime Minister to London to discuss in person the proposed amendments with the Imperial authorities.[1] It is known that on these occasions Prime Ministers did not obtain all they wished.[2]

Coinage and currency

The same consultative processes were also followed in respect of legislation affecting coinage and currency.[3] Indeed in these cases the British Treasury and sometimes the Bank of England were brought into the discussions. That these limitations could have affected Southern Rhodesian financial policies considerably is illustrated by the fact that it would have been impossible without United Kingdom consent to have tied Southern Rhodesian currency to the South African pound.[4]

Indeed it was the realization of economic realities by successive Southern Rhodesian Governments that caused much legislation relevant to financial matters to be cleared with the British Government just as if such measures were reserved. All Southern Rhodesian legislation affecting loans was cleared in advance, negotiations taking place with the British Treasury and sometimes also with the Bank of England.[5] The necessity for this was caused by the fact that not only was Southern Rhodesia concerned lest her loan terms be unacceptable to the British Government and thus in turn unacceptable to British investors, but also by the fact that in many cases she could not make international borrowings without United Kingdom intervention or the provision of a United Kingdom guarantee. Again, if she wished to raise loans from the British Government it might be necessary to show Britain her

[1] e.g. the Ministerial Titles Act 1933 discussed by Mr. H. U. Moffat in 1932, the Constitution Amendment Acts 1937 and 1938 discussed by Mr. Huggins from 1934 to 1937, the Constitution Amendment Act 1948 discussed by Sir Godfrey Huggins in 1947 and 1948, and the Constitution Amendment Acts of 1951 and 1953 discussed by Sir Godfrey Huggins during the prolonged negotiations for the creation of Federation.

[2] e.g. the 1937 amendments read with the Amending Letters Patent rejected many of Mr. Huggins' proposals. See Cmd. 5218, p. 4. In 1947 and 1948 Sir Godfrey Huggins pressed for the institution of separate African representation on the lines of the South African pattern (as established in 1936) but this was also refused.

[3] See *S.R.L.A.D.*, Vol. 26(2), col. 2790.

[4] Sir Edgar Whitehead in a personal communication has stated that at one time the South African Minister of Finance, Mr. J. H. Hofmeyr, suggested that the Southern Rhodesian currency should be pegged to the South African pound rather than to sterling, but he informed Mr. Hofmeyr that this was constitutionally impossible. Sir Edgar's real reason was that, since Southern Rhodesia's main market was the United Kingdom, it was advantageous to be tied to United Kingdom currency.

[5] e.g. the General Loans Act 1937, General Loans Act 1948 (see *S.R.L.A.D.*, Vol. 29, col. 54), the Exchange Control Act of 1948, Rhodesia Railways (E.C.A.) Loan Act 1952, and the Specific Loan Appropriation Act 1960.

proposed loan estimates as was done in 1962 to obtain the Butler loan of three and a half million pounds.[1]

Conclusions

Study of the legislative process from 1923 to 1962 reveals that the reservations played a considerable part in shaping Southern Rhodesian legislative measures.[2] They were an effective psychological barrier to legislation which Southern Rhodesian Governments considered would cause difficulty with the Imperial Government.

The most significant consequence of this procedure, which can be specifically proved, was that the African franchise in Southern Rhodesia was preserved, and that specially nominated European representatives were not substituted in its place. In addition, legislation on apartheid lines denying Africans permanent rights of residence in European areas was precluded, while measures restricting the fundamental freedom of the individual were also considerably modified.[3]

However, it must be emphasized that their effect was negative,[4] as the Imperial Government could not initiate constructive measures, repeal measures already on the Southern Rhodesian Statute Book, and could not force policies on Southern Rhodesia,[5] or initiate any proposals for African advance other than by influence and advice.[6] They could, however, discourage and control fresh Southern Rhodesian proposals. If of course a reasonable proposition and fair reasons were put forward legislation was permitted, but there is no doubt that, within their sphere, the reservations were undoubtedly effective, and, through the procedure of prior consultation, were 'on a completely different footing' from the 'theoretical' right of the United Kingdom to legislate for Southern Rhodesia.[7]

It must however be conceded that, had a head-on clash on particular legis-

[1] Personal communication from Sir Edgar Whitehead. The loan estimates were shown to Mr. R. A. Butler.

[2] Evidence to this effect was given to the 1951 Select Committee on the Southern Rhodesian Constitution by Cabinet Ministers.

[3] Compare de Smith, op. cit., p. 99, note 77, and p. 130, who considered the safeguard 'to be slight'. The reservations must surely be judged by what they prevented as well as by what they failed to prevent.

[4] National Archives NE 1/1/7, Newton to Moffat, 25 September 1930: 'Our position at present seems to me fairly strong. No legislation can be dictated to us: we have the initiative and so long as we legislate with discretion after full consultation with the High Commissioner and the Secretary of State we cannot be interfered with.'

[5] *S.R.L.A.D.*, Vol. 13, col. 2230–1, 31 May 1933, Mr. H. U. Moffat, Prime Minister. See also *S.R.L.A.D.*, Vol. 33(2), col. 2640. Compare a statement by the Leader of the Opposition in *S.R.L.A.D.*, Vol. 16(2), col. 1735 (1935), to the effect that the Land Apportionment Act had been forced upon Southern Rhodesia by the Imperial Government and that the Maize Control Act would also not have been enacted had it not been for the reservations in the Constitution.

[6] *S.R.L.A.D.*, Vol. 12, col. 1018, 26 April 1932, Moffat.

[7] *S.R.L.A.D.*, Vol. 47, col. 6007, 21 June 1961, Whitehead.

lation occurred, the British Government would have been bound to give way unless it was prepared to intervene militarily once responsible government had been conceded and once Britain had no administration or officers of her own in Southern Rhodesia to implement decisions. In the event of any serious clash of opinion, an election on the issue would have been fought and the Imperial Government would have been placed in a dilemma.[1]

The reservations were also important from the point of view of a possible amalgamation of Southern Rhodesia and Northern Rhodesia. It was made quite clear to the Southern Rhodesian Government that, should the restrictions in the Constitution be removed, closer union proposals would have no hope of success.[2]

From another point of view the secrecy of the procedure of advance consultation and agreement substituted for effective overt use of the power of reservation was extremely convenient to successive United Kingdom Governments. As Sir Godfrey Huggins percipiently pointed out in 1946: the reservations are 'a tremendous embarrassment to the Government that happens to be in power in the United Kingdom'.[3] It is for this reason that Britain was willing to dispense with the reservations in 1961. But Britain always required substituted safeguards in their place. In 1950 the Southern Rhodesian Government was informed that a second Chamber would be required.[4] Eventually, a Declaration of Rights forming part of the Constitution and subject to exceptionally rigid procedures of amendment, a Constitutional Council to act as a preliminary legal filter and delaying mechanism, and an entrenched judiciary with a right of appeal to the Judicial Committee of the Privy Council were substituted for the reservations in the Constitution of 1961.

---

[1] See *S.R.L.A.D.*, Vol. 31(1), col. 606, 3 May 1950, Huggins: 'The reservations are not serious when it comes to a real show-down.' The attitude of nearly all Southern Rhodesian Prime Ministers is epitomized by a story which Lord Malvern has related on a number of occasions: 'I once had a discussion on reservations in the Constitution with Mr. Creech Jones. I asked why they did not agree to the two Rhodesias being amalgamated because, I said, "we will accept the reservations contained in the Southern Rhodesia Constitution for the whole area. What was good enough for Southern Rhodesia in 1923 was surely good enough for the whole area!" His answer was: "What are the reservations?" To which I replied that "No racial laws differentiating between the races could be passed without the agreement of the Crown." He said: "Yes, and suppose the Crown refuses to agree, what happens then?" I said: "Well, if the Prime Minister is sure of himself he will have a general election." He said: "Yes, and he would come back with a huge majority", to which I replied: "Yes, more than likely." He said: "And what happens then?" and I said: "Then it is up to you, if you have got an army corps to spare, you could get on with it." ' See also *S.R.L.A.D.*, Vol. 17, col. 1580, Huggins on the 1937 constitutional changes, and *S.R.L.A.D.*, Vol. 3, col. 1517, Coghlan on the possibility of railway legislation being refused.

[2] *S.R.L.A.D.*, Vol. 13(1), 1950, 3 May 1950, col. 602; *S.R.L.A.D.*, Vol. 31(2), col. 2126. Lord Malvern in a personal communication has also revealed that he would not enact measures in Southern Rhodesia which would have made closer union impossible and that this acted as a restraining factor on the sort of legislation he introduced in Southern Rhodesia.

[3] *S.R.L.A.D.*, Vol. 26(2), col. 1726–7, 25 July 1946.

[4] *S.R.L.A.D.*, Vol. 31(1), col. 602, 3 May 1950.

13

THE GOVERNOR

THE Office of Governor was constituted by separate Letters Patent under the Great Seal, while Royal Instructions as to the exercise of the powers conferred on the Governor by virtue of his office and in terms of the Constitution were also issued.[1]

The Governor, who was also to be Commander-in-Chief, was to be appointed by Commission under the Royal Sign Manual and Signet and was also to hold office during pleasure.[2] His salary was payable by the Crown, but the Constitution provided that £4,000 should be payable from the Southern Rhodesian Consolidated Revenue Fund for this purpose, while such salary should not be altered during his continuance in office.[3] Indeed, the Governor's salary was protected against alteration by the Legislative Assembly as the provision relative to this could not be amended by the Legislature.[4] However, the Southern Rhodesian Government made available to the Governor additional emoluments in the form of an entertainment and personal allowance since the amount specified in the Constitution required supplementation.[5]

Since the Crown appointed the Governor, who was an Imperial officer, it was free to appoint any person it saw fit. From the grant of responsible government, however, there was informal consultation on any proposed appointment. Thus in the case of the first Governor, the Southern Rhodesian representative in London, Sir F. Newton, was informed of those persons whom the Colonial Office considered eligible and was given the opportunity to communicate with Sir Charles Coghlan, the future Southern Rhodesian Prime Minister, to obtain his views.[6] Nonetheless the future Southern Rhodesian Prime Minister could not select the Governor as the ultimate decision rested with the Crown.

By 1942 it was accepted that the Southern Rhodesian Prime Minister should be consulted on proposed appointments, largely as a result of pressure

[1] Letters Patent passed under the Great Seal of the United Kingdom constituting the Office of Governor dated 1 September 1923, and issued on 25 August 1923, and Instructions passed under the Royal Sign Manual and Signet to the Governor and Commander-in-Chief of the Colony of Southern Rhodesia on 25 August 1923. Given on 1 September 1923. The Crown expressly reserved the right to revoke, alter, or amend these Letters Patent. Clause 15.

[2] Letters Patent constituting the Office of Governor, Clause 1.

[3] Constitution Letters Patent, section 55.

[4] Constitution Letters Patent, Section 26(2).

[5] S.R.L.A.D., Vol 22, col. 273, 7 May 1942, Huggins. This amount was then £6,000.

[6] National Archives CO 8/1/1, Newton to Coghlan, 10 May 1923.

by Sir Godfrey Huggins who was able to insist on this because of the inadequacy of the emoluments specified in the Constitution.[1] However, the Prime Minister considered that there was no possibility of the United Kingdom agreeing to freedom of the Southern Rhodesian Government in nominating a Governor because of the considerable power exercisable by any Governor. On the other hand, Sir Godfrey Huggins subsequently insisted, after it had been agreed that a British High Commissioner would be accredited to Southern Rhodesia, that no further 'imperial pro-consuls' should be appointed as Governor.[2] In any event the United Kingdom Government became less concerned about the incumbent of the Governorship from the time of the High Commissioner's appointment in 1951. Eventually in 1959 a Southern Rhodesian, Sir Humphrey Gibbs, was appointed as Governor on the recommendation of the Southern Rhodesian Prime Minister, Sir Edgar Whitehead.

Provision was also made for the appointment of an Acting Governor when the Governor was unable to perform the duties of his office. Such acting Governor was appointed and removable by the Crown and was temporarily vested with the Governor's powers.[3] If the Governor was merely absent for a short period then he might appoint a Deputy-Governor who, subject to any instructions by the Governor whose powers would in no way be abridged, would perform the functions of the Governor.[4]

As an Imperial officer the Governor was, as also were any Acting or Deputy-Governors, bound to conform with any Royal Instructions which might be issued from time to time.[5] These might be varied or revoked, and be given either formally or informally. They might also be communicated to the Executive Council of the Colony if the Governor thought fit.[6] The Governor might not disregard such Instructions although disregard would not invalidate action taken by him.[7]

Functions of the Governor

Although the Governor was solely responsible to the Crown he was required to act in two capacities: that of the local head of state and that of an

[1] *S.R.L.A.D.*, Vol 22, col. 273, 7 May 1942. Sir Godfrey informed the Legislative Assembly that he had notified the British Government that if he was not consulted no additional emoluments would be provided.

[2] Personal communication by Lord Malvern relative to 1951 correspondence with the United Kingdom Government.

[3] Letters Patent constituting the Office of Governor, Clause 10 (subsequently amended in 1926). This applied where the Governor died, became incapable, or was away from Southern Africa.

[4] ibid., Clauses 11 and 12.

[5] Letters Patent constituting the Office of Governor, Clauses 2, 10, and 12.

[6] See Keith, *Responsible Government*, op. cit., pp. 80–81. Instructions to Governor of Southern Rhodesia, 25 August 1923. Clause 3.

[7] Keith, op. cit., p. 81.

Imperial officer exercising powers on behalf of the United Kingdom Government. In both such capacities, which often could not be differentiated, he enjoyed considerable discretionary authority.

The Governor as head of the Southern Rhodesian State

The Governor as head of the executive government of Southern Rhodesia was the repository of extensive reserve power.

The Letters Patent constituting the Office of Governor had established an Executive Council for the Colony over which the Governor presided and the members of which were to be appointed by him from 'Ministers or other persons'.[1] This left it open to the Governor to assert the principles of the Constitution through use of his legal powers or to prevent Ministers from obstructing constitutional government.[2]

The function of the Executive Council was to advise the Governor on the use of his executive powers. Since the Governor presided at its meetings he was associated with most of the executive decisions of the Southern Rhodesian Government and aware of important issues.[3] In addition, although he did not attend Cabinet meetings it was the practice of Southern Rhodesian Cabinets to send copies of their minutes to the Governor and also to the High Commissioner.[4]

Normally the Governor was in the execution of his powers to be guided by the advice of the Executive Council. However, the Royal Instructions provided that

if in any case he shall see sufficient cause to dissent from the opinion of the said Council, he may act in the exercise of his said powers and authorities in opposition to the opinion of the Council, reporting the matter to Us without delay, with the reasons for his so acting. In such case, it shall be competent to any member of the said Council to require that there be recorded upon the Minutes of the Council the grounds of any advice or opinion that he may give upon the question.[5]

[1] Clause 5.

[2] See Keith, op. cit., p. 108. No appointment of any person who was not a Minister was ever made to the Executive Council.

[3] The Governor's Powers Act of 1951 facilitated the transaction of routine business by providing that matters might be decided by a Committee of Executive Council and put before the Governor by the Prime Minister without the necessity for a full meeting. It is submitted that such a procedure, had it been abused by the Prime Minister, would have made the Governor less conversant with the details of policy decisions. This did not in practice occur owing to good relationships between Governors and Prime Ministers. Thus Sir John Kennedy as Governor made suggestions as to the functions of Executive Council which Ministers accepted. See *infra*, Chapter 14.

[4] *S.R.L.A.D.*, Vol. 22, col. 3106, 10 February 1942.

[5] Clause 6. Similar instructions are given to Australian State Governors and the Tasmanian Premier argued in 1950 and 1956 that Governors of Australian States now stand in the same position to State Parliaments as the Queen stands to the Imperial Parliament. This view was neither accepted nor rejected by the Governor: see A. C. Castles, *Limitations*

This gave the Governor considerable reserve power of dissenting from executive action. Such power would only have been used in the local context if Governments had suggested illegal action or excessively harsh action against Africans. In the Imperial context it would have been used if Royal Instructions were given conflicting with local wishes. In reality this reserve power was related to his functions as an Imperial officer since at the time of granting the responsible government Constitution of 1923 the Imperial authorities had determined that they should retain considerable influence over the administration of Native Affairs, and in the chain of control over the Southern Rhodesian authorities the Governor was to be an important link as he would be the only Imperial officer on the spot. After 1937 this reserve power of dissent became even more important when the Secretary of State was substituted for the High Commissioner as the controlling Imperial authority.[1]

However, successive Governors looked upon it as their function to maintain satisfactory relationships with Southern Rhodesian Prime Ministers so that in practice there were no disputes between Governors and Prime Ministers. Since all parties approached problems in a conciliatory spirit with a willingness to compromise, the typically informal British arrangements worked and there was no occasion for disagreement.[2] As a result the power was not exercised. Nonetheless it remained an important potential limitation on the independence of Southern Rhodesian Governments. Indeed, in 1942 the Prime Minister considered that no Native Commissioner could be removed without the Governor's consent.[3] Sir Edgar Whitehead has even stated that the possibility of a Governor taking a literal view of his powers in terms of this Clause was one of the factors moving him to initiate negotiations for the Southern Rhodesian Constitution 1961 which eventually removed this considerable limitation on Southern Rhodesian autonomy.[4]

In addition, the Royal Instructions envisaged that in certain circumstances the Governor was to exercise an independent judgement, irrespective of the views of his Ministers. This was the case in respect of reprieves which,

on the Autonomy of the Australian States, (1962) Public Law 175 at 181 et seq. It appears from Gluck v. The Governor, 1947 (1) S.A. 494 at 498 and from African Newspapers (Pvt.) Ltd. and Wason v. Lardner Burke and Bosman NN.O., 1964 (4) S.A. 486 (S.R.A.D.) that, as a result of the Interpretation Act 1930 (Chapter I of 1939, sec. 3) where an Act of the Legislature conferred powers on the Governor this meant 'acting by and with the advice of the Executive Council'. However it is submitted that the Governor could remain passive or refuse to act relying on the Royal Instructions even where a section empowered him to act.

[1] See infra, Chapter 14.
[2] Personal communications from Lord Howick and Sir John Kennedy. Lord Howick as Sir Evelyn Baring was Governor from 1942 to 1944. Sir John Kennedy was Governor from 1947 to 1953.
[3] S.R.L.A.D., Vol. 22, col. 274, 7 May 1942. This was not technically correct as the Constitution had been amended to allow the Governor in Council powers over the Native Department. The statement could only have reflected the power exercisable by the Governor to block Executive Council decisions if he saw fit.
[4] Statement in a Seminar at the University College in 1963. One distinguished ex-Governor had during his office pointed out to Sir Edgar the extent of his powers.

although they were considered by the Executive Council, were to be decided according to the Governor's own 'deliberate judgement'. The Governor was in all such cases to enter a detailed minute of the reasons for his decision. A similar procedure applied to pardons.[1] On a limited number of occasions the Governor in fact utilized this power to dissent from the view of the Executive Council, but such occasions arose only when the Council was split on the issue.[2] Indeed, both Lord Howick and Sir John Kennedy were always able to obtain the agreement of the Executive Council to their decisions, although Sir John reveals that in a few cases this only occurred by a majority.[3] This power was also removed after the coming into force of the 1961 Constitution as the original Royal Instructions were replaced in June 1962 by others, instructing the Governor to accept the advice of his Council on such matters.[4]

The Governor and the Cabinet

In terms of the Constitution Letters Patent the Governor was empowered to appoint a Ministry holding office during pleasure and not exceeding six in number.[5] The head of this Ministry was originally designated as Premier and subsequently as Prime Minister,[6] while each Minister was to be in charge of a Department of the Administration which would be assigned to him by the Governor as he saw fit.[7]

The Governor's discretion to appoint a Prime Minister was thus expressly retained. There was however little opportunity for Southern Rhodesian Governors to exercise discretion in making appointments. In most cases there has been no practical freedom of choice in that parties have been headed by official leaders who have been elected to the Legislative Assembly.

Only in the general election of 1946 was a party without an overall majority

[1] Royal Instructions Clauses 9 and 8. For an account of the procedure in 1949 relative to judges' reports, recommendations, Cabinet consideration, and ultimate Executive Council decisions, see *S.R.L.A.D.*, Vol. 30(2), cols. 2643–4.

[2] Personal communication from Lord Malvern.

[3] Personal communications from Lord Howick and Sir John Kennedy.

[4] S.R. Royal Instructions 1962. Procedure: Governor's Council and Capital Cases. 6 June 1962.

[5] Letters Patent, section 37. By Act 38 of 1948 this number was increased to seven.

[6] Letters Patent as amended by the Ministerial Titles Act No. 9 of 1933.

[7] At the grant of responsible government there were four main departments of the Administration. These were the Division of the Administrator, including the Native Department, that of the Treasurer, that of the Attorney-General, and that of the Secretary of Mines and Works. This system had been shaped on the Cape Colony model by Sir W. H. Milton, Administrator from 1899 to 1914. The structure was only slightly modified after the grant of responsible government as all pre-existing laws and administrative arrangements continued in force unless amended by the new Constitution: Section 63(2) Constitution Letters Patent. Subsequently, with the growth of Southern Rhodesia, Ministries expanded. By 1961 (when many Ministries had been transferred to the Federation of Rhodesia and Nyasaland) there were Ministries of the Treasury, Justice, Internal Affairs, Local Government, Native Affairs, Native Education, Roads, Irrigation and Lands, Mines, Labour and Social Welfare, and Housing held by seven Ministers, including the Prime Minister.

in the Legislative Assembly returned. The Governor then invited Sir Godfrey Huggins as the leader of the majority party to form a Government, which he was able to conduct for two years with alternative support from or abstention on different issues by the Southern Rhodesia Labour Parties and the Liberal Party.[1]

The only occasion on which the Governor exercised any element of personal choice was in his selection of Mr H. U. Moffat as Prime Minister in 1927 after the sudden death of Sir Charles Coghlan. However, Sir Charles had expressed the sentiment that Moffat should succeed him and apparently the majority of the Cabinet took a similar view.[2]

When Moffat resigned in 1934 the Rhodesia Party had already elected Mr. G. Mitchell as leader, it having been arranged that Moffat should resign at the convenience of the Party and that he would advise the Governor that Mitchell should succeed him.[3] The Governor thereupon requested Mr. Mitchell to form a government.

In respect of the appointment of Ministers much has depended on the relationship between Prime Minister and Governor. A strong Governor such as Sir John Chancellor[4] exercised influence on Mr. Moffat as Prime Minister. If the Prime Minister were inexperienced he might also seek the advice of the Governor. This apparently Mr. Huggins did when he attempted to form his first Ministry, but the Governor, Sir Cecil Rodwell,[5] declined to give him advice. In subsequent Ministries, however, Lord Malvern made such appointments as he saw fit, although if he was intimate with the Governor he might discuss the allocation of particular Ministries.[6]

Although the Governor had the reserve power of dismissing Ministers this was never used. The only occasion when a Governor could conceivably have used his power arose after Mr. Garfield Todd had received the resignation of members of his Cabinet in December 1957. It became clear that he did not enjoy the support of a majority of his caucus and that, were the Legislative

---

[1] See C. Leys, op. cit., pp. 162 et seq. for description of these parties. In 1948 Mr. Huggins accepted a Labour Party amendment to a motion of no confidence. He informed the House that he had done this because the Party had indicated confidence in his administration and said that he would otherwise have advised the Governor to send for the leader of the Opposition (Liberal Party) to form a Government: S.R.L.A.D., Vol. 27(2), col. 3177, 5 February 1948.

[2] National Archives NE 1/1/5, Fynn to Newton, 15 September 1927: 'I got back just in time to attend a meeting with the Governor when he came to the decision to invite Mr. Moffat to take the Premiership . . . Moffat . . . felt that the country was calling for him and that Sir Charles had expressed the hope that he would succeed him.'

[3] National Archives MO 13/1/1, Moffat to Downie. A similar situation arose in 1958 when Mr. R. S. Garfield Todd resigned and advised the Governor to request Sir Edgar Whitehead, who had been elected leader of the United Federal Party, to form a government. In 1964 under the 1961 Constitution when Mr. Winston Field resigned he advised that Mr. I. D. Smith be appointed by the Governor. Mr. Smith had been selected for this purpose by his party executive and parliamentary caucus although not by a party congress.

[4] 1924-8.   [5] 1928-33.

[6] Personal communication from Lord Malvern.

Assembly to meet, he would suffer an adverse vote.[1] At this time the Legislative Assembly stood adjourned from 21 August 1957 to 29 October 1957.
However, the form of the resolution adopted by the House permitted the
Speaker, if it appeared to his satisfaction 'after consultation with the Prime
Minister that the public interest required that the House should meet earlier
or later', to stand the House adjourned to a suitable time.[2] In order that he
might call a party congress to determine the issue of leadership, Mr. Todd
then twice obtained the Speaker's agreement to further adjournments, and the
House eventually met on 28 February 1958, under a new Prime Minister,
Sir Edgar Whitehead, who had shortly before been appointed on Mr. Todd's
advice. The Governor apparently did not consider that this action in continuing to govern without summoning Parliament in order to avoid an adverse
vote was a ground for dismissal,[3] although there is no doubt that a Ministry
commanding a majority could have been formed by other members of the
Legislative Assembly. Subsequently Sir Edgar Whitehead accepted the
principle that adjournments should not be permitted beyond the fixed
date.[4]

Ministers have on two occasions been 'dismissed' in a non-technical sense.
These occasions arise when Ministers disagreed with the Prime Minister and
Cabinet, but refused to resign. In both cases the Prime Minister tendered his
resignation and that of his Cabinet and thereafter the Governor reappointed
the Prime Minister who was then free to reconstitute his Ministry.[5]

During October 1943 another case of 'dismissal' occurred when Sir Godfrey
Huggins insisted that the two Labour Ministers in a war-time Coalition
Cabinet should not caucus with their party. He informed them that he could
not have Cabinet Ministers taking directions from an outside body and unless
they would undertake not to attend Labour Party caucus meetings he would
have to ask for their resignation. Both Mr. A. H. Davies and Mr. Keller then
decided to resign.[6] The Governor, however, never became involved in these
'dismissals'.

The Governor's discretion in granting or refusing a dissolution was

---

[1] *Semble* it is constitutional to dismiss a Prime Minister before an adverse vote and a
Governor may act on information received from a reliable source: *Adegbenro* v. *Akintola*,
[1963] 3 W.L.R. 63.

[2] This practice apparently originated during the Second World War. No other Commonwealth country has adopted a similar custom.

[3] Cf. Keith, op. cit., p. 123. See also E. A. Forsey, *Dissolution of Parliament*, Oxford,
1943, p. 184, who refers to the unconstitutionality of immediate prorogal of the Canadian
Parliament in 1873 for three months in order to avoid a vote of censure.

[4] See *S.R.L.A.D.*, Vol. 41, col. 362, 22 July 1958. His party had been criticized for abusing
this procedure because of dissension within its ranks. A new Standing Order No. 251A was
then introduced in February 1959 to prevent the reoccurrence of such an abuse.

[5] In 1932 Mr. R. A. Fletcher refused to resign from the Moffat Cabinet and again in 1950
Mr. R. Halsted refused to resign from the Huggins Cabinet.

[6] Personal communication from Lord Malvern. Leys, op. cit., p. 185, gives a somewhat
different version probably based on information from Mr. Keller.

expressly mentioned in the Constitution.[1] Only on two occasions does it appear that the Governor declined to grant a dissolution. The first occasion arose in 1932 when Mr. Moffat consulted the Governor on a dissolution as he anticipated difficulties in passing certain legislation. The Governor, however, informed him that until such time as he encountered difficulties with financial proposals there was no case for an appeal to the country.[2]

Subsequently Mr. Huggins had difficulties with a section of his party which declined to support him in putting through railway legislation which had been agreed with the B.S.A. Company and the British Government. He was then assured of support by the Parliamentary Opposition. Mr. Huggins thereupon requested a dissolution, but the Acting Governor, Sir Fraser Russell, who was Chief Justice, refused this request as Mr. Huggins could continue to govern with the Opposition and had not been defeated in the Legislative Assembly.[3] Shortly thereafter Mr. Huggins arranged a coalition between the loyal members of his party and the Opposition party, both groups joining in the formation of a new party, the United Party.[4] A further request in November 1934 for a dissolution was then accepted by the Acting Governor and Mr. Huggins was returned to power with a substantial majority.

The question whether a dissolution should be refused again arose in July 1948 when Sir Godfrey Huggins, who had led a minority government since 1946, suffered a defeat on a financial measure in the Legislative Assembly and requested a dissolution. Before acceding to this request the Governor, with the agreement of Sir Godfrey, assured himself that the Leader of the Opposition, Mr. J. H. Smit, whose party was almost numerically equal,[5] could not form an effective government.[6] This was a perfectly constitutional use of the Governor's powers in regard to dissolution, since it is recognized that in a House where no party has a clear majority a defeated minority government is not entitled to a dissolution if the Crown can find another cabinet willing to try to carry on with the existing House. In such circumstances the Crown may consider the 'parliamentary situation' and the possibility of an

---

[1] Letters Patent, Section 18(1): he might dissolve the Assembly 'whenever he shall think fit'.

[2] National Archives DO 1/1/6, Moffat to Downie (S.R. High Commissioner in London), 1 March 1932.

[3] Personal communication from Lord Malvern. Sir Fraser Russell obviously relied on the 1909 Australian precedent and Keith, op. cit., pp. 157–9. It is doubtful whether this decision was correct as the Opposition was agreeable to a dissolution, supply had been secured, the Government was seeking the dissolution after the first session of the Legislative Assembly, and no alternative government was possible: Forsey, op. cit., pp. 113, 269.

[4] See Gann and Gelfand, op. cit., p. 106 and Leys, op. cit., p. 138.

[5] There were eleven members in Smit's Liberal Party, while in Huggins' United Party there were thirteen out of a House of thirty members.

[6] Personal communication from Sir John Kennedy. Gann and Gelfand, op. cit., p. 206, refer to this incident and state that the Governor also required Sir Godfrey to satisfy him that, in view of the troubled international situation, his Ministry could carry on all essential business in the event of a third world war.

20—C.H.L.S.R.

alternative effective Government,[1] even if this depends on a temporary coalition.[2] When it became apparent that Mr. Smit was unable to form an alternative Government, Sir Godfrey Huggins' request was granted and his party was returned with a sizeable majority.

During the operation of the 1932 Letters Patent no need arose to exercise the Crown's reserve power entitling it to insist upon a forced dissolution.[3] Nor was it necessary to invoke the Governor's reserve power to refuse the Royal assent. This again was expressly preserved by the Constitution as was a discretionary power to reserve any legislation quite apart from that which he was bound to reserve in terms of Section 28 or the Royal Instructions.[4] Many measures were however reserved in view of Section 28 of the Letters Patent and also the Royal Instructions. Indeed, prior to giving assent to any measure the Governor considered an opinion by the Attorney-General as to the nature and effect of the measure and whether it came within the scope of the constitutional provisions for reservation.[5] On the other hand, no case of discretionary reservation or dissent arose.

The Governor was also given power to return by message to the Legislature any proposed law presented to him with any amendments which he might recommend.[6] This power was used at the instance of the Imperial authorities when provisions of the General Loans Bill 1937 were inconsistent with Section 10 of the Southern Rhodesia Loans Act 1923, which set out the terms of the first Southern Rhodesian stock issued. The Governor, Sir Herbert Stanley, then transmitted an amendment to the Legislative Assembly which 'would be acceptable to Her Majesty's Government in the United Kingdom' and these amendments were passed.[7] Had they not been accepted a case for refusal of assent would have arisen.

Again, the Governor might transmit the draft of Bills which he considered it desirable to introduce.[8] This, however, was the normal method of introducing legislation and in practice there was no occasion on which a Governor transmitted a Bill independently of the Executive.

The Governor also enjoyed the normal functions of issuing Proclamations, notifying the time and place of sessions of the Legislature,[9] proroguing the

---

[1] Forsey, op. cit., pp. 112–13. The Governor relied on Forsey in coming to his decision.

[2] Forsey, op. cit., pp. 116–18.

[3] See Forsey, op. cit., pp. 71, 270–1.

[4] Letters Patent, Section 27. Laws passed by the Legislative Assembly were to be presented for assent to the Governor 'who shall declare according to his discretion, but subject to this Constitution and any instruction in that behalf given him, under Our Sign Manual and Signet, or through a Secretary of State, that he assents in Our name, or that he withholds assent, or that he reserves the law for the signification of Our pleasure'. Pending assent, no law was to take effect: Section 30.

[5] This was standard practice in all colonies: see Keith, op. cit., p. 211.

[6] Section 29 of the Letters Patent.

[7] S.R.L.A.D., Vol. 17, cols. 1499–1500, 19 April 1937.

[8] Section 19 of the Letters Patent.

[9] Section 17.

Legislature,[1] and dissolving it at the expiration of five years from the date of its first meeting.[2] His was the responsibility furthermore of issuing without delay writs both for general elections and for by-elections.[3]

Influence of the Governor

The Governor, particularly in the early days of responsible government, was able to exercise considerable personal influence. Normally he was an Imperial Civil Servant of considerable governmental experience, well qualified to advise the relatively inexperienced local administration.[4] Later, as local politicians became more experienced, they tended to rely on their own opinions and the Governor was only able to exercise influence through advice which he tendered in his constitutional capacity and through his personal good relationships with his Prime Minister.[5] Thus Sir Herbert Stanley exercised great personal influence because of the confidence between himself and Mr. Huggins. Indeed Stanley's views that a new British Dominion should be formed in Central Africa as a counterbalance to the Union of South Africa, which was controlled by Afrikaner nationalists, influenced Mr. Huggins in his adoption of this policy.[6] Stanley in the fullest sense acted as intermediary between the local Government and the Imperial authorities.

Earlier, Sir John Chancellor, the first Governor, had exercised influence on Sir Charles Coghlan and a considerably greater degree on the second Premier, Mr. H. U. Moffat.[7] Later, Sir Charles Rodwell's advice was also valued by Southern Rhodesian governments. In addition, he advised the Southern Rhodesian Government as to the type of matter they should communicate to the Imperial authorities[8] and might propose amendments to

[1] Section 18(1).　　[2] Section 18(2).
[3] Sections 3 and 15(3).
[4] The first three Governors had had lengthy Colonial experience: Sir John Chancellor (1924–28), Sir Charles Rodwell (1928–33), and Sir H. J. Stanley (1935–42).
[5] See Cmd. 5949, p. 18, where, referring to the Southern Rhodesian Governor in 1939, it was said: 'The Governor . . . has the right to be consulted and to advise.' See also *Halsbury*, 3rd ed., Vol. 5, p. 446, and Keith, op. cit., p. 106. Lord Malvern in a personal communication has said: 'When I got to know the Governors well I used to talk to them about all sorts of things.'
[6] It also influenced the Dominions Office not to reject this policy out of hand.
[7] See *S.R.L.A.D.*, Vol. 7, col. 458: 'He has been our guide . . . in the manner in which he has assisted and advised the Premier and Ministers. No detail was too small for him to notice and discuss whether it was with the Minister or the heads of Departments.' On one occasion he advised Moffat as to the proper use of police forces in dealing with a strike. On another he induced him not to proceed with proposals for closure of the rolls to African voters. Personal communications from a confidential source. He also amongst other things advised on honours (National Archives NE 1/1/7, Moffat to Newton, 8 May 1928), the seat for which the Prime Minister should stand at the next election (ibid., 5 December 1927), on the country's coat of arms (CO 8/1/1, 29 October 1923), and on land settlement questions (NE 1/1/7). In fact in 1924 the Governor induced Moffat, who was then a Minister, not to resign from the Cabinet: MO 13/1/1, Moffat to Davis, 29 November 1924.
[8] National Archives NE 1/1/7, Moffat to Newton, 6 January 1930.

regulations.[1] Not only because he was Commander-in-Chief, but also because of the valuable advice he could give was he consulted on defence reorganization.[2]

At all times Southern Rhodesian Governments welcomed advice and comment by Governors.[3] This was particularly the case in matters in which the Imperial authorities were concerned. Here the Governor's dual functions overlapped, so that while at times he reported on events for the information of the United Kingdom Government, at other times he acted as a mediator between Southern Rhodesian and United Kingdom Governments, and yet on other occasions he acted as adviser to both governments. Indeed Lord Howick has stated: 'I regarded my main function as being that of an adviser to both Governments and I felt that my main task was to obtain agreement between them.'[4] Sir John Kennedy also states that: 'I would have regarded it as a failure in that relationship (between Governor and Prime Minister) had conflicting views been communicated to Whitehall.'[5]

Governors in practice advised Southern Rhodesian Governments as to the view which would satisfy the Imperial authorities. Thus the first Governor, Sir John Chancellor, assisted the Southern Rhodesian Government in justifying and explaining legislation such as the Native Affairs Act 1927 and the Native Juveniles Employment Act 1927,[6] while Sir Charles Rodwell similarly assisted the Southern Rhodesian Government in dealing with attacks by the Archbishop of Canterbury on the Native Marriages Ordinance Amendment Act 1927.[7]

The cordial relationship established between Governor and the Prime Minister enabled the Governor to discuss matters freely with the Prime Minister. In discharging his special responsibility for interpreting the policy and wishes of the United Kingdom Government[8] the Governor would explain the United Kingdom Government's view and then in turn notify the United Kingdom Government in despatches of the opinion of the Southern Rhodesian Cabinet. This informal method of reaching agreement was particularly important in working the reserved clauses of the Constitution, as suggestions for modifications of proposed legislation could privately be made and, in the prevailing atmosphere, these would almost invariably be regarded as helpful and be accepted in the drafting stage.[9] Sometimes the Governor himself might make suggestions for amendment, or that the Prime Minister should discuss the proposals with the Chief Justice as a member of the Board

---

[1] National Archives MO 13/1/1, Rodwell to Moffat, 11 February 1931.
[2] National Archives RO 7/1/1, Rodwell to Hudson, 19 March 1932.
[3] Personal communications from Lord Howick, Sir John Kennedy, and Lord Malvern.
[4] Personal communication in June 1964.
[5] Personal communication in June 1964.
[6] National Archives NE 1/1/7, Moffat to Newton, 5 December 1927; S.R.L.A.D., Vol. 7, col. 460.
[7] National Archives S 138/10, Rodwell to Moffat, 11 July 1929.   [8] Cmd. 5949, p. 18.
[9] Personal communication from Sir John Kennedy. See also supra, Chapter 12.

of Trustees for the Native Reserves. This was done in the late nineteen forties on the advice of Sir John Kennedy and, as a result, a draft Bill providing that no African be entitled to remain in urban areas after six months, unless he was in employment, was dropped.[1]

On administrative questions Governors' views might also have considerable effect. Thus in 1941 Lord Hailey, who had conducted a confidential survey on Native Affairs in Southern Rhodesia for the United Kingdom and Southern Rhodesian Governments, concluded that 'the development of native policy in Southern Rhodesian Reserves has been influenced by the advice given by the Governor'.[2] There is no doubt that Governors concerned themselves with the welfare of the African population. Thus Sir John Chancellor encouraged the settlement of Africans in the Sabi Reserve where land was available,[3] watched the complaints of Chiefs and also made it clear that no recruitment by the Southern Rhodesian administration of African labour except in its own employment would be permitted.[4] Subsequently Sir Cecil Rodwell concerned himself with the working of Native Boards which were the precursor of Native Councils.[5]

The Governor could also convey gentle warnings that the introduction of particular legislation would lead to clashes with the United Kingdom Government and possibly the need for resignation of the Prime Minister.[6] He might also insist that Southern Rhodesian administrative action would not receive United Kingdom approval.[7]

Acting Governors did not exercise the same influence. This was the more emphasized because the Acting Governor was usually the Southern Rhodesian Chief Justice, whose opinions did not normally carry weight with the Prime Minister as in his view Chief Justices were inclined to adopt a legalistic approach to the functions of Governor.[8]

---

[1] Personal communications from Sir John Kennedy, Sir Robert Tredgold, and Mr. W. A. E. Winterton.

[2] National Archives S 235/482, Confidential report by Lord Hailey on Southern Rhodesia, p. 3.

[3] National Archives S 138/10, Correspondence, S 138/21, Chief Native Commissioner to Secretary to Governor.

[4] R. L. Buell, *The Native Problem in Africa*, Macmillan, 1929, Vol. I, p. 230. In 1925 the Governor stated: 'Any measures taken by Government to apply compulsion to natives to secure an adequate supply of labour for private employers would be opposed to the traditional policy of His Majesty's Government and would be altogether repugnant to the sentiment of the Imperial Parliament.'

[5] See *infra*, Chapter 14.

[6] National Archives NE 1/1/1, Coghlan to Newton, 1/8/25. 'The Governor said to me that he understood from a previous conversation I rather favoured taking over the Railways and that I proposed legislation in that direction which if not assented to by the Imperial Government would involve my resignation.'

[7] National Archives LE 3/2/1/4. Cabinet Resolution 2182, 27 November 1931. Proposals requiring applicants for passports to produce certificates of payment of income tax were rejected by the Governor.

[8] Personal communication from Lord Malvern.

The Governor as an Imperial officer

The Governor from the Imperial point of view was charged with multiple functions and was certainly no mere Ministerial mouthpiece. Since originally there was no British High Commissioner appointed to Southern Rhodesia, the Governor was the local representative of the British Government. He was also the British official commissioned with the duty of reporting on events in Southern Rhodesia.[1] On other occasions the Governor was the channel of communication for the views of the Governments and in this process he enjoyed mediatory functions. The Governor was also Commander-in-Chief of the Armed Forces and had certain duties under the United Kingdom Army Act while he was responsible for seeing that Southern Rhodesian forces were not employed beyond the borders of the Colony without Imperial consent. In addition, he was required to make himself available for consultation by and advice to, the Secretary of State and the High Commissioner for South Africa in regard to the acts and proposals of the Southern Rhodesian Government, particularly in view of the continued Imperial powers of supervision over the Native Reserves, the administration of the Land Apportionment Act, and over the Native Department itself.[2] His advice could also be required on whether reserved measures should receive assent. He might even be required to exercise the reserve powers of the Crown to protect Imperial interests or to preserve the Imperial connection.[3] Finally the Governor had wider duties after the closer association of British Central African Territories from 1945 until the creation of the Federation of Rhodesia and Nyasaland, since the Southern Rhodesian Governor was Chairman of the Central Africa Council.[4]

The difficult task of reconciling these functions with his duties as constitutional head of an executive controlled by his advisers[5] was carried out by Southern Rhodesian Governors without conflict arising in practice. Indeed

---

[1] The Governor was intended to 'take the place of the Resident Commissioner': Jollie, op. cit., p. 247. Governors until 1951 wrote regular and lengthy despatches on political and economic events in Southern Rhodesia. I have also been informed by a confidential source that early Governors' activities were almost akin to those of Imperial 'spies' on Southern Rhodesian events. See also National Archives RO 7/1/1, Rodwell to Harding, 6 April 1933, reporting on the state of the parliamentary parties and 20 April 1933 commenting that if the election were lost this would 'place the country at the mercy of a set of irresponsibles'. That this occurred without breach of good relations between Southern Rhodesian Prime Ministers and Governors is a tribute to their tact and discretion, and was only possible in a situation where there were not considerable or deeply felt differences of policy between the Governments.

[2] The two former powers persisted until 1962 while the latter disappeared in 1937. The Governor was always appointed by the Secretary of State as Chairman of the Board of Trustees of the Reserves to administer the Reserves Trust. See Chapter 14, infra.

[3] No question of the use of such power however arose in practice.

[4] See infra, Chapter 15. Earlier the Hilton Young Commission has suggested that the Governor of Southern Rhodesia should also be appointed High Commissioner for Southern Rhodesia, Northern Rhodesia, and Nyasaland but this suggestion was not adopted.

[5] Governors could obtain information from any department. Thus Governors obtained information from the Native Department in particular: see RO 7/1/7, folios 442ff. The

the Governor was able with his intimate knowledge of the situation in the country and the administration[1] to give the United Kingdom valuable information which no High Commissioner could provide. But this intimate knowledge also assisted Southern Rhodesian Governments, as the Governor was able to act in a more informal way with understanding of their problems and thus secure agreement with the United Kingdom Government.[2] Indeed the Southern Rhodesian Governor was able to advise the Commonwealth Relations Office on its dealings with Southern Rhodesia which were sometimes tactless on the official level.[3] The measure of Governors' success in this respect is that Governors were locally considered to have identified themselves with the country.[4] Indeed Sir John Kennedy, as an ex-Governor, was invited in 1960 by the Prime Minister, Sir Edgar Whitehead, and the organizers to be Chairman of a National Convention to make proposals for the future development of Southern Rhodesia.

Nonetheless, as Southern Rhodesia began to reach out to independence, such a position became anomalous and the functions of the Governor gradually diminished. Thus in 1951 after the appointment of a British High Commissioner the Governor was relieved from the duty of acting as channel of communication between the Governments and also from the duty of writing personal despatches to the Secretary of State on political and economic affairs. There was however no change in the functions of the Governor under the Constitution, so that a Governor could still give advice to the Imperial authorities on reserved matters and questions touching on any exercise of the Secretary of State's powers. Governors also kept in close touch with the High Commissioner.[5]

Subsequently it seems that there was a tendency for Governors' views to be considered as less important since the Imperial authorities had now their own diplomatic representative to perform such functions. Ultimately under the 1961 Constitution, the position was accepted that the Governor was to exercise his powers in accordance with the constitutional conventions obtaining in the United Kingdom, retaining only certain reserve powers which could be invoked by him as guardian of the Constitution in the event of unconstitutional action or some grave crisis in which Imperial interests were at stake.

Governor in 1934 was watching the operation of levies of 2s. 6d. per head on native cattle, and the reaction of the African population as expressed through Native Boards. The Native Department had been responsible for restraining the Cabinet from raising this levy to 10s. per head.

[1] 'The really onerous part of his duty consists in his watching that portion of colonial politics which touches on the connection with the mother country': Jenkyns, op. cit., p. 106, quoting Merivale.

[2] Personal communication from Lord Howick.

[3] In 1950 the Governor wrote a memorandum, which was circulated to the British Cabinet, on the correct approach to be adopted towards the S.R. Government.

[4] Sir Edgar Whitehead considers Sir Herbert Stanley did this to a very great extent.

[5] Personal communication from Sir John Kennedy.

14

NATIVE ADMINISTRATION AND CONSTITUTIONAL CHANGES 1925–62

> We accept fully the proposition that there is an Imperial responsibility
> for the protection of native races not represented in legislative
> assemblies.[1]

UNDER the 1923 Letters Patent, Britain reserved to herself considerable powers in respect of native administration since the Buxton Report, which preceded the grant of responsible government, had recommended that 'the natives are entitled to be secured in their existing position and to be ensured against discriminatory disabilities or restrictions'.[2] The Commission had advised that the procedure under the Southern Rhodesia Order in Council 1898 whereby the High Commissioner and the Secretary of State had 'considerable powers of control over the Administration insofar as it affects the natives . . . should be altered and disturbed as little as possible'.[3] Accordingly a large number of the provisions contained in the Southern Rhodesia Order in Council 1898 were adopted and inserted in the Southern Rhodesia Constitution Letters Patent 1923. In addition, to the extent that there was no repugnancy between the Letters Patent and the Order in Council, the 1898 Order in Council remained in force.[4] Although the Order might be repealed or amended by the Legislature those provisions in the Order which related to and affected the sections in the Letters Patent dealing with Native Administration could not be amended. It was expressly provided that neither the sections in the Letters Patent nor the relevant sections in the 1898 Order could be amended by the Legislative Assembly.[5]

The High Commissioner's powers of control remained an integral feature of the new Constitution.[6] He continued to exercise on behalf of the Imperial Government his functions of control over native affairs, although other powers such as the power of legislating by Proclamation were withdrawn,[7] while all

---

[1] W. S. Churchill, *H.C. Deb.*, 4th ser., Vol. 152, col. 1232, 28 February 1906. Cp. The Southern Rhodesian attitude—Newton (High Commissioner in London) to Moffat (Prime Minister): 'We had a damn sight too much of this trustee business': National Archives NE 1/1/7, 1 July 1929.

[2] Cmd. 1273, § 61. See *S.R.L.A.D.*, Vol. 17, col. 1619, 12 October 1937, Huggins. Lord Buxton had informed the Prime Minister that if this had not been agreed upon, responsible government would not have been granted.

[3] Cmd. 1273, § 63.   [4] Letters Patent, Section 63(2).   [5] Letters Patent, Section 26(2).

[6] Stanley had suggested this in his Memorandum: African 1085, No. 3, Encl., 21 July 1920. In *H.C. Deb.*, Vol. 183, col. 1425, 11 May 1925, Ormsby-Gore acknowledged the control reserved to the High Commissioner for South Africa.

[7] Section 58(1).

powers previously exercisable by him in terms of any Ordinance or Proclamation were transferred to the Governor in Council unless specially reserved to him.[1]

Control over Native Affairs Department officials

As before, appointments, salaries, and disciplinary proceedings in the Native Department were subject to the High Commissioner's approval.[2] He could require the suspension of any officer of the Native Department, while any suspension ordered by the Governor in Council was to be reported to him for his confirmation, disallowance, or general discretionary decision.[3]

The High Commissioner (now the Governor-General of South Africa) also had the power to intervene at any time if he considered that officials in the Native Affairs Department were not maintaining proper standards of administration. There is, however, no evidence that this was necessary.[4] This is not surprising since the Native Department had been established on a proper basis since 1897 and all its appointments had been subjected to Imperial scrutiny. Furthermore, a local Public Services Board to advise on appointments of all civil servants had been set up in 1927 and formally established in 1933.[5] Indeed, the Department had high traditions of service of its own.[6]

[1] Section 58(ii). This meant that he no longer exercised control of the Military Police forces when they were on active service (S.R. Order in Council 1898, Section 48, as amended). The other powers were minor: he was no longer responsible for granting warrants for apprehension and expulsion of dangerous persons (Proclamation, 30 June 1891, Peace Preservation Ordinance, Section 1), for confirming the sentences of special courts established under the Volunteer Regulations (Ordinance 2 of 1902, Section 48), for establishing tariffs for witnesses from neighbouring territories (Proclamation 1 July 1898, Sections 1 and 2), in regard to the removal of criminal lunatics (Ordinance 3 of 1908, Sections 24 and 26), for confirming sentences on juvenile offenders in capital cases (Ordinance 4 of 1910, Section 1), controlling monies held by the Custodian of Enemy Property (Ordinance 2 of 1915, Section 6), or for declaring whether maintenance orders should be enforced (Ordinance 20 of 1921, Sections 1 and 2).

[2] Sections 39(i) to (iii) of the Letters Patent.

[3] Section 40(i) to (v).

[4] The Native Affairs Department files up to 1934 are available for inspection in the National Archives. On the other hand, correspondence with the Governor-General went through the Governor's office and these files are not open to inspection.

[5] Under Section 4 of the Public Services Act 1931. See S.R. Government Notice 117 of 24 February 1933 for Civil Service Regulations. As early as 1912 the Company had established an Advisory Committee to scrutinize the appointment of all civil servants. In certain cases Public Services Board recommendations might be preferred by the Cabinet to those of the Chief Native Commissioner, e.g. the Chief Native Commissioner's views as to his successor were overruled: see Chief Native Commissioner to Secretary for Premier, 27 August 1930, National Archives S 138/6, MSS.

[6] Native Affairs Department files in the National Archives reveal the way in which the Department attempted to further the national welfare of the African people, particularly by improvement of water supplies and agricultural advice in the Reserves. See S 138/7, MSS. A Department of Native Education was also established. See, too, Reports of the Chief Native Commissioner, 1924–62. National Archives S 138/32, MSS. Superintendent of Natives, Bulawayo, to Chief Native Commissioner, 13 March 1931, shows how Native

However, the Governor-General watched the calibre of recruits,[1] on one occasion, after approving Native Affairs Department promotions, suggesting that a proportion of public school boys be taken in.[2] The procedure of securing the High Commissioner's approval was, in fact, fully observed[3] and when appointments had been approved by the Executive Council they were then submitted to the High Commissioner for his approval. Even such matters as the approval of the Acting Native Commissioners *vice* others who were going on leave were processed with the assurance that the Acting Native Commissioner was 'fully qualified to act',[4] while transfers, promotions, and salary increases were also cleared.[5]

In fact in 1931, when salary decreases for Native Commissioners were proposed as a result of the economic crisis, the High Commissioner at first refused to commit himself, demanding full particulars of all deductions and eventually giving permission only on the 'understanding that deductions at the same rates will be applicable to all other branches of the Public Service'.[6]

The High Commissioner also refused to appoint a new Chief Native Commissioner on mere telegraphic request and insisted on a formal despatch from the Governor incorporating the last Chief Native Commissioner's recommendation.[7] The appointment of a new Chief Native Commissioner in 1928 was in fact confirmed by the Secretary of State,[8] who associated himself with an appreciative minute to the ex-Chief Native Commissioner by the High Commissioner commenting how invaluable the help of the Chief Native Commissioner had been 'in the discharge of our responsibilities in respect of the administration of native affairs in Southern Rhodesia'.[9] Similarly when

Commissioners were accused by the public of being 'negrophilist'. From the mid-nineteen-fifties the Department was subjected to heavy criticism as being separatist and paternalistic. See Report of the Commission appointed to inquire into and report on Administrative and Judicial Functions in the Native Affairs and District Courts' Departments. C.S.R. 22–1961, Government Printer, Salisbury.

[1] National Archives S 138/6, Telegraph Governor to High Commissioner, 27 May 1927, stating qualifications and lack of qualifications of Native Commissioners.

[2] National Archives S 138/6, Athlone to Chancellor, 8 February 1927. This suggestion was made informally. The Prime Minister then told the Governor that this policy was already followed: Coghlan to Chancellor, 21 March 1927.

[3] On one occasion only the Governor wrote to enquire how a Director of Native Development had been appointed without the High Commissioner's approval: National Archives S 138/125, 2 January 1926.

[4] National Archives S 138/6, Governor to High Commissioner, 16 November 1926. See also Governor to High Commissioner, 11 January 1929; Telegram High Commissioner to Governor, 25 April 1932.

[5] National Archives S 138/6, 27 July 1927, Chief Native Commissioner to Premier requesting Prime Minister to take steps to obtain the approval of the High Commissioner for salary increases.

[6] National Archives S 138/6, Telegram High Commissioner to Governor, 18 November 1931. Telegram High Commissioner to Attorney-General, 30 October 1931.

[7] National Archives S 138/6, Telegram High Commissioner to Governor, 17 March 1928.

[8] National Archives S 138/6, Despatch from Secretary of State, Mr. Amery, to the Earl of Athlone. S.A. No. 127, 24 April 1928.

[9] National Archives S 138/6, High Commissioner to Governor, 24 March 1928.

at one time the removal of the new Chief Native Commissioner was under consideration, the Prime Minister commented that it would be necessary to refer the matter to the High Commissioner.[1]

This protection given to the Native Affairs Department largely put it beyond the reach of Southern Rhodesian Governments.[2] In fact, the Native Department was a 'Government within a Government' and for a long time this resulted in native affairs being kept out of politics. There were two completely separate civil services in practice (although transfers between them took place): there was the ordinary civil service administering matters affecting Europeans and the Native Affairs Department administering Africans. The Chief Native Commissioner enjoyed tremendous powers and only gradually came to consult the Minister responsible for African Affairs: indeed, the first Prime Minister and Minister of Native Affairs, Sir Charles Coghlan, was not even kept informed of happenings in the Native Affairs Department.[3]

However, when changes in Government occurred this external control over the Native Affairs Department and its virtual independence of Government was resented. In 1934, Mr. Huggins refused to permit sums to be voted for Native Development as the Imperial Government would not approve the appointment of a Chairman to the Native Affairs Commission proposed by him.[4] The Prime Minister therefore informed the House that he would visit the Dominions Office so that he could explain and continue with his native policy as Government was finding the control irritating, expensive, and liable to lead to friction.[5] Thus moves were initiated to have the control of the High Commissioner removed.[6]

Administrative measures and Africans

In addition to his control over the personnel of the Native Department, the High Commissioner was also able to scrutinize the effect of Native Affairs Department policies since he was entitled to demand from the Governor any information relating to Native Affairs.[7] Furthermore, the Governor in Council was compelled to refer any questions relating to natives to a High Court Judge for report if the High Commissioner so requested. Thereupon the Governor in Council was to inform the High Commissioner of the contents of the report and of any action proposed in the matter.[8] Should the

---

[1] National Archives NE 1/1/7, Moffat to Newton, 21 August 1928.
[2] *S.R.L.A.D.*, Vol. 44, col. 3142: 'The Department was placed very largely under external control.' Sir Edgar Whitehead, Minister of Native Affairs.
[3] Personal communication by Lord Malvern.
[4] *S.R.L.A.D.*, Vol. 14, col. 531, 24 March 1934.
[5] *S.R.L.A.D.*, Vol. 14, col. 1325, 10 May 1934.
[6] *S.R.L.A.D.*, Vol. 14, col. 534, 2 March 1934. This eventually occurred in 1937.
[7] Section 44. This was a new provision which had not appeared in the 1898 Order in Council.
[8] Section 45. This was not as effective as Section 86 of the Southern Rhodesian Order in

Governor in Council wish, in the event of misconduct by Chiefs or tribes, to impose reasonable fines on the offenders, this also required the High Commissioner's consent.[1]

The Native Reserves

The Native Reserves, as set apart for the sole use of the African population by the Southern Rhodesia Order in Council 1920, continued to vest in the High Commissioner. Indeed all the provisions of the Order were to continue in force.[2] Thus no alteration in the conditions on which non-Africans occupied land in the Reserves could be made without the High Commissioner's assent to any changed regulations.[3] Nor could any land be taken from the Reserves for administrative purposes without the High Commissioner's consent, while when cases arose the High Commissioner required to be satisfied and given full explanation as to why large areas were being taken.[4] Later in 1928, as a result of intervention by the High Commissioner, safeguards were introduced in respect of deforestation of the Reserves where European miners were cutting timber.[5] The High Commissioner also required to be satisfied that a proper Native Reserves Trust Fund was established to deal with the revenues accruing from Native Reserves, insisting that his approval be obtained for estimates of expenditure from such funds[6] and that one of the objects of the Trust must be 'native education and industrial training'. He also demanded and obtained an undertaking from the Government that the establishment of such a fund would not preclude further general funds being voted for African development, the Government in fact undertaking to make other sources available in addition. The High Commissioner's powers to protect African interests in respect of water rights and irrigation schemes were also continued.[7]

Council 1898 since in the earlier section the High Commissioner was himself authorized to take any action on such report as he saw fit.

[1] Section 46. This was slightly stronger than Section 88 of the Southern Rhodesia Order in Council, which only permitted the High Commissioner to remit such fines.

[2] Section 42(i).

[3] Southern Rhodesia Order in Council 1920. Article 4 provided for regulations which were issued by S.R. Government Notice 206 of 18 May 1923, while in terms of Sections 14 and 16 the Governor was required to act under these regulations in accordance with the High Commissioner's instructions. The provisions requiring the High Commissioner's assent were rigidly observed: see National Archives S 138/10, High Commissioner to Governor, 8 September 1928, agreeing to minor modifications in the conditions.

[4] National Archives S 138/259. Governor's Minutes 149, 225 of 1925. The Governor assured the High Commissioner that the interests of inhabitants would not be adversely affected: Governor to High Commissioner, 20 April 1925. The High Commissioner would only consent after full details were given and assurances given that Africans' access to water supplies would not be affected adversely: High Commissioner to Governor, 18 May 1925.

[5] See National Archives LE 3/2/1/2, Cabinet Resolution 810 of 19 April 1928 laying down that in future no excessive amounts of timber were to be cut and that payment must be made for all amounts cut.

[6] See National Archives S 235/344 MS.

[7] Letters Patent, Section 42(ii): see S.R.L.A.D., Vol 14, col. 534, 24 March 1934, where

At the same time Section 83 of the Southern Rhodesia Order in Council 1898 was incorporated into the Letters Patent as Section 43. This entrenched the right of Africans to acquire, hold, encumber, and dispose of land on the same conditions as non-Africans but afforded Africans protection by invalidating contracts for the disposal or encumbrance of land unless certified by a Magistrate to have been made in his presence, that the African understood the transaction, and that the consideration was reasonable.[1]

Finally, the High Commissioner was required to approve the establishment by Proclamation by the Governor in Council of Native Councils in Native Reserves.[2] Any regulations governing such Councils' powers and proceedings were also to be subject to the High Commissioner's approval.[3] In practice from 1924 the Native Department started holding meetings with Chiefs and Headmen, which it considered as the precursor to proper Native Councils.[4] Ultimately a draft Native Councils Bill was prepared and printed,[5] but the Secretary of State cabled the Governor to warn the Southern Rhodesian Government that such a Bill would be void in terms of Section 26(2) read with Section 47(1) of the Letters Patent as this was within the High Commissioner's exclusive sphere.[6] Accordingly the Bill was dropped.

Delegated legislation

One of the most important provisions of the Constitution was that more extensive protection against discriminatory delegated legislation and administrative action was afforded Africans, as the High Commissioner's approval was necessary where any condition, disability, or restriction was imposed on Africans which did not equally apply to persons of European descent,[7] unless the enabling law explicitly defined and prescribed such restrictions.[8]

Mr. Huggins complained about the necessity for obtaining the High Commissioner's permission to allow the Chief Native Commissioner to appear in the Water Court to obtain a water right in a Reserve: 'It is stretching our patience too far when they want to interfere with such trivial things.'

[1] This was effective until Letters Patent of 26 March 1930 permitted the enactment of a law permitting Africans alone to acquire and hold land in certain parts of the Colony and Europeans alone in other specified parts. Cp. new Section 43(2)(a). The Land Apportionment Act 1930 then made such provisions. See *supra*, Chapter 12.

[2] The section was inserted as a result of the High Commissioner's suggestion that Native Councils be established on the lines of those established under the Union of South Africa Native Affairs Act 23 of 1920 or analogously to the Basutoland Council: African 1085, No. 3. High Commissioner to Secretary of State, 6 August 1920.

[3] Section 47.

[4] Report of the Chief Native Commissioner for the year 1924. Salisbury, Government Printer. C.S.R. 7, 1925, p. 2.

[5] A.B. 18 of 1929.

[6] National Archives S 235/444, Minute 253 of 1929, 5 June 1929.

[7] Section 41 of the Letters Patent. Compare Section 80 of the Southern Rhodesia Order in Council 1898. This applied only to Ordinances, and was the equivalent of Section 28(a) of the Letters Patent.

[8] See *Mabelreign Town Management Board* v. *James Chamboko*, 1962 R. and N. 493

In interpreting the effect of this section and also Section 28 of the Constitution, the courts made a clear distinction between differentiation—a simple distinguishing between the races—and discrimination—unfavourable differentiation between the races.[1] However, Section 41 did not permit either differentiation or discrimination unless the Secretary of State consented to the regulation or the enabling law had provided for it.[2] Naturally, once authority to differentiate was given by the Secretary of State, a differentiating regulation was permissible. However, authority to differentiate, although permitting of 'intangible discrimination' (i.e. psychological consequences only would ensue since equal facilities were provided) would not permit of 'tangible discrimination' (unequal facilities),[3] as power to discriminate had to be specifically given either in express terms or by necessary implication. In practice this meant that even though regulations might differentiate and permit separate facilities, there would have to be impartiality and equality of treatment, unless express authority to discriminate was given.

The need for consent could not be evaded by the enactment of a regulation which did not differentiate but merely provided the opportunity to differentiate.[4] Similarly although there was no law providing for the reservation of administrative instructions for approval before such restrictions became operative, the delegation of an absolute discretion to an official could not be permitted as this would 'frustrate the purposes of Section 40 of the Constitution by permitting action to be taken in an informal way in respect of a matter which, if it were to be done with the ordinary and proper formalities, e.g. by-law or regulation, would require the approval of the Secretary of State'.[5]

(F.C.) at pp. 496–7 per Clayden C.J.: 'There is a clear policy in the Constitution. Any legislation differentiating between European and African has to receive assent in Britain and the differentiation has to be apparent to Her Majesty's advisers. If there is potentiality for differentiation in the enabling Act it has to be reserved; if there is differentiation in subordinate legislation under that Act it requires no further approval if its form was apparent under the Act, for that form has already been approved. But if the differentiation has come about under powers generally conferred the form of the differentiation enacted has to be approved in its turn.'

[1] *Chamboko* v. *Mabelreign Town Management Board*, 1962 R. and N. 450 at 453 per Beadle C.J.

[2] This was recognized by the Government. When requested to discriminate on Central African Airways the Prime Minister replied, after referring to Section 40, that 'in public concerns in the Colony differential treatment is *ultra vires* our Constitution': *S.R.L.A.D.*, Vol. 30(1), col. 993.

[3] Beadle C.J. in *Mehta* v. *City of Salisbury* at pp. 918–19, citing *R.* v. *Abdurahman*, 1950 (3) S.A. 136 (A.D.) at 149 per Centlivres J.A.; *Rex* v. *Lusu*, 1953 (2) S.A. 484 (A.D.) per Centlivres C.J. at 490; *Bindura Town Management Board* v. *Desai & Co.*, 1953 (1) S.A. 358 (A.D.) at 363 per van den Heever J.A. and at 369 per Hoexter J.A. (the latter was a case on appeal from Southern Rhodesia).

[4] Per Clayden C.J. in *Mabelreign Town Management Board* v. *Chamboko, supra* at 497.

[5] Briggs F.J. in *City of Salisbury* v. *Mehta, supra* at 703. (The reference in this case is to Section 40, not 41, because in 1937 the section was renumbered). See also Beadle C.J. at p. 681. Cp. *Pillai* v. *Mudanayake*, [1953] A.C. 514. However, in practice, discrimination by

In comparison with Section 28 there was no alternative in respect of delegated legislation permitting a suspending clause or reservation as advance consent of the High Commissioner had to be obtained. Another distinction between Sections 41 and 28(a) was that there could be no doubt that Section 41 imported 'practical application' by the use of the words 'equally apply'. However, in dealing with subordinate legislation Governments, in practice, relied on their legal advisers and, if they received advice that legislation did not discriminate, would not submit the subordinate legislation for consent of the Imperial authorities.

That the Southern Rhodesian Government found this control irksome was proved by the fact that in 1928 the Attorney-General (then a member of the Cabinet) complained to the Secretary of State about the High Commissioner's powers in respect of legislation affecting Africans.[1] Nevertheless this safeguard (with the substitution in 1937 of the Secretary of State for the High Commissioner) remained in the Constitution until it was replaced by the Southern Rhodesia Constitution 1961.

Constitutional amendments, 1925–62[2]

Attempts to gain higher status

No sooner was responsible government established than attempts to improve the status of Southern Rhodesia began.

The first attacks were directed against the protections given to the British South Africa Company and in particular against the 'railway reservation', while the Prime Minister went so far as to have a draft Bill prepared to evade Section 28(e).[3] After negotiations with the British South Africa Company and the Imperial Government this reservation was transposed into the Railway Act 1927 in a slightly less restrictive form, where, since it had been deleted from the Constitution,[4] it attracted less hostility.

The 'mineral reservation' was also eliminated in 1934[5] after a Government purchase of the British South Africa Company's mineral rights but, until that time, it had been completely effective in barring legislation.

executive and administrative discretion certainly occurred. See National Archives LE 3/2/1/4/, Cabinet Resolution No. 2430 of 8 April 1932, which shows that the Cabinet was annoyed that a mining prospecting lease had been granted to an African. They resolved that special notice should be given to all officials that applications for such licences must be submitted to the Minister of Mines and that none were to be issued without his approval.

[1] National Archives NE 1/1/4, Newton to Fynn, 13 December 1928.

[2] Other than the establishment of the Federation of Rhodesia and Nyasaland which is dealt with in Chapters 15 and 16.

[3] National Archives CO 8/1/2, Newton to Coghlan, 22 April 1926. Apparently the Colonial Office was very anxious to see the draft though the Prime Minister decided not to proceed with the Bill until he had had negotiations with the British South Africa Company.

[4] Letters Patent of 28 May 1927. See Proclamation No. 11 of 1927.

[5] Letters Patent of 6 April 1934. See Proclamation No. 4 of 1934.

Increased local control over Native Affairs

The 'native reservation' was also subjected to an attempt at removal when the Secretary of State visited Rhodesia in 1927 but the Prime Minister's request for this was refused,[1] and the reservation in fact remained fully effective until 1962. Nonetheless the United Kingdom Government agreed after the Land Commission Report of 1925 and prolonged negotiations to permit the enactment of a law permitting segregated land ownership in Southern Rhodesia. This occasioned a constitutional amendment in 1930.[2] Amendment of the Letters Patent[3] was also made to permit the establishment of Native Councils in areas outside the Reserves as it was envisaged that in the new native purchase areas to be created under the Land Apportionment Act Native Councils in native village settlements might be established.[4]

The constitutional amendments of 1937

By 1934, although a slight increase in the powers of the Legislature had occurred, pressures for higher status were strengthened by the election of Mr. Huggins. From 1934 to 1937 he visited the Dominions Office annually, requesting higher status for Southern Rhodesia—although not dominion status—and considerable correspondence passed between the Governments.[5] Negotiations settled details of draft changes in the Constitution and also in legislation and statutory instruments. When assured that adequate safeguards existed for the Native Reserves the Imperial Government permitted their relatively direct control of native administration through the High Commissioner[6] to be eliminated in favour of remote control by the Secretary of State.[7] Although the High Commissioner's control was eliminated, he was to

[1] Personal communication from a confidential source. Mr. Amery refused the request on 20 August 1927.

[2] Letters Patent of 26 March 1930. African rights to hold land on the same conditions as Europeans as set out in Section 43 were finally repealed by Letters Patent of 25 March 1937.

[3] Letters Patent of 22 July 1931, amending Section 47.

[4] National Archives S 138/55, Private Secretary to Premier, to Secretary to Law Department, 10 January 1931. In fact two native village settlements were proposed. Ultimately in 1936 Luveve Village Settlement at Bulawayo and in 1937 Highfield at Salisbury were established. In practice these provisions were not utilized and Native Boards, purely advisory to the Native Commissioner and non-elective, were established from 1931 onwards. By 1933 there were Native Boards in all districts except Sebungwe: Report of the Chief Native Commissioner for 1933, C.S.R. 9, 1934.

[5] See *S.R.L.A.D.*, Vol. 15, col. 58.

[6] From 1935 styled the High Commissioner for Basutoland, the Bechuanaland Protectorate, and Swaziland and not for South Africa as formerly. From the appointment of Lord Clarendon in 1930 the Governor-General of South Africa was no longer High Commissioner but a separate Imperial official was appointed.

[7] *S.R.L.A.D.*, Vol. 17, col. 2204, 26 October 1937, Huggins: 'We do not want anybody messing about with our affairs who understands too much about them. We simply want someone who can satisfy a section of the House of Commons. The less he knows, I think, the better.'

be furnished with such information relating to the Colony's native affairs as in the Governor's opinion would help him in discharging his duties. He was also entitled to request any information.[1]

There were also alterations in the Royal Instructions to the Governor, who need not now reserve laws dealing with divorce or imposing any differential duty. In other cases, however, he was still to reserve Bills as the British Government thought consultation with them was necessary on the remaining reservations which might affect other than purely local interests—e.g. legislation affecting neighbouring territories, treaty relations or currency.[2] Insofar as the need for consultation and consent under Sections 28(a) and 41 of the Letters Patent were concerned, the British Government stated that Southern Rhodesian native policy might have repercussions beyond its borders.[3]

The Blue Book setting out the proposed changes emphasized that Imperial control was to be retained but that, because the administrative intervention of the High Commissioner between the Government of the Colony and the Secretary of State was felt to be anomalous, the method of exercise would be reconsidered. This 'did not imply any radical departure from the main principle upon which the relevant provisions of the Constitution had been framed'.[4] Nonetheless, although Imperial scrutiny of Bills and the requirement of Imperial consent to discriminatory subordinate legislation remained, the substitution of Secretary of State and Governor in Council to exercise the powers formerly exercised by the High Commissioner in matters affecting Native Administration naturally diminished the effectiveness of Imperial control.[5]

In the legislative sphere, however, Britain retained entire control. Indeed, since discriminatory legislation required the consent of the Secretary of State, there was on such matters considerable correspondence between the Governments. The Imperial Government's insistence that it be satisfied that such legislation was not unjust to the African people caused immense inconvenience to the Southern Rhodesian Government on occasions.[6] In certain cases

[1] Additional Instructions to the Governor of 25 March 1937. See Proclamation 16 of 1937.

[2] Cmd. 5218. Despatch from the Governor of Southern Rhodesia relating to the Proposed Amendment of the Southern Rhodesia Constitution, p. 4.

[3] Cmd. 5218, p. 6. The Ministers of Southern Rhodesia acquiesced 'in a decision which it was not in their power to alter'.

[4] Cmd. 5218, p. 9, Mr. J. H. Thomas, Dominions Secretary. Mr. Huggins stated that the proposed reforms were of 'a milk and water nature': S.R.L.A.D., Vol. 17, col. 1580, 11 October 1937.

[5] Cf. Mr. Huggins' later statement that he was now satisfied 'we are masters in our own house': S.R.L.A.D., Vol. 17, col. 1619, when he was being attacked by the Opposition for not having secured complete removal of Imperial control.

[6] See S.R.L.A.D., Vol. 23, cols. 503, 507, and 2358, disclosing difficulties in respect of the establishment of war-time rationing schemes. On the one hand butter (which Africans hardly used) could not be rationed, while on the other sugar (which Africans consumed in very much larger quantities than Europeans) could also not be rationed. Eventually after

21—C.H.L.S.R.

the British Government altered the proposals and imposed conditions before it would permit any regulations. This was usually done in order to secure equal facilities when segregatory regulations were requested.[1] In other instances, the Constitution acted as a deterrent to the introduction of discriminatory regulations.[2] In 1962 the Prime Minister of Southern Rhodesia declined to answer a parliamentary question as to whether any proposed subordinate regulations were refused assent by the Secretary of State.[3] He similarly refused to answer whether any proposed regulations or amendments were suggested by the Secretary of State[4] or whether any were withdrawn after consultations.[5] The Prime Minister, however, made it clear that many statutory instruments had been forwarded for the assent of the Secretary of State often on the advice of the Law Officers.[6]

Again, although Sections 79, 80, and 82 to 89 inclusive of the Southern Rhodesia Order in Council 1898 and the Southern Rhodesia (Native Reserves) Order in Council 1920 were revoked, their contents were adapted and re-enacted in the Southern Rhodesia Constitution Letters Patent 1923, as amended.[7]

The Reserves were now vested for the sole use of the indigenous[8] African population with a Board of Trustees[9] exercising most of those powers formerly exercised by the High Commissioner, such as correction of boundaries, powers under the Water Act 1927[10] and the Native Reserves Forest

---

lengthy negotiations the Imperial Government agreed to permit the enactment of the Emergency Powers (Defence) Amendment Act.

[1] Although this was an Act and not a regulation, a pertinent example was the Municipal Act No. 13 of 1940, Section 113(7)(c), which provided that by-laws might be made permitting the provision of separate omnibuses or portions of omnibuses for the use of white persons, or natives, of Asiatics, or of other Coloured persons. (This is now Section 270(51)(c) of the Municipal Act No. 34 of 1952.) Lord Malvern in a personal communication stated that after lengthy correspondence it was agreed that segregation would be permitted on condition that equal facilities were provided for all races, even if not on the same vehicle.

[2] In 1961 and 1962 the question whether these should be permitted in respect of Municipal and Town Management Board swimming baths was hotly argued in Southern Rhodesia as a result of the decisions in *City of Salisbury* v. *Mehta, supra* and *Mabelreign Town Management Board* v. *Chamboko, supra.* After public pressure Sir Edgar Whitehead enquired from the Secretary of State, Mr. Sandys, whether such a regulation would be permitted. He was informed that when it was drawn up it would then be considered. No such regulation was ever drafted. (It is doubtful whether Sir Edgar wished to proceed, but in any case he knew that had he wished to do so the answer would have been negative.)

[3] *S.R.L.A.D.*, Vol. 51, col. 2037, 22 August 1962, on the grounds that intergovernmental discussions were confidential.

[4] ibid., col. 2038.   [5] ibid., col. 2205.   [6] ibid., cols. 2205–6.

[7] Letters Patent of 25 March 1937. See Proclamation No. 15 of 1937.

[8] There had previously been no limitation to indigenous Africans. The Secretary of State accepted that immigrant labourers had no right to the Reserves: Cmd. 5218, p. 12.

[9] Section 42(1).

[10] Lord Malvern states that Sir Edward Harding refused to allow these powers to be eliminated even though it was put to him that at that time a High Court judge sat in the Water Court and would take into consideration African interests. Such a judge's decision could be set aside by the Board if it substantially affected the water supply of any Reserve.

Produce Act 1929, and the removal of Africans from land required for mineral development, railways, townships, or public works (subject to just compensation elsewhere).[1] Imperial control was to some degree maintained by the fact that the Chairman was nominated and appointed by the Secretary of State who in practice appointed the Governor as Chairman. The other Board members were the Chief Native Commissioner (who had originally been appointed with the Secretary of State's approval and who could only be removed with his approval) and the Chief Justice of the Colony.[2] The Board of Trustees could make rules governing their proceedings subject to the secretary of State's approval.

The Board was, however, limited by its trust. Thus no portion of any Reserve could be alienated unless in special circumstances the Secretary of State consented in writing (with the right to impose such conditions as he saw fit) while, in any case of alienation, adequate compensation in land was to be provided.[3] These provisions were completely effective and the Imperial Government always carefully scrutinized any exchanges of Reserve land. In practice, Southern Rhodesian Prime Ministers met with no difficulties because they were generous in the exchanges suggested, but they realized that had they not been equitable the exchanges would have been refused.[4]

Again although regulations might now be made by the Governor in Council for the utilization of Crown revenue produced by the Native Reserves, these required the approval of the Secretary of State.[5] Similarly regulations for the administration of Reserves were to be approved by the Secretary of State.[6] Again persons other than indigenous Africans could only be permitted in the

[1] Sections 44, 42(3), and 43(2). No Reserve could be materially affected or diminished thereby.

[2] Section 41(1).   [3] Section 43(1).

[4] Personal communications by Lord Malvern and Sir Edgar Whitehead.

[5] Section 42(4). See also S.R. Government Notice 714 of 1937 regulating the Native Reserves Trust Fund. Expenditure was to be devoted to improving services in the Reserves —water supplies, roads, bridges, soil conservation, &c. This according to Lord Malvern was also the origin of the Native Development Fund Act 1948, which imposed Levies on African produce and in return provided dipping and market services, afforestation, improvement of irrigation, water supplies, roads and bridges, and soil conservation. This latter legislation is in fact discriminatory as it means that African producers obtain less for their produce. Arguments in favour and against are complex. Africans receive a uniform price irrespective of the expense of forwarding such produce lengthy distances to the rail head. Excess sums are used for African development. It can be argued that the latter is a general State responsibility, while Africans near to transport facilities subsidise those further away, although this should be done by Government. The general attitude of condemnation of the Act is justified by the remarks made during its passage by a member of the governing party who subsequently became Deputy Federal Prime Minister. The Bill he said (with approval) was aimed at dealing with 'the problem of the native who in the opinion of the Native Department might be receiving too much for his products': S.R.L.A.D., Vol 29, col. 2488, Caldicott.

[6] As part of the negotiations all the regulations governing the occupation of Reserves by non-indigenous Africans, mining in the Reserves, the lease of store trading and mission sites, any other lease of land in a Reserve, and also the regulation of all funds derived from the Reserves were completely re-drawn by agreement. See Cmd. 5218, pp. 31–43.

Reserves under regulations approved by the Secretary of State.[1] These powers did not merely remain paper powers. They were exercised[2] and the United Kingdom would enquire if there was any apparent irregularity in the conduct of affairs in the Reserves.[3]

Africans might not be removed from Reserves save under any law (which in any event would either have been reserved or have been subject to the Secretary of State's approval as a discriminatory regulation) unless the Governor in Council, after full enquiry, made such order.[4] Although this power previously lay in the High Commissioner, the Governor could dissent if he saw fit from Executive Council advice under Clause VI of the Royal Instructions.[5] In fact large powers of Imperial control over the Reserves remained. This in practice meant that two-thirds of the rural African population were protected by the Imperial authorities. In December 1957 it was estimated that 1,598,208 of the estimated rural African population of 2,263,617 lived in the Reserves.[6]

Governors also were very conscious of their duties as Trustees for the Reserves. Sir Evelyn Baring and Sir John Kennedy, as Governors, visited the Reserves frequently to examine conditions and the former, in particular, concerned himself with detailed points of administration.[7]

The High Commissioner's powers under the Land Apportionment Act 1930 to approve of alterations in the boundaries or exchanges of land in the Native area, to assign or lease land in the unassigned area, to approve non-African occupation of land in the Native area, to appoint a member of the Land Board and to approve any regulations under the Act (e.g. removal of natives, prevention of squatting, &c.) were similarly vested in the Secretary of State.[8] At the same time Section 43 of the Constitution was finally repealed[9] and in its place a new paragraph (d) was added to Section 28. This provided

[1] See Southern Rhodesia Government Notice 715 of 1937 governing the grant of trading, mission school, and business sites in Reserves.

[2] See National Archives S 11 S.R. 48, Eden to Stanley, 16 February 1940, approving changes in the regulations governing mission sites in the Reserves.

[3] e.g. in 1940 the Dominions Office enquired from the Governor as to why there were discrepancies in the Native Reserves Fund Accounts: National Archives S 11 S.R. No. 287, Dominions Office to Governor, 15 October 1940.

[4] Section 45(1). Cp. Section 85, Southern Rhodesia Order in Council 1898.

[5] However under a responsible government constitution it would be a serious matter for the Governor to disagree with the Executive Council and such action might well provoke a crisis. Two distinguished ex-Governors have informed me that they never had any occasion on which to dissent from Executive Council advice.

[6] Second Report of the Select Committee on Resettlement of Natives, L.A.S.C. 3—1960, p. 40. The Reserves covered approximately 22 per cent of the total area of Southern Rhodesia: see p. 15. By 1957 there had been considerable urbanization of the African population, but prior to 1940 the vast majority of Africans lived in the rural areas.

[7] Personal communication from Professor K. Kirkwood.

[8] Land Apportionment Amendment Act No. 35 of 1937, Section 3.

[9] Except for the protection given to Africans that contracts for alienation or encumbrance of their land required witnessing and certification by a magistrate that the transaction was fair and understood by the native. This was retained in Section 46 as substituted.

that any law which repealed, altered, amended, or was in any way repugnant to or inconsistent with the Land Apportionment Act 1930 was to be reserved.[1]

Control over Native Department officials, however, largely fell away, the justification for this being the creation of the Public Services Board statutorily regulated by the Public Services Act of 1931: the Legislative Assembly was at last permitted to legislate on the duties to be performed by Native Affairs Department officials. Two safeguards for the Department still remained. Firstly the Chief Native Commissioner could not be removed from his office without the consent of the Secretary of State.[2] Secondly, since the Governor was in exceptional circumstances permitted to disregard Executive Council advice, and since salary increases or decreases and removals from office of Native Commissioners required the approval of the Governor in Council, there was the reserve right of an Imperial official intervening to prevent the taking of decisions considered by him to be wrong.

Yet another change was that Section 47 providing for the High Commissioner's control over the conditions of establishment of Native Councils was repealed. The Legislative Assembly thereafter passed the Native Councils Act of 1937[3]—legislation which would previously have been *ultra vires* in terms of Section 26(2).[4] This was cleared and approved by the Dominions Office as it was reserved legislation. However, as Native Councils were only in 1943 given powers to raise taxes with the consent of the Governor in Council while expenditure required the Native Commissioners' permission, they did not become effective instruments of Government.[5] Furthermore, the Councils were composed of Government-appointed Chiefs and other members selected by the population and appointed by the Governor on the Native Commissioners' recommendations. In 1940 there were only twenty such Councils and these were financially paralysed.[6] Although in 1942 Councils were given minor powers of taxation the Council system did not work well.[7] Ultimately by Act 19 of 1957[8] the system was revised in order to

[1] Letters Patent of 25 March 1937; see Proclamation No. 15 of 1937.

[2] Section 39(3). Shortly before the implementation of the 1961 Constitution it was suggested that the section should be invoked to remove a Chief Native Commissioner who had opposed progressive Government policy and that the Secretary of State would readily consent. No such action was in fact taken.

[3] Act No. 38 of 1937. (Chapter 74 of 1939.)

[4] Cp. the decision in 1929 not to proceed with legislation as the result of a warning from the Secretary of State that it would be void.

[5] See Cmd. 8235, Central African Territories: Comparative Survey of Native Policy, § 53 and § 144–51.

[6] National Archives S 235/482, Confidential Report by Lord Hailey on Southern Rhodesia, pp. 16–17.

[7] In 1951 there were 57 Councils, 40 of which had exercised their taxing powers but 10 subsequently changed their minds and did not collect tax. See R. Howman: *African Local Government in British East and Central Africa*. University of South Africa, 1963. Part III, Section 1, para. 155.

[8] Now known as the African Councils Act (Chapter 95) Statute Law of Southern Rhodesia (Revised Edition 1963).

encourage organized communal self-help. However, in 1958 there had been no growth from 1953 in the number of Native Councils there still being fifty-eight only which covered at most only a quarter of the African population.[1] Neither its predecessor nor the 1957 Act have been effective instruments of local Government.[2]

A definition of 'native' was also added to Section 62 of the Constitution. This had already been used in a number of reserved measures such as the Native Affairs Act to make it clear that persons of mixed descent who lived among and after the manner of natives were also classified as natives. Such persons if they lived otherwise were not to be so classified.

It is apparent from the aforegoing that, while from 1923 to 1937 Southern Rhodesia had hardly been self-governing in respect of Native Affairs, in 1937 considerable constitutional changes occurred in the direction of increased local autonomy and diminished Imperial control. Nonetheless Imperial control remained even if it was of a less direct character, and, although Southern Rhodesia could control her own native administration without the High Commissioner's scrutiny, the Secretary of State and the Governor retained considerable powers, which could have been invoked if any cause for intervention had arisen, while legislation always remained subject to scrutiny and delegated legislation imposing discrimination required the Secretary of State's consent.[3] The grant of 'complete self-government', the Imperial authorities insisted, was not 'practical politics'.[4] In any event the Prime Minister of Southern Rhodesia was still an amalgamationist and he accepted these limitations on Southern Rhodesia's power of complete self-government in order to make amalgamation with Northern Rhodesia possible.[5] The opinion of a learned academic writer that the powers in respect of native administration were 'inoperative in practice' cannot be accepted.[6]

Further diminution of Imperial control

Pressure for increased Southern Rhodesian status abated during the Second World War years. In any event, the Prime Minister of Southern Rhodesia

[1] See *A Handbook on the Federation of Rhodesia and Nyasaland*, Ed. by W. V. Brelsford. Cassell, 1960. Chapter 40, African Local Government, p. 702. For a detailed analysis of the failure of one Council see Report of the Mangwende Reserve Commission of Enquiry, 1961, § 328–84.

[2] Report of the Commission Appointed to Inquire into and Report on Administrative and Judicial Functions in the Native Affairs and District Courts Department, C.S.R. 22, 1961, Government Printer, Salisbury, pp. 20–21. In October 1964 only fifty-five Councils were functioning, sixty-two in all having been appointed: *S.R.L.A.D.*, Vol. 58, col. 1715, 14 October 1964.

[3] For a summary of remaining powers see Cmd. 5949, Rhodesia–Nyasaland Royal Commission Report (The Bledisloe Report), pp. 13–18.

[4] Cmd. 5949, p. 115, quoting a Despatch from the Secretary of State to the Governor of Southern Rhodesia of October 1936.

[5] *S.R.L.A.D.*, Vol. 21(1), col. 561, 22 May 1941, Mr. Huggins: 'It is worth that price to keep them, if we can get amalgamation.' Lord Malvern confirmed this in a personal communication in November 1962.

[6] M. Wight: *British Colonial Constitution, 1947*. Oxford, 1952, p. 62.

was not in favour of the achievement of Dominion Status at that time.[1] By 1947 attitudes had, however, changed and in that year the Prime Minister requested the Imperial Government to consider granting Dominion Status.[2]

Eventually in 1949 it was agreed that the Governor's powers to dissent from the decisions of the Executive Council should be modified. In future the Governor should be solely the representative of the Queen except in respect of his constitutional responsibility for exercising a discretion in terms of the Constitution, while his diplomatic and reporting functions would be transferred to a British High Commissioner to be appointed to Southern Rhodesia. The Royal Instructions were accordingly amended and came into force in 1950. The Additional Instructions[3] revoked the existing Clause VI and substituted a clause that permitted the Legislature to make provisions for the manner of the Governor's exercise of any powers conferred under any Act, or regulation, or rule under any Act. Thus in conferring powers on the Governor, an Act could now specify that the Governor should act on the advice of the Cabinet or any particular Minister, in effect removing his reserve discretion. In all other cases (i.e. where no such provision was made) the Governor was as before to be guided by the advice of the Executive Council and could, if he saw fit, dissent from such advice, reporting the matter without delay to the King through the Secretary of State.[4] In practice, however, no such provisions were made by any Act.[5]

[1] See Gann and Gelfand, op. cit., p. 169. Earlier in 1929, 1930, and 1933, Mr. Moffat when Prime Minister had disclaimed any desire to seek Dominion Status: National Archives NE 1/1/7, 24 September 1929 and 8 March 1930, Moffat to Newton. See also DO 1/1/6, Moffat to Sir E. Harding, 18 January 1933.

[2] S.R.L.A.D., Vol. 27(1), col. 1187, 28 May 1947, Fletcher. Sir John Kennedy, however, states that Sir Godfrey Huggins did not want Dominion Status in so far as this entailed financial responsibility for the conduct of external affairs. Personal communication, 17 February 1965.

[3] Additional Instructions passed under the Royal Sign Manual and Signet to the Governor and Commander-in-Chief of the Colony of Southern Rhodesia dated 24 November 1949, brought into force on 31 August 1950, by Governor's Proclamation No. 48 of 1950 of 31 August 1950.

[4] My view of this change was confirmed by Sir Robert Tredgold in a personal communication.

[5] However the Interpretation Act (Chapter I of 1939), Section 3 defined the 'Governor' as 'the officer for the time being administering the Government of the Colony acting by and with the advice of the Executive Council'. In African Newspapers (Pvt.) Ltd. and Wason v. Lardner Burke and Bosman NN.O., 1964 (4) S.A. 486 (S.R.A.D.), Beadle C.J. held that where the word 'Governor' was used in legislation—even before this change apparently—it must be read with the Interpretation Act which means 'that the Governor must at all times do what his Ministers are lawfully empowered to advise him to do'. This view was also adopted in Gluck v. The Governor, supra. Beadle C.J. considered that Clause VI of the Royal Instructions did not apply in respect of Governor's functions conferred by Act of the Legislature. Furthermore if there was any conflict between Royal Instructions and legislation the latter was to prevail. Indeed Beadle C.J. considered 'that there is no distinction between the functions of the Governor as defined in Section 45 of the Constitution', i.e. the 1961 Constitution which makes the following of Executive Council advice mandatory, and the 1923 Constitution. It is submitted, however, that until 1962 the Royal Instructions

Thereafter the Governor's Powers Act[1] provided for a Committee of the Executive Council consisting of those members of the Executive Council who were Ministers. The Prime Minister might bring any proposal that the Governor should exercise any of his powers before such Committee and, if approved, submit it to the Governor without any need for a meeting of the Executive Council. As the Prime Minister explained in the Legislative Assembly this Act was merely intended to facilitate routine business, which now need not go to the Executive Council. But in practice it meant that the Governor was not always present at discussions on the use of his powers. Proposals that he should exercise these powers would be put to him thereafter by the Prime Minister. However, even under this new dispensation it was the duty of Ministers to supply him 'with sufficient information to enable him to exercise his recognized advisory, mediatory, and residual discretionary functions'.[2] Owing to the good sense of those who had to work this procedure and to the satisfactory personal relationships of Southern Rhodesian Prime Ministers and Governors, no difficulties arose. Indeed Sir Godfrey Huggins informed the Governor, Sir John Kennedy, that the Governor was free to raise any matters for discussion and that Ministers welcomed the remarks of the Governor. However, there is no doubt that the procedure could have been used to diminish the influence of the Governor, just as it meant that certain Ministers were excluded from consideration of matters which were decided without their participation.[3]

In 1951 the first British High Commissioner for Southern Rhodesia was appointed.

As a result of these changes possibilities of intervention by an Imperial officer could be reduced by the passage of an Act by the Legislature dealing with the topic in dispute and providing that powers in respect of that topic were to be exercised on Ministerial advice only. Furthermore, the British Government now had to rely for information as to the general course of events in Southern Rhodesia on a 'diplomatic representative' who, however close his relationships might be with the Administration, was not in the inner counsels of Government. Naturally, insofar as the Governor still had constitutional responsibility to the Secretary of State, e.g. on reserved legislation and wherever he enjoyed any discretion, he continued to communicate with the Secretary of State on such matters.[4]

would apply where the Governor remained passive or refrained from acting: see Keith, *Responsible Government*, op. cit., Vol. I, p. 108.

[1] Act No. 13 of 1951.

[2] *Halsbury*, 3rd ed., Vol. 5, p. 466; and A. B. Keith: *The Dominions as Sovereign States*, Macmillan, 1938, p. 218.

[3] Correspondence between the Governor and Lord Malvern took place on certain aspects of this procedure, as the Governor thought it undesirable to settle too many matters by minutes on files, particularly if they touched on the rights of the individual citizen. A suggestion that such matters be always discussed in full Council was adopted. Personal communication from Sir John Kennedy.

[4] Governors also kept the High Commissioner fully informed on all matters requiring co-ordination or mutual consultation. Personal communication from Sir John Kennedy.

Insofar as Dominion Status was concerned, it became Southern Rhodesian Government policy from 1950 not to proceed with this request as this would make amalgamation with Northern Rhodesia impossible.[1] Although the Government agreed in May 1950 to the appointment of a Select Committee on the Constitution, which would make recommendations leading towards Dominion Status, it did this tongue-in-cheek as the Prime Minister already knew that the British Government was prepared to appoint a committee of officials from the Governments of the United Kingdom, Southern Rhodesia, Northern Rhodesia, and Nyasaland to examine the question of federation. Apparently the Southern Rhodesian Government was in 1952 given an option to elect between going ahead with Federation or abandoning such a scheme and achieving Dominion Status for Southern Rhodesia.[2]

Subsequently when amendments to the Letters Patent affecting the reservations were being negotiated in 1955, the then Prime Minister, Mr. Todd, raised the question of removal of the reservations, but was told by the Imperial Government that this must be deferred until immediately before the review of the Federal Constitution destined to take place between 1960 and 1963.[3]

Other constitutional amendments

The other amendments to the Constitution during this period were of a more technical nature designed to facilitate its operation in the light of circumstances prevailing in Southern Rhodesia.

Thus in 1925 it was found necessary to amend the Constitution to permit members of Parliament to have a direct pecuniary interest in contracts with the Government despite the fact that such contract was not with a company composed of more than twenty-five members. It was argued that had this not been permitted, in view of the small European population, there would not have been sufficient adequately qualified persons, and certainly persons of substance, who would have been prepared to sit as members of Parliament. Accordingly Section 22(2) was deleted[4] so that such a member should not vacate his seat.[5]

[1] *S.R.L.A.D.*, Vol. 32(2), col. 2126, Sir G. Huggins: 'I know from the very highest source that should the Colony obtain Dominion Status in anything like the near future, the question of amalgamation with Northern Rhodesia can be written off completely.'

[2] *S.R.L.A.D.*, Vol. 59, col. 422, 27 October 1964: Mr. Smith, Prime Minister.   Sir John Kennedy, Governor at that time, has however stated that there are no firm grounds for believing that Southern Rhodesia could have had Dominion Status as an alternative to Federation. Personal communications of November 1964 and 17 February 1965.

[3] *S.R.L.A.D.*, Vol. 45, col. 922, Minister of the Treasury. See also *S.R.L.A.D.*, Vol. 39, col. 1414, Mr. Todd: 'We should long ago have had these reservations removed from our Constitution'; and *S.R.L.A.D.*, Vol. 40, col. 483. Mr. Todd predicted that the reservations would be eliminated in 1960. In a speech reported in the *Rhodesian Herald*, 19 July 1957, Mr. Todd said that he had conveyed his views to the British Government and would be discussing the removal of the reservations later that year with the Secretary of State.

[4] Constitution Letters Patent Amendment Act No. 7 of 1925.

[5] The only occasion on which such contracts have occasioned parliamentary comment

Again in 1926 the Letters Patent Constituting the Office of Governor were amended to make it clear that, if the Governor left the Colony (rather than South Africa), his powers could be vested by the Crown in an Acting Governor, and that the Governor retained his powers if he visited territories south of the Equator (i.e. Northern Rhodesia and Nyasaland in particular), whereas previously this applied only to South African visits.[1] The Governor was also precluded from leaving the country for periods exceeding six weeks per annum unless for reasons of ill health.[2]

In 1933 the Ministerial Titles Act changed the title of the head of the Ministry from 'Premier' to 'Prime Minister'.[3]

In 1940 a temporary National Emergency Constitution Act, expiring six months after the termination of the War, permitted seven Ministers and a Parliamentary Secretary to the Prime Minister to be appointed.[4] In 1948 the Constitution Further Amendment Act of 1948 made this number of Ministers permanent,[5] while the section dealing with the Ministry was rationalized in 1953 to eliminate reference to the first general election under responsible government[6] and the Constitution generally was amended to eliminate lapsed and obsolete provisions, particularly in respect of the qualifications and disqualifications of voters, the holding of elections, the application of electoral laws generally, the qualifications of candidates, the sessions of the Legislature,

---

was reported in the Second Report of the Select Committee on Public Accounts, March 1959. *L.A.S.C.* 6, 1958. See also *S.R.L.A.D.*, Vol. 42, col. 2670, for comments on a lease of property to a member in 1935 which was renewed in 1953, when the member had become a Minister of the Crown, without any tenders being invited. This renewal and subsequent oral variations thereof were condemned by the Select Committee, which recommended that Parliament should immediately be informed of such contracts and that the Auditor-General should comment on such contracts in his Report. There is also a safeguard in that the Powers and Privileges of Parliament Act, Section 11, makes it an offence for any member to vote or take part in the discussion of any matters in which he has a direct pecuniary interest. This is also reflected in S.O. 107 (1964 ed.). A ruling by the Speaker that this meant 'a personal pecuniary advantage . . . separately belonging to the person whose votes are questioned, and not in common with the rest of His Majesty's subjects' was given in 1942. The Speaker considered that 'on a matter of State policy . . . constituents . . . must not lightly be disenfranchised": *S.R.L.A.D.*, Vol. 22, col. 1370.

[1] Letters Patent of 30 August 1926, in force from that date. See Proclamation No. 11 of 1926.

[2] There was previously no aggregate limit. See Clauses 10, 11, and 12 as amended.

[3] Act No. 9 of 1933 amending Section 37(1) of the Southern Rhodesia Constitution Letters Patent 1923. The Act also provided that the 'Treasurer' should be called the 'Minister of Finance', the 'Colonial Secretary' the 'Minister of Internal Affairs', and that there should be a 'Minister of Justice' vested with the powers of the 'Attorney-General'.

[4] Act No. 15 of 1940. It was not necessary to specify the appointment of a Parliamentary Secretary because this appointment could in any event be made. A Parliamentary Secretary to the Prime Minister was appointed from 1941 to 1946, and a Parliamentary Secretary for Native Affairs was appointed from 1957 to 1960. The Southern Rhodesia Constitution 1961, sec. 46 specifically provided for the appointment of Parliamentary Secretaries of whom there were three at the end of August 1965. This section has now been repealed and provision has been made for the appointment of Deputy Ministers.

[5] Act No. 38 of 1948.   [6] Act No. 23 of 1953.

Standing Rules and Orders of the Legislative Assembly, and the privileges of Members.[1]

Delimitation provisions

Prior to 1938 Delimitation Boards had been appointed in 1927 and 1937 to make recommendations for the redivision of the Colony into electoral districts,[2] but implementation of their recommendations required an Act of Parliament.

In 1938 it was recognized that a Delimitation Commission was necessary to redivide the Colony into electoral districts from time to time on the same principles previously recognized, such as community of interests, physical features, means of communication, existing electoral boundaries, and sparsity and density of population, permitting of a variation of 15 per cent more or less than an equal number of voters[3] but avoiding the necessity for Parliamentary intervention on each occasion. This was done by the Constitution Amendment Act[4] which provided for the quinquennial appointment of a Delimitation Commission appointed by the Governor and consisting of the Chief Justice and two other members selected by the Chief Justice.[5] The decisions would be automatically implemented by the Governor and need not be ratified by the Legislative Assembly, while the former provision for the Legislature to make laws from time to time for the redivision of electoral districts was repealed.

Official language

A constitutional amendment in 1951 laid down that the English language was to be the only official language of the Colony.[6] Earlier until 1937 there had been express legislative provision that Dutch should be an official language in the Courts.[7] The 1951 constitutional amendment was aimed at Afrikaans but would also apply to African languages such as Sindebele or Shona. However, a proviso permitted the publication of all legislative

---

[1] ibid., Sections 5, 6, 7, 9, 10, 12, and 13.

[2] As a result of the 1927 Commission the Electoral Districts Delimitation and Voters Lists Act No. 7 of 1928 provided for twenty-six single-member seats. In addition in Salisbury and Bulawayo two dual-member constituencies were retained. After the 1938 Commission of Enquiry the Electoral Delimitation Act 1938 provided for thirty single-member electoral districts.

[3] It had previously been 20 per cent when Delimitation Boards recommended on proposed delimitation.

[4] Act No. 31 of 1938.

[5] Section 8 of the Southern Rhodesia Constitution Letters Patent 1923, as amended.

[6] Act No. 6 of 1951.

[7] As a result of the Dutch Language Judicial Use Act No. 21 of 1884 (as amended of the Cape Colony). This was repealed by the General Law Amendment Act No. 25 of 1937.

measures, orders, and notices in native languages for the information of Africans, while in native courts proceedings in African languages were permitted.[1]

Changes in respect of the Reserves

In 1955 yet other amendments occurred as a result of further Letters Patent making changes in respect of the exchange of Reserve Land for Crown Land.[2] These amendments made it easier for the Government to make exchanges, although the Secretary of State's approval was still necessary. Land could now be taken for defence purposes or any other public purposes (previously only for public works) and there was no longer a limitation that, if townships or areas for purposes of mineral development were taken, this must be for the exploitation of an important mineral discovery.[3] Any such land was to become part of the European Area under the Land Apportionment Act, while Crown land exchanged would become part of the Reserves and vest in the Board of Trustees.[4] Again, although natives who were removed were to be justly compensated the compensation need not necessarily be alternative land.[5] Compensation was now payable to an individual African not to the community as a whole.[6] Furthermore, land set aside in the Reserves for townships was now to be vested in the Governor and to become part of the Native Purchase Area, and it was therefore removed from the control of the Board of Trustees.[7]

Changes in the composition of the Legislative Assembly

Other constitutional changes were occasioned by increases in the size of the Southern Rhodesian electorate after the War. This led to proposals for enlargement of the Legislative Assembly. In 1948 a motion requesting an increase in the size of the Legislative Assembly was moved in order to permit of the election of forty members instead of thirty.[8] Eventually the Constitution was amended in 1951,[9] after lengthy negotiations with the Imperial

[1] Section 60(3) and (4) of the Letters Patent as amended.

[2] Letters Patent of 7 March 1955. See Proclamation No. 17 of 1955. See Sections 42 and 43 of the Southern Rhodesia Constitution Letters Patent as amended.

[3] Section 43(2) as amended.   [4] Section 43(5) as amended.   [5] Section 43(3) as amended.

[6] Section 43(2), (3), and (4). This was the result of the implementation of the Native Land Husbandry Act 1951 which permitted individual land holdings in the Reserves.

[7] It must be remembered that under the Land Apportionment Act the Secretary of State had to approve exchanges between the Native Areas and European Areas and also regulations so his control was still retained.

[8] S.R.L.A.D., Vol. 28, col. 632, 2 June 1948, Sir Godfrey Huggins used this occasion to advocate closure of the voters' rolls to Africans and the substitution of Europeans who would represent African interests.

[9] Constitution Amendment Act No. 6 of 1951, amending Sections 3 and 8 of the Letters Patent.

Government, by the introduction of a new principle in order to secure a minimum rural representation despite the increase in urban voters. The Constitution now provided that the number of Members of the Legislative Assembly should be equal to the number of electoral districts fixed by a Delimitation Commission established under Section 8 of the Letters Patent. The Commission was to divide the Colony into forty electoral districts of which at least fourteen were to be rural electoral districts. Urban electoral districts would be created on the basis that no electoral district would contain 15 per cent more or less than an equal number of voters. If this made it necessary to increase the number of districts above forty this could be done. In practice this would have meant a House of about forty gradually increasing with increases in the size of the electorate.

However, with the establishment of the Federation of Rhodesia and Nyasaland and the consequent transfer of many functions to the Federal Legislative Assembly, the Southern Rhodesian Constitution was again amended to reduce the House to a membership of thirty, still, however, retaining the departure principle.[1] In practice, therefore, the membership of the House remained at thirty from 1924 to 1962, as an election was not held during this period when the Constitution provided for the election of a larger number of members.[2]

Ultimately in 1960 the size of the House was increased to fifty seats.[3] The purpose of this was dual: it was due partly because of the increase of work anticipated as a result of the probable recommendations of the Review Commission on the Federal Constitution (it was envisaged that functions would be returned to Southern Rhodesia); and it was also done in order to make possible the election of one or two Africans to the Legislative Assembly in electoral districts (which would now be smaller) where there was a concentration of African voters.[4]

In addition, during the period there were minor constitutional amendments clarifying points of definition such as persons falling within the category of

[1] Constitution Amendment Act No. 23 of 1953. For a general account, see Leys, op. cit., p. 193.

[2] The life of the Parliament elected in 1948 was extended for one year in spite of Section 18(2) of the Constitution by Section 2 of Act 23 of 1953. This was done owing to the delay in the negotiations for the creation of Federation and the establishment of the Federal Legislative Assembly. Earlier Section 3(3) of the Prolongation of Parliament Act of 1943 had permitted the prolongation of Parliament's life beyond the five years' period specified in Section 18(2) of the Constitution provided a two-thirds majority of the total membership of the House voted in favour of such a proposal. The Act was used to extend Parliament's life after the War to 3 May 1946: see *S.R.L.A.D.*, Vol. 24, col. 1828.

[3] Constitution Amendment Act No. 37 of 1960. The departure principle was still retained but the basic number of rural electoral districts was now to be 18.

[4] See *S.R.L.A.D.*, Vol. 45, cols. 1484 to 1489, Sir Edgar Whitehead, 17 August 1960. The United Kingdom Government also held this view: *H.C. Deb.*, Vol. 642, col. 1701, 22 June 1961. The United Kingdom Government discussed this matter with the Southern Rhodesian Government during the course of the negotiations for the Southern Rhodesia Constitution 1961; *S.R.L.A.D.*, Vol. 45, col. 704, 28 July 1960.

'native',[1] or comprehensively stating the grounds for (and excuses for not) vacating a parliamentary seat.[2]

Changes in the franchise qualifications

The Southern Rhodesian Constitution merely provided that voters' qualifications and disqualifications should be those prescribed by the existing electoral laws as at the grant of responsible government or as amended by any laws passed by the Legislature.[3] Since the franchise therefore was in the hands of the Legislature important changes to voters' qualifications were possible and these occurred in 1951 and 1957. It is essential to examine both the formal provisions and the practical consequences of these changes, since without an examination of the franchise laws and their effectiveness in maintaining control of the Legislature by a predominantly European electorate, bare statements of the constitutional machinery would be meaningless, and unrelated to the realities of the racial situation in Southern Rhodesia.

Until 1951 the voters' qualifications remained at the level that had been prescribed in 1912. In 1951, however, voters' qualifications were raised. Property occupied was to be valued at £500 (not at £150 as laid down in 1912) and income, wages, or salary was to be £240 per annum (instead of the £100 prescribed in 1912). In addition, applicants for the vote had now to be able to speak and write the English language, quite apart from the necessity of filling in the enrolment form without assistance. Southern Rhodesian citizenship was made a further requirement as a Citizenship Act had just been introduced.[4] A re-registration of voters was also prescribed—although persons already on the roll were entitled to re-register despite lack of the new qualifications. In the event the new electorate was predominantly European.[5]

Thereafter a Commission was appointed at the end of 1956 to consider and report on a system for the just representation of the people of the Colony in the Legislative Assembly 'under which the Government is placed and

[1] Constitution Amendment Act No. 26 of 1948, Section 2.
[2] Constitution Amendment Act No. 23 of 1953, Section 11.
[3] Southern Rhodesia Constitution Letters Patent 1923, Section 4. In 1953 this was amended so as to be those prescribed by the Colony's electoral laws: Section 5 of Act 23 of 1953.
[4] Electoral Amendment Act 1951 and the Consolidated Electoral Act No. 27 of 1951.
[5] See Leys, op. cit., p. 192, who quotes the post-registration figures as 45,111 Europeans, 380 Africans, 444 Asians, and 500 Coloureds. In 1928 there had been 62 African voters as opposed to approximately 22,000 Europeans: S.R.L.A.D., Vol. 7, col. 224. In 1933 there were 58 Africans and over 24,000 European voters: S.R.L.A.D., Vol. 13, col. 528, 26 April 1934. By 1939 there were only 39 African voters out of a total electorate of 24,626 (Cmd. 5949, p. 15), while by March 1948 there were 258 African voters and 47,840 European voters: S.R.L.A.D., Vol. 28, col. 322. Prior to the Electoral Act 1951 there were 453 Africans on the roll: Leys, op. cit. By November 1956 out of a total electorate of 52,184 only 560 were Africans. Leys, op. cit., p. 196, estimates that ten times more Africans than did could have registered, relying on a Southern Rhodesian Government statement that 5,000 Africans in April 1957 had incomes of £240 per annum.

remains in the hands of civilized and responsible persons . . .'.[1] The Commission produced the most reasoned statement so far made in Southern Rhodesia for justifying high franchise qualifications as a means of maintaining a society which would give every 'individual the opportunity to lead the good life as he sees it'. High qualifications, the Commission considered, were the best way of determining the capacity to vote intelligently. The Commission made proposals for raising the franchise generally but at the same time for introducing a category of voters with special qualifications (£15 per month income and literacy), whose vote should not count for more than one-half of the total votes cast by voters with ordinary qualifications in the same constituency. Had this been accepted Africans would have been given immediate and substantial voting power. However, the existing system was ultimately perpetuated of 'a common roll that is nominally a common roll, but in which the qualifications for the franchise are fixed so high that, in effect, the African is virtually excluded'.[2] This the Commission considered was the position obtaining under the franchise laws then in force and condemned, but the system, in fact, 'though not in name, a system of racial representation',[3] was to continue.

Although the Government adopted the Report's proposals for raising the franchise, it substituted other proposals, which were more difficult of attainment, for the special voting qualifications. At the same time it dropped the Report's proposal for devaluation of the votes cast by special voters, but provided that once the special voters reached 20 per cent of the total number of registered ordinary voters, no further enrolment of special voters might take place.

The Electoral Act of 1957 eventually provided for complex changes in the franchise the effect of which, it is submitted,[4] was to provide for an immediate

---

[1] Report of the Franchise Commission 1957, Government Printer, Salisbury, p. 1. The Commission was composed of Sir Robert Tredgold, Chief Justice of the Federation, Sir John Murray, Chief Justice of Southern Rhodesia, and Sir Charles Cumings, a former Chief Justice of the Sudan. For a detailed criticism of the Report see Leys, op. cit., pp. 217–29. Despite this criticism the Tredgold Report would, if fully implemented, have given Africans a considerable say in electing the Legislature. Its proposals in the context of Southern Rhodesian history and politics were enlightened and represented a change from the previous approach of changes with the sole purpose of raising the franchise qualifications.

[2] Report of the Franchise Commission 1957, p. 6.

[3] ibid.

[4] Proof cannot be afforded as the only true test would be a statistical examination of the numbers of Africans who would have been eligible under the pre-existing franchise and the 1957 franchise. Such figures are not available. The Minister, introducing the Bill, took the view that there was 'a stiffening up in the franchise qualifications', viz. higher education qualifications, stiffer enrolment forms, stricter stability tests, outright ownership of property and no longer occupation, clothing to employees no longer to be regarded as income, preferential voting, automatic changes in means qualifications according to the cost of living and the fact that provision for special voters was temporary: *S.R.L.A.D.*, Vol. 40, cols. 537 et seq., especially at 547.

increase in the number of African voters, but thereafter to put ultimate control beyond the reach of the African because the new method of entrance to the roll would fall away once special voters had reached 20 per cent of the electorate, i.e. in effect 16·6 per cent of the total electorate, at which stage the African electorate would more or less remain fixed until Africans could meet the raised franchise qualifications which, by virtue of the combination of education and means qualifications prescribed, would be unattainable by the vast majority of Africans for many years. Compliance with the educational qualifications in particular would be difficult.[1]

The aspect of the changes which made it possible for more Africans to register was the introduction of the special qualification of £120 per annum income earned for an unbroken period of two years plus two years' completed secondary education.[2] The other special qualification was the annual income specified for the franchise in 1951 (i.e. £240). Once these voters totalled 20 per cent of the ordinary voters, this method of qualification would be abrogated.[3] Although this seemed generous, the barrier of two years' secondary education would be difficult to overcome. In fact most Africans with that degree of education would in any event have been earning virtually the amount of the pre-existing means qualification. Figures given by the Division of Native Education in 1961 disclose that at the end of 1960 in Southern Rhodesia there were only 9,776 Africans who had completed three years' secondary education.[4] An extension of the franchise, however, occurred in that the senior wife of a man married under a polygamous system was now deemed to possess the same means qualification as her husband (but not his educational qualifications).

The other aspects of the franchise were extremely unfavourable to the prospects for increased African registration as voters. Various combinations

---

[1] See Appendix, Table J. In 1957 there were at most 900 Africans who had completed four years' secondary education: Table J read with Note 9.

[2] Table J shows that in 1957 about 2,890 Africans had such qualifications. By the end of 1964 this figure had risen to approximately 23,360. Had every qualified African registered this method of entry to the roll would have lapsed in 1962.

[3] A number of Coloureds and poorer Europeans would also enrol in terms of these qualifications so that it cannot be assumed that all voters with special qualifications were African.

[4] These figures were privately obtained. Unfortunately figures showing the number of Africans who had acquired two years of secondary education were not available. The figures quoted relate to candidates who passed the examinations for the S.R. Junior Certificate (4,187), the University Junior Certificate of South Africa (810), the Primary Teachers' Lower Certificate (3,473), the Elementary Industrial Certificate (1,183), and the Elementary Industrial Teachers' Certificate (113). There is a correlation between this figure and the figures disclosed in Table J, read with Note 5, which is based on information obtained from the Central Statistical Office. This shows 9,153 Africans as the figure. The discrepancy is caused by the fact that the Departmental figures show a larger number of persons as having passed the S.R. Junior Certificate—4,187—than do the Central Statistical Office figures which show only 3,597 as having passed Junior Certificate examinations exclusive of the Union Junior Certificate.

of education and ownership of property (not merely occupation of property, as previously) or earning of income (which now had to be earned over an unbroken period of two years) were required. The pre-existing franchise means qualification in fact became merely a special qualification, which would eventually fall away. Indeed the general effect was to raise the qualifications and to keep control in the hands of those with the higher qualifications (in practice, non-Africans) even though a number of Africans could come on to the roll by means of the special qualifications, viz. up to one-sixth of the electorate.

The qualifications are shown in the following Table:

TABLE I

Ordinary qualifications	Special qualifications
(a) £720 p.a. income salary or wages or ownership of property valued at £1,500 *or* (b) £480 p.a. income, &c. or ownership of property valued at £1,000 *and* completed primary education *or* (c) £300 p.a. income, &c. *or* ownership of property valued at £500 *and* four years' completed secondary education.	(a) £240 p.a. income, &c. *or* (b) £120 p.a. income, &c. *and* two years' completed secondary school education. (N.B. This category to fall away when numbers of voters with special qualifications equalled 20 per cent of those with ordinary qualifications. No further registrations were then to be permitted.)

In addition an alternative vote system (or multiple preference voting system) was introduced whereby, after first preference votes had been counted, second preference votes would be transferred, firstly from the candidate who polled the least votes and thereafter from the next least successful candidate, until such time as one candidate obtained an absolute majority of all votes cast. This was designed to avoid the danger of a split European vote, which might permit the African voters to win seats for their candidate.[1] In fact this system employed in the 1958 general election decisively affected the issue. The United Federal Party Government was returned to power as a consequence of winning four seats on the re-distribution of second preference votes in seats where the Government candidate was not top of the poll before the re-distribution of preferences.[2]

A further new principle was introduced whereby, in order to avoid the need

[1] See *Alternative Proposals for the Franchise* by H. D. Wightwick (Southern Rhodesia Legislative Assembly Library). Mr. Wightwick was the most ardent advocate of this policy and was instrumental in obtaining its adoption. He avowed this as the reason for his policy.

[2] In two other seats Government candidates headed the poll without an absolute majority and were elected after the distribution of preferences, while in four seats Dominion Party (Opposition) candidates headed the poll without absolute majorities but were elected after a re-distribution of preferences.

22—C.H.L.S.R.

to amend monetary qualifications owing to future fluctuations in the value of money (inevitably in a downward direction and thus resulting in a raising of the qualifications), a commission would triennially enquire into the value of money and in accordance with a prescribed formula the franchise qualifications would be automatically adjusted to accord with its findings.

Although the figures of enrolment of African voters are distorted by the decision of African political parties to advocate a policy of non-enrolment, by the end of November 1960 there was a total of 3,129 Africans (1,861 with special qualifications and 1,268 with ordinary qualifications) out of a total electorate of 75,061.[1] By November 1961 there were 5,177 African voters out of a total electorate of 88,820.[2]

Negotiations leading to the Southern Rhodesian Constitution
1961

In 1958 Sir Edgar Whitehead, then the Prime Minister of Southern Rhodesia, commenced negotiations with the Secretary of State for Commonwealth Relations on the possibility of revision of the Southern Rhodesian Constitution so as to transfer to Southern Rhodesia the powers reserved to the United Kingdom Government.[3] Subsequently in March 1959 the Secretary of State for Commonwealth Relations, Lord Home, visited Southern Rhodesia when further discussions ensued.[4] Since the Federation of Rhodesia and Nyasaland was in existence the talks were however limited to matters within the competence of the Southern Rhodesian Legislative Assembly in respect of which the United Kingdom retained ultimate control.

The first proposals by Sir Edgar Whitehead involved the substitution of a Senate as 'an alternative to the Secretary of State's veto'.[5] Inter-governmental talks then occurred in London in November 1959 when Sir Edgar was requested to prepare a draft for consideration by the United Kingdom. Detailed discussion of the scheme then followed in London in April 1960 but although certain points of agreement were reached correspondence on this scheme continued. The newly appointed Secretary of State for Commonwealth Relations, Mr. Sandys, then insisted that when a final conference was held it

---

[1] Report of the Commission Appointed to Re-divide the Colony into Electoral Districts, 1960. C.S.R. 10, 1961.

[2] See Passmore and Mitchell, op. cit., p. 8.

[3] Personal communication from Sir Edgar Whitehead, who had decided that such approaches would be made so that by the time the Federal Review Conference was held in 1960 removal of the reservations in the Southern Rhodesia Constitution would have preceded any Federal changes. See also *S.R.L.A.D.*, Vol. 41, col. 274, 16 July 1958, Whitehead.

[4] *S.R.L.A.D.*, Vol. 42, col. 2974, 3 April 1959, Whitehead. See also *H.C. Deb.*, Vol. 642, col. 1698, 22 June 1961. From 1959 'long and detailed discussions with the Southern Rhodesian Government followed'.

[5] *S.R.L.A.D.*, Vol. 44, col. 3050, 1 March 1960, Whitehead.

should be a fully representative one.[1] Indeed, at the outset of his negotiations, Mr. Sandys made it clear that 'the British Government would not feel able to give up its reserve powers unless there was a significant alteration of the franchise and a substantial increase in African representation in the Legislature'.[2] Nor would a mere increase in the size of the Legislative Assembly bringing in African members to represent electoral districts where African voters were concentrated satisfy the United Kingdom Government so as to induce it to relinquish its reserve powers.[3] At first it was tentatively agreed that the United Kingdom's powers should primarily, but not entirely be transferred to a Senate with special powers in respect of constitutional amendment.[4] However, the United Kingdom insisted on reserving certain negative powers so that Southern Rhodesia should not become a republic,[5] while on the other hand, the Southern Rhodesian Government requested that the provisions in the Constitution relating to Native Affairs should be changed.

As part of the bargain it was then agreed that the Southern Rhodesian Government would make changes in the Land Apportionment Act 1941, as amended.[6] Discriminatory legislation in Southern Rhodesia was likewise discussed.[7] Indeed one of the United Kingdom's main reasons for deciding to implement the Southern Rhodesia Constitution 1961 was that it was considered that 'things are definitely moving in the right direction in Southern Rhodesia',[8] and that the Government was engaged in a 'systematic review of their Statute Book'.[9]

[1] *S.R.L.A.D.*, Vol. 45, col. 240, 6 July 1960, Whitehead; and *S.R.L.A.D.*, Vol. 45, col. 708, 28 July 1960.

[2] *H.C. Deb.*, Vol. 644, col. 171, 21 July 1961, Sandys: 'In reply to specific enquiries from Sir Edgar Whitehead I informed him that the British Government would not regard the adoption of a declaration of rights and other constitutional safeguards as adequate substitutions by themselves for the British Government's existing reserve power.'

[3] *S.R.L.A.D.*, Vol. 45, col. 1720, 24 August 1960, Whitehead. The Secretary of State suggested that the introduction of a Bill of Rights subject to judicial review and a right of appeal to the Judicial Committee of the Privy Council would be a better safeguard against discriminatory laws than the present system whereby the decision was left to the particular Secretary of State in power at any time. Personal communication from Sir Edgar Whitehead. It was, in any event, Sir Edgar's intention to repeal all discriminatory laws over a period of time.

[4] The proposals were extremely fluid and no common agreement on powers or composition was reached: *S.R.L.A.D.*, Vol. 45, cols. 1669–70, 23 August 1960, Whitehead. M. Hirsch, *Focus on Southern Rhodesia*, Stuart Manning, Bulawayo, 1964, at p. 4, reveals Whitehead's proposal that the Senate be chosen by an electoral college elected from occupational groups.

[5] *S.R.L.A.D.*, Vol. 45, cols. 700–1, 28 September 1960, Whitehead. The United Kingdom also discussed the future method of constitutional amendment: *H.C. Deb.*, Vol. 623, col. 31, 9 May 1960.

[6] See *H.C. Deb.*, Vol. 623, col. 31, 9 May 1960, and Vol. 642, col. 1814.

[7] *H.C. Deb.*, Vol. 623, col. 31, 9 May 1960.

[8] *H.C. Deb.*, Vol. 637, col. 734, Sandys. Cp. Cmnd. 1148, pp. 75–76. It seems in retrospect that the new Constitution was granted on the basis that a particular party, that of Sir Edgar Whitehead, would remain in power and that this party would bring about a relatively

Footnote 9 on next page.

During 1960 a group of influential Southern Rhodesian citizens organized a National Convention or 'indaba' held at Salisbury in early November under the chairmanship of Sir John Kennedy to discuss the participation by all races in all spheres of the country's life and the elimination of racial discrimination. This Convention was attended by representatives of all races and occupational groups. The Convention, which was unofficial, but enjoyed the support of the governing party[1] put forward proposals for the election of ten to fifteen African representatives, an increase in the size of the Legislative Assembly, and a broadening of the franchise to secure African participation in government. The Convention also recommended the incorporation of a Bill of Rights in the Constitution, the abolition of the Native Affairs Department, the progressive repeal of the Land Apportionment Act and the legislative prohibition of public social discrimination.[2] Many of these suggestions were taken up at the subsequent Constitutional Conference which followed.

In December 1960 a Constitutional Conference to be held immediately

smooth change to majority rule over a period of years. Political assumptions of this nature are no basis for deciding constitutional questions, especially if they turn out to be mistaken. Sir Edgar Whitehead's policy as put to the United Kingdom Government and as partly revealed to the electorate was to remove all discriminatory legislation relatively rapidly and, in particular, the Land Apportionment Act. He maintained, however, that time before a hand-over was necessary in order to train African civil servants and that this would take at least ten years as the Civil Service had only been opened to Africans in 1960. The franchise he proposed would, in his view, lead to an African majority in fifteen years as a result of expanding African education and opportunities for advancement for Africans in the Civil Service and the Railways, and of the right to buy individual Purchase Area farms. His aim was to create an African middle class which would eventually take over political power and exercise it responsibly. He could not go further than this as he had to consider the opinion of his electorate, which was predominantly European. In fact, Sir Edgar Whitehead went too far in the view of his electorate and, in the general election of 14 December 1962 he was defeated.

[9] *H.C. Deb.*, Vol. 648, col. 1045, 6 August 1961, Under Secretary of State for Commonwealth Relations. At this time the Government of Southern Rhodesia had either introduced or prepared a series of measures lessening discrimination, viz. Public Services Amendment (No. 2) Act No. 42 of 1960 opening the Civil Service to all races, the Pass Laws (Repeal) Act No. 50 of 1960 (but it must be noted that other laws still required Africans to carry registration certificates which, in practice, operated as Passes), the Land Apportionment Amendment Act No. 54 of 1960 modifying the laws relating to native urban areas, the Local Government Act No. 4 of 1961 to provide for Local Boards in African townships, the Liquor Amendment Act No. 15 of 1961 permitting all races to buy liquor, the Immorality and Indecency Suppression (Repeal) Act 42 of 1961 (repealing an Act which had imposed heavy penalties on Africans who cohabited with European woman and lesser penalties on such women, no penalties being inflicted on European men and African women who cohabited), the Repeal of Laws Act No. 35 of 1961 (repealing a number of discriminatory laws, e.g. Settlement of Colonial Natives in Kaffir Kraals Prohibition Act (Chapter 95), and Native Adultery Act (Chapter 96)), and the Land Apportionment Amendment Act No. 37 of 1961 creating a category of land open to all races.

---

[1] See Report of the National Convention of Southern Rhodesia, Salisbury, 1960, p. 49. Cabinet Ministers attended as observers and information from Civil Service departments was made freely available.

[2] ibid., pp. 7–31.

after the Federal Review Conference and to which two African Nationalist leaders were invited at the insistence of the United Kingdom Government[1] was arranged. However, the African Nationalist delegates were not permitted to be present at the Southern Rhodesian Conference by Sir Edgar Whitehead on the grounds that they had earlier boycotted the Federal Review Conference. At this Southern Rhodesian Conference Mr. Sandys emphasized the need for safeguards replacing British powers, which should be acceptable both to the House of Commons and the majority of Southern Rhodesians of all races. Local agreement should be reached, preferably by a broadly representative conference or on a government to government basis, the final proposals requiring to be accepted by the African people.[2] After procedural discussions the Conference then adjourned. In view of Mr. Sandys' remarks and also threats by other delegates not to attend, Sir Edgar Whitehead then invited the Nationalist leaders to return to the Conference when re-assembled. A joint statement was issued by him as Prime Minister and by Mr. Nkomo, leader of the National Democratic Party, the African nationalist party of Southern Rhodesia, denouncing violence and agreeing to work together for a new constitution.[3]

In January 1961 the Conference re-convened in Salisbury under the chairmanship of Sir Edgar Whitehead. Discussions leading to agreement then occurred between the delegates representing the local political groupings in respect of non-controversial matters and those affecting United Kingdom powers.[4]

From 30 January to 7 February 1961, the Conference then re-assembled in Salisbury under the chairmanship of Mr. Duncan Sandys, the Secretary of State for Commonwealth Relations, who insisted on increasing African 'participation in government at a reasonable rate'.[5] At the end of the Conference after intense pressure by Mr. Sandys, who consulted with the political groups separately, delegates of all shades of political opinion reached agreement on proposals for a new constitution and agreed to invite the

---

[1] Personal communication. Mr. Sandys insisted on a fully representative conference. Only two of the nineteen delegates to London were African Nationalists.

[2] See Hirsch, op. cit., p. 6. The author was a delegate to the Conference, and played a part in formulating the governing party's proposals.

[3] *The Rhodesia Herald*, 20 December 1960.

[4] Agreement was reached on the method of appointment and removal of judges, that separate Ministers would be responsible for law and order on the one hand and courts on the other, that there would be no executive interference with the courts, that magistrates would no longer have general administrative functions, that Native Commissioners would no longer exercise criminal jurisdiction, that the Native Commissioner would in future be a district administrator charged with encouraging local government on a democratic basis, and that a declaration of rights which would later be discussed in detail would be inserted in the new constitution. The significance of these discussions is that some of these changes, e.g. taking away the criminal jurisdiction of Native Commissioners, were embodied in subsequent legislation.

[5] Hirsch, op. cit., p. 16.

United Kingdom Government to implement the recommendations of the Conference.[1] The aim of the new constitution was to bring about transition to African majority rule over a period of years.[2] As agreed at the Conference, the basic features of the new constitution were that the United Kingdom Government would surrender its powers of reservation of Bills and general disallowance, the Governor's power to dissent from Executive Council advice, its controls over matters relating to the Native Department, and its powers to revoke or amend the vital sections of the constitution conferring legislative power. The Legislature of Southern Rhodesia would also be permitted to enact laws having extraterritorial operation. In return for the removal of these elements of subordination, a Declaration of Rights subject to judicial review with a right of ultimate appeal to the Judicial Committee of the Privy Council would be inserted in the constitution. In addition, a Constitutional Council with delaying and advisory functions in respect of Bills and subordinate legislation would be created. The major consideration for the constitutional changes, however, was that the Southern Rhodesians agreed to alterations in the franchise, in the composition of the Legislature, and in the method of election of members. The franchise would, to a certain extent, be enlarged by the creation of a new 'B' roll qualification.[3] Voters could be enrolled on either the 'A' or the 'B' Roll, the 'A' Roll voters electing fifty members representing constituencies and the 'B' Roll voters electing fifteen members for electoral districts, the Legislative Assembly membership being thereafter increased to sixty-five. As between the Rolls there was to be cross-voting except that, when the proportion of 'B' Roll votes cast for an 'A' Roll constituency amounted to more than 25 per cent of the votes cast, such votes would be proportionately devalued and *vice versa* in the case of 'A' Roll votes cast for a 'B' Roll electoral district. In addition a rigid procedure for constitutional amendment was prescribed in the majority of cases—a two-thirds majority of the total membership of the Legislative Assembly— while in cases where amendment of certain basic clauses of the constitution was sought majorities of each of the European, African, Asian, and Coloured communities voting separately or the approval of the United Kingdom Government were required in addition. Indeed certain provisions of the constitution would not be capable of amendment except by the Crown in Council. These related to the formal position of the Governor as the Sovereign's

[1] However the Dominion Party which was subsequently merged in the present Southern Rhodesia Government party, the Rhodesian Front, did not agree to these proposals. Once the proposals were converted into the new Constitution, the leader of the Rhodesian Front, Mr. Field, stated that his party would uphold the Constitution. The present Prime Minister, Mr. Field's successor, Mr. Smith, now supports this Constitution, although initially he resigned from the United Federal Party because of its backing for the 1961 Constitution.

[2] Estimated by Sir Edgar Whitehead to be about fifteen.

[3] However, certain voters already registered (those with 'special qualifications' under the 1957 franchise) came within this category, the practical result of this change being to make their votes less significant by taking them off the common roll. See *infra*, Part II, Chapter I.

representative and the Sovereign's power to disallow Acts affecting Southern Rhodesian undertakings in respect of stocks registered under the Colonial Stock Acts or Acts inconsistent with the United Kingdom's international obligations in respect of Southern Rhodesia.[1]

All groups stated that they reserved their position on the franchise and parliamentary representation.[2] However, shortly after the conclusion of the Conference the leaders of the National Democratic Party (the African nationalist party in Southern Rhodesia at that time) stated that they could not accept the constitutional proposals as agreed upon, and that they were not prepared to recognize a new constitution based on the Conference proposals.[3] Despite strenuous opposition both by the National Democratic Party and the British Labour Party, the United Kingdom Government decided to implement the agreement reached at the Constitutional Conference.[4]

Drafting of detailed proposals then went ahead and in May delegates, except for the nationalist leaders who boycotted these discussions after attending the opening session, met to discuss proposals relating to the Native Reserves, the Land Apportionment Act and the creation of Tribal Trust areas.[5] Thereafter government to government talks were held and on 1 June final agreement on the draft proposals was reached. This had been preceded by tense negotiations as Sir Edgar Whitehead insisted on formal acknowledgement by Britain of a convention that Parliament at Westminster would not legislate on matters within the competence of the Southern Rhodesian Legislative Assembly. Only after he had threatened to reject the whole constitutional settlement did the British High Commissioner notify him that the United Kingdom Government would acknowledge this convention.[6] On 13 June White Papers detailing the proposals were published, and in July 1961 these were approved by the House of Commons.[7]

In the interim the Southern Rhodesian Legislative Assembly had passed

[1] See Cmnd. 1291.   [2] Cmnd. 1291, p. 5.

[3] *The Times*, 18 February 1961. As a historical fact, however, the leaders had agreed to the introduction of a new constitution as outlined in the White Paper. Their repudiation occurred after violent attacks on them by members of their Party. It must be remembered that the nationalist leaders did not have expert advisers to assist them and that they were considerably influenced by a powerful Secretary of State in reaching agreement. See *H.C. Deb.*, Vol. 637, col. 737, 23 March 1961, where Mr. Sandys read out a letter from the Secretary-General of the National Democratic Party acknowledging their agreement.

[4] The United Kingdom Government informed Sir Edgar Whitehead that he need not consider himself bound by the proposals in view of this repudiation but the Prime Minister elected to proceed with the new constitution. Personal communication from a confidential source.

[5] To offset the nationalists' withdrawal and in order to show some African backing for the constitutional changes Sir Edgar Whitehead assembled over 500 Chiefs and Headmen at a meeting in Gwelo in May 1961, where resolutions supporting the Government were passed. See Alport (Lord), *Sudden Assignment*, Hodder & Stoughton, 1965, pp. 53-4.

[6] Personal communication from a confidential source.

[7] Cmnd. 1399, Cmnd. 1400. *H.C. Deb.*, Vol. 644, col. 171, 21 July 1961.

the Referendum Act[1] providing for a referendum for the purpose of determining whether the voters of Southern Rhodesia were in favour of, or against the draft proposals which would be placed before them for the introduction of the new constitution. On 26 July 1961 the Southern Rhodesian electorate approved these proposals.[2]

The Southern Rhodesia (Constitution) Act 1961

On 23 November the Southern Rhodesia (Constitution) Act 1961, enabling Her Majesty by Order in Council to revoke the Southern Rhodesia Constitution Letters Patent 1923 and to grant a new constitution in its place received the Royal Assent.[3] The Act provided that the Order might confer power on the Legislature of Southern Rhodesia to enact laws having extraterritorial operation.[4] The Order in Council might also

authorize the amendment or revocation of any of the provisions of the Order in any manner specified by the Order in relation to those provisions respectively but nothing in this Act shall authorize any other amendment or revocation of any of the provisions of the Order.

In terms of the Southern Rhodesia (Constitution) Act, no amendment could therefore be made except in terms of procedures authorized by the Constitution Order in Council. The wording of the Act did not, however, derogate from other powers of amendment which might be in existence.[5]

The Southern Rhodesia (Constitution) Order in Council

Thereafter the Southern Rhodesia (Constitution) Order in Council 1961[6] was made on 6 September 1961. The new Constitution did not, however,

[1] No. 25 of 1961 passed in May and the Referendum Amendment Act No. 32 of 1961 passed in June. It was argued in respect of the Referendum Act that it created new constitutional machinery for consultation of the electorate and therefore was a constitutional Bill, which should have been passed by a two-thirds majority of the total membership of the Legislative Assembly under Section 26(2) of the 1923 Letters Patent. This argument was rejected by the Speaker of the Legislative Assembly: S.R.L.A.D., Vol. 47, col. 5274, 2 May 1961.

[2] 42,004 voters (65·79 per cent of votes cast) were in favour of the proposals, and 21,846 against (34·12 per cent). The total electorate was 83,486. The percentage poll was 76·48 per cent. See Passmore and Mitchell, op. cit. The African nationalist party, the National Democratic Party, advocated a boycott of the official referendum, holding its own referendum on 23 July. It claimed that 457,189 votes were cast against the new constitution and 584 in its favour.

[3] Under Section 61 of the 1923 Letters Patent the right of revocation of the whole Constitution was not reserved so that an Imperial Act was necessary for such a purpose.

[4] 10 Eliz. II, c. 2, Sec. 1.

[5] It is submitted that there remained powers of amendment under the Rhodesia and Nyasaland (Federation) Act 1953 (1 & 2 Eliz. II, c. 30).

[6] S.I. 1961, No. 2314.

come into force immediately, although certain sections of the Order making transitional provisions came into effect on 7 December 1961.[1] Thus the Legislative Assembly was authorized to pass a Bill amending the Southern Rhodesian Electoral Act No. 27 of 1951 in order to provide for new franchise qualifications set out in the Second Schedule to the Constitution in accordance with detailed provisions prescribed in the Order,[2] to make provisions for a General Election for the purpose of constituting a Legislative Assembly composed of sixty-five members elected from fifty constituencies and fifteen electoral districts according to a delimitation procedure laid down in the Constitution, and to provide for the keeping of two voters' rolls for each constituency and electoral district to be known as an 'A' Roll and a 'B' Roll, on which existing voters were to be placed according to their qualifications. Special provisions for cross-voting and devaluation of votes after a certain proportion had been reached were also to be inserted, while a voluntary single 'preferential vote' was to be substituted for the existing 'multiple' preferential vote.[3]

Once the projected Electoral Act had been enacted the Governor, in order to afford sufficient opportunity for any newly qualified persons to claim registration as voters, was to allow a period not being in excess of six or less than three months for this purpose. Thereafter he was to bring into effect the provisions relating to the establishment of a Delimitation Commission charged with the duty of dividing Southern Rhodesia into fifty constituencies and fifteen electoral districts.[4] After the report of the Delimitation Commission and any proclamation implementing its report, the Governor was as soon as possible by proclamation to dissolve the existing Legislative Assembly, to appoint a date for a General Election to elect the new Legislative Assembly prescribed in the new Constitution, and to bring into force on the same date as the dissolution of the existing Legislative Assembly the remainder of the Constitution.[5] As from that date the Southern Rhodesia Constitution Letters Patent 1923 and the Letters Patent constituting the Office of Governor were revoked, while powers reserved to Her Majesty by the Order in Council to amend, add to, or revoke the Order, except as specified in Section 111 of

[1] S.R. (Constitution) Order in Council, section 20.

[2] There are slight discrepancies between the detailed provisions in the Order and the Second Schedule. Thus those provisions incorporated in the Electoral Act, which are not also set forth in the Schedule, may be changed by simple majority of the Legislature, e.g. the preferential vote, while others set out in the Schedule were not put in the Electoral Act. Cp. Schedule, Item 8, with the Electoral Act, Chapter 2, section 14(4), which does not permit the wives of Chiefs and Headmen to register by virtue of their husband's qualifications. The preferential vote was in fact eliminated by Electoral Amendment Act No. 30 of 1964 which was passed by a simple majority of the Legislative Assembly.

[3] S.I. 1961, No. 2314, sections 2 and 3.

[4] Section 4. From the date of the Proclamation by the Governor establishing the new Delimitation Commission, sections 8 and 9 of the Southern Rhodesia Letters Patent 1923 were revoked: S.I. 1961, No. 2314, section 21(1).

[5] Section 5.

the Constitution, fell away.[1] By Royal Instructions of 6 June 1962, it was provided that the previous Royal Instructions to the Governor should be revoked as from the appointed day and that from that time onwards he should accept the advice of the Governor's Council in respect of the prerogative of mercy.

In August 1962 the Electoral Amendment (No. 2) Act No. 16 of 1962 was passed by the Legislative Assembly. It contained provisions required by the Order in Council. Thereafter the Delimitation Commission was set up, and, when it had presented its report, the Governor proclaimed the names and boundaries of the constituencies and electoral districts recommended by the Commission, thereupon also proclaiming dissolution of the existing Legislative Assembly, appointing the 14 December 1962 as the date for a General Election,[2] and bringing the remaining provisions of the new Constitution into force as from 1st November 1962.[3]

In the intervening months prior to the dissolution the Legislative Assembly of Southern Rhodesia had continued in terms of the 1923 Constitution and during that period had passed stringent security laws, many of which would have conflicted with the Declaration of Rights contained in the new Constitution, had it been in force.[4] At the same time the African nationalist leaders, who had decided to boycott elections under the new Constitution, and to discourage registration of voters,[5] had carried their opposition to the forum of the United Nations. Here the position in Southern Rhodesia was investigated by the Special Committee on Colonialism in March, April, May, and June 1962, while a Sub-Committee of that Committee had talks in London with the British Government in April 1962. The matter was also debated by

[1] Sections 21(2) and 22. M. Hirsch, op. cit., p. 33 reveals that the Southern Rhodesian Government was concerned as a result of vociferous African opposition both inside and outside Southern Rhodesia that such powers might be utilized. The powers were a factor in the Whitehead Government's decision to hurry the processes required to bring the new Constitution into operation.

[2] In the Election of 14 December 1962 the Rhodesian Front won thirty-five of the 'A' Roll constituencies, all of these Members of Parliament being European. The United Federal Party won twenty-nine seats, of which fifteen were 'A' Roll constituencies represented by fourteen European members and one Coloured member, while fourteen were 'B' Roll electoral districts represented by fourteen African members. In addition, one electoral district returned an Independent European sympathizing with African political interests. There were 91,272 'A' Roll voters, of whom 1,920 were African and 10,497 'B' Roll voters of whom 9,585 were African at the time of the election. The African nationalists boycotted the election and the 'B' Roll votes cast were only 24 per cent of the potential.

[3] Southern Rhodesia Proclamation No. 42 of 1962.

[4] The Law and Order (Maintenance) Amendment Act No. 35 of 1962 and the Unlawful Organizations Act No. 28 of 1962. These, the former Federal Chief Justice, Sir Robert Tredgold, described as 'provisions more appropriate to a police state'. The United Kingdom Labour Party alleged that enactment of these provisions was a breach of faith.

[5] They felt that had they operated the Constitution they would have been considered by world opinion to have accepted it. Furthermore the franchise was so designed to permit only an African elite to vote. Had they been defeated it would have appeared as if the African people had rejected them and their policy.

the General Assembly in June and in October 1962, and by the Trusteeship Committee in October 1962.

On 20 September 1962 under the Law and Order (Maintenance) Act as amended, many African leaders were restricted to tribal areas under police surveillance, while others were restricted to small areas in the urban centres. The Zimbabwe African People's Union, which had now become the African nationalist party,[1] was proscribed on the 20 September under the Unlawful Organisations Act. Thereupon the Trusteeship Committee and the General Assembly both expressed concern at 'the explosive situation obtaining in Southern Rhodesia' and urged Britain to intervene to secure the lifting of restrictions on nationalist leaders and the ban on Z.A.P.U. Thereafter, on 30 and 31 October, Sir Edgar Whitehead addressed the Trusteeship Committee as a British delegate.[2] Nonetheless, on 31 October 1962 the Committee and the General Assembly both passed resolutions calling on Britain to suspend the Constitution of 6 December 1961, to cancel the forthcoming elections, to convene a conference to formulate a new constitution, to extend the franchise immediately to all inhabitants, and to establish equality among them. Britain abstained from voting on this resolution, as she did on all other occasions when Southern Rhodesia was debated. When the final vote was taken in New York, all provisions of the 1961 Constitution had already come into force in Southern Rhodesia.[3] Southern Rhodesia had therefore obtained a constitution couched in largely non-racial terms which could eventually lead to majority rule but, in practice, meant that European control was to continue for a lengthy period,[4] although in that period new discriminatory measures would be difficult to introduce in view of the constitutional safeguards contained in the new Constitution.

[1] The Nationalist Democratic Party had been proscribed on 8 December 1961, and Z.A.P.U., formed within a fortnight of the N.D.P.'s proscription, was its successor with virtually the same leadership.

[2] By the invitation of the United Kingdom Government. Sir Hugh Foot, the United Kingdom delegate for Colonial and Trusteeship questions had resigned on the 11 October as he felt he could no longer support his Government's policy in Central Africa: H. Foot, *A Start in Freedom*, Hodder & Stoughton, 1964, pp. 215–26.

[3] It is interesting to speculate whether Britain disregarded a resolution of the General Assembly at a time when she still had power to intervene in Southern Rhodesia—acknowledging, however, that Britain did not recognize the competence of the Assembly on Southern Rhodesian matters. The resolution in New York was passed shortly after midnight of 31 October by Southern Rhodesian time, but by Greenwich Mean Time it was passed before midnight. If expressions as to date and time at which the Constitution (brought into force under United Kingdom instruments) was to come into force were to be taken to intend G.M.T. then the Constitution was not in force at the time of the General Assembly resolution. See the Statutes (Definition of Time) Act 1880, 43 & 44 Vict. c. 9.

[4] See *infra*, Part II, Chapter 1, on the franchise and its effects.

15

MOVES TOWARDS CLOSER UNION WITH
THE NORTHERN TERRITORIES

The arguments for and against closer union

ARGUMENTS urging closer union between Southern Rhodesia and Northern Rhodesia have been expounded at various times for over fifty years, the basic arguments remaining the same but the emphasis changing depending on political circumstances and the particular standpoint of the protagonist. The main arguments originally put forward were both economic—economies of administration to the British South Africa Company—and political—an appeal to imperialist emotion with a plea for a white British Dominion in Central Africa. In fact, this was Rhodes' desire manifested in his early attempts to retain control of Nyasaland and to keep it within the Company's sphere.

Subsequently the political arguments changed in their emphasis. Although at one time the Imperial Government had considered some form of closer union desirable for purposes of Imperial consolidation in Central Africa, this was supplanted by a desire to create a liberal British counterpoise to the white Afrikaner nationalism of South Africa. By the early nineteen-fifties this attitude changed its emphasis to the ideal of the establishment of a multi-racial society interposed between the white racialism of South Africa and the black nationalism of the rest of the African continent. Furthermore, it was even thought that if a federation were created Southern Rhodesian Africans would be afforded political opportunities which could not otherwise have been available to them.[1]

Although Imperial aims were largely idealistic the aim of many European politicians who urged the creation of Federation was to secure European control 'for the foreseeable future' by extending Southern Rhodesian influence over all British Central Africa and by eliminating Colonial Office control.[2] On the other hand, other Europeans feared that closer union would lead to too rapid an increase in the political power of Africans, that the

---

[1] e.g., *H.L. Deb.*, Vol. 181, col. 517, 1 April 1953, Lord Hailey.

[2] See African fears to this effect outlined in Cmnd. 1148, at p. 18. See also C. Leys, 'The Case against Federation in Central Africa', *Public Law*, Spring 1960, pp. 18 and 19, suggesting that the prime object of a Federation was to place Northern Rhodesia as well as Southern Rhodesia under local European control. See also T. R. M. Creighton, *The Anatomy of Partnership*, Faber, 1960, p. 39, who brings out the divergent views of the various groups creating and participating in any scheme for closer union. See also E. P. Dvorin, 'Central Africa's First Federal Election: Background and Issues', *The Western Political Quarterly*, Vol. 7, 1954, at pp. 377-9, for a description of the attitude of the European electorate of Southern Rhodesia.

Colonial Office (viewed by them with suspicion) would be given more power, and that Dominion status for Southern Rhodesia under the type of constitution implemented in 1923 would not be granted.[1]

African opinion in the Northern Territories insofar as it was articulate was from the beginning intensely opposed to closer union as Africans feared the extension of Southern Rhodesian native policy and discriminatory practices to Northern Rhodesia and Nyasaland. There can be no doubt that closer union was imposed against their wishes.[2] The Africans of the Northern Territories in fact reversed the European argument that Federation would be to the detriment of Southern Rhodesian Europeans: they argued that closer union would lead to the withdrawal of Imperial protection from the Northern Territories and to increased white domination through a largely white central Legislature.

Economic arguments also played a great part, particularly in the era of the post-war planners. These arguments rested largely on economies of scale, on the creation of a common market, on a powerful credit-worthy central government, and the complementary nature of the three Territories.[3] The mineral wealth of Northern Rhodesia was also a great attraction for Southern Rhodesia[4] which, although it did not have a mono-economy such as that of Northern Rhodesia, was largely dependent on its tobacco crop at that time. Economic arguments appealed therefore to Southern Rhodesian self-interest and at the same time in a more altruistic fashion to the Imperial Government which wished 'to try an experiment to see whether the forces released, the pent-up pressures can be harnessed and directed towards the good of all these races'.[5]

[1] Southern Rhodesian politicians have stated that Southern Rhodesia could have obtained dominion status in 1952 as an alternative to Federation (e.g. the present Prime Minister, Mr. Smith: S.R.L.A.D., Vol. 59, col. 422, 27 October 1964) implying that the United Kingdom would have agreed to this and that the terms would have been acceptable to the predominantly European electorate. However Sir John Kennedy, Governor at the time, in a personal communication in November 1964 has stated that 'there are no firm grounds for assuming that Southern Rhodesia could have had dominion status at that time if they had not favoured closer union'.

[2] Lord Salisbury and Mr. Lyttelton openly admitted this, stating that their overriding duties as trustees forced them to overrule the wishes of their beneficiaries, the views of the latter not being in the Africans' own best interests. It was also considered that the pros and cons of a conception such as Federation could not be understood by the uneducated African masses, but that if Federation were imposed and thereafter a statesman-like approach were adopted, African opinion would see the advantages of federation.

[3] Cmnd. 1148, p. 23. Nyasaland was considered as not being economically viable. See also A. Hazlewood and P. D. Henderson, Nyasaland: The Economics of Federation, Blackwell, 1960, which has an opposing point of view. Europeans in Northern Rhodesia have also opposed closer union on the basis that Northern Rhodesian copper resources would subsidize the other Territories to the detriment of Northern Rhodesia.

[4] See Gann and Gelfand, op. cit., for the Southern Rhodesian Prime Minister's point of view. This wealth and its significance were pointed out in 1938: Report of the Commission appointed to enquire into the financial and economic position in Northern Rhodesia. Colonial No. 145, H.M.S.O., London, 1938—The Pim Report.

[5] H.C. Deb., Vol. 516, col. 2047, 24 June 1953, Lyttelton.

Even after the dissolution of Federation, certain common services have been maintained for economic reasons and it is still the United Kingdom policy to seek to assist in the evolution of effective new forms of collaboration between the Territories and to preserve and to promote in particular the economic prosperity of all.[1]

One of the two decisive factors in the Imperial Government's decision to accede to the pressure of local European politicians in power and to create Federation was best described by Sir Arthur Benson, who was intimately involved in the negotiations leading to Federation as Secretary of the Central Africa Council and subsequently as Governor of Northern Rhodesia. He wrote in 1961 to *The Times* that Federation came about as a result of recognition that there was 'a great opportunity, perhaps the last opportunity, to create an influential State in Africa where colour or race were to become of no account'.[2]

The other decisive factor was Britain's fear that Southern Rhodesia would join the Union of South Africa,[3] a fear that was accentuated by the relatively high proportion of Afrikaners in Southern Rhodesia in 1951.[4]

---

[1] Cmnd. 2093, paras. 31–33. The arguments, political and economic, for closer union can be found in the works mentioned in the aforegoing footnotes and also in K. Kirkwood, 'The Proposed Federation of the Central African Territories', New Africa Pamphlet No. 21, South African Institute of Race Relations, Johannesburg, 1951; E. Clegg, *Race and Politics, Partnership in the Federation of Rhodesia and Nyasaland*, Oxford, 1960; R. C. Pratt and C. Leys, *A New Deal in Central Africa*, Heinemann, 1960; P. Mason, *Year of Decision: Rhodesia and Nyasaland in 1960*, Oxford, 1960; C. Sanger, *Central African Emergency*, Heinemann, 1960; G. Jones, *Britain and Nyasaland*, Allen & Unwin, 1964; and H. Franklin, *Unholy Wedlock*, Allen & Unwin, 1963. Some of these works are frankly polemical. Indeed 'the debate which preceded Federation at Westminster was the most intense on any Colonial subject within memory': 'The Debate on Central African Federation in Retrospect', W. F. Gutteridge, *Parliamentary Affairs*, Vol. X, pp. 210–19 at 211. The creation of the Federation has been compared with abandonment of Britain's trust in 1909 when the natives of South Africa were handed over to the Government and Legislature of the Union of South Africa. The same fate that was predicted in the debates on the South Africa Act was also predicted for Africans in the United Kingdom pre-Federation debates. For the general political reasons for federalism and the circumstances in which it is possible see K. C. Wheare, *Federal Government*, Oxford, 3rd ed., pp. 35–54; K. C. Wheare, 'Federalism and the Making of Nations', in *Federalism, Mature and Emergent* (ed. McMahon), Doubleday, 1955, and Part I generally. For the application of federalism in underdeveloped countries, see F. G. Carnell in *Federalism and Economic Growth in Underdeveloped Countries* (ed. U. Hicks), Allen & Unwin, 1961; M. Beloff, 'The Federal Solution in its Application to Europe, Asia and Africa', *Political Studies*, 1953, pp. 114–31; W. S. Livingston, *Federalism and Constitutional Change*, Oxford, 1956, esp. Chapter 1; and W. S. Livingston (ed.), *Federalism in the Commonwealth*, Cassell, 1963, which gives an extensive bibliography of works on federalism.

[2] *The Times*, 20 February 1961. Sir John Kennedy, Governor of Southern Rhodesia at that time and Chairman of the Central Africa Council, has confirmed that this was an important factor in the British Government's final decision. Personal communication, November 1964.

[3] Personal communication from Sir John Kennedy in November 1964. See also Viscount Chandos (O. Lyttelton), *The Memoirs of Lord Chandos*, Bodley Head, 1962, p. 387.

[4] See Leys, *European Politics*, op. cit., p. 95, who shows that Afrikaners formed 24·5 per

History of the closer union movement

Had it not been for the ill-fated Jameson Raid both Southern and Northern Rhodesia would have been governed by the Company Administrator and Council in Southern Rhodesia as an Order in Council making such provision had been prepared. However, the Raid led to a different solution whereby the High Commissioner exercised control over Company officials in Northern Rhodesia, who were responsible to him and not to the Administrator and Council in Southern Rhodesia, although the Company was itself responsible for administering both Territories.[1]

With the increasing tempo of European settlement in both Territories moves to establish closer links between the countries were initiated. Holding strong views on the desirability for creating a South African Federation, Lord Selborne as High Commissioner suggested in 1907 that the Europeans of Southern Africa should federate to develop the area as far as Lake Tanganyika in a development comparable to that of the United States of America.[2] In particular he considered that the Northern railway belt should be united to Southern Rhodesia.[3]

As early as 1909 the suggestion that Southern and Northern Rhodesia should amalgamate to form a 'great British community in the heart of Africa under its own government' became common property. Indeed, by 1911 the High Commissioner found this idea being widely mooted.[4] Subsequently in 1913 the British South Africa Company put forward a scheme on these lines in order to economize on administration, which was made public by Sir Starr Jameson, now Chairman of the Company.[5] When a draft Order in Council had been prepared the Company formally put such a scheme to the Legislative Council in 1917. Although a motion in favour of amalgamation was passed, the majority of the elected representatives voted against it as they feared they would not gain responsible government if 'the Black North' were added to Southern Rhodesia, while the future of the white man would be rendered insecure by the relatively large numbers of African clerks and artisans of the North. Nor did they wish to assume the financial burden of Northern Rhodesia which, at that time, could not balance its budget.[6]

cent of the rural European population which was significant when related to the Southern Rhodesian system of delimitation of electoral districts with heavy urban loading. According to Leys the over-all percentage of Afrikaners was 13·5 per cent. These figures are probably too low as they are based entirely on Dutch Reformed Church Membership. From 1952, when immigration restrictions were imposed in Southern Rhodesia, to 1955 immigration quotas were so filled as to exclude Afrikaners as far as was possible.

[1] See L. H. Gann, *The History of Northern Rhodesia*, Chatto & Windus, 1964, for an authoritative account of early government in Northern Rhodesia.

[2] *The Selborne Memorandum*, op. cit.

[3] African 872, No. 118, 17 June 1907.

[4] African 948, No. 68, Encl., 19 May 1911.

[5] See *Rhodesia Herald*, 24 December 1913.

[6] See *S.R. Legco Deb.*, 1917, col. 309 et seq., for the views of Sir Charles Coghlan.

The Colonial Office then informed the Company that under these circumstances amalgamation could not be proceeded with.[1] Rejection by the settlers of amalgamation in fact saved the Colonial Office any embarrassment in rejecting the proposals.[2] The Company, however, subsequently appointed its Administrator as Administrator of both Territories in order to effect economies.[3]

By 1925 the Southern Rhodesian attitude began to change: responsible government had been attained and Northern Rhodesia, it was clear, would become a financially attractive proposition when its vast copper resources publicized in that year were exploited. Tentative enquiries were then made by the Southern Rhodesian High Commissioner in London. After informal discussions with the Colonial Office, Newton informed the Prime Minister that the Colonial Office would be prepared to carve up Northern Rhodesia, giving the eastern side to Nyasaland and leaving Barotse territory as a reserve enclave, probably giving the middle portion to Southern Rhodesia.[4] By this time, Colonial Office attitudes towards the desirability of forcing Southern Rhodesia into the Union of South Africa had begun to alter and the Colonial Office was envisaging the counterpoise of a British white Dominion in East and Central Africa.[5] The idea of a wider East and Central African federation encouraged a degree of coolness towards the idea of Southern Rhodesia acquiring power over Northern Rhodesia.[6] As a result of Newton's enquiries,

[1] B. K. Long, op. cit., pp. 216–17, quoting a private letter of December 1917 from Walter Long, Secretary of State, to Drummond Chaplin, the Administrator. This is worth quoting at length as it reveals the dilemma of the United Kingdom Government in dealing with elective assemblies: 'I cannot ignore the fact that whether for good or for evil you have got an elective body in Southern Rhodesia. Once you allow a country to elect representatives it is impossible in my judgement for H.M. Government to ignore the opinions of the elected members or to go in direct opposition to the majority of them. I am confident that to do this would land any Secretary of State in grave difficulties, would impose upon him responsibilities which would, I think, be impossible for him to bear, and—I cannot help thinking— would create difficulties for the people responsible for government, which might be of the most formidable kind.'
[2] That the Colonial Office was reluctant that amalgamation should occur was manifested when it rebuked the High Commissioner for stating in 1916 that no Imperial interest was involved and that amalgamation depended on the settlers' wishes. Personal communication from a confidential source. For the remarks in question see *S.R. Legco Deb.*, 1917, cols. 319–20, 25 April 1917, where these were quoted.
[3] See Rhodesia (Administrator) Order in Council 1921.
[4] i.e. the railway strip, National Archives CO 8/1/2, Newton to Coghlan, 20 July 1925.
[5] Cmd. 2387. Report of the East African Commission, pp. 8–9. The Commission found federation premature on grounds of lack of communications, expense and administrative impracticability, but it suggested co-ordination by conferences, both technical and administrative, and the regular holdings of Governors' conferences attended by the Governors of Northern Rhodesia and Nyasaland for the discussion of matters of common interest. See also National Archives CO 8/1/2, Newton to Coghlan, 3 December 1925.
[6] See National Archives LE 3/2/1/1, Newton to Coghlan, 20 February 1925, in regard to the possibilities of linking with the Protectorates and amalgamation with Northern Rhodesia. The Colonial Office professed to be afraid of difficulties with South Africa, the natives, and the Aborigines Protection Society.

Sir Charles Coghlan discussed amalgamation of Northern Rhodesia and Southern Rhodesia with Amery, Secretary of State, in London in 1926 and again in 1927 on a visit by Amery to Southern Rhodesia. These requests were rejected as the Colonial Office now had plans for an East African Federation.[1]

Meanwhile Southern Rhodesian pressure continued from 1927 to 1933, when Mr. H. U. Moffat was Prime Minister. In 1927 the Cabinet resolved to propose a Conference between representatives of Northern Rhodesia and Southern Rhodesia to discuss amalgamation, but the British Government refused to permit this pending the visit of the Hilton Young Commission.[2] In 1928 the Cabinet had discussions with unofficial members of the Northern Rhodesian Legislative Council, but the majority of elected members of Northern Rhodesia at that time opposed amalgamation.[3] Moffat also put his views on amalgamation to the Hilton Young Commission.[4]

Thereafter in 1929 the majority report of the Hilton Young Commission, despite a minority report in favour by the Chairman, rejected proposals for any further territory being added to Southern Rhodesia until she had demonstrated her ability to settle the native problem.[5] At the same time it made it clear that Northern Rhodesia and Nyasaland could not feasibly be linked with East Africa.[6] The Commission emphasized, on the other hand, the need for a consistent native policy in Britain's East and Central African territories.[7] Although the Southern Rhodesian Prime Minister protested to the Imperial Government, the majority view of the Commission was upheld.[8]

Subsequently in 1930, when the Passfield Memorandum affirmed the United Kingdom's responsibility as trustee for the African people in Northern Rhodesia as elsewhere and stated that 'the interests of the African natives

---

[1] For Colonial Office attitude see NE 1/1/1, Newton to Coghlan, 2 June 1927. Apparently the Dominions Office favoured amalgamation but was 'afraid of the House of Commons on native questions': National Archives NE 1/1/7, Newton to Moffat, 9 August 1928. Amery personally favoured amalgamation: personal communication from a confidential source. The beginnings of development on the Northern Rhodesian copper belt in 1925 probably made the Colonial Office more reluctant to part with Northern Rhodesia.

[2] National Archives LE 3/2/1/2. Cabinet resolutions 684 of 8 December 1927, and 710 of 5 January 1928.

[3] For record of meetings, see National Archives LE 3/1/1, 12 March 1928. See also J. W. Davidson, *The Northern Rhodesia Legislative Council*, Faber, 1948, pp. 90 et seq., and Gann, op. cit., *A History of Northern Rhodesia*, pp. 245–50. At that time Northern Rhodesian settlers did not fear Imperial control but considered Southern Rhodesian control would be a disadvantage.

[4] National Archives LE 3/1/1, Confidential speech by Moffat to the Hilton Young Commission, 30 March 1928.

[5] Cmd. 3234, Report of the Commission on Closer Union of the Dependencies in Eastern and Central Africa, pp. 89–95, which condemned the grant of responsible government to immigrant minorities. See also p. 96 which criticized elected European majorities. The Chairman, however, favoured a partition of Northern Rhodesia with the rail of line being added to Southern Rhodesia, North-Eastern Rhodesia to Nyasaland, with Barotseland a Native Reserve, all to be under a High Commissioner who would also be Governor of Southern Rhodesia.

[6] Cmd. 3234, pp. 281–2.   [7] Cmd. 3234, p. 7.   [8] See Gann, op. cit., p. 248.

must be paramount',[1] a fresh impetus was given to moves for closer union and a further unofficial Conference took place at the Victoria Falls between Northern and Southern Rhodesian parliamentarians. When a formal Conference was requested, the Imperial Government offered the Prime Minister of Southern Rhodesia such unacceptable terms that he was forced to reject the offer.[2] Subsequently Passfield informed the Southern Rhodesian Government that amalgamation was at that time out of the question although His Majesty's Government did not reject the principle. Co-operation between the Territories should, however, be increased.[3] Mr. J. H. Thomas, the new Colonial Secretary, affirmed this and said it must be made clear at the outset that when amalgamation came about 'definite provisions for the welfare and development of the native population' must be made.[4] After the joint Parliamentary Select Committee on closer association in East Africa had slurred over Passfield's views, Moffat spoke to the Dominions Office again in 1932.[5] However, he received no encouragement.

Once more Northern Rhodesian unofficial members met the Southern Rhodesian Cabinet in 1933, and in July 1934 Mr. Huggins, the new Southern Rhodesian Prime Minister, accompanied by his Chief Native Commissioner, put to the Colonial Office a scheme for the incorporation into Southern Rhodesia of the Copperbelt, for the creation of separate white and black areas, and proposals for African opportunities for advancement to the highest levels in the African areas, while areas outside the railway belt should, he considered, remain under Colonial Office control.[6] This scheme was rejected by the Colonial Office.

[1] Cmd. 3573, Memorandum on Native Policy in East Africa. Lord Passfield has been accused of 'siring' federation, because of the fears his Memorandum stimulated in European settlers. See also Cmd. 3574, Statement of the Conclusions of H.M. Government of the United Kingdom as regards Closer Union in East Africa (June 1930), p. 8: 'Establishment of a common roll is the object to be aimed at and attained with an equal franchise of a civilization or education character open to all races.' Earlier in 1923 the Duke of Devonshire had recorded H.M. Government's 'considered opinion that the interests of the African natives must be paramount and if and when those interests and the interests of immigrant races should conflict, the former should prevail': Cmd. 1922, Indians in Kenya—Memorandum.

[2] Personal communication from a confidential source. National Archives NE 1/1/7, Newton to Moffat, 2 August 1929, stated that 'Passfield would agree to amalgamation if it were possible to secure for the Imperial Government some greater control of the native question that would involve some diminution of the powers at present possessed by Southern Rhodesia'. *Contra* Gann, op. cit., p. 249, who states that the Conference was refused by Her Majesty's Government. This was, in fact, its public attitude.

[3] National Archives MO 13/1/1, Secretary of State to the Governor, 1 July 1931.

[4] H.C. Deb., Vol. 254, col. 1471, 22 July 1931.

[5] National Archives DO 1/1/6, Moffat to Downie, 25 April 1932, requesting the High Commissioner to arrange an informal interview on this matter with the Secretary of State and also on Southern Rhodesia's claim to Northern Bechuanaland.

[6] See C. L. Carbutt, 'The Racial Problem in Southern Rhodesia', N.A.D.A., No. 12, 1934, p. 6, for the Chief Native Commissioner's views. See Gann and Gelfand, op. cit., pp. 99–102 and p. 116 for details of Huggins' proposals. See also 'Southern Rhodesia, Recent

Pressure for amalgamation of the Territories, however, continued from both Southern Rhodesian and Northern Rhodesian parliamentarians, who met at an unofficial Conference at the Victoria Falls in 1936, and also from certain large financial interests.[1] At the same time the Southern Rhodesian Governor, Sir Herbert Stanley, from 1935 onwards strongly advocated in memoranda to the Colonial Office a Central African union of Northern Rhodesia and Southern Rhodesia as a counterpoise to the Afrikaner Union of South Africa.[2] To these pressures the Imperial policy-makers gradually began to capitulate.

Early consultative mechanisms and common services

The first formal mechanism for closer consultation was the decision to hold annual Governors' Conferences, the first of which was held in 1935, at which closer relations between the Territories in regard to defence, common currency, customs, communications, education, research, trade representation mining laws, dual taxation of Africans, and the creation of a common court of appeal were discussed. From these discussions proposals for co-ordinated common services and common consultation emerged.[3] As a result the Rhodesian Court of Appeal was created in 1939.[4]

However, these measures were regarded as insufficient by the advocates of closer union—among them many senior United Kingdom civil servants in the Dominions Office. Further discussions occurred in 1936 and 1937 in

Progress and Development'—Address by G. M. Huggins, 18 July 1934, Empire Parliamentary Association, London, pp. 12–13, where Huggins informed his audience of these schemes and that they had been put to the British Government.

[1] See Gann and Gelfand, op. cit., p. 117 et seq., referring to Sir Ernest Oppenheimer's views. But the British South Africa Company and other mining houses were opposed to amalgamation, particularly because of the introduction of colour bar practices from Southern Rhodesia, and increased labour costs as a result. Apparently they still had this attitude in 1937. Personal communication.

[2] See Gann and Gelfand, op. cit., p. 118. Also personal communications from confidential sources. Sir Hubert Young, Governor of Northern Rhodesia, favoured further co-operation between the Central African territories and some public United Kingdom announcement that Southern Rhodesian, Northern Rhodesian and Nyasaland interests were closely linked. The latter request was refused by the Colonial Office.

[3] e.g. The Inter-Territorial Labour Conference with a Standing Committee was created, as was the Inter-Territorial Communications Board. Common currency also came into use with Northern Rhodesia and Nyasaland enjoying representation on the Southern Rhodesian Currency Board.

[4] Act No. 33 of 1938. The Court heard criminal appeals from the High Courts of Northern Rhodesia and Southern Rhodesia. It was to be composed of at least three judges drawn from the High Courts of Northern Rhodesia and Southern Rhodesia, the President being the Chief Justice of Southern Rhodesia. Appeals from Southern Rhodesia still lay at the option of the accused to the Appellate Division of the Union of South Africa. By Act 14 of 1947 appeals from Nyasaland were also directed to this Court which was renamed the Rhodesia and Nyasaland Court of Appeal. Appeals from Nyasaland had previously lain to the East African Court of Appeal.

London.[1] Ultimately the United Kingdom Government appointed the Bledisloe Commission to investigate the possibility of closer association, although it had been decided that amalgamation was not at that time possible.[2] The Commission reported that amalgamation would be advantageous to the Territories, that the Territories would 'become more and more closely interdependent in all their activities and that identity of interests would lead them sooner or later to political unity', and that amalgamation should be accepted in principle.[3]

However, the Commission felt that the time for amalgamation was not yet ripe mainly owing to the 'inherently different' and 'divergent'[4] native policies and 'the fears and suspicions at present prevalent among the natives',[5] despite its favourable comment, on the extensive social services provided for Africans in Southern Rhodesia in comparison with those provided in the Northern Territories.[6] Nonetheless it recommended that an Inter-Territorial Council should be created composed of the Southern Rhodesian Prime Minister and the Northern Governors, and that attempts should be made further to co-ordinate technical services and planning.

As a result of objections by Mr. Huggins to the Report when he was told

[1] In 1937, during the Coronation celebrations, the Colonial and Dominion Secretaries, the three Governors, and the Southern Rhodesian Prime Minister met to discuss the problems involved. Britain's dilemma was that Southern Rhodesian native policy was diverging so rapidly from native policy in the North that closer union would become impossible at a later stage. If it were now refused impetus would be given to the creation of increased ties between Southern Rhodesia and South Africa. At the same time the United Kingdom had to consider how to maintain its trust to the Africans of Northern Rhodesia.

[2] See National Archives SM 4/1/1, ff. 69–84, for draft of Huggins' letter to Mr. Malcolm Macdonald, Secretary of State. Huggins insisted that amalgamation should not be excluded from the Commission's terms of reference as this would further the Unionist cause while the Imperial Government would in no way be bound by the Report, as it had forewarned the Southern Rhodesian Prime Minister that amalgamation would not be permitted. Gann, op. cit., pp. 273–4, makes the Imperial attitude of no further surrender of native responsibilities clear. The Commission was regarded as a delaying device by the Colonial Office—personal communication from a confidential source—but they could not reject the demands outright as this might lead to a clash and difficulties in obtaining an alternative Ministry in Southern Rhodesia. On the other hand, the Colonial Office would not permit its trusteeship obligations to be diminished by allowing Southern Rhodesia control. In addition, Northern Rhodesian copper mines were strategically important while political considerations in the United Kingdom would not permit a change in the United Kingdom policy: Gann and Gelfand, op. cit., p. 119. The biography of the then Chief Secretary of Northern Rhodesia, C. Dundas, *African Crossroads*, Macmillan, 1955, pp. 176–9, shows the reasons for opposition by officials from the Colonial Office.

[3] Cmd. 5949, Rhodesia–Nyasaland Royal Commission Report at 214. However, there were dissentient notes by Mr. W. H. Mainwaring and Mr. T. Fitzgerald, and qualifications and conditions by Mr. I. Orr-Ewing and Mr. E. Evans. (Four of the six members.) For a full discussion of the Report see R. Gray, *The Two Nations*, Oxford, 1960, pp. 150–96. This book is an admirable social history of Southern Rhodesia from 1918 to 1953.

[4] Lord Bledisloe on 31 July 1939: *H.L. Deb.*, Vol. 114, col. 704. Nonetheless, Southern Rhodesian policy was not 'less favourable' to Africans.

[5] Cmd. 5949, p. 218.

[6] These findings were borne out in the Pim Commission Report on Northern Rhodesia: Colonial No. 145 of 1938.

that Southern Rhodesia's native policy precluded closer union,[1] the Secretary of State for the Colonies agreed to send out Lord Hailey to conduct an independent and expert survey of native policy in the Central African Territories.[2] However, the outbreak of war in 1939 put an end to the possibility of any important decisions being taken at that time, although Lord Hailey, in fact, reported in 1941.[3] But, as a result of the need to co-ordinate the war effort of the Central African Territories, an Inter-Territorial Secretariat, confined to easing wartime problems and co-ordinating economic effort, was established in Salisbury. Other consultative bodies were merged in the new Secretariat.

The Central Africa Council

In 1944 the Colonial Office proposed an advisory and consultative Inter-Territorial Council with a permanent Secretariat under the chairmanship of the Governor of Southern Rhodesia.[4] The establishment of the Central Africa Council was announced in October 1944 and first met in June and July 1945. The Governor of Southern Rhodesia was Chairman, and the Governors of Northern Rhodesia and Nyasaland and the Prime Minister of Southern Rhodesia were *ex-officio* members.[5] Each of the three Territories appointed three ordinary members for two-year periods. In practice, these were the Chief Secretaries of Northern Rhodesia and Nyasaland and two unofficial members from each of these Territories, while Southern Rhodesia was represented by three Cabinet Ministers.[6] These members were nominated by the Governors of Northern Rhodesia and Nyasaland and the Prime Minister of Southern Rhodesia.[7]

The Chief Secretary and officers of the Secretariat were to be appointed by

[1] See Rotberg, 'The Federation Movement in British East and Central Africa, 1889–1953', (1964) *Journal of Commonwealth Studies*, Vol. 2, p. 141.

[2] Gann, op. cit., p. 279; Gann and Gelfand, op. cit., p. 121.

[3] Copies of his confidential reports on the individual territories are in the National Archives. S 235/482, Report on Southern Rhodesia, at p. 28, states that there was a growing recognition of the native as an integral part of society and that there was much promise of increased attention to measures for the material conditions of Africans. His published conclusions are printed as *Note on the Bearing of Native Policy on the Proposed Amalgamation of the Rhodesias and Nyasaland*, London, H.M.S.O., 1941. Lord Hailey pointed out that the divergence in native policies 'though not necessarily conclusive', would have great bearing on any scheme for closer association.

[4] For Colonial Office attitude of this period, see Gann, op. cit., pp. 356–8. The *Bledisloe Report*, Cmd. 5949, at p. 221, had made a similar suggestion.

[5] Article 2, The Constitution of the Central Africa Council. Agreement between the Governments of Southern Rhodesia, Northern Rhodesia, and Nyasaland, National Archives.

[6] Apparently the Southern Rhodesian Prime Minister invited the leader of the Opposition to attend as one of the Southern Rhodesian members but he declined to participate in the working of the Council: *S.R.L.A.D.*, Vol. 27(2), col. 3170, 5 February 1948.

[7] Article II(2).

the Chairman with the concurrence of the Governors of Northern Rhodesia and Nyasaland and the Prime Minister of Southern Rhodesia,[1] and were to perform not only all secretarial work required by it, but were also to be available to the Governments for facilitating co-operation in administrative and technical services or in the advancement of the Territories' joint interests.[2] To finance the Council a common fund was established which was to be audited by the Auditor-General of Southern Rhodesia, while estimates and supplementary estimates were prepared by the Chief Secretary and approved by the Council.[3]

The Council was to meet at least twice in each calendar year as decided by the Chairman in consultation with the Governments,[4] while any Territory might request a special meeting to discuss a specific matter within the competence of the Council, the Chairman being required to convene a meeting as soon as possible.[5] Alternatively, if no meeting was necessary or the matter was so urgent that it could not await a meeting, the opinion in writing of the members might be obtained.

The Council was 'consultative and advisory in character'. All decisions were taken by the Territorial Governments and Legislatures and Council decisions could not be enforced. Indeed the Council's constitution might be varied from time to time by agreement between the Governments after consultation with the Council.[6]

The basic function of the Council was the promotion of co-operation between the three Governments. It was to consider communications, economic relations, education, soil and water conservation, agriculture, veterinary and forestry matters, medical and health matters, tsetse control, currency, archives, African labour, research, joint services, public relations, and such other matters as might be agreed upon.[7]

For the purpose of carrying out its functions, the Council was empowered to appoint standing committees keeping under continual review the subjects within the Council's competence,[8] and in addition might convene special conferences and appoint special committees to deal with technical and special aspects of subjects within its purview. Such committees need not be composed of Council members, but the Chief Secretary would be a member *ex officio* of all such committees.[9] A number of standing committees dealing with particular problems were then appointed.[10]

---

[1] Article III.   [2] Article XII.

[3] Article III(3)(5) and Article IV(1). Southern Rhodesia paid ten parts, Northern Rhodesia seven, and Nyasaland three.

[4] Article V, as amended in February 1946.   [5] Article VI.   [6] Article XIII.

[7] Article VIII.   [8] Article IX.   [9] Articles X and XI.

[10] Cmd. 7987, The British Territories in East and Central Africa, 1945–50, p. 29. The sub-committees dealt with research (Standing Research Advisory Committee), meteorology, economic development and planning, currency, customs, public relations, education, agriculture, health, veterinary science, forestry, legal questions, and migrant labour. See also Cmd. 7715, The Colonial Territories 1948–49, and Cmd. 8243, The Colonial Territories,

Common services soon began to emerge. As a result of recommendations by the Council's Civil Aviation Committee, the Central African Airways Corporation and the Central African Air Authority were created by legislation of the three Territories.[1] An African Broadcasting Advisory Board and a Central African Instructional Film Unit were also established. A Central African Statistical Office giving all three Territories services was created, while the Southern Rhodesian Archives became the Central African Archives.[2] In addition, a Hydro-Electric Power Commission, controlled by the Central Africa Council, was established to investigate the possibilities of hydro-electric power (their reports among others led to the Kariba scheme being initiated after Federation).

However, by January 1950, the Southern Rhodesian Government gave notice that it would cease to be a member of the Central Africa Council after twelve months had elapsed.[3] The Committee then made recommendations for changing the machinery and recommended a Rhodesia–Nyasaland Inter-Territorial Secretariat under the control of a consultative Inter-Territorial Conference meeting at least once a year. In the interim, decisions would be taken by officials of the Government without any necessity for Inter-Territorial discussions. If such proved necessary a meeting of the Conference would be summoned.[4] These recommendations were accepted but never implemented, as negotiations to create a federation covering the British Central African Territories had commenced.

The negotiations for federation

By 1948 the Colonial Office and Dominions Office began to take the possibility of a federation in British Central Africa seriously and a number of official memoranda favoured such a federation. These argued that the creation of a strong Central African British state would be a counter to Afrikaner nationalism and any closer association of Southern Rhodesia with

1950. As a result of the Council's work, agreement on the care and control of migrant labourers between the Territories was reached: see Central Africa Council Report 1947. C.S.R. 42–1947.

[1] For Southern Rhodesia, see the Central African Air Services Act No. 11 of 1946.

[2] See the Archives Amendment Act No. 44 of 1946.

[3] The Central Africa Council was politically unpopular in Southern Rhodesia. The 1948 General Election, although this was in fact actually desired by Sir Godfrey Huggins, came about as the result of a defeat in the Legislative Assembly on the Currency Board Bill of 1948, which was a measure that had been agreed upon at a meeting of the Central Africa Council. Mr. Creech Jones considered that the Southern Rhodesian Government 'deliberately destroyed the Central Africa Council for the purpose of clearing the deck in order that amalgamation or federation ... should be introduced': H.C. Deb., Vol. 668, col. 1024, 3 December 1962. The Southern Rhodesian Government's attitude however was that the Council suffered from a lack of constitutional authority and that its dissolution would be a constructive and not a destructive act making greater powers for co-operation in the form of federation possible. Personal communication from Sir John Kennedy in November 1964.

[4] Cmd. 7987, pp. 30–31.

the Union of South Africa.[1] Furthermore, it was felt that association with Northern Rhodesia would influence policy towards Africans in Southern Rhodesia and bring Southern Rhodesia policy more into line with the policies of trusteeship followed in the Northern Territories, and that this would afford the opportunity of re-introducing Imperial native policies in Southern Rhodesia.[2] In addition, economic arguments, strategic considerations, the general tendency towards regional associations evident after the war, the ideal of forming a multi-racial state neither prey to white nor black nationalism, and the co-operativeness of Southern Rhodesia in collaborating with the Northern Territories, as well as changes in Southern Rhodesia's native policy during and after the war, all induced the Colonial Office to favour federation.[3]

Sir Godfrey Huggins, the Southern Rhodesian Prime Minister, and Mr. Roy Welensky, Leader of the Northern Rhodesian Unofficial Members, were at this time still seeking amalgamation, but they were informed when attending the British Africa Conference of September 1948 that union could not be permitted while a federal scheme could be considered.[4] After suggestions to this effect by Creech Jones and Oliver Stanley, Huggins and Welensky called a Conference of unofficials from the three Territories at which no Africans were present. This Conference, held in February 1949, at the Victoria Falls, produced a federal draft scheme reflecting Sir Godfrey's political aims of

[1] Personal communication from a confidential source. See also Viscount Chandos (previously Mr. Oliver Lyttelton, Secretary of State for the Colonies): *The Memoirs of Lord Chandos*, Bodley Head, 1962, p. 387, for a lengthy statement of this aspect of policy. It was felt that Afrikaner policy towards the native races was counter to British conceptions of United Kingdom responsibilities: 'If our way of leading these nations to self-government and independence was to prevail, federation seemed to us to be essential. It had the effect of immediately diverting Afrikaner influence.' See Gann and Gelfand, op. cit., p. 209 and pp. 218–20; Leys and Pratt, op. cit., pp. 50–51. Whenever the negotiations for federation seemed to be lagging, the Southern Rhodesian Prime Minister would judiciously drop a hint that Southern Rhodesia would have to look South.

[2] Gann, op. cit., p. 403, Personal communications from a confidential source. See also Hailey, *An African Survey*, revised edition, Oxford, 1959, p. 152, suggesting that constitutional development in Southern Rhodesia would be increasingly influenced by a federal legislature including African representatives. This has proved true. Lord Hailey was in favour of amalgamation provided the Southern Rhodesian Industrial Conciliation Act was not extended to the North. See also Gann and Gelfand, op. cit., p. 208.

[3] See generally Gann and Gelfand, op. cit., pp. 208–20; Gann, op. cit., pp. 397–404; and also Clegg, op. cit., pp. 164–5, for a full account of the attitudes leading to Federation and the mechanics of its creation. See also Creighton, op. cit., pp. 37–38, for an account which is marred by over-statement. However, the counter-arguments to Federation are clearly set forth.

[4] R. Welensky, *Welensky's 4,000 Days*, Collins, 1964, pp. 23–26. See also D. Taylor, *The Rhodesian: The Life of Sir Roy Welensky*, Museum Press, 1955, pp. 103–7. Leys in 'The Case against Federation in Central Africa', *Public Law*, Spring, 1960, p. 18, sums up the position: 'The constitutional device of federation was adopted by the local European leadership in Central Africa not for its own sake but as one better calculated to win acceptance by the British Government than the scheme for outright amalgamation of the two Rhodesias which had long been their aim.'

amalgamation and his franchise views. It proposed a House of Representatives, from which Africans would be excluded, and suggested that minimal powers be given to the Territorial legislatures. African land rights should be guaranteed by the Federal instead of the United Kingdom Government.[1] These proposals were not, however, formally put to the Imperial Government.

After the United Kingdom General Election in 1950 when Mr. Griffiths became Colonial Secretary and Mr. Gordon Walker Commonwealth Relations Secretary, Sir Godfrey Huggins resuscitated a suggestion originally made by Mr. G. H. Baxter, Assistant Under-Secretary for Commonwealth Relations, that a committee of officials should investigate the problems of closer association.[2] Mr. Griffiths accepted this suggestion announcing on the 8 November 1950, that the problem would be examined afresh.[3] A Conference of Officials of the three Central African Territories, of the United Kingdom Government, and of officials of the Central Africa Council then met in March 1951 in the United Kingdom and a series of Command Papers followed.[4]

The Conference's findings on native policy were the most vital: they pointed to differences 'in political development (particularly the representation of Africans in central politics), land allocation, certain aspects of the employment of Africans and the recognition of trade unions for Africans'. However, they believed that 'these differences, although important, relate largely to method and timing and that the ultimate objective of all three Governments is broadly the same, namely, the economic, social, and political advancement of the Africans in partnership with the Europeans'.[5] The Conference of Officials unanimously considered closer association to be necessary. They advocated urgent action to this end producing a federal scheme rejecting both amalgamation (including any division of Northern Rhodesia) and a confederation.[6] They favoured a federation in which Territorial and Federal Governments were to be allocated functions in such a manner that matters most closely affecting the life of the African would come within the Territorial

---

[1] Franklin, op. cit., p. 38; also Gann and Gelfand, op. cit., p. 216; Gann, op. cit., p. 405; and Rotberg, op. cit., p. 155, who quotes Sir Stewart Gore-Brown, a delegate from Northern Rhodesia, as stating that Huggins suggested that the Territorial legislatures should be the equivalent of British County Councils.

[2] Gann and Gelfand, op. cit., p. 218; Gann, op. cit., p. 410.

[3] It seems that in reality a private agreement was reached in March 1950, as civil servants from all the Territories commenced working on a comparative survey of native policies long before this official announcement: Leys and Pratt, op. cit., p. 19.

[4] Cmd. 8233, Central African Territories, Report of Conference on Closer Association, London, March 1951; Cmd. 8234, Central African Territories: geographical, historical, and economic survey; Cmd. 8235, Central African Territories: Comparative Survey of Native Policy. The latter found that Southern Rhodesia spent more in total on social services for its African population than the two Northern Territories together: p. 24. It also stated that although there were fundamental theoretical differences, in practice policies towards Africans had more nearly approached each other over the last five years: p. 9.

[5] Cmd. 8233, § 18, Cp. Kirkwood, op. cit., who points out that these were the vital differences which made a Federation impossible to operate in practice.

[6] Cmd. 8233, pp. 13–15.

and not the Federal sphere, although economic matters would come within the Federal sphere. In addition, safeguards for African interests were proposed, such as representation of Africans in the Federal Legislature, an African Affairs Board, and a Minister of African Interests. The Territorial constitutions should, except as affected by the establishment of the Federation, continue in operation with the United Kingdom Government still retaining its responsibility for the government of and for constitutional change in Northern Rhodesia and Nyasaland.[1]

Despite a visit by both Colonial and Commonwealth Relations Secretaries to Central Africa in August and September 1951, and attendance at a further Conference at the Victoria Falls in September 1951, which was attended by members of all the Governments concerned, the British Government did not commit itself to the principle of Federation. The final communique of the Conference, issued when it adjourned,[2] carefully reserved the various Governments' position and made it clear that no binding decisions were being reached,[3] although it was apparent from the communique that the Secretaries of State were prepared to agree to Federation on certain conditions.[4] However they could not commit the British Government on so important an issue even had they wished to do so, as, when the Conference assembled, the British Prime Minister, Mr. Attlee, had just requested a dissolution. In the ensuing election the Attlee Government was defeated.

The final decision to go forward with a Central African Federation was taken by the newly elected Conservative Government. On the 21 November 1951, Mr. Oliver Lyttelton, the Colonial Secretary, announced governmental approval of the principle of federation of the Central African Territories.[5] Thereafter the processes of constitution-making followed.

The making of the Federal Constitution

In January 1952 an unofficial Conference was assembled in London, where in private discussions the main outlines of the future Constitution were

[1] Cmd. 8233, p. 15.

[2] It was stated that it would probably re-assemble in the middle of 1952, Cmd. 8573, Annex II.

[3] Cmd. 8573, Annex II, § 5. See Franklin, op. cit., pp. 59–61, for an account of the deadlock on the questions of African representation, amalgamation, and Southern Rhodesia's desire that Nyasaland be excluded. See also Pratt and Leys, op. cit., pp. 31–32, for another account of the deadlock that was reached since the United Kingdom Ministers were not prepared to override African opposition to the proposals.

[4] Cmd. 8573, Annex II, § 7 and 11, viz. the overcoming of African apprehensions, the total exclusion of amalgamation, control of political advancement and safeguarding of African land rights in the Northern Territories by the United Kingdom, and the application of 'partnership' between Europeans and Africans. Southern Rhodesian and Northern Rhodesian delegates considered the Secretaries of State accepted the principle of Federation: Gann and Gelfand, op. cit., p. 223; Gann, op. cit., 413; Welensky, op. cit., p. 42—particularly Mr. Gordon Walker.

[5] Cmd. 8411. Closer Association in Central Africa: Statement by Her Majesty's

agreed upon. The United Kingdom Government made its rejection of amalgamation quite clear,[1] and also insisted that Nyasaland become part of the Federation.[2] In addition, it refused to allow any reduction in the number of African representatives in the Federal Legislature and declined to permit a unified Civil Service for the Territories and the Federation. It also declined to permit the Federal Government to veto legislation in conflict with the Preamble to the Federal Constitution.[3] On the other hand, the Imperial Government agreed to the relaxation of certain of the safeguards proposed by the Conference of Civil Servants. Thus, the Federal Legislature was now, except of course for the first election, permitted to make provision, subject to certain safeguards, for a Federal franchise whereas the officials had suggested that this was undesirable.[4] In addition, constitutional amendment by the Federal Legislature was to be permitted, although the officials had suggested that no major constitutional changes should occur within the first five years of Federation.[5] Any Bills providing for constitutional amendments were however subject to approval by a two-thirds majority of the total membership of the Legislature and to reservation. Should the African Affairs Board or any Territorial Legislature object to the measure, assent would have to be signified by Order in Council, so that the Imperial Parliament could pronounce upon the issue. On the other hand, another increase in status was conceded, as a proposed reservation in the Governor-General's Instructions that he reserve laws relating to currency was removed.[6]

Yet another significant change was that Sir Godfrey Huggins succeeded in eliminating a proposed Minister of African Interests, who would be a member of the Cabinet, appointed by the Governor-General in his discretion subject to the Secretary of State's consent, from any of the members representing African interests. Such Minister would not have been responsible to his colleagues.[7] The African Affairs Board as now proposed was to be entirely

Government in the United Kingdom, 21 November 1951. The Conservatives accepted the reasoning of the Colonial Office outlined above. See Chandos, op. cit., p. 390: 'The judgement of Ministers and of the highly trained Colonial Service, both at home and overseas, may have been wrong but at least the motives underlying the policy of federation were enlightened, liberal, and unselfish.'

[1] See Cmd. 8573, Southern Rhodesia, Northern Rhodesia, and Nyasaland, Draft Federal Scheme prepared by a Conference held in London in April and May 1952, § 8.

[2] Welensky, op. cit., p. 43, states that British initiative led to Nyasaland's inclusion. T. Franck, *Race and Nationalism*, Fordham, 1960, p. 323, states that Mr. Lyttelton later insisted on its inclusion.

[3] See Gann, op. cit., pp. 413–14.   [4] Cp. Cmd. 8233, pp. 24 and 40, with Cmd. 8573, p. 14.

[5] Cp. Cmd. 8233, p. 26, § 100, with Cmd. 8573, p. 33. This change and the former change permitted the Federal Constitution Amendment Act No. 16 of 1957 and the Federal Electoral Act No. 6 of 1958.

[6] Cp. Cmd. 8233, p. 24, with Cmd. 8573, p. 20.

[7] See Cmd. 8233, p. 17. See also Annex III. This Minister could report on any action detrimental to African interests, and the Governor-General could then refer the question to the Secretary of State, who would be enabled to withhold approval. Unless the matter was urgent no action could be taken pending the Secretary of State's decision. Southern Rhodesian politicians described the proposal as one for 'a cuckoo Minister'.

outside the Legislature. Previously the officials had suggested a Board consisting of the three Territorial Secretaries of Native Affairs, one elected or unofficial member and one African drawn from each Territory, while the Chairman would be the Minister of African Interests with a seat in the Federal Cabinet.[1] All legislation was to have been scrutinized by this Board before publication and if, after passing through the Legislature, any Bill was considered as detrimentally affecting African interests it was to be reserved. In addition, the Board proposed by the officials, would have held a watching brief and had power to report on all representations made to it on matters affecting African interests in the administration of the unified services. Not only was the Minister eliminated, but the composition and functions of the Board were redesigned to exclude all Members of Parliament and public officers, and to make it smaller. Each Governor was now to appoint one African and one European whose membership could be revoked by the Governor-General with the consent of the Secretary of State.[2] The Board as now designed could comment on differentiating measures, which imposed disabilities on Africans but could not, as the officials had suggested, comment on the wide field that would have been opened to it by permission to comment on legislation 'detrimental to African interests'.[3]

A further change was that, although it had originally been proposed that the representatives for African interests for Southern Rhodesia in the Federal Parliament should be nominated by the Governor, they were now to be elected by the predominantly European Southern Rhodesian electorate.[4]

The full Lancaster House Conference was held in April and May 1952 and was boycotted by the African delegates from the Northern Territories, who did not wish to be associated in any way with Federation. In discussing the proposals the United Kingdom Government was still firm on the issue that the Secretary of State should retain full responsibility for recruitment in the Colonial Service,[5] rejected Southern Rhodesian requests for a bicameral Legislature at this stage,[6] declined to permit the creation of a unified police force to enforce Federal and Territorial laws,[7] and rejected the name of the new state proposed by the Southern Rhodesian delegation—'the Kingdom of Rhodesia and Nyasaland'.[8]

Further changes from the officials' proposals, however, occurred since many matters, which were in the officials' scheme to have been beyond the competence of the Federal Legislature, were now made concurrent matters, viz. town planning, prisons, roads, co-operatives (except where the majority

[1] Cmd. 8233, pp. 16–17.   [2] Cp. Cmd. 8233 and Cmd. 8573, pp. 23–26.
[3] Cp. Cmd. 8573, p. 24, with Cmd. 8233, p. 31. See *H.C. Deb.*, Vol. 504, col. 8812, 24 July 1952, where this was pointed out by the Labour ex-Secretary of State.
[4] Leys and Pratt, op. cit., p. 27.   [5] Cmd. 8753, p. 21.
[6] Both in Cmd. 8573 and in the draft scheme there was power to amend the Constitution to create a Second Chamber of the Federal Legislature.
[7] See Cmd. 8573, p. 13.   [8] See Gann, op. cit., p. 414.

of the members were African), and health, while income tax and marketing were made exclusively Federal.[1] Indeed, the need for concurrent powers had not been seen by the officials and their introduction must have been the work of Professor K. C. Wheare, who was Constitutional Adviser and assisted in the preparation of the Federal scheme.[2] The officials had, in fact, suggested mutually exclusive Territorial and Federal legislative lists.

The Conference issued a draft federal scheme[3] and this, in order to make provision for technical matters outside the competence of the Conference, provided for the establishment of a Judicial Commission to consider the establishment of a Federal Supreme Court, a Fiscal Commission to report on the financial arrangements for the Federation and the Territories, and a Civil Service Preparatory Commission to work out how the Federal Public Service was to be established.[4]

After the reports of the three Commissions[5] and a visit by the Minister of State for the Colonies, Mr. Henry Hopkinson, to Central Africa in August and September 1952, a final Conference, again boycotted by the African representatives from the North, met in London in January 1953—the Carlton House Terrace Conference. Here the proposed safeguard of the African Affairs Board was made less effective and further modified to bring it within the Federal Legislature as a Standing Committee consisting of specially appointed and elected European members and a specially elected African member from each of the Territories elected by majority vote of all the representatives of African interests.[6] As Members of Parliament, the Board members would no longer be removable by the Governor-General with the consent of the Secretary of State. The power of the Board to strike out at legislation was also cut down by a change in the definition of what constituted discriminatory legislation: previously legislation which 'might' subject Africans to disabilities was to be reported on by the Board, whereas the new draft provided that actual discrimination was necessary by substituting the words 'will . . . have such an effect'.[7] On the other hand, the Governor-General could only assent to a measure which he was satisfied did not differentiate and to which the Board had objected 'if he satisfied himself . . . that the reasons given by the Board . . . were of an irrelevant or frivolous nature'.[8]

---

[1] Cp. Cmd. 8233 with Cmd. 8573. See Franklin, op. cit., p. 67.

[2] See *Federal Government*, op. cit., pp. 79 et seq., where the author illustrates the necessity for concurrent powers in federations.

[3] Cmd. 8573, Southern Rhodesia, Northern Rhodesia, and Nyasaland, Draft Federal Scheme, prepared by a Conference held in London in April and May 1952.

[4] See respective terms of reference in Cmd. 8573, pp. 31–32, 26–27, and 29.

[5] Cmd. 8671, 8672, and 8673, presented to Parliament on the 29 October 1952.

[6] Cmd. 8753, § 26. This affected the character of the Board as, in practice, some of its members were chosen by an 'electoral college' which was itself elected by a predominantly European electorate.

[7] Cp. Cmd. 8573, p. 24, and Cmd. 8574, p. 26.

[8] Cp. Cmd. 8233, p. 24, with Cmd. 8574, p. 27.

The provision relating to police was also modified to permit the Federal Government to maintain a Federal Police Force for use in any Territory at the request of the Governor, in addition to, or in substitution for, the Territorial police force.[1] Furthermore, European agriculture in Southern Rhodesia including veterinary services was transferred to Federal control, and provisions were made for the possible transfer of such agriculture in the Northern Territories.[2] As a result the Federal Government would be enabled to exercise greater power in Southern Rhodesia than in the Northern Territories, unless they agreed to the transfer of similar powers.

The change which was to have the most far-reaching consequences was a provision that for the first ten years there could be no re-allocation of powers as between Federal and Territorial Governments and Legislatures except with the consent of all three Territorial Legislatures. This was secured by providing that no draft Bill amending the Legislative Lists providing for the allocation of powers as between Federal and Territorial Legislatures, could be introduced in the Federal Legislature until resolutions of approval had been passed by the Territorial Legislatures.[3] This for a fixed period precluded changes in the direction of amalgamation or, conversely, of loosening the Federal links. On the other hand, it was provided that at the end of the ten-year period there would be a review of the Federal Constitution by the United Kingdom Government and the four Governments of Central Africa.[4] The United Kingdom Government further insisted that no secession clause could be permitted and that no Territory could have this right.[5] A further provision designed to prevent attempts to test Federal laws was also omitted.[6] On the other hand the final form of the Preamble to the Constitution was agreed upon and this contained words which could subsequently be relied upon as justification for

[1] See Cmd. 8753, § 20.

[2] Cmd. 8753, § 20.

[3] Cmd. 8753, § 37, later Section 98 of the Federal Constitution. It is interesting to speculate what constitutional crises this section prevented. Had the section not been inserted the onus of rejecting constitutional Bills, which had been reserved, would have been on Her Majesty's Government. In the last years of Federation this section made amendment of much of the Federal Constitution impracticable.

[4] It was at this Conference, held in 1960, that it became apparent that the Federal Constitution could not continue.

[5] See *H.L. Deb.*, Vol. 245, col. 1165, 19 December 1962, Lord Salisbury; col. 1208, Viscount Chandos; col. 1209, Viscount Boyd; col. 1180, Lord Colyton; col. 1171, Viscount Malvern. See also *Federation of Rhodesia and Nyasaland: The British Government's Broken Pledges and the Consequences*, published by the Federal Government of Rhodesia and Nyasaland, 1963, pp. 4–5, giving detailed extracts from the Minutes of the Conference and referring to Sir Roy Welensky's personal knowledge of these statements. See also Franck, op. cit., p. 323, reporting Mr. Lyttelton's attitude as revealed in a personal interview with Lord Malvern. *Contra* Cmnd. 1949.

[6] Cmd. 8573, Chapter IX, § 4 (The May 1952 Draft Constitution) had proposed that Federal laws should be laid upon the Table of each Territorial Legislature and, if within six months thereof, no Legislature had resolved that the law did not relate only to Federal matters, such law could not be questioned in any Court, on the ground that the law related to matters other than Federal matters.

dissolving the Federation when it ceased to have the consent of its inhabitants.[1]

Minor modifications and additions were also made as a consequence of the Judicial, Fiscal, and Civil Service Commission Reports. The final Conference Report and Federal Scheme were published in February 1953,[2] and again emphasized that amalgamation of the Territories in whole or part would not be permitted.[3] It was also made clear that United Kingdom responsibility for constitutional advance in the two Northern Territories would remain, subject to consultation with the Federal Government.[4]

The House of Commons approved the principle of Federation in March.[5] Soon thereafter the Southern Rhodesian Legislative Assembly passed the Federation Poll Act[6] to provide for a referendum on the issue of federation. It was suggested that the Act should provide for a two-thirds majority at the proposed referendum, but this was rejected, as was a proposal for delay until the final form of the Constitution was made public.[7]

---

[1] The statement that the Federation would go forward to independence when this was desired by its 'inhabitants' subsequently became a brake to Federal Government pressures for independence without African consent. This phrase was inserted at the insistence of the Attorney-General for Northern Rhodesia, Mr. Unsworth, later Sir Edgar Unsworth, Chief Justice of Nyasaland: see Franklin, op. cit. Gann and Gelfand, op. cit., however infer, without expressly stating this, that Sir Godfrey Huggins was responsible for its insertion.

[2] Cmd. 8753, Southern Rhodesia, Northern Rhodesia, and Nyasaland: Report by the Conference on Federation held in London, January 1953; Cmd. 8754, Southern Rhodesia, Northern Rhodesia, and Nyasaland: The Federal Scheme prepared by a Conference held in London in January 1953.

[3] Cmd. 8753, p. 7.

[4] The Southern Rhodesian delegation attempted to provide that changes should be 'agreed' but the Conference rejected this: S.R.L.A.D., Vol. 46, col. 2652, 1 November 1960, Sir Edgar Whitehead.

[5] H.C. Deb., Vol. 513, col. 801, 24 March 1953.

[6] No. 9 of 1953.

[7] S.R.L.A.D., Vol. 33(2), col. 4203-38 and col. 4430. The latter rejection was insisted upon by the United Kingdom Government by cable. In respect of the former plea the legal point was not properly considered whether a referendum, even though it be merely consultative, is a new constitutional mechanism or procedure and an addition to the constitutional machinery of the country. (Cp. The creation of Advisory Councils of State or of a Bill providing for the use of referenda generally.) If it were so classified, it would have been a constitutional measure and the question would have arisen whether Section 26(2) of the Southern Rhodesian Constitution Letters Patent required that any Bill creating a new constitutional mechanism be passed by a two-thirds majority of the members of the Legislature. Section 26(2) was, however, narrowly drawn, giving the Legislature power to 'repeal or alter any of the provisions of these our Letters Patent ... provided further that no provisions of these our Letters Patent as may be repealed or altered by the Legislature as aforesaid, shall be valid', unless a two-thirds majority of the total membership of the Legislature affirmed the Bill. Section 28(b) providing for reservation of constitutional Bills was similarly drafted. If a Bill providing for the holding of a referendum was a constitutional measure, it would appear that, as an addition to the Constitution, it would have been an alteration (if it were not an alteration it would apparently have been beyond the competence of the Legislative Assembly) and could have been construed as an amendment to Section 4 (dealing with elections) as it would have provided an additional method of popular consultation. It would therefore require a two-thirds majority and reservation. This was not the

On Thursday, 9 April 1953, a referendum in terms of the Federation Poll Act was held in Southern Rhodesia. The total vote in favour of Federation was 25,570 with 14,729 against.[1] The die had now been cast in favour of Federation. The electorate of Southern Rhodesia had taken a decision that would extend Southern Rhodesian influence over the Northern Territories, at the same time permitting a degree of reciprocal influence from these Territories.[2]

The Rhodesia and Nyasaland Federation Act 1953

In May 1953 the Rhodesia and Nyasaland (Federation) Bill was debated in the House of Commons[3] and eventually on the 14 July the Rhodesia and Nyasaland (Federation) Act 1953[4] became law.

The Act permitted the Crown by Order in Council to provide for the Federation of the Territories, for the establishment of all such Federal authorities as might appear expedient, and for the conferment on such authorities of powers and duties.[5] In addition, the Crown might make provision for restriction of the right to petition for special leave to appeal from Territorial High Courts to the Privy Council after establishment of the Federal Supreme Court.[6] The Act also permitted the Crown to amend the Letters Patent or Orders in Council relating to the government of the Territories in such a manner as might appear expedient or necessary, having regard to the Federation.[7] There were, however, two limitations on this power: an Order made under the Act was to be laid before each House of Parliament and addresses were to be moved by each House praying Her Majesty to make such an Order[8]; and, when such Order was made, unless it specified the method whereby it was to be amended or revoked, it was not to be capable of amendment other than by Act of Parliament.[9]

Furthermore, any incidental, consequential, and transitional provisions

view taken in 1953 or subsequently in 1961 by the Southern Rhodesian Government's legal advisers, while the Speaker, without reasons, overruled a point of order to this effect: *S.R.L.A.D.*, Vol. 41, col. 5274. Cp. *The King* v. *Nat Bell Liquors Limited*, [1922] A.C. 128 (P.C.) where Lord Sutherland left open the question whether the Direct Legislation Act of Alberta providing that the Legislature was required to pass legislation approved by popular vote was *ultra vires*.

[1] *Rhodesia Herald*, 10 April 1953. The Legislative Councils of Northern Rhodesia and Nyasaland passed resolutions in favour of the proposed Federal Scheme in April 1953.

[2] Federation was criticized by European opponents in Southern Rhodesia as letting in Colonial Office influence by the back door since two members of the Federal Assembly were nominated by the Governors of Northern Rhodesia and Nyasaland.

[3] See *H.C. Deb.*, Vol. 515, cols. 407 et seq., and also Vol. 516. The creation of Federation was one of the bitterest political issues between the parties in Britain. Until 1959 there were constant recriminations over each issue of policy affecting the Federation. The question was even discussed at the Fourth Committee of the United Nations at the end of 1953, when the Rev. Michael Scott wrote to the United Nations about African objections to the Federation.

[4] 1 & 2 Eliz. II, c. 30.   [5] Section 1(1)(a)(i) and (ii).   [6] Section 1(1)(a)(iii).
[7] Section 1(1)(b).   [8] Section 1(4).   [9] Section 1(2).

which appeared necessary in respect of any enactments, Orders in Council, and any other instruments relating or referring to any of the Territories could be made.[1] These powers were used to create the Federation of Rhodesia and Nyasaland and are still in existence.[2]

Under this Act, on 1 August 1953, the Federation of Rhodesia and Nyasaland (Constitution) Order in Council 1953 was made.[3] This provided for the establishment of a Federation whose Constitution was contained in an Annex to the Order in Council. Under the Federation of Rhodesia and Nyasaland (Commencement) Order in Council, provisions of this Constitution dealing with the Governor-General and Executive Government were brought into force from 3 September 1953,[4] while the first Governor-General of the Federation, Lord Llewellin, assumed office on 4 September, subject to Royal Instructions.[5] On 7 September, the Governor-General appointed the first Prime Minister, Lord Malvern, and two other Ministers of the Federal Government.[6]

During this short transitional period the Governor-General was vested with both the executive and legislative powers of the Federation. In exercising these powers he was to act in accordance with the advice of the temporary Ministry, but was empowered to disregard their advice in his own discretion, in which event he was required to report his views to the Secretary of State and to act on the Secretary of State's instructions.[7] The Governor-General's legislative powers were exercisable by regulations, which were to continue in effect until such time as they were revoked by the Federal Legislative Assembly,[8] while special provisions for initial financial expenditure were made.[9] The remaining provisions of the Constitution were brought into

---

[1] Section 1(1)(c).

[2] The Act is still on the Statute Book as it was not repealed by the Rhodesia and Nyasaland Act 1963, 11 & 12 Eliz. II, c. 34. In fact, the Federation of Rhodesia and Nyasaland (Constitution) Order in Council 1953 (S.I. 1953/1199) is still in force other than for the Annex (the Federal Constitution). It has been slightly amended in Section 13 by the Federation of Rhodesia and Nyasaland (Dissolution) Order in Council, S.I. 1963, No. 2085, Section 75 and Schedule III, Item 1.

[3] S.I. 1953, No. 1199. Before the Order was issued there were in June 1953 differences of opinion as to the form of Article 68(3) but these were settled—in a way which meant that, if the African Affairs Board were divided on an issue, the Chairman would exercise his vote so as to have the measure reserved: S.R.L.A.D., Vol. 34, col. 1612, 23 September 1953.

[4] S.I. 1953, No. 1200. Certain other provisions were also brought into force. See S.I. 1953, No. 1199, Section 1(2).

[5] Instructions to our Governor-General and Commander-in-Chief of the Federation of Rhodesia and Nyasaland or other person for the time being performing the functions of that Office, made on 1 August 1953.

[6] A temporary Minister was permitted to retain his seat in any Territorial Legislative Assembly until such time as he became a Member of the Federal Assembly. By virtue of these provisions, Sir Godfrey Huggins and Mr. Roy Welensky retained their seats in the Territorial Legislatures.

[7] S.I. 1953, No. 1199, Section 2(4). Several disagreements arose between the Governor-General and the temporary Ministry. Personal communication.

[8] S.I. 1953, No. 1199, Section 2(1) and (3). See also Cmd. 8754, p. 45.   [9] Section 2(5).

operation on 23 October 1953 by Governor-General's Proclamation,[1] and on 15 December 1953 the first Federal General Election was held.

Departures from the final Draft Scheme

The final Federal Constitution departed, except in one respect, only to a minor degree from the Federal Draft Scheme. The major departure was the insertion of an Article, which preserved the powers of the Crown conferred by Act of Parliament (as opposed to the prerogative) to legislate by Order in Council for the Federation or any of the Territories.[2] This was intended to make it clear that Crown power under the Foreign Jurisdiction Act was preserved, should it be argued that the ratio of *Campbell* v. *Hall* was applicable so that such powers would disappear if no reservation were made.[3] However, the Article did not refer specifically to the Foreign Jurisdiction Act and stated that powers under any Act (both present and future) were preserved.

Another variation in the Constitution was that the powers of External Affairs entrusted to the Federal Government did not include 'relations between the United Kingdom and any of the Territories'. The White Paper had not made this clear nor given a complete picture of the detailed limitations that would be imposed in respect of the Federal Government's power to conduct External Affairs, although it had indicated that arrangements similar to those already existing with the Southern Rhodesian Government would be made.[4]

Finally, although the Federal Government was given power to maintain a Federal police force for service in the Territories and this might be used on the request of the Governor of any Territory, such police force was to be 'under the operational control of the Governor of that Territory'.[5]

[1] Federal Proclamation No. 2 of 16 October 1953.
[2] Article 29(7).
[3] *Contra* the view of Luxmore J. in the North Charterland Case.
[4] Second Schedule, Part I, Item 1. Cp. Cmd. 8754, pp. 10 and 23, Note 20.
[5] Second Schedule, Part I, Item 36. Cp. Cmd. 8754, p. 12. The limitations put on the use of Federal police forces effectively prevented their creation.

16

THE FEDERATION OF RHODESIA AND NYASALAND

General characteristics of the Federal Constitution

THE Constitution of the Federation of Rhodesia and Nyasaland, incorporated as an annex to a United Kingdom Order in Council, was stamped with the 'federal principle'[1] so that the Territorial Constitutions and the institutions under them continued, subject to the amendments necessitated by the creation of the Federal Legislature and Government. The division of power between the Federation and the Territories was made effective by the fact that the Constitution was subject to judicial review so that Acts *ultra vires* the powers exercisable by the Legislatures could be invalidated.[2]

The principle on which powers were allocated between the Federal State and the Territories was designed to secure that 'services which have a specially close relation to the day to day life of the African people should remain the responsibility of the Territorial Government'.[3] Although this racial principle was adopted as the basis of allocation of functions, it was done in order both to placate African opposition to Federation in the two Northern Territories and to leave powers of political advancement and the major regulation of the life of the African people in the hands of Colonial Office Governments in the Northern Territories. Indeed the Federal Constitution was unique in that it permitted its units to be of different constitutional status with differing degrees of external control over such units.[4] Division of power based on such

---

[1] See generally K. C. Wheare, *Federal Government*, Oxford, 3rd ed. and at p. 15 quoting the Report of the Royal Commission on the Australian Constitution (1929) at p. 230: 'A form of government in which sovereignty or political power is divided between the central and local governments so that each of them within its own sphere is independent of the other'. See also McMahon, *Federalism, Mature and Emergent*, Doubleday, 1955; D. V. Cowen, *The Foundations of Freedom*, Oxford, 1961, pp. 156–76; A. P. Newton, *Federal and Unified Constitutions*, Longmans, 1923; B. Schwartz, *American Constitutional Law*, Cambridge, 1955; and W. S. Livingston, *Federalism and Constitutional Change*, Oxford, 1956.

[2] *Mutasa and Others* v. *Minister of Law*, 1959 R. and N. 251, was an unsuccessful attempt to invalidate certain provisions of the Federal Prisons Act No. 9 of 1955. Cp. *Marbury* v. *Madison*, 1 Cranch. 137, 177 (U.S. 1803).

[3] Cmnd. 8233. See E. P. Dvorin, *Emergent Federalism in Central Africa* in G. M. Carter and W. O. Brown (Eds.), *Transition in Africa, Studies in Political Adaptation*, Boston, 1958. The author's comments are directed towards the mechanical problems of Federation rather than the political difficulties of applying federalism in a plural society. This can be explained by the date of writing.

[4] Whereas Southern Rhodesia remained a Colony enjoying responsible government, Northern Rhodesia and Nyasaland remained protectorates in which Her Majesty's Government continued responsible for constitutional advance: preamble.

a racial principle could not, however, be satisfactory. Since a Federation directly operates on all persons and property within its limits [1] it was obvious that African affairs could not be entirely beyond the reach of the Federal Legislature as Africans would also be affected by Federal laws. A further principle of division employed was that major powers of economic regulation were to be granted to the Federal Government so that an effective central authority could take economic decisions in the interests of the whole area. [2]

In this division of governmental and legislative powers between the Federation and the Territories, the Constitution categorized certain powers as exclusive to the Federation [3] and others as concurrent, both Federation and Territories enjoying rights to legislate in the latter field. On the other hand, certain powers were made exclusively Territorial. A notable feature was that the allocation of powers as between exclusive and concurrent lists was specified in great detail—seventy-six items in all. Examination of the vast field within which the Federal Legislature and Executive could act justifies the first Federal Prime Minister's description of his country as a Federation 'on the brink of amalgamation . . .. It was as near a United (sic unitary) Government as possible except that Native Affairs was kept out.' [4] In fact, the Southern Rhodesian Legislature surrendered somewhat more power to the Federal State than did the Northern Territories since three items relating generally to Southern Rhodesian non-African agriculture and agricultural research were made exclusively Federal, while the Northern Governments retained these powers. [5]

Since the Federal Government was a 'government of enumerated powers' [6] it could only exercise the powers granted to it, and all residual powers belonged to the Territories except insofar as the grant of enumerated powers implied incidental powers consistent with the letter and spirit of the Constitution. [7]

To resolve conflict between the Federation and the Territories, provisions for the supremacy of Federal laws in spheres in which such legislation was

---

[1] Schwartz, op. cit., p. 35.

[2] See A. H. Birch, 'Inter-Governmental Financial Relations in New Federations' in *Federalism and Economic Growth in Underdeveloped Countries*, op. cit.

[3] In fact potentially exclusive. See *infra*.

[4] Commission of Enquiry into the Siting of the Territorial Capital. Record of Evidence, p. 19. See also the Southern Rhodesian Prime Minister's comment in 1954: 'The Constitution we have been given is a constitution which takes us as far as we can go on the road to amalgamation without actually dispensing with the federal system and substituting for it a unitary system of government . . .. My own belief is that our constitution is leading us along the road towards amalgamation': *S.R.L.A.D.*, Vol. 36, col. 2892, 23 November 1954.

[5] Only in 1955 by the Non-African Agriculture (Transfer to Concurrent List) Ordinance of Northern Rhodesia was this transferred to the Federation with the exception of Forestry and Irrigation. The Nyasaland Government always refused such transfer: *Rhodesia Herald*, 4 January 1956.

[6] *Kansas* v. *Colorado*, 206 U.S. 46 at 81 (1907).

[7] Cp. *McCulloch* v. *Maryland*, 4 Wheat. 316, 405–6, and 421 (U.S. 1819).

competent were made, while on the executive side Federal and Territorial Governments were enjoined to consult and co-operate. The Territories were also to exercise their executive powers so as not to prejudice Federal authority. However, judicial enquiry into whether executive power had been exercised in accordance with these injunctions was precluded. On the other hand judicial definition of the limits of the fields of Federal executive and legislative competence was necessary in order to determine whether any particular exercise of power was *ultra vires*.[1]

Regionalism was taken account of in the composition of the Federal Legislative Assembly, which was to be composed of specified numbers of African and European Members drawn from each Territory, and certain Members of any race again elected by and allocated to the Territories.[2] Regard was also paid to regionalism in that power to amend the Constitution so as to alter the legislative power of the Federal Legislature was restricted for ten years after the coming into force of the Constitution. During that period Territorial Legislatures could block amendments. Insofar as all other constitutional amendments were concerned, if the Legislature of any Territory objected to a constitutional Bill within sixty days of its passage, external safeguards requiring United Kingdom consent by Order in Council were brought into play.

Regional powers were again respected in that Federal laws implementing treaties could not, unless the subject matter of such laws was in any event within Federal competence, come into effect in any Territory unless the Governor of the Territory, acting on Territorial Cabinet advice, declared such laws to be in force.

Regional independence was also secured by carefully devised financial provisions both in respect of taxing and borrowing powers, while the allocation of funds raised was to be reconsidered from time to time in the light of changing needs by a Commission containing representatives of all four Governments.

Territorial courts established under the Territorial constitutions were also to continue in existence and to enforce both Federal and Territorial laws. Although the Constitution provided for the establishment of a Federal Supreme Court, which was to be endowed with appellate and certain original jurisdiction, until such time as the Federal Legislature provided otherwise Federal Laws would be enforced by the Territorial Courts.

Finally, no right of secession was written into the Constitution. The only way in which secession could be effected would be by Act of the United Kingdom Parliament.[3]

[1] See *Mutasa and Others* v. *Minister of Law, supra*.

[2] In practice the convention also developed that Federal Cabinets should contain Ministers from all Territories although there was no provision for this in the Constitution.

[3] Cmnd. 1148, pp. 98 et seq. This section of the Monckton Report led to charges by the Federal Prime Minister that the British Government had given assurances that secession

As already indicated the safeguarding of the federal principle and Territorial powers necessitated a degree of constitutional rigidity. Even where these were not at stake a restrictive amending procedure was prescribed: a two-thirds majority of the total membership of the Federal Legislature and reservation were necessary for all constitutional amendments while in certain circumstances assent by Order in Council was an additional requirement. To a significant extent the major topics of constitutional concern were incorporated in the Federal Constitution, e.g. composition and powers of the Legislature, the executive, the judiciary, and the franchise. On the other hand, delimitation of constituencies was subject to laws of the Legislature as were the whole gamut of individual rights from citizenship and immigration to freedom of speech and property rights (except African land). Indeed there was no Bill of Rights, but merely a preamble which was, in the main, directed to repudiating amalgamation and re-stating United Kingdom authority for political advancement and guaranteeing African land rights in the Northern Territories.

However, two politically significant statements were made in the preamble. The first was that association of the Territories in a Federation 'would conduce to the security, advancement, and welfare of all their inhabitants and in particular would foster partnership and co-operation between their inhabitants'. This concept of 'partnership' subsequently became a bitter political issue in British Central African politics: criticism came from the African side because of failure to implement the principle both in daily life and in the form of the Constitution, and it came from certain Europeans, who considered it would lead to rapid African political advance.[1]

The second political statement was that the Federation would 'when those inhabitants so desire . . . go forward . . . towards the attainment of full membership of the Commonwealth'. Again this condition for Federal independence caused bitter controversy. The United Kingdom Government took the view that this required not merely a majority of voters, but consent of 'a majority of all the inhabitants',[2] whereas the Federal Government considered that the original intention of the preamble had been perverted.[3] The preamble was in fact held up as a bar, both in 1956 and 1957, when Lord Malvern, and later Sir Roy Welensky, sought independence for the Federation.

would not be dealt with in the Report and had not stood by these assurances. See also *Fed. Parlty. Deb.*, Second session, Second Parliament, cols. 3144–5, 25 October 1960. See also *infra*, Part II, Chapter 6.

[1] Cmnd. 1148, pp. 19–21. The word 'partnership' was chosen both because it avoided necessity either for strict equality or for European or African subordination. The concept, however, ultimately implied equality. See Leys, *European Politics*, op. cit., pp. 272–4. See also Clegg, op. cit., Sanger, op. cit., pp. 46–50, Creighton, op. cit., pp. 101–6, Leys and Pratt, op. cit., pp. 170–4, Mason, *Year of Decision*, pp. 51 et seq.

[2] *H.C. Deb.*, Vol. 516, col. 1969, 24 June 1953, Lyttelton.

[3] Gann and Gelfand, op. cit., p. 251, quoting Lord Malvern's views. *Contra* Pratt and Leys, op. cit., p. 186.

The only specific rights legally secured by the Constitution were African land rights, and the right not to be excluded from the Federal Public Service on racial grounds. The laws relating to African land, which conferred special protections, were to continue in existence, so that the only purpose for which the Federal Government could acquire such land might be for public works, and other specified purposes laid down in those laws. In addition, a specific limitation was imposed that no such land should be used for the purpose of settling immigrants. Barotse land was even more strictly protected, since only the Secretary of State and the Chief of the Barotse could consent to its alienation.

Although laws with regard to the franchise which might disqualify any person from voting other than because of an election offence were subject to the constitutional amendment procedure, this did not prevent the enactment of voters' qualifications which in fact enfranchised the majority of Europeans and excluded the majority of the Africans. Indeed, although the Federal franchise qualifications as introduced in 1958 were couched in non-racial terms, they were clearly designed with this object in view.

Again, relative to the electoral system, minority voters (viz. the few Africans who had acquired a vote and the few European opposition voters) were not given any special protection either in the form of proportional representation or of a transferable vote. However, the latter system was introduced in 1957 for elections to the Southern Rhodesian Territorial Legislature.

On the other hand, there was an institutional safeguard in the form of the African Affairs Board, responsible for reporting on subordinate legislation (which in the event of such report would be subject to disallowance by the Secretary of State), making representations as to African interests, reporting on differentiating measures, and causing differential Bills to be reserved.

Communalism was also seen in the composition of the Legislative Assembly which was, apart from a certain number of Members of any racial group, to consist of specified numbers of Europeans and Africans. Racial composition was also stipulated for the African Affairs Board.

Quite apart from these special provisions, the usual features seen in constitutions granted to British territories enjoying responsible government were to be found. There was to be cabinet government on United Kingdom principles with a Ministry and Executive Council appointed from Ministers and others.[1]

The Governor-General was in nearly all cases to follow Executive Council advice, while in those cases where he retained a discretion the Royal Instructions required him to act in accordance with relevant United Kingdom conventions.

The Cabinet was responsible to a unicameral assembly enjoying legislative

---

[1] In practice the Cabinet was always limited to Ministers.

power.[1] An early case made it clear that this legislative power could be delegated to the Executive.[2]

The party system was employed in conjunction with cabinet government.[3]

In addition, independence of the Federal judiciary was secured by provision that judges could not be dismissed without a resolution to this effect by the Federal Legislative Assembly.[4]

On the other hand, the Federation enjoyed considerable powers not normally granted to British dependencies. It was given considerable entrustments in respect of external affairs; in particular it enjoyed the right to negotiate trade agreements and agreements with neighbouring territories; its Prime Minister had a standing invitation to Commonwealth Prime Ministers' Conferences; its affairs were handled by the Commonwealth Relations Office and not by the Colonial Office; it had full powers in regard to internal defence; it had the right to raise loan funds, to establish a central bank (instead of being dependent on a Currency Board) and to maintain its own currency; and it was permitted to enact its own citizenship legislation.

In spite of these features it could not, however, be described as self-governing, since responsibility for the two Northern Protectorates was vested in the Colonial Office,[5] while in addition considerable external controls remained. These included United Kingdom power to legislate by Act which might revoke the Constitution, allow for secession or make other provisions, Crown power to legislate by Order in Council under the Foreign Jurisdiction or any other Act,[6] Crown power to suspend the Constitution, disallowance by the Crown of any Bill within twelve months of its passage, the rule of repugnancy, the appointment of the Governor-General on United Kingdom advice, the right of the Crown to give him Royal Instructions, the duty resting on the Governor-General to reserve Bills amending the Constitution, or reported on by the African Affairs Board, or affecting the franchise qualifications for assent by the Crown on United Kingdom advice, general discretionary reservation of Bills by the Governor-General, reservation of certain specified

---

[1] Although the Constitution provided that it might be amended so as to establish a second chamber of the Federal Legislature, this was never done.

[2] *R. v. Christopoulos*, 1957 R. & N. 251 (S.R.). Extensive powers to legislate were delegated to the Governor-General, as the Federal Assembly could not enact vast numbers of laws immediately upon the commencement of Federation. In accordance with the principles laid down in *R. v. Burah, supra,* and *Hodge* v. *The Queen, supra,* the delegation was upheld.

[3] Although the Constitution made no provision for a Leader of the Opposition, he was paid a salary from the start of the Federation.

[4] At that time, Colonial Office constitution-makers had not hit on the expedient of Judicial Commissions as the method for removal of judges. See Roberts-Wray, 'The Independence of the Judiciary in Commonwealth Countries' in *Changing Law in Developing Countries,* op. cit.

[5] This was the official United Kingdom view, see *H.L. Deb.,* Vol. 245, col. 1221, 19 December 1962, Lord Dilhorne L.C. The Federation was a dependency enjoying responsible government but was not self-governing.

[6] Article 29(7).

Bills under the Royal Instructions, and the Judicial Committee's power to grant appeals by special leave.[1] There were also other automatic features of subordination inevitably ensuing from the Federation's dependent status. Thus the Federal Government had no right to be consulted as to changes in the Royal succession or Royal style and titles, while the Federal Legislature could not enact laws having extra-territorial operation, and its power in respect of external affairs was limited to the entrustments made to it from time to time. These inequalities of status vis-à-vis the United Kingdom became during the short history of the Federation an important political issue, and Federal Governments, spurred on by similar Opposition demands, sought to have the 'elements of subordination' removed from the Federal Constitution.

The interesting point arises as to whether the Federation was anything more than an agglomeration of two Protectorates and one Colony. The Order in Council creating the Federation made provision for this difficulty insofar as United Kingdom Statutes were concerned. It was provided that references in any Act to the expressions 'British possession' and 'part of Her Majesty's Dominions' should be construed as including a reference to the Federation as a whole. Similarly in the numerous enactments where the expression 'Colony' appeared, this was to be construed as referring to the Federation.[2] Nonetheless, from the point of view of common law, the Federation was not a Colony. It was a hybrid created by statute, but without merger of its component parts. Indeed the Federal Supreme Court held that in a Federation 'the Territorial states do not merge their identity into that of the Federal State. Some sovereignty is surrendered but the Territorial Governments remain as entities separate from that of the Federal Government.'[3] In fact before the enactment of the Federal Citizenship Act No. 12 of 1957 there was no such thing as 'Federal nationality': the inhabitants of Southern Rhodesia were Southern Rhodesian citizens and British subjects, while those of the Northern Territories were British Protected Persons.

Similarly, it is submitted that the Federation did not have a 'common law',[4] the Federal Supreme Court in hearing appeals being required to apply the law of the Territory from which the appeal originated.[5] Although Federal statutes were of application throughout the Federal area there might have

---

[1] See *infra*.

[2] Section 13 of the Federation of Rhodesia and Nyasaland (Constitution) Order in Council.

[3] *Ranger* v. *Greenfield and Wood*, NN.O 1963 (1) R. & N. 127 (F.C.) at 142 per Conroy C.J. (N.R.). The Southern Rhodesian Government was held to be a 'Government' for the purpose of giving information under the Immigration Act No. 37 of 1954 to the Federal Government in Order that the Federal Governor-General might deem a person in respect of whom such information had been given to be a prohibited immigrant.

[4] The point was raised but left open in *Chassay Brothers* v. *Shaw and Macintyre*, NN.O. 1956 R. & N. 188 (F.C.).

[5] Federal Supreme Court Act 1955, Section 8.

been difficulties in interpreting such statutes, since English Law was adopted in the Northern Territories[1] and Roman–Dutch Law in Southern Rhodesia.[2] Anomalies would certainly have arisen if rights and duties had been differently interpreted in each Territory.[3] However, the problem of the interpretation of Federal statutes and common law rights of the Crown in respect of its Federal Government might have been solved by consideration of the fact that the Federal Constitution was of United Kingdom origin and was framed in the light of the English common law. Clearly the Constitution should have been interpreted in this light quite apart from specific application in Section 12(8) of the Order of the Interpretation Act of 1889.[4] It would seem, therefore, that Federal statutes required interpretation in accordance with English canons.

Yet another problem relating to choice of law in a Federation was not settled—the law to be applied in respect of litigation between Territorial Governments. One view would permit of such disputes being decided in accordance with the rules of Private International Law if the dispute was classifiable as relating to contract, tort, property, &c. On the other hand, if the matter has a constitutional or public character it should probably be decided in accordance with Public International Law, which has been applied in disputes between the American States.

Comparison of the Federal Constitution and the Southern Rhodesian Constitution 1923 reveals that the Constitutions were basically similar except for the special features exhibited by the Federal Constitution owing to its federal nature. Neither gave full independence, although in respect of the matters within their sphere the Federal legislative and executive organs were less limited. The main difference was in the machinery for exercising Imperial control over discriminatory legislation: in Southern Rhodesia either advance consent was necessary or the Bill required a suspending clause or reservation, whereas in the Federation the safeguard lay in the discretion of the African

---

[1] The Northern Rhodesia Orders in Council 1924 to 1960 Section 27(2) and the British Central Africa Order in Council Section 15(2) as amended applied the Common Law and doctrines of Equity in force in England on the 17 August 1911 and the 11 August 1902 in Northern Rhodesia and Nyasaland respectively.

[2] See *infra*, Part II, Chapter 3.

[3] To some extent this could have been met by applying the principle that unless there are compelling reasons to the contrary the earlier decision should be followed: *Abbott* v. *Philbin*, [1959] 3 All E.R. 590 at 601 per Lord Evershed M.R. In addition the Legislature obviously intends a statute to have the same meaning throughout its sphere of competence. Revenue statutes in particular should be uniformly interpreted and the Courts might have utilized the rule that the technical meaning should be ignored and the practical meaning applied: *I.T.C.* v. *Gibbs*, [1942] A.C. 402 per Lord Simon at 414–15.

[4] Cp. *Smith* v. *State of Alabama* (1888), 124 U.S. 465 at 478: 'The interpretation of the Constitution of the United States is necessarily influenced by the fact that its provisions are framed in the language of the English common law and are to be read in the light of its history.' In South Africa it has been held that in constitutional issues the Crown prerogative rests on English law: *Union Government* v. *Estate Whittaker*, 1916 A.D. 194 at 203.

Affairs Board,[1] which was empowered to request reservation in which event the Secretary of State was required to consider whether or not to advise assent. If, however, the reservation procedure was not invoked by the Board, the Act in question could not be tested in the Courts, whereas if the Governor did not follow the procedure outlined in the Southern Rhodesian Constitution, the Act in question would have been void. Furthermore under the Federal Constitution the safeguard against discriminatory subordinate legislation was possible subsequent nullification by the Secretary of State if the African Affairs Board reported adversely on any instrument, whereas in Southern Rhodesia advance approval of the Secretary of State was necessary. There was a further difference in that an additional safeguard appeared in the Federal Constitution—that the Federal Public Service must be open to all races, whereas in Southern Rhodesia Africans were excluded from the Public Service. In one last respect the Federal Government and Legislature enjoyed more power than the Southern Rhodesian Government, since, with the advent of Federation, the financial restrictions previously imposed on Southern Rhodesia disappeared: there was to be no reservation of Bills affecting currency, and the Federation could establish its own central bank, whereas Southern Rhodesia had merely been permitted a Currency Board in line with other dependencies.[2]

Analysis of the Federal Constitution
The Federal Governor-General

The Monarch was represented in the Federation by the Governor-General and Commander in Chief appointed by Her Majesty and holding office during Her Majesty's pleasure.[3] Although the Federal Government were as a matter of courtesy consulted on the appointments of the two Governors-General[4] they had no right to give advice on this matter, which was tendered by Her Majesty's Government in the United Kingdom.

The Governor-General was, unless an express reference was made to his discretion, to act in accordance with the advice of his Executive Council, but the Crown retained the right to give him Instructions as seen fit from time to time.[5] The only published Instructions to the Governor-General were issued on 1 August 1953.

Any Acting Governor-General, necessary owing to the absence or incapacity of the Governor-General, would also be appointed by the Crown and

---

[1] Unless it was a constitutional Bill or one amending the franchise qualifications. Here the Federal safeguard was wider, there being compulsory reservation of such Bills.

[2] See *S.R.L.A.D.*, Vol. 43, col. 859, 29 July 1959, Sir Edgar Whitehead.

[3] Article 2(1). The Governor-General's salary might not be reduced during his continuance in office: Article 2(4).

[4] Lord Llewellin (1953–7) and the Earl of Dalhousie (1957–63).

[5] Article 39 read with Article 2(2). No court could enquire whether the Governor-General had observed such Instructions or on whose advice he had acted.

would be subject to similar Instructions.[1] A Deputy to the Governor-General, who might be appointed by the Governor-General if he was away from the seat of the Federal Government or the Federation, or ill for a period of short duration, was subject not only to the Royal Instructions, but also to the instructions of the Governor-General, whose powers were not in the meanwhile abridged.[2]

The Governor-General's discretion to assent or declare that assent was withheld from any Bill was set out in the Constitution. In addition, it was expressly stated that he might reserve any Bill for the signification of Her Majesty's pleasure,[3] while under clause 2 of the Royal Instructions he was required, unless prior Instructions were given or a suspending clause was inserted, to reserve any Bill appearing to him to be inconsistent with the Crown's treaty or international obligations, or any Bill whereby any grant of land or money or other donation might be made to him, or any Bill containing provisions which had either been previously dissented from or disallowed. The Constitution also required the Governor to reserve any Bill amending the Federal Constitution, any Bill making provision for qualifications or disqualifications as voter, candidate, or Member where these prescribed disqualifications other than election offences, and any Bill where reservation was requested in writing by the African Affairs Board on the grounds that it was a differentiating measure, unless in the latter case he was satisfied after representations by the Prime Minister that it was essential in the public interest that the Bill be brought into immediate operation or unless he was satisfied both that the Bill was not a differentiating measure and that the Board's reasons were irrelevant or frivolous.[4] A power in relation to the African Affairs Board itself was that the appointment of the chairman and deputy chairman was in the Governor-General's discretion.[5]

In addition to the Governor-General's discretion to dissolve and prorogue the Federal Assembly, to appoint a Prime Minister and other Ministers holding office during pleasure, and to appoint, on the Prime Minister's recommendation, members of the Executive Council holding office during pleasure, was expressly reserved.[6] However, in exercising his discretion the Governor-General was 'so far as may be' to act in accordance with the constitutional conventions applying to dissolution, prorogual, and appointment of Prime Ministers in the United Kingdom.[7] The degree of adaptation of United Kingdom conventions by the Governor-General and their observance or otherwise could not, however, be enquired into in any court.[8]

---

[1] Article 3.   [2] Royal Instructions and Article 4 of the Constitution.   [3] Article 24(1).
[4] Articles 10(2), 97(1), and 75. The Minister of Law once ventured an example of what he considered would be a frivolous objection. If a Bill provided that all cyclists travelling on Rhodesia's strip roads should give way whenever they were in competition with a motor car, objection on the grounds that the vast majority of cyclists are African and the majority of car drivers European would, he considered, have been frivolous.
[5] Article 67(2).   [6] Article 67(2).   [7] Royal Instructions, Clause 3.   [8] Article 39.

Clashes between the Governor-General and his Executive Council were not publicized, but apparently there were considerable disagreements between the first Governor-General, Lord Llewellin, at the beginning of his term of office and the Federal Cabinet.[1] Later in 1963 the second Governor-General, the Earl of Dalhousie, was required by his Cabinet to read a remarkable Speech from the Throne attacking the British Government and accusing it of betraying the people of the Federation and doing them irreparable harm. The speech also stated that the Federal Government had not been consulted by the United Kingdom Government when decisions relative to the future constitutional advance of the Territories were being made.[2] Despite misgivings the Governor-General delivered this speech.[3]

Executive powers of the Federation were vested in Her Majesty and might be exercised on her behalf by the Governor-General or other persons authorized by him, or by any law of the Federal Legislature.[4] Executive authority was defined to extend to the maintenance and execution of the Constitution and to all matters within the legislative competence of the Federal Legislature.[5] However, in exercising the powers so conferred the Federal Government was bound to observe the provisions of any international or Commonwealth agreement relative to any Territory entered into by Her Majesty's Government prior to Federation.[6]

[1] Personal communication from a confidential source.

[2] *Fed. Parlty. Deb.*, Vol. 20, cols. 2–3, 8 April 1963.

[3] The Governor-General was disturbed about this speech. Personal communication from a confidential source. Had he refused to deliver it his only course would have been to submit his resignation which in the stormy atmosphere prevailing would have provoked a crisis. The speech was not such as to have justified the dismissal of the Federal Ministry. The speech involved allegations that the United Kingdom Government had dishonoured an undertaking that the Federal Government would be consulted on any such changes. That this pledge was honoured is apparent from the many opportunities given to the Federal Government to put an opposing point of view when changes were suggested, and its ability on a number of occasions to modify the proposals in a direction desired by it. Sir Roy Welensky's autobiography is itself an implicit refutation of these charges as it outlines the lengthy discussions he had with the United Kingdom Government. Consultation was not to be equated to necessity for Federal Government advance agreement. Sir Roy reveals that the Federal Government was consulted about constitutional change in Northern Rhodesia in 1953, in 1958, 1961, and 1962. Similarly it was consulted in relation to Nyasaland constitutional changes in 1959 and later.

[4] For the degree to which personal prerogatives of the Monarchy are extended to a Governor-General see H. V. Evatt, *The King and His Dominion Governors*, Oxford, 1936; A. B. Keith, *Responsible Government in the Dominions*, op. cit., Vol. 1, pp. 80–104, and Hood Phillips, op. cit., 3rd ed., pp. 668–70. The Federal Governor-General was given no special protection against frivolous and vexatious claims. This was probably because in terms of the Federal Supreme Court Rules all proceedings were commenced by application when the Court's original jurisdiction was invoked. However, this would not protect the Governor-General in his personal capacity. The Southern Rhodesian Governor on the other hand could not have any civil process issued out against him except by leave of the Court on motion: Rules of the High Court, Order 3, Rule 14—see *Gluck* v. *The Governor*, 1947 (1) S.A. 494 (S.R.).

[5] Article 36.

[6] Article 44. This also applied to the use of Federal legislative power. Such a provision

Through the Governor-General it is clear that the Crown retained certain powers of control although these were not exercised in practice. In addition to the powers expressly given him the Governor-General was also the repository of reserve powers as guardian of the Constitution,[1] while he had the normal powers and rights in respect of advice, information, and consultation which all Governors-General enjoy in order to perform their residual advisory functions.[2]

Cabinet system

The Governor-General was required to appoint a Prime Minister and other Ministers holding office during pleasure. From the Ministers, the Governor-General, on Prime Ministerial recommendation, appointed an Executive Council to advise him on the government of the Federation. In all cases unless express reference to his discretion was made the Governor-General was required to follow the advice of his Executive Council.[3] This also applied to the prerogatives of mercy, pardon, and respite in respect of offences against Federal laws.[4]

A cabinet system on United Kingdom lines taking policy decisions and co-ordinating and directing the machinery of government was instituted

was necessary as the United Kingdom remained internationally responsible for the Federation. Whether this article was intended to cover treaties has been doubted by D. P. O'Connell in 'State Succession and the Effect upon Treaties of Entry into a Composite Relationship' (1963), 39 *B.Y.I.L.* 54 at 127. O'Connell comments that, from the list of pre-Federation treaties and their application (as enumerated by the Federal Department of External Affairs prior to Federal dissolution), it is impossible to discern any coherent doctrine adopted by the Federal Government on the functional succession of the Federation in the execution of the treaties of the Territories. The list disclosed that thirty-two extradition treaties applied to all the Territories and none to the Federation as a whole although extradition was within the exclusive legislative competence of the Federation.

[1] Such powers might have been relevant during the existence of the Federation owing to frequent mentions by responsible Federal Ministers, including the Prime Minister, Sir Roy Welensky, of a 'Boston Tea Party' and a 'unilateral declaration of independence'. The latter is no new concept in Southern Rhodesian public life: it was first raised during the Federation campaign by Mr. Roy Welensky who referred to a 'historical tea party' (see W. F. Gutteridge, op. cit., 217) and again by Lord Malvern in 1956 who emphasized the complete local control over Federal Defence Forces and hoped that these Forces would not have to be utilized against a foolish United Kingdom Government in the same way that the North American Colonists had had to use theirs. In the 1958 Federal General Election the then leader of the Federal Opposition, Mr. Winston Field, again raised the question, while in 1962 such a possibility was actually canvassed by Sir Roy Welensky. Somewhat earlier he had a complete plan of action for such a course drawn up by his military advisers: *S.R.L.A.D.*, Vol. 59, col. 735, 29 October 1964. The present agitation in Southern Rhodesia directed to the same end has its 'intellectual origins' in these statements.

[2] The first Governor-General, as an administrator of long experience, was able to give valuable advice to the Federal Government. Personal communication from a confidential source.

[3] Articles 37, 38, and 39.

[4] Article 43. This contrasted with the Royal Instructions to the Governor of Southern Rhodesia.

from the creation of Federation. Whereas initially only five Ministers were appointed, by 1958 there were seven Cabinet Ministers including the Prime Minister and two Parliamentary Secretaries (the latter were not members of the Executive Council).[1] In April 1959 the incumbent of the Parliamentary Secretaryship to the Ministry of Home Affairs was promoted to the Federal Cabinet and an African appointed in his place. In June 1962, a second African Parliamentary Secretary was appointed, by which time there were eleven Cabinet Ministers and four Parliamentary Secretaries. However, at the end of 1962 Mr. Savanhu, the first African Parliamentary Secretary, resigned on the issue that 'partnership' had not been implemented in respect of the Federal Civil Service,[2] and another African Parliamentary Secretary was shortly thereafter appointed in his place. However, no African ever became a member of the Federal Cabinet.

The history of Federal Executive government was otherwise unclouded by public disputes. When the Cabinet was reconstituted from time to time, Ministers who had expressed their willingness to continue were omitted only on the grounds of age.

The federal principle and the Executive Government

The Federal character of the Constitution left its marks on certain aspects of executive power. A provision exhorting the Governments of the Territories and of the Federation to consult on all matters of common interest and concern was inserted.[3] Apparently in respect of Southern Rhodesia at least the provision was not observed in spirit since considerable disputes arose between the Federal and Territorial Prime Ministers as to the degree of consultation necessary. The Southern Rhodesian Prime Minister considered that a consultative Economic Council should be established while the Federal Prime Minister considered a formal body unnecessary.[4] However, since the

[1] There were numerous Ministries, but Ministers were often appointed to hold several portfolios. The Ministries were the Prime Minister's Office and Ministry of External Affairs, the Ministry of Defence, of Home Affairs, of Power, of Economic Affairs, for the Public Service, of Transport, of Education, of Posts, of Health, of Agriculture, of Law, of Finance, of Commerce and Industry, and of Works.

[2] See *Fed. Parlty. Deb.*, Vol. 19, cols. 1840 et seq., 7 November 1962, explaining his views. No African was appointed to the Federal Civil Service Commission and few Africans were appointed to Branch I of the Service, while those who were appointed were required to serve in areas where they would have little contact with Europeans. Cp. Article 43 of the Constitution which stated that regard should be had to the circumstances of the locality in which a civil servant would be employed. At the beginning of January 1963, partly as a result of this unfavourable publicity, regulations for a new structure for the Federal Public Service on a non-racial basis were introduced.

[3] Article 41(2).

[4] This was reflected in statements in the Southern Rhodesian Legislative Assembly by the then Prime Minister, Mr. Garfield Todd. Gann and Gelfand, op. cit., pp. 232 et seq., reveal the disagreements which arose between Sir Godfrey Huggins as Federal Prime Minister and Mr. Todd as Southern Rhodesian Prime Minister. Mr. Todd maintains that his

governing party in Southern Rhodesia and that in the Federation were in fact, although not technically until 1957, one and the same, there were not, except for personality clashes, serious difficulties between Federal and Territorial Governments.

Nonetheless, accusations as to the lack of machinery for permanent and satisfactory consultation by the Southern Rhodesian Prime Minister[1] seem to be borne out by the report on 'The Machinery of Inter-Governmental Co-operation' contained in the 'Survey of Developments since 1953' prepared by a committee of civil servants for the use of the Federal Review Commission.[2] From the outset of Federation it was laid down that questions of policy should not be exchanged between individual Ministers, but between Governments, i.e. in Southern Rhodesia between the Departments of the Federal and Southern Rhodesian Prime Ministers. However, only four meetings of the Heads of Governments as a whole took place before 1960, although informal meetings took place from time to time.[3]

Indeed, the major machinery of consultation which came into existence was either necessarily established in terms of the Constitution—the Apportionment Commission, the Loans Council, the Fiscal Review Commission—or in terms of statutes which required Federal representation on Territorial statutory boards or vice versa, or for a particular joint development project such as Lake Kariba.[4] Persistent requests by the Southern Rhodesian Government to establish a Standing Economic Council were refused by the Federal Cabinet, which was only prepared to hear representations from time to time: at most it would agree to a special meeting of Ministers if a subject for consideration arose—despite Southern Rhodesia's desire for a Council to operate on some fourteen major subjects including broad planning on economic development.[5] Indeed, the Southern Rhodesian Prime Minister complained that although the Southern Rhodesian Government had requested an Economic Council in April 1954, it was only in July 1956 that the first meeting of a committee of civil servants occurred: 'We should not have to ask for Federal

---

subsequent downfall was engineered by Sir Roy Welensky, the following Federal Prime Minister.

[1] *S.R.L.A.D.*, Vol. 37, cols. 1019 and 1045, 21 July 1955, Prime Minister; Vol. 38, col. 2143, 21 March 1956, Prime Minister; and Vol. 39, cols. 329 and 340, 20 July 1956, Prime Minister. Apparently co-operation occurred at lower levels in the Civil Service: Vol. 39, cols. 847–8, 9 August 1956. Cp. Canadian Provincial Dominion Conferences and Australian State and Dominion Premiers Conference. For the opposite point of view—that the Southern Rhodesian Prime Minister was attempting to interfere in Federal matters— see Gann and Gelfand, op. cit., p. 232.

[2] Cmnd. 1149. Lord Alport, then the British High Commissioner, reveals that from 1961 onwards contacts between the Southern Rhodesian and Federal Governments were perfunctory and that there was no proper liaison or consultation, op. cit., p. 37.

[3] By 1961 'Heads of States' meetings had ceased: Alport, op. cit., p. 41.

[4] The Inter-Territorial Consultative Committee on Labour was established as a consequence of difficulties in making satisfactory arrangements for the workmen on the Kariba project: E. P. Dvorin, op. cit., at pp. 69–70.

[5] *S.R.L.A.D.*, Vol. 39, col. 19, 5 July 1956, Ministry of the Treasury.

consultation and at least we should be given full information on any matter which concerns the Federation. After all, we are a responsible government and there is nothing which happens, particularly on the constitutional side, in any other part of the Federation which does not have its real effects on Southern Rhodesia . . . we should not be looked upon as just a junior government.'[1]

However, Territorial Governments were given advance information in cases in which the Federal Government adjudged them to have an interest: this was done in concurrent subjects, but not normally in regard to exclusively Federal matters. In most cases draft Bills were sent to Territorial Governments to comment on Federal Bills which had legal implications for the Territories.

One of the major disputes during 1957 between the Federal and Territorial Governments related to the proposed Federal franchise: the Southern Rhodesian Government was determined to uphold the principle of a common roll whereas the Federal Government sought to introduce two separate rolls and to proceed with their legislation before the Tredgold Commission, appointed by the Southern Rhodesian Government to enquire into the franchise, had reported. Eventually agreement was reached whereby the Federal Government awaited the Commission's report and both groups of proposals were thereafter, to a considerable degree, aligned.[2] There was apparently also some disagreement on the proposals put forward by the Federal Government in 1957 in respect of the creation of a Central Africa Office in London to deal with all Federal problems and the Territorial Prime Minister refused to permit the Federation to intervene as between the Southern Rhodesian Government and the Commonwealth Relations Office.[3]

On the other hand consultations with all the Territories on internal security of the Federation were held in 1955 when it was agreed that this was a matter more proper for the Territorial Legislatures than for the Federal Assembly, and that all Territories would so far as possible introduce uniform legislation. Thus it was that the Southern Rhodesian Public Order Act of 1955 imposing severe limitations on civil liberties was introduced.[4]

By 1957, however, a merger of the Southern Rhodesian and Federal Government parties was arranged. As a result, difficulties between the parties were smoothed over and the Southern Rhodesian Prime Minister was able to announce that his Government had had 'very close consultations on many subjects from time to time' with the Federal Government.[5] Nonetheless, if the Federal Government wished to take action in any field it would override Territorial views. In 1958, the Territorial Legislature, having been consulted

---

[1] *S.R.L.A.D.*, Vol. 39, col. 329, 20 July 1956.
[2] Leys, op. cit., pp. 141–2 and 213.   [3] *S.R.L.A.D.*, Vol. 39, col. 1419, 3 May 1957.
[4] See *S.R.L.A.D.*, Vol. 38, cols. 1425 and 1429. At the third reading four Government supporters voted against the measure. The Public Order Act was the precursor of the present Law and Order (Maintenance) Act.
[5] *S.R.L.A.D.*, Vol. 40, col. 484, 31 July 1957.

by the Southern Rhodesian Prime Minister for its views on the introduction of a public holiday, Federation Day, expressed the view through the majority of its members that such action would be premature and would provide the occasion for violent incidents in the Northern Territories.[1] The Federal Government, however, ignored the views of the Assembly and the Southern Rhodesian Prime Minister and introduced such a public holiday.

Despite these differences between the Southern Rhodesian and the Federal Governments they were not of great moment. The real difficulties of the Federation occurred when in the last years of Federation the Governments of the two Northern Territories came into the joint hands of Colonial Civil servants and African parties opposed to Federation.

Apart from the duty of the Federal and Territorial Governments to consult each other the Constitution provided that executive authority of the Territories was not to be exercised so as to impede or prejudice the exercise of Federal authority. Such exercise was not, however, a justiciable issue.[2]

Special provision was also made for the Governor of a Territory to confer on the Governor-General or a Federal officer or authority, with the Governor-General's consent, Territorial executive functions, if such functions were in his opinion ancillary or related to any matter in respect of which the Federal Government enjoyed executive authority.[3] Similarly the Governor-General might entrust to a Territorial Governor, Federal functions in any Territory, while a Federal law might confer powers or impose duties on a Territorial Governor, official, or authority in respect of any matter within Federal legislative competence, even if exclusively Federal, provided that the Governor declared by notice in the official Territorial Gazette that such provision should have effect.[4] Of this latter provision considerable use was made, as by January 1963, fifty-six Federal Acts conferred duties on Southern Rhodesian authorities.

The policy of the Federal and Southern Rhodesian parties in power was in fact to amalgamate the offices of Federal Governor-General and Southern Rhodesian Governor.[5] This design was not in fact executed except when the Federation was in its last stages and the Governor of Southern Rhodesia was appointed as Acting Governor-General of the Federation. There were, however, several objections to such a course being followed as the incumbent of these two offices would be vested with multiple constitutional capacities and would owe loyalty to four authorities—Her Majesty, the United Kingdom Government, the Federal Government, and the Southern Rhodesian Government. Embarrassing situations could have arisen owing to conflicting advice being tendered. Even if the incumbent acted completely

---

[1] S.R.L.A.D., Vol. 41, cols. 36–41, 2 July 1958.
[2] Article 42(3).   [3] Article 42(3).   [4] Article 41(1) and (2).
[5] S.R.L.A.D., Vol. 43, cols. 402–3, 17 July 1959, Whitehead. The same attitude was adopted towards the police forces: Vol. 43, cols. 1228–35, Whitehead.

constitutionally accepting the relevant binding advice the absolute confidence which should have existed between him and his respective Cabinets would necessarily have become impaired.[1]

The Federal Civil Service

At the establishment of Federation, provision was made for the Governor-General to appoint an Interim Federal Public Service Commission to advise on matters connected with the Federal Civil Service, which Commission would be composed of a Chairman nominated by him and three members nominated by the Governors of the Territories. Provision was made for a five-year period of secondment, two years of which were to be compulsory, for Territorial civil servants, and also for specially generous provisions for abolition of office and pensions.[2] During this five-year period the Civil Service Commission established a European Pensionable Branch of the Service and evolved conditions of service for European officers who would transfer to this from the Territorial Governments. African employees, however, retained their varying Territorial conditions of employment.[3]

In 1956 four branches of the Service were established, Branch I being at that stage entirely European with salaries rising to a high level, and Branches II, III, and IV being in effect entirely non-European consisting of a small number of African professionals, nurses, and numerous clerks, messengers, cleaners, &c. The Federal Public Service Act 1959 then provided for the promotion of non-Europeans to Branch I, while Branch II was to serve as a proving ground for Africans with academic and technical qualifications other than medical ones. By September 1959 four non-European doctors, an information officer attached to the High Commissioner's office in London and fifteen teachers who were Africans had been appointed to Branch I.[4] Civil servants in both Branches I and II enjoyed security of tenure as under the terms of the Federal Public Service Act 1959 their contracts were binding on the Crown.[5]

[1] e.g. advice by the Federal Government to the Governor-General to terminate Territorial legislative power under Article 29(2) with the Territorial Government at the same time objecting; Territorial advice to decline to give a law implementing a treaty effect in a Territory under Article 34; Territorial advice to decline to have rights and duties imposed on him under Article 41(2); differing advice as to exercise of executive authority bearing in mind Article 42(4) which provided that Territorial executive advice should not be exercised in such a way as to impede Federal Executive authority; and conflicting advice whether to assent to either Territorial or Federal Bills outside the field of the particular Legislature's competence. (*Quaere* whether since in terms of Article 35(1) the Bill would be void the Governor-General should assent and leave the matter to the Courts.)

[2] S.I. 1953, No. 1199, Sections 6–11.

[3] Cmnd. 1149, p. 59, gives the reason that uniformity of wages paid to African civil servants would in view of the lower wage rates prevailing there have disrupted the Nyasaland economy.

[4] Cmnd. 1149, pp. 59–60.

[5] No. 19 of 1959. This limited the Crown prerogative by providing that Branch I and Branch II officers could only be dismissed in terms of the Act or in terms of their contracts.

Eventually by the beginning of 1963 the Federal Civil Service Regulations were made fully non-racial, but in practice the administrative Civil Service remained European while junior clerical and menial posts were filled by Africans. Although the Federal Constitution provided that no person should be ineligible for employment in the Federal Public Service on the grounds of race the requirement that regard should 'be had only to his competence, experience, and suitability' was a factor excluding the majority of Africans from employment as a result of their educational history.[1] However, by implication from Article 40(3) in European areas Europeans should in the main have been employed, while in African areas the reverse should have been the case.[2] Such a provision was certainly not in accordance with the 'partnership' mentioned in the preamble to the Constitution.

The hub of the Civil Service was Salisbury in Southern Rhodesia which became not only the Southern Rhodesian capital, but also the Federal capital until such time as the Federal Legislature otherwise provided.[3] Eventually a Select Committee to enquire into the siting of the capital reported in favour of Salisbury.[4] This decision 'undoubtedly caused dissatisfaction and suspicion in the Northern Territories'.[5] Although the Federal Government took over an area adjacent to Salisbury for the creation of a Federal capital in which the Federal legislature could make special laws overriding all Territorial laws[6] the Federal Government did not proceed with the erection of buildings in this area and the Federal Legislative Assembly and Government offices remained in the centre of Salisbury.

Limitations on Federal competence in respect of external affairs

Prior to Federation a degree of autonomy in respect of external affairs had been permitted to the Southern Rhodesian Government by the United Kingdom Government on the basis of a delegation, the United Kingdom Government remaining responsible and, therefore, requiring prior consultation before the Southern Rhodesian Government might enter into any commitments which it was competent to negotiate, viz. trade agreements relating to the treatment of goods with foreign governments, local agreements, and representational arrangements with neighbouring territories, and membership

---

[1] Article 40(2). See de Smith, op. cit., p. 135.

[2] As de Smith points out from 1962 onwards only African Federal civil servants were suitable for posts in Nyasaland.

[3] Article 6.

[4] Votes and Proceedings of the Federal Assembly, First Session, First Parliament, p. 70.

[5] Cmnd. 1148, para. 263. The capital of a multi-racial state was thus situated in an area practising racial discrimination. The Monckton Report suggested that although Salisbury should for a time remain the administrative capital, the Legislature should perambulate between the Territories and possibly consider the establishment of a new capital.

[6] Article 6(3).

of international organizations which contemplated Southern Rhodesian membership.[1]

The Federal Constitution permitted the Federal Legislature to enact laws with respect to external affairs as defined in Item I of Part I of the Second Schedule thereof.[2] These were defined so as to permit of legislation in respect of such external relations as might from time to time be entrusted to the Federation by Her Majesty's Government in the United Kingdom, and the implementation of conventions, treaties, and other obligations affecting either the Federation or any Territory (whether entered into before or after the creation of Federation by Her Majesty's Government on behalf of the Federation or Territories, or by the Territories before the coming into force of the Federation, or by the Federation thereafter with the authority of Her Majesty's Government in the United Kingdom). External affairs, however, did not include the relations between the United Kingdom and any of the Territories, while a subsequent proposal for a Federation Office between Southern Rhodesia and the Commonwealth Relations Office was rejected in 1957.[3]

Since the Federal Government enjoyed executive authority in respect of all matters within the competence of the Federal Legislature[4] the previous authority enjoyed by the Southern Rhodesian Legislative Assembly and Cabinet was to that extent diminished.[5] Indeed, Article 29(2) of the Constitution was invoked. This authorized the Governor-General of the Federation by notice in the official Gazette of any Territory to prescribe that any Territorial legislative power enumerated in Part I of the Second Schedule should cease. Territorial legislative and executive power was accordingly terminated in 1953 in respect of External Affairs.[6] From this time the sole power retained by the Territories in this respect was to prevent the implementation of any treaty, convention or agreement relating to a matter which was not included in the Federal or Concurrent Legislative Lists. Federal Laws dealing with such matters could not have effect in relation to any Territory until the Governor of the Territory declared by notice in the Gazette that such law was to have effect.[7]

Similar powers to those previously entrusted to Southern Rhodesia were delegated to the Federal Government by the United Kingdom Government

---

[1] Cmnd. 1149, p. 22.   [2] Article 29(1).

[3] *S.R.L.A.D.*, Vol. 39, col. 1419, 3 May 1957, Mr. Todd, Prime Minister.

[4] Article 36(2).

[5] Article 42(1): 'subject to the provisions of this Constitution the executive authority of each of the Territories shall continue in accordance with the constitution of that Territory'.

[6] S.R.G.N. 903 of 1953. Powers in respect of duties of Customs and Excise, and Taxes on Income and Profits were subsequently terminated by S.R.G.N. 345 of 1961.

[7] Article 34. Thus if the Federation agreed to exempt diplomatic representatives from municipal rates, municipal parking laws, and death duties any Federal legislation making such provision would have required Territorial approval indicated in the manner above outlined.

by an Agreement of October 1953. In addition, the Federal Government was permitted to enter into direct consultation with the Governments of Commonwealth countries and to make arrangements for the exchange of representatives. Prior consultation, information as to the progress of negotiations, and agreement of the United Kingdom was necessary except in respect of minor matters of purely mutual interest arranged with a Commonwealth country.[1] Subsequently in November 1956, arrangements for the treatment within the Federation of representatives of governments and organizations outside the Federation were entrusted to the Federal Government.

In April 1957, further delegations of authority to the Federal Government were made. In a joint communique issued by the Secretary of State for Commonwealth Relations and the Federal Prime Minister,[2] the United Kingdom Government announced that the Federation was to be entrusted with 'responsibility for External Affairs to the fullest extent possible consistent with the responsibility which Her Majesty's Government must continue to have in International Law, so long as the Federation is not a separate international entity'. The Federation was to be free to conduct all relations with members of the Commonwealth directly, to make agreements of any kind, and to exchange High Commissioners with such countries. It could also enter into negotiations and agreements with any foreign country 'subject in each case to the need to safeguard the responsibility which Her Majesty's Government must have in International Law so long as the Federation has not a separate international entity'.[3] The Federation was also to be free to appoint diplomatic agents, or consular or trade representatives in countries willing to receive them in order to deal with matters within Federal competence and to receive such representatives from other countries. In addition to the Federal representatives already on the diplomatic staffs of the British Embassies in Washington and Lisbon, the Federation could associate representatives with any United Kingdom diplomatic mission. Finally the Federation, insofar as it did not already possess authority, was permitted to acquire in its own right membership of international organizations which contemplated Federal membership. In all these cases the United Kingdom Government expected to be informed as to the initiation and progress of negotiations so as to be enabled to inform other Commonwealth Governments on matters of concern to them and so as to be able to advise on the international aspects of any agreement.[4]

[1] Cmnd. 1149, p. 22.
[2] For Text see Keesings Contemporary Archives 1957–8, 15529–30.
[3] Comnd. 1149, p. 23.
[4] Cmnd. 1149, pp. 24–26, reveals the extent to which the Federation by 1959 had participated in International and Commonwealth organizations and entered into representational agreements with other countries. This did not include the United Nations Organization, or the International Labour Organization, to the latter of which it sent observers and also to numerous other organizations.

Thus, although the Federation was not independent, it enjoyed a remarkable degree of freedom to conduct its external affairs. This was particularly marked in the conduct of its relations with Commonwealth countries. From 1935 to 1953 the Prime Ministers of Southern Rhodesia had been invited to attend Imperial Conferences and the great majority of Commonwealth Prime Ministers' Conferences.[1] After the establishment of Federation the Federal Prime Minister took the place of the Southern Rhodesian Prime Minister at these Conferences: in practice this meant that Sir Godfrey Huggins continued to attend in a changed capacity. At the Commonwealth Prime Ministers' Conference in 1956 the Federal Prime Minister was then issued a special standing invitation to attend future Conferences. The communique issued at the conclusion of the Conference stated that:

taking into account the twenty years attendance firstly by the Prime Minister of Southern Rhodesia and now by the Prime Minister of the Federation, they agreed that they would welcome the continued participation of the Prime Minister of the Federation of Rhodesia and Nyasaland in meetings of the Commonwealth Prime Ministers.[2]

His successor, Sir Roy Welensky, continued to attend Commonwealth Prime Ministers' Meetings and to take a full part in discussions. However, he was not present when questions of Commonwealth membership were discussed.[3]

In fact, during its existence, the Federation was for the most part treated as a Member of the Commonwealth vis-à-vis other Members. Thus, in 1957, when the Indian Government presented a memorandum on the treatment of diplomats in the Federation, the United Kingdom Government adopted the attitude that this matter should be dealt with by the two Governments concerned,[4] while in 1958 the United Kingdom Government declined to intervene in respect of the Federal Immunities and Privileges Act and Orders issued thereunder, stating that these powers and consequent diplomatic arrangements were now the responsibility of the Federal Government as a result of its enhanced status.[5]

---

[1] See *supra*, Chapter 11.

[2] See *Documents and Speeches on Commonwealth Affairs 1952 to 1962*, edited by N. Mansergh, Oxford, 1963, p. 132, quoting an extract from the final communique from the Commonwealth Prime Ministers' Meeting held in London 27 June to 6 July 1956. Cp. Cmnd. 1149 at p. 21 where it is suggested that 'this invitation was extended in recognition of Sir Godfrey Huggins' personal qualities as a Commonwealth statesman and was repeated on the same basis'.

[3] e.g. in the case of the discussions relative to South Africa's membership.

[4] See Fawcett, op. cit., p. 114, who considered that British authority was attenuated. Fawcett also mentions possible Federal intervention in Katanga. Welensky, op. cit., pp. 211–13, however, makes it clear that he was in consultation with United Kingdom Ministers and could not act without their authority in respect of Katanga. See also *H.L. Deb.*, Vol. 225, col. 287, 14 July 1960, Lord Home.

[5] *H.C. Deb.*, Vol. 585, col. 1358, 3 April 1958.

The Federal Legislature

Composition

As in all British Territories the Crown was part of the Legislature which consisted of Her Majesty and a Federal Assembly.[1]

The Assembly was originally composed of a non-member Speaker entitled to a casting vote,[2] and thirty-five members. Twenty-six of these were to be 'elected members' of any race of whom fourteen were to be elected in Southern Rhodesia, eight in Northern Rhodesia, and four in Nyasaland. There were, in addition, to be six 'specially elected African members' each Territory electing two. Finally, three European[3] members charged with special responsibility for African interests completed the membership of the Assembly. Of the latter the Southern Rhodesian electorate chose the Southern Rhodesian specially elected European member, while the two other members were to be 'specially appointed European members', each Northern Governor appointing one.

Those 'elected members' who were to be elected from Northern Rhodesia and Southern Rhodesia were for the first general election to be elected under the respective Territorial laws subject to necessary modifications made by regulations issued by the Governor-General, such regulations being approved by the Secretary of State,[4] while the Nyasaland 'elected members' were to be elected under regulations made by the Governor-General with the agreement of the Governor of Nyasaland and approved by the Secretary of State.[5] The effect of these laws was that the twenty-six 'elected members' in the first Federal Assembly were all Europeans elected by predominantly European electorates.[6]

[1] Article 8.

[2] Articles 9(2) and 19(2). If any member was elected Speaker he was thereupon to vacate his seat: Article 16. The Deputy Speaker was, however, to be a member: Article 17.

[3] This did not include a Eurafrican or Asian. Such a person must be 'unquestionably of European extraction and not only half a European': *Thornicroft* v. *Federal Minister of Internal Affairs*, 1954 (1), S.A. 519 (R. & N. C.A.) in which case the nomination of a prominent member of the Coloured community was disallowed.

[4] Article 11. In Southern Rhodesia the only changes were in respect of the number of Electoral Districts required—fourteen instead of the thirty for the Legislative Assembly. The effect of the franchise qualifications was that in Southern Rhodesia there were 48,870 European, 594 Asian, 570 Coloured, and 441 African voters, while in Northern Rhodesia there were 14,487 European, 892 Asian and eight African voters (Cmnd. 1149, p. 11). The Northern Rhodesian qualifications were an income of £200 per annum, or occupation of a house or building valued at £250, plus the status of a British subject. This last requirement excluded Africans who were only British Protected Persons unless they were naturalized.

[5] Article 12. The position in Nyasaland was provided for by the Nyasaland Federal Electoral Regulations of 1953 which were subsequently amended in 1955. No elections properly so-called had previously taken place in Nyasaland. These Regulations permitted United Kingdom citizens who were Nyasaland residents with an income of £200 per annum or property of £250 in value to vote. As a result there were 981 Europeans and seventy-seven Asian voters.

[6] This was also the case in the second Federal Assembly while in the final Assembly one

The specially elected European member and the two specially elected African members from Southern Rhodesia were also to be elected under regulations made by the Governor of Southern Rhodesia.[1] These applied the existing electoral law. Accordingly twenty-nine members out of the total membership of thirty-five were elected in practice predominantly by Europeans.

The two specially elected African members from Northern Rhodesia were however to be elected by a body designated by the Governor of Northern Rhodesia as being representative of Africans.[2] Similar provisions applied in respect of the Nyasaland specially elected African members.[3]

Standard disqualifications both for election and subsequent vacation of seats by the elected, specially elected and appointed members were laid down (viz. bankruptcy, office under the Crown, insanity, etc.) except that in the Northern Territories British Protected Persons were eligible for election.[4] A special provision was inserted that any person who was a member of a Territorial Legislature and was elected to the Federal Assembly was required to resign his Territorial membership before he could take his Federal seat.[5] The reason for this provision was that there was in fact a translation of a large number of members from the Southern Rhodesian Legislative Assembly to the Federal Legislative Assembly. The first Prime Minister and four of his Cabinet were in fact members of the Southern Rhodesian Legislative Assembly prior to their translation to the Federal Assembly and a large number of Federal members of Parliament also left the Territorial Assembly in order to become members of the Federal Legislative Assembly. In fact eleven of the

Coloured Member was elected. For accounts of the first Federal general elections, see E. P. Dvorin, *Central Africa's First Federal Election, Background and Issues*, op. cit., pp. 369–90; and Leys, op. cit., pp. 195–212. Even after the second Federal general election, which was held in December 1958, there was still a tremendous imbalance between the number of registered African and European voters. The only figures which are available are quoted in Cmnd. 1149 at p. 11 and relate to the 31 August 1959. These show that in the Federation as a whole there were then 85,834 European, 7,132 African, 3,194 Asian, and 881 Coloured voters. At the time of the last Federal election in 1962, figures released by the Central African Statistical Office still show this imbalance. There were then 103,896 European, 4,504 Asian and Coloured, and 10,958 African voters of whom at least 6,000 were registered on a special roll and were not, therefore, entitled to vote for the forty-four 'elected members' who in terms of the Constitution Amendment Act of 1957 replaced the original twenty-six 'elected members', whereas the great majority of European voters were on the general roll and were entitled to vote for these 'elected members'. See Figure I *infra*, pp. 394–5.

[1] Article 13(1).

[2] Article 13(2). See Northern Rhodesia G.N. No. 309 of 30 October 1953 specifying the African Representative Council of Northern Rhodesia as the elective body.

[3] Article 13(3). See Nyasaland Government Notice No. 180 of 23 October 1953 providing that specially elected African members should be elected by the African Protectorate Council of Nyasaland.

[4] Articles 14 and 15.

[5] Article 10(3). This provision was applied in March 1956 when Mr. R. Williamson, a Member of the Southern Rhodesian Legislative Assembly, was elected at a Federal by-election. He thereupon resigned his Southern Rhodesian seat.

fourteen Southern Rhodesian 'elected members' had previously been members of the Southern Rhodesian Assembly.

The Federal Legislature after the first election was empowered to make all provisions in respect of 'elected members' necessary for the conduct of elections, the qualifications and disqualifications of voters and candidates, delimitation, and vacation of seats by such members. However, if an Electoral Bill in the opinion of the Speaker laid down qualifications or disqualifications for voters, candidates, or members, other than being concerned in an election offence, such Bill had to be passed by not less than two-thirds of the total membership of the Assembly, endorsed to this effect by the Speaker, and reserved by the Governor-General.[1]

It was the subsequent use of this provision, viz. the enactment of the Federal Electoral Act 1958 combined with the Citizenship of Rhodesia and Nyasaland and British Nationality Act 1957 and the Constitution Amendment Act 1957, that made the eventual dissolution of Federation, unless major constitutional changes occurred, inevitable. This combination of Acts made it impossible for Africans to participate to any great extent in the election of any Federal Government and further altered the balance of communal representation by increasing the absolute majority of members elected by a largely European electorate as opposed to those representing Africans despite the fact that the increase in membership was proportionate. The changes made it clear to African politicians in the Northern Territories that they could not in their lifetime hope to gain control of the Federal Legislature under the Federal franchise introduced in 1958.[2]

Procedure

In respect of procedure in the Federal Assembly the standard provisions for the conduct of legislative business in British exported constitutions were inserted. Thus the usual oaths of allegiance were to be taken, while proceedings were to be conducted in English which was to be the Federation's official language.[3] Again, although the Federal Parliament might legislate in respect of privileges of Federal Members of Parliament, these were not to exceed those enjoyed by the House of Commons while in the interim these were prescribed by Governor-General's Regulation.[4] The Constitution also empowered the Governor-General to draft Standing Orders which would be effective until amended by the Assembly. A quorum of twelve members was laid down in the Constitution and the usual restrictions as to the introduction

[1] Article 10(2).

[2] See *infra* (constitutional changes in the Federation) and also Figure 1.

[3] Article 7. Other languages might be used for the purpose of bringing matters to the attention of persons concerned therewith.

[4] Federal Assembly (Privileges, Immunities, and Powers) Regulations 1953 (F.G.N. 50/53). These were never altered as the Federal Legislature did not legislate on this topic.

of money votes applied, while penalties for unqualified persons sitting were also inserted.[1] Again it was laid down that the Assembly should meet at least once in every year, that the first session should be held within twelve months of the coming into force of the Constitution, and that twelve months should not intervene between any subsequent sessions.[2] Whereas the Governor-General might at any earlier time prorogue or dissolve the Assembly he was required to dissolve it at the expiration of five years from the date of its first meeting after any general election,[3] and not later than three months after any dissolution a general election was to be held.[4]

In the main the procedure followed in the Assembly was similar to that in the United Kingdom except for differences occasioned by the relative size of the two Legislatures, e.g. Bills were dealt with in Committee of the whole House and not referred to Standing Committees unless a special Select Committee was appointed for the purpose.[5] Since the Standing Orders required reference to the procedure and privileges obtaining in the Commons when no express provision existed on the point in question, reference to Commons practice was often made. Extensive use was also made of the Select Committee system[6] and Sessional Committees were appointed by the Committee on Standing Rules and Orders[7] for various purposes. In particular a Select Committee on Public Accounts responsible for reporting on and investigating cases where parliamentary grants had been misused or applied for other purposes than those prescribed was sessionally appointed.[8]

As in the Southern Rhodesian Legislative Assembly the Government caucus was extremely important in the conduct of business and was used as the place to air opposition to Government proposals. However, since Federal Governments always had large majorities they could permit their backbenchers great latitude in debate and from time to time even permitted attacks from the floor of the House.[9]

Legislative powers

As indicated earlier the legislative powers accorded to the Federal Assembly were allocated on the basis that matters affecting the day to day life of Afri-

---

[1] Article 18–22.   [2] Article 26.
[3] Article 27.   [4] Article 28.
[5] This procedure was followed in the case of the Federal Companies Bill intended to introduce a uniform company law for Central Africa. Unfortunately it was not enacted before Federal dissolution.
[6] To report on the desirability of introducing decimal coinage; to report on the most desirable situation for a Federal capital; to scrutinize delegated legislation.
[7] The Committee responsible for arranging the affairs of Parliament, chaired by the Speaker and consisting of the Prime Minister, the Leader of the Opposition, the Leader of the House, the Chairman of Committees and other senior members of the Opposition.
[8] See Leys, op. cit., pp. 58–59, for details of other Sessional Committees.
[9] Leys, op. cit., p. 62.

cans should be Territorial whereas other matters and economic questions should be Federal.

The Federal Legislature was given powers for the peace, order, and good government of the Federation with respect to any powers allocated to it. It was also given powers in respect of any matter incidental to powers conferred on any of the three arms of government in the Federation.[1] It might also legislate for part of the Federation only or make different provisions for different parts except in respect of taxes on income and profits and emergency taxes.[2] Apart from a detailed enumeration in the Second Schedule to the Constitution of fields in which the Legislature was competent, the Federal Legislature was given powers in respect of certain specified matters, e.g. to provide for a Federal Supreme Court, to provide for judges' salaries, to provide for electoral laws, to provide for the salary of the Auditor-General, to make amendments to the Constitution, to legislate for the seat of government and in that area even to override laws exclusively within Territorial competence.[3]

The Federal legislative powers were enumerated in detail (seventy-six items in all) in Parts I and II of the Second Schedule to the Constitution. Part I, the Federal Legislative List, consisted of numerous matters which were described as being exclusively Federal, whereas Part II, the Concurrent Legislative List, contained matters in respect of which both Federal and Territorial Legislatures had power to make laws.[4] However, even in respect of the Federal Legislative List Territorial legislative power continued until such time as the Governor-General by notice in the Territorial Gazette prescribed that such legislative power should cease, as until such time the matter was 'deemed to be included in the Concurrent List'.[5] In fact it was only in respect of Items 1 (External Affairs), 11 (Duties of Customs and Excise), and 12 (Taxes on Income and Profits), that such power was exercised.[6] The effect of these notices was, it is submitted, the extinction of such Territorial powers and their elimination from the Territorial Constitutions.

The Federation of Rhodesia and Nyasaland (Constitution) Order in Council in Section 14(1) provided for the continuance in force of Territorial Constitutions subject to the Federal Constitution[7] while Article 29(4) of the

---

[1] Article 29(1). The extent of the incidental power was not investigated. Item 75 of the Concurrent List permitted the Federal Legislature to legislate for Commissions of Enquiry and this avoided the difficulties encountered on this point in Australia (see *Attorney-General for the Commonwealth* v. *Colonial Sugar Refining Company*, [1914] A.C. 237). A Federal Commissions of Enquiry Act No. 15 of 1955 was passed and amended by Act 31 of 1960.

[2] Articles 29(6), 80(3), and 81(2).

[3] Article 6(3). See the Seat of Government (Special Laws) Act 1956 and regulations thereunder: F.G.N. 163/56.

[4] See Appendix, Table I.   [5] Article 29(2).

[6] See S.R.G.N. 903/53 relating to External Affairs, and S.R.G.N. 345/61 relating to the other matters in respect of which Territorial legislative power was extinguished.

[7] The Rhodesia and Nyasaland (Federation) Act 1953, section 1(1)(b) and (c) permitted

Constitution laid down that 'save as provided by or under this Constitution the legislative powers of the Legislature of any Territory shall continue in accordance with the constitution of that Territory'. The necessary implication is that legislative powers, to the extent that the Constitution otherwise provided, did not continue in accordance with the pre-existing Territorial constitutions.[1]

The provisions made by the Federal Constitution were that power to make laws 'to the exclusion of any power of the Legislature of a Territory' was conferred on the Federal Legislature when the Governor-General gave the requisite notice in terms of Article 29(2). The Article stated that Territorial 'power shall not cease . . . until such time as the Governor-General may by notice . . . prescribe'. Consequently if the Governor-General did so prescribe Territorial power would 'cease'.[2] This view is supported by Australian *dicta* on the effect of the Commonwealth Constitution on State legislative powers.[3] Furthermore there is no doubt that in the case of ordinary statutes where power in respect of the same subject is conferred by an earlier Act on one public body and by a later Act on another there is an inconsistency, and the powers conferred by the earlier Act are *pro tanto* repealed.[4] There seems no reason why this rule of construction should not be applied to conflicts of this nature between an Order in Council and earlier Letters Patent even though they may be constitutional instruments. If this view is correct the Southern Rhodesian Constitution was amended so that any powers made exclusive in terms of Article 29(2) which were previously exercisable by virtue of the amendment of the Letters Patent or Orders in Council relating to the government of the respective Territories while Section 14(1) of the Federation of Rhodesia and Nyasaland (Constitution) Order in Council 1953 provided that the Territorial constitutions were to have effect 'subject to the provisions of this Order'. (The Marginal Note reads: 'Amendment of Territorial Constitutions'.)

[1] Implied amendment of constitutions is permissible: *Krause* v. *C.I.R.*, 1929 A.D. 286 per Wessels J.A. and *McCawley* v. *The King*, [1920] A.C. 691.

[2] The same word is used in Article 35(4) which states that Territorial laws enacted 'before the date when that matter *ceased* to be within the legislative competence of that Legislature' should continue in effect until amended by the Federal Legislature. Reference is also made to the 'exclusive' competence of the Federal Legislature in Articles 29(2) and 35(4), to laws 'not within the competence' of a Legislature in Article 29(5), and to the fact that such laws 'shall be void' in Articles 29(5) and 35(1).

[3] See *D'Emden* v. *Pedder* (1904), 1 C.L.R. 91 per Griffith C.J. at 111: 'As from the point at which the quality of exclusiveness attaches to the Federal power the competency of the State is altogether extinguished.' *Pirrie* v. *Macfarlane* (1925), 36 C.L.R. 170 at 191–2 per Isaacs J.: 'Where, however, a power such as defence or customs is "expressly" by sections 106 and 107 *eliminated from* State Constitutions because made exclusive by section 52, its control is necessarily by force of the very words of the Constitution placed outside the ambit of the State Constitution and beyond any power of the State to affect.' (Italics and underlining by the Court.) See also *Amalgamated Society of Engineers* v. *Adelaide Steamship Co. Ltd.* (1920), 28 C.L.R. 129 at 154 per Knox C.J., Isaacs, Rich, and Starke JJ.: 'it is a fundamental and fatal error to read section 107 as reserving any power from the Commonwealth that falls fairly within the explicit terms of an express grant in Section 51, as that grant is reasonably construed, unless that reservation is expressly stated'.

[4] *Daw* v. *Metropolitan Board* (1862), 31 L.J.C.P. 223 at 225 per Willes J.

conferment of powers for the peace, order, and good government of Southern Rhodesia under the Letters Patent were extinguished.[1]

This position, it is submitted, continued throughout the existence of the Federation and was not affected by the coming into force in 1962 of the Southern Rhodesia Constitution 1961. Although the 1961 Constitution conferred powers to legislate for the peace, order and good government of Southern Rhodesia on the Legislature,[2] such a grant would have to be construed in accordance with the Federal Constitution.[3] Indeed if the construction is adopted that the Southern Rhodesian Legislature was granted powers to legislate on exclusively Federal matters, the grant of these powers would have amounted to a partial repeal of Article 29(2) of the Federal Constitution, which, it is submitted, was not intended.[4]

Since many matters were placed within the exclusive competence of one or other Legislature provision for the voidness of laws enacted by the other Legislature were inserted. Just as Territorial laws trenching on the exclusively Federal field were void, so conversely was the Federal Legislature prohibited from making laws other than those enumerated in the Federal and

---

[1] There is however an alternative view that the Southern Rhodesian Constitution was not amended by the Federal Constitution, the grant of general legislative power to the Southern Rhodesian Legislative Assembly merely requiring to be 'read down' by reference to the Federal Constitution.

[2] Section 20(1). Power to legislate in respect of External Affairs would not be construed as being included in such a grant as Southern Rhodesia was still a dependency. Cp. de Smith, op. cit., pp. 57 and 59, who suggests that where a country is internally self-governing the Constitution should indicate expressly or by implication that general control over external relations is withheld from that government.

[3] S.I. 1961 No. 2314 Annex Section 117(1) sets out a rule of construction to this effect. The provision should also be considered in the light of section 14(2) of the Federation of Rhodesia and Nyasaland (Constitution) Order in Council 1953 which provides that amendments to Territorial Constitutions 'inconsistent' with the provisions of that Order are to the extent of such inconsistency to be void. By interpreting powers for 'peace, order, and good government' as excluding powers made exclusively Federal there would be no inconsistency between the Federal Constitution and the Southern Rhodesian Constitution 1961. In a federation powers for peace, order, and good government must be construed in accordance with any enumerated powers. Each law must be passed in relation to a granted subject and those affirming the validity of any law must show that 'the challenged law is truly one with respect to any enumerated subject matter': see *The Trustees and Executors and Agency Co. Ltd.* v. *The Federal Commissioner of Taxes* (1933), 49 C.L.R. 220 per Evatt J. at 236. This reasoning applies equally to Territorial legislation and a general grant of powers for peace, order, and good government to a Territorial Legislature would have to be construed in connection with the powers permitted to that Legislature in terms of the Federal Constitution.

[4] Particularly because the Southern Rhodesian Constitution 1961 was designed to complement the Federal Constitution and was constructed round it: viz. Sections 14(1)(i)(j), 43(1)(c), 49, 67(3), 68(2)(a), 70(3), 71(4)(5), 74, 76(b), 77(1)(a) and (2)(c)(e), 96(b)(i), 108(2)(a), 116(1), 117(1), and the Second Schedule Item 5(a). In any event when a Legislature has vested powers of a special character in one body for a particular purpose 'no subsequent statute in merely general terms giving powers which by their generality apply to the special powers conferred by the former Act, will override the special provisions thereby delegated to the particular body': *The London & Blackwall Railway Co.* v. *The Board of Works for the Limehouse District* (1856), 69 E.R. 1048 per Page Wood V.C. at 1050.

Concurrent Legislative Lists or laws authorized by other provisions in the Constitution.[1] The Federation was in fact specifically excluded from the industrial conciliation sphere and forbidden to legislate in connection with trade unions except in respect of its own employees.[2] Finally it was made quite clear that neither Legislature could act outside its sphere of competence by provision that any law made by either a Federal or Territorial Legislature that was not within the competence of that Legislature at the date of its making was declared to be void.[3]

Difficulties always arise in Federations as to the characterization of particular laws and whether any particular law falls within an enumerated head of power. The question was raised in *Mutasa and Others* v. *The Minister of Law*,[4] whether the Federal Prisons Act No. 9 of 1955 was entirely within the scope of Item 60 of the Concurrent List. The Court held that in interpreting the Constitution narrow and pedantic constructions were to be avoided, and when powers were conferred unless there were express indications to the contrary they were intended to be comprehensive.[5]

On another occasion the Federal Government were concerned to regulate the manufacture of goods within the country and considered that Item 10 did not give them this power. Accordingly the Territorial Legislatures were requested to pass legislation.[6]

A special limitation designed to preserve the Territorial constitutional provisions and Orders in Council dealing with African land rights was also inserted: powers of the Federal Legislature to make provision for the acquisition of African land were to be exercised in accordance with the special protective African land laws of the Territories.[7] However any provisions in

---

[1] Article 29(4).

[2] Article 30(1). Disputes in relation to the Federal Public Service were exclusively within Federal competence: Article 30(2).

[3] Article 29(5). The decision in *R.* v. *Christopoulos*, 1957 R. & N. 787 (S.R.) per Murray C.J. can only be justified on the basis that legislation under Item 10 of the Federal Legislative List was competent, even if the Governor-General had not in fact specified certain commodities thereunder, such specification relating either to the future or the past. It had been suggested that the legislation was *ultra vires* the Federal Legislative Assembly, as no Order had been made at the time legislation was enacted. The Court stated this argument and then without any adequate reasons rejected it.

[4] 1959 R. & N. 251.

[5] At p. 255 per Tredgold F.C.J. Clayden F.J. also adopted the same view. The result was that persons who had committed no offences and had been preventively detained under Territorial laws could be held in Federal prisons which were considered to be prisons generally and not merely 'prisons . . . for the treatment . . . of offenders against any law'. This was not a construction in favour of liberty. The Territorial Governments would, had another construction been adopted, have had to make legislative provision for persons who had not offended against any law and they would have suffered considerable inconvenience.

[6] *S.R.L.A.D.*, Vol. 39, col. 1076. The Southern Rhodesian Legislature passed the Standardization of Soap Act 1957 in accordance with this request.

[7] viz. the provisions in the Southern Rhodesia Constitution Letters Patent 1923, the Land Apportionment Act 1941 and the relative Orders in Council in Northern Rhodesia

such a law for the purpose of settling immigrants on African land was to be of no effect.[1] Barotseland was particularly protected as no alienation in the area reserved from prospecting might be made without the consent of the Chief of the Barotse and the approval of the Secretary of State.[2]

Since Territorial legislative powers continued in terms of Article 29(4) all residual powers were reserved to the Territories. The major powers thus reserved were constitutional and electoral change in the Territorial sphere, legislation and control over Territorial civil services, taxation other than income tax, sales tax, customs and excise duties,[3] the maintenance of law and order, Territorial police forces, administration of justice in Territorial courts, labour matters including industrial conciliation,[4] factories, work-men's compensation, housing, rent control, social welfare and relief services, liquor legislation, betting, lotteries and pools, African affairs generally, in-cluding African primary and secondary but not technical and higher educa-tion, African agriculture,[5] land laws, mines and minerals, the conservation of natural resources, forestry, water conservation, irrigation, non-major irri-gation schemes, game preservation, game reserves, and fishing rights.

Except for these residual Territorial powers, a vast sphere of operation was permitted to the Federal Government and Legislature. In fact during Federa-tion most of the concurrent field was covered by Federal legislative and administrative action. Indeed in respect of sixteen of thirty-one matters enumerated in the Concurrent List Southern Rhodesia was by 1963 no longer administratively active, while in respect of five further matters she was barely active, whereas the Federal Government was administratively active in all but five matters on the Concurrent List and had entirely taken over the sixteen fields in which Southern Rhodesia was not active. Similarly, in respect of seventeen of the matters specified in the Concurrent List Southern Rhodesia

and Nyasaland. Federal public purposes were now to be included as grounds for transfer of such land.

[1] Article 33(1).

[2] Article 33(2). In addition all rights reserved to Africans under the Lewanika Concession were to continue in full force and effect, the rights thus being incorporated into the Federal Constitution and further recognized.

[3] But in these cases including powers relative to motor spirit in respect of which the Federal Legislature had no competence. Motor spirit was in Southern Rhodesia an im-portant source of taxation. By the end of Federation 2s. per gallon excise duty was levied. Death duties, transfer duties, stamp duties, licence fees, personal tax and poll taxes, etc., were Territorial taxes.

[4] Article 30(1). Disputes in relation to the Federal Public Service were exclusively within Federal competence: Article 30(2).

[5] In Nyasaland non-African agriculture was also Territorial, while African agriculture in Southern Rhodesia was to be designated by Order of the Governor-General and Governor of Southern Rhodesia and such Order could not subsequently be varied or revoked. See Part III D of the Second Schedule to the Federal Constitution. The African Agriculture Designation Order was issued in S.R. Government Notice 292/54. Until this was issued the Federal Government had no legislative power in respect of European agriculture in Southern Rhodesia: Second Schedule, Part III B.

passed no legislation after the creation of Federation, whereas in respect of twenty-four of the thirty-one matters the Federal Government legislated.[1]

In respect of the potentially exclusive sphere, Southern Rhodesia at no time either legislated or acted administratively although in respect of the construction and maintenance of international roads she exercised power on an agency basis on behalf of the Federal Government. In 1961, however, the Southern Rhodesian Government, which was being hindered in its development programme by inadequate revenues, suggested imposing a Territorial income tax. The Federal Government then promptly made income tax, and customs duties and excise exclusively Federal.[2]

Not only did the Southern Rhodesian Legislature and Executive lose power as a result of the creation of Federation but the Legislature virtually debarred itself from debating topics which were Federal matters. In 1955 the Speaker adopted the rule applied in the United Kingdom in regard to debates in the Commons and Lords, that allusions to debates in the other House are out of order, the justification being that the rule prevents fruitless arguments between members of two distinct bodies unable to reply to each other, and also because such debates were supposed to be not known and therefore not capable of being noticed. Members of the Southern Rhodesian Legislative Assembly were therefore prohibited from quoting from or alluding to Federal debates.[3] This rule became so rigid that in 1959 a motion was moved that the restrictions on the scope of debate permitted in the Territorial House should be reconsidered. The Government then adopted the attitude that such matters could be discussed, but not criticized in detail if their administration was a Federal responsibility.[4] No vote was taken but in practice from that date the Speaker permitted greater latitude.

Delegations of legislative power

Just as there were special provisions for the delegation of executive power, so there was provision for the delegation by Federal and Territorial Legislatures to each other of powers within their respective competence. Some of these provisions applied to all while others applied only to certain Territories. Thus in view of the exclusion of non-African agriculture, animal health and plant pests in the Northern Territories from Federal competence, the Legislatures of these Territories were empowered by the Federal Constitution to pass

[1] See generally Appendix Table I outlining the legislative and administrative position as at the end of 1963. Unitary forces were so marked at the commencement of Federation that the Southern Rhodesian Minister of Roads and Immigration announced in 1954: 'We are going to work ourselves out of a job': *S.R.L.A.D.*, Vol. 35, col. 93. Dvorin in *Emergent Federalism in Central Africa* at p. 75 estimates that 60 per cent of the Territorial services were handed over to the Federal Government.

[2] S.R.G.N. 345/1961.

[3] *S.R.L.A.D.*, Vol. 37, col. 3025, 5 June 1955.

[4] *S.R.L.A.D.*, Vol. 42, cols. 2171 and 2188, 4 March 1959.

laws conferring concurrent legislative power in respect of these matters on the Federal Legislature. Once transferred, such powers could not be diminished.[1] Only Northern Rhodesia, however, acted in terms of this Article.[2]

In respect of residual matters Territorial Legislatures might confer upon the Federation, subject to their Constitutions, i.e. their own powers of constitutional amendment, powers for specified purposes. The unitary principle could here be seen, since such powers could be utilized to create or regulate any authority 'to exercise functions in respect of more than one Territory'. For narrower purposes powers might be conferred for establishing and regulating schools for special categories of pupils, for tsetse control and necessary tsetse control services, and for transferring any specified powers for the purpose of a matter included in either Legislative List.[3]

The Federal Legislature was less limited in its power of conferring legislative power on Territorial Legislatures as it might confer power in respect of any matter on the Federal Legislative List. Delegations by either Federal or Territorial Legislatures might be general, limited, or subject to conditions, and were subject to revocation by any subsequent law of the conferring Legislature, such law however only taking effect six months after its enactment. While such delegated powers were in existence the relevant matters were deemed to be included in the Concurrent List.[4] The only Federal delegation in fact occurred at a time when it was already clear that the Federation would be dissolved: the Taxes (Authorization) Act No. 12 of 1963 which permitted the Territorial Legislatures to make laws providing for taxes on sales of goods and duties of excise on opaque beer.

The 'federal principle' again manifested itself in provisions safeguarding the Territories against legislation affecting them mainly by virtue of Federal power to implement treaties and international obligations, such legislation not otherwise being within Federal legislative competence. No law of such a nature could have effect in any Territory until such time as the Governor thereof declared by notice in the Gazette that the law should come into force.[5] Under these provisions by 1963 two Acts had been brought into force in Southern Rhodesia, and fifteen Orders thereunder, relating to immunities and privileges of Commonwealth and foreign diplomats, had been issued.

Provisions relating to conflict between Federal and Territorial laws were also inserted, the principle being that wherever the Federal Legislature was competent, whether in terms of the Legislative Lists or as the result of the delegation of legislative power for the time being by a Territory, Federal law

---

[1] Article 31.

[2] Non-African Agriculture (Transfer to Concurrent List) Ordinance 1955.

[3] Article 32(2). Acting under this Article the three Legislatures conferred authority on the Federal Legislature to create a National Art Gallery and to make provision for the furthering of fine and applied arts generally. See Art Gallery (Authorization) Act 1957 of Southern Rhodesia followed by the Federal Rhodes National Gallery Act No. 3 of 1958.

[4] Article 32(1)(3)(4).   [5] Article 34.

should prevail over Territorial law, which should to the extent of any inconsistency be void. Laws enacted at a time when any Legislature was competent should continue in force until such time as they were repealed by the Legislature having competence at that later time.[1]

In relation to Federal legislative power, it must be remembered that all laws passed by the Federal Legislature were within twelve months of their assent subject to disallowance by the Secretary of State.[2] Although such power was never invoked, it was accepted as being fully operative should it ever have been required.[3]

In addition, quite apart from the powers of the British Parliament to legislate for the Federation, the Crown retained power to legislate by Order in Council in terms of any United Kingdom Act conferring power on Her Majesty.[4] Thus Orders under the Foreign Jurisdiction Acts or any other enabling Acts could still be issued and might override Federal laws.

Constitutional amendment

The Federal Legislature was empowered to amend any of the provisions of the Constitution.[5] There were however two types of amendment outside Federal competence. Article 1 of the Constitution stated that the Federation should consist of Southern Rhodesia, Northern Rhodesia, and Nyasaland,[6] but similar provision was made in Section 1(1) of the Federation of Rhodesia and Nyasaland (Constitution) Order in Council. Although revision of Article 1 was within Federal competence, such amendment could not, because of the Colonial Laws Validity Act, conflict with Section 1(1) of the Order in Council. In these circumstances both Federal dissolution and provision for the secession of any Territory were outside Federal legislative competence.[7]

The Federal Legislature was, however, specially empowered to add to the constitutional machinery a second chamber, to prescribe its functions, and to make any consequential amendments.[8]

The amending procedure required that all constitutional Bills be passed at the third reading by not less than two-thirds of the Members of the Assembly. Thereafter such a Bill was to be reserved by the Governor-General for the Royal assent given in the normal way through a Secretary of State. Even so, such assent might not be given until sixty-five days after the passage of the

---

[1] Article 35.   [2] Article 25.

[3] The Monckton Commission commented on the 'twelve-month period of uncertainty' as to whether any Bill will be disallowed: Cmnd. 1148, para. 333.

[4] Article 29(7).   [5] Article 97(1).

[6] This provision led to the decision by the Monckton Commission that secession was a subject for consideration at any Review Conference on the Federation: Cmnd. 1148, para. 288(f).

[7] This attitude was adopted in 1962 by the British Government: see *H.L. Deb.*, Vol. 245, cols. 1218 et seq., Lord Dilhorne L.C.

[8] Article 97(5).

Bill unless the Legislatures of all three Territories passed resolutions that they did not object to the Bill.[1] If either any Territory by resolution objected to such a Bill within sixty days of its passing or the African Affairs Board requested that the Bill be reserved as a differentiating measure, then the Crown could only assent to the measure by Order in Council. A draft Order assenting to any such Bill was to lie before both Houses of Parliament in the United Kingdom for a period of forty days and might only then be presented to Her Majesty, provided that no resolution was passed by either House requesting that the draft be not submitted.[2] Although the African Affairs Board objected to the Constitution (Amendment) Act No. 16 of 1957, no Territorial Legislature objected to any of the three constitutional amending Bills which were enacted. This is explicable on the basis that the Southern Rhodesia Legislature was controlled by what was in reality the same political party as that which controlled the Federal Government, whereas while the Colonial Office through the use of its nominated members could have passed such resolutions in the two Northern Legislative Councils, the United Kingdom Government of the time instructed its officials against making such a move.

Amendments which would alter either the legislative competence of the Federal Legislature, the section providing for a review of the Constitution within seven to nine years of the establishment of the Federation, or that imposing the restriction in question, required not only a two-thirds majority but for the first ten years of the coming into force of the Federal Constitution resolutions by each Territorial Legislature that they did not object to the introduction of such a Bill in the Federal Assembly.[3] This provision could have been effectively utilized to prevent the amendment of Item 40 of the Federal Legislative List in 1959.[4] During the existence of the Federation no other amendment in respect of the allocation of powers was made. The value of the provision was, however, in its negative and deterrent aspects, rather than in its actual use.[5]

The United Kingdom made it clear that the whole Constitution was subject to review within seven to nine years of its coming into force, by a Conference consisting of delegations chosen by the respective Governments, namely, the Federal Government, the United Kingdom Government, and the three Territorial Governments.[6] Although the Constitution contained no

---

[1] Article 97(1) and (4).   [2] Article 97(2)(3).   [3] Article 98.

[4] Act No. 27, 1959. The amendment was not constitutionally significant. According to the original Item 40, the Federal Legislature could only legislate in respect of professional qualifications. As amended it could legislate generally with respect to any professions, provided, however, the Governor of any Territory consented.

[5] In the early years of Federation nominated members of the Colonial Office predominated in the Legislative Councils of the two Northern Territories, although from 1959 in Northern Rhodesia there was a majority of elected members. By the end of Federation African majorities controlled both the Northern Legislatures.

[6] Article 99. As de Smith, op. cit., p. 42, comments, this makes it clear that the United Kingdom Government 'would play an active part in the shaping of a new Constitution for the Federation if and when the occasion arose'.

limitations on the scope of such Review Conference, the Federal Government subsequently adopted the attitude that no changes could be made in the Federal Constitution as a result of such Conference without Federal Government consent. This was based on the announcement in 1957 of a convention that the United Kingdom Government would not initiate legislation on matters within the competence of the Federal Legislature without a prior request by the Federal Government.[1] Quite apart from the convention the Federal Constitution could not be revoked by Order in Council, although express saving (unnecessary in fact) was made of the United Kingdom Parliament's right to amend or revoke the Constitution at any time.[2]

Public finance and the Constitution

The difficult problem of allocating financial resources so as to secure the independence of the Territories and of the Federal Government was met by detailed provisions in the Constitution.[3]

Assets and liabilities originally belonging to the Territories were to be examined by an Apportionment Commission consisting of a chairman appointed by the Governor-General with the approval of the three Territorial Governors, and five other members, two of whom would be appointed by the Governor-General, while the other three would be appointed one by each Territory.[4] The Commission would designate assets and liabilities, excluding the outstanding public debts of the Territories, for transfer to the Federal Government and these would then be transferred to the Federation in accordance with directions and regulations made by the Governor-General. The Apportionment Commission would, subject to certain minimum sums, also determine the proportions of the outstanding Territorial public debts which ought to be transferred to the Federation in view of its taking transfer of Territorial assets and the need to see that no Territory was left with an excessive volume of debt in relation to its remaining assets and revenues. Regard was also to be had to the need for interest and amortization charges.[5] Appointed in September 1953, by the end of June 1954 the Commission had completed its work and made detailed recommendations on the basis of the functions assumed by the Federal Government.[6] The sums apportioned to the

[1] See infra.   [2] Rhodesia and Nyasaland (Federation) Act, Section 1(2).
[3] See generally, K. C. Wheare, Federal Government, op. cit., Chapter 6; A. H. Birch, Federation, Finance and Social Legislation in Canada, Australia and the United States of America, Oxford, 1955; A. H. Birch in Federalism in Undeveloped Countries, op. cit., at p. 113, and U. K. Hicks, Development from Below: Local Government and Finance in Developing Countries in the Commonwealth, Oxford, 1961.
[4] S.I. 1955, No. 1199, Sections 3 and 4.
[5] Section 5.
[6] Report of the Apportionment Commission, Government Printer, Salisbury, 1954. C. Fed. 6 and also C. Fed. 6 (Appendices). £87,604,109 of Southern Rhodesia's public debt was transferred to the Federal Government, whereas £20,373,415 and £6,228,488 of the

Federation in respect of the Territorial public debts were charged on the Consolidated Revenue Fund of the Federation.[1]

Revenues and monies received by the Federation were to form a Consolidated Revenue Fund from which no money might be withdrawn except by appropriation made by a Federal law.[2] An Auditor-General of the Federation was to be appointed who could only be removed by the Governor-General on an Address from the Federal Assembly praying for his removal on the ground of misbehaviour or of infirmity of body or mind. During his period of office his salary might not be reduced while he would retire at the normal retiring age for civil servants. The duties of the Auditor-General were laid down in the Audit and Exchequer Act 1954—audit of and enquiry into the accounts of all public officers and duties of reporting on deficiencies to the Ministry of Finance. He was also given considerable powers of enquiry, access to records, &c., in the possession of any Federal official and the right to surcharge.[3] The Federal Auditor-General could also be entrusted with the same functions of auditing Territorial public accounts by the Governor of any Territory with the consent of the Governor-General. This was done by Southern Rhodesia and Nyasaland.[4]

Although the Federal Legislature was given potentially exclusive power to legislate in respect of taxes on income and profits, and on the sale of goods (other than motor spirit) and to impose duties of customs and excise including export duties (subject to the like restriction in regard to motor spirit) the Federation did not retain all these funds for its sole use. Based on the investigations of the 1953 Fiscal Commission, provision was made that taxes on income and profits and export duties were to be allocated on a fixed basis: 64 per cent to the Federation, 13 per cent to Southern Rhodesia, 17 per cent to Northern Rhodesia, and 6 per cent to Nyasaland.[5] Although the Federa-

---

Northern Rhodesian and Nyasaland public debts respectively were transferred. The Southern Rhodesian amount was so much greater than the other amounts because it represented heavy expenditure on railways, electricity undertakings, and heavily capitalized agricultural statutory commissions which were transferred. These however were largely self-remunerative.

[1] Article 93.

[2] Article 78. The Federal Legislature might also provide for making sums available for unforseen expenditure or to cover a period of up to four months before the coming into force of the next Appropriation Act. This was done by the Audit and Exchequer Act No. 9 of 1954 limiting the period to three months, the monies to be used for purposes authorized in the preceding financial year and the total not to exceed half a million pounds.

[3] Though no express provision to this effect was contained in the Constitution, the mechanisms of parliamentary control of finance in the United Kingdom were to a large measure adopted. Expenditure was considered in Committee of Supply and taxation by the Committee of Ways and Means. A Select Committee on Public Accounts using the Auditor General's annual report as the basis for its investigations was also appointed each session. On the other hand, there was no Select Committee on Estimates and there were lengthy debates on individual Loan and Revenue Votes in Committee of the whole House.

[4] S.R.G.N. 308/54, Nyasaland G.N. 78/54.

[5] Articles 80 and 83. Transitional provision was made for allocation by the Governor-

tion collected these taxes, the respective proportions were to be paid out of the Federal Consolidated Revenue Fund to the Governors of the respective Territories. All the proceeds of customs and excise duties and fees levied by the Federal Government for services were however retained by the Federation.

During wartime or a state of emergency proclaimed by the Governor-General with the consent of the three Territorial Governors, the Federal Legislature was empowered to levy an emergency tax on income or profits or both. In these circumstances the proceeds could all be retained by the Federation.

The Territories as indicated earlier, enjoyed residual powers of taxation.[1] They were also empowered by law of their Legislatures to authorize the Federal Governments to levy and collect a Territorial surcharge on income and profits up to a percentage not exceeding 20 per cent of the basic tax payable under Federal income tax laws by individuals resident in the Territory, while in the case of a resident body corporate the levy might be at the rate of one-fifth of the basic tax on all profits liable to such basic tax.[2] The Federal Legislature was empowered to provide by law for the levying and collecting of Territorial surcharge on behalf of any Territory that had provided for it. The Territorial Surcharges Act No. 23 of 1954 was accordingly enacted, making provision for determining the place of residence of individuals and bodies corporate.[3] The proceeds of any Territorial surcharge were handed over to the Governor of the relevant Territory. Southern Rhodesia, from the beginning of Federation, made full use of her powers of imposing a Territorial surcharge, whereas such powers were only utilized by Northern Rhodesia in the last years of Federation.

In addition the Territories were entitled, should any sales tax be imposed on goods by Federal law, to an aggregate proportion of not less than two-thirds of the proceeds, the allocation between the Territories to be prescribed by the Federal law.[4] The Federation itself did not make use of this provision, but in 1963 in terms of Article 32(1) of the Constitution passed the Taxes (Authorization) Act,[5] which authorized the Territorial Legislatures to provide for sales taxes and duties of excise on opaque beer. This the Southern Rhodesian Legislature did by the Sales Tax Act.[6]

General, after consultation with the Territorial Governors of sums raised by such taxes under Territorial laws before the enactment of Federal laws: Article 85.

[1] They could impose duties on motor spirit, personal tax, poll tax, stamp duties, transfer duties, death duties, dog tax, licence fees, etc.

[2] Article 82.

[3] In *Commissioner of Taxes* v. *John Howard and Company (Africa) Ltd.*, 1959 R. & N. 151, it was held that Section 6(5) of this Act which prohibited the body corporate from deducting losses incurred in one Territory from its taxable income accrued from sources in another Territory was *ultra vires* Article 82.

[4] Article 84.   [5] No. 12 of 1963.

[6] No. 43 of 1963. It also provided for a tax on the hire of goods by virtue of Southern Rhodesia's residuary taxing power.

External borrowing (except in respect of monies advanced by Her Majesty's Government in the United Kingdom) by the Federation and the Territories was to be co-ordinated and rationalized. A Loan Council, consisting of a Federal Minister nominated by the Governor-General and a representative of each Territorial Government nominated by the respective Governors was established.[1] The Loan Council was to consider the external loan programme of each Government including its statutory corporations, which programmes were to be formulated after consultation with the other Governments. The Council was empowered by unanimous decision either to approve the programmes suggested or to approve a smaller aggregate amount, taking into account the economic interests of the Federation and the Territories. If a smaller aggregate amount were approved, the allocation between the Governments could either be made by unanimous agreement, or failing this, in the same specified proportions applied in the case of revenue from income tax.[2] The raising of external loans (except in the event of special loan provisions essential in a state of Federal emergency, which provisions did not require approval by the Loan Council) either without the approval of the Council or in excess of the amount allocated was prohibited.[3]

Although similar provision was not made in respect of internal loans, in accordance with the injunction to the Governments to consult together in matters of common concern, the four Governments in practice agreed upon the regulation and allocation of internal loans.[4]

Finally in view of possible changes in relative needs of the Governments the Constitution provided that further Fiscal Commissions should be appointed from time to time. The first was to be appointed not less than three nor more than four years after the coming into force of the Constitution and thereafter at periods not in excess of five years, except by unanimous agreement of the Governor-General and the Territorial Governors. Such Commissions would after consultation between the Governor-General and the Governors be appointed to consider whether the allocations in respect of taxes on income and profits, export duties, and external loans were satisfactory. The Constitution, however, merely provided that the Commission's report should be laid before the Federal Assembly and not for its automatic implementation.[5] In 1957 (the Southern Rhodesian Government had been pressing for its appointment in 1956[6]) a Fiscal Commission was appointed in terms of this section,[7] and after its report the Federal Assembly passed the Constitution Amendment Act No. 13 of 1958 which altered the shares of income tax and export duties,[8] with effect from 1 July 1957.[9] At the same

---

[1] Article 88. The Federal Minister was to have a casting vote.   [2] Articles 89 and 90.
[3] Articles 91 and 92. If emergency loans were raised Federally, the Loan Council was to be informed and might take that amount into account in agreeing to the loan programme.
[4] See Article 42(2) and Cmnd. 1449, p. 144.   [5] Article 96.
[6] S.R.L.A.D., Vol. 39(3), Speech from the Throne, 4 July 1956.
[7] F.G.N. 11/57. Report C. Fed. 56.
[8] Never in practice imposed.
[9] See Articles 80 and 83 as amended. Southern Rhodesia's share was increased from 13

time the Federal share of external borrowings was decreased and the Southern Rhodesian proportion increased, while the share of the Northern Territories remained stationary.[1]

Apart from provisions dealing with allocation of resources, further provisions were inserted to deal with the particular problems of a federation. Thus the Governor-General was empowered by proclamation in the Territorial Gazettes to prohibit the imposition of Territorial taxes which would have the effect of restricting the freedom of goods between Territories.[2] In addition, since the Territories might need the credit-worthiness of the larger unit as a prop in raising loans, the Federal Legislature was empowered to authorize the Federal Government to guarantee any Territorial loans, and also to give financial assistance to any Territory on such terms and conditions as the enabling Act might prescribe.[3]

The difficulties of deciding whether the doctrine of 'the immunity of instrumentalities' applied in the Federation were also avoided in respect of taxing powers enjoyed by the Federation and Territories. All the Governments could expressly impose taxes with respect to the property or monies of any of the other Governments within their respective jurisdictions.[4] Subsequently the doctrine was in general rejected by the Federal Supreme Court, when it held that legislation could bind the Crown in respect of the Federation and *vice versa*: all statutes were to be construed on ordinary principles, and the Crown would be bound either if express provision was made or such an implication was necessarily intended.[5]

Despite the precise constitutional provisions for public finance they can be criticized because of their effect on the economic development of the Territories: the allocation of funds as between Federation and Territories placed the major sources of wealth and the lion's share thereof in Federal hands, whereas the main needs for development funds were in spheres administered

to 14 per cent, Northern Rhodesia's from 17 to 18 per cent, Nyasaland's remained stationary, and the Federal share was reduced from 64 to 62 per cent.

[1] Article 90(3)(a) and (b) as amended. Southern Rhodesia's proportion increased from 13 to 16 per cent while the Federal proportion was reduced from 64 to 61 per cent.

[2] Article 86. Such a law would be void unless it related to motor spirit.

[3] Articles 94 and 95. These Articles were discussed in a Southern Rhodesian debate in 1955 when it was maintained that the allocation by the original Fiscal Commission had been so inadequate that Southern Rhodesia's independence was being threatened. It was suggested that the Federal Supreme Court should decide disputes on this matter in terms of Article 53(a) of the Constitution. However, the Minister of the Treasury rejected the proposals, reverting to the Government's suggestion of an Economic Council and possibly an early review: *S.R.L.A.D.*, Vol. 37, cols. 817 et seq.

[4] Article 87. But monies did not include the proceeds of any tax.

[5] *Attorney-General for Southern Rhodesia* v. *Jones*, 1962 R. & N. 187 per Clayden F.C.J. distinguishing the Australian and Canadian cases. Briggs F.J. at 200 concurred, reserving his views on the position where legislation imposed penalties on the Crown itself as opposed to Crown servants. In this case a Federal civil servant acting within the scope of his employment was found guilty of breaching the Southern Rhodesian Roads and Roads Traffic Act.

by the Territories. If Federation was to succeed, vast sums required spending on African advancement, African education and industrial training, African agriculture, water development in African areas, African housing in the developing urban centres, and on social welfare measures. These sums were not available to the Territories, and Southern Rhodesia in particular was short of funds even though she used her residuary powers of taxation far more extensively than Northern Rhodesia and Nyasaland.[1]

The African Affairs Board

As indicated earlier, an institutional safeguard to preclude racial discrimination against Africans, the African Affairs Board, was created. The Board was to be a Standing Committee of the Federal Assembly.[2] Since the Board was composed of Federal parliamentarians its members could utilize the forum of the Assembly to voice their views publicly. This was perhaps an advantage over the earlier proposals that the Board should be outside the Assembly. However, mere ability to voice opposition in a public forum would be of little value in the face of a large parliamentary majority holding different views.

The Board was composed of three African Members and the three European Members of the Assembly representing African interests, viz. the two specially appointed members from Northern Rhodesia and Nyasaland, and the specially elected member from Southern Rhodesia, the latter in practice being a member of the governing United Federal Party and being, as indicated above, elected by the predominantly European electorate of Southern Rhodesia. The African Board members, one from each Territory, were elected by majority vote of the six specially elected African members and the three European members charged with special responsibility for African interests. From these six members of the Board the Governor-General was in his discretion to appoint a chairman and a deputy chairman.[3] The chairman[4] was

---

[1] From 1958 Southern Rhodesia adopted the principle of deficit budgeting essential in an underdeveloped territory. This was done, however, not because of economic theories but because without such provision Southern Rhodesia could not have maintained the standard of services she had done in the past in addition to her large commitments for police forces.

[2] Article 67(1). It might even act while the Assembly stood adjourned or prorogued, while in the event of a dissolution the members of the Board were to continue sitting and acting until the first meeting of the new Assembly: Article 69. The Standing Orders of the Federal Assembly (S.O. 193 and 197) provided that except as otherwise provided in the Federal Constitution the Board should be treated as a Select Committee and should therefore make a report on its work each session to the Assembly.

[3] Article 67.

[4] The chairmen were Dr. J. F. Haslam, 3 February 1954 to 20 December 1954 (Northern Rhodesian nominated European who resigned owing to ill health), Rev. P. Ibbotson to 3 April 1955 (Southern Rhodesian elected European who died in office), Sir John Moffat to April 1959 (Northern Rhodesian nominated European), Mr. J. L. Pretorius,

entitled to a casting vote as well as his deliberative vote, the casting vote to be exercised so as to enable further deliberation to be given to the matter.[1] Decisions of the Board were in fact sometimes taken by a majority vote.[2] The effect of these provisions and the composition of the electorates was that the first African Affairs Board contained four independent members from the Northern Territories, and two members of the United Federal Party from Southern Rhodesia.

Functions of the Board

The Board was to make to the Prime Minister, or through him to the Executive Council, any representations it considered desirable in the interests of Africans in relation to matters within Federal legislative and executive competence. On a request by a Territorial Government it would also assist such Government in the study of matters affecting Africans and in the exchange of information relating to such matters.[3]

Unfortunately soon after its creation the Board adopted a self-denying principle that it would not make representations on behalf of individuals. It reported that its 'functions do not include enquiries into the complaints of individuals with a view to representations being made on their behalf as individuals unless such complaints have wider implications'.[4] However it did consider many matters. Amongst those considered by the first Board and in respect of which certain representations were made, were requests to the Government to modify its policy so as to establish African cadet units, on treatment of prisoners, equal facilities for Africans in railway dining cars and restaurants, and in Government institutions, especially Post Offices,[5] higher and technical education for Africans with special reference to the training of African nurses and nursing orderlies, defence conditions of service, Federal conditions of service for African civil servants and those with professional qualifications, and university facilities for Federal Africans in South Africa.[6] Continuous representations were made in respect of Federal conditions of service for African civil servants and those with professional qualifications. The same action was taken in respect of higher and technical education.[7] However it cannot be said that the representations on many of these

appointed on 6 April 1959, who resigned early in 1961 (Nyasaland nominated European), and Mr. H. E. Davies, appointed on 9 February 1962 until the Federal dissolution (Southern Rhodesian elected European).

[1] Article 68(3). This was inserted at the United Kingdom's request so that if the Board was evenly divided reservation would occur: *S.R.L.A.D.*, Vol. 34, col. 1612.

[2] The Board was not unanimous in reaching decisions: *Fed. Parlty. Deb.*, col. 2083, 29 July 1959. A United Federal Party member dissented in respect of the Board's reports on the Federal Constitution Amendment Bill (Fed. A. 18) and the Electoral Bill (Fed. A. 23).

[3] Article 70. Its reports do not indicate that this latter provision was ever utilized.

[4] Report of the Board for the First Session of the First Parliament, 2 June 1955. Fed. A. 1; see also Fed. A. 6.

[5] Fed. A. 6, 1955–6 Report.   [6] Fed. A. 17, 1956–7 Report.

[7] Fed. A. 25, 1957–8 Report. Fed. A. 30, 1958–9 Report.

matters were successful as it was evident that Government not only resented the existence of the Board [1] but was also antagonistic to members of the Board who had been outspoken against Government action. [2]

The Board was reconstituted in 1959. Reports of its work indicate that few representations were made by the new Board. Nonetheless, after these changes in the composition of the Board, when Mr. J. L. Pretorius became chairman and established good relations with the Federal Prime Minister, a great deal of good work was done on an informal level. [3] The Government continued to pay regard to representations, whether made formally or informally, by the succeeding chairman, Mr. H. E. Davies. [4] It is, however, submitted that, although the re-constituted Board was doing valuable work by making such informal representations, the fact that this had to be done informally in order to achieve results in a sense derogated from its status as an institutional safeguard, i.e. as long as it did not officially take action the Government was prepared to co-operate, but once the Board made a formal stand the Government became hostile.

The Board was also empowered to report within thirty days of its publication on any subordinate legislation made under any Federal law. If the Board within that period [5] reported to the Prime Minister giving reasons for its description of the measure as differentiating, the Prime Minister was, unless the Board should within the next thirty days have withdrawn its report, to send the report and his comments to the Governor-General for transmission to the Secretary of State. Within twelve months of the receipt of such a report the Secretary of State might disapprove of the measure in question and instruct the Governor-General to publish notice of his disapproval in the Federal Gazette, in which case the measure would be annulled as from the date of publication. [6]

The Board, acting under this Article, reported on the Defence (Regular Forces) (African Members) Regulations 1956, [7] which did not provide for promotion of Africans through the ranks to commissioned rank as did the parallel Regulations governing European regulars. However, after corres-

---

[1] See the attitude of the Minister of Law, *Fed. Parlty. Deb.*, col. 2085, 29 July 1959.

[2] See *Fed. Parlty. Deb.*, col. 1166, 1 July 1959, for an attack on Sir John Moffat.

[3] Although this was done on an informal basis, it was effective because the chairman could always place matters before the Board formally at a later stage. The Federal Prime Minister even invited the chairman of the Board to attend the 1960 Review Conference as a delegate. Personal communication from the Hon. Mr. Justice Davies.

[4] Personal communication from the Hon. Mr. Justice Davies.

[5] The Board considered the period too short to permit of proper scrutiny of all instruments and suggested that the Constitution be amended to allow a two months period for objections to be taken: Report 1955–6, Fed. A. 6.

[6] Article 77. In the Federation the procedure was subsequent disallowance after a report by the Board, whereas in Southern Rhodesia advance approval of discriminatory subordinate legislation had always to be obtained. If this was not done, the regulation or by-law was *ultra vires*. See *supra*.

[7] F.G.N. 79/56. For Board's action see Fed. A. 6 and Fed. A. 7.

pondence with the Prime Minister's Office, the report was withdrawn in the light of an assurance that it was the Federal Government's intention to promote Africans as and when suitable material became available.[1] Subsequently, as a result of these discussions, certain amendments were made to the Regulations in question.[2]

The Board's most important deterrent function, however, was that it was to draw the attention of the Federal Assembly to any Bill which was in its opinion a differentiating measure and to have power to cause such Bill to be reserved.[3] A differentiating measure was a Bill or instrument

by which Africans are subjected or made liable to any conditions, restrictions, or disabilities disadvantageous to them to which Europeans are not also subjected or made liable, or a Bill or instrument which will in its application have such an effect.[4]

The Board interpreted this section as having reference to 'discrimination' in the technical sense, as it only reported on measures which differentiated and were disadvantageous to Africans.[5] It also stated that it would only decide whether a measure was legally discriminatory but would not pronounce on the desirability of discrimination.[6]

If the Board did not cause a Bill to be reserved the Act could not, in contrast with discriminatory measures passed by the Southern Rhodesian Assembly, be tested in the courts. On the other hand, it was clear that the Board could take cognizance of the definite practical effect of measures whereas it was doubtful whether such measures in Southern Rhodesia required reservation. However the way in which a differentiating measure was defined precluded the Board from protesting if it was not clear that a Bill would differentiate as opposed to the possibility of differentiation. Nor could it object if non-Africans (Europeans, Asians, and Coloureds) were discriminated against. This latter position was made quite clear by the negative form in which the definition was couched. There was no question of declaring a Bill discriminatory if

[1] Lord Malvern's version of this incident is that the Regulations considerably improved existing conditions for African regulars, and that if the Board persisted with its objections to the measure he would have withdrawn the Regulations including all the benefits they conferred. This he told the Board. Personal communication from Lord Malvern.

[2] Report 1956–7, Fed. A. 17. In September 1964, although the regulations are now non-racial, the highest ranking African regular in the Southern Rhodesian army, which succeeded to the Federal army, was a Warrant Officer Class I: *S.R.L.A.D.*, Vol. 58, col. 404, 16 September 1964.

[3] Articles 74 and 75.

[4] Article 71(2).

[5] Cp. the Southern Rhodesian Constitution under which Bills required reservation if they merely differentiated.

[6] See Report of the Board on the Electoral Bill, Fed. A. 23 (also printed in Cmnd. 362). It has been submitted that discrimination may be desirable to remedy social and economic imbalance: see Y. P. Ghai, 'The Kenya Council of State and the African Affairs Board of the Central African Federation: an experiment in the protection of minorities' (1963), *I.C.L.Q.*, Vol. 12, p. 1089 at 1122–8.

it discriminated in favour of Africans.[1] On these grounds it could not be said that the Defence Act 1955, which provided for compulsory military training in the Territorial forces for European, Asian, and Coloured male persons but not for Africans, should have been reported on by the Board, which took no action against the Bill. Members explained that they considered the Board should only intervene where there was 'major' discrimination against Africans.[2] Nor did the Board take action against the Rhodesia and Nyasaland Cadet Corps Bill 1955, which made no provision for the training of African cadet corps. Instead it merely made representations.[3] On an earlier occasion, however, the Board had made representations to the responsible Minister that a Bill appeared to have a differentiating effect and the Minister thereupon agreed to amendment of the Bill.[4]

The manner in which the Board was to function was laid down in the Constitution. Before any Bill was introduced in the Federal Assembly a copy of the proposed Bill was to be sent to the Board. If however the Governor-General in his discretion certified in writing that the proposed Bill was of such a nature that in the public interest it should not be published before its introduction in the Assembly,[5] or that it was so urgent that it would not be in the public interest to delay its introduction, this provision could be overridden.[6] The purpose of giving the Board adequate time for consideration was to enable it to discuss clauses with the responsible Minister at an early stage so that it could be amended at Committee stage. The Board therefore attempted to consider all Bills before their second reading.[7]

At any stage during the passage of the Bill the Board might lay before the Assembly a report that the Bill was a differentiating measure and its reasons

---

[1] In the Southern Rhodesia Constitution 1961 these points have been clarified. Discrimination occurs where any race is granted privileges or advantages not granted to another racial group. See *infra*, Part II, Chapter 4.

[2] See Comment by R. A. Hasson and L. A. J. Armour in *Public Law*, Summer, 1960, at p. 142, that this was an 'unwarranted abdication of responsibility resulting from a narrow conception of what is "desirable in the interests of Africans"'.

[3] See the Report of the African Affairs Board, 26 June 1956, Fed. A. 6. The position still is that there are no cadet corps in African schools: see *S.R.L.A.D.*, Vol. 58, col. 405, 16 September 1964, where the Prime Minister, Mr. Smith, refused to introduce such training in the African schools on the grounds that money available for African education should not be diverted in order to instruct African cadets.

[4] Report of the African Affairs Board, 2 June 1955, Fed. A. 1.

[5] Clearly envisaging urgent financial measures or laws providing for emergency powers.

[6] Article 73. So far as is known the power was not used. It is noteworthy that the Governor-General was required to act in his discretion whereas under the Southern Rhodesia Constitution 1961 the Prime Minister of Southern Rhodesia certifies Bills as urgent thereby permitting a politician to avoid the delaying powers of the Constitutional Council.

[7] Report of the Standing Committee, African Affairs Board, First Session of the First Parliament, Fed. A. 1. This kept the Board very busy. In 1954–5 the Board met on 55 occasions, on 37 occasions in 1955–6, on 29 occasions in 1956–7, 26 occasions in 1957–8, 13 occasions in 1958–9, 16 occasions in 1959–60, 18 occasions in 1960–1, 6 occasions in 1961–2, and 8 occasions in 1962–3.

for this conclusion. Subsequently if the Board was satisfied that the objectionable provisions had been removed, a further report to that effect might be laid.[1] If when the Bill was finally passed the Board was still dissatisfied, it might in writing, stating its reasons and the fact of any dissentient views, present to the Federal Speaker a request that the Governor-General reserve the Bill.[2] In these circumstances the Governor-General was required to reserve the Bill, which was to be sent, together with the Board's request, to a Secretary of State.[3] If their request related to a constitutional Bill instead of assent being given in the normal way by communication by a Secretary of State, an Order in Council would be required.[4]

There is no doubt that the mere existence of the Board caused the Federal Government to exercise great care in the drafting of legislation, both principal and subsidiary.[5] However, the Board was also intended to reassure Africans that they would not be discriminated against and in this respect public action by the Board was necessary. The Board's ability or otherwise publicly to check discriminatory measures was put to the test by the Constitution Amendment Bill 1957 and the Electoral Bill 1957.[6] During the passage of both of these Bills the Board laid reports in terms of Article 97 before the House. However both Bills were passed without amendments to meet the Board's objections, and when the Secretary of State was forced to consider whether the Bills should be assented to or not, as a result of requests made by the Board for reservation in terms of Article 75(1), both Bills were assented to on his advice.[7] Although the Board was able to cause the measures to be reserved, this was the limit of its powers. The decision thus rested with the United Kingdom Government which, should it consider the 'merits of the measures outweighed any possible disadvantages',[8] could advise Her Majesty to assent. Thereafter the legislation could not be further questioned.

In the two cases in question prior to introduction of the measures and even

---

[1] Article 74.   [2] Article 75(1).

[3] Article 75(4) permitted the Governor-General in his discretion to assent to a Bill, either if he was satisfied that it was not a differentiating measure and the Board's reasons were irrelevant or frivolous, or if he was satisfied, after Prime Ministerial representations, that it was essential in the public interest that the Bill be immediately brought into operation. If the Governor-General assented by virtue of these provisions he was forthwith to send the Secretary of State the Bill, the Board's request and a statement of his reasons for assenting. Disallowance would then have been the course open to the Secretary of State, which makes it clear that the power of disallowance inserted in the Federal Constitution was to be used if the occasion arose.

[4] Article 97.

[5] Personal communication from the Hon. Mr. Justice Davies.

[6] F.B. 1 of 1957 and F.B. 21 of 1957.

[7] See Fed. A. 18, Report on the Constitution Amendment Bill and Fed. A. 21, A Communication from the Secretary of State for Commonwealth Relations on the Constitution Amendment Bill. See also Fed. A. 23 on the Electoral Bill and Fed. A. 24, A Communication from the Secretary of State for Commonwealth Relations on the Electoral Bill.

[8] The comment of the Federal Minister of Law on the United Kingdom Government's action in the two cases in question: *Fed. Parlty. Deb.*, cols. 2083–4, 29 July 1959.

before their preparation in Bill form, responsible British Ministers had committed the British Government to agreement on the proposals. On 8 January 1957 Mr. Lennox Boyd, the Colonial Secretary, agreed with Sir Roy Welensky that the Federal Assembly could be enlarged and the composition of the African Affairs Board altered. The agreement to permit enlargement of the Federal Assembly was publicly affirmed in a joint communique issued by the Prime Minister of the Federation and the Secretary of State for Commonwealth Relations in London in April 1957. In fact a 'package deal' had been arranged[1]: the Federal Government would introduce a Federal Citizenship Bill which would allow British Protected Persons to become Federal citizens; at the same time the Federal Assembly would be enlarged—the proportion of special representatives remaining the same; and a Federal Electoral Bill would also be introduced which would permit British Protected Persons to become voters.[2] In return for approval of these arrangements, the Federal Prime Minister agreed that his Government would abandon its former aim of ultimate amalgamation. Indeed, he considered that permitting British Protected Persons to acquire the Federal franchise, provided they satisfied the other qualifications, was a great concession by his Government. The net result was that considerable changes in the composition of the Federal Assembly were now agreed upon which would involve an increase in size and the creation of further special seats to be occupied by Africans, although the United Kingdom Government insisted that the existing specially elected African members in Northern Rhodesia and Nyasaland should be elected virtually on the old basis.[3] The African Affairs Board had not been consulted in respect of these measures.[4]

[1] This clearly emerges from Sir Roy Welensky's autobiography, *Welensky's 4,000 Days*, pp. 74–84. It had been agreed first between Welensky and Lennox Boyd, the Colonial Secretary, and subsequently with Lord Home, the Commonwealth Relations Secretary. See also Keesing's Contemporary Archives 1957–8, 13524, where Mr. Lennox Boyd is reported as having discussed franchise and citizenship changes with the Federal Government in January 1957. See also 15529 to 15530, where the British Government in April 1957 announced their agreement in principle to enlargement of the Federal Assembly and stated that franchise, citizenship and Assembly increase proposals had been discussed with the Territorial Governments and agreement reached on proposals for the increase in the Assembly.

[2] It must be remembered that although the British Government had control of the franchises in the two Northern Territories, they had not at that time extended it to British Protected Persons. In 1957 in Northern Rhodesia there were only eleven Africans on a common roll of approximately 20,000 voters. Only in 1959 were British Protected Persons allowed the vote: see the *Northern Rhodesian General Election 1962*, D. C. Mulford, Oxford, 1964.

[3] Franklin, op. cit., pp. 125 et seq. The only change made was that African voters would have a say in their election and the electoral regulations were accordingly changed to permit this.

[4] H. Franklin, op. cit., pp. 122 et seq. The author's informant was Sir John Moffat. The Federal Government never consulted the African Affairs Board in drafting Bills, but privately negotiated any Bills which might be questioned with the Commonwealth Relations Office before introduction. This was understandable in view of Sir Godfrey Huggins' long experience of Southern Rhodesia's reserved clauses and was probably the reason why

The Constitution Amendment Bill provided for an increase in the total size of the Assembly from 35 to 59 Members. Instead of 26 'elected members' there were now to be 44 'elected members', of whom 24 were to be elected by Southern Rhodesia, 14 by Northern Rhodesia, and 6 by Nyasaland. (The previous figures had been 14, 8, and 4 respectively.) In addition, there were now to be '8 elected African members', 4 coming from Southern Rhodesia, 2 from Northern Rhodesia, and 2 from Nyasaland,[1] while the '4 specially elected African members' (2 from Northern Rhodesia and 2 from Nyasaland) were retained. The three Europeans charged with special responsibility for African interests also remained.

In addition a 'fade-out' principle was introduced whereby whenever an African was elected as an 'elected member' thereafter at the next General Election the number of 'elected members' would be increased by one whereas the number of representatives for African interests would be correspondingly reduced, the reduction being first made from among the 'specially elected African members', and finally from specially elected European members in respect of the particular Territory.

The Federal franchise proposals were announced shortly thereafter so that a complete picture could be obtained. Apart from normal qualifications as to residence,[2] citizenship, or the status of a British Protected Person, and age, a combination of means and educational qualifications was required. Voters could become either general voters or special voters enrolled on two separate rolls, the general voting qualifications being much higher than the special voters' qualifications. The general voters in Southern Rhodesia were entitled to vote for an 'elected member', an 'elected African', and the Southern Rhodesian European member charged with special responsibility for African interests.[3] Special voting qualifications were lower, but special voters might only vote for an 'elected African member' and in the case of the Northern Territories participate in an electoral college system for the 'specially elected African members'. In Southern Rhodesia special voters

the practice arose. However, it defeated the whole purpose of the African Affairs Board if real agreement was reached beforehand. The Hon. Mr. Justice Davies has also confirmed that the Board was not consulted in the drafting of legislation: personal communication, 8 August 1964. See also Dvorin, op. cit., who declared, even before these measures, that the Federal Government had had frequent conversations with the United Kingdom Government on Bills but had refused to consult the African Affairs Board.

[1] The two specially elected African members previously elected by Southern Rhodesia were now designated as 'elected African members', see *infra*, and this explains the discrepancy.

[2] The period of residence required for candidates was specified as five years, so that large numbers of European immigrants who arrived after the creation of the Federation were not eligible until at least the third Federal general election.

[3] i.e. every Southern Rhodesian general voter had three votes and could vote for candidates for three types of seat. In Northern Rhodesia and Nyasaland the general voters only had two votes, as the Europeans charged with special responsibility for African interests were nominated by the Governors.

might also vote for the European charged with special responsibility for African interests.[1]

Provision was made for the appointment from time to time of a Delimitation Commission, chaired by the Federal Chief Justice, which would observe the same principles as those applicable to the Southern Rhodesian Delimitation Commission, except that the variation as between seats might not be in excess of 15 per cent or less than an equal number of voters unless the Commission deemed it necessary to increase this figure to 25 per cent, in which case a 50 per cent discrepancy would be possible as between the smallest and largest seats.

The franchise qualifications[2] in practice meant that the majority of special voters would be African and the great majority of general voters Europeans.[3]

Reporting on the Constitution Amendment Bill, the African Affairs Board pointed out that although there had been an approximately proportionate increase in size as between the number of elected members and the total number of members representing African interests,[4] the measure differentiated in that it increased the difference in the size of groups from seventeen to

[1] i.e. in Southern Rhodesia special voters could vote for an 'elected African Member' and for the European charged with special responsibility for African interests, whereas in Northern Rhodesia and Nyasaland the special voters could only vote for an 'elected African', as the European members were nominated, and have some say in the election of the 'specially elected African members'.

[2] Combinations of means and educational qualifications required:

General voters

	Income p.a. for two years preceding registration	or	Ownership of immovable property and valued at	Educational qualification
1.	£720		£1,500	—
2.	£480		£1,000	Completed primary education.
3.	£300		£500	Four years' secondary education.

4. Ministers with university degree or five years' training at a theological school or two years at school and three years' service, and Chiefs deemed to have means qualifications.

Special voters

1.	£150		£500	—
2.	£120		—	Two years' secondary education.

Note: Every applicant was required to have an adequate knowledge of the English language, viz. ability to speak, read, write, and comprehend it subject to testing. He was also required to complete the claim form unassisted in his own writing.

Provision was made to permit the Minister of Law, if a Commission appointed at five-yearly intervals reported a fall or rise in the purchasing power of money in comparison with its value at the date of the Electoral Act, to alter the monetary qualifications so that inflation or deflation would not affect the requirements.

[3] See Appendix Table J, Educational Qualifications of Southern Rhodesian Africans obtained from the Central Statistical Office. No figures are available for the Northern Territories but until recently better and more provision was made for the education of Southern Rhodesian Africans than for those of Northern Rhodesia and Nyasaland. Table K shows incomes earned by Africans in the Federation.

[4] The ratio was formerly 26:9. It was now to be 44:15.

twenty-nine. As the Board said: 'In Parliament it is the size of the majority that is important.'[1] Furthermore whereas Africans under the original Constitution absolutely controlled four members in a House of thirty-six, under the Constitution as amended they would control the same number in a House of fifty-nine, since they did not control the appointment of the European representatives nor did they control the election of the new 'elected Africans' as the latter would be elected by both rolls on which European voters were likely to predominate. Although the Board pointed out the need for 'honest racial representation' once the principle of racial representation was recognized, this was not accepted. In fact the elected Africans were in practice to be elected in the main not by the people they were meant to represent but by the largely European electorate.

Reporting on the Electoral Bill[2] the Board pointed to the fact that general voters would in the main be European and special voters African. They emphasized that European voters would control at least forty-nine and probably fifty-three members under the new proposals,[3] whereas the African voters would on the other hand retain control over four members. The proportion of racial control over members was therefore being altered to the detriment of Africans.

The Board's protests at the introduction of the Bills in the Federal Assembly were ignored,[4] and when the Bills were reserved, although the Secretary of State for Commonwealth Relations, Lord Home, privately pressed Sir Roy Welensky to liberalize the franchise, he accepted Sir Roy's statement that he had gone 'to the limit of liberalization with our electorate'.[5] Lord Home then informed the Board that the proposals in the Constitution Amendment Bill 'represent a necessary, desirable, and substantial advance on anything which has gone before'.[6] Similarly in February 1958 he advised assent to the Electoral Bill because the new franchise provisions 'mark a distinct advance on those now operating because they will largely increase the number of Africans eligible to register and thus to cast a vote for the election of members to the Assembly and by the reinforcement of the principle of a non-racial common basis for the franchise'.[7]

[1] Report Fed. A.18, 29 July 1957, also printed in Cmnd. 298.

[2] Fed. A.23, also printed in Cmnd. 362.

[3] The effect of the proposals would be that the forty-four 'elected members', the four Southern Rhodesian 'elected African members', and the Southern Rhodesian European representing African interests, i.e. forty-nine, would be elected by predominantly European electorates. In addition this would probably apply to the four new 'elected African members' from Northern Rhodesia and Nyasaland. The latter assumption was borne out in practice as a result of the failure of Africans to register as voters: Cmnd. 1149, p. 11. See Figure I.

[4] The Federal Government's replies were published in Cmnd. 298 and Cmnd. 362. They ignored the real issue—that African influence in the Assembly had been substantially diminished.

[5] Welensky, op. cit., p. 81. These discussions took place in the Federation in October 1957.

[6] Special Report of the African Affairs Board, Fed. A.21, 9 December 1957.

[7] Special Report of the African Affairs Board, Fed. A.24, 24 June 1958.

The Federal .

As originally composed under the Constitution and Territorial
Electoral Laws as adapted from 1953 to 1958

Total membership   35 plus non-member Speaker with casting vote.

26 'elected members'	14 S. Rhodesia 8 N. Rhodesia 4 Nyasaland	'Non-racial', but in practice all Euro elected by a predominantly European electo
6 'specially elected African members'	2 S. Rhodesia 2 N. Rhodesia 2 Nyasaland	Elected by predominantly European elector African elected
3 'European members charged with special responsibility for African interests'	1 S. Rhodesia 1 N. Rhodesia 1 Nyasaland	Elected by predominantly European elector Appointed by Governors

Effect

29 members elected by predominantly European electorate, 27 of whom were Europeans and
    necessity Africans.
 4 Africans elected by Africans of Northern Rhodesia and Nyasaland.
 2 Europeans nominated by Colonial Office.

Notes:

1. At the first Federal election in 1953 there were 64,338 European, 448 African, and 2,133 Colo
   and Asian voters. See Cmnd. 1149, p. 11.
2. At the second Federal election in 1958, including general and special voters there were 8?
   European, 7,132 African, and 4,057 Coloured and Asian voters. See Cmnd. 1149, p. 11.
   At the third Federal election in 1962, including general and special voters, there were 10?
   European, 10,959 African, and 4,505 Coloured and Asian voters. (Figures released by Ce
   Statistical Office.)

e Assembly

As composed after the Constitution Amendment Act 1957 and the
Federal Electoral Act 1958, from 1958 to 1962

---

l membership   59 plus non-member Speaker with casting vote.

lected members'	24 S. Rhodesia	'Non-racial', but in practice all European elected by a predominantly European electorate of general voters
	14 N. Rhodesia	
	6 Nyasaland	

lected African Iembers'	4 S. Rhodesia	Elected by general and special voters, the great majority of whom were European [2]
	2 N. Rhodesia	
	2 Nyasaland	

| specially elected frican Members' | 2 N. Rhodesia | African elected |
| | 2 Nyasaland | |

European members harged with special esponsibility for frican interests'	1 S. Rhodesia	Elected by general and special voters, the majority being Europeans.
	1 N. Rhodesia	Appointed by the Governors
	1 Nyasaland	

Effect

3 members elected by predominantly European electorate, 45 of whom were Europeans and 8 of necessity Africans.
4 Africans elected by Africans of Northern Rhodesia and Nyasaland.
2 Europeans nominated by Colonial Office.

---

hese figures are to some extent distorted by boycotting of the rolls by Africans qualified to egister. This was a feature of the situation later in the history of the Federation. However, nce such voters could in the main only have registered as special voters, African participation ould merely have affected the election of 'elected African members', 'specially elected African iembers', and the Southern Rhodesian European charged with special responsibility for African iterests. This could not greatly have affected the Parliamentary situation.

Thus on the only two occasions on which the Board requested that Bills be reserved the responsible Secretary of State had committed himself and his Government in advance and was forced to disregard the Board's views, even though he clearly had second thoughts on the agreement reached with the Federal Government.

Although the Board had been designed to allay African suspicions aroused by the creation of Federation, the fact that on the first two and only two occasions on which it requested reservation its views were overruled by the British Government justified the comments that as a safeguard it was value-less.[1] In fact the Rev. A. B. Doig, the European nominated member for Nyasaland, resigned from the Federal Assembly and Board on the grounds that it had proved ineffective and that African representatives would no longer be effective.[2] Not only had the safeguard been ineffective, but the Board itself was to be fundamentally changed in composition partly as a result of the constitutional amendments but also as a consequence of the changes in the composition of the Federal Assembly.

Yet another consequence was that the two-thirds majority of the total Assembly necessary for constitutional change became easier to obtain in practice. The actual Constitution Amendment Bill was only passed by 25 to 9 votes, 24 votes being needed for a two-thirds majority in the House as originally composed.[3] A two-thirds majority of the increased membership would be 40 and this could easily be obtained from the 44 'elected members', even if all the members in any way representative of African interests, how-ever they might be brought into the House, voted solidly against the measure.

---

[1] See the Monckton Report's remarks that the Board had lost African confidence and that its prestige and usefulness had been injured by the fact that its objections had been overruled: 'In the eyes of many this was a convincing proof of the Board's ineffectiveness as a safeguard': Cmnd. 1148, para. 233.

[2] See his views before the United Kingdom Government announced its decision on the Bill as expressed in a letter to Mrs. Castle: *H.C. Deb.*, Vol. 578, col. 888.

[3] The Government majority of twenty-five was composed of twenty-two 'elected members', the Southern Rhodesian European charged with special responsibility for African interests, and the two 'specially elected African members' from Southern Rhodesia. The opposition was made up by the two Europeans from Northern Rhodesia and Nyasa-land charged with responsibility for African interests, three 'specially elected Africans' from the North (one Northern Rhodesian 'specially elected African member' was not present), an independent European 'elected member' from Northern Rhodesia, and three European 'elected members' of the Dominion Party (right wing). Had the two 'specially elected African members' from Southern Rhodesia voted against the Bill the necessary two-thirds majority would not have been obtained. Mr. Savanhu, one of these 'specially elected Africans' from Southern Rhodesia, decided to vote with the Government, salved his conscience by resigning his seat and was immediately re-elected at an unopposed by-election by the predominantly European electorate. For his statements see Keesing's Contemporary Archives 1957–8, 15781. This voting position recurred on the third reading of the Electoral Bill: see Sanger, op. cit., pp. 125–7, for the dilemma of the two 'specially elected African members' from Southern Rhodesia, who were members of the governing party and who voted for the Bill on the basis that a concession had been made in lowering the special voters' income qualification from £180 to £150 per annum.

In the event all the Board's arguments proved true. In the Federal Assembly elected under the Federal Constitution as amended and the Electoral Act 1958,[1] out of a total membership of 59 only four members were chosen predominantly by Africans,[2] while 53 were elected by a predominantly European electorate.[3] The remaining two members were the nominated European members for Northern Rhodesia and Nyasaland.

The long term significance of these changes was vast, quite apart from the increased disparity in numbers in the Assembly as at that time between Europeans and Africans. It became clear that with the high Federal franchise Africans in the Territories would not for many years be able to enrol in sufficient numbers to enable them to win the 44 seats for 'elected members', which could always control the Assembly.[4] Even if a few such seats were won, the 'fade-out' principle would counteract this victory in the next election by correspondingly reducing the number of representatives of African interests. Furthermore even those Africans who registered on the special roll were to a large extent rendered impotent by the fact that although they could vote for 'elected African members', the general roll (consisting largely of Europeans), would for a long period counteract their votes, since general roll voters could also vote for the 'elected African members'. African control of the Federal Legislature was therefore indefinitely postponed. Finally, by agreeing to this Federal franchise, the United Kingdom had made it impossible to affect the future composition of the Assembly, by progressively lowering Territorial franchises in the Northern Territories, so that 'elected members' of the Federal Parliament would become more representative. Although one of the motives of Federation had been to bring influence from the north to bear at the centre, this concept had now been abandoned. These changes made politicians realize that Federation must be dissolved, if they were to obtain full powers of government over their own people.

The changes were also reflected in the composition of the Board itself.

[1] No. 6 of 1958. The Act also made detailed provisions for the conduct of elections, election offences, qualifications and disqualifications for voters and candidates, and the circumstances in which a seat should be vacated. Except in respect of the means and educational qualifications required the rest of the Electoral Act reflected standard practice in countries which adopted the United Kingdom system of elections.

[2] The Nyasaland 'specially elected African members' were unrepresentative of African feeling, because it was decided to boycott the election and they were chosen mainly by members of African Provincial Councils in Nyasaland, and the few Africans who had registered as voters with United Federal Party support. In the election held in 1962, the boycott had extended. The Southern Rhodesian 'elected African members' were elected by a predominantly European electorate, while in those cases where their seats were contested the 'specially elected African members' from Northern Rhodesia and Nyasaland represented themselves and a few dozen voters from the Provincial Councils and persons on the Federal special voters' rolls who were prepared to vote.

[3] See *supra* and Figure I.

[4] See Cmnd. 1148, para. 87. In 1960 the Monckton Commission felt that 'the African vote ... cannot for an indeterminate period exercise any significant influence in the election of three-quarters of the Federal Assembly'.

Although its membership was to remain at six the three African members in the Territories were now to be elected by all the members representing African interests, however elected.[1] The election of the second Board held on 2 April 1959 was extremely revealing, both as to the way in which voting occurred and as to the fundamental changes in the composition of the Board as a combined result of the constitutional changes and the Electoral Act. The Board was now converted into a reflection of the Assembly and was no longer a safeguard for a largely unenfranchised group of the society.

Mr. Robert Moffat[2] informed the Assembly that in electing the members for each Territory there was block voting by the United Federal Party— the governing party.[3] As a result the new Board was composed of four members of the United Federal Party (including the Southern Rhodesian European representative for African interests) and the two European appointed members from Northern Rhodesia and Nyasaland. Even if the Board as now composed acted honourably in all respects, as a safeguard it lost all psychological value because at best it no longer had the appearance of independence and at worst the Government had now packed the Board with its supporters in order to destroy its embarrassing powers, at the same time maintaining the facade of a safeguard. It was not surprising that Mr. Yamba, one of the 'specially elected Africans' from Northern Rhodesia, put forward a motion calling for the setting up of an independent body to replace the African Affairs Board and to assume its functions under the Constitution.[4]

It is difficult to believe that these consequential changes in the composition of the Board were not deliberately planned by the Federal Government and that the British Government and its legal and Commonwealth Relations advisers did not forsee these consequences when examining the proposals for change in detail, more particularly as these changes effectively prevented any obstruction by the Board without the odour of abolishing it. From Sir Roy Welensky's book it is implicit that Mr. Lennox Boyd agreed to such changes.[5]

The Board as reconstituted operated until the close of Federation. As before it perused all subordinate legislation and Bills. Only on one occasion did it consider a Bill potentially differentiating. When, however, it had heard

[1] Article 67 as amended by Section 10 of the Constitution (Amendment) Act No. 16 of 1957.

[2] The brother of Sir John Moffat. Sir John declined renomination to the Assembly in view of the rejection of the Board's views by the Federal and United Kingdom Governments.

[3] Fed. Parlty. Deb., cols. 6024–5, 29 July 1959: 'The members of the United Federal Party voted to give one political party a majority on the Board. I think it was obvious to all of us who took part in the election that the matter had been arranged beforehand. I think that the Government had decided who were to go on to the Board and issued their instructions and the members of the Board acted accordingly.' U.F.P. members denied the allegation that a prior arrangement to this effect had been made and that they had discussed the matter in caucus. They may well have discussed it outside caucus.

[4] Fed. Parlty. Deb., col. 1153, 1 July 1959.   [5] Op. cit., p. 74.

evidence, the Board was satisfied that in the light of existing circumstances the provisions of the Bill (dealing with the method of grading and sale of African grown tobacco on Trust land) were justified. Accordingly reservation was not requested.[1] However, effective intervention occurred by the Board in 1961 and 1962 in two cases where subordinate legislation differentiated.[2]

As indicated above, the Board apparently made few formal representations to the Federal Government. The only ones disclosed in its reports were representations on matters affecting African interests such as the marketing of African produce in Northern Rhodesia and Southern Rhodesia, restrictions on imports and import duties on goods bought by the African population, and the conditions of service of Africans in the regular Defence Force.[3]

A new development also occurred in 1960–1 when the draft of a proposed regulation was sent by one Ministry for prior advice by the Board. Changes were suggested, accepted, and a non-differentiating measure was then produced.[4]

Conclusions

Any final assessment of the value of the Board as a safeguard must be guided by two considerations: the actual work it performed and its effect on legislation was one of its aspects, but equally important was its other aspect—its public image. From the first point of view the Board did a considerable amount of valuable work, had a great psychological effect on the Federal Government and the drafting of legislation, and made important and sometimes effective representations to the Government.[5] However from the public point of view it was a failure.[6] This failure was occasioned by the political decision of the United Kingdom Government to ignore the Board's protests. Since the ultimate safeguard was meant to be Imperial control exercised by the British Cabinet after reservation, measures were consequently dependent on varying Cabinet interpretations of what trusteeship involved. Although the notion of a Board was valuable the weakness of the procedure was its dependence on decisions taken by United Kingdom political Ministers. Thus

[1] Fed. A.45 dealing with the Tobacco Marketing and Levy Bill F.B. 34A of 1960.

[2] Relative to the control of maize sales by African producers in the Eastern Province of Northern Rhodesia and to special rules for African witnesses in the Federal Supreme Court. See Fed. A.45, A.46, and A.62. The Board reported on both these measures and the offending laws were either withdrawn or amended.

[3] See Fed. A.37, Report 1959-60.   [4] Fed. A.45.

[5] As a political judgement it is probably true that the representations made by the second and third African Affairs Boards received a more sympathetic hearing from the Federal Government as the Board was by then dominated by Government party members: *supra*. In addition an unfortunate personality clash between Sir John Moffat as chairman of the Board and the Federal Prime Minister no longer impeded the Board's work.

[6] cf. the Report of the Monckton Commission; Leys and Pratt, op. cit., p. 117; Hasson and Armour, op. cit. The manner in which these criticisms are couched occasionally makes it seem as if the Board itself was the target. This was probably not the intention of the writers.

the Board itself was in no sense an ultimate safeguard and cannot be criticized for its failure: the failure was that of the United Kingdom Government.[1]

Judicial powers within the Federation

The existence of the High and inferior Courts of the Territories was not affected by the establishment of Federation. Such Courts were however to be invested with jurisdiction in civil and criminal proceedings arising under the Federal Constitution or any Federal law until such time as the Federal Legislature either created Federal courts[2] or provided otherwise. Federal laws were to be enforced by the Territorial courts as if they were laws of the particular Territory,[3] while Territorial and other authorities throughout the Federation were to enforce the judgements of the Federal Supreme Court.[4] Alteration of the composition or powers of the Courts in respect of Territorial laws was not within Federal legislative competence.

Provision was made for a Federal Supreme Court to replace the Appellate Division of the Union of South Africa (which heard appeals from Southern Rhodesia) and the Rhodesia and Nyasaland Court of Appeal (which heard criminal appeals from all the Territories).[5]

The Federal Supreme Court was to be composed of a Federal Chief Justice, from two to six Federal Justices appointed by the Governor-General, and the Chief Justices of each of the Territories.[6] Provision was also made for an acting Chief Justice or acting Federal Justices.

The Federal judges enjoyed security of tenure, subject to removal by the Governor-General after an address from the Federal Assembly praying for their removal on the grounds of misbehaviour or infirmity of body or mind.[7]

---

[1] The arguments in favour of constitutional safeguards are strongly urged by D. V. Cowen, op. cit., pp. 113–25. He makes the telling point that the entrenched sections of the South Africa Act, although they were ultimately avoided by ingenious strategems, had considerable value in attracting world publicity to the attempts to disenfranchise the South African Coloured voters. As the author points out, it is relatively easy to devise stronger safeguards than those in the South Africa Act. The same argument applies to the African Affairs Board.

[2] The Federal Special Court for Income Tax was a court constituted by Federal law. Cp. *Commissioner of Taxes* v. *Pan-African Roadways Ltd.*, 1957 (2) S.A. 539 and 541, where it was held that the Southern Rhodesian Special Tax Court was a 'court'.

[3] Article 45.   [4] Article 58(1).

[5] Article 62. See *Commissioner of Taxes* v. *Pan-African Roadways Ltd.*, *supra*, in which it was laid down that prior to the establishment of the Federal Supreme Court, appeals to the Appellate Division of the Union of South Africa could be noted and that all pending appeals were saved: Articles 64 and 65.

[6] Article 46. In practice there were never more than two Federal judges and the Federal Chief Justice appointed. The Court relied on making up the quorum of three judges by calling in Territorial Chief Justices if necessary. Such Chief Justices sat in cases from any Territory and there was no tendency to secure that the Southern Chief Justice sat in Southern Rhodesian appeals in particular.

[7] Article 47(6)(b).

Salaries of judges in amounts prescribed by Federal legislation[1] were to be paid out of the Consolidated Revenue Fund and might not be reduced during their tenure of office.[2]

The Federal Supreme Court Act[3] conferred on the Court jurisdiction to hear civil and criminal appeals from the High Courts of the Territories, made provision for the officers of the Court, laid down rules for the procedure and practice to be applied by the Court in the exercise of its jurisdiction, and generally provided for the exercise of its powers.[4]

On 1 August 1955 the Federal Supreme Court assumed its functions by virtue of a Governor-General's Proclamation.[5]

The Court so established was mainly an appellate civil and criminal court, and the Constitution gave it an exclusive appellate jurisdiction from the High Court to determine appeals involving the interpretation of any provision of the Federal or Territorial Constitutions.[6] However certain exclusive original jurisdiction was also conferred on the Court. If any question as to the interpretation of the Federal Constitution arose in proceedings in the Territorial High Court, the latter might refer the question directly to the Federal Supreme Court while if such question arose in any other Court, the person presiding might apply to the High Court for an order referring the question to the Federal Supreme Court and was required, unless the request was frivolous or vexatious, to make such application if requested to do so by any party to the proceedings.[7] More importantly, the Federal Supreme Court, to the exclusion of all other courts, had exclusive original jurisdiction—

    (a) in any dispute between the Federation and a Territory or between Territories, if and in so far as that dispute involves any question (whether of law or fact) on which the existence or extent of a legal right depends;

    (b) to hear and determine—

        (i) any question whether by reason of circumstances prescribed by a law of the Federal Legislature or this Constitution a vacancy exists in the Federal Assembly; or

        (ii) a petition complaining of an undue return or an undue election of a member of the Federal Assembly by reason of want of qualification or by

---

[1] Federal Supreme Court (Judges' Salaries, Pensions, and Allowances) Act 8 of 1955 as amended by Act 50 of 1962.

[2] Article 50.   [3] Act No. 11 of 1955.

[4] The Act in Section 9 stated that the practice and procedure of the Court should in civil and criminal appeals, except as provided by Rules, be exercised as nearly as may be in accordance with the law and practice for the time being observed in the Court of Appeal and the Court of Criminal Appeal respectively. This provision was interpreted in *Mehta* v. *The Master*, 1958 R. & N. 570. Clayden F.J. considered whether this Section covered judicial precedent and held that the Federal Supreme Court was free to depart from its own decisions in the same circumstances as was the Judicial Committee. Nor was it bound by decisions of its predecessors such as the Appellate Division of the Union of South Africa. See my article 'Stare Decisis and the Federal Supreme Court', *R. & N.L.J.*, July 1962, pp. 126–52, in which a different view is taken on the former point.

[5] Article 66, F.G.N. 148/55.   [6] Article 55.   [7] Article 54.

reason of disqualification, corrupt or illegal practice, or irregularity or by reason of any other cause whatsoever;

(c) in any matter in which a writ or order of mandamus or prohibition or an injunction or interdict is sought against an officer or authority of the Federation as such.[1]

During the existence of the Federation no disputes were referred to the Court in terms of Article 53(a) or (b).[2] But Article 53(c) was used whenever such claims were brought against an officer or authority of the Federation.[3] However the Article only conferred original jurisdiction in the particular circumstances specified: if an action involved a vindicatory claim as in *Codron* v. *Macintyre and Shaw* NN.O.[4] the Court did not possess original jurisdiction and the claim would require to be asserted in a Territorial High Court.[5] The Court, however, was at liberty to disregard the mere formality of the wording of any order sought and could refuse to allow a litigant to determine which Court would hear the matter by attaching a quite inappropriate label to his action.[6]

The Federal Legislature was empowered to confer in any class of case a right of appeal to the Judicial Committee of the Privy Council. Until such law was passed there were to be no appeals as of right. Eventually, as a result of the new Southern Rhodesian Constitution which came into force in 1962,

---

[1] Article 53 as amended by section 9 of the Constitution Amendment Act of 1957. The original jurisdiction relative to the right of persons to be or remain members of the Federal Assembly was more clearly defined by this Act.

[2] There were two cases involving parliamentary elections to the Federal Assembly but they were both decided before the establishment of the Federal Supreme Court. See *Thornicroft* v. *Federal Minister of Internal Affairs*, 1953 S.R. 143 (heard by the Rhodesia and Nyasaland Court of Appeal in terms of the transitional provisions in Article 64(1)) and *D'Enis* v. *Federal Minister of Internal Affairs*, 1954 (1) S.A. 117 (S.R.). In the latter case the Court held at that stage no action could lie against a Government official in the absence of any law governing proceedings against the Crown or its Federal servants, or liability of the Crown. One of the first Acts passed by the Federal Parliament was the Federal Crown Proceedings Act No. 14 of 1954.

[3] e.g. *Ranger* v. *Greenfield and Wood* NN.O., *supra*; *Chassay Brothers* v. *Shaw and Macintyre* NN.O., *supra*. The article also applied to Federal statutory commissions which were held to be bodies empowered to carry out part of the functions of Federation: *Southern Rhodesia Electricity Supply Commission and Minister of Power* v. *Chamber of Mines, Rhodesia*, 1960 R. & N. 348.

[4] 1960 R. & N. 418.

[5] The point that the court had no jurisdiction was not even taken in *Kantor (Pvt.) Ltd.* v. *Macintyre N.O. and the Controller of Customs and Excise*, 1957 R. & N. 780. The Court realized that it had decided the matter *sub silentio* three years later. See also *Ex parte Goodair*, 1955 (4) S.A. 78 (S.R.) at 81, where Morton A.C.J. queried whether Article 53 precluded the courts of Southern Rhodesia from issuing a writ or order of mandamus or prohibition against a Federal prisons officer and whether the High Court had accordingly been deprived of the power of ordering the release of any prisoner no matter where he be detained within the country. It is submitted that the section did not apply to a writ *de homine libero exhibendo*, the Roman–Dutch Law equivalent of *habeas corpus*, as it referred only to the two aforementioned writs.

[6] *Codron* v. *Macintyre and Shaw* NN.O. at 427.

the Federal Supreme Court (Amendment) Act[1] provided for an appeal as of right to Her Majesty in Council from any determination of the High Court of Southern Rhodesia in relation to a claim by any person that the provisions of the Declaration of Rights contained in the Southern Rhodesia Constitution 1961 had been contravened in relation to him.[2]

Special leave to appeal could still be granted[3] except where the law of a Territory or a Federal law provided in respect of any High Court decision that it was to be final. In such event neither the Federal Supreme Court nor the Privy Council could hear an appeal.[4]

In cases where no appeal to the Federal Supreme Court was permitted and no provision made that the High Court decision was to be final, appeal by special leave would lie.[5] This was intended as a precautionary measure lest there be circumstances in which there was no right of appeal.

Constitutional changes in the Federation

During the ten years of its existence the Federal Constitution was amended on four occasions. In addition in 1956 and 1957 the Federation's authority in the field of external affairs was increased by additional entrustments from the United Kingdom, while the Federal Prime Minister obtained a standing invitation to Commonwealth Prime Ministers' Conferences in 1956 instead of mere *ad hoc*, even if almost continuous, participation as an observer. The final change was the recognition in 1957 by the United Kingdom Government of a convention relating to the exercise of United Kingdom legislative powers relative to the Federation.

The first amendment[6] was made soon after the establishment of the

---

[1] Act 46 of 1962.

[2] See the original Section 71 of the Southern Rhodesia Constitution 1961 prior to its amendment in 1964 by the Constitution Amendment Act No. 13 of 1964, Section 8.

[3] The first appeal by special leave was *Mungoni* v. *Attorney-General of Northern Rhodesia*, [1960] A.C. 336. There was only one case originating in Southern Rhodesia during the existence of the Federal Supreme Court which proceeded to the Judicial Committee, viz. *R.* v. *Mapolisa*, 1963 R. & N. 808 (F.S.C.), a case under Section 33A of the Law and Order (Maintenance) Act 1960 as amended. The appeal was dismissed: Privy Council Appeal No. 19 of 1964 (as yet unreported).

[4] Article 63 read with Section 1(a)(iii) of the Rhodesia and Nyasaland (Federation) Act 1953 as interpreted in *Gonthi* v. *R.*, 1958 R. & N. 35. In the case in question the Nyasaland Legislative Council had not declared High Court decisions on fact in criminal cases originating in subordinate courts to be 'final'. This was successfully done in respect of appeals on fact and sentence from the Nyasaland High Court by Section 60 of Nyasaland Ordinance No. 26 of 1958. See *Pindeni* v. *R.*, 1959 (2) R. & N. 475.

[5] Per Tredgold F.C.J. in *R.* v. *Gonthi, supra*. Dicta by Clayden F.J. in *R.* v. *Gonthi* are, it is submitted, too wide as it can be inferred from his decision that appeal by special leave could only be given in cases where no appeal lay to the Federal Supreme Court, i.e. the only case preserved would be an appeal from the original Federal Supreme Court jurisdiction. Tredgold F.C.J. did not take this view.

[6] In terms of the Constitution Amendment Act No. 18 of 1954.

Federation in order to clarify the power of Territorial Governments to impose a Territorial surcharge and was occasioned by slipshod drafting of the original Constitution.[1] The third amendment made in 1958, resulted from the Report in 1957 of the Fiscal Commission,[2] established in terms of Article 96, recommending a reallocation of revenue and loan funds. In effect Southern Rhodesia's share of external borrowings was raised from 13 per cent to 16 per cent of the total at the expense of the Federal share, while the Southern Rhodesian and Northern Rhodesian shares of monies raised from taxes on income and profits and export duties were each raised 1 per cent, again at Federal expense.[3]

The final amendment made it clear that the Federation was empowered to deal with any matter relating to professions and callings designated by the Governor-General by Order approved of by the Governor of any Territory concerned.[4] Previously Item 40 had related only to professional qualifications so that it was impossible for professions or callings generally to be regulated by the Federal Legislature and Government, making uniformity throughout the Territories difficult of attainment. At the request of professional bodies this amendment was therefore made.[5]

The significant constitutional amendments during the existence of Federation were, however, those contained in the Constitution Amendment Act 1957[6] (already discussed in connection with the African Affairs Board), whereby the membership of the Assembly was increased from 35 to 59, the 'fade-out' principle was introduced, and the additional 'elected African members' were to be chosen by the same electorate that chose the 'elected members', except that certain special voters were also entitled to vote.[7] The effect of these changes was that in the second and subsequent Federal Assemblies 53 members of the House were elected by a predominantly European electorate. Of these 53 members 45 were European,[8] while eight were necessarily African. The Africans in the Northern Territories continued to elect four 'specially elected African members' while the Colonial Office through its Northern Governors continued to nominate two Europeans.[9]

---

[1] The Constitution provided that surcharge could be levied on different bases either on physical persons or on bodies corporate whereas the real intention had been that both persons and bodies corporate should be liable.

[2] C. Fed. 56.

[3] Constitution Amendment Act No. 13 of 1958 amending Articles 90, 80, and 83.

[4] Constitution Amendment Act No. 27 of 1959, amending Item 40 of the Federal Legislative List.

[5] The Accountancy profession, and the Medical and Dental professions were then federalized.

[6] No. 16 of 1957.

[7] The combined effect of the Constitution Amendment Act 1957 and the Electoral Act 1958.

[8] In 1962 the governing party supported a Coloured candidate as an elected member. Thus there were only forty-four Europeans elected to the house.

[9] See Fig. I, *supra*. All the African Nyasaland members from 1959 were representative of

Other than as one of the four 'specially elected African members' any African participation in the Federal Government or Legislature except as a protegé of the Government party and European electorate was by these changes made impossible until such time as large numbers of Africans obtained the vote through increasing education and economic development.[1]

Another fundamental constitutional change occurred as a result of the reservation of the Electoral Act by the Governor-General. Somewhat earlier the Governor-General had reported to the Commonwealth Relations Office on a dispute with the Federal Prime Minister involving a matter of precedence. He had been informed that, as personal representative of the Queen, it was not his function, unless his discretion was involved, to write political despatches.[2] When the Electoral Bill was reserved, the Acting Governor-General, Sir Robert Tredgold (who was the Chief Justice of the Federation) considered it his duty to report on the measure as he considered once a measure was reserved it was his duty to comment on it. Sir Robert was, however, informed by the Secretary of State for Commonwealth Relations that the United Kingdom attitude was that since there was a United Kingdom High Commissioner, the Governor-General should not report on Bills even when they were reserved. The Federal Prime Minister also gave this as his view. Both the United Kingdom authorities and the Federal Prime Minister in fact relied on the earlier precedent, which had no application to such a situation.[3] However this was one of the few occasions on which the Governor-

---

the governing party as the Nyasaland African National Congress, later the Malawi Congress Party, boycotted anything relating to Federation including the election of 'specially elected African members'. In the parliamentary election held on 27 April 1962, there were only fifteen seats contested as African Nationalist parties and European right-wing parties both boycotted the last Federal election. As a result the United Federal Party held fifty-four out of the fifty-nine seats. In addition, one European right-wing Independent, two appointed Europeans representing African interests for Northern Rhodesia and Nyasaland, and two specially elected Independent Africans from Northern Rhodesia were elected. In the Federal Assembly prior to 1962 there had been an opposition of fourteen and forty-five Government supporters.

[1] The policy of the Territorial Governments was to provide the majority of the population with some primary schooling rather than to divert their funds to secondary education for fewer people. See the effect of this policy in Southern Rhodesia: Leys, op. cit., pp. 239-40; and also Appendix Table 'J' in relation to Southern Rhodesia.

[2] Part of the despatch is probably quoted in S. Weinberg, *An Outline of the Constitutional Law of the Federation of Rhodesia and Nyasaland*. For the use of the Department of the Controller and Auditor-General published for private circulation (by a member of the Federal Attorney-General's Department), at p. 86 where the author, quoting, says that the constitutional functions of the Governor-General had 'been decisively settled on the basis that when the Governor-General's discretion is not involved it is improper for him to offer advice to the Secretary of State save on the advice of the Executive Council'.

[3] Personal communication from Sir Robert Tredgold. The version given in Franck, op. cit., at p. 310, is somewhat misleading as it does not indicate that Sir Robert sent a copy of his despatch to the Federal Prime Minister and that the Commonwealth Relations Office replied in a courteous fashion to Sir Robert when it gave this ruling. The Federal Prime Minister also interviewed Sir Robert because he was extremely concerned about the whole matter.

General had a discretion, since Article 75(4) gave the Governor-General a discretion to assent despite a request for reservation by the Board. There is no doubt that the ruling given in these circumstances was an incorrect one probably dictated by the fact that Sir Robert's advice to the United Kingdom Government was highly embarrassing as it supported the view of the African Affairs Board so that the United Kingdom Government, in observing its prearranged bargain with the Federal Government, would then have had to overrule not only the African Affairs Board but also the Governor-General. The long-term consequence was that, in practice, the Governor-General although theoretically in terms of the Constitution entitled to exercise a limited discretion was now to be a mere channel of communication for Federal Ministers and had no right to comment on those messages forwarded by him.

In combination with these changes the most significant other change was the joint announcement by the Secretary of State for Commonwealth Relations and the Federal Prime Minister on 27 February 1957, of a Convention relating to United Kingdom legislative powers in respect of the Federation. In 1956 Lord Malvern (formerly Sir Godfrey Huggins) had attempted to negotiate arrangements with the United Kingdom Government whereby the Federation would become independent. These arrangements envisaged the repeal of the restrictive provisions relative to disallowance and reservation and the abolition of the African Affairs Board. In return, the Federal Government would enter into a treaty with the United Kingdom Government whereby it would undertake not to enact any discriminatory measures and generally to observe the limitations on its powers previously imposed by the Constitution. In addition the Territories would be entitled to veto constitutional amendments increasing Federal powers or interfering with Territorial governmental and legislative rights. This scheme was rejected by the United Kingdom Government, which took up the attitude that the Federation could not go forward to independence unless its 'inhabitants' so desired. Relying on the preamble, the United Kingdom Government insisted that African approval (not forthcoming) was required for any change in status. Furthermore it considered that at this time changes would prejudice the future constitutional Review to be held between 1960 and 1963.[1] The subsequent debate in the Federal Parliament disclosed no details of the scheme.[2]

---

[1] See Gann and Gelfand, op. cit., pp. 251–4. The authors present Lord Malvern's view that the United Kingdom Government was distorting the original meaning of the preamble, which had been inserted to reassure Southern Rhodesian Europeans that Federation would not stop the attainment of Dominion status. Its purpose was not to 'rule out independence without consent expressed in some unspecified fashion through a black plebiscite'. See also Welensky, op. cit., p. 71, and *The Constitutional Status of the Federation of Rhodesia and Nyasaland*, by G. H. Baxter and P. W. Hodgens, (1957) International Affairs, Vol. 33, p. 442 at 449. The former author, a previous Under-Secretary of State for Commonwealth Relations, was a close associate of Lord Malvern.

[2] *Fed. Parlty. Deb.*, col. 916, 2 August 1956, Lord Malvern explaining his motives.

Negotiations, however, were continued for increased Federal status. As has been pointed out by Leys, the object was not to secure increased international status and external diplomatic representation, but to obtain 'a free hand in regard to native policy' and to preclude intervention in internal affairs of the country.[1] This, in particular, would have meant that African advancement could not have been forced upon the Federation by any future United Kingdom Government wishing to implement such a policy.

The discussions on enhanced Federal status were taken further by the new Federal Prime Minister, Sir Roy Welensky,[2] and in January 1957 when Mr. Lennox Boyd, the Colonial Secretary, visited the Federation, there were extensive discussions on higher status for the Federation, greater powers for the Federation in respect of external affairs and on the United Kingdom's power to legislate by Order in Council.[3]

In mid-April 1957 the Federal Prime Minister, Sir Roy Welensky, and the Minister of Law, Mr. Greenfield, then had discussions in London with Lord Home, Commonwealth Relations Secretary, and Mr. Lennox Boyd. At these discussions a considerable advance in status was accorded to the Federation, and a joint statement was issued by the Governments on 26 April 1957.[4] The Federation was now to be entrusted with 'responsibility for external affairs to the fullest extent possible consistent with responsibility which Her Majesty's Government must continue to have in International Law so long as the Federation is not a separate international entity'.[5]

The United Kingdom agreed also that the Federal Legislature should have power to legislate with extra-territorial effect and agreed that legislation would be introduced at Westminster to permit this.[6]

The enhanced status of the Federation was further recognized by permitting the Prime Minister direct access to the Sovereign on Federal matters affecting the Sovereign personally, on the award of honours for services to the Federation, and on a number of ceremonial matters. From that time the Federation was given a separate honours list.[7]

Although in 1953, when Britain's considerable power to legislate was raised in the Southern Rhodesian Assembly, the future Federal Prime Minister, Sir Godfrey Huggins, had dismissed these fears, his Government sought to

[1] Op. cit., p. 50–52.
[2] In public speeches in December 1956 and June 1957, which are reprinted in Keesing's Contemporary Archives 1957–8, 15324, Sir Roy Welensky revealed part of the content of these discussions.
[3] See Welensky, op. cit., p. 74. As mentioned above the 'package deal' in regard to constitutional amendment, citizenship and the franchise was also discussed, it having already been put in December 1956 to the Territorial Governments.
[4] For text and explanations by the Federal Prime Minister see Keesing's Contemporary Archives 1957–8, 15529–30.
[5] See supra for the additional entrustments relating to foreign affairs made as a consequence of this announcement.
[6] In practice this promise was not implemented.   [7] See The Times, 1 June 1958.

28—C.H.L.S.R.

have Britain's powers in this respect fettered. Despite the fact that the United Kingdom Government had informed the British Council of Churches that 'it would in any foreseeable circumstances be morally and politically indefensible for Parliament to enact amendments (to the Federal Constitution) which had not been ... agreed',[1] Huggins sought assurances on this point and on Britain's general power to legislate. These questions were again raised in 1957 when the Colonial Secretary visited the Federation. Ultimately at the London talks in April the Federal Government secured a concession of fundamental significance.

The Secretary of State and the Federal Prime Minister in announcing the decisions at the talks stated:

The Federal Prime Minister drew attention to doubts which had arisen in regard to the purpose and effect of Article 29(7) of the Federal Constitution and to the subject of legislation in the United Kingdom for the Federation. United Kingdom Ministers made it clear that the United Kingdom Government recognize the existence of a convention applicable to the present stage of the constitutional evolution of the Federation, whereby the United Kingdom Government in practice does not initiate any legislation to amend or to repeal any Federal Act or to deal with any matter included within the competence of the Federal Legislature, except at the request of the Federal Government.[2]

Not only did this convention inhibit the use of any powers conferred on Her Majesty by any Act of the United Kingdom Parliament to legislate for the Federation but it also restrained the use of the United Kingdom Parliament's power to legislate on matters within the competence of the Federal Legislature. The recognition of this convention by the United Kingdom Government was construed in the Northern Territories and by opponents of the Federal regime as 'British willingness to give virtually unreserved support to a European-controlled Federal Government'.[3]

Apart from this advance in status the Federal Government also obtained the permission already mentioned for changes in composition and size of the Federal Assembly and the establishment of a uniform Federal franchise. In addition, it achieved yet another of its objects: it had long sought recognition of the principle that all civil services in the Federation, whether Federal or Territorial, should be locally based[4] and the United Kingdom Government now agreed to work towards this objective and examine the question of interchangeability of officers. Even a proposal that a separate Central Africa Office dealing with all relationships with the Federal Government and Territories

---

[1] *S.R.L.A.D.*, Vol. 34, col. 1896, 30 October 1953, Huggins.
[2] Joint Announcement quoted in Cmd. 1149, p. 20.
[3] Leys and Pratt, op. cit., p. 117.
[4] This had been rejected prior to the establishment of Federation and early in 1955 Lord Malvern's proposals for a common service were again rejected by the Secretary of State: Gann and Gelfand, op. cit., p. 236.

should be created and be responsible to both Secretaries of State for Commonwealth Relations and the Colonies jointly was not rejected out of hand. (This would, if accepted, have tended to diminish Colonial Office control.)

Finally, the United Kingdom Government agreed to hold the Review Conference on the Federation at the earliest possible date, viz. 1960, in order to review the Constitution and to agree on further constitutional advance. The Conference would 'consider a programme for the attainment of such status as would enable the Federation to become eligible for full membership of the Commonwealth'. In return for these considerable advances in status, the Federal Prime Minister explicitly renounced intentions of pressing for amalgamation, but the British Government made an equal concession by reaffirming that it was opposed to secession of any Territory from the Federation. Sir Roy also announced a 'concession' that British Protected Persons should be entitled to the Federal franchise and in his autobiography considered that enlargement of the Federal Assembly was a similarly generous move.[1]

As viewed in 1957 the Federal Government had achieved a marked success —an advance in status which almost compromised the United Kingdom Government and made it difficult, unless circumstances changed considerably, for the United Kingdom not to agree to a further advance in status in 1960. However the very success attained by the Federal Government in consolidating its powers and constitutionally perpetuating the power of the predominantly European electorate contained the seeds of Federal destruction. African leaders in Nyasaland and Northern Rhodesia, certain that the United Kingdom Government would accede in 1960 to Federal demands for independence, totally and permanently rejected Federation, started militant political action, and set out at all costs to achieve political power in the two Northern Territories and to destroy the Federation.[2]

[1] Welensky, op. cit., pp. 76 et seq. Cp. the views of the African Affairs Board. In the light of the present situation the British Government's attitude seems inexplicable: an autobiography on the lines of Sir Roy Welensky's revelations by a British Cabinet Minister justifying the United Kingdom attitude at that time is somewhat unlikely.

[2] See Sanger, op. cit., pp. 178–81; D. C. Mulford, op. cit., p. 9.

PART II

THE CONSTITUTIONAL LAW OF SOUTHERN RHODESIA

1

THE LEGISLATIVE ASSEMBLY, THE FRANCHISE, LEGISLATIVE POWER, THE LEGISLATIVE PROCESS, AND THE CONSTITUTIONAL COUNCIL

General characteristics of the Southern Rhodesian Constitution 1961

THE Southern Rhodesia Constitution 1961 is based on the concepts of British parliamentary democracy,[1] the British Cabinet system, and constitutional guarantees of human rights.[2] In some ways it is typical of the new series of constitutions produced for dependent territories on the way to independence, yet in certain respects it is unique in that it confers a remarkable degree of self-government on Southern Rhodesia in the external sphere by allowing the Southern Rhodesian Legislature powers of extraterritorial legislation and by the large entrustments in practice made in respect of external affairs. Internally there is self-government, complete except for the fact that certain powers of constitutional amendment are in the hands of the Crown, while a residual power of disallowance and reserve powers in respect of Royal Instructions, suspension, and revocation of the Constitution remain.[3]

On the other hand, there is a typical exportation of the Cabinet system and the British constitutional conventions pertaining thereto. There is a Governor to represent the Monarch, who is a constituent part of the Legislature, and to exercise executive power on Her behalf. The unicameral Legislature, although somewhat unorthodoxly elected, observes the procedure of the House of Commons, the same machinery of control of national finance, and has the same privileges. In addition, the new method has been adopted of securing the judiciary by providing for a judicial tribunal to enquire into cases where removal of a judge is sought.[4]

---

[1] This remains true despite the fact that the present Electoral Act in effect allows a predominantly European electorate to elect the majority of members of the Legislature. See *infra.*

[2] For an impassioned plea for such an approach see Cowen, op. cit. The recent great change in the attitude of the constitution-makers of the Colonial and Commonwealth Relations Offices is described by Professor S. A. de Smith in 'Fundamental Rights in Commonwealth Constitutions', *Journal of the Parliaments of the Commonwealth* (1962), Vol. XLIII, pp. 10 et seq., in his *The New Commonwealth and its Constitutions*, op. cit., in 'Fundamental Rights in the New Commonwealth' (1961), *I.C.L.Q.*, Vol. 10 at pp. 83, 215, and by Professor A. Gledhill, 'Fundamental Rights', in *Changing Law and Developing Countries*, op. cit., pp. 81 et seq.

[3] See *infra*, Chapter 7.

[4] The Privy Council is not however involved as an additional safeguard.

All the new safeguards devised by Imperial constitution-makers are found in some form or another in the Constitution. Thus there is the institutional safeguard of the Constitutional Council empowered to delay legislation in conflict with the Declaration of Rights. There is the lengthy enumeration, subject to detailed exceptions, of fundamental human rights set out in the Declaration of Rights which is buttressed by judicial review with an appeal as of right to the Privy Council. There are special land provisions securing Tribal Trust Land for the sole and exclusive use and occupation of tribesmen.[1] There are provisions securing the pensions of civil servants. Furthermore, there is an exceptionally rigid procedure of constitutional amendment, while the franchise is dealt with in the Constitution and an amendment to this is treated as if it were a constitutional amendment. There are also constitutional provisions to secure proper delimitation of electoral districts and constituencies, and there are special procedures providing for cross-voting, which, although couched in non-racial language, are designed to secure that both major racial groups shall have some say in the election of those members of the Legislature who will in effect be elected by an electorate predominantly consisting of the other race.[2]

It is noticeable that for the most part the Constitution is couched in non-racial terms, thus the Legislature, executive, and judiciary[3] are defined and constituted without any reference to race. However, the procedure for amendment of the specially entrenched provisions of the Constitution is racial in character, as is the composition of the Constitutional Council, the composition to some extent of the Board of Trustees of Tribal Trust Land, and the trust imposed upon the Board, while certain exceptions to the Declaration of Rights are based on the application of African Customary Law.

The Legislature

Composition and election

The Legislature of Southern Rhodesia consists of Her Majesty the Queen and a Legislative Assembly.[4]

The Legislative Assembly is composed of sixty-five Members, fifty of whom are elected by constituencies and fifteen of whom are elected by electoral districts.[5] There is also provision for the election of a Speaker, who may be a

[1] Cp. the provision for Reserves in the Southern Rhodesia Constitution 1923 and special land provisions in the Constitution of the Federation of Malaya.

[2] See infra.

[3] Which stand in relation to one another in much the same way as in the United Kingdom, except that the Southern Rhodesian judiciary may declare statutes unconstitutional.

[4] Section 6. This section cannot be amended by the Southern Rhodesian Legislature, but only by Her Majesty by Order in Council or by the United Kingdom Parliament: Sections 105 and 111.

[5] Sections 7 and 37. Members of Parliament are equal in status whether elected by a constituency or by an electoral district. All are comparatively poorly paid when account

non-Member, provided he is not disqualified from election as a Member of the Assembly.[1]

The provisions for election to and membership of the Legislative Assembly are in fact extremely complicated, involving the division of the country as a whole into fifty constituencies and a second delimitation involving the division of Southern Rhodesia into fifteen electoral districts.[2] Voters are placed on an 'A' Roll or on a 'B' Roll, the voting qualifications for the 'A' Roll being higher than those for the 'B' Roll.[3] Voters on both Rolls can vote for a member for their particular constituency and for their electoral district. However, the Members representing constituencies are prodominantly elected by 'A' Roll voters and those representing electoral districts predominantly by 'B' Roll voters. This is effected by provision for devaluation of 'B' Roll votes cast for a constituency, once the number of 'B' Roll votes is in excess of one-fourth of the total number of votes cast by 'A' Roll voters. Similarly in electoral districts once the number of 'A' Roll votes cast is in excess of one-fourth of the total number of 'B' Roll votes cast, then the 'A' Roll votes are proportionately devalued so that each candidate is treated as having received such number of votes by the 'A' Roll voters as bears the same proportion to the number of votes actually received by that candidate as one-fourth of the total number of votes cast by the 'B' Roll voters bears to the total number cast by the 'A' roll voters.[4] In effect, this means that the 'A' Roll voters can have up to 20 per cent influence in an electoral district and

is taken of general salaries prevailing in Commonwealth Parliaments: see the Ministers', Speaker's, and Members' of Parliament (Salaries and Allowances) Act, Chapter 3.

[1] Section 10. The present Speaker was elected in July 1964 as a sitting member but resigned his seat soon after election. His predecessor was similarly elected under the 1923 Constitution and was re-elected as Speaker not being then a Member at the first session of the new Legislative Assembly as constituted under the 1961 Constitution. The Speaker's salary may not be reduced during his continuance in office: Section 12(1). It is governed by the Ministers', Speaker's and Members' of Parliament (Salaries and Allowances) Act.

[2] This is done by a Delimitation Commission appointed every five years and presided over by the Chief Justice and two other persons nominated by him. The same principles of division as those specified in the 1923 Constitution are enjoined on the Commission. It is to attempt to see that the number of voters in each constituency are equal and similar provision is made in respect of electoral districts. The principle of rural and urban constituencies is retained, it being provided that there should be not less than eighteen rural constituencies. The first Delimitation Commission set up in terms of these provisions adopted the attitude that an equality of voters meant in respect of each constituency an equality of 'A' Roll voters and in respect of each electoral district an equality of 'B' Roll voters, no regard being paid to the numbers of 'B' Roll voters in a constituency and the number of 'A' Roll voters in an electoral district. As a result, although there is comparative equality of 'A' Roll voters in constituencies and 'B' Roll voters in electoral districts, there is great inequality between the numbers of 'A' Roll voters in electoral districts and 'B' Roll voters in constituencies: see Report of the Commission Appointed to Divide the Colony into Constituencies and Electoral Districts, 1962, Government Printer, Salisbury. C.S.R. 34 1962.

[3] See Figure I, infra, for Voters' Qualifications.

[4] Electoral Act, Chapter 2, Section 81(2) passed in terms of the Southern Rhodesia (Constitution) Order-in-Council Sections 2 and 3 and the Second Schedule to the Constitution, Item 10.

80 per cent influence in a constituency, while 'B' Roll voters can have up to 80 per cent influence in an electoral district and 20 per cent influence in a constituency.[1] However, 'A' Roll voters have a greater say in the election of the Legislative Assembly as a whole, since there are fifty constituencies in which they predominate and only fifteen electoral districts in which 'B' Roll voters predominate.

These voting provisions were further complicated by the fact that each voter was permitted to exercise a single transferable vote.[2] However, by the Electoral Amendment Act 1964[3] this system has been eliminated.[4]

Voters' qualifications

Prior to the implementation of the new Constitution an Electoral Amendment Act[5] was passed in accordance with provisions set out in the Southern Rhodesia (Constitution) Order-in-Council. This Act provided for the keeping of an 'A' and a 'B' Roll and set out 'A' Roll voters' qualifications, which were the same as the 'ordinary' qualifications for the voters' rolls introduced in 1957,[6] with the addition of persons holding office as Chiefs or Headmen. It also specified the 'B' Roll qualifications, which were the same as the 'lower' qualifications with certain additions and concessions, viz. the period required for consistent earning of income was reduced from two years to six months, a property ownership qualification which included hire-purchasers was inserted, kraalheads and ministers of religion were to be qualified, and special qualifications for persons over thirty years of age were introduced.[7] Persons who had gained entry to the former common voters' roll by means of the 'lower' qualification were to be transferred to the 'B' Roll, while persons

---

[1] If there are two candidates contesting a particular seat and it is assumed that all 'B' Roll voters will vote against a particular candidate for a constituency, that candidate will require 62·53 per cent of the 'A' Roll votes cast to win the seat. Conversely, if in an electoral district all 'A' Roll voters vote against a particular candidate, he will require 62·53 per cent of the 'B' Roll votes cast to win. This is on the assumption that there are sufficient voters registered on each Roll so that they may count for their full percentage when cross-voting occurs.

[2] Electoral Act (Chapter 2), sections 60 (4), 81 (5) and (8).

[3] Act No. 30 of 1964, section 7.

[4] It seems that there was a strange oversight by the drafters of the Constitution since the Southern Rhodesia (Constitution) Order-in-Council in Section 3D stipulated that, amongst other requirements, a new electoral law should provide for this preferential voting system, whereas the Second Schedule to the Constitution, which sets out all the other requirements so enumerated as a measuring rod for amendments to the Electoral Act, does not mention this. The effect of Section 9 of the Constitution is that these other requirements in respect of the Electoral Act may not be amended except by a two-thirds majority or, in certain cases by the same procedure followed in the case of amendment of a specially entrenched provision of the Constitution, whereas the preferential vote could be and was eliminated by a simple amendment to the Electoral Act by a majority of Members of the Legislature.

[5] No. 62 of 1961.

[6] See *supra*, Part I, Chapter 14.

[7] See Cmnd. 1291, Annex A.

who had enrolled on the 'ordinary' qualification were transferred to the 'A' Roll.[1]

All the provisions contained in the Electoral Act except for those relative to Chiefs, Headmen, and Kraalheads are couched in non-racial language. It is, however, unreal to abstract the bare qualifications from their application to the racial groups in Southern Rhodesia. As can be seen from Figure I the franchise qualifications contain standard citizenship, age, and residence requirements.[2] However, certain alternative combinations of income or property and educational requirements are in addition required, except in the case of duly appointed Chiefs and Headman, who do not even need to be able to sign the voter's registration form and are to be automatically enrolled.[3] Special provision is also made for the registration of persons over the age of thirty years who are considered to be more mature.

The basic principle of the franchise qualifications is that the lower the income or property requirement, the higher must be the educational qualifications of the applicant. Since there is normally a direct relationship between the level of education and earning capacity, the alternatives are, in practice, not as generous as they might at first sight appear. Either the highest educational qualification could serve as the sole requirement or the higher property or income qualification could have sufficed.[4] In fact it is submitted that the number of potential registrants is determined by the Southern Rhodesian educational system.[5]

[1] In effect, 3,231 Africans were transferred to the 'B' Roll and 1,397 were put on the 'A' Roll. This led to criticism since all these voters had been on the common roll while when earlier changes in the franchise had been made, existing rights had been preserved. Analogies were drawn in the Legislative Assembly of the transfer of South African Coloured voters to a special roll: see *S.R.L.A.D.*, Vol. 49, col. 338, 11 December 1961.

[2] There are also standard disqualifications—the commission of electoral offences, mental disorder, imprisonment without the option of a fine within five years, &c.: see Electoral Act (Chapter 2), Section 17.

[3] The framers of the franchise considered that, whereas other persons required certain minimal educational qualifications, Chiefs and Headmen, who in Southern Rhodesia are Government appointed or removable by Government, are by virtue of their office sufficiently responsible to exercise the franchise. Section 8(1) of the Electoral Act read with Section 3E of the Southern Rhodesia (Constitution) Order in Council provided for the compulsory registration by the Chief Registering Officer of such persons as 'A' Roll voters, and as soon as the new Electoral Act came into force these persons were registered without being consulted. Some of them objected since they sympathized with a boycott of the voters' roll by Africans generally. See *S.R.L.A.D.*, Vol. 49, col. 943 and col. 950–1, 16 and 20 March 1962. As at 31 May 1964 there were 209 Chiefs and 342 Headmen registered (figures from the Central Statistical Office).

[4] viz. persons who earn £528 or more p.a. are likely to have four years' secondary education, whereas persons who earn less than this amount are unlikely to have had such an educational background, although there may be exceptional cases where this does not apply.

[5] See Appendix, Table J, for figures of educated Africans in Southern Rhodesia, and Tables Q and R for African property owners in Southern Rhodesia, the numbers of whom are so small that they do not materially affect the issue. In any event many of them are likely to have the requisite educational or income qualifications and would therefore be double-counted.

FIGURE I

Southern Rhodesia Voters' Qualifications

(See Sections 8, 9, 10, 11, and 15 of the Electoral Act)

Qualifications common to both Rolls

1. Citizenship of Rhodesia and Nyasaland.

2. Twenty-one years of age or over.

3. Two years' continuous residence in the Federation and three months' residence in the constituency and electoral district concerned immediately preceding application for enrolment.

4. Adequate knowledge of the English language and ability to complete and sign the registration form except in the case of duly appointed chiefs and headmen.

5. The following additional qualifications are required:

'A' Roll

(a) Income of not less than £792 during each of two years preceding date of claim for enrolment or ownership of immovable property of value not less than £1,650; *or*

(b) (i) Income of not less than £528 during each of two years preceding date of claim for enrolment or ownership of immovable property of value not less than £1,100;
    and

   (ii) completion of a course of primary education of pre-scribed standard; *or*

(c) (i) Income of not less than £330 during each of the two years preceding date of claim for enrolment, or owner-ship of immovable property of value not less than £550;
    and

'B' Roll

(a) Income at the rate of not less than £264 per annum during the six months preceding date of claim for enrolment or ownership of immovable property of value of not less than £495; *or*

(b) (i) Income at the rate of not less than £132 per annum during the six months preceding date of claim for enrolment, or ownership of immovable property of value of not less than £275;
    and

   (ii) two years' secondary education of prescribed standard; *or*

(c) Persons of over 30 years of age with—

   (i) Income at the rate of not less than £132 per annum during the six months preceding the date of claim for enrolment, or ownership of immovable property of value not less than £275;

(ii) four years' secondary education of prescribed standard; *or*

(d) Appointment to the office of Chief or Headman.

and

(ii) completion of a course of primary education of a prescribed standard; *or*

(d) Persons over 30 years of age with income at the rate of not less than £198 per annum during the six months preceding the date of claim for enrolment, or ownership of immovable property of value not less than £385; *or*

(e) All kraal heads with a following of twenty or more heads of families; *or*

(f) Ordained ministers of religion with university degree or five years' full-time training or two years' training and three years' service.

Notes:

1. In terms of Section 13 of the Electoral Act (which provision was permitted by Section 9(3) of the Constitution) the Governor has prescribed that the means qualification as enacted in the Act and the Second Schedule to the Constitution should be increased by 10 per cent. See Governor's Proclamation No. 32 of 31 August 1964 in Southern Rhodesian Government Notice 658/64. The Electoral Act does not therefore reflect the present franchise qualifications.

2. Note that 'owner', for purposes of the 'B' Roll only, includes a hire-purchaser if such person has been in continuous occupation for three years, is not in arrears, and has paid not less than 10 per cent of the purchase price of such property (Section 11).

3. The value of board and lodging may be included in computing salary (Section 12).

4. Except in the case of wives of Chiefs and Headmen, a married woman is deemed to have the same means qualifications as her husband. However, only the first wife under a system permitting of polygamy is deemed to have such qualifications (Section 14).

It is necessary in order to obtain the franchise for any applicant to have completed varying periods of 'primary' or 'secondary' education. The Electoral Act does not define these terms, but has provided for an Educational Qualifications Board, from which there is no appeal, to determine the required standards of education. The Board consists of three members who 'shall be persons having wide experience in matters of education' plus the Chief Justice as Chairman. The Board's rulings are of great significance as is shown by its decision that for a period of education to have been 'completed' an applicant must have acquired a certificate, i.e. passed and not merely have attended the course.[1] Another ruling although taken on educational grounds and the present organization of the school system[2] in effect discriminates against Africans. Whereas in the case of pupils of European, Coloured, and Asian schools the attainment of a Standard 5 pass is considered by the Board to amount to the completion of primary schooling, in the case of African school pupils a pass of Standard 6 is the point at which it has ruled primary schooling is completed.[3] Similarly it would be necessary for a pupil from an African school to have passed Standard 8 (Southern Rhodesian Junior Certificate) in order to have completed two years secondary education, whereas a pupil at a European, Asian, or Coloured School would have completed such education after passing Standard 7. Yet other significant decisions of the Board have been given in respect of teacher and nurses' training, neither of which strictly speaking amount to secondary education. Passing the Nurses Final Examination or the Primary Teachers' Higher Certificate (undertaken after passing Junior Certificate) has been equated to four years of secondary education, whereas passing the Primary Teacher's Lower Certificate (undertaken after passing Standard 6) is not counted as secondary education at all.[4]

The effect of the franchise requirements is at present to place control of the constituencies in the hands of Europeans, who form the vast majority of 'A' Roll voters, and to place control of the electoral districts in the hands of Africans who form the large majority of 'B' Roll voters. The most recent registration of voters in Southern Rhodesia is shown in tabular form in Figure II.

The position in January 1965 was that out of a total of 97,284 'A' Roll voters, 92,405 were European and 2,330 were African. In respect of the 'B' Roll, the position was that there were 11,577 voters in all, of whom 10,689 were African and 587 were European.

These figures are distorted by virtue of the fact that Africans have boycotted

---

[1] Minutes of the Educational Qualifications Board Meeting chaired by Sir John Murray on 20 January 1961. Available for inspection in the office of the Chief Registering Officer.

[2] African primary schools continue to Standard 6 whereas non-African primary schools continue to Standard 5, Standard 6 being the first year of non-African secondary education.

[3] Minutes of 20 January 1961.

[4] All the decisions of the Educational Qualifications Board on equivalent qualifications are reflected in the Notes to Table J in the Appendix.

FIGURE II

Registered Voters in Southern Rhodesia

(Source: Central Statistical Office and *S.R.L.A.D.*, Vol. 57, col. 301, 5 August 1964
and Vol. 61, cols. 1213–14, 21 July 1965)

		31 May 1961[1]	31 August 1962[1]	31 May 1964[1]	31 January 1965
Europeans:	'A' Roll	77,717	86,720	89,278	92,405
	'B' Roll	429	614	608	587
Asians:	'A' Roll	972	1,151	1,231	1,242
	'B' Roll	55	147	114	120
Coloureds:	'A' Roll	999	1,281	1,308	1,307
	'B' Roll	63	151	176	181
Africans:	'A' Roll	1,397	1,920	2,263	2,330
	'B' Roll	3,231	9,585	10,466	10,689
	Total	84,863	101,569	105,444	108,861

[1] These figures are relevant for comparative purposes as they show the number of registered voters who could vote under the old franchise prior to the new Constitution, who could have participated in the 1961 and 1964 Referenda, and who could have participated in the 1962 and 1965 general elections.

the voters' rolls from at least the beginning of 1961 and probably earlier. However, the effect of the boycott, it is submitted, has only been marked in respect of the 'B' Roll, for which large numbers of Africans would probably be eligible.[1] Another consequence of the boycott has been that cross-voting was not effectively used either in the 1962 or the 1965 General Elections. In fact the number of 'B' Roll votes registered did not nearly approach one-fourth of the number of 'A' Roll votes in the majority of constituencies,[2] which varied in 1965 from 2,509 in the largest constituency to 1,595 in the smallest.[3] Furthermore only approximately 24 per cent of the registered 'B' Roll voters cast votes in the 1962 election and 13·7 per cent in the 1965 election.

[1] See Appendix, Tables J and K read with Figure I. Estimates have varied from 60,000 potential registrants in 1961 by Sir Edgar Whitehead (*S.R.L.A.D.*, Vol. 49, cols. 366–8, 11 December 1961) to over 100,000 in 1964 (Statement submitted to the Secretary General of the United Nations by the United Kingdom Delegation on behalf of the Government of Southern Rhodesia in June 1964). See also Appendix, Table P. Table P read with Table J indicates that the figure would have been a maximum of 70,000 on the assumption that Africans complete primary education at sixteen years of age.

[2] See Appendix, Table L, for numbers of 'B' Roll votes in the constituencies as at 30 April 1963 and 28 February 1965. Only in twenty-two of the fifty constituencies did 'B' Roll votes reach three figures. In the May 1965 election only in nine constituencies could the full effect of 'B' Roll voting (had it occurred) have been felt because only in nine were the 'B' Roll votes one fourth or more of the number of 'A' Roll votes.

[3] *S.R.L.A.D.*, Vol. 61, cols. 1497–1500. These figures relate to 28 February 1965. In the largest constituency there were also thirteen 'B' Roll voters, eight voters in all being African. In the smallest constituency there were 268 'B' Roll voters, 301 Africans in all being on the Rolls.

In respect of the 'A' Roll, it is submitted that, even if every potential African registrant were to enrol, the total number could not at present be in excess of 8,500.[1] It has, however, been suggested that the present franchise qualifications will ensure the emergence of a majority of African voters in a relatively short period of time. This is correct in respect of the 'B' Roll but not necessarily correct in respect of the 'A' Roll. Only if there is a rise in African incomes and an increase in the number of Africans able to obtain four years of secondary education, will there be a rapid increase in the number of potential African 'A' Roll registrants. Table J shows that the Southern Rhodesian African education system has not in the past produced many Africans with the requisite educational qualifications. Even assuming an expansion in the present rate of growth of African schooling the African education system will between 1966 and 1971 only have produced a further 35,482 potential African 'A' Roll registrants.[2] On the other hand, if there were a great expansion in secondary school education, and provided increased employment for a greater number of better educated Africans

---

[1] Estimate as at 31 July 1965. See Appendix, Table O, for estimates relative to September 1961. Table J read with notes 7, 8, and 9 discloses that in 1965 the cumulative figure of Africans who had four years of secondary education was approximately 6,300. This represents an increase of 2,994 Africans on the 1961 educational figures of 3,306 (obtained from Table J and notes 7, 8, and 9) but some of these would not have reached the age of twenty-one. Even on the assumption that all were of age and earned the required income (now £27 10s. 0d. p.m.—see Figure I) the total potential number of registrants as at 31 July 1965 was 8,494, with a large element of double-counting, the unlikely assumption being made that none of those with educational qualifications had already acquired the franchise by virtue of the income qualification. Average annual earnings of employees in 1964 as compared with those in 1961 have not risen sufficiently to indicate that larger numbers of Africans could qualify by virtue of their income qualifications alone. (Monthly Digest of Statistics, May 1965, Central Statistical Office, Salisbury, p. 9.) Neither is it likely that many Africans with primary education earn sufficient to meet the franchise requirements. Whereas the required income is £44 per month if the applicant has primary education, the average income of African household heads residing in Salisbury's main African townships and possessing such education was £19 15s. 11d. per month. Furthermore, in 1964 it appears that only 1 per cent of African family units (irrespective of the degree of education of the head of family and therefore including all those with a higher standard of education) had an income of £36 per month or over: Report on Urban African Budget Survey in Salisbury 1963/64. Central Statistical Office, Salisbury, July 1965. Table 7, p. 10, and Table 10, p. 13. The Southern Rhodesian Government estimated the potential figure in June 1964 as then being at least 10,000. Statement to Secretary General, supra. Table J read with Table O, however, shows a maximum then of 7,239. It also appears from figures quoted by the Southern Rhodesian High Commissioner in London in July 1964 that the Ministry of Education gave him figures which indicated that at that time there were a potential 6,969 voters. Personal communication from a confidential source.

[2] See Table M which, in the assumption that the Southern Rhodesia education system will continue to expand and that there will be places for African children, gives the maximum potential number of Africans with four years of secondary education. Such persons will not all qualify for the vote as numbers will not be twenty-one years of age, while unless there is an expansion in the job opportunities available to Africans not all of them will be able to find employment: see 'The Requirements and Supply of High Level Manpower in Southern Rhodesia, 1961–70', Occasional Paper No. 3, Department of Economics, Salisbury, 1964, p. 16, Table 16.

could be found, Africans could in twelve years (1977) reach the present total of 'A' Roll European registered voters.[1]

A further factor affecting the potential number of registrants is the difficult type of claim form for registration. The current claim form contains 38 questions, requiring applicants to state such technicalities as whether they are citizens by registration.[2] The Minister of Internal Affairs has explained that, since the Electoral Act in section 15 requires claimants to be able to speak, read, write, and comprehend the English language, administrative instructions have been given to registering officers to ensure that applicants have such knowledge and that they should if necessary test an applicant's understanding of English. He contended that the Act required persons to possess not merely a small and limited vocabulary but a 'reasonably extensive vocabulary'. The Minister acknowledged that 'the very purpose of this form is itself to be restrictive in its effect. It is a test. It is a filter . . .'[3] The Government thereupon refused to simplify the form as this would enable persons with lower standards to pass the test.

Yet another factor that affects the franchise is that section 13 of the Electoral Act provides for an automatic percentage increase in franchise property and income qualifications if a Commission, which is to be appointed triennially, reports that in comparison with the 'purchasing power of money in Southern Rhodesia' at 1 July 1957 there has been an increase of not less than ten per centum.[4]

Whatever may be the future—and such predictions depend on political and economic variables—the present position is that the Southern

---

[1] See Table N for such a projection. This assumes that all qualified Africans would earn salaries of over £330 p.a. and would have reached the age of majority, and that the total number of European registrants would not have increased. There are however approximately 3,800 European school-leavers per annum with the requisite educational qualifications who would, assuming a balance of European emigration and immigration, have swelled the European vote by a further 41,800.

[2] In 1937 eleven questions required answering, in 1946 twelve, in 1952 fifteen, and in 1958 twenty: *S.R.L.A.D.*, Vol. 61, cols. 1228–9, 21 July 1965.

[3] *S.R.L.A.D.*, Vol. 61, cols. 1262–3, Mr. Harper, 21 July 1965.

[4] If the decrease is greater than 20 per cent there is a corresponding increase in the amount of the monetary qualifications. There is again a proportionate increase if there is a 30 per cent or more decrease. The second Commission appointed in terms of this section (see S.R.G.N. No. 324/64) reported on 6 July 1964, that there had been a 10·5 per centum decrease in the purchasing power of money in comparison with its initial power. The Commission reached its findings by weighting average indices of the Consumer Price Index for Europeans and Africans in urban areas only. Its report, however, discloses that there had been no rise in the cost of living of Africans in rural areas where 82 per cent of the African population reside, largely outside the money economy. If the figures relate to Southern Rhodesia and to the population of Southern Rhodesia as a whole, the overall rise in the cost of living has only been 1·84 per cent. However, section 13 refers to 'the purchasing power of money' and the fact that the majority of the population has not been affected by decreases as it lives outside the money economy is irrelevant to the operation of the section. Consequently inflation in urban areas and the cash economy may result in rendering persons outside the cash economy ineligible for the franchise.

Rhodesian Legislative Assembly is elected by a predominantly European electorate.[1]

Qualifications for election as members and vacation of seats

The Legislative Assembly constituted under the 1923 Constitution was empowered by the Southern Rhodesian (Constitution) Order in Council to provide for the conduct of elections for Members of the new Legislative Assembly in terms of the 1961 Constitution,[2] while the 1961 Constitution permits laws of the new Legislature to make general provisions for the qualification and disqualification of candidates and for the holding of elections.[3] In practice, however, the major part of the existing law was retained. In particular, the provision continued whereby the qualifications of a candidate were equated to those of a voter.[4] This meant that the new voters' qualifications were required by candidates for election. Standard disqualifications were laid down, viz. office under the Crown, mental disorder, imprisonment within five years without the option of a fine,[5] bankruptcy, &c.[6] while similar provision was made in the Constitution itself for the vacation of seats by Members who are absent from twenty-one consecutive sittings during any session of the Assembly without leave, who cease to be British subjects, who are sentenced to a term of more than six months' imprisonment, &c.[7] Provision is also made complementing the disqualifications by rendering any person who sits and votes knowing that he is disqualified liable to penalties.[8] However, proceedings of the Assembly are nonetheless valid.[9] Unless it can

---

[1] This can be seen in its present composition (July 1965). All fifty members representing constituencies are members of the Rhodesian Front (a right-wing European Party). The electoral districts are represented by ten African members who are members of the United Peoples Party (formerly the Rhodesia Party née the United Federal Party) and three African independents, one Asian and one European independent.

[2] S.I. 1961, No. 2314, Section 2(1)(c).

[3] Section 8(1)(a).

[4] See Electoral Act, Section 51(11).

[5] This provision will, unless it is changed, exclude a large number of African leaders who have received such sentences for political offences under the Law and Order (Maintenance) Act, Chapter 39, e.g. for making subversive statements—Section 44 of this Act prescribes imprisonment as the punishment for this particular offence. The Rev. N. Sithole is ineligible for election on this basis, as is Mr. J. Nkomo.

[6] Electoral Act, Section 51(12).

[7] Sections 14 and 15. During the course of 1963 concern was occasioned by the fact that one of the Members representing an electoral district was charged under the Law and Order (Maintenance) Act for making a statement which would bring the police force into contempt and disesteem. He was, however, acquitted.

[8] Section 16 of the Constitution.

[9] Section 18. Quaere whether this would relate to a situation where all 'Members' were disqualified, since there might be no 'Legislative Assembly' in terms of Section 7(1) but merely a body of persons purporting to act as such. Section 18 was probably inserted to make it clear that consequences such as those which arose in Strickland v. Grima, [1930] A.C. 285 could not follow.

be argued that on general principles of judicial review where there is a written constitution, the courts have jurisdiction, it seems that the Legislature is the sole judge of qualifications of its members,[1] and that even though a Member may be disqualified the courts may not pronounce on this.[2]

The meeting of the Legislative Assembly

The Governor may appoint the place and time for the meeting of the Legislative Assembly.[3] There must, however, be a session beginning in every calendar year so that a period of twelve months shall not elapse between the last sitting of the Assembly in one session and its first sitting in the next session.[4] Again, the Governor may at any time prorogue the Assembly,[5] whereas adjournments are provided for by the Standing Orders.[6]

The Assembly is likewise liable to dissolution at any time by Proclamation of the Governor acting in his discretion in accordance with constitutional conventions observed in the United Kingdom,[7] while it must be dissolved at the expiry of five years from the date of its first meeting after any general election.[8] Thereafter a general election shall be held within such period not being in excess of four months, as shall be prescribed by the Governor by Proclamation.[9]

Procedure

The procedure of the Assembly is, with certain modifications, similar to that in the United Kingdom.[10] It is governed by Standing Orders which are

---

[1] Section 8(1)(c) permits the Legislature to provide by law for the hearing of election petitions and this has been done in the Electoral Act, but this does not relate to subsequent vacation of seats.

[2] See Keith, *Letters on Imperial Relations, 1916–1935*, Oxford, 1935, pp. 290–2. There is no express provision in the Constitution permitting the courts to pronounce on the composition of the Legislature as there was in Section 56(b)(i) of the Federal Constitution, which gave the Federal Supreme Court exclusive original jurisdiction to determine whether a vacancy existed. Cp. *Strickland* v. *Grima*, *supra* at p. 297 and *Senanayake* v. *Navaratne*, [1954] 3 W.L.R. 336. Cp. also Section 71(1) of the Constitution which gives the High Court jurisdiction to enquire into contraventions of the Declaration of Rights, and Section 115(1) which relates to the validity of 'Acts'. The only section in the Constitution which might conceivably give the High Court jurisdiction is Section 53(3), as amended, which gives the General Division of the High Court 'full jurisdiction . . . over all matters within Southern Rhodesia'.

[3] Section 33(1). It has, however, always met at the Legislative Assembly building in Salisbury.

[4] Section 33(2), as amended. Section 9 of the Constitution Amendment Act 1965 was introduced as a consequence of a motion arguing that the original section required the Assembly to begin and end a session pursuant to a prorogation or a dissolution once at least in every calendar year. The motion was negatived by the Legislative Assembly, the House at that time having continued in the same session for more than twelve months: *S.R.L.A.D.*, Vol. 60, cols. 102 et seq., 24 February 1965.

[5] Section 34(1).   [6] S.O. 19 to 30.   [7] Section 34(2) and Section 45(1).

[8] Section 34(3).   [9] Section 19.

[10] Some of the departures from United Kingdom procedure are occasioned by the special

altered from time to time by the Assembly[1] which provide that these are in case of doubt to be interpreted in the light of relevant practice in the House of Commons, while gaps shall be filled by such practice except that restrictions introduced in the Commons by Standing Order are not applicable.[2] A considerable difference in procedure is however occasioned by the size of the House, which does not appoint Standing Committees to consider Bills, so that the Committee stage always occurs in Committee of the whole House. Another important difference is that Speaker's rulings may be challenged and that a division shall then be called.[3] There is also a special Private Members' afternoon (Wednesday) on which motions moved by Private Members take precedence over Government business. Private Members do not move Private Members' Bills but rely on this procedure to advance their views. Special provision is also made that the House may not proceed on any Bill or motion infringing Crown prerogatives unless the Governor signifies his consent.[4] Another difference is that a motion for closure does not require a minimum number of members to vote in favour before it can be carried.[5]

Standing Orders provide that no member may refer to any matter on which a judicial decision is pending,[6] and on one occasion an unsuccessful attempt was made to persuade the Courts to intervene in the conduct of parliamentary business on this account. That the Courts are not prepared to enforce such a Standing Order appeared from *Ex parte Wilson*.[7] In this case the Speaker had ruled that although ownership of the British South Africa Company's mineral rights was the subject of litigation in the High Court, debate was permissible as it merely involved the question of the payment of royalties. Thereafter, in an application to Court for an Order directing the Registrar to place before the Speaker the fact that such a case was pending, the Court refused to grant the application as 'there can be no doubt the matter of the

---

institutions created by the Constitution. Thus special provisions have been made in Standing Orders 161 to 171 to deal with relations between the Legislative Assembly and the Constitutional Council, while provision has been made for motions to the Crown in terms of Section 109 of the Constitution.

[1] At present the 7th edition (1964) is in force. There are two volumes, one relating to public business and the other to private bills. There is also a Private Bill Procedure Act (Chapter 6). For Speaker's rulings as to whether a Bill is private or not, and the tests to be applied, see *S.R.L.A.D.*, Vol. 27(2), col. 2989.

[2] Standing Order 236. Erskine May's *Parliamentary Practice* is always referred to when any point for decision arises.

[3] S.O. 99.

[4] S.O. 98. This is an Order which survived the 1923 Constitution. Until 1962 the Governor was required in terms of the Royal Instructions to reserve such Bills.

[5] The closure has infrequently been used: the last occasion was on 6 August 1958; see *S.R.L.A.D.*, Vol. 41, col. 998. Earlier the closure had been used for the first time on a financial measure: see *S.R.L.A.D.*, Vol. 41, col. 884, 1 August 1958, and comment in col. 995, 6 August 1958, which led to the closure being used a second time. Provision for the guillotine exists (S.O. 63) but has never been utilized.

[6] S.O. 57(iv).

[7] 1933 S.R. 76.

bounds of discussion, of the scope of discussion, is entirely within the jurisdiction of the House itself, exercised, probably, through Mr. Speaker'.[1]

The Legislative Assembly is presided over by the Speaker or, in his absence,
by the Deputy Speaker,[2] who is the Chairman of Committees.[3] When presiding, neither enjoys an original or casting vote.[4] For the transaction of
business a relatively small quorum of ten members is required.[5]

The Legislature may also provide for the privileges, immunities, and powers
of the Legislative Assembly and its Members. These are largely governed by
the Powers and Privileges of Parliament Act,[6] which is to some extent a restatement of powers and privileges as interpreted in the Commons, but is not
a codification. The Act provides that the Assembly and its members shall
enjoy the like privileges, immunities, and powers as were enjoyed on the
24 September 1923, by the House of Commons.[7] It also gives Parliament the
powers of a court of record[8]; and it permits Parliament by resolution to
authorize the Attorney-General to prosecute in the High Court for contravention of the Act which sets out a number of offences such as contempts of
Parliament.[9] By the end of July 1965 there had only been three Committees
of Privilege appointed by the Legislative Assembly during the whole of its
existence.[10]

---

[1] Per Russell C.J. at 79. The Court considered such action would amount to interference
with the object of influencing the course and scope of debate in the Assembly.

[2] Section 23. Further provision is made for the election of a Member to preside in their
absence. At the beginning of every session the Speaker nominates two Members who, with
the Chairman of Committees and the Deputy Chairman of Committees, constitute the
Chairman's panel, and any one of the members of this panel can be called on to take the
Chair: S.O. 9(3)(4).

[3] S.O. 8.

[4] Constitution, Section 25(2). S.O. 34 reflects this provision and also lays down that if
the House is equally divided, a motion shall be lost.

[5] Section 24.   [6] Chapter 4.   [7] Chapter 4, Section 33.

[8] Section 5. Under this section Committees of Privileges have heard evidence on oath,
while Section 10 permits Parliament to impose fines and fees for contempts. This power is
dealt with in S.O. 201–4. However, it may be that the provision for such powers is *ultra
vires* as Chapter 4 was enacted in terms of Section 25(1) of the 1923 Constitution, which
provides that the privileges and powers of Parliament shall not exceed those for the time
being held, enjoyed, and exercised by the House of Commons. The Commons has not
exercised the power to impose fines since 1666, while Lord Mansfield in *James* v. *Randall*,
1 Cowp. 17 held that the Commons was not a court of record and that it had no power to
impose fines in *R.* v. *Pitt* and *R.* v. *Mead*, 3 Burr. 1335. See also Erskine May's *Treatise on
the Law, Privileges, Proceedings and Usage of Parliament, 16th Ed.*, Butterworths, 1957, p. 90.
Apparently in Canada where a similar limitation existed, an Act passed in 1873 was disallowed, since it purported to confer power on Committees of the Canadian Senate and
House of Commons to examine witnesses on oath. Such powers were subsequently
accorded by an Imperial Act. See Keith, *Responsible Government*, Vol. II, op. cit., p. 766.
An Imperial Act would not now be necessary in Southern Rhodesia as the 1961 Constitution
in Section 26 authorizes the Legislature to make provision to determine and regulate the
privileges, immunities and powers of the Assembly without any limitation that these shall
not exceed the powers enjoyed by the Commons.

[9] Section 10.

[10] The Assembly has recently become conscious of its privileges. The three Committees

On earlier occasions the Speaker has ruled that there have been breaches of privilege but has left the question to the House, which has accepted apologies instead of appointing Committees of Privilege.[1] On yet another occasion two Members, one of them the Leader of the Opposition, were found guilty of a contempt of the House, by vote of the whole House, and were suspended for seven days for refusing to attend meetings of the Select Committee on Public Accounts.[2] On a limited number of other occasions breaches of privilege were also raised.[3]

Extensive use is made of the committee system. At the commencement of every session, the Speaker appoints certain sessional committees, viz. the

were appointed in 1964 and 1965. In the first case, it was found that the conduct of a journalist, who challenged a member to repeat remarks outside the Chamber, did not constitute a breach of privilege: Report of the Committee of Privileges, L.A.S.C. 9–1964. In the second case, where there was an allegation that a false and scandalous libel on Members of the Opposition had been published by the Organizing Secretary of the Governing Party, the Committee found that the libel did not touch on their conduct as members, but that there had been a misrepresentation of the proceedings of Parliament which it deplored. In view of its desire to preserve freedom of speech in matters of political controversy the Committee thought that Parliament should only take note of gross and scandalous misrepresentations and they considered that the particular statement complained of did not have this character and thus did not amount to a contempt: L.A.S.C. 12–1964 and *S.R.L.A.D.*, Vol. 58, col. 1384, 7 October 1964. In the third case, after a Member of Parliament had described UNESCO as 'an evil organization' and deplored the fact that UNESCO representatives were teaching young people, the Professor of Education at the University College challenged the Member to substantiate what he had said about UNESCO representatives who were attached to his department. He also said 'One does not normally look for earnest seekers of the truth among politicians, but one does expect a man with some education, like Mr. Owen-Smith, to make sure of his facts, especially before making a maiden speech in Parliament.' The Committee found that publication of this statement in a newspaper report constituted a breach of privilege: L.A.S.C. 4–1965.

[1] Thus after a newspaper report had stated that the Chairman of Committees, then Mr. W. J. Harper, had adopted a partisan approach in the chair the House accepted an apology from the Editor of the *Bulawayo Chronicle*: *S.R.L.A.D.*, Vol. 43.

[2] See *S.R.L.A.D.*, Vol. 22, col. 1506 et seq., 10 June 1942. The Members had refused to attend as they considered a convention had been breached by the election of a government member as Chairman of this Committee. One of them had then asked the Committee on Standing Rules and Orders to release him from membership of the Public Accounts Committee but this request was refused. The other Member did not wish to act 'on what might prove to be a purely white-washing committee of the government' and also failed to attend the meetings of the Select Committee. After a letter of complaint by the Chairman of the Public Accounts Committee, the Speaker found that they had failed to fulfil duties imposed on them by the House. *Quaere* whether the House or the Speaker should not first have warned them to attend the Committee. See *S.R.L.A.D.*, Vol. 22, cols. 1910 et seq., 26 June 1942, quoting O'Brien's Case.

[3] See *S.R.L.A.D.*, Vol. 24, col. 988, 12 May 1944, where the Speaker ruled that wartime censorship of Members' letters was not a breach of privilege. In October 1961 a Member refused to vacate the Members' Lobby, this having been set aside on the Speaker's instructions for a meeting of the Council of Chiefs, as he considered the Lobby was reserved for Members only. The Member, when warned that the Speaker intended to raise this as a breach of privilege, apologised and no proceedings were initiated. Personal communication. On another occasion a Commission of Inquiry's terms of reference were drafted so as to 'enquire into the speech' made by a Member whose remarks gave rise to the appointment of the Commission: see *S.R.L.A.D.*, Vol. 46, cols. 3928–30, 29 November 1960.

Committee on Standing Rules and Orders, the Printing Committee, the Parliamentary Library Committee, and the Internal Arrangements Committee.[1] Select Committees are frequently employed. There are three sessional select committees—the Select Committees on Public Accounts, Pensions, Grants and Gratuities, and that on Estimates. Others are appointed on an ad hoc basis to investigate problems[2] while, on several occasions, Bills have been referred to select committees after second readings.[3]

Financial procedure

The standard British principles of parliamentary control of public finance are observed by the Southern Rhodesian Legislative Assembly, so that the sanction for expenditure and sole power of authorizing the raising of funds is vested in Parliament.[4] The same principles of Treasury control as in the United Kingdom are applicable so that the Treasury adjusts competing claims by Departments and approves votes on the estimates.[5] After Cabinet approval the various revenue and loan votes are placed before and approved by the Assembly when sitting in Committee of Supply under the Chairman of Committees. Eighty-five hours are allotted to the business of supply on the main Estimates[6] and a convention operates that the Opposition in consultation with the Leader of the House may place on the Order Paper those votes which it wishes to debate.

The Estimates are preceded by a motion by the Minister of Finance to go into Committee of Ways and Means when he delivers his Budget speech, after which the economic and financial as well as general policy of the

[1] S.O. 13(1). The Standing Rules and Orders Committee is presided over by the Speaker and is responsible for advising Mr. Speaker on appointments to select committees and the general management of Parliament. The Prime Minister and Leader of the Opposition are members.

[2] They have often been used as a vehicle for putting forward a point of view when the Government wishes to introduce particular legislation, viz. the Select Committee on Resettlement of Natives, and the Select Committee on Betting and Lotteries, both of which preceded legislation on the topics in question.

[3] e.g. The Land Husbandry Bill 1951 and the Industrial Conciliation Bill 1957.

[4] Certain powers of taxation have been delegated under the Municipal Act, Town Management Act, and other local government Acts to local authorities, but these taxes nonetheless rest on parliamentary authorization, and such delegation could be revoked at any time.

[5] Shortly before the dissolution of Federation the Treasury was re-named the Ministry of Finance. In 1942 the then Prime Minister insisted on United Kingdom Treasury practice being observed: see *S.R.L.A.D.*, Vol. 21(1), col. 3102. The Treasury on two recent occasions had no option but *ex post facto* to ratify heavy expenditures incurred by Ministers. In the one case the Prime Minister had given a Government guarantee in respect of a bank overdraft in excess of half a million pounds, the estate of the debtor at that time being under provisional sequestration. The incidents were deplored by the Minister of Finance who insisted that 'control must be exercised by the Treasury': *S.R.L.A.D.*, Vol. 61, col. 430, 18 June 1965.

[6] S.O. 82(1).

Government are debated.[1] Later the Committee of Ways and Means approves the various taxation proposals and thereafter specific Bills are brought up authorizing the imposition of various taxes.[2]

The same procedure, except that no Budget statement is made and that detailed debate occurs in Committee of Supply is followed if supplementary Estimates are brought forward later in the year to cover items for which Departments have failed to estimate. Special provision is also made for unforeseen expenditure, which cannot be postponed: the Governor may by special warrant authorize the issue of sums for this purpose provided that the total of sums issued under the section does not at any time exceed £500,000 and that the sums are submitted to Parliament for appropriation not later than the next ensuing sitting.[3] Special provision is also made for advances.[4] Except in these cases and cases where expenditure is charged on the Fund by the Constitution, by an Appropriation Act, or by a law of the Legislature no money may be withdrawn from the Consolidated Revenue Fund.[5]

An unusual procedure was adopted during 1963 and 1964 as a result of Federal dissolution. Since there was an extraordinary situation in which it was extremely difficult to estimate expenditures in view of the return of Federal functions, the expedient of a Vote of Credit of £25 million was adopted.[6] Normal budgetary practices have, however, since been resumed.

Financial proposals can only originate from the Government, as section 28 of the Constitution provides that Bills, motions, or petitions providing for charges on the public revenue, unless introduced by a Minister or Deputy Minister, may only be proceeded with upon the recommendation of the Governor signified by a Minister. Eventually, once the procedures outlined above have been observed, an annual Appropriation Act is passed authorizing the issue from the Consolidated Revenue Fund of specified sums for services detailed in the Estimates. Provided the Minister of Finance agrees, virement is permitted so that savings on a sub-head of a vote may be used to meet excess expenditure on any other sub-head of the same vote.[7]

Parliamentary control of expenditure is further ensured by the appointment

---

[1] The Speech from the Throne—Debate on the Motion for an Address in reply to the Governor's speech, see S.O. 14—is the proper occasion for general policy to be debated.

[2] e.g. the Stamp Duties Amendment Act 1963, the Vehicle Tax Amendment Act 1964, &c.

[3] Audit and Exchequer Act (Chapter 144), section 23. The use of the word 'sitting' has in practice been interpreted to mean 'session': S.R.L.A.D., Vol. 54, col. 2158, 3 October 1963.

[4] Chapter 144, section 24 as amended by section 11 of Act 42 of 1963.

[5] Section 113(3) as amended.

[6] See S.R.L.A.D., Vol. 54, cols. 1673 et seq., 30 September 1963.

[7] Provision for virement is normally made in the annual Appropriation Act, see e.g. the Appropriation Act No. 40 of 1962, section 6(1). The Select Committee on Public Accounts has criticized too generous an interpretation of the principles of virement, which it set out at length and which it considered should be used with caution. See First Report of the Select Committee of Public Accounts, Government Printer, Salisbury, L.A.S.C. 1–1959.

of two Select committees: the Select Committee on Public Accounts,[1] and the Select Committee on Estimates[2] which has several sub-committees which investigate Departments. The latter Committee is empowered to report on how the policy implied in the Estimates and any Supplementary Estimates may be carried out more economically and on the principal variations and the form of the Estimates, but it may not examine or report on Government policy or recommend deduction of amounts in the Estimates.[3] The Select Committee on Public Accounts considers the Report made by the Controller and Auditor General[4] and examines this and Departmental accounts and investigates whether the Administration has been negligent. This Select Committee can be an important instrument in checking waste and inefficiency in the Administration and its reports have on occasion led to considerable controversy,[5] but its reports are normally implemented by the responsible Ministries. One result of its criticism is that whereas previously the Estimates gave no indication[6] of contingent liabilities which might arise out of Government guarantees and contractor finance,[7] the practice has now been adopted of including this information in the Estimates.

The Auditor General, who holds office during good behaviour subject to removal on an address by the Assembly[8] is charged with ensuring the

---

[1] Appointed on the Southern Rhodesian High Commissioner's (Sir Francis Newton) suggestion from 1930 onwards. No convention has been established that the Chairman should be a financial spokesman from the Opposition, largely because in the past the Assembly was too small. From 1958 to mid-1964 an Opposition Member was appointed as Chairman, but recently a Government back-bencher has again been elected Chairman.

[2] Appointed for the first time in 1964.

[3] S.O. 193.

[4] Provided for in the Audit and Exchequer Act, Chapter 144. The Auditor General assists the Committee with advice and by pointing out administrative irregularities in his Report.

[5] In 1941 and 1942 there was a wrangle between the Committee and the Government, occasioned by the Minister of Finance, who refused to return certain papers to the Auditor-General: see *S.R.L.A.D.*, Vol. 21(1), col. 3103. In 1943 the Committee reported that the Government had contravened the Audit and Exchequer Act by excessive drawings on Governor's warrants: see *S.R.L.A.D.*, Vol. 24, col. 2831. Difficulties on this score had already occurred in 1940: *S.R.L.A.D.*, Vol. 20, cols. 970–6. In 1944 another dispute arose out of a refusal by the Minister of Agriculture to allow the Auditor-General to examine the books of a Statutory Commission: see *S.R.L.A.D.*, Vol. 24, col. 728. In 1960 the Select Committee recommended Government immediately to institute an independent enquiry into the organization of the Division of Native Affairs and a bitter debate ensued, in which Government refused to adopt the report but had it referred for consideration. The latter procedure only occurs when questions of policy are involved: see *S.R.L.A.D.*, Vol. 44, cols. 3077–146. Eventually at the end of 1960 the Robinson Commission was appointed to enquire into the administrative and judicial functions of the Native Department—for its Report see C.S.R. 22–1961. There is in fact a departure from House of Commons practice because it is normal in the Southern Rhodesia Legislative Assembly to debate the report of the Select Committee on Public Accounts, whereas this is not frequently done in the Commons.

[6] See First Report of the Select Committee on Public Accounts, L.A.S.C. 1–1959, p. 4.

[7] Criticized from the point of view of weakening parliamentary control of finance: First Report of the Select Committee on Public Accounts, L.A.S.C. 4–1958, pp. 5–6.

[8] Chapter 144, Section 5(1). In 1944 the Auditor General was attacked by Mr. T. W. H. Beadle for involving himself in policy and thus in politics: *S.R.L.A.D.*, Vol. 23, col. 511.

proper audit of public accounts. At the same time he enjoys absolute independence to criticize the administration of public funds and to report to Parliament. In addition, the Auditor General enjoys power to surcharge the person responsible for public moneys where any deficiencies have occurred.[1]

Legislative power and the legislative process

The Constitution stipulates that it is to be the fundamental and supreme law of Southern Rhodesia since Section 115(1) provides that:

Any provision of any Act (or of any instrument having the effect of law made under the authority thereof) . . . which is inconsistent with any provision of this Constitution shall be invalid to the extent of the inconsistency.

This section makes it clear beyond doubt that the courts have power of judicial review to strike down legislation inconsistent with the Constitution,[2] quite apart from the 'manner and form' provision in Section 5 of the Colonial Laws Validity Act.[3]

Subject to the Constitution, the Legislature has plenary power to make laws for the peace, order, and good government of Southern Rhodesia,[4] and such laws may also operate extraterritorially.[5] However, there are a limited number of matters in respect of which the Southern Rhodesia Legislature is incompetent. These are certain constitutional amendments which are reserved to the Crown to provide for by Order in Council.[6]

As a result certain sections of the Constitution have been placed beyond the

---

[1] Chapter 144, Section 13. He is also given this power in respect of local authorities: see the Town Management Act (Chapter 134), Section 182, and the Local Government Act (Chapter 124), Section 56. The African Councils Act (Chapter 95), Section 95 allows an audit officer to levy a surcharge.

[2] *Nkomo and Others* v. *Minister of Justice and Others*, 1965 (1) S.A. 498 at 501.

[3] It is submitted that in any event on the authority of *R.* v. *Ndobe*, 1930 A.D. 484 and *Harris* v. *Minister of Interior*, *supra* at 470 the Courts would have had such power. See also *Bribery Commissioner* v. *Ranasinghe*, [1964] 2 W.L.R. 1301.

[4] Section 20(1). 'Within the limits of the Constitution the Legislature is "mistress in her own house". . . . If they are valid enactments it is not for the courts to adjudicate upon their wisdom, appropriateness and the necessity for their existence': Quenet J.P. in *Gundu and Sambo* v. *Hayward and Bosman NN.O.* Judgment No. A.D. 97/65 at pp. 9 and 10.

[5] Section 20(2). These powers were utilized in the Preservation of Constitutional Government Act (Chapter 45), Section 2, to make it a criminal offence for a Southern Rhodesian resident either within or outside S.R. to advocate the establishment of an organization to overthrow the Government by unconstitutional means or to coerce the Government, while Section 3 gives extraterritorial operation to Sections 29, 31, 44, and 48 of the Law and Order (Maintenance) Act (Chapter 39). This makes it an offence for any resident outside Southern Rhodesia to make statements threatening or encouraging violence or inciting a strike in an essential service in Southern Rhodesia, to make a subversive statement (one likely to excite disaffection against the Government or Constitution of Southern Rhodesia), or to publish news which is likely to cause fear, alarm, or despondency amongst the Southern Rhodesian public.

[6] Section 105 read with Section 111.

reach of the Southern Rhodesia Legislature, viz. those sections relating to the office of Governor and to his powers and duties,[1] to the Governor's assent or refusal of assent to Bills,[2] to disallowance,[3] to the prerogative of mercy,[4] to the composition of the Legislature,[5] to the definition of the authority in whom executive power for Southern Rhodesia is vested and how such power is to be exercised,[6] and to the section reserving this power to the Crown in Council. Even the Crown in Council may not amend Section 111 or add a reference to a section not embodied in it, as this power is exercisable only by the United Kingdom Parliament.[7]

At the time of their coming into operation the powers of the Legislative Assembly were further limited by the Federal Constitution, since there was express provision that in so far as the Federal Constitution related to the peace, order, and good government of Southern Rhodesia as a Territory of the Federation, the 1961 Southern Rhodesian Constitution was to be read and construed, subject always to the Federal Constitution's express provisions as amended from time to time.[8] The effect of this provision was that until Federal dissolution, Southern Rhodesian legislative power was subject to potential exclusion in respect of matters enumerated in the Federal Legislative List and was, in fact, excluded in certain cases (viz. external affairs, taxes on incomes and profits, and duties of customs and excise.[9]

---

[1] Sections 1, 2, 3, and 5.   [2] Section 29.   [3] Section 32.
[4] Section 49.   [5] Section 6.   [6] Section 42.
[7] Section 111 proviso. As a result of this section and the proviso a motion was moved and carried with the support of the Southern Rhodesian Government on 24 March 1964 (see *S.R.L.A.D.*, Vol. 56, cols. 1274–1310) in order to secure to a two-thirds majority of the Southern Rhodesian Legislative Assembly the power of amendment of these sections. The effect of the motion had it been acceded to, would have been to have permitted Southern Rhodesia to turn itself into a Republic and to amend fundamental sections of the Constitution on a mere two-thirds majority accompanied by a request to the British Government. The latter would have been duty-bound to implement the request by Order in Council. In addition the motion made it clear that any British legislation by Order in Council in respect of Southern Rhodesia would not be permissible unless this were requested by the Southern Rhodesian Government after a two-thirds majority of the Legislative Assembly had indicated its approval. Mr. Smith on becoming Prime Minister in June 1964 did not pursue this motion which requested the Governor 'to submit to Her Majesty a petition humbly praying Her Majesty in Her Parliament in Great Britain to amend Section 111 of the Constitution of Southern Rhodesia, 1961, so that the power and authority of Her Majesty to amend, add to or revoke by Order in Council the provisions of the Constitution presently specified in that section shall be exercised by Her Majesty at the request of the Government of Southern Rhodesia and may be exercised by Her Majesty only with the consent of the Government of Southern Rhodesia. Provided that a request shall be deemed not to have been made by the Government of Southern Rhodesia unless such request is accompanied by a certificate under the hand of the Speaker that the Legislative Assembly, by the affirmative votes of not less than two-thirds of the total membership of the Assembly, has passed a motion for the making of such a request': *S.R.L.A.D.*, Vol. 56, col. 1310.
[8] S.I. 1961/2314 Annex Section 117(1).
[9] See *supra*, Part I, Chapter 16. It will be submitted that as a result of certain constitutional anomalies the latter position still obtains in respect of Southern Rhodesian legislative competence: *infra*, Part II, Chapter 7.

In all other respects the Legislature enjoys full competence, although in a limited number of cases special procedures are enjoined upon it if it wishes to enact particular legislation.[1] Thus where any Bill would vary the terms of the trust imposed on the Board of Trustees for Tribal Trust Land and its powers and functions,[2] or would impose racial limitations on land ownership or occupation more restrictive than limitations in the Land Apportionment Act in force at the time of coming into effect of the Constitution, the same[3] procedure must be followed as that applicable to amendment of a specially entrenched provision of the Constitution. Furthermore, legislation which would vary the qualifications or disqualifications of voters at elections for the Legislative Assembly cannot be passed unless at the third reading the Bill is approved by a two-thirds majority of the total membership of the Assembly,[4] while any Bill which would render ineligible for registration as a voter any person who possessed the voters' qualifications specified in the Second Schedule in the Constitution, can only become law if the same procedures are followed as in the case of amendment to a specially entrenched section of the Constitution.[5] Finally any Bill which would, if enacted, amend the provisions for cross-voting as reflected in paragraph 10 of the Second Schedule must also be subjected to the same procedure for amendment to a specially entrenched constitutional provision.[6] Thus although the provisions to the Electoral Act are not technically part of the Constitution, they require for their amendment the observance of similar procedures.

The Constitution is drafted in such a way that it would seem that legislation inconsistent with the Declaration of Rights set out at length in the Constitution cannot be enacted even by these special procedures, unless the measure is expressed to be a constitutional amendment Bill.[7] This provision must have been inserted in order to direct the attention of the Legislature and the public to the nature of the enactment in question, as constitutional amendments are not lightly made.

[1] 'A legislature has no power to ignore the conditions of law making that are imposed by the instrument which itself regulates its power to make law. This restriction exists independently of the question whether the legislature is sovereign': *Bribery Commissioner* v. *Pedrick Ranasinghe*, [1964] 2 W.L.R. 1301 per Lord Pearce at 1310. See also p. 1312 where the learned Lord of Appeal stated that the observance of procedural provisions was 'a necessary part of the legislative process' and that 'no question of sovereignty arises'.

[2] Tribal Trust Land is composed of the Reserves plus the Special Native Area created in terms of the Land Apportionment Act and any other land set aside for the occupation of tribesmen by a law of the Legislature: Section 103(a)(b).

[3] Section 103(c).   [4] Section 9(1).

[5] Section 9(2).   [6] Section 9(4).

[7] Section 70(1)(a) provides that laws in respect of which Section 107 is applicable are not subject to the Declaration. Section 107 deals with specially entrenched constitutiona l provisions and constitutional Bills, while Section 105 proviso prohibits amendment of the Constitution by implication, stating that amendments must be in express terms. Had it not been for this proviso it would otherwise have been arguable from *Krause* v. *C.I.R.*, 1929 A.D. 286 and *McCawley* v. *The King*, [1920] A.C. 691 that amendment by implication was permissible.

All constitutional amendments require special procedures to be followed, in some cases the procedure being more rigid than in others. Every constitutional Bill requires a vote of not less than two-thirds of the total membership of the Southern Rhodesian Legislative Assembly at the final vote thereon.[1] This at present means that forty-four members must be in favour of the final vote on any Bill.[2] In addition there are certain specially entrenched constitutional provisions (enumerated in the Third Schedule) which require for their amendment not only passage by a two-thirds majority of the Legislative Assembly but also referenda by each of the four principal racial communities (viz. European, African, Asian, and Coloured) at which a majority of each group, voting separately, approves the change.[3] An alternative to this latter procedure is a motion to the Governor asking him to submit the Bill to Her Majesty for assent, but such a motion may only be moved (again by a two-thirds majority) after the Governor has indicated to the Assembly that Her Majesty (in this case advised by the British Cabinet) has agreed to the moving of the motion.[4]

The specially entrenched provisions cover the major topics of constitutional significance.[5] All the provisions, which specify as being necessary procedures similar to those required for constitutional amendment of specially entrenched provisions of the Constitution (e.g. amendments raising the franchise qualifications) are themselves safeguarded. The constitution of both the Appellate and General Divisions of the High Court, the appointment, qualifications, salary, and removal[6] of judges, the Roman–Dutch Law as the common law, and the right of the Legislature to provide for special leave to appeal to the Privy Council are all likewise safeguarded. The same is applicable to the Declaration of Rights, the Constitutional Council's composition and functions, the duties and powers[7] of the Board of Trustees of Tribal Trust Land, the powers of the Legislature in regard to land, the provision for constitutional amendment, the pensions of civil servants, and the provision for supremacy of the Constitution.

---

[1] Sections 106 and 110.

[2] Section 117(7) as amended. This also applies to motions requiring a two-thirds majority.

[3] Sections 107, 108, and 110. This safeguard was advocated in the Monckton Report, Cmnd. 1148, § 260, where, however, a three-quarters majority of the total membership of the Legislature was specified as being desirable.

[4] Section 109. The effect is that a two-thirds majority of the Legislature is required on two occasions during the passage of the measure. This procedure was utilized to pass the Constitution Amendment Act No. 13 of 1964.

[5] See the sections enumerated in the Third Schedule and also the Second Schedule. Most of these were specified as necessary in the Monckton Report, Cmnd 1148, § 261–2.

[6] Although it is provided that judges may only be removed after a recommendation to this effect by an independent tribunal (Section 56B(1)), the composition of the tribunal (at present judicial) is not specially entrenched (Section 56B(2)–(4) read with the Third Schedule as amended by Section 20 of Act 13 of 1964).

[7] But not the composition which is an ordinary constitutional provision (see Third Schedule read with Section 94).

Bills amending any other provisions of the Constitution cannot be passed unless they receive at their third reading a two-thirds majority of the votes of the total membership of the Legislative Assembly.[1] Thus the composition of the Legislative Assembly (that is, the number of constituencies and electoral districts and the ratio between these), the provisions for delimitation, legislative procedure, and numerous other provisions may be altered more easily than may the specially entrenched provisions, which in many circumstances would in practice be incapable of amendment unless the United Kingdom Government were prepared to permit the procedure of reservation to be employed as an alternative to four separate racial referenda.

Quite apart from these special provisions specifying particular majorities, nearly all Bills after their final reading have to be submitted for report to the Constitutional Council, which has powers of delay if the Bill is inconsistent with the Declaration of Rights. If, however, the Bill in question has not been adversely reported upon by the Council, it shall be presented to the Governor for assent.[2] The Governor's discretion to refuse to assent is in fact preserved by virtue of express reference thereto,[3] but no powers of reservation remain except in respect of Bills amending specially entrenched provisions of the Constitution where an address praying the Governor to submit the Bill to Her Majesty for assent has been moved and passed by a two-thirds majority of the total membership of the Legislative Assembly, in which case the Governor is required to reserve the Bill.[4]

After assent each Act is enrolled in the Office of the Registrar of the High Court but the validity of any Act does not depend on this enrolment.[5] Even after assent and enrolment a limited category of Acts is subject to disallowance within six months of the Governor's assent.[6]

The Constitutional Council

As indicated above, the large majority of Bills before they can be converted into Acts by virtue of the Governor's assent are subjected to scrutiny and possible delay by a body intended as a check on the Legislature and as a filtering mechanism to separate Bills which are inconsistent with the Declaration of Rights from those which may be enacted without further ado. This

---

[1] Section 106.

[2] Section 29(2).　　[3] Section 28(3)(a).　　[4] Section 30(1).

[5] Section 31(3). This must have been inserted to preclude any possible application of the enrolled Bill rule: see *Edinburgh and Dalkeith Railway Company* v. *Wauchope* (1842), 8 Cl. and F. 710 at 724–5; G. Marshall, *Parliamentary Sovereignty and the Commonwealth*, Oxford, 1957, pp. 23–24 and Appendix II, p. 251. Opinion by Professor E. C. S. Wade; *contra* R. F. V. Heuston, *Essays in Constitutional Law*, Stevens, 1961, pp. 17–22. See *Bribery Commissioner* v. *Pedrick Ranasinghe*, [1964] 2 W.L.R. 1301 (P.C.) for the view that where the Constitution prescribes procedures to be followed as part of the legislative process these must be complied with.

[6] Section 32. See *infra*, Chapter 7.

body is the Constitutional Council, established in terms of the Southern Rhodesia Constitution 1961.

The Council, to a considerable extent, reflects the recommendations of the Monckton Report for the introduction of Councils of State in the Federal and Territorial Constitutions[1] although the notion of such an institutional safeguard was first to be found in the Federal African Affairs Board, while it was subsequently developed through the Kenyan Council of State system.[2] However the Southern Rhodesian Constitutional Council is a far more effective body than either of these institutions and has been given even more extensive functions than those proposed in the Monckton Report.[3]

Composition

The Constitutional Council is a non-political and multi-racial body with a distinct judicial flavour. The present (first) Council was elected by an Electoral College consisting of the Chief Justice and puisne Judges of the High Court and any resident retired judges, while the President of the Council of Chiefs was an additional member.[4] Of these members six were elected for six years and five for three years.

Subsequent Councils are to be elected by secret ballot by an Electoral College again consisting of Judges, ex-judges, and the President of the Council of Chiefs, but also including the Chairman and members and ex-members or ex-chairmen of the Constitutional Council.[5] Such a College must be presided over by the Chairman of the Constitutional Council, who shall not be entitled to vote, and it must elect members to fill any vacancies from the names of duly qualified candidates submitted to it by the Constitutional Council, and from any further candidates nominated by the Chief Justice after consultation with the puisne Judges.[6] A degree of continuity of membership of the Council is secured by the staggering of elections to the Council, as at the end of every three years either five or six members complete their terms of office, while the

[1] Cmnd. 1148, § 242–62.

[2] See Ghai, op. cit.

[3] A major difference between the Report and the Council as established is that the Report suggested that the Council should be concerned only with the prevention and removal of unfair discrimination and that questions relative to liberties set out in any Bill of Rights should be left to the Courts alone.

[4] Southern Rhodesia (Constitution) Order-in-Council, Section 13(2). The President of the Council of Chiefs is elected by the Council in terms of the Council of Chiefs and Provincial Assemblies Act (Chapter 111), Section 7(4).

[5] Sections 80(1) and 81(2). Late in 1965 an election was held to replace the five members whose terms of office had expired in December. Objections to the method of election were voiced in the Legislative Assembly: *S.R.L.A.D.*, Vol. 61.

[6] Section 81(4) and (5). The Council must put forward the names of at least two duly qualified candidates for each vacancy.

others continue to complete their six-year terms.[1] However, no member can be re-elected for a second term to the Constitutional Council.[2]

Not only was the first Council of eleven members and a Chairman judicially elected from a list prepared by the Governor and approved by the Secretary of State of thirty-three persons qualified as candidates and willing to stand for election[3] but its composition has also a legalistic flavour. Both in respect of the first Council and all future Councils, it is specified that two of the Council's eleven elected members shall be either advocates or attorneys of the High Court of not less than ten years' standing, while its Chairman, holding office for seven years,[4] and appointed by the Governor on the advice of the Chief Justice after consultation with the puisne Judges, must be either an ex-judge of the High Court or of a superior court in a country in which the common law is Roman–Dutch or a retired advocate or attorney of not less than fifteen years' standing.[5] It was probably because of this 'legal' character of the Council that Hawthorn J. in considering whether a Ministerial certificate that provisions in the Unlawful Organizations Amendment Act No. 9 of 1963 should be accepted in a society which has a proper respect for the rights and freedoms of the individual considered that it was 'well worthy of note' that the Council had not adversely reported on this measure.[6]

Of the eleven elected members of the Council while two, as indicated above, must be persons with legal experience, three can be persons of any race and the remaining six must be selected to secure a multi-racially balanced composition—two requiring to be European, two African, one Asian, and one Coloured.[7]

[1] Section 75(3). The filling of casual vacancies is also provided for. A casual vacancy was filled in January 1965 in consequence of the death of the Asian member of the Council.

[2] Section 77(1)(f). This is probably because the Council is a self-perpetuating body. On the other hand it seems wrong that persons who enjoy public confidence should be precluded from a second term of office. There is no limitation precluding a member from subsequently becoming Chairman, provided he is qualified and appointed, although the Chairman may not be reappointed in that capacity. Conversely, it seems that someone who has been Chairman could thereafter become a member for one term.

[3] A number of influential Southern Rhodesians were approached to permit their names to go forward but declined. Thus Sir Robert Tredgold, Mr. Josiah Chinamano, Mr. Nathan Shamuyayira, and others declined to allow their names to go forward as they considered the Constitution as a whole was unacceptable to the African population. Personal communications from confidential sources.

[4] The Chairman may only be removed for inability to discharge the functions of his office or for misbehaviour and the identical procedure required for the removal of the Chief Justice in Section 56B(2) of the Constitution applies to his removal: Section 74(4).

[5] Constitution. Sections 73 and 74. By chance this legalistic composition of the Council has been increased as one of the ordinary members was an ex-judge of the High Court.

[6] *Musururwa* v. *Attorney-General Southern Rhodesia*, 1963 (4) S.A. 720 (S.R.) at 726. It is submitted that this was an irrelevant consideration: see *Nkomo* v. *Lardner-Burke Judgement*, A.D. 164/65 per Quènet A.C.J. at pp. 6–7.

[7] Constitution. Section 73. There are in fact five African members of the Council, five Europeans including the Chairman, one Asian, and one Coloured member. If a question arises as to the racial community to which any person shall be deemed to belong, the Chairman shall decide the matter finally and his decision may not be questioned in any Court of law: Section 88(4).

Qualifications and also disqualifications (including the requirement of vacation of seats) for members are laid down. These not only set out the standard type of disqualification for election to a public body,[1] but also include a number of requirements that render many Southern Rhodesians ineligible for membership. No person is eligible for election to the Council unless he is of the age of thirty-five or over.[2] Furthermore, not only must a member be a citizen of Southern Rhodesia but a long association with the country is required, since a member must have resided in Southern Rhodesia for a period of not less than ten out of the fifteen years immediately prior to his election.[3]

Finally provisions are inserted which have the purpose of excluding many persons who have been active in politics in the last five years preceding their election. Thus any person who within that period has been a member of the Legislative Assembly or of the Federal Assembly, or who has been a candidate for election to either of these Assemblies, is excluded.[4] Similarly, if a member of the Council becomes a candidate for election to the Legislative Assembly he shall vacate his seat.[5] Provision for removal of members is also made where any member of the Council discloses any proceedings of the Council without the authority of the Chairman[6] or acts improperly in his capacity as a member.[7] Whether this general provision for removal on grounds of having

---

[1] e.g. bankruptcy, insanity, imprisonment, and the holding of public office. With reference to the last disqualification it is specially provided that the office of Chief shall not be deemed to be a public office, so that an African Chief is at present a member. Chiefs would, were it not for this section, be considered officers in the service of the Crown in right of Southern Rhodesia (Section 116(1)) since they receive salaries and allowances from the Crown. See African Affairs (General) (Amendment) Regulations 1965 (No. 6), R.G.N. 479/65.

[2] This provision effectively excludes the majority of educated Africans. Only since 1949 has much in the way of secondary education been available to Africans. See Appendix Table J. Most persons receiving secondary education after that date would be too young to be eligible.

[3] This provision excludes a large number of Europeans who are S.R. citizens (the residence requirement for citizenship is two years for British subjects) and excluded from election to the first Council any person who had not settled in Southern Rhodesia before Federation. Migration figures (obtained from the Monthly Digest of Statistics, September 1964 and Leys, op. cit., p. 74) reveal that from 1952 to 1962 there were 118,926 European immigrants and 72,000 emigrants with a net immigration gain of 46,626. It cannot be assumed that all the emigrants came from the group of new immigrants so that the figure of Europeans who arrived between 1952 and 1962 and are still resident in Southern Rhodesia is probably in excess of 50,000, whereas the total Southern Rhodesian population as at 31 December 1962 was 224,000, including children. In addition, the proportion of adults amongst immigrants is normally high, so that a large proportion of the European adult population was ineligible for membership of the Council. This lengthy residence requirement does not, however, apply to the Chairman of the Council.

[4] Section 77(1)(a).   [5] Section 77(2)(e).

[6] Section 79(1). The Chairman takes an oath of secrecy not to reveal or to authorize members to reveal directly or indirectly any matter debated in the Council unless satisfied that to do so would be contrary to the public interest: First Schedule, Item 5. Members take similar oaths not to reveal matters except with the express authorization of the Chairman: First Schedule, Item 6.

[7] Section 79. If this is alleged the Governor sets up a Commission of Enquiry and is required to act in terms of their recommendations.

30—C.H.L.S.R.

acted improperly as a member comprises taking an active part in politics other than as a candidate has been debated in the Legislative Assembly. Chief Kaisa Ndiweni, a member of the Constitutional Council, was the leading speaker at an 'indaba' of the Chiefs held in October 1964 at which he spoke on some of the most contentious political issues in Southern Rhodesia and advocated the grant of independence under the present Constitution.[1] The Government however rejected a motion requesting that the Government appoint a Commission of Inquiry to inquire into whether he had acted improperly, maintaining that there was nothing in the Constitution 'which forbids the participation of a member of the Constitutional Council in politics'[2] and that since there was no express prohibition on engaging in politics this was permissible. Indeed by implication the Minister of Justice regarded even active entry into party politics by a Member of the Council permissible unless the member stood as a candidate.[3] It is submitted that this attitude is not in accordance with the spirit of the Constitution.

Council procedure

The Council meets[4] on the summons of the Chairman, who presides, and who has both an original and a casting vote.[5] The Chairman must appoint a Deputy Chairman who shall carry out the Chairman's duties in his absence.[6] For the regulation of its proceedings the Council may make rules with the approval of the Governor.[7]

Council meetings require a quorum of seven members, including the person

[1] Independence, the franchise, the tribal system and its structure in relation to the administration, the unsatisfactory character of the leaders of nationalist political parties, the political, legal, and administrative powers and authority of the Chiefs, the attitude of the United Kingdom Government, and representation of the Chiefs in Parliament were amongst the topics on which the Chief spoke: S.R.L.A.D., Vol. 59, cols. 560–1, 28 October 1964. His speech (unacknowledged) is reprinted in The Demand for Independence in Rhodesia. Consultation with the African Tribesmen through their Chiefs and Headmen. The Domboshawa 'Indaba'. Government Printer, Salisbury, 1965, pp. 26–30.

[2] S.R.L.A.D., Vol. 59, col. 572, 28 October 1964. The Minister also irrelevantly justified the Chief's conduct on the basis of the powers of the Council of Chiefs and Provincial Assemblies Act (Chapter 111) which requires Provincial Assemblies of Chiefs to bring any matter of national interest to the notice of the Council of Chiefs and of the Minister. However the 'indaba' was not authorized in terms of any law as it was neither a meeting of Provincial Assemblies nor of the Council of Chiefs, being merely a meeting arranged by the Minister of Internal Affairs, at which over 400 Headmen, who do not feature in the Act, attended with all S.R.'s Chiefs and many officials of the Internal Affairs Department.

[3] S.R.L.A.D., Vol. 59, col. 571.

[4] In the ten months of its active existence in 1963 the Council had thirteen meetings, consisting of thirty-seven sitting days: Annual Report of the Constitutional Council for the year 1963: C.S.R. 1–1964, Government Printer, Salisbury, p. 2. In 1964 it had thirteen meetings involving twenty-three sitting days: Annual Report for the Year 1964: C.S.R. 3–1965, para. 3.

[5] Sections 88(2)(3) and 89(3).

[6] Section 88(1).   [7] Section 89(7).

presiding, while decisions are made by a majority.[1] It is in fact stipulated that the Council must report whether its opinion was unanimous and, if not, the number of votes for and against the decision.[2] The degree to which the Council has managed to obtain general agreement for its decisions emerges from its published reports, which are despatched by the Council to the Speaker of the Assembly and laid on the table on the next sitting day after receipt.[3] In the majority of cases the Council has so far reached unanimous decision but in respect of one Act, enacted under a certificate of emergency, one Bill, four statutory instruments, and two existing Acts there have been majority decisions.[4]

It was probably in order to give the public some information as to the Council's activities that the provision for disclosure of Council voting was inserted, and that it was stipulated that an annual report by the Council on its work must be presented to the Governor and be laid before the Legislative Assembly without undue delay.[5] Despite the fact that the public are kept informed of the work of the Council they are entirely excluded from its proceedings. Although written representations and evidence may be sent to it 'the Council shall not be entitled to hear objections or to examine witnesses in regard to any Bill or law which is being considered by the Council'.[6] This prohibition impedes the Council in discharging its duties. Unless Council Members make use of their personal knowledge (which seems invidious and allows much scope for their personal opinion and bias) they are not in a position to make informed decisions involving factual issues, e.g. where the decision in question involves taking a view of a particular factual situation, such as whether the state of public order in the country makes it necessary for the enactment of a particular law, which infringes a freedom set out in the Declaration of Rights. Indeed, the Council commented in its First Annual Report:

. . . unless the Council has the right to receive evidence it is not fully in a position to discharge its duties. For example the Declaration of Rights states that 'No written law shall contain any discriminatory provision'. To this rule there are a number of exceptions, and, to quote only one of them, a law may be discriminatory

---

[1] Section 89(1)(a).   [2] Section 89(5)(a).

[3] S.O. 168, which was made in terms of Section 90(1) of the Constitution. For the conduct of business between the Council and the Assembly, the Governor is entitled to make rules: Section 90(2).

[4] The Law and Order (Maintenance) Amendment Act No. 12 of 1963 (9-2), the Deportation Amendment Bill 1964 (9-1), Government Notices 1234, 1235, and 1242 of 1960, made in term of Section 7 of the Law and Order (Maintenance) Act 1960 (7-4, 8-3, and 10-2, respectively), Government Notice No. 252 of 1965 made in terms of the Local Government Act, the African Wills Act, Chapter 108 (6-4), and the Criminal Procedure and Evidence Act, Chapter 31 (8-2).

[5] The Council's report is published as a Southern Rhodesian Command Paper. The first report gave a valuable and full picture of the work of the Council but the second report was largely formal in character.

[6] Section 89(4).

if, in consideration of the state for the time being of the economy of Southern Rhodesia such law is reasonably justifiable in the interests of Southern Rhodesia as a whole. How is the Council to determine the state of the economy if it is not permitted to enquire into the economy?

Again, restrictions on freedom of assembly and association are permissible in the interests of defence, public safety, public order, or public health. It is only by receiving the evidence of experts that the Council can determine whether a particular provision is in the interests of, say, defence or public health.

It would seem to be very much in the interests of everyone if the Council were permitted to enquire into and receive evidence upon the reasons why a particular law is deemed to be necessary although it otherwise infringes the Declaration of Rights.[1]

The difficulties under which the Council laboured in coming to a decision on such a matter is probably part of the explanation why the Council did not report adversely on the Law and Order (Maintenance) Amendment Act No. 12 of 1964, which in Section 9 provided for an extension from three to twelve months in the power of the Minister of Law and Order to restrict persons to a specified area in Southern Rhodesia.[2] In respect of this Act the Council had to decide whether infringement of the right to personal liberty and the right to freedom of assembly were interfered with. However, it seems that the Declaration of Rights is so worded that it permits a law of the Legislature to require persons to remain within specified areas in Southern Rhodesia.[3] Nevertheless such restriction must also infringe the right of freedom of association with persons outside the area and in these circumstances the Council should have examined whether such right was curtailed. Exceptions to this right are only permitted if necessary in the interests of public safety, public order, &c.[4] To have decided that the Act infringed this right would have involved the Council in making a decision on a matter of great political consequence, soon after it had been violently attacked by a Cabinet Minister[5]

[1] Annual Report of the Constitutional Council for the year 1963, Govt. Printer, Salisbury, C.S.R. 1–1964, p. 5.

[2] Nor did it report on the Law and Order (Maintenance) Amendment Act 1965, Section 2 of which extended the period of restriction to five years. Restriction areas have been the subject of litigation in the General and Appellate Divisions of the High Court: *The Minister of Justice and Law and Order and Attorney-General* v. *Musururwa and Others and Nkomo and Others*, 1964 (3) S.A. 209 (S.R.A.D.). The former matter is now on appeal to the Privy Council. Large numbers of African Nationalists are restricted to remote areas of Southern Rhodesia, including Mr. Nkomo who was successively leader of the National Democratic Party, the Zimbabwe African Peoples' Union, and the Peoples' Caretaker Council, prior to their proscription. He was first restricted and from October 1964 was preventively detained until the Appellate Division of the High Court declared this to be unlawful: *Nkomo and Others* v. *Minister of Justice and Others, supra*. He was again restricted after this decision was delivered. The five-year period of restriction has been challenged in criminal proceedings against restrictees for breaking the terms of their restriction orders.

[3] Section 58(2)(k) read with Section 72(1), definition of 'law' and 'lawful'. There is no 'freedom of movement' set out in the Declaration of Rights.

[4] Section 66(2)(a).   [5] See *infra*.

and it is not surprising that the Council apparently avoided putting itself in the position of arbiter as to what was necessary in the interests of public order and safety.[1] In fact, the Constitution imposes an exceptionally difficult and invidious task on the Council which is made more difficult by the fact that it cannot hear evidence on these contentious matters.

A further limitation on the Council is that it may not make recommendations for amendment to any measure on which it reports adversely. Although the Council criticized this limitation on its powers,[2] this seems a correct limitation as if this were not the case the Council might later have to report on the effect of its own suggestions.

Council functions

The major functions of the Council are to report whether the provisions of Bills, Acts assented to after a certificate of urgency by the Prime Minister, and statutory instruments are inconsistent with the Declaration of Rights in the Constitution. The Council may also, but is not required to,[3] examine existing Acts and subordinate legislation for the same purpose. Finally, the Council is charged with the duty of making it possible for a litigant who tests an infringement of the Declaration of Rights to be partially indemnified against legal costs, provided the Council considers he has brought a proper and suitable test case. However, the Council has not the functions of the African Affairs Board to make representations on matters desirable in the interests of Africans, and suggestions in the Monckton Report[4] that it be permitted to make any representations on unfairly discriminatory trends were not accepted. On the other hand, its scope of action is far broader than that of the Board, as it is concerned with legislation infringing any of the freedoms set out in the Declaration and these apply to all persons, not only to Africans.

Bills

Immediately a Bill has passed its third reading the Speaker of the Legislative Assembly is required to transmit the Bill to the Council for its consideration.[5] The Council must then within thirty days [6] report to the Governor

---

[1] In respect of the Unlawful Organizations Amendment Act No. 9 of 1963 the Council was in similar difficulties and reported non-adversely, but somewhat exculpatorily it stated that it wished 'it to be known that it gave careful consideration to Section 2 of the said Act in relation to Section 66(2) of the Constitution': Report received by the Speaker on 8 April 1963. In one sense it did make itself arbiter by making non-adverse reports: in effect, this meant that it found the laws in question were necessary.

[2] Annual Report, 1963, pp. 5–6.

[3] Cp. Cmnd. 1148, § 250 which suggested that the Council should be required to recommend the introduction of legislation to remove existing discriminations.

[4] Cmnd. 1148, § 250(c).   [5] Section 84(1).

[6] Or within any extended period granted by the Speaker on the application of the Council's Chairman, if he considers complexity, or the quantity of Council business or sufficient reasons exist to justify an extension: Section 84(4).

and the Speaker whether the Bill would, if enacted, be inconsistent with the Declaration of Rights.[1]

A Bill cannot be presented to the Governor for assent unless the Speaker certifies that the Council is of the opinion that none of its provisions will infringe the Declaration of Rights, or that the Council, by virtue of its not having reported within the required period, is presumed to be of such an opinion.[2]

If the Council has reported adversely on any Bill, legislation is not, however, completely blocked. The measure can be proceeded with immediately if, on receipt of an adverse report by the Council, a motion for presentation to the Governor for assent of the impugned Bill is passed by a two-thirds majority of the total membership of the Assembly.[3] If this procedure is not followed the effect of an adverse report is to delay the enactment of the measure for at least six months after its third reading, at which stage (unless it is a constitutional Bill or one amending the franchise) the Assembly can pass it by a simple majority.[4] However, up to the present,[5] the Constitutional Council has not found anything in any Bill forwarded to it in terms of Section 84 to occasion it to make an adverse report.[6]

There are, however, two exceptional categories of Bills to which the whole procedure outlined above does not apply, thus permitting the Constitutional Council to be by-passed, as such Bills may be assented to without having

[1] Section 84(2). The Council has not adopted a narrow approach to its task and, even though it has not adversely reported, it has on several occasions commented on discriminatory features of measures which, although not inconsistent with the Declaration because of certain exceptions or other special provisions, are possibly undesirable, e.g. in reporting on the Land Apportionment Bill (A.B. 60/1963), the Council indicated that it could not report adversely on the measure but that it considered that the use of the power contained in subsection (3) of the new section 41 I could result in discrimination and prejudice. It has also indicated that the use of powers of subsidiary legislation must be in accordance with the Declaration of Rights, e.g. Report on the High Court Bill (A.B. 2A/1963) where the Council pointed out that use of the Court's rule-making power must be in accordance with Section 63(9)(10) of the Constitution, so as to secure that proceedings are held in open court.
[2] Section 84(6) and (5).
[3] Section 84(6)(c). The Monckton Report, Cmnd. 1148, §§ 353–4 advocated much greater powers of delay—a nine months' interval, passage by a three-quarters majority, and thereafter separate racial referenda of each racial community passed by two-thirds of those voting in each of the separate racial groups.
[4] Section 84(6)(c)(i).   [5] November 1965.
[6] In 1963 the Council reported non-adversely on thirty-three Bills, although in two cases it made comments on Bills. Thus in its Report on the Casino Bill (A.B. 86/1963) the Council states that 'it notes that an opportunity may have been lost to encourage respect for the Declaration of Rights of the Constitution of Southern Rhodesia by not making it a specific condition of the leasing of national land for a Casino that discrimination shall not be permitted on the grounds of race, tribe, place of origin, political opinions, colour, or creed'. Again in respect of the Land Apportionment Amendment Bill, No. 60 of 1963, it commented that discrimination and prejudice could result through use of power envisaged in Section 43(I) of the section, even though section 104(2) of the Constitution authorized such a provision. In 1964 the Council reported non-adversely on sixty-nine Bills. However it added a rider to its report on the Deportation Amendment Bill (No. 64B, 1964).

been scrutinized by the Council. These categories cover Money Bills and Bills certified by the Prime Minister to be so urgent that it is not in the public interest to delay their enactment. In the latter case, the Council has no power to delay such a measure[1] but a special procedure for a subsequent report by the Council exists,[2] and the Declaration of Rights still applies to the measure so that it can be tested in the Courts. Understandably, Bills amending the specially entrenched provisions of the Constitution do not go to the Council, as Bills passed in terms of the procedure required for this purpose can themselves amend or repeal any provision of the Declaration of Rights.

The exclusion from Council scrutiny of Money Bills is, however, significant, particularly since Money Bills are widely defined to include both taxation Bills and Appropriation Bills.[3] Although such measures can be 'vehicles of seriously unfair discrimination', the provisions in the Constitution relative to the Council and the Declaration of Rights nonetheless are in all cases inapplicable.[4]

Urgent Bills

Although Bills enacted on a certificate of urgency by the Prime Minister do not go to the Council for scrutiny prior to assent, a copy of the Act must, as soon as may be, be sent by the Speaker to the Council for report. Thereupon the Council must within seven days make a report.[5] In 1963 the Council only had occasion to report adversely on one such Bill[6]—the Law and Order (Maintenance) Amendment Act No. 12 of 1963, Section 2 of which was found to be inconsistent with the rights of freedom of association by a nine to two majority. The section in question prohibited public gatherings on Sundays, except gatherings permitted by the Minister of Law and Order or described in a Schedule to the Act. (The Schedule in the main excluded gatherings of a sporting or of a religious character.) In order to meet this criticism by the

---

[1] Suggestions have been made that this procedure has been abused. In 1963 fourteen certificates of urgency were granted. At independence negotiations in June 1963, the British Government raised the question with the Southern Rhodesian Prime Minister whether such a certificate should not only be granted where circumstances analogous to a state of emergency made the passage of the measure urgent (cp. Cmnd. 1148 § 257). The Prime Minister then stated in the Legislative Assembly that, except on the rarest of occasions, he would not issue certificates of urgency, although he did not accept the British contentions: *S.R.L.A.D.*, Vol. 53, col. 9, 18 June 1963. During 1964 seven certificates of urgency were used, two relating to security measures and one to secure a rapid assent to the Referendum Act 1964.

[2] See *infra*.

[3] See Cmnd. 1148 § 256 which recommended that taxation Bills, although not Appropriation Bills, should be subject to Council scrutiny.

[4] Cmnd. 1148 § 256. Thus, large expenditure on European schools in comparison with African schools, or conversely, heavy transfer duties on immovable property in the European area as defined in the Land Apportionment Act would be permissible.

[5] Section 85(2). In terms of Section 90(2) the period has been prescribed as seven days by Section 3 of the Constitutional Council Rules, 1963 (S.R.G.N. No. 79 of 1963).

[6] This procedure was used on fourteen occasions in 1963, seven of these occurring at the end of 1963 in respect of legislation urgently required because of impending Federal dissolution.

Council an amending Bill was then introduced into the Legislative Assembly but before it could be debated an African trade union leader, Mr. J. T. Maluleke, initiated proceedings in the High Court to test the validity of the Act. The Court thereupon issued a rule nisi, calling on the Minister of Law and Order to show cause why section 6A of the Act, as amended, should not be declared *ultra vires* the Constitution.[1] Since the matter was now *sub judice* the Legislative Assembly agreed to the Bill being discharged.[2]

Again in March 1964 the Council adversely reported on an Act which was assented to by the Governor after a certificate of urgency had been given— The Preventive Detention (Temporary Provisions) Amendment Act 1964. The principal Act enacted in 1959 expressly provided that it should expire at the end of a five-year period[3] whereas the amendment purported to extend its operation by substituting the word 'ten' for the original 'five' year expiry period. The consequence of this decision was that it was doubtful whether the Southern Rhodesian Government had any powers of preventive detention except in terms of Emergency Regulations authorized by the Emergency Powers Act (Chapter 33) and section 69 of the Declaration of Rights.[4] However, in mid-October 1964 the Minister of Law and Order purporting to act in terms of the Preventive Detention (Temporary Provisions) Act on the

[1] *Maluleke* v. *The Minister of Law and Order and Another*, 1963 (4) S.A. 206 (S.R.).

[2] *S.R.L.A.D.*, Vol. 53, cols. 1694–5, 20 May 1964. The matter is still *sub judice* as lengthy affidavits and replying affidavits have been filed, while the applicant also petitioned for leave to continue the proceedings *in forma pauperis*: see *Maluleke* v. *Dupont N.O. and Others*, 1964 (2) S.A. 692 (S.R.).

[3] See Constitutional Council Report No. 31 of 18 March 1964. The Report unanimously resolved that the Act infringed section 58(1) of the Declaration of Rights, which provides for personal liberty. The Council considered that the Act did not fall within the exempting provisions as amounting to a re-enactment of a law which was in force at the time of coming into effect of the new Constitution, since the operation of the original Act had been limited to a period of five years and this limitation was a fundamental feature of that Act.

[4] This is probably one of the reasons why in August 1964 the Minister of Law and Order declared a State of Emergency in the Government African Township of Highfield, and a subsequent state of emergency in October in the Municipal Township of Harare, both parts of Salisbury. Earlier the Minister of Law and Order had attempted to evade the Council's decision by utilizing Section 50 of the Law and Order (Maintenance) Act (Chapter 39), which provides for restriction in conjunction with the Protected Places and Areas Act (Chapter 76) to achieve the same result as detention of African nationalists. The General and Appellate Divisions of the High Court, however, declared orders made in terms of these Acts, whereby a protective area was declared round the area in which the persons were restricted, in effect creating an 'internment camp', to be *ultra vires*—although the Appellate Division found that the Minister had acted in good faith. See *Minister of Justice and Law and Order and Attorney-General* v. *Musururwa and Others and Nkomo and Others*, 1964 (3) S.A. 209 at 223, where Beadle C.J. held that the 'pith and substance' of the action taken by the Minister resulted in preventive detention and even though the separate use of two Acts might each in itself be lawful if the real objective (which the Minister admitted to in his pleadings) was by their joint effect to achieve an unlawful result then such action was unlawful. Hathorn J.A. at pp. 226–7 also laid it down that the Protected Places and Areas Act could not be used for the purpose of creating an internment camp whether or not in combination with the Law and Order (Maintenance) Act as the powers were not given for that purpose. The matter is now on appeal to the Judicial Committee of the Privy Council.

basis that he might do so until successfully challenged in the Courts,[1] detained African nationalist leaders.

Statutory instruments

The Council must also consider every statutory instrument after its publication in the Gazette,[2] and report within ninety days to the Speaker and the Secretary for Justice[3] whether it is inconsistent with the Declaration.[4]

It is important to note that statutory instrument is defined[5] so as not to include delegated legislation issued in terms of Federal laws or United Kingdom laws such as the Federation of Rhodesia and Nyasaland (Dissolution) Order-in-Council.[6] The Council has in fact reported to this effect and held that new regulations, issued in terms of the Federal Education Act, which with its regulations was continued in force by the Order in Council, are not made in the exercise of a power conferred by the Legislature of Southern

---

[1] When questioned whether this Act would be utilized despite the Constitutional Council's Report the Minister of Justice blankly stated: 'Government is proceeding to use this Act': *S.R.L.A.D.*, Vol. 59, col. 158, 21 October 1964. This was immediately challenged in the Appellate Division of the High Court (by virtue of its original jurisdiction in relation to any infringement of the Declaration of Rights) and the Court thereupon ordered the detainees to be released, holding that the Preventive Detention Act was in conflict with Section 58 of the Declaration, and was not saved by Section 80(1)(c) as it was an amendment to and not a re-enactment of provisions in the Act since it made material changes in the existing law: *Nkomo and Others* v. *Minister of Justice and Others, supra.* The Minister continued to hold the detainees for several days after the judgement pending the lodging of an appeal to the Judicial Committee, with the approval of the Appellate Division, which agreed that the detainees might be held for a week until an application for leave to appeal had been lodged. The Minister adopted the same attitude in respect of the combined use of the Law and Order (Maintenance) Act and the Protected Places and Areas Act and continued to act in terms of these measures, pending an appeal from the General Division to the Appellate Division of the High Court in *Minister of Law and Order* v. *Musururwa and Nkomo, supra,* even though the lower Court had declared his action unlawful. The justification for this attitude was presumably that in civil cases the lodging of an appeal suspends the operation of the judgment.

[2] Gazetting is compulsory: Section 86(1). The Interpretation Act (Chapter 1), Section 18(1), provides that statutory instruments come into operation on the date of their publication unless some other date is fixed for the coming into operation thereof.

[3] Prescribed as the authority to whom such report must be made in terms of Section 86(2) of the Constitution and Sections 6 and 7 of the Constitutional Council Rules 1963.

[4] Again the Council has not adopted a narrow view of its functions and has indicated that, although a statutory instrument does not on the face of it infringe the Declaration, a particular use of its provisions could be employed to infringe Section 68 of the Constitution: see Constitutional Council Report No. 30 of 29 January 1964 on S.R.G.N. 600 of 1963— the Bellevue Swimming Bath By-laws.

[5] Section 83 of the Constitution defines statutory instrument as ' "statutory instrument" means any Proclamation, rule, regulation, by-law, order, notice, or other instrument having the force of law, made by the Governor, or any other person or body under the authority of any Act of the Legislature for the time being in force'.

[6] Statutory instruments issued under Federal laws not only are not defined as such, but Section 70(3) of the Constitution specifically excludes anything done under the authority of any Federal law from the Declaration.

Rhodesia.[1] The Council has 'pointed out the anomalies of such a position' and the situation which, in course of time, will arise when Southern Rhodesian and Federal laws become so intermingled as to make any distinction between them unrecognizable. However the Constitution has not been amended to bring Federal laws or statutory instruments made in terms thereof under the jurisdiction of the Council.[2]

Once the Council issues an adverse report on a statutory instrument the Governor must publish a notice of annulment of the particular provision and this has the effect of revocation as from that date, unless the provision is either amended or revoked by the authority which issued it or the Assembly passes a resolution confirming the instrument within twenty-one days of the Council's report being presented to it.[3]

During 1963 the Council examined and reported on 708 statutory instruments and adversely reported on 37[4] but in each case the instruments were either repealed or amended. That great attention is paid to these reports is apparent, since the Council's reports on these topics were even raised by the First Secretary of State during Southern Rhodesian independence discussions in London in June 1963.[5] Furthermore these had an affect on the draftsmen as subsequent statutory instruments were so drafted as to be consistent with the Declaration of Rights. Thus in 1964 the Council examined 522 statutory instruments, none of which was found to be inconsistent with the Declaration.[6]

Although the Council may not comment on trends in society it clearly may comment on trends which emerge from measures it is required to examine. Thus, after having adversely reported on nine Southern Rhodesian Government Notices, issued by regulating authorities under Section 7 of the Law and Order (Maintenance) Act in order to control public meetings, as having infringed the freedoms of assembly and expression, the Council commented that:

It is apparent to the Council that the directions contained in the aforesaid notices all follow a common pattern. When considered as a whole, the common pattern creates a strong impression in the mind of the Council that some regulating autho-

[1] See Report on the Education (Tuition and Accommodation) Regulations 1964, S.R.G.N. 191 of 1964. The Council did not actually comment on its own competence but held that since these were not 'laws' as defined in Section 72(a) of the Constitution they could not be in conflict with the Declaration of Rights—see Constitutional Council Report No. 32 of 30 July 1964. The effect is that African children whose school fees have not been paid may be excluded from school, whereas European children in respect of whom similar circumstances prevail, cannot be excluded.

[2] Annual Report 1964. C.S.R. 3–1965 para. 8.

[3] Section 86(4). The resolution can be passed by a simple majority. Cp. Cmnd. 1148, § 259 which advocated a three-quarters majority.

[4] See Report, p. 3. From the individual reports it emerges that the majority of these infringed freedom of assembly and of expression, while some involved discrimination.

[5] S.R.L.A.D., Vol. 53, col. 175.

[6] C.S.R. 3–1965, para. 6. Two draft statutory instruments were submitted to the Council for examination prior to them being made.

rities may not have applied themselves to the question whether the directions which they issued were appropriate to the circumstances existing within their areas or were reasonably necessary to achieve the objects of subsection (1) of section 7 of the enabling Act in their areas. . . . The Council is of the opinion that there is a real danger that in some areas such directions may go beyond the objects sought to be achieved by subsection (1) of section 7 of the empowering Act and that there is every likelihood that they will have the effect of inhibiting rather than controlling public gatherings if they continue to take the form in which they are at present.

Pre-existing legislation

The Council is empowered to examine any Act or statutory instrument (excluding Federal Acts or anything done under the authority of any Federal law)[1] in force prior to the coming into effect of the 1961 Constitution and to give an advisory report whether such measure is inconsistent with the Declaration of Rights as if the Declaration applied to the measure, despite the fact that no pre-existing laws can be tested against the Declaration.[2] Any such report must be sent without delay to the Speaker and to the Governor, while the Speaker must without undue delay cause the report to be laid before the Legislative Assembly. The Council has utilized this power to report on a number of occasions, mainly in respect of Acts but also in respect of a statutory instrument.[3] As a result a number of these measures have been debated in the Legislative Assembly.[4] On the first two occasions an attempt was made to persuade the Government to accept a convention that where the Council reported adversely on an existing Act or statutory instrument the Government should normally act on such an adverse report, and if it found itself unable to

[1] Section 70(3).   [2] Section 87.

[3] The Acts on which the Council had reported adversely as at 30 June 1965 were the Native Education Act No. 8 of 1959, which it found discriminatory against all races, the African Law and Courts Act (Chapter 104), which it found discriminatory as against Africans, the Native Affairs Act (Chapter 92), which it considered discriminated against Africans and infringed freedoms of assembly and expression, the Land Apportionment Act which discriminated against all races, the African Wills Act (Chapter 108), which discriminated against Africans, the Criminal Procedure and Evidence Act (Chapter 31), which it considered discriminated against Africans and also against Asians and Coloureds, the Unlawful Organisations Act (Chapter 81), which it considered infringed the constitutional right to protection from deprivation of property, the African Development Fund Act (Chapter 96), which it considered potentially prejudiced African farmers, the Africans (Registration and Identification) Act (Chapter 109), and the African Labour Regulations Act (Chapter 100), both of which it found discriminated against Africans, the National Registration Act (Chapter 136), which discriminated against non-Africans, the Town and Country Planning Act (Chapter 133), which infringed the protection afforded personal liberty, and the Municipal Act (Chapter 125), and the Town Management Act (Chapter 134), both of which discriminated against all races. The statutory instrument which received an adverse report was the Southern Rhodesian Government Notice 1020 of 1962, an order in terms of Section 7 of the Law and Order (Maintenance) Act, which the Council considered infringed freedom of association.

[4] See *S.R.L.A.D.*, Vol. 53, cols. 509 et seq., 24 July 1963; Vol. 53, cols. 521 et seq., 24 July 1963; Vol. 53, cols. 542 et seq., 4 September 1963; Vol. 56, cols. 306 et seq., 4 March 1964; Vol. 58, cols. 370 et seq., 16 September 1964; Vol. 60, cols. 842 et seq.

remove the anomaly to which the Council had drawn attention, to bring the matter and its reasons before the Legislative Assembly. The Government, however, declined to accept such a convention.[1] Somewhat later the Minister of Internal Affairs accepted that 'if there is nothing inimical in the report (of the Council) and it is not against the public interest or law and order . . . in general those reports should be adopted'.[2] However, another Minister has subsequently violently attacked the Constitutional Council for exercising its power of examining and reporting on the existing law, since it is not 'required' to report on such measures. The Minister of Local Government in fact suggested that the Council should not report on existing measures if its report might be 'ill-timed'. Indeed he accused the Council of having a mischievous purpose and a discriminatory approach and of lacking balanced judgement and practical understanding.[3] These heated accusations against the Council arose from its report on the Land Apportionment Act 1941,[4] which gave a lengthy and balanced assessment of the effect of the Act and its historical background.[5] It is significant that such statements were made in the Legislative Assembly under the cloak of Parliamentary privilege, since the Council enjoys 'the same immunities and privileges *mutatis mutandis* as the Legislative Assembly and the members thereof'[6] and such statements if not protected would have amounted to contempts of the Council.[7] It will be interesting to see whether the Council has been intimidated by these attacks, for it will be a brave Council that reports again on controversial legislation in conflict with the Declaration, even though this be its proper function.[8] The Council in a recent report has stated that

The Council considers it is to be its duty and function to draw attention to provisions in any existing law which would be inconsistent with the Declaration of Rights if such Declaration applied thereto.[9]

[1] *S.R.L.A.D.*, Vol. 53, col. 525, 24 July 1963.

[2] *S.R.L.A.D.*, Vol. 54, col. 578, 4 September 1963, Howman.

[3] *S.R.L.A.D.*, Vol. 56, cols. 568 et seq., 10 March 1964.

[4] Constitutional Council Report No. 29 of 5 February 1964.

[5] The Council adopted a legal approach, relying on and quoting at length from Beadle C.J.'s dicta on tangible and intangible discrimination set out in *Mehta* v. *City of Salisbury*, 1961 R. & N. 911. The Minister (*S.R.L.A.D.* Vol. 56, col. 577) maintained that the Council had no authority to assess such 'nebulous, unascertainable, and varying features', which could only be determined by a particular complainant.

[6] Section 89(8).

[7] Section 10(e) and (1) of the Powers and Privileges of Parliament Act, Chapter 4. It would also seem that the Minister's statement could be considered as a disrespectful speech reflecting on the Council or as a statement tending to bring it into odium, contempt, or ridicule or to lower its authority, and even as attempted intimidation of members to execute their duties in a certain way. See note on this particular breach by O. Hood Phillips (1947), 10 M.L.R., p. 420.

[8] Should the Council report on the Law and Order (Maintenance) Act 1960 which clearly is in conflict with numerous sections of the Declaration, the Council will probably be subjected to a similar attack.

[9] Constitutional Council Report No. 36 of 18 November 1964. In its 1964 Annual Report

Legal assistance in testing the Declaration of Rights

The final function enjoyed by the Council is that of being the arbiter whether a litigant, who challenges legislation or administrative action as being an infringement of the Declaration of Rights in relation to him should be entitled to assistance in paying his legal costs. If the Council is of the opinion that the case constitutes 'a proper and suitable test case for determining the validity of that law or provision', it may certify in writing to this effect and then refund him costs certified by the Court as having been reasonably incurred in connection with the proceedings.[1]

However, the provisions for legal assistance are carefully hedged and qualified and in practice are not as generous as they might at first sight appear. Firstly, the litigant, even if he succeeds in obtaining such a certificate from the Council, is only entitled to be 'refunded' costs: he will therefore, unless he secures the services of attorneys willing to await the refund, have to expend moneys in advance and thereafter recover these from the Council. Secondly, costs 'reasonably incurred' have been restrictively interpreted as meaning party and party costs and not attorney and client costs, although it was strongly argued that this might result in an aggrieved person being denied the full benefit of the Declaration of Rights through inability to afford the whole expense of the necessary litigation to establish his rights in Court.[2] Furthermore, unless the Council has adversely reported on a measure, or unless the issue has been raised either in proceedings in the General Division or in an inferior court and referred by the presiding officer to the Appellate Division, an applicant may not obtain legal assistance for these proceedings[3] (e.g. one who applies to the Appellate Division in the exercise of its original jurisdiction under the Constitution). Only if he proceeds to appeal from the Appellate

---

the Council stated that 'it was and is the intention of the Council to examine in terms of Section 87 of the Constitution in due course all existing legislation': C.S.R. 5–1965, para. 7. The Council explained that it was bound to ensure that every person in Southern Rhodesia enjoyed the fundamental freedoms of the individual as set out in the Declaration and that 'news reporting' was 'responsible for the public gaining the impression that the sole task of the Constitutional Council is to search in legislation for racial discrimination': para. 11.

[1] Section 71(6).

[2] See *Maluleke* v. *the Minister of Law and Order and Others, Dupont N.O. and Others,* 1964 (2) S.A. 692 (S.R.) per Lewis J. In Southern Rhodesia there is no legislation as in England providing for legal assistance in civil cases and no inherent power of the Court to grant such aid. The only way in which the Court can grant such aid is by granting an application for leave to sue *in forma pauperis* in terms of Order 36 of the Rules of the High Court. The Rules are extremely restrictive in this respect as the petitioner must successfully show that he is not possessed of property to the value of £50 excepting household goods, wearing apparel, and tools of trade. He must also show his income, his receipts, and necessary charges thereon. This, in most cases, makes it impossible for petitioners to obtain aid as poor persons even though they have not got the means to continue litigation.

[3] Section 71(6).

Division to the Judicial Committee may assistance in respect of these latter costs be given.

Conclusions

Although it is too soon after the establishment of the Council to make any final judgement, it is apparent that the Council has so far been a valuable new addition to the constitutional machinery, and that within its sphere it can safeguard individual liberty. In those cases where the Constitutional Council has been ineffective, this has been either because of the limitations imposed on its powers, and the narrow definition of its functions, or a consequence of the drafting of the Declaration of Rights with its extensive exceptions to the rights enumerated.[1]

[1] See *infra*, Chapter 4.

2

THE EXECUTIVE

The Governor [1]

THE executive authority of Southern Rhodesia is vested in Her Majesty and may be exercised on Her Majesty's behalf by the Governor. [2]

As indicated earlier, all the constitutional provisions relating to the appointment, the powers and duties of the Governor and the appointment of any Acting Governor [3] as well as the Governor's salary and allowances are beyond the competence of the Southern Rhodesian Legislature and may only be amended by the Crown by Order in Council. [4] The Governor's salary and allowances may however from time to time be prescribed by a law of the Legislature although they may not be reduced during his continuance in office. His salary is paid out of the Consolidated Revenue Fund and is at present £8,500 per annum. [5] In addition, the annual Appropriation Act provides for certain grants and allowances. [6] This means that the position and actions of the Governor are only debated on the Estimates. Furthermore, it is a convention in the Southern Rhodesian Assembly in so doing only to raise major points of policy on appropriations for the Governor, while the Standing Orders of debate further protect him, as his name may not be irreverently used in debate or be used for the purpose of influencing the House in its deliberations. [7]

The Governor is also safeguarded against frivolous litigation by Order 3, Rule 14 of the Rules of the High Court of Southern Rhodesia, which stipulates that no civil process may be sued out against him without the leave of the Court upon motion made for that purpose. [8]

The Cabinet system

The Constitution spells out the cabinet system of government by specifying that the Governor is to appoint a Prime Minister and must, on the advice of

---

[1] The Governor and his relationship to remaining reserve powers of the United Kingdom are dealt with in Chapter 7 *infra*. It is therefore not proposed at this point to deal with the appointment of the Governor, the question of Royal Instructions to the Governor, or his reserve powers.

[2] Section 42. [3] But not of a Deputy Governor. [4] See *supra* Part II, Chapter 1.

[5] Section 5 of the Constitution and Governor's Salary Act No. 3 of 1963, section 2(b).

[6] Under the Prime Minister's Revenue Vote a provision of £31,300 is made for salaries of personnel employed by the Governor, incidental expenses and a grant to the Governor of £26,752 to cover the cost of his staffs and maintenance of his residences etc. See Estimates of Expenditure for the year ending 30 June 1965, C.S.R. 17–1964, Government Printer, Salisbury.

[7] S.O. 57(ii) (7th ed., 1964). [8] See *Gluck* v. *The Governor, supra.*

the Prime Minister, appoint other Ministers and Deputy Ministers holding office during pleasure.[1] From these Ministers the Governor is required on the advice of the Prime Minister to appoint an Executive Council which shall include the Prime Minister.[2] Thereafter in the exercise of his functions the Governor must act in accordance with the advice of this Council or the appropriate Minister unless the Constitution or any other law so requires.[3]

The Executive Council as thus specified is a different body from the Cabinet although in practice the composition of the two is identical, except for the fact that the Governor is not a member of the latter body. The Executive Council seldom meets[4] and is a rubber stamp for Cabinet decisions, while the Governor in nearly all cases exercises his powers either on the advice of a committee of the Executive Council or on that of an individual Minister.

Certain discretion is expressly reserved to the Governor as the Constitution specifies that the Governor shall act in accordance with his own discretion in two matters viz. the power of dissolution of the Legislative Assembly and the appointment of a Prime Minister.[5] In both cases the Governor must, however, observe the constitutional conventions applicable in such matters in the United Kingdom.[6] The observance or non-observance of such conventions and the question of on whose advice if any, or its nature, the Governor has acted, are not justiciable issues as the Constitution prohibits Courts from enquiring into such matters.[7]

In relation to the summoning, prorogation and dissolution of Parliament it is clear that it is only in the case of dissolution that the Governor has a discretion. When his discretion is reserved express reference is made to the power of dissolution conferred on the Governor by Section 34(2) of the Constitution but no reference is made to Section 34(1) which gives him the power of prorogual or to Section 33(1) which confers on him the power of summoning the Assembly. It is therefore clear that the Governor has no discretion in the use of the two latter powers and that the statutory rules requiring him to act on advice apply to his power to summon or to prorogue Parliament.

Although the provision dealing with the relationship of the Governor and the Prime Minister merely specifies that the Governor has a discretion in the

[1] Section 43(1) as amended by the Constitution Amendment Act 1965. Formerly a maximum of eleven Ministers could be appointed and there was no provision for Deputy Ministers, Parliamentary Secretaries being utilized instead.

[2] Section 44(1).

[3] This safeguards the issuing of Royal Instructions under section 2 or the enactment of a law giving the Governor a discretion.

[4] Its main purpose for meeting is to discuss reprieves.

[5] Section 45(1) proviso.

[6] Section 45(1) proviso specifies that 'the constitutional conventions which apply' in the United Kingdom shall be observed. There is no margin for adaptation or modification as the phrase 'as nearly as may be' is not inserted.

[7] Section 45(2).

appointment of a Prime Minister, nothing is said about his discretion in relation to dismissal of the Prime Minister or to the removal of Ministers.[1] However, since Section 43(3) states that any Minister of the Crown shall hold office during pleasure, it seems that the reserve power of exercising a discretion in such matters remains.[2]

Cabinet government in practice in Southern Rhodesia

To a large degree the system of cabinet government in Southern Rhodesia has been patterned on the British model, although there have been occasions on which it has tended to break down, either where governments have had unstable majorities, or alternatively where Cabinet dissension has occurred and there has been an unwillingness to observe the conventional restraints. Nonetheless, for the most part the British tradition has been followed. In fact one ex-Cabinet Minister in several of Sir Godfrey Huggins' Cabinets stated that Sir Godfrey 'used Jennings as his Bible', while Lord Malvern himself stated that he considered Jennings a valuable guide to which he frequently referred.[3]

The choice of the Prime Minister

Although the Governor has a discretion in the appointment of the Prime Minister, in the case of the three Prime Ministers who have so far held office under the 1961 Constitution the Governor has had little discretion. The first, Sir Edgar Whitehead, was Prime Minister under the 1923 Constitution at the time of the coming into force of the 1961 Constitution and formed a caretaker government during the election period before the new Legislative Assembly was chosen. The second, Mr. Field, was leader of the Rhodesian Front which won the 1962 general election. Subsequently, a Cabinet revolution confirmed by the Rhodesian Front party caucus, led to Mr. Field's resignation. Mr. I. D. Smith had in the meantime been chosen by caucus (there was no election within caucus as no alternative candidate was nominated) to be the next Prime Minister, and the resigning Prime Minister advised that Mr. Smith should be appointed. Even had Mr. Field attempted to govern with the aid of the Opposition he would not have commanded a majority in

---

[1] It is expressly stated that there is no discretion in the appointment of Ministers: Section 43(1).

[2] See also *Adegbenro* v. *Akintola, supra* for the explanation that if such questions were spelt out the Governor would have to act on Prime Ministerial advice. It seems difficult however to apply this argument to the Southern Rhodesian Constitution, as it could quite easily have specified a discretion in this matter by adding words to this effect to Section 45(1) proviso.

[3] In a personal communication after referring without prompting to Jennings' comments on whether the Prime Minister was *inter stellas luna minores*, he particularly approved of Jennings' description of the Prime Minister as a sun around which planets revolve: see W. I. Jennings, *Cabinet Government*, Cambridge, 1947 ed., p. 150.

31—C.H.L.S.R.

the House, as he had only one supporter and one doubtful member who might have followed him.[1]

A practice developed under the 1923 Constitution on the advice of General Smuts[2] to the effect that the Prime Minister might resign for the purpose of reconstituting his Government, thus indicating readiness to continue in office with some new colleagues. If, however, he simply resigned this would give the Governor a free hand in calling a new Prime Minister.

A departure from normal Cabinet practice occurred after the May 1965 general election in that the Prime Minister did not reconstitute his caretaker Government until two weeks after the announcement of the election results. When suggestions were made that the delay had been occasioned by the refusal of two of his Cabinet to resign, the Prime Minister announced that the cause of the delay was a wish to reorganize Ministries before a Cabinet reshuffle. The two Ministers in question were both subsequently dropped from the Cabinet and appointed to diplomatic posts.

The composition of the Cabinet

Provision similar to that in the 1923 Constitution exists whereby a person may hold office as a Minister for up to four consecutive months without also being a member of the Legislative Assembly. Should there be a dissolution before this period has elapsed the Minister can continue in office until the Assembly meets, but he can only continue thereafter if he has been elected at that general election.[3] This provision was used on a number of occasions under the 1923 Constitution,[4] and has continued in use. It was employed during the period between the dissolution of the last Legislative Assembly elected under the 1923 Constitution and the general election of 1962, when the Minister of the Treasury was not a member of the outgoing Assembly. It was again used between 15 September and 1 October 1964 when Mr. C. W. Dupont, the Deputy Prime Minister and Minister of External Affairs, sat for a short time outside the House, having resigned as a sitting member to contest a by-election against Sir Roy Welensky.

One remarkable departure from normal Cabinet practice in respect of Cabinet composition occurred from February to April 1958, when an ex-

---

[1] Personal communications from various confidential sources.

[2] See National Archives MO 13/1/1, Smuts to Moffat, 28 August 1928. Moffat had written to Smuts asking him for advice on the method of making changes in his Government.

[3] Section 43(4). Section 43(5) precludes abuse of this provision by short breaks in the appointment.

[4] Thus in 1958 Sir Edgar Whitehead became Prime Minister and sat as such outside the House. When he unsuccessfully contested a seat at a by-election the 1958 general election followed. It was also used in 1934 when Mr. F. Harris was appointed Minister of Agriculture from outside the House and in 1962 when Mr. Ellman Brown was appointed Minister of the Treasury. In both these cases the appointments were made shortly before a general election.

Prime Minister, Mr. Garfield Todd, became a member of Sir Edgar White-head's Cabinet even though this was not a coalition cabinet and he had just been forced to resign as Prime Minister in favour of Sir Edgar by his party congress.[1]

Under the 1923 Constitution there were a small number of occasions on which a Minister without Portfolio was appointed.[2] These precedents have been followed under the 1961 Constitution and for a short time Mr. Dupont was Minister without Portfolio.

All Ministers have always been members of the Cabinet, but although Parliamentary Secretaries have been appointed from time to time they are not and never have been members of the Cabinet.

The selection of Ministers

The Governor is bound to accept the advice of the Prime Minister in the selection of Ministers.

Whether in tendering advice the Prime Minister is absolutely free in his choice depends partly on political factors as to what will be acceptable to his party[3] and partly on his own personality. If the Prime Minister is determined to be entirely independent, as apparently was the case with Mr. Field, he can exercise unfettered choice in his selection of Ministers.[4] On the other hand his successor, Mr. Smith, in choosing his first cabinet was not only fettered by the fact that Cabinet Ministers who had assumed office under Mr. Field continued in office upon his resignation, but also adopted the attitude that his appointments should be acceptable to his party caucus. In choosing his second Cabinet he was able to exercise more freedom and to drop two Ministers who had been the subjects of much public criticism.

Occasionally Cabinet Ministers have attempted to stipulate that they should hold particular portfolios, and it is understood that Mr. Smith refused to accede to one such demand.[5] There have also in the past been attempts, sometimes successful, to lay down conditions for accepting office.[6] On other

---

[1] Although A. J. Balfour assumed Cabinet office he had not immediately beforehand been forced by his party to resign as Prime Minister.

[2] e.g. Sir Percy Fynn and Mr. J. W. Keller.

[3] It is often difficult to leave out certain personalities. Earlier Sir Charles Coghlan against his wishes took a certain Minister into his Cabinet: National Archives CO 8/1/1, Coghlan to Newton, 1 September 1924 and 31 December 1923.

[4] It has been suggested that Mr. Field had a confidante in Mr. Dupont whom he consulted. The first Prime Minister of Southern Rhodesia, Sir Charles Coghlan, consulted Sir Francis Newton at length on proposed Cabinet appointments: see National Archives CO 8/1/1, Coghlan to Newton, 18 August 1923 and 24 August 1923.

[5] Under the 1923 Constitution Mr. T. W. H. Beadle in 1946 successfully demanded as a condition of his service that he be appointed Minister of Justice. Personal communication from Lord Malvern.

[6] One leading barrister who accepted the office of Minister of Justice in the early nineteen-thirties successfully demanded that he should not lose his chance of appointment to the bench as in any case he was next in line for appointment to a judgeship.

occasions the Prime Minister has himself attached conditions to offers of office.[1]

A matter to which Prime Ministers have devoted attention is the holding of directorships by Cabinet Ministers. Sir Godfrey Huggins laid it down that the Prime Minister of the day was to be the final judge of the propriety or otherwise of continuing to hold any particular directorship, and that he should be informed before their appointment by prospective Ministers of their directorships. These they would resign, whether of private or of public companies, except in the case of concerns dealing with family affairs, where the company was not primarily engaged in trading, or if the directorship related to a philanthropic undertaking.[2] The question was again raised during the Prime Ministership of Mr. Todd, who informed Parliament that he had asked his Ministers to give up directorships in public companies and also certain directorships in private companies.[3]

The status of the Prime Minister

The status of the Prime Minister in relation to his Cabinet and his parliamentary caucus varies greatly depending upon the personality of the particular man. Those with a more autocratic temperament seek to exercise greater power, demand more freedom to negotiate, and tend to be more overbearing and less attentive to advice.

Nearly all Southern Rhodesian Prime Ministers have from time to time been accused of being autocrats: H. U. Moffat, the second Prime Minister, was accused by his Cabinet of failing to consult them and of keeping too much to himself;[4] Mr. Godfrey Huggins was accused in 1934 of destroying the Reform Party because he demanded freedom to negotiate a new Railway Agreement for the country;[5] Mr. R. S. G. Todd was accused by his Cabinet of autocracy and failure to consult on vital measures;[6] and Mr. W. J. Field was similarly accused of failing to consult his Cabinet and of overriding both their views and those of his caucus.[7]

---

[1] Thus in the case of certain Ministers Mr. Field demanded undertakings that they would at any time tender their resignations without any difficulty if asked by him to do so.

[2] *S.R.L.A.D.*, Vol. 32(2), col. 3685, Huggins.

[3] *S.R.L.A.D.*, Vol. 39, col. 1420, 3 May 1957, Todd.

[4] National Archives LE 3/1/2 (Leggate to Eaton, 9 September 1930).

[5] See Leys, op. cit., p. 137.

[6] *Rhodesia Herald*, 10 February 1957 and *Sunday Mail*, 9 February 1957.

[7] In all such cases only time and the documents will prove the correctness of such allegations. Thus in Mr. Todd's view he allowed complete freedom to his Ministers. Similarly Lord Malvern in a personal communication stated that he was permitted by his Ministers a great deal of independence to negotiate on important questions and also allowed them similar independence, only requiring that he be kept fully informed of events. It would be invidious to state the sources of information on more recent events and recent Cabinet practice, as my informants are actively engaged in politics. Names of informants on recent events are therefore not given.

Again the character of the question at issue may determine the degree of freedom permitted to the Prime Minister, as on matters of magnitude no deviations from party principles will be permitted.[1]

Whether the Prime Minister will permit himself to be overruled also depends on his personality. Certain Prime Ministers have even disregarded decisions taken by the Cabinet, whereas other Prime Ministers approach matters in a spirit of compromise and are prepared to accept a Cabinet majority view. On yet other occasions Prime Ministers have been voted down by their Cabinets.[2] However, a strong Prime Minister might, if he considered the issue important enough, insist on having his own way.[3]

The Prime Minister has always demanded that he has the right to be kept fully informed. When dealing with technical subjects Ministers have however been permitted more independence and less information has been required.[4] Indeed the Prime Minister may sometimes feel that far too much is brought forward to the Cabinet and that many matters should be decided by the relevant Ministers without further ado.[5]

Up to the present Southern Rhodesian Cabinets have been too small for an inner Cabinet to have developed. There is no doubt, however, that Prime Ministers tend to have some advisers with whom they are more intimate than others. Indeed a recent Prime Minister was criticised by his Cabinet for having a confidante (subsequently he changed his confidante) with whom he discussed his decisions, and for frequently not putting these matters before the whole Cabinet.

Prime Ministers have since 1944 avoided the duty of arranging the business of the House. Since April of that year a Leader of the House has been appointed by the Prime Minister to relieve himself of such duties.[6] A heavy responsibility may fall on the Leader of the House if snap amendments arise. If these are of substance there is consultation with the Prime Minister and the Minister concerned.[7] If they are not substantial, the present practice is for the

---

[1] It was for this reason that Mr. Field was forced by his Cabinet to resign, as it was considered that in his 'independence' negotiations with the British Government he had departed too far from the principles of his party in respect of the Land Apportionment Act and other matters relating to discrimination.

[2] e.g. Moffat was overruled by his Cabinet and forced by them to raise with the United Kingdom Government the question of testing the British South Africa Company's mineral rights: National Archives DO 1/1/6, Moffat to Downie, 22 December 1932. Later Moffat stated that there was 'an air of unreality . . . . I have the feeling that my opinion does not really matter': National Archives DO 1/1/6, Moffat to Downie, 13 February 1933.

[3] This was Lord Malvern's attitude expressed in a personal communication.

[4] Lord Malvern in a personal communication. He considered that only on two occasions during his twenty years of office was he not kept properly informed. Mr. Todd in a personal communication thought that he had allowed too much latitude to his Ministers and had not required sufficient information from them.

[5] This is the attitude of the present Prime Minister, Mr. Smith.

[6] *S.R.L.A.D.*, Vol. 24, col. 185, 20 April 1944.

[7] Lord Malvern comments: 'We often agreed by nodding our heads'.

relevant Minister, the Leader of the House, and the Government Whip[1] to consult. If, however, the matter is one of moment, the relevant measure may be postponed or placed down the Order Paper so that consideration can either be given by the Cabinet or by caucus.[2]

The question of the removal of Ministers has also once arisen under the 1961 Constitution. The Prime Minister, Mr. Field, demanded that Mr. Gaunt, then the Minister of Mines, should honour a promise to resign at any time and should state that he had done so on grounds of ill health. This Mr. Gaunt at first agreed to do, but thereafter declined to specify ill health as the reason, refusing also to state that impending Federal dissolution was the ground for his decision. Ultimately Mr. Field withdrew his request that Mr. Gaunt resign. Subsequently the issue was again brought to a head by further differences between Mr. Field and Mr. Gaunt and the question resolved itself into a decision by the Cabinet whether to retain Mr. Field or Mr. Gaunt. The Cabinet then decided that Mr. Field himself should resign.

So far, under the 1961 Constitution, no issues have arisen on which a Minister has stipulated that if the Cabinet did not change its policy he would resign.[3]

Cabinet power

The Cabinet is the policy making body and can and does quite frequently overrule Civil Service proposals put forward to it—very often on political grounds. This tendency has recently been emphasized. Until 1962 the same governing party had been in office for a continuous period of almost thirty years, and as a result the new Government had to some extent to 'tame' the Civil Service which had become accustomed to the views of the former Government.[4] Accordingly a great deal of policy revision and also of administrative work has fallen on the shoulders of Ministers so that to some extent present Ministers have turned themselves into super civil servants overseeing the actions of the administration. The extent to which the Service directs a particular Minister and the Minister the Service however again depends on

[1] The Whip is consulted so that the feelings of back benchers can be assessed.

[2] Important amendments to the Law and Order (Maintenance) Amendment Act 1963 exempting women and juveniles from compulsory hanging who breached clause 33A of that Act, as originally put forward in the Bill, were decided upon at Cabinet level.

[3] This occurred under the 1923 Constitution on at least one occasion, when the Cabinet abandoned a proposed maize levy as Mr. W. M. Leggate would otherwise have resigned: National Archives NE 1/1/7, Moffat to Newton, 10 June 1930. It also occurred in 1957 when the Prime Minister, Mr. Todd, publicly threatened to resign if his franchise legislation was not approved: see Leys, op. cit., p. 229. This was one of the matters about which his Cabinet Ministers publicly complained when they eventually resigned in 1958: see *Sunday Mail*, 9 February 1958.

[4] Personal communication from a Cabinet Minister.

personality.[1] Particularly powerful civil servants may in fact obstruct the Minister.[2] On the other hand, even recommendations by the Treasury or the Public Services Board (charged with recruitment, decisions on establishments, and control of the Service) may occasionally be overruled.

Topics for Cabinet decision

Formerly the tax proposals but not the whole budget were brought to Cabinet a few days before the Budget Statement, while the whole budget was discussed between the Minister of Finance and the Prime Minister.[3] At that time when tax proposals came before Cabinet there might even be changes in incidence or amount. Indeed if the imposition of a tax was likely to be highly controversial even caucus might be consulted.[4] At the present time discussions normally only take place between the Minister of Finance and the Prime Minister. However in specific cases discussions occur with Ministers whose portfolios will be affected by any proposals. The possibility of budget leaks has by this procedure been diminished.[5]

The question of senior appointments in the Civil Service usually goes to Cabinet, although on occasion the Prime Minister has acted in such matters without consulting the Cabinet.[6] Among the senior appointments which are normally considered by the Cabinet are the appointment of chairmen and members of statutory Boards, the appointment of permanent heads of Ministries and Departments, and of the High Commissioner, the last having on several occasions been an avowedly political appointment.[7]

The Speech from the Throne is also a matter that is decided upon at

---

[1] Unfortunately in Southern Rhodesia there has at times been a marked tendency to give office to loyal party supporters who have no ministerial ability.

[2] This has often been alleged with reference to the Chief Native Commissioner. (This office is now designated Secretary of Internal Affairs.)

[3] Personal communication from Lord Malvern.

[4] Lord Malvern in a personal communication stated that in 1949 he consulted his caucus in advance on a tobacco levy on tobacco sales which he introduced: 'Caucus agreed and then ratted within a week.'

[5] Nonetheless a Minister recently stated in a personal communication that he realised there were always small leaks which did not matter so long as they did not reach the press. In 1948 allegations of such a leak were made, it being alleged that the budget speech had been sent in a sealed envelope to the press one week before its delivery with instructions not to open this until the time of the budget speech: S.R.L.A.D., Vol. 28, col. 256. A Select Committee in an exculpatory report found that no leak had occurred because of this. But, because it was necessary to overstamp cigarette boxes with a new surtax in advance of the budget proposals, the tax had to some extent become known. No action was taken against the responsible Minister.

[6] The Southern Rhodesia High Commissioner in London from 1964 to 1965 was appointed by the Prime Minister without prior consultation with his Cabinet.

[7] On two occasions in the early thirties appointments were made to get rid of particular Cabinet Ministers. Recently two diplomatic posts have been filled by former Ministers dropped from Mr. Smith's reconstituted Cabinet.

Cabinet, each Minister submitting a draft of those portions of the Speech which concern his portfolios.[1]

The exercise of the prerogative of mercy is also more fully discussed at Cabinet particularly in view of the introduction of the 1961 Constitution. The use of this power is the only occasion on which Ministers may record their dissent, and on at least one occasion a Minister has at Executive Council insisted on recording that he disagreed with a particular decision.

Criminal prosecutions and the use of the Minister of Law and Order's powers in this respect have not been discussed by the present Cabinet.[2] On the other hand, the question of whether or not persons should be preventively detained has been brought to Cabinet.

Matters not normally brought to Cabinet include the question of the composition of the Cabinet.[3] Owing to a misunderstanding by several Ministers when the present Prime Minister suggested that the Cabinet might reconsider existing administrative arrangements Cabinet composition was discussed.

The award of Honours is also not normally discussed at a full Cabinet, although it is usual for the Prime Minister to ask Ministers to submit recommendations and to consult Ministers out of courtesy.[4]

Two major topics on which Ministers are not kept fully informed are security questions and matters affecting external affairs.

Dissolutions are also not discussed at Cabinet, this being the prerogative of the Prime Minister, who may however discuss the matter with his more senior colleagues.[5]

Cabinet procedure

The Southern Rhodesian Cabinet Secretariat was first established in 1948. Prior to that time there had not been any secretarial organization other than the services provided by the Secretary to the Prime Minister, and all that was done in the way of recording Cabinet meetings was to send written resolutions relating to the main subjects discussed at Cabinet meetings to all Ministers whether present or not. Indeed these resolutions went not only to Ministers, the Governor, and the High Commissioner, but to all Departments of the Civil Service. They were not even confidential to the heads of Depart-

---

[1] This occurred from quite early in the history of cabinet government in Southern Rhodesia: National Archives LE 1/1/1, Cabinet resolutions 352, 365 and 816.

[2] It is clear that these matters were discussed with the Minister of Justice in the Whitehead Cabinet. See *infra*, Chapter 3.

[3] On at least one occasion under the 1923 Constitution the Prime Minister had discussed this with his Cabinet: National Archives LE 1/1/7, Downie to Newton, 30 October 1927.

[4] On a recent occasion these precedents were disregarded.

[5] Lord Malvern informs me that having decided the time was favourable for him to hold a general election he made his defeat on the Currency Board Bill of 1948 a matter of confidence without consulting his Cabinet and that certain Ministers took umbrage while others had 'such cold feet' that they declined to stand for election when a dissolution occurred as a result of defeat on the measure.

ments until 1933 when Mr. Huggins first became Prime Minister.[1] As Sir Godfrey Huggins said in 1948: 'In the past we have followed the system in vogue before Lloyd George became Prime Minister in the United Kingdom . . .. The Prime Minister when he had time and could remember it jotted down what the Cabinet decisions were and these were sent round to the various Ministers merely as a reminder.'[2] Since 1948 however a Cabinet Secretariat, modelled on the United Kingdom system, has been in operation with full documentation and records.[3]

The Southern Rhodesian Cabinet formally meets at least once a week, normally on Tuesday mornings. In addition it meets informally (attendance at such meetings not being compulsory) once a week at 5 p.m. Furthermore, if any urgent business arises the Cabinet may be summoned to a special meeting. There are of course also many personal meetings of individual Ministers with the Prime Minister.

The agenda is prepared by the Secretary to the Cabinet and is thoroughly documented, each Minister submitting items for the agenda and memoranda on the subject in question. However, urgent business not on the agenda (described as 'under the line' business) is also taken, the difference being that there is normally no documentation and prior circulation to the Ministers of such matters.

There is no special seating at Cabinet meetings, though there is a tendency for the more senior Ministers to sit nearer to the Prime Minister.

Prior to Cabinet meetings there is a certain amount of pre-arrangement and, as is natural with all politicians, agreements for mutual support occur. Lobbying may be important when inter-departmental disputes between Ministers arise as these are normally settled by the Cabinet.[4] Sometimes it even becomes necessary for the Prime Minister to decide the issue if the Cabinet is divided on such a matter.

There are often lengthy debates at Cabinet, particularly on agricultural matters.[5] To these debates expert advisers are sometimes called in, although they do not normally attend Cabinet meetings. The same thing applies to Parliamentary Secretaries when matters which are their responsibility are discussed.[6]

---

[1] Personal communication from Lord Malvern.

[2] S.R.L.A.D., Vol. 28, col. 497, 31 May 1948.

[3] In fact a United Kingdom official was brought out to initiate the Secretariat and he spent some time at the United Kingdom Cabinet Office before establishing the system in Southern Rhodesia.

[4] Such disputes have often occurred in Southern Rhodesia, e.g. between the Central Mechanical Equipment Department and user departments (S.R.L.A.D., 1950, col. 767) and between the Department of Lands and the former Department of Native Affairs.

[5] Sometimes there have even been scenes: see National Archives 1/1/7, Moffat to Newton, 28 September 1929.

[6] The Parliamentary Secretary for Information was virtually Minister of Information in Mr. Smith's first Cabinet and was occasionally invited to attend Cabinet to discuss matters affecting the Information Services. The same thing applies to the present Parliamentary Secretary for Mines.

Sometimes votes are taken by show of hands at Cabinet, although there is no recording of votes in favour of or against any decision and no question of recording a dissent.[1]

After the meeting minutes are drawn up and sent to Ministers. These not only incorporate the final decision but give a precis of the discussion which took place. Minutes are still sent to heads of Ministries for their information. However not all matters are recorded in the minutes as these may be highly confidential. Such matters are then recorded in 'the standing file' and a record is sent only to the particular Minister concerned. Difficulties as to interpretation of decisions do not normally arise as the first item of business at every Cabinet meeting is confirmation of the minutes of the previous meeting so that any ambiguities are resolved.

One of the difficulties under which Cabinets labour is that all the previous Cabinet's minutes are destroyed, outgoing Cabinet Ministers taking their memoranda and minutes with them on leaving office.[2] The only guide to decisions is administrative or legislative action taken by the previous Cabinet.

The system of appointing Cabinet Committees not all of which are purely Ministerial has been adopted. There are certain standing Cabinet committees and also *ad hoc* committees appointed from time to time. The first Cabinet committee to be appointed was a War Committee which operated during the last world war.[3] Subsequently from 1948 when the Cabinet Secretariat was established, it was provided that the Cabinet secretary should be chairman of all the larger departmental committees and secretary to all Ministerial committees and inter-departmental co-ordinating committees which would co-ordinate matters before they came to Cabinet. Soon thereafter a Committee of Ministers presided over by the Minister of Finance was established,[4] which by 1951 had developed into a Ministerial Economic Co-ordinating Committee examining all questions before they came to Cabinet.[5]

At present there is a Committee Co-ordinating Economic Affairs consisting of the Ministers whose portfolios impinge on these matters.

A further committee is the Appeal Committee on Estimates which consists

[1] In 1942 the Minister of Finance asked to record his dissent and Sir Godfrey Huggins then told him if he insisted on this he must resign. Personal communication from Lord Malvern.

[2] Lord Malvern on leaving office took virtually the whole Prime Minister's Office documentation with him. He has however donated the material to the National Archives but it will not be open for thirty years.

[3] For its working and composition see *S.R.L.A.D.*, Vol. 20, col. 967. See also Vol. 21(1), col. 3079. The War Committee was not a separate Cabinet, as all main issues of policy were submitted to the whole Cabinet which received the minutes of the daily meetings of the War Committee. One of the reasons for the resignation in 1942 of the Minister of Finance was that he resented his exclusion from this Committee. Lord Malvern in a personal communication stated that it was impossible to have him on the Committee as he was 'a Victorian financier' and in war time 'all finance goes mad'.

[4] *S.R.L.A.D.*, Vol. 29, col. 326, 25 November 1948.

[5] *S.R.L.A.D.*, Vol. 31(2), col. 3033.

of the Minister of Finance and another Minister to hear appeals when a departmental request has been rejected by the Treasury.

A new Cabinet Co-ordinating Committee on Community Development with power to call for or to review plans of all Ministries to implement local government has recently been established.[1]

There is also an important committee, the Security Council, which was established soon after the Field Government came to power. This consists of some Ministers, some heads of Ministries, and certain security officers. As its name indicates, it is concerned with matters affecting the security of the country.

Ministerial responsibility

Perhaps the biggest departures from strict United Kingdom practice have been in the field of Ministerial responsibility, both collective and individual. However, the need for collective responsibility has always been recognized and Ministers may bring any matters before Cabinet, although it is unusual to bring forward minor matters in the Department of another Minister.[2] Furthermore, when regulations are made by the Governor in Council all Ministers express their views thereon.[3] On the other hand, the tradition that Ministers should defend decisions even if they disagree, should not discuss their differences outside Cabinet, should not disagree in public,[4] should abide by Cabinet decisions, and cannot insist on recording their dissent, have occasionally broken down. Most of these incidents occurred either during 1942 when the Minister of Finance disagreed so radically with the rest of the Cabinet that he resigned (breaking another rule thereafter by discussing Cabinet differences in public)[5] or during the period when there was a National Government formed by the governing United Party and certain members of the Rhodesian Labour Party who resigned from their party in 1940 to form the Labour Party and to remain in office as part of a war-time coalition.[6] It

[1] Report of the Secretary of Internal Affairs for the year 1963, C.S.R. 16–1964, p. 2.

[2] This rule was enunciated by Sir Charles Coghlan when Mr. Moffat insisted on discussing the retirement of the old and the appointment of the new Chief Native Commissioner: National Archives MO 13/1/1, Coghlan to Moffat, 12 January 1926.

[3] S.R.L.A.D., Vol. 43, col. 1126, 5 August 1959.

[4] On one occasion the Prime Minister had to order a Minister to resign or to stay silent as he would not tolerate anything in the shape of an attack on the Government's policy from the Minister: see National Archives NE 1/1/7, Moffat to Newton, 6 March 1930.

[5] The ex-Minister of Finance was accused of a multitude of sins against the doctrine of Cabinet responsibility: see S.R.L.A.D., Vol. 21(1), col. 3105 et seq., 10 February 1942, Huggins (for not consulting the Prime Minister—at this stage the Prime Minister obtained permission from the Governor to disclose Cabinet minutes in order to contradict statements by the former Minister), cols. 3366–7, 3423–4, and S.R.L.A.D., Vol. 25(2), cols. 2378–80, 6 July 1945 (for revealing Cabinet secrets).

[6] According to Sir Godfrey Huggins, each party 'reserved its own ideological ideas' and the Labour members were given rather more liberty: S.R.L.A.D., Vol. 23, 572, 11 May 1943. Indeed on one earlier occasion one Labour Minister and the Minister of Finance voted against the Government on a motion which the Minister of Air had stated the Government could not accept: see S.R.L.A.D., Vol. 20, cols. 1494–5, 24 October 1940.

also broke down again in January 1958 when members of Mr. Todd's Cabinet resigned, stating that they were not kept informed of certain major decisions relative to subordinate legislation providing for an increase in the minimum wages payable to African industrial workers.[1]

On yet another occasion the limits of the doctrine were reached when the Prime Minister resigned in 1950 to get rid of the Minister of Trade, Industry and Development who had on Cabinet instructions implemented an unpopular policy.

More recently a breakdown in collective responsibility occurred when Mr. Field repudiated an attack by Mr. Gaunt on the Southern Rhodesian Minister in Washington for certain statements he had made in a newspaper article, and yet did not force Mr. Gaunt's resignation.

Behaviour of the Cabinet in the House is today more rigidly controlled. There is not as there was in 1940 to 1943 any question of the Cabinet not supporting all Government proposals. Ministers may not abstain, let alone cross the floor as was then permitted, and they must be present for votes unless paired.

In regard to individual responsibility, there have also been departures from strict doctrine, the Minister of Justice stating on one occasion that where a senior civil servant had made errors in a memorandum on a Bill before the House, he should be criticised.[2] On another occasion a Parliamentary Secretary denied any political responsibility of Ministers for mistakes by their Departments, their only duty, according to him, being to put such mistakes right after the Public Accounts Committee had pointed them out.[3] Again in 1960 the Minister of Justice refused to accept responsibility when a Commission appointed to enquire into allegations of interference with the courts found that there had been an attempt by the Executive to interfere with the discretion of magistrates on two occasions.[4]

On the other hand, a Minister was recently submitted to continuous attack for making an incorrect statement as to certain American financial assistance for Rhodesian industry. Only when, during the course of a by-election campaign, this matter was used as election advertisement material, did the Minister make a public statement to the effect that his speech had been prepared by a senior civil servant and that he had not answered criticism until

---

[1] *Sunday Mail*, 9 February 1958. According to ex-Cabinet Ministers Mr. Todd had ignored the advice of Ministers and caucus and Cabinet meetings had become a farce. Mr. Todd however maintained in a personal communication that these matters had been before every Cabinet meeting for approximately nine months and the challenged decision had been taken by the whole Cabinet.

[2] It was immediately pointed out to the Minister that this was his own responsibility: see *S.R.L.A.D.*, Vol. 17, cols. 2091, 2144.

[3] *S.R.L.A.D.*, Vol. 23, col. 511, Beadle.

[4] C.S.R. 7–1961, pp. 5 and 11, and *S.R.L.A.D.*, Vols. 4290–2 and 4351–61. In the United Kingdom such allegations, to some extend found to be proved by a Commission, would certainly have led to the resignation of the Minister concerned.

that stage as a Minister must take responsibility for the acts of his officials unless they been been guilty of wilful misconduct.[1]

Other oddities affecting Cabinet and party government have also occurred in Southern Rhodesia. During the war, an independent Member, who won a by-election, was treated as 'a National Member', was allowed to attend party caucuses, to enquire into governmental matters and was yet permitted to remain a free agent.[2] Again, owing to instability of his majority, the Prime Minister would allow free votes of the House on important measures, including financial measures, and would even permit Cabinet Ministers as well as back benchers to vote against major proposals.[3]

The same sort of thing occurred again during the Todd Government when Ministers and Members disagreed with certain measures, it being agreed when the Government enjoyed an absolute majority in favour of a measure that members of the governing party could voice their opposition from the floor of the House.[4]

Another feature was, during the existence of a minority government from 1946 to 1948, excessive use of the Select Committee system. Indeed, the Prime Minister described the system as executive government by Select Committee, the powers of control in effect being taken out of the hands of Government and being placed in those of Select Committees.[5] In order to remain in power, the Government was even prepared to accept amendments to motions of confidence,[6] which placed the Government at the mercy of the Labour Opposition.[7]

Subsequently, when it became obvious that Government would be defeated

[1] See Southern Rhodesia Information Department Statement 971/64/DTMW.
[2] S.R.L.A.D., Vol. 21(1), cols. 2501–2, Leggate.
[3] See S.R.L.A.D., Vol. 24, col. 1828 for a motion urging the extension of the life of Parliament where the Minister of Agriculture and Defence voted against this motion—a free vote was permitted; S.R.L.A.D., Vol. 23, col. 1903, 17 June 1943 where a Parliamentary Secretary and three Ministers crossed the floor to delete a clause in the Excess Profits Bill; S.R.L.A.D., Vol. 21(1) where four back benchers after political meeting mandates voted against the Government on a motion of confidence; and S.R.L.A.D., Vol. 30(2) where a clause in the Tobacco Marketing Bill providing for Ministers by regulation to allocate tobacco quotas as between different classes of grower was defeated, the Cabinet being in the minority.
[4] e.g. in 1955 four Government supporters voted against the third reading of the Public Order Bill: S.R.L.A.D., Vol. 38, col. 1838. Two Ministers on a free vote voted against a motion on the siting of the Territorial capital: S.R.L.A.D., Vol. 38, col. 2092, 2 December 1955. On 'matters of principle and conscience' the Prime Minister agreed to a free vote when the Land Apportionment (Amendment) Act 1954 was passed: S.R.L.A.D., Vol. 36, col. 2599. In this case six Members crossed the floor to vote against amendments to the Act which allowed the multi-racial university to operate, to allow an African advocate to have chambers in a European town, to permit inter-racial clubs and to allow non-indigenous Africans to stay at international hotels provided they obtained a permit. Nor was the whip applied on the Electoral Bill 1957 when five Government Members were permitted to cross the floor: S.R.L.A.D., Vol. 40, col. 1088.
[5] See S.R.L.A.D., Vol. 31(1), cols. 1238 et seq.
[6] Another unusual procedure first introduced in 1942.
[7] S.R.L.A.D., Vol. 27(2), col. 2176, 5 February 1948.

by its own supporters, it was even prepared to withdraw the Budget proposals against what was obviously its own better judgement.[1]

Political pressures and power in the Cabinet system

Leys in his *European Politics in Southern Rhodesia*, published in 1959, has
cogently argued that there was a 'one-party system' in Southern Rhodesia,
using the phrase in an unconventional fashion to indicate that one and the
same party had always been in power.[2] This contention could perhaps be
better stated by saying that in Southern Rhodesia there is at any point of
time only one political party which enjoys massive support from the European
electorate. In 1962 the permanent Opposition came to power, but it has now
become the sole effective party enjoying support by the European electorate,
as the former governing body has in large measure disintegrated, losing
many supporters to the new Government. Indeed between July 1964 and May
1965 four of the twelve Cabinet Ministers including the Prime Minister were
formerly Members of Parliament representing the United Federal Party, the
United Party, or the United Rhodesia Party.[3] Leys, writing in 1958, foresaw
that

if the Opposition party were to dislodge the Government and establish itself firmly in
office . . . there is no reason to think that this would herald the end of the one party
system and the beginning of an alternating two-party mechanism like that in Britain.
On the contrary, the one-party system would be likely to be more firmly entrenched
than ever, although the complexion of the policies of Government and Opposition
will be reversed.[4]

This is precisely what has happened in Southern Rhodesia, where the more
conservative elements in the European population have gained control of
the Government, while those who are more disposed to a multi-racial solution have become the somewhat ineffective opposition.[5] However, such
statements relate only to European politics and take no note of African
politics. Leys was writing before changes in the Constitution made it possible
for African nationalist politicians to enter the Southern Rhodesian Legislative Assembly. Although they have not so far participated actively in the

[1] See *S.R.L.A.D.*, Vol. 33(1), cols. 1553 et seq., 1650 and 1641. A proposed purchase tax
was withdrawn and changes in the incidence of personal tax were also made. The Prime
Minister stated: 'I am very disappointed that honourable Members have not been prepared
to lead on this occasion but have followed the crowd': *S.R.L.A.D.*, Vol. 33(1), col. 843.
[2] Op. cit., p. 173.
[3] The United Federal Party and the United Rhodesia Party were the Federal and Territorial descendants of the United Party which decided, on the creation of Federation, to
divide into a Territorial and a Federal Party, simultaneous membership of both parties
being possible. See Leys, op. cit.
[4] Leys, op. cit., p. 176.
[5] This is not the place to analyse Southern Rhodesian politics, which would be a lengthy
task for a political scientist.

parliamentary mechanism the growth of the African nationalist movement makes minor modifications in Leys' thesis necessary. However, in the light of the present franchise provisions even if the African nationalists participated they would be condemned to the role of 'permanent Opposition' for many years to come although they could form the official Opposition, as they could win at least fifteen electoral districts and probably one constituency.[1]

Despite the refusal of the African nationalists to participate and the fact of Southern Rhodesia's 'one-party system' the parliamentary mechanism is in operation, with two parties[2] and a few independents.[3] It can of course be argued that such a parliament is unreal in that it does not represent the political opinion of the whole population. However it is very real in that it exercises legislative power.[4]

Leys[5] points to the importance of the Government caucus and its value in constructive self-criticism. This latter comment was no longer applicable in the period from 1958 to 1965 as the parliamentary parties were differently composed, the Government party having a smaller majority and consisting of more 'loyal supporters'. There have been no cases, as in past Legislative Assemblies, of Government party members being freed from the party whip. At present the Cabinet controls the caucus, which only asserts itself against the Cabinet if an attempt is made to depart from party policy.[6]

To a considerable extent the influence of caucus depends on the personality

---

[1] The Minister of Internal Affairs has announced his Government's intention to have a re-registration of all voters: *S.R.L.A.D.*, Vol. 59, col. 790, 2 December 1964. If, when this occurs, African voters boycott the re-registration as seems very likely, the number of African voters could well be reduced from the total of 12,929 on both 'A' and 'B' Rolls at 31 May 1964 to about 2,500. If this occurs the Government will be reinforced in its demand to substitute Chiefs' seats for the fifteen electoral districts and may even without doing this possibly be able to win electoral districts by virtue of its powers of patronage in seats where the number of 'B' Roll voters would be just over 150 in all.

[2] The party system proper only started in Southern Rhodesia in 1927. Shortly thereafter the Leader of the Opposition was first recognized: *S.R.L.A.D.*, Vol. 6, col. 950, 967–8. For a history of European political parties the authoritative work is Leys, op. cit. The present governing party is the Rhodesian Front descended from the Dominion Party and consisting of fifty European members representing constituencies. The official Opposition consists of ten African members of the United Peoples Party which was formed as a vehicle for its African Members of Parliament when the Rhodesia Party, formerly the United Federal Party, disbanded in May 1965 after all its European candidates in the General Election of that month had been defeated.

[3] There are at present (July 1965) two Independent Members who put forward the Nationalist point of view. They are however too few in numbers to do more than this and occasionally to obstruct procedure. There are also three other Independent Members who represent electoral districts. Of these it has been alleged that two enjoy Government (Rhodesian Front) support.

[4] In Southern Rhodesia since Governments maintain strict control of their parliamentary parties legislative powers are exercised at the dictate of the executive.

[5] Op cit., at pp. 62–3.

[6] Some observers consider caucus controls Cabinet, but others consider the party executive controls both Cabinet and caucus. The information in the text comes from Cabinet Ministers and caucus members.

of the Prime Minister in office. Thus the present Prime Minister is more amenable to caucus opinions and holds the view that since caucus represents the party, he should consult it on important issues.[1] A recent development has been the establishment of permanent caucus committees appointed to advise and consult with each Minister on legislation relative to his portfolio.[2] Legislation is referred to these committees after it has been to Cabinet. The Committees then indicate their views and the measure thereafter goes back to Cabinet a second time for final decision. So far no decisions have been forced on Cabinet by caucus.

Individual Members of Parliament sometimes influence decisions, but this greatly depends on the personality of the Member of Parliament. Individuals can, however, have nuisance value to Government, particularly if they are 'leaked' information by civil servants and thus enabled to speak with authority on Government's administrative failures.[3]

The Opposition has exercised influence on Government policy in a negative sense, as the Cabinet was unlikely to introduce measures, unless they involved major principles of party policy, that would cause violent adverse criticism by the Opposition. The positive effect of the Opposition has always been small, even though on non-political and non-controversial measures its views were considered.[4] Much also depends on the Leader of the Opposition, who is officially recognized and paid a salary, and the degree to which he is prepared to co-operate with the Government.[5] However, on procedural matters there is normally agreement and co-operation between the party whips. Since May 1965 the Opposition, except for one Independent European, has consisted entirely of non-Europeans while the Government party has consisted entirely of Europeans. In these circumstances opposition may be discounted by the governing party (itself representing one section of the community) on the basis that the opposition represents only sectional and racial interests.

Outside pressure groups exercise more influence on Ministers, particularly

[1] Care must be taken in consulting caucus, as there are inevitably 'leaks'. As Sir Godfrey Huggins once said: 'I do not think I have ever attended all the time I have been in this House where there was not a leakage': *S.R.L.A.D.*, Vol. 33(2), col. 3914, 9 February 1953.

[2] It is understood that Ministers bring civil servants with them when they meet caucus committees in order to explain technical points involved in the measures. It is submitted this is an unorthodox use of civil servants.

[3] Ordinary Members of Parliament may not request information from civil servants, but must go through a Minister.

[4] In 1930 the Government adopted policies which were first advocated by the Opposition e.g. the Industrial Conciliation Act, the Workmen's Compensation Act, and factories legislation.

[5] At present pairing arrangements are in operation although at first this was refused. In the past Leaders of the Opposition have been criticised for too willing co-operation with the Prime Minister. Sir Edgar Whitehead in particular used to 'hamstring' the Opposition as a whole by taking the Leader of the Opposition personally into his confidence on controversial issues.

the major interests of agriculture, mining, commerce, and industry.[1] In fact one Minister has said 'Ministers are showered with advice, particularly on agricultural matters and by commerce, and industry.' As a result of these intense pressures it is normal for Ministers to consult affected interests before decisions are made.[2]

Government Departments

The Government Departments provide the administrative machinery whereby effect is given to Government policy and legislative measures, and execute the multifarious tasks of administration in a modern state. Southern Rhodesian Departments are unaffected by changes in Government, except that where considerable policy shifts occur these may to a certain extent be reflected in reorganization of the administration.

Of recent years the structure of Government Departments in Southern Rhodesia has undergone a great change, partly as a result of the dissolution of Federation and the return of former Federal functions to the Southern Rhodesian Government. However, some of the more important modifications followed from the Robinson Report, on the organization and functions of the Native Affairs Department and the District Courts Department,[3] and from a series of reports by Dr. T. Paterson, who advised the Southern Rhodesia Government on reorganization of the civil service.[4]

There were at the end of July 1965 twenty-one Ministries in Southern Rhodesia,[5] while within the Ministries were various Departments and Branches. At the head of each Ministry is a political Minister who may in practice hold several portfolios. The permanent civil service head of the

---

[1] Described in Leys, op. cit., pp. 98–111. The large mining corporations do not exercise so great an influence on the present Government, which is politically opposed to their colour policies.

[2] If this is not meticulously done the interests in question complain. See *S.R.L.A.D.*, Vol. 58, cols. 841–8, 25 September 1964, where it appears that the Rhodesia National Farmers Union complained that it had not been consulted on a minor measure—the Pig Industry Amendment Bill.

[3] C.S.R. 22–1961.

[4] C.S.R. 9–1962; C.S.R. 35–1962 (Local government), and C.S.R. 2–1963 (Job evaluation). These are most unusual reports which contain a remarkable amount of sociological and psychological jargon and several 'theoretical' chapters in respect of which the Commissioner laid claim to 'the copyright'. It is not surprising that the reports were enthusiastically supported by civil servants—the Secretaries of Ministries and other senior officials received a 22·5 per cent salary increase as a result of the Commissioner's recommendations. See Third Report of the Estimates Committee 1964. L.A.S.C., 14–1964, p. 2.

[5] viz. Department of the Prime Minister, and the Ministries of External Affairs, of Defence, of Internal Affairs, of the Public Service, of Justice, of Law and Order, of Information of Local Government and Housing, of Labour and Social Welfare, of Finance, of Posts, of Commerce and Industry, of Transport and Power, of Roads and Road Traffic, of Mines and Lands, of Water Development, of Agriculture, of Immigration and Tourism, of Health and of Education.

Ministry is designated Secretary and is assisted by a Deputy Secretary.[1] An unusual feature of Southern Rhodesian administration is the fact that the Secretary of each Ministry and also the heads of certain important Departments write annual reports on the work of their Ministries which are published as Southern Rhodesian Command Papers and presented to the Legislative Assembly shortly before Committee of Supply on the main Estimates. Civil servants have been permitted a remarkable degree of independence in writing these reports and at times such reports have even criticised Government policy.[2]

Establishments as between the various Departments are recommended by the Public Services Board and confirmed by the Treasury which controls all expenditure and exercises a general supervisory power to secure that public funds are properly expended.

The Public Service

The Civil Service is governed by the Public Services Act, Chapter 90, and enjoys a great deal of independence. In terms of the Public Services Act there has been established a Public Services Board which is responsible for making regulations as to recruitment, appointment, promotion, conditions of service, transfer and retrenchment of officers, the formation of new Departments, and proposals to effect economies and to promote efficiency.[3]

The Public Service greatly influences the composition of the Board, even though the Governor has an absolute discretion in the appointment of members, as it is provided that before exercising his discretion he shall consult the

[1] Some Ministers have two Deputy Secretaries, something of a 'troika' system having been adopted after recommendations to this effect in the Paterson Report, C.S.R 9–1962, pp. 114 et seq. The system has not been fully implemented, and the Estimates Committee has commented that its adoption was precipitate and unwarranted: L.A.S.C. 14–1964, para. 6.

[2] e.g. the Report of the Chief Native Commissioner for the year ending 31 December 1961—C.S.R. 28–1962, strongly attacked aspects of the implementation of policy by the Whitehead administration then in office. It was also a highly political document and criticized Members of Parliament. Again, the report of the Commissioner of Roads and Road Traffic for the year 1963, C.S.R. 13–1964, pp. 17 and 21, criticized 'unenlightened authority which constantly suggests and presses for changes in the constitution and structure of the Ministry', and complained of 'this persistent interference'.

[3] Chapter 90, Section 11. The Board was informally established in March 1928 and formalized in the Public Services Act 1931. Under the B.S.A. Company a standing Advisory Committee, to which 'all matters relating to the appointment, promotion and pay of officers shall be referred' was established at the end of 1912 as a result of a 1909 Board of Inquiry into the working of the Public Service: G.N. 380, 5 December 1912. From time to time as a result of various Commission Reports, increases in the powers of the Board and provision for additional security and benefits for public servants have been made by amendments to the Act, e.g. by Act 18 of 1944 considerable changes were made implementing a Report by the Godlonton Commission in 1938, and by Acts 39 of 1948, 55 of 1949, and 18 of 1956 the Plewman Commission Report of 1945 (Report of the Public Services Inquiry Commission) was implemented.

representatives of any Public Service Associations in regard to the appointment of a chairman and one other member of the Board if the total membership of the Board is four, whereas if it is five then the Association shall be consulted in respect of the chairman and two members.[1] As a result the Board is predominantly composed of members of the Service. At present it consists of a chairman and four members, one of whom is part-time. The chairman and full-time members are civil servants. Indeed, the Estimates Committee of the Legislative Assembly considered it necessary to recommend that the Board's constitution should be changed so that neither the chairman nor a majority of members of the Board should be civil servants or retired civil servants. Service representation, the Committee recommended, should be reduced to one member.[2]

The Board exercises considerable power as Board recommendations are difficult to reject. Although the Governor in Council may within six months vary or reject any recommendation on furnishing reasons to the Board, the Board must reply to this statement and their reply must be considered by the Governor in Council.[3] Any rejections of Board recommendations are also to be fully reported on by the Board to the Legislative Assembly and are to be laid upon the table. Consequently in practice the Government is extremely hesitant to reject Public Services Board recommendations, and this seldom occurs.

Although both Roman–Dutch Law and English Law are similar on this point since English Law governs any matters relative to the Crown's 'constitutional position in regard to matters of government',[4] it seems that at common law all Crown servants hold office at pleasure.[5] It also seems that the Crown apart from statute (viz. the Public Services Act and the Police Act) may curtail its powers of dismissing its employees at pleasure by contract.[6]

[1] Chapter 90, Section 3(3). Terms of office are also subject to consultation with the Public Services Association.

[2] Third Report of the Estimates Committee 1964, L.A.S.C. 14–1964, para. 8. It is doubtful whether these recommendations will be implemented, as the Civil Service is one of the most powerful pressure groups in Southern Rhodesia. There were approximately 9,150 established posts held by non-Africans at the end of July 1964 and in March 1964 there were approximately another 8,915 unestablished posts so held. The total of non-Africans employed amounted to 18,066 (information by courtesy of the Central Statistical Office). If wives were taken into account, the civil service vote amounts to at least one-third of the 'A' Roll electorate. Such figures do not include any of the serving personnel of the British South Africa Police, the Southern Rhodesian Army, or the Royal Rhodesian Air Force.

[3] Chapter 90, Section 14.

[4] *Union Government* v. *Whittaker*, 1916 A.D. 194 at 203 per Innes C.J. *Contra* J. P. Verloren van Themaat T.H.R.-H.R., Vol. 16 (1953), pp. 69 et seq. See, however, B. Beinart T.H.R.-H.R., Vol. 15 (1952), p. 162.

[5] For an illuminating analysis of both English and Roman–Dutch Law and a full examination of the questions involved see B. Beinart, 'The Legal Relationship Between the Government and Its Employees'. 1955, *Butterworths South African Law Review*, pp. 21 et seq.

[6] See Beinart, op cit. at pp. 54 et seq. Beinart effectively disposes of *Anning* v. *The Colonial Secretary*, 1931 S.R. 95 where one of the *rationes* for dismissal of an unestablished servant engaged for a fixed term was that the Crown could still dismiss at pleasure.

However, the legal relationship between the Administration and its servants has been considerably modified by the Public Services Act[1] and although the relationship of servants on the fixed establishment is based on the common law the statute and regulations thereunder exclude many of its consequences. Where however, the Act is silent, or where the employee is not on the fixed establishment, and therefore not governed by the Act, the common law applies.[2]

Civil servants on the established staff enjoy security of tenure in that the grounds of discharge are specified in the Public Services Act, while no officer may be discharged without a recommendation from the Board.[3] Where misconduct—specified in detail—is alleged, the Board either enquires into the matter or a committee of three officers nominated by the Minister of the Public Service headed by a judicial officer of at least fifteen years' experience enquires into the charges.[4]

Political activities of civil servants are strictly limited by the definition of 'misconduct', since it is 'misconduct' for any officer to become a member of any political organization or to take an active part in political matters.[5] This limitation also applies to employees in unestablished posts as there is a similar condition in their terms of service. Apparently it does not apply to employees on contract terms, as during a recent by-election campaign in September 1963 the information adviser to the Government was requested by the Prime Minister to address a private party political house meeting.[6]

Civil servants are also given certain constitutional protection. This relates

[1] For an analysis of the Public Services Act and its effect on the relationship between the Crown and its employees see Beinart, op. cit. In *Davis* v. *Colonial Secretary*, 1931 S.R. 94, it was held that the Crown's right to dismiss at pleasure had been abrogated by the Act.

[2] *Anning* v. *Colonial Secretary*, 1931 S.R. 95.

[3] The grounds of discharge are continued ill-health, abolition of office, reorganization to facilitate improvements of organization and efficiency and economy, unfitness or incapacity to perform duties, failure to become a citizen six months after the earliest possible date or after appointment whichever may be the later, and misconduct.

[4] Chapter 90, Section 41(3). If a committee investigates the matter the Board then considers its findings and may direct further evidence or the submission of further reports.

[5] Section 39(h). This provision has not prevented civil servants adopting political attitudes. On one occasion the Director of the Medical Services was reprimanded for refusing to allow a clinic to be opened by the wife of an Opposition Member of Parliament: *S.R.L.A.D.*, Vol. 22, col. 1889. On yet another occasion a leading civil servant proposed giving a public lecture on closer association which was cancelled by the Prime Minister: *S.R.L.A.D.*, Vol. 32, col. 2605. An unusual feature of Southern Rhodesian public life is the introduction of 'closed meetings' for civil servants which are arranged by the leaders of the main political parties and where, after speeches, civil servants ask questions from the floor. In 1964 such a meeting was held by the Prime Minister at the request of the Public Services Association to explain his attitude to a unilateral declaration of independence.

[6] The Prime Minister accepted personal responsibility for this conduct and explained that electors had requested to meet this individual so that they might be satisfied that his views on racial issues were not as they had been represented. He accepted the general principle however that such an employee was in a position where he should not take part in party politics: *S.R.L.A.D.*, Vol. 58, cols. 896 et seq. However the Minister of the Public Service contended that such an employee was only bound by the terms of his contract: cols. 900–1.

to their pensions and gratuities which are safeguarded by a section of the Constitution, whereas the Public Services Act and the rights which it confers can be amended by a simple majority of the Legislative Assembly. The Constitution in Section 114 provides that any person holding public office is entitled to have his claim to a pension or gratuity or that of his wife or dependents governed by the law in force at the time of his appointment, or alternatively he may elect to have his pension governed by any subsequent law. It is also provided that all pensions and gratuities are to be charged upon and paid out of the Consolidated Revenue Fund. Section 114 is a specially entrenched provision of the Constitution and is therefore not easily susceptible of amendment.

The racial composition of the Civil Service to a large extent reflects that of the electorate. Only in 1960 were established posts in the Civil Service opened to Africans as prior to that time Africans could merely hold the more menial unestablished posts available to temporary Government employees.[1] By mid-1963, as a result of this change, there were ninety-three established African civil servants, all occupying very junior positions, out of a total establishment of 2,247.[2] At present there are approximately 1,652 African civil servants out of the total number of officers of 9,905.[3] However, this increase in numbers of African civil servants is almost entirely a result of the transfer of Federal civil servants on Federal dissolution, included amongst whom were a large number of lower grade African civil servants.[4] Considerable numbers of Africans are employed by the Government as unestablished employees and as casual labour.[5] That African civil servants do not hold any key positions emerges from the Southern Rhodesian Government List 1964,[6] which lists all senior and relatively senior public servants. Only three Africans are listed, one of whom is at the Washington Mission, and two of whom are attached to the Natural Resources Board which is concerned with the conservation of resources in African and European areas of the Colony alike.[7] The only other Africans listed are African members of the

[1] See Public Services Amendment (No. 2) Act No. 42 of 1960, which deleted the prohibition on entry to the service of 'any native or coloured person' inserted in 1931. Removal of racial aspects from Government employment was only completed in 1964. The rules governing the appointment and conditions of service of various categories of employees are now publicised in Public Service Board Circulars 37A/1, 35A 43/3 and 44A.

[2] See *S.R.L.A.D.*, Vol. 50, cols. 358–9, 4 July 1962.

[3] *S.R.L.A.D.*, Vol. 61, cols. 1213–14, 21 July 1965.

[4] 1,250 of the 1,652 African civil servants are officers from the Federal Service who now occupy unestablished posts in the Southern Rhodesian Service. Almost all of these are on salary scales between £150 and £420 per annum: *S.R.L.A.D.*, Vol. 61, col. 566.

[5] In July 1965 there were 19,625 Africans and 1,317 Europeans employed on unestablished conditions of service, while there were a further 14,811 ungraded casual employees all of whom were African: *S.R.L.A.D.*, Vol. 61, cols. 1213–14 and 1506.

[6] Government Printer, Salisbury, June 1964.

[7] Section 19(3) of the Public Services Act provides that the Minister, in appointing or promoting to any post in the Service 'may have regard to the circumstances of the locality and the sphere of duties of such posts'.

public nominated to statutory boards, it being necessary in most cases for there to be one African representing the African Farmers Union.[1]

The Chiefs

The Chiefs are Government officials, appointed in terms of Sections 4 and 17 of the African Affairs Act by the Governor. They hold office during pleasure, and contingent upon good behaviour and general fitness.[2]

Although Chiefs are envisaged as hereditary holders of the office, it is only official recognition that carries with it the title of Chief. In practice the Governor frequently appoints the person holding traditional title to the chieftainship, but this is not always done.[3] In other cases where the tribe (reference is here to the Mashona, who have a complicated system of collateral succession) have been unable to agree on a successor, the Government have made the decisions and in the last ten years have on twelve occasions arranged for some form of election.[4] Furthermore, not all traditional chieftainships are recognized as from time to time Government has carried out a general

[1] These figures are borne out by the fact that no African is employed in a higher position in the Civil Service than Band C, Grade 6 whereas grades rise to Band E, Grade 10: *S.R.L.A.D.*, Vol. 61, cols. 1213–14, 21 July 1965.

[2] Between 1935 and the present, twenty-one Chiefs have been deposed by the Government. Six of these were deposed for unsuitability or for drunkenness, and the others because of criminal convictions: *S.R.L.A.D.*, Vol. 59, col. 160, 21 October 1964. Between 1928 to 1935 a further eleven were deposed (see Reports of the Chief Native Commissioner for the years 1928–34).

[3] The Governor is entitled to exercise an unfettered discretion in the appointment of Chiefs and the creation, amalgamation or subdivision of tribes. Formerly Section 10 (now repealed) of the Native Affairs Act (Chapter 72 of 1939) implied that the Governor should have regard to native opinion and native customary succession as investigated by the Chief Native Commissioner, but once that investigation (now no longer necessary) had been made he was 'free to act as he thinks best in the interests of the good government of the natives': *Muwuungani* v. *Minister of Native Affairs*, 1957 (2) S.A. 544 (F.C.) at 546 per Tredgold C.J. See the Report of the Mangwende Reserve Commission in 1961, para. 132, where a more junior member in the line of succession was appointed in order to secure a more progressive Chief. This Chief was subsequently deposed by Government on the grounds that he had been convicted of perjury and in 1964 was restricted to the Gonakudzingwa Restriction Area. Three of the seven Ndebele Chiefs on the Chiefs' Council were not heirs at customary law. Chief Simon Sigola, one of Southern Rhodesia's leading Ndebele Chiefs, was not a hereditary Chief, as he succeeded his father, who was a Government messenger appointed to the office of Chief. Similarly, Chief Kaisa Ndiweni was not the heir apparent at customary law to his chieftainship. He was however pushed forward 'by the people' as being more educated. Again, Chief Ngungumbana succeeded a distant agnate. Indeed one of Southern Rhodesia's leading officials in the Department of Internal Affairs has said: 'It is a most extraordinary fact that very often the administration may miss the rightful successor': R. Howman in 'Chiefs and Councils in Southern Rhodesia', *From Tribal Rule to Modern Government*, Rhodes-Livingstone Institute, Lusaka, 1949, p. 41. The Government nonetheless professes that: 'The Chiefs are born with the blood of Chiefs': *S.R.L.A.D.*, Vol. 59, col. 1103, 4 December 1964.

[4] *S.R.L.A.D.*, Vol. 59, cols. 158–9, 21 October 1964.

reorganization of chieftainships reducing the numbers of recognized Chiefs. Thus in 1951, eighty-nine out of approximately 323 chieftainships were abolished.[1] Chieftainships were 'amalgamated' thus different ethnic tribes were placed under one Chief.[2] The fact that the 'Government Chief' may not be the 'real Chief' may lead to difficulties and the Africans in the area may still take their disputes to be settled by the person whom they regard as the proper incumbent of the chieftainship.[3]

In fact in recent litigation counsel for the Government argued that 'the African tribes in Rhodesia today are in no way identifiable with the tribes which existed prior to the conquest of Rhodesia in 1893 but are essentially administrative units created by administrative action under the African Affairs Act'.[4] Indeed Davies J. held that 'the tribes of Rhodesia no longer consist of ethnic groups but of administrative units created by action under the (African Affairs) Act'.[5] Furthermore the learned judge considered that in present-day circumstances it was impossible in law for Shona customary law to operate to confer a corporate personality on a tribe so that it was capable of acquiring rights or obligations.[6]

Chiefs are charged with duties of tax collection, prevention of crime in their tribal areas, and oversight of the general good conduct of Africans under their charge.[7] Chiefs rank as constables within their tribal areas.[8] They also possess civil jurisdiction and are *ex officio* members of the African Councils in their areas.[9] Chiefs have, however, gradually been converted into minor administrative officers of Government, supporting the authority of the District Commissioner in rural areas.[10] More recently, they have been used

[1] *S.R.L.A.D.*, Vol. 59, para. 60. This had been recommended in the Report of the Native Production and Trade Commission 1944: C.S.R. 2–1945, Government Printer, Salisbury. The number of Chiefs recognized has varied. In 1902, fifty were recognized. In 1911 there were 271 and in 1921 there were 330. Dr. Kingsley Garbett in a personal communication informed me that in 1914 in the Darwin district out of twenty-one traditional Chiefs only six were recognized as such by the administration. As at 21 July 1965, there were 217 recognized Chiefs in all Southern Rhodesia: *S.R.L.A.D.*, Vol. 61, col. 1217.

[2] This had also occurred in earlier years ; e.g. in *Muwuungani* v. *Minister of Native Affairs* it was stated that in 1903 the Samriwo Chieftainship had been extended to cover two other ethnic groups.

[3] The Robinson Report, C.S.R. 22–1961, para. 183.

[4] *Zihumbga* v. *Harper, Robertson and Dodd*, NN.O Judgement GD/CIV/20/65 at p. 4.

[5] At p. 5 following *Muwuungani* v. *Minister of Native Affairs*, 1957 (2) S.A. 544 (F.C.).

[6] Ibid., at p. 7.

[7] Chapter 92, section 18. It is a criminal offence for a Chief to fail to carry out these duties: section 19.

[8] Section 17. This section provides the justification for the recent Government statement that: 'Guns are being made available to the Chiefs and Headmen. They have the power to arrest persons who try to undermine their authority': *S.R.L.A.D.*, Vol. 59, col. 1103, 4 December 1964.

[9] See African Councils *infra*, Chapter 5.

[10] e.g. they were used when the Land Husbandry Act was being implemented to assist in the allocation of farming and grazing rights. Chiefs had formerly enjoyed the sole responsibility for allocating land to applicants in tribal areas and the Ndebele Chiefs particularly resented their loss of control over tribal land: C.S.R. 22–1961, para. 198. The

for political purposes to bolster the Government claim to independence when they were brought by Government to a meeting of 196 Chiefs and 426 Headmen and invited to state their views on the question of independence for Southern Rhodesia.[1]

At present Chiefs are paid a small salary and much larger allowances, depending on whether they co-operate with Government and have a satisfactory personality.[2] These salaries and allowances were increased in 1961, and again increased in 1965.[3] Chiefs, Headmen, and Kraalheads can also be

Secretary of Internal Affairs has now prophesied that 'Chiefs and Headmen will have made available to them a much greater part to play in the control and allocation of tribal land': C.S.R. 27–1963, p. 7. A Tribal Land Authorities Bill 'formally recognizing and establishing the traditional tribal authorities as the land authorities in the tribal areas, with powers to control the allocation of land in their areas' has been delayed owing to difficulties arising out of the Constitution: C.S.R. 39–1965, pp. 9–10.

[1] The Secretary of Internal Affairs stated that 'The unanimous support for Government at this meeting will probably be a milestone in the history of this country': C.S.R. 39–1965, p. 4. The Government view is that, despite the absence of any institutionalized consultation with their people or any formal device parallel to 'the vote', the Chiefs do not express personal views, but only express views after consultation with their people. See *infra*, Chapter 7. Chiefs and their families are under constant police and military protection: *S.R.L.A.D.*, Vol. 159, col. 711, 29 October 1964, Minister of Internal Affairs. This unfortunately is necessary as Chief Charewa of Mtoko, a member of the Council of Chiefs, died when his house was set alight in October 1961, while a Headman was shot in 1964 and Chiefs are subject not only to political pressures but also to threats of physical violence.

[2] *S.R.L.A.D.*, Vol. 54, col. 185, 29 August 1962. The personal allowance depends on 'the personal attributes of the Chief concerned, his administrative ability, his co-operation with the administration, his tribal importance, leadership, control, and authority over his people'. Allowances until October 1964 ranged from nothing to £30 per month in the case of the administration's favourite Chief, and salaries from £8 to £20 per month: *S.R.L.A.D.*, Vol. 52, col. 135, 13 March 1963. Apparently there are statistically significant differences in the remuneration of Shona and Ndebele Chiefs. 42 per cent of Ndebele Chiefs get salaries of £20 per month or more as compared with 23 per cent of non-Ndebele Chiefs. 19 per cent of Ndebele Chiefs receive £20 per month or more in allowances as compared with 6 per cent of non-Ndebele Chiefs. Personal communication from Dr. Kingsley Garbett whose figures are based on 209 Chiefs for whom information was available in *S.R.L.A.D.*, Vol. 52. The salaries of Chiefs have since July 1965 been increased with retrospective effect from 1 October 1964 to £420 per annum for 188 Chiefs with followings of over 500. The remaining twenty-nine Chiefs with lesser followings receive £240 per annum. In addition fifty-four Chiefs each received a personal allowance ranging from £6 to £240 per annum. The Minister of Internal Affairs has refused to disclose the recipients of this patronage, declining on three occasions to answer parliamentary questions as to the names, tribal origins, sizes of followings, salaries, and allowances of all Southern Rhodesian Chiefs. In 1961 the Report of the Mangwende Reserve Commission stated that it 'failed to see how a modern Chief can possibly maintain his position on his officially recognized income alone'. Since then salaries and allowances of Chiefs have twice been increased. Even disregarding a Chief's income from his agricultural enterprise and a variety of traditional tributes, tokens, fees, and ritual payments received from his followers, Chiefs have an infinitely larger income than the average rural African. It has been estimated that the total income of the average sized family of seven living in a Reserve is £53 per annum derived from all sources, including their joint agricultural enterprise in the subsistence economy, wages, sales of beer, and income earned by migratory labour: R. W. M. Johnson, 'An Economic Survey of Chiweshe Reserve' (1964), *Rhodes-Livingstone Journal*, Vol. 36, p. 104.

[3] Report of the Secretary for Native Affairs and Chief Native Commissioner for the year

allocated larger farming areas and can be given the right to graze additional numbers of cattle in Tribal Trust areas, whereas this is not permitted to other Africans.[1] They also receive court hearing fees of 5s. per case in their tribal courts.

Government policy towards Southern Rhodesian Chiefs has not been consistent. Originally the policy was to replace the traditional system of rule by Chiefs with 'direct rule' of the central Government through Native Commissioners, leaving the Chiefs as minor administrative instruments of the central Government.[2] In fact the African people in rural areas were until the nineteen-thirties 'left alone' under the traditional system and their Chiefs subject to the supervision of Native Commissioners.[3] Indeed the number of recognized Chiefs even increased until 1951 when a reduction in their numbers was made.[4]

Later when Government policy began to encourage agricultural development in the African areas no definite policy of associating the Chiefs with this was adopted.[5] On the other hand Chiefs and Headmen were associated with Native Councils by the 1937 Native Councils Act,[6] and the 1937 Native Law and Courts Act gave statutory recognition to civil jurisdiction continuously exercised by Chiefs and Headmen from the time of the European occupation. Nonetheless such statutory recognition of the right of certain Chiefs and Headmen to hear civil cases did not in practice increase their powers.[7] In fact, although Government had by this time adopted the policy that the Chiefs' powers and status should be enhanced, little in the way of practical consequences ensued from this policy.

Even during the late nineteen-forties when Government was clear that it should 'increase by all possible means the prestige, status and powers of

1961, C.S.R. 28–1962, p. 17. See also the African Affairs (General) (Amendment) Regulations 1965 (No. 6), R.G.N. 479/65.

[1] African Land Husbandry Act, Chapter 103, Sections 38(1) and 15(1).

[2] Southern Rhodesian Chiefs were never used as instruments of 'indirect rule' as in other British African Territories.

[3] The interference related to maintenance of law and order, the prohibition of 'tribute labour . . . together with a few abhorrent customs': Howman, *African Local Government in British East and Central Africa*, University of Pretoria, 1963. Mimeographed. Part III, para. 156(a).

[4] According to Shona custom, if there were serious disputes as to the succession to a chieftainship, the rival groups might split and a new chieftainship might be established. In 1949 the Government proposed to abolish 142 chieftainships. 'Confidential Survey of Southern Rhodesian Native Policy 1950'. Unpublished, p. 31.

[5] For a summary of the changed attitude towards African development see Report of the Secretary for Native Affairs and Chief Native Commissioner for the year 1961. C.S.R. 28–1962, pp. 21–3.

[6] They had earlier been associated with Native Boards and from 1924 had held informal meetings with District Commissioners. See *infra*, Chapter 5.

[7] The Native Law and Courts Act gave Chiefs no power to enforce their judgement while the fact that cases 'on appeal' from Chiefs' courts were re-trials, the Chiefs' decisions being disregarded, tended to derogate from their status. See *infra*, Chapter 3.

Chiefs'[1] little had been done to implement this other than the abolition of certain minor chieftainships in 1951 and the introduction of 'a £1 10s. per mensem' personal allowances for Chiefs. In fact one of the consequences of the 1951 Land Husbandry Act was the diminution of Chiefs' powers since the allocations of farming and grazing rights were made by assessment committees and not by the Chiefs who by customary law allocated all land to their people, in some cases directly or through their subordinates.

However, from the late nineteen-fifties the Government policy of 'building up' the Chiefs began to be implemented in legislation. In 1959 the Native Affairs Act and in 1960 the Law and Order (Maintenance) Act gave the Chiefs special protection against being brought into disrepute or contempt, and penalized remarks that were likely to impair their authority. Thereafter Chiefs were appointed to influential positions. Thus, Chief Simon Sigola was nominated by the Southern Rhodesian Government to be a member of the Monckton Commission. Subsequently Chief Kaisa Ndiweni was sent as a Southern Rhodesian delegate for the Chiefs to the Federal Review Conference in 1960 and to the Southern Rhodesian Constitutional Conference held early in 1961. Since 1961, with the creation of the Council of Chiefs and the formalization of Provincial Assemblies of Chiefs, Chiefs have obtained even higher status and are consulted by Government on legislative measures affecting the African people.[2] Further increases in power in the tribal areas and in the law-making process have recently been promised the Chiefs.[3]

The additional powers and responsibilities, which have been 'grafted' by legislation onto the indigenous tribal system,[4] have however resulted in a situation which occasions conflict between those responsibilities and those inherent in their traditional position.[5] Their position is most aptly described in the Report of the Mangwende Reserve Commission of Enquiry:

> It is the Chiefs' unenviable lot to be both the bottom of the European upper half of the pyramid [of Southern Rhodesian administration], and the top of the lower

[1] Confidential Survey, op. cit., p. 29.

[2] See C.S.R. 16–1964, p. 5, C.S.R. 27–1963, p. 7, C.S.R. 28–1962, p. 17. For the Whitehead Government's policy of building up the Chiefs to offset African nationalist leaders, see Alport, op. cit., pp. 53–4.

[3] Speech by the Minister of Internal Affairs on 26 October at the Chiefs' 'indaba': *Rhodesia Herald*, 27 October 1964. See also the Report of the Secretary for Internal Affairs and Chief Native Commissioner for the year 1962, C.S.R. 27–1963, p. 7. The Government have undertaken not to make any changes in the Constitution until 'after consultation with the Chiefs as the leaders of the people': *S.R.L.A.D.*, Vol. 59, col. 1103, 4 December 1964. The same statement confirms that 'after independence, the Government would like to see Chiefs represented in Parliament so that they can reflect the views of the ordinary people and so assist in the making of laws'.

[4] *The Domboshawa 'Indaba'*, Government Printer, Salisbury, 1965, p. 42, §25.

[5] *The Domboshawa 'Indaba': The Views of Some Sociologists and Anthropologists in Rhodesia.* Salisbury, 1 February 1965. Mimeographed.

part of the structure. This dual position is fraught with difficulties because it involves a reconciliation between two inherently conflicting roles (and loyalties): that of faithful servant of an essentially foreign and superimposed Administration, and that of head and representative of an autonomous African tribal community whose support is equally vital to him. When the aims of the Administration and of the tribal community coincide, reconciliation is no problem; but when these aims diverge (as they often do) the Chief is in the unhappy position of seeking to satisfy one master without incurring the displeasure of the other.[1]

The Chiefs are assisted by Headmen responsible for different wards (dunhu) of the chieftainship. Headmen are appointed by the Secretary for Internal Affairs, normally acting on chiefly advice. However, according to customary law Headmen would more correctly have been described as subchiefs and their offices would have been hereditary. This position has been partially abandoned.[2] Headmen are also charged with the good conduct of Africans under their care and with the notification of all crimes in their area to the Chief and District Commissioner.[3] They are also to act as constables.

Under the Headmen are heads of kraals,[4] charged with the duty of reporting crime, the arrival of newcomers in their area and any unauthorized building or tilling of land.[5] It is again a criminal offence for a head of kraal to fail to notify such occurrences or the sojourn at his kraal for seven days or more of any African.[6]

Provision is also made for African messengers with the powers and duties of constables who are attached to the office of District Commissioners. Messengers are non-traditional officials and are charged with conveying messages

---

[1] Report of the Mangwende Reserve Commission of Enquiry 1961, para. 166. The Chief whose activities occasioned this Enquiry was in fact deposed by the Government.

[2] Personal communication from Dr. Kingsley Garbett.

[3] Chapter 92, Section 26. Headmen receive a small subsidy. As at 28 July 1965, 359 persons held the office of Headman: S.R.L.A.D., Vol. 61, col. 1501.

[4] Kraals are collections of huts and residences of Africans and the Kraalhead is the African who according to African customary law is the senior member or is recognized as such by the other members of the kraal: Chapter 92, Section 2, definitions. For an outline of Mashona political and social structure see the Mangwende Report, paras. 26–62; *The Dombashawa 'Indaba'*, Annexure A; and *The Dombashawa Indaba: The Views of Some Sociologists and Anthropologists in Rhodesia*, op. cit., p. 2.

[5] No African may move from one district to another or erect new huts or cultivate new ground without the permission of the District Commissioner. Breach of this provision is a criminal offence: Chapter 92, Section 37. 178 Africans were charged with this offence between 1958 and 1963: S.R.L.A.D., Vol. 53, col. 312.

[6] Section 28. Section 41 imposes a duty of reporting on crimes on all Africans. There is no such offence as misprision under the Roman–Dutch common law except in respect of high treason, in which case a person who fails to report that high treason is being or is about to be committed is himself guilty of treason: Gardiner and Lansdown, *South African Criminal Law and Procedure*, Juta, 6th ed., p. 993. These statutory duties of notification resting only on Africans have been found to be discriminatory by the Constitutional Council: see Report No. 28 of 14 August 1963, pp. 3–6. From 1958 to July 1963 four such charges have been brought against Chiefs and seven against Headmen: S.R.L.A.D., Vol. 53, cols. 310–11, 17 July 1963.

to Chiefs and Headmen from District Commissioners, summoning parties to civil cases and reporting on crimes to the District Commissioner, who is a member (in practice a European) of the Public Service.[1]

It will be apparent from the aforegoing that except for changes in terminology from 'Native' to 'District' Commissioner and from 'Native' to 'African', the African Affairs Act maintains almost the identical administrative structure for African rural areas that was set up by the Southern Rhodesian Native Regulations in 1898. The only practical administrative difference is that in 1964 approximately eighteen per cent of Africans were resident in the urban areas of Southern Rhodesia and were therefore not subject to this system of control.[2]

All officials of the Southern Rhodesian Government are protected against criticism by Section 41 of the Law and Order (Maintenance) Act, which provides that

any person who, without lawful excuse, the proof whereof lies on him, utters any words or does any act or thing whatever which is likely to undermine or impair the authority of any public officer or class of public officer (which for this purpose includes a Chief, Headman or Kraalhead); to engender feelings of hostility towards any public officer or class of public officer; or to expose any public officer or class of public officer to contempt, ridicule or disesteem shall be guilty of an offence and liable to a fine not exceeding £100 or to imprisonment for a period not exceeding one year.

A similar Section 44 in the African Affairs Act makes it an offence for an African to bring any officer of the Southern Rhodesian Government or a Chief, Headman, or Kraalhead 'into disrepute or contempt' or to do any act which is likely to undermine his authority.[3] However, in respect of the African Affairs Act, no provision is made for 'lawful excuse'.

The forces

Neither the Police Force nor the Army form part of the Public Service, the Army being governed by the Federal Defence Act 1955 which is

[1] Sections 30 and 31. The Government has recently stated that Chiefs 'have been provided with specially-trained messengers who know how to deal with trouble makers': *S.R.L.A.D.*, Vol. 59, col. 1103, 4 December 1964. It does not seem as if this reference is to the messengers in terms of the Act, as the Minister of Internal Affairs acknowledged that the latter had been replaced by these new messengers: *S.R.L.A.D.*, Vol. 60, col. 380, 5 March 1965. It has been suggested that they would act as bodyguards to Chiefs: ibid., col. 354.

[2] Report of the Secretary for Internal Affairs 1963, C.S.R. 16–1964, p. 4, discloses that of the total African population of 3,830,000 as at 31 December 1963, 2,100,000 were in tribal areas, 110,000 in Purchase areas, 890,000 in European farming areas (where there would still be Kraalheads), and 690,000 in urban areas. Approximately 430,000 are non-indigenous Africans and these would be almost entirely in the towns and in the European farming area.

[3] From 1959 when this Section came into force, to mid-1963, there were 174 prosecutions

still in force in Southern Rhodesia, and the Police by the Police Act 1964.[1]

The Southern Rhodesian Army is composed of regulars,[2] territorials and cadet forces. There is also provision for the compulsory call-up of the non-African adult male population up to the age of 50,[3] and for compulsory military training ('peace training') of non-Africans for a maximum period of four years between the ages of 18 and 30.[4] The potential of the Southern Rhodesian armed forces is larger than appears from the number of regular soldiers (3,405) as there are a further 3,405 territorials and cadets and there is a large potential reserve to be called upon in times of emergency as a result of the provisions for compulsory call-up. There are a further 941 regulars, cadets, territorials, and other staff in the Royal Rhodesian Air Force.[5]

No constitutional problems have occurred in respect of annual Army Acts, as there is no question of annual re-enactment of the Defence Act. Appropriations for defence purposes merely form part of the general estimates of expenditure being provided for in the annual Appropriation Act and in any supplementary estimates.

Difficulties may however arise as to the legal position of the Army when called in aid of the civil power as this not infrequently occurs in Southern Rhodesia. The position has to some extent been covered by the Law and Order (Maintenance) Act which deals with the dispersal of public assemblies and protects any person who aids a police officer in dispersing a gathering.[6] If such person uses 'all such force as is reasonably necessary for overcoming . . . resistance (he) shall not be liable in any criminal or civil proceedings for having by the use of such force caused death or harm to any person'. However, the dilemma of whether to obey superior orders and whether these will in any given circumstances be a defence still remains, as there has been no statutory interference with the common law on this point.[7] However, members of the

and 148 convictions under this section, which was still used even after the implementation of the Law and Order (Maintenance) Act, 115 prosecutions and ninety-five convictions occurring since 1961: *S.R.L.A.D.*, Vol. 53, col. 311, 17 July 1963.

[1] The Public Services Act, Chapter 90, Section 18(5)(g), expressly excludes the Police Force. Their position is dealt with *infra*, in Chapter 3.

[2] Regulars may be African or European but receive different pay and allowances and are governed by different regulations according to their race. See *infra*, Chapter 4.

[3] Defence Act No. 23 of 1955, Section 27A as amended by Section 2 of Act 2 of 1961 read with the definition of 'resident' in Section 2.

[4] In practice only those of up to twenty-four years of age are required to undergo such training which involves three-and-half months' full-time training and part-time service for the next three years.

[5] Establishments are those shown in the Estimates for the year ending 30 June 1965. C.S.R. 17–1964.

[6] Chapter 39, Section 15(5). An objective test is adopted.

[7] See *R. v. Smith* (1900), 17 S.C. 561. Cp. *R. v. van Vuuren*, 1944 O.P.D. 35, where an entirely objective test of legality is adopted.

forces can expect that an Indemnity Act will be passed to safeguard them, as occurred in 1959.[1]

Provision is made in the Defence Act for the establishment of courts martial while the appellate division of the High Court is to be constituted by the Chief Justice as a Courts Martial Appeal Court.

Statutory bodies

There is a great deal of State participation in various sections of the economy, particularly in respect of the marketing of agricultural products. Indeed at one time the State participated actively in statutory industrial corporations, particularly during the war years and immediately thereafter. However, the governing party changed its policy and became 'firmly committed to a policy of endeavouring to get across to private enterprise as many of the statutory undertakings as we possibly can'.[2] As a result, although the Government still controls a number of important public utilities through statutory boards, it has for the most part disposed of public corporations which operated major industries.[3]

In the public utilities field the Government still participates through statutory corporations, most of which were formerly administered by the Federal Government. On Federal dissolution, Federal statutory corporations were wound up but agreements were entered into for the transfer of their property rights and liabilities to new Territorial corporations established by means of regulations modifying and adapting Federal laws and applying them to the Territories.[4] Other corporations were dissolved, re-established and charged with the provision of common services shared in by Southern Rhodesia by the Dissolution Order in Council.[5] These for the most part related to transport and power.[6] Broadcasting is no longer a common service and is entirely under Southern Rhodesian control.[7]

---

[1] Public Order (Amendment) Act No. 41 of 1959, Sections 4(1)(f) and (2), where an indemnity was conferred in respect of 'any act or thing whatsoever in good faith advised, commanded, ordered, directed or done' in connection with the state of emergency in Southern Rhodesia in early 1959.

[2] *S.R.L.A.D.*, Vol. 37, col. 1021, 21 July 1954, Minister of the Treasury. See also Leys, op. cit., pp. 66 et seq. and 251-4.

[3] It still maintains certain services to industry, e.g. the gold roasting plant at Que Que and the Cotton Industries Research Board.

[4] S.I. 1963, No. 2085, Section 17.

[5] See *infra*, Chapter 6.

[6] viz. the Central African Power Corporation, Central African Airways, and the Rhodesian Railways. The Agricultural Research Council of Central Africa was also maintained.

[7] The degree of governmental control exercised over the Board of the Southern Rhodesia Broadcasting Corporation has in fact become a political issue there being many allegations, repudiated by Government, that the R.B.C. has become a propaganda service of Government: see *S.R.L.A.D.*, Vol. 58, col. 989, 29 September 1964. Somewhat earlier, the Parlia-

Apart from these bodies there are a large number of statutory corporations concerned with the agricultural sphere, viz. the Land and Agricultural Bank, the Cold Storage Commission, the Pig Industry Board, the Dairy Marketing Board, the Grain Marketing Board, the Tobacco Export Promotion Council of Rhodesia, the Rhodesia Tobacco Marketing Board, the Tobacco Research Board, the African Labour Supply Commission and the Forestry Commission.

The remarkable feature of Southern Rhodesian agricultural statutory commissions is the degree to which participation by the agricultural industry has been permitted in the various boards. Not only are associations of the industry recognized by the Government, and given an assured income by legislation imposing levies on produce or imposing licence fees which are to be paid to their managing bodies[1] but the composition of the statutory commissions is made up of representatives of the industries involved chosen by the responsible Minister from a panel of names submitted by the industries in question. In most cases the chairman is a senior civil servant, often chosen after consultation with the relevant industrial association.[2]

The other public corporations are either local government bodies[3] or public boards or commissions for regulating national cultural assets[4] and in other cases sports.[5]

The degree of governmental control over statutory corporations and their

mentary Secretary for Information 'advised' the Chairman of the Board that it would in Government's view be undesirable if certain statements explaining a visit to England to put views about Southern Rhodesia to the United Kingdom Government and leading politicians and industrialists by an ex-Member of Parliament opposed to Government were reported. The Corporation then refused to broadcast the ex-Member's statement: *Rhodesia Herald*, 1 May 1964. Further controversy resulted from Government statements that it intended to acquire control of Rhodesia Television Limited, a public company which by contract with the R.B.C. provides television services. The contract and the Broadcasting Act provide for interference by the R.B.C. and by the Government. The Government was nonetheless dissatisfied and insisted on obtaining 51 per cent of the shares in the Television Company. See *S.R.L.A.D.*, Vol. 59, cols. 797–858, 2 December 1964. At the end of 1964 control was acquired by the R.B.C. through a purchase of the totality of founders', i.e. voting shares of the television company. This purchase was made largely from Lord Thompson and was partly financed by a Government loan: Rhodesia Information Service Press Statement 219/65/BB.

[1] e.g. the Cotton Levy Act, Chapter 182, Section 6, provides for finance for the Rhodesia Cotton Growers Association, the African Farmers Licensing Act, Chapter 98, Section 5, provides that the African Farmers Union shall be paid licence fees, the Rhodesia National Farmers Union receives a levy under the Federal Agricultural Products Levy Act 1957 and the Rhodesia Tobacco Association a similar levy on the sale of flue and fire cured tobacco under the Federal Tobacco Levy Act 1960. See Leys, op. cit., pp. 99 et seq.

[2] See Leys, op. cit., pp. 62 et seq.

[3] See *infra*, Chapter 5.

[4] The Commission for the Preservation of National Historical Monuments and Relics, the National Art Gallery, the Board of Trustees of National Museums and the National Trust.

[5] The Boxing and the Wrestling Control Boards.

activities has not recently been a political issue in Southern Rhodesia.[1] Ministers have always been prepared to accept responsibility for the acts of corporations, as they have been able to exercise influence through their civil servants nominated to such boards. There is also a certain amount of control by virtue of provision in the Audit and Exchequer Act which permits the Legislative Assembly by resolution to direct the Auditor General to audit the accounts of any statutory body established by Act of the Legislature,[2] in which event full power to examine all books, accounts and vouchers of a statutory corporation may be exercised.

There are also statutory provisions governing private corporations.[3]

In addition the Royal prerogative of chartering corporations that may operate in Southern Rhodesia still remains. This has not been delegated to the Governor. However, the only such chartered corporations at present operating in Southern Rhodesia are the British South Africa Company, which is now entirely financial and commercial,[4] and the University College of Rhodesia and Nyasaland, which is a multi-racial university college offering courses which lead to degrees of the University of London.[5]

Litigation against the Crown

Although the Roman–Dutch Law permitted litigation against both sovereign and state subject to certain limitations[6] the Cape Supreme Court held in 1887 that the Crown was not liable for wrongful acts of its servants since English Law governed Crown liability.[7] Consequently the Cape

---

[1] This may change in view of the creation of a Sabi-Limpopo Authority created by the Sabi-Limpopo Authority Act 1964. The Authority has been given full powers to construct dams, bridges, roads, buy lands, develop townships and oversee the economic development generally of nearly one-quarter of the area of Southern Rhodesia. It is governed by a Board of Directors nominated by the Governor. These directors are large property owners, industrialists and farmers in the area. They are empowered to override the views of local authorities and are placed in control of large sums voted by Parliament or borrowed by the authority. No mechanisms of control are written into the Act. Amendments seeking to exclude persons with pecuniary interests in that area from directorships were rejected by the Government: *S.R.L.A.D.*, Vol. 59, col. 1152, 4 December 1964.

[2] Audit and Exchequer Act (Chapter 144), Section 10. In the mid-1940s considerable debate occurred in Parliament as the result of a demand by the Auditor-General who was supported by the Public Accounts Committee, to audit the accounts of certain statutory commissions. At that time the Act did not specify that a parliamentary resolution was necessary.

[3] The Companies Act (Chapter 223) and the Co-operative Companies Act (Chapter 181).

[4] Early in 1965 the B.S.A. Company became a subsidiary of Charter Consolidated Ltd.

[5] For the University College Charter see F.G.N. 103/55.

[6] See C. P. Joubert in (1952) 15 T.H.R.-H.R. 7 and E. Kahn in *Annual Survey of South African Law*, Juta 1957, pp. 10–11.

[7] *Binda* v. *Colonial Government* (1887), S.C. 284. de Villiers C.J. suggested that this rule could also preclude contractual actions against the Crown. The case has since been criticized as not being in accordance with the Cape Articles of Capitulation 1806 which pro-

Colony passed the Crown Liabilities Act No. 37 of 1888. Subsequently the Southern Rhodesian Legislature passed its own Crown Liabilities Act No. 7 of 1932 which is modelled on the Union Crown Liabilities Act No. 1 of 1910. Section 2 of the Southern Rhodesian Act provides that:

Any claim against Her Majesty in her Government of Southern Rhodesia which would, if that claim had arisen against a subject, be the ground of any action in any competent court, shall be cognizable by any such court, whether the claim arises or has arisen out of any contract lawfully entered into on behalf of the Crown or out of any wrong committed by any servant of the Crown acting in his capacity and within the scope of his authority as such servant.

Although the Act makes claims against the Crown 'cognizable' and does not expressly impose liability on the Crown, in practice liability has been imposed. However, there are *dicta* that the Act did not confer 'any substantive right of holding the Crown to any contract'.[1] Jurisdiction has been exercised in respect of all civil claims against the Crown since the Act relates to 'any claim' against Her Majesty, which would have, 'if that claim had arisen against a subject, been the ground of an action'. Thus the Courts have entertained claims both contractual and quasi-contractual, delictual and quasi-delictual.[2] But although 'the Act gives a right of action against the Crown and to that extent the prerogatives of the Crown must be taken to have been abrogated ... all other prerogatives and rights of the Crown remain'.[3]

A marked difference between English Law and the consequences of the Act as interpreted by the Courts is that the Courts have considered that they are not confined to giving judgements sounding in money. Innes J.A. analysing the South African Crown Liabilities Act said that the Courts had been given statutory jurisdiction to issue a mandamus and that such jurisdiction 'may be exercised not only in respect of claims for damages, but also in cases where relief is sought by way of declaratory or mandatory order'. However, 'no decree granted, whether sounding in money or not, can be enforced against the Crown. The Legislature has been content to rely upon the moral obliga-

---

vided that 'the burghers and inhabitants shall preserve all their rights and privileges which they have enjoyed hitherto'. See J. P. Verloren van Themaat, *Straatsreg.* Butterworth's, 1956, pp. 57 et seq.

[1] *Waterfalls T.M.B.* v. *Minister of Housing*, 1957 (1) S.A. 336 (S.R.) at 341 per Murray C.J. *Contra* Watermeyer C.J. in *Sachs* v. *Donges*, 1950 (2) S.A. 265 (A.D.) at 279 that the Act 'in effect, imposes liability on the Crown in respect of contracts lawfully made on its behalf by its authorized servants and in respect of torts committed by its authorized servants'.

[2] For a summary of the cases see L. A. Rose Innes, *Judicial Review of Administrative Tribunals in South Africa*, Juta, 1963, p. 230. K. Neethling in 'The Legal Position of the State in Relation to Payment of Interest A Temporae Morae', (1956) 73 *S.A.L.J.* at 409 argues that this does include liability for *mora* interest as it is a principle of Roman–Dutch Law that the Crown should not be so liable.

[3] *S.A.R. & H.* v. *Smith's Coasters (Prop.) Ltd.*, 1931 A.D. 113 per de Villiers C.J. at 124.

tion which such decrees are bound to exercise upon all concerned.'[1] None-theless it was subsequently held that not only interdicts but orders of specific performance can be granted against the Crown.[2]

The Courts have also granted declaratory orders and permitted review pro-ceedings on motions against the Crown. Conversely the Crown may institute proceedings in the same fashion as a natural person, although it has been held that the state may not sue for defamation.[3]

Crown liability for the wrongful acts of its servants

The Crown, just like any other master, is held vicariously responsible for the wrongful acts of its servants committed in the course of their employ-ment.[4] In practice this liability may be more extensive than in England because in Southern Rhodesia the police are Crown servants and thus Southern Rhodesian Law allows an action against the Crown for wrongful acts com-mitted in the course of their duty by members of the police force. However, anomalies and fine distinctions in applying the principles of vicarious responsibility have arisen relative to police conduct. In *B.S.A. Co.* v. *Crick-more*[5] a police constable in the Company's employ had wrongfully arrested the plaintiff, but the Company was held not liable since the constable in effecting the arrest was not under the control of the Company, but was carry-ing out a duty entrusted to him by the Legislature and could not be regarded *pro hac vice* as the Company's servant. The scope of this decision was sub-sequently restricted by later decisions that the Crown escapes liability only if the duty the policeman is engaged upon 'is such that it takes him out of the category of servants for the time being'.[6] The mere fact that the duty is a statutory duty is not enough. To take the case out of the Act there must be a lack of one or more of the essentials of the law relating to a master and a servant, such as that the police officer was performing a personal duty of a personal nature (whether ministerial or discretionary) which made him independent of the control of the Crown *pro hac vice*. However, difficulties have persisted and in *David* v. *Minister of Justice and Others*, it was held that a policeman who commits an unlawful assault in the course of arresting an

---

[1] *Minister of Finance* v. *Barberton Municipal Council*, 1914 A.D. 335 at 355. In this case the mandatory interdict was granted against the Minister in his personal capacity. In *Schierhout* v. *Union Government*, 1926 A.D. 99 it was accepted that such an order may be made against the Crown itself.

[2] *Codron* v. *Macintyre and Shaw NN.O.*, 1960 (3) S.A. 419 (F.C.) at 427.

[3] *The Spoorbond* v. *South African Railways*, 1946 A.D. 999. This decision was reached on grounds of public policy.

[4] See Rose Innes, op. cit., pp. 231–6 for a discussion of all the South African cases.

[5] 1921 A.D. 107.

[6] *Union Government* v. *Thorne*, 1930 A.D. 47 at 51. See also *Swarts* v. *Minister of Justice*, 1941 A.D. 181 and *Sibiya* v. *Swart N.O.*, 1950 (4) S.A. 515 (A.D.) at 520.

accused whom he has a personal discretion to arrest or not, does not render the Crown liable.[1] On the other hand it seems that if the policeman is acting under superior orders the state is then liable,[2] as it clearly is if after an arrest has been made an assault then occurs.[3]

Contractual liability of the Administration

Although the Crown may enter into binding contracts, there is doubt whether it may contract in such a fashion as to fetter its future executive action. In *Waterfalls T.M.B.* v. *Minister of Housing*, Murray C.J. held that as the Crown prerogative was no more restricted in the Colony than it was in the United Kingdom the Court should follow the decision in *Rederaktiebolaget Amphitrite* v. *The King*.[4] But the Court did not determine the *ratio decidendi* of that case or examine it critically, despite differing interpretations of the principle involved by writers on constitutional law.[5] Subsequent remarks by the learned judge however indicated that his judgement was based on the principle that an authority to whom 'discretionary administrative powers' are entrusted cannot 'fetter his right, if circumstances connected with his administration require it, to exercise his discretion in some other way'.[6]

'The Amphitrite' has also been accepted without criticism in various *dicta* by van den Heever J.A.[7] There is no doubt that the principle that the Crown cannot fetter its future executive action has been adopted in Roman–Dutch Law.[8] However there are *dicta* that even if the Crown is 'compelled by state

---

[1] 1961 (2) S.A. 626. For a prediction that this would occur and criticism of the position see E. Kahn (1951) 68 S.A.L.J. 6 at 7. It may be that a different approach might be adopted in Southern Rhodesia in view of Section 3(2) of the Law and Order (Maintenance) Act which imposes a duty on every police officer as such to apprehend offenders. When a policeman exercised his discretion to arrest as a peace officer he would therefore be acting also as a police officer. See Section 9(1) of the Police Act 1964 which imposes on police the duty of exercising such powers and performing such duties as are by law conferred or imposed on a member.

[2] *Ingram* v. *Minister of Justice*, 1962 (3) S.A. 225 where the accused as a member of a police force had been ordered to make an arrest in the course of his duty.

[3] *Sibiya* v. *Swart N.O.*, *supra*.

[4] [1921] 3 K.B. 500.

[5] 1957 (1) S.A. 336 (S.R.) at 341. The remarks of the learned judge were *obiter* as he had already reached a decision on the ground that the alleged undertaking on which the plaintiffs relied was *ultra vires* of the Minister. For criticism of his judgement see E. Kahn in *Annual Survey of South African Law*, Juta, 1957, pp. 6–11.

[6] *Supra* at p. 342. The test proposed by Murray C.J. as to when an administrative discretion cannot be fettered was very favourable to the Minister viz. if this is required by circumstances connected with his administration. Cp. J. D. B. Mitchell, *The Contracts of Public Authorities*, George Bell, 1954, p. 60.

[7] *Sachs* v. *Dönges*, 1950 (2) S.A. 265 (A.D.) at 309–11 while Centlivres C.J. at 296 considered the rule in 'the Amphitrite' to be a part of the wider principle that the Crown cannot fetter its future executive action.

[8] *Fellner* v. *Minister of the Interior*, *supra* at 536 per Centlivres C.J. See also van den Heever J.A. in *Sachs* v. *Dönges*, *supra* at 315 et seq.

necessity to breach contracts or commit torts, ... if it does so it is not acting lawfully and must suffer the legal consequences, unless it is indemnified by Parliament'.[1] A further ruling which in effect supports the rule that an administrative discretion cannot be fettered has been given in Southern Rhodesia. In *Salisbury City Council* v. *Donner*, Murray C.J. ruled that 'estoppel cannot be raised in matters concerned with the exercise of a statutory public duty'.[2]

Statutory limitations of Crown liability and that of its servants

The Crown is exempted from liability for its acts by certain legislation. Thus the Federal Posts and Telegraphs Act No. 20 of 1954, still in force in Southern Rhodesia, exempts the Crown and its officers for defaults or negligence in respect of any postal article or telegram.[3] Other Acts give indemnities to Crown servants.[4] It is also stipulated in the Crown Liability Act that special periods of limitation of action and pre-conditions for the institution of action against the Crown for liability occasioned by the acts of its servants are to be unaffected.[5]

The Crown may bind itself by statute, but when this is done it must be either by express words or by necessary intendment.[6]

Rights of action against Crown servants may also be limited by reference to conditions as to notice or as to the institution of action within a limited

---

[1] Watermeyer C.J. in *Sachs* v. *Dönges N.O.* at 276. See also authorities cited in Hahlo and Kahn, op. cit., p. 198 with reference to accrued rights.

[2] 1958 (2) S.A. 368 (S.R.) at 372.

[3] Again Section 80 of the African Land Husbandry Act (Chapter 103) indemnifies the Government, Ministers and officers for anything in good faith done under the terms of this Act.

[4] e.g. Section 54 of the Police Act 1964, exempts members of the force from liability, other than in legal proceedings for unlawful arrest or detention, for acts done in obedience to an irregular warrant. Section 48 of the Criminal Procedure and Evidence Act (Chapter 31) provides that when a peace officer or private person in arresting any person who is on reasonable grounds suspected of having committed any offence mentioned in the First Schedule to that Act kills that person, such person being unable to be apprehended or prevented from escaping by other means, such killing shall be deemed in law justifiable homicide. See *R.* v. *MacDonald*, 1963 (1) S.A. 851 (S.R.). In this case an African was shot by a European Police reservist who suspected that the African was obstructing the police in the execution of their duty. Despite what amounted to a very strong direction to convict the accused a Special Jury (*infra*, Chapter 3) returned an acquittal.

[5] Section 2 proviso.

[6] *Attorney-General* v. *Jones*, 1962 R. & N. 187 (F.C.), per Clayden F.C.J. at 189. According to *Evans* v. *Schoeman N.O.*, 1949 (1) S.A. 751 (A.D.), such an implication will only be drawn, in the absence of express wording, where the 'beneficent purpose must be wholly frustrated unless the Crown were bound'. See Kahn's caustic comment in Hahlo and Kahn, op. cit., p. 199. See L. C. Steyn in *Die Uitleg van Wette*, Juta, 1952, 2nd ed., pp. 68–69.

period.[1] Since such limitations must be strictly construed[2] the provisions do not affect the state and where specific limitations are imposed by statute the state remains liable subject to the common law rules of prescription.[3]

Execution may not be levied against the Crown nor may Crown property be attached as the Crown Liabilities Act prohibits such proceedings.[4]

Procedure in litigation against the Crown

The Crown Liabilities Act in Section 3 provides that in proceedings against the Crown the applicant may make the Minister who is the head of the Department concerned nominal defendant or respondent. Thus Ministers are cited by their names with the addition of the words *nomine officio*, e.g. *Stumbles N.O.* v. *New Zealand Insurance Co. Ltd.*[5]

The decision in *Duncan* v. *Cammell Laird & Co. Ltd.*[6] has been adopted.[7] This was inevitable in view of Section 33 of the Civil Evidence Act, Chapter 18 of which provided for questions of privilege on grounds of public policy to be decided as if the matter were depending in the Supreme Court of Judicature in England. However *dicta* by Maisels J. in *Faber* v. *Barrow* indicate that the Court can investigate the *bona fides* of a Minister in giving a certificate that he objects to producing an official document on grounds of public policy.[8] Presumably when further litigation involving state privilege arises the courts will follow *In re Grosvenor Hotel, London (No. 2)*.[9]

There appears to have been an extension of this principle in *Taylor* v. *The Prime Minister and Minister of Internal Affairs*.[10] The Court cited the Cammell Laird decision and then accepted that where the Minister had stated

---

[1] e.g. the Federal Customs Act No. 16 of 1955 (still in force in Southern Rhodesia) in Section 179, provides that actions against Customs officers must be commenced within three months of the cause of action, while no such action can be commenced until one month after written notice of intention to commence action has been given to the officer concerned. Similar provision, except that the period for institution of action is six months, appears in Section 57 of the Police Act 1964.

[2] *Benning* v. *Union Government*, 1914 A.D. 180.

[3] In *Pycroft* v. *Field N.O.* (an unreported decision of the Southern Rhodesia High Court in 1963), action was brought for an assault committed in 1940, the Common Law rule being that the period of prescription is thirty years.

[4] Crown Liabilities Act, Section 4.

[5] During the existence of Federation certain Departments were transferred to the Federal Government and there was no Southern Rhodesian Minister responsible for such a Department which had, when under the Southern Rhodesian Government, incurred liability. In such cases action was brought against the Southern Rhodesian Prime Minister e.g. *Pycroft* v. *Field N.O.*, there then being no Minister of Health or of Defence.

[6] [1942] A.C. 624.

[7] *Ex parte Zelter*, 1951 (2) S.A. 54 (S.R.) and *Faber* v. *Barrow* (1), 1963 (1) S.A. 422 (S.R).

[8] *Supra* at 429. Maisels J. stated that in such a case the Minister would have an opportunity of filing a further affidavit but concluded that in the case before the Court there were 'no grounds for not regarding the Minister's affidavit as conclusive'.

[9] [1964] 3 W.L.R. 992.

[10] 1954 (3) S.A. 956 (S.R.).

that it was essential in the interests of security on confidential information available to him that the applicant should forthwith be removed from the Colony, such a statement must also be accepted by the court in deciding whether to grant a stay of deportation pending an appeal.

Costs are awarded in favour of the Crown or against it on the same principles that apply to an ordinary litigant. This also includes the rule whereby in special circumstances a successful party may be deprived of his costs.[1]

[1] *Palley* v. *Knight N.O.*, 1961 (4) S.A. 633. In this case the Minister of Justice exercised power to ban meetings and announced reasons for his action which would have rendered it *ultra vires*. After proceedings had been commenced to set aside the ban he then announced his real reasons in a replying affidavit. These brought his action within the terms of the section authorizing such conduct and the proceedings were then withdrawn. The Minister was deprived of his costs.

3

THE SOUTHERN RHODESIAN LEGAL SYSTEM

The law of Southern Rhodesia

THE law to be applied in Southern Rhodesia has depended on a series of provisions going back to the establishment of the British South Africa Company. Although the Charter imposed on the Company the duty of appointing such judicial officers and establishing such courts as were from time to time necessary for the administration of justice,[1] it did not prescribe what general law the Company was to administer. Nonetheless the Company was enjoined that in administering justice to the inhabitants of its territories

careful regard shall always be had to the customs and laws of the class or tribe or nation to which the parties respectively belong, especially with respect to the holding, possession, transfer, and disposition of lands and goods and testate or intestate succession thereto, and marriage, divorce and legitimacy and other rights of property and personal rights, but subject to any British laws which may be in force in any of the territories aforesaid, and applicable to the peoples or inhabitants thereof.[2]

As soon, however, as the Company established the rudiments of an administration in Mashonaland, the Company's Administrator, A. R. Colquhoun, declared that the laws of the Cape Colony were to be applicable in the Company's territory.[3] But it was only in June 1891 that proper provision for the establishment of a legal system was made. In May of that year the South Africa Order in Council 1891 had authorized the High Commissioner for South Africa to provide by proclamation for the administration of justice, although in so doing he was enjoined to

respect any native laws or customs by which the civil relations of any native chiefs, tribes, or populations under Her Majesty's protection are now regulated, except so far as the same may be incompatible with the full exercise of Her Majesty's power and jurisdiction.[4]

Acting in terms of this power, the High Commissioner then established a system of magistrates' courts in Mashonaland, exercising civil and criminal

---

[1] Article 22.
[2] Article 14.
[3] Administrator's Proclamation No. 1, 28 September 1890. See *supra*, Part I, Chapter 3.
[4] Order in Council of 9 May 1891, Section 4.

jurisdiction except in matters in which natives only were concerned.[1] It was provided that in any proceedings in such courts

the law to be administered shall as nearly as the circumstances of the country will permit, be the same as the law for the time being in force in the Colony of the Cape of Good Hope: provided no Act passed after this time by the Colony of the Cape of Good Hope shall be deemed to apply to the said territory.[2]

Subsequently, when Company jurisdiction was extended to Matabeleland, fuller provision was made for the application of the law of the Cape Colony, as at the commencement of the Order, in the High Court of Matabeleland and all magistrates' courts throughout the whole of the future Southern Rhodesia.[3] However, customary law was specifically preserved in civil cases between natives.[4] Some flexibility was afforded by the insertion of the phrase 'as nearly as the circumstances of the country permit', so that it was subsequently held that neither Cape revenue laws nor jury trial in civil cases were introduced.[5]

When the judicial system was placed on a sound basis in 1898 the original time of application of Cape Colonial law—10 June 1891—was reinstated, and 'so far as not inapplicable' such law was to be applied by all courts.[6] Later this provision was re-enacted as Section 13 of the High Court Act (Chapter 8 of 1939).

The provision for the applicability of Cape Colonial law was inserted in the Constitution in 1961, and, in 1964, when the sections relating to the judicature were re-enacted, applicability of Cape Colonial law became a specially entrenched provision making it unsusceptible of amendment.[7]

Section 56D of the Southern Rhodesia Constitution 1961 now reads:

subject to the provisions of any law for the time being in force in Southern Rhodesia relating to the application of customary law, the law to be administered by the High Court and by any courts in Southern Rhodesia subordinate to the High Court shall be the law in force in the Colony of the Cape of Good Hope on the 10th day of June, 1891, as modified by subsequent legislation having in Southern Rhodesia the force of law.

---

[1] High Commissioner's Proclamation of 10 June 1891, Sections 3, 4, and 8. Jurisdiction over natives might be exercised if 'necessary in the interests of peace or for the punishment of acts of violence to persons or property'.

[2] Section 19.

[3] Matabeleland Order in Council of 18 July 1894, Section 26. 'Matabeleland' here covered all Southern Rhodesia. The date of commencement of the Order was its date of publication in the Cape of Good Hope Government Gazette (Sections 56 and 3 of the Order). This was 5 October 1894 (High Commissioner's Notice No. 38 of 1894).

[4] Section 27.

[5] *Stevenson* v. *B.S.A. Co.*, *supra* and *Salisbury Reef Gold Mining Co.* v. *B.S.A. Co.*, *supra*.

[6] Southern Rhodesia Order in Council 1898, Section 49(2). No subsequent statute of the Cape Colony was to be of effect unless specifically applied to Southern Rhodesia: Section 49(4).

[7] Southern Rhodesian Constitution 1961, Section 56E and the Third Schedule, as amended by Sections 4 and 20 of the Constitution (Amendment) Act of 1964.

The effect of this provision is that, subject to changes introduced by statute and the preservation in certain spheres of African customary law, the Roman–Dutch Law as it had evolved[1] in the Cape Colony by 1891 is the common law of Southern Rhodesia. Later statutory developments in the Cape do not concern Southern Rhodesia.[2] However, subsequent interpretation by the Cape courts of the Roman–Dutch Law should be looked to in order to determine the position. This issue was raised in *Central African Airways Corporation* v. *Vickers Armstrong Ltd.*[3] Until 1931 there had been conflicting decisions in the Cape Colony on attachment to found jurisdiction and, had a decision been given in 1891, a different view from that confirmed by the Cape Courts in 1931 might have been adopted. Clayden F.J. who followed the 1931 Cape decision, laid it down that

a practice, later shown to be erroneous, cannot be regarded as the law in force in 1891; the true law must be looked to.[4]

This, however, does not mean that Southern Rhodesian courts are bound to follow Cape courts in their decisions on the Roman–Dutch Law. Indeed the Southern Rhodesian High Court assumed that it was not, after such appeal had been abolished, bound to follow decisions of the Cape courts, given even at a time when the Cape Supreme Court was that to which appeal was made from the Southern Rhodesian High Court.[5] However, as Beadle C.J. recently stated: 'The tradition of our courts has been to follow the decisions of the Cape Provincial Division rather than of any other Province of the Republic (where other considerations are equal).'[6] Nor will the Southern

[1] For the history of its evolution see H. R. Hahlo and E. Kahn, *The Union of South Africa: the Development of its Laws and Constitution*, Stevens, 1960, pp. 10–21 and 28–51. See also *Cambridge History of the British Empire*, Vol. 8, 2nd edition, Cambridge, 1963, Chapter XXXI, The Roman–Dutch Law in South Africa, by the late Rt. Hon. Chief Justice E. F. Watermeyer, and J. W. Wessels, *History of the Roman–Dutch Law*, Grahamstown, African Book Co., 1908.

[2] Section 49(4) of the Southern Rhodesia Order in Council 1898 expressly excluded the application of subsequent Cape statutes unless specifically applied by proclamation, order, or regulation, but this was not expressed in subsequent re-enactments of Section 49. Certain *obiter dicta* in *Nkambule* v. *The King*, [1950] A.C. 379 at 393 and 399 (a case relative to Swaziland which had taken over Transvaal law in 1907) are relevant in view of this omission. The Court felt that alterations or amendments to Transvaal law or subsequent consolidations were binding in a territory which had received such law. For a refutation of this view see A. J. Kerr, 'The Reception and Codification of Systems of Law in Southern Africa' (1958), *J.A.L.*, Vol. 2, p. 82 at pp. 87–89.

[3] 1956 (2) S.A. 492 (F.C.).

[4] At pp. 493–4. See also *R.* v. *Goseb*, 1956 (2) S.A. 696 (S.W.A.) at 699, where, interpreting somewhat similar provisions in relation to South West Africa, Claasen J.P. held that the territory could not be saddled 'for ever' with decisions that might have been wrongly decided in the Cape of Good Hope. A decision interpreting the common law has retrospective effect: see *Mineworkers' Union* v. *Prinsloo*, 1948 (3) S.A. 831 (A.D.) at 852.

[5] *R.* v. *Chavendera*, 1939 S.R. 218 per Russell C.J. at 225–7.

[6] *Hickey* v. *R.*, 1963 R. & N. 932 at 936 where the Court overruled a decision by a magistrate that he should follow a decision of the Divisional Court of the King's Bench in preference to a decision of the full bench of the Cape Provincial Division in its appellate jurisdiction. In any event the Court found the Cape Court's reasoning preferable.

Rhodesian courts necessarily follow other South African courts on the Roman–Dutch Law. Thus in *Salisbury Bottling Co. (Pvt.) Ltd.* v. *Central African Bottling Co. (Pvt.) Ltd.* Clayden F.J. refused to follow a leading Transvaal case as it did not correctly represent the Roman–Dutch Law as it should have been applied in the Cape Colony in 1891.[1]

It would also seem that, since Roman–Dutch Law is a growing system and changes in accordance with 'the prevalent moral and political theories and intuitions of public policy',[2] the law as it develops in Southern Rhodesia may eventually differ considerably from the common law of the Cape Province, which now forms part of the Republic of South Africa. Such an attitude was in fact adopted by Tredgold C.J. when interpreting whether the words 'surviving spouse' in the Southern Rhodesia Death Duties Act of 1929 include the wife of a polygamous marriage. He considered that it was 'quite unrealistic to affirm that it is contrary to the policy of our law when the majority of marriages in the Colony are under a polygamous system recognized for all civil purposes'.[3] However in *R.* v. *Ncube* it was held that the Roman–Dutch Law had not been altered by this statutory recognition in certain circumstances of polygamous marriages and that in so far as the criminal law of bigamy was concerned the contracting of two customary marriages would not be an offence.[4]

The main development of Southern Rhodesian common law will be through the decisions delivered by the General and Appellate Divisions of the High Court.[5] The doctrine of judicial precedent has been adopted in the

---

[1] 1958 R. & N. 17 at 31. He disagreed with the second proposition in *Patz* v. *Greene*, 1907 T.S. 427 at 433 that where an act is prohibited 'in the public interest, then any member of the public who can prove that he has sustained damage is entitled to his remedy'.

[2] *Daniels* v. *Daniels*, 1958 (1) S.A. 513 (A.D.) at 522–3 per Schreiner J.A. adopting the words of Mr. Justice Holmes. Compare Lord Tomlin's remarks on the character of Roman–Dutch Law in *Pearl Assurance Co.* v. *The Union Government*, 1934 A.D. 560 (P.C.) at 563: 'That law is a living, virile system of law, ever seeking, as every such system must, to adapt itself, consistently with its inherent basic principles to deal effectively with the increasing complexity of modern organized society.'

[3] *Estate Mehta* v. *The Master*, 1958 R. & N. 570 (F.C.) at 588–9. In *Mehta* v. *City of Salisbury*, 1962 (1) S.A. 675 Beadle C.J. at 686–7 considered that in interpreting a Southern Rhodesian statute regard must be had to 'the surrounding circumstances when it was passed ... In considering a statute in a country whose racial policies are quite different from those of the Republic of South Africa it might however be quite wrong to draw a similar inference.' See also *Nordenfelt* v. *Maxim Nordenfelt Gun and Ammunition Co.*, [1894] A.C. 535 at 553 per Lord Watson.

[4] 1959 (2) R. & N. 460 (S.R.). Perhaps somewhat inconsistently it has been held that conclusion of an unregistered native customary marriage during a Christian marriage is bigamy: *R.* v. *Muzanenamu*, 1952 S. R. 35 and *R.* v. *Tarasanwa*, 1948 (2) S.A. 29 (S.R.) following *R.* v. *Nkabi*, 1918 S.R. 160 where it was held that it is bigamous if one or other marriage is by Christian rites even if the first be customary. There are numerous Southern Rhodesian decisions that such conduct is bigamous. See criticism of these decisions in H. R. Hahlo, *The South African Law of Husband and Wife*, Juta, 1963, 2nd edition at p. 90 ('Choice of Law' by E. Kahn).

[5] Decisions on the law of Southern Rhodesia are to be found in the Southern Rhodesia

modern Roman–Dutch Law, except that the rule applied by the House of Lords and the Court of Appeal that courts are absolutely bound by their own previous decisions [1] has not been accepted. [2] As Centlivres C.J. has said, in comparing Roman–Dutch and English practice on this point, 'there is . . . nothing in Roman–Dutch Law to justify the practice as far as the Appellate Division is concerned. The judicial tradition—if such it may be called—of reverence for precedents is, therefore, different in England from what it is in the Union.' [3]

Privy Council decisions, if given on appeal from Southern Rhodesia, are absolutely binding on all courts in Southern Rhodesia. [4] Similarly, a decision on the Roman–Dutch Law, providing that Roman–Dutch authorities were referred to and discussed, is binding. [5] Again, a Privy Council decision on the interpretation of a similarly worded statute in another country is binding, provided that there is no relevant difference in the common law of the two countries. [6] Authority also exists that a Privy Council decision on a statute involving public policy should be followed. [7]

If, however, a particular statute requires courts to apply English law, [8] it seems that in such instances courts must follow decisions of the House of

Reports 1899 (one volume only), in the series of Cape Supreme Court Reports from 1896 to 1911, in the Southern Rhodesia Reports 1911 to 1955, in the Appellate Division Reports of the Union of South Africa from 1911 to 1946 (Southern Rhodesian decisions are often quoted on appeal), in the South African Law Reports from 1947 onwards and in the Rhodesia and Nyasaland Law Reports from 1956 onwards. Certain criminal cases are reported in the Rhodesia and Nyasaland Court of Appeal Reports from 1939 to 1955 while African Customary Law cases can be found in the reports of the Southern Rhodesia Native Appeal Court. Tax cases are reported in the South African Tax Cases series of reports.

[1] For the basis of exceptions to and possible invalidity of this rule see R. Cross, *Precedent in English Law*, Oxford, 1961; A. W. B. Simpson, 'The Ratio Decidendi of a Case and the Doctrine of Binding Precedent', in *Oxford Essays on Jurisprudence*, Oxford, 1961; and G. Dworkin, 'Stare Decisis in the House of Lords' 1962, *M.L.R.*, 163.

[2] See *Harris* v. *Minister of the Interior*, *supra* at 452–4 and *R.* v. *Sillas*, 1959 (4) S.A. 305 (A.D.) at 311 for a full discussion of the principles applied in South Africa which for the most part apply equally to Southern Rhodesia. See Hahlo and Kahn, op. cit., pp. 29–34.

[3] *Fellner* v. *Minister of the Interior*, 1954 (4) S.A. 523 (A.D.) at 530.

[4] Compare *Estate Cato* v. *Estate Cato*, 1915 A.D. at 303 per Innes C.J. where this rule was laid down with reference to South Africa.

[5] *McCullogh* v. *Fernwood Estates*, 1920 A.D. 204 at 208 per Innes C.J. and *Conradie* v. *Rousseau*, 1919 A.D. 279 at 286 per Solomon A.C.J.

[6] *R.* v. *Nkala*, 1961 (4) S.A. 177 (F.C.) per Beadle C.J. (S.R.).

[7] *Patz* v. *Salzburg*, 1907 T.S. 526 at 528. However the *dicta* by Beadle C.J. in *Mehta* v. *City of Salisbury*, 1962 (1) S.A. 675 (S.R.) at 686–7 and those by Tredgold C.J. in *Estate Mehta* v. *The Master*, *supra* at 589 make it clear that when interpreting statutes in a country whose racial policies are different from those of the Southern Rhodesian Legislature it might be quite wrong to draw similar inferences.

[8] The Civil Evidence Act (Chapter 18), in Sections 18, 21, 24, 29, 30, 31, 33, and 34 provides that evidence is admissible if it would be admitted 'if the case were depending in the Supreme Court of Judicature in England'. Similar provision is made in the Criminal Procedure and Evidence Act (Chapter 31), Sections 285–6, 291, 295 and 340. The General Law Amendment Act (Chapter 20), also provides that except for statutory enactments passed after 11 September 1879, the law in relation to maritime and shipping law and actions in respect of fire, life and marine assurance, stoppage in transitu, and bills of lading shall

Lords even if these conflict with Privy Council decisions.[1] Similarly, if express reference is made to the Supreme Court of Judicature in England or to decisions of the Courts of Appeal and Criminal Appeal the same should apply.[2] If such express provision is not made and there is no conflict, House of Lords decisions are of persuasive authority. In fact it has been held that if a decision of the House of Lords on an English statute not in identical terms is very similar to a Federal statute the case will be decisive unless a difference in the law or facts can be found.[3]

The practice of the Appellate Division of the High Court in regard to judicial precedent has not yet been settled, but the position is probably governed by a statutory provision. Section 9 of the High Court Act reads:

So far as concerns records, practice and procedure the appellate jurisdiction vested in the Appellate Division shall be exercised in accordance with this Act and rules of court, and where no special provision is contained in this Act or in rules of court, as the case may be, with reference thereto, any such jurisdiction in relation to criminal and civil matters shall be exercised as nearly as may be in conformity with the law and practice for the time being observed in England by the Court of Criminal Appeal and the Court of Appeal respectively.

During the existence of the Federal Supreme Court, in respect of which similar provision was made, the Court held *obiter* that if this section applied to questions of precedent (which it doubted) then in considering its previous decisions, the Court should

adopt the rule which applies in the Privy Council which is the ultimate Court of Appeal . . . to differ from previous decisions only with the greatest hesitation, and so, to exercise jurisdiction as nearly as may be with the English courts mentioned in Section 9 if that section applies.[4]

be 'the law administered by the High Court of Justice in England for the time being'. Much other English Law has been adopted through the medium of statutes which are in many respects replicas of English legislation, e.g. the Bills of Exchange Act (Chapter 218) and the Companies Act (Chapter 223). English Law is not specifically adopted in these measures and certain provisions have been inserted in the light of the Roman–Dutch common law, e.g. recognition of pre-incorporation contracts, judicial management to avoid winding up, and special statutory remedies as a substitute for conversion which does not exist in Roman–Dutch Law.

[1] See *Ex parte Zelter*, 1951 (2) S.A. 54 (S.R.), where Beadle J. (as he then was) held himself bound by *Duncan* v. *Cammell Laird*, [1942] A.C. 624, and not by *Robinson* v. *State of South Australia (No. 2)*, [1931] A.C. 704. *Ex parte Zelter* was followed in *Faber* v. *Barrow (No. 2)*, 1962 R. & N. 657 (S.R.).

[2] Compare *R.* v. *L.*, 1951 S.R. 106 at 119 where Beadle J. held that 'although the Privy Council is not part of the Supreme Court of Judicature in the event of conflicting decisions of the Court of Criminal Appeal and the Privy Council, the Court will be bound by the latter'. This point was expressly left open when the case went to the Appellate Division : see 1951 (4) S.A. 614 (A.D.) per Centlivres C.J. at 619. It is submitted that the approach adopted by Beadle C.J. in *R.* v. *L.* was incorrect in view of the wording of the statute.

[3] *Umtali Finance Co.* v. *The Commissioner of Taxes*, 1962 R. & N. 277 (F.C.) at 283.

[4] *Estate Mehta* v. *The Master*, 1958 R. & N. 570 per Clayden F.J. at 577–80. The point was taken by the court *mero motu*. For criticism of these views see my article in the *Rhodesia and Nyasaland Law Journal*, Vol. 2, p. 126 at 144 et seq.

It is probable that the Appellate Division of the High Court will take the same view of its powers and consider itself entitled to overrule its previous decisions. The question will also arise as to powers of the Appellate Division in respect of decisions of courts to which it is a successor. Again the decision in *Estate Mehta* v. *The Master* will probably guide the Appellate Division, as it was then laid down that the Federal Supreme Court was free to depart from decisions given by courts to which it was a successor such as the Appellate Division of the then Union of South Africa.[1] Similarly the High Court will probably adopt the same view as that taken by the Federal Supreme Court to decisions given *per incuriam*.[2] It is also likely to adopt the attitude of the Federal Supreme Court towards decisions of lower courts, viz. that it is free to disagree with such decisions and that it is not restricted by any rule that the decision of the lower court must clearly be shown to be wrong.[3]

The General Division of the High Court is bound by decisions of the Privy Council, the Appellate Division of the High Court,[4] and decisions of former appeal courts given while such courts were courts of appeal for Southern Rhodesia.[5] However, if two conflicting decisions of equal standing are cited, the High Court considers itself free as to which of the decisions to follow.[6]

A single judge is also bound by a decision of a full bench, but one High Court judge is not bound by an earlier decision by a single colleague, and may depart from such a decision if satisfied that the previous decision was wrong and ought not to be followed.[7] Southern Rhodesian judges have not so far

---

[1] It is submitted that in this respect the Mehta Case was correctly decided. Thus the Appellate Division of the High Court will be able to overrule decisions given by the Federal Supreme Court during its existence. See also *R.* v. *Chavendera, supra* where the High Court held that it was not bound to follow the decisions of Cape courts given at a time when appeals were made to such courts from Southern Rhodesia.

[2] See *Attorney-General of Northern Rhodesia* v. *Dimakopoulos*, 1961 R. & N. 833. See also *Codron* v. *Macintyre and Shaw NN.O.*, 1960 R. & N. 418 at 421, where a question which had passed *sub silentio* was raised. In *R.* v. *Nkala*, 1961 (4) S.A. 177 (F.C.) at 181 the Court held that it was not bound by decisions based on a concession made by counsel.

[3] *Central African Airways Corporation* v. *Vickers-Armstrong Ltd.*, 1956 R. & N. 4 at 8 per Clayden F.J.

[4] Decisions by higher courts are binding on lower courts in the same hierarchy: *R.* v. *Lusu*, 1953 (2) S.A. 484 (A.D.) at 491–2.

[5] The High Court of Southern Rhodesia has stated that it has no power to overrule South African Appellate Division decisions given while the latter was court of appeal for Southern Rhodesia: *Acting Master of the High Court* v. *Estate Mehta*, 1957 (3) S.A. 727 (S.R.) at 737 per Morton J., approved by Hathorn J. in *R.* v. *Nkala*, 1961 (2) S.A. 429 at 433; left open by Murray C.J. in *Commissioner of Taxes* v. *H. W. Strong (Pvt.) Ltd.*, 1958 R. & N. 324 at 334. This point was expressly left open by Beadle C.J. in *R.* v. *Nkala* on appeal to the Federal Supreme Court. Beadle C.J. still regarded the point as an open one in *Mehta* v. *City of Salisbury*, 1961 R. & N. 911 at 934. Compare *R.* v. *Chavendera, supra*. In *R.* v. *Masuka and Others*, 1965 (2) S.A. 40 (S.R.) at 43 Young J. without adducing any reasons held that he was not bound by decisions of the Federal Supreme Court.

[6] *Commissioner of Taxes* v. *H. W. Strong (Pvt.) Ltd.*, 1958 R. & N. 324 at 334 and *R.* v. *Nkala, supra* at 433.

[7] *Mockford* v. *Gordon and Abe Gordon (Pty.) Ltd.*, 1949 (3) S.A. 1173 at 1174 per Clayden J. (as he then was); cp. *R.* v. *Bilse*, 1952 (2) S.A. 30 (O.) at 32.

been involved in difficulties of determining the precise *ratio decidendi* of an earlier decision. The difficulties that can occur where it is the habit of all the members of an appellate court to state their own reasons are illustrated in *Fellner* v. *Minister of the Interior*.[1] It would however be hazardous to guess which attitude would be adopted as in this case four judges gave differing decisions on the effect of *Sachs* v. *Donges N.O.*[2] in which four judges had given reasons which differed, two being dissenting judgements, while there was one concurrence.

The aforegoing discussion relates only to binding precedents, but, even where decisions are not binding, the Southern Rhodesian courts will take guidance from the decisions of other courts. Thus decisions of the Appellate Division of the Republic of South Africa and of the various Provincial Divisions given on matters of Roman–Dutch Law are of great persuasive authority. English law reports are also frequently referred to,[3] while decisions in the United States, Australia, and Commonwealth countries, such as Canada and India, are also occasionally relied upon.[4]

Statute law in Southern Rhodesia

For the most part statutes in force in Southern Rhodesia consist of laws passed by the Legislature of Southern Rhodesia, although a small number of Acts of the United Kingdom Parliament extending to all colonial territories, several Orders in Council and a considerable number of regulations thereunder,[5] and constitutional provisions in British instruments are of application in Southern Rhodesia.

---

[1] 1954 (4) S.A. 523 (A.D.) Centlivres C.J. and Fagan J.A. (concurring) held that a *ratio decidendi* which is only the majority of a majority is not binding, whereas Schreiner J.A. held that an expressed reason may be a *ratio* although it has not the support of a majority of the whole Court, and that where several major reasons for a decision are advanced each is a *ratio decidendi*.

[2] 1950 (2) S.A. 265 (A.D.).'

[3] A typical Southern Rhodesian case, *Turner & Company (Pvt.) Ltd.* v. *Arcturus Road Council*, 1957 R. & N. 775, dealing with questions of interpretation of statute involved the quotation of five English decisions, three English texts, and five South African decisions.

[4] Australian and Canadian cases were heavily relied on in deciding whether Southern Rhodesian legislation bound persons in the service of the Federal Government (see *Attorney-General for Southern Rhodesia* v. *Jones*, 1962 R. & N. 187 (F.C.)); American cases were quoted in *Mehta* v. *City of Salisbury, supra*; and in litigation on the Declaration of Rights—see *Maluleke* v. *Minister of Law and Order*, 1963 R. & N. 554 in which one Southern Rhodesian case, two Privy Council decisions, one American, one Australian, and one Indian decision were referred to.

[5] These have provided for the continuation in force of all Federal laws (which term includes subsidiary legislation under such laws) except to the extent that these have either been amended or repealed at any time by the Legislature of Southern Rhodesia or by the Governor prior to 1 July 1964: see Federation of Rhodesia and Nyasaland (Dissolution) Order in Council 1963, S.I. 1963 No. 2085, Section 2. A large body of Federal law enacted from 1953 to 1963 is thus still in force by virtue of U.K. statutory provision to that effect.

Once a Southern Rhodesian Act has been passed by the Legislative Assembly and assented to by the Governor, it must be published in the Southern Rhodesian Government Gazette and comes into operation either on the date of its publication or on the date specified in the Act.[1] Thereafter statutes are published in annual volumes, each law being given a serial number (e.g. No. 37 of 1962). However, for ease of reference Southern Rhodesia has twice appointed Statute Law Revision Commissions to prepare revised editions of the statute law—once in 1937 and again in 1962.[2] These Commissions were given considerable powers to omit, consolidate, and alter the statute law in force, provided that they might not make any major alteration or amendment in the substance of any law. In addition, as a consequence of their deliberations, considerable numbers of old statutes were repealed by the Legislature.[3] The result of the labours of the first Commission was the publication in 1940 of a five-volume Revised Edition of the Statute Law of Southern Rhodesia which became the sole authentic edition of, and conclusive evidence of the provisions of, the statutes in force in Southern Rhodesia on 1 January 1939.[4] Individual Acts were numbered as Chapters and are referred to by their short title followed by the Chapter number.[5] Subsequently, the statutes passed between 1939 and 1949 were collected and printed in a three-volume edition.[6]

In view of the mass of legislation passed since the 1939 Revised Edition, in 1961 it was considered essential that the statute law be again revised and legislation authorizing the appointment of another Statute Law Revision Commission was enacted in 1962.[7] Ultimately in 1964 the Revised Edition 1963 of the Statute Law of Southern Rhodesia was brought into force. This set out the statute law in eight volumes containing 313 Chapters,[8] and

---

[1] Constitution, Section 30(3).

[2] See Revised Edition of the Laws Acts No. 8 of 1937 and No. 34 of 1962.

[3] See Statute Law Revision Act 1937, General Law Amendment Acts of 1937 and 1938, and the Repeal of Laws Act No. 14 of 1962. (Pending legislation to establish the 1962 Commission, a committee commenced the work of revision and recommended the repeal of many laws.)

[4] See Section 10, Revised Edition of the Laws Act 1937. This provision was in conflict with Section 35 of the Southern Rhodesian Letters Patent 1923 which provided that the copy of a law enrolled in the office of the Registrar of the High Court was to be conclusive evidence. The point never arose for a decision in practice.

[5] e.g. The Insolvency Act (Chapter 53). Since 1964 reference is made to Chapter 53 of 1939, to distinguish the 1939 edition from the 1963 edition.

[6] The Statute Law of Southern Rhodesia containing Acts of Parliament from 1 January 1939 to 31 December 1949. C. F. Roworth Ltd. London, 1950.

[7] Revised Edition of the Laws Act No. 34 of 1962.

[8] e.g. The Electoral Act (Chapter 2). No reference is made to the date of the edition in referring to these Chapters. From a lawyer's point of view the system is undesirable, as confusion results owing on some occasions to reference being made to Acts as Chapters and on others to their year of passage. Furthermore, in order to interpret legislation it is often necessary to have recourse to the legislative history of the Act in question, which cannot be determined from the Revised Edition, while case law for the most part refers to the sections of any Act as amended and not to the Chapter in the Revised Edition.

containing virtually all Acts passed by the Legislature of Southern Rhodesia.[1]

The law as stated is to be conclusive evidence of the provisions of any statute.[2] There is, however, special provision in the Amendments Incorporation Act No. 71 of 1959 which permits the Minister of Justice at any time to order the reprinting of a measure as amended. Such a reprinted Act is *prima facie* evidence of the provisions of the laws so reprinted.

Since the Revised Edition, except as indicated above, is conclusive evidence of the Statute Law of Southern Rhodesia, any statutes not stated in the Revised Edition are accordingly no longer law. In fact many old statutes were repealed in 1937 and 1938, when meticulous consideration was given to Cape Ordinances and Acts, and further repeals occurred in 1962. Consequently numerous Acts of the Cape Colony which were in force on 10 June 1891 are no longer of application. Difficulties however may arise in respect of Dutch statutes prior to the British occupation of the Cape Colony in 1806. If these were in force as 'any other legislative enactments'[3] having in the Colony the force of law, no evidence of their provisions may be given. If, however, they had been absorbed into the Roman–Dutch Law, then they would still be receivable as part of the common law.[4] It is doubtful whether the definition in the Revised Edition of the Laws Act 1937 was intended to change the common law that such Dutch statutes had become part of the common law and it is therefore submitted that 'legislative enactment' must be narrowly construed so as not to include all law statutory in origin.[5]

An important point that is open to doubt as a result of the various Revised

---

[1] Provision was made for the omission of certain scheduled laws, notably financial measures, which were nonetheless to have the force of law: Revised Edition of the Laws Act 1962, Section 6. Much statute law is still in force in the form of Federal statutes continued under the Rhodesia and Nyasaland Act 1963. Federal statutes are gradually being re-enacted by the Southern Rhodesian Legislature.

[2] Section 10. This is so despite Sections 34 and 35 of the Southern Rhodesia Letters Patent 1923, which were in force at the time of the Third Reading of the Bill as the Letters Patent were revoked by the time the measure received assent, this being given in November 1962 in terms of the Southern Rhodesia Constitution 1961, Section 31(2) of which authorized the Legislature to provide that such a Revised Edition should be the sole and authentic version of such laws and conclusive evidence thereof.

[3] Definition of 'statute' in the Revised Edition of the Laws Act 1937 read with definition of 'laws' in Section 2 of the Revised Edition of the Laws Act 1962.

[4] *Estate Heinamann* v. *Heinamann*, 1918 A.D. 84 at 114 and *R.* v. *Harrison and Dryburgh*, 1922 A.D. 320 at 326. There can be no question that Justinian's *Corpus Juris Civilis*, although statutory in origin, has been incorporated into the Roman–Dutch common law and those parts of the Code which are still of application have operation as part of the common law and not as statute. The same applies to the Political Ordinance of 1580: *Spies* v. *Lombard*, 1950 (3) S.A. 469 (A.D.) at 483 per van den Heever J.A. See R. H. Christie, *Rhodesian Commercial Law*, Juta, 1961, at p. 28.

[5] However, because the definition expressly excludes Imperial enactments and is so broad in its terms, it is arguable that it has reference to Dutch statutes. Considerable changes in the common laws of succession, lease, law of property, &c. would on this interpretation have occurred.

Editions and the Constitution is whether abrogation of statutes or common law by disuse can now occur in Southern Rhodesia. According to the Roman–Dutch common law, which adopted Justinian's view as set out in the Digest, both statutes and common law could be abrogated by disuse.[1] However, Section 56D of the Constitution read with Section 7 of the Southern Rhodesia (Constitution) Order in Council 1961, which was preceded by the various Orders in Council and the High Court Act stipulating that the law of the country was to be the law in force in the Cape Colony in 1891 'as modified by subsequent legislation', may have altered the position in relation to the abrogation of common law by disuse.

Although previously a law might be rendered obsolete either by contrary usage or by non-enforcement for a very long period 'in face of circumstances calling for its enforcement'[2] it has now been provided that 'all laws in force in Southern Rhodesia' prior to the 1961 Constitution are to remain of force and effect subject to the power of the Legislature or other authority to amend or repeal these, while 'the law in force' in the Cape Colony except 'as amended by subsequent legislation' is to have in Southern Rhodesia the force of law. If 'law' or 'laws' in either of these provisions includes the common law, then there can no longer be abrogation by disuse. A provision in Section 135 of the South Africa Act 1909 similar to that contained in Section 7 of the Southern Rhodesia (Constitution) Order in Council 1961 was interpreted in *Webster* v. *Ellison*, and the Court there held that the Legislature 'meant statutes and never intended that the section should apply to judge made law'.[3]

In *R.* v. *Detody* it was held by Innes C.J. that this rule of non-abrogation of statutes applied not only to those on the statute book at the time of Union but to all future statutes.[4] These decisions are not however of application to section 56D of the Constitution where the word 'law' was used to bring in the Roman–Dutch common law. Even though 'law' in this sense might include the doctrine of abrogation by disuse itself[5] the express wording of Section 56D that only subsequent legislation may modify the 'law' amounts to a repeal of the doctrine. The result is, it is submitted, that there can be no abrogation by disuse of either statute or of common law in Southern Rhodesia.

[1] The Roman text relied on was D.1.3.32.1. Constantine took a different view: C.8.52.2. For the Roman–Dutch position see *R.* v. *Detody*, 1926 A.D. 198 at 224 per Kotze J.A. Abrogation by disuse does not apply to legislation introduced under British administration. See also *Seaville* v. *Colley* (1891), 9 S.C. 39 at 44 per de Villiers C.J.

[2] *Green* v. *Fitzgerald*, 1914 A.D. 88 at 111 per Innes J.A.

[3] 1911 A.D. 73 at 99 per Solomon J. See also *R.* v. *Detody*, 1926 A.D. 198 at 201 per Innes C.J. followed by Beadle C.J. in *African Newspapers and Another* v. *Lardner-Burke and Another*, *supra* in interpreting Section 70(1)(b) of the Southern Rhodesian Constitution which provided that laws 'in force' before the coming into operation of the Constitution could not be tested against the Declaration of Rights. See, however, Section 72(1) definition of 'law', para. (c).

[4] 1926 A.D. 198 at 201. This point was, however, left open by Kotze J.A. at p. 225.

[5] See D. Pont, 'Die Wet-afskaffende Krag van die Gewoonte' (1937) 1 *T.H.R.—H.R.* 49 at pp. 54–57.

There have, however, been a number of cases in which it has in *dicta* been assumed, this point passing *sub silentio*, that it would be possible for the common law to have been abrogated by disuse in Southern Rhodesia after 1891.[1]

There is also a vast mass of subsidiary legislation in Southern Rhodesia which is published in Government Notices annexed to the Southern Rhodesia Government Gazette. Such subsidiary legislation (which may be tested by the courts[2]) is only to come into operation on the date of publication in the Gazette unless some other date is fixed. In any event it may not come into operation before the enabling Act.[3] Such legislation is of course subject to the procedural safeguards in the Constitution which provide for scrutiny by the Constitutional Council.[4] An additional safeguard exists in that all regulations must be laid on the table of the Legislative Assembly within thirty days of their publication, or if the Legislative Assembly is not then sitting, within thirty days after the commencement of the session.[5]

The application of African customary law in Southern Rhodesia

From the beginnings of European settlement in Southern Rhodesia the British South Africa Company had been enjoined in Article 14 of the Charter to pay careful regard to the customs and laws of the local tribes. When the future Southern Rhodesia became a protectorate the Order in Council of May 1891, Section 4, made similar provision and the High Commissioner's Proclamation thereunder of 10 June 1891 in Section 9 provided that where jurisdiction was exercised over natives

the decisions shall follow the laws and customs of the natives concerned, in so far as they are applicable; provided that if such laws or customs conflict or are not clearly proved or if such laws or customs should be found to be incompatible with peace, order and good government, the court may decide in accordance with the law which would regulate the decision if the matter in dispute concerned persons of European birth or descent.

In 1894 the basis of applicability of African customary law, which has lasted in much the same form until the present day, was set out by the Matabeleland Order in Council 1894. This stipulated that it was to be preserved only in civil cases between natives. Section 27 provided that

---

[1] See *R. v. Fuleza*, 1951 (1) S.A. 519 (A.D.) per van den Heever J.A. at 522 and 529 and per Fagan J.A. at 532; *R. v. Chipo and Others*, 1953 (3) S.A. 602 (S.R.); and *R. v. Chipo and Others*, 1953 (4) S.A. 573 (A.D.).

[2] See *infra*.

[3] Interpretation Act (Chapter 1), Sections 18(1) and 21.

[4] See *supra*, Part II, Chapter 1.

[5] Interpretation Act (Chapter 1), Section 30. In 1950 a Select Committee was appointed to scrutinize delegated legislation. However no great need was apparently felt for such a Committee and it did not survive.

in civil cases between natives the High Court and the magistrates' courts shall be guided by native law, so far as that law is not repugnant to natural justice or morality, or to any Order made by Her Majesty in Council, or to any Proclamation or Ordinance. In any such case the court may obtain the assistance of one or two native assessors, to advise the court on native law and customs, but the decision of the court shall be given by the judge or magistrate alone. In all other respects the court shall follow as far as possible the procedure observed in similar cases in the courts of the Colony.[1]

From that period onwards the Roman–Dutch criminal law applied to Africans as did all statute law unless specifically excluded.

These provisions were re-enacted by Sections 50 and 51 of the Southern Rhodesia Order in Council 1898, which provisions were subsequently reincorporated, subject to one considerable modification, in the Native Law and Courts Act No. 33 of 1937, when the position of African customary law was strengthened. The Act, which was passed to settle doubts, arose out of two conflicting cases decided in the High Court in 1935 and 1936.[2] Previously the courts had been enjoined that 'they be guided by native law', but by the Native Law and Courts Act it was provided that 'in the determination of civil cases between natives by any court of law the decision shall be in accordance with native law and customs'. As the High Court subsequently held: 'within its own limits the native law has been substituted for the previously existing common law'.[3]

It is clear, however, that the sphere of operation of African customary law is a limited one. It is in the first place inapplicable in the realm of criminal law.[4] Thus the common law of crime and crimes established by statute govern Europeans and Africans equally.

Secondly, African customary law is applicable only to cases 'between Africans', so that where there is a European plaintiff or defendant, the matter is governed by the Roman–Dutch common law.[5] No provision exists, as in

---

[1] Bigamous marriages were to be treated as valid for all civil purposes in so far as recognized by native law and custom: Section 28.

[2] *Komo and Leboko* v. *Holmes N.O.*, 1935 S.R. 86 and *Vela* v. *Mandinika and Magutsa*, 1936 S.R. 86.

[3] *In re Robert*, 1953 (3) S.A. 97 per Tredgold C.J. at 100.

[4] See e.g. *Wiri* v. *Mashayangombe*, 1939 S.R.N. 54 where it was held that although 'Incest was in native law regarded as a crime against the State—that is, the Chief, and was sometimes punished by death', this was today of no application. In *R.* v. *Tshipa*, 1957 R. & N. 751 it was held that African customary rules as to relationships by affinity had not been incorporated into the Roman–Dutch Law. If this had been done, 'the criminal courts of the Colony would have been administering one law of incest in respect of natives and another law of incest in respect of Europeans'. See also *R.* v. *Ncube*, 1959 R. & N. 466 at 469, where it was held that although polyandry was a crime by native law and custom, the common law did not recognize customary marriages and therefore 'to punish the contracting of such a marriage would be in effect to incorporate into the Roman–Dutch Law something found only in native customary law'.

[5] However, there may still be anomalies as the rights of the African may depend on customary law. Thus in litigation against a European where a claim is made by an African

many former British colonial territories, for the application of customary law where a substantial injustice would otherwise be occasioned by strict adherence to the common law.[1]

Thirdly, it is provided that where custom 'is repugnant . . . to the provisions of any statute law' in force it shall not apply.[2] In addition, in several instances the statute law of Southern Rhodesia makes express provision which cuts across African customary law.[3]

Fourthly, if African customary law 'is inapplicable to the matter or cause before the court' then the Roman–Dutch common law must be applied.[4] This means that the transaction must be one known to customary law and that there must be rules of the particular customary law available for the decision of the dispute.[5] It is difficult to rationalize and extract principles from the decisions of Southern Rhodesian courts given in terms of this provision, since they have not always been consistent in deciding when customary law is inapplicable or even what inapplicability means, it having been held in

widow against a tortfeasor for loss of support occasioned by the wrongful killing of the claimant's spouse, the courts test the widow's claim to support by African customary law. As this does not give a wife a claim for maintenance against her husband (apparently her father may claim from the husband's father—*Mada* v. *Skudamedzi*, 1942 S.R.N. 193) she may not claim against a tortfeasor: see *Ex parte Seti and Others*, 1963 R. & N. 681, following *Santam* v. *Fondo*, 1960 (2) S.A. 467 (A.D.). In this case the marriage was a customary marriage not registered in terms of Section 3 (1) of the African Marriages Act (Chapter 105) but the same would probably apply to registered marriages. It may be that in civil or Christian marriages an action would lie, since the courts will, where Africans enter into a legal relationship inconsistent with customary law apply the ordinary law of the land in regard to disputes between them (*Dokotera* v. *The Master*, 1957 (4) S.A. 468 (S.R.) at 470 per Murray C.J.) unless this is excluded by statute. It is submitted that Section 2 of the African Law and Courts Act does not exclude the application of the common law duty of support between spouses or of the Deserted Wives and Children Protection Act (Chapter 173).

[1] e.g. The Subordinate Courts Ordinance (Chapter 4), Northern Rhodesia, Section 16.

[2] African Law and Courts Act, Section 2, definition of 'African law and custom'.

[3] Thus the African Marriages Act (Chapter 105), Section 11, prohibits pledging of African girls under the age of twelve years for future marriage and makes this a criminal offence, while Section 15 prohibits compulsion of African women to marry, and Section 16 provides that no customary marriages may be dissolved except by a court of competent jurisdiction. The African Law and Courts Act (Chapter 104), Section 4(2) provides that the Roman–Dutch common law on the prohibited degrees of relationship relative to marriage shall prevail over African custom in the case of civil marriages. Section 70 of the Administration of Estates Act also applies the ordinary law of administration of deceased estates to Africans who have contracted civil or Christian marriages. The African Wills Act (Chapter 108), Section 2, allows Africans who have entered into a civil or Christian marriage by will to provide for the guardianship of their children, while Section 5 allows any African to dispose by will of his rights to immovable property. Finally the Prescription Amendment Act (Chapter 25) relating to limitation of actions applies to all races (*Yobe Jere* v. *Chadzuza Gamaliel and Jairosi Lungu*, 1959 S.R.N. 652) despite the fact that customary law knew no prescription (*Vimba* v. *Tali*, 1942 S.R.N. 161).

[4] African Law and Courts Act, Section 3(1).

[5] A. N. Allott, 'The Judicial Ascertainment of Customary Law in British Africa' (1957), 20 *M.L.R.* 244 at 245. In *Dokotera* v. *The Master*, *supra* at 469 Murray C.J. held that this meant 'a concept entirely unknown to native law and custom in this colony', and at 471 considered that this referred to relationships 'foreign to native law and custom'.

one case that inapplicability must be tested on the basis of repugnancy to natural justice.[1] A further complication has been that where decisions by the courts have tended to withdraw certain fields from the operation of customary law (e.g. decisions have applied to a civil or Christian marriage all the common law proprietary consequences of such a marriage, as such a legal relationship is inconsistent with customary law)[2] the Legislature has intervened. Thus it has provided that

the solemnization of a marriage between Africans in terms of the Marriage Act (Chapter 177) shall not affect the property of the spouses, which shall be held, may be disposed of, and, unless disposed by will, shall devolve according to African law and custom.[3]

However, it is submitted that, as a consequence of Section 2 of the African Law and Courts Act, customary personal law is scarcely touched by legislation. In the definition of 'African law and custom' it is provided that

nothing in the Statute Law of Southern Rhodesia relating to the age of majority, the status of women, the effect of marriage on the property of the spouses, the guardianship of children, or the administration of deceased estates shall affect the application of African law and custom except in so far as such Statute Law has been specifically applied to Africans by statute.[4]

Indeed, as Murray C.J. has said, 'a special code has been provided by the Legislature to deal with succession, either testate or *ab intestato* to the

---

[1] *Chakawa* v. *Goro*, 1959 S.R.N. 644.

[2] *Komo and Leboko* v. *Holmes*, 1935 S.R. 86. The parties in this case were held to be married in community of property, the marriage having been entered into before the Married Persons Property Act (Chapter 178) had laid down that future marriages should be out of community of property. See also *Vela* v. *Mandinika and Magutsa*, 1936 S.R. 171 and *Flora Sebetsa* v. *Maxwell Sebetsa Rathuso*, 1946 S.R. 49. Contra, *Chiduku* v. *Chidano*, 1922 S.R. 55 where the right of a woman married by Christian rites as natural guardian of her children on her husband's death intestate were overridden by customary law. In view of this and of earlier decisions it seems that common law consequences relative to guardianship do not follow. However the decisions were based on absence of repugnancy and the point that customary law was entirely inapplicable to the relationships resulting from Christian marriage was not taken.

[3] African Marriages Act (Chapter 105), Section 13. This section refers only to marriages 'in terms of the Marriages Act'. It is submitted that it does not apply to marriages contracted outside Southern Rhodesia, since when the Legislature is referring to all non-customary marriage whatever the *locus celebrationis* it clearly indicates this fact: cp. Section 2 of the African Wills Act (Chapter 108) which refers to 'a Christian or other civilized marriage'. Section 13 applies only to movable property as there is 'no native law or custom dealing with the devolution of immovable property': *Dokotera* v. *The Master, supra* at 471.

[4] It has been held that this proviso does not mean that the Married Persons Property Act No. 10 of 1928, which was not in express terms said to be applicable to marriages between Africans, is not applicable to Africans who have contracted a Christian marriage. If Africans contract such a marriage they have entered a relationship unknown to customary law thereby incurring the necessary proprietary consequences of the ordinary law of the land which was altered by statute in 1928. They are thus married out of community of property: *Dokotera* v. *The Master, supra* at 473.

property of a deceased native'.[1] Thus it has been provided that although customary law is inapplicable to the devolution of immovable property by will[2] customary law shall apply in the case of intestacy in respect of such property.[3] In respect of movable property owned by an African it seems that there can be no valid will under the African Wills Act, but, dependent on the method of its acquisition, certain movable property may be disposed of *inter vivos* or by will at customary law.[4]

Similar inconsistency by the courts themselves has been shown in decisions on the law of contract. Although there have been general *dicta* that in mercantile transactions customary law is inapplicable and that the common law should be applied,[5] in certain cases which are not mercantile transactions common law has been applied,[6] while in others which have involved such a transaction customary law has been preferred to the common law.[7]

The same inconsistency emerges in relation to the law of delict. In some cases the courts have adopted the attitude that where customary law did not give an action, common law should be applied,[8] or alternatively that customary law was not static and that therefore it should be developed to cover

---

[1] *Dokotera* v. *The Master* at 472.

[2] *Dokotera* v. *The Master, supra* and *Gwebu* v. *Gwebu*, 1961 R. & N. 694. This is because individual ownership of immovable property was unknown to customary law.

[3] African Wills Act (Chapter 108), Section 6 which states that the heir at African law shall succeed: *Dokotera* v. *The Master, supra* at 471F. This special code excludes the application of the general statutory provisions regarding intestate succession contained in the Deceased Estates Succession Amendment Act No. 26 of 1954. However since Act 26 of 1954 was not a reserved measure and it was the invariable habit under the 1923 Constitution to reserve discriminatory measures (Beadle C.J. in *Mehta* v. *City of Salisbury*, 1961 R. & N. 911 at 925) it is arguable that the measure should be interpreted as applying to all members of the community. Compare *dicta* by Briggs F.J. in *Mehta* v. *City of Salisbury, supra* (on appeal) at 1013A: 'If an Act has not been reserved there may be justification for construing its provisions in case of doubt in such a way that it would not have been necessary to reserve it by giving words a non-discriminatory sense which they can fairly bear.'

[4] *Dokotera* v. *The Master*, 1957 (4) S.A. 468 at 470C and 471A. See Chapter 108, Sections 2, 5, 9(1), and 12. The latter section expressly saves the rights of general heirs at customary law.

[5] *Bangure* v. *Muwirimi*, 1946 S.R.N. 84 (mitigation of damages on common law principles required by plaintiff in action for breach of contract), *Chitiyo* v. *Hlupane*, 1940 S.R.N. 85 (common law applied to breach of contract of carriage), *Kakoma* v. *Chikono*, 1946 S.R.N. 135 (common law applied to partnership), *Tangwara* v. *Tlili*, 1960 S.R.N. 680 (common law liability applied to African public carriers), and *Tasara* v. *Agnes Manjaya*, 1958 S.R.N. 581 (an African woman licensed trader treated as a *femme sole* for purposes of litigation).

[6] *Ndewere* v. *Magwede*, 1960 S.R.N. 682 (common law liability only for gross negligence or fraud applied to gratuitous deposit).

[7] *Taruwasha* v. *Ngwuse*, 1934 S.R.N. 66 (customary law applied to make an agent personally liable for defaults of depositary), *Imbwadzawo* v. *Manondo*, 1948 S.R.N. 191 (an agent introducing a principal is personally liable by customary law and is therefore entitled to pay his principal's debt and reclaim), and *Saniso and Marume* v. *Masora*, 1941 S.R.N. 127 (where the common law of a tender to protect against liability was rejected—in fact a lobolo case, but the principle would relate to mercantile transactions).

[8] In *Keresiah and Jack* v. *Martha and Mugweni Masimba*, 1958 S.R.N. 551 an action for assault according to common law was given although customary law did not recognize this.

accusations not known to it.[1] In other cases the courts have held that the absence of a remedy was not to be tested by reference to the 'inapplicability' of customary law but by enquiring whether the absence of a remedy was repugnant to natural justice.[2] Conversely if customary law gave an action while common law gave none, the test for its survival has been repugnancy to natural justice.[3] In other cases decisions have been given without analysis and requirements for an action as stipulated by customary law have been demanded even though this would result in no remedy being available in many cases.[4] Even in regard to the assessment of damages there has been similar inconsistency at times applying customary law[5] and in another case the view being adopted that the common law must be applied in the assessment of damages.[6] A remarkable attitude has in fact been adopted by the courts who have held that in such cases they should award 'an arbitrary sum, regard being had to differences in culture and in the scale of civilization in arriving at an appropriate solatium'.[7]

Again, in respect of the law of persons there has been no consistency, on one occasion the courts declaring customary law to be applicable despite the changed circumstances of modern African society,[8] on other occasions allowing African women rights that are enjoyable in terms of common law only.[9] At other times extension has been made of customary law to fit new

---

[1] *Soffa and Hilda* v. *Gondwe*, 1946 S.R.N. 87 (defamation extended to cover accusation of seduction).

[2] See *infra* for the rules as to repugnancy. In *Chakawa* v. *Goro*, 1959 S.R.N. 644 pauperian liability for the acts of domesticated animals was excluded as being unknown to customary law and the absence of such a remedy was not considered immoral.

[3] See *Matiyenga and Mamire* v. *Chinamura and Others*, 1958 S.R.N. 553 in which parents were held liable under customary law for delicts of their minor children committed in their absence.

[4] See *Marufu* v. *Ephraim*, 1938 S.R.N. 40 where it was held that in customary law in order for there to be liability for slander there must be express malice and the statement complained of must have been made to a person occupying a position of authority. In *George* v. *Gabaza*, 1948 S.R.N. 187 it was held that for liability for personal injury in African law there must be either malice or rough conduct, mere negligence being insufficient.

[5] *Mashako Pembi* v. *Stephen Chinombe*, 1953 S.R.N. 412—no loss of earnings recoverable in the case of seduction.

[6] *Nyovare* v. *Mungwara*, 1956 S.R.N. 503.

[7] *Keresiah and Jack* v. *Martha and Mugweni Masimba*, 1958 S.R.N. 551 following *Jojo* v. *William Bain & Co. Ltd.*, 1941 S.R. 72. This conclusion is remarkable in view of the judgement in *Radebe* v. *Hough*, 1949 (1) S.A. 380 (A.D.), a decision in which the South African Appellate Division had overruled Jojo's case, while still Southern Rhodesia's ultimate court of appeal, and had laid down that damages for pain and suffering cannot be determined by reference to race or to social, cultural, or financial status. As Hoexter A.J.A. at 385–6 stated: 'The fact that the appellant is a native earning only £2 a week, is not evidence that he is insensitive to pain.'

[8] In *Maria* v. *Nyamayaro*, 1950 S.R.N. 237 an African unmarried woman in an urban area was sued for return of money left in her custody, but the court held that she could only be sued assisted by her guardian.

[9] *Mzondiwa* v. *Maguta*, 1947 S.R.N. 147 recognized that unmarried women in towns could own bicycles and that a wife would own what she brought into the marriage.

situations,[1] while on the other hand in certain cases the courts have hesitated to extend customary law.[2] Customary law may be abrogated by disuse and will then be displaced by common law.[3]

Sensibly, in procedural matters the courts have laid down that proceedings should not be unduly hampered by formalities, subject to the parties not being prejudiced.[4] However, although the practice and procedure and law of evidence in African cases, other than for regulations made to the contrary, is to be regulated by customary law,[5] certain common law rules of evidence have been imported.[6]

Repugnancy of customary law

Customary law may not be applied if such law or custom 'is repugnant to natural justice or morality'.[7] The meaning that should be attached to this phrase has been elucidated in a number of cases. Tredgold S.J. in interpreting these words, said:

> Whatever these words may mean, I consider they should only apply to such customs as inherently impress us with some abhorrence or are obviously immoral in their incidence.[8]

Another test propounded is that the custom 'so outrages accepted standards of ethics as to create a sense of revulsion'.[9]

[1] Thus women can own cattle as they could in limited circumstances by customary law: see *Katsandi* v. *Chuma*, 1947 S.R.N. 6 and *Nyongwana* v. *Mapiyi*, 1947 S.R.N. 182.

[2] See *Mutizgwa* v. *Hilda and Tafira*, 1958 S.R.N. 565, where, although the court ruled that on dissolution of a marriage by customary law a wife might keep her pots and utensils, this did not apply to metal pots, pans, and crockery of value purchased by the husband for the benefit of the home.

[3] *Zaba* v. *Tolongo*, 1944 S.R.N. 52 where it was held that the custom that Chiefs were entitled to the skins of leopards killed in their area had been abrogated and that the common law relating to the ownership of wild animals by their captor applied.

[4] *Dayimano* v. *Kgaribaitse*, 1931 S.R. at 136.

[5] African law and Courts Act, Section 7.

[6] In practice the hearsay rule has been applied: *Ida* v. *Mbala*, 1946 S.R.N. 143 and *David* v. *Mary*, 1956 S.R.N. 514. It has also been laid down that in seduction cases there must be corroboration (*Maduba* v. *Taruva*, 1947 S.R.N. 167) but proof is only required on a balance of probability (*Andrew* v. *Gabriel*, 1959 S.R.N. 665). However, the African Marriages Act, Section 14 provides that a marriage by customary law, unless such marriage is registered, will not render either spouse incompetent to give evidence against the other party.

[7] Section 2, African Law and Courts Act.

[8] *Chiduku* v. *Chidano*, 1922 S.R. 55 at 58 in which the right of the eldest brother of a deceased husband to claim guardianship and custody of the latter's children, as opposed to their mother, even in a Christian marriage, was held not to be repugnant. See also *Duma* v. *Madidi*, 1918 S.R. 59. This was followed in *Vela* v. *Mandinika and Magutsa*, 1936 S.R. 161 at 174 per Russell C.J. who held that the right of a husband to claim the children of his wife by another man was not repugnant, but that it would be repugnant if he refused to release those rights on being paid adequate damages.

[9] *Matiyenga and Mamire* v. *Chinamura and Others*, 1958 S.R.N. 553 in which case customary law was applied to render parents liable for the delicts of their minor children.

There have been few cases in which the courts have in practice considered that customary law has been immoral and repugnant to justice, while those instances where custom has been found repugnant have for the most part related to the status of women,[1] particularly if the woman is a party to a Christian marriage,[2] the grounds of divorce,[3] and the welfare of children.[4] Finally one interesting case laid down that slavery and any payment for release from slavery as a captive in war cannot be countenanced.[5]

The repugnancy rule has in practice operated to drive cases involving superstition and taboos away from the formal courts, although these matters may still be taken by African Chief's courts. As an experienced Southern Rhodesian administrator has said: 'an important aspect of native law becomes unknown and out of reach of control or explanation, whose very existence is not suspected until a serious crime blows up'.[6]

The possibility of Africans wishing to come entirely under the common law in respect of the civil law has been envisaged by the Legislature and provision has been made for individual Africans to apply to the Secretary of Internal Affairs who, subject to the approval of the Minister, may grant such an applicant a certificate deeming him for the purpose of the application of customary law and the jurisdiction of African courts not to be an African.[7]

Another problem which has come before the courts on a number of occasions in relation to African customary law is the question of conflict of laws. Such problems can arise either as a result of differing customary laws within Southern Rhodesia or as a result of dealing with alien Africans of whom considerable numbers are present in Southern Rhodesia as migratory

[1] *R.* v. *Gutayi*, 1915 S.R. 49 at 61, where it was held that a widow is emancipated by marriage from her guardian's power and on widowhood does not revert to him: otherwise there would be 'a species of traffic in the womenkind' of Africans, 'a kind of perpetual obligation that such women should fall back into servitude as domestic servants and workers in the fields'. In *Katsandi* v. *Chuma*, 1947 S.R.N. 6 at 7 it was held that a woman is as free after divorce as death, being emancipated by marriage.

[2] In *Sikwela* v. *Sikwela*, 1912 S.R. 168 it was held that repudiation of such a wife is prohibited, although allowed by customary law. A wife is also allowed an action for damages for adultery if married by Christian rites, even though this was not recognized by customary law. See *Iden* v. *Philemon*, 1918 S.R. 140 and *Zakariah* v. *Dzwiti*, 1945 S.R.N. 68. See also *Beatrice and Njambwa* v. *James*, 1944 S.R.N. 46, *Dayimano* v. *Kgaribaitse, supra*, and *Ellen* v. *Jim*, 1931 S.R. 118.

[3] In *Chawa* v. *Bvuta*, 1928 S.R.N. 98 it was held that in a customary marriage sterility should be permitted as a ground for divorce although this was not recognized by customary law.

[4] Customary law is applicable, but the overriding test must be what is beneficial to the moral and material welfare of minor children: *Dayimano* v. *Kgaribaitse*, 1931 S.R. 134, *Jeremiah* v. *Salome*, 1932 S.R.N. 43, *Jamu* v. *Jim and Takaziweyi*, 1939 S.R. 49 at 52, and *Rhodia* v. *Mandala*, 1942 S.R.N. 179 at 183.

[5] *Mabigwa* v. *Matibini*, 1946 S.R.N. 117.

[6] *Report on Native Courts for Southern Rhodesia*, by R. Howman, 1953, para. 117. Copy in Southern Rhodesia Legislative Assembly Library.

[7] African Law and Courts Act, Section 12.

labourers. The only statutory provision is in the African Law and Courts Act, Section 3(2) of which reads:

Where the parties to a civil case between Africans reside in areas where different African laws and customs are in operation, the African law and custom, if any, to be applied by the court shall be that prevailing in the place of residence of the defendant.

In cases not covered by this provision the rules of private international law have for the most part unconsciously been adopted. The decisions have sometimes involved proper statements of principles[1] but frequently correct decisions have only accidentally been reached.[2]

The reason for the haphazard application or non-application of customary law and the absence of consistency in applying legal principles is explicable on the basis that only in 1958 was the Native Court of Appeal (now the Court of Appeal for African civil cases) properly constituted under a President, who was required to have considerable legal experience, whereas previously the President and members of the Court had consisted solely of members or ex-members of the Native Department.[3] Of recent years, a tendency to encourage the application of common law or mercantile law can be seen, while the District Commissioner's Courts have 'been formalizing their procedures and gradually eliminating the old and informal "settlement of a dispute under a tree"'.[4]

---

[1] Thus it was held in *Tom* v. *Raina and Ben*, 1952 S.R.N. 294 that a woman domiciled in Southern Rhodesia who married a man domiciled abroad acquired her husband's domicile on marriage. Conversely, a woman domiciled abroad who married a Southern Rhodesian domiciled African acquired a Southern Rhodesian domicile: *Kapeta and Mairesi* v. *Mugwagwa*, 1954 S.R.N. 464. Similarly the question whether a valid marriage has been contracted has been decided by reference to the *lex loci celebrationis* (*Rhodia* v. *Mandala*, 1942 S.R.N. 179—*contra*, *Leya and John Phiri* v. *Masuiso Banda*, 1958 S.R.N. 605, where Northern Rhodesian customary law was applied in determining the validity of a marriage of such foreigners in Southern Rhodesia). Guardianship of children of such a marriage has been determined on the principle of the best interests of the children (*Reya Kapita* v. *Zuze*, 1951 S.R.N. 269). However, difficult problems as to guardianship of children where the father comes from a patrilineal tribe entitled to such guardianship and the mother from a matrilineal tribe which considers her entitled to guardianship have not been discussed, rulings having been given that the consequences of marriage must be determined by reference to the *lex loci celebrationis* (see *Kapeta and Mairesi* v. *Mugwagwa*, *supra*), but the ultimate basis being the best interests of the children.

[2] *Sigonquo* v. *Matombi and Pameti*, 1958 S.R.N. 585 where lobolo was reclaimed from an African settled with another tribal group. The rule was laid down that all disputes in such cases should be decided in accordance not with his personal law but with the law of the tribal group with which he was resident. (If the problem were characterized as involving the proprietary consequences of marriage, this decision would be correct as the law of the husband's domicile was applied.)

[3] See the Native Affairs Amendment Act No. 16 of 1958, Section 17(2).

[4] Report of the Secretary for Internal Affairs 1963 (C.S.R. 16–1964, p. 20). The Secretary reports that of 8,812 cases heard in the District Commissioners' Courts in 1963, 3,386 were based on common or mercantile law and 5,426 were based on African customary law.

The Courts of Southern Rhodesia

The most noticeable feature of the system of courts established in Southern Rhodesia is not, as in the United Kingdom, the distinction between civil and criminal courts,[1] but the provision of separate courts for Europeans and for Africans in respect of most civil litigation.

The history of these provisions has been somewhat chequered. When the first magistrates' courts in Southern Rhodesia were established by High Commissioner's Proclamation in 1891, magistrates were precluded from hearing matters in which natives only were concerned unless this was 'necessary in the interests of peace or for the prevention or punishment of acts of violence to persons or property'.[2] However, when in 1894 a High Court of Matabeleland was established and magistrates' courts were set up on a proper basis, these Courts were given jurisdiction over all persons in Southern Rhodesia subject to the provision that in hearing cases involving Africans they might at their discretion summon one or two native assessors to act in a purely advisory capacity.[3] These provisions were repeated in the Southern Rhodesia Order in Council 1898,[4] and when in 1899 Native Commissioners were for the first time permitted judicial powers, they were given jurisdiction over all races similar to that exercised by magistrates.[5]

In 1910 the first differentiation was made when the magisterial jurisdiction exercised by Native Commissioners was confined to Africans only.[6] However both the High Court and magistrates' courts retained concurrent jurisdiction over Africans.

In 1927 a fundamental change occurred when Native Commissioners were given exclusive inferior jurisdiction to hear civil cases between Africans, the magistrates courts' jurisdiction in this respect being abolished.[7] Furthermore Native Commissioners were given exclusive criminal jurisdiction over pro-

[1] Such a distinction was made in 1965 between Regional Courts which exercise only criminal jurisdiction (but in theory may be given civil jurisdiction also) and between courts of provincial and senior magistrates and magistrates which exercise both criminal and civil jurisdiction. See the General Law Amendment Act No. 18 of 1965.

[2] Section 8. Magistrates in hearing such cases had power to call in advisory assessors: Section 11.

[3] Matabeleland Order in Council 1894, Sections 26, 27 and 36.

[4] Sections 49 (1), 50 and 79.

[5] See High Commissioner's Proclamation of 12 June 1899 issued in terms of Section 78(3) of the Southern Rhodesia Order in Council 1898. Nine out of the twenty-four Native Commissioners were appointed as special Justices of the Peace. Previously certain Special Justices of the Peace had been appointed in terms of Cape Act 10 of 1876, which was assumed to be part of the law of the country. The first Special Justice of the Peace was appointed at Tuli on 27 April 1894 (see *Statute Law of Southern Rhodesia, The Charter to 1899*, p. 794). After the appointment of Native Commissioners from 1899, no further appointments of other persons to exercise such powers were made.

[6] High Commissioner's Proclamation No. 55 of 1910, Section 14. In practice since many N.C.'s were also appointed as Assistant Magistrates, they heard European cases.

[7] See Native Affairs Act, Chapter 72 of 1939, Sections 14 and 15. For amendments see Native Affairs Amendment Act No. 14 of 1927.

ceedings for contraventions of the Native Affairs Act.[1] High Court jurisdiction over all persons, however, remained. At this stage, therefore, Africans could go before a completely separate set of inferior courts in respect of criminal offences and were forced to go before these courts in respect of civil cases. This position in fact lasted until 1962 and the differentiation in respect of civil cases still remains.

Yet a further change occurred when in 1937 the African Chiefs and Headmen were for the first time in Southern Rhodesia officially given judicial powers. Although the High Commissioner's Proclamation of 1891 had in Section 10 given the Resident Magistrate power, subject to the High Commissioner's approval, to appoint Chiefs to exercise civil and criminal jurisdiction over the natives, this provision was never utilized. Nor was much use made of the provisions inserted in the 1894 and 1898 Orders in Council for the calling in of native assessors. In practice, however, customary courts continued to operate as they had done before European occupation of the country.[2] This position was to some extent given statutory recognition by the Native Law and Courts Act 1937, which provided for the establishment by Governor's warrant of courts to be held by Chiefs and Headmen which would enjoy a limited civil jurisdiction over Africans only.[3]

Subsequently in 1958, as a consequence of a committee chaired in 1956 by the Southern Rhodesian Chief Justice,[4] magistrates' courts were again given concurrent jurisdiction in civil matters concerning Africans, provided both parties consented thereto, or one of the parties was an African who had been granted a certificate of exemption from customary law.[5] At the same time the extensive civil jurisdiction without any upper monetary limit formerly enjoyed by the Native Commissioners' courts, was put on the same basis as that enjoyed by magistrates.[6]

Finally, in 1963 all criminal jurisdiction, except in respect of contempt of court, was taken away from Native Commissioners (now termed District Commissioners) and criminal jurisdiction in inferior courts was made the exclusive prerogative of magistrates' courts.[7]

[1] Section 15.

[2] See Howman, op. cit., para. 27. At para. 91, the author considered that in 1953 many unauthorized courts were operating. See also the Robinson Report (C.S.R. 22–1961), paras. 81 and 83.

[3] See infra. The Native Law and Courts Act has since the Revised Edition of the Statutes 1963 been designed as the African Law and Courts Act. The same applies to the former Native Affairs Act and other Acts in which the word 'native' was used. There may in the text, therefore, be occasions on which reference is made to 'African' and others in which reference is made to 'native'.

[4] Report of the Committee on Inferior Courts in Southern Rhodesia 1956.

[5] Magistrates Court Amendment Act No. 4 of 1958, Section 4. Africans licensed under the Licence Control Act may litigate on contracts arising out of businesses to which their licenses relate: Magistrates Court Amendment Act 1965, Section 2(a).

[6] Native Affairs Amendment Act No. 16 of 1958, Section 3.

[7] Native Affairs Amendment Act No. 22 of 1963. This resulted from the Robinson Report's recommendations, supra, and agreement at the 1961 Constitutional Conference.

The position at present[1] is that the same criminal courts enjoy jurisdiction over all races viz. the High Court and the magistrates' court, but in civil matters unless Africans consent to the jurisdiction, hold business licences, or have been exempted there are different inferior courts—the magistrates' court for Europeans and the District Commissioners' and Chiefs' courts for Africans. In addition the system of appeal is different, as an additional court of appeal, the Court of Appeal for African civil cases, formerly the Native Appeal Court, is interposed in the case of Africans, who must first proceed through this Court before they may appeal to the Appellate Division of the High Court, whereas Europeans may go on appeal to the latter Court directly from the magistrates' court.

Another distinctive feature of the Southern Rhodesian legal system is that in the case of criminal trials in the superior courts a modified jury system is available to non-Africans, whereas Africans have no right to trial by jury.[2] Furthermore non-Europeans (Africans, Asians, and Coloureds) are not eligible for membership of juries.

The Magistrates' Courts

The main inferior civil and criminal courts of Southern Rhodesia, the magistrates' courts, were first established in 1891 and reconstituted in 1894, 1898, 1911, and 1931, during which time and also on subsequent occasions their powers were increased, extended, and redefined. At present they are governed by the Magistrates' Court Act (Chapter 15).

Magistrates' courts are established for each province[3] or regional division[4] by the Minister of Justice, who determines the number of courts required and then by notice in the Government Gazette specifies the places where such courts are to be held.[5] In July 1965 there were seven provincial magistrates' courts and three regional courts for Southern Rhodesia.[6] In addition the

---

[1] November 1965. Proposals have been made that Chiefs should be given criminal jurisdiction in minor matters involving Africans. A similar suggestion was rejected by the Robinson Commission, *supra*, para. 187 and by the Report of the Committee on Inferior Courts in Southern Rhodesia, para. 20. It is nonetheless being pursued by the Government and a draft Tribal Law and Courts Bill was prepared, but ran into difficulties in view of the provisions against discrimination in the Declaration of Rights (Section 67): see Report of the Secretary for Internal Affairs for the year 1963. Government Printer, Salisbury, C.S.R. 16–1964, p. 3.

[2] See *infra*.

[3] Provinces are administrative units created in terms of the General Administration Act No. 19 of 1962. There are seven administrative provinces in Southern Rhodesia in which Government Departments are regionally organized. The provinces are divided into a total of fifty districts. See S.R.G.N. 254 and 255 of 1963.

[4] Regional divisions are created by the Minister of Justice from one or more provinces or portions of provinces: General Law Amendment Act 1965, Section 4(1).

[5] Magistrates' Court Act, Chapter 15, Sections 4 and 5 as amended.

[6] There are regional courts at Salisbury, Bulawayo, and a third circuiting court which visits Umtali, Gwelo, Fort Victoria, and Sinoia.

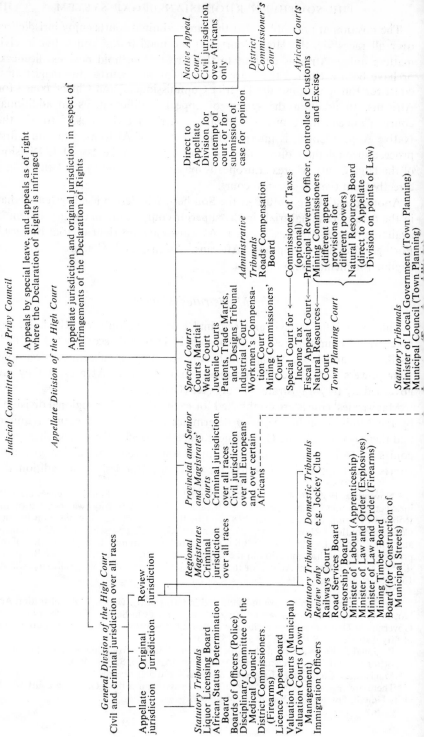

FIGURE 1

Southern Rhodesian Legal System as at 31 October 1965

provincial courts may from time to time sit at another place appointed for the periodical holding of such courts.[1]

The courts are staffed by a chief magistrate, regional magistrates, provincial magistrates, senior magistrates, magistrates, and persons acting in these capacities.[2]

Provision exists for the Minister of Justice, with the approval of the Chief Justice to appoint a chief magistrate of Southern Rhodesia and regional magistrates. The Minister may without approval, but after consultation, appoint senior magistrates, from whose ranks provincial magistrates may be appointed. However, the appointment of mere magistrates requires neither the approval of nor consultation with the Chief Justice.[3] The designation of office is important since powers of sentence in criminal cases depend on the post occupied by the magistrate. Thus sentencing powers enjoyed by provincial or senior magistrates are double those enjoyed by magistrates,[4] while regional magistrates can exercise even more extensive powers.[5]

Provision has recently been made whereby a magistrate may before any evidence has been led, in any criminal trial, provided he obtains the approval of the Minister of Justice, summon to his assistance one or two assessors who have in his opinion experience in the administration of justice or skill in any matter which may have to be considered at the trial.[6] In cases where the

---

[1] Chapter 15, Section 3. This provides for something akin to a circuit system for the remote areas. There are seventy periodical courts held at different villages in the country.

[2] Chapter 15, Section 3, definition of 'magistrate' as amended by the General Law Amendment Act 1965, Section 3.

[3] Chapter 15, Section 7B.

[4] Chapter 15, Section 49(2)(a) and 3(a). In summary trials magistrates' jurisdiction is six months' imprisonment and/or a fine of £50 and/or a whipping of ten strokes, which may be combined with imprisonment but not with a fine. Only in the case of persons under nineteen years of age may a whipping be administered in combination with a fine: Chapter 31, Section 374. A recent change in the law allows whipping of a juvenile to be combined with a suspended sentence. In the case of senior or provincial magistrates the jurisdiction is increased to twelve months' imprisonment and a fine of £100. In the event of a remittal to a magistrate's court after a preparatory examination has been held, the sentencing powers of all magistrates are doubled: Sections (2)(b) and (3)(b). Legislation sometimes confers special powers of sentence, e.g. the Law and Order (Maintenance) Act (Chapter 39), Section 58(1) authorizes magistrates on summary trial to impose a £500 fine or three years' imprisonment, and empowers regional, provincial, or senior magistrates to impose a £1,000 fine and/or five years' imprisonment. In certain cases Section 59(1) read with the Second Schedule to this Act requires a senior, provincial, or regional magistrate to impose a minimum sentence of five years' imprisonment. Again the Protected Places and Areas Act (Chapter 76), authorizes such magistrates to impose a £1,000 fine and/or five years' imprisonment. The chief magistrate possesses the powers and jurisdiction of a regional magistrate in a regional division and of a provincial magistrate in any province: Chapter 15, Section 7C(1).

[5] Regional magistrates may either in summary trials or on remittal impose sentences of imprisonment for five years, fines not exceeding £500 and whippings not exceeding twelve strokes: Chapter 15, Section 49(4) as amended by the General Law Amendment Act 1965, Section 6(a).

[6] Magistrates' Court Amendment Act 1964, Section 2.

magistrate invokes this provision he remains sole judge of law, but on matters of fact the finding of a majority of members of the court is to be its finding.[1] In questions of sentence the magistrate may consult assessors, but the sole responsibility remains his.[2]

Magistrates' jurisdiction in criminal cases

The jurisdiction enjoyed by magistrates in criminal cases is of a fourfold character: they enjoy summary jurisdiction in less serious cases; they hold preparatory examinations to investigate allegations that an accused has committed a serious crime; they conduct, after the holding of a preparatory examination, trials on remittal by the Attorney-General either under their ordinary or increased jurisdiction[3]; and they may sentence accused persons who at their preparatory examination have pleaded guilty and have been remitted to them for sentence by the Attorney-General after he has considered the record of the preparatory examination.[4]

In respect of summary trials generally only crimes committed within the province or the regional division or within two miles of its boundaries fall within the jurisdiction of the court, but special provision exists that if the offence was begun or completed or one of the elements of the crime was committed within the province or regional division the court shall have jurisdiction.[5] All crimes except treason and murder and those where by statute a mandatory death penalty is imposed are within the jurisdiction, but except in the case of a regional magistrate who can try rape cases summarily, rape can only be tried on remittal by the Attorney-General after a preparatory examination has been held.[6] If, however, on summary trial, it appears to the court that from its nature the case is more proper for the cognisance of the High Court, or the public prosecutor so requests, the magistrate must stop

---

[1] ibid., Section 2(3)(d) 'provided that when only one assessor sits the decision . . . of the magistrate shall be the decision . . . of the court'.

[2] ibid., Section 2(3)(e).

[3] Criminal Procedure and Evidence Act (Chapter 31), Section 96(1)(d) and (e). When an accused had been remitted to be tried under the increased jurisdiction, he could formerly demand, when required to plead, that his case should be tried before the High Court: Section 244(1). After a ruling by the High Court that the Attorney-General could not seek to deprive an accused of this right by revoking a notice to try him under the increased jurisdiction and substituting a notice of trial under the ordinary jurisdiction—*Sibiya* v. *R.*, 1963 R. & N. 421—the section giving this right was repealed by the General Law Amendment Act 1965, Section 27.

[4] Chapter 31, Section 96(f) and (f1), and Sections 166 and 242.

[5] Chapter 15, Section 52, as amended. The section contains other provisions extending the jurisdiction. Thus if it is expedient owing to the number of accused or with a view to avoiding excessive inconvenience or the disturbance of public order the Attorney-General may in writing direct trial at a specified place and time in any province or regional division: Section 52(9) read with Section 90(5)(a) of Chapter 31.

[6] Chapter 15, Section 49(6). On remittal to the court of other magistrates such trial must take place under the increased jurisdiction: Chapter 31, Section 96(1)(e).

the proceedings, remand the accused, and submit a report to the Attorney-General together with a copy of the record.[1] The Attorney-General may either direct that the proceedings be converted into a preparatory examination, that the case be continued by the magistrate, or that the proceedings be commenced afresh in the Court of a regional magistrate.[2]

When a serious crime has been committed, or it is considered desirable that the accused (often with a long list of convictions) should come before the High Court, which has unlimited powers of sentence, a preparatory examination is held. Again, preparatory examinations are held in the province where the crime or some of its elements has been committed, but the Attorney-General may in special cases authorize the preparatory examination to be held in another magisterial province.[3] The procedure is similar to the preliminary enquiry of English law, as the accused is not on trial and the Crown case against him is disclosed. However, the Attorney-General at any stage during a preparatory examination, whether or not any evidence has been led, may serve notice on the accused of his intention to indict the accused for trial before the High Court on a specified offence. Such notice is also served on the magistrate who shall then forthwith commit the accused for trial and grant a warrant for his committal. This section could be applied so as in effect to deny an accused the opportunity of having a full preparatory examination. However, when this is invoked the Crown must inform the accused of the names of the witnesses it intends calling and give a brief summary of the evidence it intends leading.[4] At the end of the preparatory examination the magistrate may either discharge the accused, commit him for further examination, commit him for trial, or, if the accused has confessed, for sentence.[5] Thereafter the Attorney-General will decide whether to prosecute the accused, and if so whether to indict him in the High Court for trial or sentence or to remit the accused to the magistrate's court either under the increased or the ordinary jurisdiction, to the court of a regional magistrate who conducted the preparatory examination, or to that of another regional magistrate for fresh trial.[6]

On remittal, trial is conducted in the same way as if it were a summary trial, with the difference that where the magistrate is the same magistrate who conducted the preparatory examination, it is sufficient to hand in the depositions of witnesses made at the preparatory examination.[7] In certain circum-

---

[1] Chapter 15, Section 51(1) as amended.

[2] Chapter 31, Section 260A.

[3] Criminal Procedure and Evidence Act (Chapter 31), Section 90 as amended.

[4] Section 106 of Chapter 31. This section had within a short period of its introduction been invoked on eleven occasions: *S.R.L.A.D.*, Vol. 60, col. 746, 12 March 1965. Allegations were made during debate that the section would be used in such a way as virtually to eliminate preparatory examinations.

[5] Chapter 31, Sections 83, 84, 85, and 88.

[6] Chapter 31, Section 96. He may also direct the reopening of the preparatory examination.

[7] Chapter 31, Section 243(2).

stances where witnesses at the preparatory examination are not available, their depositions may be put in.[1] If remitted for sentence on a plea of guilty, the accused may be sentenced without any further evidence unless he desires to adduce evidence which the court may or may not permit.[2]

Magistrates' civil jurisdiction

Provincial magistrates, senior magistrates and magistrates may exercise civil jurisdiction, but courts of regional magistrates have no jurisdiction in civil matters except as may be specially provided.[3]

In general, magistrates' civil jurisdiction is confined to cases concerning Europeans (which term includes all non-Africans) only, or to cases between a European and an African.[4] The court's jurisdiction is also limited to persons resident, employed, or carrying on business within the province, to persons who have themselves initiated proceedings, to partners whose business premises are situated within the province or whose partner resides therein, and to cases where the cause of action arose wholly within the province.[5] The courts may adjudicate on matters where the amount in dispute is not in excess of £200, where ejectment is claimed, provided the value of the right of occupation is not in excess of this sum, and in cases where claims are made on liquid documents to an amount of £500 and any interest due thereon.[6] Jurisdiction is increased by provisions permitting the parties to agree by a signed memorandum to give the court a greater jurisdiction, by allowing a party to abandon part of his claim to bring the matter within the jurisdiction, and by permitting the court to try any matter for the balance of an account even if the whole matter if tried would have been beyond the jurisdiction.[7]

Jurisdiction is expressly prohibited in cases where divorce or judicial separation is sought, the validity or interpretation of testaments is involved, the status of persons relative to mental capacity will be affected, specific performance is claimed unless accompanied by an alternative claim for payment of damages except in cases where the value of the property claimed does

---

[1] Chapter 31, Section 287(1). This applies when a witness is dead, ill, or kept away by the accused.

[2] Section 242.

[3] Chapter 15, Section 7 as amended.

[4] If both parties are Africans over whom the court has jurisdiction, it may nonetheless transfer the matter to the District Commissioner's court: Chapter 15, Section 10(3).

[5] Chapter 15, Section 10(1)(a).

[6] Chapter 15, Section 10(1)(b).

[7] Chapter 15, Section 10(1)(e), (h), (j). The magistrate's court is a creature of statute and has no jurisdiction beyond the statute creating it. It has no inherent jurisdiction such as that possessed by the High Court: *Hatfield Town Management Board* v. *Mynfred Poultry Farm (Pvt.) Ltd.*, 1962 R. & N. 799.

not exceed £200, a decree of perpetual silence is sought, provisional sentence is claimed,[1] and where rights in future can be bound.[2]

There is considerable advantage in being able to pursue matters in the magistrates' court, since cases are brought to trial relatively more speedily than in the High Court. Furthermore, there are magistrates' courts in all the larger towns of Southern Rhodesia whereas the High Court sits for the most part in Salisbury or Bulawayo, and even its circuits are restricted to Umtali, Fort Victoria, and Gwelo. Finally, the scale of costs is far lower in a magistrate's court, where attorneys have rights of audience, than in the High Court, where it is necessary to employ both an advocate and an attorney unless the litigant appears in person.[3]

The General Division of the High Court

Since 1894 when the High Court of Matabeleland was established, which was thereafter succeeded to by the High Court of Southern Rhodesia in 1898 in terms of the Order in Council of that year, there has been a High Court exercising jurisdiction over all persons and all matters in Southern Rhodesia. The High Court was safeguarded in the Southern Rhodesia Constitution 1961, which in a specially entrenched provision dealt with the constitution and powers of the Court, matters which had previously been dealt with only in the High Court Act (Chapter 8 of 1939). Subsequently in 1964 the Constitution was amended to provide that there should be a General Division of the High Court, which would be 'a superior court of record with full jurisdiction, civil and criminal, over all persons and over all matters within Southern Rhodesia' and an Appellate Division, which would have powers conferred upon it by the Constitution and by law of the Legislature.[4] The reason for the establishment of the Appellate Division was the necessity after Federal dissolution to create a court of appeal in Southern Rhodesia to replace the Federal Supreme Court.[5]

[1] Provisional sentence or namptissement is a speedy remedy afforded by the Roman–Dutch Law to the possessor of a liquid document who is entitled to obtain a provisional judgement and the right of immediate execution, subject to the right, for one month, of the defendant to force the plaintiff to go to trial on the matter, provided that the defendant has paid the plaintiff in full, the latter being bound to give security for restitution. It is dealt with in the Rules of the High Court, Order 4. See also J. Herbstein and L. de V. van Winsen, *Civil Practice of the Superior Courts in South Africa*, Juta, 1954.

[2] Reference here is to permanent definitions of status, such as married status, legitimacy, &c.: see Section 12.

[3] It seems that a company cannot appear 'in person' through the medium of a representative: *S.A. Cultivators (Pty.) Ltd. v. Flange Engineering Co. (Pty.) Ltd.*, 1962 (3) S.A. 156.

[4] Southern Rhodesia Constitution, Sections 50, 52(3), and 53(3).

[5] The Southern Rhodesian Government, prior to dissolution, introduced a Bill to make this provision, but objections were made that a constitutional amendment was required (*S.R.L.A.D.*, Vol. 55, cols. 898 et seq. and 1033 et seq.) to give the court any greater status than that of a statutory tribunal. It might well have been that the appointment of such a tribunal would have been held to be an unconstitutional encroachment upon the judicial power which was reserved to the High Court in terms of the Constitution: see *Bribery*

The Government however declined to set up an entirely separate appeal court on financial grounds,[1] and the analogy of the Court of Criminal Appeal in the United Kingdom was used to justify the division of the High Court.[2]

The General Division of the High Court is the old High Court in another guise except that for the most part it has been shorn of appellate powers which it previously possessed in respect of appeals from magistrates' courts, special courts, and the majority of special statutory tribunals, these powers having been transferred to the Appellate Division. Its main functions therefore are the exercise of original civil and criminal jurisdiction and revisory jurisdiction. However, it still hears appeals from a small number of statutory tribunals.

The seat of the High Court and its principal registry is at Salisbury, but there is a branch at Bulawayo, while judges from Salisbury proceed on circuit to Umtali and Fort Victoria, and the Bulawayo High Court has sessions in Gwelo.[3]

The General Division is composed of the Chief Justice, and such puisne judges as may from time to time be appointed, there at present being six puisne judges who sit with the Chief Justice. In addition the Judge President of the Appellate Division and the Judge of Appeal may sit with the consent of the Judge President, although this has not occurred in practice.[4]

In exercising its original jurisdiction in civil cases the Court hears matters beyond the jurisdiction of magistrates' and District Commissioners' courts (in the latter case enforcing customary law in so far as it is not inapplicable or repugnant). It may also hear matters within the jurisdiction of such courts, although, unless the 'action from its nature or circumstances was fit to be brought' in the High Court, such action is sanctioned by special provisions as to costs.[5] The only limitation on its powers is in relation to the original jurisdiction granted to the Appellate Division by Section 71(4) of the Constitution to hear applications relating to infringement of the Declaration of Rights.

The High Court normally sits when dealing with civil cases as a one-judge

Commissioner v. Ranasinghe, [1964] 2 W.L.R. 1301. The Government withdrew the measure, but in 1964 secured constitutional amendments to permit the creation of the appellate division. If the reasoning in Bribery Commissioner v. Ranasinghe is correct it would not be possible to remove aspects of its jurisdiction from the High Court and confer these on a special tribunal, e.g. to create a special court for treason trials or sabotage trials.

[1] S.R.L.A.D., Vol. 55, col. 888, 10 December 1963.

[2] There are, however, considerable practical differences owing to the small number of judges in Southern Rhodesia and also because they are also judges of fact, the jury system rarely coming into operation. The new Appellate Division of the High Court not only acts as a court of criminal appeal but is also the court of civil appeal.

[3] This is done in terms of Section 45 of the High Court Act which provides that the General Division shall sit at such times and such places as may be directed by the Chief Justice.

[4] Section 53(1) of the Constitution.

[5] Chapter 15, Section 38. The High Court may on the application of a defendant transfer a case for trial to a magistrate's court if the plaintiff is unlikely to be able to pay costs (Chapter 15, Section 16) and may also remit cases in forma pauperis unless jurisdiction in the issues at stake is denied to the magistrate's court.

court. However, if difficult matters of law arise, more than one judge may sit, and the Chief Justice has the right to direct that such matter shall proceed before a larger number of judges.[1]

There is no jury system in civil trials. For the most part procedure is similar to that in the United Kingdom—the High Court Rules are very similar to the Cape Colony Supreme Court Rules, which were originally modelled on English procedure and were first promulgated on 1 September 1829. English authorities on procedure are frequently cited. However, remedies such as provisional sentence (the nearest English equivalent being summary judgement, which is also available in Southern Rhodesia), wider powers of attachment to found jurisdiction, and wider powers of imprisonment for debt exist. Perhaps the major procedural difference is that there are no officials who are the equivalent of Masters so that preliminary orders and decisions on interlocutory matters are given by the Judges in many cases in Chambers. In recent years proceedings by way of notice of motion have to a great extent displaced trial proceedings.[2]

Criminal trials in the High Court

When exercising its original criminal jurisdiction, the composition of the Court depends on whether the accused is an African or a European. Prior to 1927 Africans were subject to trial by Ordinary Jury just as most Europeans were, but in this year the judge and assessors system was introduced by the Criminal Trials (High Court) Act. If the accused is an African, the trial is conducted before a judge and two assessors selected by the judge from persons who are or have been Native Commissioners (now District Commissioners) for a period of not less than ten years.[3] In such trials whereas the judge is sole judge of law and decides whether a matter is one of law or fact and also has sole responsibility for sentence, the decision of a majority of the members of a court on questions of fact is to be the finding of the court.[4]

Where the accused is a European, he is normally tried by a judge and an Ordinary Jury. The principles of trial by jury have, however, been departed from in two respects in Southern Rhodesia: a jury consists only of nine

[1] High Court Act No. 22 of 1964, Section 30(4). Cases concerning interpretation of wills, or cases where there have previously been conflicting decisions are those in which at least two judges sit in practice. Section 30(1) provides that the majority decision shall be that of the court, but Section 30(2)(b) states that if the court is equally divided a third judge must be called in.

[2] See G. Findlay, Application versus Trial (1951), 68 *S.A.L.J.* 20.

[3] See Chapter 31, Section 223. If Africans are charged jointly with Europeans who do not agree to trial by assessors, they are then triable by jury: Section 228. No such trials have been held.

[4] Chapter 31, Section 225. The system is quite different from that of the purely advisory assessors who are called in by judges in former British African Territories: see J. D. Jearey, 'Trial by Jury and Trial with the Aid of Assessors in the Superior Courts of British African Territories' (1961), *J.A.L.*, Vol. 5, pp. 36, 82.

jurors, who must be European male citizens with property qualifications (equivalent to the 1951 franchise requirements)[1]; and a jury can return a majority verdict of seven to two after it has deliberated for at least two hours.[2]

A further departure was occasioned by the unsatisfactory nature of early jury trials in which the accused had been charged with committing a serious offence against an African.[3] From 1912 Special Juries have been required to sit where the accused is a European charged with murder, culpable homicide, rape, robbery, or an attempt to commit any of these crimes or with an assault with any special intent in respect of an African.[4] A Special Jury is composed of five jurors only, who are chosen from a list of persons designated by the Governor and approved by the Legislative Assembly.[5] Again a majority verdict may be given, in this case by four to one after deliberation of not less than two hours.[6]

From an analysis of ordinary and special jury trials it is interesting to note that there is a greater tendency to acquit or alternatively convict the accused of a less serious offence than that charged when the offence has been committed against an African than there is when he has committed an offence against a non-African.[7]

Provision also exists if sufficient qualified jurors for either an Ordinary or Special Jury trial are not available, for the judge to call in up to four advisory assessors who may be persons of either African or European descent. In the event of this provision being utilized, the judge is to be sole judge of law and

---

[1] Chapter 31, Section 174. Prior to 1908, every male registered voter who could read or write was qualified to be a juror (Sections 2 and 7 of Ordinance 4 of 1899). No Africans were ever summoned in practice. In 1908 Section 2 of the Jury Law Amendment Ordinance No. 10 of 1908 inserted the provision that jurors should be European. The Constitutional Council in its 34th Report of 11 September 1964 considered that this section derogates from the status of Asians and Coloureds as they may be tried by jury but may not sit on a jury.

[2] Chapter 31, Sections 171, 204. These provisions were also inserted by Ordinance No. 10 of 1908, Sections 3 and 5. From 1958 to 1964 there were only 32 ordinary jury trials: S.R.L.A.D., Vol. 58, col. 1370, 7 October 1964.

[3] See *supra*, Part I, Chapter 8.

[4] Chapter 31, Section 216. These provisions were originally inserted in Ordinance 13 of 1912.

[5] Chapter 31, Sections 217 and 218. In practice such juries are usually composed of men of substance who are well known citizens, often with a commercial background. There are at present 216 special jurors for the country: S.R.G.N. 721/64.

[6] Section 217. From 1958 to 1964 there have been only nine special jury trials: S.R.L.A.D., Vol. 58, col. 1370. A further joint trial was held in October 1964 subsequent to the statement in Hansard.

[7] See S.R.L.A.D., Vol. 58, cols. 1711–12, 14 October 1964. In thirty-two ordinary jury trials between 1958 to 1964, four accused were acquitted, nineteen were convicted as charged, and nine were convicted in terms of sections of the Criminal Procedure and Evidence Act which permit the return of other verdicts. However in nine special jury trials involving ten accused, five were acquitted, one was convicted as charged and four others were convicted on verdicts of having committed less serious offences than those charged. Thus in the case of Special Juries there has been a 50 per cent acquittal rate but in the case of Ordinary Juries only a 12·5 per cent rate.

fact and any dissent of the assessors is merely to be recorded.[1] This is similar to the provision for trial by assessors in former British African Territories. However, the provision is academic, since it has apparently not been used since 1899.[2]

Notwithstanding these provisions for jury trial, any non-African may elect to be tried by a judge and two assessors. In such event the assessors are selected by the judge from persons who have experience in the administration of justice or skill in matters to be considered at the trial. Such assessors are judges of fact jointly with the judge, decisions being taken by a majority.[3] In practice this is the method of trial most frequently employed in the case of non-Africans.[4]

The modifications in the jury system and the introduction of the system of trial by judge and assessors is perhaps the most notable procedural difference between the English and Southern Rhodesian systems of criminal procedure. The reason for similarity in other respects is that criminal procedure is based on the English model. English criminal procedure was first adopted by the Cape Colony in 1828,[5] while the English law of evidence is observed except as modified by statute.[6] Furthermore, preparatory examinations are conducted in the same fashion as are preliminary enquiries and the *cursus curiae* is similar. All proceedings are held in open court,[7] and the accused must be present.[8]

---

[1] Chapter 31, Sections 172, 173, and 221. The provision for advisory assessors has survived from Ordinance No. 4 of 1899. It had previously been in the High Commissioner's Proclamation of 23 July 1895 (see *Statute Law from the Charter to 1899*, p. 105). From 1895 to 1899 prior to the introduction of jury trial in Southern Rhodesia, the High Court judge had sat with advisory assessors in criminal cases.

[2] Report No. 34 of the Constitutional Council, para. 8.

[3] Chapter 31, Sections 222 and 225. On rare occasions judges have been in the minority. The provision for judge and assessors to sit was first made by the Criminal Trials (High Court) Act No. 18 of 1927.

[4] Whereas in 1959 there were eight jury trials, there were 157 trials of non-Africans by judge and assessors. In 1960 there were seven jury trials as opposed to 136 by judge and assessors: see Report of the Secretary for Justice and Internal Affairs, C.S.R. 9–1961, read with *S.R.L.A.D.*, Vol. 58, col. 1370.

[5] The Criminal Procedure Ordinance No. 40 of 1828 as amended by Ordinance No. 73 of 1830. Rules of Court made provision for trial procedure.

[6] See Criminal Procedure and Evidence Act, Chapter 31, numerous sections of which expressly state that the test for admissibility is whether evidence would be admissible in a similar case depending in the Supreme Court of Judicature in England. These provisions were first introduced in the Cape by Ordinance No. 72 of 1830.

[7] In limited circumstances the Court may be cleared: Chapter 31, section 232(4) allows the General Division to clear a court whenever it thinks fit, but inferior courts may do so only if it appears to the court that it would be in the interests of good order or public morals or of the administration of justice that a trial should be held behind closed doors. Sections 232(7) and (9) provide for the exclusion of the public when a person under the age of nineteen years is on trial or is giving evidence.

[8] If the accused so misconducts himself that it is impossible to continue in his presence the court may order his removal and the trial can proceed in his absence: Chapter 31, Section 232(1). In *Matimba* v. *Aylward N.O. & R.*, 1962 R. & N. 571 a conviction was set

A major point of difference is that all prosecutions are initiated either by the Attorney-General, by a member of his staff, or by a public prosecutor attached to an inferior court as the Attorney-General's representative.[1] Only if the Attorney-General declines to prosecute may a private prosecution be brought and this differs from the English private prosecution in that not only is it brought in the name of the individual bringing the prosecution, but only a person who can show some substantial and peculiar interest which he individually has suffered from the commission of an offence may bring such proceedings. However, the protection afforded injured individuals is wider, since the Crown, by issuing a nolle prosequi cannot prevent such proceedings being brought.[2]

Another difference in trial procedure is that the prosecutor sums up the Crown case at the end of all the evidence and thereafter the accused or his legal representative may address the court. Only if a new matter of law is raised by the accused or his representative may the prosecutor reply, and even then he is confined to that matter of law. Accordingly the accused normally has the last word, whether or not he adduces evidence.[3]

Yet a further difference from the English position is that special provisions exist for the purpose of prosecuting corporations and associations, and these effectively impose vicarious liability on corporations for the acts of their servants and directors in advancing or attempting to further the interests of the corporation or association in the performance of their powers and duties.[4] These provisions also impose individual liability on all persons and servants of corporations and members of associations unless it is proved that such persons did not take part in the commission of any offence committed by the corporation or association.[5] Again, the court's power to award compensation payable by the accused to victims is wider.[6] Finally, the powers of sentence of the court in respect of corporal punishment are very wide, applying to all common law offences and to numerous statutory offences, e.g. to all offences

aside when the court proceeded with a trial in which, after an unsuccessful application that the Magistrate should recuse himself, the accused had then left the court. An exceptional procedure exists whereby an enquiry may be conducted and persons may be required to give evidence on pain of committal to prison for seven days despite the fact that no accused person is before the court. Chapter 31, Section 102(1) allows magistrates a discretion to require the attendance of any person who is likely to give material evidence as to any supposed offence whether or not it be known or suspected by whom the offence has been committed. However it is the duty of magistrates to ensure that members of the public are not unduly harassed by inquisitions: *Parker* v. *R.*, *The Times*, 22 December 1965.

[1] Chapter 31, Sections 9, 11, 13, and 18.

[2] Indeed a *nolle prosequi* is a condition precedent to the bringing of such action, the Attorney-General being required to give a certificate that he declines to prosecute: Chapter 31, Section 22. The only way for the Crown to prevent a private prosecution would be to exercise the prerogative of pardon.

[3] Chapter 31, Section 236.

[4] Section 401(1).

[5] Section 401(5) and (7).

[6] Section 386—up to £200.

committed under the Law and Order (Maintenance) Act.[1] On the other hand the courts have lost much of their discretion in sentencing offenders who have committed offences against 'public order' as the Law and Order (Maintenance) Act specified that minimum sentences must be imposed when certain sections of that Act have been breached.[2]

In certain circumstances, apart from cases heard on appeal or review, where sentences are not lightly altered, the High Court may sentence accused persons who have not appeared before them for trial. This occurs when such an accused has been convicted, but, before sentence has been passed, the magistrate, being of the opinion that the accused has previous convictions and that a sentence in excess of his jurisdiction is justified, has adjourned the case and reported on the proceedings to the Attorney-General. The Attorney-General may then direct that the case be transferred to the General Division for sentence, in which event, if a judge in chambers considers the proceedings to be in accordance with real and substantial justice, he shall cause the accused to be brought before him in open court to receive sentence at his hands.[3] Furthermore, if an accused has on the direction of the Attorney-General been committed for sentence to the High Court, after having pleaded guilty at a preparatory examination, the Court may enter a plea of guilty if the accused fails to plead guilty and may sentence him without hearing any evidence.[4]

Review jurisdiction

Powers of reviewing the proceedings of administrative tribunals, public authorities and officials, domestic tribunals, and of inferior courts of law are vested in the General Division of the High Court wherever such tribunals,

---

[1] Chapter 39, Section 60.

[2] See Chapter 39, Section 26 (intimidation), 28 (boycotting), 45 (throwing articles at motor vehicles), 37 (injuring or attempting to injure or set fire to persons or residential or occupied property by the use of inflammable liquid or explosives—the death penalty), and certain other common law offences such as arson, malicious injury to property, or theft, if the charge has been instituted on the written authority of the Attorney-General (Section 59, Second Schedule). Sir Robert Tredgold, the Federal Chief Justice, resigned in protest when this Act was passed stating that 'it outraged almost every basic human right and is an unwarranted invasion by the Executive of the sphere of the Courts'. Statement of 1 November 1960 reported in the *Rhodesia Herald*.

[3] Chapter 15, Section 51(2), and Chapter 31, Section 260A(b). Where an accused is in such circumstances brought before the judge he shall not be called upon to plead to the charge but shall be dealt with as if he had been convicted by the General Division of the offence concerned: Section 260C. Another occasion on which sentence may be passed on an accused despite the fact that the presiding officer did not try the accused arises in terms of Section 358(5) of Chapter 31, where it is provided that in the magistrates' court if the judicial officer who convicted the accused is absent any other judicial officer, after consideration of his record, may pass sentence on the offender. However, in the magistrates' court less serious offences are under consideration.

[4] Chapter 31, Sections 96(1)(b), 166, and 301(a).

officials, or inferior courts[1] are guilty of irregularity or illegality in the performance of their duties. The source of such review is not to be traced in the Roman–Dutch Law,[2] although the High Court with reference to review of the proceedings of public bodies has spoken of its 'indisputable common law power . . .'.[3] The true explanation of review powers is twofold. Review power of the proceedings of public bodies is inherent in the full jurisdiction 'over all persons and all matters within Southern Rhodesia', which is conferred upon the General Division of High Court of Section 53 of the Constitution.[4] Secondly, Section 31(1) of the High Court Act No. 22 of 1964 provides that

The general division shall have power, jurisdiction, and authority to review all proceedings of all inferior courts of justice and tribunals established by law within Southern Rhodesia.[5]

Review is clearly to be distinguished from appeal as the characteristic of review is that it attacks the method of reaching the decision and not its merits, with the reservation that even though the procedure may have been success-fully impugned in criminal cases a conviction or sentence may not be quashed unless the court considers that 'a substantial miscarriage of justice has actu-ally occurred'.[6]

Review proceedings are initiated by application on notice of motion sup-ported by affidavits as to the facts justifying review.[7] These proceedings are the Roman–Dutch equivalent of an application for an order of certiorari. Control over administrators, inferior courts, and tribunals can also be exercised either by prohibitory or mandatory interdicts, and Clayden F.J. has held that the interdict in its prohibitory and mandatory sense 'is sub-stantially the equivalent' of injunction, mandamus, and prohibition.[8] It is also possible for the Courts to grant a declaratory order as 'the General

---

[1] There is no review of High Court proceedings, the only remedy being an appeal: *Ex parte Scott* (1909), 26 Juta 520.

[2] *Ellis* v. *Morgan*, 1909 T.S. 576 at 583 per Mason J.

[3] *L. and B. Holdings* v. *Mashonaland Rent Appeal Board*, 1959 (3) S.A. 466 (S.R.) at 468 per Murray C.J.

[4] This provision was formerly in Section 2 of the High Court Act, Chapter 8 of 1939. See *Pilossof* v. *Greenfield N.O.*, 1951 (2) S.A. 525 (S.R.) at 526 and *Johannesburg Consoli-dated Investment Co.* v. *Johannesburg City Council*, 1903 T.S. 111 per Innes C.J. at 115: 'It is a right inherent in the Court which has jurisdiction to entertain all civil causes and proceedings. Non-performance or wrong performance of a statutory duty by which third persons are injured or aggrieved is such a cause as falls within the ordinary jurisdiction of the Court.' *Contra*, L. A. Rose Innes, *Judicial Review of Administrative Tribunals in South Africa*, Juta, 1963, pp. 7–8, and 18. It would be more correct to say that the principles upon which such review will be granted have been evolved by the Courts independently of statute and to this extent review is governed by common law.

[5] This section formerly related only to inferior courts of justice: see Section 15 of the High Court Act, Chapter 8 of 1939.

[6] High Court Act, Section 31(2) proviso.

[7] Rules of the High Court, O.25, R. 6.

[8] *Codron* v. *Macintyre & Another*, 1960 (3) S.A. 419 (F.C.) at 414. The term *mandamus* is used in Roman–Dutch practice.

Division may, in its discretion, at the instance of any interested person, enquire into and determine any existing, future, or contingent right or obligation, notwithstanding that such person cannot obtain any relief consequent upon such determination'.[1] However, there is no question of any relator action being available as in English law, or any question of the Court having jurisdiction to grant an injunction or declaration at the suit of the Attorney-General in his capacity as guardian of the public interest.[2] Nor is the *actio popularis* of the Roman–Dutch Law available as this is obsolete.[3]

It seems that in general the requirements for *locus standi* in review proceedings are more generous in Roman–Dutch than in English Law, since the interest required of an applicant on review need not be more special than that of other members of the public, provided he has a direct personal interest.[4] Differences of interpretation between South African and Rhodesian courts have arisen in respect of *locus standi* in suits following conduct prohibited by statute. In *Patz* v. *Greene & Co.*[5] it was held that any member of the public who can prove damage is entitled to seek the intervention of the Courts to enforce such a prohibition by interdict or may claim relief by way of review or an action for damages. However Clayden F.J. in *Salisbury Bottling Co. (Pvt.) Ltd.* v. *Central African Bottling Co. (Pvt.) Ltd.* held that not only was it necessary for such an applicant to have suffered damages in order to be entitled to claim an interdict[6] but that also mere breach of the statute and damage were insufficient unless 'proceedings for an interdict were a remedy contemplated by the Act'.[7] He considered a declaration of rights would not be available either, but thought that a private prosecution might be competent.[8]

Statutory exclusion of the High Court's power of review has been effected

---

[1] High Court Act 1964, Section 33. This remedy was first introduced in 1956 by Section 19 of Chapter 8 of 1939 as amended by Section 3 of Act 25 of 1956. The section is modelled on and is in material terms identical with Section 102 of Union of South Africa Act 46 of 1935. South African decisions on the construction of their Act give guidance: see *Turner & Co. (Pvt.) Ltd.* v. *Arcturus Road Council*, 1958 (1) S.A. 409 (S.R.) at 410 per Murray C.J. The court requires a concrete dispute to have arisen; the plaintiff must be a person interested in the existing right; a declaratory order must be binding, in the sense of being *res judicata* on the persons concerned; and finally the balance of convenience in deciding the issue at that or at a later stage must be considered.

[2] *Salisbury Bottling Co. (Pvt.) Ltd.* v. *Central African Bottling Co. (Pvt.) Ltd.*, 1958 R. and N. 17 at 26.

[3] *Dalrymple* v. *Colonial Treasurer*, 1910 T.S. 372 at 380.

[4] *Director of Education* v. *McCagie*, 1918 A.D. 616 at 628–9. Compare de Smith, *Judicial Review of Administrative Action*, Stevens, 1959, pp. 305–13, 343 et seq.

[5] 1907 T.S. 427 at 433.

[6] 1958 R. & N. 17 at 29. In *Patz* v. *Greene* it was held that damage would be presumed where an act was prohibited in the interest of a particular class of persons. Where, however, this was done in the public interest loss must be proved. See also *Chassay Bros.* v. *Shaw & Macintyre NN.O.*, *supra*.

[7] *supra* at 32.

[8] At 26–27.

by various statutes in relation to particular cases. There is, however, a 'recognized presumption against construing a statute so as to oust the jurisdiction of the ordinary courts of law'.[1] Nonetheless statutes may effectively do this. Thus the Law and Order (Maintenance) Act provides that any order by the Governor declaring a publication to be prohibited 'shall be final and may not be varied or set aside in any court of law'.[2] However it seems that, despite this phraseology, 'if there were a manifest absence of jurisdiction or if an order were made or obtained fraudulently a competent court would be entitled to interfere and would interfere'.[3]

Whether review is excluded by the addition of a special statutory remedy in the Act will depend upon interpretation of the statute in question, but unless it is clear that the Legislature has confined the party complaining of a breach of a statutory obligation to a particular remedy the new remedy will be cumulative to the old.[4] Where there are cumulative remedies an aggrieved party may not normally proceed on review until he has exhausted the remedies provided by the statute. However there are numerous exceptions to this statement and there is no general rule that while there is a possibility of extra-judicial redress or if further administrative action is provided for, no review may lie.[5]

---

[1] *Turner & Co. (Pvt.) Ltd.* v. *Arcturus Road Council, supra* per Murray C.J. at 411. In *Rhodesian Publications Ltd.* v. *Servicemen's Reinstatement Board*, 1945 S.R. 73 it was held that even if provision is made that a decision is to be 'final' it must be made in terms of the regulations.

[2] Chapter 39, Section 18(6). The Unlawful Organizations Act, Chapter 81, Section 3(3) states that proclamations declaring organisations to be unlawful 'shall not be open to question in any court of law'. The Preventive Detention (Temporary Provisions) Act, (Chapter 74), Section 13, which has expired and was not effectively extended by Act No. 1 of 1964 (*Nkomo and Others* v. *Minister of Justice and Others, supra*) provided that 'save as is expressly provided in this Act, a detention order and a restriction order shall not be subject to any appeal, review or other proceeding in any court of law nor shall any action, suit, or other legal proceeding or remedy be available to any detained person in respect of his detention or restriction'.

[3] *Union Government* v. *Fakir*, 1923 A.D. 466 per Innes C.J. at 469–70. For a discussion of the cases see Rose Innes, op. cit., pp. 58 et seq.

[4] *Madrassa Anjuman Islamia* v. *Johannesburg Municipality*, 1917 A.D. 718. This is relevant in S.R. where there is sometimes an appeal afforded by a statute from the decisions of an administrative body, e.g. an appeal from decisions of the Liquor Licensing Board on questions of law and fact lies to the High Court: The Liquor Act (Chapter 234), Section 21(1). See *Lowenthal* v. *Liquor Licensing Board*, 1956 (1) S.A. 227 (S.R.). However even though an appeal lies, since it is from the decision of an administrative tribunal enjoying a discretion, it is not a rehearing on the merits, and the High Court will only interfere 'if it finds that the decision was not based on reasonable grounds, that some wrong principle was applied, that matters were taken into account that should not have been considered, or that matters were not considered that should have been taken into account': Quènet J. (as he then was) in *Jackson* v. *Adams*, 1958 (4) S.A. 78 (S.R.) at 82. See also *McCormick* v. *Liquor Licensing Board*, 1956 (1) S.A. 471 (S.R.), *Vainona Estates Ltd. and Others* v. *Anderson and Anderson*, 1960 R. & N. 395, and *Tselentis* v. *City Council of Salisbury*, Judgement A.D. 119/65.

[5] See *Bindura T.M.B.* v. *Desai*, 1953 (1) S. A. 358 (A.D.) 363, an appeal from S.R., where it was held that review was not precluded immediately upon refusal of the granting of a

Grounds for review where competent may also be severely restricted by specific statutory provision. Thus the Law and Order (Maintenance) Act markedly curtails the right of the Court to review administrative decisions taken in the interests of law and order, by empowering officials to exercise discretionary powers of prohibiting processions, public gatherings, and meetings if they are 'of opinion that by reason of particular circumstances existing . . . serious public disorder may be occasioned',[1] and by providing that if the Minister 'considers that it is desirable for the maintenance of law and order to do so' he may prohibit public gatherings and prohibit particular persons from attending public meetings.[2] Similar subjective powers are conferred on the Minister to restrict persons to particular areas, to prohibit them from entering specified areas, and to provide that they shall notify their movements to the authorities.[3] Furthermore the *audi alteram partem* rule is excluded in respect of the latter powers by provision for representations to the Minister within seven days after delivery of any order in terms of Section 50.[4] These provisions were drafted in the light of and to exclude the consequences of *R.* v. *Ngwevela* which attempted to uphold fundamental liberties in the face of statutory encroachment.[5] This method of avoiding the *audi alteram partem* rule by implication was indicated in *Sachs* v. *Minister of Justice*.[6] However, *ex abundante cautela* lest this decision be wrong, provision has been made in the Act that orders made against persons restricted after a conviction 'shall not be subject to any proceedings in any court of law on the grounds

licence by a Town Management Board, even though the Governor had an executive discretion to enquire into the decision and to order the issue of a licence when one had been refused. See Rose Innes, op. cit., pp. 76–88 for a full discussion of the exceptions.

[1] Sections 10(1) and 11(1).

[2] Sections 12(1) and 13(1).

[3] Sections 50 and 51. Both sections now provide for orders to be applicable for up to five years. However orders under Section 51 may only be imposed on persons convicted of offences under security legislation or offences under the common law committed in circumstances which in the Minister's opinion are associated with public disorder. Another Act conferring discretionary powers is the Emergency Powers Act No. 48 of 1960 which authorizes the Governor to issue a proclamation of emergency if 'it appears' to him that the public safety is endangered.

[4] Section 50(6). Similar provision is made in respect of certain prohibited immigrants by Section 10 of the Immigration Act. In *Taylor* v. *The Prime Minister*, 1954 (3) S.A. 956, Beadle J. at 963 held that it was clear that the Legislature did not intend the *audi alteram partem* rule to apply to undesirable visitors, who on information received from any Government had been declared by the Governor to be undesirable immigrants. If allowed to enter the Colony to make representations one of the objects of the Legislature might well be defeated.

[5] 1954 (1) S.A. 123 (A.D.) followed in *Saliwa* v. *Minister of Native Affairs*, 1956 (2) S.A. 310 (A.D.). Compare *Laubscher* v. *Native Commissioner Piet Retief*, 1958 (1) S.A. 546 (A.D.)—a retreat from this position. Decisions given by the South African Appellate Division during the early nineteen fifties should go down in history both to the honour of the judges and to the ineffectiveness of any judiciary in ultimately withstanding a Legislature that is determined to overrule each decision vindicating individual liberty by new and ingenious legislation.

[6] 1934 A.D. 11.

that the person against whom it was made was not afforded an opportunity of making representations to the Minister before it was made'.[1]

The grounds on which administrative action and delegated legislation may be impeached have been developed under the influence of English decisions and, as in English law, the scope of review may depend upon the appropriate classification of a particular statutory power. Although the courts have warned against characterizing functions and then deriving legal rules from the particular classification,[2] they have themselves characterized particular functions as being administrative or quasi-judicial and held that differing legal consequences ensue.[3] If a function is found to be ministerial, quasi-judicial, or purely administrative, the courts will apply different considerations in testing the validity of the exercise of a discretion. Similarly in testing the exercise of delegated legislative powers they apply slightly different tests.[4] de Smith has cynically pointed to the realities: 'The truth of the matter is that the mode of classifying statutory functions is determined by the scope of review that the courts deem to be desirable or practical.'[5]

Statutory grounds for review in terms of Section 31 of the High Court Act are specified in the Act as absence of jurisdiction, interest in the cause, bias,

---

[1] Section 51(6). The type of case in which Section 51(6) is employed is illustrated by the history of Mr. Moton Malianga, who was restricted for five years to a 1,500 acre area known as Wha Wha. He had been convicted on four counts under the Law and Order (Maintenance) Act for certain subversive statements but on appeal all but one of these convictions were upset: *Malianga* v. *R.*, 1963 (4) S.A. 226 (F.C.). Immediately after serving a sentence of one year's imprisonment, a further year being suspended, an order in terms of Section 51(1) was served on him: S.R.N. 1597/1964, 23 October 1964. Under Sections 50 and 51, 418 persons were restricted in Southern Rhodesia as at 19 November 1964. (Information by courtesy of the Department of Justice.) Between 1962 and July 1965 restriction orders were served on 1,319 persons, of whom only eight were Europeans. Fifty-two of the orders were for five-year periods: *S.R.L.A.D.*, Vol. 61, col. 1777, 4 August 1965. Not all the orders restricted persons to remote areas of the country, a proportion restricting persons to a small radius of the town in which they were resident.

[2] *Pretoria North Town Council* v. *A.1 Ice Cream Factory Ltd.*, 1953 (3) S.A. 1 (A.D.) per Schreiner J.A. at 11: 'The classification of the discretions and functions under the headings of "administrative", "quasi-judicial", and "judicial" has been much canvassed in modern judgements and juristic literature; there appears to be some difference of opinion, or of linguistic usage, as to the proper basis of classification, and even some disagreement as to the usefulness of the classification when achieved. I do not propose to enter into these interesting questions to a greater extent than is necessary for the decision of this case; one must be careful not to elevate what may be no more than a convenient classification into a source of legal rules. What primarily has to be considered in all these cases is the statutory provision in question, read in its proper context.'

[3] *Minister of the Interior* v. *Mariam*, 1961 (4) S.A. 740 (A.D.) at 751–2. See also *Brits Town Council* v. *Pienaar N.O.*, 1949 (1) S.A. 1004 (T.) at 1019 and *Hotel Association of Southern Rhodesia* v. *Southern Rhodesia Liquor Licensing Board*, 1958 (1) S.A. 426 (S.R.) at 429–30.

[4] For a succinct summary of the position see *Hahlo* v. *Kahn*, op. cit., pp. 186–94. See also Rose Innes, op. cit., Chapters 6–17. B. R. Bamford, *The Law of Partnership and Voluntary Associations in South Africa*, Juta, 1958, at pp. 106–22 summarizes the law relating to judicial review of domestic tribunals.

[5] Op. cit., pp. 50–51. The learned author puts in a caveat for precedent.

malice or corruption on the part of the person presiding, and gross irregularity in the proceedings.[1] However common law grounds[2] for review are wider.[3]

Validity of a decision may depend on whether the tribunal or authority followed the correct procedure in reaching its decision, whether it was properly constituted, whether action has been taken on the requisite jurisdictional facts,[4] whether the exercise of such a power has been authorized[5] either expressly or impliedly (thus bringing in the requirement of reasonableness which is applied to Ministerial legislation in the same way as it is to all other subordinate legislation such as by-laws),[6] whether a delegation has been authorized,[7] whether a discretion has been exercised on extraneous grounds,[8] whether mistake of law has precluded the exercise of the discretion owing to a mistake as to its nature,[9] whether improper motive,[10] *mala fides*,[11] or bias[12] vitiated the exercise of the power, whether non-compliance with the maxim *audi alteram partem* has invalidated the proceedings,[13] whether the Act en-

---

[1] Section 32(1).

[2] These are saved by Section 2(2).

[3] They are enumerated in *Edwards Ltd.* v. *Stumbles N.O.*, 1963 R. & N. 68 at 73.

[4] *Le Roux* v. *Grigg Spall*, 1946 A.D. 244.

[5] *Roberts & Letts* v. *Fynn*, 1920 A.D. 23 (an appeal from S.R.).

[6] *R.* v. *Campbell (Pvt.) Ltd.*, 1956 (1) S.A. 256 at 262. Compare *Sparks* v. *Edward Ash Ltd.*, [1943] K.B. 223 at 230 per Scott L.J.

[7] *R.* v. *Nyandoro*, 1959 (1), S.A. 639 (S.R.) 640; *Waterfalls T.M.B.* v. *Minister of Housing*, 1957 (1) S.A. 336 (S.R.) at 339; and *R.* v. *Nkomo*, 1963 (4) S.A. 166 (S.R.) at 177 et seq. A sub-delegation of a discretion is permissible in two exceptional cases: where a skilled officer is required to form a judgement in a complicated situation not capable of being decided in advance; and when an officer on the spot is required to decide in the light of actual circumstances of the moment, a particular question requiring immediate decision.

[8] *Touriel* v. *Minister of Internal Affairs*, 1946 A.D. 535 at 547 (on appeal from S.R.).

[9] Mere wrong interpretation of a statutory provision is by itself not a sufficient ground for review: *Doyle* v. *Shenker*, 1915 A.D. 233. Only if an official fails to exercise his discretion at all through misreading an Act and thus failing to appreciate the nature of his discretion will the Court intervene: *Johannesburg City Council* v. *Chesterfield House*, 1952 (3) S.A. 809 (A.D.) at 825 per Centlivres C.J. and *L. & B. Holdings (Pvt.) Ltd.* v. *Mashonaland Rent Appeal Board*, 1959 (3) S.A. 466 (S.R.) per Murray C.J. In the former case Centlivres C.J. at p. 825, discussing *Lee* v. *Showmen's Guild of Great Britain*, [1952] 1 All E. R. 1175, held that a mistaken view of the law adopted by a domestic tribunal was not in Roman-Dutch Law *per se* a ground for setting aside its decision. If in addition the *dicta* by Denning L.J. in this case and in *Barnard* v. *National Dock Labour Board*, [1953] 2 Q.B. 18 at 47 are correct (see de Smith, op. cit., p. 410) there is a considerable difference from the attitude of English courts. Again mere error of law on the face of a record which did not go to the jurisdiction (see *R.* v. *Northumberland Compensation Appeal Tribunal, ex parte Shaw*, [1951] 1 K.B. 711, and [1952 1 K.B. 338 (C.A.)) would not on the present state of South African authorities be regarded as a ground for review.

[10] *Van Eck* v. *Etna Stores*, 1957 (2) S.A. 984 (A.D.); *Palley* v. *Knight N.O.*, 1961 (4) S.A. 633 (S.R.); and *Minister of Justice* v. *Musururwa and Nkomo*, 1964 (3) S.A. 209 at 226–7.

[11] *Adams Stores (Pty.) Ltd.* v. *Charlestown Town Board*, 1951 (2) S.A. 508 (N.) at 517.

[12] For the test of pecuniary interest see *Olley* v. *Maasdorp*, 1948 (4) S.A. 657 (A.D.) (on appeal from Southern Rhodesia).

[13] See *Ex parte Zelter*, 1951 (2) S.A. 54 (S.R.) at 55, *Pilossof* v. *Greenfield N.O.* (2), 1951 (2) S.A. 529 (S.R.) at 529; and *Taylor* v. *Prime Minister*, 1954 (3) S.A. 956 (S.R.) at

joined is specified with sufficient certainty,[1] or whether refusal to give reasons should be regarded as indicative of improper purpose.[2]

Unreasonableness as a ground for invalidating administrative decisions has received particular attention. The leading South African case on this point held that even though racial differentiation might not be expressly authorized it could not be invalidated on grounds of partiality provided substantial inequality or partiality did not result.[3] However, Beadle C.J. in *City of Salisbury* v. *Mehta, supra*, refined this rule, drawing a distinction between tangible discrimination and intangible discrimination.[4] He considered that if Rasool's Case laid down the principle that no express authority was required to 'discriminate intangibly' between the races, provided that there was no 'tangible discrimination', he could not approve of the decision, which he in any event distinguished. Indeed, in Southern Rhodesia in view of Sections 28(a) and 40 of the 1923 Constitution Letters Patent, unless either differentiation or discrimination on racial grounds was expressly authorized, it was impermissible.[5] However once a questioned enactment fell clearly within the terms of the grant 'there is no room for the argument that the power was unreasonably exercised'.[6] Thus once express authority to 'differentiate' on racial grounds was given, i.e. permitting mere 'distinguishing between' or 'discrimination coupled with equality', then differentiating regulations would be *intra vires*, notwithstanding the fact that they amounted to 'intangible discrimination' so long as there was no 'tangible discrimination'.[7] In order to issue valid regulations which 'tangibly discriminated', i.e.

960 in which case Beadle J. considered the rule could be applied after the making of an order but before it came into effect, whereas Hathorn J. held it must be observed before the making of the order. According to *Monckten* v. *B.S.A. Co.*, 1920 A.D. 324 the maxim is not applicable to purely contractual rights.

[1] *R.* v. *Jopp*, 1949 (4) S.A. 11 (N.).

[2] *Pretoria North Town Council* v. *A.1 Ice Cream Factory, supra* at 16.

[3] *Minister of Posts and Telegraphs* v. *Rasool*, 1934 A.D. 167.

[4] This distinction was based on psychological factors dealt with in *Brown* v. *Board of Education, Topeka* (1953), 98 L. Ed. 873.

[5] Compare *R.* v. *Abdurahman*, 1950 (3) S.A. 136 (A.D.) at 149 for the view that there must at common law be express authorization to allow of discrimination.

[6] Quènet J.P. in *Gundu and Sambo* v. *Hayward and Bosman NN.O.* Judgement No. A.D. 97/1965 at p. 10. Hahlo and Kahn, op. cit., at p. 190 have described the willingness of the courts to find delegated powers specific as 'a grand abdication of jurisdiction'. A similar abdication of jurisdiction is to be found in *Mustapha* v. *Receiver of Revenue, Lichtenburg*, 1958 (3) S.A. 343 at 357 where Ogilvie Thompson J. held that if an official exercises a right to cancel a contract, the power to contract being authorized by regulations, this is the exercise of a contractual right and not a statutory power, and, even though its exercise may have been occasioned by racial prejudice, it cannot be attacked as being unreasonable. The dissenting judgement of Schreiner J.A. at 350 'that the contractual element must not be allowed to obscure the fact that the Minister's powers are statutory' is more realistic and to be preferred.

[7] Beadle C.J. considered that provided the facilities afforded the different races were 'substantially equal' there would be no discrimination. However, on appeal to the Federal Supreme Court, Briggs F.J. was not 'satisfied that it must be a sufficient answer to say that separate amenities of equal quality reserved for the respondent's community exist in another

were unequal in their operation, express authority to discriminate was necessary. The practical significance of this question has become less important as the situation will now for the most part be covered by Sections 67 and 68 of the Declaration of Rights, except in respect of subordinate legislation in terms of Federal Acts still in force in Southern Rhodesia and Southern Rhodesian subordinate legislation in force before the coming into operation of the 1961 Constitution.[1]

Unreasonableness *per se* is not sufficient ground for review and even if there is no evidence upon which a decision could reasonably have been reached the decision must be so grossly unreasonable to indicate either that the tribunal did not apply its mind to the matter or that there was *mala fides* or an improper motive.[2] Where a matter has been left to the discretion of a public officer and this has *bona fide* been exercised, the Court cannot interfere with his decision by substituting its own conclusions for his, even if it considers that the decision reached by the officer was wrong and inequitable.[3]

If the Court finds that a body has rendered its proceedings reviewable on any of the aforementioned grounds, it may set aside or correct the proceedings in a civil case, and in a criminal case hear further evidence, alter or quash the conviction, substitute another sentence, or remit the case to the magistrate with instructions as to further proceedings.[4]

Automatic review

A valuable safeguard—review in the ordinary course, more frequently referred to as automatic review—exists in addition to the statutory provisions for review and the inherent power of the Court to entertain reviews. In criminal cases where any court imposes a sentence of imprisonment in excess of three months or a fine exceeding £25 or any whipping (except one inflicted on a juvenile) the record of the proceedings must be sent within one week

place': 1961 R. & N. 1000 at 1016. For comment on this decision, see 'The Reservation of Separate Amenities: The Southern African Experience', L. A. J. Armour and R. A. Hasson (1963), *Public Law*, pp. 275 et seq.

[1] An interesting point arises whether there may be discrimination in terms of the prerogative. Passports are not granted by virtue of any written law, but by virtue of the prerogative (*Sachs* v. *Dönges N.O.*, 1950 (2) S.A. 265 (A.D.)), whereas Section 67 of the Constitution only applies to discrimination by virtue of written laws. It is practice of the Southern Rhodesian passport authorities to refuse passports to non-Europeans unless they make a deposit of £120 avowedly for the purpose of paying for their return fare should they be deported from the country of their destination, or to demand a suretyship for this amount from some person of substance.

[2] *Clan Transport Co. (Pvt.) Ltd.* v. *Rhodesia Railways and Another*, 1956 (3) S.A. 480 (F.C.).

[3] *Shidiack* v. *Union Government*, 1912 A.D. 643.

[4] High Court Act, Section 31, read with Section 56 of Chapter 15. If on an application for review two judges cannot reach agreement, the application is deemed to be dismissed: High Court Act, Section 30(2)(a).

to the Registrar of the High Court, who places the papers before a judge in chambers for his confirmation of the proceedings as being in accordance with natural justice.[1]

Furthermore in any case not subject to automatic review the accused may within three days, if he considers the sentence not in accordance with real and substantial justice, deliver to the clerk of the court written statements setting out his reasons. If this is done, the same procedure as in the case of automatic review is brought into operation.[2]

Where automatic review has come into effect in either of these ways, an accused may within three days after the date of his sentence deliver a statement as to why the sentence imposed on him is excessive and if the reviewing judge considers the ends of justice will be met by a less sentence, he may reduce or vary the sentence as he thinks fit.[3]

When the General Division reviews any proceedings it has considerable power to alter, quash, vary, or confirm them and also the sentence, and it may even direct that the case be argued by the Attorney-General and counsel appointed by the Court.[4]

Continuous use is made of these valuable provisions and there is no doubt that automatic review is a considerable check on any misuse of power by magistrates, and in a number of cases secures justice to persons who have either been wrongly convicted or excessively punished.[5] Review in terms of these sections does not preclude an appeal from the magistrate's decision, but the review proceedings viz. the giving of a certificate that the proceedings were

[1] Chapter 15, Section 55(1) and (3).

[2] Chapter 15, Section 55(2).

[3] Chapter 15, Section 58.

[4] Chapter 15, Section 56. The reviewing judge may not impose a sentence more severe than that imposed by the magistrates' court.

[5] Analysis of reports of review judgements (unreported but circulated for information by the Registrar of the High Court) delivered from January to September 1964 by the High Court in Salisbury (this does not include Bulawayo judgements) shows that in six cases both convictions and sentences were set aside, and in fifteen cases sentences were reduced, this being done in several cases on the grounds that the sentence induced a sense of shock in the court (e.g. R. v. Patero and R. v. Hosiah Tumidzayi). In yet another case it was too late to alter the sentence as it had already been undergone. In one case sentence was altered, while another sentence was criticized as being too lenient. Yet another case was remitted to the magistrates' court for further evidence. A reported review which shows the type of decision involved is R. v. Mawena, 1964 (3) S.A. 779 (S.R.) where a condition of a suspended sentence—that the accused attend no gatherings—was struck out. In three of these cases the court set the matter down for argument in terms of Chapter 15, Section 56. Since many of these cases involved joint trials, the number of accused involved is greater than appears. See also Report of the Secretary for Justice for the year ended 31 December 1963, C.S.R. 29–1964, p. 14, which shows that in 1962 there were 6,834 cases confirmed and perused by the judges and 178 in which they altered convictions, or sentences, or set aside the verdict. In 1963 there were 7,377 cases confirmed and 198 cases in which the judges intervened on review, while in 1964 there were 8,687 cases confirmed or perused and 201 in which they intervened: Report of the Secretary of Justice for the year ending 31 December 1964, C.S.R. 34–1965, p. 18.

in accordance with real and substantial justice, are not themselves appeal-able.[1]

Special courts and special tribunals

In accordance with the modern trend to establish courts of special jurisdic-tion and numerous tribunals, the Southern Rhodesian Legislature has created an extensive system of such bodies. With few exceptions the General Division of the High Court has power of review of their proceedings, but the question whether an appeal is also available depends in each case on construction of the particular statute establishing the body.

The legal system of Southern Rhodesia is diagrammatically illustrated in Figure I [2] which makes it clear how little uniformity has been adopted towards the question whether there should be appeals from statutory tribunals, and if so whether the appeal should lie to the General Division or to the Appellate Division. Thus in some cases appellate jurisdiction is exercised by the General Division of the High Court while in others appeals go directly to the Appellate Division. In many cases no appeals are permitted, but in all cases the pro-ceedings of such courts and tribunals are reviewable, unless review is speci-fically excluded, while in many cases the statute provides for statutory review. In other cases optional routes of appeal are provided.[3] Whether appeal, if it lies, permits appeal on fact as well as on law again depends on the particular statute.[4]

The composition of these special courts again varies greatly—from the Water Court, the Industrial Court and the Town Planning Court, each composed of a president with lengthy legal experience and two assessors, to Mining Commissioners' Courts composed of a Mining Commissioner who has technical skill but little legal knowledge.

Provisions for arbitration largely modelled on a Cape copy of the United

[1] *Salah* v. *R.*, 1962 R. & N. 429 (F.C.). The point was expressly left open whether appeal from a judgement given after consideration of papers sent for review and confirmation was possible.

[2] The source was the *Revised Edition of the Statute Law of Southern Rhodesia 1963*, as amended at 31 October 1965. All statutory tribunals where express reference to review or appeal has been made have been inserted in this diagram. However, it does not give a com-plete picture of administrative bodies subject to review as Ministers and officials exercise quasi-judicial or administrative powers under many Acts and there has been no attempt to set out all such provisions. It should be noted that where there is a special statutory 'review' provided for, the High Court has greater powers than is the case where it exercises powers of review over public bodies and inferior courts, and possesses not only the powers of a court of review, but also has 'the functions of a court of appeal': *Johannesburg Consolidated Invest-ment Co.* v. *Johannesburg Town Council, supra* at 117 per Innes C.J. Cp. *Tselentis* v. *City Council of Salisbury*, Judgement No. A.D. 119/65.

[3] As in the case of decisions by the Commissioner of Taxes and by Factory Inspectors.

[4] e.g. appeal from the Workmen's Compensation Court or the Industrial Court lies on law only, whereas there is no such limitation in respect of appeals from the Water Court.

Kingdom Act of 1889 exist.[1] There is, however, a major difference in that the decision of an arbitrator may not be set aside as in England for a mistake as to the law, unless this is so gross as to amount to evidence of misconduct.[2] Apart from voluntary arbitration, various statutory provisions exist for arbitration on compensation questions in the case of expropriation of property or where compulsory powers are utilized by public authorities.[3]

Special courts for Africans
Chiefs' and Headmen's courts

Since 1937 statutory African courts of first instance have been constituted by Governor's warrant.[4] Such courts are presided over by Chiefs or Headmen who must be assisted by at least two advisory counsellors who have been approved for service by the District Commissioner. No distinction is made in the jurisdiction given to Chiefs and Headmen, although this is not in accordance with customary law, in which a Chief's court is superior to that of a Headman and hears appeals from the latter. At present there are over 200 Chiefs and a considerable number of Headmen empowered to hold such courts.[5] However, the statutory courts are outnumbered by the customary African courts which have continued to try cases and settle disputes between Africans just as they did before the European entered the colony.[6]

The procedure of statutory courts (and also of non-statutory unauthorized ones) is that of customary law and is lengthy and informal. Little has been done to formalize court procedure and there are no court clerks and no proper records kept. Customary procedure is designed to restore the social balance and harmony by efforts to get the parties to agree. Indeed the characteristic feature of such courts is that judgement is in many cases obtained by arriving at a general consensus of opinion and a decision which both parties are prepared to accept, rather than the giving of oracular judgement by decree.[7]

---

[1] The Arbitration Act (Chapter 8).

[2] *Dickinson and Brown* v. *Fisher's Executor*, 1915 A.D. 166.

[3] See the Lands and Arbitration Clauses Act (Chapter 14), which sets out the standard procedure for fixing compensation. Statutes providing for authority to expropriate land or materials must be read with this Act: Section 2.

[4] In terms of Section 5(1) of the African Law and Courts Act (Chapter 104).

[5] *S.R.L.A.D.*, Vol. 58, col. 1714, 14 October 1964. In 1953 180 Chiefs' courts and nineteen Headmen's courts were officially recognized: Howman, op. cit., para. 91.

[6] Robinson Report, para. 179. The Commission recommended that this *de facto* position should be regularized, para. 183.

[7] See Howman, op. cit., para. 54 and J. H. Holleman, *Shona Customary Law*, Oxford 1952, pp. 14, 17–18. See also the Robinson Report, para. 180, where the Commission found that the aim of such courts was 'to arrive at a decision that will bring the litigants together again as friends and remove the friction which might occur in the community if this were not done'. Even if Africans proceed to the Native Commissioner's court, this 'is often used as an outside criterion and the parties then proceed to return to their own customary courts to re-adjudicate in the light of the native commissioner's decision in order to restore social harmony'.

In cases where the counsellors or the majority of such counsellors disagree with the Chief, it is provided that he must report this disagreement to the District Commissioner.[1]

A serious limitation on the powers of these courts is their inability to enforce their judgements other than by a request by the Chief to a District Commissioner for assistance, or through a criminal prosecution initiated by the Crown against an African who has contravened the African Law and Courts Act by not obeying a Chief's summons or by disregarding procedure laid down by Governor's regulations.[2] Chiefs themselves have no powers to punish for contempt of court. As far as the unrecognized customary courts are concerned, they have only moral and social sanctions of the tribal community to enforce their decisions. In practice 'some headmen have been punished for enforcing their judgements in the manner approved by custom'.[3]

Certain minor court fees (5s.) are paid by both parties, the successful party being refunded his fee. However, customary tokens accepting the jurisdiction of the court, which are also payable at other stages during the procedures, still survive. All such fees are payable to the Chief and remain his personal property, including the formal fees, which in other British African Territories have to be paid over to the local African Council.[4]

The jurisdiction enjoyed by the African courts is very limited, although not by the stipulation of monetary limits, there being no monetary limit imposed on such Courts by the Act and apparently none in terms of their warrants.[5] Such courts may only exercise jurisdiction if all the parties are African, if the defendant is ordinarily resident, and at the time of summons is actually resident, in the court's jurisdiction, and if the action is capable of decision according to African customary law.[6] No criminal jurisdiction is permitted nor can action be brought if it arises from any act or omission (other than an act of adultery) which is punishable as an offence.[7] Accordingly many delictual actions are excluded from the court's jurisdiction. Furthermore, no action for divorce may be heard.[8] However, the limits of this jurisdiction are in practice often ignored and African courts adjudicate in civil

---

[1] African Law and Courts Act (Chapter 104), Section 5(4).

[2] Chapter 104, Section 8(2) and (11). See also Howman, op. cit., para. 27.

[3] Robinson Report, para. 185, viz. 'Compelling the defendant to work for the Chief or plaintiff until he satisfied the judgement or by forcibly or stealthily removing cattle from the defendant and giving them to the plantiff.' The Commission found that failure to allow enforcement of their judgements stultified the functions of African courts.

[4] See Holleman, op. cit., pp. 17–18 and Howman, op. cit., paras. 141–5.

[5] S.R.L.A.D., Vol. 58, col. 1715, 14 October 1964.

[6] Chapter 104, Section 6(1). If this is not possible, the African court must state all proceedings in the case to the District Commissioner for a decision or transfer by him to a competent court: Section 3(1)(a).

[7] Chapter 104, Section 6(2)(b) and (3). Adultery is specifically mentioned as until 1962 the Natives Adultery Act prohibited adultery by Africans.

[8] Chapter 104, Section 6(2)(a).

cases arising out of criminal acts.[1] For the most part, however, cases heard in such courts concern the recovery or return of lobola, damages for adultery or seduction, succession and inheritance, maintenance for and custody of children, the effect of marriage on the property of the spouses, and defamation.

District Commissioners' courts

District Commissioners' courts are the next in the hierarchy of courts entrusted with civil jurisdiction over Africans. The District Commissioner who adjudicates may call in any Chief to act as an advisory assessor in matters concerning customary law.[2]

District Commissioners have the same financial limits to their jurisdiction as those imposed on magistrates. However, they are not precluded from dealing with African divorces or cases involving the interpretation of testaments.[3] Since 1963 they have, however, had no criminal jurisdiction except in respect of contempts of court.

The civil jurisdiction administered by the District Commissioners is both original and revisory. In respect of his revisory jurisdiction, the District Commissioner may at all times have access to African courts and their records, and may on his own initiative revise proceedings in such court or intervene at any stage of the proceedings and transfer the case to his own or to any other competent court.[4] District Commissioners also exercise appellate jurisdiction, as any party who is dissatisfied with the judgement of an African court may appeal to the District Commissioner's court. There are no Chief's appeal courts established on the models of those in British African Territories. Appeals made to the District Commissioner are not really appeals but retrials, as the judgement of the African court becomes of no force or effect and the matter is reheard *ab initio*. Part of the reason for this is that no proper records are kept by African courts, and the Act provides that the judgement of the African court is not even to be taken into consideration. As a result, new witnesses may be produced, and this makes the proceedings subject to abuse, as the African court can be used merely to discover an opposing party's case.[5] From a District Commissioner's court appeal lies as of right to the Court of Appeal for African civil cases.

The Court of Appeal for African civil cases

Next in the hierarchy of courts for Africans is the Court of Appeal for

---

[1] Robinson Report, para. 181. African customary law is concerned primarily to compensate the individual or family injured by the crime, rather than to inflict punishment on the criminal, although the customary law sometimes imposed punishments.

[2] African Affairs Act (Chapter 92), Section 9(4).

[3] African Affairs Act (Chapter 92), Section 9(2).

[4] African Law and Courts Act (Chapter 104), Section 9.

[5] Howman, op. cit., para. 135(e) makes this criticism.

African civil cases which was first established in 1928 when the Chief Native Commissioner was required to sit with two assessors. Since 1958 the court has been composed of a president, who must be a retired judge or advocate of not less than twelve years' standing, sitting with two assessors selected by the president from a list of persons who are or have been Native Commissioners or District Commissioners nominated by the Minister of Internal Affairs.[1] Decisions of the court are taken by a majority.[2]

It is this court which has been most responsible for attempting to set out coherent principles of law which will serve as a guide to lower courts for the future, and since its establishment its decisions have been reported.[3]

Since the Court of Appeal for African civil cases has the same power to hear appeals as the Appellate Division of the High Court from magistrates' courts, appeals may freely be lodged from District Commissioners' courts except in respect of interlocutory matters.[4]

Further appeal as of right lies from the Court of Appeal for African civil cases to the Appellate Division of the High Court.[5]

Appeals in Southern Rhodesia

A system of appeals was first established in Southern Rhodesia when the Matabeleland High Court was in 1894 given jurisdiction to hear appeals from magistrates' courts.[6] In 1898 the High Court of Southern Rhodesia as its successor was given similar powers.[7] Appeals from the High Court itself, however, lay from 1896 to the Cape Supreme Court, first in terms of the Matabeleland Order in Council and later of the Southern Rhodesia Order in Council.[8] In civil cases appeals might only be brought if the amount in dispute exceeded £100, unless leave of the High Court was obtained, while in criminal cases appeal was only permitted if a special entry on the record alleging irregularity or illegality in the proceedings had been made, or a question of law had been reserved and entered by the Court on the record.[9] There was

---

[1] African Affairs Act (Chapter 92), Section 10(1), (2), and (4).

[2] Chapter 92, Section 10(5).

[3] As Reports and Decisions of the Native Appeal Court, Southern Rhodesia. These are cited as e.g. Robert v. Mugwagwa, 1954 S.R.N. 438.

[4] African Affairs Act (Chapter 92), Section 10(6) read with Section 36 of Chapter 15.

[5] African Affairs Act (Chapter 92), Section 10(8) as amended by Section 54 of Act 22 of 1964.

[6] Matabeleland Order in Council, Section 40.

[7] Southern Rhodesia Order in Council, Section 74. This included power to hear appeals from the decisions of Native Commissioners exercising judicial powers.

[8] Matabeleland Order in Council 1894, Section 35, implemented by Cape Act 35 of 1896, Sections 44 to 49, and Southern Rhodesia Order in Council 1898, Sections 58 and 60, implemented by the Cape Colony's Supreme Court Extended Appellate Jurisdiction Act No. 22 of 1898.

[9] Southern Rhodesia Order in Council 1898, Sections 60–64.

no appeal on fact. Further appeal as of right to the Judicial Committee lay on the same conditions as appeal lay from the Supreme Court itself.

Subsequently when the Appellate Division of the Union of South Africa was constituted, Section 103 of the South Africa Act 1909 provided that appeals from the Southern Rhodesian High Court (except in cases of orders or judgements given by a single judge on application by way of motion or petition, or on a summons for provisional sentence, or judgements as to costs only, in which cases jurisdiction was concurrent) were to proceed to that Court. Only in 1931 did the Southern Rhodesian Administration of Justice Act[1] repeal Sections 58–68 of the Southern Rhodesia Order in Council of 1898 and stipulate that all appeals should lie to the Appellate Division.[2]

In 1938 the Rhodesia Court of Appeal Act,[3] which established the Rhodesia Court of Appeal, provided that criminal appeals might either proceed to that court or to the Appellate Division. However, civil appeals all went to the Appellate Division.

This remained the position until 1955 when the Federal Supreme Court was established,[4] and appeals to the Appellate Division were, in terms of the Federal Constitution, no longer permitted.[5] Until April 1964 the Federal Supreme Court continued in operation, although it could not hear appeals lodged after 31 December 1963. It then became essential after Federal dissolution to establish a new appellate court for Southern Rhodesia.

The Appellate Division of the High Court

Established by Sections 50 and 52 of the Southern Rhodesia Constitution as amended, the Appellate Division of the High Court is composed of the Chief Justice, the Judge President, such other judges of appeal as the Governor deems necessary (at present one), and puisne judges of the High Court designated by the Chief Justice with the consent of the Judge President to act as judges of the Appellate Division. In practice the Appellate Division when hearing appeals has for the most part so far been composed of the Judge President, the Chief Justice and an acting judge of appeal.[6]

[1] No. 14 of 1931. In practice most Rhodesian appeals from 1911 onwards went to the Union Appellate Division.

[2] This was confirmed by a Union Act, the Rhodesia Appeals Act No. 18 of 1931.

[3] Act 33 of 1938, Section 4 saved the question of special leave to appeal to the Judicial Committee which no longer lay as of right.

[4] In terms of articles 45 and 66 of the Federal Constitution as implemented by the Federal Supreme Court Act No. 11 of 1955.

[5] Article 62B: see Commissioner of Taxes v. Pan African Roadways Ltd., 1957 R. & N 258 (F.C.).

[6] In a number of cases there have been two acting judges of appeal sitting with the Judge President. This is inevitable in view of the small number of permanent members of the Court. It is submitted that it is most undesirable for puisne judges to sit for some cases in the General Division and then the next week to sit in the Appellate Division where they may have to pronounce on the judgements of their brethren, thereafter again returning to the General Division.

The jurisdiction of the Appellate Division is for the most part appellate, but in terms of section 71(1) and (4) of the Constitution it has original jurisdiction to hear and determine applications by any person alleging that the provisions of the Declaration of Rights have been or are being contravened in relation to him, and also to hear any matter involving such a question if referred to it by any person presiding in any court who shall, if so requested by any party to the proceedings, refer the matter.[1] An alleged contravention of the Declaration may also come before the Appellate Division when exercising its appellate jurisdiction notwithstanding the fact that the point had not been raised in the court *a quo*.[2] Such a case is determined under Section 71 of the Constitution and not under the High Court Act.[3] If a point could and should have been raised at a trial, or later on appeal, and was not so raised the Court cannot then entertain an application under Section 71(1).[4] Indeed it will be *functus officio*.[5] It does not appear from the wording of Section 71(1) and 71(4) that the jurisdiction of the Appellate Division in such matters is exclusive but in *Zihumbga* v. *Harper, Robertson and Dodd NN.O.* it was held that jurisdiction in cases where it is alleged that the Declaration has been contravened is confined to the Appellate Division, the General Division having no power to deal with such an allegation.[6] In the first year of its existence the Appellate Division entertained five applications in terms of Section 71.[7]

Other original jurisdiction may be conferred upon the Appellate Division from time to time by law of the Legislature, but this may not be exclusive, as

---

[1] Section 71(2).

[2] Section 71(3). See *Chikwakwata* v. *Bosman N.O.*, Judgement No. A.D. 133/65 per Beadle C.J. at p. 3 and *Gundu and Sambo* v. *Hayward and Bosman NN.O.*, Judgement No. A.D. 97/65 at 4–5 and 15–16.

[3] *Chikwakwata* v. *Bosman N.O.*, *supra*.

[4] Section 71(3) precludes an application under Section 71(1) in these circumstances. This position is not affected by the proviso to Section 71(4), viz. that the Court may not exercise its powers under that sub-section 'if it is satisfied that adequate means of redress for the contravention alleged are or have been available to the person concerned under any other law'. See *dicta* by Lewis A.J.A. in *Gundu and Sambo* v. *Hayward and Bosman NN.O.*, *supra* at p. 15 where he considered that the proviso merely referred 'to the exercise of the Courts' power to *enforce* the provisions of the Declaration of Rights, i.e. by the issue of orders . . . writs, . . . and . . . directions' and that the effect of the proviso is simply that where, for example, a person has complained of wrongful arrest or imprisonment the Court will not make any special order to give him redress under Section 71(4) of the Constitution if he can obtain his redress by action for damages in the ordinary way.

[5] *Gundu and Sambo* v. *Hayward and Bosman NN.O.*, *supra* per Lewis A.J.A. at p. 16.

[6] Judgement No. GD/CIV/20/65 (as yet unreported) at p. 2 per Davies J. The decision was based on a concession on this point by counsel. *Dicta* by Quènet J.P. in *Gundu and Sambo* v. *Hayman NN.O.* at p. 4 are to the same effect.

[7] *African Newspapers (Pvt.) Ltd. and Wason* v. *The Minister of Law and Order, supra*, in which case the application was dismissed; *Maluleke* v. *The Minister of Law and Order*, which is still pending; *Joshua Nkomo* v. *Lardner-Burke N.O. and the Attorney-General*, *supra*, in which the application was successful; *Gundu and Sambo* v. *Hayward and Bosman NN.O.*, Judgement No. A.D. 97/65 in which the application was rejected both on the merits and on the ground that the court had no jurisdiction; and *Chikwakwata* v. *Bosman N.O.*, *supra* where an appeal on the merits was dismissed.

the General Division has full jurisdiction, civil and criminal, over all persons and matters within Southern Rhodesia.[1] However, it may hear points of law submitted to it directly by courts of District Commissioners and by the Natural Resources Board.[2]

Appellate jurisdiction may be conferred on the Court by law of the Legislature. Pursuant to this authorization the High Court Act 1964 has conferred on the Appellate Division both criminal and civil appellate powers in respect of appeals from the General Division, magistrates' courts, the Court of Appea for African civil cases, and various special courts and statutory tribunals (see Figure I, *supra*). The Court has no powers of review, which are the prerogative of the General Division, but it may still hear appeals from reviews.[3]

The Appellate Division has inherited not only the appellate powers of the Federal Supreme Court in respect of Southern Rhodesia but has taken over most of the appellate functions previously exercised by the Southern Rhodesian High Court as constituted prior to the creation of the Appellate Division. Thus appeals from the magistrates' court, the Court of Appeal for African civil cases, the special courts and many of the special tribunals no longer lie to the High Court as General Division but lie directly to the Appellate Division. The effect has been to cut out a step in the hierarchy of courts of appeal as formerly appeals from such courts lay first to the High Court and then to the Federal Supreme Court. The result could possibly be more frequent use of the ultimate court of appeal, the Judicial Committee.

Criminal appeals which fall within the jurisdiction of the Appellate Division comprise questions of law, of fact, of mixed law and fact, and appeals against sentence.[4] Where a question of law alone is involved appeal from the General Division is as of right. Where, however, fact, or mixed law and fact, in respect of a decision of the General Division is involved, leave to appeal is required either from a judge of that Court or from the Judge President, except in the case of a man sentenced to death.[5] No similar limitations requiring leave to appeal, however, apply to appeals from magistrates' courts.[6] It is not only the accused who enjoys a right of appeal, as the Attorney-General may appeal against judgements of the General Division and of magistrates' courts on points of law.[7] Furthermore, the Attorney-General may take sentences 'on

---

[1] Constitution, Section 52(3) read with Section 53(3). See *Bribery Commissioner* v. *Ranasinghe, supra*.

[2] African Affairs Act (Chapter 92), Section 50 and the Natural Resources Act (Chapter 264), Section 17.

[3] Section 25—appeals lie in any civil case subject to limited exceptions.

[4] Since the Court enjoys powers not only to reduce but to increase sentences on appeal, frivolous appeals on sentence are discouraged: see High Court Act 1964, Section 14(4).

[5] High Court Act, Section 13.   [6] Chapter 15, Section 59(1).

[7] High Court Act, Section 13(3) and Magistrates Court Act, Section 61. In the latter Act this procedure is somewhat inaptly named 'review'. However such appeals shall not affect the verdict in the particular case but merely provide guidance on the law for the future. The accused has a right to be represented at such an appeal.

review' if he considers the sentence to be inadequate. In this case, however, the Appellate Division may pass such sentence as it thinks ought to have been passed.[1]

Appellate civil jurisdiction of the Appellate Division is also extensive, as the court may hear any civil appeal from the General Division except for certain interlocutory orders, preliminary orders, and judgements by consent. Leave to appeal may be given in interlocutory matters either by a judge of the General Division or by the Judge President, and the same applies to judgements as to costs.[2] Interlocutory matters in which the liberty of the subject is involved, where an interdict has been refused or granted, or where a special case has been stated under the arbitration laws are, however, subject to appeal without leave.[3]

From the Appellate Division any further appeal lies to the Judicial Committee of the Privy Council.

The Judicial Committee of the Privy Council

Although Section 56E of the Southern Rhodesian Constitution empowers the Southern Rhodesian Legislature by law to provide for appeal as of right to the Judicial Committee, this provision has not as yet been utilized.

However Section 71(5) of the Constitution provides for an appeal as of right to the Judicial Committee where any person is aggrieved by a determination of the Appellate Division in respect of an alleged contravention of the Declaration of Rights in terms of Section 71, unless such appeal is merely frivolous or vexatious.[4] Rule 2 of the Judical Committee Rules 1957 (No. 2224) provides that either special leave must be obtained from the Judicial Committee itself or that leave must be obtained from the court *a quo* before any appeal can be proceeded with. In *Chikwakwata* v. *Bosman N.O.*, *supra*, it was held that even where appeal lies as of right application for leave to appeal must first be made to the Court from which the appeal is to be brought and it is the duty of the Court to form a judgement whether the appeal does or does not lie and to express that opinion so that the Privy Council will be relieved from the duty of itself making the enquiry.[5] Once the Court has decided that a right of appeal exists it has, however, no discretion to refuse leave to appeal.[6]

---

[1] Chapter 15, Section 62.

[2] High Court Act 1964, Sections 25 and 26.

[3] High Court Act, Section 26(d).

[4] An argument that the Appellate Division in determining appeals alleging contravention of the Declaration of Rights was not acting in terms of Section 71 was rejected in *Chikwakwata* v. *Bosman N.O.*, *supra* at pp. 3–4 by Beadle C.J. who took a broad view of the intention of the draftsmen of the Constitution holding that a determination under Section 71 meant every determination which concerned the question of whether or not Sections 57–68 of the Declaration of Rights had been contravened. He considered that 'it must be the substance of the matter with which the Constitution is concerned, not the particular procedure by which the matter happens to have been determined'.

[5] Adopting *Halsbury*, 3rd edition, Vol. 5, p. 684, para. 1460.

[6] In an unreported judgement of 20 November 1964 (*Lardner-Burke and Bosman NN.O.*

Since Section 71(5) allows 'any person aggrieved' by the determination of the Appellate Division to appeal it apparently permits appeal by persons other than the person who has alleged the Declaration of Rights has been contravened in relation to him. Included among such persons in most instances would be the unsuccessful party to the litigation. However, the mere fact that a litigant is disappointed or annoyed at the decision does not bring him within the category of persons aggrieved.[1] Nor does the mere fact that persons who are public bodies have been frustrated in the performance of their public duties render such persons or bodies aggrieved persons.[2] Indeed unless a litigant has had an order made throwing a burden upon him it seems that he is not a person aggrieved.[3] Accordingly it may well be that the person who is alleged to have contravened the Declaration of Rights and had an order against him will not be an aggrieved person even though he has been respondent in the action. This point passed *sub silentio* when the Appellate Division of the High Court ordered that leave be granted to the Minister of Justice and the Attorney-General to appeal against its decision in the case of *Nkomo* v. *Lardner-Burke N.O. and Attorney-General*.[4] It may therefore be that the Minister of Justice, when an order has been made against him declaring statutory powers invoked by him to be invalid in terms of Section 115 of the Constitution is not 'a person aggrieved' so as to be entitled to appeal as of right.[5] However, it appears from the decision of Lord Denning in *Attorney-General of the Gambia* v. *N'Jie* that the Attorney-General has in some cases sufficient interest as representing the Crown as guardian of the public interest to have *locus standi*.[6] Whether the term includes persons other than parties to the litigation has also to be determined.

---

v. *Nkomo and Others*, Judgement No. A.D. 140/64) Beadle C.J. left it open whether the Appellate Division had any discretion in the matter. Cp. *Halsbury*, 3rd edition, Vol. 5, p. 684, where it is stated that the function of the court is restricted to deciding whether an appeal lies as of right. In *Chikwakwata* v. *Bosman N.O.*, *supra* at pp. 5–6 Beadle C.J. accepted that once the Court had decided an appeal lay as of right it had no discretion to withhold permission and that it was in no way concerned with the likelihood of success of such an appeal.

[1] *R.* v. *London Quarter Sessions, ex parte Westminster City Council*, [1951] 1 All E.R. 1032 at 1033 per Lord Goddard C.J.

[2] *Ealing Borough Council* v. *Jones*, [1959] 1 All E.R. 286 at 288 per Lord Parker C.J.

[3] ibid. per Lord Parker C.J.

[4] Order by Beadle C.J. of 20 November 1964, Quènet J.P. and MacDonald A.J.A. concurring.

[5] In each case what is involved is interpretation of the particular statute (*Sevenoaks U.D.C.* v. *Twynam*, [1929] 2 K.B. 440 per Lord Hewart C.J. at 443). It appears from Section 71(1) that the purpose of the section is to confer rights of redress and appeal on persons who allege their rights have been infringed rather than on persons who are found by the Court to have contravened the rights of others.

[6] [1961] A.C. 617 at 634—a decision interpreting Section 31 of the West African (Appeal to Privy Council) Order in Council 1949. Lord Parker C.J. in *R.* v. *Boldero, ex parte Bognor Regis U.D.C.* Knight's Local Government Reports, Vol. 60 (1962), 292 at 296 stated that the *dicta* by Lord Denning must be confined to the particular facts of that case.

Apart from the provisions of Sections 71 the Appellate Division has no power to grant leave to appeal to the Judicial Committee 'because there is nothing in any law of this territory which provides for this Court giving leave to appeal to the Privy Council'.[1] This position is not affected by the somewhat ambiguous wording of Rule 2 of the Judicial Committee Rules 1957. As the Lord Chancellor indicated:

> In criminal cases unless there is some express provision of the law of the country from which the appeal comes authorizing an appeal in pursuance of leave from the court appealed from, an appeal will only lie under special leave granted by the Judicial Committee.[2]

The power of the Judicial Committee to grant special leave to appeal still remains. In addition *ex abundante cautela* a saving provision (Section 56G of the Constitution) has been inserted.[3] However the limitations which the Judicial Committee imposes on itself in granting special leave to appeal may mean that unless legislation is enacted in terms of Section 56E, further appeal from the Appellate Division will rarely be permitted.[4] Quite apart from the stringent tests it demands to be satisfied when leave is sought to appeal in civil and criminal matters, the Judicial Committee has imposed special restrictions when dealing with cases which originated from that Dominion when it was ultimate appellate court for South Africa. It laid down in respect of South African appeals that 'the prerogative should be exercised in a very restricted sense'.[5] Indeed it stipulated that only when matters of

[1] Beadle C.J. in *Chikwakwata* v. *Bosman N.O.*, *supra* at 5.

[2] Communication from the Lord Chancellor's Office quoted in *Chikwakwata* v. *Bosman N.O.*, *supra*.

[3] See *infra*, Part II, Chapter 7.

[4] In civil cases special leave to appeal will only be granted 'where the case is of gravity involving a matter of public interest or some important question of law, or affecting property of considerable amount or where the case is otherwise of some public importance or of a very substantial character': *Prince* v. *Gagnon* (1882), 8 App. Cas. 103 at 105. Even if a case is of public importance and of a substantial character, if the judgement appears to the Council clearly right they will refuse special leave to appeal (*Le Cité de Montreal* v. *Les Ecclésiastiques de St. Sulpice* (1889), 14 A.C. 662). Special leave will not be granted to determine academic or speculative questions (*Attorney-General for Ontario* v. *Hamilton State Railway*, [1903] A.C. 520) or merely abstract rights (*R.* v. *Louw, ex parte Attorney-General for the Cape of Good Hope*, [1904] A.C. 412); nor from a decision which is not 'judicial' (*Moses* v. *Parker*, [1896] A.C. 245 and *Lovibond* v. *Governor-General of Canada*, [1930] A.C. 717). It is also reluctant to grant leave to appeal on questions of fact, more particularly where two colonial courts have reached the same decisions on those facts (*Srimati Bibhabati Devi* v. *Kumar Ramendra Narayan Roy*, [1946] A.C. 508). In criminal cases jurisdiction is exercised even more sparingly and the court will not grant leave to appeal on questions of fact, while in other cases it has said that it will not grant leave unless it is prima facie 'shown that by a disregard of the forms of legal process, or by some violation of the principles of natural justice or otherwise, substantial and grave injustice has been done': *In re Dillett* (1887), 12 App. Cas. 459 at 467. See also *Arnold* v. *The King Emperor*, [1914] A.C. 644 at 650, where the test laid down is that 'justice itself in its very foundations has been subverted'.

[5] *Whittaker* v. *Durban Corporation* (1920), 90 L.J. (P.C.) 199. This attitude was however to some extent affected by Section 106 of the South Africa Act which authorized the Union Parliament to abolish such appeals by a Bill, subject to reservation.

paramount difficulty or importance arose should leave to appeal be granted.[1]

Even if the Judicial Committee hears an appeal, it is reluctant to over-rule the appellate court of a colony on a constitutional question. Furthermore, much will depend on the composition of the Judicial Committee at any point of time, whether a restrictive or liberal interpretation of a constitutional provision will be adopted.[2]

The personnel of the Law

The judiciary

In accordance with the recent trend to fetter the hands of the executive in appointing members of the judiciary, the Constitution inserts special safe-guards to safeguard proper appointments.[3] Section 55 provides that no puisne judge may be appointed by the Governor on the Prime Minister's advice unless the Chief Justice has agreed. Similarly no Judge of Appeal may be appointed unless both the Chief Justice and the Judge President have agreed, while in the case of appointment of the Judge President the agreement of the Chief Justice is necessary. The appointment of a Chief Justice is not subject to such safeguard, as the Chief Justice is appointed by the Governor on the Prime Minister's advice. If, however, it is proposed to appoint a person who is not already a judge of the High Court, the former Chief Justice, the Judge President, and the other judges of the High Court must be consulted. Their agreement is not, however, essential. Accordingly, a determined Prime Minister could alter the nature of the judiciary by making an appointment from outside, as the Chief Justice is the key to control. Indeed, the personality and character of the Chief Justice is all important, as he is the main safe-guard against bad appointments through the necessity for his consent.

The qualifications for appointment to a judgeship are either that the appointee has, for not less than ten years, been qualified to practise as an advocate in Southern Rhodesia or in a country in which the common law is

[1] See the remarks of Lord Haldane in *Hull* v. *McKenna and Others*, 1926 I.R. 402: 'In the case of South Africa, which is a unitary state, counsel will observe that the practice has become very strict. We are not at all disposed to advise the Sovereign, unless there is some exceptional question, such as the magnitude of the question of law involved, or it is a question of public interest in the Dominion to give leave to appeal. . . . In South Africa, we take the general sense of that Dominion into account, and restrict the cases in which we advise His Majesty to give leave to appeal.'

[2] Compare the attitude that the Canadian Constitution was 'a living tree capable of growth and expansion within its natural limits' (Lord Sankey in *Edwards* v. *Attorney-General for Canada*, [1930] A.C. 124 at 136) with the restrictive attitude adopted towards any encroachment of Dominion powers on provincial legislative powers (*Attorney-General for Canada* v. *Attorney-General for Ontario*, [1937] A.C. 326 at 354) where Lord Atkin referred to the 'water-tight compartments' of the ship of state.

[3] All that the 1923 Constitution specified in respect of the appointment of judges was that they were to be appointed by the Governor in Council: Section 38(1).

Roman–Dutch and English an official language, while an ex-judge of a superior court in such a country is also eligible. No limit is placed on the number of judges who may be appointed, so that there is nothing other than the requirement of the Chief Justice's agreement to prevent 'bench packing' if the Government wished to adopt such a policy.

Although the first judges of the Southern Rhodesian High Court were drawn from outside the country,[1] a tendency has gradually developed to appoint locally qualified advocates to the Bench. There have been three methods of entry to the Bench by local advocates. One of these has been the holding of the office of Minister of Justice (until 1933, Attorney-General) as a political Minister. In fact four of the country's Chief Justices, including the present Chief Justice, were appointed to the Bench as puisne judges, having immediately beforehand resigned their offices as Ministers of Justice.[2] Another method of entry has been appointment after holding office of Attorney-General.[3] The final method has been membership of the local Bar other than as a political minister. At present six of the puisne judges of the High Court have been appointed in this way, but the first such appointment was made in 1956. Of these judges, two have been Members of Parliament.[4]

Judges are still imported from the South African Bar owing to the shortage of judicial material in a country with such a small population as Southern Rhodesia,[5] while two distinguished South African judges from the Transvaal Provincial Division were appointed in 1955—Sir John Murray as Chief Justice of Southern Rhodesia and Sir John Clayden as a judge of the Federal Supreme Court, the latter subsequently becoming Federal Chief Justice. However, this tendency to import judges is less noticeable than in former years.

[1] Vincent J., the country's first judge, was in fact a colonial civil servant who was Crown Prosecutor in Bechuanaland until the time of his appointment by the British South Africa Company.

[2] Sir Robert Hudson, Sir V. A. Lewis, Sir Robert Tredgold, and Sir Hugh Beadle.

[3] Reference is to the chief civil servant entrusted with the prosecution of crimes and the preparation of legislation. Before the grant of responsible government in 1923 the Attorney-General was charged with all administration of justice. Attorneys-General promoted to the bench include Sir Clarkson Tredgold S.J., Sir W. E. Thomas, Sir Ralph Morton, and the Hon. Mr. Justice Jarvis. Sir Robert MacIlwaine was a former Solicitor-General. Indeed it is almost a convention that the Southern Rhodesia Attorney-General should on retirement be appointed to the bench. Mr. Justice Blakeway was Attorney-General for the High Commission Territories prior to his appointment.

[4] The Hon. Mr. Justice Dendy Young was Leader of the Opposition in the Federal Parliament when he was appointed a judge by the Southern Rhodesian Governor. The Hon. Mr. Justice Davies had been a member of the Federal Parliament and after Federal dissolution was appointed a judge of the High Court by the Southern Rhodesian Government, to which he had been politically opposed.

[5] The present Judge President of the Appellate Division, Sir Vincent Quenet, was a member of the Johannesburg Bar before accepting appointment as a puisne judge, while the Hon. Mr. Justice Hathorn was a leading member of the Natal Bar. For a short time the Hon. Mr. Justice I. A. Maisels, formerly of the Johannesburg Bar, was a puisne judge before he resigned in 1963.

There have also been frequent appointments of acting judges (who must have the same qualifications as judges) in order either to clear congestion on the rolls or more frequently to act in place of judges who are away on commissions or on leave. The Chief Justice in particular is frequently away as he is often appointed Acting Governor. He is also occupied with commissions and with sitting *ex officio* on Boards. He is Chairman of the Delimitation Commission in terms of Section 36(1) of the Constitution. He is Chairman of the Board of Trustees for Tribal Trust Land in terms of Section 94(1) of the Constitution, and he has just been Chairman of a Commission appointed in terms of Section 13 of the Electoral Act, to enquire into the purchasing power of money in Southern Rhodesia in order to determine whether the franchise qualifications ought to be raised. The present Chief Justice was also, while a puisne judge, a member of the Monckton Commission and Chairman in 1959 of the Review Tribunal established in terms of the Preventive Detention (Temporary Provisions) Act, while the Chief Justice of Southern Rhodesia, Sir John Murray, and the Chief Justice of the Federation, Sir Robert Tredgold, also sat on a commission to enquire into the franchise. It has been suggested by Sir Robert Tredgold, a former Southern Rhodesian and Federal Chief Justice, that it is undesirable that the Chief Justice should be so intimately concerned with matters that may become politically controversial. There can be no doubt that even though this has been standard colonial practice, it is most undesirable that a Chief Justice should act as Governor and assent to legislation which may subsequently be the subject of litigation.[1] Again, in politically sensitive areas such as electoral delimitation and the safeguarding of the Tribal Trust Land, it seems somewhat unfortunate that the Constitution requires his participation.[2] However, there can be no criticism of the use of judicial commissions to make recommendations for changes in the law,[3] or in other cases to enquire into or ascertain facts.[4]

The safeguards for judicial independence of judges once appointed are designed on the new model adopted since 1957 by the Commonwealth Relations and Colonial Office constitution makers. Section 56C of the Con-

---

[1] Chief Justices are on occasion consulted by the Governor for legal advice. This again is a highly undesirable practice, particularly if it involves advice on the Governor's powers, which may subsequently be the subject of litigation in which a decision is given by the Chief Justice. Again, the Chief Justice is from time to time consulted on the drafting of legislation and was recently consulted in respect of certain provisions of the controversial Referendum Act of 1964; see *S.R.L.A.D.*, Vol. 58, col. 1706, 13 September 1964.

[2] This was apparently the result of decisions taken at the Southern Rhodesian Constitutional Conference 1961: see *S.R.L.A.D.*, Vol. 55, col. 190, 10 December 1963, Whitehead.

[3] e.g. the 1956 Commission to Enquire into the Inequalities or Disabilities as between Men and Women, which was chaired by the Hon. Mr. Justice Beadle.

[4] e.g. Report of the Commission to Investigate the Grievances which gave rise to the Strike amongst the African Employees of the Rhodesia Railways. Government Printer, Salisbury, 1946 (Sir Robert Tredgold), and Report of the Commission of Inquiry into Allegations of Interference with the Courts. Government Printer, Salisbury, C.S.R. 7-1961. (The Hon. Mr. Justice Lewis.)

stitution provides that judges' salaries and allowances shall be charged upon and paid out of the Consolidated Revenue Fund. Consequently they are not debated on the annual estimates. Judges are also expressly excluded from membership of the Civil Service.[1] Furthermore a judge's salary may not be reduced during his continuance in office, while his salary is governed by the High Court Judges' Salaries and Allowances Act.[2]

Although neither the Constitution nor the Legislative Assembly's Standing Rules and Orders of Debate contain any provision preventing parliamentary criticism of a judge except on a substantive motion, since, where no provision is made United Kingdom practice must be followed, the conduct of the judges may not be debated except by a substantive motion. No such motion has in fact been moved, and the only criticism of judges has been in respect of their views when reporting as members of commissions.[3]

A judge of the High Court is not only immune from liability for acts done or words spoken in his judicial capacity,[4] but is protected against the issue of any civil process unless the leave of the General Division of the High Court is granted on a special application made for that purpose.[5] The law of contempt of court which permits either summary punishment or the initiation of subsequent criminal proceedings, similarly protects the judges against defiance of authority and from conduct calculated to bring them into contempt.[6]

Judges' security of tenure is safeguarded by provision for retirement at the age of 65 years,[7] and provision that the office of a judge may not be abolished

[1] Public Services Act (Chapter 90), Section 18(5)(b).

[2] Act No. 16 of 1964. The Chief Justice receives £5,600 per annum, the Judge President £5,500, and judges of appeal and puisne judges £5,200 per annum. Judges also receive such allowances and privileges as may be approved by the Governor. These include either Government housing or a housing allowance and Government transport. No judge has, as in South Africa, attempted to claim that liability to pay income tax amounted to a reduction in salary: see *Krause* v. *Commissioner of Inland Revenue*, 1929 A.D. 286.

[3] There was considerable implied though not express criticism when the Southern Rhodesian Government in 1960 introduced the Law and Order (Maintenance) Act, which contained a large number of minimum sentence provisions in respect of offences against public order. It was in protest against this Act that the former Federal Chief Justice, Sir Robert Tredgold, resigned, considering it 'an unwarranted invasion by the Executive of the sphere of the courts'.

[4] The same rule applies to magistrates. For the principles see *Penrice* v. *Dickinson*, 1945 A.D. 6. In respect of acts not within his jurisdiction he can be held responsible and also if he acted with improper motive: see *Cooper* v. *The Government*, 1906 T.S. 436.

[5] Rules of the High Court of Southern Rhodesia, O.3, R.14.

[6] See *R.* v. *Torch Printing and Publishing Co. Ltd. and Others*, 1956 (1) S.A. 815 (C.) for the nature of a criminal contempt. The Court adopted Lord Russell's words in *R.* v. *Gray*, [1900] 2 Q.B. at 40 and accepted the right of individuals to criticize as set out in *Ambard* v. *Attorney-General of Trinidad*, [1936] 1 All E.R. 704 (P.C.) at 709. In the case of magistrates Sections 6(4) and 69 of the Magistrates' Court Act permit magistrates to order persons who disturb the peace of the court to be detained until the rising of the court. The latter section allows imprisonment for up to seven days or a £5 fine for contempt *in facie curiae*, and one month's imprisonment and/or a £25 fine for noncompliance with magisterial orders.

[7] An invidious provision states that a judge may elect to continue until 70 'subject to the submission to and acceptance by the Governor of a medical report as to the judge's

37—C.H.L.S.R.

during his tenure of office without his consent.[1] The major safeguard, however, is that a judge may only be removed from office for inability to discharge the functions of his office or for misbehaviour, and even then may not be removed unless the question of his removal has been referred to an independent tribunal which has recommended his removal on these grounds. Requests for initiation of such proceedings are by the Chief Justice in respect of puisne judges, the Judge President in respect of Judges of Appeal, and by the Prime Minister in respect of the Chief Justice or the Judge President. Thereupon the Governor shall appoint a tribunal of at least three persons who have held office as judges of the High Court or of a superior court in the United Kingdom or in a country in which the common law is Roman–Dutch and English is an official language. Pending its report, the Governor, acting on advice of the persons who are empowered to request the appointment of such a tribunal, may suspend the judge whose removal is subject to investigation. The tribunal then reports to the Governor, who is empowered to act on its report but is not, however, bound to remove the judge in question even if the commission reports adversely.[2] No provisions for reference of the adverse report to the Judicial Committee of the Privy Council for a binding decision exist, as they do in a number of other recent Commonwealth constitutions. Most of the provisions relative to the dismissal of judges are specially entrenched clauses of the Constitution and are therefore subject to the remarkably rigid amendment procedure, but the composition of the tribunal is not one of the specially entrenched sections, and this could accordingly be changed by a two-thirds majority of the Legislative Assembly.

The Presidents of special courts

There are also a number of provisions for judges of special courts. Thus the Water Act provides for the appointment of Water Court judges holding office till the age of 65 years, subject to dismissal by the Governor for proved misbehaviour.[3] Again, the President of the Natural Resources Court is to be a Water Court judge appointed by the Governor for such period and on such conditions as he may determine. The Presidents of the Town Planning Court, of the Industrial Court, of the Workman's Compensation Court (who is to be the President of the Industrial Court), of the Fiscal Appeal Court, of the Special Court for Income Tax, of the Court of Appeal for African civil cases, and the President of the Patents Tribunal, however, enjoy no security of

mental and physical fitness so to continue in office': see Section 56A(1). The submission of an adverse medical report will be a delicate task.
[1] Constitution, Section 56A(3).
[2] Section 56B(2)(c) read with Section 56B(1).
[3] Chapter 268, Sections 64 and 67.

tenure and are subject to appointment on terms determined by the Governor.[1] In all these cases the appointee is required to be an advocate of at least ten years' standing, or a judge or ex-judge of a superior court in a country in which Roman–Dutch is the common law and English an official language. In respect of the Water and Town Planning Courts it is laid down that private practice shall amount to misbehaviour but there is no such stipulation in respect of the other courts and senior members of the Bar are appointed to head these courts with the right of private practice.

The magistracy

Magistrates are members of the civil service appointed by the Minister of Justice.[2] They are required to have passed the civil service lower law examination prior to appointment,[3] but the principle has in practice been adopted that a magistrate should have passed both the civil service lower law and the higher law examination or some other equivalent examination.[4] As civil servants they are generally speaking subject to the same provisions as to promotion, transfer, pay, increments, and Departmental discipline as any other civil servant and fall under the District Courts Department, which is a branch of the Department of Justice. As a result, much dissatisfaction has arisen amongst magistrates.[5] In fact the Magistrates' Association felt that 'the independence of a magistrate as a judicial officer is affected by the freedom of the Government to promote, transfer, or dismiss him and . . . urged that they should be placed in a different position to other civil servants with respect to these matters'.[6] They therefore sought the appointment of a judicial service commission.

The relationship between the magistracy and the Executive has in fact been publicly discussed on several occasions.[7] Ultimately in 1961 a judicial

---

[1] The Natural Resources Act (Chapter 264), Section 22(3); the Town and Country Planning Act (Chapter 133), Section 3(3); the Industrial Conciliation Act, Section 6(3); the Workmen's Compensation Act, Section 13(3); the Fiscal Appeal Court Act 1965, Section 3(2); the Income Tax Act 1954, Section 57(1); the African Affairs Act (Chapter 90); and the Patents Act 1957, Section 71.

[2] In terms of Section 7(1) of Chapter 15, read with the Public Services Act (Chapter 90).

[3] Chapter 90, Section 36.

[4] Robinson Report, *supra*, para. 175. These examinations are conducted by officers on the staff of the Attorney-General.

[5] See Memorandum prepared by the Magistrates' Association to be presented to the Commission appointed to Inquire into the Judicial and Administrative Functions of District Courts and the Native Affairs Department. Government Printer, Salisbury, 1961. Annexure 'A', The Independence of the Judiciary.

[6] Robinson Report, para. 125.

[7] See *S.R.L.A.D.*, Vol. 25 (1), col. 760–75, 17 May 1945, where any executive interference with the courts was condemned. See also *S.R.L.A.D.*, Vol. 31, col. 854, 9 May 1950 where the Minister of Justice stated that if the sentences of a particular magistrate were consistently wrong he was transferred to another branch of the service and that this had occasionally happened. The correct course was direction by Parliament in changing the type of sentence to be imposed, which would indicate the view it took of the gravity of the offence.

commission found that the Executive attempted to interfere with the discretion of magistrates on two occasions in 1960 in regard to the granting of bail, by querying magistrates' decisions after they had released two African National- ist leaders. It also found that police had been keeping records of sentences imposed by magistrates, which were forwarded with comments to the Secre- tary for Justice and (according to the commissioner) accidentally found their way to the magistrates.[1] Furthermore, a letter was sent by a senior police officer suggesting that a magistrate be reprimanded for a sentence imposed by him. It was also found that magistrates were called upon to explain their sentences, but that from 1953 (with the comment that magistrates found this irksome) it was recognized that such explanations might be called for, pro- vided this was done sparingly and not in a manner suggestive of directions being given to the magistrates. The report exculpated Government on the basis that these actions were taken in time of public disorder, and that, since heavy penalties for offences against the police and a right on the part of the Attorney-General to appeal against sentences had been introduced subse- quently by the Law and Order (Maintenance) Act, such police complaints as to inadequacy of sentence would be unlikely to recur. Nonetheless, in view of the adverse publicity occasioned by the report, it is unlikely that there will be further interference with magistrates.

Magistrates are still civil servants subject to the same Departmental dis- cipline as before, despite recommendations by the Robinson Commission that a judicial service commission be appointed.[2] Indeed Section 7B(5) of the General Law Amendment Act 1965 has specifically applied to the Public Services Act to the appointment of all magistrates.

District Commissioners

District Commissioners (formerly Native Commissioners) are also civil servants who before appointment must have passed the civil service lower law examination and certain examinations in African customary law.[3] Their lack

[1] These comments included the following: 'Please see and note the disgusting leniency of the sentence. The magistrate was Mr. X.' 'Inadequate sentence.' 'Much better—a good magistrate.' See Report of the Commission of Inquiry into Allegations of Interference with the Courts, C.S.R. 7–1961, p. 7.

[2] An astounding report by a lay commissioner—the First Report of the Commission of Inquiry into the Organisation and Development of the Southern Rhodesian Public Services, C.S.R. 9–1962 at p. 145, rejected this recommendation. At p. 145 the Commissioner con- sidered that magistrates would give the best decisions if they knew that these were being scrutinized by a chief magistrate who was an administrative officer with a view to deciding promotion on merit, while at p. 147 the commissioner went out of his way to state that the chief magistrate must explain to the magistrates the reason why 'a law has been passed and the intentions of the Legislature, planning in terms of the good of the whole'. For- tunately these recommendations have not been accepted either!

[3] Chapter 92, Section 36. The customary law examinations are a Departmental require- ment.

of independence from the Executive has become less important since, except in respect of certain offences under the African Affairs Act, they no longer enjoy criminal jurisdiction as they formerly did.[1] Furthermore, since a recommendation by the Robinson Commission has been accepted that ultimately all jurisdiction should be transferred either to the magistrates' courts or to tribal courts,[2] their remaining judicial powers will largely disappear.

The Officers of the Law

The Attorney-General, unlike the United Kingdom Attorney-General, is a civil servant vested with the responsibility for prosecuting all crimes in Southern Rhodesia. The Attorney-General also acts as law adviser and is charged with the preparation of legislation. In all these activities, however, he is subject to the control of his political Minister, the Minister of Justice.[3] The Deputy to the Attorney-General is the Solicitor-General, who is likewise a civil servant. The Attorney-General is also assisted by a staff of professional assistants, who appear in the High Court, and by public prosecutors, who are attached to magistrates' courts and are charged with the duty of prosecuting there.[4] The Attorney-General, like other civil servants, is safeguarded against dismissal by the provisions of the Public Services Act which secures that no public servant may be dismissed except on the recommendation of the Public Services Board.[5] The Act, however, may be amended at any time by the Legislature, so that the Attorney-General does not enjoy any special constitutional protection.

There has recently been appointed a State Attorney assisted by professional staff to perform work for the State which has in the past been performed by private practitioners. Nonetheless, a considerable amount of Government work is still handled by such practitioners.

There are also numerous court officials, including a Registrar of the High Court and deputy and assistant registrars as well as clerks. The responsibility of the registrars is to administer the court and they are also responsible for taxing bills of costs, as Taxing Officers.[6] A sheriff and assistant sheriffs are

[1] In the Report on Allegations of Interference with the Courts at p. 12 there was a suggestion that an Assistant Native Commissioner had been upbraided by the police for lenience in sentencing an African accused convicted of housebreaking.

[2] Report of the Secretary for Internal Affairs (1963), C.S.R. 16–1964, p. 20.

[3] Criminal Procedure and Evidence Act (Chapter 31), Sections 9 and 12. Allegations of interference with the Attorney-General by the Prime Minister were debated at length in *S.R.L.A.D.*, Vol. 48, cols. 1201–54 and 1349 et seq. and 1373 et seq. There have also been allegations that this occurred on one occasion in respect of the prosecution for a criminal offence of a sitting Member of Parliament of the governing party at a time when it had a narrow majority in the Legislative Assembly.

[4] Chapter 31, Section 18(1).

[5] Chapter 90, Section 32(1) proviso. The grounds for dismissal are either misconduct, abolition of office, unfitness or failure to acquire citizenship.

[6] Rules of the High Court, O.33, R.1.

also appointed, their duties comprising the service of process and the execution of court orders.[1] The sheriff is also concerned with the running of criminal sessions.

Other civil servants are responsible for certain functions of a judicial character. The Master of the High Court, and the additional and assistant Masters,[2] are charged with functions in respect of the administration of deceased estates, in respect of the winding up of companies under the Companies Act (Chapter 223), and in respect of the Insolvency Act (Chapter 53), and the Death Duties Act (Chapter 146). The office of the Master is an office of record for Southern Rhodesia.

Yet other civil servants exercising powers of a judicial character are mainly concerned with statutory registration and lodging of documents. Most of their decisions can be taken on appeal to the General Division, but in some cases they proceed to a special tribunal. The most important of these officials concerned with the lodging of documents are the Registrar of Deeds and the Registrar of Companies.[3]

The Police

The early history of the control over police forces in Southern Rhodesia has earlier been outlined.[4] After 1923 the B.S.A. Police came under the command of the Commissioner of Police, subject to the direction of the Governor in Council. In 1930 the Minister of Defence became responsible for administration of the Police but these duties were later assigned to the Minister of Justice. At present the Minister of Law and Order is the responsible Minister.

As the Police are not members of the Public Service they do not come under the control of the Public Services Board.[5] There is, however, a Police Advisory Board, with a status similar to that of the Public Services Board, on which a Chairman, who must be either a retired judge or legal practitioner of at least ten years' standing, sits with two other members nominated by the Government. This Board may enquire into and report to the Minister on grievances of members of the force, and report to the Minister on appeals against dismissal and demotion.[6]

Since 1964 a Police Conditions of Service Board has been established, consisting of a chairman appointed by the Minister, the Deputy Secretary for the Ministry of Law and Order, a member of the Public Services Board, and

---

[1] High Court Rules, 5, 30, 35, 41, 42, and 49.

[2] Appointed in terms of the Administration of Estates Act (Chapter 51), Section 3.

[3] Deeds Registries Act (Chapter 253) (Southern Rhodesia has a system of land registration) and the Companies Act (Chapter 223). There are also Registrars of Patents, of Designs, and of Trademarks.

[4] See *supra*, Part I, Chapter 10.

[5] Public Services Act, Chapter 90, Section 18(5)(g).

[6] Police Act 1964, Section 40 read with Section 37. The Commissioner would also come within these provisions if he were dismissed or demoted: Section 4.

two Deputy Commissioners of the Force.[1] This Board is responsible for enquiring into and reporting on conditions of service in the Force and any matters affecting its welfare and efficiency. It may hear representations from the Minister, the Commissioner, and executive committee of the B.S.A.P. Association which is established in terms of regulations made by the Governor under the Act.[2]

As a result, although the Police Forces do not enjoy protection by virtue of provisions in the Constitution, something akin to a Police Service Commission has been established by law of the Legislature. However, the Force does not enjoy the same degree of security as do civil servants, since the Police Advisory Board is purely advisory to the Minister and there is no requirement that before a dismissal can occur the Board should have made a recommendation to this effect. Detailed provisions for police discipline are set out in the Police Act and members may be tried for misconduct either before the General Division, the magistrates' court, a board of officers, or by a commissioned officer if the accused is of a junior rank.[3] Misconduct is specified at length in a schedule to the Act and renders any active participation in politics an offence. Such active participation includes membership of a trade union or employers' association other than the B.S.A.P. Association established under the Act.[4]

The duties of a policeman were the subject in 1960 of definition. These were then prescribed as being:

> The general duty of maintaining law and order in Southern Rhodesia, of taking all steps which on reasonable grounds appear to him to be necessary for preserving the peace, for preventing crime, for protecting property from malicious injury, for the detection of crime, for apprehending offenders and for suppressing all forms of civil commotion or disturbance that may occur in any part of Southern Rhodesia.[5]

The powers of the police were in 1960 considerably extended by the Law and Order (Maintenance) Act. Statutory provisions (Section 17) now incorporate the law as stated in *Thomas* v. *Sawkins*,[6] and avoid the limitations

---

[1] Section 43.   [2] Section 45(1).   [3] Sections 17 and 21.
[4] First Schedule.
[5] Law and Order (Maintenance) Act (Chapter 39), Section 3(2). A proviso to this section insists that no police officer may disobey the lawful order or direction of a person placed in authority over him. This proviso was inserted as the result of an incident in which two senior police officers were suspended from duty for attempting to arrest African Nationalist leaders in spite of contrary instructions from the Attorney-General and through him from the Cabinet. These leaders had confessed to making statements inciting a strike of African workers. The police officers were brought before a Police Board of Enquiry, but the Board discharged them as also did the magistrate's court when they were charged under the Police Act. The matter was debated at length in Parliament: see *S.R.L.A.D.*, Vol. 48, cols. 1201–54, 1349 et seq. and 1373 et seq. The reason for the amendment was that the law as it stood before that date imposed a duty on police officers to act, and they therefore considered that they were entitled to disregard contrary commands.
[6] [1935] 2 K.B. 249, followed in South Africa in *Wolpe* v. *Officer Commanding the South*

on police interference with meetings inherent in *Beatty* v. *Gillbanks*,[1] and restrictions on police powers to remain on property as set out in *Davis* v. *Lisle*.[2]

There are no Judges' Rules in Southern Rhodesia so that limitation on police powers of questioning suspects and accused persons depend on the law of evidence alone. It has therefore been held that 'If the police in taking a statement from an accused break something in the Judges' Rules in force in England or in the Republic (of South Africa), the Court must determine whether this was improper on the merits and not by consideration of whether or not the Rules were observed.' Even if something improper is done so long as this did not influence the accused or affect his volition the statement is not inadmissable as observance of the Judges' Rules in these countries is not the determining factor.[3]

Minor officials

No provision exists for coroners in Southern Rhodesia but in their place magistrates conduct inquests in terms of the Inquests Act (Chapter 12).

Justices of the Peace are also appointed who have power and are required to preserve the public peace.[4] The office, however, is largely honorary, except that solemn oaths and declarations may be made before a Justice of the Peace, and any person who makes a false statement in such circumstances is guilty of an offence and renders himself liable to the penalties for perjury.[5]

Commissioners of Oaths are also appointed by the Minister of Justice and have the same power in respect of oaths as Justices of the Peace.[6] In addition, a number of persons such as notaries public, District Commissioners, senior police officers, and other persons in public positions (e.g. Members of Parliament) are *ex officio* Commissioners of Oaths.

The legal profession

A remarkable feature in Southern Rhodesia is that although only a small proportion of the population can afford to patronize lawyers, the country has persisted in having a divided profession.

African Police, Johannesburg, 1955 (2) S.A. 87 (W.). For an analysis of this case see B. Beinart, 'Police Powers', *Butterworths South African Law Review 1955*, pp. 157–65.

[1] (1882), 9 Q.B.D. 308.

[2] [1936] 2 K.B. 435.

[3] *R* v. *Tapeson*, 1965 (2) S.A. 761 (S.R.A.D.) and *R.* v. *Ananias*, 1963 (3) S.A. 486 (S.R.).

[4] Justices of the Peace Act (Chapter 13), Section 3. Justices of the Peace have power to preserve the public peace and to call to their assistance constables, peace and military officers, and all subjects to quell riots, brawls, disturbances, and to lodge rioters, brawlers, vagrants and disturbers of the peace in any prison to be dealt with according to law. These powers have not been used in practice since the beginning of this century.

[5] Oaths and Declarations Act (Chapter 16).

[6] Commissioners of Oaths Act (Chapter 9), Section 4.

Advocates in Southern Rhodesia are required to be qualified and admitted to practice in accordance with the Advocates Act (Chapter 207), and in terms of the Rules of the High Court. To be admitted an applicant must either be a barrister in the United Kingdom or South Africa or have obtained a United Kingdom or South African LL.B. degree or the Oxford B.A. in Jurisprudence or the B.C.L. In addition local examinations in statute law must be written, while those who have not acquired these qualifications in South Africa must also pass examinations in Roman–Dutch Law. Within the six months preceding the application the prospective advocate may not have had any connection with the profession of an attorney either in Southern Rhodesia or elsewhere.[1] There is at present no system of pupillage and an advocate may immediately commence practice. Nor is a Chambers system akin to that in the United Kingdom permitted, as the Rules of the Bar prohibit any relationship in the least degree resembling partnership.[2]

Advocates have the exclusive right of audience in both Divisions of the High Court and a right of audience concurrent with attorneys in inferior courts, and District Commissioners' courts. Their work also consists of settling and drafting pleadings and giving opinions. However counsel may not accept briefs from persons other than from an attorney except in special circumstances, e.g. dock briefs, cases undertaken at the request of the court, or when appearing for the Crown.[3] Strict rules of etiquette govern the relationships of counsel and attorneys.

The Bar of Southern Rhodesia is very small, there being in August 1964 thirty-two practising advocates. Patents to Queen's Counsel are granted by the Governor acting on the advice of the Minister of Justice, who consults the Chief Justice and on occasions applications for patents have been refused. A patent is generally granted to the Attorney-General. Once silk has been taken a Queen's Counsel may not appear without a junior in any matter originating in the High or Magistrates' Courts, although he may appear alone in special courts. This is infrequently done in practice.

Attorneys must be qualified and admitted in terms of the Attorneys, Notaries, and Conveyancers Act. The period of training required for an attorney varies, depending on whether he has a university degree and whether he has practised as a member of the Bar. In other cases five years of articles and the Attorneys Admission Examination (in three parts) must be passed.

---

[1] Advocates Act (Chapter, 207) Section 4. This rule of quarantine discourages attorneys from moving to the Bar.

[2] A rule more honoured in the breach is that it is improper for Counsel to hand on a brief received by him to anyone else except with the authority of the instructing attorney. Counsel must seek instructions from his attorney if it is impossible for him to attend to the brief. Implied authority to hand on a brief is often relied on in practice.

[3] Advocates may accept briefs directly from a District Commissioner to defend an African accused if the D.C. has confirmed in writing that the accused is unable to provide more than twenty-five guineas for the defence.

To be admitted as a notary or a conveyancer, attorneys require to pass further examinations.

Attorneys have a right of audience concurrent with counsel of appearing in magistrates' courts and special courts and tribunals. An important part of their work is the drafting of documents, the taking of statements, preparation of briefs, and giving legal advice directly to members of the public. It is a criminal offence for unqualified persons to perform these services.[1]

Proceedings against attorneys for dishonourable conduct are largely initiated by the Law Society of Southern Rhodesia which is constituted by Private Act.[2] The Society makes application to the General Division for the striking off or suspension of attorneys and appears in all proceedings relative to attorneys.[3] There were in August 1964 171 practising attorneys in Southern Rhodesia, including the two Government Attorneys.[4]

Legal advice and representation

The provisions for free legal advice in Southern Rhodesia are unfortunately inadequate. Legal advice to poor persons is only made available through a voluntary arrangement between the Bar and Side Bar in Salisbury and the Citizens' Advice Bureau whereby persons without financial means are referred by the Bureau on a roster basis to attorneys who may further refer the matter to an advocate who has volunteered to participate in the scheme.

Legal representation is on a somewhat different basis as it is available in a circumscribed category of cases. In criminal matters in which an accused person is standing trial in any court or in cases where an accused is appearing before a magistrate to undergo a preparatory examination, the Legal Assistance and Representation Act (Chapter 40), which was passed in 1948, provides that 'if it appears in the interests of justice' and that such person's means are insufficient, a judge, magistrate, or registrar may certify that he should have legal assistance. The court may then assign the accused a legal representative.[5] However the provision is little used as the Act provides that it must be 'practicable' to procure the services of an advocate or an attorney, and this is not always the case. Furthermore it is difficult for a court to decide whether 'it is desirable in the interests of justice' to secure such representation unless evidence has first been led. Finally the public are ignorant of the existence of these provisions and there are few attempts to invoke them.

---

[1] Attorneys, Notaries, and Conveyances Act (Chapter 229), Sections 23 and 24.

[2] The Law Society of Southern Rhodesia (Private) Act (Chapter 213).

[3] Attorneys, Notaries, and Conveyancers Act (Chapter 229), Sections 31 and 33.

[4] Of these one was African, one was Asian, and the others were European.

[5] Fees ranging from £3 to a maximum of £12 are payable in respect of each case by the registrar of the court from public funds. In addition expenses may be reimbursed: G.N. 290/1949. Rules under the Legal Assistance and Representation Act.

A further provision is contained in Section 4 of the Act which permits the Attorney-General, if he has indicted an accused for trial before the High Court or remitted him to any other court, to certify on similar grounds that the accused should have legal assistance. The Attorney-General utilizes these powers when an accused has been charged with a serious crime such as murder, rape, or breach of Section 37 of the Law and Order (Maintenance) Act.[1]

In terms of the Bar Rules it is also provided that counsel must accept dock defences on the instructions of the prisoner in person.[2] However, little use can be made of this facility as counsel do not attend Court on the opening day of the criminal sessions.

A further possibility of obtaining legal assistance arises out of an arrangement between the Bar and the Ministry of Internal Affairs. In terms of this agreement advocates may accept briefs directly from District Commissioners if the District Commissioner has certified that the accused is unable to pay more than 25 guineas for his defence, provided that the fee for the brief is not less than 7 guineas.[3]

The High Court has also an inherent power to appoint counsel and attorneys to appear *pro deo* for an undefended accused, but such power is usually only invoked if the matter involves difficult points of law or if the death sentence is a possible penalty and the accused has not been assigned counsel under the Act.

No provision is made in the Legal Assistance and Representation Act for aid in the conduct of criminal appeals. However the Rules of the Appellate Division allow an application to be made to the Registrar of the Court who enquires into the appellant's means and then refers his report to a judge who may grant legal aid for the preparation of the record and also for the assignment of counsel. This may be given subject to conditions and subject to part payment by the appellant depending on his means. If it appears desirable in the interests of justice a judge may assign assistance to any appellant whether or not he has applied for legal aid in the conduct of his case.[4]

Despite these provisions the majority of persons brought before the criminal courts are unaware of their rights to obtain legal aid so that the majority of cases are undefended. Should a case be undefended it is however the duty of the court to go out of its way to assist the unrepresented accused and to explain the burden of the charge to him.[5]

---

[1] For such appearances counsel are paid a nominal fee and are normally chosen from a roster of juniors. However senior counsel occasionally appear *pro deo* at the request of the Court as in *Mapolisa* v. *R.*, 1963 R. and N. 808 (F.C.).

[2] At a minimum fee of two guineas and at a maximum of seven guineas.

[3] The Bar Council in 'exceptional' circumstances may authorize a minimum fee of two guineas.

[4] Rule 21(5), S.R.G.N. 380/64.

[5] This is not always observed. See *R.* v. *Mukwacha*, 1962 R. & N. 842 (S.R.) in which a

The Constitution in Section 67(2)(d) ironically reflects the position:

Every person who is charged with a criminal offence . . . shall be permitted to defend himself in person or at his own expense by a legal representative of his own choice.

In civil cases the position is also unsatisfactory. In High Court actions legal assistance can be obtained by *in forma pauperis* proceedings in which leave of the Court to sue or defend is sought. A safeguard for the opponent is that the Court will not grant leave unless counsel has certified that the petitioner *prima facie* has a good case, and will only do so after the opposite party has had an opportunity to show cause why such relief should not be granted. Furthermore the means test is strict (the petitioner must not be possessed of £50 property, excluding household goods, wearing apparel, and tools of trade).[1] The provisions of the Rule must be strictly complied with since it affords a privilege which may work hardship on an opponent who would in the event of his success be unable to recover costs from the assisted pauper.[2]

Similar provision exists in terms of the Magistrates Court Rules which allow the court if satisfied that an applicant has a *prima facie* case but is not possessed of means or earnings sufficient to enable payment of court fees and messengers' charges to exempt the applicant from such costs and to order the clerk of the court to assist him in the procedural aspects of the case or to appoint an attorney to represent him.[3]

The Appellate Division Rules now allow civil appellants to apply for leave to prosecute or defend an appeal *in forma pauperis*.[4] Formerly there was no such provision in the Rules but the High Court (before its reconstitution in 1964) held that in any event it had an inherent power to allow any proceedings to be brought before it *in forma pauperis* and that the procedure laid down in the Rules dealing with leave to bring or defend actions should *mutatis mutandis* apply.[5]

In District Commissioners' Courts there is no provision for free legal representation although court officials may in practice assist a plaintiff to draft a summons initiating action. Neither is any free assistance available in the Court of Appeal for African civil cases.

Although the legal assistance provisions may on paper appear satisfactory it is submitted that in practice they are inadequate not only because of the

conviction and sentence were set aside on automatic review because the magistrate had not explained to the accused what would be a sufficient defence to the charge.

[1] G.N. 612/1963. Until the end of 1963 the amount was £10, a quantum arrived at at the beginning of this century, and with reference to which Murray C.J. commented that this was 'obviously a trifling sum and hopelessly little to permit any person to embark on litigation': *Joseph* v. *Joseph*, 1958 (4) S.A. 85 (S.R.) at 86.

[2] *Joseph* v. *Joseph*, *supra* at 87 per Murray, C.J.

[3] S.R.G.N. 1/1932 Order V.

[4] S.R.G.N. 380/1964. Rule 38.

[5] *Mapalala* v. *Guter*, 1958 (3) S.A. 679 (S.R.).

limited circumstances in which they are available,[1] but also because of the fact that the majority of the population are uneducated and have had a foreign legal system, which operates formal courts conducted in a foreign language,[2] imposed upon them. These criticisms are even more justified when regard is had to the possibility of miscarriages of justice in criminal cases.

[1] Poor persons of all races are affected by the strict provisions.

[2] All proceedings before any division of the High Court and in the Magistrates' Courts and the pleadings thereof shall be in the English language: High Court Act No. 22 of 1964, Section 47, and Magistrates Court Act, Section 6, as amended by the General Law Amendment Act 1965, Section 4. The Rules of the High and Magistrates' Courts provide for the services of interpreters who are sworn truly to interpret. But this is not sufficient guarantee that issues are properly communicated to an accused person.

4

THE STATE, THE INDIVIDUAL, AND THE DECLARATION OF RIGHTS

Nationality and aliens

SHORTLY before the establishment of Federation, the unusual step was taken of permitting Southern Rhodesia, which was not a dominion, to pass her own nationality and citizenship laws.[1] Consequently from 1949 the Southern Rhodesian Citizenship and British Nationality Act as amended from time to time provided for Southern Rhodesian citizenship, while that Act and the British Nationality Act 1948 stipulated that Southern Rhodesian citizens should also be British subjects.[2]

The same privilege was permitted by the United Kingdom Government to the Federation and early in 1958 the Citizenship of Rhodesia and Nyasaland and British Nationality Act 1957 came into force, Federal citizenship being substituted for Southern Rhodesian citizenship.[3] This Act as amended from time to time governed the position until the Federal Laws (Cesser) Order[4] provided that it should, on the dissolution of Federation, cease to have effect as respects Southern Rhodesia. Shortly before dissolution the Southern Rhodesian Legislature after close consultation between the Southern Rhodesian and British Governments passed an agreed measure, the Citizenship of Southern Rhodesia and British Nationality Act No. 63 of 1963, which was to come into operation on the date of dissolution of the Federation.[5] The Bill was intended to confer Southern Rhodesian citizenship on all Southern Rhodesian residents who were former Federal citizens and also generally to replace the Federal legislation.

The Act proceeds on the principles which have commonly been adopted by Commonwealth countries in their citizenship laws. Thus Southern Rhodesian citizens are by virtue of their Southern Rhodesian citizenship also British subjects. There is nothing to preclude citizens from being dual or even multi-

---

[1] *Supra*, Part I, Chapter 11.

[2] See C. Parry, *Nationality and Citizenship Laws of the British Commonwealth and the Republic of Ireland*, Stevens, 1957, for a commentary on this legislation.

[3] The Southern Rhodesian Citizenship and British Nationality (Repeal) Act No. 1 of 1958 repealed the earlier Southern Rhodesian legislation. Parry, op. cit., Vol. II, comments on the Federal Citizenship legislation.

[4] S.R.G.N. 786/63 issued in terms of Section 2(2) of the Federation of Rhodesia and Nyasaland (Dissolution) Order in Council.

[5] The use of a certificate of urgency employed in this case was justified so that this Bill could become law before Federal dissolution.

nationals except for the provision that a citizen of full age who, while outside Southern Rhodesia, by some voluntary and formal act other than marriage, becomes a national of another country thereupon ceases to be a Southern Rhodesian citizen.[1]

The Act provides for the standard methods of acquiring nationality, viz. birth, descent and adoption, registration and naturalization. Acquisition by either of the last two methods, however, is entirely at the discretion of the Minister of Internal Affairs after the fulfilment of specified requirements.[2]

The position of married women and children is for the most part also dealt with in the standard way. However, the attitude of the Southern Rhodesian Legislature (an attitude similar to that of the South African Legislature) towards polygamous marriages has necessitated special provision. Thus women married outside Southern Rhodesia under a system permitting of polygamy are not, if they cease to be British subjects by virtue of their marriage, to be deemed such even though this is the case with women married under non-polygamous systems.[3] Similarly, children born outside Southern Rhodesia of a father who was a citizen otherwise than by descent are not, if children of a marriage solemnized outside Southern Rhodesia under a system permitting of polygamy, citizens by descent.[4] Again, wives of Southern Rhodesian citizens married outside Southern Rhodesia under a system permitting polygamy are not entitled to claim citizenship by registration.[5]

There are also provisions in what has come to be common form for the refusal of citizenship and for power of the Minister to refuse to give reasons for his refusal of any application made under the Act.[6]

Deprivation of citizenship by registration or by naturalization is also possible on certain specified grounds, viz. obtaining citizenship by fraud, for disloyalty, disaffection, trading with the enemy, a sentence of imprisonment of not less than one year, or a sentence of not less than six months imprisonment without the option of a fine under Southern Rhodesia's security laws or for certain common law offences.[7] However, before he may exercise such power, the Minister must be satisfied that 'it is not conducive to the public good that the person should continue to be a citizen', shall inform him in

[1] Act 63 of 1963, Section 23 read with 'foreign country' in Section 3(1).

[2] Sections 6–16. Citizens of Commonwealth and ex-Commonwealth countries require a two-year period of residence to become eligible, while aliens and British Protected Persons must have been resident for a total period of four years or longer apart from any other requirements as to language, &c.

[3] Section 26(2).   [4] Section 7(1).   [5] Section 10(1)(b).

[6] Section 32(1). Ministerial decisions are not subject to appeal or review in any court.

[7] Section 18(1)(b). It is hazardous for naturalized and registered citizens actively to participate in African nationalist politics. If they possess publications relating to an unlawful organization, whether or not it has ceased to exist, they may be sentenced to a term of imprisonment in excess of six months in terms of Section 9 of the Unlawful Organizations Act 1959 as amended, while if they are convicted of making or possessing a subversive statement, which is widely defined in terms of Section 39 of the Law and Order (Maintenance) Act 1960 a sentence of compulsory imprisonment is entailed.

writing of the grounds on which such an order is proposed, and shall refer the case for enquiry and report to a commissioner appointed for him for this purpose, who shall be a judge or ex-judge or advocate of at least ten years standing.[1] The significance of deprival of citizenship is that once this has occurred the ex-citizen may be declared a prohibited immigrant and forced to leave the country. Citizens may not be declared prohibited immigrants unless a deportation order has been made against them,[2] while deportation orders against citizens can only be made in the event of the person in question having been convicted of a scheduled crime,[3] and subject to the further limitation that persons born in Southern Rhodesia or those who have been resident in the country for more than seven years may not be deported.[4] There is no safeguard requiring observation of the *audi alteram partem* rule and the appointment of a legally trained commissioner as in the case of deprivation of citizenship, the only right exercisable by the deported person being the right to draw the Minister's attention to mitigating circumstances.

Provision also exists for automatic deprivation of citizenship in the case of naturalized and registered citizens who are absent from Southern Rhodesia for a continuous period of seven years.[5]

A somewhat unusual provision relates to renunciation of citizenship which, although this right is generally permitted to dual nationals, requires the authority of the Minister in the case of renunciation of Southern Rhodesian citizenship by citizens of Commonwealth countries, of Eire and of South Africa, who are ordinarily resident in Southern Rhodesia.[6]

Citizenship legislation does not form part of the Constitution,[7] while questions relating to immigration, citizenship, or deportation do not come directly within the scope of the Declaration of Rights. Indeed there is no special provision relative to legislative competence in these spheres other than for the fact that the Declaration of Rights states that the provisions relative to discrimination shall not apply in respect of 'restrictions on entry into . . . Southern Rhodesia . . . in the case of persons who are neither citizens . . . by virtue of their connection with, or regarded by virtue of a written law as permanently resident in Southern Rhodesia'.[8] There being no provision in the Constitution relative to freedom to move into the country the Southern

---

[1] Section 18(2)(3)(4).

[2] Federal Immigration Act No. 37 of 1954 as amended by Act 9 of 1959. See Section 13(1)(e) as amended read with Section 5(1)(i). This Act is still in force.

[3] The scheduled convictions for the most part relate to serious crimes or attempts or incitements to commit such crimes, but they also include political offences.

[4] Federal Deportation Act No. 36 of 1954 which is still in force in Southern Rhodesia.

[5] Section 22(1). This period may be extended by the Minister while absence for certain specified purposes is not taken into account in determining the length of absence.

[6] Section 17(3).

[7] Compare the Nigerian Constitution of 1960: S.I. 1960 No. 1652, Sections 7–16, where constitutional amendments were required to change the citizenship laws.

[8] Constitution Section 67(3)(d).

Rhodesian Legislature may pass any legislation or authorize the taking of any administrative action regulating immigration, the grant of residence permits, permanent or otherwise, the grant, refusal or deprivation of citizenship and may pass laws relative to deportation without such laws being subject to the anti-discrimination provisions in the Declaration of Rights. Once, however, an alien or non-citizen was granted a residence permit under any law for the time being in force relative to immigration[1] he could not then be subjected to discrimination, although prior to the grant of such permit discrimination would be competent.[2]

Aliens once lawfully within Southern Rhodesia by virtue of a permanent residence permit are entitled to the same protection afforded by the laws of the country to all inhabitants and also to the constitutional protections set out in the Declaration of Rights. Aliens on temporary permits are similarly entitled to protection of the laws and the Declaration of Rights with the exception that laws may discriminate against their entry into Southern Rhodesia, their employment in, acquisition of or interest in immovable property in Southern Rhodesia, or their enjoyment of services provided out of Southern Rhodesia public funds.[3] A liability to which only aliens[4] are subject arises from the power of the Minister of Internal Affairs to direct any alien to leave Southern Rhodesia within a specified period or by warrant to authorize his removal if it is 'in his opinion in the public interest'.[5] Such alien may be held in prison pending his removal.

The Declaration of Rights

Inserted in the middle of the Southern Rhodesian Constitution 1961 is a preamble to Chapter VI, the Declaration of Rights. This reads as follows:

Whereas it is desirable to ensure that every person in Southern Rhodesia enjoys the fundamental rights and freedoms of the individual, that is to say, the right, whatever his race, tribe, place of origin, political opinions, colour or creed, but

---

[1] viz. Section 29 of the Immigration Act 1954.

[2] In practice there is discrimination in application of the immigration laws. Acting in terms of Section 5(1)(a) of the Immigration Act the Federal Minister responsible deemed all non-Europeans to be unsuited to Federal (now Southern Rhodesian) requirements and to be undesirable immigrants on account of their standard or habits of life. See Summary of Federal Immigration Requirement for Immigrants and Settlers from the Union of South Africa, Government Printer, 6105–20,000, 9 July 1959, p. 4: '(29) non-Europeans are not normally admitted either as immigrants or on temporary employment permits. Any non-European wishing to visit the Federation should first apply to the Federal Chief Immigration Officer.' An exception to this rule was made to allow Dr. S. B. Ngcobo to accept employment as a lecturer at the University College. The rules are also not applied to migratory labourers or to African labourers recruited for employment in Southern Rhodesia's mines or on farms.

[3] Constitution Section 67(3)(d).

[4] Aliens are persons who are neither British subjects, British Protected Persons from Northern Rhodesia or Nyasaland, or citizens of South Africa or Eire: Section 2, Deportation Act 36 of 1954.

[5] Section 3(1) as amended by the Deportation Amendment Act 1964.

38—C.H.L.S.R.

subject to respect for the rights and freedoms of others and for the public interest, to each and all of the following, namely—

(a) life, liberty, security of the person, the enjoyment of property and the protection of the law;
(b) freedom of conscience, of expression, and of assembly and association; and
(c) respect for his private and family life.

the following provisions of this Chapter shall have effect for the purpose of affording protection to the aforesaid rights and freedoms subject to the limitations of that protection contained in those provisions.

The recent change in attitude of the 'indefatigable constitution-mongers of the Colonial and Commonwealth Relations Officers' from cynicism and hostility to relative enthusiasm about the insertion of fundamental rights provisions in their products has been the subject of much comment.[1] Formerly scepticism as to the value of such provisions was widespread among English constitutional lawyers, this attitude being best expressed in the Simon Report of 1931 on the situation in India.[2] Even assuming in the words of the Simon Commission Report, 'the will and the means' to make such a declaration effective, fundamental guarantees may be vitiated by the need in defining the protected rights to avoid placing embarrassing and unnecessary restrictions on the power of legislatures. As Professor Wheare has said: 'no realistic attempt to define the rights of the citizen can fail to include qualifications', but unfortunately only too often in practice, Professor Wheare continued, 'when we see the result it is difficult to resist making the question "What of substance is left after the qualifications have been given full effect"'.[3] This comment, it will be submitted, might be the epitaph of the Southern Rhodesian Declaration of Rights.

Yet another factor that in large measure determines the effectiveness of any Declaration of Rights and in particular that in the Southern Rhodesia Constitution 1961 is the attitude adopted by the Government in power to the Constitution. This becomes all the more important when, although judicial review may be available, there is no proper provision for legal aid to secure

[1] See S. A. de Smith, 'Fundamental Rights in the New Commonwealth' (1961), 10, *I. C.L.Q.* 83, 215; 'Fundamental Rights in Commonwealth Constitutions' (1962), 43, *Journal of the Parliaments of the Commonwealth*; and *The New Commonwealth and its Constitutions*, Stevens, 1964. See also A. Gledhill, 'Fundamental Rights', in *Changing Law and Developing Countries*, op. cit., and Cowen, op. cit., pp. 113 et seq. The arguments for and against Bills of Rights are fully set out in these works.
[2] 'Many of those who came before us have urged that the Indian Constitution should contain definite guarantees for the rights of individuals in respect of the exercise of their religion and a declaration of the equal rights of all citizens. We are aware that such provisions have been inserted in many constitutions, notably in those of the European states formed after the war. Experience, however, has not shown them to be of any great practical value. Abstract declarations are useless unless there exists the will and the means to make them effective.' Cmd. 3569 (1930), 22–23.
[3] *Modern Constitutions*, Oxford, 1962, p. 57.

that the constitutional machinery for enforcement is brought into action. If a Government is prepared to 'take chances' on the law and to take controversial action possibly inconsistent with the fundamental rights provisions until such time as this action is specifically declared to have contravened the Constitution, there can be considerable interference in practice with fundamental freedom. This is the more marked if the persons who are the objects of governmental action are ignorant of their legal rights and unable to obtain legal aid. How such an attitude by a Government may operate in practice is best illustrated by reference to governmental action taken in respect of Mr. Nkomo and certain other leading African nationalists from March to November 1964. Despite warnings in Parliament that such action might be unlawful, the Minister evolved a scheme by which with the use of the Law and Order (Maintenance) Act 1960 and the Protected Places and Areas Act, he effectively held Mr. Nkomo and others in effective detention in the Gonakudzingwa Restriction Area. Once this action was declared unlawful by the courts, the Minister nonetheless continued to enforce his orders pending a decision on appeal, the applicants at that time having insufficient funds to apply for a writ *de homine libero exhibendo* or a declaration that they were entitled to their freedom in the light of the ruling by the General Division of the High Court. When the Appellate Division invalidated the Minister's scheme, he then invoked the Preventive Detention (Temporary Provisions) Act 1959 as amended in 1964, despite an adverse report on it by the Constitutional Council and further warnings to the Minister in Parliament that this would be unlawful. As a result, the nationalist leaders were detained in Gwelo prison until mid-November, when the Appellate Division of the High Court declared that the Act contravened the Declaration of Rights. The Court, however, adopted an unusual attitude and agreed to postpone granting an order for the applicants' release for one week, pending an appeal against the decision by the Minister to the Judicial Committee. Within this period, however, the Minister re-restricted the appellants to the Gonakudzingwa Area. It will be seen, however, that Mr. Nkomo and others were for eight months effectively detained.[1]

Yet another instance illustrating the ineffectiveness of the Declaration in

[1] A further step open to the Minister would be the declaration of a state of emergency in the Nuanetsi area which includes the Gonakudzingwa area, and by virtue of emergency regulations the detention of the nationalist leaders. To have done this immediately after the Appellate Division judgement might however have been suggestive of *detournement de pouvoir*. Time having elapsed on 28 May 1965 the Governor declared a state of emergency in the Nuanetsi area. The Minister of Justice declared that the main objects of the action had been 'to stop the dissemination of subversion to tribal and other areas, to bring the activities of the restrictees under control and to restore law and order in the area . . . (and) to arrest and detain those emissaries of Nkomo who were operating in the emergency area': *S.R.L.A.D.*, Vol. 61, col. 34, 10 April 1965. Those persons formerly unlawfully detained are in terms of Section 58(5) of the Constitution entitled to compensation. Thus retrospective legislation granting an indemnity to the Minister of Law and Order is only possible if it takes the form of a constitutional amendment. See *supra*, p. 434, n. 7.

such a situation relates to the position of persons detained in terms of the Emergency (Harare and Highfield) Regulations 1964.[1] Although the Declaration of Rights in Section 69 provides that in cases of detention a tribunal shall be established by law, the Minister of Justice, despite requests for the appointment of such a tribunal, both by detainees and in Parliament, where he undertook to do so, failed to establish such tribunal, apparently taking the view that he need not do so until twelve months had elapsed from the date of the detentions, although there is little in the Section to justify such a view.[2] Again, the only method to enforce action on the Minister would be by an application for a mandamus. However until such action is taken the Minister, relying on a doubtful interpretation of the law, can in effect render the constitutional protection valueless. As already indicated[3] there is little provision for legal aid generally, while the narrowly drafted constitutional provisions relating to certificates by the Constitutional Council for test cases on the Declaration do not permit of aid in such an action since a certificate can only be granted if an adverse report has been made on the Act or law, or if the issue has been referred to the Appellate Division by a court in any proceedings, or in an appeal from the Appellate Division under its original jurisdiction.[4] Furthermore, detained persons cannot be seen by members of the public and may not communicate with or be communicated with by other persons except in terms of rules made by the camp superintendent. It is also an offence either to send a letter from such a camp or to receive one unless the removal of such a letter has been authorized by the camp superintendent.[5] Under these circumstances it is in practice extremely difficult to advise such detainees to commence legal proceedings against the Minister by way of an application for leave to sue *in forma pauperis*. In fact this particular example shows that the combination of the laws as to *locus standi* (this is narrowly defined), the lack of legal aid, and the Emergency Regulations themselves may render impotent the protections conferred by the Declaration of Rights. A Government can fairly be criticized if it embarks on dubious legislative schemes, since governments should be the upholders of the Constitution both in letter and in spirit and should not adopt an attitude which would more befit tax avoidance experts.

The attitude of the Courts towards their function in interpreting the scope of the fundamental rights provisions may also considerably affect the application of the Declaration of Rights. It is too early yet to say whether the Courts will adopt a narrow positivist approach or whether they will take a purposive view of the constitutional provisions. Should they wish to take the

[1] S.R.G.N. No. 620 B and No. 718 B of 1964.
[2] There is a clear drafting error in the section on which the Minister may have taken this view. See *infra*.
[3] *Supra*, Part II, Chapter 3.
[4] *Supra*, Part II, Chapter 1, and Section 71(6) of the Constitution.
[5] See the Emergency (Harare) Regulations, Sections 25, 34, and 35.

latter view, *dicta* on the Federal Constitution in *Mutasa* v. *Minister of Home Affairs, supra,* may assist them.[1] However, four of the judgements so far given on the Declaration of Rights seem to indicate a tendency to treat the Constitution as a statute to be interpreted according to ordinary canons.[2] Furthermore, another tendency has emerged of assuming in favour of challenged legislation that every possible presumption should be made in favour of the validity of such a law.[3] Indeed the position has been reached where in interpreting the same phrase in laws *in pari materia* a wide interpretation was adopted so as not to invalidate the Unlawful Organizations Amendment Act No. 9 of 1963,[4] but a narrow meaning was given to the identical phrase in interpreting Section 19 of the Law and Order (Maintenance) Act, Chapter 9. In the latter case, where an accused was charged with having a banned publication in his possession without lawful excuse, the Court considered that if a wide meaning were taken the purpose of the law would be defeated.[5] It seems invidious that the Courts should adopt dual standards for interpreting the extent of and elements of statutory crimes depending on whether the legislation in question is sought to be invalidated in terms of the Declaration or whether the proceedings merely involve an accused who raises the defence that his conduct is not covered by the Act in question.

Again, in deciding whether a law has been changed so as not to be safeguarded as an existing law and thus exempted from the provisions of the Declaration, the Courts have taken a restricted view of their powers, holding that they may not examine questions of how the laws are administered in deciding whether they are valid or not, the validity of challenged laws requiring to 'be decided by purely legal considerations'.[6]

[1] They should be extremely careful in utilizing foreign decisions to interpret the Southern Rhodesian Declaration. A timely warning on the use of such cases without full appreciation of the whole stream of legal decisions in interpreting provisions incorporating fundamental guarantees was given by D. A. Grove in 'The Sentinels of Liberty: the Nigerian Judiciary and Fundamental Rights' (1963), *J.A.L.*, Vol. 7, at 164–7.

[2] This is apparent from the meticulous examination of the provisions of the Constitution by the Courts and the care with which they have examined what constitutes a re-enactment of a law so as to come within the provisions of Section 70(1)(c) thus being exempted from the application of the Declaration.

[3] *Maluleke* v. *Minister of Law and Another,* 1963 (4) S.A. 206 (S.R.) at 211 per Beadle C.J. Where wide delegated powers are conferred 'the Legislature must have intended that when the Minister exercised his powers he would observe the Constitution and exercise the powers delegated to him lawfully and not unlawfully': *Nkomo and Others* v. *Minister of Justice and Others,* 1965 (1) S.A. 498 (S.R.A.D.) at 503. Cp. the position in Nigeria where a similar attitude has been adopted: Grove, op. cit., at 163 and criticism at 165.

[4] *Musururwa* v. *Attorney-General, Southern Rhodesia,* 1963 (4) S.A. 720 relative to the use of the words 'without lawful excuse' in Section 9(1)(bb) of Act 38 of 1959 as amended.

[5] *R.* v. *Mackay,* 1964 (1) S.A. 304 (S.R.) at 310.

[6] *African Newspapers (Pvt.) Limited and Another* v. *Lardner-Burke and Another,* 1964 (4) S.A. 486 (S.R.A.D.) at 490. In this case it was alleged that prior to the coming into force of the new Constitution the Governor might dissent from the view of his Cabinet and enjoyed a discretion to refuse to ban a newspaper, but that from the time of coming into force of the new Constitution he was obliged to act on the advice of his Government. It was then

However in *Chikwakwata* v. *Bosman N.O.*, *supra* at p. 4, Beadle C.J. took a generous view of the provisions permitting appeal as of right to the Privy Council and held that a commonsense view of what the Constitution's drafters must have intended should be adopted. He considered in deciding whether appeal lay as of right for contraventions of the Declaration, that the Constitution was concerned with the substance of the matter and not with the particular procedure by which the matter happened to have been determined. Accordingly in interpreting ambiguous wording, which the Crown contended did not allow appeals as of right from appellate decisions of the Appellate Division, Beadle C.J. rejected this contention and held that appeal to the Privy Council lay as of right.

One last point made by many constitutional writers must be reiterated. In the final analysis every constitution depends on popular acceptance. If community attitudes do not support the fundamental rights provisions they will become ineffective either through the required amending majority or by revolution. Indeed this is the reason why many lawyers have little faith in paper constitutions, every revolution being legal when it succeeds, new law being substituted and the old constitution being cast into the wastepaper basket. Thus it is the people who are the ultimate safeguard for discouraging and correcting abuses. As the late Mr. Justice Jackson wrote in his essay on the American judiciary:

> I know of no modern instance in which any judiciary has saved a whole people from the great currents of intolerance, passion, usurpation, and tyranny which have threatened liberty and free institutions ... I doubt that any court, whatever its powers, could have saved Louis XVI or Marie Antoinette. None could have avoided the French Revolution, none could have stopped its excesses, and none could have prevented its culmination in the dictatorship of Napoleon. It is not idle speculation to enquire which comes first, an independent and enlightened judiciary or a free and tolerant society—it is my belief that the attitude of a society and of its organized political forces, rather than its legal machinery, is the controlling force in the character of free institutions.[1]

General characteristics of the Southern Rhodesian Bill of Rights

As one of the recent series of colonial constitutions containing a Bill of Rights, the Southern Rhodesia Constitution 1961 is basically similar to the models from which it has been adapted, having in particular many affinities

---

argued that there had been a 'fundamental alteration in the law' as it existed before the coming into force of the new Constitution and that the law should not therefore be saved as a law in force immediately before the appointed day which had continued in force at all times since that day. The Court however held that 'the law as it existed in the statute book has remained unaltered. That the manner in which the law is administered may have altered is not a matter of which this Court can take cognisance.' Cp. *R.* v. *Detody*, 1926 A.D. 198 at 201 where Innes C.J. held that a law in force meant one 'in existence on the statute book'.

[1] R. H. Jackson, *The Supreme Court in the American System of Government*, Harvard University Press, 1955, pp. 80–81.

to the Nigerian Constitution of 1960, and, through that, to its progenitor the European Convention for the Protection of Human Rights and Fundamental Freedoms to which the United Kingdom acceded in 1951 as a member of the Council of Europe. In view of the quantity of writing comparing various Bills of Rights[1] little purpose would be served by a detailed analysis of the Southern Rhodesian Bill of Rights in relation to similar Constitutions. Suffice it to say that as in the case of other recent Colonial and Commonwealth Relations Office constitutions, there has been meticulous drafting in carefully qualified language[2] of the Declaration of Rights which forms part of the text of the Constitution; detailed exceptions which are intended to be an exhaustive enumeration of the circumstances in which the provisions shall not apply, have been incorporated; the specific rights enumerated are by virtue of the provisions for constitutional amendment treated as analogous to restrictions on legislative competence[3]; and the Declaration is buttressed by judicial review, Section 115 providing for the invalidity of any law enacted after the coming into force of the new Constitution which is inconsistent with any of its provisions, while Section 71 gives original jurisdiction in respect of alleged contraventions of the Declaration to the Appellate Division of the High Court and a right of appeal to the Judicial Committee.[4] Like most other British colonial constitutions containing Bills of Rights, there is no reference to social and economic freedoms, other than the right of compensation where property is expropriated, and no reference to the duties of the individual towards the State.[5]

However, certain points of difference are worth noting, the Southern Rhodesian Declaration of Rights in some particulars giving wider protection than the Nigerian guarantees on which it is for the most part modelled, while in others it is more restrictive. Thus the protection of the Southern Rhodesian Declaration is, except in respect of certain types of discriminatory laws, extended to citizens and non-citizens alike, whereas this was not the case in Nigeria.[6] It is also apparent from the absolute language used in prohibiting infringements of the fundamental rights that the Declaration applies to cases where administrative action derogating from the freedoms is taken.[7] However

---

[1] See the various writings by de Smith cited above.

[2] There are no vague formulations such as those in the American Bill of Rights which have enabled the United States Supreme Court to set out on their judicial policy-determining role.

[3] The Rights enumerated in the Declaration are specially entrenched provisions of the Constitution and may not be amended other than by the specified procedures outlined in Part II, Chapter 1. Furthermore, it appears that no law inconsistent with the Declaration may be enacted, unless the measure is expressed to be a Constitutional Amendment Bill and is passed in the requisite fashion.

[4] See *supra*, Part II, Chapter 3.

[5] See de Smith, *The New Commonwealth and its Constitutions*, p. 184.

[6] S.I. 1960 No. 1652, Section 26.

[7] e.g. 'No person shall be subjected to torture, to inhuman or degrading punishment';

there are respects in which the Nigerian guarantees were more generous. Freedom of movement was there a guaranteed freedom[1] whereas in Southern Rhodesia there is no recognition of such a freedom. Similarly, certain freedoms are recognized in other constitutions which find no place in the Southern Rhodesian Declaration, viz. there is no safeguarding of the right of parents freely to choose the method of their children's education.[2] Likewise, there is no mention of such recognized freedoms as the right to marry,[3] freedom of choice of occupation[4] and freedom of choice of residence.[5]

alternatively 'no person shall be hindered in the enjoyment of his freedom of conscience'. In addition, the subsections dealing with exceptions to the Declaration and with the *onus* of proof in litigation alleging its contravention refer to things 'done under the authority of any law', i.e. lawful administrative action.

[1] S.I. 1960, No. 1652, Section 27, but this only applied to citizens.

[2] Schools can become centres of indoctrination, cp. 'Christian National Education' in South Africa. This the Government has recognized by insisting on strict control of African schools in terms of Section 11 of the African Education Act (Chapter 97). It has refused to recognize certain 'community schools' started by members of the public with nationalist sympathies, the decision by the Minister in such a case being 'final'. The same arguments could be applied in reverse to Government schools. The only possible method of attacking 'indoctrination' in schools and allowing freedom of choice would be by reliance on Section 65(1) of the Declaration, which provides that 'no person shall be hindered in his freedom of expression, that is to say freedom . . . to receive . . . ideas and information with interference'. However, the African Education Act and action taken under it is saved as a law in force before the Constitution came into effect. There is no guarantee of free primary education. Cp. the position under the Cyprus Constitution.

[3] The absence of such a provision when taken in conjunction with Section 67(3)(b) of the Declaration, which exempts laws relative to marriage from the prohibition against discrimination, makes possible the introduction of a Prohibition of Mixed Marriages Act similar to Union Act No. 55 of 1949.

[4] Possibly the prohibition in respect of future laws against requiring persons to perform 'forced labour' partly covers this freedom. However, the Master and Servants Act (Chapter 247), Sections 30 and 40, and African Labour Regulations (Chapter 100), Section 23, both of which statutes are preserved as existing law, make it a criminal offence for a servant to depart from his employment. Between 1960 and 31 May 1965, 5,694 Africans were prosecuted for this offence: *S.R.L.A.D.*, Vol. 51, cols. 2039–40, and Vol. 61, cols. 1779–80, 4 August 1965. In Kenya there is a guarantee of freedom to follow one's chosen occupation.

[5] The Land Apportionment Act 1941 effectively prevents Africans from leasing, acquiring or occupying property in European areas and Europeans from doing the same in African areas. The provisions in the Constitution relative to Tribal Trust Land prevent Europeans from acquiring or occupying such land. See generally *infra*, Chapter 5. In practice, if Southern Rhodesian laws are enforced it will be difficult for more Africans to become town dwellers. Because of the provisions of the Land Apportionment Act unless they are employed as domestics or their presence is necessitated on their employers' premises, they may not live in the European area of which the greater part of most of the towns is comprised. The African urban area consists of municipal and Government African townships. The occupation of premises and accommodation in municipal townships is rigidly controlled by township superintendents in terms of the Native Urban Area By-laws of the various towns issued in terms of Section 38 of the Land Apportionment Act No. 11 of 1941. See e.g. S.R.G.N. 178/53 for the Salisbury By-laws, which provide that no unauthorized persons may occupy accommodation in such a township, that certificates of occupation must be obtained from the township superintendent, and that such certificates may be cancelled if the holder is unemployed for a period in excess of one month or is not 'a fit and proper person', having committed certain crimes. Government townships are also subject to control as strict 'lodgers' regulations' make it unlawful for occupants or owners of premises in

It is to be hoped that the Declaration will not be envisaged by the Legislature as setting maximum standards for safeguards[1] as it is not an exaggeration to say that in some respects the existing statute and common law is more generous than are the provisions of the Declaration. An example of such a discrepancy is the statement in the Declaration that a person shall not be considered to have been unlawfully killed if this results from the use of force reasonably justifiable in the circumstances of the case for the defence of property,[2] whereas, according to the Roman–Dutch common law killing in defence of property is unlawful.[3] Again, the Declaration permits killing to prevent the commission of a criminal offence, whereas the Criminal Procedure and Evidence Act, Section 49(2) limits this right to killing persons accused or suspected of having committed an offence listed in the First Schedule. Again, the Criminal Procedure and Evidence Act, Section 111, provides that when a court exercises its discretion to grant bail, no person shall be required to give excessive bail, whereas the provisions of the Declaration of Rights which 'secure the protection of law' and those relating to personal liberty only mention bail when a person is not brought to trial within a reasonable time, in which event he is to be released upon 'reasonable conditions'. It therefore appears that in terms of the Declaration a law authorizing excessive bail would be permissible provided this had no application to cases where the delay in bringing the accused to trial was unreasonable. There is, however, no question of any right to bail, either in terms of existing law or of the Declaration, except in the event of an accused being brought to trial after an unreasonably long time.[4] Again, the Criminal Procedure and Evidence Act, Section

such townships to have unauthorized lodgers resident with them, all lodgers, i.e. persons residing for more than one night in a township otherwise than as owner or lessee of the whole premises, requiring to be registered with the township manager. Lodgers are severely restricted in numbers. See the Local Government Areas General Regulations 1962, S.R.G.N. 569/62, as amended by S.R.G.N. 257/64 and 659/64. The declarations in 1964 of states of emergency in Highfields and Harare were partly motivated by a Government decision to rid the townships of unauthorized lodgers.

[1] See de Smith, *The New Commonwealth*, op. cit., at p. 169.

[2] Section 57(2)(a).

[3] See *R. v. Detsera*, 1958 (1) S.A. 762 (F.C.) at 767 per Tredgold C.J. See also A. V. Lansdown, *Outlines of South African Criminal Law and Procedure*, Juta, 1960, at p. 64. However, it is permissible to use a reasonable degree of force to prevent removal of or injury to one's property, and, depending on the circumstances, the situation may so change that a killing in self-defence may arise.

[4] Section 145(2) of the Criminal Procedure and Evidence Act is again more generous than the Declaration, stating that in the case of High Court trials if the person has not been brought to trial within six months of his commitment, he shall be discharged from his imprisonment, there being no provision for his release subject to conditions, as is provided in the Declaration. However, in one respect the Declaration is more generous than the existing statute law, as release or release subject to conditions applies to all trials, whether in the High or Magistrates' Courts, whereas the Criminal Procedure and Evidence Act, Section 150, only placed such a restriction on trials in the High Court. Thus trials in the Magistrates' Court can be indefinitely postponed by a series of postponements, provided each is not in excess of fourteen days at any one time. This provision, being an existing law, is still in force.

229, provides that every trial shall be in open court subject to limited exceptions, which are far more widely drafted in the Declaration.[1] A much more serious encroachment in the Declaration, however, is the right of any Minister of the Crown to put in a certificate that it would not be in the public interest for a matter to be disclosed in public. If this is done courts and tribunals are required to make arrangements for the hearing of evidence *in camera* and to prevent disclosure of such matters.[2]

A surprising feature of the Declaration of Rights is that it either envisaged further legislation imposing capital punishment or it failed to take account of decisions on other Declarations of Rights. It is however difficult to assume that the decisions in *Gopalan* v. *The State of Madras*[3] and the Irish Supreme Court decision of *In re Article 26 of the Constitution and the Offences against the State (Amendment) Bill 1940*[4] were unknown to the draftsmen. At all events the protection afforded to the right to life is scanty, as a person may be deprived of his life 'in execution of the sentence of a court in respect of a criminal offence of which he has been convicted'. Thus the Constitution does not preclude the Legislature from stipulating that the death sentence shall be mandatory in any class of offence, e.g. subversion.[5]

Yet another feature of the Declaration is that it expressly permits the enactment of new laws providing for the restriction of persons to specified areas in Southern Rhodesia and for prohibition of entry into other areas although the Law and Order (Maintenance) Act, which makes extensive and detailed provisions for restriction was saved as an existing law.[6]

The rights dealt with in the Southern Rhodesian Constitution 1961 are the rights to life, to personal liberty, to protection from slavery and forced labour, to protection from inhuman treatment, to protection from deprivation of property, to privacy of home and other property, to protective provisions to secure the observance of proper legal procedure, to freedom of conscience, to freedom of expression, to freedom of assembly and of association, and of protection from discrimination by written laws or by administrative action.

[1] Compare Section 229(4)(a) with Section 63(10) of the Declaration which permits a trial to be held *in camera* in the interests of defence and of public safety as well as of public order.

[2] Constitution, Section 63(10).　　　[3] 1950 S.C.R. 88.　　　[4] [1940] Ir. R. 470.

[5] That this view is correct was shown by the amendment in 1963 of the Law and Order (Maintenance) Act 1960, Section 33A, of which now provides for a mandatory death penalty for offences which under common law might only amount to malicious injury to property. The Constitutional Council did not adversely report on the measure, the Judicial Committee pronounced on it in *R*. v. *Mapolisa*, without any possibility of upsetting the conviction on this ground being canvassed, and this view was upheld in *Gundu and Sambo* v. *Hayward and Bosman*, NN.O. Judgement No. A.D. 97/65 (as yet unreported). Nor did the Appellate Division hold that the section imposing a mandatory death penalty contravened Section 60 of the Constitution which prohibits 'inhuman or degrading' punishment as they considered the Section had no bearing on the proportionality of punishment but merely prohibited types or modes of punishment not hitherto recognized under the law prior to the appointed day which were themselves inhuman or degrading.

[6] Constitution, Section 58(2)(k), read with Section 72(1) definition of 'law'.

All of these rights are supplemented by provisions for judicial review and enforcement.

Although in respect of the new series of constitutions containing Bills of Rights the generalization has been made that 'of the guaranteed rights some are expressed in absolute terms' while others are subject to various qualifications,[1] the only 'absolute' right in terms of the Southern Rhodesian Declaration is the right that no criminal offences may retrospectively be created and that no penalty more severe than that competent at the time when an offence was committed may be imposed. Excepted from this provision would appear to be judicial decisions which retrospectively define the law, as the rule of the common law that decisions operate retrospectively would be saved as an existing law. However the power to legislate retrospectively in such matters has not survived as an existing law, since Section 70(1)(b) read with Section 72(1) shows that the saving of existing laws related only to provisions of laws passed by the Legislature or to instruments thereunder or to the common law. The Constitution for such purposes is not a law and therefore new laws passed in pursuance of the grant of legislative power in terms of the Constitution would not come within Section 70(1)(c). Consequently no retrospective legislation can be passed, if it creates criminal offences or imposes more severe penalties.

Rights not to be subjected to degrading punishment, to be held in slavery or servitude, or to be compelled to perform forced labour are in Southern Rhodesia subject to qualifications. The major qualifications on all these rights is contained in Section 70(1)(b) and (c) of the Declaration. This not only saves from the provisions of Section 57 to 68 all rules in force immediately before the coming into operation of the Constitution which have at all times since continued in force, but also saves any new written law to the extent that it repeals or re-enacts any such provision. Within the short period the 1961 Constitution has been in force[2] in four of the six cases so far heard involving provisions of the Declaration, Section 70 has been involved for the justification of laws which would otherwise have contravened the Declaration. In the *African Daily News Case, supra* the application was unsuccessful, as the Court held that the action challenged was taken under a law saved by Section 70(1)(b) of the Declaration. However, in *Nkomo and Others* v. *Minister of Justice and Others, supra* the law was struck down as not falling within the saving provisions of Section 70(1)(c), as being a re-enactment. In the latter case the Court assumed in favour of the Minister that 're-enactments with modifications' were possible, and then examined at length the meaning of a 'modification' which it found to be 'something which does not change the essential nature of or character of the repealed enactment'.[3] It

[1] de Smith, 'Fundamental Rights in Commonwealth Constitutions', op. cit., p. 16.

[2] Three years as at the date of writing—November 1965.

[3] At p. 505. See also *Nkomo* v. *Lardner-Burke* Judgement A.D. 164/65 per Quènet A.C.J. at pp. 6–7.

then held that the challenged law had effected a 'radical transformation' in the law. In *Maluleke* v. *the Minister of Law and Another*[1] the Court rejected the view that new hindrances which are the equivalent of restrictions in force at the time of the coming into operation of the Constitution are saved by Section 70. The Court declined to take what it described as a 'practical approach' to such a problem and ruled that it is concerned with the section under which a hindrance is imposed, not one under which it might also have been imposed. Furthermore, a law which was in force at the appointed day when the new Constitution came into operation, which has continued in force thereafter, and which has remained in force until after the passage of a new restrictive measure will not be saved unless it has continued in force 'at all times since that day'.[2]

The only provision in the Declaration which is to override existing law is that providing for safeguards relative to detention and actions which may be taken during a state of emergency. Sub-sections 69(2) and (3) of the Declaration provide that a tribunal shall be established of persons included amongst whom must be one holding or who has held high judicial office or a Southern Rhodesian legal practitioner of seven years' standing. However, there is no provision as to the minimum period within which a request for review of an order of detention must be heard by the tribunal,[3] and the detention of an individual may not again be reviewed earlier than a twelve-month from the preceding request made by the detainee.[4] Furthermore, the authority by whom the detention was ordered is not obliged to act in accordance with such a tribunal's recommendations. As indicated above, the Minister of Justice despite the declaration of states of emergency in Highfield township in August 1964 and in Harare in October 1964 failed to establish a tribunal.[5] The Highfield emergency was twice extended to 'consolidate the present atmosphere of peace and calm and to rebuild', but no tribunal was established.[6]

Suspension of the Declaration of Rights during periods of public emer-

---

[1] 1963 (4) S.A. 206 (S.R.) at 217.
[2] 1963 (4) S.A. 206.   [3] Cp. one month in Nigeria: Section 29.
[4] Cp. six months in Nigeria. There appears to be a drafting error which states that the review shall not be earlier than twelve months after the detainee 'last made such a request' Clearly what was meant was the meaning given in the text.
[5] This drafting error mentioned above may be the Minister's justification for his view that he is not bound to appoint a tribunal earlier than twelve months after receiving a request for a tribunal to recommend whether the person concerned should be continued in detention.
[6] *S.R.L.A.D.*, Vol. 59, col. 592, Minister of Law and Order, 28 October 1964. The Minister admitted that 'thugs' detained would continue to be detained and hoped that, provided the period of detention were 'long enough', they would have learnt a lesson. When it was argued in Parliament that there had been an abuse of power the emergency being extended not because there was a danger to public safety, or disturbance of public order, or interference with essential services (Emergency Powers Act (Chapter 33), Section 3(1)), the Minister contended that if the emergency were lifted there would be an immediate threat of danger to the public safety, and that 'there does exist, although it is underground, perhaps, a potential for the development of the conditions which are covered in Section 3(1) of the Act': see col. 604.

gency, which can last for three months,[1] is also permitted. During any emergency all the enumerated rights may be suspended except for the provisions as to the detention tribunal, retrospective legislation concerned with criminal offences and penalties, and those giving protection from slavery, forced labour, and inhuman treatment as well as the right to life.[2] It is apparent that the framers of the Southern Rhodesian Constitution paid little heed to the warning given by the United States Supreme Court soon after the Civil War against suspension of the American Bill of Rights:

> No doctrine involving more pernicious consequences was ever invented by the wit of man than that any of its provisions can be suspended during any of the great exigencies of government. Such a doctrine leads directly to anarchy or despotism.[3]

The safeguard against reckless declaration of a state of emergency is very slight, the Emergency Powers Act, Chapter 33, governing the situation, as the Constitution provides for such a declaration either by virtue of a law of the Legislature for the time being in force relating to emergency powers, or by resolution of the Legislative Assembly.[4]

The present law in force relating to declaration of states of emergency, the Emergency Powers Act, provides that a declaration of emergency may be made if at any time it appears to the Governor that action is being taken or is immediately threatened by any persons or body of persons of such nature and on so extensive a scale as to be likely to endanger the public safety, to disturb or interfere with public order, or to interfere with the maintenance of any essential service.[5] It is a notable feature that a state of emergency can either relate to Southern Rhodesia as a whole or to part thereof,[6] and it is quite possible to declare different areas successively under states of emergency as was done in the case of the Salisbury townships of Highfield and Harare.

Such declarations may be extended from time to time for further periods not exceeding three months by the issue of a fresh proclamation, provided, by a mere resolution of the Legislative Assembly, it is so determined.[7]

---

[1] Cp. Cmnd. 1148, para. 257, where the Monckton Commission recommended that states of emergency should not be permitted to last for more than two-month periods.

[2] Constitution, Section 69(1). A possible case of inhuman or degrading treatment not covered by the exceptions in Section 60(2) relating to 'reasonably justifiable' methods to prevent persons escaping from custody arose out of the method by which persons detained or restricted during the recent states of emergency were moved from one place to another. They were transported in military aircraft, some being handcuffed to the body of the aircraft or by handcuffs which passed through the seat structures. The responsible Minister justified this by saying that if there were a crash guards had the keys to release the detainees: S.R.L.A.D., Vol. 59, col. 117, 20 October 1964.

[3] Ex parte Milligan (1866), 18 L. Ed. 281.

[4] Section 72(2). When Her Majesty is at war until the declaration of peace a state of emergency also exists.

[5] Chapter 33, Section 3(1).

[6] Chapter 33, Section 3(1) read with the Constitution, Section 72(2)(b).

[7] Constitution, Section 72(2)(c) and Chapter 33, Section 3(2). Cp. the Nigerian Constitution, Section 65, which, in the case of a state of emergency, required resolutions by both

Furthermore, even when a period of public emergency has been terminated, it seems that for specified purposes the emergency may be extended.[1]

The only safeguard against reckless administrative action is that when a state of emergency is declared to exist, the reasons for the issue of such a proclamation must be communicated to the Legislative Assembly as soon as possible. Furthermore, the Legislative Assembly may within the next twenty-eight days of any regulations made under a state of emergency being laid before it, resolve that such regulations be annulled.[2] If not annulled such regulations may, in terms of the Emergency Powers Act, be inconsistent with any Southern Rhodesian law and may amend, suspend the operation of, and apply any law, with or without modifications.[3] There is little likelihood of the Legislative Assembly rescinding action taken by the Cabinet. Indeed the fact that such a safeguard is of little avail against a Government determined to exercise emergency powers was shown when the Highfield emergency was twice extended to the 25 May 1965, despite Ministerial admissions that the area was calm and peaceful.

Unless it infringes one of four specified freedoms, no law making provisions with respect to the taking of action in an emergency can be invalidated. However, action taken under such law must not exceed 'anything which, having regard to the circumstances prevailing at the time, could reasonably have been thought to be required for the purpose of dealing with the situation in question'. Administrative action can therefore be impugned if it exceeds anything which could reasonably have been thought to be required.[4]

Houses of Parliament (a safeguard not possible in Southern Rhodesia) or recommendations by two-thirds majorities of each House declaring that democratic institutions were threatened with subversion.

[1] Constitution, Section 72(3). It seems that this sub-Section may permit of detention to be extended although the emergency in the area from which such persons were taken for detention may have been terminated.

[2] Chapter 33, Section 4(5).

[3] Section 69(1) of the Constitution provides that 'nothing contained in any law shall be held to be inconsistent with or in contravention of any of the fundamental freedoms not saved during time of emergency'.

[4] Cp. Section 28(1) of the Nigerian Constitution, where it is stipulated that the measures challenged should be 'reasonably justifiable for the purpose of dealing with the situation that exists'. It is submitted that the Southern Rhodesian wording allows more latitude to the administration than the Nigerian wording, the latter being objective and testing the action of the administration by the views of the court as to what is reasonable. The Southern Rhodesian wording does not permit the court to substitute its view of what was reasonable, but requires it to examine the action in the light of what could reasonably have been thought to be required by any person in that position. de Smith has pointed to distinctions in the scope of review resulting from the adoption of different phraseology and these views have been criticized by Grove, op. cit., pp. 167–8. It is however submitted that Grove's somewhat emotive views are incorrect and, despite certain *dicta*, the attention of the courts not being specifically directed to these points, there is a difference in the scope of review permitted by such phrases. Indeed there can be no doubt that there is a great difference between things 'reasonably done under' the authority of any necessary law (which is the normal type of action to which the Declaration does not apply) and 'action . . . which . . . could reasonably have been thought to be required'.

Further derogation from the rights protected by the Declaration is possible in the case of persons who are members of a disciplined force, only the rights of protection from slavery and forced labour and from inhuman treatment being applicable to such persons when action is taken against them in terms of the written disciplinary laws providing for the regulation of their discipline.[1]

Since only 'laws' of the Southern Rhodesian Legislature or action taken under such 'laws' may be invalidated by the Declaration[2] action taken under United Kingdom Acts and statutory instruments may not be tested against the Declaration. That the Declaration is similarly inapplicable to Federal laws and action thereunder is expressly provided.[3] For these reasons Federal laws and statutory instruments issued thereunder which are still in force in Southern Rhodesia by virtue of regulations under the Rhodesia and Nyasaland (Dissolution) Order in Council 1963 may not be adversely reported on by the Constitutional Council. Similarly, fresh statutory instruments can be issued under the Federal laws continued in force without being subject to the Constitutional Council's powers to scrutinize and possibly invalidate them.[4]

In addition to the general qualifications and circumstances already outlined in which nearly all rights can be circumscribed, certain of the rights can be overruled for prescribed purposes, viz. public safety, public order, public morality, public health, or for the purpose of protecting the rights and freedoms of other persons.[5] Laws interfering with rights to protection against deprivation of property, of privacy of home and other property, of freedom of conscience, freedom of expression, of assembly and of association are thus permissible, provided that the law infringing these freedoms makes provisions necessary for these prescribed purposes. Furthermore, special additional exceptions are written into the relevant rights, e.g. town and country planning justifies inroads into the right of protection from deprivation of property and the right of protection of privacy of persons' dwelling houses.

The fundamental rights into which new laws may make greatest inroads are the rights to protection from discrimination either by law or by administrative action. A major opportunity to enact discriminatory measures arises from the fact that these protections do not apply in the case of money Bills

---

[1] Section 70(2) read with Section 72(1). 'Disciplined force means a naval, military, or air force, or a police force, or a prison service, or any other body established for public purposes by a written law providing for the regulation of the discipline of that body and declared by that law to be a disciplinary force for the purposes of this chapter.' Since a law providing for disciplinary regulations of a body established for public purposes may be declared to be a disciplinary law it appears that a law regulating the conditions of service and discipline of public servants as a body could be passed and would be exempted from the provisions of the Declaration relative to discrimination.

[2] Section 72(1), definition of 'law' and *African Newspapers and Another* v. *Lardner-Burke and Another*, *supra* at 491. The Constitution is not a 'law' for this purpose.

[3] Section 70(3).   [4] *Supra*, Part II, Chapter I, and *infra*, Chapter 6.

[5] Beadle C.J. in *Maluleke* v. *Minister of Law and Order*, 1963 (4) S.A. 204 (S.R.) at 209 considered that the exceptions in the case of public safety and public order were the equivalent of the American and Australian 'police powers'.

as defined in Section 83. The definition of a money Bill will therefore become important if a measure containing financial provisions is challenged.[1] It is stipulated in the Constitution that public Bills which contain 'only provisions' dealing with financial matters (which are specified in detail) are money Bills. Consequently 'tacking' will not avoid the constitutional safeguards. Nonetheless, as the Monckton Report commented, money Bills may be 'vehicles of serious unfair discrimination' and therefore discrimination can in practice result.[2]

Again, laws or administrative action may not be invalidated for discrimination in so far as these relate to 'adoption, marriage, divorce, burial, devolution of property on death or other matters of personal law'.[3] As already indicated, this would permit the enactment of a Prohibition of Mixed Marriages Act, refusal of an application to adopt a child of another racial or religious group, a provision that all European property should on death of the owner devolve on the *fiscus*, or that devolution of European property is subject to heavy succession duties, or of any provision which could be characterized as a matter of 'personal law'.

Furthermore, common law and statute law may be excluded in respect of Africans in such spheres as are covered by their customary law.[4] Thus there is nothing to prevent a law of the Legislature denying Africans common law rights conferred on them by the law of delict and confining them to such actions as were recognized by customary law.[5] Whether these powers to discriminate apply only in respect of Africans indigenous to Southern Rhodesia is somewhat ambiguous as the phrase 'Africans of a particular race or tribe indigenous to Southern Rhodesia', has been employed. On a restrictive interpretation, it is submitted 'race' should also be qualified by 'indigenous to Southern Rhodesia', thus precluding the passages of such discriminatory laws in relation to non-indigenous Africans.

It is also permissible to enact and to apply discriminatory restrictions to non-citizens who have not acquired permanent residence.[6] These restrictions may relate to entry into, or employment in Southern Rhodesia, or on the acquisition of, or of interests in, or rights over immovable property in Southern Rhodesia, or on the enjoyment of services supplied out of Southern Rhodesian public funds.[7] The point arises whether a corporation would be

[1] For purposes of the Declaration of Rights Speaker's rulings on money Bills are irrelevant although in relation to the Constitutional Council his rulings cannot be challenged: Section 84(8) and (9).

[2] Cmnd. 1148, para. 256, and see *supra*, Part II, Chapter 1.   [3] Section 67(3)(b).

[4] Section 67(3)(c). This to some extent reflects the provisions of Section 2 of the African Law and Courts Act (Chapter 104), the latter however only excluding the application of certain statute law to Africans unless expressly applied to them.

[5] See *supra*, Part II, Chapter 3. It appears from decisions there quoted that negligence was not sufficient for the imposition of liability in customary law, recklessness or *dolus* being required.

[6] See *supra*.   [7] Section 67(3)(d).

protected against these discriminations, particularly if a discriminatory law were enacted prohibiting the acquisition of immovable property in Southern Rhodesia. It is submitted that by virtue of its incorporation in terms of the Companies Act (Chapter 224), a company has Southern Rhodesian nationality [1] and Southern Rhodesian domicile [2] (even though it cannot be a citizen [3]) and therefore by virtue of a written law, i.e. the law which provided for its incorporation, it is permanently resident in Southern Rhodesia. Even though it may be argued that it is common law which determines the residence of a company [4] it is suggested that a liberal interpretation of the provisions in the Declaration should be adopted so as to treat a Southern Rhodesian incorporated company as being permanently resident in the country by virtue of a written law. This view is strengthened by the fact that the Interpretation Act 1889, which applies to the Declaration, defines persons to include corporations, while the fact must have been known to the constitutional draftsmen that certain Southern Rhodesian legislation characterizes corporations as being of a particular race, viz. the Land Apportionment Act (Chapter 257), Section 2(1) of which defines 'African' and 'European' to include corporations depending on whether the persons who have a controlling interest therein are either African or European. [5]

Yet another case where discrimination is permissible occurs where a law sets out qualifications 'for service as a public officer or as a member of a disciplined force or for the service of any public authority or of any body corporate established directly by a law'. [6] Such qualifications however may not be qualifications by way of race, tribe, colour, or creed. It seems that the purport of this somewhat obscure section is to permit administrative action and determination of qualifications which would in effect discriminate against certain racial or religious groups and thus to allow the application of certain oaths and loyalty tests without conflicting with the provisions of the Declaration.

The introduction of further new discriminatory laws is also possible provided that these do not result in the law 'affording greater difference of treatment of different descriptions of persons than immediately before the date of the making of the law in question'. [7] When such discrimination is permitted

---

[1] *Janson* v. *Driefontein Consolidated Mines Ltd.*, [1902] A.C. 484 at 497. See also *Attorney General* v. *Jewish Colonization Association*, [1900] 2 Q.B. 556.

[2] See *Gasque* v. *Commissioners of Inland Revenue*, [1940] 2 K.B. 80.

[3] See A. Gledhill, *Fundamental Rights in India*, Stevens, 1956, p. 38.

[4] Cp. the test of central control: *de Beers Consolidated Mines Ltd.* v. *Howe*, [1906] A.C. 455.

[5] Even though the Land Apportionment Act places racially restrictive limitations on land acquisition, ownership and occupancy, it would not be invalidated even were this view adopted since it was a law in force at the time of the new Constitution.

[6] Section 67(3)(e).

[7] Section 67(4) proviso. If this proviso is construed as relating to practical application of treatment before the day in question, it might be possible to legalize existing social discriminations. It is submitted, that, despite the ambiguity of the section, 'than' relates to 'the laws

39—C.H.L.S.R.

it must be reasonably justifiable in the interests of Southern Rhodesia as a whole, or in order to secure the protection in an equitable manner as between the various descriptions of persons affected and their respective interests. The Court in determining whether a law is permissible must pay regard to the nature of the condition, restriction, disability, privilege or advantage, to any special circumstances appertaining to persons of that or any other description, to the stage of social or economic development for the time being reached by the various descriptions of persons and to the state for the time being of the economy of Southern Rhodesia.[1]

The discretion of persons vested with powers to regulate the institution, conduct or discontinuance of any civil or criminal proceedings is also saved against invalidation by the provisions prohibiting discriminatory action.[2]

Finally, it is provided that the Section invalidating discriminatory legislation cannot invalidate a law which, although it derogates from the protections afforded to privacy of home and property, to freedom of conscience, expression of assembly or of association, has been upheld by virtue of its being a law required in the interests of defence, public safety, public order, &c. It would seem therefore that there is nothing to prevent security legislation aimed against a particular racial group, and that, provided such security legislation was considered necessary, it could not be challenged.[3]

It should be noted that the anti-discrimination provisions apply only to written laws and to persons acting in a fashion which has either expressly or impliedly been authorized by a written law. There is nothing to prevent discrimination which is authorized by virtue of the common law, which is in any case preserved. The Roman–Dutch common law affords persons of different colour or different religion equal status and treatment to that afforded to all other inhabitants 'for it preserves equality and binds the citizens equally'.[4] However, freedom to contract and the right to refuse to contract with members of the public or with particular classes of persons, as well as the law relating to servitudes which permits the registration of racially restrictive covenants, may permit of discrimination.[5]

This situation is impliedly recognized by the Declaration, there being no provisions prohibiting private discrimination in places to which the public resort.[6]

---

in respect of the matter in question' and that new discriminations cannot be greater than old 'legal' discrimination.

[1] Section 67(4).

[2] Section 68(3). Thus if the Attorney-General were to prosecute only Africans for certain offences his actions would be unchallengeable.

[3] See Section 67(5).

[4] See *Minister of Posts and Telegraphs* v. *Rasool*, 1934 A.D. 167 and 177 quoting Voet 1.3.5.

[5] See *infra*, Chapter 5, where the enforceability and importance in practice of restrictive covenants is examined.

[6] Cp. the position in Kenya: S.I. 1963 No. 791, Section 13(7). In Roman–Dutch Law

Yet another limitation on the scope of the anti-discrimination provisions is that although practical application of laws must be taken into account in deciding whether there has been discrimination, unless the imposition of any disability, condition, or restriction, or the granting of privilege, or advantage to others 'is wholly or mainly attributable to the *description* by race, tribe, colour or creed of the persons concerned' the law will not be regarded as discriminatory.[1]

Furthermore, it is not sufficient to show the possibility of prejudice when a law is sought to be invalidated: there must be actual prejudice or it must be clear that 'as an inevitable consequence of that provision' persons will be prejudiced.[2]

Procedural provisions[3]

The procedure to be adopted in an attempt to challenge legislative or administrative action has partly been laid down in the Declaration and has partly been established by the Courts.

Before any applicant can succeed in his claim to invalidate a law or action taken in terms of a challenged law, he must show that he has been hindered in the exercise of his rights. *Locus standi* to approach the Courts is narrowly defined as an applicant must show that the Declaration of Rights has been or is being 'contravened in relation to him' and only then may he apply to the

there are no duties attached to public callings such as those of innkeepers or of carriers to provide services to all members of the public.

[1] Section 67(2). This was probably why the Constitutional Council did not report on the Citizenship of Southern Rhodesia and British Nationality Act No. 63 of 1963, which denies citizenship to children of Southern Rhodesian citizens who are born outside Southern Rhodesia of a potentially polygamous marriage. This law was not saved by Section 70(1) as it was more restrictive than the former Federal law which applied to marriages outside the Federation only. Polygamy is not a description by race, colour, tribe, or creed. In practice polygamy is of no concern to Southern Rhodesian Europeans, is permissible for Mohammedans, and is regularly practised by Africans, very frequently because of the rules of customary law relating to the levirate. Similar considerations must have caused a majority report by the Council that the Local Government Areas General (Amendment) Regulations 1965 (No. 6) were not inconsistent with the Declaration. These regulations require occupiers of premises in certain local government areas to pay fees in respect of lodgers residing in their premises. The main Regulations give arbitrary powers to township managers and impose criminal sanctions. Of those townships which have been declared as Local Government Areas all are African townships but for the township of Westwood (a 'multi racial' township, designated under the Land Apportionment Act, but which is in reality entirely African). The fees are therefore not payable by races other than Africans. The majority of the Council held that 'the regulations do not contain discriminatory provisions within the meaning of Section 67 of the Constitution': Letter of the Chairman of the Council to the Speaker of the Legislative Assembly, 6 July 1965.

[2] Section 67(2).

[3] It is not here proposed to deal with the original jurisdiction of the Appellate Division of the High Court to entertain applications in respect of alleged contraventions of the Declaration. This has been dealt with in Part II, Chapter 3 *supra*. Similarly the question of legal aid from the Constitutional Council has been dealt with in Part II, Chapter 1 *supra*.

High Court 'for redress'. As Beadle C.J. said, this does not confer a general right of action of 'any member of the Public: the Declaration envisages relief for particular grievances'.[1]

Furthermore, it appears that there must have been 'an actual illegal infringement of the applicant's rights' and that an anticipated infringement will not entitle persons to apply to Court.[2] However, this view might have to be qualified. If a contravention was clearly about to occur and the person whose rights would be contravened expected irreparable injury to ensue he should have *locus standi* to restrain such a contravention of the Declaration.[3]

Once the complainant has satisfied the court that he has *prima facie* been hindered in the enjoyment of his rights a Minister of Government may then file a certificate signed by him to the effect that he is of opinion that the challenged law or restriction is necessary on any of the exceptional grounds which permit derogation from the guarantees. The effect of such a certificate is that the restrictions on the right which the applicant is seeking to assert are

deemed to be so necessary unless the court decides as a result of hearing the complainant that in a society which has a proper respect for the rights and freedom of the individual, the necessity of that law on the grounds specified in the certificate or, as the case may be, the necessity of those restrictions cannot reasonably be accepted without proof to the satisfaction of the court.[4]

Once the Minister has produced a certificate, the Court must then determine whether or not it should require proof to its satisfaction that the law is necessary[5] and whether it should go behind the Minister's certificate. Of the three occasions where the filing of such a certificate has been relevant, the Minister has on one occasion 'made a generous and . . . very proper concession', making 'no attempt to shelter behind the certificate and to argue that a section such as Section 6(A) of the Law and Order (Maintenance) Act is the

---

[1] *Maluleke* v. *Minister of Law and Order, supra* at 214.

[2] Ibid. Cp. the position in Nigeria discussed by Grove, op. cit., at 161 where a similar attitude was adopted.

[3] See Section 60(1) of the Declaration which states that no person shall be subject to inhuman punishment or degrading treatment. In *Gundu and Sambo* v. *Hayward and Bosman*, NN.O., *supra*, where Section 37(1)(c) of the Law and Order (Maintenance) Act was challenged by persons sentenced to death in terms of that Section although the court rejected the application on grounds of lack of jurisdiction (having earlier heard an appeal from the applicants and therefore having exhausted the jurisdiction conferred by Section 71 of the Constitution) it did not question whether a person sentenced to death could apply to court to test the law before he had actually been executed. It could however be argued that his rights had been infringed by the mere passing of such a sentence.

[4] Provisions to this effect appear in Section 61(3) relative to deprivation of property, in Section 62(3) relative to privacy of home and other property, in Section 64(5) relative to freedom of conscience, in Section 65(3) relative to freedom of expression, and in Section 66(3) relative to freedom of assembly and of association.

[5] The question has not so far been raised whether 'is necessary' relates to the time of enactment or to the time when the law is challenged. The latter construction favours freedom but would result in uncertainty.

sort of section that would normally be found in a society which has a proper respect for the rights and freedoms of the individual'.[1] However, in *Musururwa* v. *Attorney-General, supra* the Minister was not prepared to make a similar concession, putting in a certificate that the challenged law was necessary. The court then refused to go behind the certificate, and Hathorn J. gave some important guidance on the attitude of the Courts to such a certificate. He considered that 'the test to be applied is objective in two respects: (a) as to the standard of the society by which the matter is to be judged, and (b) as to whether the Minister's certificate can or cannot be reasonably accepted'.[2] The learned judge than proceeded to analyse the nature of sedition and concluded that conduct of that character is recognized as criminal. He considered that the fact that sedition was a crime in so many countries was 'of the greatest importance ... particularly when one of the criteria against which the law ... in question must be measured is a society which has a proper respect for the rights and freedoms of the individual'. The judge concluded that 'a proper respect for the rights and freedoms of the individual recognizes the need for the infringement or limitation of these rights in the interest of the police powers and, in particular in relation to the present case the need for the prohibition of sedition in order to preserve the security and existence of constitutional government. An organization declared under the Act should be taken to be one whose objects are subversive.' In such circumstances the challenged law could reasonably be accepted in the interests of public safety and public order, no case having been made out for going behind the Minister's certificate, it being 'normal' to prohibit sedition in a democratic society.[3]

The Minister has also put in a certificate on another occasion, but did not in that case require to rely on it, as the Declaration was found to be inapplicable to the challenged action.[4]

Procedure, according to Beadle C.J., falls into two stages. At the first stage the Court determines two issues: whether the applicant has *locus standi*, having been hindered in the enjoyment of his rights, and also whether it should accept the Minister's certificate or go behind it.[5] If the Court decides

---

[1] *Maluleke* v. *Minister of Law and Order, supra* at 218.

[2] 1963 (4) S.A. 720 (S.R.) at 724.

[3] At 726. Cp. a similar decision in *D.P.P.* v. *Obi*, 1961 1 All N.L.R. 182 (Federal Supreme Court) discussed by Grove, op. cit., at pp. 157–8. The learned judge also considered it 'well worthy of note' that the Constitutional Council had not commented adversely on the measure. That this was an irrelevant consideration and that the Courts must not abdicate to the Council's view of democracy appears from *Nkomo* v. *Lardner-Burke* Judgement A.D. 164/65 at p. 7. It is also submitted that the learned judge erred in stating that an organization declared to be subversive under the Act should be deemed to have had subversive objects. Assuming that the Court finds the legislation to be necessary in the interests of public order, &c., it must then pursue a separate and further enquiry as to whether the administrative action taken in terms of that law was reasonably done under its authority. See *infra* p. 891.

[4] *African Newspapers and Wason* v. *Lardner Burke and Bosman NN.O., supra*.

[5] *Maluleke* v. *Minister of Law and Order, supra* at 210.

to call on the Minister for proof it will then issue a rule *nisi* calling on the Minister to show cause and to satisfy the Court that the law is in fact necessary.[1] The Court, however, may not make a final order until it has given the Minister an opportunity to be heard as it cannot deny the Minister the right to be heard 'simply because the Court may think that it may not be possible for the Minister . . . to place any proof before it which may satisfy it'.[2]

However, the provision allowing the Minister to put in a certificate does not relate to whether things 'done under the authority of any law' have been reasonably done. The Minister's certificate may be given either for the purpose of showing that 'the law in question is necessary' or for showing that 'any restrictions imposed by the law in question upon public officers are necessary in the public interest'. If administrative action is challenged a Ministerial certificate would be competent in respect of the necessity for the law in terms of which the challenged action was taken, but would be incompetent so far as it purported to relate to the further question whether the action was 'reasonably done under the authority of' any law (assuming that the Court finds such law to be necessary). Whether such action was 'reasonably done' is a separate question for investigation by the Court in relation to which the various sub-sections permitting the Minister to put in certificates have no application. The further problem arises whether the phrase 'reasonably done' relates to the method of 'doing' or whether it relates to the circumstances in which action is taken. The latter interpretation is a more liberal one favouring individual rights, while the other merely restates the common law that statutory power must be reasonably exercised. If the view that the doing must relate to the circumstances in which action is taken a wide field of judicial review is opened.[3]

The realities of civil rights in Southern Rhodesia

Despite the statement in its preamble that the Declaration of Rights is intended 'to ensure that every person in Southern Rhodesia enjoys the fundamental rights and freedoms of the individual', it is submitted that the preservation of existing laws and the carefully qualified fashion in which the fundamental rights have been drafted in practice leaves little room for the operation of the Declaration. It is submitted that even if new legislation infringing freedoms were to be invalidated existing legislation gives the

---

[1] This is a more generous attitude than that adopted by the Nigerian courts, which have taken the line that in view of the presumed constitutionality of every statute, the burden of proving that a law is not reasonably justifiable rests on the person who so alleges: Grove, op. cit., p. 160.

[2] *Maluleke* v. *Minister of Law and Order, supra* at 215.

[3] Even though the enabling law would itself be valid. In any event the onus of showing unreasonability would rest on the applicant as the presumption *omnia praesumuntur rite esse acta* would apply.

administration so much power that it can achieve nearly all its objects in other ways.[1] To support such a generalization it is essential to give some idea of the existing legislation of Southern Rhodesia in relation to the conventionally recognized fundamental freedoms, and some idea of the factual place in society occupied by Africans as a result of economic and social restraints which have resulted from legislative and administrative policies.[2]

Protection of the right to life

In practice, except for Section 33A of the Law and Order (Maintenance) Act decreeing mandatory hanging, the provisions of Southern Rhodesian law relative to capital punishment are similar to those in many other countries. Thus capital punishment must be imposed in the case of a conviction for murder unless extenuating circumstances are found to exist. Capital punishment may also, at the discretion of the Court, be imposed despite extenuating circumstances in the case of murder, in the case of attempted murder, and in cases of high treason, rape or attempted rape.[3] Since 1964 it has also been a permissible sentence for offences involving the possession of grenades and manufactured bombs.[4]

A person will not be held responsible if, in defending himself, force is justifiably used resulting in death. Furthermore, when a person who is on reasonable grounds suspected to have committed an offence enumerated in the First Schedule flees or resists arrest and cannot be apprehended and prevented from escaping by other means, a peace officer or private person authorized to arrest him who kills the person so fleeing or resisting arrest is deemed to have committed justifiable homicide.[5] The provisions in the Declaration and in Southern Rhodesian statute law authorizing killing in the dispersal of crowds allow the police more latitude than does the law in England, as such force is permissible as is reasonably necessary for overcoming resistance during the dispersal of an unlawful gathering (i.e. three or more persons in a public place having been ordered by a police officer to disperse, such officer having had reasonable grounds to believe that a breach of the peace was likely to occur).[6]

[1] e.g. when preventive detention was held unlawful, restriction in a remote area could be employed, or a state of emergency could be declared for a small part of the country, e.g. the Salisbury African townships.

[2] To give a complete picture of these consequences would provide a thesis topic for a political scientist.

[3] Criminal Procedure and Evidence Act (Chapter 31), Sections 360(1), 384(1).

[4] Law and Order (Maintenance) Amendment (No. 2) Act 1964.

[5] Criminal Procedure and Evidence Act, Section 48(1), which corresponds with Section 57(1)(b) of the Declaration, the latter however being somewhat wider.

[6] Chapter 39, Section 15. Compare the classic statement by Bowen L.J. in the Report of the Select Committee on the Featherstone Riot 1893, C. 7234: 'The taking of life can only be justified by the necessity for protecting persons or property against various forms of

Personal liberty

Provisions similar to those standard in most countries exist relating to sentencing persons who have committed crimes to imprisonment. Sentences of imprisonment may also be imposed for contempt of court[1] and for contempt of Parliament. Detention is also permitted of diseased,[2] insane,[3] or alcoholic[4] persons, as well as of prohibited immigrants,[5] deportees, or persons who are the subjects of an extradition order.[6] In addition a person under twenty-three years of age who has been detained by a court order for educational or welfare purposes may have his liberty restricted.[7]

However, special provisions in existing laws seriously derogate from personal freedom. The Law and Order (Maintenance) Act (Chapter 39), in Sections 50 and 51, allows the Minister of Law and Order to restrict persons to particular areas of Southern Rhodesia for periods up to five years. It has been held by Young J. that 'the area specified must be a reasonable area, such that in it an ordinary man can support himself and his family and lead a normal life generally. It must not have the attributes of a concentration camp.'[8] However, although the learned judge held that the Gonakudzingwa Restriction Area was malarial, was an 'inhospitable' tract, was 'marginal even for purposes of subsistence agriculture, which is the only economic potential at the moment', since it consisted of 400 square miles, since furthermore the hardships of the restrictees had been mitigated by the practice of the Government in supplying the restrictees 'with all of their essential requirements free of charge'[9] and since in his view the Legislature contemplated

violent crime, or by the necessity of dispersing a riotous crowd which is dangerous unless dispersed, or in the case of persons whose conduct has become felonious through disobedience to the provisions of the Riot Act and who resist the attempt to disperse or apprehend them.'

[1] Magistrates' courts have been given power to commit persons for up to seven days who have misbehaved in court (Chapter 15, Section 69(1)) while the High Court may summarily deal with contempts. Contempt of court as a consequence of defying a High Court order is dealt with in the Rules of the High Court, Order 42, proceedings being initiated by the aggrieved party on notice of motion or *mero motu* by the Court. The Constitutional Council adversely reported on the Town and Country Planning Act (Chapter 133), since it provides that an investigator holding a local enquiry under that Act may be punished for contempt or refusal to appear before the investigation. The investigation is neither a court of record nor a court of law and the Act therefore contains provisions which would be contrary to Section 58 of the Declaration of Rights were this applicable. (The Act is an existing law.) See Report No. 40, 7 April 1965.

[2] Public Health Act (Chapter 167), Sections 23 and 27, and the Leprosy Act (Chapter 163), Section 2.

[3] Mental Disorders Act (Chapter 164), Sections 11, 16, and 17.

[4] Inebriates Act (Chapter 38).   [5] Immigration Act 1954.

[6] Extradition Act (Chapter 34), and Extradition and Fugitive Offenders Act (Chapter 35). See also Deportation Amendment Act 1964, which is intended to supplement these powers.

[7] Children's Protection and Adoption Act (Chapter 172), Section 31.

[8] *Nkomo and Others* v. *Lardner-Burke N.O.*, Judgement No. G.D. 31/1965 at p. 13.

[9] In fact at least one restrictee has been found to be suffering from pellagra and mild

merely that the restrictee would be viable in the area (viability in his opinion referring to an individual such as 'the typical African peasant'), he concluded that this was an area for purposes of Sections 50 and 51. There were in August 1965, 604 persons restricted in Southern Rhodesia to this and to two other areas, of which one, Sikombela, is similar in nature to Gonakudzingwa.[1]

The Vagrancy Act (Chapter 49), allows vagrants (those unable to show they have employment or visible and sufficient means of subsistence) to be arrested without warrant. Thereafter, pending an enquiry they are held in reception centres and may at the enquiry be committed to re-establishment centres for their rehabilitation. This Act has for the most part been used against Africans and when introduced was announced as being part of the Whitehead Government's security legislation.[2] Again, as already indicated, the Government may invoke its emergency powers to make inroads on personal liberty. Thus in 1959 and again in 1964 and 1965 the Government utilized powers to make regulations during a state of emergency providing for detention of persons.[3]

The provisions of Sections 30 to 38 of the Criminal Procedure and Evidence Act and recent legislation make it probably correct to state that in the majority of statutory offences where a security offence is involved and in the case of all serious common law offences arrest can be effected without a warrant. Peace officers[4] have particularly large powers of arrest without warrant,[5] and even private persons may arrest without warrant in specified circumstances. The latter powers are exercised either on the private person having a reasonable suspicion that a specified offence has been committed[6]

---

scurvy. Personal communication from physician. No special provision is made for the maintenance of their dependants who are dwellers in urban African townships or their children who are at schools in such areas, whereas when persons were restricted under the Preventive Detention (Temporary Provisions) Act (Chapter 74) (now lapsed) the Curatorship (Detained Persons) Act (Chapter 62) made provision for the care and administration of the property and affairs of detained persons and for the care, maintenance, and general welfare of their dependants.

[1] S.R.L.A.D., Vol. 62, col. 229, 13 August 1965. There were 464 at Gonakudzingwa, 76 at Sikombela, and 64 at Wha Wha.

[2] See an article on the Vagrancy Act entitled 'The Great Fraud' in the Central African Examiner, 5 November 1960, which alleges that the Act was intended for security purposes. The Act in Section 4(1) makes it an offence for any person to permit a vagrant to reside on his premises.

[3] See S.R.G.N. 122/59 Emergency (Temporary Detention) Regulations 1959, S.R.G.N. 718 B/64 Emergency (Harare) Regulations 1964 and S.R.G.N. 804 B/64 Emergency (Highfields) Regulations 1964 (No. 2). From 1 January 1964 to 4 August 1965, 1,791 Africans and two Coloureds were detained either in prisons or in camps without trial in terms of such regulations, whereas no Europeans or Asians were detained during the same period: S.R.L.A.D., Vol. 61, col. 1778, 4 August 1965.

[4] Who are widely defined so as to include not only policemen and immigration officers but also any person designated by the Minister by notice in the Gazette, e.g., location superintendents etc.

[5] Criminal Procedure and Evidence Act (Chapter 31), Sections 31, 32.

[6] Chapter 31, Section 36.

or if an offence has been attempted or committed in his presence.[1] The powers of peace officers are, however, much wider. If a person is wrongfully and unlawfully arrested he may bring an action against the person who has infringed his civil rights, but, since arrest is permitted wherever a person is 'reasonably suspected' of having committed an offence listed in the First Schedule or in Section 32, there is little scope for actions for wrongful arrest as police officers can usually point to reasonable grounds for suspicion.[2]

The grant of bail to an accused which is a matter considerably affecting personal liberty, is normally at the discretion of the court with a right of appeal to the general division of the High Court. However, major changes in the law were introduced by the Law and Order (Maintenance) Act 1960, the present position being that if the Attorney-General certifies that it is likely that public security would be prejudiced if the accused were admitted to bail, the court has no power to grant bail.[3]

Another type of imprisonment which is becoming progressively less acceptable in modern countries is imprisonment for civil debt, which is possible in Southern Rhodesia in certain limited circumstances. However, no decree of civil imprisonment may be made against a debtor who proves that he has no means of satisfying the judgement debt either wholly or in part, either out of present means or future income unless he has wilfully made away with property to defeat the judgement creditor, is able to earn sufficient, but refuses to do so in order to defeat the creditor, or is squandering his money and is apparently living beyond his means.[4]

Protection from slavery, servitude, and forced labour

Only in the case of convicted prisoners is there in practice any forced labour in Southern Rhodesia. Imprisonment with hard labour is a competent sentence by any court in respect of common law offences where this is so provided.[5] Such sentences are exempted from the provisions of the Declaration. Nor does the term 'forced labour' include labour required from lawfully detained persons, viz. detainees, restrictees, and lunatics, &c., if such labour is reasonably necessary in the interests of hygiene, for the maintenance of

[1] Chapter 31, Section 33.

[2] Cp. the views expressed by John Adolphus in 1824 in 'Observations on the Vagrant Act': 'A police officer always thinks that he has just reason to suspect that a felony has either been committed or meditated: he lives to suspect, and if he ceased to suspect, he must find some other employ, or cease to live.'

[3] Chapter 31, Section 107(2) as amended by Section 14 of Act 12 of 1964, and Section 113 as amended. See also the High Court Amendment Act 1964, Section 2.

[4] Magistrates Court Act (Chapter 15), Section 23. Cp. Section 35 of the High Court Act No. 22 of 1964 which does not refer to these exceptional circumstances in which a decree can be granted. Civil imprisonment is dealt with in Order 41 of the Rules of the High Court.

[5] Chapter 31, Section 360(2)(a).

the place where they are detained, or if it is required for purposes of any detained person's rehabilitation, education, or welfare.[1]

Labour required by their disciplinary laws from persons in the armed services is also not considered as being forced.[2]

The Constitution also exempts 'any labour which forms part of normal communal or other civil obligations' from the application of the Declaration.[3] Existing laws which are saved in fact make such provision. Thus the African Councils Act (Chapter 95), Section 61, provides that

A council may by resolution declare that the labour for any minor undertaking of the council shall be provided on a communal basis by the inhabitants of the area, and may make by-laws requiring able-bodied inhabitants of the area to perform work on a communal basis in such undertaking for a period not exceeding six days in any quarter.

Again the African Land Husbandry Act (Chapter 103), Sections 61 and 63, provides that Africans under the age of fifty-five who have been unemployed for a period of one month or longer (African farmers on the Tribal Trust Lands are for this purpose unemployed) may once a year be ordered by their Chiefs, Headmen, Kraalheads, or African Councils 'to perform labour in the direct interests of the African inhabitants of such area in connection with the conservation of natural resources of such area or the promotion of good husbandry'. Thereafter the Africans so called up must attend before the District Commissioner where they are entered into the employment of the Government for a period not in excess of ninety days and are paid not less than the ruling current wages in the African district concerned for the class of work required.[4] To fail to comply with such an order is a criminal offence, while Africans who are so engaged become liable to the Masters and Servants Act and the African Labour Regulations Act both of which provide criminal penalties for deserters and for failure to obey an employer's commands.

Indeed, perhaps the most important aspect of forced labour in Southern Rhodesia is the imposition of criminal sanctions on defaulting employees, which are provided for by existing laws, in particular by the African Labour Regulations Act, by the Africans (Identification and Registration) Act and by the Masters and Servants Act. Thus,

any African labourer who without lawful cause deserts or absents himself from his place of employment, or fails to enter upon or carry out the terms of his contract of employment, is guilty of an offence and is liable to a fine not exceeding £10 or to imprisonment for a period not exceeding two months.[5]

---

[1] Constitution, Section 59(2)(b). Thus the regulations under the Vagrancy Act 1960 make provision for vagrants to perform labour which is considered to form part of the rehabilitatory process.

[2] Constitution, Section 59(2)(c).   [3] Section 59(2)(e).   [4] Sections 64 and 65.

[5] Chapter 100, Section 23(1)(a). From the beginning of 1962 to 31 May 1965, 1,047 Africans were prosecuted for breach of this Section: *S.R.L.A.D.*, Vol. 61, col. 1779–80,

Again,

any African who, while under contract of service to one employer, knowingly enters the service of another employer, shall be guilty of an offence and liable to a fine not exceeding £10 or, in default of payment, to imprisonment for a period not exceeding three months.[1]

The Masters and Servants Act also imposes penal sanctions on any servant who

without leave or other lawful cause, absents himself from his master's house or premises or other place proper and appointed for the performance of his work; during working hours, or at any time if resident on his master's premises, becomes or is intoxicated; ... refuses to obey any command of his master, or of any other person lawfully placed by his master in authority over him, which command it was his duty to obey; ... is abusive or insulting, either by language or conduct, to his master or his master's wife or children, or to any person lawfully placed by his master in authority over him; ... or without lawful cause, departs from his master's service with intent not to return thereto.[2]

Servants are so defined that in practice they are almost all African, while masters are almost all non-African.[3] This is shown by the statistics of prosecutions under various provisions of the Act.[4]

Again, the African Juveniles Employment Act applying to African juveniles provides for punishment, including whipping, of juveniles who breach their duties of service. Furthermore, unemployed juveniles may be contracted for a period of service not exceeding six months by the District Commissioner.[5]

4 August 1965. The African Labour Regulations Act covers all recruited Africans, skilled and unskilled and unrecruited Africans except those in domestic service and those who are skilled workmen: Section 2 definition of 'African labourer'. Governor's regulations controlling labourers do not, however, unless specifically applied, govern non-recruited labourers: Section 30(3). Section 23 has been found by the Constitutional Council to be discriminatory: Report No. 38, 20 January 1965.

[1] The Africans (Registration and Identification) Act (Chapter 109), Section 14(1). Cp. the *dicta* by Lord Atkin in *Nokes* v. *Doncaster Amalgamated Collieries*, [1940] A.C. 1014: 'I had fancied that ingrained in the personal status of a citizen under our laws was the right to choose for himself whom he would serve, and that this right of choice constituted the main difference between a servant and a serf.'

[2] Chapter 247, Sections 30(1)(b)(c)(f)(h) and (l).

[3] Chapter 247, Section 2: 'servant includes any person employed for hire, wage, or other remuneration ... to perform any handicraft or other bodily labour in domestic service, mining, agriculture, husbandry, trade, or manufacture, or as coachman, driver, groom, stable-keeper, gardener, or any other similar occupation; (and) any person performing bodily labour in any work or undertaking of what ever kind it may be, without exception, in the capacity of labourer, but not also in that of a skilled workman'.

[4] From January 1960 to 31 May 1965, 13,166 Africans, four Europeans, one Asian, and one Coloured were prosecuted under the subsections quoted. Conversely during the same period only sixty-one Africans were prosecuted under Section 38(1) which penalizes employers who fail to pay a servant's wages whereas 508 Europeans and eight-eight Coloureds and Asians were so prosecuted: *S.R.L.A.D.*, Vol. 51, cols. 2039–40, 22 August 1962, and Vol. 61, col. 1779–80, 4 August 1965.

[5] African Juveniles Employment Act (Chapter 89), Section 7. See *supra*, Part I, Chapter 12, for comment on the passage of this measure in relation to the reserved clauses in the 1923 Constitution.

Freedom of movement

As indicated earlier the Declaration of Rights fails to safeguard or even to recognize freedom of movement. Had such a freedom been specified, existing Southern Rhodesian laws would have rendered the provision virtually nugatory. Such a law is the African Affairs Act (Chapter 92), which in Section 37 provides that no African shall move from one district to another without the consent of the District Commissioners of the districts concerned. Africans so moving commit a criminal offence and may be ordered to return from whence they came.[1] Furthermore, Section 45 of the African Affairs Act prohibits all persons other than indigenous Africans from entering any Tribal Trust Land or tribal area without the written permission of officials of the Department of Internal Affairs, subject to exceptions in the case of persons who must necessarily travel through such areas, persons such as civil servants and Members of Parliament, and persons exercising powers and carrying out duties imposed on them by law.[2] Furthermore, Section 45(4)(a) allows the Minister to exclude any African with land or property rights or occupying land in a tribal area from such areas after full enquiry, while Section 45(4)(b) allows any person to be excluded from such areas after enquiry by the Secretary for Internal Affairs.[3]

Furthermore, the Protected Places and Areas Act (Chapter 76), Section 5(1), allows the Minister, if it appears 'necessary or expedient', to control the movement and conduct of persons in areas which he may declare prohibited. Beadle C.J. has commented that

> It is well to note here that the Minister's powers to declare a protected area are not as limited as the use of the word 'protected' might indicate. He can declare an area to be protected even though the purpose of the order is not to protect any physical thing but really to control the movement of persons within that area.[4]

Areas may also be declared closed labour areas if 'the supply of native labour in the area exceeds the demand for native labour in that area'. In such a case non-Southern Rhodesian Africans are prohibited from seeking work or entering the service of persons in such an area.[5]

The Law and Order (Maintenance) Act, Section 49, also makes provisions for the imposition of a curfew by regulating authorities,[6] if any public disorder

---

[1] The Minister of Justice, on the basis of administrative difficulties, refused to answer a question as to how many charges had been preferred under this section: *S.R.L.A.D.*, Vol. 52, cols. 1360 and 1346, 13 March 1963.

[2] These provisions were used from 1960 to 1962 to prevent numbers of Europeans from visiting restrictees in the Gokwe Area.

[3] As at 13 March 1963, 457 Orders in terms of Section 45(4)(b) had been made and 254 were still in force: *S.R.L.A.D.*, Vol. 52, col. 1359, 13 March 1963.

[4] *Minister of Justice and Attorney-General* v. *Musururwa and Nkomo*, 1964 (4) S.A. 209 (S.R.A.D.).

[5] Foreign Migratory Labour Act 37 of 1958, Section 4(1).

[6] These are usually senior police officers appointed for an area or in some cases District Commissioners.

is apprehended or occurs. Persons found out of doors without permission within the hours specified commit an offence and are liable to a fine not exceeding £50 or to imprisonment for a period not exceeding six months.

A major limitation on freedom of movement is that in terms of Section 50 of the Law and Order (Maintenance) Act the Minister may, if he considers it desirable for the purpose of maintaining law and order, make an order against any person to secure that he shall not be in any area in Southern Rhodesia specified in the order for a period not exceeding four years, that he shall remain in such area as may be specified, or that the person so named must notify his movements in such manner, in such terms and to such authorities as may be specified.[1] These provisions are used for purposes of restriction and it is in terms of orders under this Section that 448 African nationalists were restricted as at the end of November 1964 to either the Gonakudzingwa or Wha Wha restriction areas in Southern Rhodesia.[2]

Yet another Section permits similar restrictions to be imposed for a five-year period on persons convicted of an offence under the Law and Order (Maintenance) Act, the Unlawful Organizations Act, and of common law offences committed in certain circumstances, such persons having been sentenced to pay a fine exceeding £25 or having been sentenced to imprisonment for a period exceeding three months.[3]

There is no right enjoyed by any citizen over fifteen years of age to leave Southern Rhodesia, unless he is in possession of a valid travel document and leaves through a prescribed port.[4] Any person who leaves in contravention of these provisions or any person who conveys such a person out of Southern Rhodesia commits an offence.[5] An additional disability applies in this respect to Africans, as no African may leave Southern Rhodesia unless he is in possession of a permit from a District Commissioner or a registering officer granted for this purpose.[6]

---

[1] The latter section, at that time giving the Minister such powers for three-month periods, was used in respect of two European members of the staff of the University College of Rhodesia and Nyasaland who were confined to an area within three miles of the University in 1962 and required to report daily to the Police. It has been employed against many hundreds of Africans.

[2] *S.R.L.A.D.*, Vol. 59, col. 791, 2 December 1964.

[3] A suspended sentence in terms of Section 382(1)(b) of the Criminal Procedure and Evidence Act (Chapter 31), i.e. a sentence the operation of which is suspended conditional upon good conduct, etc., is for this purpose a sentence of imprisonment: *Nkomo and Others* v. *Lardner-Burke N.O.*, Judgement G.D. No. 31/1965, pp. 16–20.

[4] Departure from Southern Rhodesia (Control) Act No. 25 of 1964, Section 3(1). Prescribed ports have been specified as particular border posts: S.R.G.N. 485/64, Departure from Southern Rhodesia (Control) Regulations 1964, Second Schedule.

[5] Sections 8 and 4. The possible penalty is a £500 fine and/or two years' imprisonment. It is a defence for a carrier to show that he did not know, had no reason to believe and could not reasonably ascertain that the person conveyed by him was not a citizen in possession of a valid travel document.

[6] Africans (Registration and Identification) Act (Chapter 109), Section 16. Between January 1958 and July 1965, 364 Africans were prosecuted for leaving Southern Rhodesia

Africans may also be prohibited by the Minister of Internal Affairs from entering areas within twenty-five miles of Southern Rhodesia's boundaries. Africans who then enter such areas commit an offence. Such a prohibition however does not apply to Africans resident in such areas, to those in Government employment, to those with passes issued by a District Commissioner authorizing entry into such an area, or to African foreigners who are in possession of valid passports to enter Southern Rhodesia for the purpose of proceeding beyond its limits, it being necessary for such foreigners to pass through that area. [1]

Protection from inhuman punishment and treatment

Except for the mandatory imposition of the death penalty under Section 33A of the Law and Order (Maintenance) Act 1960 and for the fact that death is a possible sentence in the case of rape or attempted rape [2] punishments imposed on criminals in Southern Rhodesia are for the most part similar to punishments imposed in other countries, viz. imprisonment with or without hard labour, and with or without solitary confinement and spare diet, declaration as a habitual criminal, fines, whipping, and putting the accused under recognisances with conditions. [3]

Whipping is a punishment that is still extensively imposed, and it is competent not only in respect of common law offences but in respect of all statutory offences against the Law and Order (Maintenance) Act. [4]

Thus convictions for political offences render an offender liable to corporal punishment. However Magistrates' courts may not impose a sentence of whipping in the case of first offenders unless they have committed serious criminal offences, a statutory offence for which whipping has been prescribed as a permissible penalty, the theft of a bicycle or vehicle, or the theft of maize on the cob. [5]

The only arguable case for invoking Section 60(1) of the Declaration in

without such a permit: *S.R.L.A.D.*, Vol. 15, col. 1961–2, 15 August 1962, and Vol. 61, col. 1777–8, 4 August 1965.

[1] African Labour Regulations Act (Chapter 100), Section 26. The Constitutional Council has found this section to be discriminatory but stated that in practice no action had been taken under it. Since the Act was in force before the 1961 Constitution the Declaration of Rights is not applicable to it. See Constitutional Council Report No. 38, 20 January 1965.

[2] Chapter 31, Section 360(1).   [3] Chapter 31, Section 360(2).

[4] Chapter 39, Section 60—except where a person is sentenced under Section 37, i.e. Section 33A of the 1960 Act as amended.

[5] Magistrates Court Act (Chapter 15), Section 49(8)(a). This last circumstance in which whipping can be inflicted on a first offender reflects the power of European agricultural interests to secure the introduction of legislation. Such provision was introduced in 1958. Whipping may also be imposed under Section 10(b) of the Stock and Produce Theft Act (Chapter 48). There are a number of other occasions on which whipping can be imposed while limitations also exist on the imposition of whipping on second offenders. Special provisions govern whippings of juvenile offenders: Chapter 31, Section 374 as substituted.

respect of Southern Rhodesian laws was in relation to the mandatory imposition of the death penalty under Section 33A of the Law and Order (Maintenance) Act 1960.[1] This was not a law in force at the time of coming into
operation of the new Constitution and could therefore be tested against the
Declaration. It has however been ruled by the Southern Rhodesian Appellate
Division that the section in the Declaration prohibiting torture, inhuman or
degrading punishment or other treatment relates only to kinds, types, or
methods of punishment or treatment which are in themselves inhuman or
degrading and not to the severity, quantum, or appropriateness of a punishment in particular circumstances.[2]

Nonetheless it is submitted that the word 'punishment' incorporates a
reference to the offence in respect of which it is being inflicted and that therefore regard can be paid to the relationship between the offence and the degree
of punishment imposed and whether it is excessive.[3]

If this view is correct it is then necessary to determine whether it would be
'inhuman' to impose such a punishment for such an offence. It is submitted
that a mandatory imposition of the death sentence for action which might
only amount to malicious injury to property is an inhuman punishment
particular where the section also comprehends any *socius criminis*.[4]

It may however be that Section 60(3) saves this punishment, as although the
offence and punishment in question were enacted in 1963 after the coming

[1] Cp. the South African General Law Amendment Act 1962 (generally known as the
Sabotage Act) which does not impose a mandatory death penalty but gives the courts a
discretion to impose the death sentence in respect of similar and possibly even more serious
offences than those dealt with in Section 33A of the Law and Order (Maintenance) Act
1960.

[2] *Gundu and Sambo* v. *Hayward and Bosman, NN.O., supra.* The matter is now on appeal
to the Judicial Committee of the Privy Council. The Appellate Division refused to follow
the majority decision in *Weems* v. *The United States*, 217 U.S. 349; 54 Law. Ed. 793 and
followed the minority opinion and other cases such as *The State of Louisiana* v. *Resweber*,
91 Law. Ed. 429 and *The Territory* v. *Ketchum*, 10 N.M. 718 in which it was held that somewhat similar phraseology in the Philippine Constitution (identical in wording with the U.S.
Eighth Amendment) only prohibited the legislature or judiciary from inflicting cruel bodily
torture. If this view is correct it would be permissible for a law to impose the death penalty
for a minor offence but not a public flogging (assuming the latter to be degrading punishment).

[3] It is also submitted that since Section 57 expressly deals with the death penalty and
authorizes its imposition in respect of any criminal offence, Section 60 must have reference
to something other than the mere imposition of a penalty of that nature, viz. to its character
as a punishment in relation to the offence.

[4] In *Gundu and Sambo* v. *Hayward and Bosman NN.O., supra* Lewis A.J.A. at p. 17
found that Section 37(1)(c) of the Law and Order (Maintenance) Act could result in cases
'where the death sentence would be so disproportionate to the offence as to shock public
feeling'. The judge conceded that in a wider sense (than the words were used in Section
60(1) of the Declaration) a punishment, though not necessarily degrading *per se*, might
become inhuman or degrading when it was excessive in relation to the offence for which
it was prescribed. Guidance can be obtained from the Roman–Dutch common law as it
has been modified because it is only in the case of murder that such a penalty is mandatory
and even then statutory modifications have rendered the imposition of this penalty discretionary where there are extenuating circumstances.

into force of the new Constitution, Section 60(3) permits the doing of anything by way of punishment 'which might lawfully have been so done' before
the coming into operation of the new Constitution. If this is merely interpreted as saving existing laws it would be superfluous, as this has already
been done by Section 70(1)(b). It is however possible to give different shades
of meaning to Sections 60(3) and 70(1)(b) thereby rendering Section 60(3)
not otiose. Section 70(1)(b) saves laws only if they were both in force at the
time of coming into operation of the new Constitution and have also 'continued in force at all times since that day'.[1] Similarly Section 70(1)(c) permits
repeal and re-enactment of written laws to the extent that the law re-enacts a
provision 'which has been contained in a written law at all times since
immediately before that day'. Accordingly a re-enactment of a repealed law
would, if there were an interval before its re-enactment, not be saved by
either Section 70(1)(b) or (c). Section 60(3) would however save a provision
stipulating a punishment in these circumstances.

   An indication that Section 60(3) refers not merely to types of punishment
which could have been inflicted prior to the new Constitution is given by the
use of the word 'so'. Section 60(3) saves only action done under laws authorizing the doing of anything by way of punishment 'which might lawfully have
been so done . . . immediately before the appointed day'. It is submitted
that this wording relates the doing of such an act to the circumstances in
which it could have been performed before the new Constitution. If this view
is correct a punishment such as mandatory hanging for breach of Section 33A
of the Law and Order (Maintenance) Act could not be imposed, there being
no law at the time when the Constitution came into operation permitting
such a punishment in such circumstances.

   This approach was however rejected by Quènet J.P. in *Gundu and Sambo* v.
Hayward and Bosman NN.O., *supra*. He considered that such a view could not
have been intended by the framers of the Constitution as 'the necessary consequence of such an interpretation would be to drastically restrict the field of
future legislation—the punishment for offences in future enactments would
have to be limited to punishments for like offences in laws in existence
immediately before the appointed day'.[2] Whether the Judicial Committee
will endorse this attitude remains to be seen.

Protection from deprivation of property

   For the most part the Southern Rhodesian Legislature has, as is shown by
its legislation, a respect for individual property rights.[3] Its legislation provides

[1] *Nkomo and Others* v. *Minister of Justice and Others*, *supra*.

[2] At p. 11. It is however submitted that the ambiguity in a provision intended to protect
individual liberties should permit of an interpretation favouring individual freedom rather
than one enhancing legislative power to infringe individual rights.

[3] This is even shown by its taxation policy, there being no succession duty in Southern

for compensation when land is taken for public purposes or when materials are removed from such land for these purposes. In fact the standard provisions for arbitration as to compensation are written into every Act unless specifically excluded.[1] Similar provisions for compensation are contained in the Municipal Act,[2] while under the Town and Country Planning Act compensation is determined by the Town Planning Court.[3] On the other hand, provisions exist for requisitioning property without compensation in the case of an epidemic.[4] This would also be permitted in terms of regulations issued under the Emergency Powers Act.

Special provision is made for compensation for any loss suffered by Africans who are removed from Tribal Trust Land which is required for setting aside as an African township, for the purposes of conservation of natural resources, or for other purposes in African interests. Such compensation is to be prescribed by regulations.[5]

Political considerations have however influenced the African Affairs Act (Chapter 92), which in Section 45(7) provides that when an African is prohibited from remaining in Tribal Trust Land or in any other tribal area, on the grounds that in the opinion of the Minister of Internal Affairs the presence of such a person in the Tribal Trust Land or area is undesirable in the public interest, all the land rights he has in such area shall be cancelled, the African being given three months to dispose of his rights to another African approved of by the District Commissioner. In the event of failure to do so, such compensation as the Minister may determine is payable, such amount not to be less than the current value of such rights.[6]

Power to deprive an African of his rights to occupy accommodation provided in a Municipal African township is also given to the superintendent of such township, either if the occupant is unemployed for a period in excess of one month or if he is not 'a fit and proper person', having been convicted of offences against the Southern Rhodesia security laws or certain other crimes.[7]

Rhodesia, while the Death Duties Act (Chapter 156), imposes relatively low duties on deceased estates.

[1] Lands and Arbitration Clauses Act (Chapter 14), Section 2.

[2] Chapter 125, Section 274.

[3] Chapter 135, Section 43. However, by virtue of certain sections, in this Act, there can be considerable interference with private rights, e.g. particular use of land may be prohibited if it does not conform to surrounding amenities (Section 32), while where townships are established in approving subdivisions a proportion may be reserved for public purposes, endowments demanded for future local authorities, and roads and streets may be required to be set aside and vested in local authorities (Sections 81, 82, 83 and 96).

[4] Public Health Act (Chapter 167), Section 40.

[5] African Land Husbandry Act (Chapter 103), Section 53. Compensation also relates to rights to graze stock and cultivate land granted in terms of the African Land Husbandry Act. These provisions are repeated in Constitution in a somewhat wider form. See *infra*, Chapter 5.

[6] Section 45(7)(8).

[7] Salisbury Native Urban Areas By-laws 1953. S.R.G.N. 178/53, Section 10(1).

Finally, the Constitutional Council has reported that provisions in the Unlawful Organizations Act (Chapter 81), would have contravened Section 61(1) of the Constitution had the Unlawful Organizations Act not been an existing law. Section 9 of that Act provides that property of an unlawful organization is to be confiscated to the Crown, but does not provide, even assuming that such acquisition is exempted as being necessary in the interests of public order, for any compensation or for any right of access to 'an adjudicating authority to declare the legality of the taking and the amount of compensation which should be paid'.[1]

Protection of privacy of person and home

Although the fine sounding statement has been made that 'no one has a right to enter the house of another against his will', except in terms of Section 54 of the Criminal Procedure and Evidence Act,[2] and the general rule is that search of or entry into premises requires a warrant, it is nonetheless necessary to give police powers of taking immediate action either in the case of search for a person known or suspected to have committed any offence and suspected to be on such premises[3] or if delay would defeat a search.[4] In addition much other legislation confers rights of entry onto property.[5] Some of the legislation authorizing entry is however discriminatory, thus the Africans (Urban Areas) Accommodation and Registration Act (Chapter 110), provides in Section 47 that

any member of the British South African Police shall have the right at all times to enter upon any land included in an African residential area for the purpose of ascertaining whether or not the provisions of this Act or any other law are being complied with and for the purpose of preserving the peace and preventing the commission of crimes therein and generally performing all such other duties as may achieve or assist in achieving such purposes.

Section 48 allows any member of the police at all reasonable times to inspect any premises in an African residential area. The consequence of these

[1] Constitutional Council Report No. 35. Amendments to Sections 8 and 9 by Act 9 of 1963 providing for seizure of property belonging to an unlawful organization before its declaration as such were invalidated in *Nkomo* v. *Lardner-Burke* Judgement A.D. 164/65.

[2] *R.* v. *Nkomo and Others*, 1963 (4) S.A. 166 (S.R.) at 171 per Beadle C.J. The learned Chief Justice upheld the duty of the police when acting without a warrant audibly to demand admission and to notify the purpose for which entry was sought before entering premises. He held that police entry without observance of such duties was unlawful. See Chapter 31, Section 46.

[3] Criminal Procedure and Evidence Act (Chapter 31), Section 46.

[4] Chapter 31, Section 54. Section 55 authorizes search by an occupier of property of any premises including huts, kraals, and enclosures on his property if he is satisfied that there is reason to suspect that any stolen stock or produce is there concealed.

[5] viz. the Municipal Act, Section 273; the Local Government Act, Section 59; the Town and Country Planning Act, Section 113(1); the Town Management Act, Section 187; the Housing and Building Act, Section 21(1) and the African Beer Act, Section 24(1).

provisions is to exclude the necessity for search warrants in African townships. There is no similar provision relative to European residential areas.

Apart from these specific powers, the Law and Order (Maintenance) Act, Section 17(1)(b) provides that

for the proper exercise of his preventive powers and the proper execution of his preventive duties, a police officer may . . . enter and remain on any premises including private premises, in which three or more persons are gathered whenever he has reasonable grounds for believing that a breach of the peace is likely to occur or that a seditious or subversive statement is likely to be made.[1]

Furthermore, powers without warrant to search all motor vehicles and persons in such vehicles have been conferred upon the police by the Governor, who has declared that he is of the opinion that such action was desirable in the interest of public safety.[2]

Safeguards for the accused in criminal procedure

Criminal procedure in Southern Rhodesia as set out in the Criminal Procedure and Evidence Act and Magistrates Court Act was very much the same as it is in other parts of the English speaking world until 1960, when the Law and Order (Maintenance) Act was enacted. Before that Act, precedents for onus-shifting provisions could be found in the Stock and Produce Theft Act (Chapter 48), Sections 4 and 5 of which shifted the onus on to persons in possession of stock or produce with regard to which there was a reasonable suspicion that it had been stolen, to give a satisfactory account of such possession, while persons who received stolen produce were required to prove to the court's satisfaction that they had reasonable cause for believing that the person from whom they had acquired it was authorized to deal with or dispose of it. As a result of the Law and Order (Maintenance) Act, however, numerous offences were introduced and old statutory offences were re-enacted so as to shift the burden of proof in respect of certain facts on to the accused.[3]

---

[1] As indicated in Part II, Chapter 2, *supra* the enactment of this provision was intended to avoid any difficulties which might have resulted from some of the *dicta* by Avory J. in *Thomas* v. *Sawkins*, [1935] 2 K.B. 249, that such entry could only occur if seditious speeches 'would' be made or if a breach of the peace 'would' take place.

[2] This has been done in terms of Chapter 39, Section 56(3).

[3] Thus Section 41 prohibits the doing of any act or uttering of any word likely to impair the authority of any public officer or to expose him to contempt, ridicule or disesteem 'without lawful excuse, the proof whereof lies on him'. Again, Section 19(2) renders it criminal for any person 'without lawful excuse the proof whereof lies on him', to have a prohibited publication in his possession. See *R.* v. *Mackay*, 1964 (1) S.A. 304 (S.R.) in which the editor and publisher of a banned publication who had kept one copy for accounting purposes was found guilty under this section. Again, Section 26 creates an offence where any person 'without lawful excuse, the proof whereof lies on him, watches any premises or the approach to such premises, persistently follows some other person, does any other act or behaves in a manner likely to make some other person apprehensive as to what may happen

In yet other sections of that Act it is provided that an offence is committed and that ignorance of relevant facts, which would otherwise have vitiated *mens rea*, is irrelevant as mere conduct in certain circumstances is an offence.[1] Furthermore, Section 55 provides that where any person

has acted or conducted himself in such a manner, or has spoken or published such words, that it might reasonably be expected that the natural and probable consequences of his act, conduct, speech, or publication would, in the circumstances, be the commission of public violence by members of the public generally or by persons in whose presence the act or conduct took place,

he shall be deemed to have committed the common law offence of incitement to public violence, thus dispensing with the duty of the Crown to prove *mens rea*.

Freedom of conscience

No existing laws of the Southern Rhodesian Legislature can be construed as infringing religious freedom.[2] However, the effect of certain municipal by-laws may well be to hinder this freedom. Gatherings in townships may only take place at specified places, e.g. a gathering solely for religious purposes takes place at a church site.[3] If this is taken in conjunction with the rule that in municipal townships applicants for sites for religious purposes must furnish proof to the Council's satisfaction that the particular religious denomination concerned 'has a substantial enrolment of active members in the area under

---

to such other person or to any member of such other person's family or any dependant of such other person or to any property, business or interest of such other person, or does any act or behaves in a manner which is likely to compel or induce such other person to do some act which such other person is not legally obliged to do'. There is a similar onus-shifting in Section 28 (boycotting), Section 30 (hiding tools or clothes, or jeering or jibing at people), Section 31 (inciting a strike in an essential service), Section 36 (the carrying of offensive weapons), and Section 37 (injury by inflammable materials or explosives to property used for residential purposes or to any property in which a human being is present irrespective of the knowledge of the accused).

[1] See Section 6(6) penalizing any person who takes part in a procession for which a permit has not been obtained. Section 7(4) penalizes any person who attends a public gathering on a public holiday or a Sunday except of a class described in a schedule to the Act or authorized by permit of the Minister. Section 10(3) penalizes any person who takes part in a prohibited procession. Section 11(3) is to the same effect in respect of prohibited gatherings. Section 17(3) penalizes persons who either enter or leave an area around which a cordon has been established. Section 44(2)(f) makes it an offence merely to possess a publication containing a subversive statement. The seller of any publication containing an extract from a public prohibited publication also commits an offence: 19(1).

[2] Possibly Africans might construe the Witchcraft Suppression Act (Chapter 50), as interfering with their traditional beliefs. The Act imposes heavy penalties on persons who advise how to bewitch any person or property, or undertake to find thieves or accuse others of being wizards. Persons who use the services of sorcerers or witch finders are similarly punished.

[3] S.R.G.N. 254/61. Salisbury Native Townships Meetings By-laws 1961, issued under Section 67 of the Local Government Act 1961.

the jurisdiction of the Council' and has 'established or maintained a college or similar institution for the training of its ministers', or that they are 'similarly otherwise adequately trained'[1] it appears that small denominations may be discriminated against.[2]

Protection of freedom of expression

Apart from the normal limitations on speech imposed by the civil law relating to defamation, the common law of sedition and the criminal law relating to defamatory libels[3] and obscene publications[4] modern statutes from 1936 onwards have increasingly made inroads into the right of freedom of speech. The first of these laws was the Sedition Act 1936, subsequently supplemented by the Subversive Activities Act 1950 and the Public Order Act 1955. In 1959 lacunae in these Acts were filled out by the Unlawful Organizations Act, the Preventive Detention (Temporary Provisions) Act, and by amendments to the Public Order Act and the Native Affairs Act, all of which Acts placed considerable limitations on individual freedoms. Eventually in 1960 the Law and Order (Maintenance) Act which purported to be a consolidation of the Subversive Activities Act and the Sedition Act, was passed. However, in almost every case the safeguards and provisions of the old legislation were abandoned while penalties were doubled. At the same time the Public Order Act was repealed and re-enacted as the Emergency Powers Act and the Vagrancy Act was introduced.

The freedom of the press is far from secure as the Law and Order (Maintenance) Act contains provisions which permit the executive to prohibit publications. Thus the Governor may declare a publication to be prohibited if he is of the opinion that 'the printing, publication, dissemination or posession of any publication or series of publications is likely to be contrary to the interests of public safety or security'.[5]

Unless a contrary intention is expressed in the prohibition order, it applies not only to all subsequent issues of the publication but also to any other publication if such publication is in any respect a continuation of or in substitution for the prohibited publication. If such an order relates to all publications by a specified person or association then the prohibition applies not only to all past but to all future publications by that person or association. Such an order may not be varied or set aside by any court of law.[6] The sole

---

[1] Salisbury Urban Area By-laws 1953 S.R.G.N. 178/53, Section 83.

[2] This applies to African separatist churches which have in earlier times in Southern Rhodesia served as a substitute for nationalist parties. Dr. T. O. Ranger in an unpublished lecture at the University College of Rhodesia and Nyasaland in 1961 on 'The Separatist Churches of Southern Rhodesia' has proved this point.

[3] See the Libel Act (Chapter 41), which is a restatement of Cape Act 46 of 1882.

[4] Obscene Publications Act (Chapter 43).   [5] Chapter 39, Section 18(1).

[6] Section 18. Sale, distribution, dissemination, reproduction or even possession of such a publication is an offence: Section 19.

safeguard against abuse of this power is that in the case of newspapers registered before the 2 December 1960 as newspapers in terms of the Printed Publications Act (Chapter 75), the order must be authorized by the Legislative Assembly.[1]

There is no press censorship in Southern Rhodesia and no control over the registration of newspapers except that every newspaper must be registered with the Director of the Archives.[2] Nonetheless, the Section of the Law and Order (Maintenance) Act making it an offence to publish subversive statements, which are widely defined, and the provisions which make it an offence to expose the police or any public officers to contempt, ridicule, or disesteem, make the reporting of much political news a dangerous operation.

Newspapers must taken great care in selecting the news they print as

any person who makes, publishes or reproduces any false statement, rumour or report which is likely to cause fear, alarm, or despondency among the public or to disturb the public peace shall be guilty of an offence and liable to imprisonment for a period not exceeding seven years, unless he satisfies the court that before such making, publication, or reproduction, as the case may be, he took reasonable measures to verify the accuracy thereof.[3]

Any person who utters, writes, circulates, or displays a subversive statement or has in his possession a publication containing such a statement is guilty of an offence and liable to imprisonment for five years.[4] Subversive statements include not only the sort of statements which would be regarded as seditious in other countries but also any statement which 'is likely . . . to engender or promote feelings of hostility to or to expose to contempt, ridicule, and disesteem any group, section, or class in or of a community on account of race, religion, or colour'.

This provision makes it extremely difficult for African nationalist leaders to condemn the present system by which the organs of Government are controlled by a predominantly European electorate, whereas Africans form 94·4 per cent of the population[5] without infringing this section.[6]

---

[1] The only newspaper so far banned has been the *African Daily News*, a newspaper which was owned by the Thompson Organization and which catered for African aspirations. See S.R.G.N. 620 E of 23 August 1964. For the Government's justifications for so acting and criticism thereof see *S.R.L.A.D.*, Vol. 57, cols. 1276–1308 and 1341–1416.

[2] Printed Publications Act (Chapter 75), Section 5(1).

[3] Chapter 39, Section 48. One of Rhodesia's major papers, the *Chronicle*, has recently been prosecuted under this section for publishing an inaccurate report of events at a public gathering at which there was a bomb explosion, and the proprietors of the banned *African Daily News* have similarly been prosecuted for inaccurate news reports.

[4] Chapter 39, Section 44(2).

[5] Figures derived from the Monthly Digest of Statistics, July 1965, Central Statistical Office.

[6] See *R. v. Mackay*, 1964 (3) S.A 176 (S.R.) for the sort of statement which falls within the prohibition. The accused, a European journalist, was found guilty of possessing a circular letter sent from Dar es Salaam shortly before the 1962 general election to a number of

Furthermore, a person who utters any words or does any act or thing whatsoever which is likely to undermine or impair the authority of any public
officer or class of public officer or to expose him to contempt, ridicule or
disesteem is guilty of an offence and liable to a fine not exceeding £100 or to
imprisonment for a period not exceeding one year.[1] A similar section imposes
liability for action which is likely to undermine police authority or to engender feelings of hostility towards or to expose the police or any section
thereof to contempt, ridicule, or disesteem.[2]

Southern Rhodesian citizens by the Rev. N. Sithole, who was on his return convicted and
sentenced to a term of imprisonment for publishing such statements. Relevant parts of the
statement on which the High Court relied in convicting the accused read as follows: 'Sir
Edgar Whitehead is a European leader. He looks after the interests of the whites only. Those
Africans who think Sir Edgar Whitehead cares for their interests might as well think that a
leopard cares for the interests of a goat. Sir Edgar was chosen by whites and he is therefore
responsible only to whites. Make no mistake about this. In 1959 they asked him to ban the
A.N.C. and he did it. In 1961 they asked him to ban the N.D.P. and he did it. In 1962 they
asked him to ban ZAPU and he did it. Why? Because the whites elected him and he is responsible to them. Sir Edgar has never tried to remove the political grievance of the franchise
which worries the Africans so much. Europeans do not want the majority of the Africans to
have the vote, and therefore their leader acts accordingly . . .. The European minority, led
by Sir Edgar, is the real "enemy of law and order" since they do not want the vote to
be extended to the 4,000,000 Africans in Southern Rhodesia. They want it to remain the
monopoly of only 250,000 whites.' Clayden F.C.J. on appeal took the view that these
statements were not subversive but found that a subsequent statement in the letter was subversive, viz. that the Europeans were prepared 'to go to any lengths to oppress the African
majority in order that the white minority might rule Southern Rhodesia indefinitely. They
are the oppressors, the Africans are the oppressed': *Mackay* v. *The Queen*, 1964 (3) S.A.
176 (F.C.). The Chief Justice held that every judge, lawyer, or police officer who held the
document in his possession at any time committed an offence as no *mens rea* was required,
mere possession of such a subversive statement constituting an offence. In *R.* v. *Takawira
and Others*, Judgement No. A.D. 78/65, Quènet J.P. held that such an interpretation would
result in an absurdity so glaring that it could never have been contemplated by the Legislature.
It is submitted that this argument also applies to the appearance of such a statement in a
law report and in constitutional law text book exemplifying the type of statement considered by the courts to be subversive.

  [1] Section 41(1).
  [2] Section 39. Thus an accused was convicted under this section for describing African
police reservists as 'girl guides' because they wore a blue uniform and a hat similar to those
worn by girl guides. In *Mukahlera* v. *R.*, 1961 R. & N. 872 an accused was convicted for
having told a political meeting of 400 or 500 Africans, at which the police were present,
that they must not have ill feelings against the police who had been sent to the meeting by
others but that the police were 'small boys' and that the meeting must 'treat them as small
boys'. Again in *Haddon* v. *The Queen*, Judgement A.D. 106/65, the editor of the *Central
African Examiner* was convicted for having published a sonnet entitled 'Men and Beasts'
which drew attention to a dog's admirable qualities, lamented the fact that men had subverted these qualities, and in particular, that the police had trained their dogs 'to hate the
smell of black: The dispossessed, the people of the land'. These statements are given for the
purpose of exemplifying the type of statement found by the courts as likely to engender
feelings of hostility to the police. That such a statement is circulated to a 'sophisticated'
section of the public is no defence as such persons are equally capable of emotion. The
question in each case is whether such statement is likely to have the effect of occasioning
hostility not whether in fact it did have that result: *Haddon* v. *The Queen*, *supra* and *R.* v.
Nkomo, 1964 (4) S.A. 452 (S.R.A.D.) at 454.

Yet another section penalizes 'any person who uses any opprobrious epithet or any jeer or jibe to or about any other person in connection with the fact that such other person has undertaken, continued, returned to or absented himself from work or refused to work for any employer, or undertaken duties as a member of any police reserve or any Government department'.[1]

Finally, any police officer is given considerable preventive power as he may at any gathering either public or private 'forbid any person from addressing such gathering ... whenever he has reasonable grounds for believing that a breach of the peace is likely to occur or that a seditious or subversive statement is likely to be made'.[2]

Freedom of assembly and of association

For greater clarification of existing law it is hereby declared that the freedom commonly called the freedom of public assembly does not confer on any individual the right to be at any place situated on land belonging to or vested in the Crown or a local authority or any other person; roads, streets, lanes, paths, pavements, sidewalks, thoroughfares and the like exist for the free passage of persons and vehicles along them, not for the exercise by any individual of the freedom of public assembly.[3]

When Dicey's analysis of the freedom of assembly as consisting in the right of people to assemble and 'meet together in any place where otherwise they each have a right to be for a lawful purpose and in a lawful manner'[4] is applied to the legal position in Southern Rhodesia there is neither individual nor collective freedom to assemble, both being subject to severe limitations. The Law and Order (Maintenance) Act prohibits the holding of or any participation in a public procession unless a permit has first been obtained from a regulating authority, who may impose any conditions as to date, time, duration, and any other matter designed to preserve public order.[5] Similar restrictions apply to public gatherings, which are so defined as to include gatherings of twelve or more persons in a public place and also gatherings of more than 200 persons irrespective of where such gathering occurs and irrespective of whether it is confined to particular persons invited, or to members of an organization.[6] Regulating authorities, in most cases a senior police officer for the area or the District Commissioner, may impose conditions on public meetings.

Standard conditions imposed require seven days advance notice of such a meeting, a copy of the agenda, the name and address of the chairman, and

[1] Chapter 39, section 32.
[2] Chapter 39, section 17 (1) (a).
[3] Law and Order (Maintenance) Act (Chapter 39), Section 4.
[4] Dicey, Law of the Constitution, 9th edition, Chapter 7.
[5] Section 6.   [6] Section 2. Definition of 'public gathering'.

names and addresses of all speakers before permission is granted.[1] The Act also provides that facilities other than equipment for recording the proceedings must be made available by the convenors.[2]

Powers to prohibit all or any class of public processions and public gatherings for up to three months in an area are vested in District Commissioners subject to confirmation of any prohibition within seventy-two hours by the Minister of Law and Order.[3] The Minister may also prohibit particular public gatherings, all public gatherings throughout the Colony, gatherings by specific organizations, and gatherings on particular days.

He may also specify the hours at which gatherings may be held and may impose conditions either in respect of all public gatherings or relative to public gatherings convened by specific organizations or persons.[4] The Minister may also, if he considers it is desirable for the maintenance of law and order to do so, by notice prohibit any person from attending any public gathering in Southern Rhodesia or any part thereof.[5] Disregard of any of these prohibitions or the conditions imposed are serious offences, the convenors being liable either to a fine not exceeding £100 or to imprisonment for a period not exceeding one year, as is any person who takes part in a prohibited procession, while any person who is present at such a prohibited gathering is liable to a £50 fine or six months imprisonment. All the powers conferred on the Minister and District Commissioners have frequently been invoked in practice.

Section 6A of the Law and Order (Maintenance) Act as amended in 1963 provides that 'no person shall organize a public gathering to be held on a Sunday or other public holiday or convene, hold, address, or attend a public gathering on a Sunday or other public holiday'. These provisions do not apply to the gatherings listed in the Third Schedule to the Act, viz. for *bona fide* religious, educational, and recreational purposes, meetings by associations or organizations not of a political nature where the matters dealt with are non-political, meetings of registered trade unions[6] and meetings held for other similar purposes.

---

[1] See e.g. S.R.N. 1020/62. Direction No. 4 requires the convenor of any gathering to confine the speakers to those persons named in the notification of the gathering previously supplied to the regulating authority. Subsequent Government Notices issued after the coming into force of the 1961 Constitution have been invalidated by the Constitutional Council for containing such a direction. See Constitutional Council Report on S.R.N. 131/63 published in the Gazette of 15 February 1963.

[2] Section 8(5). The police attend all major African political gatherings and take tape recordings thereof. They also attend certain European political meetings for the same purpose. The Constitutional Council has invalidated conditions imposed after the coming into force of the new Constitution, which required convenors of meetings to provide a minimum of two suitable tables and five suitable chairs for use by the police. See e.g. Report on S.R.N. 172/63, 197/63, &c.

[3] Sections 10(1) and 11(1).

[4] Section 12(1).   [5] Section 13(1).

[6] African trade unions with nationalist sympathies are for the most part unregistered

The Minister may also permit any particular public gathering.[1] It should be noted that many of these powers have been duplicated in the African Affairs Act (Chapter 92), except that in Tribal Trust Land and tribal areas permission for gatherings of twelve or more Africans requires the written consent of the District Commissioner given after consultation with the Chief of the area,[2] while particular persons may be prohibited from attendance at gatherings generally or at a particular gathering by the District Commissioner after consultation with the Chief.[3]

Furthermore, powers of control of meetings in urban areas have been duplicated by the municipalities and the town management boards through by-laws issued under the Local Government Act 1961, Section 67 of which authorizes the issue of by-laws for control of African townships. These by-laws impose restrictions similar to those of the regulating authorities on the holding of public meetings.[4]

Control of crowds is secured by authorization to any police officer to give such instructions as may appear to him to be necessary or expedient in the circumstances for the proper maintenance of public order in any public place, and in particular for preventing the obstruction of roads and pavements in any place where they are liable to be obstructed, or in the vicinity of the Legislative Assembly, Courts of Law, Government offices, diplomatic offices, Ministerial residences, or that of the Governor, and in the vicinity of theatres, cinemas, or other places of public resort.[5]

Provision for dispersal of crowds is also made. Section 15(1) of the Law and Order (Maintenance) Act reads:

> If three or more persons are assembled in a public place or at a public meeting and conduct themselves in such a manner that a police officer has reasonable grounds for believing a breach of the peace is likely to occur or that public disorder is likely to be occasioned, he may call upon the persons assembled to disperse and for that purpose he shall endeavour to obtain the attention of those persons by such lawful means as he deems most suitable, and then in a loud voice order them to depart forthwith from the place of assembly. Such order shall be repeated by him three times. If any person fails so to depart immediately after an order is so given and repeated, the persons so remaining shall be deemed to be an unlawful gathering, and to have taken part in an unlawful gathering.

and therefore cannot have meetings on Sundays which is virtually the only day convenient for African workers. See *infra* in regard to trade unions.

[1] Law and Order Maintenance Amendment Act No. 12 of 1963, Section 2.

[2] Chapter 92, Section 46(1). Out of 101 applications to hold meetings in reserves or tribal areas between May 1959 and May 1963, sixty-seven were refused: *S.R.L.A.D.*, Vol. 53, col. 26, 19 June 1963.

[3] Chapter 92, Section 47. Only two notices prohibiting persons from addressing or holding meetings in such areas were served from 1959 to June 1963: *S.R.L.A.D.*, Vol. 53, col. 26. However, there were many bans on public meetings generally in the African Reserves.

[4] See, e.g. the Salisbury Native Townships By-laws 1961, S.R.G.N. 254/61 and also the Gwelo Meetings By-laws S.R.G.N. 16/62.

[5] Chapter 39, Section 16(1).

Persons who fail to disperse, or reassemble elsewhere, commit an offence, and a police officer and any other person acting in aid of him may do all things reasonable for their dispersal.[1]

Power to declare organizations to be unlawful whether incorporated or unincorporated and also sections, branches, or committees, or any subsidiary body forming part of an association are given by the Unlawful Organizations Act (Chapter 81). Such powers are to be exercised by the Governor if it appears to him that the activities of such an association are likely to endanger public safety, disturb the public order, to raise disaffection among the inhabitants or to promote feelings of ill will or hostility between or within different races in the Southern Rhodesian population.[2] Successor organizations, organizations descended from the same parent organization as an unlawful organization, and any organization composed substantially, though not necessarily predominantly of, or directed or controlled directly or indirectly by persons who have been or are officers of an unlawful organization, may also be prohibited, while persons who take part in the activities of an unlawful organization or carry on any activity in its direct or indirect interests commit an offence.[3]

The Preservation of Constitutional Government Act (Chapter 45), provides that any person who breaches its provisions is guilty of an offence and liable to a period of imprisonment not exceeding twenty years. The Act is breached when a Southern Rhodesian citizen either within or outside Southern Rhodesia

Organizes or sets up or helps to organize or set up, or advocates, urges or suggests the organization or setting up of, any group or body with a view to that group or body overthrowing or attempting to overthrow the Government by unconstitutional means; or taking over or attempting to take over the Government by unconstitutional means or usurping the functions of Government in Southern Rhodesia; or coercing or attempting to coerce the Government; or supports or assists any such group or body in doing or attempting to do any of the things described (above) . . . or in any manner seeks to enlist the aid of any person, group or

---

[1] Section 15(2)(3) and (5). In dispersing them the police officer and those assisting him may use all such force as is reasonably necessary for overcoming such resistance and shall not be liable in any civil or criminal proceedings for having by the use of such force caused harm or death to any person.

[2] Chapter 81, Section 3(1).

[3] Section 10(b). Numerous other offences relative to unlawful organizations are also created by the Act. Furthermore, any person who was an office bearer of an unlawful organization or an officer may by written notice be asked to resign as an office bearer or member from any organization or class of organizations, and may be prohibited from becoming such for a period not exceeding three years if the Governor is satisfied that the activities of such a person are such or would be likely to endanger public safety, public order, or to prejudice the tranquillity or security of the Colony, or would result in other similar consequences: Unlawful Organizations Act 1959, Section 5A as amended by Act 9 of 1963.

body, whether such person, group or body is within or outside Southern Rhodesia in doing or attempting to do any of the things (above) described.[1]

Limitations on the activities of trade unions are imposed by the Industrial Conciliation Act which prohibits both trade unions and any employers' organization[2] from employing any of their funds for political purposes or for assisting any body which is authorized to use its funds for such purposes in terms of its constitution. Trade unions are in fact entirely prohibited by the Industrial Conciliation Amendment Act 1964 from participating either directly or indirectly in 'politics'.[3]

The right to strike has also been carefully regulated and may only be employed after a conciliation process has first been followed.[4] Breach of these provisions constitutes an offence.[5]

Quasi-military organizations and unlawful drilling are also prohibited and heavy penalties can be imposed, viz. imprisonment for up to ten years.[6]

Freedom from discrimination

Despite the prohibition against discrimination contained in the Declaration of Rights, the saving of all laws in force before the coming into operation of the new Constitution has preserved numerous discriminatory provisions. In addition to legalized discrimination in terms of these provisions, much legislation couched in non-discriminatory language has its main effect on Africans who are subjected to its penal provisions, whereas such Acts are in practice virtually inapplicable to Europeans. Furthermore, even though there may at present be no legislation which results in economic differentiations in the positions of Europeans and Africans, such differentiations have resulted from earlier legislation only relatively recently repealed, from governmental policy in relation to the sums devoted to African education and the type of education provided,[7] and from the fact that Government recruiting policy to the various posts within its patronage has virtually excluded certain racial groups.[8] Discrimination in Southern Rhodesia as a result of legal provisions

[1] Chapter 45, Section 2. Mr. Smith and his Ministers could be charged under this Section.
[2] But not large public corporations who are the worst offenders.
[3] In a sense all issues with which trade unions are concerned are political. These prohibitions ensure that there cannot be a Southern Rhodesian Labour Party.
[4] Chapter 246, Section 122.
[5] The Law and Order (Maintenance) Act, Section 40, makes it an offence to do any act calculated to induce any member of a police force to withhold his services. Police regulations in the First Schedule to the Police Act 1964 make it a criminal offence for any member to discuss conditions of service except in terms of the provisions of that Act which provide for a British South Africa Police Services Association. Any strike by police would be unlawful.
[6] Sections 22 and 23 of Chapter 39.
[7] See Appendix, Table J.
[8] Former legislative prohibition and Government's recruiting policy to the Civil Service and unestablished Government posts in respect of non-Africans has resulted in few Africans

can in fact be examined on a number of levels: it can be looked at from the point of view of legislation designed for and expressed to be for Africans only. It can be extracted from general legislative measures which for the most part govern all races but at the same time contain discriminatory provisions. Finally, it can be found as a consequence of legislation, which, although couched in non-discriminatory language, has its effect on particular racial groups only. As a consequence of these provisions and of Government policy major economic differentiations between Africans and non-Africans have resulted.

Legislation applicable to Africans only

An unusual feature of Southern Rhodesian legislation is that general provisions which apply to all races are to a considerable extent duplicated in measures applicable to Africans only, thus making it possible for Africans either to be prosecuted under the ordinary law of the land or alternatively under a special law applicable to them alone. The African Affairs Act (Chapter 92) in particular contains such provisions. Section 44 of that Act makes it an offence for an African to make any statement or do any act whatsoever which is likely to undermine the authority of any Government officer or any Chief, Headman, or head of kraal or to bring such persons into disrepute or contempt.

Similarly regulations under that Act may be made in terms of Section 53(1)(b) prohibiting, restricting, controlling, and regulating the carrying of assegais, knives, knobkerries, sticks, or other weapons by natives,[1] although the Law and Order (Maintenance) Act penalizes any person who has in his possession an offensive weapon. Again, municipal by-laws for African townships may have the same effect of permitting control of public meetings as has Section 8 of the Law and Order (Maintenance) Act, thus the Salisbury Native Townships Meetings By-laws 1961 [2] impose control and restrictions on public meetings virtually identical to those generally imposed by regulating authorities by virtue of their powers under Section 8 of the Law and Order (Maintenance) Act.

Although the Constitutional Council has adopted the attitude that such provisions, viz. those in the African Affairs Act, 'viewed as part of the whole body of law have little or no discriminatory effect' it then proceeded to point out that

to the ordinary man who has no specialized knowledge of the remainder of our law, they must appear to be discriminatory. This effect is emphasized by the continual

occupying responsible posts: see *supra* Part II, Chapter 2. Again, there is no recruitment of Coloureds and Asians to the British South African Police: *S.R.L.A.D.*, Vol. 52, col. 20–32, 19 June 1963. There were no African commissioned officers in the Army or the Police.

[1] No such regulation has in fact been made and the Constitutional Council therefore considered it only potentially discriminatory: Constitutional Council Report No. 28, 14 August 1963, p. 15.

[2] S.R.G.N. 254/61. Other municipal councils and town management boards have passed similar by-laws for their townships.

use of these provisions in prosecutions of Africans . . .. When an African is so prosecuted, the fact that he is an African is a necessary averment of the charge on trial; this is apt to create in his mind a sense of injustice in that he believes that his race is one of the reasons for his prosecution, and that a member of any other race would have gone scot free. The Council is aware that in the minds of those against whom discrimination applies, it is the fact rather than the degree of discrimination which counts. The mere fact of being singled out as members of a particular race for special treatment under a particular law is considered an affront to dignity and is not assuaged by pointing out that the degree of discrimination is negligible, or that under another law all races are subjected to the same or similar treatment.[1]

In addition to such measures which duplicate the general law, there is a great deal of legislation which applies only to Africans as is manifest from the special title 'African Affairs' in the Revised Statute Law of Southern Rhodesia 1963, there being twenty-four Acts applying almost entirely to Africans, the majority of which create numerous criminal offences.[2] The major Acts provide for the administration of Africans under the control of District Commissioners, Chiefs, Headmen, and of Kraalheads in the rural areas,[3] for local government by African Councils for Africans in rural areas[4] and by African Advisory Boards in urban municipal areas,[5] for special courts for Africans held by District Commissioners, Chiefs, and Headmen in respect of African civil cases (these being excluded from magistrates courts),[6] for the preservation of African customary personal laws,[7] for regulating African employment and imposing penal sanctions on Africans who break their contracts of service[8] for regulating African education,[9] for the acquisition of rights over land in Tribal areas,[10] for regulating the marketing of African products and for providing for levies on such products for the development

---

[1] Constitutional Council Report No. 28, 14 August 1963, pp. 15–16.

[2] The practical applications of some of these Acts can be seen by an examination of prosecutions or convictions for their breach. S.R.L.A.D., Vol. 50, col. 1320, 13 August 1962, discloses that from January 1959 to June 1962 two Europeans were charged with offences under the African Affairs Act, while 1,047 Africans were so charged. In the same period one European was prosecuted under the African Land Husbandry Act while 4,316 Africans were so prosecuted, 4,160 being convicted.

[3] The African Affairs Act is dealt with in Part II, Chapter 2, supra.

[4] The African Councils Act is dealt with in Chapter 5 infra. The Council of Chiefs and Provincial Assemblies Act is also dealt with at that point as providing for African advisory bodies for African interests.

[5] The Africans (Urban Areas) Accommodation and Registration Act, is dealt with in Chapter 5 infra.

[6] The African Law and Courts Act is dealt with in Chapter 3 supra.

[7] The African Law and Courts Act, the African Affairs Act, the African Wills Act and the African Marriages Act. See Chapter 3 supra.

[8] The African Labour Regulations Act, the African Juveniles Employment Act, the African Labour Supply Commission (Declaratory) Act and the Foreign Migratory Labour Act.

[9] African Education Act.   [10] The African Land Husbandry Act.

of African areas,[1] and for laws compelling Africans to carry registration certificates or certificates of identity.[2]

Of these Acts, five have already been reported on by the Constitutional Council and have been found to be discriminatory, but since they are existing laws the Declaration of Rights does not affect their validity.[3]

The relevant provisions of most of these Acts in relation to the structure of administration, the legal system and freedom from forced labour have already been examined. It remains, however, to make more detailed comment on the Africans (Identification and Registration) Act (Chapter 109), and Acts which affect the economic rights of Africans such as the marketing and levy legislation and the African Land Husbandry Act.

Although at the end of 1960 certain of the African 'pass' laws had been repealed by the Land Apportionment Amendment Act No. 54 of that year,[4] the Africans (Identification and Registration) Act 1957 (now Chapter 109 of the statute law), which repealed but also in large measure re-enacted the Native Passes Act (Chapter 77, of 1939), makes provision for the registration of Africans, for the issue to them of certificates of registration, registration books or identification cards, and for the imposition of criminal liability on any African who

is found in any district without a certificate, book, identity card, or permit issued or deemed to have been issued under this Act; (or) being obliged by law to possess or carry a certificate, book, identity card or permit, refuses or neglects to produce it when required to do so by any police officer or other authorized official.[5]

Every African male on attaining the age of sixteen years is required to register himself at a registration office to be issued either with a registration certificate or a registration book.[6] Chiefs, Headmen, and Kraalheads who fail to see that every African living or being within the area over which they exercise

[1] The African Cattle Marketing Act, the African Development Fund Act read with Section 27 of the Federal Grain Marketing Act No. 23 of 1957.

[2] The Africans (Registration and Identification) Act.

[3] viz. the African Law and Courts Act, the African Affairs Act, the African Wills Act, the Africans (Registration and Identification) Act, and the African Labour Regulations Act: Constitutional Council Reports Nos. 27, 28, 33, 37, and 38. Regulations issued under the African Education Act relating to conditions of service of African and European teachers employed by the Division of African Education and the regulations providing for the exclusion of African children from schools if their fees are unpaid have also been found discriminatory: Constitutional Council Report of 26 June 1963 and Constitutional Council Report No. 32 of 30 July 1964.

[4] The repealed laws were the Natives Registration Act (Chapter 76 of 1939), the Native Urban Locations Act (Chapter 84 of 1939), and the Town Locations Regulations Act (Chapter 85 of 1939), which provided for the carrying of various documents by Africans.

[5] Chapter 109, Section 21(d) and (e). Between January 1958 and July 1965, 34,790 Africans were prosecuted under this provision. After the repeal of the pass laws in the period January 1961 to July 1965 the number prosecuted was 20,457 Africans: S.R.L.A.D., Vol. 51, cols. 1761–3, 15 August 1962, and Vol. 61, cols. 1777–8, 4 August 1965. The Constitutional Council has found this section to be discriminatory: Report No. 37, 20 January 1965, p. 4.

[6] Chapter 109, Section 4.

control appears before a registration officer commit an offence.[1] Instead of the necessity for carrying a registration book, certain classes of Africans can be authorized to carry identity cards. Such classes are prescribed by the Minister of Internal Affairs, and Africans of such a group are entitled to apply for an identity card to the Secretary of Internal Affairs. If such an African is over twenty-five years of age, and if in the opinion of the Secretary for Internal Affairs he is 'by reason of his character, record, qualifications, and standing a fit and proper person' to receive an identity card he may be granted a card.[2]

The possible number of holders of identity cards is not very great in relation to the size of the African population, as the Natives (Registration and Identification) Regulations 1958 as amended merely permit Chiefs, Headmen, owners of property, or hire-purchasers of property who have held such property for five years, university graduates, Africans with standard VI education who have for ten years carried on a trade or profession, licensed traders for five years, master farmers who have farmed continuously for five years, messengers of the Department of Internal Affairs who have been employed for twenty years, and African non-commissioned officers and constables of the British South African Police with twenty years' service, as well as African Members of Parliament, and voters to apply for identity cards.[3] However, even the holding of an identity card does not confer great advantages. Although such persons are exempted from the operation of municipal by-laws or regulations requiring Africans to be in possession of a pass and from compulsory vaccination and medical examinations in terms of regulations under the Africans (Urban Areas) Accommodation and Registration Act (Chapter 110), they must always carry such cards and can still be required by any police officer to produce their identity card. Unless they do so they commit an offence.[4]

Non-indigenous Africans are also required to register unless such an African is visiting the colony for a period not exceeding ninety days and is a Member of Parliament or occupies an equivalent position and has been invited to visit the Colony by the Southern Rhodesian Government.

It is however possible for other Africans to apply for exemption before their entry.[5]

Registration certificates or registration books not only serve as documents of identity but are also records of the employment history of Africans and

[1] Chapter 109, Section 7.
[2] Chapter 109, Section 9(2)(d).
[3] S.R.G.N. 208/58, as amended. As at 28 July 1965, 6,229 Africans had been issued with identity cards: S.R.L.A.D., Vol. 61, col. 1501. The Secretary of Internal Affairs if he has reasonable grounds for thinking that the holder of an identity card is no longer a fit and proper person to hold such a card, may after written notice calling on such holder to show cause why it should not be cancelled and after due enquiry, cancel such a card and demand its surrender: Section 11(1) and (2).
[4] Chapter 109, Section 10, read with Section 21.
[5] S.R.G.N. 208/58, Section 11.

41—C.H.L.S.R.

every employer of an African must enter in his registration certificate the date of commencement of his employment and the amount of wages stipulated.[1] Any African who mutilates, adds to, or alters any material particular on his registration certificate commits an offence and is liable to imprisonment for a period not exceeding three months or a fine not exceeding £10.[2] The Act also creates a number of miscellaneous offences such as making use of the certificates of other Africans and general contraventions of the Act.[3]

Yet another discriminatory provision in this Act which results in numerous convictions of Africans for trespass is Section 20(2) of the Act. This provides that

no African shall enter or be upon the property of any other person unless he is in the employ of such other person; he has the permission of the person in charge of such property to enter or be upon it; he enters or is upon such property for the purpose of seeking employment at any reasonable and proper time; or has other reasonable and satisfactory excuse therefor. Possession of an open delivery note relating to the goods of a merchant, shopkeeper or tradesman shall be regarded as a sufficient excuse.[4]

It will be seen therefore that the effect of this Act is to turn a considerable number of African male adults into petty offenders.[5]

Other legislation restricts freedom of Africans in the economic sphere. Some of this legislation still remains as re-enacted from before the grant of responsible government viz. the African Cattle Marketing Act, which was intended to protect Africans from exploitation. This Act provides that no non-African may buy any African cattle other than at a sale organized by the Department of Internal Affairs, or in terms of a permit issued by a District Commissioner, nor may any person sell any such cattle except as so provided.[6]

Free participation at sales is not permitted as the Minister of Internal Affairs may prescribe by written directions to a District Commissioner persons,

---

[1] Chapter 109, Section 12(1). It is an offence for an African to engage himself to another employer while under contract of service: Section 14(1). It is also an offence for an employer knowingly to engage such an African.

[2] Section 21(f). Between January 1958 and July 1965, 610 Africans were convicted under this section: *S.R.L.A.D.*, Vol. 51, cols. 1761–2, 15 August 1962, and Vol. 61, cols. 1777–80, 4 August 1965. Any person who does such an act also commits an offence: Section 22(c).

[3] In the period above mentioned a further 2,202 Africans were convicted of offences under such other provisions: *S.R.L.A.D.*, Vol. 51, cols. 1761–2, and Vol. 61, cols. 1777–80, 4 August 1965.

[4] In the period between January 1958 and July 1965, 57,989 Africans were convicted of an offence under this section: *S.R.L.A.D.*, Vol. 51, cols. 1761–2 and Vol. 61, cols. 1777–8. The Constitutional Council has commented on the discriminatory character of this section: Report No. 37, 20 January 1965, p. 4.

[5] See *S.R.L.A.D.*, Vol. 51, cols. 1761–2 and Vol. 61, cols. 1777–8. In the seven-and-a-half year period between January 1958 and July 1965, there were 95,340 convictions of Africans under this Act.

[6] Chapter 94, Section 4. Breach of the provisions of the Act renders the offender liable to a fine not exceeding £50 or to imprisonment not exceeding six months: Section 13.

or classes of persons, or both, who alone may purchase cattle at Departmental sales. He may also fix quotas for the purchasers of African cattle and prescribe the percentage, class and grade of cattle allowed to purchasers.[1] The result is that there is no free market for the sale of African cattle which may well in time of demand operate to the disadvantage of African sellers, although in times of excessive supply African sellers are protected against themselves should they wish to sell cattle privately.

A measure of even more consequence to African farmers is the African Development Fund Act which in Section 15 authorizes the Minister of Internal Affairs annually to impose levies on any type of African produce of up to fifteen per cent of the price paid by the buyer for the African produce.[2] The Act is made relatively easy in its administration by provisions for compulsory registration of buyers who are made responsible for payment of the levy (and who therefore take this into account in fixing the price paid), the conduct by the Internal Affairs Department of sales of cattle, and by provisions in the Federal Grain Marketing Act 1957, Section 27 of which stipulates that the prescribed price fixed by the Board for all purchases of grain shall be paid to African producers less any sums due in terms of the African Development Fund Act.[3]

In 1964 the Minister of Internal Affairs imposed a levy of ten per cent on the knock-down bid of cattle sold at public auction, and in the case of other sales ten per cent of the amount received by the African seller.[4] A similar ten per cent levy is payable on African produce[5] while maize, munga, kaffir corn, and ground nuts have levies payable on them at fixed rates per bag.[6] It should also be noted that African producers are required to pay transport levies and a handling margin charge, as well as a charge for the cost of any bags in respect of their maize sales.[7] The reason for this is that African maize is collected by traders in rural areas and not delivered directly to the Grain Marketing Board, although provision exists for any African producer to make deliveries of twenty-six bags or more direct to the Marketing Board and thus to receive the full prescribed price less the African Development Fund levy only. The practical effect of these provisions is that European farmers, after

---

[1] Section 10.   [2] Chapter 96, Section 15.

[3] The latter provisions are also used to collect levies payable by non-African farmers in terms of the Agricultural Produce Levies Act No. 19 of 1957. The principles on which these levies are imposed are entirely different.

[4] S.R.G.N. 782/63, Native Cattle Levy Order 1964. S.R.G.N. 70/64, The Native Pig Levy Order imposed a levy of 1d. per lb. on the cold dressed weight of slaughtered pigs.

[5] S.R.G.N. 333/64, African Development Fund (African Produce Levy) Order 1964. Such produce includes beans, cotton, fruit and vegetables, rupoko, sesame, sun hemp seed, and vegetable seeds.

[6] S.R.G.N. 311 D/64, Native Development Fund (Native Maize, Munga, Kaffircorn, and Groundnuts) Levy Order 1964. The payment on shelled groundnuts was 7s. per bag and that on maize 3s. 3d. per bag, &c.

[7] In terms of the Grain Marketing Act and the regulations thereunder. These provisions were originally in the Southern Rhodesian Maize Control Act.

taking into account the cost of the bags, receive 13s. 3d. per bag of maize more than Africans unless such Africans are able to sell directly to the Grain Marketing Board, in which case they receive 3s. 3d. per bag less than European farmers.[1] Insofar as the agricultural levies applied to the inhabitants of the African Purchase Areas they were however abolished in 1964.[2]

Justification of the African Development Fund levy is that such levies are paid into a trust Fund and are to be used for paying persons employed either by the Fund, or as dip attendants (to secure proper dipping of African cattle), and are also to be used in African areas to

construct works, dams, roads, boreholes, buildings, dipping tanks, structures or fences; carry on pasture improvement and management; carry out afforestation schemes; carry out soil conservation works; advertise African produce; (and to) initiate marketing schemes for African produce and establish markets for such produce.[3]

The objection can however be made that there is no similar levy for development in European agricultural areas which enjoy the benefit of much public expenditure, being for the most part adjacent to the Colony's railway lines, better roads, and electricity supplies, whereas African areas are for the most part more remote and undeveloped.[4] Nor is there any realistic comparison that can be made between levies made under the African Development Fund Act and levies imposed under the Federal Produce Levies Act No. 19 of 1957, which provides for levies on European produce, since the latter levies can only be imposed after agreement in a referendum of members of the appropriate producers' association, proceeds of such levies being payable to the producers' association concerned for the interests of producers of a particular agricultural product. Indeed legislation, the African Farmers' Licensing Act (Chapter 98), provides for similar revenue for the African Farmers' Union by means of licence fees required to be paid by African Native Purchase Area Farmers. In fact, it is submitted that the levies payable in terms of the African

---

[1] The effect of these laws from time to time and the justification for the policy of equalization of transport charges to African producers have been examined by R. W. M. Johnson in *African Agricultural Development in Southern Rhodesia 1945–1960*, Food Research Institute, Stanford, 1964, pp. 199 et seq. The sum of 13s. 3d. is composed of 3s. 3d. African Development Fund levy, 7s. transport levy, and 3s. handling margin paid to the trader.

[2] This resulted in withdrawal of grants made by the African Development Fund to African Councils in such areas. These had been receiving approximately £40,000 *in toto per annum* from the Fund, and had come to rely on this money for most of their basic development. As the subvention has not been replaced, nine Councils have requested that the levies be reimposed: C.S.R. 39–1965, p. 29.

[3] Chapter 96, Section 6(k)–(p). For a recent explanation of the Act's beneficial purposes see Report of the Secretary for Internal Affairs for the Year 1964. C.S.R. 39–1965, pp. 10, 11, and 42.

[4] See Franck, op. cit., pp. 299–300. The insistence on dipping of African cattle is not entirely altruistic as if African owned cattle are diseased, such disease tends to spread to European-owned cattle.

Development Fund are really sums which should be found out of public revenues.[1]

The Constitutional Council has so far only reported on Section 22 of the African Development Fund Act, but has found that this provision is discriminatory and would be inconsistent with Section 67(1) of the Declaration of Rights if this were applicable to existing laws. Section 22 gives the Minister of Internal Affairs power to prohibit the purchase of prescribed African produce in certain areas if he considers such prohibition

is desirable in order to (a) conserve African produce owing to a crop failure; or (b) (to) encourage the production of a particular type of African produce in any particular area by discouraging the production of other types of produce in that area.

The Council justified the first ground of prohibition as securing the protection of the interests of some Africans as Section 67(4) of the Constitution prescribes that provisions may be made to 'secure the protection in an equitable manner as between the various ... respective interests'. However it felt that the second ground of prohibition could be prejudicial as

it may be asked why Africans should be subjected to the disadvantage that the sale of any crops which they grow, or may have grown, can be prohibited merely because they are Africans? If the prohibition were common to all farmers in the same area no prejudicial discrimination on the grounds of race would arise.[2]

Rights over land held by African farmers are not of the same character as are the rights enjoyed by Europeans in respect of land which they are enabled to purchase. Since the land rights in terms of the Land Husbandry Act and Land Apportionment Act were until recently the only land rights available to Africans,[3] comparison must be made between the statutory tenure available to Africans and the common law ownership which most Europeans acquire over their land. The African Land Husbandry Act (Chapter 103), imposes considerable restrictions on the right of African farmers in the Tribal Trust Land either to farm as they please or to dispose of their holdings. The African Land Husbandry Act is designed to secure good farming practices so that if

[1] Cp. the attitude adopted by the Government that 'the main purpose of the Fund is to carry out what is not a normal function of Government, namely to apply to capital and servicing purposes, through a trust fund, money which in a more advanced society would be applied by the producers themselves: C.S.R. 39–1965, p. 42. Central Government makes grants-in-aid to the African Development Fund for development activities which it considers governmental responsibilities and for implementation of the Agricultural Development Plan and of the African Land Husbandry Plan, the latter involving servicing of international loans.

[2] Constitutional Council Report No. 36, 18 November 1964. The Council noted that no action had ever been taken under the Section. The Section could be relevant in view of possible overproduction of tobacco.

[3] Even at the end of 1964 the area of Unreserved Land in which Africans could obtain absolute ownership was relatively small. See *infra* Chapter 5.

an African is three times convicted of contravening Sections 5 and 7 of that Act which Sections provide for limitations on the stock carrying capacity of land and permit regulations for the enforcement of good farming practices, his rights of grazing cattle may be cancelled.[1] Similarly, if he is so convicted or disregards the conditions as to farming attached to his farming rights, the District Commissioner may, after giving notice to the farmer and an opportunity for representations to be made, cancel his farming (cultivation) rights.[2] Yet another restriction on the rights of Africans in respect of their holdings in the Tribal Trust Land is that a District Commissioner has a discretion, after consultation with the African Council in the area, or the Chief if there is no African Council, to refuse to transfer a grazing right, transfer of which must be registered with the District Commissioner.[3] A similar restriction applies to the transfer of farming rights.[4] Furthermore, both farming and grazing rights expire on the death of the holder,[5] and although the holder may record with the District Commissioner the name of the person to whom he wishes a new grant to be made upon his death, the District Commissioner has a discretion to disregard this nomination, the ordinary laws of succession thereby being excluded.

It is extremely significant that land holdings under the African Land Husbandry Act, whatever their value, do not qualify the holder for the franchise, as the Electoral Act stipulates that an applicant must be 'the owner of immovable property', owner meaning the person in whose name the property is registered in the Deeds Registry, or, in respect of the 'B' Roll only, a hire-purchaser who will on fulfilment of the conditions of the agreement be entitled to claim such registration.[6]

Somewhat similar restrictions on transfer *inter vivos* and on death extend to the land rights of Native Purchase Area farmers. The Land Apportionment Act (Chapter 257), Section 11, prohibits any owner of land in the Native Purchase Area from disposing, alienating, leasing or encumbering his land without the approval by the Rural Land Board[7] of the transferee and of the terms and conditions of such disposal, alienation, lease or encumbrance. Furthermore, the African Wills Act (Chapter 108), Sections 7 and 8, applies this rule to testamentary and intestate succession to such land, requiring that if any transfer is refused, the property shall be sold and the proceeds paid to the heirs. This Act has been found by a majority report of the Constitutional Council to be discriminatory.[8]

---

[1] Chapter 103, Section 26.
[2] Chapter 103, Section 33.
[3] Section 21.   [4] Section 46.
[5] Sections 23, 24(1), 48, and 49(1).
[6] Chapter 2, Section 10(1) and (2) and Section 11(2).
[7] Established by the Rural Land Act 1963.
[8] The Council in its 33rd Report found that despite Section 67(3)(b) of the Declaration, since the Act did not relate to a matter of devolution of property which was peculiar to the

General legislative measures containing discriminatory provisions

Apart from those measures which are intended to have their major application to Africans, general legislation of the country designed to apply to persons of all races also contains discriminatory provisions. Some of these Acts discriminate against both Africans and non-Africans, e.g. the Land Apportionment Act, which divides Southern Rhodesia into a European Area, an African Area, an Unreserved Area and National Land, and provides for segregated land ownership and occupation.[1] But many others contain provisions which are aimed at Africans and a few which are aimed at Asians and Coloureds in addition to Africans.

Among such measures are the Municipal Act, which allows municipalities to regulate African eating houses, to prohibit non-Africans from being present in such eating houses,[2] and to regulate pedestrian traffic in public streets including the use thereof by Africans.[3] The Municipalities may also appoint separate omnibuses or portions of omnibuses for the use of white persons, of Africans, of Asians, and of other Coloured persons respectively, and may restrict the use of such omnibuses and portions thereof to such persons.[4]

---

personal law of Africans, it was nonetheless discriminatory, although it could not be invalidated since it was an existing law. African personal law did not recognize individual land ownership, but only rights of occupation to land.

[1] See Constitutional Council Report No. 29 of 5 February 1964 to this effect. The Land Apportionment Act is discussed at length in Chapter 5 *infra*. It is not therefore discussed at this point. See also *supra* Part I, Chapter 12, for comments on its enactment.

[2] Chapter 125, Section 277 (32). Eating houses are premises where food or drink is served to Africans for consumption on such premises. This provision was adversely reported on by the Constitutional Council: Report No. 41, 19 May 1965. They stated that the refusal of a right to non-Africans to enter an African eating house 'results in differential treatment by law and could readily create feelings of humiliation, insult, and inferiority in the African mind by the veiled suggestion that he is not a fit person to have members of other races associate with him when taking a meal'. Similar provision exists in the Town Management Act (Chapter 134), which was also adversely reported on by the Constitutional Council: Report No. 43, 28 May 1965.

[3] Chapter 125, Section 277(48). Under a similar section in the former Municipal Act a by-law of the Bulawayo Municipality forbidding Africans to 'use' pavements was declared *ultra vires*: R. v. *Sikupa*, 1934 S.R. 94. However differently phrased by-laws are in force in other municipalities and were approved in this case, e.g. the Gatooma by-laws (G.N. 438/1939), Section 20: 'No native shall make use of, walk, stand or loiter on any footpath, or any path used solely or mainly for pedestrian traffic within the limits of the Municipality except for the purpose of crossing the same to enable such Native to enter any shop, store or place of business or dwelling house to make *bona fide* purchase, or to transact *bona fide* business on his own behalf or that of his master or employer. Natives in charge of European children shall be allowed to walk on footpaths when actually in attendance on such children.' The Constitutional Council has reported on the discriminatory character of this provision: Report No. 41, 19 May 1965.

[4] Chapter 277, Section 51(c). Segregation on 'buses was observed until 1961, when African demonstrators began to use 'buses which were on certain routes in practice used only by Europeans. No restrictions have been enforced. This provision and a similar provision in the Town Management Act (Chapter 134), were reported on by the Constitutional Council: Report No. 41, 19 May 1965, and No. 43, 28 May 1965.

Municipalities may also control and supervise the housing of African servants and prevent annoyance arising therefrom to other persons.[1]

Yet another discriminatory measure is the Criminal Procedure and Evidence Act. Africans are discriminated against by this measure and so are Asians and Coloureds, the latter groups by virtue of the fact that they may not be jurors while the former are discriminated against in that jury trial is not available to Africans. Africans are tried by a judge and two officials or ex-officials of the Department of Internal Affairs sitting as assessors whereas other races in cases where there is trial by judge and assessors appear before assessors experienced in the administration of justice or skilled in matters to be considered at the trial and not before administrators of African Affairs.[2] The same Act gives European policemen powers not given to African policemen, whatever their rank.[3]

A further discriminatory measure is the Children's Protection and Adoption Act, which gives protection to non-African children under the age of seven years who are kept apart from their guardians but does not give similar protection to infants who are African.[4]

Another social welfare protection that is not available to Africans is the grant of old age pensions. No African is entitled to an old age pension although such pensions are provided for Europeans and also granted to Asians and Coloureds, individuals of the latter two groups receiving only two-thirds of the amounts which may be granted to European pensioners.[5]

A measure of great economic importance which provides opportunities for discrimination is the Industrial Conciliation Act. Although in 1959 the Industrial Conciliation Act No. 29 of that year was for the first time made applicable to all races, the Act still permitted a certain amount of racialism. Thus, despite a stipulation that the constitution of registered trade unions or employers' organization shall not contain any provision whereby any person is excluded on grounds of race, colour or religion from membership, its constitution may permit its membership to be divided into branches on the basis of the race or colour of the members.[6] Furthermore, if the Registrar who administers the Act considers that the provisions in the constitution of any trade union or employers' organization in relation to the protection of skilled or minority interests or the voting rights of members are inadequate, he may

---

[1] Chapter 277, Section 277(70).   [2] See *supra* Part II, Chapter 3.
[3] Constitutional Council Report No. 34, 11 September 1964.
[4] Chapter 172, Section 8. Until this Act was amended in 1960 African juveniles did not enjoy the protection of juvenile courts, while provisions to prevent their ill-treatment by parents and guardians were inapplicable.
[5] See the Old Age Pensions Act (Chapter 103), Sections 2, 3, and 8. Pensions to Europeans may not exceed £150 per annum and to Coloureds and Asians £100 per annum. For a picture of the various disabilities of Eurafrican, Coloured, and Asian communities see three Select Committee reports between 1959 and 1960 which resulted in some of their disabilities being removed by legislation.
[6] Chapter 246, Section 47(3)(b).

require such provision to be amended with a view to the better protection of those interests or rights.[1] In practice nearly all skilled workers in Southern Rhodesia are Europeans, as it was only by the Apprenticeship Act 50 of 1959 that the apprenticeship system was opened to Africans.

In spite of this legislation which makes African industrial advancement possible, there are few African skilled workers and few being trained.[2] The provisions in the Industrial Conciliation Act which relate to the protection of skilled workers therefore in practice relate to the protection of non-African interests.

Furthermore, many African trade unions are unregistered, as no trade union may be registered if it was formed, or exists for the purpose of furthering the interests of its members on a basis of race or colour,[3] while if a trade union has already been registered to represent the industrial interests of the area in which the applicant union seeks registration, the application must be refused.[4] In practice, European unions of long standing were already registered when the 'non-racial' Act was introduced and when any racial provisions in their constitution had been eliminated, continued to represent the industrial interests concerned.

African nationalist trade union leaders also allege that where no trade union was already registered, trade unions sponsored by Africans prepared to co-operate with Government were registered, thus precluding the registration of nationalist sponsored unions.[5] Unregistered unions are nonetheless controlled by the Act and precluded from striking unless an industrial board, or council, or conciliation board has considered and reported on the matter. Strikes or lock-outs other than in terms of these provisions are unlawful.[6]

The Firearms Act is a measure which is openly couched in discriminatory language prohibiting Asians, Coloureds, and Africans from possessing any firearms or ammunition, except when they have obtained a special conditional permit or have obtained a letter of exemption from the Secretary of Internal Affairs.[7] Although the Explosives Act is not couched in openly discriminatory

[1] Chapter 246, Section 247(4).

[2] See *S.R.L.A.D.*, Vol. 49, col. 579, 7 March 1962, where in reply to a question how many European and African apprentices were registered in Southern Rhodesia's main industries it was stated that as at 28 February 1962 there were in all five years of training in the respective industries 1,195 European apprentices, and 30 African apprentices, there being no African apprentices in the electrical engineering industry, the mining industry, or the printing industry. As at 28 July 1965, this position had improved to the extent that there were 55 African apprentices, one of whom was in the printing industry and four of whom were in the electrical industry: *S.R.L.A.D.*, Vol. 61, col. 1505

[3] Chapter 246, Section 37(1)(e).   [4] Chapter 246, Section 36(1)(2).

[5] Personal communications from Mr. J. T. Maluleke.

[6] Chapter 246, Section 122. In addition the Law and Order (Maintenance) Act (Chapter 39), Section 31, penalizes any person who advises, encourages, incites, commands, aids, or secures any act likely to hinder or interfere with the carrying on of an essential service, the latter including all public utilities and also services relating to the production, supply, delivery, and distribution of food.

[7] Chapter 250, Sections 24 and 30.

language, the Government may make regulations relative to the possession and use of explosives which may differentiate between various classes of persons.[1]

Yet another Act potentially permitting discrimination is the Federal Control of Goods Act, which provides for the control of the supply and distribution of goods. The Act permits the making of regulations for these purposes and the regulations may differentiate between classes of persons.[2]

A further discrimination is that in terms of the Defence Act, although provision is made for compulsory non-African war time service and for Europeans to undergo peace training, no African is liable to render such services.[3] The major discrimination in matters military, however, occurs by virtue of subordinate legislation, which makes considerable differentiations between the conditions of service of European and African members of the armed forces.[4]

Education is another sphere in which there is considerable discrimination. Non-African education is governed by the Education Act,[5] whereas African education is governed by the African Education Act.[6] Segregated schools are the rule, although provision exists for the establishment and control of private schools which may admit pupils of all races.[7]

Apart from the provisions of the Acts which secure segregation of African and non-African pupils, the operation of the Land Apportionment Act prohibits African pupils from occupying land in the European area and vice versa except in the case of private schools. In addition, within the category of non-African Government schools there is further segregation. Certain schools are restricted to European pupils only, Asian and Coloured pupils attending unrestricted schools.[8]

Schooling for Europeans is compulsory,[9] whereas this is not the case with

---

[1] Chapter 249, Section 27(2).

[2] Act 12 of 1954, Section 5. This means that if rationing were introduced differential rationing would be possible.

[3] Federal Defence Act No. 23 of 1955, Section 2.

[4] Compare F.G.N. 145/61, Defence (Regular Forces) (European Members) Regulations 1961 and F.G.N. 374/62, Defence (Regular Force) (African Members) Regulations 1962. e.g. an African staff sergeant receives 11s. 6d. per day whereas a European of the same rank receives £1,023 18s. per annum. The European also receives special allowances and increased medical, pension and leave benefits, children's, quarters' and servants' allowance, and a native languages gratuity, &c.

[5] Federal Act No. 15 of 1956 as amended by Act 19 of 1962.

[6] Southern Rhodesian Act No. 8 of 1959 as amended by Act 18 of 1962, now Chapter 97.

[7] Land Apportionment Amendment Act 53 of 1962, Section 47A. There are in practice scarcely a dozen such schools and the number of Africans who can afford to send their children to such schools is negligible. Schools require governmental approval to admit African pupils and in August 1965 it was announced that no further such pupils would be permitted.

[8] See F.G.N. 290/56. In practice a few Asian children are permitted to attend European schools. These are usually the children of foreign diplomats.

[9] See Section 41 of the Education Act.

African children. Furthermore, the Constitutional Council has drawn attention to the fact that, although it cannot adversely report on these Acts and laws thereunder,[1] discrimination results from the Acts and from regulations issued by virtue of the powers therein contained. One of the major resulting differentiations is that if an African pupil's school fees are unpaid, such pupil may be excluded from a Government school, whereas European children cannot be similarly excluded.[2]

Perhaps the most marked discrimination in the education field is however the annual amount spent by Government per head on the education of African and non-African pupils. For the year ending June 1965 the average expenditure per head on European, Coloured, and Asian pupils will be £99 and that on African pupils £9 9s.[3]

Acts couched in non-discriminatory language affecting Africans

Much Southern Rhodesian Legislation is couched in non-discriminatory language and is applicable to all races. In practice however its main application is to the African population, as it results in Africans either being subject to liabilities or unable to secure privileges whereas the majority of members of other races are not in practice subjected to the penal provisions of such measures or alternatively qualify for the privileges conferred by these Acts.

As has already been indicated, the most important measure of this type is the Electoral Act, which in effect renders eligible for the franchise the majority of the non-African population and renders ineligible the majority of the African population.[4] Similarly, the Municipal and Town Management Acts, when taken in conjunction with the Land Apportionment Act, which makes it impossible for Africans to reside in such areas, and with local boundaries, which are so devised as to prevent the creation of any African ratepayers, retain the local government franchise almost entirely in European hands.[5] In addition they provide that a spouse married under systems permitting of polygamy shall not be deemed to possess the same qualifications as

[1] The African Education Act was an existing Act and the Federal Education Act is not a 'law' on which the Council can pronounce and to which the Declaration applies: Section 72.

[2] Compare S.R.G.N., 504/64, the African Education (Schools) (Amendment) Regulations 1964 (No. 1), Section 29A and 29B with S.R.G.N. 191/64, The Education (Tuition and Accommodation Fees) Regulations 1964. See Constitutional Council Report No. 32, 30 July 1964.

[3] Source: Estimates of Expenditure, Government Printer, C.S.R. 17-1964, pp. 128 and 133, the total available for non-African education being £5,802,797 and the total for African education being £6,185,000. There were in July 1964 58,769 non-African school children and 623,140 African pupils. The figures are slightly weighted as the non-African education structure includes a high proportion of secondary school pupils who are more expensive to educate. 21,743 non-Africans and 12,872 Africans receive post-primary education: see *Monthly Digest of Statistics*, October 1964, Central Statistical Office, pp. 8-9.

[4] See *supra* Part II, Chapter 1.

[5] Report by the Constitutional Council on the Land Apportionment Act 1941, No. 29 of 5 February 1964.

his or her spouse, this provision in effect excluding Asian women but no European women.[1]

Legislation penalizing political offences has its main operation on the African population. Thus from 1960 to the end of May 1965 6,301 Africans were prosecuted under the Law and Order (Maintenance) Act whereas only fifty-eight Europeans, nine Asians, and thirteen Coloureds were so prosecuted.[2] Similarly in the same period 1,610 Africans were prosecuted under the Unlawful Organizations Act whereas only four Europeans, one Asian, and four Coloureds were so prosecuted.[3] Again the Emergency Powers Act has its main application to Africans as under regulations made under that Act, 1,791 Africans were served with detention orders and preventively detained without trial during 1964 and the first half of 1965, whereas no Europeans, no Asians, and two Coloureds were detained in the same period.[4]

Similarly, the main application of the Masters and Servants Act is to Africans,[5] while the Vagrancy Act has its major application to the African population.[6]

The Prison Regulations[7] again in practice provide methods whereby discrimination is effected, as prisoners are graded in four grades, each grade being placed on different diet scales, receiving different clothing issues and different clothing issues and different cell equipment.

In practice all Europeans are classed as grade I prisoners, Asians and Coloureds as grade II prisoners and Africans as grades III and IV prisoners, although an occasional African, if he can prove he was for a six months'

[1] African women are not at present affected as they may not reside in such areas owing to the provisions of the Land Apportionment Act. See generally *infra*, Chapter 5.

[2] *S.R.L.A.D.*, Vol. 61, col. 1781–2, 4 August 1965. Twenty-six Europeans, one Coloured, and 3,448 Africans were convicted. As at 28 July 1965, no Europeans, Asians, or Coloureds were serving prison sentences for convictions under the Law and Order (Maintenance) Act whereas 1,129 Africans were serving such sentences: *S.R.L.A.D.*, Vol. 61, col. 1504.

[3] *S.R.L.A.D.*, Vol. 61, col. 1781–2, 4 August 1965.

[4] *S.R.L.A.D.*, Vol. 61, col. 1778, 4 August 1965.

[5] See *supra*.

[6] Figures of vagrants arrested without warrant in its first week of operation show that 6 Europeans, 3 Coloureds, and 686 Africans were so arrested. *S.R.L.A.D.*, Vol. 46, cols. 2613–4, 28 October 1960. *S.R.L.A.D.*, Vol. 50, cols. 1319–20, 3 August 1962, shows that from January 1959 to June 1962, 24 Europeans were prosecuted for having committed offences against the Act—such as escaping from custody and breaching regulations thereunder—while 875 Africans were so charged. There are a number of genuine non-African vagrants. The danger that Africans may be mistakenly treated as vagrants is twofold: most Africans are migratory labourers; and there is considerable African unemployment. The Act uses the terminology of the National Assistance Act 1948 (11 & 12 Geo. 6, c. 29), but there is a considerable difference in that in the United Kingdom only persons who claim state assistance may in lieu of a grant be sent to rehabilitation centres whereas in Southern Rhodesia the initiation of action depends on whether a policeman arrests any person 'unable to show that he has employment or visible and sufficient means of subsistence'.

[7] F.G.N. 42 of 1956. For court sentences imposed on offenders see C. A. Rogers and C. Frantz, *Racial Themes in Southern Rhodesia*, Yale, 1962, pp. 143–5. See also *R.* v. *Kafakarotwe*, 1951 S.R. 162 for the view that the more serious social and economic consequences for Europeans of imprisonment should be considered in sentencing.

period earning an income of a relatively high amount, may be regarded as a grade II prisoner. The practical discrimination can be quite considerable.[1]

Practical consequences of discrimination

It would be unrealistic to end this Chapter without a comment on the consequences which have ensued as a result of Southern Rhodesian legislation and administrative and educational policies.[2]

Control of political institutions as already indicated is predominantly in European hands, while in the economic sphere the position of the non-African is predominant. Few Africans own immovable property,[3] whereas the majority of adult Europeans own such property. Again, the other indicator of wealth— liability to income tax—shows that there were only 255 Africans in Southern Rhodesia liable to such tax.[4] Again, higher and secondary education which is the main means to advancement, is not available to any great numbers of Africans because of the structure of the African education system, whereas there are no limits on the availability of places to Europeans.[5]

Perhaps the most convincing figures proving the differences in the circumstances of Africans and non-Africans are the annual average earnings of such groups. In 1963 the average earnings (including earnings from the subsistence economy) per head of adult Africans was £61·2 per annum whereas for non-Africans the figure was £979 per annum.[6]

[1] See the Fourth Schedule to the Regulations. Grade I prisoners receive 12 ounces of meat per day whereas grades III and IV prisoners receive 16 ounces per week. Grades III and IV prisoners are also prohibited from wearing shoes.

[2] For a full analysis of the economic and social consequences of Southern Rhodesian legislative and administrative policies and the development of these policies from 1918 to 1953, see R. Gray, *The Two Nations*, Oxford, 1960.

[3] See Appendix Tables Q and R.

[4] See *S.R.L.A.D.*, Vol. 57, col. 304, 5 August 1964. The Minister did not think that there was any reason to suspect that substantial numbers of Africans who should be making returns of income were failing to do so.

[5] For the effects of this on African education see Appendix Table J. See also *Monthly Digest of Statistics, October 1964*, Central Statistical Office, Salisbury, pp. 8–9, which shows that 1,734 Europeans were in VIth forms in 1964 whereas only ninety-three Africans were in such forms. In forms IV and V there were a further 4,088 Europeans and 655 Africans.

[6] Figures are derived from the *National Accounts and Balance of Payments of Northern Rhodesia, Nyasaland, and Southern Rhodesia, 1954 to 1963*, Central Statistical Office, Salisbury, pp. 151–2. Total African earnings in Southern Rhodesia were made up of £68·6 million in wages, £25·2 million from the subsistence economy, and £3·8 million from self employment totalling £97·6 million. Non-African earnings were £107 million from wages, and £27·5 million from self-employment, totalling £134·5 million. A further £10 million from income from property, which would accrue almost entirely to non-Africans, has been disregarded since a proportion would accrue to non-residents. The African adult population over 21 years of age was 1,593,000 and the non-African equivalent population was 137,600 (information by courtesy of the Central Statistical Office).

Conclusions

In a recent short comment, the Bulletin of the International Commission of Jurists stated that:

The Constitution of Southern Rhodesia is a striking example of the futility of laying down human rights in the Constitution and thereafter subjecting those same human rights to the sway of a legislature which does not adequately represent the people of the country; an examination of Southern Rhodesian legislation in relation to the human rights proclaimed in the Constitution makes one wonder why the trouble was ever taken to put those human rights in the Constitution.[1]

It is difficult in the light of the present legislative position in Southern Rhodesia to disagree with the views expressed in this quotation.

This situation has resulted partly from the widely drafted exceptions to the application of the Declaration, but more from the preservation of existing law. Despite the fact that the Declaration may give a small measure of protection in respect of laws enacted from 1963 onwards,[2] such judicial action can have little effect on the whole field of Southern Rhodesian legislation. This conclusion can scarcely be resisted in view of existing powers to restrict individual freedoms.

It is generally accepted that in time of emergency governments may require exceptional powers.[3] Nonetheless, this is the very time when, with passions running high, individual rights most need protection. If in normal times these rights are not in practice protected, there seems little purpose in inserting a Bill of Rights in the Constitution as this gives a misleading paper impression of the degree of freedom available to the inhabitants of the country.

[1] Bulletin of the International Commission of Jurists, No. 18, March 1964. 'Southern Rhodesia—Human Rights and the Constitution', at p. 44.

[2] This has been shown by the fact that of the first six suits brought before the Southern Rhodesia courts alleging contravention of the Declaration, the courts in two instances found that the Declaration had been contravened and in another found a *prima facie* contravention.

[3] *Vide* the famous judicial statement that a modern war cannot be conducted in accordance with the principles set out in the Sermon on the Mount.

5

LAND APPORTIONMENT, LOCAL GOVERNMENT, LOCAL ADMINISTRATION, AND ADVISORY BODIES

General characteristics of local government in Southern Rhodesia

THE administration of local areas in Southern Rhodesia cannot, as in developed countries, be seen in terms of a coherent pattern of local government. Many factors have occasioned this situation. Perhaps the major reason is that the Legislature in determining the form of administration of various local areas has adopted different solutions and different legislative provisions, depending on whether Africans or Europeans are concerned.[1] Again, within these categories further differentiations have been made, depending on whether industrial towns in urban areas or isolated communities in rural areas are involved. It is these criteria which have affected the decisions whether genuine local government[2] rather than decentralized administration directed by officials of the central government has been adopted in any area. They have also determined the amount of control which the central government has insisted on exercising over local action,[3] the permissive powers it has conferred on local government bodies, and the duties it has imposed upon such bodies.

Yet one more factor which until recently has increased the complexity of Southern Rhodesian local government must be mentioned. This has been the division of the country into land of different categories and the establishment within those categories of land of differing types of local government body, there however being a considerable amount of confusion and overlapping, and the position being made more difficult by the fact that central administrative control of local government bodies was (and to a certain degree still is) split between two Government Departments. Indeed, unless local government is seen in the context of the land provisions both in the Constitution and the Land Apportionment Act, it is extremely difficult to comprehend.

---

[1] In European areas the Municipal Act, the Town Management Act, and until 1961 the Village Management Act (now replaced by the Local Government Act) have been used, whereas in African areas the Native Councils Act and the Natives (Urban Areas) Accommodation and Registration Act were employed.

[2] Genuine local government might be said to occur when powers of executive action and legislative power relative to local matters are entrusted to an elected body responsible to a local electorate.

[3] Under the Local Government Act, Section 6, the Governor may make regulations for the working of local committees and under Section 61 for financial powers of boards etc. but has no such powers in respect of municipalities.

Quite apart from the effect on local government of all these factors, two characteristics of Southern Rhodesian local government in comparison with local government in the United Kingdom at once become apparent. Firstly, even in those areas where local government is developed there is no proper direct grant system in operation,[1] municipalities relying on their rating and borrowing powers and service charges for the most part, and to a certain extent being assisted in providing services by three specific Acts which authorise them to obtain additional revenue. Thus they obtain funds under the Services Levy Act (Chapter 78) from the imposition of a service levy on employers of African labour,[2] which are used for the purpose of subsidizing housing and transport services for Africans. They also obtain revenue under the African Beer Act[3] and the Liquor Act[4] from the sale and manufacture of African beer and the sale of spirits to Africans, the profits of such sales being permitted, by virtue of regulations made by the Minister of Local Government, only to be used for social welfare purposes and the betterment of social conditions generally in African townships.[5] They also obtain payments made in terms of Section 9 of the Vehicle Tax Act (Chapter 160) for licensed vehicles ordinarily kept in the area of jurisdiction of local authorities.[6] The position is similar in respect of less developed forms of local government. Thus the collective total of all grants by central government to the African Councils of Southern Rhodesia will only be £40,000 in the year ending 30 June 1966.[7]

Yet another peculiarity of Southern Rhodesian local government is that national party politics are only beginning to affect the pattern of local politics. Formerly local politics depended almost entirely on personalities, and local elections were marked by the apathy of electors. More recently there has been a tendency for candidates in municipal and town management board elections to be backed unofficially by one or other of the two main European political parties. Since there is no longer a European opposition party, this means that

[1] The Crown is exempted from rates but makes *ex gratia* payments which would be the equivalent of such amounts were they leviable.

[2] The Act applies only in designated areas, mainly to employers of industrial and commercial labour. It does not apply to domestic servants, to females, to persons earning in excess of £22 per month and to certain other categories designated by the Minister. The Act is not applied in rural areas. The policy of the present Government is to eliminate the services levy by consolidating present rent allowances into wages, by increasing wages by a pound per month, by raising rents and lodger fees in Government townships, by reviewing rent structures to aim at economic rents, by building future housing on an economic basis, and by annual reviews of bus fares: C.S.R. 19–1965, pp. 16–17.

[3] Chapter 93, Section 6 gives local authorities a virtual monopoly in native beer and prohibits home brewing.

[4] Chapter 274, Section 83.

[5] See S.R.G.N. 335/57 amended by S.R.G.N. 446/57, 457/58 and 568/59.

[6] Apart from sums raised by these specific legislative provisions all Town Management Boards and local authorities under the Ministry of Local Government will, in the year ending 30 June 1966, receive collectively the sum of £25,664: C.S.R. 21–1965, p. 53.

[7] C.S.R. 21–1965, p. 97. African Councils receive certain payments from the African Production and Marketing Development Fund but this is derived from special levies paid on African produce and livestock.

candidates may compete for the support of the governing party.[1] Similarly in respect of African Advisory Boards and to a lesser extent in the case of African Councils, there has been a tendency for candidates backed by African nationalist parties[2] to win elections. Indeed in Advisory Board elections in African townships in Bulawayo in 1962, African nationalist candidates were elected in every case. Conversely, part of the reason for the breakdown of African local government has been nationalist feeling, all the members of the Bulawayo Advisory Board having resigned while in certain other cases members of African Councils have had to be nominated by District Commissioners, as either voters have refused to elect councillors, or sufficient candidates have not come forward for election.[3]

Finally, a particular note of warning must be sounded. Although from an inspection of the statute book an ideal legislative framework may have been enacted in Southern Rhodesia, this to a large extent remains little more than enabling legislation barely implemented in practice outside the urban areas. Thus the Local Government Act 1961, which makes possible a flexible and non-racial local government system, had in November 1965 only partially been implemented in European areas and not at all in African areas in the sense of providing elective local government.

Land and the Constitution

One of the constitutional changes effected by the Southern Rhodesian Constitution 1961 was the vesting of the Southern Rhodesian Native Reserves described in the Southern Rhodesia Constitution Letters Patent 1923 and

[1] This occurred in Salisbury's 1965 municipal elections where candidates allowed their political affiliations to be advertised. Leys, op. cit., p. 65, discounts politics as playing a great role in local government, but the position has changed considerably since 1958 when Leys was writing. In municipal elections from 1958 onwards the majority of the supporters of the one candidate have in fact been supporters of the one major political party, and the majority of the supporters of the other candidate members of the opposition political party, e.g. in by-elections held in the Mount Pleasant Town Management Board in July 1964, the two candidates who headed the poll were unofficially supported by the Rhodesian Front, the governing party. Since the disappearance in May 1965 of any European opposition party, this tendency has been obscured e.g. in Salisbury's 1965 municipal elections in some cases the opposing candidates belonged to the same party while in one case no party supporter was sponsored. In the latter case the poll was the lowest known, viz. c. 9 per cent. Until this occurred percentage polls had been increasing. Whereas in the past they were almost 20 per cent of the electorate, they had in some cases risen to 40 per cent.

[2] Banned under the Unlawful Organizations Act (Chapter 81), but continuing to operate in practice as an amorphous mass movement.

[3] This occurred in the Mangwende Reserve in 1960. The tendency of African political parties—the Reformed Industrial and Commercial Workers Union was a precursor of such parties—to capture all seats on Advisory Boards could however be seen as early as 1953. See R. Howman, *African Local Government in British East and Central Africa*, op. cit., Part VII, paras. 71–72.

the Special Native Area established under the Land Apportionment Act 1941[1] in a Board of Trustees of Tribal Trust Land for the sole and exclusive use and occupation of tribesmen. The consequence of this provision was that an additional area of over nineteen million acres[2] was in effect added to the Reserves and brought within the constitutional protection given them.[3] The reason for this change was that under the 1961 Constitution the Legislature was given the power to amend the Land Apportionment Act and to make provision for the opening up of land to all races, amendments to the Act being no longer reserved measures in view of the alterations in the Constitution. It accordingly became necessary to safeguard the Special Native Area for exclusive occupation by Africans, and it was therefore treated on the same constitutional basis as the Reserves. As at the end of 1963 the Tribal Trust Land of Southern Rhodesia amounted to 40,020,000 acres out of Southern Rhodesia's total acreage of 96,600,000 acres.[4]

The Board of Trustees of Tribal Trust Land is vested with all Tribal Trust Land and is charged with the duty of securing to the tribesmen the sole and exclusive use and occupation of such land.[5] The Board's trust does not, however, extend to administration of such areas or their development, as this is the responsibility of the Southern Rhodesian Government.[6] In fact by virtue of various provisions, such as Section 37(2) of the African Affairs Act (which gives District Commissioners the right to assign lands for huts, gardens, and grazing grounds) and the African Land Husbandry Act (which provides for allocation of farming and grazing rights to individual Africans) distribution

---

[1] The Special Native Area was established by Act No. 11 of 1941 as amended by Act 25 of 1950 after recommendations by the Danziger Committee appointed in 1948 'to enquire into the question of additional land for native occupation': see L.A.S.C. 3–1960, pp. 12 et seq.

[2] See Act No. 23 of 1962, Section 13(e) for the increase of the Special Native Area immediately before the implementation of the Southern Rhodesian Constitution 1961.

[3] Prior to the 1961 Constitution the Special Native Area had, in terms of the Land Apportionment Act, been kept exclusively for the occupation of Africans and the consent of the Secretary of State had been necessary if its boundaries or extent were to be altered, but amendments to the regulations governing land-holding in the special Native Area could, in terms of the Land Apportionment Act, be made without parliamentary intervention by the Governor with the consent of the Secretary of State, while the Act itself could be amended by simple majority subject to reservation of the Bill. In the case of the Reserves although exchanges and alterations in their boundaries could occur, after the written consent of the Secretary of State subject to adequate compensation in land elsewhere, the provisions in the 1923 Constitution dealing with the Reserves were unalterable by the S.R. Legislature.

[4] Report of the Secretary for Internal Affairs for the year 1963, C.S.R. 16–1964, p. 7. This area was occupied by 2,100,000 of Southern Rhodesia's total African population of 3,830,000 as at that time.

[5] However, the dominion in the right of searching and mining for and disposing of all minerals, mineral oils, and natural gases is vested in the Governor: Section 93(2) proviso. It has been held that it is the rights of tribesmen and not tribes that are protected by the Constitution: *Zihumbga* v. *Harper, Robertson and Dodd NN.O.*, *supra* at p. 6.

[6] Section 95(2). To the extent that responsibility has been devolved on the Sabi Limpopo Authority by the Sabi Limpopo Authority Act 1964, its provisions are, it is submitted, in conflict with Section 95(2) and therefore invalid in terms of Section 115(1).

of land to tribesmen in such areas occurs at the instance of Government officials, and not at the behest of the Board.[1]

The Board is chaired by the Chief Justice of the High Court, who has a casting vote. There are five other members who hold office for five years, one being a Chief appointed by the Council of Chiefs, another the Chairman of the Natural Resources Board, and three members appointed by the Governor, one experienced in African agriculture, another in financial matters, and the last in local government in Tribal Areas.[2]

The provisions relative to the Reserves in the 1923 Constitution have been adapted, amended, and incorporated as the provisions governing Tribal Trust Land. Thus Section 96 strictly limits the purposes for which regulations may permit non-tribesmen[3] to occupy any portion of Tribal Trust Land.[4] However, an escape clause allows the Board to make an agreement or regulations permitting non-Africans to occupy Tribal Trust Land for any purpose which the Board considers to be in the interests of tribesmen 'or in the public interest'. In view of this provision and the fact that 'the public interest' may well conflict with that of tribesmen, the interests of the latter can be overridden depending on the Board's view of the circumstances.[5]

[1] Allocations of land under the Land Husbandry Act have been suspended pending the introduction of a proposed Tribal Land Authority Bill which will establish the traditional tribal authorities as the land authorities in the tribal areas with powers to control the allocation of land in their areas: C.S.R. 39–1965, pp. 9–10. As at the end of 1964, 15,928,243 acres of the 29,343,700 acres of Tribal Trust Land which had been proclaimed under the Act, had been finally allocated: do., Table 2, p. 41.

[2] Section 94. This is not a specially entrenched provision and could be altered by a two-thirds majority of the Legislative Assembly, whereas the other provisions relative to Tribal Trust Land are either specially entrenched or it is provided that any Bill containing any provision which would if enacted diminish the powers or functions in respect of the Board's various responsibilities or would vary the terms of its trust, shall be subject to the same procedure as if it were a specially entrenched constitutional Bill: Section 103.

[3] The difficult problem of whether an African can cease to be a tribesman has not yet arisen. A tribesman is defined in Section 92(1) as 'a person who, under tribal law and custom, is recognized as a member of a community under the control or leadership of a Chief appointed and holding office under the law for the time being governing the appointment of chiefs'. Many Africans in the urban areas have cut adrift from the tribal system but presumably their genealogy could be traced, and they would then in terms of African customary law be recognized as being under the control of a particular Chief. However, by customary law children of marriages between an indigenous mother and a non-indigenous father would not be under the control of a Southern Rhodesian Chief.

[4] viz. for governmental or administrative purposes, religious or educational purposes, purposes in the interests of tribesmen, for the purpose of attending hospitals, clinics and other establishments for the benefit of tribesmen, for the purpose of cemeteries or burial grounds, for the exercise of rights under the Mining Laws, and rights in respect of forest produce and natural resources, and for the purposes of hotels and similar establishments for travellers.

[5] Cp. Section 101(b) under which the Governor with the consent of the Board may make regulations for the control of all moneys received under agreements made with the Board and for the application of such moneys 'in the interests of the tribesmen'. In 1965 the Board provided £10,000 towards the cost of a foreign tour by Chiefs including a visit to South African Bantustans: see C.S.R. 39–1965, p. 53. It is submitted that it is questionable whether the application of such moneys was 'in the interests of tribesmen'.

The Board is given similar discretion in respect of the exchange of Tribal Trust Land for Crown Land, provided again that the exchange is 'in the public interest'. If, however, such an exchange is made, the terms and conditions of the exchange must provide for the assigning of alternative land to any tribesman who is dispossessed, and the payment of compensation to him for permanent improvements and his removal from land formerly occupied by him.[1] Again, the Board may consent to an order by the Governor declaring the Tribal Trust Land to be Crown land no longer vested in the Board, if the Governor certifies that the land is required for any public purpose including mineral development, defence and the improvement of communications.[2] Again there is provision for compensation of dispossessed Africans but assignment of alternative land is not here compulsory.

Yet another way in which land can be removed from the control of the Board and vested in the Crown of Southern Rhodesia is in the eventuality of a scheme for the irrigation of Tribal Trust Land. If the Board is satisfied that such a scheme would be to the benefit of tribesmen and that it is necessary to provide security by way of a mortgage of the land for moneys advanced in carrying out the scheme the Board may so certify. Thereafter the Governor may declare that the land in question shall be Crown land for the purpose of granting freehold title to the person undertaking the irrigation scheme. However, it is to be a condition of each such grant that the occupation of the land be reserved exclusively for tribesmen and that terms and conditions of tenure be approved by the Governor.[3]

Provision is also made for the conversion of Tribal Trust Land into land held on individual freehold tenure. If, after having consulted the Chief concerned, and having duly considered the interests of other tribesmen who might be affected, the Board is satisfied that it is the general wish of the tribesmen living in a substantial area of Tribal Trust Land that their rights should be so converted and that this will be in the general interests of tribesmen, the Board may consent to the Governor declaring the land in question to be Crown land no longer vested in the Board. However, such land shall be granted only to the tribesmen concerned, subject to any limitations on future disposal of such land as a law of the Legislature may prescribe.[4]

Finally, land, which has by law been set aside for the establishment with the consent of the Board of a township, village, or business centre for the use and occupation by tribesmen, shall, at the time prescribed in the law in question, cease to be part of the Tribal Trust Land and become vested in the Governor, who shall make it available for purchase and lease as if it were Native Purchase Area as defined in the Land Apportionment Act.[5]

---

[1] Section 97.
[2] Section 98.
[3] Section 99.   [4] Section 100.
[5] Section 101(1)(a).

The Land Apportionment Act and the Constitution

Under the 1923 Constitution as amended every amendment to the Land Apportionment Act required either to be reserved or to contain a suspending clause or to have been given prior approval by Her Majesty.[1] With the coming into operation of the 1961 Constitution the Imperial controls disappeared and in their place were substituted other procedural safeguards.[2] Thus legislation which imposes any racial limitation on the ownership or occupation of land in Southern Rhodesia which is more restrictive than any limitation contained in the Land Apportionment Act as in force at the time of coming into effect of the 1961 Constitution cannot be passed unless the procedure applicable to amendment of the specially entrenched provisions of the Constitution has been followed.[3]

A further limitation is that although land may be derestricted without any special procedure being observed, there is an absolute prohibition on increasing the European area of land beyond its extent at the time of the coming into force of the new Constitution.[4] The Native Purchase Area, however, may be added to, subject only to the limitation that the total acreage in that area may not exceed the aggregate of the amount of the Tribal Trust Land and the Native Purchase Area at the time of coming into force of the Constitution.[5]

The Land Apportionment Act[6]

The Land Apportionment Act 1941 (perhaps Southern Rhodesia's most frequently amended statute) at present divides Southern Rhodesia into the European Area, the Native Area,[7] National Land, and Unreserved Land.

[1] See *supra* Part I, Chapter 12.

[2] See *supra* Part II, Chapter 1.

[3] See Section 103(c). It is submitted that this provision would also strike at delegated legislation or administrative provisions. *Dicta* by Briggs F.J. in *City of Salisbury* v. *Mehta*, *supra* at 703 are relevant as the learned Judge of Appeal held that if informal action were permitted in respect of a matter which, if it were to be done with the ordinary and proper formalities, would require the following of a particular procedure (in that case approval of the Secretary of State) such permission would frustrate the purposes of the Constitution.

[4] Section 102(2)(e).

[5] Section 102(2)(d). An African Government could, therefore, provided it followed the procedure set out in Section 103(c) add a further considerable acreage to the Native Purchase Area, which was 4,215,784 acres as at the appointed date, while the Reserves were in excess of 20,000,000 acres. The Native Purchase Area has not, since the appointed date, been considerably added to. If such changes were made, Europeans could be excluded from such areas. Furthermore, provided the procedure is followed, there is no limitation on additions to Tribal Trust Land: Section 102(1)(b)(iv).

[6] Originally enacted in 1930, see Part I *supra*, Chapter 12, re-enacted as Act 11 of 1941. It was found by the Constitutional Council in its 29th Report of 5 February 1964, to be a discriminatory measure which would have been inconsistent with Section 67 of the Declaration of Rights had that Section not been inapplicable to it as an existing law.

[7] This term was still used by Act 47 of 1963, which amended the Land Apportionment Act.

European land is the residuary category consisting of all land that is not Tribal Trust Land, Native Land, National Land, or Unreserved Land.[1]

Whereas Unreserved Land[2] may be leased or alienated either to Southern Rhodesian Africans or to Europeans individually or to bodies corporate, and, whereas National Land is reserved for the purposes of forestry and nature reserves, conservation of wild animal and fish life, and national parks and may not be alienated[3] both European and Native areas are subject to racially restrictive conditions as to occupancy, acquisition, lease, ownership, and in some cases, even as to use. Thus, except as specially provided, no person other than an indigenous African[4] may acquire, lease or occupy land in the Native Purchase Area.[5] Permission of the Governor is required and may in special circumstances be given if a non-indigenous African wishes to acquire, lease or occupy land in the Native Purchase Area. Similar provisions pro-

[1] As amended by Section 2 of Act 33 of 1964. As at the end of 1963 the distribution of land in Southern Rhodesia was as follows: Tribal Trust Land 40,020,000 acres, African Purchase Area 4,220,000 acres, Unreserved Land 5,870,000 acres, European Area 35,950,000 acres, National Land 10,540,000 acres, making a total in all of 96,600,000 acres. See the Report of the Secretary for Internal Affairs for the year 1963, C.S.R. 16-1964, p. 7.

[2] A category of land established only in 1961, when a new concept of land open to all races was introduced by Act No. 37 of 1961. Land may be declared Unreserved by the Governor by proclamation on application by the owner after consultation with any local authority in the area: Chapter 256, Section 6 as amended.

[3] Act 47 of 1963, see Second Schedule (K): Land Apportionment Act, Section 19 as amended. In fact approximately 36,000 Africans are in occupation of such land by virtue of permits formerly granted by the Governor, their rights being preserved by Section 63(2) of the Rural Land Act: see Constitutional Council Report No. 29, p. 8. Section 44(1) of the Rural Land Act allows the Minister of Agriculture to permit persons to occupy such land on conditions prescribed by the Minister or fixed by him in any particular case. Such land may also be occupied under leases to establish shops, hotels, and restaurants in a park (National Parks Act 1964, Section 8(d) and (e)) or under Section 29(2) of the Land Apportionment Act). The Minister of Law and Order has no power to alter the general law governing the occupation of National Land by designating National Land as a restriction area for the purposes of Section 50 of the Law and Order (Maintenance) Act: *Nkomo and Others* v. *Lardner-Burke N.O.* Judgement No. G.D. 31/1965 per Young J. In this case an Asian was restricted to National Land in the Gonakudzingwa Area, Section 96 of the Constitution precluding his restriction to the Tribal Trust Land forming the rest of the Area. The Minister remedied his oversight immediately after the decision by fixing conditions on which this Asian might occupy National Land in terms of Section 43 of the Rural Land Act, and by issuing a fresh restriction order to that area.

[4] Section 2(1) defines an indigenous African as 'an African who is descended through the male line from a member of one of the tribes ordinarily resident in Southern Rhodesia'.

[5] Chapter 257, Section 7. Section 16 as amended provides that the Governor after consultation with the Rural Land Board may permit a European to occupy such land for educational, religious or other purposes for the benefit of Africans, for governmental administrative purposes, and for hotels for travellers or for trading or like purposes. In the last case it is not stipulated that such uses must be for the benefit of Africans. The Rural Land Board consists of nine members appointed by the Minister of Agriculture, five of whom must be chosen from a panel of names submitted by the Natural Resources Board and farming associations or other public bodies approved of for this purpose by the Minister: Rural Land Act No. 47 of 1963, Section 5. Another special exemption allows Europeans to hold land for the purpose of security for the repayment of monies expended or to be expended on the development of such land: Chapter 257, Section 17.

hibit non-Africans from owning, occupying, or leasing land in the African Townships Area, although statutory bodies may own, occupy, or lease land in townships for the carrying out of any functions for which they have been established.[1]

In respect of the European Area, the provisions are even more stringent, although in recent years there has been a tendency to create new exceptions to the operation of the Act. No African shall acquire, lease, or occupy land in the European Area and it is a criminal offence for owners or occupiers to permit, suffer, or allow any African to occupy such land, or to lease, or attempt to dispose of it to an African.[2] However, there is a long list of exceptions to this provision.[3] Nonetheless, breach is still a criminal offence and the Act is enforced by prosecutions. Furthermore, the Act has important effects in the field of contract, as contracts which contravene the Act are clearly illegal.[4]

Even more severe restrictions are placed on occupation by Africans of land in areas under the jurisdiction of local authorities. Once a local authority has established an African township, subject to certain exceptions, 'no African may lease, use or occupy any land outside that area which falls within the area under the jurisdiction of the local authority'.[5] Recently new

[1] Section 26. Special provision however exists for declaration by the Governor that land in townships is open to European acquisition and lease: Section 27.

[2] Section 42.

[3] Africans who are employees whose presence is necessitated on the land and Africans under labour agreements are exempted. The former exemption is reflected in an important measure which revolutionized the position of Africans in Southern Rhodesia's urban areas —the Natives (Urban Areas) Accommodation and Registration Act No. 6 of 1946, which first forced employers to supply free accommodation to African employees and certain of their wives. The Act was consolidated by Act 20 of 1951 and is now Chapter 110. Other exceptions allowing African occupation of European land include the cases of Africans occupying land for educational, religious or other purposes considered by the Minister of Internal Affairs to be for the benefit of Africans, and of Africans carrying on business for the benefit of Africans. Occupation is also permitted for treatment at Government and local authorities' hospitals and clinics, for instruction at Government educational institutions, and for governmental purposes. Mission land may also be occupied for educational and religious purposes. Special provisions permit African professors, lecturers, research workers, and students to use the premises of the University College of Rhodesia and Nyasaland. Furthermore, families of the aforementioned categories of persons are also permitted to occupy property unless the Governor makes a contrary declaration.

[4] *Reynolds* v. *Kinsey*, 1959 (2) R. & N. 289 (F.C.). Such contracts would in Roman–Dutch Law be sanctioned by unenforceability and inability to obtain restitution, the latter sanction depending on the court's assessment of conflicting principles of public policy, viz. the need to discourage illegality and the need to secure simple justice between man and man: *Jajbhay* v. *Cassim*, 1939 A.D. 537.

[5] Section 63(1). The exceptions are as follows: African employees engaged upon work necessitating their presence on the land (this would include all domestics) are excepted from this provision, as are university staff in respect of the University College premises, and any African advocate who obtains a permit from the Minister of the Interior, the latter being satisfied that the grant of such permit is necessary for the practice of the former's profession. A non-indigenous African *bona fide* visiting Southern Rhodesia may be granted a permit to stay at an hotel in the European area, provided a hotel owner is willing to accommodate him (this is unlikely in Southern Rhodesia's smaller urban centres). In addition, it is

permissive provisions which create potential exceptions to the Act were passed. These allow the Governor to declare land owned for industrial purposes or for business purposes to be an area in which Africans may acquire, lease, use or occupy such land for the aforegoing purposes.

In the former case the Governor need only consult the local authority concerned, but in the latter case, such a declaration can only be made on the application of the local authority itself.[1] A further extension, in order to facilitate private enterprise developing African townships, provides that the Governor may on the application of the owner of any land reserved for African housing purposes, declare the area an African township, wherein Africans may lease, use or occupy land.[2] Recently provision has been made whereby the Governor may, after consultation with any local authority concerned, declare land zoned as residential to be an area which Africans might acquire with a view to occupying.[3] This has made it possible for multi-racial areas to be created. All that has resulted in practice is the designation of a residential area known as Westwood which was formerly occupied by Europeans and which was adjacent to a large African township. No Europeans are resident in this area so that it is in fact entirely African and is governed under the Local Government Areas General Regulations, which the Constitutional Council reported apply in practice only to African townships.

The employment in Section 63(1) of the word 'use' when prohibiting

possible for hotels to be declared hotels in which any African indigenous or non-indigenous may be accommodated, thus avoiding the necessity in each case for the grant of a permit. However, there are only three hotels in Southern Rhodesia which have applied for such declarations—the Jameson and the Ambassador Hotels in Salisbury and the Victoria Falls Hotel. Southern Rhodesia's major international hotel, Meikles, avoiding the odium of becoming known as a multi-racial hotel, is still relying on the permit system, it being illegal for indigenous Africans to be accommodated there as they do not come under the permit system. Furthermore, a declaration permitting land to be used for training courses or educational facilities of a specialized character for which governmental provision is not made may be made if the Minister of Education recommends this and the owner or occupier of such land has applied for such a declaration. Similar provision exists to permit private schools to be attended by Africans. But in 1965 Government announced a policy of refusing the admission of new pupils. It also rejected any new multi-racial hotel applications. Finally, an association which in the opinion of the Minister of Internal Affairs would promote good race relations may be permitted to carry on cultural, welfare, religious, recreational, or sporting activities and to provide accommodation subject to conditions for a short period. See Chapter 257, Sections 46, 63(1)(d), 66, 67, 68, 81, 82, 83, and 84.

[1] Sections 69 and 70. No action has been taken under Section 69. See Annual Report by the Secretary for Local Government and Housing for the year ending 31 December 1963, C.S.R. 20–1964, p. 6. However, a small multi-racial business area was proclaimed in Bulawayo on the fringe of the main business area and in the proximity of the main approaches to the African Townships on the western commonage. Annual Report of the Secretary for Local Government and Housing for the year ending 31 December 1964, C.S.R. 19–1965, pp. 3–4. In 1965 the police threatened to prosecute landlords who leased property in any other parts of the European business or residential areas to Africans. Consequently all African tenants were evicted.

[2] Again no action has been taken as no developers have invoked the section: C.S.R. 20–1964, p. 6.

[3] Act 55 of 1963, Section 41 I.

African 'use' of such land has made the ambit of this Section difficult of definition, and the problem has been exacerbated by the various amendments to the Act creating exceptions. Some of these exceptions, notably Section 65(2) which permits Africans who are *bona fide* guests of members of clubs to occupy or use the club premises and Section 82, which permits clubs and associations to permit persons to occupy or use their premises, would appear to give the word a very extended meaning.

That 'use' is employed in a very wide sense is made even clearer by Section 41(B) of the 1941 Act as amended by Section 7 of Act 51 of 1954. This provided that if a person attended or took part in a function or activity given or provided by or under the auspices of a cultural, welfare, or religious association he, 'shall not be deemed . . . to use such land'. If 'use' is taken in this sense[1] it would exclude any 'use' by Africans of land in areas of local authorities who had established an African township. The consequences of such a view were evident to Beadle C.J. in certain *obiter dicta* in *Mehta* v. *City of Salisbury, supra*. He considered that—

the word 'use' is sandwiched in between the words 'lease' and 'occupy' and . . . must be construed *eiusdem generis* with these words. In this context the word 'use' must mean 'use' by virtue of some interest in the land, as for example a partnership agreement involving the use of a particular piece of land. The word 'use' cannot mean merely 'being on' the land. If 'use' means this, extraordinary results would follow. A native would not be allowed to use the public parks, the public streets, or to make purchases from a shop in the European area.[2]

Despite these *dicta* by Beadle C.J. it is submitted that the amendments to the Act clearly show that 'use' was intended to have its normal wide and untechnical meaning. In any event, the law is still not settled on the point, thus leaving it open to the Attorney-General to initiate prosecutions for breach of this Section in circumstances which are still undefined. Indeed, the Constitutional Council has commented how prejudicial to both Africans and Europeans alike the present situation is, as it is difficult to regulate conduct

---

[1] See e.g. *R.* v. *Sikupa*, 1934 S.R. 94, where regulations of the Bulawayo Municipality were held *ultra vires* as being unreasonable, since they prohibited the 'use' by Africans of sidewalks, which would have meant that an African could not even cross the sidewalk to enter a shop.

[2] Beadle C.J. considered that his view was supported by *Powell* v. *Kempton Park Racecourse Company*, [1899] A.C. 143 at 159–60. He also adopted the view that since there had been no prosecutions for such 'usage', *subsecuta observatio* justified the adoption of such a meaning (he may not have been aware that the Law Officers had consistently advised the Government for a twenty-year period that 'use' had this wide meaning and that the Section was invoked by the municipalities to reject potential applications in the European Area to build cinemas designed for Africans. However, Departmental practice is not a good guide to interpretations of statutes). He also justified his interpretation on the basis that the wording of what was formerly Section 41(B) relative to 'native guests' (since amended—but this would not affect the interpretation) was inserted *ex majori cautela*. Finally he considered the word in its context as ambiguous and that it should therefore be construed so as to interfere as little as possible with civil liberties. The Federal Supreme Court when the case went on appeal declined to deliver itself of any *obiter dicta* on this issue.

precisely in accordance with the Act, as even judges are uncertain of the meaning of these words.[1]

Until 1960 the Land Apportionment Act had been even more racially restrictive, as prior to amendment of the Act in that year, Africans might only acquire the freehold of land in the Native Purchase Area or in native townships in the Special Native Area, and could at most acquire leaseholds in African townships in the European area, i.e., all townships adjacent to European towns. By Sections 17 and 23 of Act 54 of 1960, it was however provided that the land in native townships might be owned on conditions approved either by the Governor or the Minister of Internal Affairs, depending on the method of establishment of the township. As a result of this change the Southern Rhodesia Government in 1963 established the Kambazuma Township in Salisbury, where Africans can obtain freehold title, and has also transferred certain property in Highfield to Africans,[2] while the Bulawayo Municipality has been converting its leasehold township schemes to freehold.

It should however be mentioned that quite apart from legislative provisions which make it impossible for Africans to acquire land in many areas of Southern Rhodesia, particularly in the urban areas, an extensive practice of inserting racially restrictive title deed conditions has been established.

Thus one of the conditions of title inserted in many title deeds to immovable property is that the land in question shall be reserved for the ownership of or occupation by persons who are wholly of European descent. Such conditions in Roman–Dutch Law are not based on an analogy with the rule in *Tulk* v. *Moxhay*,[3] but arise from an application of the law of contract and property. In Roman–Dutch Law it is permissible to enter into a *stipulatio alteri* and the courts have held that when a racially restrictive condition is contained in the deeds of sale of townships, such a condition may be interpreted as a *stipulatio alteri* whereby the purchaser—

agreed to subject his holding to the burden of this restriction for the benefit of each and every present and future holder of other lots and agreed to accept the benefit of the same restriction imposed or to be imposed upon all the holdings for his own advantage. Each contract with the common . . . (seller) was for the benefit of third parties and each involved an acceptance of similar benefits from time to time by those parties.[4]

Thereafter if these conditions are registered against the title the result is a negative praedial servitude which all successors in title to the original purchaser have the same right to enforce.[5]

---

[1] Report No. 29 of 5 February 1963, p. 24.
[2] There are also a small number of wealthy Africans who own houses at Marimba Park, a special township near Salisbury, but their situation does not reflect that of the ordinary African citizen.
[3] 41 E.R. 1143 (H.L.).   [4] *Alexander* v. *Johns*, 1912 A.D. 431 per Innes A.C.J. at 443.
[5] *Eiffel Mansions (Pty.) Ltd.* v. *Cohen*, 1945 W.L.D. 200 at 204 per Ramsbottom J. Because of the system of land registration and registration of servitudes in Roman–Dutch

Difficulties may however arise as to whether a condition contained in a contract of sale was intended merely as a personal servitude in favour of the township owner or whether the restriction was intended for the benefit of all stand holders and not the township owner alone. Only in the latter case could any stand holder enforce the condition, it being no longer open to the township owner to waive such a condition. The test to be applied in deciding such cases has been set out in *Norbrick (Pty.) Ltd.* v. *Rand Townships Registrar*.[1]

In Southern Rhodesia it was until recently the practice for applicants for sub-divisions to request and for the Minister of Local Government in approving townships to impose racially restrictive conditions. This was clearly *ultra vires* the powers granted to the Minister in terms of the Town and Country Planning Act.[2] However, the Town Planning Court in a later decision left it open for individuals to continue the practice of inserting restrictive conditions as it considered that conditions could be incorporated by the township owner or anyone else in their titles quite apart from the statutory power to impose conditions granted to the Minister.[3]

The Court considered that such a condition would be enforceable, although breach of the condition would not be punishable as a criminal offence since it had not been imposed by the Minister in terms of the Act.[4]

Private sellers have taken advantage of the law in this respect and racially restrictive conditions of title have been inserted in the title deeds of most peri-urban townships stands in Southern Rhodesia.[5] The practical significance of this is that whereas the municipalities occupy relatively small central areas in the main towns, the peri-urban areas are the dormitories of a large

Law restrictive covenants are always enforceable as registration in the Deeds Registry is notice to the world and there would be no possibility of a purchaser without notice. Even if the covenants were unregistered, there is no provision analogous to the Land Charges Act 1925 (15 & 16 Geo. V), Ch. 22, Section 13(2), and a purchaser with notice would be bound.

[1] 1948 (1) S.A. 1037 (T) per Clayden J. (as he then was), who adopted the principles set out in *Elliston* v. *Reacher*, [1908] 2 Ch. 374.

[2] Act No. 19 of 1945, Section 52(2). See *Sampson and Others* v. *The Minister* (T.904–13 November 1961), an unreported decision of the Town Planning Court where it was held that the Minister had no power to impose such a condition. In addition under the 1923 Constitution he could not impose such a condition or regulation unless he had obtained prior approval of the Secretary of State. See *Mehta* v. *City of Salisbury*, *supra* and *Chamboko* v. *Mabelreign Town Management Board*, *supra*.

[3] For the Minister's powers, see Section 52(2) and the Fourth Schedule to the Town and Country Planning Act.

[4] *Coronation Investments (Pvt.) Ltd.* v. *Greendale Town Management Board and Others* (T.P.) reported in (1962) R. & N. L.J., Vol. 2, p. 192. Section 117 makes breach of conditions imposed by the Minister punishable.

[5] See Third Report of the Select Committee on Disabilities of Eurafrican, Coloured, and Asian Communities. L.A.S.C. 2–1960, p. 13. In Fort Victoria and Umtali all peri-urban stands contain restrictive conditions and in Que Que all but one such stand contains a racially restrictive condition. In Salisbury 92 per cent of stands in peri-urban areas have such conditions and in Bulawayo 44 per cent.

residential population and for the most part these dormitory areas cannot be occupied by non-Europeans. It should be noted that in this context non-Europeans would include Asians and Coloureds as well as Africans.

Even if no racially restrictive conditions are inserted in any title deed and also within the municipalities where such conditions have hardly been used, 'because of the reluctance of Europeans to sell or to rent property to members of these communities' non-Europeans for the most part are restricted to certain small areas made available to them by the municipalities.[1]

It may be that new racially restrictive covenants entered into after the coming into force of the Declaration of Rights in the Southern Rhodesia Constitution 1961 will be struck down by Section 68 as in terms of that Section no public officer could register such a condition, nor would the Courts enforce it.[2] On the other hand since the Registrar of Deeds in registering servitudes acts in terms of the Deeds Registries Act, which was a law in force prior to the coming into operation of the new Constitution, action done under the authority of that law cannot be held to be inconsistent with the provisions of Section 68. Even if it is doubtful whether new restrictive convenants may be registered, there seems no reason why such covenants, provided they were in force prior to the coming into effect of the Declaration of Rights, cannot be enforced, since Section 70(1)(b) of the Constitution provides that the Declaration shall not apply to anything contained in or done under the authority of any law in force immediately prior to the coming into operation of the Constitution and which has continued in force at all times since that date. Since the law includes the Roman–Dutch common law[3] such servitudes would be saved and would be enforceable.[4]

---

[1] L.A.S.C. 2-1960, p. 14. The Committee, however, did not recommend removal of freedom to impose racially restrictive conditions in covenants as it would 'not be advisable to forgo the principle of private contractual arrangements between private individuals'.

[2] Both Registrar and judges are public officers (see Section 116 (1)) and therefore cannot perform any executive or administrative act in such a manner that any person of a particular description by race, tribe, colour or creed is prejudiced by being subject to restrictions or disabilities or being denied privileges or advantages which persons of other descriptions are not subject to or are accorded, if the imposition or denial is wholly or mainly attributable to the description of such a person by race, tribe, colour or creed: Section 68. Action by the Registrar in registering servitudes is clearly administrative, while even though a pronouncement by the Courts would be judicial any enforcement of the judgement would be administrative. Compare *Shelley* v. *Kraemer*, 334 U.S. 1 (1948), contra *Corrigan* v. *Buckley*, 271 U.S. 323 (1926). It seems voluntary adherence to the terms of covenants is permissible—see *Shelley* v. *Kraemer, supra* at 13 per Vinson C.J.

[3] Section 72(1) definition of law: '(c) any unwritten law in force in Southern Rhodesia'. Alternatively such action was taken under the Deeds Registries Act which as an existing law is also saved by Section 70(1)(b).

[4] Before the 1961 Constitution came into force it was clear that discriminatory laws could be passed by the Legislature, that discriminatory subordinate regulations could be made, and that these would be enforced by the Courts: Clayden C.J. in *City of Salisbury* v. *Mehta, supra*. The same analogy would apply to restrictive covenants if they were within the law.

Local government in the European urban area
The history of local government

The first organs of local government in Southern Rhodesia were the *ultra vires* Sanitary Boards established in 1891 by Dr. Jameson.[1] Eventually the Sanitary Boards were properly established in terms of the Town Management Ordinance No. 2 of 1894 and their regulations were confirmed.[2] In addition the Town Management Ordinance provided for the Administrator to apply its provisions to all towns, villages or communities.

Subsequently as part of the constitutional and administrative reconstruction of Southern Rhodesia after the Jameson Raid and the Matabele and Mashona Rebellions, the Municipal Law of 1897, which was based on the Cape Municipal Act,[3] was passed in the form of Regulations by the Administrator and Council. The new Municipal Law, however, applied initially only to Salisbury and to Bulawayo.

Soon thereafter the Village Regulations No. 182 of 1898 gave the Administrator power to provide for the good government of communities not subject to Municipal Regulations or to other legislation providing for their government. Not only could the Administrator make rules for various purposes but he could appoint Village Boards consisting of two or more persons holding office for such time as he thought fit, to carry out such rules.

By 1898 therefore the three major legislative measures providing for local government in European areas were on the Southern Rhodesian statute book. Since that time they have of course been considerably amended. This is most apparent in regard to provisions as to the constitution and powers of such bodies. At present the basic Acts are the Municipal Act (Chapter 125),[4] the Town Management Act (Chapter 134),[5] and the Local Government Act (Chapter 124).[6]

---

[1] *Supra* Part I, Chapter 5. The Salisbury Sanitary Board was established by G.N. 6 of 1891 and an election was held at the end of that year. The Board then levied rates. In 1892, the Victoria Sanitary Board was appointed.

[2] Ordinance 2 of 1894, Section 37. The old Boards were brought under the Ordinance by G.N. 25 of 1895. Regulations imposing public health duties on the Sanitary Board of Salisbury and permitting the Administrator to apply these to other townships were also passed: The Townships Sanitary Regulations No. 109 of 1895.

[3] Section 2 provided that the Municipal Act 1882 of the Cape of Good Hope, should not be in operation in the Company's territories. This provision was not necessary as up to that time Cape law had not been imported as such law would only be applied 'as nearly as the circumstances of the country permit': Matabeleland Order in Council 1894, Section 37. See also *supra*, pp. 136-7. The history of Southern Rhodesian local government contained in Brelsford, op. cit. at p. 694, is somewhat misleading.

[4] The Municipal Act was first consolidated by Act No. 36 of 1930, and thereafter was again consolidated by Act 34 of 1952. It is the subject of frequent amendment.

[5] This was re-enacted and put on a more modern basis by Act 21 of 1926. It was thereafter consolidated by Act 36 of 1953 and has also been subsequently amended.

[6] Act 4 of 1961 which repealed and replaced the Village Management Act (Chapter 99 of 1939), the latter being a virtual restatement of the Village Regulations of 1898. However, the

Government supervisory bodies

Two Government Ministries are responsible for supervising local government in Southern Rhodesia: the Ministry of Internal Affairs, which is responsible for supervising Africans in the rural areas—Native Purchase Areas and the Tribal Trust Land—and the Ministry of Local Government,[1] which is responsible for all local government in urban areas, whether African or European, and also for European rural local government. This division of functions is recent, as until July 1961 all African local government, urban and rural, was handled by the Ministry of Internal Affairs (formerly the Native Affairs Department).

These Ministries give technical advice (particularly the Ministry of Local Government) and are responsible for supervising such matters as estimates, applications for loan monies, etc. The Ministry of Local Government always adopted the principle of consultation with interested local government bodies and a Local Government Advisory Committee has been established. It contains a number of private citizens and is charged with advising the Ministry on the form of local government, the establishment of local government where so far not established and the suitability or otherwise of existing forms of local government.[2] The Government consults the local authority concerned in any particular matter, but on policy matters deals also with the Local Government Association, which represents all elected local authorities and which makes numerous representations to Government on changes in the law, sometimes even obstructing Government policy.

Municipalities

Municipalities as constituted in Southern Rhodesia are local government authorities which can be compared with similar urban bodies in the United Kingdom, except that they are not charged with such extensive duties in relation to responsibility for education and health services. On the other hand, they have greater duties in respect of the provision of housing for Africans resident in urban areas and great powers of administering and legislating for African townships, despite the fact that the inhabitants of such areas do not enjoy the municipal franchise.

Southern Rhodesian municipalities are all established in terms of the

---

Local Government Act went further than the Village Management Act, as it set out to provide a potential framework for a comprehensive and flexible system of urban and rural local government in both African and European areas in Southern Rhodesia.

[1] The Ministry of Local Government has within it the Town Planning Department and the Department of Public Works, which also manages Government real estate matters.

[2] Report of the Secretary for Local Government for the year 1961, C.S.R. 30–1962, p. 11, for full terms of reference.

Municipal Act. There are at present seven municipalities,[1] Salisbury and Bulawayo however being dignified with the status and title of 'city'.[2]

Municipalities are constituted in his discretion by the Governor.[3] Once constituted, a municipality is a body corporate with perpetual succession and is governed by a Council composed of a mayor and councillors.[4]

The municipal franchise in Southern Rhodesia is at first sight generous, as all persons of full age, unless disqualified,[5] who either own or occupy immovable property which is liable to be rated (i.e. in the municipal area) and which is shown in the valuation roll as having a value of not less than £50, are entitled to be registered provided their rates are not in arrear.[6] Furthermore a spouse, unless married under any system permitting of polygamy, is deemed to possess the same qualifications as his or her spouse.[7] This provision enfranchises virtually all adult Europeans living in municipal areas, but does not enfranchise Africans who are resident in urban areas under the control of the municipalities. Even though amendments to the Land Apportionment Act in 1960 creating the African Townships Area permitted Africans to own land in municipal townships,[8] and although many Africans occupy property which would be of the requisite rateable value, they may not be registered as voters because of the fact that African townships have by deliberate policy not been incorporated into the municipal area.

Consequently, there are African townships owned and controlled by the municipalities, surrounded by a municipal area and yet not forming part of the

[1] Annual Report of the Secretary for Internal Affairs and Housing for the year ending 31 December 1964, C.S.R. 19–1965, Government Printer, Salisbury, p. 6, viz. namely, Bulawayo, Fort Victoria, Gatooma, Gwelo, Que Que, Salisbury, and Umtali.

[2] The City of Bulawayo (Private) Act (Chapter 119), and the City of Salisbury (Private) Act (Chapter 120). However, the Municipal Act is equally applicable to the two cities.

[3] Section 9. Sections 11–16 deal with the question of the exercise of his powers, petitions for the constitution of municipalities, counter petitions, publications of petitions, investigations as to matters connected with petitions, etc.

[4] Sections 7 and 8(1). Mayor and councillors are unpaid, although the Mayor of Salisbury receives £2,000 per annum hospitality allowance, and Salisbury councillors also receive £10 per month allowance. 'Alderman' is an honorary title which may be conferred on a councillor who has held office for ten years. Section 6 of Act 73 of 1964, allows the payment of pensions in special circumstances to councillors who have held office for twenty years.

[5] Disqualifications are of the normal type, viz. mental disorder, a five-year period after discharge from imprisonment without the option of a fine (this includes a suspended sentence), and persons who are in arrears with their rates within three months before the elections: Sections 32 and 33.

[6] Section 2. Special provision exists for the Governor to apply proportional representation and the transferable vote to municipal elections if a poll of voters or a majority of voters at a general meeting of enrolled voters has so resolved: Section 65. This Section has not so far been invoked.

[7] Section 29(5).

[8] Land Apportionment (Amendment) Act No. 54 of 1960, Section 23. Of the municipalities, only the Bulawayo Municipality has introduced a scheme of freehold home ownership in its townships, in accordance with the amended Act. Even then there are not many African owners of property, but numbers are in the process of purchasing their houses over a twenty-five-year period.

municipal area.[1] If such townships were incorporated on the present municipal franchise, large numbers of Africans would enjoy the vote since occupiers of municipally owned immovable property are entitled to be enrolled although improvements made by the Council on its land are not taken into account in determining the value of such property.[2] Nevertheless, in practice most stands without improvements would be valued at £50 were they within the municipality and the occupiers would thus qualify for the vote.

The combined effect in practice in 1964 of the Land Apportionment Act and the way in which the boundaries of the municipalities are drawn is that the only Africans in Southern Rhodesia eligible for the municipal franchise are two African advocates who have leased chambers in Salisbury.

Another feature of the municipal franchise in Southern Rhodesia is that if any municipality is divided into wards, there is no limitation on voters being enrolled on more than one roll as occupiers or owners of property in each ward. It is frequently found that persons have votes in different wards owing to their occupancy of business premises as well as of residential accommodation.[3] Furthermore, they may be able to exercise votes as representatives of a company, since where property is owned by a company, the manager, secretary, or other person in actual occupation may be enrolled to vote in respect of such property.[4]

Elections are held annually on the first Wednesday of August of each year, but only one-third of the total number of councillors retire by rotation, so that one-third come up for election at any time. Where a municipality has been sub-divided into wards, councillors retire and new councillors are elected in equal numbers by every ward. If however there are four councillors in a ward, only one-quarter of the councillors shall be re-elected annually.[5] Provision is also made for by-elections.

Councils are composed of from six to twenty-four councillors, the number in each case being specified by the Governor.[6] Councillors' qualifications are somewhat more stringent than those of voters, since the value of the property owned or occupied by a candidate must be of the yearly value of not less than £20 and such property must have been owned or occupied not less than six months before any election.

The procedure to be followed in Council business which is based on the Cape model, is specified at some length in the Act. Among these provisions

[1] e.g. in Bulawayo the African townships have not been incorporated into the municipality, nor have railway townships in the heart of the municipality. The same thing applies to Salisbury townships.

[2] See Municipal Act, Section 127, read with Sections 28 and 29(2).

[3] See Sections 29(4) and Section 39 which permit this.

[4] Section 31(1).

[5] Thus for example in Salisbury councillors in various wards hold office for four-year terms. In most municipalities there are usually three councillors to a ward, but the Governor may declare that the number of councillors for each ward shall be four.

[6] Section 68(1) and Section 9(1)(g).

is the rule that Council meetings shall be open to the public. However, it is competent for the Council to resolve itself into committee, and to exclude the public from any meeting if it is deemed that the subject can be more conveniently and advantageously discussed in private.

Meetings of occasional and standing committees are not open to the public.[1] Another special provision stipulates that if a councillor has a pecuniary interest, direct or indirect, in any contract or proposed contract, he must, if present at a meeting where this is the subject of consideration, disclose this fact immediately, and is also prohibited from taking part in the consideration, or discussion of, or vote on any question with respect to the matter.[2]

The powers enjoyed by Councils are considerable. Generally they may pass all by-laws required for maintaining good rule and government in the municipality.[3] In addition a larger number of topics on which by-laws can be made are detailed in the Act.

An extension of municipalities' by-law making powers arises from the fact that municipalities are empowered to make special by-laws and to extend the application of their ordinary by-laws to areas outside their boundaries and to the municipal commonage.[4] Municipalities are also expressly authorized by the Local Government Act to make by-laws for their African townships.[5]

[1] Section 92.

[2] Section 71(1). Knowing breach of this Section is a criminal offence. The councillor however, may only be prosecuted for such an offence with the consent of the Attorney-General: Section 72. The Section applies if either he or his spouse is a member of a company concerned in such a contract, or he is a partner or is in the employment of a person who has himself a pecuniary interest in the transaction. The interest of a spouse is also included for this purpose. Previously it was provided that no person could become or continue as a councillor who had any direct or indirect pecuniary interest in a contract with the municipality: Section 17(2) of Chapter 97 of 1939. As a result a city councillor married to a surveyor who as an independent contractor had obtained certain contracts with a municipality was declared incapable of holding office as a councillor at the time of her election: *Olley* v. *Maasdorp and Another*, 1948 (4) S.A. 657 (A.D.).

[3] Section 277(78).

[4] Sections 280–82. The commonage is the area adjoining the limits of a municipality which is vested in the municipality. In respect of the commonage, the power does not include the imposition of rates.

[5] Chapter 124, Section 67. Sections 280–82 of the Municipal Act in any case allow this in respect of municipally owned townships. However, the Local Government Act would have to be invoked in townships with African home ownership. Formerly, Section 38 of the Land Apportionment Act 1941 authorized municipalities to make any laws 'for the good rule, government control, use and occupation of townships within their control'. By-laws issued under this enabling Section are still in force having been saved by Section 44 of Act 54 of 1960, e.g. the Salisbury Native Urban Areas Regulations 1953 (S.R. G.N. 178/53), still lay down strict rules for the occupation of municipal housing, it being a criminal offence for unauthorized occupiers to reside in such housing. Certificates of occupation are normally only granted to employees and such certificates may be cancelled if Africans are unemployed for one month or more or are considered not fit and proper persons having committed certain crimes.

43—C.H.L.S.R.

A copy of all by-laws which have been passed by a Council must be deposited at the Council's office not later than seven days before the confirmation of the by-law, where it shall be open to inspection by any person at all reasonable times.

A notice setting out the purport of the proposed by-law and that it is available for inspection shall also be published in a newspaper generally circulating in the neighbourhood. After the period of inspection has elapsed by-laws are submitted for the approval of the Governor, whereupon, if approved, they are published in the Gazette and thereafter have the force of law.[1]

Municipalities also have extensive rating powers. Only if the rate imposed is in excess of 4d. in the £ on the value, or 1s. 4d. on the annual value of rateable property, or a special rate is intended to be levied need a Council take special steps. In such a case notice must be published by the Council for not less than seven days, any ten ratepayers within seven days thereafter being entitled to demand that the proposal be submitted to a poll of ratepayers.[2] No governmental assent is required for Council Estimates, as is the case with lesser local authorities in Southern Rhodesia.[3]

The executive powers of municipalities are also extensive. They largely relate to powers to establish and maintain undertakings and public services, e.g. sewage works, electricity services, water supplies (including the building of major water works), housing schemes, construction of streets, footpaths and gutters, railway sidings, aerodromes, and also to provide maternity and child welfare services, creches, ambulances, fire brigades, omnibuses, and other vehicular services, recreation grounds, parks, art galleries, parking places, buildings, abbatoirs, fruit and vegetable markets, and African eating houses.[4] Yet other powers are given them in terms of the Town and Country Planning Act (Chapter 133), which makes local authorities their own planning authorities responsible for the preparation and enforcement of town planning schemes in their areas,[5] and which also permits the Minister of Local Government to delegate to such authorities powers and duties in respect of areas for the planning of which he is responsible.[6] Furthermore there are many Acts which confer specific powers on and sometimes impose duties on local authorities to take action in specialized fields.[7]

---

[1] Sections 278 and 279.

[2] Section 164. Similar provision exists that twenty voters in writing may request a poll if the council proposes to borrow monies other than for refunding operations: Section 118. For any proposed borrowings for permanent works public notice in the Gazette and in newspapers must be given at least one month before the proposal is adopted: Section 117.

[3] It is, however, the practice to send the Estimates to the Minister of Local Government for his information.

[4] Section 256(1)–(20), as amended by Section 16 of Act 20 of 1964.

[5] Sections 18 and 39.   [6] Chapter 133, Section 41.

[7] e.g. the Shop Hours Act (Chapter 238), the Cemeteries Act (Chapter 118). The Public Health Act (Chapter 167), is particularly important as imposing numerous duties on munici-

Municipalities are even permitted to maintain their own police forces[1] although in practice they rely on the British South African Police. Furthermore, they may employ parking supervisors to assist the police in the enforcement of any by-laws relating to the use of roads,[2] and the larger municipalities have utilized this provision, thus having their own force of what might loosely be termed 'traffic police'.

Municipalities may employ a Town Clerk and also such other officers and servants as may be necessary to assist in the execution of their powers. Provision is made for their appointment and dismissal, while special safeguards are given to Town Clerks and other senior local government employees in that they may not be dismissed except upon a majority vote of the whole number of councillors at a meeting specially convened for such a purpose.[3]

The most important power, however, possessed by municipalities is their power to establish African townships with the approval of the Governor.[4]

Such townships are heavily populated, having residential accommodation both in the form of hostels for single men and houses and flats for married Africans,[5] which have been erected by the municipalities who are by law bound to supply hostels for work seekers and African visitors.[6] Furthermore, the Minister of Internal Affairs under the Land Apportionment Act may by written notice require municipalities to provide residential accommodation for Africans whether living under family conditions of life or not. In the event of failure by the municipalities to comply with such an order, the Minister may himself undertake such works and recover the amount from the Municipality.[7] Indirectly, municipalities are also therefore obliged to provide such accommodation.

Any such townships form part of the African Townships Area, but although they are outside municipal boundaries, they are subject to the control of municipalities. As indicated above, the municipalities enjoy in respect of such

palities, viz. Sections 7, 10, 14, 19, 38, 84, 101, and 102, relating to the appointment of Medical Officers of Health and Sanitary Inspectors, notification of infectious and epidemic diseases, the furnishing of water supplies and the supervision of sanitation and housing.

[1] Section 196.   [2] Section 197.   [3] Section 195.

[4] Land Apportionment Act (Chapter 257), Section 54. Many of these townships were established under legislation which is now repealed. Formerly there was great confusion of terminology. Townships now include all 'native urban areas' established by the Governor under Section 36 of the Land Apportionment Act 1941 and 'locations' set aside in terms of the Native Urban Locations Act (Chapter 84 of 1939). Salisbury 'location' dates back to the city's first Sanitary Board in the early eighteen nineties.

[5] Before the war there was a far greater proportion of hostel accommodation for male migratory labourers. Today much more family accommodation is available, but the amount of accommodation available in any particular municipality will depend on its policy. Thus Bulawayo in 1964 provided accommodation for 15,967 married couples and accommodation for 13,303 single persons, whereas Salisbury provided accommodation for 8,109 married couples and for 25,578 single Africans: C.S.R. 19–1965, p. 23.

[6] Africans (Urban Areas) Accommodation and Registration Act (Chapter 110), Section 40(1).

[7] Land Apportionment Act (Chapter 257), Sections 59 and 60 read with Section 54.

townships the same plenary, administrative and legislative powers that they enjoy within their boundaries.[1] Thus large numbers of people are governed by elected local authorities in whose election they have no say.

It should also be noted that adjacent to the municipalities and their townships there are in many cases Government African townships over which the municipalities have no control, and which are centrally administered by the Department of Local Government and Housing. These townships were either established under the Native Urban Locations Act (Chapter 84 of 1939) as native urban locations, or as native village settlements established by the Governor under Section 34 of the Land Apportionment Act 1941.[2] At present there is no local government at all in such townships, the only sign of advance being that the Minister of Local Government has in respect of Highfield (which was from August 1964 to May 1965, declared an emergency area in terms of the Emergency Powers Act (Chapter 33)) declared that he intends to appoint a nominated Board chosen after consultation with the community. The Minister has stated that 'this body will be given a reasonable amount of autonomy, especially in regard to financial responsibility . . . . If this experiment is successful and an atmosphere free from intimidation is established . . . elections will be held and a formal authority inaugurated'.[3] However, the Secretary for Local Government reported in 1965 that his Department had been investigating the establishment of local authorities in African townships and that such bodies would require executive and decision-making functions, a sound financial basis, African participation, and intensive training of Africans who entered the employ of African local authorities. He concluded 'it is quite clear therefore, that local authorities in African townships, cannot appear overnight, but will develop and extend over a period. The Ministry is, however, anxious to start the process as soon as the population of the townships can rid themselves of the fear of reprisals by extremists on 'co-operators' or 'stooges'.[4] As at the end of 1964 the Department of Local Government was administering thirty-three African townships either through town managers or through District Commissioners of the Department of Internal Affairs.[5] The local population have no voice in their local government, even though a considerable number of the occupants are 'home owners', the Government having since 1955 introduced home ownership schemes whereby Africans could obtain property on a 100-year lease.

There are also a number of African townships established with the permis-

---

[1] However, such property may not be rated. The Municipality of Salisbury controls three large townships outside its boundaries, Harare, Mufakose, and Mabvuku. Bulawayo has six townships, only one of which—Pumula—is outside the commonage.

[2] Highfield at Salisbury, Luveve at Bulawayo, and Senka at Gwelo are native village settlements.

[3] Southern Rhodesia Press Statement 909/64 PT. 14 September 1964.

[4] C.S.R. 19–1965, p. 1.

[5] C.S.R. 19–1965, pp. 5–6.

sion of the Governor by statutory boards for employees and their families.[1] These townships are adjacent to municipalities but again do not form part of them,[2] being administered by the statutory commissions concerned. Again there is no local government within the area though it is theoretically possible for the Minister of Local Government to invoke the Local Government Act and to grant certain powers of local government.

This unsatisfactory position in respect of African representation in urban local government, both in government and municipal townships, was reported on by the Plewman Commission in 1958.[3]

The problem has not yet been solved and has been complicated by controversy over the last three years whether a 'two-tier' system of local authorities should be adopted with each local authority enjoying autonomy subject to co-ordination of their activities by a regional authority,[4] or whether urban Africans should be given representation within the existing Councils.[5] Legislation—the Local Government Act—exists which could be used to impose a solution,[6] but the present Government is unlikely to coerce the municipalities or to insist on the provision of more local self-government for Africans. In fact the provisions of the Local Government Act have been used

---

[1] Land Apportionment Act (Chapter 257), Section 51(1).

[2] e.g. Rugare African township established by the Rhodesia Railways near Salisbury, Sizinda and Matshobana in Bulawayo. Similar townships have been established by Rhodesia Railways at Wankie, Banket, and Lalapanzi. The Cold Storage Commission has established one at Bulawayo, while the Cotton Research and Industries Board has established one at Gatooma. Such townships still form part of the European area although they are occupied by Africans and their families.

[3] Report of the Urban African Affairs Commission, *supra*, paras. 506 et seq. At para. 509, the Commission recommended in respect of Salisbury and Bulawayo that two Africans either be nominated to or elected to the municipal standing committees on Finance and African Administration in order to provide representation in respect of the African section of the urban communities.

[4] This is the solution favoured by the present Government. The debate on two-tier government is only partly occasioned by the need to give African urban communities some representation. The major reason is the proliferation of local authorities in the greater Salisbury area, where there are seven Town Management Boards as well as the City Council. For an analysis of the need for integration of services see 'The Local Government Structure in Greater Salisbury' by B. J. Neale, Town Clerk of Salisbury, City of Salisbury, 1962. Mimeographed.

[5] The City of Bulawayo appointed a panel to investigate this problem. The panel recommended that African areas should be incorporated and that a franchise based on responsible occupation of prescribed property should be introduced: see Representation in Local Government in the Area under the Jurisdiction of the City Council of Bulawayo, City of Bulawayo, February 1963. Mimeographed.

[6] The Governor may by a Gazette notice declare any area to be a Local Government Area. Such powers can be exercised in respect of a township established by a municipality or Town Management Board after consultation with such body. The Governor can then appoint a Local Committee or Board. If this is done in respect of an area belonging to a municipal Council or to a Town Management Board, the Governor may make an apportionment of property, assets, rights and liabilities and give directions so as to do justice between the Local Board and the Council if they are unable to reach agreement: Section 3(1)(2)(4).

to secure central government control of African townships or to allow non-Governmental European Local Committees to manage such areas.

A noticeable feature of municipal government is that the degree of governmental control over municipalities is much less than in the case of other local government authorities. Nonetheless, there are numerous mechanisms of control. As indicated, not only do all by-laws require the approval of the Governor, but in addition every by-law in force in any municipality may be repealed by him.[1] Financial control over loans is extensive, since if municipalities wish to borrow sums in excess of one-sixth of the value of the rateable property within the municipality, permission is necessary from the Governor, who may investigate the matter and may authorize the borrowing if satisfied that the permanent undertaking proposed to be built with such money will be self-remunerative and that taking into account previous loans and sinking funds, permission can safely be granted.[2] In addition, since 1947 the Government has controlled local authority borrowing by establishing a common pool for loans to local authorities, and by allocating varying sums from this pool to each authority depending on priorities. Both Bulawayo and Salisbury may float separate loans of up to £750,000 per annum on the local market in addition to any shares they may receive from the pool. However, in recent years, owing to political uncertainty, such loan funds have not been available. Furthermore, it is the Minister who appoints auditors to municipalities, in each year appointing an auditor from a list submitted by the particular Council of persons approved by the Minister.[3] The Governor also has power to appoint any person to examine the accounts of any municipality.[4]

Again, municipalities may not alienate or permit to be built upon, enclosed or cultivated, any land vested in the Council without the consent of the Minister of Local Government to such proposed arrangement.[5] Conversely, Councils may not expropriate property without the consent of the Governor.[6] Furthermore, certain action may only be taken with Ministerial consent and objections must be heard by the Minister.[7]

In exceptional circumstances yet another power exists—the Governor may even appoint councillors e.g. when a vacancy cannot otherwise be filled.[8] This provision, however, has never been utilized in practice.

Finally the Governor is given large discretionary powers exercisable either on petition by the municipality or without such petition provided the Governor has given notice for three consecutive weeks in the Gazette and a

[1] Section 284. [2] Section 123.

[3] Section 101 as amended by Section 11 of Act 20 of 1964. The Minister may at any time remove any auditor upon the Council's request: Section 104.

[4] Section 113. [5] Section 191. [6] Section 274.

[7] e.g. the construction of private streets and footpaths and sewerage works: Sections 227 and 252.

[8] Section 66.

local newspaper stating his intention to exercise his power. If within a month after the last publication of a notice in the Gazette, no sufficient case is shown to the Governor why this power should not be exercised, it is lawful for him to alter the boundaries of municipalities, to add to or to exclude land from their areas, to sever a municipality into two separate municipalities, to determine or alter the number of councillors assigned to a municipality, and in cases where he had included any area within the municipality, to require the municipality to extend all or any of its by-laws, to waive rates and to exercise considerable discretionary powers.[1]

The central Government may also interfere in the event of default by municipalities. Thus if municipalities fail to set aside and develop African townships with all necessary services and to provide residential, shop or office accommodation in such areas, the Minister of Internal Affairs may undertake such works and recover the cost from the municipality. Other default powers apply in respect of public health matters. Similarly, the municipalities can be forced to propose town planning schemes under the Town and Country Planning Act, which are to be approved by the Governor,[2] and again in the event of failure the Minister may act in the place of and at the expense of the defaulting municipality. Alternatively after the holding of a local enquiry the Minister may by mandamus require the authority to execute any scheme.[3] Furthermore, the Minister can control the establishment of all townships by the municipality, as no township may be established without his permission.[4] An unusual feature of the Town and Country Planning Act should however be noted: persons aggrieved by administrative decisions in town planning matters are given a right of appeal to a Town Planning Court and not to the responsible Minister.

Town Management Boards

Town Management Boards are local government authorities with a lower status than that enjoyed by municipalities. Not only are they subjected to more governmental control, but they are not entrusted with so wide a range of powers and functions as are the municipalities. There were in December 1964, twenty-five Town Management Boards in Southern Rhodesia.[5]

Another major difference between municipalities and Town Management

---

[1] Sections 9 and 15. The latter powers were intended to relate to the incorporation of African townships in municipalities if this should occur.

[2] Chapter 133, Sections 18 and 35.

[3] Chapter 133, Section 50(2). The Section also confers default powers on the Minister which are the Southern Rhodesian equivalent of United Kingdom default powers in relation to sewerage disposal, lighting and water supplies.

[4] Chapter 133, Section 60. Nor may sites be offered for sale or lease unless such township has been approved.

[5] C.S.R. 19–1965, p. 7.

Boards lies in their franchise qualifications. In Town Management Boards not only must a prospective voter either be the owner or occupier of immovable property in the Board area, but it is provided that he must also be enrolled on a roll of voters under the Electoral Act, thus importing the national franchise requirements.[1] Spouses, except those married under a system permitting polygamy are deemed to possess the same qualifications as their spouses.[2] The effect of these qualifications is that a considerable number of residents in Town Management Boards who may even own property are disqualified from voting in local government elections. The qualifications, however, make no difference to Africans who are in any event ineligible for the Town Management Board franchise because of the effect of the Land Apportionment Act, which provides that no African can acquire, occupy or lease land in the European Area in which all Town Management Boards are situate.

Town Management Boards are smaller than municipalities and are composed of from six to twelve members, holding office for three years and retiring in rotation.[3] Provisions similar to those relating to municipalities as to the conduct of elections, the retirement of members, proceedings, appointment of officers, etc., are made by the Town Management Act. However, the powers and duties of Boards are not as wide as those of municipalities, e.g. Boards require Ministerial consent to operate omnibuses or to construct general undertakings where a specific power is not explicitly given.[4]

Town Management Boards' Estimates of revenue and expenditure must be submitted to the Minister, who may order the Auditor-General to enquire into them. Unless Ministerial permission is obtained, Boards after submission of their Estimates may not increase items or place new items on any Estimates.[5] Indeed, financial control over Town Management Boards is even stricter than in the case of municipalities, in that the Minister may send auditors' reports to the Auditor-General, who has power to raise surcharges on any responsible individual where money has been improperly paid, where charges have improperly been incurred or where deficiencies have occurred.

Again, Town Management Boards are not permitted to be their own town planning authorities as are the municipalities. Town Management Boards use instead the services of the central Government's Town Plannning Department, which is part of the Ministry of Local Government. Nor are Town Management Boards owners of large areas of land (except for streets and public buildings) as are municipalities, since it is only the latter which were generously endowed with commonages by the British South Africa Company. There is no unalienated land vested in Town Management Boards, as land

---

[1] Town Management Act (Chapter 134), Section 13(1).
[2] Section 13(2). This might exclude Asian women.
[3] Section 9. The number is determined by the Governor: Section 4(1)(e).
[4] First Schedule, Items 18 and 48. Boards may not operate a police force.
[5] Section 166 (3).

in Board areas is either in private ownership or reserved for governmental purposes by the Crown.

Again, Town Management Board by-law making powers are not so extensive, while the Governor is free to refuse assent, to approve part only of a by-law, and even to amend proposed by-laws.[1] Furthermore, although Town Management Boards are authorized to impose rates and do not require Ministerial permission such rates may not exceed 4d. in the £ of the aggregate value of land and improvements unless approval from the Minister is obtained, there being no provision for a poll of voters similar to that applicable to municipalities.[2] On the other hand Town Management Boards are not normally charged with the duty of maintaining African townships, since many of them do not maintain townships.[3]

The Local Government Act

The Local Government Act (Chapter 124), is designed to provide for local government in areas where the community is not sufficiently large or developed to warrant a Town Management Board, but the central Government considers that powers of local government should nonetheless be given to the community. Unfettered discretionary powers in assessing the needs of any community for local government and the form this should take are given to the Cabinet, which may by virtue of the Act impose either of two forms of local government authority, while within these forms there may be infinite permutations of authority permitted, this again depending on the Government's decision whether to delegate particular powers or not.

The Act envisages two methods of local government: the appointment of Local Boards and the appointment of Local Committees. In an area which is neither a municipality nor Town Management Board area, where it is impracticable to appoint a Local Committee or Local Board, the Minister of Local Government may appoint Local Government Area Officers. Such appointments do not result in local government, however, but in decentralized administration, the Minister appointing public servants to perform duties in relation to an area which he has declared to be a Local Government Area.[4] In a small number of cases persons other than civil servants have been appointed in that Local Committees have been allowed to manage African townships in their area.[5] The Minister may make such regulations as he deems necessary for the control, government, and management of the Area.[6] It is

---

[1] Section 105.

[2] Chapter 134, Section 142.

[3] If they do maintain townships, Sections 54, 59, and 60 of the Land Apportionment Act are equally applicable to them.

[4] Chapter 124, Section 64.

[5] Section 64 as amended by Section 6 of Act 67 of 1964. See C.S.R. 19–1965, p. 2.

[6] Section 65(1). See S.R.G.N. 569 of 1962 which contains the Local Government Areas General Regulations. These empower the Minister to appoint managers for Local Govern-

these powers that are now used to control Government townships.[1] It should be noted that in reality all the townships which have been declared as Local Government Areas are African townships.[2]

Local Committees are the 'lowest' form of local government. Although such bodies are nominated, being composed of three or more persons holding office during the pleasure of the Governor, they may number ordinary citizens amongst their members and in practice the Minister consults local interests before nominating a Local Committee. In fact the Local Committees are the old Village Management Boards, enjoying more or less similar powers, having however suffered a name change. Their powers include the taking of necessary steps for the preservation of public health, the provision of a proper and adequate water supply, of other essential services and of amenities for the inhabitants. The Minister may from time to time assign other functions to Local Committees. However, powers enjoyed by such Committees are purely administrative and they enjoy no power to impose rates,[3] nor can they exercise any legislative power, although they are to be consulted by the Governor, who may make regulations in order to enable the Committee to carry out its functions and on matters similar to those in respect of which municipalities and Town Mangement Boards may make by-laws.[4] As at the end of September 1964, there were six Local Committees in operation in Southern Rhodesia.[5]

Local Boards, the next form of local government, are bodies corporate enjoying far greater powers than Local Committees. Some Boards even have an elective element holding office for three years, Board members consisting

ment Areas, and also deal with control of public meetings, streets, public health and other matters. By S.R.G.N. 257 of 1964, considerable powers of control over occupiers and lodgers in such townships were assumed.

[1] Such townships were formerly governed by the Native Urban Locations Act (Chapter 84 of 1939), Section 10. This was repealed by Section 46 of Act 54 of 1960, but regulations under the Act were saved.

[2] The township of Westwood is also declared to be such an Area. Westwood was formerly a European township but it was in 1964 zoned as an Area in which Africans might also acquire land, i.e. as a multi-racial residential area under Section 41(I) of the Land Apportionment Act. In fact there are no longer any Europeans resident in Westwood. A minority of the Constitutional Council on 6 July 1965, reported on the fact that, although on a strict legal interpretation the Local Government Areas General Regulations did not discriminate against Africans, when the Amendment (No. 6) Regulations of 1965 were considered against the factual position that they applied only to Africans it was clear that they were discriminatory and prejudicial and imposed disabilities on Africans. These disabilities were the payment of fees by occupiers in respect of lodgers residing in their premises in those areas. In fact the Local Government Areas General Regulations as a whole seriously discriminate against Africans in practice as they confer considerable 'police powers' on township superintendents and provide for penal sanctions.

[3] They may with the Minister's approval charge for services or amenities provided by them: Section 5(2).

[4] Section 6(1).

[5] S.R.L.A.D., Vol. 58, cols. 677–8, 23 September 1964, viz. Essexvale, Karoi, Melsetter, Odzi, Victoria Falls, and Tengwe. All these Committees are entirely European.

of both elected and nominated members are prescribed in different numbers for each Board.[1]

It is even possible for the Governor to prescribe by Gazette notice that a Board may consist solely of elected members. Conversely, it is possible for Boards still to be entirely nominated. Three Local Boards had been established at the end of November 1964, the Penhalonga Board consisting of five members, of whom two were nominated, the Woodville Board of six appointed members,[2] and the Fern Valley Board of five appointed members.[3]

The franchise for Local Boards is widely drafted and covers adult citizens who are owners or occupiers for a six-months period of immovable property, while spouses are deemed to be similarly qualified, except that only the senior wife of a polygamous marriage is deemed to possess the same qualifications as those of her husband.[4] Similar qualifications are demanded for candidature, while elaborate provisions are made for the election of members, for the procedure of Boards, for their powers, and for securing proper control of Board's finances (Estimates and loans have to be approved by the Minister). Most of these provisions are modelled on the Town Management Board Act.

The powers of Boards are far greater than those of Committees. Depending on authorization by the Minister, Local Boards may make by-laws for virtually the same purposes as those open to Town Management Boards,[5] such by-laws being subject to approval, disapproval, or amendment by the Governor.

They may also be empowered to levy rates.[6] Their executive powers are also wider than those of Committees but not quite as wide as those of Town Management Boards, although they can construct any public works with the Minister of Local Government's permission.

The Minister has a great deal of power to act if the Board fails to take action: he may require the Board to exercise all or any of the powers set out in the First Schedule to the Act and may in the event of default exercise such power himself.[7] Similarly, he may even levy a rate within a Board area if the Board has failed to meet interest on loans or payments or to meet any deficit.[8]

Rural local administration

Both Local Committees and Local Boards are bodies appointed in small towns and villages in rural European areas. However, in many areas centres are not sufficiently large to justify the establishment of Boards or Committees. In such circumstances powers of local administration have been to a

---

[1] Section 7.
[2] *S.R.L.A.D.*, Vol. 58, col. 678, 23 September 1964. All members of the Boards are European.
[3] S.R.N. 1738/64.   [4] Section 9.
[5] Chapter 124, Section 40 and Second Schedule.
[6] Chapter 124, Section 36(1).   [7] Section 35.   [8] Section 36.

large extent exercised either by Road Councils established under the Roads and Road Traffic Act or by Intensive Conservation Area Committees appointed under the Natural Resources Act. The latter are Committees appointed by the holders of land in an area which has been declared by the Ministry of Agriculture to be an Intensive Conservation Area. They consist of up to seven members and are responsible for inaugurating and undertaking the construction of works and measures for soil and water conservation and improvement of soil and water resources in their areas.

Such Committees are given power to execute all necessary works and to raise funds by assessing owners, who will benefit therefrom, with the costs of such work.[1] In addition, I.C.A. Committees may borrow monies from Government and be given grants in aid. They may also, if two-thirds of the owners of more than fifty acres of land have at a special meeting approved a resolution to this effect, which has also been approved by the Natural Resources Board, impose a tax on land owners of more than fifty acres of land in their area.[2] In December 1964 there were ninety-nine Intensive Conservation Area Committees in operation in the European Area and sixty in the African Purchase Area and other African rural areas.[3]

The other type of body which to some extent carries out local government functions is the Road Council, of which there were forty-nine at the end of 1964.[4] These are established under the Roads and Road Traffic Act (Chapter 289), Section 64, by the Minister of Roads. Each Road Council is composed of a chairman appointed by the Minister and six elected members. The franchise is somewhat limited as the qualifications are either ownership of land within the area of the Council, ownership of a mine within the area,[5] the holding of a dealer's licence for that area, or ownership of a public service vehicle operating within the area, coupled in the last case with residence in that area.[6]

The main purpose of such Councils is that they have power to make roads and bridges in their areas,[7] and are entitled to levy rates for these purposes on those persons who have the voter's qualifications specified above.[8] The sums raised by Road Councils are supplemented by Government block grants and by a Government grant of three-quarters of the amount raised through local taxation.[9]

---

[1] Sections 53–56.   [2] Section 60.

[3] Annual Report of the Natural Resources Board of Southern Rhodesia 1964. C.S.R. 18–1965, Government Printer, Salisbury, pp. 2–3.

[4] Report of the Commissioner of Roads and Road Traffic 1964. C.S.R. 9–1965, Government Printer, Salisbury, p. 8.

[5] Only certain mines with a specified output and labour force come within this qualification.

[6] Section 68(1)

[7] Sections 28(2) and 31. Councils are not concerned with main roads, which are a Government responsibility.

[8] Section 90(2)(a).

[9] 54·25 per cent of Road Council funds came in 1963 from central Government sources.

It is clear from this outline that rural local government is little developed in Southern Rhodesia, but this is understandable in view of the smallness of the European population and its scattered character.

Recently the Government has introduced a policy of encouraging the creation of local authorities to cover the European rural areas, the basis of this extension being the concept of community development. As at the end of 1964 twenty-four advisory Local Government Commissions were in the process of establishment. Such Commissions are however appointed by the Minister of Local Government from nominations made through the District Commissioner and are merely advisory—'the idea being to give the Minister some notion of how they would like their affairs handled'.[1] Whether extensive powers will be entrusted to these nominated bodies is as yet unknown.

Local government in African rural areas

The historical background

The first suggestion that some form of local government[2] should be extended to Africans in the rural areas was made by the High Commissioner for South Africa prior to the framing of the 1923 Constitution and resulted in Section 47 of that Constitution, which permitted Native Councils to be established in any Native Reserve by the Governor in Council, subject to the approval of the High Commissioner. Such councils might discuss matters of direct interest to the native population generally and in addition the Governor in Council might make regulations 'conferring on such Council such powers of management in connection with local matters affecting indigenous natives as can in his opinion be safely and satisfactorily undertaken by them'.

In practice this Section of the Constitution was not invoked and although in 1929 the Moffat Government drafted a Native Councils Bill which they thought might be used in projected village settlements they intended to establish after the passage of the Land Apportionment Act, they did not proceed with this measure as it was found to conflict with Section 47 of the Constitution.[3]

Instead, in 1931 the Letters Patent were amended to permit the establishment of Councils in terms of the Constitution in Native Purchase Areas defined by the Land Apportionment Act and in any other area set apart for the use and occupation of natives. Again, this provision was not implemented.

---

[1] C.S.R. 19–1965, p. 5.

[2] It can be argued that local self-government existed and still exists in tribal areas in the form of 'Tribal Government'—see R. Howman, *African Local Government in British East and Central Africa*, op. cit., Part III, para. 186. In this Chapter, however, institutional local self-government with elective institutions is being examined.

[3] *Supra* Part I, Chapter 14.

However, from 1924 onwards the Native Affairs Department had established a system of meetings of Chiefs and Headmen with the Native Commissioner of their district to discuss matters of moment, the goal of the Department being to establish local native councils.[1] These informal consultative and advisory meetings with Native Commissioners continued until 1930, when, after a recommendation by a Native Affairs Departmental Committee, it was decided to establish Native Boards. Such Boards, the Chief Native Commissioner said, 'must be regarded as a preparatory step for the inauguration of the more formal Native Councils contemplated in the Constitution Letters Patent of the Colony'.[2]

Each district was to have a Board under the chairmanship of the Native Commissioner. Chiefs and Headmen would be *ex officio* members[3] and a number of elected members would be chosen 'by popular voice in such manner as the Native Commissioner may decide', such number not to be in excess of the number of *ex officio* members. In 1931 Native Boards were first established and by the end of 1932 the Chief Native Commissioner could report that in nearly all districts such Boards had been formed.[4] Eventually, in 1933, the constitution of these Boards was made more formal, although no statutory authority existed, and the Chief Native Commissioner circularized all Native Commissioners on the constitution and duties of Native Boards.[5] Such Boards were to 'advise the Government on all and any matters affecting the advancement, welfare or other interests of the native community . . . and the development of native reserves'. However, they were given no power to take any action, being merely consultative bodies. Nonetheless, Boards opened an opportunity of advancement to some Africans as it was laid down that the membership of Boards should include the secretary of the Board 'who shall be a native if a sufficiently qualified one be available'.[6]

In 1937 as part and parcel of the constitutional changes initiated in that year, the Native Councils Act was passed, while Section 47 was eliminated from the 1923 Constitution. The Councils so established were composed of all Chiefs[7] and Headmen, and so many other indigenous natives residing within the area of any Council as might be appointed by the Governor, provided that before such nomination

[1] Report of the Chief Native Commissioner, Salisbury, for the year 1924, C.S.R. 7–1925, Government Printer, p. 2.

[2] Chief Native Commissioner's circular letter No. C.559/4464/N. of 16 September 1930.

[3] These two categories were to receive a small Government subsidy but this was not because of their Board membership but rather because of their other administrative duties.

[4] Report of the Chief Native Commissioner for the year 1932, C.S.R. 9–1933. Government Printer, Salisbury.

[5] Chief Native Commissioner's Circular No. 43. Annexure to Addendum of 17 May 1933.

[6] Ibid., para. 4(b).

[7] The purpose of the Prime Minister in passing this Act and a companion Act, the Native Law and Courts Act, was 'to restore authority to the Chiefs and to educate the Africans in administration . . . .. If we are successful with Native Councils I anticipate that the Chief's

the natives of the area shall be given an opportunity to nominate any suitable person to represent their interests and a complete list of persons so nominated shall be submitted to the Governor, together with the recommendations of the Native Commissioner and the Chief Native Commissioner thereon.[1]

Even though appointed for terms not in excess of two years, the nominated members' offices were terminable at the Governor's pleasure. Owing to these new provisions the elective element in the old Boards was perhaps greater than it was in the case of the later formal Councils.[2] The local Native Commissioner was to be chairman of any Council, was to preside at its meetings, and was to act in an advisory capacity to it. He was vested with all the executive powers of the Council.[3] Councils were further subject to control in that the Chief Native Commissioner might attend any meetings of a Council and address it, while all appointments to a Council and their tenure, and approval of, amendment of, and repeal of all Council by-laws were at the mercy of the Governor, who was also vested with further considerable regulatory powers and might abolish a Council at any time.

However, the potential powers of the Councils were far greater than those of the Boards. They might construct and maintain roads and bridges, conserve and augment water supplies, engage in soil conservation, provide facilities for education, and generally take action in public health questions and matters affecting conservation and natural resources. In addition, in respect of such matters they might make by-laws,[4] although these might be amended and added to by the Governor if he thought it 'advisable and not opposed to the true spirit and intent of the by-law as submitted by the Council'. All by-laws required his approval and he might at any time repeal a by-law.[5]

However, the Councils established under the Act were unable to exercise their powers in practice because they were given no financial powers, their only revenue consisting of any grants which might be made to them, and of

authority, guided by his elders, will pass into the hands of the Chief subject to the advice of his elected Council', quoted in 'Government of Southern Rhodesia: Confidential Survey of Native Policy, 1950'. Unpublished, p. 33.

[1] Native Councils Act (Chapter 74), Section 4(1).

[2] The Native Department in the '1950 Confidential Survey' at p. 40, stated that in practice the later system was no less democratic than the other and that all persons voted for by the local inhabitants were thereafter nominated to Councils except on the grounds that a particular person was unqualified or was at the bottom of the poll and that to have appointed him would have made the number of Council members excessive.

[3] Chapter 74 of 1939, Section 5(1).

[4] Act 38 of 1937, Sections 6 and 7(1).

[5] Section 7(3) and (4). In practice it was extremely difficult to pass by-laws as they had 'to survive the scrutiny of the law officers and run the gauntlet of the Government up to the Governor and Executive Council before they were finally gazetted'. Delays were sometimes interminable. A leading Native Commissioner instanced the Mrewa (Chitowa) Native Purchase Area Council By-laws suggested on 17 November 1949, submitted by the Native Commissioner on 4 January 1950, gazetted on 15 December 1950, and commented 'no local authority can maintain an interest in such circumstances': Howman, op. cit., Part I, para. 49.

donations and fees.[1] Indeed at the end of 1940 when twenty-three such Councils had been established, the Chief Native Commissioner wrote that the Councils did not differ greatly from the Boards and that the point of difference was that whereas Boards could merely discuss matters Councils *could* progress to local government status.[2] Similarly, Lord Hailey, writing a confidential report for the United Kingdom and Southern Rhodesian Governments on Southern Rhodesia, considered that Councils were not functioning properly as they were suffering from financial paralysis.[3] The position was somewhat changed in 1943 by the passage of legislation empowering Native Councils to impose taxation on certain adult males in order to obtain funds to carry out schemes which fell within the scope of their powers.[4] These powers were further amended in 1949 and by the end of that year there were fifty-eight Councils in existence, forty-one of which were imposing taxation.[5]

Nonetheless, loan funds were not made available to Native Councils and even in respect of revenue only if Councils decided to impose taxes were central Government grants made available to them in proportion to the amounts raised voluntarily. A noteworthy feature of the attachment of Councils to the administration is the fact that in 1955 over twenty-five per cent of the members of Councils were still Chiefs or Headmen.[6]

Yet another interesting point is that although in 1929 the Southern Rhodesia Government had envisaged establishing Councils in native village settlements to be established near the European urban centres, when Highfield, near Salisbury, was established in 1937 and Luveve near Bulawayo in 1936 they were not given Native Councils. Even at the end of 1964 Government African townships had no formal local governmental bodies composed of local inhabitants.

Despite the increase in power of Councils, they were for the most part an

---

[1] Chapter 74 of 1939, Section 10(1).

[2] Report of the Chief Native Commissioner for the year 1940, C.S.R. 13–1941. Government Printer, Salisbury, p. 11.

[3] National Archives S.235/482, Confidential Report by Lord Hailey in 1940, on Southern Rhodesia, p. 17.

[4] Act No. 25 of 1943.

[5] Taxes imposed by Councils vary. Most impose a dog tax (in which case no dog tax is payable to the central Government). They may also impose a poll tax of £1 (or more) on adult male land holders and this is usually done in Purchase Area Councils. Others impose a vehicle licence fee on bicycles and animal drawn vehicles. Yet others impose fees for dipping services: see e.g. S.R.G.N. 413 of 1956, and S.R.G.N. 17 of 1955 for typical Native Council by-laws, the former being passed by a Native Council in the Marirangwe Purchase Area and the latter by that in the Ndanga Reserve. Other Council revenue comes from water rates, hire charges for transport, school fees, rentals of leased premises, and milling and hulling fees.

[6] See R. Howman, 'Chiefs and Headmen in Southern Rhodesia', in *From Tribal Rule to Modern Government*, ed. R. Apthorp, Rhodes-Livingstone Institute, Lusaka, 1959 at p. 45. In 1955 there were 218 Chiefs and headmen who were members of Councils and nearly 600 elected members.

unsuccessful experiment. Accordingly in 1957, as it was felt that a new approach must be adopted so that the Councils would be identified with the wishes and desires of the African community, the Legislature passed a new Native Councils Act.[1] The principles underlying the Act were those of 'community development', which has subsequently been adopted by the Whitehead, Field, and Smith Governments as their 'philosophy' of local government.[2] In fact, a Project Agreement was entered into between Southern Rhodesia and the United States Government, as a result of which Southern Rhodesia received assistance for this purpose from the Agency for International Development.[3]

Before any Council may be established under the Act

the Minister shall cause enquiries to be made and shall have satisfied himself that there is among the inhabitants of the area concerned a general wish that the Council shall be established.[4]

while in establishing the Council the Minister shall have regard to

(a) the needs and community interests of the inhabitants of the area or areas concerned; (b) the financial resources which shall be available to the council or councils by way of rating or otherwise; and (c) the physical features and natural resources of the area or areas.

Having established the Council, the Minister confers powers on it by warrant, but in so doing he must not only have regard to the matters above mentioned, but must also consider whether an Act or thing being done by a Council is likely to

(a) foster the sense of community and citizenship of the inhabitants of the area; (b) promote initiative and a sense of responsibility; or (c) promote the development of the economic progress of the area with the active participation of the inhabitants.

The Act also establishes an African Councils Board to advise the Minister of Internal Affairs as to the exercise of his powers under the Act and gives it power to investigate Council matters if directed to do so by the Minister.[5]

---

[1] Act No. 19 of 1957.

[2] Community development as it is known in Pakistan, Ghana, and other underdeveloped countries is intended by this phrase. Unfortunately the term has in recent years in Southern Rhodesia been employed by politicians of various parties including members of the governing party in such a way that it has become suspect. Indeed, if the policy is applied in a particular way it has been considered capable of leading to apartheid and 'polite Bantustans'. See the Report of the Secretary for Internal Affairs for the year 1960, C.S.R. 16–1964, p. 6, for comment on public confusion and 'misrepresentation' on this subject.

[3] This assistance was normally in the form of training of personnel. The Southern Rhodesian Government has established the Community Development Training School for African Officers at Domboshowa.

[4] Section 9 of the African Councils Act (Chapter 95).

[5] Act 19, 1957, Section 5. The Board is bound to review and report on the system from time to time and such reports to the Minister must be laid before Parliament: Section 6. The Board's reports are published at the back of the Secretary for Internal Affairs' Annual

44—C.H.L.S.R.

The Board is composed of the Secretary for Internal Affairs as Chairman and one other officer of the Department of Internal Affairs nominated by the Minister, an officer of the Treasury nominated by the Minister of Finance, one by the Minister of Local Government, and any others nominated by the Minister of Internal Affairs.

After advice by the Board, the Minister may by notice in the Gazette establish Councils and the areas for which they can act. He may in his discretion confer on them powers to make by-laws for all or any of the purposes for which a Town Council or Town Management Board may make by-laws or regulations. He may confer similar powers to levy licence charges and fees for services rendered and, subject to such restrictions or modifications as he considers necessary, may confer all or any of the powers enjoyed by such bodies on a Native Council.[1] After establishment the power of, composition of, and franchise for Native Councils are set out in a warrant issued, revocable and amendable by the Secretary for Internal Affairs under the directions of the Minister.[2]

As before all Chiefs and Headmen are members unless the latter are specifically excluded by the warrant, while Chiefs are also *ex officio* vice-presidents of these Councils unless it is specifically directed otherwise. However, the local District Commissioner is still president of every Council and until warrants provide otherwise is also Chairman. In 1964 in twenty-five of the fifty-two Councils then functioning there was provision for an African chairman.[3] The franchise is also determined by the warrant but in practice adult taxpayers in the area are permitted to vote,[4] while the qualifications for candidates are equated to those of voters.[5] Normal disqualifications relative to convictions, and election offences are also prescribed.

A noticeable feature of the new Councils Act is that an attempt has been made to associate the traditional authorities more closely with the local Councils. Not only are Chiefs and Headmen members as was formerly

Report, but since the Secretary for Internal Affairs is Chairman of the Board, they are really *addenda* to his Report.

[1] Section 7. No Native Council has as yet been entrusted with these extensive powers.

[2] Section 11.

[3] Report of the Secretary for Internal Affairs for the year 1963, C.S.R. 16–1964, p. 86. Warrants vary considerably. In the Native Purchase Area Councils are composed of six to twelve members and only two of these Councils have Chiefs or Headmen on them. In the Tribal Trust Land Councils contain as many as twenty-four members and in the largest Council of twenty-four members there are four Chiefs and ten Headmen.

[4] In general in the Tribal Trust Land the voters' qualifications are specified merely as being an inhabitant of the area, although women are generally excluded, whereas in Native Purchase Areas it is only owners or lessees who qualify for a vote. This information was obtained from Mrs. G. Passmore, who has prepared a detailed summary of 'Local Government Legislation in Southern Rhodesia', and has been kind enough to allow me to use her manuscript.

[5] Section 38 provides that the District Commissioner may nominate Council members if insufficient candidates offer themselves for election. This power was used in the Mangwende Reserve in recent years.

provided but a duty has now been imposed on Chiefs to attend Council meetings.[1] Chiefs, Headmen and Kraalheads are identified with the Council by being bound to publish all Council by-laws, directions and notices, by being charged with the collection of all rates and fees imposed by the Council, by being charged with enforcement of Council by-laws and by being bound to enforce communal services provided for in such by-laws.[2]

This attempt to make Councils in the tribal areas work closely with the tribal leaders has been occasioned by earlier conflicts and suspicions between traditional leaders and elected councillors which had resulted in the refusal of some Chiefs to allow the establishment of local government in their areas.[3]

It should be noted that within the African rural areas are several ' African townships' where purely African 'urban' centres have been artificially laid aside for the acquisition by Africans of stands with registered freehold title for residential, trading or industrial purposes.[4]

Some of these townships fall within the area of Native Councils but they have not had a noticeable effect on the composition of Councils, because they have remained small and undeveloped, partly owing to the artificiality of their creation.[5]

Study of the African Councils Act shows that the Act is in reality an elaborate enabling Act, which sets out at length model provisions for the proceeding of Councils, for appointment of Council officers, for strict financial control and audit of accounts,[6] and numerous other provisions for the grant of permissive powers to Councils and the methods of control exercisable by Government. In fact as has been partly indicated the Administration still retains considerable control over the Councils, quite apart from its power to establish and abolish them. It may define the powers of Councils, narrowly or widely delegating by-law making powers. The Governor approves, repeals, and amends by-laws. The Minister defines the rate-making powers of Councils.

[1] Act 19 of 1957, Section 15(3).

[2] Section 61 allows Councils to declare by resolution that work for minor undertakings shall be provided on a communal basis, and to pass by-laws requiring able-bodied inhabitants to provide such service for a period not exceeding six days in any quarter. This has not been invoked in practice. In addition Section 62 authorizes discharge of obligations to pay rates or fees by doing communal work instead.

[3] C.S.R. 39–1965, p. 28. Comment by the Secretary of Internal Affairs is apt: 'the problem is a universal one in all societies with institutions of inherited leadership'. He also stated that in African Purchase Areas, where the society was more individualistic, there were no complications due to the presence of traditional authorities and that the Council system had been better received.

[4] This was first authorized by Section 12 of Act 11 of 1941.

[5] Report of the Urban African Affairs Commission 1958, p. 56. In 1958 there were six such townships, only three of which had developed to any extent, these three being dormitories for Salisbury, Bulawayo, and Umtali.

[6] Depending on the Council's warrant, estimates must be prepared and approved by the Native Councils Board or a person nominated by the Board: Section 80(1). If the warrant does not direct the preparation of estimates, no expenditure can be incurred without a resolution by the Council and the approval of the District Commissioner: Section 81(1).

The District Commissioner is still normally president and also chairman. The Provincial Commissioner may appoint a vice-chairman for the Council. The Secretary for Internal Affairs may attend and speak at any Council meeting. The Minister may rescind any rates passed by the Council and levy any rates if he considers it necessary (as may the District Commissioner in certain circumstances). The Minister may make regulations for numerous purposes relative, amongst others, to qualifications of voters and candidates, electors, Council business, duties of Council employees, financial procedure and Council contracts, while the Native Councils Board has supervisory power in respect of Council estimates which it must approve.

Special provision for auditing and inspection of Council books is also made, and these must be open at all reasonable times to inspection by Internal Affairs Department officials. There is a necessity for Councils to establish proper reserves and sinking funds, and, where no estimates are necessary, the cash books of the Council must be produced at every meeting.

Despite this new enabling Act, the Council system has not worked well. The Chief Native Commissioner reported in 1960 that 'the very existence of Councils is threatened' and subsequently the whole system was scrutinized by the Robinson and Mangwende Reserve Commissions, although they considered the Act provided ideal machinery.[1] Quite apart from the fact that the Act was implemented at the worst possible time, when rural African dissatisfaction was at a maximum,[2] difficulties have arisen because the position of Chiefs in relation to their Councils and to the Native Commissioners has been unsatisfactorily defined so that conflicts have developed.[3] Since these

---

[1] C.S.R. 22–1961—the Robinson Report—and Report of the Mangwende Reserve Commission of Enquiry (Mimeographed).

[2] The Mangwende Report in para. 117 found that probably 'the greatest set-back which the new Native Councils Act could possibly suffer was that its proclamation fell in the period when all available administrative staff were marshalled for the speediest possible implementation of the Land Husbandry Act'. The latter was an Act designed to prevent fragmentation of African held land and to place, by the allocation of individual farming and grazing rights, the responsibility for the essential conservation of land and water on individually accountable people. The Act though agronomically ideal 'has become one of the most contentious matters passed by the Southern Rhodesia Parliament and a target for bitter attack from the African side. One reason is that the Act completely ignores (if not deliberately rejects) the customary basis of African land tenure, for instance by introducing the principle of individual _and negotiable_ rights to strictly demarcated registered holdings. Another reason is, that during its wholesale implementation, the tide of industrial prosperity, which could have provided expanding horizons, turned. Instead, a recession took place which left many with the unhappy sense of insecurity of not knowing from where to derive their immediate and future livelihood': Mangwende Report, para. 78. In the Mangwende Reserve 'more than two-fifths _of the adult males_ who had documentary proof of their membership of a rural village community, _have been rendered landless by these allocations_': Mangwende Report, para. 411 (Commission's underlinings).

[3] See Report of the Secretary for Native Affairs and Chief Native Commissioner for the year 1959, C.S.R. 18–1960, pp. 158–9 for conflict resulting from the confused position of Chief and Council. The Mangwende Report, paras. 177–82 commented on the friction resulting from the juxtaposition of Chiefs and Native Commissioners on Native Councils,

Reports Government policy has been to enhance the status of Chiefs further and measures to this end are in preparation.[1]

At the end of 1964 only fifty-two Councils were in existence,[2] seven having been abolished 'due to lack of interest' between 1961 and 1962. A further three are providing no services to the public, and four more 'although moribund', continue to provide such things as firearms and Council halls but spend no money on providing services.[3] Indeed, Councils only cover approximately half the African population in the rural areas.[4]

The only other form of local government that exists in African rural areas is the Intensive Conservation Area Committee, of which there were at the end of 1963, forty-six in operation.[5]

The future of local government in African rural areas is uncertain, as according to the Secretary for Native Affairs in his capacity as chairman of the Native Councils Board, the continued existence of Councils was threatened. Although subsequently he felt that the Councils, 'which like withering yellow plants appeared to be dying off, are showing signs of revival',[6] there is little concrete to show any change. At the end of 1964 he still felt there was 'no reason for undue optimism and that the road ahead would be a long, and very hard one'.[7]

Local government in African urban areas

In urban areas there were no traditional authorities to control those Africans who originally came as migratory labourers to the towns. Even when numbers of Africans became permanent town dwellers no provision

while the Robinson Report, p. 21, found that some Chiefs regarded Councils as a threat to their own authority and wished them to be advisory to the Chief.

[1] Report of the Secretary for Internal Affairs and Chief Native Commissioner for the year 1962, C.S.R. 27–1963, Government Printer, Salisbury, p. 7. These laws will give Chiefs and Headmen 'a much greater part to play in the control and allocation of tribal land and in the advising and adjudication of their system of tribal law and custom'.

[2] A peak of sixty-one Councils was reached in 1959: C.S.R. 18–1960, pp. 161–2.

[3] C.S.R. 27–1963, p. 90. This was still the position in October 1964: S.R.L.A.D., Vol. 58, col. 1715, 14 October 1964.

[4] Howman, op. cit., Part II, para. 156(f). The number of Councils has not increased since the time when Howman wrote, so the same position obtains.

[5] C.S.R. 27–1964, p. 3.

[6] C.S.R. 16–1964, p. 89. However, the Secretary made a revival conditional on encouragement and assistance by Government, the provision of adequate finance, local leadership, and a sense of responsibility.

[7] C.S.R. 39–1965, p. 27. He urged that 'unless responsibility for such services as primary education, minor health facilities, feeder roads and secondary water supplies were vested in local government we can never expect to see Councils established on a firm and enduring basis'. Clear cut decisions on the financial support to be given to Councils was most urgent as 'Councils cannot be expected to assume additional responsibilities without knowing how they can face them': C.S.R. 39–1965, pp. 28–29. For the year ending 30 June 1966, all African Councils and Community Boards will receive in toto £40,000 by way of grants from the central authorities: C.S.R. 21–1965, p. 97.

was made either to place them under any tribal authority or to allow them some local self-government—they remained under the control of either the central administration or of the European municipalities and Town Management Boards which had established African townships.

The only method of conveying the opinions of the African location dwellers to the administering authorities was through the African location Headmen first appointed by the Administrator and subsequently by the Governor under Section 9(1)(a) of the Native Urban Locations Ordinance No. 4 of 1906.[1] Depending upon the character of the particular appointee, a Headman might serve as an intermediary between the inhabitants and the European local authority.

Much later certain Councils introduced informal Advisory Boards. Thus in 1940 the Bulawayo Municipality established an Advisory Board for its first and oldest township.[2] According to the Native Affairs Department other informal Advisory Boards as channels for communication of grievances were also in operation.[3]

The need for some participation in urban local government was eventually recognized by the Legislature in 1946 and the Natives (Urban Areas) Accommodation and Registration Act provided that in every native residential area the local authority was to establish a Native Advisory Board, which was to consist of not less than three natives resident within the area in addition to a chairman who might be European or African. The Act, however, only applied to African residential areas under the control of the municipalities or of the Town Management Boards and did not apply to Government townships or to those of statutory undertakings. Indeed, even at the end of 1964 both of the latter categories of townships were still without any form of local government available to their inhabitants.[4] In the local authority townships, however, Advisory Boards have been functioning since 1946.

The franchise and candidates' qualifications for Advisory Boards have been laid down by the Governor. These qualify occupiers of property who have resided in the area for a continuous period of twelve months and are not in arrears with their rent, providing they have not been sentenced during the

---

[1] Associations have been formed from time to time from the beginning of this century to give expression to African views, but these were not formally recognized and were discouraged by the authorities.

[2] Representation in Local Government in the Area under the Jurisdiction of the City of Bulawayo. February 1963, City of Bulawayo. Mimeographed, p. 1. In 1930, a Report of Enquiry into the Bulawayo location had recommended the creation of such Boards: see National Archives S.235/477 and 478.

[3] 'Confidential Survey of Native Policy 1950,' p. 56. The Native Affairs Department considered African welfare societies and tribal societies more suitable for this purpose. It thought that the Federation of African Welfare Societies, which was largely directed by Europeans, was the ideal body to make representations on behalf of Africans.

[4] At the end of 1964, there were thirty-three African townships administered in this fashion by the central Government: C.S.R. 19–1965, p. 5.

preceding three years either to imprisonment without the option of a fine or to a period of imprisonment in excess of three months with such option.[1] The number of Board members to be elected by these voters is determined by and the chairman is appointed by the local authority.[2] In practice the chairmen are city councillors.[3]

The functions of these Boards are to consider and report on

Any by-laws or regulations which the local authority proposes to make or apply under the provisions of Section 67 of the Local Government Act; any matter referred to it by the Minister or by the local authority; and any matter specially affecting the interests of Africans in the local authority area upon which the Board may consider it useful or desirable to report.[4]

The Board may also recommend to the local authority

the making or the application of any by-laws or regulations which it considers necessary or desirable in the interest of the Africans in the African residential area.[5]

Copies of any report by the Board are to be transmitted to the Governor when any by-laws or regulations are submitted to him for approval.

In addition to the duties imposed on them by the Act, it is the duty of Board members

to interest themselves in the welfare of the residents of the area and to acquaint themselves with and advise the residents of the area of any laws applicable to such area.[6]

However, as Salisbury's Director of African Administration stated in his 1963 Annual Report

the 'Advisory' Board system as has previously been stated is an outmoded mechanism. The fact that the body is 'advisory' carries with it no responsibility and any actions taken by the governing body, viz. the Council itself, if unpopular or contentious, are never the concern of the Board, even though the Board itself may have supported a particular policy. Attempts have been made at administrative level to delegate more responsibilities to the Board but unless there is an enlightened and dynamic approach to this matter, it is more than conceivable that 1964 will see the end of these Boards.[7]

[1] See S.R.G.N. 524 of 1952. Natives (Urban Areas) Advisory Board Regulations 1952, Section 6.
[2] e.g. the Harare Advisory Board in Salisbury has eight members and a chairman with a casting vote only.
[3] In Salisbury the councillor chosen is usually the chairman of the African Administration Committee and in Bulawayo the chairman of the Housing and Amenities Committee. A vice-chairman shall also be appointed by and hold office during the pleasure of the local authority. In Bulawayo the practice has been to allow the vice-chairman to be elected by the Board. Information from Mrs. Passmore, op. cit.
[4] Chapter 110, Section 35(4).
[5] Chapter 110, Section 35(5).
[6] Natives (Urban Areas) Advisory Board Regulations 1952, Section 11.
[7] Annual Report of the Director of African Administration for the year ending 30 June 1963, City of Salisbury, 1963, Mimeographed, p. 62, para. 307.

These words are borne out by the complete failure of the Advisory Board system in Bulawayo, where all six Boards have resigned,[1] and in Salisbury where only one out of three Boards is functioning. In fact, out of thirteen Boards in six municipalities, seven were not working in 1964.[2]

These purely consultative bodies have not met the need for local government,[3] while since the Advisory Board franchise is open to many Africans, Board elections have become obvious occasions on which African nationalist groups can demonstrate their strength.

African advisory bodies

Although Africans by virtue of the system of government are unable to take any considerable part in central or in local government, it would be misleading not to give a picture of the role played by African advisory bodies which have recently been established by the Government to advise it on matters affecting the African population. These bodies are the recently formalized Provincial Assemblies of Chiefs and the Council of Chiefs.

From 1951 onwards the Native Affairs Department adopted the policy of holding regular Provincial Chiefs' Assemblies. By 1959 these Assemblies were meeting two or three times a year and putting forward proposals for legislative and administrative change to the Native Affairs Department.[4]

In 1961, at the joint insistence of Mr. Duncan Sandys, Secretary of State for Commonwealth Relations and that of Sir Edgar Whitehead who was then Prime Minister,[5] a national assembly of Chiefs, the Council of Chiefs,

[1] Bulawayo, of all Southern Rhodesian municipalities, gave most encouragement to her Boards, consulting them closely on the framing of estimates and accepting Board recommendations on details on the estimates. The failure of the Boards must be explained on political grounds.

[2] *S.R.L.A.D.*, Vol. 58, col. 676, 23 September 1964. This shows the existence of only thirteen Boards. However, according to the report of Salisbury's Director of African Administration, there was in 1963 another Board in Salisbury, that for Mufakose Township. The Director stated: 'There was a complete boycott in respect of Mufakose and Mabvuku and no nominations nor elections were held for either of these townships . . .. There were obvious political pressures.': para. 306.

[3] The central Government has acknowledged this: 'It is generally recognized that the advisory board system which has hitherto been followed has outlived its usefulness. An advisory body, without executive and decision making functions, will rarely develop a proper sense of responsibility': Report of the Secretary for Local Government and Housing for the year ended 31 December 1964. C.S.R. 19–1965, p. 13.

[4] Report of the Secretary for Native Affairs and the Chief Native Commissioner for the year 1959, C.S.R. 18–1960, p. 17. According to the Chief Native Commissioner, amendments to the Native Affairs Act in 1959 which restricted public meetings in Tribal Trust Land were requested by the Chiefs.

[5] Confidential Memorandum by the Secretary for Internal Affairs for the Parliamentary Committee Investigating the Method of Consultation of African Opinion on the Independence Issue. September 1964. See also *The Dombashawa 'Indaba'*, op. cit., para. 29, where it is stated that Mr. Sandys insisted on the enactment of legislation providing for the formal establishment of a Council of Chiefs and for Provincial Assemblies of Chiefs.

was established.[1] In fact, the Council of Chiefs, although not part of the Constitution, is assumed to exist in a number of constitutional provisions which make reference to it.[2]

Shortly before its formal establishment the Government had arranged for a meeting of all the Chiefs and their Headmen in May 1961 at Gwelo,[3] where after two days of discussions the Chiefs drew up a list of resolutions which were presented to the Prime Minister.[4] It was then agreed to establish a national Council of Chiefs. The Chiefs also elected twenty-one Chiefs as an Interim Council which met in May and October 1961.

The Council of Chiefs and Provincial Assemblies Act subsequently established the national Chiefs' Council and provided for an Assembly of the Chiefs in each province.

These 'provinces' were to be determined by the Minister on the recommendations of the Inaugural Council elected at Gwelo, which would recommend the division of all the Tribal Trust Land of Southern Rhodesia into seven provinces.[5] The provinces were eventually defined in 1962.[6]

---

[1] See the Council of Chiefs and Provincial Assemblies Act No. 58 of 1961.

[2] Although the Council of Chiefs is not part of the Constitution, its President is a member of the electoral college to elect the Constitutional Council (Section 80(1)(c)) and the Council of Chiefs appoints a Chief as a member of the Board of Trustees of Tribal Trust Land (Section 94(1)(a)). The President of the Council of Chiefs also participated in the election of the first members of the Constitutional Council (Order in Council, Section 13(2)(d)). Southern Rhodesia's two leading Ndebele Chiefs and one Shona chief, Chief Enoch Mangwende (who owes his position to a Government appointment when ex-Chief Mangwende was deposed) are on constitutional bodies. Chief Kaisa Ndiweni was elected to the Constitutional Council and Chief Simon Sigola was nominated by the Governor to the Board of Trustees of Tribal Trust Land. Chief Sigola has also been nominated by Government to a non-constitutional body, the Natural Resources Board, while Chief Mangwende was elected by the Chiefs to the Board of Trustees for Tribal Trust Land.

[3] Over 500 Chiefs and Headmen attended: Report of the Secretary for Native Affairs for the year 1961. C.S.R. 28–1962, p. 16. The meeting was not open to Members of Parliament, except to the Leader of the Opposition for a short period: S.R.L.A.D., Vol. 59, col. 710, 29 October, 1964.

[4] Legislation which, according to the Chief Native Commissioner, was repealed on Chiefly requests made on these occasions, was the Natives Adultery Act, which had made adultery by Africans liable to criminal penalties, and the removal of a £20 ceiling on lobola transactions. One has some scepticism about the origin of the requests. Certainly no repeals would have been effected if this had been contrary to Government policy.

[5] 'Provinces' under the Council of Chiefs and Provincial Assemblies Act are not to be confused with the 'provinces' established in terms of the General Administration Act No. 19 of 1962, which divides the whole of Southern Rhodesia into provinces and districts. S.R.G.N. 254 and 255 of 1963, issued in terms of the General Administration Act, divided Southern Rhodesia into seven provinces and a total of fifty districts within those provinces. Thus Government Departments are regionally organized within the various provinces, e.g. in the Department of Internal Affairs there are Provincial Commissioners, while magistrates in the Department of Justice have jurisdiction in a particular province. However, the seven 'provinces' of Tribal Trust Land coincide with the seven administrative provinces to the extent that each falls within the administrative province of the same name, but merely consists of the Tribal Trust Land in such administrative province.

[6] S.R.G.N. 474/62. Council of Chiefs and Provincial Assemblies General Regulations 1962. The provinces are Matabeleland South, Matabeleland North, Mashonaland South, Mashonaland North, Victoria, Manicaland, and Midlands.

The Provincial Assemblies were first to meet in November 1962,[1] and thereafter at least twice a year, so that a six-month period should not intervene between the conclusion of one and the commencement of the next meeting. This provision was subsequently amended so that the Provincial Assemblies need meet only once a year.[2] However, one-third of the number of Chiefs in any province may requisition the Minister to call a meeting.

The functions of these Provincial Assemblies are both electoral and advisory. Each Provincial Assembly must elect a number of its members to be members of the Council of Chiefs this number being prescribed by the Minister of Internal Affairs.[3] Assemblies must also consider and report on any matters referred to them by the Minister, the Trustees for Tribal Trust Land, the Council of Chiefs or a member of the particular Assembly. Each Assembly is also

responsible for bringing to the notice of the Council of Chiefs any matter of national interest and to the notice of the Minister any matter of local interest which affects the inhabitants of the province or any part thereof which concerns their interests or well being.[4]

The Chiefs' Council at present consists of twenty-six Chiefs[5] elected by the Provincial Assemblies and holding office for five years, while retiring Chiefs are eligible for re-election. The Council meets twice yearly without an interval of more than six months between meetings, and similar provision to that applicable to Provincial Assemblies exists for Chiefs to requisition a meeting.

The Chiefs at their first meeting in November 1962, elected a President, Chief Shumba Chekayi. There was originally no provision for the removal of the President. However, Chief Shumba subsequently signed a petition to be forwarded to the Queen opposing independence for Southern Rhodesia under a Government elected by a minority of the population. When the Council of Chiefs met in May 1963, Chief Shumba was required to resign as President. Various allegations have been made ranging from a report that the Ndebele Chiefs refused to participate in the Council so long as he was President,[6] to a Government statement that the other Chiefs no longer wanted him as President, as they did not want the Council of Chiefs to be involved in politics.[7]

---

[1] S.R.G.N. 474/62, Section 3.   [2] Act 58 of 1963, Section 2.

[3] A total of twenty-six Chiefs in all are elected, the seven provinces above electing 4, 3, 4, 3, 5, 4, and 3 Chiefs respectively, seven coming from the Ndebele areas. Section 6(1) requires the Minister to prescribe 'equitable representation for each province with due regard to the total number of tribesmen in each province'. However, there seems to be a disproportionate number of Ndebele Chiefs having regard to their smaller population and smaller number of taxpayers. Personal communication from Dr. Kingsley Garbett who has been doing an analysis of the prominent part played by Ndebele Chiefs.

[4] Council of Chiefs and Provincial Assemblies Act (Chapter 111), Section 5(3).

[5] This is the number prescribed by the Minister by S.R.G.N. 474 of 1962.

[6] African Daily News, 23 May 1963.

[7] Rhodesia Herald, 25 May 1963, reporting a statement from the Southern Rhodesia Information Department. It will be noted that Chief Shumba opposed independence under the present Constitution. The Council of Chiefs apparently did not in October 1964 think

Soon thereafter the Act was amended to provide that 'the president or the deputy president of the Council may be removed from office by a majority vote of the members of the Council present at a meeting of the Council'.[1]

Both the Minister and the Board of Trustees for Tribal Trust Land are entitled to nominate representatives who may put forward their views at meetings of the Council of Chiefs or at Provincial Assemblies. All meetings of the Chiefs whether at Provincial Assemblies or in Council of Chiefs are to be held in private,[2] except for the right of the Minister or his representative to attend, but not to vote at such meetings.[3]

The Minister has considerable regulatory power relative to these bodies and may make regulations providing for committees of Provincial Assemblies, procedural matters, quorums, etc.

Major powers of affecting the composition of the Assemblies are also given the Minister allowing him to prescribe the disqualifications for membership of a Provincial Assembly and the Council of Chiefs, the circumstances in which vacation of office in a Provincial Assembly or the Council of Chiefs shall occur and to provide for the filling of vacancies in membership.[4] The Minister has further powers whereby he may prescribe allowances for the Chiefs and he has utilized these in respect of the Council.[5] He also has a residual regulatory power 'to enable the Council of Chiefs to carry out any function or duty which may be conferred or imposed upon it under any other law'.[6]

The functions of the Council of Chiefs are

to make representations to the Minister with regard to the needs and wishes of the tribesmen living on Tribal Trust Land; to consider any representation made to it by a Provincial Assembly and in its discretion to report thereon to the Minister; and

that support for independence involved them in politics. See *infra*, Chapter 7. The Report of the Secretary for Internal Affairs for 1963, C.S.R. 16–1964, at p. 5, merely states that Chief Shumba tendered his resignation. In *S.R.L.A.D.*, Vol. 54, at col. 187, 29 August 1963, the responsible Minister gave the explanation that the Chief gave press interviews without securing the approval of the Council.

[1] Act 58 of 1963, Section 3. The words 'present at a meeting' may be important. At the same time as the clash with Chief Shumba several African Chiefs from Manicaland were unceremoniously sent back to their homes after disagreements with Government. These Chiefs, however, were not members of the Council of Chiefs. See *African Daily News*, 23 May 1963 and *S.R.L.A.D.*, Vol. 54, cols. 180 et seq., 29 August 1963.

[2] It is an offence for a person to interrupt their proceedings or to refuse to leave a meeting of Chiefs, either in Provincial Assembly or in Council, when requested to do so: Section 14(1)(2).

[3] A savings clause provides that meetings may be held even if the Minister or his representative are not present: Section 12(4).

[4] Section 15(1)(f)(g)(h).

[5] S.R.G.N. 750 of 1964 provides for a small salary for the members of the Council of Chiefs and special allowances for Chiefs when on Government business.

[6] Section 15(j)

to consider and report on any matter referred to it by the Minister or the Board of Trustees for consideration.[1]

Already there has been a change in the Government conception of the role to be played by the Council of Chiefs. When it was established in 1961 the Secretary for Native Affairs declared that 'there is no intention of turning Chiefs into politicians nor of establishing the Chiefs' Council as a political body',[2] but two Ministers have subsequently declared that the Chiefs are by law required 'to concern themselves with politics' and that 'there is a part in politics which must be played necessarily by the Chiefs'.[3] In fact the Council of Chiefs was allowed to meet the Lord Chancellor, Lord Gardiner, and Mr. Bottomley, the Commonwealth Relations Secretary, in March 1965, to demand from them, independence for Southern Rhodesia under the present Constitution, and to condemn the African nationalist movement.[4]

The future of the Council of Chiefs is assured under the present Government. Indeed the questions still to be decided are whether additional functions will be conferred upon the Council and whether it will be converted from the merely advisory body it at present is, to a body exercising more extensive powers. This will depend on constitutional and policy changes introduced by the Southern Rhodesian Government.[5]

Changes in the status of the Council of Chiefs have been mooted, either in the direction of turning the Council into a second chamber of the Legislative Assembly (which would require an Order in Council) or by substituting fifteen seats to be filled by representatives elected by the Chiefs for the fifteen electoral districts (this would require only a two-thirds majority of the Legislative Assembly).

The Southern Rhodesian Government has recently stated that

after independence, the Government would like to see Chiefs represented in Parliament so that they can reflect the views of the ordinary people and so assist in the making of laws. Any change in the Constitution of Rhodesia will be carried out

[1] Council of Chiefs and Provincial Assemblies Act (Chapter 111), Section 8.

[2] Report of the Secretary for Native Affairs and Chief Native Commissioner for the year 1961. C.S.R. 28–1962, p. 2. See also *S.R.L.A.D.*, Vol. 54, col. 187, 29 August 1963, the Minister of Internal Affairs: 'It is certainly not Government's intention . . . to use the Chiefs in any political capacity.' Cp. the Southern Rhodesia Command Paper on 'The Domboshawa Indaba' where the Chiefs and Headmen were used to press the Government's demand for independence for Southern Rhodesia. See especially pp. 16–33 and 53–61.

[3] *S.R.L.A.D.*, Vol. 59, col. 572, 28 October 1964, the Minister of Law and Order and col. 574, the Minister of Internal Affairs.

[4] *Rhodesia Herald*, 3 March 1965.

[5] Even matters such as the Tribal Law and Courts Bill giving all Chiefs criminal jurisdiction have met with drafting difficulties because of Section 67 of the Declaration of Rights. Although the Government is prepared to allow Chiefs criminal jurisdiction over Africans, they are not prepared to concede this to them over Europeans.

only after consultation with the Chiefs as the leaders of the people. The Government and the traditional leaders are moving together as one team. Throughout the country great numbers of people are rallying to their Chiefs. Now that you know what Government policy is, you also must rally to your Chief. Those who argue will be brushed aside.[1]

[1] *S.R.L.A.D.*, Vol. 59, col. 1103, 4 December 1964.

6

FEDERAL DISSOLUTION, REMAINING COMMON SERVICES, AND CONSEQUENT CONSTITUTIONAL ANOMALIES

AFRICAN opposition to the Federation, strengthened by the desire of the majority of the inhabitants of Northern Rhodesia and Nyasaland to establish their countries as two independent African states, reached such proportions that in 1959 states of emergency were declared to exist in all three Federal Territories.[1] These events and the Devlin Report on the emergency in Nyasaland[2] forced the United Kingdom Government to change its policy and take account of African opposition. The Secretary of State for Commonwealth Relations, Lord Home, then announced that

as power is transferred from the British Government in respect of the Northern Territories it will be transferred not to the Federal Government but to the Governments of the two Northern Territories, which will progressively become more and more representative of Africans until they have African majorities.[3]

In preparation for the 1960 Review of the Federal Constitution, the United Kingdom Prime Minister announced in July 1959 that an Advisory Commission would be appointed to advise the five Governments as to the constitutional programme and framework best suited to achievement of the objects contained in the Federal Constitution and its preamble.

Appointed in November and December 1959[4] the Monckton Commission

[1] For the growth of African nationalism in Southern Rhodesia, see Sanger, op. cit., and R. I. Rotberg, 'The Rise of African Nationalism: The Case of East and Central Africa, *World Politics*, 15 (1962), 75–90, and 'African Nationalism in East and Central Africa', *International Affairs*, 36 (1960), pp. 464–75.

[2] Cmnd. 814. Report of the Nyasaland Commission of Enquiry (1959), §§ 43 and 44. For accounts of these events see Sanger, op. cit.; Jones, op. cit.; Pratt and Leys, op. cit.; Mason, *Year of Decision*; Franck, op. cit. See also Review Tribunal, Preventive Detention (Temporary Provisions) Act 1959. Report. Salisbury, Government Printer, 1959, for a report by the Southern Rhodesian Chief Justice, Sir Hugh Beadle, justifying Southern Rhodesian detentions. Certain detainees were held for agitating against legislation which was, within a short period, condemned by the Select Committee on Resettlement of Natives (L.A.S.C. 3–60) and by the Robinson Commission (C.S.R. 22–1961).

[3] *H.L. Deb.*, Vol. 218, col. 596, 27 July 1959.

[4] After long consultation with the Governments involved. See Welensky, op. cit., pp. 137 et seq. There were disputes on the terms of reference and the proposed membership, Sir Roy refusing to accept a Malayan. There were afterwards heated exchanges that the Commission had exceeded its agreed terms and disregarded private United Kingdom assurances that the question of secession would not be pronounced on by the Commission in its Report. Other disputed points were dealt with in the Report, §§ 9–10 dealing with the scope of the evidence and § 11 dealing with immunity of witnesses. The Commission was composed of eleven United Kingdom members selected by the United Kingdom Government, an

reported in October 1960.[1] It advocated considerable changes, since it considered that the Federation could not be maintained in its present form, while at the same time it rejected dissolution as this 'would be an admission that there is no hope of survival for any multi-racial society on the African continent'.[2]

The Monckton Report was not accepted by the Federal Government while a Review Conference, held in December 1960 in London and attended by representatives of the five Governments, was adjourned after fruitless discussions. It was not reconvened.

Changes in the Territorial constitutions of Northern Rhodesia and Nyasaland had already occurred in 1958 and 1959 and the rate of change designed to secure African advance was thereafter to be increased. In 1960 it was agreed that Nyasaland would be given a more advanced constitution,[3] while in 1962 it was agreed to introduce internal self-government in 1963.[4] Northern Rhodesia also made considerable constitutional advance under an extremely complicated constitution in 1962.[5]

Thereafter in March 1962 United Kingdom Ministerial responsibilities for the Federation and its constituent Territories were vested in the First Secretary of State, Mr. Butler,[6] who in May announced his intention of appointing a team of advisers to examine the consequences of secession for Nyasaland. During the rest of 1962, continuous discussions between the United Kingdom Government and the Federal Government ensued, the Federal Government seeking to obtain an overall settlement of the problems in Central Africa,[7] the British Government seeking also alternative forms of association, but recognizing African opposition, in particular that of Nyasaland which was

Australian, a Canadian, and thirteen other members, some suggested by the Federal Government and others by the Territorial Governments.

[1] Cmnd. 1148, 1149, and 1150. There were certain notes of reservation on particular points by varying members and a minority report by two of the twenty-six members.

[2] Cmnd. 1148, p. 111. See pp. 111–21 for summary of proposed changes. However, as the Commission acknowledged: 'The wisdom of Solomon himself, were we able to command it, would not suffice to make any constitution work, without the good will of the people. We cannot create this good will. Unless both races genuinely wish to make the association succeed, unless they are prepared to understand and to meet each other's point of view, and unless both sides are ready to make some sacrifices, the new forms will do no better than the old': Cmnd. 1148, p. 34.

[3] Cmnd. 1132 (1960) implemented by S.I. 1961 No. 1189.

[4] Cmnd. 1887. This was done by S.I. 1963 No. 883. On 26 September 1963 it was stated that Nyasaland would become independent on 6 July 1964. This has been implemented by the Malawi Independence Act, 13 & 14 Eliz. II, c. 46.

[5] S.I. 1962 No. 1874. The constitutional proposals were subjected to considerable vicissitudes as a result of Federal Government intervention. See Welensky, op. cit., and Franklin, op. cit. It has since 24 October 1964 become the independent state of Zambia.

[6] H.C. Deb., Vol. 655, cols. 1545–7, 15 March 1962, Mr. Macmillan. Relevant staffs from the Colonial Office and Commonwealth Relations Office would be brought together as a unit as from 19 March 1962.

[7] These discussions are detailed from the Federal Government's point of view in The Issue of Nyasaland's Secession, Government Printer, Salisbury. C. Fed. 231.

already virtually a self-governing state.[1] Eventually on 19 December 1962, Mr. Butler announced that the United Kingdom Government would permit Nyasaland to secede from the Federation.[2] Thereafter on the 28 February 1963, Mr. Butler announced the appointment of a working party under the chairmanship of Sir George Curtis to consider the practical problem of Nyasaland's secession. Finally on 29 March 1963 it was announced that Northern Rhodesia would also be permitted to secede.

Many accusations were levelled by the Federal Government at the British Government, among them those of broken pledges that secession would not be permitted,[3] and that the British Government would not initiate any legislation dealing with any matter included within the competence of the Federal Legislature.[4] On the other hand, the United Kingdom Government consistently denied both that it had broken any pledges or breached the convention which, it alleged, did not apply either to the secession of any Territory or to the dissolution of the Federation.[5]

The United Kingdom Government advanced several alternative arguments as to why legislation providing either for secession of a Territory or for Federal dissolution was in accordance with the convention, which they stated they were honouring. Firstly they maintained that such a convention did not relate to dependencies which had responsible government type constitutions but only to those which actually had self-government.[6] Since the United Kingdom Government remained responsible for government and constitutional change in the two Northern Territories it could not be said that the Federation was self-governing. Secondly they maintained that such a convention applied only to concurrent legislative power and not to constituent power so that although the passage of ordinary legislative measures by the United Kingdom Parliament would be in breach of the convention the power of making constitutional changes remained unfettered.[7] Finally they argued that,

---

[1] The advisers, headed by Sir Roger Stevens, visited Central Africa in July and September 1962. No report of their advice was published. The Federal Government was apparently suspicious of the Report: Alport, op. cit., p. 177.

[2] *H.C. Deb.*, Vol. 669, col. 1267. Lord Alport, then the British High Commissioner in the Federation, has subsequently stated that in his view it was the victory of the European Rhodesian Front party in the Southern Rhodesian General Election of 14 December 1962 which resulted in the dissolution of the Federation by making its continuance a political impossibility: op. cit., p. 184. Alport's autobiography gives an account of relations between the Federal, Southern Rhodesian, and British Governments between 1961 and 1963, of attempts to preserve the Federation, and of events which led to its ultimate dissolution.

[3] *Federation and Nyasaland: The British Government's Broken Pledges and the Consequences.* Published by the Federal Government.

[4] *The Constitutional Convention*, Government Printer, 1962. C. Fed. 232. See also *Fed. Parlty. Deb.*, cols. 2033, 2170, 17 December 1962, and col. 11, 8 April 1963.

[5] *H.L. Deb.*, Vol. 238, col. 957–8, 27 March 1962, Viscount Kilmuir L.C.; *H.L. Deb.*, Vol. 245, col. 1221, 19 December 1962, Lord Dilhorne L.C.; and Cmnd. 1948.

[6] Southern Rhodesia was instanced as an example of the latter class of colony.

[7] This is a variant of the argument as to the effect of *Campbell* v. *Hall*, set out at length by Roberts-Wray, op. cit.

even if such a convention extended also to powers of constitutional amendment, it only related to amendments within the competence of the Federal Legislature. Although Article 1 of the Federal Constitution stated that the Federation should consist of the three Territories, since Section 1(1) of the Federation of Rhodesia and Nyasaland (Constitution) Order in Council stated that 'Southern Rhodesia, Northern Rhodesia, and Nyasaland . . . shall be associated in a Federation' the Federal Legislature could not amend the Constitution to permit of secession or of Federal dissolution as the consequence would be repugnancy to the Order in Council, and this was not possible in view of the Colonial Laws Validity Act. It is submitted that the first and third of these arguments were valid.

It can also be argued that Article 99 of the Federal Constitution by providing that the United Kingdom Government should participate in a review of the Federal Constitution envisaged that the United Kingdom 'would play an active part in the shaping of the new Constitution . . . if and when the occasion arose'.[1]

On 8 May 1963, the United Kingdom announced its intention to dissolve the Federation[2] and eventually on 18 June 1963, after correspondence and discussions with the Prime Minister of Southern Rhodesia, Mr. Field, who had declined to attend unless Southern Rhodesia were first promised independence, the First Secretary announced that the Governments of the Federation, of Southern Rhodesia, and of Northern Rhodesia, had agreed to attend a Conference on the orderly dissolution of the Federation. The Nyasaland Government would only be represented by advisers as Dr. Banda had refused to attend. The Conference was held in June and July 1963 and it agreed to establish machinery to implement Federal dissolution, consisting of two general committees composed of officers of the four Governments, each presided over by a United Kingdom chairman.[3] Committee 'A' was concerned with arrangements for the transfer of authority and functions from the Federal to the Territorial Governments, while Committee 'B' was concerned with arrangements for the continuation of joint Territorial administration of certain common services. These Committees then proceeded to make arrangements for the orderly transfer of Federal functions to the Territorial Governments.

---

[1] de Smith, op. cit., p. 42.

[2] For this decision see Alport, op. cit., p. 177.

[3] Cmnd. 2093, § 9. The United Kingdom Government had suggested the appointment of an Interim Commissioner acting on British instructions charged with the duty of administering and winding up services, creating or abolishing public offices in the service of the Federation, applying and adopting Federal laws to the Territories, and vested with all Federal assets and liabilities as in the case of the Interim Commissioner appointed to supervise the dissolution of the Federation of the West Indies under the West Indies Act 1962 and Orders in Council thereunder. The Federal and Southern Rhodesian Governments strongly objected to such a procedure being followed.

45 – C.H.L.S.R.

The Rhodesia and Nyasaland Act 1963

Thereafter the Rhodesia and Nyasaland Act 1963[1] was passed by the United Kingdom Parliament to make provision for the dissolution of the Federation and the consequential distribution of functions of the Federal Government and Legislature among the Territories. Such arrangements were to be made by Orders in Council, which could be varied or revoked by a subsequent Order. Prior to 1 October 1963, Orders so issued were subject to amendment in pursuance of Resolutions of either House of Parliament, while subsequent Order could only be made if drafts were laid before the United Kingdom Parliament and approved by Resolution of each House.[2] Such Orders could not amend the constitution of any of the Territories.[3]

In terms of this Act the Federation of Rhodesia and Nyasaland Order in Council 1963 was issued in September implementing decisions made by the two committees of civil servants.[4] The Order transferred legislative and executive powers in respect of specified matters from the Federation to the Territories at varying dates from 1 October to 1 December 1963. It also made provision for the continuance in force of existing laws on these topics and their adaptation and modification by the Governor of any Territory. In addition, it purported to confer power to legislate in respect of duties of customs and excise, and taxes on income and profit in respect of which the Federal Legislature had exclusive legislative power.[5]

It is arguable that this Order was *ultra vires* in so far as it purported to confer such powers on the Southern Rhodesian Legislature, though it was not *ultra vires* in respect of Northern Rhodesia and Nyasaland, since, although the Order in Council was issued under the Rhodesia and Nyasaland Act 1963, it was also issued under all other enabling power possessed by the Crown.[6]

The Rhodesia and Nyasaland Act in Section 1(2)(e) prohibited amendment of the Southern Rhodesia Constitution by virtue of that Act and it is doubtful whether alternative powers of amendment could be relied on.[7]

---

[1] 11 & 12 Eliz. II, c. 34. The Act received the Royal Assent on 31 July 1963.

[2] 11 & 12 Eliz. II, c. 34, Section 2.

[3] Section 1(2)(e).

[4] S.I. 1963, No. 1635.

[5] S.I. 1963, No. 1635, Section 1(2) and 2, which purported to provide that, notwithstanding Articles 29(2) and 35(1) of the Federal Constitution, Territorial Legislatures might after the dissolution of the Federation, exercise legislative power in respect of these matters which had been declared exclusively Federal.

[6] Section 3(3) of the Act preserved powers under the Foreign Jurisdiction Act 1890 and prerogative powers in respect of Northern Rhodesia and Nyasaland. See *Buck* v. *Attorney-General*, [1964] 2 All E.R. 663 at 668.

[7] It is doubtful whether in view of Section 1(2) of that Act the Rhodesia and Nyasaland (Federation) Act 1953 permitted these changes while the Southern Rhodesia (Constitution) Act 1961 gave no powers of amendment other than those specified in the Southern Rhodesia Constitution 1961 so could not be invoked in aid. The Royal prerogative would not have

It has already been submitted[1] that to the extent that legislative powers were declared to be exclusive to the Federal Legislature such powers were eliminated from the Southern Rhodesia Constitution and the general grant of legislative power was to that extent amended. This occurred in respect of external affairs, power to legislate on duties of customs and excise and taxes on income and profits. It has also been argued that this position was not affected by the grant of the Southern Rhodesia Constitution 1961.[2] If this is correct then the return of such power to the Southern Rhodesian Legislature required a constitutional amendment, and this it is submitted was not competent in terms of the Rhodesia and Nyasaland Act or of any other enabling Act, requiring the passage by the United Kingdom Parliament of further legislation.

The arguments against this view are that the declaration of powers as being exclusively Federal in terms of Article 29(2) of the Federal Constitution did not effect an amendment to the Southern Rhodesia Constitution, merely requiring the grant of legislative powers to Southern Rhodesia to be 'read down' by reference to the Federal Constitution and to be construed subject to that Constitution as it existed from time to time.[3] If this view is correct then no constitutional amendment would be required to restore such powers to the Southern Rhodesia Legislature. It is however submitted that the Southern Rhodesia Constitution was amended by action in terms of Article 29(2)[4] and that it is clear from scrutiny of the various documents that the Federal Constitution was not merely a temporary limitation on Southern Rhodesia's legislative powers, so that with dissolution limitations on Southern Rhodesia's powers would 'automatically disappear'.[5] Nor did it merely create an exemption or exception from their operation,[6] or modify Southern Rhodesian legislative powers in their application to particular cases so as to permit of revival free from modifications on its repeal.[7] In fact the Federal and Southern Rhodesian Constitutions were to be construed as if contained in one instrument,[8] and since they were incorporated the 'repeal of the first Act (i.e. the Federal Constitution) will not take away the effect of the words which are so repeated in the second Act (i.e. the Southern Rhodesia Constitution 1961) by

been available in view of the failure of the Crown to reserve powers of amendment other than those specified in Section 111 of the Southern Rhodesia Constitution 1961 read with Section 1(2) of the Southern Rhodesia (Constitution) Act 1961.

[1] Part I, Chapter 16, *supra*.

[2] Part I, Chapter 16, *supra*.

[3] Such a rule of construction is in fact set out in Section 117(1) of the Southern Rhodesia Constitution 1961.

[4] *Supra*, Part I, Chapter 16.

[5] See *Federal Outlook*, August 1963—Official organ of the United Federal Party, the governing party of the Federation.

[6] Craies on *Statute Law*, 5th ed., Sweet & Maxwell, 1952, at pp. 346-7.

[7] *Glaholm* v. *Barker* (1866), 1 Ch. App. 223.

[8] Cp. *Canada Southern Railway Company* v. *International Bridge Company* (1883), 8 A.C. 723 at 727.

incorporation'.[1] Indeed Parliamentary exposition by taking into account the aims and provisions of the subsequent statute[2] shows that there was no automatic revival as it was considered necessary to provide for 'consequential distribution of functions of the Federal Government and Legislature amongst the Territories'.[3]

A further argument, somewhat more difficult to meet, is that despite sub-Section 1(2)(e) since sub-Section 1(1) of the Rhodesia and Nyasaland Act 1963 empowers Her Majesty in Council to provide for 'the consequential distribution of functions of the Federal Government and Legislature among the Territories' and since sub-Section 1(2) specifies that detailed powers relative to such distribution shall be 'without prejudice to the generality of the foregoing sub-section' constitutional amendment of Territorial constitutions is permissible to the extent that it is necessary as a consequence of Federal dissolution.[4] This contention can however be resisted in view of the express wording of sub-Section 1(2)(e), which specifically states that, although powers to modify instruments having effect under any United Kingdom Act of Parliament are given (the Southern Rhodesian Constitution 1961 is such an instrument having effect under the Southern Rhodesia (Constitution) Act 1961), the 'section'—note not the 'sub-section'—shall not authorize constitutional amendment of any of the Territorial constitutions. This is reinforced by the fact that the Act clearly differentiates between 'sections' and 'sub-sections'[5] so that sub-Section 1(2)(e) must be read, despite the generality of the opening words of sub-Section 1(2) and the general conferment of powers by sub-Section 1(1), as limiting all powers conferred in terms of Section 1.

It is submitted that the Federation of Rhodesia and Nyasaland Order in Council did not and could not amend the Southern Rhodesian Constitution and that Southern Rhodesian legislative power was still limited by virtue of the amendments to the Southern Rhodesian Constitution effected by action taken under Article 29(2) of the Federal Constitution.

The repeal of the Federal Constitution did not alter this position so as impliedly to amend the Southern Rhodesian Constitution. Nor did mere repeal of that Constitution revive these powers as they were not in force at the time the Federal Constitution was repealed.[6] Nor would such powers be

---

[1] *The Queen* v. *Smith* (1873), L.R. 8 Q.B. 146 per Cockburn C.J. at 149.

[2] See *Ormond Investment Co.* v. *Betts*, [1928] A.C. 143 at 146.

[3] Section 1(1) of the Rhodesia and Nyasaland Act 1963.

[4] I am indebted to Professor S. A. de Smith for this argument.

[5] 1(1) refers to 'section'; 1(2) refers to 'the foregoing sub-section', and then to 'this section'; 1(2)(d) and 1(2)(e) to 'this section'; 1(3) to 'this section' and 'the foregoing sub-section'; 1(4) to 'sub-section (1) of this section', and thereafter to 'section'; 2(3) refers to 'sub-section'. The draftsman was meticulous in using 'section' where this was required and 'sub-section' where this was necessary. Meaning and purpose must be given to these differing words.

[6] Section 38(2) of the Interpretation Act 1889, 52 & 53 Vict. c. 63, was specifically applied to the repeal of the Federal Constitution by S.I. 1963, No. 2085, Section 76(3).

automatically transferred to the Southern Rhodesian Legislature by the mere fact of Federal dissolution.[1]

It is also doubtful whether despite Section 5 of the Colonial Laws Validity Act,[2] the Southern Rhodesian Legislature may itself amend Section 20(1) of the Constitution so as to confer upon itself power even though Section 105 authorizes it to amend or add to any of the provisions of the Constitution. Limitations on the power of legislatures cannot be removed by the legislatures themselves. As van den Heever J.A. said: 'Parliament cannot expand its mandate by deleting the inhibition of its powers . . .. One must keep in mind that this inhibition is in restraint of power and not a regulation of method. No legislative organ can perform an act of levitation and lift itself above its own powers by the bootstraps of method.'[3]

However in practice, the Southern Rhodesian Legislature and the Law Officers have not considered the arguments outlined above to be valid, as it has been assumed that the Legislature possesses power in all these fields and legislation dealing with such matters has been passed during 1964.[4]

Subsequently this Order was revoked by the Federation of Rhodesia and Nyasaland (Dissolution) Order in Council 1963[5] approved by both Houses on 17 December 1963. This provided for the dissolution of the Federation of Rhodesia and Nyasaland and with it the Federal Government and Legislature and all Federal Authorities, except such as were specially continued in existence. The Federal Constitution from immediately before 1 January 1964 was, except as so provided, thereupon to cease to have effect.[6]

Laws enacted both by the Federal Legislature and Territorial Legislatures and any subsidiary legislation in terms of such laws were to continue in force subject to amendment either by the Territorial Legislatures or by modification and adaptation by regulations, appearing expedient as a consequence of the Order and made by the Governor of a Territory before 1 July 1964.[7]

---

[1] Cp. *dicta* in relation to a suggested analogous assumption of power in *Usif Patel* v. *The Crown*, quoted in Jennings in *Constitutional Problems in Pakistan, supra*, at pp. 244–5. Muhammed Munir C.J. here held, on the assumption that the Constituent Assembly of Pakistan was lawfully dissolved, that 'the effect of the dissolution can certainly not be the transfer of its powers to the Governor-General . . . he himself is not the Constituent Assembly and on its disappearance he can never claim powers which he has never possessed nor claim to succeed to the powers of that Assembly'.

[2] This must be construed as having given power to representative legislatures to diminish or restrain that authority. See *Attorney General for New South Wales* v. *Trethowan* (1931), 44 C.L.R. 394 at 440. *Dicta* in *Hoani Te Heuheu Tukino* v. *Aotea District Maori Land Board, supra*, are however against this view.

[3] *Minister of the Interior and Another* v. *Harris and Others*, 1952 (4) S.A. 769 at 790.

[4] e.g. The Customs and Excise Amendment (No. 3) Act No. 51 of 1964.

[5] S.I. 1963 No. 2085, Section 77—without prejudice to any law or regulation made or other thing done by virtue of that Order.

[6] Section 1.

[7] Section 2(1), (3), and (6). Such gubernatorial regulations could have effect from the time specified therein so long as it was not earlier than the dissolution of the Federation: Section 2(5). See, e.g. the Southern Rhodesian Statutes (General) (Modification and Adaptation) Regulations, S.R.G.N. 801 of 1963. See also the Amendments Incorporation (Modifica-

Territorial Governors might, before the dissolution, declare that any laws enacted by the Federal Legislature should cease to have effect on the dissolution of the Federation.[1] Despite the reference to 'any law' it has been held that Governors did not enjoy a power to declare a cesser of legislation affecting currency and exchange control, this power being precluded by the provisions in the Dissolution Order in Council for a temporary Committee of Ministers to regulate such matters and for amendment of such measures by the Governor of the Bank of Rhodesia and Nyasaland acting with the concurrence of this Committee.[2]

Liquidating agencies

A Liquidating Agency, composed of the Secretaries to the Treasury of Southern Rhodesia and Nyasaland and the Permanent Secretary to the Ministry of Finance of Northern Rhodesia, was appointed as a body corporate charged with winding up the affairs of the Federation and with the disposition of its assets and liabilities in terms of the Order.[3] The Liquidating Agency was to apportion by agreement of the Territories the assets and liabilities of the Federation, and to collect income tax and Federal revenues until 31 March 1965.[4] It was vested with all movable Federal Government property including currency and securities.[5] Loan liabilities of the Federation were apportioned in the Order to the Territories.[6] Sinking funds of the Federation's internal debt were also transferred to the Territories, but those in respect of the external debt were to continue to be administered by the existing trustees on the existing terms and conditions until the stock for which such funds were established should have been redeemed.[7] The Liquidating Agency would also terminate when it was satisfied, with the concurrence of the Territorial Governments, that it had completely performed its functions. It would, on certifying to this effect, cease to exist.[8]

tion and Adaptation) Regulations 1964, S.R.G.N. 352 of 1964, giving the Minister of Justice power to print Acts originally enacted by the Federal Assembly with all amendments incorporated.

[1] Section 2(2). See the Federal Laws (Cesser) Order, S.R.G.N. No. 786 of 1963.

[2] *R. v. de Kock*, 1965 (2) S.A. 380 (S.R.). Young J. held that in so far as the Federal Laws (Cesser) Order declared a cesser of the Exchange Control (Temporary) Act 1961 it was *ultra vires*. This view was partly based on Sections 66 to 69 and partly on an argument *ab inconvenienti* since there would have been no exchange control legislation in force if the provision in the Order had been declared valid.

[3] Sections 3, 4, and 6.   [4] Section 6.

[5] It was also vested with the assets of Federal statutory corporations: Section 17(3).

[6] Section 12 refers to the internal debt and Section 16 to the external public debt. See Schedule I for the actual apportionment. Southern Rhodesian Act No. 66 of 1963 empowered the Southern Rhodesian Government to undertake the discharge of International Bank loans. The United Kingdom Government had refused to guarantee any stocks: *H.L. Deb.*, Vol. 254, cols. 196 et seq., 17 December 1963. The Lord Chancellor.

[7] Section 16(5). These trustees will therefore operate until 1981. See Schedule I, Part D.

[8] Section 9. None of the Territories could legislate to alter these provisions in view of the Colonial Laws Validity Act.

A Temporary Staff Authority was also established to control and exercise the functions formerly enjoyed by the Governor-General in relation to the employment of Federal civil servants who might be seconded to the Territories, while a Temporary Staff Commission was to exercise all former Federal supervisory powers in respect of such officers which were not formerly enjoyed by the Governor-General. The Staff Commission was also to have general responsibility for their welfare.[1] The Staff Commission and Staff Authority ceased to exist on 1 June 1964.

Permanent agency appointed to safeguard Federal civil servants' pensions and benefits

The Order also established a Central African Pension Fund to vest in Trustees domiciled in the United Kingdom and appointed by the five Governments. The Trustees are vested with the former Federal Pension Fund and such sums as may be provided by the United Kingdom Government as well as certain other sums for the payment of pensions, gratuities and commutations of pensions, etc., to former Federal civil servants. The Trustees must invest such funds, report on the state of the fund (which is to be actuarially valued every five years), make available such sums as are necessary to the Pensions Agency charged with actual payment of the pensions, gratuities, and other benefits mentioned, and secure the audit of the accounts of the Pension Agency.[2]

The actual payments from time to time are to be made by the Pensions Agency, which consists for the time being of the officer performing the functions of Pensions Officer of the Southern Rhodesian Government, who is also to receive any contributions and to pay over any balance not required for outgoing payments to the Trustees. The Pensions Agency has all powers previously held by various Federal authorities in relation to payment, discontinuance, suspension, forfeiture and commutation of pensions and benefits.[3] Although the provisions setting up the Pensions Agency and the Trust Fund may not be varied by the Territories, the provisions of the Schedule may be varied by the Pensions Agency with the concurrence of the Governments of the Territories, provided, however, that no variation diminishing any benefits set out in the Schedule may be made.[4]

Transitional common services

Although the major Federal institutions were dissolved at the same time as the Federation itself, special provision was made for the continuance of the

---

[1] Sections 21 and 22.
[2] Sections 24, 25, 26, 28, and 32. Schedule II.   [3] Sections 27, 29, 30, and 31.
[4] S.I. 1963/2085, Schedule II, Clause 38. See S.R.G.N. 351 of 1964 for Variation (No. 1) of Schedule II to the Federation of Rhodesia and Nyasaland (Dissolution) Order in Council 1963.

Federal Supreme Court and other Federal courts (the Court Martial Appeals Court, the Special Court for Income Tax Appeals and the Patents Tribunal) to continue in existence until such courts had disposed of all proceedings pending before the Federal dissolution.[1]

When the Federal Chief Justice was satisfied that these courts had disposed of all business in terms of the Order he was by writing under his hand so to certify, whereupon such court should cease to exist. The Federal Supreme Court ceased to exist on the 30 April 1964.[2]

Another common service continued on a temporary basis was the currency of the Federation. Federal currency continued to be legal tender in the Territories until 1 June 1965. In the meanwhile the value of one Federal pound was tied to one pound sterling until the date of demonetization.[3] During this period the respective Ministers of the Treasury (or of Finance) of the three Territories constituted a Committee of Ministers who could only act on the basis of unanimity and who exercised the powers previously enjoyed by the Governor-General and the Federal Minister of Finance in terms of the Federal Bank of Rhodesia and Nyasaland Act 1956, the Banking Act 1959, the Exchange Control Act 1954, and the Currency and Exchange Control (Temporary) Act 1961, subject to modifications in such Acts made before dissolution of the Federation by the Governor of the Bank with the concurrence of the Committee of Ministers.[4]

The Bank of Rhodesia and Nyasaland (the Central Bank) was also to continue exercising all its functions until 31 December 1965, unless earlier dissolved by the Committee of Ministers. When the Bank was dissolved the gold, cash, securities, loans, and financial assets of the Bank were allocated among the Central Banks established in the Territories in proportion to the amount of Federal money handed in by each Central Bank to the Bank of Rhodesia and Nyasaland before the date of demonetization.[5] The Territories in terms of the Colonial Laws Validity Act were not permitted to alter these provisions. In anticipation of demonetization Southern Rhodesia established her own Central Bank and introduced a new currency.[6]

Remaining common services

At the Dissolution Conference held in July 1963, the Governments recognized the need for certain forms of inter-Territorial co-operation. It was

---

[1] Section 19(1)—except in respect of Nyasaland.

[2] Section 19(6). The other courts ceased to exist somewhat earlier.   [3] Section 66.

[4] Sections 68 and 69. See e.g. Bank of Rhodesia and Nyasaland (Modification and Adaptation) Regulations, 1963. S.R.G.N. No. 956 of 1963. See *R.* v. *de Kock*, 1965 (2) S.A. 380 (S.R.) where it was held that the provisions of Sections 66–69 precluded the Governor having power under Section 2(2) to declare the cesser of any of these Acts.

[5] Section 70.

[6] Reserve Bank of Rhodesia Act, No. 24 of 1964, which gives it powers similar to those exercised by the former Bank of Rhodesia and Nyasaland, viz. banker to the Government,

agreed that, in the event of such collaboration occurring, constitutional responsibility for the functions involved would rest with the Territorial Governments and that any joint arrangements would be based on agreement between the Territories each exercising their separate powers.[1]

After the Conference negotiations followed and four Agreements were reached. Two of the Agreements, that relating to the Central African Airways Corporation[2] and that relating to the Agricultural Research Council,[3] were between all three former Federal Territories. The two Agreements relating to Rhodesia Railways and the Central African Power Corporation were, however, merely between Northern Rhodesia and Southern Rhodesia.[4]

As a result Southern Rhodesia has made arrangements to participate in four common services, while these arrangements have been reflected in subsequent Southern Rhodesian legislation.[5] These arrangements were also incorporated in the Federation of Rhodesia and Nyasaland (Dissolution) Order in Council.

The Higher Authority for Power and the Central African Power Corporation

The Order established for Northern and Southern Rhodesia[6] a Higher Authority for Power composed of two members of the Government of

the sole right to issue bank notes and coins, power to determine the rate of purchase and sale of sterling and other currencies and, with the authorization of the Minister, to issue instructions which are binding on bankers.

[1] Cmnd. 2093, para. 35 and 36.

[2] See S.R.G.N. No. 750 A of 1963 for text and annexures. The Agreement was concluded on 4 and 5 December 1962.

[3] See S.R. Information Service Press Statement 294/63/RL of 11 December 1963.

[4] See S.R.G.N. 657A of 1963. The Central African Power Corporation Agreement was concluded on 25 November 1963, while the Rhodesian Railways Agreement was concluded on 10 December 1963. See S.R.G.N. 750B of 1963. A subsequent Agreement was entered into between the Governments of Southern Rhodesia, Northern Rhodesia, and the Bechuanaland Protectorate relating to Rhodesia Railways (S.R.G.N. No. 773 of 1963) by which it was agreed that the interests of Bechuanaland would be regarded in respect of the operations of the system in Bechuanaland, and that the Government of Bechuanaland would be consulted on proposals adversely affecting traffic on the section of the system passing through Bechuanaland.

[5] The Rhodesia and Nyasaland Common Services Guarantee Act No. 64 of 1963 empowering the Government to guarantee the discharge of their obligations by the Central African Airways Corporation, the Central African Power Corporation and the Rhodesia Railways. See also the Central African Power Act No. 62 of 1963, the Central African Civil Air Transport Act No. 69 of 1963, the Air Services Act No. 70 of 1963, and the Rhodesia Railways (Modification and Adaptation) Regulations (S.R.G.N. No. 800 of 1963).

[6] Although Northern Rhodesia has now become the independent state of Zambia, Nyasaland, the state of Malawi, and Southern Rhodesia is referred to by its Government as Rhodesia (see *infra* Chapter 7). The former nomenclature has been employed in this work, since in the Order, in legislation as originally enacted, and in inter-Territorial Agreements this has been used. By the Zambia and Malawi Titles Act No. 90 of 1964 it is provided that

Northern Rhodesia and two of the Government of Southern Rhodesia. The Higher Authority was, after consultation with the Central African Power Corporation (also established by the Order), to give general directions to the Corporation as to the carrying out of its functions, but only unanimous decisions of the Higher Authority were to have effect.[1] The Agreement between the Territories provided that, in the event of inability of the Higher Authority to reach a decision, such matter should be submitted to an arbitrator. If any agreement on an arbitrator were impossible the President of the International Bank for Reconstruction and Development would be requested to recommend an arbitrator whose award would be implemented by the Higher Authority. Any disagreement between the two Governments on the terms of the Agreement would be similarly settled.[2]

The Central African Power Corporation would also be a body corporate consisting of a Chairman (appointed on the first occasion by the Governments of Northern Rhodesia and Southern Rhodesia and subsequently by the Higher Authority) and seven other members (one appointed by the Higher Authority with the approval of the Commonwealth Development Corporation and three by each of the Governments of Northern Rhodesia and Southern Rhodesia). Such persons were not to be members of the Legislature of either Territory and were subject to the same sort of disqualifications rendering candidates ineligible for Parliament or causing Members to vacate their seats.[3] This Corporation, decisions of which are taken by majority vote, is vested with all assets and liabilities of the former Federal Power Board and is charged with supplying electricity to undertakings within the Territories.[4]

The Governments of Southern Rhodesia and Northern Rhodesia agreed to enact legislation conferring on the Higher Authority, the Territorial Ministers responsible for Power, and the Corporation, all powers and functions set out in the Agreement and the Order in Council and not to alter such legislation without the consent of the other Governments. The Governments also agreed to assist the Corporation to carry out Stage II of the Kariba project, to refrain from entering into agreements for the purchase outside their Territories of power which could be more economically provided by the Corporation, to refrain from expanding power without the approval of the Higher Authority and to prepare annually five-year development plans.[5] Finally, they agreed to keep each other and the Corporation informed of and to consult on proposals for the abstraction of water from Lake Kariba or the impounding or abstrac-

'Zambia' and 'Malawi' shall be substituted in any enactment where 'Northern Rhodesia' and 'Nyasaland' respectively appear.
    [1] S.I. 1963 No. 2085, Sections 33, 34, and 35.
    [2] S.R.G.N. 657A. Agreement, Article 20.
    [3] Sections 36, 37, 38, and 39.   [4] Sections 41, 42, and 43.
    [5] See S.R.G.N. No. 657A. Agreement, Article 4. Cp. the Southern Rhodesian Central African Power Act No. 62 of 1963 enacted in pursuance of this provision.

tion of water from its sources for irrigation or other purposes.[1] All the provisions of the Order in respect of each Territory may be amended or revoked by a law of the Territorial Legislature.[2]

The Higher Authority for Civil Air Transport

A similar Higher Authority for Civil Air Transport was created by the Order, except that the Authority consisted only of three Ministers, one appointed by each of the three former Federal Territories. Similar rules as to unanimity of decisions and arbitration on matters incapable of being decided were applied, except that in this case an arbitrator might be recommended by the Director-General of the International Air Transport Association. The Air Authority was to give the Central African Airways Corporation directions as to its functions, and was to be responsible for the grant of rights or concessions in connection with air services and consultations with the United Kingdom Government in respect of air traffic rights until independence of any of the Territories.[3] After independence of any country the United Kingdom Government would entrust the Higher Authority with its rights to conduct negotiations with other Governments on air traffic rights, subject to prior consultation and agreement of the United Kingdom on matters of concern to it while the Higher Authority would be responsible for approving I.A.T.A. resolutions subject to the overall authority of the United Kingdom, pending such entrustment.[4] The Higher Authority has a Secretariat consisting of officers seconded from the Public Services of the Territories as agreed by the Governments and approved by the Higher Authority.[5]

The Agreement is subject to major review within three years of its commencement on three months' notice by any Government.[6]

The Central African Airways Corporation was also constituted by the Order and a previous Corporation of the same name dissolved. The assets and liabilities of the former Corporation were vested in the new Corporation.[7] Provisions similar to those applicable in the case of the Central African Power Corporation were made in respect of the appointment and removal of members.[8] The Corporation was charged with the duty of supplying the needs of the Territories for air services within, into, from, and through the Territories.[9]

[1] Article 17.   [2] S.I. 1963/2085, Section 45.
[3] S.I. 1963 No. 2085, Sections 47, 48, and 49. S.R.G.N. No. 750A of 1963, Articles 34 and 12. Malawi and Zambia are both now independent.
[4] Agreement, Articles 13 and 16.   [5] Agreement, Article 18.
[6] S.R.G.N. No. 750 A, Article 35.   [7] Section 57.
[8] The first Chairman was to be appointed by the Territorial Governments jointly, but subsequent Chairmen were to be appointed by the Higher Authority. There were to be five other members (two appointed by each of Northern Rhodesia and Southern Rhodesia, one by Nyasaland) and also a further member to be appointed by the Higher Authority with the approval of the Commonwealth Development Corporation: Sections 51, 52, 53, and 54.
[9] Section 57.

Its decisions are taken by majority vote.[1] The Corporation was also to establish in each Territory a private limited company, which would be vested with all immovable property and chattels (other than aircraft) of the Corporation. These companies which have been established operate internal Territorial air services, traffic handling services, and Territorial managerial and sales functions.[2]

Again the Governments agreed to implement the Agreement entered into by legislation.[3] However, these provisions of the Order may be amended in respect of each Territory by its Legislature.[4]

The Rhodesia Railways

The Order and the Agreement between the Northern Rhodesian and Southern Rhodesian Governments provided for the continuance of the body corporate known as the Rhodesia Railways. Again a Higher Authority, consisting of two Members of the Northern Rhodesian and two of the Southern Rhodesian Governments, was constituted. The functions and powers of this body were set out in the Southern Rhodesian Rhodesia Railways Act 1949 and the Northern Rhodesia Railways Ordinance 1949, both of which it was agreed would be amended in accordance with a draft attached to the Agreement.[5]

The Rhodesia Railways was to be governed by a Board of Management comprising a Chairman appointed by the Higher Authority and six members, three of whom would be appointed by the Government of Southern Rhodesia and three by the Government of Northern Rhodesia.[6] The Board's powers were governed by the railway legislation above mentioned.

In addition a Railways Court for Northern Rhodesia, Southern Rhodesia and Bechuanaland was established to hear appeals and industrial disputes on matters concerning the railways. Such decisions were not subject to any appeal.[7] The Court is composed of a President (appointed by the Governments of Southern Rhodesia and Northern Rhodesia after consultation with the Government of Bechuanaland) and four members appointed by the President. Again such provisions may be amended and revoked by the Territorial Legislatures.[8]

---

[1] Section 55(4).   [2] Agreement, Articles 5, 6, and 8.
[3] See the Central African Civil Air Transport Act and the Air Services Act Nos. 69 and 70 of 1963, passed by the Southern Rhodesian Legislature.
[4] Section 65.
[5] This was done in Southern Rhodesia by the Rhodesia Railways (Modification and Adaptation) Regulations: S.R.G.N. No. 800 of 1963.
[6] S.I. 1963 No. 2085, Section 71(2).
[7] They may be subject to judicial review by the General Division of the Southern Rhodesian High Court by virtue of its inherent right to review the proceedings of all tribunals performing administrative duties imposed on them by statute: *L. and B. Holdings* v. *Mashonaland Rent Appeal Board*, 1959 (3) S.A. 466 (S.R.).
[8] Section 73.

The Agreement also makes important provisions that will make it difficult for the Territories to develop independent railway systems. New developments or proposals contemplating the diversion of traffic or the denial of new traffic to the Railways, must be approved by the Higher Authority if the Railways are to be ordered to construct them. A Government may make alternative arrangements for construction but, if the result of these would be to divert traffic or cause loss to the existing Railways, compensation for any loss must be paid to Rhodesia Railways by the Government concerned.[1] These provisions probably render Northern Rhodesia liable for large sums of money in compensation should her Government develop new railway lines connecting Northern Rhodesia with Tanganyikan ports or attempt to double the present Benguela Railway Company's lines in Northern Rhodesia.

Finally the Governments have agreed to special arrangements for settlement of railway labour and trade union relations. These have been effected by amendments to their respective railway legislation.[2] In addition a further revision after joint consultations will be undertaken by the Governments in order to remove differential procedure in the existing legislation.[3]

Whether the unitary railway system will survive is open to doubt as there have been disagreements on the Board of Management and the vice-Chairman, with the knowledge of the Southern Rhodesian Minister of Transport, has made public statements on the fact that the Board was divided.[4] The Minister of Transport then requested a meeting of the Higher Authority but the responsible Northern Rhodesian Minister refused to attend the meeting.[5] The Order in Council contains no provision dealing with the meeting of the Higher Authority and until the end of October 1965 no meetings of the Authority were held.[6]

The Agricultural Research Council

The Order also provided that the existing Federal Agricultural Research Council should be dissolved and its assets and liabilities vested in a new

[1] See S.R.G.N. 750 B of 1963, Agreement, Articles 34–47. If agreement on any sum payable as compensation is impossible the matter is subject to arbitration and if agreement on an arbitrator cannot be reached, the President of the International Bank for Reconstruction and Development shall be asked for a binding recommendation.

[2] S.R.G.N. 750 B of 1963, Agreement, Articles 32 and 4. Appendix VI provides that all differentiations with race as the criterion should be removed.

[3] See S.R.G.N. No. 800 of 1963. The Appendix lays down principles to be observed in the review.

[4] S.R.L.A.D., Vol. 62, cols. 1–4, 10 August 1965.

[5] Rhodesia Herald, 12 August 1965. The issues of disagreement involve the effect on running costs of a policy of rapid Africanisation of employees which is being followed by the Northern Rhodesian (Zambian) Government and which according to the Southern Rhodesian view has resulted in an increased accident rate and consequent expense and delays. Further expense has been occasioned by the necessity to provide 'inducement pay' for expatriate employees in Northern Rhodesia and from the reluctance of Southern Rhodesian European employees to be transferred there.

[6] None of the Higher Authorities (viz. for Railways, for Power, and for Civil Air Transport) had met as at the end of August 1965. The Order also fails to make any provision

Agricultural Research Council, which would be a body corporate established by the Order. The Council is composed of a Chairman, appointed by the Governments of Northern Rhodesia, Nyasaland, and Southern Rhodesia jointly, and six other members, two being appointed by each Government as well as any additional members agreed on by all Governments. Tenure and conditions of service are determinable by the Governments jointly.

The Council is charged with promotion, direction, and control of agricultural, veterinary, and tsetse research in the Territories. It is particularly concerned with research into soils, vegetation, crop, lisvestock, forestry, hydrology, wild life, and fisheries, while it conducts its research in accordance with programmes approved by the Territorial Governments and co-operates with Territorial or other research organizations. It is envisaged that the Council will employ persons engaged in research.[1] By agreement the Territories may confer other functions connected with such research on the Council, while on the other hand the Territorial Legislatures may amend or revoke the provisions of the Order in relation to each Territory.

Conclusions on common services

The great differences in political complexion between Governments of Northern Rhodesia, Nyasaland, and Southern Rhodesia make further co-operation at present unlikely. This is the more so now that Northern Rhodesia (Zambia) and Nyasaland (Malawi) have become independent republics in the Commonwealth. Although it is the United Kingdom Government's declared policy to seek to assist in the evolution of effective new forms of collaboration between the Territories, particularly in respect of shared economic arrangements and common services,[2] Britain no longer has the power to implement such a policy. Only if changes in the complexion of the respective Governments occur, making political co-operation easier, is inter-Territorial collaboration likely to increase or are further common services likely to be established.

Constitutional anomalies as a result of Federal Dissolution

Although the Federation of Rhodesia and Nyasaland (Dissolution) Order in Council made provision for the consequences of Federal Dissolution, certain anomalies remain. As a consequence of the limitation in the enabling Act that Territorial constitutions might not be amended,[3] neither any Order under the Act nor any regulations made under powers conferred by the

for the meeting of the latter two Authorities, merely providing that, subject to the rule that their decisions shall be unanimous, these Authorities shall determine their own procedure: Sections 35 and 49. In November 1965 the Railways Higher Authority first met.

[1] See S.I. 1963 No. 2085, Sections 61 to 65.
[2] Cmnd. 2093, paras. 31–33.
[3] The Rhodesia and Nyasaland Act 1963, Section 1(2)(e).

Order may amend any Territorial constitution or make provision inconsistent with it.

The Southern Rhodesia Constitution 1961 as originally enacted postulated the continuance of the Federal Constitution: thus Members of the Southern Rhodesia Legislative Assembly were to vacate their seats if they became Members of the Federal Assembly or members of the Federal Government[1]; persons might not simultaneously be Southern Rhodesian and Federal Cabinet Ministers[2]; Members of or candidates for election to the Federal Assembly within the past five years were ineligible for election to the Constitutional Council, while Members of the Council who either became candidates for election to or Members of the Federal Assembly were to vacate their seats[3]; Tribal Trust Land might be occupied by the Federal Government for administrative purposes[4]; the Constitution was to be construed always subject to the express provisions of the Rhodesia and Nyasaland (Constitution) Order in Council 1953 as amended from time to time[5]; the Governor's prerogative of mercy extended only to offences against laws in force in Southern Rhodesia other than Federal laws[6]; and the Declaration of Rights did not apply to laws other than those passed by the Southern Rhodesian Legislature or instruments thereunder, while Federal laws were expressly exempted (in fact, protection against discriminatory laws and administrative action did not apply even to Southern Rhodesian laws providing for persons of a particular description, if the Federal Legislature had legislated with respect to persons of other descriptions or had or was entitled to assume exclusive power so to legislate)[7]; the Southern Rhodesian High Court's jurisdiction was diminished by the exclusive original jurisdiction of the Federal Supreme Court; right of appeal from the High Court to the Privy Council on determinations on the Declaration of Rights was precluded while the Federal Constitution provided for an appeal to the Federal Supreme Court[8]; and, finally, citizenship of the Federation of Rhodesia and Nyasaland was a necessary qualification for the Chairman and members of the Constitutional Council, for African voters entitled to vote in a referendum amending the entrenched provisions of the 1961 Constitution, and for voters.[9] In addition, if any Member ceased to possess Federal citizenship he was to vacate his seat.[10]

---

[1] S.I. 1961 No. 2314, Annex Sections 14(1)(i)(j).

[2] Section 43(1)(c).   [3] Section 77(1)(a) and 2(c) and (e).

[4] Section 96(b)(i).   [5] Section 117(1).   [6] Section 49.

[7] Sections 67(3) and 68(2)(a), i.e. Southern Rhodesian laws dealing with African education and agriculture were exempted from the protection of Sections 67 and 68 because the Federation had legislative power in respect of non-African primary and secondary education and non-African agriculture in Southern Rhodesia.

[8] Section 71(4) and (5).

[9] Sections 74, 76(b), 108(2)(a), and the Second Schedule to the Constitution Item 5(a) read with Section 8(1)(a) of the Electoral Act 1951 as amended by Section 3 of Act No. 62 of 1961.

[10] Section 14(1)(h) read with Section 52(4) and Section 8(1)(a) of the Electoral Act as amended.

Although many of these provisions became obsolete and the need to invoke them in practice fell away as a result of Federal dissolution, some still form part of the Southern Rhodesia Constitution.

The disappearance of the Federal Supreme Court occasioned the first amendments to the Southern Rhodesia Constitution 1961, whereby all the provisions relating to the judicature were amended and re-enacted and an Appellate Division of the High Court was created to replace the Federal Supreme Court.[1] Section 71 was also amended to take this into account and to provide that appeals on determinations by the Appellate Division of the High Court on the Declaration of Rights should lie as of right to the Judicial Committee of the Privy Council.[2] At the same time the provisions as to joint membership of the Federal and Territorial Assemblies and combined holding of Ministerial posts in both Governments were deleted from the Constitution,[3] while the Federal citizenship requirement for African voters in referenda was replaced by one of Southern Rhodesian citizenship.[4] Indeed many of the provisions referred to above were amended.[5]

However, certain vital provisions were not amended, despite the fact that the Bill, as introduced[6] made provision to amend one of these, since the Government, at committee stage, withdrew the proposed constitutional amendment. In addition, no provision was made for either the Declaration of Rights or the Constitutional Council to operate in respect of Federal laws or statutory instruments issued under such laws either before or after dissolution. Since the Constitutional Council is only permitted to report on 'Acts' and 'statutory instruments' as defined in the Constitution, it cannot examine or give an advisory report on laws enacted by or with the authority of the Federal Assembly.[7] In fact, it is submitted that Federal laws continued in force in Southern Rhodesia by virtue of Section 2 of the Federation of Rhodesia and Nyasaland (Dissolution) Order in Council 1963[8] are no longer 'Federal laws', but are British laws and equally beyond the power of the Constitutional Council to examine. Nor has the Council power to scrutinize or report adversely on, and possibly cause invalidation of, fresh statutory instruments issued under such laws.[9] Large bodies of new law can therefore

[1] See The Constitution Amendment Act No. 13 of 1964, Section 4.
[2] Section 8.
[3] The Constitution Amendment Act No. 13 of 1964, Section 2(a) and Section 3.
[4] The Constitution Amendment Act No. 13 of 1964, Section 16.
[5] Amendments to Sections 67(3), 74, 76, 77, 96, 116, and 117(1) were made in order to provide for the changes and to make adaptations as a result of the dissolution of the Federation.
[6] A.B. 10 of 1964. See Clause 20.
[7] Section 87 read with Section 83 (definition of 'statutory instrument'), Section 116(1) (definition of 'Act') and Section 70(3) (exemption of Federal laws).
[8] Section 2 of the Federation of Rhodesia and Nyasaland (Dissolution) Order in Council and Section 1(2)(d)(e) of the Rhodesia and Nyasaland Act 1963.
[9] See Section 86 read with Section 83, definition of 'statutory instrument'.

be introduced by subordinate legislation but will not be subject to the filtering mechanism of the Constitutional Council.[1]

On the other hand if the Federal laws continued in force in Southern Rhodesia are still 'laws of the Federal Legislature', and this they might well be as meaning must be given to the phase, the Governor of Southern Rhodesia may not then remit sentences, grant pardons or generally exercise the prerogative of mercy in respect of any offences against such laws.[2] If this is the case the position cannot be changed other than by the issue of further Royal Instructions instructing the Governor to exercise the prerogative in respect of such offences or more properly by an Order in Council, amending Section 49(2) so as to permit the Governor a discretion to exercise the prerogative of mercy in respect of all laws in force in Southern Rhodesia.[3]

Another serious consequence already indicated is that powers eliminated from the Territorial constitutions, because such powers were exclusively conferred on the Federation were not, it is submitted, restored to Southern Rhodesia since the Dissolution Order in Council could not in terms of the enabling Act amend the Southern Rhodesian Constitution. If this view is correct the Southern Rhodesian Legislature is at present without powers of imposing taxes on incomes and profits, or customs and excise duties.[4]

The consequences having most political significance relate, however, to the extinction of Federal citizenship and its replacement in Southern Rhodesia by Southern Rhodesian citizenship.[5] Whereas Federal citizenship was replaced

---

[1] e.g. in terms of the Federal Defence Act No. 23 of 1955, the Prisons Act No. 9 of 1955, the Education Act No. 15 of 1956. These were the major acts whereby discrimination was effected by the Federal Government. The Education Act permitted separate schools for Europeans on the one hand, and Asians and Coloureds on the other hand. Regulations under the Prisons Act were couched in non-discriminatory language but, in practice, all Europeans are classed as Grade I prisoners, Coloureds and Indians and a very small number of Africans are treated as Grade II prisoners, and the vast majority of Africans are, in practice, graded as Grade III prisoners, each Grade of prisoner being entitled to different clothing and allowances and rations, the Grade I prisoners getting very much more in the way of rations and proper clothing, etc. Under the Federal Defence Act a large number of discriminatory regulations were issued making quite different provisions for remuneration, accommodation, and allowances of African and European troops.

[2] Section 49.

[3] The wording of Section 49(2) would seem to preclude the issue of Royal Instructions as the issue of such Instructions would be tantamount to amendment of Section 49(2) and this cannot be done other than by an Order in Council. See Section 111 read with Section 1(2) of the Southern Rhodesia (Constitution) Act 1961. Section 49 may not be amended by the Southern Rhodesia Legislature: Section 105.

[4] It will also be submitted that it has no power to legislate in the field of external affairs (using this term in an unorthodox sense): *infra* Chapter 7.

[5] See the Southern Rhodesian Citizenship and British Nationality Act No. 63 of 1963 and the Federal Laws (Cesser) Order 1963, S.R.G.N. No. 786 of 1963, made in terms of sub-Section 2 of the Dissolution Order in Council, which repealed the Federal Citizenship Act in respect of Southern Rhodesia from the date of Federal dissolution. In any event, as a matter of International Law, the dissolution of the Federation 'immediately before 1 January 1964' (S.I. 1963 No. 2085, Section 1) extinguished Federal nationality. See P. Weis, *Nationality and Statelessness in International Law*, Stevens, 1956, p. 140. This rule,

by Southern Rhodesian citizenship as a requirement for the eligibility of the Chairman and members of the Constitutional Council and in respect of the African voters entitled to vote in a referendum, no such alteration was made to the Second Schedule to the Constitution.[1] The Second Schedule is a measuring rod by which amendments to the electoral laws must be judged; if any Bill will, if enacted, vary the qualifications of voters so as to make any person ineligible, who possessed the qualifications set out in that Schedule, such Bill is to be treated as a constitutional Bill amending a specially entrenched provision of the Southern Rhodesian Constitution (i.e. it requires for its passage a two-thirds majority and approval by four separate racial referenda or reservation).[2] Since the Second Schedule specifies Federal citizenship[3] and two years' continuous residence in the Federation, amendment of the Electoral Act 1951, which now reflects the Schedule, to provide for Southern Rhodesian citizenship and residence qualifications, will have the effect of rendering ineligible for the franchise a number of persons possessing the qualifications set out in that Schedule (i.e. former Federal citizens formerly resident in the Northern Territories who have at the time of any amending Act been resident for three months in a Southern Rhodesian constituency or electoral district). In view of the rigid amending procedure, it may be difficult to procure the passage of such a measure either as a result of failure to obtain a majority in any one racial referendum or as a result of United Kingdom refusal to permit the alternative reservation procedure to be utilized.[4]

If no amendment occurs difficult consequences ensue whichever of two differing legal interpretations be adopted. Either the position is that such voting qualifications are impossible of fulfilment,[5] in which event they fall

not being inconsistent with statute law or judicial decisions, would have been municipally applied had there been no repeal: *Chung Chi Cheung* v. *The King*, [1939] A.C. 160; *West Rand Central Gold Mining Co.* v. *The King*, [1905] 2 K.B. 391 (C.A.).

[1] The Constitution Amendment Bill A.B. 10 of 1964, Clause 20, was withdrawn at Committee stage. The Bill did not contain provisions eliminating ex-membership of the Federal Legislative Assembly or candidature for that Assembly within the last five years as a disqualification for Constitutional Council Membership and it was obviously intended that this should remain as a disqualification in the Constitution. It cannot therefore be assumed that, wherever there is any reference to the Federation of Rhodesia and Nyasaland, or its institutions these references should automatically fall away.

[2] Constitution, Section 9(2) read with Sections 106, 107, 108, 109, and 110.

[3] Second Schedule, The Franchise, Item 5: 'The following requirements shall be common to both an 'A' Roll and a 'B' Roll: (a) Citizenship: Citizenship of Rhodesia and Nyasaland. (b) Age: 21 years or over. (c) Residence: Two years' continuous residence in the Federation and three months' residence in the constituency immediately preceding application for enrolment.'

[4] A United Kingdom Government might, in the light of present Commonwealth feeling and United Nations interest, be reluctant to be concerned in a Bill amending the Southern Rhodesia franchise (even though this might be occasioned by technicalities) without amending the educational and means qualifications, which bar the majority of the population from qualifying for the vote.

[5] There is no authority on such a point and the only approach can be by analogy that the maxim *lex non cogit ad impossibilia* applies. See Broom's *Legal Maxims*, 9th ed., at

away: there can be no automatic substitution of Southern Rhodesian citizenship or residence in their place.[1] Therefore persons may qualify as voters without any citizenship qualifications or two-year residence qualifications. Indeed, in the case of candidates for election to the Legislative Assembly such person need never have been a Southern Rhodesian or Federal citizen or even resident in Southern Rhodesia or the Federation.[2] This result is absurd as aliens could become voters and Members of Parliament.[3]

The alternative attitude is that the provision remains of force and effect and that applicants for registration must be Federal citizens. Legal advice to this effect seems to have been proffered to the Government. Not only was this indicated by the statements of the Minister of Internal Affairs (the Minister responsible for the administration of the Electoral Act), but the Minister of Law and Order has told a public meeting that the effect of the Second Schedule of the Constitution was 'that citizens of the former Federation who might be citizens of Zambia or Malawi, could qualify to be registered as voters in Rhodesia. . . .. By the dissolution of the Federation, this expression now becomes meaningless as it *could be* that no citizen qualification is required to become a voter.' Accordingly the Minister considered a constitutional amendment 'essential'.[4]

pp. 171–2, where the author states that the maxim 'has been adopted and applied by the law of England under various and dissimilar circumstances'. See also *dicta* by Greenberg J.A. in *R. v. Hargovan*, 1948 (1) S.A. 764 (A.D.) at 770 that 'the performance of a statutory obligation is excused if it is rendered impossible by the operation of a subsequently enacted statute'. Craie's *Statute Law*, 5th ed., Sweet & Maxwell, 1952, p. 228, states that the maxim applies to a statutory duties compliance with which is excused if impossible. See also *The Queen v. The Justices of Leicestershire* (1850), 117 E.R. 391 at 392.

[1] The word Federal citizenship does not include Southern Rhodesia citizenship, which is not a species of Federal citizenship. Indeed the history of the Electoral Act makes this clear as Section 8 originally specified Southern Rhodesian citizenship as a requirement (Act 27 of 1951). Thereafter the Act was amended to provide in the alternative for Southern Rhodesian or Federal citizenship (Act 38 of 1957). Finally it was amended so as to delete Southern Rhodesian citizenship as an alternative qualification (Act 62 of 1961). When a specific item is deleted, in construing the remaining part such item is not included in general words even if those words would otherwise have included such an item: *Attorney-General v. Lamplough* (1878), 3 Ex.D. 214.

[2] The Electoral Act 1951, Section 52(4) read with Sections 8(1) and 9(1) and (2). Candidates need not have any residence qualification.

[3] In practice, although there has been no amendment to the Electoral Act by S.R. Government Notice No. 865 of 1964 issued under Section 172 of Chapter 2, the Governor has prescribed that on the form of application for registration as a voter, the voter must state whether he is a Southern Rhodesian citizen, and the replacement of Southern Rhodesia, wherever Federation previously occurred, has been prescribed. See Electoral (Amendment) Regulations 1963 (No. 1). However the Minister of Internal Affairs stated on 21 July 1965 that 'this form must necessarily be a reflection of the requirements contained in the Electoral Act which themselves stem from the Constitution in many respects. Until the Constitution is changed it is not possible to change the Electoral Act and if the Electoral Act is not changed then this form must continue to reflect the requirements in the Electoral Act': *S.R.L.A.D.*, Vol. 61, col. 1263. See also col. 1265 where the Minister considered that it was necessary to enquire on the form whether persons were citizens of the Federation.

[4] Extracts from a speech by Mr. Lardner-Burke to a meeting at Sinoia on 23 April 1965.

If Federal citizenship is to be treated as a requirement, there can be no further registration of voters,[1] as the Electoral Act requires that a person 'is', not 'was', a Federal citizen.[2] Until the Electoral Act is amended no candidates would, on this argument, be eligible.[3] The latter difficulty could easily be avoided by altering candidates' qualifications, which do not form part of the Constitution, through an amendment to the Electoral Act to replace Federal citizenship as a requirement with Southern Rhodesian citizenship. This could have been done either before or after the date of Federal dissolution by the Legislative Assembly or in terms of Section 2(3) of the Federation of Rhodesia and Nyasaland (Dissolution) Order in Council 1963 by the Governor, who was empowered by regulations made before the 1 July 1964 to modify any Territorial or Federal law in force immediately before dissolution in so far as this appeared expedient as a consequence of Federal dissolution. Such powers have not however been exercised.

Furthermore, it is submitted that on this view all Members of the Southern Rhodesian Legislative Assembly vacated their seats 'on the dissolution of the Federation'. This situation was occasioned by the joint effect of the Citizenship of Rhodesia and Nyasaland British Nationality Act which ceased to have effect at that time as regards Southern Rhodesia,[4] by the constitutional provisions for the automatic vacation of seats by Members of Parliament if they cease 'to be qualified for election to the Assembly',[5] and by the further fact that candidates' qualifications were equated to voters' qualifications, which demand Federal citizenship.

This view is however only valid if the maxim *lex non cogit ad impossibilia* is not applicable. The decision whether the maxim is to be invoked should not be influenced by the fact that the result might be highly inconvenient or politically hazardous as 'such considerations are irrelevant in a court of law'.[6] It is submitted that what is at issue is the interpretation of two statutes, viz. the Constitution read with the Electoral Act. Whether the maxim is to be applied

---

Roneoed Statement on Proposed Amendments to the Constitution. Supplied by courtesy of the Rhodesian Front.

[1] If this approach is adopted even more embarrassing consequences would ensue as a result of the combined effect of the Electoral Act and the Constitution.

[2] Section 52(4) of the Electoral Act read with Section 8(1).

[3] In fact four by-elections occurred during 1964 and in 1965 a General Election, but this objection has not been raised in respect of any of the candidates.

[4] The Federal Laws (Cesser) Order, *supra*.

[5] Constitution, Section 14(1)(h). 'The seat of a Member of the Legislative Assembly shall become vacant . . . (h) if he ceases to be qualified for election to the Assembly under any law for the time being in force in Southern Rhodesia'.

[6] *Ex parte Mwenya*, [1960] 1 Q.B. 241 at 308 per Sellers L.J. Sellers L.J. was referring to the deprival of the right of *habeas corpus*. The analogy can be applied that Southern Rhodesian inhabitants have the right not to be governed by a Parliament not functioning in terms of the Constitution. Compare *Sabally and N'Jie* v. *H.M. Attorney-General, supra*, where it was necessary for either a subsequent Order in Council or an Act of the United Kingdom Parliament retrospectively to validate elections in Gambia Protectorate and thus provide for a Legislative Assembly.

involves the true construction of the statutes.[1] An examination of the nature of the provisions requiring Federal citizenship reveals that the Constitution imposes an absolute liability[2] of a sitting Member to vacate a parliamentary seat if he ceases to possess the requisite qualifications.[3]

The cases in which the maxim has been applied relate to non-compliance with statutory duties and cases in which breaches of positive duties have occurred,[4] whereas continuance as a Member is a privilege dependent on fulfilment of certain conditions but is not a duty. The maxim has definitely been excluded in cases where what is in issue is a condition precedent to the exercise of the jurisdiction of a tribunal, in which cases compliance may not be dispensed with.[5] The situation is analogous in that it is a condition precedent to registration as a voter, or nomination as a candidate, that one be a Federal citizen.

It is also submitted that since the Rhodesia and Nyasaland Act 1963 prohibited amendment of the Territorial Constitutions, application of the maxim in interpreting the joint effect of the Dissolution Order in Council and the Constitution would in effect have the same consequence as a constitutional amendment, so that such an interpretation would be inconsistent with the enabling Act.

A precondition for the application of the maxim is that the impossibility must always have existed,[6] whereas from the implementation of the Southern Rhodesia Constitution on 1 November 1962 to 31 December 1963 it was possible to be a Federal citizen. In addition, all practical endeavours must have been used to surmount the difficulties,[7] whereas, despite the fact that the possibility of such automatic vacation in the event of Federal dissolution and its avoidance by means of an amendment to the Electoral Act had been debated in Parliament,[8] the Members of the Southern Rhodesia Legislative Assembly acting collectively did nothing to prevent this situation by amending

---

[1] *J. J. Makin* v. *London and North Eastern Railway*, [1943] K.B. at 471; Halsbury, 3rd ed., Vol. 36, §*704; and Maxwell, 11th ed., at p. 375.

[2] It is a liability to vacation that is in question not a qualification, since qualifications for Members are dealt with in Section 7(1) of the Constitution—incidentally also incorporating Sections 52(4) and 8(1) of the Electoral Act.

[3] See *River Wear Commissioners* v. *Adamson* (1877), 2 A.C. at 750 per Lord Cairns L.C. to the effect that where an absolute liability is imposed by Act of Parliament, the party is still liable irrespective of acts of God or man. Maxwell, 11th ed., p. 374, also applies the principle to liabilities.

[4] This is the way in which Craies describes the maxim, op. cit., p. 228. See also *R.* v. *Hargovan, supra.*

[5] See *Jones* v. *The South Western Railway Co.* (1872), L.R. 7 Ex. 287 at 293, where the Court held that it could not 'dispense with what the legislature made the indispensable foundation' despite impossibility both in law and in fact.

[6] *The Richmond Gas Co.* v. *Richmond Surrey Corporation*, [1893] 1 Q.B. 56—a case of supervening impossibility precluding the performance of statutory duties, in which the plea was not upheld.

[7] Broom's Legal Maxims, 9th ed., at p. 170.

[8] *S.R.L.A.D.*, Vol. 55, col. 171, 13 November 1963.

the qualifications specified for candidates in the Electoral Act before Federal dissolution.

Finally, since the question is one of statutory interpretation, application of the ordinary canons of construction is decisive against application of the maxim, as the language is clear and explicit in demanding Federal citizenship.[1] This requirement must be given effect whatever the consequences.[2] This rule of interpretation applies also to constitutional instruments.[3] Although the literal interpretation be mischievous it is decisive, and absurdity, even to the extent of unseating all the members of the Legislature, could only be looked to if the Constitution were ambiguous, which it is not.[4] Even if it be considered possible to consider the question of inconvenience this must be looked at in the light of the state of affairs as at the date of passing the statute and not in the light of subsequent events.[5] Indeed a statute must be construed as if the Court were interpreting it the day after it was passed [6] and since there was nothing inconvenient in 1962 in providing that Members of the Southern Rhodesian Legislative Assembly should vacate their seats if they ceased to be Federal citizens, inconvenience cannot now be considered. If there is now inconvenience as a result of unforseen contingencies or omissions, these must be remedied by the competent legislature.[7] The competent legislature is in this case either the United Kingdom Parliament, the Crown in Council acting under the Rhodesia and Nyasaland (Federation) Act 1953,[8] or the Crown acting by virtue of the prerogative.[9]

---

[1] This is particularly explicit by virtue of the Second Schedule to the Constitution (as much a part of the Constitution as any other part: *Attorney-General* v. *Lamplough, supra*), which states a series of qualifications all of which must be complied with in order to become a voter: there is a citizenship requirement, an age requirement, a residence and a language requirement. The Schedule repeats the concept of citizenship by specifying the particular citizenship which is required, viz. 'Citizenship: Citizen of Rhodesia and Nyasaland'.

[2] *Warburton* v. *Loveland* (1831), 2 B. & C. 480 at 489; *Abbey* v. *Dale* (1851), 20 L.J.C.P. 233 at 235; *In re Robb's Contract*, [1941] Ch. 463 at 470 per Lord Green M.R. and at 478-9 per Clauson L.J.

[3] *Attorney-General for Ontario* v. *Attorney-General for Canada*, [1912] A.C. 571 at 483 per Lord Loreburn: 'In interpretation of a completely self-governing Constitution founded upon a written organic instrument . . . if the text is explicit the text is conclusive alike in what it directs and what it forbids.'

[4] See Maxwell, 11th ed., p. 4.

[5] *Attorney-General* v. *Prince Ernest Augustus of Hanover*, [1957] A.C. 436 (H.L.).

[6] The Longford (1889), 14 P.D. 34 at 36.

[7] *Magor and St. Mellons R.D.C.* v. *Newport Corporation*, [1952] A.C. 189 at 191 per Lord Simmonds: 'It is the least justifiable when it is guesswork with what material the legislature would, if it had discovered the gap, have filled it'.

[8] There would be no validly constituted Southern Rhodesia Legislative Assembly, and no Crown powers either under the Foreign Jurisdiction or British Settlement Acts (which are irrelevant to Southern Rhodesia) or under the Rhodesia and Nyasaland Act 1963 by virtue of Section 1(2)(e). Powers under the Rhodesia and Nyasaland (Federation) Act of 1953 are, however, probably spent.

[9] Lord Denning M.R. has stated that when 'legislative institutions set up by the Crown cease to exist or are for any reason incapable of functioning, then the Crown must be able to resolve the impasse. It can in that event resort to its prerogative power to amend the

It must, however, be remembered that Courts frequently take into consideration the practical effects of their decisions and that this may result in a Court rejecting the aforegoing arguments.[1]

If however, the views outlined above are correct all members of the Southern Rhodesia Legislative Assembly vacated their seats on the dissolution of the Federation, while no further voters can be registered, and no candidates are eligible for election as members. Furthermore, any Acts passed by the Legislative Assembly since 1 January 1964 are invalid.[2]

constitution' which it may do retrospectively by Order in Council: *Sabally and N'Jie* v. *H.M. Attorney-General*, [1964] 3 W.L.R. 732 at 744. See also *dicta* by Harman L.J. at 747 and Russell L.J. at 749.

[1] See *R.* v. *Paddington Valuation Officer*, [1964] 3 All E.R. 200 at 208. However Widgery J.'s *dicta* that 'administrative chaos and public inconvenience' would be caused related to the grant of a discretionary remedy. See also Lord Dunedin's *dictum* in *Murray* v. *Commissioners of Inland Revenue*, [1918] A.C. 541 at 553 that 'nothing short of impossibility should in my judgement allow a Judge to declare a statute unworkable'.

[2] See *Sabally* v. *Attorney-General, supra*. The reason for invalidity is that there were no members representing either constituencies or electoral districts: see *dicta* by Lord Denning M.R. at 742–3. This is not affected by Section 18 of the Constitution, which provides for the validity of proceedings of the Legislative Assembly, despite any vacancy or the participation of a person not entitled to sit, as there would be no Legislative Assembly consisting of duly elected persons (Section 7(1)) and in any event such a provision could not be interpreted so as to extend to a situation where no 'members' were present. Cp. the position in Malta where Acts passed by the Legislative Assembly by virtue of the votes of people illegally present as Members were invalidated: Cmd. 3993, pp. 71–72.

7

THE LIMITATIONS ON SOUTHERN RHODESIA'S SOVEREIGNTY[1]

The United Kingdom's power to legislate

THE Parliament of the United Kingdom has an inherent power to legislate for any part of Her Majesty's Dominions. However, the Statute of Westminster 1931, provided that no United Kingdom Act passed after its commencement was to extend or be deemed to extend to a Dominion as part of its law unless the Act in question expressly recited that the Dominion concerned had requested and consented to its enactment.[2] Since the Statute of Westminster has no application to Southern Rhodesia, and neither the Southern Rhodesia (Constitution) Act 1961[3] nor the Rhodesia and Nyasaland Act 1963[4] affect this position, Parliament at Westminster has unfettered legal power to legislate for Southern Rhodesia. As Mr. Sandys said, when discussing Southern Rhodesia: 'Nothing we can do, no assurance I can give, not even an Act of Parliament here, can remove the inalienable power of this Parliament to legislate.'[5]

This power is buttressed by the rule of repugnancy expounded in the Colonial Laws Validity Act 1865.[6] Accordingly the Southern Rhodesian Legislature may not pass an enactment in conflict with any Act of the United Kingdom Parliament or any Order, Rule, or Regulation made under any such Act which has been extended to Southern Rhodesia. A considerable number of United Kingdom Acts apply to Southern Rhodesia, e.g. the Official

[1] This does not, except in one instance, refer to procedural requirements which must be complied with in order to amend the Constitution or the Electoral Act. '"A state can be unquestionably sovereign, although it has no legislature which is completely sovereign." As Bryce points out in his *History and Jurisprudence*, ". . . legal sovereignty may be divided between two authorities . . . such a division of legislative powers is no derogation from . . . sovereignty" ': *Harris and Others* v. *Minister of the Interior*, 1952 (2) S.A. 428 per Centlivres C.J. at 464 and at 468.

[2] 22 & 23 Geo. V, c. 4, sec. 4. See K. C. Wheare, *The Statute of Westminster and Dominion Status*, Oxford, 1938, pp. 153–75. The Statute does not diminish the power of the United Kingdom Parliament to legislate for the Dominions, but merely provides in Section 4 for a rule of construction. See the *dicta* by Lord Sankey that Section 4 could be disregarded by the Imperial Parliament in *British Coal Corporation* v. *The King*, [1935] A.C. 500 at 520. See also K. C. Wheare, *Constitutional Structure of the Commonwealth*, Oxford, 1960, p. 27. Cp. S. A. de Smith, *The New Commonwealth and its Constitutions*, Stevens, 1964, pp. 4–9 for the view that this is only necessarily correct in English law. See also G. Marshall, *Parliamentary Sovereignty and the Commonwealth*, Oxford, 1957, pp. 76 et seq. and pp. 145 et seq.

[3] 10 Eliz. II, c. 2.   [4] 11 & 12 Eliz. II, c. 34.
[5] *H.C. Deb.*, Vol. 637, col. 729, 23 March 1961.   [6] 28 & 29 Vict. c. 63, Sec. 2.

Secrets Act 1911.[1] However, by virtue of the announcement in 1961 by the United Kingdom Government of its recognition of 'an established convention for Parliament at Westminster, not to legislate for Southern Rhodesia on matters within the competence of the Legislative Assembly of Southern Rhodesia, except with the agreement of the Southern Rhodesian Government',[2] this power of positive legislation, though not of course the operation of the Colonial Laws Validity Act, has been limited by convention.

Acknowledging that convention is not law and that the Courts will not enforce it[3] successive British Governments[4] would be anxious not to break such a constitutional convention and would, in the political sphere, attempt to exercise British legislative powers within the limits defined by the convention so as not to breach its clearly agreed upon terms.[5] However 'emergencies may cause rules to be broken. Improper action by the colonists might compel Parliament to legislate in disregard of the ordinary maxims of policy',[6] but

[1] 1 & 2 Geo. V, c. 28. Power by Order in Council to exclude any British possession having similar legislation has not been exercised in spite of the enactment of the Southern Rhodesian Official Secrets Act (Chapter 137). Section 21 of this provides that 'this Act shall not affect the application of the Official Secrets Act 1911 of the United Kingdom to acts committed in the Colony to which the said Act applies'.

[2] Cmnd. 1399, p. 3. See *supra*, pp. 232–4 and 317.

[3] Cp. *British Coal Corporation* v. *The King*, [1935] A.C. 500 where, in interpreting the Statute of Westminster and the British North America Act 1867, the Privy Council took into account two conventions: see W. I. Jennings, 52 L.Q.R. 177–9.

[4] This can be seen in the change in attitude of the Labour Party, now that it forms the Government of the United Kingdom. When in opposition it stated that 'No constitution is defensible which fails to allow the people of those territories to control their destinies. We have bitterly attacked the Southern Rhodesian Constitution for that and a Labour Party would therefore alter it—we've made that very, very plain'—Mr. Harold Wilson in a B.B.C. broadcast of 13 March, reported in the *Rhodesia Herald*, 14 March 1963. Indeed the Labour Party consistently stated, when in opposition, that it would not consider itself bound by assurances and declarations by a Conservative Government. It has since done a *volte face*, first recognizing the 1961 Convention on 3 March 1965, in a joint statement by Lord Gardiner and Mr. Bottomley, *Rhodesia Herald*, 4 March 1965. The Ministers declared that 'any attempt by the British Government to impose unilaterally a solution of these problems (transition to majority rule) would violate the 1961 Constitution and the established convention that Parliament at Westminster does not legislate on matters within the competence of the Legislative Assembly of Rhodesia except with the agreement of the Rhodesia Government'. Furthermore they had informed Nationalist leaders that 'Britain would not herself act unconstitutionally, whether by armed force, or otherwise, to change the constitution, and that it would be useless for her to call a constitutional conference unless all parties concerned were willing to attend it'. This acknowledgement of the convention was repeated in the House of Commons on 8 March 1965; *H.C. Deb.*, Vol. 708, col. 37.

[5] See *H.L. Deb.*, Vol. 238, cols. 957–8, 27 March 1962, the Lord Chancellor, Lord Kilmuir, and *H.L. Deb.*, Vol. 245, vol. 1218, 19 November 1962, the Lord Chancellor, Lord Dilhorne. See also de Smith, op. cit., p. 42, who states that the United Kingdom is 'constitutionally bound (in the absence of a fundamental change of circumstances) by the limitations that it has expressly accepted'.

[6] Jenkyns, op. cit., p. 12. This principle is correct even though the author was writing at the beginning of this century. See Mr. Bottomley, Secretary of State for Commonwealth Relations in *H.C. Deb.*, Vol. 708, col. 38, 8 March 1965: 'I made it quite clear that so long as there was no unconstitutional action this Government would respect the convention.' See also *H.C. Deb.*, Vol. 708, col. 197, 15 March 1965.

in all normal circumstances the United Kingdom Government would observe the convention. On the other hand, once the limits of the convention were defined, no United Kingdom Government would feel obliged to interpret the powers of the United Kingdom Parliament as being restricted beyond the necessary scope of the convention. This was the attitude of the Lord Chancellor, Lord Kilmuir, to a similar convention in respect of the Federation of Rhodesia and Nyasaland. On 27 April 1957 in a joint communique issued by the Secretary of State for Commonwealth Relations and the Prime Minister of the Federation, it was announced that

United Kingdom Ministers made it clear that the United Kingdom Government recognizes the existence of a convention ... whereby the United Kingdom Government in practice does not initiate any legislation to amend or repeal any Federal Act or to deal with any matter included within the competence of the Federal Legislature, except at the request of the Federal Government.[1]

In discussing whether provision by Act of the United Kingdom Parliament for the Federation or secession of a constituent Territory was a breach of such convention, the Lord Chancellor indicated that 'the important point ... is that as to those matters that fall outside that understanding and are not included within the competence of the Federal Legislature, the legal position must clearly be ... that the legislative power of this Parliament is free from any restriction'.[2] It is therefore necessary to examine the scope of the Southern Rhodesian convention and to define its limits.

Scope of the convention

Unfortunately the convention seems to have been rather loosely worded as it refers to 'matters within the competence of the Legislative Assembly of Southern Rhodesia'. Strictly speaking, no matters other than the provision for the Legislative Assembly to make its own Standing Rules and Orders are within the competence of the Legislative Assembly. In truth the convention should have referred to the Legislature of Southern Rhodesia,[3] viz. the Crown and the Legislative Assembly. This was the meaning ascribed to the phrase by the United Kingdom Attorney-General in July 1963, when he stated that

[1] For text, see Cmnd. 1149, Advisory Commission on the Review of the Constitution of the Federation of Rhodesia and Nyasaland. Appendix VI. Survey of Developments since 1953, p. 20, and see *supra*, Part I, Chapter 16.

[2] The Lord Chancellor maintained that such action was 'a matter solely within the legislative competence of the United Kingdom': *H.L. Deb.*, Vol. 238, col. 957, 27 March 1962. See also *supra*, Part II, Chapter 6.

[3] This convention was announced during the currency of the Southern Rhodesian Constitution Letters Patent 1923 which in Sections 1 and 2 provided that the Legislative Assembly should be the Legislature, but since Section 26(1) provided that laws must be made by the Crown acting 'by and with the advice and consent of the Legislature', it would appear that the Legislative Assembly acting alone had no competence.

the United Kingdom Parliament should not legislate for matters 'within the competence of the Legislature of Southern Rhodesia'.[1]

Yet another point which has received interpretation is the question of on whose advice the United Kingdom Parliament should act in determining Southern Rhodesian consent to British legislation for Southern Rhodesia. Cmnd. 1399 states that 'the agreement of the Southern Rhodesian Government' is required, but the Attorney-General has stated that it is 'the consent of the Southern Rhodesian Parliament' which should be obtained.[2] An analogy may be drawn from the Statute of Westminster, which provides with reference to Australia that the request and consent that is required is that of both the Parliament and the Government of the Commonwealth.[3] Similarly, amendment of those provisions of the Canadian Constitution which require to be amended by United Kingdom legislation, is requested by the Government of the Dominion by the method of forwarding addresses from both Houses of the Dominion Parliament.[4] It is unlikely that a United Kingdom Government would introduce major legislation without the request and consent of the Southern Rhodesian Legislative Assembly. On the other hand, if the matter were technical or, in the case of an Order in Council making provision for Southern Rhodesia (where power to issue such an Order remains), the United Kingdom Government might act on Southern Rhodesian Government consent alone. It seems that the view of Mr. Wilson's Labour administration is that it is the consent of the Southern Rhodesian Government that must be obtained.[5]

A further point of interpretation has arisen as to whether the convention covers powers of constitutional amendment in addition to ordinary concurrent legislative power or whether it merely relates to normal legislative acts, e.g. the imposition of a tax on bicycles. If the analogy of the Federal convention is followed (and there is nothing in the wording of the relative conventions to indicate any difference[6]), it would appear that such a convention does not relate to matters other than to internal legislation and 'ordinary

---

[1] *H.C. Deb.*, Vol. 681, col. 415, 16 July 1963, Sir John Hobson.

[2] ibid.

[3] Section 9(3).

[4] Wade and Phillips, *Constitutional Law*, 6th edition, Longmans, 1960, p. 414. See also Jennings and Young, *Constitutional Laws of the Commonwealth*, Oxford, 2nd edition, 1952, p. 134, referring to the position in New Zealand where by Section 3 of the New Zealand Statute of Westminster Adoption Act 1947 it is required that the request and consent should be that of the New Zealand Parliament.

[5] *H.C. Deb.*, Vol. 708, col. 197, 15 March 1965, Mr. Bottomley.

[6] It is, however, arguable that since Article 99 of the Federal Constitution provided that at the Review of the Federal Constitution the United Kingdom would be represented by a delegation it was envisaged that the United Kingdom would have a real say in the future development of the Constitution: de Smith, op. cit., p. 42. On the other hand a similar argument could be applied to the Southern Rhodesia Constitution 1961, which in Section 111 expressly refers to the power of the Crown in Council to amend certain sections of the Constitution.

normal legislative acts'.[1] The Lord Chancellor, in debating the similar Federal convention, declared that, despite the fact that the Federal Legislature enjoyed powers of constitutional amendment and that such action was therefore within its competence, the convention did not inhibit the British Parliament from legislating so as to amend the Federal Constitution. The same argument, if correct, is applicable to the Southern Rhodesian Constitution.[2]

It is however submitted that this differentiation between concurrent and constituent powers is irrelevant when examining the conventional relationships between the United Kingdom and her self-governing territories in view of the further convention that Britain does not legislate to change the constitutions of self-governing territories if such changes are within the competence of the local legislature unless the consent of that legislature has first been obtained. That such a convention exists was acknowledged by Lord Dilhorne, who attempted to meet any arguments based on this convention by putting forward an alternative justification: the Federation had a responsible-government type constitution but did not enjoy self-government, particularly in view of Britain's powers in the Northern Territories. On the other hand in respect of Southern Rhodesia Lord Dilhorne accepted that such a convention applied.

Even so, the formulation of this latter convention leaves constitutional amendments which are beyond the competence of the local legislature outside the scope of the convention, thus permitting of Imperial legislation on such matters without breach of convention.

This attitude was adopted by the Attorney-General in 1963 when he intervened in a debate to correct the First Secretary, Mr. Butler, who had stated that 'the Government takes the line that there has been a forty-year convention since 1923 with Southern Rhodesia that we should not intervene in their constitutional matters'.[3] The Attorney-General stated that not only was the convention 'first recognized in 1961' but that 'the only position

---

[1] *H.L. Deb.*, Vol. 245, col. 1221, 19 December 1962, the Lord Chancellor, where this attitude was adopted towards the Federal convention. For the Federal Government's point of view see *The Constitutional Convention*, Salisbury, Government Printer, 1962, C. Fed. 232; *The Issue of Nyasaland's Secession*, Salisbury, Government Printer, 1962, C. Fed. 231; *Federation of Nyasaland: the British Government's Broken Pledges and the Consequences*, published by the Federal Government. See also *Fed. Parlty. Deb.*, cols. 2033 et seq., 19 December 1962, Sir Roy Welensky; and col. 2170, 20 December 1962; and cols. 205 et seq. 19 December 1962; and col. 327, 17 April 1963, the Minister of Law. For the British Government's repudiation of these allegations that pledges had been broken see Cmnd. 1948.

[2] Although no specific convention was relied upon to prevent the dissolution of the Federation of the West Indies the same argument applies since the United Kingdom does not normally legislate for self-governing territories. Against the wishes of the Federal Government dissolution of the Federation of the West Indies was provided for by Orders in Council under the West Indies Act 1962 (10 & 11 Eliz. II, c. 19). Prior to the dissolution a Commissioner was permitted to disregard the advice of the Cabinet.

[3] *H.C. Deb.*, Vol. 681, col. 412, 16 July 1963, Butler.

which has been taken' was that 'it would not be right for this Parliament to legislate for matters which are within the competence of the Legislature of Southern Rhodesia without the consent of the Southern Rhodesian Parliament'.[1] Indeed, it is very doubtful if the convention, when announced in 1961, was intended to affect powers of constitutional amendment which were clearly possessed by the United Kingdom at that time[2] as the Secretary of State for Commonwealth Relations, Mr. Sandys, when first questioned about the announcement of the Convention stated that he had entered into no new commitment: 'whatever the constitutional position is, nothing that I have done has altered it in any way'.[3]

Nonetheless, responsible Ministers in the United Kingdom have considerably glossed the convention and extended its original meaning from that given to it in 1961.[4] Thus the Under Secretary of State for Commonwealth Relations, relying on the convention, informed the House of Commons that if it became desirable to amend the Southern Rhodesian Constitution in any way not authorized by the Order in Council so that further United Kingdom legislation was necessary 'there would of course be no question of the British Government asking Parliament to legislate in a situation like that without the agreement of the Southern Rhodesian Government'.[5] Mr. Sandys has also stated that the Convention made it 'constitutionally improper and impracticable for us without the consent of Southern Rhodesia to impose upon it a new Constitution with a much wider representation to Africans'.[6] Mr. R. A.

[1] *H.C. Deb.*, Vol. 681, col. 415, 16 July 1963, Sir John Hobson.

[2] Cp. the prerogative powers of the Crown specially reserved in terms of Section 61 of the Southern Rhodesia Constitution Letters Patent 1923.

[3] *H.C. Deb.*, Vol. 641, col. 1395, 8 June 1961.

[4] This has probably been done with developments at the United Nations Organization in mind, e.g. Sir Patrick Dean's speech at the United Nations on 28 June 1962, which stated that the United Kingdom had 'no power to intervene in Southern Rhodesia's internal affairs without the consent of the Government of that territory', a similar speech by Mr. C. King on 21 March 1963 at the Committee of Twenty-four, Mr. Jacklin's statement on 7 March 1963 that Britain 'had neither the right in law nor the means in practice to intervene in Southern Rhodesia', the British Government's Statements to the Special Committee that it 'had no power to intervene in the internal affairs of Southern Rhodesia either constitutionally or physically' (Report of 30 July 1963) and Sir Patrick Dean's speech on 10 September 1963 emphasizing the 'freedom of the Southern Rhodesian Government to conduct their own internal affairs is no fiction but an inescapable constitutional and political fact'. It is the 'political fact' that has been decisive in Britain's adoption of this attitude: see Mr. Sandys' statement that 'I hope that those outside who always tell us that we ought to interfere and do this or that in Southern Rhodesia will realize that there is not a single official or soldier in Southern Rhodesia responsible to the British Government': *H.C. Deb.*, Vol. 684, col. 585, 15 November 1963. The attitude of Mr. Wilson's administration has also been conditioned by this 'political fact' and by its belief that the employment of force against Southern Rhodesia would 'result in economic and war developments which might spread far beyond Rhodesian borders' and even in a second 'Congo': for these views on the impossibility of using force against Southern Rhodesia see a statement made by Mr. Bottomley at Accra on 10 August 1965 quoted in the *Rhodesia Herald*, 13 August 1965.

[5] *H.C. Deb.*, Vol. 648, cols. 1049–50, 6 August 1961.

[6] *H.C. Deb.*, Vol. 648, col. 1110, 8 November 1961.

Butler has also extended its scope. He announced that, except in respect of the Queen and the Governor, the amendment of the Southern Rhodesian Constitution was a matter for Southern Rhodesian legislation and that Britain had no power to change the Southern Rhodesian Constitution.[1] Indeed, he considered that the convention meant British 'non-interference in the internal affairs of Southern Rhodesia'.[2] On the other hand Mr. Butler maintained that the United Kingdom Parliament retained 'power to legislate with regard to the Federation and so indirectly with regard to Southern Rhodesia'.[3] However, the First Secretary subsequently, in answer to a request for full independence by the Southern Rhodesian Prime Minister, Mr. Field, replied that the United Kingdom Government agreed 'that in the light of the recognized convention it would not be right for the United Kingdom themselves to enact any changes in the Constitution. Nonetheless our Government would wish to discuss with yours whether and in what respect the powers of amendment (conferred in the 1961 Constitution) . . . should be exercised'.[4] Thereafter Mr. Butler announced Southern Rhodesian and British agreement 'that any changes in the Southern Rhodesian Constitution will be effected by the Southern Rhodesian Parliament and not by Parliament at Westminster'.[5]

When, at the end of May 1963, the Southern Rhodesian Prime Minister discussed the question of the grant of independence to Southern Rhodesia, he received 'repeated assurances in writing and by word that Her Majesty's Government cannot and will not interfere in our affairs',[6] while Mr. Sandys extended the meaning to the fullest possible extent when in November 1963 he stated that Southern Rhodesia enjoyed 'complete internal self-government' and that Britain had 'long ago accepted the principle that Parliament at Westminster does not legislate for Southern Rhodesia except at her request'.[7]

Despite these statements it is submitted that Britain is only limited in respect of matters within the scope of the convention (it is accepted that this encompasses constitutional amendments which are within the competence of the Southern Rhodesian Legislature). If this view is correct certain types of constitutional amendment which are not within the competence of the Legislature of Southern Rhodesia are outside the scope of the convention. Section 111 of the Southern Rhodesian Constitution reserves power to the

---

[1] *H.C. Deb.*, Vol. 667, col. 1375, 22 November 1962.

[2] *H.C. Deb.*, Vol. 659, col. 237, 8 May 1962, Butler, and *H.C. Deb.*, Vol. 668, cols. 969–70, 3 December 1962. These statements were in fact welcomed as an extension of the convention by Sir Edgar Whitehead in *S.R.L.A.D.*, Vol. 56, col. 684, 11 March 1964. Mr. Bottomley has also stated that 'we undertook not to interfere in the internal affairs of Rhodesia': *H.C. Deb.*, Vol. 708, cols. 37–38.

[3] Cmnd. 2000. Correspondence between Her Majesty's Government of the United Kingdom and Her Majesty's Government of Southern Rhodesia, Butler to Field, 9 April 1963.

[4] Cmnd. 2000, Butler to Field, 2 May 1963.

[5] Cmnd. 2000, Butler to Field, received 16 May 1963.

[6] *S.R.L.A.D.*, Vol. 53, col. 14, 18 June 1963, Field.

[7] *H.C. Deb.*, Vol. 684, col. 585, 15 November 1963.

Crown by Order in Council to amend, add to or revoke sections of the Constitution dealing with the office of Governor and his powers and duties (Sections 1, 2, 3, and 5), the Governor's assent or approval of assent to Bills (Section 29), disallowance (Section 32), the prerogative of mercy (Section 49), the composition of the Legislature (Section 6), and the definition of the authority in whom executive power for Southern Rhodesia is vested and how such power is to be exercised (Section 42). In addition, the Legislative Assembly is prohibited by Section 105 of the Constitution from legislating on these topics.[1] In the light of these provisions it is submitted that not only would a United Kingdom Order in Council be permissible but that Parliament could legislate on these topics without breach of convention.

Indeed, as a result of the possibilities inherent in Section 111 the Southern Rhodesian Government accepted a motion asking the Governor to submit a petition to the Queen requesting her to secure the passage by the United Kingdom Parliament of an Act amending Section 111 of the Constitution, so as to make it clear that the power of the Queen by Order in Council to amend various provisions in the Constitution should only be exercised with the consent of a two-thirds majority of the Southern Rhodesian Legislative Assembly and furthermore that this power must be so exercised on any resolution passed by a two-thirds majority of the total membership of the Legislative Assembly.[2]

Section 111 has been attacked as not being a true reflection of the White Paper which preceded the grant of the 1961 Constitution[3] since paragraph 78 of Cmnd. 1400, which preceded Section 111, declared that only the 'formal functions within the Constitution of the Sovereign and of the Governor in his capacity as the Sovereign's representative' would not be subject to amendment by the Legislature. Although it is questionable whether Section 111 reflects the views embodied in the White Paper, it is submitted that Section 111 is unambiguous and that therefore any regard to the White Paper as illuminating 'the subject matter with which the Legislature was dealing'[4] is impermissible.[5] Only 'where the meaning of an Act is doubtful' are the Courts 'at liberty to recur to the circumstances under which it passed into law'.[6]

---

[1] de Smith, op. cit., p. 43, considers that none of these provisions is of first rate practical importance.

[2] *S.R.L.A.D.*, Vol. 56, col. 630, 11 March 1964, and col. 1010, 18 March 1964. See text of the motion quoted in Part II, Chapter 1.

[3] *S.R.L.A.D.*, Vol. 56, col. 640, and col. 665, 11 March 1964.

[4] Per Lord Halsbury L.C. in *Herron* v. *Rathmines and Rathgar Improvement Commissioners*, [1892] A.C. at 502.

[5] 'In the interpretation of a completely self-governing constitution founded upon a written organic instrument ... if the text is explicit the text is conclusive alike in what it directs and what it forbids.' *Attorney-General for Ontario* v. *Attorney-General for Canada*, [1912] A.C. per Lord Loreburn at 583.

[6] *South Eastern Railway Co.* v. *The Railway Commissioners* (1880), Q.B.D. 217 per Cockburn C.J. at 236. If Section 111 were ambiguous it seems that Cmnd. 1400 could be examined. See authorities cited in Jennings and Young, op. cit., pp. 127–8. *Dicta* that a White

It is similarly submitted that in interpreting the ambit of the powers conferred by Section 111 the convention that Britain will not legislate for Southern Rhodesia without her consent is equally irrelevant as the section is unambiguous.[1]

The extent to which the exercise of such powers could, without breach of convention, affect the Constitution is quite considerable. Accepting that an amendment to any of the enumerated sections, which also had the effect of consequentially amending any other section not so enumerated would be a breach of convention, it is submitted that many amendments of consequence would not have this effect and would be permissible.

Minor amendments would be possible to sections 1, 2, and 49, thus Section 1 could be amended so as to exclude any consultation with the Prime Minister of Southern Rhodesia, which is now required in respect of the appointment of a Governor. Section 2 could be amended to give the Governor executive powers to be exercised in his personal discretion. Section 49 could be altered so as to confer the prerogative of mercy on the Governor acting in his discretion, or on the advice of the British Cabinet.[2]

A possible major amendment would be to increase the power of negative control by adding further categories of laws of the Southern Rhodesian Legislature which could be disallowed by the Queen acting on the advice of Her Majesty's Government in the United Kingdom. At present Section 32(1) merely specifies two categories of laws subject to disallowance. There is no reason why further categories could not be added, e.g. land laws, security laws, discriminatory laws. It is submitted that such additions would not impliedly or consequentially amend any other provisions of the Constitution: they would not interfere with the functions of the Legislative Assembly, which is concerned with the passing of Bills and the making of laws.[3] Nor would such provisions interfere with the giving of assent to Bills as disallowance is a procedure relative to Acts after they have been made and no other part of the Constitution is concerned with this.

Another major change which would not breach the convention would be amendments to Sections 6 and 29(2) making provision for an Upper House or Senate (composed or elected in any way specified in the Order creating it) as part of the Legislature, and further providing that the Governor should only assent to Bills after approval by the Senate, which should consider Bills after they had been duly passed by the Legislative Assembly. The insertion of

Paper is inadmissible evidence to assist in construction (in this case of the Second Schedule to the Buganda Agreement of 1955 which had the force of law) in *Katikiro of Buganda* v. *Attorney-General*, [1960] 3 All E.R. 849 (P.C.) at 855–6 are *obiter*.

[1] Were it ambiguous then the convention could have been called in to aid in interpretation: see *British Coal Corporation* v. *The King, supra*, as interpreted by W. I. Jennings in 52 L.Q.R. at 177–9.

[2] In fact this could even be done without any constitutional amendment by the giving of Royal Instructions under Sections 2 and 45(1).

[3] Section 20(1): 'The Legislature shall have power to make laws (to be entitled Acts).'

a new step in the legislative process and a further element in the composition of the Legislature does not either expressly or impliedly amend any section of the Constitution which is within the competence of the Southern Rhodesian Legislature.

Thus, without breach of convention, either the Crown by Order in Council or the United Kingdom Parliament could make major amendments to the Southern Rhodesian Constitution. The practicability of enforcing such constitutional powers belongs, however, to the realm of politics and not to that of law.[1]

Specific legislative powers afforded the Crown under United Kingdom Acts

Specific powers of legislation conferred on the Crown by Acts of the United Kingdom Parliament are not subsumed under the convention, which provides that 'Parliament at Westminster' does not legislate for Southern Rhodesia in matters within the competence of the Southern Rhodesian Legislative Assembly. In fact, the surviving powers conferred on the Crown by particular statutes relate either to provisions consequential on the establishment or dissolution of Federation, which at the time of their conferment and at the time when the convention was recognized, were for the most part beyond the competence of the Southern Rhodesian Legislature.

Although the Rhodesia and Nyasaland (Federation) Act remains on the statute book it is arguable that since the dissolution of Federation any powers conferred by that Act are spent.

However, there is no doubt that the Federation of Rhodesia and Nyasaland (Constitution) Order in Council 1953 is still in force. This is clear from the Federation of Rhodesia and Nyasaland (Dissolution) Order in Council 1963, which provides for minor amendments to the 1953 Order in Council.[2]

Section 14(9)(b) of that Order permits the Crown by Order in Council to—

make such adaptations and modifications of any further enactment or of any Order in Council, Order, regulation or other instrument, being an enactment or instrument relating or referring to any of the Territories and passed or made before the making of this Order, as appear to Her Majesty to be necessary or expedient by reason of the provisions of this Order.

The effect of this would seemingly be to preserve Crown power to amend enactments relating or referring to the Territories, if made before the Federation

---

[1] Compare Mr. Sandys' reference to the fact that 'there is not a single official or soldier in Southern Rhodesia responsible to the British Government', supra. See also H.C. Deb., Vol. 713, col. 1558, Mr. Bottomley: 'The Rhodesian Government have not been staffed or controlled by the Colonial Office. Their police forces, armed forces, and administration have all been under the control of the Rhodesia Government. These are the realities which must be borne in mind in any consideration of this difficult problem.'

[2] S.I. 1963 No. 2085, Section 75, Schedule III, Item 1.

47 — C.H.L.S.R.

of Rhodesia and Nyasaland (Constitution) Order in Council, in the light of the provisions of that Order.

Much greater power is given by the Rhodesia and Nyasaland Act 1963 which permits the Crown by Order in Council to make any incidental, supplemental, and consequential provisions as a result of the dissolution of the Federation of Rhodesia and Nyasaland,[1] although this Act does not itself authorize amendment of the Territorial Constitutions.[2] So far two Orders in Council have been issued under this Act[3] but all Orders may be varied or revoked by a subsequent Order in Council subject to laying such Draft Order before Parliament and approval by Resolution of both Houses.[4] The Crown, therefore, retains considerable power to make provision relating to the functions previously exercised by the Federal Government and Legislature, e.g. the Crown may make provision 'as to the armed forces and public service of the Federation and persons being members or former members thereof'.[5]

The Crown is not empowered to legislate for Southern Rhodesia under the British Settlements Act 1887[6] since the Act only gives the Crown legislative powers in respect of any British possession 'which has not been acquired by cession or conquest and is not for the time being within the jurisdiction of the legislature, constituted otherwise than by virtue of this Act or of any Act repealed by this Act, of any British possession'.[7] As Southern Rhodesia is within the jurisdiction of the Southern Rhodesian Legislature which, prior to 1962, was constituted by the Southern Rhodesia Constitution Letters Patent 1923 and thereafter under the Southern Rhodesia (Constitution) Act 1961, Southern Rhodesia is not a British settlement in respect of which the Crown can exercise the powers conferred by the Act. Furthermore, since Southern Rhodesia is a colony acquired by conquest and not by settlement or occupation,[8] the British Settlements Act cannot be of application.

Similarly, no power exists under the Foreign Jurisdiction Acts, which only empower the Crown to legislate by Order in Council in areas out of Her Majesty's dominions, i.e. in foreign countries. As Southern Rhodesia has been a colony since 1923, powers under this Act cannot be invoked either.

Although until 1961 the Crown enjoyed considerable powers of prerogative legislation to amend the Southern Rhodesian Constitution by virtue of the

---

[1] 11 & 12 Eliz. II, c. 34, Section 1(1).

[2] ibid., Section 1(2)(e).

[3] S.I. 1963 No. 1635 and S.I. 1963 No. 2085.

[4] Rhodesia and Nyasaland Act 1963, Section 2(1) and (2).

[5] Section 1(2)(b). Literally interpreted this would confer the right on the Crown by Order in Council to alter the present arrangements relating to armed forces and to place them under its own control, or to place former Federal civil servants under Crown control for purposes of creating an administration.

[6] 50 & 51 Vict. c. 54.

[7] Section VI.

[8] See *In re Southern Rhodesia, supra,* at 215–16, at 221, and at 239–40.

reservation contained in the Southern Rhodesia Constitution Letters Patent 1923, this power was virtually suspended by the Southern Rhodesia (Constitution) Act 1961 and the Order in Council thereunder which provided for the methods by which the Southern Rhodesian Constitution 1961 was to be amended. Nothing in the Act authorized any other amendment or revocation.[1] Accordingly during such time as the statutory powers of constitutional amendment specified in the Southern Rhodesia (Constitution) Order in Council 1961 are in existence, to that extent the Royal prerogative is suspended.[2]

For a short period prior to the coming into force of the Southern Rhodesian Constitution 1961, the Crown's full powers to amend, add to, or revoke the Constitution and that Order in Council were reserved.[3]

However, even after the coming into force of the Constitution, Section 111 of the Constitution reserved to Her Majesty power by Order in Council at any time to add to, amend, or revoke the provisions enumerated in that section.[4]

The significance of such power is that its use is not limited by the convention previously discussed, since the Legislature of Southern Rhodesia is incompetent to amend the sections of the Constitution to which that power relates.[5]

That this attitude might be adopted is implicit from an answer of the Lord Chancellor to a question whether Section 49 of the Constitution dealing with the prerogative of mercy could be amended by the United Kingdom Parliament without reference to the Government of Southern Rhodesia. The Lord Chancellor replied that full power and authority were reserved to Her Majesty by an Order in Council to amend, add to, or to revoke Section 49 and the other sections enumerated in Section 111.[6] In practice, however, in all normal cases the Southern Rhodesian Government and Legislative Assembly would be consulted on the exercise of such power.

It seems that the Crown still retains a modicum of prerogative power as it may, to a minor degree, legislate through Letters Patent and Royal Instructions issued under the Sign Manual and Signet relating to the office of Governor.[7]

Finally, although this power is conferred by Southern Rhodesian legislation,

---

[1] 10 Eliz. II, c. 2, Section 1(2).

[2] *Attorney-General* v. *de Keyser's Hotel Ltd.*, *supra*. See, however, *dicta* by Russell L.J. in *Sabally & N'Jie* v. *H.M. Attorney-General, supra* at 749 that 'if, in conferring on the Crown powers within its prerogative, a statute imposes restrictions, limitations, conditions, or a required *modus operandi*, then the prerogative is superseded and the powers cannot be exercised otherwise than subject to such restrictions, limitations, or conditions, or in accordance with that *modus operandi*. I do not think the cases establish more than that.'

[3] Southern Rhodesia (Constitution) Order in Council, Sections 22 and 5(b).

[4] See *supra* and de Smith's comments, op. cit., at p. 43.

[5] Section 105.

[6] *H.L. Deb.*, Vol. 255, col. 6, 4 February 1964.

[7] See Roberts-Wray, op. cit., pp. 18–19 and de Smith, op. cit., p. 52, n. 49.

it should also be mentioned that in terms of Section 53(3) of the Land Apportionment Act No. 11 of 1941 any regulations under that Act require the approval of the Secretary of State for Commonwealth Relations. Such regulations may relate to the area of land holdings sold or leased to Africans in the Native Area of the Colony, and to conditions attached to such holdings, and may make provisions for the good government and general welfare of African townships, village settlements and business centres.[1] In addition restrictive regulatory powers are given permitting prohibition and restriction of the entry of undesirable persons into the Native Area and prohibition of non-Africans entering native locations. Despite the new Constitution the Act has not so far been amended to eliminate the Secretary of State's approval as a requirement for regulations.[2]

Revocation of the Constitution

When legislative institutions have been granted to a conquered colony, unless the Crown has expressly reserved the right of revoking the grant, there can be no revocation of the Constitution, i.e. rescission of or cancellation of the Constitution, 'the most drastic of all steps when self-government has once been granted'.[3] The only power of revocation reserved in the Southern Rhodesian Constitution 1961 was that mentioned in Section 22 of the Southern Rhodesia (Constitution) Order in Council 1961, which reservation has now lapsed. Therefore, during such time as the Legislature of Southern Rhodesia continues to exist, the Crown has no power of revoking the Constitution. However, on the analogy of the early cases relating to the revocation of Royal Charters, it is arguable that the Crown may resume a Government granted under a constitution that has been abused.[4]

Indeed there have been *dicta* that indicate that the Royal prerogative to legislate for conquered territory to which representative legislative institutions have been granted, revives when the representative legislature begins to func-

---

[1] The latter power is not now invoked in practice as the Local Government Act 1961, Section 65, gives similar powers to make regulations which do not require the consent of the Secretary of State. See also *supra*, Chapter 5.

[2] It might be argued that if the Act were amended to eliminate the reference to the Secretary of State all regulations under the section as amended could be tested against Section 67 of the Declaration of Rights as the law would be changed and would no longer be saved by Section 70(1)(b) as being in force before the time of coming into effect of the new Constitution, a clear discretion and power formerly given to the Secretary of State having been removed: see *African Newspapers (Pvt.) Ltd. and Wason* v. *Lardner-Burke and Bosman NN.O.*, *supra*, in which a somewhat similar argument was advanced on different facts. This is probable the reason why the section has not been amended to eliminate the Secretary of State's power.

[3] Malta: Report of Constitutional Commissioner (Sir Harold MacMichael), Colonial No. 207 (1947), p. 33.

[4] See Forsyth, op. cit., pp. 381 et seq. for the Crown's right to revoke a Charter that has been abused and to provide a new form of government. Such a power in Forsyth's view does not extend to altering enactments or making laws.

tion illegally, i.e. in a manner different from the one in which it is intended to function.[1] Should the legislative institutions which have been established cease to exist or for any reason become incapable of functioning the Crown may 'resort to its prerogative power to amend the Constitution or set up a new one'.[2]

There is no doubt that the Imperial Parliament retains full power to authorize the revocation of any constitution by Act, as in the case of Malta in 1936,[3] in which event the Crown's prerogative power of legislation would, after revocation, revive.[4] Such drastic action would clearly only be taken in exceptional circumstances, such as the failure of legislative institutions or where it was necessary to dispense with the wreckage of the old constitution.

Suspension of the Southern Rhodesia Constitution

Suspension of the constitution is, however, 'a temporary process of a less definitive type'.[5] In such a case, as an emergency measure, full legislative and executive authority is placed in the hands of the Governor while the existing Ministry is retained in office and is available in a consultative capacity in so far as the Governor chooses to make use of their services.[6] Such action could, if necessary, be taken in Southern Rhodesia by amendments by Order in Council to Sections 6 and 42 of the Southern Rhodesia Constitution 1961 (relating to the composition of the Legislature and in whom the executive authority of Southern Rhodesia is vested), on the analogy of the Malta (Temporary Government) Order in Council 1930 of 26 June 1930, which gave the Governor power to make laws, vested executive government in Her Majesty to be administered by the Governor as her representative, empowered him to act in opposition to the advice of the Executive Council, and provided that anything inconsistent in the Constitution should be deemed to be of no effect.

That the United Kingdom Government can exercise this exceptional power

---

[1] See the judgement of *Usif Patel* v. *The Crown* (*Federal Court of Pakistan*) quoted in W. I. Jennings, *Constitutional Problems in Pakistan*, Cambridge, 1957, at pp. 454–5.

[2] *Sabally & N'Jie* v. *H.M. Attorney-General*, *supra* at 744 per Lord Denning M.R.

[3] This was done in Malta in August 1936 by Letters Patent issued after the Malta (Letters Patent) Act, 26 Geo. V and 1 Edw. VIII, c. 29 had conferred power on the Crown to revoke or amend the Malta Constitution Letters Patent 1921. See also W. K. Hancock, *Survey of British Commonwealth Affairs*, Vol. I, *Problems of Nationality*, Oxford, 1937, pp. 406–28. Revocation of the Maltese Constitution occurred a second time after the passing of the Malta (Letters Patent) Act 1959, 7 & 8 Eliz. II, c. 14. See also Cmnd. 1261. The same thing was done in the case of British Guiana in 1928 by the British Guiana Act, 18 Geo V, c. 5. This Constitution, however, only conferred representative government.

[4] See *Sammut* v. *Strickland*, *supra*.

[5] Colonial No. 207 (1947), p. 33. See *H.C. Deb.*, Vol. 314, col. 510, 1 July 1936, Mr. Henderson, pointing out the distinction between 'killing' and suspending the constitution.

[6] *H.C. Deb.*, Vol. 240, col. 968, 24 June 1930, Mr. MacDonald, Prime Minister. This occurred in Malta in June 1930 (see Cmnd. 3993, Malta Royal Commission 1931 Report, p. 201), in November 1933 (Colonial 207 (1947), p. 8) and in 1958.

in respect of Southern Rhodesia has been recognized by United Kingdom Ministries. On occasions when requested to suspend the Southern Rhodesia Constitution 1923 and the 1961 Constitution, Ministers have not denied this power.[1] In fact in 1963 the First Secretary explicitly acknowledged the power but declined to exercise it in respect of Southern Rhodesia.[2] Again in March 1964 the Secretary of State for Commonwealth Relations impliedly recognized this power by stating the impropriety of intervening 'at an intermediate stage in the operation of the Southern Rhodesia Constitution'.[3]

There is no doubt that in a crisis the Southern Rhodesia Constitution could be suspended by Order in Council.

Disallowance

The Crown, acting on the advice of the United Kingdom Government, retains the power to disallow certain categories of Southern Rhodesian laws for a period of six months from the date of the Governor's assent to such a law.[4] In cases where such power is exercised, the Governor shall cause notice of disallowance to be published in the Gazette, and from the date of such publication the law which has been disallowed shall cease to have effect, while any enactment repealed or amended by the disallowed law shall have effect as if the latter had not been made.[5]

The first category of laws subject to disallowance is necessary in view of the United Kingdom's ultimate responsibility for Southern Rhodesia. Thus, any laws which in the opinion of Her Majesty's Government in the United Kingdom appear 'to be inconsistent with any obligations imposed on Her Majesty in relation to Southern Rhodesia by any treaty, convention, agreement, or amendment relating to any country or international or similar organization' may be disallowed.[6]

The protection of British investors is the reason for the second category of laws subject to disallowance. Thus laws may be disallowed which appear to Her Majesty's Government in the United Kingdom to alter to the injury of stockholders any undertakings given by the Southern Rhodesian Government at the time of issue in respect of Southern Rhodesian Government stocks registered under the Colonial Stock Acts. Similarly, laws which involve a

---

[1] *H.C. Deb.*, Vol. 631, col. 559, 1 December 1960; Vol. 658, col. 112, 19 April 1962; Vol. 667, col. 139, 22 December 1962; and Vol. 668, col. 1064, 3 December 1962. The last occasion is revealing as Mr. Butler in discussing this possibility did not deny its existence but merely stated that he had no intention of suspending the Constitution.

[2] *H.C. Deb.*, Vol. 681, col. 412, 16 July 1963.

[3] *H.C. Deb.*, Vol. 693, col. 884, 20 April 1964.

[4] Section 32(1) of the Southern Rhodesia Constitution 1961. The provisions for disallowance may not be amended by the Southern Rhodesian Legislature but only by Her Majesty by Order in Council: *supra*.

[5] Section 32(2) and (3).

[6] Section 32(1)(c).

departure from the original contract in respect of such stock may be disallowed.[1] However, the subsection relating to disallowance of Southern Rhodesian laws affecting Southern Rhodesian Government stock is likely to become progressively less important, in view of the provisions of the Trustee Investment Act 1961.[2] This repealed Section 1 of the Trustee Act 1925,[3] which had permitted United Kingdom trustees to invest in securities authorized in terms of the Colonial Stock Act of 1900.[4] Since its repeal fresh investments by trustees, unless such power is conferred by the trust instrument, cannot be made in Southern Rhodesian Government stock. Apparently it might even be the duty of trustees to dispose of existing investments in Southern Rhodesian Government stock in terms of section 6(1)(b).[5] On the other hand, institutional and other investors who have bought Southern Rhodesian stock will continue to require this protection, as will holders of stock issued by the Federation of Rhodesia and Nyasaland and holders of any stock issued before the dissolution of the Federation by the Territories in substitution therefor, since, despite the provisions of the Trustee Investments Act 1961, these remain stocks in which a trustee may invest.[6]

That such powers are real has been emphasized by a statement by the First Secretary, Mr. Butler, that the Crown can exercise this power if necessary.[7]

Reservation of Southern Rhodesian Bills

The Constitution provides that, except in respect of Bills amending the specially entrenched sections of the Southern Rhodesian Constitution, Bills rendering ineligible for registration as voters persons having the franchise qualifications set out in the Second Schedule, and certain Bills affecting land, no Bill shall be reserved.[8] There is accordingly no discretionary reservation such as that which existed under the 1923 Constitution.

Since the procedure for the amendment of the specially entrenched provisions of the Southern Rhodesian Constitution and passage of those Bills

---

[1] Section 32(1)(a) and (b). Cp. The Ceylon Independence Act 1947 (11 Geo. VI, c. 7). Whereas the provisions for an alternative procedure in the Colonial Stock Act 1934 (24 & 25 Geo. V, c. 47) have been extended to Ceylon, they have not been extended to Southern Rhodesia as she is not yet independent.

[2] 9 & 10 Eliz. II, c. 62.

[3] 15 & 16 Geo. V, c. 19.

[4] 63 & 64 Vict. c. 62.

[5] Despite Section 4 of the Trustee Act 1925 providing that a trustee shall not be liable for breach of trust by reason only of continuing to hold an investment which has ceased to be authorized by the general law or by the trust instrument, Section 2 of the Trustee Investment Act 1961 apparently requires a trustee to dispose of existing investments if such investment will upset the balance of the trust fund. See H. G. Hanbury, *Modern Equity*, 8th edition, Stevens, 1962, p. 679.

[6] See S.I. 1963 No. 2085, Section 16(8) and (6), Part D of Schedule I. Some of the stock matures as late as 1981.

[7] *H.C. Deb.*, Vol. 668, cols. 969–70, 3 December 1962.

[8] Section 30(1) and see *supra*, Chapter 1.

which require the observance of a similar procedure, i.e. approval by a two-thirds majority of the total membership of the Legislative Assembly and by a majority of each of the four principal racial communities of Southern Rhodesia, viz. European, African, Asian, and Coloured, voting separately in a referendum, is probably the most difficult barrier to constitutional amendment yet devised,[1] the Constitution has provided an alternative method of amendment. In this alternative procedure such a Bill requires to be passed by a two-thirds majority of the total membership of the Legislative Assembly, but in lieu of a referendum a motion, passed also by a two-thirds majority, to present an address to the Governor praying him to submit the Bill to Her Majesty for assent, may be moved by a Government Minister after the Governor, in pursuance of Instructions from Her Majesty, has signified Her Majesty's consent to the moving of such an address.[2] Upon receipt of such address the Governor is required to reserve the Bill in question for the signification of Her Majesty's pleasure while that Bill shall only come into operation on the date on which the Governor publishes a Proclamation signifying Her assent thereto.[3]

By virtue of these provisions the United Kingdom Government is empowered to advise Her Majesty as to whether such alternative procedure should be utilized for any particular constitutional amendment. The effective barrier in the procedure is the necessity for Her Majesty's Instructions to the Governor authorizing the moving of a motion for an address, as presumably once Instructions permitting the moving of an address were issued on United Kingdom Ministerial advice, the constitutional Bill, although reserved, would be assented to on similar advice. The United Kingdom through this procedure can therefore exercise the negative power of refusing to permit the passage of a constitutional amendment in this fashion.[4] Such power may be of great significance, as utilization of this procedure could break internal constitutional deadlock. Although the British Government at first indicated that such power would only be used for minor and technical amendments, it later acknowledged that major amendments could be made in this way.[5] In fact, in 1964 this procedure was utilized to recast the provisions relating to the judicature in Southern Rhodesia and to establish an Appellate Division of the High Court,[6] in lieu of the defunct Federal Supreme Court, which ceased to

---

[1] The Constitution is possibly even less susceptible of amendment than is the Cyprus Constitution.

[2] Sections 107 and 109.

[3] Section 30(1), (4), and section 29(3). See e.g. S.R.G.N. No. 367A of 1964, Proclamation of 15 May 1964 giving effect to the Constitution Amendment Act No. 13 of 1964.

[4] Cmnd. 1399, para. 54, where it was made clear that the United Kingdom Government reserved the right to state that it considered that 'it will be more appropriate for the issue to be decided by a referendum'.

[5] Cp. *H.C. Deb.*, Vol. 642, col. 1708 (where the earlier attitude is maintained) with col. 1782, 22 June 1961.

[6] Constitution Amendment Act No. 13 of 1964.

exist in April 1964, when it had heard and determined all proceedings pending before it immediately before the dissolution of the Federation.[1]

The removal from the Constitution of this alternative method of amendment of entrenched provisions is within the competence of the Southern Rhodesian Legislature, provided in so doing it follows either of the procedures provided for the amendment of a specially entrenched constitutional provision. However, such removal would place the Legislature in a position in which further constitutional amendment to such provisions as are enumerated in the Third Schedule to the Constitution might well in practice become impossible.

The Governor

The Governor of Southern Rhodesia is not appointed on the advice of the Southern Rhodesian Prime Minister but on the advice of the United Kingdom Government. However, the Constitution recognized the long-standing practice by which the Southern Rhodesian Prime Minister was consulted before any appointment was made. Thus it is provided that the Prime Minister should be consulted concerning the person to be appointed Governor, although no court may enquire into whether this provision has been observed.[2] There is no time limit to the tenure of office of the Governor, who shall hold office during Her Majesty's pleasure.[3]

The Governor, who represents the Crown, has such powers and duties as Her Majesty may from time to time be pleased to assign him and, in exercising these powers, he is required to act in accordance with Instructions given him from time to time by Her Majesty.[4] The retention of these powers was apparently insisted on at the Southern Rhodesian Constitutional Conference in February 1961, by Mr. Sandys, who pointed out that, although the Governor normally acted on the advice of the local Executive Council, the Sovereign retained power to give Instructions to Her Governor until such time as the country became fully independent.[5]

---

[1] S.I. 1963 No. 2085, Section 19(1) and (6). See *supra*, Part II, Chapter 6.

[2] Section 1(1). The appointment of an Acting Governor is made in the same way: Section 3(1).

[3] The present Governor has held office for five years. Should the Governor wish to vacate his office it might be difficult to obtain a successor to him without provoking a political crisis, as it is unlikely that one would be acceptable both to Her Majesty's Government in the United Kingdom and to Her Government in Southern Rhodesia.

[4] Section 2. No enquiry may be made in any court as to whether the Governor has conformed with such Instructions.

[5] Hirsch, op. cit., p. 30. The author charges the British Government with breaking understandings reached at the Conference, by vesting the executive authority of Southern Rhodesia in Her Majesty (Section 42) and providing that it 'may be exercised on Her Majesty's behalf by the Governor' who, in terms of Section 2, is subject to 'such Instructions if any as Her Majesty may from time to time see fit to give him'. This arrangement was clearly in accordance with the differentiation pointed out by Mr. Sandys in regard to the Governor's powers and the Sovereign's powers. However, it was somewhat inconsistent

Other than for the Southern Rhodesian Royal Instructions of 6 June 1962, which required the Governor in capital cases, from the coming into force of the new Constitution, to act on the advice of the Governor's Council, and which revoked the earlier Royal Instructions, there are no formal Instructions issued in the ordinary way under the Royal Sign Manual and Signet to the Governor.[1] As the Instructions are revocable and are subject to amendment, it would be possible for the Governor to be instructed to exercise the prerogative of mercy on the advice of the United Kingdom Government or in his own discretion as was formerly the case under the 1923 Constitution.[2] It will also be possible in the event of a fundamental constitutional crisis or action touching on Imperial interests for the Governor to be instructed not to accept the advice of his Executive Council.[3] Similarly, although the Governor

with statements made by him at a Press Conference reported in the *Rhodesia Herald*, 1 June 1961, stating that apart from a few formal matters, all Britain's reserve powers had been abandoned. See Hirsch, op. cit., pp. 31, 60, and 111.

[1] Since Instructions may, however, be given informally, even telephonically, the Governor of Southern Rhodesia may have received other secret Instructions. That further Instructions may be given is explicitly stated in the existing Instructions as Clause 6 commands the Governor to communicate not only the existing Instructions to the Governor's Council but also 'all such other Instructions as he may from time to time receive from Us'.

[2] The power of the Crown to give such instructions was debated at the United Nations early in 1964. It is particularly relevant in view of the mandatory provisions for the imposition of death in cases under Section 33A of the Law and Order (Maintenance) Act 1960 as amended by Section 4 of Act 12 of 1963 (now Section 37 of Chapter 39) and the fact that the present Royal Instructions require the Governor to exercise the prerogative on the advice of his Council. Section 33A provides that persons who, by the use of petrol or inflammable liquid, set fire to, or by the use of explosives cause or attempt to cause damage to any person or building, *shall* be sentenced to death where the offence is committed in respect of any person or any building used for residential purposes, whether or not occupied at the time, or any non-residential building in which any other person is present at the time of the offence, irrespective of the knowledge of the accused. As at the end of July 1965 twenty-four prisoners had been sentenced to death under this section. The range of operation of the section can be illustrated by *R. v. Mapolisa*, 1963 R. & N. 808 (F.S.C.) in which the High and Federal Supreme Courts and the Judicial Committee ruled that a *socius criminis* commits the same crime as the principal offender and is subject to the same minimum penalties in Roman–Dutch Law. The accused in this case assisted an unidentified third party to manufacture a petrol bomb and walked with this third party to a European dwelling, into which the bottle containing petrol was thrown. The only injury caused was the burning of a hole in a lounge carpet, breaking of some window glass, and a slight burn on the hand of the householder, who threw the bomb into his garden. The trial judge sentenced the accused to death since the law allowed him no discretion. The Lord Chancellor then refused to commit himself on the disputed question whether a residual power to intervene in the exercise of the prerogative of mercy by the Governor remains in the Crown: *H.L. Deb.*, Vol. 255, col. 7, 4 February 1964. Ultimately Mapolisa was reprieved by the Governor. Representations to this effect were made by the British Government to the Southern Rhodesian Prime Minister. No executions have been effected as at the date of writing since appeals are pending to the Privy Council in the case of *Chikwakwata* v. *Bosman N.O.* alleging contravention of Section 60 of the Declaration of Rights.

[3] Section 2 read with section 45(1) makes it clear that this would not be unconstitutional by the employment of the phrase 'except where under this Constitution or any other law . . . he is required to act in accordance with the advice of any other person or authority'. See also Jenkyns, op. cit., p. 110: 'the obligation of the Governor to act on the advice of the

in all normal situations acts on Executive Council advice in assenting to legislation he could be instructed to disregard Council advice. Such a situation could only arise if a fundamental attack was being made on the Constitution or if major Imperial interests were at issue.[1]

Quite apart from any Royal Instructions, since the Governor is guardian of the Constitution,[2] it would be his duty to exercise Crown reserve power where the preservation of the Constitution was at stake.[3] Thus a Governor faced with 'a coup d'état under the forms of law' should refuse assent.[4]

It is this very function as guardian of the Constitution that raises the vexed question of the extent of the reserve power of the Crown.[5] That such power is necessary is shown by Forsey who says: 'The danger of Royal absolutism is

Ministers on local matters is subject to the exceptions that he cannot be asked either to disobey the law or to act contrary to his instructions from the Crown'.

[1] Anson considers a Governor has a discretionary power to disregard Ministerial advice in such circumstances: Anson, *Law and Custom of the Constitution*, 5th edition, Oxford, Vol. II, Part 2, p. 79, although Keith takes the view that a Governor should only do this on Imperial instructions: *Responsible Government*, op. cit., p. 212. Assent was refused to a financial measure that was ill-advised prior to dissolution of the Federation of the West Indies: *H.C. Deb.*, Vol. 657, cols. 134–9, 2 April 1962.

[2] See A. B. Keith: *The King and the Imperial Crown*, Longmans, 1936, p. 203 and also at p. 183 where the author states that the Crown is 'charged with the final duty of preserving the essentials of the Constitution'. See also Keith, *The Sovereignty of the Dominions* Macmillan, 1929, pp. 246–7, and Hood Phillips, *Constitutional Law*, 2nd edition, Sweet & Maxwell, 1957 p. 669, where the author says 'He is the custodian of the Dominion Constitution' with reference to Dominion Governor-Generals. A. V. Dicey also stated in a letter to *The Times* of 15 September 1913 that 'the King's negative to Bills . . . may be the means of saving the Constitution itself on an occasion worthy of bringing it forth'. Further views to this effect appear in Evatt, op. cit., pp. 91–102. Such views were vindicated in *Federation of Pakistan and Others* v. *Moulvi Tazimuddin Khan* P.L.R. [1955], F.C. 435 per Muhammed Munir C.J., quoted in W. I. Jennings' *Constitutional Problems in Pakistan* at pp. 146–8, where the Court held that 'a law which strikes at the very foundation of the constitution' may be refused assent. Indeed even to introduce a measure for the purpose of constitutional, amendment without consulting the electorate is considered by Keith to be a breach of constitutional usage to which the Crown could object: *The King and the Imperial Crown*, op. cit., p. 189.

[3] See Forsey, op. cit., p. 259: 'Within the ambit of the discretion residing still in the Crown there is a responsibility as great as falls to any estate of the realm or any House of Parliament . . . The plain duty of the (Crown) . . . is to make sure that responsible government is maintained, that the rights of parliament are respected, that the still higher rights of the people are held sacred, . . . that parliament is not stifled by government, but that every government is held responsible to parliament and every parliament is held responsible to the people', quoting Mr. Meighen, the Canadian Prime Minister on the Canadian Crisis of 1926.

[4] Evatt, *The King and His Dominion Governors*, p. 200, accepted by Forsey, op. cit. at p. 104.

[5] Discussion of the reserve powers of the Crown is not merely academic since possibility of the Southern Rhodesian Government declaring independence unilaterally has become a controversial political issue: see *S.R.L.A.D.*, Vol. 57, col. 89, 29 July 1964, where a motion of no confidence in the Government was moved deploring 'statements from Government spokesmen which imply that Government is contemplating a unilateral declaration of independence; and further that the House calls on Government to state categorically that it will not initiate unconstitutional action on the independence issue'. No such categorical statement has been made by the Southern Rhodesian Government and there have been ambiguous statements by the Southern Rhodesian Prime Minister that 'for the present the

past; but the danger of Cabinet absolutism, even of Prime Ministerial absolutism, is present and growing. Against that danger, the reserve power of the Crown, and especially the power to force or refuse dissolution is in some circumstances the only constitutional safeguard.'[1] However, although such powers exist it is hazardous to dogmatize on their extent since, as Evatt says, 'there is no generally recognized or binding rule to govern each situation of crisis'.[2] Nonetheless there is no doubt that there is a reserve power in the Governor to refuse advice,[3] to refuse dissolution,[4] to force dissolutions,[5] to dismiss Ministers,[6] to dissolve a Parliament that is functioning illegally[7] and even to govern and temporarily legislate by prerogative if a situation arises necessitating Royal intervention to preserve the society from dissolution.[8]

The difficulty lies in defining when such powers may be invoked. Even though an occasion might arise which would justify the use of one reserve power, e.g. refusal of dissolution (which arises relatively frequently and in more or less normal circumstances), the use of further reserve powers might well be unjustified, e.g. dismissal. However, it is clear that a situation which would justify the use of these powers would arise where there

question of such a declaration has been dropped', and that the possibility of such action would not be renounced as this was 'one of the strong levers that we have as far as our independence is concerned': *S.R.L.A.D.*, Vol. 58, col. 1637. The Southern Rhodesia Government even went so far as to publish a White Paper on Economic Aspects of a Declaration of Independence, Government Printer, Salisbury, 1965: C.S.R. 15–1965. Mr. Wilson, the British Prime Minister, because of failure by the Southern Rhodesia Government to give him assurances that such action was not contemplated, found it necessary to warn it of the serious consequences of such action (see *The Times*, 28 October 1964), while the Lord Chancellor and Mr. Bottomley in March 1965 stated that they believed 'that the greatest danger to the peace and prosperity of Rhodesia at the present time, is this threat of a unilateral declaration' and that they had communicated these views to the Southern Rhodesia Government: *Rhodesia Herald*, 4 March 1965. In answer to the White Paper, the British Prime Minister thereupon reiterated his views on the consequences of a unilateral declaration of independence: *H.C. Deb.*, Vol. 711, col. 638, 29 April 1965.

[1] Op. cit., p. 259.

[2] Evatt, op. cit., p. 288.

[3] Keith, *Responsible Government*, op. cit., p. 108.

[4] See generally Forsey, op. cit., pp. 260 et seq., and Evatt, op. cit., pp. 50 et seq., and pp. 217 et seq. See also Jenkyns, op. cit. at p. 110.

[5] Forsey, op. cit., pp. 123 and 270; Keith, *The Constitution of England from Victoria to George VI*, Macmillan, 1940, Vol. I, pp. 99–102.

[6] Forsey, op. cit., p. 130; Anson, op. cit., Vol. I, p. 336; and Evatt, op. cit., pp. 90–109. Cp. *Adegbenro* v. *Akintola*, [1963] 3 W.L.R. 63.

[7] The removal of an illegal legislature functioning 'in a manner different from the one in which it was intended to function' is 'a clear constitutional obligation': see *Report of the Special Reference made by his Excellency the Governor-General of Pakistan*, printed in Jennings' *Constitutional Problems in Pakistan*, at pp. 290–1, which decision was followed in *Pakistan* v. *Ali Ahmed Shah* P.L.R., [1955] F.C. 522.

[8] *Report of the Special Reference made by His Excellency the Governor-General of Pakistan*, reprinted in Jennings, op. cit., at pp. 298 et seq., relying particularly on the judgement of Lord Mansfield in *George Stratton and Others*, 21 Howell's St. Tr. 1046. See also Keith, *The King and His Imperial Crown*, p. 387. Cp. R. F. V. Heuston, *Essays in Constitutional Law*, Stevens, 1961, p. 72, who considers that the Pakistan judgements go somewhat beyond the available English authorities.

was illegality admitted or beyond dispute, and no remedy was available except the prerogative of the Governor,[1] or a need to assert the principles of the Constitution,[2] or if a revolutionary measure were attempted without the backing of a popular mandate,[3] or if vital and irreparable decisions were being taken leading to 'serious domestic strife'[4] or an emergency requiring action for the safety of the Colony arose.[5] Indeed it would be the duty of the Sovereign's representative to protect the people against acts of tyranny or usurpation on the part of Government or Parliament,[6] and to intervene if a Ministry attempted to govern without Parliament.[7] In a normal situation the question of the exercise of such power would not, however, arise.

The Governor acts in his discretion in accordance with constitutional conventions obtaining in the United Kingdom when appointing a Prime Minister, who holds office during Her Majesty's pleasure, or in dissolving the Legislative Assembly.[8] Again, Royal Instructions could vary this, or the Governor could exercise his own discretion in the event of a situation which called for so drastic an exercise of the Crown's reserve power, and to which the ordinary conventions of responsible government had no application.[9]

It should be noted that the Governor is still the representative of Her Majesty and that Southern Rhodesian Ministers do not enjoy full and free access to the Sovereign directly. In most cases the normal channel of communication to the Sovereign personally is through Her Majesty's Ministers in the United Kingdom. It seems that the measure of direct access to the Sovereign accorded to the Prime Minister of the Federation 'on Federal matters affecting the Sovereign personally, on the award of Honours for

---

[1] Evatt, op. cit. at p. 173; Keith, *The Dominions as Sovereign States*, pp. 228–31; Jennings, op. cit., pp. 290–1, quoting the *Special Reference of the Governor-General of Pakistan*.

[2] Keith, *Responsible Government*, op. cit., p. 108.

[3] Forsey, op. cit., pp. 123–4, and Jennings, op. cit., at pp. 147–8, quoting *Federation of Pakistan* v. *Moulvi Tazimuddin Khan*.

[4] Keith, *The King and the Imperial Crown*, op. cit., pp. 140 and 178.

[5] Jenkyns, op. cit., p. 103.

[6] Evatt, op. cit., p. 287.

[7] Keith, *Responsible Government*, p. 123. Keith comments that 'in the Dominions the reserve power may easily be held to be more necessary in view of the fact that parties sometimes seem to have little regard for anything save their immediate advantage'.

[8] Section 45(1).

[9] It seems that in a situation of imminent and extreme necessity private individuals, with a view to preserving society, may take over the Government: *George Stratton and Others*. 21 Howells St. Tr. 1046 per Lord Mansfield at 1224. This point did not arise in *R.* v. *Sithole*, 1965 (2) S.A. 29 (S.R.) in which the Rev. N. Sithole was charged with breach of Section 29(3)(b) of the Law and Order (Maintenance) Act for making statements indicating or implying that it would be incumbent or desirable to do any acts which were likely to create public disorder. He had advised Africans to keep weapons for the purpose of opposing a unilateral declaration of independence. The Court found that although this possibility had been widely discussed in Southern Rhodesia it did not go so far as to show this was likely. It therefore acquitted the accused. The Court also found at p. 34 that a 'U.D.I.' would be an illegal act.

services to the Federation and on a number of ceremonial matters' has not been permitted to the Prime Minister of Southern Rhodesia.[1]

Limitations on Southern Rhodesian competence in respect of external affairs

It is inherent in the status of all colonies that a colony as a dependency has no status in respect of external affairs whether or not such limitation be expressed.[2] Furthermore, as a dependency Southern Rhodesia has no independent personality in International Law.[3] Any powers that Southern Rhodesia now enjoys have in fact been delegated to her by the United Kingdom. As indicated earlier, progressive entrustments of power in respect of external affairs were made from 1923 onwards, first to Southern Rhodesia, and later to the Federal Government, which was permitted the fullest responsibility consonant with the United Kingdom's international responsibility for the conduct of the country's affairs. Since the dissolution of the Federation the Government of Southern Rhodesia has assumed those powers previously exercised by the Federal Government. In fact, in respect of executive powers relating to external affairs the United Kingdom has apparently entrusted to the Southern Rhodesian Government the same executive powers that were exercised by the Federal Government, and the Southern Rhodesian Government has in practice continued to operate in the same field as the former Federal Government.[4] Indeed, the United Kingdom has invited the Southern Rhodesian Government to discuss with it any revisions and changes in the entrustments necessary as a consequence of Southern Rhodesia's assumption of these powers.[5]

In the interim Southern Rhodesia has been conducting its external relations on the lines of the entrustment formerly made to the Federal Government. To a large extent Southern Rhodesia has obtained the international and

---

[1] *S.R.L.A.D.*, Vol. 58, col. 1369, 7 October 1964, Mr. Smith, Prime Minister. Prior to Federation the position was that Honours rested on Imperial advice, although recommendations by the Southern Rhodesian Prime Minister were made and accepted. See Keith, *Responsible Government*, Vol. I, xxii. The Southern Rhodesian Honours List is not transmitted by the Governor's Office directly to Her Majesty but goes to the Secretary of State for Commonwealth Relations.

[2] See A. B. Keith, *The Dominions as Sovereign States*, Macmillan, 1938, Chapter I.

[3] See *Halsbury*, 3rd edition, Vol. 5, p. 546.

[4] Annual Report of the Ministry of External Affairs: C.S.R. 28–1965, p. 2.

[5] All despatches dealing with entrustments made to the Federal Government in 1957 and any earlier entrustments have been transmitted to the Southern Rhodesian Government but as yet the despatches have not been revised: *S.R.L.A.D.*, Vol. 58, cols. 1369–70, Minister of External Affairs, 7 October 1964. On 10 December 1963 the United Kingdom Government informed the Southern Rhodesia Government, which had insisted that any diminution of the authority enjoyed by the Federal Government would not be acceptable, that 'it is the intention of Her Majesty's Government that the powers to be entrusted to Southern Rhodesia in this sphere (i.e. external relations) should be the same in scope as those presently exercised by the Federal Government': *S.R.L.A.D.*, Vol. 61, col. 1466–7, 27 July 1965.

Commonwealth memberships of international organizations formerly possessed by the Federation.[1] It also seems that most treaties with the Federation continue to bind Southern Rhodesia.[2] The United Kingdom and Southern Rhodesian Governments have adopted the view that where treaties were entered into during the existence of Federation and signed by the United Kingdom Government, international responsibility remained with Britain and that the Territories as constituent members would remain bound. When a treaty was entered into and signed by the Federation itself (by virtue of its entrustments) the question whether the treaty continued would depend upon the intention of the other contracting party. Had the intention been to contract with a dependency for which Britain was internationally responsible, the treaty would continue to bind the Territories as dependencies. If, however, the intention was to contract solely with the Federation then the treaty might require re-negotiation with the individual territories.[3] On the diplomatic side Southern Rhodesia has continued to avail herself of the right to have a Southern Rhodesian Representative on the staff of the British Ambassador in Washington and has also been permitted to have an Accredited Diplomatic Representative in the Republic of South Africa.[4] However, the Southern Rhodesia Government announced the appointment of a Rhodesian Diplomatic Representative to Portugal in July 1965, apparently without obtaining the prior approval of the United Kingdom Government.[5] The United Kingdom Government has, however, stated that 'the British Government are responsible for Rhodesian diplomatic representation in foreign countries' and that it recognized 'the need to preserve Britain's

[1] It has obtained fifteen of the seventeen more important memberships, while at the end of 1964 negotiations were proceeding in the two outstanding cases. There were, however, certain difficulties concerning Rhodesia's participation at certain international and Commonwealth Conferences, e.g. in the case of UNESCO meetings. The UNESCO General Conference has now ruled that Southern Rhodesia shall only be invited to certain categories of meetings: C.S.R. 28–1965, p. 8.

[2] Such treaties were concluded in the name of Her Majesty. This view rests on the authority of an Opinion given by the U.K. Law Officers in March 1902 on the survival of treaties when Queensland entered the Commonwealth of Australia: McNair, *Law of Treaties* at p. 644, and D. P. O'Connell, 'Independence and Succession to Treaties' (1962), *B.Y.I.L.*, Vol. 38, p. 84.

[3] See O'Connell (1963), *B.Y.I.L.*, Vol. 39 at p. 128, where the learned author details these attitudes and reveals that in the case of a Trade Agreement between a Commonwealth country and the Federation the United Kingdom and Territorial Governments and Commonwealth Government concerned accepted that the agreement had devolved on the Territories.

[4] This appointment of such a representative to South Africa is according to the Commonwealth Secretary, Mr. Bottomley, 'no precedent'. It has historical reasons in that Southern Rhodesia was represented in South Africa when the latter was a Member of the Commonwealth. When South Africa left, Britain felt it unnecessary to make any change to the situation: *H.C. Deb.*, Vol. 717, col. 469, 28 July 1965.

[5] In the view of the Minister of External Affairs, replying on 'Despatch 23' which in April 1957, entrusted the Federal Government with additional powers in the sphere of external relations, all that the entrustment required was that the United Kingdom Government be kept informed of the progress of negotiations so that they should be in a position to

ultimate responsibility for Rhodesia's external affairs, and for its diplomatic representation in foreign countries.[1] Exchanges with the Southern Rhodesian and Portuguese Governments followed in which Portugal recognised Britain's responsibility somewhat ambiguously.[2]

As yet no legislation dealing with external affairs has been enacted, but presumably the Southern Rhodesian Legislature will consider itself competent to make laws to the same extent as the Federal Legislature was authorized to do under the Federal Constitution.[3] It is submitted, however, that the Southern Rhodesian Legislature does not enjoy legislative power in respect of external affairs.

The term 'external affairs' is here used in a somewhat unorthodox and narrow sense. It is not suggested that Southern Rhodesia cannot legislate internally to implement international agreements: this she could clearly do by virtue of her powers for peace, order, and good government. What is meant is legislation having effect externally, such legislation being not already competent by virtue of the grant of extraterritorial legislative power to the Legislature. Such a grant would only permit legislation in respect of Southern Rhodesian subjects, i.e. citizens or residents, and would not comprise other persons. If legislation purporting to apply to such persons, when outside Southern Rhodesia, were enacted, it is submitted that such legislation would not merely be a contravention of International Law, but would be *ultra vires* the powers of the Legislature as relating to external affairs.[4] The reason for this incompetence is that prior to the creation of Federation, owing to her status as a colonial dependency, Southern Rhodesia did not enjoy such powers except to the extent that there had been a specific entrustment of such power.[5] After the establishment of Federation, by virtue of action in terms of Article 29(2) of the Federal Constitution, powers in relation to external affairs were made exclusively Federal and any such powers, if they ever existed, were eliminated from the Southern Rhodesian Constitution.[6]

It is submitted that this position was not affected by the revocation of the

advise where necessary on the international aspects and not that there should be consultation or that its prior approval should be obtained: *S.R.L.A.D.*, Vol. 61, col. 1467–70, 27 July 1965.

  [1] *H.C. Deb.*, Vol. 717, col. 469, 28 July 1965, Mr .Bottomley.

  [2] It received the Representative but not in the capacity claimed by Mr. Dupont: *H.C. Deb.*, Vol. 718, cols. 115–6, 1 November 1965. Britain professed that a Southern Rhodesian misunderstanding had caused the dispute: *H.C. Deb.*, Vol. 717, col. 910, 30 July 1965.

  [3] Legislation in respect of external affairs is rare in practice.

  [4] If subversive statements circulated in the United Kingdom by United Kingdom citizens about Southern Rhodesia were made punishable by Southern Rhodesian Law it is submitted the legislation in question would be declared *ultra vires*. Similarly legislation penalizing such persons for demonstrating at or attacking Southern Rhodesian external mission premises would, it is submitted, be invalid.

  [5] Cp. de Smith, op. cit., pp. 57 and 59, who suggests that where a country is internally self-governing, the constitution should indicate expressly or by implication that general control over external relations is withheld from that government.

  [6] *Supra.* See Part I, Chapter 16.

1923 Constitution and the substitution therefor of the 1961 Constitution, as Southern Rhodesia was still a colonial dependency in terms of the Constitution. Nor was it affected by the grant of extraterritorial power to Southern Rhodesia,[1] such grant merely meaning that Southern Rhodesian courts can take cognizance of Southern Rhodesian legislation governing the acts of Southern Rhodesian subjects committed outside Southern Rhodesia.[2] As the United Kingdom Solicitor-General debating the Statute of Westminster Bill explained, all that power to legislate extraterritorially means is 'that each nation has the capacity to legislate outside the three-mile limits of its own territory in respect of its own subjects in such a way as to make them amenable to the law as administered in its own courts when they come within its jurisdiction'.[3] Power to legislate extraterritorially does not permit Southern Rhodesia to alter her boundaries and she cannot amend the Southern Rhodesia (Annexation) Order in Council 1923 defining these as such changes are made under the Colonial Boundaries Act 1895[4] either by Order in Council or Letters Patent. Indeed Southern Rhodesian consent is not necessary in terms of the Act as she is not even scheduled as a self-governing country.[5]

This position was not changed by reason of the revocation of the Federal Constitution. Since Southern Rhodesia had no powers in respect of external affairs at the time of repeal of the Federal Constitution, mere repeal of the Constitution would not devolve them on the Southern Rhodesia Legislature.[6] Neither would there be any automatic transfer of power and conferment of Federal power on Southern Rhodesia in such circumstances.[7]

Furthermore, it is submitted that the Southern Rhodesian Legislature cannot confer legislative powers relating to external affairs on itself by an amendment to Section 20(1) adding to its powers for peace, order, and good government, powers in respect of external affairs, as such powers can only be conferred on Southern Rhodesia either by the United Kingdom Parliament or by the Crown by prerogative instrument.[8] It is therefore submitted that,

[1] Section 20(2) of the Southern Rhodesian Constitution 1961 specifically authorized by Section 1(1) of the Southern Rhodesia (Constitution) Act 1961. Such a provision has not previously been inserted in the constitution of a dependent territory.

[2] K. C. Wheare, *Constitutional Structure*, op. cit., p. 43.

[3] *H.C. Deb.*, Vol. 260, col. 263. See also O'Connell, *Doctrine of Colonial Extraterritorial Legislative Incompetence* (1959), 75 L.Q.R. 318.

[4] 58 & 59 Vict. c. 34.

[5] Section 1(2) and (3), Schedule. It is difficult to envisage circumstances in which Southern Rhodesian Government consent would not in practice be obtained in advance. Discussion of the boundary between Northern Rhodesia and Southern Rhodesia occurred prior to the dissolution of Federation, when it was agreed that the midline of the Zambesi and the midline of Lake Kariba would be the boundary.

[6] Indeed the Interpretation Act 1889 (52 & 53 Vict. c. 63), Section 38(2) was specifically applied to the repeal of the Federal Constitution by S.I. 1963 No. 2085, Section 76(3).

[7] See *dicta* by Muhamed Munir C.J. in *Usif Patel* v. *The Crown, supra,* quoted in Part II, Chapter 6, *supra.*

[8] Section 5 of the Colonial Laws Validity Act conferring power to make laws respecting the constitution, powers and procedure of a representative legislature, does not envisage a

48 – C.H.L.S.R.

although the United Kingdom has entrusted executive power in respect of external affairs to Southern Rhodesia, the Southern Rhodesian Legislature has no legislative powers in respect of external affairs. Even in respect of executive power relative to external affairs the Southern Rhodesian Government does not possess complete authority. Statements by United Kingdom Ministers made during the currency of the Federation and recently reiterated, make it clear that the United Kingdom recognizes that it is 'ultimately responsible' for the external affairs of Southern Rhodesia.[1] Indeed it is on the basis of this responsibility that the United Kingdom Government refuses to recognize United Nations' resolutions relating to Southern Rhodesia. Since Southern Rhodesia is a United Kingdom responsibility, questions relating to it are 'essentially within the domestic jurisdiction' of the United Kingdom and the United Kingdom accordingly rests its attitude on paragraph 7 of Article 2 of the United Nations Charter.[2]

Britain has also argued that Southern Rhodesia is a self-governing country and that the United Nations Organization accepted this in 1946 by not querying the omission of Southern Rhodesia from the list of non-self-governing territories submitted by Britain in respect of whom information would be transmitted in terms of Article 73(e) of the Charter.[3] Nevertheless the topic of Southern Rhodesia has on a number of occasions from November 1960 to 1965 been debated by the United Nations General Assembly, the Security Council,[4] the Trusteeship Committee of the General Assembly,[5]

a dependent territory however attenuated the degree of dependence conferring on itself powers to legislate in respect of external affairs. See Keith, *Responsible Government in the Dominions*, Vol. II, pp. 1146–7. The Dominions (as at the time Keith wrote and Southern Rhodesia is not yet in that position) enjoyed no 'vital power of constitutional change, . . . change details as they will they cannot enlarge their power by any Act of their own, they cannot alter their status'. See also the *dictum* by van den Heever J.A. in *Minister of the Interior* v. *Harris, supra* at 790. See also Appendix S.

[1] *H.C. Deb.*, Vol. 667, col. 35, 13 November 1962, Heath; Vol 668, cols. 967–71 and col. 1065, 3 December 1962, Butler. *H.L. Deb.*, Vol. 268, col. 993, 26 July 1965, Lord Taylor; and *H.C. Deb.*, Vol. 717, cols. 469–70, 28 July 1965, Bottomley.

[2] See *H.C. Deb.*, Vol. 662, col. 1345–6, 11 July 1962, Godber; Vol. 661, cols. 1340–1, 28 June 1962, Butler; and Vol. 675, col. 99, 8 April 1963, Heath.

[3] See *The Contemporary Practice of the United Kingdom in the Field of International Law*, 1962, I, by E. Lauterpacht, British Institute of Comparative and International Law, pp. 103 et seq. Information is only given subject to such limitations as 'constitutional considerations may require'. Britain submits that these—Southern Rhodesia's self-government—preclude such submission. Britain argued strongly in October 1962 that Southern Rhodesia was self-governing and enjoyed 'a status which took it out of the conventional sphere of the non-self-governing territories that come under Article 73 of the Charter', at a time when this was only partially true: for Britain's arguments see *Contemporary Practice*, II, July 1–31 December 1962, at p. 248. Ironically, one of the arguments used was that it was an established custom that her Prime Minister should attend Commonwealth Prime Ministers' Conferences.

[4] On 14 September 1963 the United Kingdom was invited by a motion not to transfer any power or attributes of sovereignty or any armed forces or aircraft to Southern Rhodesia until a fully representative government had been established. Britain used her veto for the first time since the Suez crisis of 1956.

[5] The Fourth Committee was actually addressed on 30 and 31 October 1962 by the

and the Special Committee on Colonialism.[1] The official attitude of the United Nations Organization is that Southern Rhodesia has 'not yet attained a full measure of self-government' as defined by Article 73 of the Charter[2] and that accordingly Chapter XI of the Charter, 'the Declaration regarding Non-self-governing Territories' and Resolution 1514 of 14 December 1960 (i.e. the Declaration on the Granting of Independence to Colonial Countries and peoples) are applicable, so that the United Kingdom as administering State[3] must give due consideration in good faith to the resolutions suggesting British intervention in Southern Rhodesia.[4] Despite the change in Government in the United Kingdom in October 1964 and the appointment as British Minister at the United Nations of Lord Caradon, who, as Sir Hugh Foot, had resigned as Britain's colonial spokesman owing to his strong views on the Southern Rhodesian issue,[5] Britain has consistently maintained the attitude that she is not the administering authority.

Southern Rhodesian Prime Minister, Sir Edgar Whitehead, who accepted a United Kingdom invitation to a seat on the delegation in order to put forward the views of the Southern Rhodesian Government. Sir Hugh Foot, United Kingdom spokesman on Colonial questions, had shortly before resigned as he could not honestly put forward his Government's views on Southern Rhodesia. See Foot, op. cit., pp. 215–26.

[1] Appointed in terms of a General Assembly Resolution of 27 November 1961. The Southern Rhodesian question was referred to the Committee by a General Assembly Resolution of 23 February 1962. On 7 April 1962 a Sub-Committee of the Special Committee left to discuss Southern Rhodesia with the British Government at its invitation. The United Kingdom when holding discussions with the Sub-Committee informed it that Southern Rhodesia had been a self-governing colony since 1923 and that 'the reserve powers of the United Kingdom which remained after 1923 were largely negative in character and have never been exercised ... although there were sometimes consultations and the British Government was therefore able to comment. Long-standing convention precluded the United Kingdom from interfering in Southern Rhodesia's internal affairs or legislating for Southern Rhodesia without its Government's consent.' A second Sub-Committee discussed Southern Rhodesia with Mr. Butler in London during mid-April 1963. In May and June 1964 similar discussions were held. A summary of events in 1964 in the Special Committee in so far as they relate to Southern Rhodesia appears in C.S.R. 28–1965 at pp. 15–16.

[2] Report of the Special Committee set up on 22 February 1962 to consider whether Southern Rhodesia had attained such status.

[3] The United Kingdom denies that it is an administering authority—see *Contemporary Practice* II, pp. 248 et seq.

[4] See R. Y. Jennings, *The Acquisition of Territory in International Law*, Manchester University Press, 1963, pp. 81–84. Prior to Federation it was even suggested that the creation of Federation was a breach of United Kingdom obligations under Article 73 and that the question should be referred to the International Court. However, the question would not have been a justiciable issue. A petition was in fact forwarded to the Secretary-General of the United Nations by the Northern Rhodesian African National Congress Party bearing date of 20 April 1953 (see *Rhodesia Herald* of 14 April 1953) while a letter by the Rev. Michael Scott was discussed in the Trusteeship Committee later that year. See also Fawcett, op. cit., pp. 140–1, and Fawcett, 'Treaty Relations of British Overseas Territories,' *B.Y.I.L.*, 1949, pp. 86–87.

[5] On the occasion of Lord Caradon's appointment the Southern Rhodesian Prime Minister stated that in the event of the United Kingdom failing to support Southern Rhodesia at the United Nations his Government would declare independence unilaterally: *S.R.L.A.D.*, Vol. 59, 27 October 1964.

Since ultimately the United Kingdom remains responsible for Southern Rhodesia's external affairs, Southern Rhodesia has no international personality. In the last event all foreign states therefore look to the United Kingdom to implement any obligations in respect of Southern Rhodesia.

Even in the event of a Government of Southern Rhodesia repudiating any British suzerainty and professing Southern Rhodesian independence *vis-à-vis* other nations, the test whether she would be held to have title to the territory would not merely depend on full and effective occupation by that Government but upon the recognition of the new state by the international community generally.[1]

Limitations on Southern Rhodesia's powers of defence

Although since 1923[2] Southern Rhodesia has possessed full powers executively and legislatively relating to her internal defence (subject until 1 November 1962 to the Governor's power of dissenting from Executive Council advice under Clause VI of the Royal Instructions and subject, during its existence, to Federal powers in terms of the Federal Constitution) as a colonial dependency she has no powers of using her defence forces externally, unless she is authorized to do this by the United Kingdom Government. During the Second World War, the Colony was permitted to control its own defence organization,[3] to commission its own officers, to insist on exclusion from the East African Command, and to decline to have a single command for the two Rhodesias and Nyasaland. When outside the boundaries of Southern Rhodesia, Rhodesian forces, however, operated as part of the Imperial defence forces.[4]

During the existence of Federation defence was a Federal power, but in respect of possible external use of Federal defence forces there were consultations with the United Kingdom Government,[5] while in cases where forces

---

[1] Jennings, op. cit., pp. 61–3. Cp. Oppenheim, *International Law*, Vol. 1, 8th edition (1955), p. 573.

[2] From 1923 until 1926 Southern Rhodesian forces continued to be governed by provisions of the Volunteer Ordinance No. 2 of 1902, as amended, except when declared to be on active service when the Army Act applied. By the Defence Act No. 23 of 1926 the forces were authorized to be used for the internal defence of the Colony when the necessity arose owing to external attack or internal disorder. The Governor was to be advised by a Council of Defence in his administration of the measure. The Act was subsequently considerably amended.

[3] Personal communication from Sir Robert Tredgold, the Minister of Defence.

[4] See J. F. Macdonald, *The War History of Southern Rhodesia*, two volumes, Salisbury, Government Printer, 1947–50.

[5] e.g. on their possible use in Katanga: see Welensky, op. cit., pp. 211–13. In *H.L. Deb.*, Vol. 225, col. 287, 14 July 1960, Lord Home as Commonwealth Secretary made it explicit that in his view of the United Kingdom's international responsibility such forces could not enter a foreign country without the agreement of and prior consultation with Her Majesty's Government. This was accepted by Welensky: see *Fed. Parlty. Deb.*, col. 1348, 18 July 1960.

operated externally as in Malaya and in the Arabian Peninsula, this was done at United Kingdom request.

Shortly before the dissolution of the Federation, an agreement was reached whereby the former Federal forces[1] would be split between the three former Federal Territories.[2] If the grant of defence forces to Southern Rhodesia was of concern or interest to other Commonwealth countries, by convention it became the duty of the United Kingdom Government to advise and consult these countries on the arrangements made before Federal dissolution. Although the British Labour Party maintained that the allocation of the former armed forces was of concern to other Commonwealth countries, the United Kingdom Government did not concede this, arguing that allocation of forces by agreement of the Territorial Governments within the Territories of the former Federation did not concern other members of the Commonwealth.[3]

However, as before, defence forces can only be used beyond the frontiers of Southern Rhodesia with British agreement. This was recently acknowledged by the United Kingdom through Sir Patrick Dean at the United Nations,[4] while Mr. Sandys in March 1964 reiterated that the use of Southern Rhodesia defence forces outside her boundaries was a matter for the United Kingdom.[5]

Southern Rhodesia has in one respect in relation to defence forces been treated as a Dominion in that the convention that United Kingdom forces should not be stationed in her territory without the consent of her Government[6] has been observed. On the other hand, Southern Rhodesia is not (nor was the Federation) defined as a Commonwealth country under the Army and Air Force Acts of 1955.[7] Accordingly, her forces are part of Her Majesty's military forces[8] and although her Legislature may pass laws adapting or modifying these Acts for the purpose of regulating its forces,[9] the powers

---

Earlier Mr. Macmillan had been evasive as to whether agreement was required, merely stating that there had been the 'closest co-operation and consultation' and that the Governments were 'in fact in agreement': *H.C. Deb.*, Vol. 626, cols. 982–6, 11 July 1960.

[1] Cmnd. 1149, p. 7, describes the forces as they were in 1960. Thereafter, a Special Air Services Squadron, an Armoured Squadron, and an all-European Regular Battalion were established. See also *The Break-up: Effects and Consequences on the Two Rhodesias*, Government Printer, Salisbury, 1963 (C. Fed. 246), pp. 118–19.

[2] See Cmnd. 2093, paras. 43 to 46, and *The Times*, 3 October 1963, which gives the actual allocations agreed upon. This meant in practice that the Southern Rhodesian Government controlled the bulk of the Royal Rhodesian Air Force, which is armed with Hunters, Canberras, and Vampires, and the Parachute Commandos of the Special Air Services Squadron, in addition to two Brigades, part-Regular and part-Territorial, the Regulars numbering about 3,400.

[3] *H.C. Deb.*, Vol. 686, cols. 1086 and 1162.   [4] On 10 September 1963.

[5] *H.C. Deb.*, Vol. 693, cols. 1095–7, 21 April 1964.

[6] Hood Phillips' *Constitutional Law*, Sweet & Maxwell, 2nd edition, 1957, p. 667.

[7] 3 & 4 Eliz. II, c. 18 and c. 19.

[8] As defined in Section 225(1) of the respective Acts.

[9] e.g. The Defence Act No. 23 of 1955 of the Federation of Rhodesia and Nyasaland,

conferred on Her Majesty to make regulations in respect of Her military forces as to command and the circumstances in which such command should be exercised would seem to be overriding.[1]

Appeal to the Privy Council

The Constitution provides in Section 71(5) for an appeal as of right in respect of alleged contraventions of Sections 57 to 68[2] of the Declaration of Rights. If any person is aggrieved by a determination of the Appellate Division of the High Court in respect of an alleged contravention of the Declaration of Rights, he may then appeal to Her Majesty in Council, provided that no such appeal shall lie if the application is merely frivolous or vexatious. This right of appeal is set out in one of the specially entrenched provisions of the Constitution and is thus, subject to the observance of the correct procedures, within the legislative competence of the Southern Rhodesian Legislature. Therefore, provided either of the procedures prescribed in Sections 106 to 110 were followed, the Southern Rhodesia Legislature could eliminate this right of appeal.

On the other hand, special leave to appeal in terms of the Judicial Committee Act 1833[3] cannot be abolished by the Southern Rhodesian Legislature in view of the Colonial Laws Validity Act. In fact the Legislature of Southern Rhodesia is less competent in respect of the abolition of certain appeals by special leave since the repeal of the Federal Constitution as Article 63(b) of the Federal Constitution read with Section 1(1)(a)(iii) of the Rhodesia and Nyasaland (Federation) Act 1953 permitted the Southern Rhodesian Legislature by declaring a decision of the High Court to be final to prevent appeal by special leave.[4] Until express power is given by an Imperial Act or provisions similar to Section 2 of the Statute of Westminster 1931 are enacted by the Imperial Parliament, the Southern Rhodesian Legislature cannot abolish the right of Her Majesty to grant special leave to appeal.[5] In fact Section 56G

which gave the Governor-General the power of nominating a Commander in Chief of the Federal Defence Forces.

[1] Section 177(1); see generally *Halsbury's Laws of England*, 3rd edition, Vol. 33.

[2] There is no appeal as of right in respect of contraventions of Section 69 which might be litigated upon in Southern Rhodesia because of failure to set up a tribunal to hear requests of persons detained during states of emergency for the purpose of obtaining recommendations concerning the necessity of continued detention.

[3] 3 and 4 Wm. IV, c. 41.

[4] Similar provision could also be made by the Federal Legislature. See *Gonthi* v. *R.*, *supra* per Clayden F.J. at pp. 42–43. Clayden F.J. also indicated at p. 45 that there could be no appeal to the Judicial Committee if an appeal lay to the Federal Supreme Court. It is submitted that this *obiter* statement is incorrect in respect of appeals to the Federal Supreme Court which originated from a Territorial High Court. See Article 63(a). Tredgold F.C.J. at p. 38 took only the narrower view.

[5] See *Nadan* v. *R.*, [1926] A.C. 482 and *British Coal Corporation* v. *The King*, *supra*. The attainment of independence does not *per se* affect the right of the Board to entertain appeals: *Ibralebbe* v. *The Queen*, [1964] 2 W.L.R. 76 (P.C.) at 90, although an independent state may at any time modify or terminate the Privy Council appeal from the Courts.

of the Constitution as amended *ex abundante cautela* contains a savings clause stating that sections permitting the Legislature to provide for appeal by right of grant (Section 56E) and that stating that there should be no right of appeal to Her Majesty in Council from the General Division of the High Court after the establishment of the Appellate Division (Section 56F) shall not be construed as impairing any right of Her Majesty in Council to grant special leave to appeal from a decision in any Division of the High Court.

Although the Imperial Conference of 1926 resolved that 'it was no part of Her Majesty's Government in Great Britain that questions affecting judicial appeals should be determined otherwise than in accordance with the wishes of the part of the Empire primarily affected', this announcement of a virtual convention that the Imperial Parliament would, at the request of a Dominion, abolish or limit the jurisdiction of the Judicial Committee for the Dominion[1] does not apply to Southern Rhodesia, which has not as yet attained a status identical to that of the Dominions in 1926.

Habeas corpus

Yet another limitation on Southern Rhodesian autonomy is the power of the Divisional Court of the Queen's Bench in England to issue a writ of *habeas corpus* in respect of British subjects detained in Southern Rhodesia. Attention was drawn to the existence of this power in the judgement of Sellers L.J. in *In re Mwenya*.[2] Despite provisions in the Habeas Corpus Act 1862[3] that the writ may not issue 'to a colony or foreign dominion' where there is a lawfully established court with 'authority to issue the said writ' the writ can still be issued in respect of Southern Rhodesia. The reason for this is that the High Court of Southern Rhodesia has no power to issue 'the said writ' of *habeas corpus* although it has power to grant the *interdictum de homine libero exhibendo*, which by judicial interpretation almost covers the same field as *habeas corpus*.[4] Nonetheless this almost equivalent remedy is not the 'said writ' and therefore *habeas corpus* would be issuable though the issue might

---

[1] Latham, op. cit., p. 549.   [2] *Supra* at 307.   [3] 25 & 26 Vict. c. 20.

[4] See *de Kock* v. *Balie*, 1879 Buch. 45 at 64; *In re Marechane* (1882), 1 S.A.R. 27 at 29 and 31; and *Tonge* v. *Governor of Johannesburg Gaol*, 1903 T.H. 393 at 401. In Roman Law there was necessity for *dolus*: see Digest 43, 29.1. pr.: *quem libero dolo malo retines, exhibeas*; while Voet still wrote of 'ill fraud' as a requirement (Gane's Translation). This is no longer the case. However the strict English practice in respect of the writ is inapplicable and it will not be issued merely because there is a bad warrant of commitment: *Tonge* v. *Governor of the Johannesburg Gaol* at 401. Nor is the law so strict where a prisoner is removed from the jurisdiction before the writ is issued: *Li Kui Yu* v. *Superintendent of Labour*, 1906 T.S. 181 at 190, *Fein & Cohen* v. *Colonial Government* (1906), 23 S.C. 750, and *Yamamoto* v. *Athersuch and Anor.*, 1919 W.L.D. 105. It also seems that it is more easily suspended as this is the case as long as there has been a proclamation of martial law: *In re Fourie* (1900), 17 S.C. 173 in which *Wolfe Tone's Trial* (1798), 27 State Tr. 613 was distinguished. *Quaere* whether in English Law war must actually be raging: *R.* v. *Allen*, 1921, 2 I.R. 241 at 273 and *Egan* v. *Macready*, 1921, 1 I.R. 265.

be attended with difficulty.[1] As Sellers L.J. said: 'There may come times in a country's history when it may appear highly inconvenient or politically hazardous that the law should pursue its course, but in a court of law such considerations are irrelevant, and cannot serve to deprive the subject of a right which an English court could give and enforce.'[2]

The Crown and the succession thereto

The Monarch of the United Kingdom is the Sovereign of all Her 'other realms and territories' including the colonies, the inhabitants of which owe Her allegiance. Southern Rhodesia is thus part of the single realm of a single Monarch.[3]

Imperial law defines the Sovereign who derives Her title to the Crown from the Act of Settlement 1700 and His Majesty's Declaration of Abdication Act 1936, both Acts of the United Kingdom Parliament.[4] Such succession may only be changed by the Queen in Her Parliament of the United Kingdom, subject to the convention that any alteration in the law touching the succession to the Throne requires 'the assent as well of the Parliament of all the Dominions as of the Parliament of United Kingdom'.[5] Southern Rhodesia, not being an independent member of the Commonwealth, is not consulted in respect of any changes in the law relating to the succession to the Crown.

Royal style and titles

By the Royal Titles Act 1953[6] the United Kingdom Parliament prescribed the title to be used by the Sovereign in relation to the United Kingdom and to all her colonies, protectorates and trust territories for whose foreign affairs the United Kingdom was responsible. The title had been arranged at informal discussions between the members attending the Commonwealth Economic Conference in December 1952. It was agreed then by Commonwealth members that it would accord 'with the established constitutional position that each member country should use for its own purposes a form of

[1] Who would be cited as respondent? The Southern Rhodesian High Commissioner in London? The Secretary of State for Commonwealth Relations? The Home Secretary?

[2] *Quaere* whether impossibility of enforcement would cause the Court to refuse to issue the writ.

[3] There is 'no mere personal union of separate crowns'—applying L. S. Amery's words to the United Kingdom and its dependent territories. This, however, is no longer true of the Dominions. See L. S. Amery, *Thoughts on the Constitution*, Oxford, 1947, pp. 151–2.

[4] 12 & 13 Wm. III, c. 2, Section 1, and 1 Edw. VIII and 1 Geo. VI, c. 3. The Regency Acts 1937 to 1953 also apply to Southern Rhodesia. Cp. Benjamin Franklin's remark on the eve of the United States' Declaration of Independence: 'I am a subject of the Crown of Great Britain', quoted in *Survey of British Commonwealth Affairs, I, Problems of Nationality 1918–1936*, W. K. Hancock, Oxford, 1937 at p. 11.

[5] Preamble to the Statute of Westminster.

[6] 1 & 2 Eliz. II, c. 9.

title which suits its own particular circumstances but retains a substantial element which is common to all'.[1]

However, since Southern Rhodesia is not an independent member of the Commonwealth, this convention does not apply to her nor could her Legislature, owing to the Colonial Laws Validity Act, enact a title in conflict with that set out in the Royal Style and Titles Act 1953: viz. 'Elizabeth II by the Grace of God of the United Kingdom, of Northern Ireland and of Her other Realms and Territories, Queen, Head of the Commonwealth, Defender of the Faith'. To constitute Her Majesty 'Queen of Southern Rhodesia' either an amendment to the Royal Titles Act would be necessary or provision similar to that of the Statute of Westminster would have to be made.[2]

Allegiance

Although it is no longer true of the members of the Commonwealth that they are necessarily 'united by common allegiance to the Crown',[3] Southern Rhodesia, as one of the realms of the Queen of the United Kingdom, owes Her allegiance, which allegiance is owed by every subject in return for the protection afforded by the Sovereign.[4] Thus, under the English Common Law, Southern Rhodesian citizens owe the Queen allegiance.[5] In addition, in terms of the Southern Rhodesia Citizenship and British Nationality Act 1963, all Southern Rhodesian citizens are British subjects, while the British Nationality Act 1948 confers on citizens of Southern Rhodesia British subject status.[6] As

---

[1] Cmd. 8748.

[2] Local politicians and even the Southern Rhodesian High Commissioner (*Rhodesia Herald*, 28 October 1964) have suggested that the Queen will remain 'Queen of Southern Rhodesia' after a unilateral declaration of independence. Unless the British Cabinet advised the Queen to agree to be head of the 'independent' state, which would be outside the Commonwealth, thereby agreeing to a new form of personal union, this is an impossibility. Mr. Wilson has stated this will not be done (*The Times*, 28 October 1964). Nor could it be done as it would by convention be necessary to consult all Commonwealth countries, who would clearly object to such action.

[3] See Cmnd. 2678—Imperial Conference 1926, Summary of Proceedings; Wheare, *Constitutional Structure*, pp. 116–17; and de Smith, op cit., pp. 9–17.

[4] *Joyce* v. *Director of Public Prosecutions*, [1946] A.C. 347 is grounded on the assumption that allegiance is owed where protection is afforded.

[5] All British subjects owe allegiance in English law: *Halsbury*, 3rd edition, Vol. 7, p. 209. See also *Gohoho* v. *Guinea Press*, [1962] 3 All E.R. 785 (C.A.).

[6] 11 & 12 Geo VI, c. 56, Section 1(1) and (3) as amended. A considerable number of Southern Rhodesian citizens are dual nationals. In 1951 28·8 per cent of the European population were born in the British Isles: Leys, op. cit., p. 76. The large immigration into Southern Rhodesia between 1953 and 1958 brought in more United Kingdom citizens. In 1957 56 per cent of immigrants were British born. Numerous other persons must be United Kingdom citizens by descent. All civil servants are probably also constructive British subjects as office-holders in the Government of a British possession: see Parry, *Nationality and Citizenship of the Commonwealth and the Republic of Ireland*, Stevens, 1957, p. 119. The Official Secrets Act applies to Southern Rhodesia (Section 10(1)) and there have been no Orders in Council excluding Southern Rhodesia from its operation, while the

a consequence of British nationality in terms of these statutes, allegiance is again owed.

Even if the Southern Rhodesian Citizenship and British Nationality Act 1963 were amended to declare that Southern Rhodesian citizens were not British subjects, such persons would in terms of the British Nationality Act 1948 retain their British subject status,[1] and, were express provision that they should not have such a status made, since Southern Rhodesia is still bound by the Colonial Laws Validity Act, the provision would be invalid. Indeed, it is the law of the Crown of England which determines whether or not a man is a British subject.[2]

The practical consequence of this duty of allegiance is its relevance to the law of treason.[3] It is arguable that since Southern Rhodesian citizens as British subjects owe the British Crown allegiance wherever they may be,[4] breach of this duty by any act such as a unilateral declaration of independence would constitute treason under the English Common Law[5] and would be triable in the courts of the United Kingdom.[6]

Although Section 3(1) of the British Nationality Act 1948 exempts citizens of specified Commonwealth countries from criminal liability under United Kingdom laws for acts committed outside the United Kingdom they still remain liable for their acts if such conduct would have constituted an offence if committed by an alien.[7] Since aliens who owe allegiance, on a broad interpretation of the ratio in *Joyce* v. *D.P.P.*, can commit treason outside the United Kingdom it is arguable that Southern Rhodesian citizens who owe allegiance can also commit treason outside the United Kingdom. On the

Southern Rhodesia Officials Secrets Act (Chapter 137), Section 21, provides that the application of the United Kingdom Act to the Colony shall not be affected.

[1] *Murray* v. *Parker*, [1942] 2 K.B. 123.   [2] Latham, op. cit., p. 520.

[3] Hood Phillips, op. cit., p. 473.

[4] See Hood Phillips, op. cit., 2nd edition, p. 480. In terms of the Roman–Dutch Law Southern Rhodesian courts have jurisdiction to try charges of high treason committed without as well as within the territory of Southern Rhodesia as long as the offender is a person owing allegiance to the State. See *R.* v. *Neumann*, 1948 (3) S.A. 1238 (T) at 1249.

[5] The Statute of Treasons 1351, 25 Edw. 3, st. 5, c. 2, as amended is declaratory of the English Common Law.

[6] *Joyce* v. *Director of Public Prosecutions, supra*. Such action would probably be construed as compassing the King's death: *R.* v. *Maclane* (1797), 26 St. Tr. 721. Alternatively, aiding rebels in the Crown's realms is treason, while it is treason felony to seek to depose the Sovereign from any part of Her Commonwealth, or to attempt by an insurrection of whatever nature by force or constraint to compel the Queen to change Her measures or counsels, or to intimidate or overawe either or both Houses of Parliament in the United Kingdom. See *R.* v. *Gallagher and Others* (1883), 15 Cox C.C. 291: it is treason even if 'a few persons . . . devise or intend to force the King by means of violence to change his counsels, or to overawe the Houses of Parliament by violent measures or threats against the property of the King, the public property, or the lives of Her Majesty's subjects'. It appears that 'where an insurrection against a Government has become so formidable as to assume the aspect of an equally balanced civil war, the laws of war are to be observed between the Government and the insurgents, and native-born subjects taken prisoners could not be tried as traitors': Law Officers' Report, 21 August 1838, quoted in McNair, *Opinions*, Vol. II, pp. 147–8.

[7] Parry, op. cit., pp. 118–19.

other hand it can be maintained that this view is contrary to the intendment of Section 3(1). However if the latter view is correct the strange consequence would follow that Her Majesty's subjects could within Her Majesty's dominions overthrow Her Majesty's authority and this would not in law be treason.

Even if all Southern Rhodesian citizens who assisted in the implementation of a unilateral declaration of independence would not be guilty of treason a majority of her citizens would be. All dual nationals with United Kingdom citizenship and all civil servants would be guilty. In addition, in accordance with the Judges' ruling of 1707 any Southern Rhodesian citizens with homes in Britain would be guilty.[1] Furthermore any Southern Rhodesian citizen who held a Southern Rhodesian passport would commit treason. Passports are regarded in law as being issued by virtue of an exercise of the Royal prerogative in the field of foreign relations.[2] In Southern Rhodesia powers in respect of foreign affairs have been delegated by the United Kingdom Government to the Southern Rhodesia Government, the United Kingdom Government, however, still remaining internationally responsible and the Southern Rhodesian Government merely acting as its delegate. In fact in respect of passports it is the United Kingdom Government that in practice ensures protection to Southern Rhodesian citizens who travel on Southern Rhodesian passports as the Southern Rhodesian Government has no international status and few overseas missions. Holders of Southern Rhodesian passports by virtue of the protection given them by the United Kingdom Government itself and through their issue by the United Kingdom Government's delegate in this field, the Southern Rhodesian Government, owe allegiance and could commit treason when regard is paid to the decision in *Joyce* v. *D.P.P.*[3]

In any event such action would be treason in terms of the Roman–Dutch Law, which would be applied if a trial took place in Southern Rhodesia.[4]

---

[1] This ruling relative to aliens with family, effects or property in England was approved in *Joyce* v. *D.P.P.* at 367.

[2] *Halsbury*, 2nd edition, Vol. 6, para. 643, approved by Centlivres J.A. in *Sachs* v. *Donges N.O.*, 1950 (2) S.A. 265 (A.D.) at 289. At 293 Centlivres J.A. said that in the Union these should be issued by the Department of External Affairs and at 301, in dealing with the grant or refusal of a passport, based this on the Crown's power to conduct foreign affairs. See also *R.* v. *Brailsford*, [1905] 2 K.B. at 745 where Lord Alverstone stated that a passport was 'intended to be presented to the Governments of foreign nations and to be used for that individual's protection as a British subject in foreign countries'.

[3] According to the Law Officers 'the obligation of allegiance does not arise from the protection which *de facto* he has enjoyed, but from the protection to which he is entitled and which he might have enjoyed if he had thought fit': 21 August 1838, quoted in McNair, *Opinions*, Vol. II, p. 147.

[4] In such an event since treason is a species of *crimen laesae majestatis* an impairment of *majestas* would have to be alleged. *Majestas* would presumably preside in the Queen and Her Government of Southern Rhodesia. Cp. *R.* v. *Leibbrandt*, 1944 A.D. 253 at 279, where it was held that in the Union of South Africa the King and His Government of the Union were clothed with *majestas*. Whereas the fundamental basis of the English law of high treason is historically primarily directed to the preservation of the personal safety of the monarch, the Roman–Dutch Law and the Roman Law are directed entirely to the protec-

Independence

Since January 1963[1] the Government of Southern Rhodesia through visits of the Prime Minister and other Ministers to the United Kingdom[2] and also through correspondence has been attempting to obtain United Kingdom consent to the achievement by Southern Rhodesia of full independence on the basis of the present Constitution and franchise.[3] The principle that

tion of the supreme authority of the state: see *R.* v. *Gomas*, 1936 C.P.D. 223 at 231 per Davis J. The question might be raised whether the British Crown possesses sufficient internal *majestas* in Southern Rhodesia for treason to be alleged against it: see *R.* v. *Christian*, 1924 A.D. at 135. However at 119–20 it was suggested that if a territory were subject to the Imperial Parliament there could then be *majestas*.

[1] See *H.C. Deb.*, Vol. 669, col. 1269, 19 December 1962 where Mr. Butler stated that there had at that date been no negotiations for Southern Rhodesian independence. See also *S.R.L.A.D.*, Vol. 53, col. 4, 18 June 1963, where Mr. Field revealed that in January and March 1963 the Southern Rhodesian Government made it clear that they considered that Southern Rhodesia was entitled to independence, should the two Northern Territories secede from the Federation.

[2] Mr. Field as Prime Minister of Southern Rhodesia visited the United Kingdom in May 1963 and from 24 January to 2 February 1964, for this purpose accompanied on the latter occasion by the Minister of Justice. The Minister of the Treasury, Mr. Smith, also visited the United Kingdom in October 1963, and later, as Prime Minister, had discussions in London with Sir Alec Douglas Home in early September 1964. In February and March 1965, the Lord Chancellor, Lord Gardiner, and the Secretary of State for Commonwealth Relations, Mr. Bottomley, visited Southern Rhodesia to negotiate on the independence issue and in July the Minister of State for Commonwealth Relations,¦ Mr. Cledwyn Hughes visited Southern Rhodesia for the same purpose. Negotiations continued through correspondence and the intermediacy of the British High Commissioner. A visit by Mr. Smith and three of his Cabinet to London in October 1965, resulted in deadlock: see Addendum.

[3] This formulation is extremely vague. The Minister of Internal Affairs has stated that this means only the mimimum changes necessary to convert the 1961 Constitution into an 'independencce constitution': *S.R.L.A.D.*, Vol. 58, col. 1661, 13 October 1964. However, the Prime Minister has indicated that his Government would, if it had the requisite majority, provide for the elimination of cross-voting by 'A' and 'B' voters in electoral districts and constituencies respectively, and introduce a 'fade-out' principle in respect of the electoral districts similar to that in the Federal constitution: *S.R.L.A.D.*, Vol. 58, col. 1637, 13 October 1964. The Minister of Internal Affairs informed the Chiefs and Headmen of Southern Rhodesia on 26 October 1964 that the Constitution would be changed so that they could participate in the law-making process: *Rhodesia Herald*, 27 October 1964. Earlier the Government did not deny allegations that it intended creating an upper house of Chiefs as part of the legislature. In the *Bulawayo Chronicle*, 1 December 1964, the Government was reported as making public announcements that after independence Chiefs will be brought into Parliament. However, the Minister of Internal Affairs has denied any intention of bringing Chiefs into the Legislative Assembly: *Rhodesia Herald*, 9 August 1965. According to a mimeographed report of a speech by the Minister of Law and Order, and a statement by the Rhodesia Front 'the only amendments to the Constitution that the Government has in contemplation and which the Prime Minister undertook to disclose to the electorate before the General Election' of May 1965 were as follows: amendment of Section 14 to provide that the office of Chief shall not be deemed to be a public office for purpose of disqualification for Membership of the Legislative Assembly; amendment of Section 37 to increase the size of the Legislative Assembly; amendment of Item 5 of the Second Schedule to the Constitution to substitute a Southern Rhodesian citizenship requirement; amendment of Section 92(1), definition of 'tribesman', to exclude non-indigenous Africans from being allocated land even if they are absorbed into tribal communities; amendment of Item 10

Southern Rhodesia 'would proceed through the normal processes to independence' has been conceded by the British Government.[1] At first the British Government adopted the attitude that a Constitutional Conference should precede the grant of independence.[2] The British Government also stated that amendments to the Southern Rhodesian Constitution 'which would result in broadening the basis of representation in the legislature' and 'development of policy on non-discrimination'[3] should be discussed, and later the United Kingdom Prime Minister declared in respect of Southern Rhodesia that his Government accepted 'the principle that the majority should rule'.[4] These demands were described by the Southern Rhodesian Government in the Speech from the Throne in February 1964 as 'extravagant terms' and it was stated that Southern Rhodesian Ministers could initiate no further discussions.[5]

After further correspondence and discussions, although not committing

of the Second Schedule and section 9(4) which provide for cross voting by 'A' and 'B' Roll voters in electoral districts and constituencies respectively; and amendment of Section 67(3)(c) of the Constitution to permit the enactment of a Tribal Courts Bill authorizing such courts to exercise jurisdiction over non-indigenous Africans. Speech of 23 April 1965. By courtesy of The Rhodesian Front.

[1] Cmnd. 2000, Butler to Field, 9 April 1963. In a joint communiqué issued on 11 September 1964 by the United Kingdom and Southern Rhodesian Prime Ministers, the British Government stated that they 'looked forward to the day when Southern Rhodesia would take her place as an independent sovereign state within the Commonwealth. For their part they were anxious that this should come about as soon as practicable': reprinted in S.R.L.A.D., Vol. 48, cols. 253–4, 11 September 1964.

[2] Cmnd. 2000, Butler to Field, 9 April 1963: 'Her Majesty's Government, in accordance with normal precedent, would expect to convene a Conference to discuss financial, defence, constitutional, and other matters, which always have to be settled before self-governing dependencies are granted independence.' The Southern Rhodesian Government threatened not to attend the Dissolution Conference of July 1963, unless it was granted independence. Agreement was, however, reached that it would attend despite Britain's refusal to enter into any such commitment.

[3] Cmnd. 2073. Further correspondence. Butler to Field, 15 June 1963, and H.C. Deb., Vol. 681, col. 411, 16 July 1963, Butler; and H.C. Deb., Vol. 684, col. 585, 15 November 1963, where Mr. Sandys stated that a 'widening of the franchise' was required. In S.R.L.A.D., Vol. 53, col. 15, 18 June 1963, Mr. Field, the Southern Rhodesian Prime Minister, stated that the British Government had in January 1963 requested that major concessions on the franchise and the representation of the people as a whole were required, while S.R.L.A.D., Vol. 53, col. 14, reveals that an increase in the number of 'B' Roll seats, i.e. electoral districts, and a lowering of the standards for the 'A' Roll was required. See also col. 218, 21 June 1963, and col. 307, 17 July 1963, mentioning a 'blocking third' of 'B' Roll seats. There were also discussions about a certificate of urgency on the one hand and a state of emergency on the other in relation to the functions of the Constitutional Council (col. 9). The British Government's requirements that additional seats for Africans be created was confirmed by the Minister of Internal Affairs in S.R.L.A.D., Vol. 58, col. 1675, 13 October 1964.

[4] H.C. Deb., Vol. 684, col. 53, 12 November 1963. The Labour Party had the same view and will not agree to Southern Rhodesian independence 'except on the basis of democratic majority rule in that country': Mr. Wilson, reported in the Rhodesia Herald, 24 March 1964.

[5] S.R.L.A.D., Vol. 56, col. 8, 25 February 1964.

itself that no Conference need be held,[1] the British Government stated that it 'must be satisfied that any basis on which it was proposed that independence should be granted was acceptable to the people of the country as a whole'.[2] At the same time the Prime Minister of Southern Rhodesia agreed that independence should be based on general consent of the majority of the people. Subsequently the Southern Rhodesian Government formulated proposals for consulting the population which, according to the Prime Minister, would be 'as wide as possible but . . . must operate within the tribal structure, while over and above this a referendum would be held of all registered voters'.[3]

The Southern Rhodesian Government in pursuance of this policy secured the passage of the Referendum Act 1964 to enable a referendum to be held 'upon the question whether the voters are in favour of or against Southern Rhodesia obtaining independence on the basis of the Constitution of Southern Rhodesia 1961'.[4] However it was provided that only voters registered in terms of the Electoral Act might participate in the referendum. The analogy of the Constitutional provisions for referenda was not adopted, although Section 108 of the Constitution provides that until there are 50,000 registered African voters all African adults who have completed their primary education may vote in a referendum. Nor was the analogy of separate racial referenda adopted. Indeed the Referendum Act 1964 was designed to make it impossible to determine whether a majority either of Europeans or of Africans voted in a particular manner. This was secured by provision that only the number of affirmative and of negative votes should be recorded, there being no indication whether votes cast were 'A' or 'B' Roll Votes.[5] Had this provision not

---

[1] The Southern Rhodesian Prime Minister has stated that when it has 'been decided that we were entitled to independence on this constitution' but not before, a conference would be held: *S.R.L.A.D.*, Vol. 58, col. 465, 17 September 1964.

[2] Agreed communique issued by the Prime Ministers of Great Britain and Southern Rhodesia: *S.R.L.A.D.*, Vol. 58, cols. 253–4, 11 September 1964. In Cmnd. 2464 there is a significant variation. It is there stated that independence should be 'explained', not 'acceptable'. On 8 March 1965 the Commonwealth Secretary stated that 'whatever settlement was needed must be acceptable to the majority of the population of Rhodesia': *H.C. Deb.*, Vol. 708, c. 36.

[3] *S.R.L.A.D.*, Vol. 58, col. 280, 15 September 1964. A Committee to advise the Prime Minister on the method of consultation consisting of both Government and Official Opposition members was appointed. See *Rhodesia Herald*, 17 September 1964 and 18 September 1964. This Committee reached agreement that consultation should be within the tribal structure and should involve Chiefs and Headmen. The Government then held a meeting of Chiefs and Headmen, there being approximately 210 Chiefs and about 400 Headmen present. No vote was taken at the final meeting of this 'indaba' and it was stated by their spokesman *nemine contradicente* that the Chiefs and Headmen favoured Southern Rhodesian independence under the present Constitution. The Opposition considered that these consultations should be extended to the Kraalhead level (*S.R.L.A.D.*, Vol. 58, col. 1943). A justification for holding the 'Indaba' and a transcript of part of its proceedings has been published by the Government: *The Demand for Independence in Rhodesia. Consultation with the African Tribesmen through their Chiefs and Headmen. The Dombashawa 'Indaba'*. Government Printer, Salisbury, 1965.

[4] Section 3(a).   [5] Section 8.

been inserted it would have been possible to have deduced, for example, that the African population opposed independence on the basis of a large 'B' Roll vote against the proposals. No firm conclusions as to the views of African voters can be drawn from the voting in view of the provisions of the Act.

A referendum in terms of the Act was held on 5 November 1964, the votes cast in favour of the proposals amounting to 58,176 and those against to 6,101. There were 965 spoilt papers as the result of a campaign to spoil papers.[1] The figures do not disclose whether Africans participated or not but press reports of activity at polling stations in African areas revealed an almost complete boycott by African voters.[2]

The United Kingdom has, however, made 'it plain that the British Government reserved their position' and will not necessarily accept any demonstration of consent on the part of the population produced by the Southern Rhodesian Government as evidence that will satisfy them of the required consent of the people of the country as a whole.[3] So far both the outgoing Conservative Government and the present Labour Government have rejected the methods of consultation proposed by the Southern Rhodesian Prime Minister as being unrepresentative of African opinion.[4] The attitude of Mr. Wilson's administration has been stated as being that it 'will not transfer power to Rhodesia except on the basis acceptable to the people as a whole'. It has also been made clear that the considerations which guide the United Kingdom Government in deciding whether independence should be conceded and on what conditions this should be done 'are to provide guarantees that future constitutional development should conform to the principle of un- impeded progress to majority rule together with an immediate improvement in the political status of the African population and progressive elimination of racial discrimination'.[5] There has, at the date of writing, been no agreement as to the terms of Southern Rhodesian independence, although correspon- dence and discussions are continuing.[6]

In any event, before independence can be achieved, an Imperial Act analogous to the Statute of Westminster or to one of the many Independence Acts passed for recent Commonwealth members will be required to remove the remaining limitations on Southern Rhodesia's competence, and to make

[1] The number of 'Yes' votes amounted to 89·3 per cent of the total votes cast (65,342). That there were many abstentions is apparent from the fact that there was only a 61·9 per cent poll, although this is partly explained on the basis that numbers of Europeans had emigrated. 'Yes' votes amounted to 55 per cent of the total electorate of 105,444. See *supra*, Part II, Chapter 1, Figure II, for its racial composition.

[2] *Rhodesia Herald*, 7 November 1964. In Willowvale, the constituency with the largest number of African voters on both 'A' and 'B' Rolls, there being 1,595 'A' and 1,328 'B' Roll voters, there was only a 26 per cent poll, which would by and large represent the European electorate in that area.

[3] See joint communiqué of 11 September 1964, *supra*.

[4] *The Times*, 22 and 28 October 1964.

[5] *H.C. Deb.*, Vol. 717, cols. 908–9, 30 July 1965, Mr. Bottomley.   [6] See Addendum.

independence fully effective.[1] This cannot be done by the Southern Rhodesian
Legislature itself without Imperial authorization, since a colonial legislature
cannot, unless expressly authorized, alter vitally the status of the territory
for which it legislates,[2] nor can a dependency acting unilaterally sever the
Imperial connection, because, as Keith argues, an Act making such provisions
would be *ultra vires* the colonial legislature.[3]

A political announcement has, however, been made that Southern Rhodesia
is no longer to be described as a 'colony' but as the 'state of Southern Rhodesia'.[4] Such statement cannot affect the position in law as Southern Rhodesia
is clearly a colony in terms of the United Kingdom Interpretation Act,[5] and
many other United Kingdom measures, including the Southern Rhodesia (Constitution) Order in Council 1961.[6] Technically, Southern Rhodesia is a British
possession[7] and can also non-technically be described as a dependency[8]
although the Southern Rhodesian Prime Minister has objected to the First
Secretary describing Southern Rhodesia as one of the 'self-governing
dependencies'.[9]

Another example of a political announcement on the nomenclature to be
adopted in respect of Southern Rhodesia occurred when on 7 October 1964,
the Southern Rhodesian Government announced that as from 24 October
the official description of the Government of Southern Rhodesia would be
'The Government of Rhodesia' and that the colony would be known as
'Rhodesia'.[10] Subsequently the Minister of Internal Affairs announced that

---

[1] Jennings, *Constitutional Laws of the Commonwealth*, 3rd edition, Vol. 1, pp. 142–8. Mr.
Wilson has informed the Southern Rhodesian Government of this necessity: *The Times*,
28 October 1964.

[2] Keith, *Responsible Government*, op. cit., Vol. I, p. 312: 'It is created for a definite
purpose; within the terms of that purpose it can effect its aims by what means it thinks fit,
but it cannot frustrate that purpose or convert to wholly different ends its powers.'

[3] Keith, op. cit., p. 313. See *infra*, Appendix S for an examination of and criticism of a
legislative scheme suggested by the Faculty of Law of the University of South Africa to
secure Southern Rhodesian independence without United Kingdom co-operation.

[4] This was confirmed with the rider that 'this would not alter the constitutional position'
on 6 February 1964 by the Central Africa Office: see *The Times*, 7 February 1964.

[5] 52 & 53 Vict. c. 63, Section 18(3)—'Any part of Her Majesty's Dominions exclusive of
the British Islands and British India.' See also de Smith, op. cit., p. 23.

[6] Section 19(1) of the Order says 'Southern Rhodesia' means 'the Colony of Southern
Rhodesia'. The Annex (i.e., the Constitution) also refers to Southern Rhodesia as a colony,
e.g. Section 1(1) and Section 116(1). The Southern Rhodesian Interpretation Act No. 25 of
1962, Section 3(3), also refers to the Colony of Southern Rhodesia, while the Colonial
Development and Welfare Act (3 & 4 Geo. VI, c. 40) refers to Southern Rhodesia as a
colony possessing responsible government. The Southern Rhodesia (Annexation) Order in
Council 1923, Section 3, provides that Southern Rhodesia 'shall be known as the Colony
of Southern Rhodesia'.

[7] Section 18(2) of the Interpretation Act 1889—'any part of Her Majesty's dominions
exclusive of the United Kingdom'.

[8] *Re Maryon-Wilson's Estate*, [1912] 1 Ch. 55 per Farwell L.J. at 66.

[9] Cmnd. 2000, p. 4, Field to Butler, 20 April 1963, and p. 12, Butler to Field, 2 August
1963, explaining that Southern Rhodesia although self-governing was not independent.

[10] Southern Rhodesia Information Service Press Statement 980/64 A.G.C.,7 October 1964.

the 1961 Constitution would be amended to this effect.[1] In fact no amendment by the Southern Rhodesian Legislature to the Constitution can change the position since the Southern Rhodesia (Annexation) Order in Council 1923, Section 3, provides that Southern Rhodesia 'shall be known as the Colony of Southern Rhodesia'. Furthermore in terms of the Southern Rhodesia (Constitution) Act 1961 and the Southern Rhodesia (Constitution) Order in Council the country is 'the Colony of Southern Rhodesia'.

The grant of independence has in the past been considered 'a matter for the United Kingdom and the territory concerned, and for them alone'.[2] This was emphasized in discussions on possible Ghanaian independence and membership of the Commonwealth by the Colonial Secretary, Mr Lennox Boyd, who stated United Kingdom readiness to grant independence if a motion requesting this were passed by a reasonable majority in an elected legislature, but affirmed that full membership of the Commonwealth was 'a different question and . . . a matter for consultation between all existing members of the Commonwealth'.[3] That Southern Rhodesian independence was entirely a matter for the United Kingdom Government was stated by the Lord Chancellor in 1963.[4] It was subsequently reiterated by the Minister of State for Commonwealth Relations and the Colonies,[5] and has been re-stated by the Prime Minister, Mr. Wilson, in the final communiqué issued by the 1965 Commonwealth Prime Ministers' Conference.

Even if there be no obligation to consult there can be no doubt that Commonwealth members are entitled to be kept informed, since at the unofficial Commonwealth Relations Conference held in Lahore in 1954, it was agreed that, although self-government was a question for the United Kingdom and the Colony concerned, other members should be kept informed.[6]

However, recent events seem to indicate that there is a further change in Commonwealth practice evolving and that Commonwealth countries should not only be kept informed but should also be consulted in respect of the grant of independence to a dependent territory. In the case of Southern Rhodesia there has been consultation with the Commonwealth Governments on the independence of Southern Rhodesia on a number of occasions.[7] Although

---

[1] *Rhodesia Herald*, 24 October 1964.

[2] *H.C. Deb.*, Vol. 488, col. 1199, 7 June 1951, Mr. Gordon Walker, Secretary of State for Commonwealth Relations. See also *H.C. Deb.*, Vol. 502, col. 778–80, 16 June 1952, Mr. Churchill, Prime Minister; *H.C. Deb.*, Vol. 526, col. 1625–6, 28 April 1954, Minister of State at the Colonial Office; *H.C. Deb.*, Vol. 562, cols. 239–40, 11 December 1956, Under Secretary of State for Commonwealth Relations.

[3] *H.C. Deb.*, Vol. 552, col. 1558, 11 May, 1956.

[4] *H.L. Deb.*, Vol. 250, col. 957–8, 30 May 1963.

[5] *H.L. Deb.*, Vol. 258, col. 893–4, 10 June 1964. The Labour Secretary of State for Commonwealth Relations has also adopted this view: *H.C. Deb.*, Vol. 713, col. 1557, 1 June 1965.

[6] *The Multi-racial Commonwealth: Proceedings of the Fifth Unofficial Commonwealth Relations Conference*, Lahore, 1954.

[7] See *H.C. Deb.*, Vol. 679, col. 640, 20 June 1963, Home.

49—C.H.L.S.R.

the United Kingdom Prime Minister stated in relation to Southern Rhodesian independence that consultation would not take the shape of formal discussion at a Commonwealth Prime Ministers' Conference,[1] Southern Rhodesia, however, was formally discussed at the July 1964 and 1965 Commonwealth Prime Ministers' Meetings and reference to the independence issue was made in the final communiqués issued by the Prime Ministers.[2] Despite Halsbury's view[3] that the grant of responsible self-government to a colony is solely a matter for the United Kingdom and the territory concerned, it seems that a new rule of Commonwealth practice is evolving.[4] Such a rule can be justified because the relations of members with the newly-independent country will be altered as the United Kingdom Government will no longer be responsible for the external affairs of that country. Since this will affect the external relations of all Commonwealth members, it is clear this is a matter of common concern and that therefore an obligation to consult must arise.[5]

It has been suggested that it is possible for there to be an independent Commonwealth country that is not a member of the Commonwealth.[6] However, it would be impossible in political terms for a particular state to be granted independence if this were a contentious Commonwealth issue. Such a grant without consultation might 'cause grievous injury to the unity of the Commonwealth and the image it presents to the world'.[7] If, as Mr. Sandys alleged, relative to Southern Rhodesia, 'the whole Commonwealth is acutely interested', members would clearly have to be consulted and this Mr. Sandys undertook to do. Despite the fact that Sir Alec Douglas Home informed the Commonwealth Prime Ministers that 'the question of the granting of independence for Southern Rhodesia was a matter for decision for the British

---

[1] *H.C. Deb.*, Vol. 696, col. 241, 9 June 1964, Home. The Prime Minister considered that at such conferences 'we do not discuss each other's internal affairs' although outside formal meetings such discussions could take place. See also 'Meetings of Commonwealth Prime Ministers' by Lord Normanbrook (1964), *Journal of the Parliaments of the Commonwealth*, Vol. XLV, p. 248 at 251.

[2] Text of the communiqué published in *The Times*, 16 July 1964, and extracts published in the *Rhodesia Herald*, 26 June 1965.

[3] *Halsbury's Laws of England*, 3rd edition, Vol. 5, p. 457.

[4] Recently Mr. Bottomley, Secretary of State for Commonwealth Relations has said the Commonwealth must be consulted on the matter. 'We would want to make sure that we had the fullest Commonwealth co-operation and settlement on this (independence)': *Rhodesia Herald*, 26 October 1964.

[5] See Latham, op. cit. at p. 260 on the duty to consult on constitutionally significant matters of common concern.

[6] See K. C. Wheare, *Constitutional Structure of the Commonwealth*, op. cit., p. 126.

[7] *H.C. Deb.*, Vol. 684, col. 586, 15 November 1963, Sandys on Southern Rhodesian independence. See de Smith, op. cit. at p. 20. See, too, *S.R.L.A.D.*, Vol. 53, cols. 10–11, 18 June 1963, in which the Southern Rhodesian Prime Minister revealed that the United Kingdom Government had suggested that the Southern Rhodesian Constitution be amended to satisfy Commonwealth opinion. The Southern Rhodesian Prime Minister considered that members of the Commonwealth were concerned lest 'Southern Rhodesia might be the rock on which the Commonwealth might founder'.

Parliament'[1] in practice the British Government informed the Southern Rhodesian Government that Commonwealth opinion on the independence issue must be sought before they would consider the question. Indeed the United Kingdom Government suggested to the Southern Rhodesian Government that it 'have (its) affairs put before a committee of members of the Commonwealth and discuss it with them'.[2] This proposal the Southern Rhodesian Government rejected. However, such a suggestion seems to suggest a new approach and that independence of Southern Rhodesia is a matter of Commonwealth concern.

In any event 'in the Commonwealth, members decide what they want to do and then bring the rules up to date'.[3]

Membership of the Commonwealth

Until Southern Rhodesia is independent she cannot become a full member of the Commonwealth, although she participates to a great extent in the co-operative, consultative, and communicative processes that are part of the Commonwealth relationship[4] and in the majority of Commonwealth organizations.[5]

In respect of membership of the Commonwealth consultation is clearly necessary.[6] This has been explained on the basis that the accession of a new member would render the general conventions of the Commonwealth automatically applicable between it and the existing members and that this would amount to an extension of the conventional obligations of members thus requiring their consent.[7] In any event if the Members are equal in status the United Kingdom cannot enjoy an exclusive prerogative to admit to membership.[8]

Apparently all that is required is consultation with members and not consent. Unanimity has so far not become a requirement.[9]

Although from 1935 to 1953 the Prime Minister of Southern Rhodesia and subsequently the Prime Minister of the Federation were invited to attend

[1] Statement by the Commonwealth Prime Ministers, *The Times*, 16 July 1964.

[2] *S.R.L.A.D.*, Vol. 58, col. 1675, 13 October 1964. Minister of Internal Affairs.

[3] Wheare, op. cit., p. 119.

[4] See H. J. Harvey, *Consultation and Co-operation in the Commonwealth*, Oxford, 1952. For more recent developments, see K. C. Wheare, *Constitutional Structure*, pp. 128–49.

[5] See Cmnd. 1149, p. 25, for Federal memberships. Southern Rhodesia has, in effect, taken over Federal memberships.

[6] Possibly only after the Independence Act of the United Kingdom Parliament is passed: de Smith in 20 M.L.R. (1957), pp. 353–4, but see *supra*.

[7] Latham, op. cit., p. 985. However the statement of the learned author that acceptance of Southern Rhodesian representation at Imperial Conferences amounted to advance consent to admission as soon as she shall have been granted full autonomy cannot be supported. See also R. C. Fitzgerald, 'The Changing Commonwealth' in *Cvrrent Legal Problems*, 1957, at 232. The author's view at p. 233 that agreement that the Federal Prime Minister should attend future Commonwealth Prime Ministers' Conferences could reasonably be regarded as consent in advance to Federal full membership of the Commonwealth is, however, incorrect.

[8] See Wheare, *Constitutional Structure*, p. 121, quoting Dr. D. F. Malan, Prime Minister of South Africa.   [9] Wheare, *Constitutional Structure*, at p. 124.

Imperial Conferences and later the great majority of Prime Ministers' Conference, the present Southern Rhodesian Prime Minister was not invited to attend the July 1964 and 1965 Commonwealth Prime Ministers' Conferences.[1] Initially, the Prime Minister was informed (with the warning that only independent countries or countries that would be independent within weeks would probably be invited) by the United Kingdom Prime Minister that, if he wished to attend the Conference he should indicate his desire to do so and that then the necessary consultations on this matter between Commonwealth members would be held.[2] After Mr. Smith had expressed such a wish and Commonwealth members had been consulted, it was then decided that 'in view of the size of the modern Commonwealth, the meetings of Prime Ministers should in future be confined to the representatives of fully independent states'. This, the United Kingdom Prime Minister maintained, was no breach of precedent and had been decided by a 'very large majority, indeed nearly all' of the Commonwealth members.[3] As a result of Federal dissolution Southern Rhodesia is therefore no longer represented at Commonwealth Prime Ministers' Conferences, while she is further from Commonwealth membership than she was before the establishment of the Federation. The Minister of State for Commonwealth Relations and the Colonies, has, in fact stated that it would be 'highly unlikely' for Southern Rhodesia to attend a Commonwealth Prime Ministers' Conference until she had attained full independence.[4]

The Southern Rhodesian Government took exception to the fact that the Southern Rhodesian Prime Minister was not invited to the Conference and this dissatisfaction was emphasized by the fact that matters relating to Southern Rhodesia were discussed at the Conference in her absence. The views of the Conference, as expressed in their final communiqué, were subsequently in September 1964 conveyed by the United Kingdom Prime Minister to the Southern Rhodesian Prime Minister, Mr. Smith who, in reply informed the United Kingdom Government 'that he did not feel bound by any of the statements made at the Commonwealth Prime Ministers' meeting, to which he had not been invited'.[5]

When and whether Southern Rhodesia will attain independence and full membership of the Commonwealth remains an undecided question.

[1] Nor was Southern Rhodesia invited to the Finance Ministers' conference held in 1964 at Kuala Lumpur under the aegis of the Commonwealth Economic Consultative Council: C.S.R. 28–1965, p. 8.
[2] H.C. Deb., Vol. 693, cols. 1095–7, 21 April 1964, Home.
[3] H.C. Deb., Vol. 696, col. 240, 9 June 1964, Home.
[4] H.L. Deb., Vol. 258, col. 891, 10 June 1964.
[5] Joint communiqué by the British and Southern Rhodesian Prime Ministers of 11 September 1964: see S.R.L.A.D., Vol. 58, col. 254. The Southern Rhodesian Prime Minister stated on 7 August 1965 that should Southern Rhodesia obtain independence it would not remain a member of the Commonwealth not only because she would be unacceptable to Afro-Asian members but also because Southern Rhodesia would not wish to remain a member of an organization 'embracing countries which are openly communist and prepared to train saboteurs to come back here and sabotage a fellow Commonwealth country': The Times, 9 August 1965.

ADDENDUM

ON the 11 November 1965 Mr. Ian Smith and his Cabinet issued a Proclamation declaring the necessity of Southern Rhodesia's immediately attaining sovereign independence and purporting to 'adopt, enact and give to the people of Rhodesia' the 'Constitution of Rhodesia 1965' which was annexed to the Proclamation.

This unilateral declaration of independence had been preceded by intense negotiations on the question of independence between the United Kingdom and Southern Rhodesian Governments.[1] Early in October the Southern Rhodesian Prime Minister and three Cabinet Ministers held discussions in London with the United Kingdom Government. These ended in deadlock as the United Kingdom Government was not satisfied that five prerequisites for the grant of independence had been met. The principles on which they required to be satisfied before granting Southern Rhodesia independence were that there should be unimpeded progress to majority rule; that guarantees against retrogressive amendment of the Constitution would be given[2]; that there should be an immediate improvement in the political status of Africans; that there should be progress towards ending racial discrimination; and that they should be satisfied that the suggested basis proposed for independence was acceptable to the people of Southern Rhodesia as a whole.[3] Mr. Smith contended that the franchise provisions of the 1961 Constitution, the actions of his Government in removing racial discrimination and its intention to end this by an evolutionary process,[4] the creation of a Senate (composed of twelve Chiefs elected by the Chief's Council), a new procedure replacing the four racial referenda or reservation for amendment of specially entrenched provisions of the Constitution whereby a two-thirds majority of both houses of the Legislature would be required on third readings of such measures, a proposed lowering of the requirements for registration on the 'B' Roll so as to enable adult African taxpayers to vote, and his Government's consultation of tribal opinion and its mandate from the electorate in the 1964 Referendum satisfactorily met the United Kingdom Government's requirements.

Mr. Smith and his Government considered that Southern Rhodesia was entitled to independence on the basis of the 1961 Constitution by virtue of her responsible exercise of powers of self-government since 1923. They were

[1] These negotiations and earlier correspondence and discussions from June 1963 to the time of the declaration of independence are fully set out in Cmnd. 2807. See also *H.C. Deb.*, Vol. 720, cols. 523–32, 12 November 1965, Mr. Bottomley.

[2] e.g. there would be no reduction of the number of electoral districts to one, and no increase of the constituencies to say 100 by a mere two-thirds majority of the Legislative Assembly.

[3] For text of Communique of 9 October 1965 see *H.C. Deb.*, Vol. 718, cols. 646–8.

[4] His Government however declined to repeal the Land Apportionment Act.

not prepared to make concessions leading to the rapid attainment of African majority rule because in their view this would end in destroying the fabric of government which had been established between 1890 and 1965. They also maintained that the people of Southern Rhodesia had been given to understand that they would be granted independence on the 1961 Constitution and that successive British Governments had misled them. However, although certain statements by Mr. Butler in Cmnd. 2000 are susceptible of the interpretation that after the dissolution of the Federation independence would be granted to Southern Rhodesia without further changes in the 1961 Constitution, the giving of such undertakings has been denied by Lord Butler and by Sir Edgar Whitehead.[1] A further allegation that Sir Alec Douglas Home's Ministry agreed without reservations in October 1964 that independence could be granted on the basis of the 1961 Constitution, provided that Mr. Smith showed that this was acceptable to the people of the country as a whole, has been denied by both Sir Alec and Lord Dilhorne.[2]

The possibility of a Treaty between the United Kingdom and an independent Southern Rhodesia guaranteeing the observance of Britain's five principles was thereafter canvassed and at the end of October, when a unilateral declaration of independence appeared imminent, the United Kingdom Prime Minister, Mr. Wilson, flew with the Commonwealth Secretary to Southern Rhodesia, later being joined there by the Attorney-General. United Kingdom proposals for a full-scale Constitutional Conference, for a Treaty, for a Commonwealth Mission headed by the Prime Minister of Australia, Mr. Menzies, and for a Referendum either by the adult population of Southern Rhodesia or by the existing electorate with the addition of those persons whom Mr. Smith intended making eligible for registration on the 'B' Roll were rejected. For a short time it appeared that the Governments would agree on the appointment of a proposed Royal Commission of three members headed by the Southern Rhodesian Chief Justice, Sir Hugh Beadle, to decide whether or not the 1961 Constitution with adjustments to make the country independent was acceptable to the people as a whole. However, by early November it was clear that the Governments could not agree either on the scope of the task of the Commission,[3] or on the procedure it should adopt.[4]

---

[1] *H.L. Deb.*, Vol. 270, col. 260, 15 November 1965; and *S.R.L.A.D.*, Vol. 57, col. 1217, 25 August 1964.

[2] *H.C. Deb.*, Vol. 718, col. 1030, 3 November 1965; and *H.L. Deb.*, Vol. 270, col. 250, 15 November 1965.

[3] The Southern Rhodesian Government's view was that a document containing only adjustments to the 1961 Constitution rendered necessary by the acquisition of independence should be agreed upon by the Southern Rhodesian and United Kingdom Governments and that the Commission should merely ascertain whether this was acceptable to the country. The United Kingdom Government wished the Commission to hear evidence, to frame a new Constitution, and then to test whether this was acceptable.

[4] The United Kingdom Government wanted an interim report and a unanimous decision by the Commission, whereas the Southern Rhodesian Government disagreed.

Not only was there disagreement on these points but Mr. Smith informed Mr. Wilson that the views of their respective Governments were irreconcilable since Mr. Wilson would not commit his Government in advance to accepting any decision of the Royal Commission or to advocating its acceptance in the House of Commons. Last minute suggestions by Mr. Wilson for a further meeting between the two Prime Ministers which should take place in Malta, and for the visit of a senior British Minister to Southern Rhodesia to reach agreement on the work of the proposed Commission were rejected by Mr. Smith. A final concession by Mr. Wilson that the United Kingdom Government would allow the Commission to proceed on the basis proposed by Mr. Smith was ignored.

Towards the end of these negotiations the Governor of Southern Rhodesia, Sir Humphrey Gibbs, on the strength of undertakings by Mr. Smith and his Cabinet that a unilateral declaration of independence was not contemplated and acting on their advice, proclaimed a State of Emergency on the 5 November in terms of the Emergency Powers Act.[1] Under Section 4 of the Act he also made Regulations[2] which gave the Commissioner of Police and Commissioned Officers appointed by him as protecting authorities power to make orders for controlling the possession or distribution of all notices, newspapers and circulars, prohibiting or restricting publications, controlling the taking of photographs, controlling the exit, ingress, removal from, prohibition from, or restriction to any areas under their command of all or any persons, establishing cordons, imposing curfews, controlling traffic, closing both public and private places, seizing vehicles, regulating the possession of arms, and closing licensed premises. Furthermore, the Minister of Law and Order was authorized to detain any person in a prison or other place if it appeared to him 'expedient in the public interest'. Police officers were authorized without warrant to detain any persons for a period not in excess of thirty days if the officer had reason to believe there were grounds to justify such person's detention, if any person questioned by an officer failed to satisfy him as to his identity, or if any person had committed or was about to commit any offence under any law. No person arrested under the Regulations might be admitted to bail without the consent of the Minister of Law and Order. In addition any police officer might without warrant search any person, premises, or vehicles. For the accommodation of any such arrested or detained persons the Minister was authorized to establish camps and it was provided that persons who communicated with detained persons other than with the authority of the Camp Superintendent committed an offence, as did those who transmitted unauthorized letters from the camp. The Regulations also authorized protecting authorities to prohibit any communications, oral or otherwise,

---

[1] See Proclamation 51 of 1965. Sir Humphrey demanded these undertakings but was deceived by Mr. Smith and his colleagues. Personal communication from a confidential source.
[2] The Emergency (Maintenance of Law and Order) Regulations 1965, R.G.N. No. 736.

between members of the public and persons restricted under the Law and Order (Maintenance Act), or persons restricted or detained under these Regulations. Protecting authorities might also prohibit the publication of any information, pictorial or in writing, concerning such persons, and orders were in fact given by the various protecting authorities on the 8 November. Finally the Regulations penalized the making of any statement likely to cause alarm or despondency among the inhabitants of Southern Rhodesia, or some of them, or the making of any statement, comment, or suggestion with respect to any measures taken for or in connection with the State of Emergency.

These Regulations were followed on 10 November by a series of further Regulations[1] not only providing for import and export control, the tightening of Exchange Control, control of goods and services, and price control, but for control of postal and radio communications, the requisitioning of transport and equipment, the employment of Southern Rhodesian defence forces outside the country, and the control of Government employees rendering it a criminal offence for a civil servant to refuse to undertake any duties imposed on him by his Minister or to leave employment after resignation if directed by a Minister that his services should be prolonged. Despite the view of the Government that it enjoyed the support of the Chiefs it also took powers to suspend Chiefs, to appoint acting Chiefs, to remove Chiefs from the tribal areas, and to order them to remain in places specified by the Minister of Internal Affairs.[2] To preclude comment on these activities the Emergency Powers (Dissemination of Information) Regulations 1965 and the Emergency Powers (Censorship of Publications) Order 1965 were also issued.[3] These provided for censorship of all publications containing 'political or other news or articles relating thereto or to other current topics'. They also provided for controlling or prohibiting the printing or publishing of any publication, for controlling the transmission of postal articles, the use of any telegraph, telephone, or telex system, for regulating broadcasting or radio-communications services, and for controlling the entry into or exit from the country of all persons or classes of persons. These Regulations also empowered the Minister of Law and Order to authorize the taking over of printing or publishing firms, to control and direct their businesses for so long as the Minister considered expedient, and to require persons employed in such firms to continue providing their services.

Ultimately by a Proclamation which, with necessary modifications, paraphrased the Declaration of Independence by the thirteen United States of America, Mr. Smith and his colleagues purported to 'adopt, enact, and give to the people of Rhodesia' the 'Constitution of Rhodesia 1965'.[4]

[1] See Government Gazette Extraordinary, 10 November 1965. R.G.N. Nos. 737 A–M.
[2] Emergency Powers (African Affairs) Regulations R.G.N. 737 M.
[3] R.G.N. Nos. 737 J & K.
[4] The Proclamation forebore to assert 'that all men are created equal'. Nor did it allege that governmental power was derived 'from the consent of the governed'.

The 'Constitution of Rhodesia 1965'

Although the 'Constitution of Rhodesia 1965' is destitute of legal effect an analysis of its provisions is worthwhile since the 'Constitution' was at the end of 1965 the fundamental norm on which the *de facto* Government of Mr. Smith based its authority.

Despite many similarities between the 1961 Constitution and the 1965 document there are nonetheless fundamental differences. Among the changes are provisions which purport to validate the illegal seizure of independence and the adoption of the new 'Constitution' by Mr. Smith and his colleagues, to remove the limitations on 'Rhodesia's' sovereignty and remaining British powers of control, to substitute a head of state designated Officer Administering the Government, who would take the place of the Governor and would act on behalf of the Queen but on the advice of Her 'Rhodesian' Ministers, to create the possibility of political appointments to the bench, and to remove the fetters which hampered constitutional amendment. In other respects the 'Constitution' is largely modelled on the 1961 Constitution and the Southern Rhodesia Order in Council 1961. Indeed in a majority of sections there are few changes other than the substitution of 'Rhodesia' as the name of the country[1] and amendments consequential upon the creation of the office of Officer Administering the Government. Major features such as the proportion and number of constituencies and electoral districts and provisions for their delimitation have been retained; the electoral laws and the franchise provisions have barely been modified; the Declaration of Rights has been translated into the 'Constitution'; the land provisions stand almost unaltered; and the provisions for the Constitutional Council and its work remain with merely consequential amendments.[2] Nonetheless it must be emphasized that the 'Constitution' attempted to bring about fundamental changes not only by asserting 'Rhodesia's' independence and by repudiating any British sovereignty, but also by introducing methods of constitutional amendment and abolishing rights of appeal to the Judicial Committee of the Privy Council which rendered the safeguards in the 'Constitution' virtually nugatory.

Independence provisions

The provisions and the omissions had both positive and negative aspects: they were positive in that they asserted 'Rhodesia's' independence and

---

[1] This is implicit throughout the 'Constitution'. Similarly the Legislative Assembly is designated 'Parliament' by Section 12.

[2] Thus Sections 40–46 of the 1965 'Constitution' approximate to Sections 35–41 of the Constitution, Sections 66–77 are identical to Sections 57–68 of the Declaration of Rights, and Sections 82–100 are virtually identical to Sections 73–91 dealing with the Constitutional Council except that under the new provisions appeal judges in addition to puisne judges participate in the election of members of the Council and are consulted before the appointment of a Chairman.

negative in that they denied British authority. Thus Section 2 provided for the coming into operation of the 'Constitution' and declared the 1961 Constitution to be of no force and effect. It was also provided that the validity of the 'Constitution' should not be enquired into in any court and that the Legislature might pass an Act of Indemnity 'in connexion with the attainment by Rhodesia of sovereign independent status'.[1] Again analysis of the various sections reveals an attempt to remove the remaining limitations on 'Rhodesia's' sovereignty.[2] Thus Section 26 provided that no Act of Parliament of the United Kingdom passed after the coming into force of the 'Constitution' should extend to 'Rhodesia'; that from such time the Colonial Laws Validity Act should not apply to 'Rhodesian' legislation; that no subsequent laws passed by the 'Rhodesian' Legislature should be void for their repugnancy to British legislation; and that the Legislature might amend or repeal any United Kingdom legislation insofar as it was part of the law of 'Rhodesia'.[3] Section 5 provided that all Her Majesty's powers relating to 'Rhodesia' should be exercised only on the advice of the Ministers of the Government of 'Rhodesia'. Furthermore no provision, as in Section 111 of the 1961 Constitution, was made for amendment by Order in Council of sections relating to the position of the Crown and Governor. There was no provision for disallowance of 'Rhodesian' Acts. The procedure for reservation of Bills amending specially entrenched constitutional provisions as an alternative to four separate racial referenda was abandoned.[4] In place of a Governor and Commander in Chief appointed by Her Majesty, holding office during pleasure, and liable to receive Royal Instructions on the advice of United Kingdom Ministers in a limited category of cases, there was to be an Officer Administering the Government who was either to be a Governor-General appointed by Her Majesty on the advice of Her 'Rhodesian' Ministers, or, in the event of failure to appoint a Governor-General within fourteen days of Her 'Rhodesian' Ministers tendering such advice, a Regent appointed either by the Executive Council[5] or in terms of a law prescribed by the Legislature.[6] The Officer Administering the Government was to hold office for a period not exceeding five years, and might be removed by a resolution passed by two-thirds of the total membership of 'Parliament' after a report prepared by a 'Parliamentary Committee' had recommended removal on the ground of misconduct or inability to perform the duties of office.[7] Instruc-

---

[1] Sections 142 and 143.   [2] See *supra* Part II, Chapter 7, for these limitations.

[3] Although Mr. Smith's Government did not adopt the legislative scheme put forward in Appendix S, they embodied in the 'Constitution' many of the provisions suggested. These had been adapted from the Status Act 1934 of the then Union of South Africa.

[4] Cp. 'Constitution', Sections 35–36 with Sections 29, 30, 107(2)(b), 109, and 110(3) of the 1961 Constitution.

[5] The Executive Council replaced the former Governor's Council.

[6] Section 3. In October the Minister of Law and Order had indicated that his Government would consider introducing a 'Regency Act' in the event of its seizing independence.

[7] Section 6.

tions to this Officer might only be given by Her Majesty on the advice of Her 'Rhodesian' Ministers.[1] All Her Majesty's prerogative powers to conduct external and internal affairs, to enter into diplomatic relations, to enter into treaties, to declare war, to make peace, and to confer honours and precedence were conferred on the Officer Administering the Government.[2] He was also to have custody of the Public Seal of 'Rhodesia'[3] and in general was substituted for the Governor in any case where powers had been conferred upon the Governor under the 1961 Constitution. Indeed where formerly action was taken in the name of and on behalf of Her Majesty this was now to be taken by the Officer Administering the Government and reference to Her Majesty was omitted.[4] Provisions were also made for the appointment of an Acting Officer Administering the Government when the office was vacant and for the appointment of a Deputy.[5] In fact on 17 November 1965 Mr. C. W. Dupont, the former Minister of External Affairs, was appointed as Acting Officer Administering the Government.[6] The 'Constitution' also purported to introduce a new concept of allegiance to the 'Constitution of Rhodesia 1965' although it also provided for allegiance to Her Majesty. It made no attempt to alter the United Kingdom legislation relating to the Crown and the succession thereto or to the Royal Style and Titles. Finally it was provided that no appeal should lie from any judgement or order of any court in 'Rhodesia' other than to the Appellate Division, thus purporting to abolish not only appeals as of right in terms of the Declaration of Rights but also appeals by special leave of the Judicial Committee of the Privy Council.[7] It was also laid down that no court and no person in 'Rhodesia' should be bound by any judgement, order, ruling, or opinion given by any tribunal, court, person, or authority outside Rhodesia after the coming into operation of the 'Constitution'.[8]

[1] Section 4. Furthermore the possibility of Royal Instructions being used to influence the exercise of the prerogative of mercy was purportedly precluded as this Officer was given power to exercise the prerogative, it being no longer the case that he exercised this 'in Her Majesty's name and on Her Majesty's behalf': cp. 'Constitution', Section 53(1) with Section 49(1) of the 1961 Constitution.

[2] Section 47.

[3] Section 119.

[4] Cp. new Section 49(2) with Section 44(2) (members of the Governor's Council holding office during pleasure), new 51 with old 47 (public offices being created in the name of and on behalf of Her Majesty), and new 52 with old 48 (public lands being disposed of by Her Majesty).

[5] Sections 7 and 8.

[6] Subsequent 'advice' by Mr. Smith's 'Government' that Mr. Dupont be appointed Governor-General was rejected as Her Majesty could not accept such 'purported advice': *Rhodesia Herald*, 4 December 1965.

[7] Cp. 'Constitution', Sections 65(1) and 80 with Sections 56E–G and 71(5) of the 1961 Constitution.

[8] Section 65(2). Pending appeals to the Judicial Committee were saved. Were Section 65(2) effective it would render nugatory any *habeas corpus* proceedings in English courts.

Transitional provisions

In addition to those provisions removing the elements of subordination there were Sections dealing with the continuance in force of existing law, the transfer of moneys in the Consolidated Revenue Fund to a new Fund, the vesting of assets and liabilities in the new Government, the devolution of rights and obligations under conventions or agreements, and the continuance of all civil and criminal proceedings.[1] It was also stipulated that holders of public offices, members and officials of the Legislative Assembly, and the judiciary should continue in office. Many of these provisions were based on the Southern Rhodesia Order in Council 1961,[2] but it was also laid down that should any official, Member of 'Parliament' or judge refuse, on being requested by the Prime Minister, a Minister, or a person assigned thereto by such persons, to state forthwith that he accepted the 'Constitution' and to take an oath set out in the First Schedule to the effect that he would serve in accordance with the 'Constitution of Rhodesia 1965' and would 'respect and uphold' such 'Constitution', then the office of such official, Member of 'Parliament' or judge should be deemed to have become vacant immediately before the coming into operation of the 'Constitution' and such person should not be entitled to any compensation for his loss of office.[3]

Purported major changes

Quite apart from the purported acquisition of independence and removal of British limitations on 'Rhodesia's' powers the 'Constitution' attempted to make fundamental changes in the procedures for constitutional amendment of the specially entrenched clauses and to confer on the Officer Administering the Government complete freedom of constitutional amendment for a period of six months. The 'Constitution' empowered the Officer Administering the Government[4] without Ministerial advice to amend, modify or adapt any provision of the 'Constitution' to such extent as might appear to him necessary or expedient.[5] It would also seem that he was empowered to amend this Section and thus to extend the period during which he might exercise such

[1] Sections 123–4, and 134–9.

[2] The sections relating to continuance in office were based on Sections 6, 7, 9, 11, 12, 16, and 18 of the Order.

[3] Sections 125(3) and (4), 126(1) and (2), and 128(3) and (4). On 16 November 1965 the Chief Justice, Sir Hugh Beadle, refused to take such an oath. He was subsequently supported by other members of the judiciary. Personal communication from a confidential source.

[4] The Acting Officer Administering the Government had the same powers and functions: Section 7(1).

[5] Section 140(1). As this power is conferred 'notwithstanding anything to the contrary contained in this Constitution' it would appear that the Officer may exercise such power in his discretion, and that to this extent Section 50, which requires him to act on advice, is overridden.

powers.¹ On this interpretation the 'Constitution' would be at the mercy of the Officer Administering the Government. At the time of the seizure of independence it was indicated that a purpose for which such power might be employed might be a Senate of the Chiefs or their representatives, this Senate to be concerned with amendment of specially entrenched provisions of the 'Constitution'.²

Amendment of all sections of the 'Constitution' was to be within the competence of a two-thirds majority of the total membership of the 'Parliament'. In the case of amendments to specially entrenched provisions the further procedural limitation was laid down that a Bill seeking to make such amendments must not only be passed at its final vote by a two-thirds majority, but, before the Officer Administering the Government might assent, 'Parliament' must by a two-thirds majority at a subsequent sitting have resolved that an Address be presented to him praying him to assent.³ This was in fact an adaptation of the procedure formerly employed when such a measure was reserved for Her Majesty's assent on the advice of the United Kingdom Government—but with the omission of any reservation or such advice. It was also provided that 'Parliament' was competent to amend every section of the 'Constitution'.⁴ Consequently the monarchical aspects could be eliminated and a presidential regime could be introduced.⁵

Yet another section permitted 'Parliament' to override the limited protection given by Section 78 (i.e. Section 69 of the 1961 Constitution) in time of public emergency. Thus Acts of Indemnity might be passed where the provision for the establishment of a tribunal to consider cases of persons preventively detained had been disregarded, forced labour had been imposed, inhuman treatment had been inflicted, or action had been taken which 'exceeded anything which, having due regard to the circumstances prevailing at the time, could reasonably have been thought to be required for the purpose of dealing with the situation in question'.⁶

¹ Cp. Section 140(1) with the proviso to Section 111 of the 1961 Constitution which precluded the Crown from amending that Section. The Southern Rhodesian Government was aware of this proviso since in 1964 it sponsored a petition requesting Parliament at Westminster to amend Section 111: *supra* Part II, Chapter 1.

² Mr. Smith in his 'Independence Broadcast' announced his intention that the Chiefs should play a greater constitutional role: *Rhodesia Herald*, 12 November 1965. In a broadcast on 20 November the Minister of Internal Affairs, Mr. Harper, declared that the Chiefs might be employed for the purpose mentioned in the text.

³ Section 115 read with Section 116(2).

⁴ Cp. 'Constitution', Section 114 with Sections 105 and 111 of the 1961 Constitution.

⁵ There would be no difficulty in practice in amending any section of the 'Constitution' as Mr. Smith controlled fifty of the sixty-five seats in the 'Parliament'.

⁶ This section might be employed to validate the Emergency (Maintenance of Law and Order) Regulations 1965 which made it an offence to make any statement, comment or suggestion with reference to the state of emergency or any measures in connection therewith. A suggestion that the state of emergency should not be extended beyond three months or that the Legislative Assembly should meet as soon as possible in terms of the Emergency

Finally an attempt was made to remove an anomaly consequent upon Federal dissolution. Whereas the Second Schedule to the Constitution had specified 'Federal' citizenship as a requirement for the franchise it was now provided that 'Rhodesian' citizenship should be the requirement. Accordingly the Electoral Act could be amended to make such provision without following the procedure for amendment of the specially entrenched sections of the 'Constitution'.[1]

Action taken by the lawful authorities

The response by the lawful authorities to the seizure of independence was immediate. Action was taken by the United Kingdom Government both in the executive and legislative spheres. Following upon Mr. Smith's Proclamation enacting the 'Constitution' the Governor, Sir Humphrey Gibbs, acting on Her Majesty's Instructions, dismissed Mr. Smith and his colleagues,[2] and on 12 November appealed to Southern Rhodesian citizens not to assist Mr. Smith's regime.[3] The matter was also brought by Great Britain before the United Nations' Security Council for debate, and on 20 November 1965 a resolution by the Council supporting British action in the form of economic sanctions and exhorting Britain to further and more stringent action was passed.[4]

In the legislative sphere the United Kingdom Government secured the passage of the Southern Rhodesia Act 1965.[5] This had a dual purpose: it was both a declaratory Act and an enabling Act conferring full power on the United Kingdom Government to deal with the extraordinary situation which had been created. In its declaratory aspect the Act reaffirmed that Southern Rhodesia continued part of Her Majesty's dominions and that the Government and Parliament of the United Kingdom had 'responsibility and jurisdiction as heretofore' in respect of it.[6] In its enabling aspect the Act empowered Her Majesty to issue such Orders in Council with reference to Southern Rhodesia as appeared to be necessary or expedient in consequence

Powers Act to hear the reasons for the declaration would fall within such a prohibition. It is submitted that such a prohibition would be struck down by Section 78(1).

[1] Section 15(2) read with Item 5(a) of the Second Schedule to the 'Constitution'. See Part II, Chapter 6.

[2] *The Times*, 12 November 1965.

[3] As a consequence of the stand taken by the Governor, Mr. Smith requested the Governor to resign and to vacate his official residence. On the Governor's refusal, Mr. Smith issued a polemic concerning the Governor's position (Rhodesia Information Service Press Statement 1023/65, 15 November 1965), and removed all facilities and perquisites of office from the Governor, e.g. telephone services, official guards and vehicles, staff and salary. These perquisites were conferred on Mr. Dupont, who was appointed Acting Officer Administering the Government on 17 November 1965.

[4] *The Times*, 22 November 1965. The resolution was not mandatory as Article 7 of the Charter was not invoked.

[5] 13 & 14 Eliz. II, c. 76.

[6] Section 1. The Act deliberately and unprecedentedly referred to responsibility of Her Majesty's 'Government' in order to emphasize this.

of the unconstitutional action taken therein.[1] Without prejudice to the generality of Her Majesty's powers such Orders in Council might suspend, amend, revoke, or add to any of the provisions of the 1961 Constitution, might modify, extend or suspend the operation of any enactment or instrument in relation to Southern Rhodesia, and might impose prohibitions, restrictions or obligations in respect of transactions relating to Southern Rhodesia or to persons or things in any way connected with that Colony.[2] Such Orders might be revoked or varied by subsequent Orders.[3] Certain procedural safeguards to ensure parliamentary supervision of the exercise of such power and to preclude its abuse were also inserted. Thus all Orders required to be laid after their making and would expire at the end of a period of twenty-eight days beginning from the date of their making unless they were approved by resolution of each House.[4] The power to make such Orders was also to expire at the end of one year from the date of passing of the Act unless this power was extended in terms of Section 3(2) by an Order in Council for one year. If this was done a draft of such Order had to be laid and to be approved by resolution of each House.[5] It should be emphasized that the Act did not authorize revocation or suspension of the 1961 Constitution as a whole and that it was expressly provided that the Constitution should remain in force as it had been amended at the time of expiry of the powers to issue Orders in Council.[6]

The powers conferred by the Act were then exercised with three purposes in view: firstly they were employed to invalidate any action taken by the Smith regime which *de facto* continued in office despite its dismissal; secondly they were invoked to confirm and in part confer executive and legislative authority[7] on the lawful authorities, in particular conferring powers on a Secretary of State concurrent with those of the Governor; and thirdly to apply economic and other sanctions against the *de facto* regime in Southern Rhodesia with the aim of forcing a return to constitutional government.

The major instrument invalidating 'Rhodesian' action was the Southern Rhodesia (Constitution) Order 1965.[8] This provided that any action taken in purported promulgation of any Constitution for Southern Rhodesia was void and of no effect.[9] It also prohibited the making of any laws by the Legislature of Southern Rhodesia, the transaction of any business by the Legislative

---

[1] Section 2(1).

[2] Section 2(2). The Act was to have extra-territorial operation: Sections 2(2)(c) and 4(2).

[3] Section 2(4).   [4] Section 2(5).   [5] Section 3(1).

[6] Section 3(3).

[7] The Select Committee on Statutory Instruments commented adversely on the conferment of legislative power suggesting that the Act had not envisaged this: *The Guardian*, 7 December 1965.

[8] S.I. 1965 No. 1952, made on 16 November 1965. Part of the Order came into retrospective operation as from 11 November 1965 and the rest came into effect as from 18 November 1965.

[9] Section 2(1).

Assembly,[1] and the taking of any steps for the reconstitution of the Assembly or the election of any member.[2] Any law made, business transacted and steps taken in contravention of this prohibition were to be void and of no effect.[3] A Secretary of State might also prohibit or restrict the exercise of any function vested in any officer or authority of the Southern Rhodesian Government including the Governor.[4] In order to make it clear that the Governor was not bound by 'Rhodesian' Ministerial advice Sections 43–46 of the Constitution were suspended so that there would temporarily be no effective provision for the appointment of Minister, Deputy Ministers, and a Governor's Council.[5] It was also provided that neither a Secretary of State nor the Governor was, when exercising power, required to follow any advice stipulated as necessary in terms of the Southern Rhodesian law conferring the power.[6]

Complementary to the provisions invalidating 'Rhodesian' action was the conferment of power on a Secretary of State by order in writing at any time to prorogue the Legislative Assembly, and the empowering of Her Majesty to make laws by Order in Council for the peace, order and good government of Southern Rhodesia including laws having extra-territorial operation.[7] Executive authority was also conferred on a Secretary of State acting on Her Majesty's behalf.[8] Furthermore the Governor, subject to any Royal Instructions he might receive or to directions from a Secretary of State, was to act in his discretion in exercising his functions.[9]

In order to force a return to constitutional government the powers conferred under the Southern Rhodesia Act were also employed to impose sanctions. Of these the most significant were the exclusion of Southern Rhodesia from the Commonwealth Preference Area defined in the Import Duties Act 1958,[10] the imposition of embargoes on the purchase of commodi-

---

[1] This provision led to uproar in the 'Rhodesian Parliament' and the suspension of the sole European member of the opposition when it met on 25 November 1965 in terms of a Proclamation issued by the Governor prior to the seizure of independence. When objection was taken to the transaction of business in view of the provisions of the Order, the Speaker ruled that proceedings were valid in terms of the 'Constitution 1965' and that members who disagreed should withdraw. This ruling was challenged, the objecting member was removed from the Chamber by the Serjeant at Arms, and nine members of the opposition walked out in the light of this ruling, although five remained behind. After several Ministerial statements the 'Parliament' adjourned. See *Rhodesia Herald*, 26 November 1965.

[2] Section 3(1)(a).   [3] Section 6.   [4] Section 4(1)(e) and (4).
[5] Section 4(1)(b).   [6] Section 4(2) and (4).
[7] Section 3(1)(b) and (c). The provisions of the Statutory Instruments Act 1946 were to apply to such Orders.

[8] Sections 4(1)(a)(d) and (e) and 5. However the Secretary of State might not exercise judicial power. By virtue of Section 4(1)(e) the Secretary of State issued the Southern Rhodesia (Revocation of Censorship) Order 1965 on 19 November 1965 revoking the Emergency Powers (Dissemination of Information) Regulations and the Emergency Powers (Censorship of Publications) Order which had imposed censorship in Southern Rhodesia.

[9] Section 4(1)(c).
[10] 6 & 7 Eliz. II, c. 6. See the Southern Rhodesia (Withdrawal of Commonwealth Preference) Order 1965, S.I. No. 1954.

ties from Southern Rhodesia, the assumption of control over the Reserve Bank of Rhodesia,[1] the suspension of Southern Rhodesia from the sterling area, the freezing by the Bank of England of all Southern Rhodesian accounts in the United Kingdom, the imposition of an embargo on the supply of oil to Southern Rhodesia and the abrogation of Southern Rhodesian rights to a sugar quota under the Commonwealth Sugar Agreement.[2] Other sanctions of a more political character were also applied. Thus provision was made for the confiscation of passports issued by the regime in 'Rhodesia' after the seizure of independence,[3] for applying the Commonwealth Immigrants Act to persons holding United Kingdom passports by reason only of their Southern Rhodesian citizenship,[4] and for declining to return fugitive offenders to the colony.[5]

Whether the *de facto* regime in Southern Rhodesia would ultimately be recognized as the lawful government, whether a compromise between Mr. Smith's regime and the British Government would be arrived at, whether the economic sanctions imposed by the United Kingdom and other states would end in the collapse of Mr. Smith's regime,[6] or whether the situation in Southern Rhodesia would provide the occasion for military intervention either by the United Kingdom or by other powers was as at the end of 1965 uncertain.

[1] The Reserve Bank of Rhodesia Order 1965, S.I. No. 2049. By this action nominees of the United Kingdom Government were placed in control of the Bank's assets including those in foreign countries. This forced foreign states to make the choice between recognizing the validity of the British measures and acknowledging the 'Rhodesian' authorities who maintained that they continued in control of the Bank's assets.

[2] Southern Rhodesia (Commonwealth Sugar Agreement) Order 1965, S.I. No. 1953. In terms of the Sugar Act 1956 (4 & 5 Eliz. II, c. 48) annual quotas from countries which are parties to the Sugar Agreement are purchased by the United Kingdom Minister of Agriculture.

[3] Southern Rhodesia (Property in Passports) Order 1965, S.I. No. 1955.

[4] Southern Rhodesia (Commonwealth Immigrants Act 1962) Order 1965, S.I. No. 1956. On the other hand it was provided that discretionary powers to grant citizenship of the United Kingdom and Colonies to Southern Rhodesian citizens were, although they had earlier lapsed, to be revived: Southern Rhodesia (British Nationality Act 1948) Order 1965, S.I. No. 1957.

[5] Southern Rhodesia (Fugitive Offenders Act 1881) Order 1965, S.I. No. 1958.

[6] By mid-December 1965 there had already been serious repercussions on the Southern Rhodesian economy. Mr. Smith's Ministry was forced to suspend repayments of capital and interest on international loans and Southern Rhodesian stocks, to impose further restrictions in respect of exchange control and imports, and to provide relief against unemployment: *Rhodesia Herald*, 9 December 1965.

APPENDIXES

THE CONSTITUTIONAL HISTORY & LAW
OF SOUTHERN RHODESIA

APPENDIX

TABLE A—*Direct Imperial influence on Southern*

History of draft Bills prior to introduction in the Legislative Council

Year	Total number of Ordinances	Draft sent to HC with RC's report	Initiated at Imperial request	Introduced as result of conditional assent	Draft amended by HC or S/S	Protracted negotiations/draft/ principle rejected	Report by RC to HC (Sec. 12 (iii) SROC 1898)
1899	22	5	—	—	1	—	All
1900	14	—	—	—	2 (result of N/A in 1899)	2 drafts to S/S at request. 1 (N/A 1899) negotiations proceeding. 2 rejected.	All
1901	24	All	4	—	3	3 rejected	All
1902	15	Large majority	1	3	2 (1 after N/A in 1901)	1 Bill delayed 2 years before promulgation by S/S.	All
1903	21	,,	1	1	3	3 negotiations proceeding.	All
1904	22	,,	2	2	3 (1 after N/A in 1903)	—	All
1905	14	,,	1	1	—	—	All
1906	17	All major Ordinances	—	—	1 (after N/A in 1905)	Ordinance to abolish Native franchise withdrawn by Board as unlikely to be approved.	All
1907	13	,,	—	—	2 (1 disallowed and 1 threatened in 1906)	—	All
1908	15	,,	1	1	2	1 delayed 1 year while CO considered whether to agree.	All
1909	12	,,	1	—	—	2 requests for amending legislation by elected members not proceeded with by Administration knowing Imperial consent would be refused.	All
1910	14	,,	1	—	—	—	All
1911	19	,,	—	—	2	—	All
1912	15	,,	1 request. 5 indirect pressure through Native Affairs Commission Report required to be implemented. 1 on threat of legislation by Proclamation.	—	—	Company did not proceed to ask CO for permission to insist on native labour on reserve roads and on public works.	All
1913	17	,,		1	—	—	All
1914	32	,,	—	2	—	1 withdrawn by Elected members after RC warned it might be financially prejudice any settlement leading to Responsible Government.	All
1915	10	About ⅓	1	2	—	—	All
1916	19	,, ,,	1	1	—	—	All
1917	18	About ⅔	1	—	—	—	All
1918	20	,, ,,	2	1	—	—	All
1919	17	,, ,,	—	—	—	—	All
1920	22	,, ,,	—	1	—	1 not proceeded with as results of HC's requirements re Africans	All
1921	23	,, ,,	2	2	—	2 drafts negotiated.	All
1922	20	,, ,,	7	—	—	—	All
1923	11	,, 9	—	—	—	—	All

Key: HC = High Commissioner   RC = Resident Commissioner   S/S = Secretary of State   N/A = Not assented to

Rhodesian Ordinances from 1899 to 1923

History after introduction in the Legislative Council

Outright assent	Assent conditional on amend- ments	Assent conditional on delegated legislation	Assent conditional on adminis- trative remedy	Not assented to by HC	Refusal of assent by HC on S/S intructions	Disallowance	Essential character of legislation subjected to interference
16	—	2	1	3	1	1	1 financial, 2 basically affecting Europeans and 3 Africans.
10	—	1	2	1	—	—	1 financial; 1 basically affecting Europeans and 6 Africans.
18	3	—	2	2	—	CO considered disallowing 3	8 basically affecting Africans, 1 civil rights, 1 financial; 1 immigration of labourers (Asian in main).
12	3	—	—	—	—	—	4 basically affecting Africans, 2 military control, 1 immigration (Asian).
19	1	—	—	1	1	—	4 basically affecting Africans, 2 Asians, 1 financial.
21	1	—	—	—	—	—	3 basically affecting Africans, 2 Asians, 2 Imperial uniformity.
12	—	—	—	2	2	CO considered disallowing 1	1 Imperial uniformity, 1 military control, 1 financial, 2 basically affecting Africans.
16	1	—	—	—	—	1 (1 in addition not disallowed conditionally on amendment).	2 basically affecting Africans, 1 Europeans, 2 financial.
11	1	—	1	—	—	CO considered disallowing 1 but undertakings given re practice.	2 financial, 2 basically affecting Africans.
15	—	—	—	—	—	1	2 basically affecting Africans, 1 Asians, 1 military, 1 Imperial uniformity.
9	—	—	1	2	1	—	4 basically affecting Africans; 1 general; 1 Imperial uniformity.
14	—	—	—	—	—	—	1 Imperial uniformity.
19	—	—	—	—	—	1 At B.S.A. Co. & Elected Members' request.	1 affecting Africans; 1 Europeans; 1 Asian.
14	1	—	—	—	—	—	7 affecting Africans; 1 general; 1 Imperial uniformity.
15	2	—	—	—	—	—	2 affecting Africans; 1 general.
29	2	—	1	—	—	—	3 basically affecting Africans; 2 Asians; 1 financial.
9	—	—	—	1	—	—	2 affecting Asians (1 a drafting mistake); 2 Africans.
19	—	—	—	—	—	—	1 affecting Africans; 1 Asians; 1 Imperial uniformity.
17	1	—	—	—	—	—	1 general; 1 Imperial uniformity.
20	—	—	—	—	—	—	1 War measure; 1 Imperial uniformity.
14	1	1	—	1	1	—	1 affecting Africans; 1 Imperial policy; 1 military control.
19	3	—	1	—	—	—	4 affecting Africans; 1 military control; 1 general
22	—	—	1	—	—	—	3 affecting Africans, 2 Imperial; 1 military; 1 general.
20	—	—	—	—	—	—	1 affecting Africans; 2 financial; 2 Imperial.
10	1	—	—	—	—	—	1 Imperial.

CO = Colonial Office   O/C = Order in Council

APPENDIX

TABLE B

Ordinances introduced as the result of a request by the Imperial authorities

Year	Short title of Ordinance	Source
1899	—	
1900	—	
1901	No. 1 The Indemnity Ordinance	
	No. 3 The War Material Export Prohibition Ordinance	African 659, No. 148
	No. 10 The Wearing of Uniforms Ordinance	National Archives A 2/4/2, 15 March 1903
	No. 23 Ancient Monuments Protection Ordinance	National Archives A 3/21/3
1902	No. 15 The Rifle and Ball Ammunition Ordinance	African 702, No. 327
1903	No. 9 The Immorality Suppression Ordinance	African 717, Nos. 289 and 291
1904	No. 6 Electric Telegraph Amendment Ordinance	National Archives A 2/4/2
	No. 19 Deserted Wives and Children Protection Ordinance	National Archives A 2/4/2
1905	No. 2 Fugitive Criminals Surrender Ordinance	African 746, No. 237
1906	—	
1907	—	
1908	No. 6 Fugitive Criminals Surrender Amendment Ordinance	National Archives A 2/5/4
1909	No. 2 Juvenile Offenders Capital Sentence Ordinance	National Archives RC 3/3/22
1910	No. 4 Juvenile Offenders Capital Sentence Ordinance	National Archives A 2/4/5
1911	—	
1912	No. 5 Cinematograph Ordinance	National Archives A 2/4/7
	No. 6 Native Labourers (Mines) Compensation Ordinance	The Imperial Government had pressed for the appointment of a Native Affairs Commission and then pressed that its recommendations be embodied in Ordinances.
	No. 7 Native Schools Ordinance	
	No. 8 Dog Tax Ordinance	
	No. 9 Box System Ordinance	
	No. 15 Native Marriages Ordinance	
	No. 13 Special Juries Ordinance	See text on threats by Imperial authorities.
1913	—	
1914	—	
1915	No. 1 Native Labour Regulations Amendment Ordinance	*S.R. Legco. Deb.* 1915, 2nd sess., col. 75
1916	No. 4 Criminal Law Further Amendment Ordinance	*S.R. Legco. Deb.* 1916, col. 152
1917	No. 1 Marriage of British Subjects (Facilities) Ordinance	*S.R. Legco. Deb.* 1918, col. 71
1918	No. 3 Marriage of British Subjects (Facilities) Ordinance	
	No. 14 Trading with the Enemy and Enemy Subjects Ordinance	

Year	Short title of Ordinance	Source
1919	—	
1920	No. 7 Treaty of Peace Order, 1919, Application Ordinance	
1921	No. 13 Loan Ordinance	
	No. 20 Maintenance Orders (Facilities for Enforcement) Ordinance	National Archives A 3/21/4
1922	No. 3 Maintenance Orders (Facilities for Enforcement) Amendment Ordinance	National Archives A 3/21/4
	No. 4 Reciprocal Enforcement of Judgements	National Archives A 2/4/12
	No. 6 Amending the Masters and Servants Amendment Ordinance	National Archives A 2/4/13
	No. 9 Official Secrets Amendment Ordinance	National Archives A 2/4/13
	No. 11 Public Servants Agreement Ordinance	*S.R. Legco. Deb.* 1922, col. 19
	No. 12 Income Tax Ordinance	National Archives A 2/4/13
	No. 13 Public Works Loan Ordinance	*S.R. Legco. Deb.* 1922, col. 358
1923	—	

TABLE C

Ordinances amended after conditional assent or in draft
by High Commissioner and/or Secretary of State

Year	Nature of Ordinance	Nature of amendment	Source
1899	No. 7 Banking	Satisfactory financial safeguards.	African 574, Nos. 119 and 173
1900	No. 8 Dentistry	Professional objections.	B.S.A. Co. Board, Minutes of 18 October 1899
	No. 14 Land Conditions	Modifying stringent occupation conditions for land-owning companies.	National Archives RC 3/3/2
1901	No. 2 Native Marriages	Power to suspend lobola (to be exercised if the need occasioned hardship).	National Archives A 2/4/1
	No. 6 Licences and Stamps	Administrative.	National Archives A 2/4/1
	No. 12 Hut Tax	Taxable age raised from 16 to 18. Period of grace extended.	National Archives A 2/4/1. African (South) C.O. 417/319, 1901, Vol. 1, 29 March 1901, Chamberlain to High Commissioner
1902	No. 1 Masters and Servants (amending Ordinance 5 of 1901)	Requiring witness to externally recruited labourers to be a magistrate.	National Archives A 2/4/1
	No. 3 Importation of Labourers — Immigration (amending Ordinance 18 of 1901)	Protector of Immigrants to be appointed by Secretary of State. Officers of Department to have same safeguards as Native Commissioner. No notices permitting immigration from specified countries without High Commissioner's or Secretary of State's consent. (Also administrative safeguard that labour only to be recruited by Administration and not by private contractors.) Natives not to include Asians or Coloureds born in South or Central Africa.	National Archives A 2/4/1. African 694, No. 160
	No. 9 Protection of Ancient Monuments	Too widely defined. Penalties too severe.	*S.R. Legco. Deb.* 1902, col. 107
	No. 11 Natives Registration (amending Ordinance 16 of 1901)	Penalties on employers failing to give certificates heavily increased.	National Archives A 2/4/1

TABLE C 767

Year	Nature of Ordinance	Nature of Amendment	Source
1903	No. 3 Amending the Criminal Law (hanging for rape and attempted rape)	Changed to include any person committing rape not merely natives raping white women.	National Archives A 2/4/2
	No. 10 Immigration	Secretary of State's objections met — wording previously aimed directly at Asians. To be amended in accordance with the wishes of India Office.	African 702, No. 392; African 717, No. 356; African 746, Nos. 74 and 100
	No. 20 Taxation of Natives	Amount of tax reduced; only to be payable in 1904, High Commissioner to have discretion to remit.	National Archives A 2/4/2. African 717
1904	No. 2 Regulating Hawkers' Licences	At first directly aimed at Asian traders in order to discriminate in grant of licences. Right of appeal to Administrator after refusal by local authority.	National Archives A 2/4/2. African 717, No. 454
	No. 6 Electric Telegraphs	Secretary of State's request. Imperial uniformity.	National Archives A 2/4/2
	No. 12 Amending Natives Pass Ordinance (amending Ordinance 10 of 1902)	Exempting Africans in transit through S. Rhodesia. Permitting Africans to enter property when seeking work (previously criminal). No deductions from wages other than by statute or Court's order. Regulations to be approved by High Commissioner. Penalties on employers increased.	National Archives A 2/4/2. African (South) C.O. 417/373, Vol. III, 1903, Lyttelton to Milner, 18 December 1903. African 717, No. 351
	No. 13 Immigration (amending Ordinance of 1903)	To meet India Office objections and Secretary of State's views.	National Archives A 2/4/2. African (South) C.O. 417/312, Vol. II, 1903
	No. 21 Native Taxation	On lines approved by Secretary of State. Amount of tax less. Regulations to be approved by High Commissioner.	National Archives RC 3/3/9. African 746, No. 223
1905	No. 13 Volunteer Ordinance (amending Ordinance 2 of 1902)	Officers to be appointed by Secretary of State. Regulations to be approved by Secretary of State. High Commissioner's concurrence in being called out on active service.	National Archives A 2/4/2. African 746, No. 109
1906	No. 4 Native Reserve Locations in or near Urban Areas	Native inspectors to be appointed by High Commissioner. (Also in order to vindicate authority of Section 80 of the 1898 Order in Council.)	S.R. Legco. Deb. 1906, col. 3. African (South) C.O. 417/422, C.O. Minute 16 February 1906 on H.C. Despatch 78/06

Year	Nature of Ordinance	Nature of amendment	Source
1907	No. 2 Post Office Savings Bank	Financial safeguards.	National Archives A 2/4/2
	No. 6 Administration of Deceased Estates (repealing Ordinance 5 of 1906)	Safeguards on investment.	National Archives A 2/4/2
1908	No. 4 Immigration and Registration of Asiatics	High Commissioner amended certain clauses. (Ultimately Secretary of State disallowed.)	National Archives A 2/4/6
	No. 5 Stock Theft and Produce (amending Ordinance 5 of 1907)	Punishment for malicious search. Europeans' property also to be searchable.	National Archives A 2/4/5
	No. 7 Police Ordinance	Control over B.S.A. police to revert to Company. Police pensions secured.	African (South) series, from 1903 to 1908
1909	—	—	
1910	No. 4 Juvenile Offenders' Capital Sentences	Discretion re death penalty.	National Archives A 2/4/5
1911	No. 3 Municipal Law	Suppression of objectionable businesses on an objective basis not merely if 'objectionable to residents'.	National Archives A 2/4/7
	No. 17 Kaffir Beer	Drafted so that a truck system in Kaffir Beer was impossible.	National Archives A 3/18/5. African (South) C.O. 417/495.
1912	—	—	
1913	No. 3 Qualifications and Registration of Voters	Allowing appeal from the decision of a registering officer against refusal to register.	S.R. Legco. Deb. 1913, cols. 4 and 77
1914	No. 1 Water Ordinance (amending Ordinance 13 of 1913)	To protect natives affected by irrigation schemes.	S.R. Legco. Deb. 1914, col. 7
	No. 5 Native Passes (amending Ordinance 15 of 1913)	Africans in transit through S. Rhodesia to be exempted.	S.R. Legco. Deb. 1914, col. 202
1915	No. 3 Native Labour Contracts (amending Ordinance 10 of 1914)	Making convictions possible of Europeans refusing to return registration certificates to Africans.	S.R. Legco. Deb. 1915, col. 200. Administrator's files
	No. 4 Immigration (amending Ordinance 7 of 1914)	High Commissioner's consent to persons being declared undesirable on economic grounds or standard of life (the clause still used to exclude non-European immigrants). High Court to have jurisdiction. Persons born in S. Rhodesia to be admitted. One polygamous wife to be admitted.	S.R. Legco. Deb. 1914, col. 202. Administrator's files

TABLE C 769

Year	Nature of Ordinance	Nature of amendment	Source
1915	No. 14 Immigration (amending Ordinance 7 of 1914)	Birth an additional qualification despite parents' domicile elsewhere.	Administrator's files
1916	—	—	
1917	—		
1918	No. 4 Accountants (amending Ordinance 14 of 1917)	No compulsory registration of non-Southern Rhodesian accountants.	Administrator's files
1919	—	—	
1920	No. 1 Defence (amending Ordinance 10 of 1919)	Safeguarding High Commissioner's control over Commandant General and thus over military forces.	National Archives A 2/4/12
1921	No. 5 Water (amending Ordinance 8 of 1920)	No allocation of water by judge under Water Ordinance to be effective until approved by High Commissioner in order to give him opportunity to secure just provision for Native Reserves.	S.R. Legco. Deb. 1921
	No. 8 Native Cattle Dealers Licensing (amending Ordinance 12 of 1920)	Native seller not to be penalized. Dealer without licence penalized but only if he has been provided with one.	S.R. Legco. Deb. 1921, col. 38
1922	—	—	
1923	—	—	

APPENDIX

TABLE D

Assent conditional on delegated legislation clarifying difficulties

Year	Short title	Purpose	Source
1899	No. 9 The Natives Employment Ordinance	To clarify that there be no pass system for natives leaving Southern Rhodesia	African 574, No. 238, Encls.
	No. 12 S.R. Native Regulations Amendment Ordinance	Making clear appeal to High Court from Special Justices of the Peace was not abolished	African 656, No. 138
1900	No. 5 Lung-sickness in Cattle Ordinance	Regulations to provide no prosecution without Administrator's consent: Africans by customary law apparently ate diseased cattle.	African (South) C.O. 417/319, Vol. I
1919	No. 3 Leprosy Ordinance	Draft regulations in accordance with High Commissioner's wishes even though within purview of Administrator. There was previous discussion whether assent should be refused.	National Archives A 2/4/3

TABLE E

Assent conditional on administrative safeguard

1899	No. 13	Juvenile Offenders Amendment Ordinance	Judges by administrative practice must review all cases where whipping imposed on juveniles.	African 574, No. 292
1900	No. 3	Census Ordinance	Not to be put into effect until state of feeling in country was peaceful.	African (South) C.O. 417/283
	No. 5	Lung - sickness Ordinance	All regulations and instructions under the Ordinance to be submitted to Resident Commissioner or High Commissioner for scrutiny. Africans eating dead animals according to native custom not to be prosecuted.	African 659, Nos. 35 and 63
1901	No. 2	Native Marriages Ordinance	Lobola not to be enforced in districts where this would cause hardship to natives.	National Archives A 2/4/1
	No. 4	Peace Preservation Ordinance	Resident Commissioner to scrutinize all prosecutions under the Ordinance and report thereon to High Commissioner.	African (South) 1901, C.O. 417/319
1907	No. 1	Natives Employment Ordinance	No labour agents to be exempted from licensing unless effective scrutiny and control of their activity by the Administrator.	
1909	No. 3	Injurious Substances and Animals Ordinance	All notices issued by the Administrator to be reported to High Commissioner.	
1914	No. 27	Compulsory Dipping Ordinance	Administrator to exempt cattle from dipping (non-compliance was criminal) in African areas.	National Archives RC 3/3/37. African (South) C.O. 417/436
1920	No. 13	Exportation and Importation Restriction Ordinance	High Commissioner to be notified of all notices by Administra-or controlling export and import of goods.	National Archives A 2/4/12
1921	No. 3	Police Ordinance Amendment Ordinance	Doubts to be cleared by departmental circular.	National Archives Administrator's files

APPENDIX

TABLE F

Assent refused

Note: In correspondence 'disallowance' is used in a non-technical sense to indicate refusal of assent. The correspondence, however, makes it clear that on all but three occasions what was really meant was non-assent by the High Commissioner either on his own initiative or on instructions of the Secretary of State: the confusion arose as a result of Section 35 of the 1898 Order in Council which did not refer to refusal of assent but to 'disallowance or other direction' in respect of Ordinances submitted for assent.

Year	Short title	Reason	Source
1899	No. 7 Banking Ordinance	Inadequate financial safeguards. The Company wished to issue Bank Notes. (Action at instance of Secretary of State.)	African 574
	No. 10 Practice of Medicine and Dentistry Ordinance	Unsatisfactory registration provisions. Objected to by professions. Action at High Commissioner's instance.	African 574
	No. 22 Land Conditions and Title Ordinance	Onerous terms of development imposed on land-owning companies. Action at High Commissioner's instance.	African 574
1900	No. 7 Magistrates Jurisdiction Ordinance	'I do not approve of putting larger powers of flogging in the hands of magistrates': Milner (High Commissioner). Action at High Commissioner's instance.	African (South) C.O. 417, 1900. Vol. I, p. 283
1901	No. 23 Protection of Ancient Monuments Ordinance	Scope of Ordinance too large and penalties too severe. (Action at High Commissioner's instance.)	African 694
1901	No. 24 Mines and Minerals Ordinance	To allow whole law to be reconsidered. Done at request of Administrator.	National Archives RC 3/3/5
1903	No. 20 Natives Tax Ordinance	Tax quadrupled from previous years in order 'to conduce to more continuous labour by the native'—Administrator to High Commissioner. 10 September 1903. Action at Secretary of State's instance. High Commissioner in favour of legislation.	African 717. National Archives A 2/4/2/. National Archives RC 3/3/8
1905	No. 4 Establishment of Native Reserve Locations in or near Urban Areas	Imposed a new disability on Africans by forcing them to live in locations unless housed by their employers or being freeholders of property to the value of £75. From these they were to be ejected on nonpayment of rent. Secretary of State's consent	African (South) C.O. 417/408. African 763, No. 165

Year	Short title	Reason	Source
		under Section 80 of Order in Council had not been obtained. Eventually in 1906 after giving High Commissioner control over the appointment of native location inspectors, H.M.G. agreed to new Ordinance as the Ordinance was merely legalizing *de facto* segregation as applied in Southern Rhodesia and copying provisions in the Cape, while the Colonial Office had vindicated Secretary of State's authority.	
1905	No. 14 S.R. Consols and Loan Ordinance	Initiating a public debt which could impede any future settlement with the Company. Action on Secretary of State's instructions.	African 763, No. 267. National Archives RC 3/3/11
1909	No. 6 Juvenile Offenders Capital Sentence Ordinance	Not clear that judge had a discretion not to impose death sentence. Action on High Commissioner's suggestion.	National Archives R.C.'s files
	No. 9 Kaffir Beer Ordinance	Possibly permitting a truck system in beer. To be referred instead to Native Affairs Commission. Action by order of Secretary of State on Acting High Commissioner's suggestion.	National Archives RC 3/3/22
1915	No. 4 Immigration Amendment Ordinance	Excluding persons born in Southern Rhodesia of parents domiciled elsewhere. Apparently result of mistake in decoding a cable. Action on High Commissioner's suggestion.	*S.R. Legco. Deb.* 1916, col. 30
1919	No. 12 Enemy Subjects Immigration Ordinance	Not in accordance with general Imperial policy which was subsequently legislated for by Proclamation. Action on Secretary of State's instructions.	National Archives RC 3/1/80. National Archives A 11/2/12/4

APPENDIX

TABLE G

Disallowance from 1899 to 1923

Year	Nature	Reasons	Source
1906	No. 3 Post Office Savings Banks	Inadequate financial safeguards allowing up to one-quarter of assets to be on deposit with Banks.	National Archives RC 3/3/10. African (South) C.O. 417/423
1908	No. 4 Restricting Immigration of Asiatics and providing for Registration of Resident Asiatics	Secretary of State utterly opposed to such legislation. High Commissioner favoured this legislation.	National Archives RC 3/3/18. National Archives. A 2/4/6 B.S.A. Co. Minutes of 2 May 1907 Annex.
1911	No. 13 Tax on Employers of Coloured Labour	Unacceptable to substantial section of farming community. Resistance to collection. Legco. leaders and Administration agreed to request Secretary of State to disallow.	National Archives A 3/21/36. Papers laid on the Table of the Legislative Council, 13 May 1912

TABLE H

Tables A–G summarized

Total number of Ordinances	Number initiated at Imperial request	Number introduced after conditional assent	Ordinances amended after conditional assent or in draft
446	34 7·6%	18 4%	38 8%

Proposed Ordinances/ Legislation not proceeded with	Conditional assents	Ordinances not assented to	Disallowances
11	35 7·8%	13 2·9%	3 0·67%

Note: Of 446 Ordinances, 141 were directly influenced by the Imperial authorities, i.e. 31·6 per cent.

Draft Ordinances not proceeded with are not included in the percentages.

TABLE I

The legislative and administrative position as at December 1963

Part I—The Federal Legislative List

Item	Matter	Federal legislation	Territorial legislation	Federal administration	Territorial administration
1.	External affairs, that is to say— (h) such external relations as may from time to time be entrusted to the Federation by Her Majesty's Government in the United Kingdom; and (b) the implementation of treaties, conventions and agreements with, and other obligations towards, countries or organizations outside the Federation affecting the Federation as a whole or any one or more of the Territories, whether entered into— 　(i) either before or after the date of the coming into force of this Constitution, by Her Majesty, or by Her Majesty's Government in the United Kingdom on behalf of the Federation or any of the Territories; or 　(ii) after the said date, by the Federation with the authority of Her Majesty's Government in the United Kingdom; or	Immunities and Privileges Acts 31/56, 3/59, 22/62	— —	Ministry of External Affairs Exclusively Federal (SRGN 903/53).	—

TABLE I   777

(iii) before the said date, by any of the Territories with the said authority; but not including relations between the United Kingdom and any of the Territories.				—
2. Extradition, fugitive offenders, and the removal of prisoners, both as between Territories and as between the Federation or a Territory and some country outside the Federation.	FGN 584/54, Prisoners' Removal (SR) Order, making adaptations	*Pre-Federal* Prisoners Removal Act (Ch. 19 of 1939), Extradition Act (Ch. 29 of 1939), Extradition and Fugitive Offenders Act (Ch. 30 of 1939)	Ministry of Law	—
3. Defence	Defence Act 23/55, 14/56, 40/59, 14/60, 2/61, 6/61 Rhodesia and Nyasaland Cadet Corps Act 22/55	—	Ministry of Defence	—
4. Immigration into and emigration from the Federation	Immigration Act 37/54, 9/57, 9/59, 37/59, 26/61, 19/63	—	Ministry of Home Affairs	—
5. Aliens	Aliens (Registration and Status) Act 39/54, 16/61	—	Ministry of Home Affairs	—
6. Citizenship of the Federation	Citizenship of Rhodesia and Nyasaland and British Nationality Act 12/57, 13/59, 16/60, 23/62	—	Ministry of Home Affairs	—
7. Banks and banking, other than land banks as defined in item 50 in Part II of this Schedule; control of capital issues.	Bank of Rhodesia and Nyasaland Act 2/56, 24/59, 9/61	—	Ministry of Finance	—
8. Control of imports into and exports from the Federation: exchange control.	Control of Goods Act 12/54 Exchange Control Act 27/54 Currency and Exchange Control (Temporary) Act 1/61, 44/62, FGN 75/54, 77/54 making adaptations	*Pre-Federal* Produce Export Act (Cap. 178 of 1939), Cattle Export Act (Cap. 184 of 1939)	Ministry of Finance Ministry of Commerce and Industry, Ministry of Agriculture	—

Item	Matter	Federal legislation	Territorial legislation	Federal administration	Territorial administration
9.	Promotion of exports from the Federation	FGN 75/54 79/54 making adaptations	—	Ministry of Commerce and Industry	—
10.	The distribution, disposal, purchase and sale of such manufactured and unmanufactured commodities and such animals and poultry as the Governor-General may by order specify, the control of the wholesale and retail price of any commodities, animals or poultry so specified, and the payment by the Federation of subsidies in respect of any commodities, animals or poultry so specified (subject to the provisions of Part III of this Schedule), so, however, that a law of the Federal Legislature relating to animals or poultry made by virtue of this item shall not have affect in relation to any Territory unless and until the Governor of that Territory has declared by notice in the official Gazette of the Territory that it shall so have effect	The commodities and animals were specified by FGN 166/55, 242/61, 44/62. By 1963 there were 9 S.R. Governor's declarations giving effect to Federal laws in terms of this item. Grain Marketing Act 23/57, 18/58, 2/59, 17/61, 14/62. Grain Marketing (Transitional Provisions) Act 48/62, Agricultural Marketing Council Act 6/56, 11/59. Dairy Produce Marketing and Levy Act 27/61, 32/62. Agricultural Products Levy Act 19/57. Tobacco Marketing and Levy Act 30/60, 21/61. Cold Storage Commission Act 9/60, 11/62	—	Ministry of Agriculture, the Tobacco Marketing Board, Federal Grain Marketing Board, Dairy Marketing Board, Cold Storage Commission and Agricultural Marketing Council	—
11.	Duties of customs and excise (including export duties) other than duties on motor spirit, whether the proceeds of those duties are to be used for Federal or for Territorial purposes (subject to the provisions of article eighty-three of this Constitution).	Customs and Excise (Declaratory) Act 21/55, Customs and Excise Acts 16, 24/55, 10, 16, 20, 29/56; 1, 10, 20, 24/57; 15, 25/58; 7, 15, 21, 22, 44/59; 3, 4, 17, 18, 39/60; 5, 22/61; 4, 6, 25, 36, 49/62.	—	Ministry of Finance. Exclusively Federal (SRGN 345 of 1961)	

TABLE I   779

No.	Subject matter	Legislation	Authority	Note
12.	Taxes on income and profits, and taxes on amounts paid or payable on the sale of goods other than motor spirit, whether the proceeds of those taxes are to be used for Federal or for Territorial purposes (subject to the provisions of articles eighty to eighty-two and eighty-four of this Constitution)	Taxes Charging Acts (nine) Income Tax Acts (14). Tax Reserve Certificates Act 19/54, Territorial Surcharges Act 29/59	Ministry of Finance. Exclusively Federal (SRGN 345 of 1961)	*Note.* In 1961 the S.R. Govt. considered introducing a Territorial Income Tax. This led to SRGN 345 of 1961 under Article 29(2) of the Federal Constitution terminating S.R. Legislative power in this respect	—
13.	Currency, coinage, and legal tender	Bank of Rhodesia and Nyasaland Act 2/56, 24/59, 9/61	Ministry of Finance.	—	—
14.	Guarantees by the Federal Government of loans	Numerous Acts	Ministry of Finance	—	—
15.	Companies, that is to say, general provision as to the incorporation, regulation, and winding up of bodies corporate, other than bodies incorporated directly by a law of the Legislature of a Territory or incorporated under a law of such Legislature for special purposes specified in that law, and other than co-operative societies or co-operative companies	*Pre-Federal* Companies Act 1951; Companies (SR) Amendment Act 20/59, 38/63	Ministry of Law		—
16.	Insurance, other than insurance undertaken by the Government of a Territory	Insurance Act 33/56, 26/59, 33/60	Ministry of Finance	—	—
17.	Bills of exchange, cheques, and promissory notes	*Pre-Federal* Bills of Exchange Act (Cap. 209 of 1939); Cheques Act 5/59	Ministry of Finance		—
18.	Copyright, patents, trade marks, designs, and merchandise marks	*Pre-Federal* Copyright Act (Cap. 212 of 1939); FGN 169/56; Patents Act 13/57, 12/59, 36/60, 1/62; Patents (Transitional Provisions) Act 5/58. Trade Marks Act 14/57, 37/60, 2/62. Registered Designs Act 12/58. Merchandise Marks Act 17/57, 17/59	Ministry of Law (copyright, patents, trade marks and designs), Ministry of Commerce and Industry (merchandise marks)		—

Item	Matter	Federal legislation	Territorial legislation	Federal administration	Territorial administration
19.	The construction, alteration, and maintenance of all roads (in so far as they lie within the Federation) scheduled as inter-territorial in the Final Act of the Transport Conference held at Johannesburg in the year 1950, and any other roads within the Federation which may be prescribed as inter-territorial by any law of the Federal Legislature	—	—	Ministry of Transport *BUT*	Ministry of Roads territorially administered on an agency basis for and with finance provided by the Federal Government
20.	Railways and ancillary services, including ancillary transport services	Rhodesia Railway Laws Amendment Act 18/55, 12/60, 39/63, FGN 298/61. Regulation of Railways (Territorial Laws) Amendment Act 28/62	*Pre-Federal* Rhodesia Railways Act 6 of 1947. Regulation of Railways Act (Chapter 261 of 1939)	Ministry of Transport	—
21.	Shipping, harbours, and ancillary services, including transport services	Inland Waters Shipping Act 34/60, 13/61	—	Ministry of Transport	
22.	Aviation, aerodromes, and ancillary services, including ancillary transport services and the safety of aircraft	Aviation Act 10/54, 25/61. Air Services Act 10/60, Central African Airways Corporation Act 11/60, 12/61, 27/62	—	Ministry of Transport	—
23.	Meteorology			Ministry of Agriculture	
24.	In relation to Southern Rhodesia, agriculture, that is to say— (a) agriculture in general, including animal husbandry, dairies and dairy-farming, horticulture, poultry-farming, bee-keeping, fish-farming, pounds and agricultural colleges; (b) agricultural research, including pasture, tobacco, veterinary and tsetse research;	Many Acts enumerated under Item 10. Pig Industry Act 28/59, 15/60, Registration of Pedigree Livestock (SR) Amendment Act 30/62: FGN 72/54: FGN 62/54: FGN 159/60: FGN 75/54: FGN 78/54: FGN 76/54: FGN82/54: FGN 284/56: FGN 194/57: Fertilizers, Farm Feeds, Seeds, and Remedies' (SR) Amdt. Act	*Pre-Federal* Registration of Pedigree Livestock Act (Cap. 192 of 1939), Cotton Levy Act 26 of 1952. Dairy Act (Cap. 186 of 1937), Farmers Licensing Act 21/42, Maize Act (Cap. 161 of 1939), Noxious Weeds Act (Cap. 163 of 1939), Ponds and Trespasses Act (Cap.	Ministry of Agriculture	—

TABLE I

781

(c) the provision and use of specialist services in connection with agriculture and agricultural products, including veterinary services and services dealing with chemistry, entomology, and plant pathology; and (d) conservation, but not including forestry, irrigation, or such agriculture as the Governor-General and the Governor of Southern Rhodesia acting jointly shall by order have designated as African agriculture (subject to the provisions of Part III of this Schedule)	8/60; FGN 65/54	190 of 1939), Fertilizers, Farm Feeds, Seeds, and Remedies Act 21 of 1952	—
25. In relation to Southern Rhodesia, animal health, including animal pests and diseases	Animal Health Act 5/60, 15/62	—	Ministry of Agriculture
26. In relation to Southern Rhodesia, plant pests and diseases	Plant Pests and Diseases Act 11/54, FGN 69/54	*Pre-Federal* Locust Distribution Act (Cap. 177 of 1939)	Ministry of Agriculture
27. Posts, telegraphs, telephones, wireless (other than broadcasting, television, and other like forms of communication), and Post Office savings banks	Posts and Telegraphs Act 20/54, 12/56, 8/59, 27/60. Radio Communications Act 32/57, 18/62. Post Office Savings Bank and Certificates Act 29/54, 2/57, 32/59, 24/60, 11/61, 39/62	—	Ministry of Posts
28. Such irrigation works and water works as the Governor-General may by order designate as major irrigation or water works or as works ancillary to such major works (subject to the provisions of Part III of this Schedule)	SRGN 585/54	*Pre-Federal* Water Act (Cap. 251)	Ministry of Power. Only the Kariba Project was designated as a major water work. Other large schemes remained Territorial. See Major Water and Irrigation Works (Designation Order) SRGN 585/54

Item	Matter	Federal legislation	Territorial legislation	Federal administration	Territorial administration
29.	The generation, supply, and use of nuclear energy	—	—	Ministry of Power	—
30.	Primary and secondary education of persons other than Africans	Education Act 15/56, 14/58, 38/59, 19/62	—	Ministry of Education	Yes, but only if such persons were in a school the majority of whose pupils were African
31.	Higher education (including higher education of Africans), that is to say, institutions or other bodies offering courses of a university, technological, or professional character	—	—	Ministry of Education. The University College of Rhodesia and Nyasaland is an autonomous institution, incorporated by Royal Charter on 10 February 1955	—
32.	Weights and measures	Weights and Measures Act 18/59	—	Ministry of Commerce and Industry	—
33.	The Federal Public Service	The Federal Public Service Act 19/59, 46/52. Federal Pensions Fund 23/54, 3/57. Federal Provident Fund 29/60	—	Ministry for the Public Service. Ministry of Finance	—
34.	Federal Public Relations	—	—	Ministry of Home Affairs (Information Services)	—
35.	Audit of Federal public accounts	Audit and Exchequer Act 9/54, 27/56, 32/60	—	Ministry of Finance	—
36.	The establishing, training, maintenance and administration of a Federal police force for service in the employment of, for use in, any Territory at the request and under the operational control of the Governor of that Territory in addition to or in substitution for the police of that Territory; and the conditions (including conditions	—	—	The Federal Government was anxious to establish such a force but neither of the two Northern Territories was prepared to permit such a force to operate in its Territories. Although S.R. Government policy favoured fed-	—

No.				
	as to payment by the Territory) on which the Federation will make that police force available for such use or employment		—	eral training of all police, S.R. had the B.S.A.P., a well-established force
37.	The establishment, constitution, jurisdiction and powers of any Federal courts other than the Federal Supreme Court (subject to the provisions as to the jurisdiction of the Federal Supreme Court contained in articles twenty-two and fifty-three to fifty-five of this Constitution)	Income Tax Act 1954. Patents Act. Trademarks Act. Registered Designs Act. Defence Act	—	Ministry of Law administering Income Tax Special Court, Patents Tribunal. Court Martials Appeal Court
38.	Legal proceedings between the Federation and a Territory or between Territories (subject to article fifty-three of this Constitution)	Service of Process and of Judgements Act 4/56	—	Ministry of Law
39.	Legal proceedings by or against the Federation other than proceedings against or by a Territory	Crown Proceedings Act 4/54, 20/55. Government Solicitor Act 3/56, 20/62	—	Ministry of Law
40.	Subject to the provisions of Part III of this Schedule, such matters relating to such professions or callings as, and to the extent which, the Governor-General, with the consent of the Governor of the Territory concerned, may by order designate. (As amended by Section 2 of Federal Act No. 27 of 1959)	9 Designation Orders designating various professions were issued. Medical Practitioners and Dentists (Territorial Laws) Act 14/61. Medical Dental and Allied Professions (S.R.) Act 24/63. FGN 181/54	*Pre-Federal* Medical, Dental and Allied Professions Act of 1952	Ministry of Health
41.	The payment of old age pensions by the Federal Government	—	*Pre-Federal* Old Age Pensions Act (Cap. 287). This was retained as old age pensions are paid only to non-Africans. New legislation conferring less than equality would have been subjected to examination by the African Affairs Board	Ministry of Finance

Item	Matter	Federal legislation	Territorial legislation	Federal administration	Territorial administration
42.	The control of any area which may be designated as a National Park by an order made by the Governor-General with the consent of the Governor of the Territory in which that area is situated, being control with respect to such matters and to such extent as may be specified in that order (subject to the provisions of Part III of this Schedule)	National Parks (Designated Areas) Act 13/55. Designation Orders—5 in all—were only made in respect of S.R.	*Pre-Federal* National Parks Act 1949	Ministry of Home Affairs	—
43.	Any monument designated as a National Monument by an order made by the Governor-General with the consent of the Governor of the Territory in which that monument is situated (subject to the provisions of Part III of this Schedule)	—	*Pre-Federal* Monuments and Relics Act (Cap. 64)	Ministry of Home Affairs	—
44.	Any other matter, whether or not otherwise within the exclusive legislative competence of the Federal Legislature, with respect to which for the time being, under or by virtue of any provision of this Constitution, the Federal Legislature has, and the Legislature of the Territory has not, power to make laws, or in relation to which reference is made in this Constitution to a law of the Federal Legislature but not to a law of the Legislature of a Territory	Numerous Acts either incidental or specified, e.g. Interpretation Act 3/54. Federal Supreme Court Act 11/55. Constitution Amdt. Act 18/54 and fifteen other amending or similar Acts as well as fifty-five financial measures to 1 January 1963	*Pre-Federal* Numerous Acts	—	—

TABLE I

785

Part II—The Concurrent Legislative List

Item	Matter	Federal legislation	Territorial legislation	Federal administration	Territorial administration
45.	Deportation	Deportation Act 36 of 1954	—	Ministry of Home Affairs	—
46.	Naturalization	Citizenship of Rhodesia and Nyasaland and British Nationality Act 12/57, 13/59, 16/60, 23/62	—	Ministry of Home Affairs	
47.	Control of the voluntary movement of persons between Territories	—	Inter-Territorial Movement of Persons (Control) Act 36/54, 54/59, 7/61, 42/61, 2/63	—	Ministry of Justice
48.	Control of movement of goods and animals between Territories	Animal Health Act 5/60	—	Ministry of Commerce and Industry; Ministry of Agriculture (certain functions)	—
49.	Development of Industries	Cotton Industry Agreement Act 2/60	Industrial Development Act 55/59	Ministry of Commerce and Industry. Ministry of Agriculture	Ministry of the Treasury
50.	Land Banks, that is to say, government institutions or institutions set up by or under a law of the Federal Legislature or of the Legislature of a Territory, being institutions of which the main purpose is the granting of credits for housing or agricultural purposes	FGN 266/57	S.R. Land Bank Act 28/ 47/ 48/53, 53/57	Ministry of Finance	Ministry of Housing
51.	Co-operative societies and co-operative companies, being such societies and companies with objects connected with agriculture, except where a majority of members are African	FGN 61/64	S.R. Co-operative Companies Act (Cap. 172), 16/53, 62/54	Ministry of Agriculture	—

Item	Matter	Federal legislation	Territorial legislation	Federal administration	Territorial administration
52.	Bankruptcy and insolvency; assignments to and compositions with creditors	Insolvency (Income Tax) Act 17/58. Insolvency (SR) Amendment Act 34/59	*Pre-Federal* Insolvency Act (Cap. 53)	Ministry of Law	—
53.	Hire Purchase	Federal Hire Purchase Act 34/56, 14/59	—	Ministry of Finance	—
54.	Roads, other than those referred to in Item 19 in Part I of this schedule	—	S.R. Roads and Roads Traffic Act, 50/53, 37/54, 55/54, 18/55, 15/56, 25/56, 34/58, 7/59, 20/59, 47/59, 79/59, 13/60, 19/61, 65/61, 8/62, 24/62	—	Ministry of Roads
55.	Rail-road crossings	Rhodesia Railways Laws Amendment Act, 18/55	S.R. Rhodesia Railways Act 1949	Through Railways Higher Authority and Ministry of Transport	—
56.	Regulation of road traffic	—	S.R. Roads and Roads Traffic Act, 1953, see *supra*		Ministry of Roads
57.	Electricity	Electricity Act, 8/56, 45/59. Power Surcharge Development Fund Act 16/62	—	Ministry of Power	—
58.	Scientific and industrial research, including in relation to Northern Rhodesia and Nyasaland, agricultural, veterinary and tsetse research	Research Act 4/59, Tobacco Research Act 1/55, 17/56, 15/47	—	Ministry of Economic Affairs	—
59.	The service and execution in any Territory of the civil and criminal processes, judgements, decrees, orders and decisions of the courts of any other country and the attendance of persons from any Territory at the courts of any other country, whether that other country is within or outside the Federation	Federal Service of Process and Execution of Judgements Act 4/56	Maintenance Orders Act (Cap. 154). Maintenance Orders Miscellaneous Provisions Act 13 of 1959. Rules of the High Court under the High Court Practice and Procedure Act (repealed by High Court Act 1963, but Rules preserved). S.R. Magistrates Court Act. Reciprocal Enforcements	Ministry of Law	Ministry of Justice

TABLE I

787

60.	Prisons and other institutions for the treatment of, and methods of treating, offenders against any law, whether or not that law is within the legislative competence of the Federal Legislature or, as the case may be, of the Legislature of the Territory	Federal Prisons Act 9/55, 8/57, 42/59, 24/62	of Judgements Act (Cap. 22), 43/62, S.R. was here legislatively active	Ministry of Law	Ministry of Justice
61.	Care and protection of minors	FGN 36/55 (amending SR Legislation as to reformatories)	Children's Protection and Adoption Act 41/49, 46/54, 28/59, 49/50, 40/61, 43/62, 49/62	Ministry of Law (reformatories only)	—
62.	Fingerprints, identification and criminal records	—	Police Act (Cap. 113) 58/54/ 25/56, 8/58	—	Ministry of Justice (later Law and Order)
63.	Security information	—	Police Act (Cap. 113) 58/54, 25/56, 8/58	Federal Government had its own security arrangements under the Department of the Prime Minister	Ministry of Justice (later Law and Order) Information was passed on to Federal Government.
64.	Health (other than silicosis in Northern Rhodesia)	FGN 148/154. Public Health (SR) Amendment Act 18/57. FGN 157/54. Prisons Act 9/55/ FGN 153/54, FGN 156/54. Dangerous Drugs Act 28/55, 7/58. FGN 180/54, FGN 155/54, FGN 152/54. Human Tissue Act 47/62	*Pre-Federal* Public Health Act (Cap. 140). Public Health Amendment Act 1 of 1953. Leprosy Repression Act (Cap. 142). Mental Disorders Act (Cap. 141). Nursing Homes Registration Act (Cap. 144). Pharmacy Poisons and Dangerous Drugs Act 50/52. Quilika Act (Cap. 147). Sale of Food and Drugs Act (Cap. 145). *Post-Federal* Pneumoconiosis Act 39/60	Ministry of Health	Silicosis Control. Ministry of Mines only.

Item	Matter	Federal legislation	Territorial legislation	Federal administration	Territorial administration
65.	Promotion of tourist traffic	—	—	Federal Tourist Board under Ministry of Home Affairs	—
66.	Town planning	—	S.R. Town and Country Planning Act 19/45, 54/54/ 1/55, 17/57, 7/58, 54/59, 14/62	—	Ministry of Local Government
67.	Geological, trigonometrical, topographical, and cadastral surveys	Geological, Trigonometrical, and Topographical Survey Act 2/58	S.R. Lands Survey Act (Cap. 244), 35/57, 80/59, 40/62. Mines and Minerals Act 38/61	Trigometrical, Topographical, and Cadastral surveys administered by Department of Surveys under Ministry of Commerce and Industry	Ministry of Lands Geological Survey
68.	Production and distribution of Government films	—	—	Federal Central African Film Unit. Ministry of Home Affairs	Ministry of Native Affairs. (Film distribution services)
69.	Broadcasting, television and other like forms of communication	Broadcasting Act 31/57, 21/58, 28/60. Broadcasting (Transitional Provisions) Act 20/60	—	Ministry of Home Affairs	—
70.	Archives	National Archives Constitution Act 16/58. National Archives Act 4/58	—	Ministry of Home Affairs	—
71.	Census and statistics	Census and Statistics Act 10/55	—	Ministry of Economic Affairs	—
72.	Indemnity in respect of acts or omissions, so, however, that the Federal Legislature shall not have power to make laws with respect to indemnity in respect of acts or omissions in breach of a law of the Legislature of a Territory which is within the exclusive legislative competence of the Legislature of that Territory	Numerous Acts of both Legislatures			
73.	Registration of births and deaths	The Births and Deaths Registration (S.R.) Act, 35/62	—	Ministry of Home Affairs	(Until 1963 registration of African births and deaths)

TABLE I   789

No.	Matter	Federal legislation	Federal Ministry	S.R. legislation	S.R. Ministry
74.	Registration and record of printed publications	(Registration and record of such publications)	Ministry of Law	Printed Publications Act (Cap. 55). Obscene Publications Act (Cap. 39)	Ministry of Justice
75.	Commissions of inquiry	Federal Commissions of Inquiry Act, 15/55, 31/60	Ministry of Law	Commissions of Inquiry Act 1941	Relevant Ministry
76.	Any other matter, whether or not otherwise within the legislative competence of the Federal Legislature or, as the case may be, of the Legislature of the Territory, with respect to which under or by virtue of any provision of this Constitution both the Federal Legislature and the Legislature of the Territory have for the time being power to make laws, or in relation to which reference is made in this Constitution to laws both of the Federal Legislature and of the Legislature of a Territory	Numerous provisions in aforementioned Acts	Relevant Ministry	Numerous provisions in S.R. legislation	Relevant Ministry

Notes:

1. Certain Territorial laws in the Federal Legislative sphere were left in force subject to adaptation by Federal Government Notices containing Orders issued under the Territorial Laws Amendment Act No. 6 of 1954 of the Federal Legislature, which delegated power to the Governor-General to issue Orders amending and adapting Territorial laws where they dealt with matters within the competence of the Federal Legislature, e.g. FGN 83/54.

2. The allocation of matters to various Ministries is in accordance with the position in 1960—Cmnd. 1149, pp. 12–14.

3. Amendments made to Southern Rhodesian legislation before the commencement of Federation have not been indicated as the purpose of the table is to indicate the degree of legislative activity after the commencement of Federation. Reference to Chapters is to the 1939 edition of the *Statute Law.*

4. Where Southern Rhodesia was legislatively active in the concurrent sphere it was usually because such matters related either to matters left exclusively to Southern Rhodesian administration or to African Affairs.

5. Laws providing for matters as a result of proposed dissolution of the Federation do not feature in the table.

Conclusions:

(a) By 1963 Southern Rhodesia was no longer administratively active in sixteen of the thirty-one matters enumerated in the Concurrent List and barely active in five others.

(b) In respect of the potentially exclusive Federal sphere (forty-four items), Southern Rhodesia had entirely abandoned both legislative and administrative functions to the Federal Government, except in respect of International Roads, the Ministry of Transport having delegated its duties of maintenance and construction to the Southern Rhodesian Ministry of Roads.

(c) Only in respect of five matters in the concurrent sphere was the Federal Government not administratively active.

(d) Only in respect of seven matters in the concurrent sphere had the Federal Legislature not been legislatively active.

TABLE J

African education in Southern Rhodesia

Year	1 Standard VI	2 S.R. Junior Certificate	3 External Junior Certificate	4 Primary Teachers' Lower	5 Other E.I.T.C.	6 Total with two years secondary (cols. 2 to 5)	7 Cumulative total with two years secondary	8 Cambridge School Certificate	9 Primary Teachers' Higher	10 Other E.I.C.	11 Total with four years secondary (cols. 8 to 10)	12 Cumulative total with four years secondary	13 Higher School Certificate
1928 to 1945	6,442	—	—	—	—	—	—	—	—	—	—	—	—
1946	1,292	—	—	—	—	—	—	—	—	—	—	—	—
1947	1,527	—	—	—	—	—	—	—	—	—	—	—	—
1948	1,511	—	—	—	—	—	—	—	—	—	—	—	—
1949	2,197	—	—	—	—	—	—	33	—	—	33	33	—
1950	1,896	—	—	—	—	—	—	47	—	—	47	80	—
1951	2,237	—	—	—	—	—	—	30	—	—	30	110	—
1952	2,354	—	—	—	—	—	—	25	—	—	25	135	—
1953	2,542	—	—	—	—	—	—	66	—	—	66	201	—
1954	3,372	—	—	—	—	—	—	58	—	—	58	259	—
1955	4,020	—	—	—	—	—	—	61	—	—	61	320	6
1956	4,860	—	—	517	274	791	791	61	107	—	168	488	4
1957	5,156	534	—	632	346	1,512	2,303	75	133	—	208	696	6
1958	6,343	533	—	860	310	1,703	4,006	92	211	—	303	999	4
1959	6,870	807	—	764	124	1,695	5,701	180	276	—	456	1,455	4
1960	9,083	883	—	732	187	1,802	7,503	260	209	80	549	2,004	9
1961	11,420	1,041	205	804	194	2,244	9,747	281	306	116	703	2,707	15
1962	11,460	1,373	502	803	105	2,783	12,530	252	308	227	787	3,494	14
1963	21,063(a)	1,677	384	999	78	3,138	15,668	360	349	243	952	4,446	16
1964	23,061(a)	2,095	1,090	689	19	3,893	19,561	535	491	229	1,255	5,701	16
	128,706	8,943	2,181	6,800	1,637	19,561	—	2,416	2,390	895	5,701	—	94

Notes:

1. *Sources:* Information obtained from the Central Statistical Office, the Annual Reports of the Secretary for African Education, and *S.R.L.A.D.*, Vol. 61, cols. 1206–14, 1501–6, 1776, and 1781–2.

2. The figures show the numbers of persons who passed examinations. These are relevant, and not enrolments, as the Educational Qualifications Board has ruled that for a period of education to have been 'completed' an applicant for the franchise must have acquired a certificate at the end of his course. Since 1963 a new system has been introduced in respect of Standard VI (see (a)) as all candidates have been awarded certificates in various divisions of pass.

3. With reference to column 1, it should be noted that in addition to those who have passed the Standard VI examination there must be added persons who have obtained certain Army Certificates of Education, the old Elementary Teachers' Certificate (up to 1938) or have passed certain South African Standard VI examinations. There are twenty-seven Africans with the requisite Army Certificate, 1,102 with the E.T.C., and 300 who have passed equivalent Standard VI examinations, i.e. a further 1,429 persons should be added.

4. Column 5 includes a number of vocational examinations which have been equated by the Educational Qualifications Board to two years' secondary education. These are the three-year Elementary Industrial Certificates for Building, Carpentry, and Needlework, and the Elementary Industrial Teacher's Certificate (Domestic Science). These were not recognized by the Federal Educational Qualifications Board as the equivalent of two years' secondary education, and therefore must be disregarded in estimating potential registrants for the Federal franchise.

5. Columns 6 and 7 do not reflect Africans who have obtained certain other qualifications equated by the Educational Qualifications Board to two years' secondary education. To the figures given must be added 810 who have passed the South African Universities' Junior Certificate, 253 who have passed the South African National Junior Certificate, 587 who obtained Goromonzi J.C. equivalence (up to 1956), 218 who have passed the Hygiene (Health) Demonstrators' (Domboshawa) Examination, 61 who passed the Native Department Interpreters' Examination, 1,317 who passed the Medical Orderlies' Examination, 753 who passed the General and Midwifery Courses for Assistant Nurses at Mission Schools, and approximately 100 (36 passed through Epworth College between 1954 and 1964) who have passed the Methodist Church's three-year course in Theology, viz. approximately 4,099 persons must be added.

6. Columns 6 and 7 do not reflect Africans who have obtained the qualifications dealt with in column 10, and will therefore have had four years' vocational education equated to four years' secondary education for franchise purposes. They do, however, include Africans who have gone on to complete the qualifications listed in columns 8 and 9, and in calculating the potential registrants, account must be taken of this, e.g. by the end of 1964 there were 4,806 with C.S.C. or P.T.H. and these must be deducted from those with two years' secondary education, assuming the others to have the 'A' Roll qualifications. Similarly in estimating potential registrants it should be realized that persons noted in columns 2–13 and in notes 3, 5, 7, 8, 9, are included in column 1 so they would have completed their primary education before their later qualifications.

7. Column 8 reflects those who have passed the Cambridge School Certificate. To these must be added 296 Africans who were candidates for the General Certificate of Education and have to merit credit the equivalent of School Certificate (*S.R.L.A.D.*, Vol. 61, col. 1211).

8. Column 10 reflects Africans who have passed the four-year Elementary Industrial Certificate in agriculture, building, and carpentry, and nurses who have passed the Nursing examination of the S.R. Medical Council (three-year post-J.C. course). It does not include 25 Nurses who passed other equivalent examinations.

9. Columns 11 and 12 do not reflect 50 Africans who have passed the Joint Matriculation Board Examination or 154 Africans who have passed the National Senior Certificate examination of the Republic of South Africa, both of these examinations being the equivalent of four years' secondary education. Neither of these examinations has been written in recent years. Nor does it reflect some of the 74 Africans who have between 1943 and 1964 passed the Chishawasha Course in Scholastic Philosophy which is treated as an equivalent of four years' secondary education. There is some double counting here as in recent years C.S.C. has been the entrance qualification for this course.

10. Column 13 does not reflect 18 African candidates for the G.C.E. who have to merit the equivalent of Higher School Certificate. Nor does it reflect 33 Africans who obtained 'A' levels in the A.E.B. Examinations, having attended the University College of Rhodesia and Nyasaland's Advanced Level Courses.

11. In calculating the number of potential voters from this table, it should be remembered that no account has been taken of deaths, nor of the fact that recent school leavers may be under the voting age of 21. It is assumed that all earn sufficient income to comply with the franchise requirements.

Wage distribution of African employees according to September 1961 census

Annual cash income			Federation	S. Rhodesia
£120–£179	19	0	123,447	65,067
£180–£239	19	0	50,751	20,939
£240–£299	19	0	19,210	11,582
£300–£359	19	0	6,037	3,430
£360–£479	19	0	3,468	1,703
£480–£599	19	0	1,066	398
£600–£719	19	0	402	208
£720–and over			603	403
		Total	204,984	103,730

Notes:

1. Source: information published by the Central African Statistical Office in April 1962.
2. There is a margin of error here as Section 12 of the Southern Rhodesian Electoral Act (Chapter 2), provides that in the computation of income the value of board and lodging can be included, and these may help to make applicants eligible for the vote.
3. There are probably a number of African professional and self-employed persons earning the requisite income who are not included in these figures but virtually all these persons would be qualified in terms of the educational qualifications and would be included in the figures which can be extracted from Table J.
4. These figures are confirmed by an answer by the Minister of Finance on 5 August 1964 (*S.R.L.A.D.*, Vol. 57, col. 304), that 255 Southern Rhodesian Africans, employed and self-employed, are taxable (Income Tax being effectively levied on a single man from £400 p.a.), and that 555 Africans had made returns, but had been assessed as not taxable.

TABLE L   793

TABLE L

'B' Roll voters registered in each constituency as at 30 April 1963 and 28 February 1965
(Source: *S.R.L.A.D.*, Vol. 53, cols. 25–26, 19 June 1963; Vol. 61, cols. 1497–1500, 28 July 1965.)

Arundel	12	13	Hillside	9	8
Avondale	13	14	Jameson	18	22
Bellevue	8	8	Lomagundi	338	350
Belvedere	13	12	Mabelreign	8	8
Borrowdale	26	27	Marandellas	356	362
Braeside	29	31	Marlborough	14	13
Bulawayo Central	45	45	Matobo	385	478
Bulawayo District	724	739	Mazoe	475	500
Bulawayo East	17	14	Milton Park	17	17
Bulawayo North	32	35	Mtoko	498	521
Bulawayo South	47	50	Queens Park	22	23
Central	458	503	Que Que	119	126
Charter	864	978	Raylton	44	46
Eastern	511	529	Rusape	603	609
Gatooma	255	268	Salisbury Central	23	24
Greendale	200	203	Salisbury City	41	44
Greenwood	10	10	Salisbury North	68	74
Gwebi	274	274	Shabani	463	463
Gwelo	24	22	Umtali East	13	17
Gwelo Rural	154	176	Umtali West	169	183
Hartley	335	339	Umzingwane	456	468
Hatfield	22	21	Victoria	883	899
Highlands North	10	12	Wankie	556	561
Highlands South	20	21	Waterfalls	59	62
Hillcrest	16	18	Willowvale	1,301	1,348
			Total	11,057	11,589(a)

Note: (a) Of the 'B' Roll voters 10,700 were African and 589 were European.

TABLE M

Projection showing possible output by the present Southern Rhodesian African education system of persons with four years' secondary education 1962–71

FORM	Cumulative total prior to 1962 (b)	1962 (a)	1963 (a)	1964 (a)	1965 (a)	1966	1967	1968	1969	1970	1971	Cumulative totals, four years' secondary education	Ministry estimates (l)	Minister's estimates (m)
Standard IV	—	29,388	35,827	40,979	45,137	(41,530)	—	—	—	—	—	—	—	—
Standard V	—	22,434	27,219	33,011	36,737	(34,170)	—	—	—	—	—	—	—	—
Standard VI	—	17,832	21,962	25,140	29,056	—	(38,622)	—	—	—	—	—	—	—
Form I	—	2,819	3,407	4,108	5,478	(13,080)	(15,380)	(17,380)	—	—	—	—	—	—
Form II	—	2,200	2,447	3,041	3,720	(5,478)	(13,080)	(15,380)	(17,380)	—	—	—	—	—
Form III	—	489	724	949	1,255	(1,560)	(2,300)	(5,490)	(6,460)	(7,300)	—	—	—	—
Form IV/V	949	352	386	655	876	(1,255)	(1,560)	(2,300)	(5,490)	(6,460)	(7,300)	27,583	25,149	22,700
E.I.C.	196	217	190	179	168	Course ceased						950	1,723	⎫
Nurses	25	10	53	50	[60](c)	[60](c)	[90](c)	[90](c)	[90](c)	[120](c)	[120](c)	768	778	⎬ {3,100}
London G.C.E., National Senior Certificate, Matriculation	—	—	—	500(d)	[90](e)	[100](e)	[110](e)	[120](e)	[130](e)	[300](e)	[800](e)	2,150	2,200	6,000 (by 1964)
Teacher Training (PTH final)	1,242	308	349	491	582	[1,000](f)	[1,200](f)	[1,400](f)	[1,600](f)	[1,800](f)	[2,000](f)	11,972	12,529	8,300
Total											10,220	43,423	42,379	40,100

Notes:

1. The cumulative totals prior to 1962 reflect those who passed the examinations concerned. See Table J, notes 7, 8, and 9, for a small further number who have other equivalents of four years' secondary education.

2. (a) represents actual enrolments: *Southern Rhodesia Monthly Digest of Statistics*, June 1965, p. 11, and *S.R.L.A.D.*, Vol. 61, cols. 1206–12. These figures do not reflect those who passed the examination.

3. (c) represents estimates of places available as estimated in figures obtained from the Southern Rhodesia High Commissioner in London in July 1964.

4. (d) is a cumulative total and is obtained from *S.R.L.A.D.*, Vol. 61, cols. 1206–12.

5. (e) represents estimates apparently given by the Ministry of African Education to the Southern Rhodesian High Commissioner. It will be noted that a considerable increase is estimated between 1969 and 1971 of approximately 515%. The assumption that this increase will occur is generous.

6. (f) represents estimates for teacher training from 1966 to 1971. These are based on figures estimated by the Ministry of Education in 1964, as reflecting teacher requirements for Upper Primary Schools. It should be noted that there is a considerable jump in the estimated places between 1965 and 1966. Subsequently it has been announced that there will be a 15 per cent drop in the number of places available in 1966: Ministry of Education Circular No. 34 of 1965, 6 September 1965.

7. The figures in rounded brackets are given as significant figures to the nearest ten and are derived from the following assumptions regarding pass, failure, drop-out, and continuation rates per centum:

	Pass rate, per cent	Failure rate, per cent	Drop out rate, per cent	Continuation rate, per cent
Standard IV to V	—	—	8 (g)	92 (g)
Standard V to VI	—	—	7 (g)	93 (g)
Standard VI to Form I	100 (h)	—	55 (i)	45
Form I to Form II	—	—	—	100
Form II to Form III	70 (j)	30 (j)	—	42
Form III to Form IV/V	—	—	40 (k)	100

Sources: Annual Reports of the Secretary for African Education 1961–64 and the *Monthly Digest of Statistics*, June 1965, p. 11.

(g) is based on experience in 1962, 1963, 1964, and 1965, and is obtained from the *Monthly Digest of Statistics*, June 1965, p. 11.

(h) Since 1963 all candidates for Standard VI have been awarded a school-leaving certificate in various divisions of pass but the Secretary for African Education reported that only those who obtained first or second grade passes were suitable for further secondary academic courses. In 1963 this represented 24·4 per cent of the candidates and in 1964, 25·9 per cent: C.S.R. 15–1964 and C.S.R. 20–1965. At para. 397 the Southern Rhodesian Education Commission reported that there were places for all Grade I's and 72 per cent of Grade II's in Form I: C.S.R. 32–1963.

(i) has arbitrarily been assumed on the basis of economic restraints which force young Africans to go into the labour market. In fact from 1962–3, 1963–4, and 1964–5, the drop out rates from Standard VI to Form I were 74, 75, and 70 per cent respectively.

(j) is derived from the Reports of the Secretary for African Education. In 1961, 1962, 1963, and 1964 it was 68, 69, 70, and 71 per cent respectively.

(k) assumes a considerable improvement in the drop out rate. From 1961–2, 1962–3, 1963–4, 1964–5 this was 66, 72, 60, and 58 per cent respectively.

8. (l) is obtained from estimates gives by the Ministry of African Education on a series of generous assumptions in 1964 to the High Commissioner in London.

9. (m) is obtained from estimates given by the Minister of African Education in a letter of 26 November 1964, published in the February 1965 issue of the *Central African Examiner.*

10. It is assumed that the present educational system remains unaltered except for the removal of one restraint which at present operates from Standard VI upwards, viz. the availability of school places and teachers. Economic restraints forcing young Africans to take employment are assumed to continue. It is also assumed that the present ratio of examination passes to failures will continue. These two assumptions counteract each other since even if there is improvement in economic conditions, more less-intelligent students will proceed through the school system. The assumption in respect of the present educational system is, however, subject to government policy which may result in lesser or greater numbers having secondary education made available to them.

TABLE N

Estimate of costs of expanding African secondary education and the number of secondary school places required to produce 68,000 with Form IV or P.T.H. passes by the end of 1974

	1963	1964	1965	1966	1967	1968	1969	1970	1971	1972	1973	1974
Enrolment in Form I	—	4,108	5,478	6,500	8,000	9,000	10,000	10,000	10,000	10,000	10,000	10,000
Enrolment in Form II	—	3,041	3,720	5,400	6,000	8,000	9,000	10,000	10,000	10,000	10,000	10,000
Enrolment in Form III and P.T.H.	—	1,574	1,983	3,500	5,000	6,000	8,000	9,000	10,000	10,000	10,000	10,000
Enrolment in Form IV and P.T.H.	—	1,170	1,447	1,900	3,500	5,000	6,000	8,000	9,000	10,000	10,000	10,000
Cumulative output	5,045 (a)	6,215	7,662	9,600	13,100	18,100	24,100	32,100	41,100	51,100	61,100	71,000
New places required per annum	—	—	2,735(b)	4,700	5,200	5,500	5,000	4,000	2,000	1,000	—	—
Extra recurrent cost of £94 per pupil (£'000s)	—	—	—	441	488	517	470	376	188	94	—	—
Total recurrent costs of secondary education and Teacher Training per annum (£'000s)	—	1,042	1,183	1,624	2,112	2,629	3,099	3,475	3,663	3,757	3,757	3,757
Total Recurrent costs of African education (all levels) (£'000s), assuming no expansion in primary education, all expansion occurring as indicated in this Table	—	6,185	6,450	6,891	7,379	7,896	8,366	8,742	8,930	9,024	9,024	9,024
% Budget increase per annum	—	—	4·2	6·8	7·0	6·9	6·0	4·4	2·1	1·0	—	—

Notes:

1. (a) was obtained from Table J and includes all Africans with four years' secondary education or its equivalent.
2. The figures for enrolment in 1964 and 1965 are taken from the Monthly Digest of Statistics, June 1965, and from the Reports of the Secretary for African Education.
3. (b) is the actual increase in places provided from 1964 to 1965.

4. The figures for recurrent expenditure are extracted from the Estimates of Expenditure for the year ending 30 June 1966 (C.S.R. 21–1965, p. 148). In deriving the recurrent cost per pupil of secondary education, viz. £94, the total secondary school and teacher training enrolment in 1965 was divided into the total recurrent cost even though the former relates to a calendar year and the latter to a financial year. No account has been taken of administrative costs, but this is offset by the fact that the cost of teacher training includes the cost of P.T.L. training (which is not equivalent to four years' secondary education).

5. Only in 1966 and 1967 has any allowance been made for failures. The Table is therefore optimistic as regards output, quite apart from the speculation that the requisite funds will be made available. The average failure rate between Forms II and III has been 30 per cent: see Table N, Note 7.

6. Figures of places required, except for 1964 and 1965, have been rounded off.

7. The total number of new places required would be *c.* 27,400 over nine years. No provision has been made for the capital cost of buildings to house these additional pupils. This might well involve the building of 55 new schools each with 500 pupils. In former years the Southern Rhodesia Government has been forced to halt its building programme owing to lack of funds (see C.S.R. 10–1962, p. 4. Report of the Director of Native Education for the year 1961). The position was bridged by the ' Butler loan ' but this loan money from the British Government has now been fully spent (C.S.R. 20–1965, p. 4). However the missions and parents of children have without any Government aid, built new schools. Thus in 1964, 8 new secondary schools were built in this way. The Estimates for the year ending 30 June 1966 provide for £270,000 for capital works for African Education. According to the National Development Plan 1965, Government Printer, Salisbury, 1965, at p. 29, the Government intends to spend a total of £940,000 for such purposes by the end of 1968.

8. The total additional recurrent cost from 1966 to 1974 is £16,906,000.

9. A forecast made by the Southern Rhodesia High Commissioner in *The Spectator* of 7 August 1964 that within ten years 68,000 Africans will have received the equivalent of four years' secondary education is thus possible, provided that funds for this purpose are made available. See also *S.R.L.A.D.*, Vol. 57, col. 862, 18 August 1964, Minister of Education, that the Government ' hope to provide the equivalent of 173 new (African) Secondary Schools in the next nine years '. These, however, will not all provide four years' of secondary education. Cp. *S.R.L.A.D.*, Vol. 57, col. 195, 30 July 1964, Minister of Finance: the annual growth in African education could not be sustained by the Exchequer. However in a letter to the *Central African Examiner* of February 1965, the Minister of Education has estimated that by 1972, 40,100 Africans will have four years' secondary education or its equivalent. Nonetheless it should be emphasised that in 1964 and 1965 the Prime Minister, Mr. Smith, refused offers of British funds for expanding African secondary education since in his view such funds were being given merely for the purpose of expediting African political advancement: *H.L. Deb.*, Vol. 270, col. 236, 15 November 1965, Lord Gardiner.

10. This table was prepared with the assistance of Mr. T. R. C. Curtin.

TABLE O

Potential number of Africans eligible for registration on the 'A' Roll as at 26 September 1961

(a) Income of £720 p.a. for two years—September 1961 Census of employees gives 403 Africans earning £60 or more per month. All assumed to be literate   403

(b) Income of £480 p.a. for two years plus primary education: limiting factor is income. September 1961 census gives about 1,150 employees earning either £40 per month or more in cash plus kind   1,150

(c) Income £300 p.a. for two years plus four years' secondary education of whom there are about 3,306 adults (Table J, end of 1961 figures, read with notes 7, 8, and 9). All such adults are assumed to possess the requisite income   3,306

(d) Chiefs and Headmen (Native Department Estimate)   587

	5,456
say	5,500

Notes:

1. Except for Chiefs and Headmen estimates are confined to African employees. There are however some African professional and self-employed persons other than purchase area farmers. Most of the former would be in categories (a) and (b) or (c). The latter would not meet the educational qualifications required in the lower bracket nor the financial qualifications for the higher brackets of the 'A' Roll but they would go onto the 'B' Roll.

2. In calculating (a) no account has been taken of ninety-four Africans who earn between £50 to £50 19s. 11d. as salary and who receive in addition housing and/or rations. Full allowance for housing and/or rations has however been made in calculating (b).

3. In calculating (c) no deduction has been made for numbers of these who appear in categories (a) and (b). It is unlikely that such relatively highly educated Africans would only be earning £300. Many of them would probably be in (a) or (b) above. There is therefore some double-counting.

4. In fact as at 31 May 1964, there were 209 Chiefs and 342 Headmen on the Roll, all automatically being enrolled by virtue of their office in terms of Section 8(1) of the Electoral Act. As at 28 July 1965, 217 persons were appointed Chiefs and 359 persons occupied the office of Headman: *S.R.L.A.D.*, Vol. 61, cols. 1217 and 1501.

5. The actual number of Africans registered on the 'A' Roll as at 31 May 1961, was 1,397.

6. Prepared from information made available by the Central Statistical Office, and from Table J.

TABLE P

Potential number of Africans eligible for Southern Rhodesian ' B' Roll as at 26 September 1961

(a) Income £240 per annum for six months: September 1961 Census gives 20,000–25,000 African employees earning £20 or more per month: assumed they could all complete application form	20,000–25,000
(b) Income £180 per annum for six months and over thirty years of age. September 1961 Census gives 50,000 to 55,000 employees earning £15 per month or more. Deducting numbers qualifying under (a) gives 30,000. Assumed one-third of these are under thirty(x) leaving balance of	20,000
(c) Income of £120 per annum for six months plus two years secondary education. Limiting factor is numbers (about 12,000) with two years' secondary education—deduct numbers qualifying for 'A' Roll with four years' secondary education—balance say	10,000
(d) Income £120 per annum for six months plus primary education and thirty years of age: Persons aged thirty or more with primary education estimated at roughly 11,000 to 12,000, but many of these would already be included under (c). Balance left arbitrarily assumed to be	5,000
(e) Kraalheads with twenty or more families who are able to complete the application form (twenty-four were registered as at 31 May 1964)	50
(f) Ministers of Religion (161 were registered as at 31 May 1964) (y)	200
Say total	55,000–60,250

Notes:

1. These figures have been prepared from information obtained from the Central Statistical Office.
2. Except for Kraalheads, estimates are confined to employees.
3. With reference to (x) the Central Statistical Office estimates that there were in May 1962, 1,042,500 Africans over the age of thirty, of whom 505,200 were male (those likely to have education or income) and 462,000 Africans between the ages of twenty-one and thirty (of whom 298,700 were male), i.e. 30 per cent of adult Africans were under thirty years of age while 37 per cent of male African adults were under thirty. It is the younger better educated Africans who earn higher incomes so that the assumption (x) that two-thirds of the Africans who earn the requisite income of £180 p.a. are over thirty is generous.
4. With reference to (y) it should be noted that most of these would have the equivalent of two years' secondary education and would be included in (c) above, or would have the equivalent of four years' secondary education if educated at Chishawasha and would therefore be included in the 'A' Roll estimate.

APPENDIX

TABLE Q

Number of Africans in the Native Purchase Area owning farms as at 31 July 1964

	Number of owners	Held for more than three years	More than 10% of purchase price paid
Purchase price between £250 and £349	31	20	12
£350 and £449	14	1	Nil
£450 and £499	1	Nil	Nil
£500 and £999	3	Nil	Nil

Notes:

1. In addition there are 6,852 farms in the Native Purchase Area owned by Africans, the original purchase price of which was less than £250.
2. These values do not include permanent improvements effected by owners since purchase.
3. 'Owner' includes those holding leases with an option to purchase.
4. Source: *S.R.L.A.D.*, Vol. 57, cols. 302–3, 5 August 1964.
5. The total number of farms allocated was 7,008 as at 31 December 1963, of which a considerable number are on leases: Report of the Secretary for Land and Natural Resources. C.S.R. 12–1964, p. 6.

TABLE R

Number of Africans who have entered into contracts for the purchase in Government townships of immovable property as at 31 July 1964

Value	Total	Acquired more than three years	Paid 10% or more of purchase price
£250–349	3,159	2,400 approx.	2,400 approx.
£350–449	1,021	950 approx.	930 approx.
£450–499	36	—	2 approx.
£500–999	8	—	—
£1,000–1499	2	1 approx.	1 approx.
£1,500–and above	5	—	—
	4,231	3,351 approx.	3,333 approx.

Notes:

1. In respect of the first two categories of property only approximate figures can be given in the third and fourth columns as the records which are maintained do not readily show the information and it has not been possible in the time available to examine each account in order to provide completely accurate figures.
2. Negligible quantities of land are available for purchase other than in such townships and Native Purchase Areas (reflected in Table Q).
3. Source: *S.R.L.A.D.*, Vol. 57, cols. 303–4, 5 August 1964.

APPENDIX S

The invalidity of a legislative scheme to secure independence without United Kingdom co-operation

A complicated and ingenious legal scheme to secure Southern Rhodesia independence in the sense of freedom from any legislative, executive or judicial control by the United Kingdom [1] has been proposed by the Faculty of Law of the University of South Africa.[2] If this scheme is adopted it may well set the Southern Rhodesian Government on a collision course with the Courts and end in invalidation of the proposed legislation as in the first two 'Coloured Vote' cases in South Africa. Even so the case put forward by the Faculty is arguable and all their suggestions cannot be dismissed out of hand. They are clearly based on certain *dicta* in *British Coal Corporation* v. *The King*,[3] *Harris* v. *Minister of the Interior*,[4] views put forward by J. G. Latham in 1928,[5] arguments in *Commonwealth* v. *Limerick Steamship Co. Ltd.*,[6] and the fact that Southern Rhodesia may legislate extraterritorially. The proposals themselves are adaptations of two South African statutes.[7]

It must be assumed that the Faculty is referring only to amendments which would be effective in Southern Rhodesian Law but not according to English Law as not even a Dominion Act can amend United Kingdom Acts as part of the law of the United Kingdom.[8]

The scheme proposed by the Faculty involves a series of constitutional amendments. They suggest that the Legislature of Southern Rhodesia should pass by a two-thirds majority a Constitution Amendment Bill amending Section 20(2) (conferring extra-territorial legislative power) by adding the words 'and of laws repealing or amending laws of the United Kingdom in so far as such laws are applicable to Southern Rhodesia'. At the same time additional sections should be added providing that the Statute of Westminster is applicable to Southern Rhodesia as if 'Southern Rhodesia' were included in the term 'dominion' in Section 1. The amending Bill should state too that no Act of the United Kingdom Parliament passed after a

---

[1] The scheme does not purport to secure Commonwealth membership.

[2] *Faculty of Law of the University of South Africa. Southern Rhodesia: Declaration of Independence. Brief Survey of the Legal Aspects.* Mimeographed (undated). A short release appeared in the *Rhodesia Herald*, 3 November 1964. The full text merely outlines the steps in the scheme without indicating any authorities on which the views of the Faculty were based.

[3] [1935] A.C. 500 at 516 explaining the ratio of *Nadan* v. *The King*, [1926] A.C. 482.

[4] 1952 (2) S.A. 428 (A.D.) at 465.

[5] *Australia and the British Commonwealth*, MacMillan, 1928, pp. 89–90. The author subsequently became Chief Justice of Australia. At the time of writing, he was the Attorney-General of the Commonwealth.

[6] (1924), 35 C.L.R. 69 at 95.

[7] The Status Act No. 69 of 1934 and the Royal Executive Functions and Seals Act No. 70 of 1934 (both repealed by the Republic of South Africa Constitution Act No. 32 of 1961).

[8] W. I. Jennings, *Constitutional Law of the Commonwealth*, Vol. I, 'The Monarchies', Oxford, 1957, pp. 134 and 147, and see Wheare, *The Statute of Westminster and Dominion Status*, 5th edition, Oxford, 1953, p. 167.

specified date 'shall extend or be deemed to extend to Southern Rhodesia as part of the Law of Southern Rhodesia unless extended thereto by an Act of the Legislature of Southern Rhodesia'. It should also amend Sections 47 and 48 of the Constitution to provide that the Governor shall act on the advice of Her Majesty's Southern Rhodesian Ministers. Furthermore a Royal Great Seal and Signet should be instituted and a Constitutional Bill passed which provides:

(i) that Her Majesty's executive acts pertaining to Southern Rhodesia shall be sealed with the Royal Great Seal and Signet for Southern Rhodesia, and shall be in the custody of its Prime Minister;
(ii) that Her Majesty's will and pleasure shall be expressed in writing and countersigned by a Minister of Southern Rhodesia;
(iii) that Southern Rhodesia Ministers shall have direct access to Her Majesty;
(iv) that such Ministers advise Her Majesty and Her Majesty acting by Order in Council in all matters pertaining to Southern Rhodesia;
(v) that, whenever for any reason Her Majesty's signature cannot be obtained or the delay in obtaining such signature would, in the opinion of the Governor, either frustrate the object thereof, or unduly retard the despatch of public business the Governor shall execute the relative instrument himself, subject to such instructions as he may receive from Her Majesty acting on the advice of Her Southern Rhodesia Ministers.

The Faculty also suggests that Section 71 of the Constitution may be amended by a mere two-thirds majority so as to exclude appeals to the Judicial Committee by the addition of a proviso to sub-Section (5) viz:

Provided further that questions relating to the constitutionality or validity of legislation duly passed by the Assembly and assented to by the Governor shall not fall under the classes of cases in respect of which an appeal lies to Her Majesty in Council.

They then submit that 'the Governor will have to assent to the various legislative measures set out' and that it is only 'in theory' that either he may refuse or the Queen may give instructions not to assent. They maintain that this 'would not be in accordance with the constitutional usage and draw Her Majesty into a political controversy'.

Finally when these measures have been approved the Southern Rhodesia Government would advise Her Majesty to exercise her powers under Section 111 to amend Sections 1, 2, 3, 5, 6, 29, 32, 42, and 49 as desired.[1]

It is submitted that the Governor should at the very outset refuse to assent to these measures as it is his duty as guardian of the Constitution to assert the principles of the Constitution, and to refuse assent to a measure which effects 'a coup d'état under the forms of law'.[2]

Even assuming that the Governor assented to the measures it is submitted that they would be invalidated by the Courts.

[1] The Faculty has not taken the point that Section 111 itself may not be amended by the Crown by Order in Council but only by the United Kingdom Parliament: see the proviso to Section 111.
[2] Evatt, *The King and His Dominion Governors*, p. 200, accepted by Forsey, op. cit. at p. 104. See *supra*, Part II, Chapter 7. Keith *The Constitutional Law of the British Dominions*, MacMillan, 1933, p. 160 commenting on a somewhat similar Irish situation, considered that assent might properly be withheld.

Before detailed analysis of the scheme the general principle that a Legislature cannot do indirectly what it cannot do directly must be reiterated. If 'legislation, though framed so as not to offend directly against a constitutional limitation of the powers of the legislature, may indirectly achieve the same result . . . in such circumstances the legislation would be *ultra vires*'.[1] In such a case the character of the legislative scheme must be tested by its 'pith and substance'.[2]

Furthermore it must be remembered that 'No legislative organ can perform an act of legislation and lift itself above its own powers by the bootstraps of method' and that no parliament can 'expand its mandate by deleting the inhibition of its powers . . ... One must keep in mind that this inhibition is in restraint of power and not a regulation of method.'[3]

The Faculty have probably based their view that it is competent for the Southern Rhodesian Legislature to amend the Constitution so as to provide for amendments and repeal of Imperial Acts by Southern Rhodesian legislation on an argument set out by J. G. Latham.[4] The argument is that amendments to a Constitution are in a different position from laws passed under the Constitution, the former becoming part of an Imperial Statute, powers of amendment of which have expressly been given. Any amendment therefore becomes part of an Imperial statute and is not itself in the position of a law made by the Legislature under the powers conferred by the Constitution. If repugnant to an earlier Imperial statute, being a later statute it prevails and is not struck down by the Colonial Laws Validity Act.[5] Furthermore it was even decided, before the passage of the Statute of Westminster, that in the case of conflict between legislation, passed under the Constitution of the Commonwealth of Australia, and Orders in Council issued under an Imperial Act expressly applying to Australia, the former must prevail as being a later Imperial enactment.[6]

It was also argued that if the Constitution created a new source of power it was unaffected by the Colonial Laws Validity Act and it would give plenary power to the local Parliament to repeal Imperial legislation extending to that colony upon the subject matter within the ambit of those provisions.[7] However the High Court of Australia rejected the implication of this argument that the Constitution operated as a *pro tanto* repeal of the Colonial Laws Validity Act. As Knox C.J. said:

if this contention were correct . . . the Colonial Laws Validity Act would have no application to laws enacted by the legislature of a colony in which a constitution in the usual form —i.e. giving power to make laws for the peace, order and good government of the colony—

[1] *Pillai* v. *Mudanayake*, [1953] A.C. 514 at 528. See also the dissenting judgement of Schreiner J.A. in *Collins* v. *Minister of the Interior*, 1957 (1) S.A. 552 (A.D.) at 575 et seq., *Minister of Justice, Law and Order, and Attorney-General* v. *Musururwa and Nkomo*, 1964 (3) S.A. 209 (S.R.A.D.) per Beadle C.J. at 215.

[2] *Minister of Justice etc.* v. *Musururwa and Nkomo, supra*, at 217.

[3] *Minister of the Interior* v. *Harris*, 1952 (4) S.A. 769 (A.D.) at 790 per van den Heever J.A.

[4] *Australia and the Commonwealth*, op. cit., pp. 89–90.

[5] See *The Commonwealth* v. *Kreglinger and Fernau Ltd. & Bardsley*, (1926), 37 C.L.R. 393 at 411 where Isaacs J. with reference to the Australian Constitution and the Judicial Committee Act held that if two Imperial enactments conflicted the later must prevail.

[6] *Commonwealth* v. *Limerick Steamship Co. Ltd.* (1924), 35 C.L.R. 69.

[7] See Keith, *Responsible Government*, 1st edition, pp. 412–23, 1190–94. Lefroy, *Canada's Federal System*, pp. 57–58.

had been conferred by an Act of the Imperial Parliament passed after 1865 . . . . In my opinion the Colonial Laws Validity Act applies to laws passed under a power given by an Imperial Act passed after that Act, as much as to laws passed under a power given by an Imperial Act passed before it.[1]

Isaacs J. also held that where there is repugnancy between an existing Imperial Act and an existing Colonial Act 'the constantly speaking Section 2 of the Colonial Laws Validity Act 1865 determines the matter'.[2] In each case it is a question of construction of the particular constitution and it may well 'be at the very threshold simply *ultra vires* of the local legislature from the standpoint of the constitution alone . . .'.[3] If such powers are permissible on the wording of the constitution:

It is not sufficient in order to avoid repugnancy to say in every case that the constitution taken by itself would authorise the local Act. There may, at the time the local Act is passed, be in existence another Imperial Act dealing with the subject matter and so applying to the Dominion that the power contained in the Constitution must be read as subject to the provisions of the Imperial Act. If that is the case, a local statute which looks only to the affirmative power appearing in the Constitution and disregards the other Imperial Act by transgressing its limitations would be repugnant to the last mentioned Act and so fall within the operation of Section 2 of the Colonial Laws Validity Act. In that case the other Imperial Act would, on the assumption made, if anterior, be still in force and if posterior, be overriding in relation to the Constitution.[4]

However if the constitution explicitly gives powers, which are repugnant to certain statutes, as a later Imperial statute it would override them. There is nonetheless confusion in Australia, as a result of conflicting decisions, whether powers conferred on the Commonwealth Parliament by the Constitution are limited by prior provisions of other Imperial Acts.[5] If the view that the later constitution overrides is accepted, it can be seen how the Faculty arrived at their view: they must have felt that the combined operation of legislative power (Section 20(1)), extra-territorial legislative power (Section 20(2)) and power to amend, add to or repeal any of the provisions of the Constitution (Section 105—subject to specified exceptions) allows provision to be made overriding Imperial Acts applying to Southern Rhodesia. Reliance has also probably been placed on the *dicta* in *Harris* v. *Minister of the Interior*[6] that the Colonial Laws Validity Act is inapplicable so far as power is given to amend the Constitution and that in the case of the South Africa Act (the Southern Rhodesian Constitution being assumed to be similar) 'unrestricted' powers of amendment were given provided that when dealing with certain matters the Legislature functioned in accordance with procedural requirements. They must also have considered that there is no statute law, other than the Colonial Laws

---

[1] *Union Steamship Co. of New Zealand* v. *The Commonwealth* (1925), 36 C.L.R. 130 at 140 per Knox C.J.; and also the views of Stark J. at 164.

[2] The wording of Section 2 is very clear: 'is or *shall be* in any respect repugnant'—see the remarks of Higgins J. at pp. 153–4 in the *Union Steamship Case*.

[3] *The Commonwealth* v. *Kreglinger and Fernau Ltd. and Bardsley* (1926), 37 C.L.R. 393 at 410 per Isaacs J.

[4] Ibid. at 410.

[5] W. A. Wynes, *Legislative, Executive and Judicial Powers in Australia.* The Law Book Company of Australia, 3rd edition, 1962, pp. 79–82.

[6] 1952 (2) S.A. 428 (A.D.) at 465 per Centlivres C.J.

Validity Act, applying to Southern Rhodesia which either expressly or by necessary intendment is repugnant to such a provision, while the Colonial Laws Validity Act itself as part of the Constitution could be amended by following the constitutional amendment procedure. Finally they may have relied on the statement that the Act is a Colonial Laws Validity Act, not a Colonial Laws Invalidity Act.[1]

It is however submitted that unless legislation analogous to Section 2(2) of the Statute of Westminster is passed applying to Southern Rhodesia, the Southern Rhodesian Legislature has no power to amend or repeal any Act of the Imperial Parliament[2]—and even thereafter would only have power in so far as any Act was part of Southern Rhodesian Law. It is submitted that there is nothing to indicate that power to override Imperial Acts has been given in any of the sections of the Southern Rhodesian Constitution or that power to amend the Colonial Laws Validity Act has been delegated[3] and that therefore the adding of such words would be repugnant to Section 2 of the Colonial Laws Validity Act. Since 'the obvious purpose and meaning of that statute was to preserve the right of the Imperial Legislature to legislate even for the Colony, although a local legislature had been given',[4] there would be repugnancy between the Act and such a proposed amendment, repugnancy arising not only where there is a 'direct collision'[5] but also where two sets of provisions aimed at one thing apply, and both set up a complete system assuming to 'cover the whole field . . .'.[6]

An even more powerful argument is that the Southern Rhodesian Constitution is only an annex to a United Kingdom statutory instrument and is not a United Kingdom Act so that any amendments to it would at most operate as part of a statutory instrument and could not therefore be inconsistent with any earlier or later United Kingdom Acts unless this had specifically been authorized by the enabling Act under which it was issued. There is no indication that in terms of the

---

[1] D. L. Keir and F. H. Lawson, *Cases in Constitutional Law*, 4th edition, Oxford, 1953, p. 79: it was 'an enabling Act, not a restrictive or disabling Act'.

[2] *Moore and Others* v. *Attorney General for the Irish Free State and Others*, [1935] A.C. 484 at 498: 'Before the passing of the Statute of Westminster it was not competent for the Irish Free State Parliament to pass an Act abrogating the treaty because the Colonial Laws Validity Act forbade a Dominion legislature to pass a law repugnant to an Imperial Act.' See also *dicta* by Isaacs J. in the *Union Steamship Case* at 150 that 'a colonial parliament cannot repeal Imperial legislation except where Imperial law so permits it'.

[3] Section 105 allows amendment of 'the provisions of this Constitution'. The Act is in a broad sense part of the Constitution, as it is of the Constitutions of all dependent territories (*McCawley* v. *The King* (1918), 26 C.L.R. 9 at 52 per Isaacs and Rich JJ.), but it is not part of the Southern Rhodesia Constitution 1961 as annexed to S.I. 1961 No. 2314. Sections 116 and 117 make it clear that where the phrase 'this Constitution' is employed reference is to the 1961 Constitution only. The grant of plenary legislative power in Section 20(1) will not validate constitutional amendments made otherwise than in terms of Section 105 since it is clear that a grant of legislative power does not comprise powers of constitutional amendment: *Chenard & Co.* v. *Joachim Arissol*, [1949] A.C. 127 per Lord Reid at 132.

[4] *R.* v. *Marais*, [1902] A.C. 51 at 54: 'This statute reconciles the two principles of giving local legislation, but, nevertheless, still leaving open to the Imperial Legislature by express legislative provision the power to do something in the Colony.'

[5] *Union Steamship Company of New Zealand Ltd.* v. *The Commonwealth*, *supra* at 156. It is submitted that there would be a 'direct collision' in this case.

[6] *Union Steamship Company Case* at pp. 147 et seq. per Isaacs J.

Southern Rhodesia (Constitution) Act 1961 this was permissible. This meets a possible argument that the Order in Council itself amended the Colonial Laws Validity Act.[1]

In any event it is submitted that the passage of such a Bill would be a clear case of a Legislature seeking to do what it had no power to do—attempting to increase the area of its power. No Legislature can increase its own status.

Even if such an amendment could be passed, Latham himself conceded that laws passed under it would still be subject to the Colonial Laws Validity Act while in addition the Imperial Parliament could get rid of such an amendment by legislation directed to that object.[2]

The second proposed amendment—that it should be provided that the Statute of Westminster should be applied to Southern Rhodesia as if 'Southern Rhodesia' were included in the term 'dominion'—is, it is submitted, also not competent. Although the Statute of Westminster is not expressed to apply to Southern Rhodesia it applies by necessary intendment to Southern Rhodesia so as to exclude it from its provisions.[3] Alternatively the Statute of Westminster and the Interpretation Act 1889 must be read together as applicable to Southern Rhodesia. Accordingly any Southern Rhodesian measure providing that Southern Rhodesia should be a 'dominion' would be repugnant to these measures and thus invalid. Finally the fundamental argument that a legislature may not enhance its own status and lift itself up by its own bootstraps would, it is submitted, invalidate such a proposed amendment.

Again the third amendment proposed—that no law 'shall extend or be deemed to extend to Southern Rhodesia as part of the law of Southern Rhodesia unless extended thereto by an Act of the Legislature of Southern Rhodesia'—is, it is submitted invalid on grounds of repugnancy to the Colonial Laws Validity Act which asserts the United Kingdom's power to legislate for Southern Rhodesia.[4] Indeed the similar provisions contained in Section 2 of the South African Status Act No. 69 of 1934 were held to be an amendment to the Statute of Westminster.[5] Probably the Faculty bases its views on Ndlwana v. Hofmeyr[6] where it was held that this provision deprived the United Kingdom Parliament of its power to legislate for South Africa. However this decision could not have been given before the passage of the Statute.[7] In any case, as

[1] In favour of such a construction it would presumably be argued that in interpreting the Constitution regard should be paid to the convention that the United Kingdom Parliament will not legislate within the Southern Rhodesian sphere of competence. However, British orientated courts are reluctant to call in aid conventions.

[2] Latham, op. cit., p. 89: 'If such an amendment conferred powers to make laws, laws made under it would be subject to the Colonial Laws Validity Act and might therefore be invalid for repugnancy to earlier and later Imperial statutes.'

[3] Contra, Wheare, The Statute of Westminster and Dominion Status, 5th edition, Oxford, 1953, p. 140. It is true there may be 'dominions' which are not dealt with in the Statute, but they then have their own Independence Acts.

[4] This purpose is inherent in the American Colonies Act 1766, 6 Geo. III, c. 12 and the Taxation of Colonies Act 1778, 18 Geo. III, c. 12. Both these Acts could be considered as statutory assertions of the right to legislate for colonies thus such an amending Bill might also be repugnant to these measures.

[5] Harris v. Minister of the Interior, supra at 467.

[6] 1937 A.D. 229.

[7] See R v. Ndobe, 1930 A.D. 484 at 492–3.

Centlivres C.J. held in *Harris* v. *Minister of the Interior* [1] 'the Status Act carried the matter no further' than the Statute of Westminster and if the Statute did not have the effect of repealing or modifying certain provisions (*sic* in this case authorizing certain legislation) then the Union Parliament could not by means of an Act do those things.

The fourth amendment—that the Governor shall act on the advice of Southern Rhodesian Ministers in respect of powers exercisable under Sections 47 and 48—must it is assumed be based on *dicta* in *British Coal Corporation* v. *The King*. It was there held in interpreting the ratio of *Nadan* v. *R.* that if plenary powers had been given to a Dominion it might even before the Statute have made legislative provision in respect of the prerogative in its application to that country, and that lack of extra-territorial legislative power and any contrary Imperial Statutes were the sole barriers to legislation affecting the prerogative. [2] Nonetheless the decision makes it clear that the colony which attempts to limit the prerogative must have 'been endowed with the requisite power by an Imperial Act likewise giving the power'. [3] The Faculty apparently must have based its opinion, that the Legislature has been endowed with such power, on the grant of plenary legislative power and of extra-territorial legislative power, on the absence of any express legislation with regard to the exercise of the prerogative, and on the assumption that powers to amend the Constitution granted under Section 105 cover the prerogative.

It is however submitted that although the Southern Rhodesian Legislature has been endowed with powers of constitutional amendment and with extra-territorial legislative power it has not been expressly endowed with power to affect the prerogative in relation to giving advice or taking executive action This appears from the Constitution as the sections dealing with the Queen's power to give Instructions, to issue Orders in Council, and the fact that She is vested with executive power are not alterable by the Legislature. [4] There is however one flaw in this argument in that Section 42 authorizes the Legislature to pass a law authorizing persons other than the Governor to exercise executive authority. However this does not affect Section 2 which commands that the Governor shall execute all things belonging to his office according to such Instructions as Her Majesty may from time to time see fit to give him, and that the Queen Herself is vested with executive authority. Indeed Section 42 merely provides that executive authority 'may' be exercised by persons authorized by law of the Legislative. Accordingly any provision making it mandatory would to this extent be *ultra vires*. Furthermore *dicta* in *In re the Initiative and Referendum Act* [5] are to the effect that the office of Governor and

---

[1] At p. 464.

[2] Cp. the dicta in *Nadan* v. *R.*, *supra* at 493 and at 495 relative to the abrogation of power vested in the Crown. However, it is arguable that the *Coal Corporation Case* merely meant in relation to Privy Council appeals that no question of the prerogative at Common Law was involved as this had been merged in Imperial legislation viz. the Judicial Committee Acts, and that the *dicta* in *Nadan's Case* still stand—see *Moore* v. *the Attorney-General for the Irish Free State, supra* at 499.

[3] [1935] A.C. at 519. See also *Attorney-General for Ontario* v. *Attorney-General for Canada*, [1947] A.C. 127 at 149, which indicates that the Statute of Westminster made a 'vital difference' and permitted legislation conflicting with the prerogative. The judgement also made the point that such legislation must be authorized.

[4] Sections 105 and 111 which relate to Sections 2, 111, and 42.   [5] [1919] A.C. 935.

'his position as directly representing the Sovereign in the Province, renders natural the exclusion of his office from the power conferred on the Provincial Legislature to amend the constitution . . .'. Indeed there is 'impropriety, in the absence of clear and unmistakable language of construing Section 92 (*sic* Sections 20(1) and 105) as permitting the abrogation of any power which the Crown possesses through a person who directly represents it'. The Court then held that in so far as an Act purported to alter the position of the Lieutenant Governor in relation to assent to Acts and to render him powerless from preventing a measure becoming law it was *ultra vires*.[1] It should however be noted that there has been a change in the Royal Instructions since November 1962, which may indicate that the grant of legislative power envisaged the passage of laws affecting the prerogative. Whereas the Royal Instructions under the 1923 Constitution required the Governor to reserve all Bills whereby the Royal Prerogative might be prejudiced, the 1962 Instructions, which revoked the earlier ones, made no such provision.

Similar arguments apply to the introduction of a Royal Great Seal and Signet for Southern Rhodesia. Furthermore the Royal Instructions to the Governor clearly provide that 'the Governor shall keep and use the public seal for sealing all things whatsoever that shall pass the said seal',[2] and in view of these Instructions the Governor could not assent to legislation repugnant to them.

Finally the proposal that Orders in Council shall be issued on the advice of Southern Rhodesian and not on that of United Kingdom Ministers would be ineffective on the ground that Orders in Council are issued by the Queen of Great Britain in Her Privy Council either under the English Common Law or in terms of English statutes and even a Dominion has no power to amend the law of the United Kingdom.[3] The Queen would accordingly still act on United Kingdom advice.

Assuming that these contentions are upheld and that the Courts held this to be a legislative scheme to achieve power which was not within the competence of the Legislature it would be a clear case for the Courts to refuse to sever any provisions and to refuse to uphold any found to be valid as 'the offending provisions are . . . so interwoven into the scheme that they are not severable'.[4]

On the other hand if the Courts were to uphold these provisions there would then have been a legal revolution and the Southern Rhodesia courts 'would have thrown off their allegiance to the United Kingdom Parliament'.[5]

The suggestion made by the Faculty that Section 71 of the Constitution may be amended by a mere two-thirds majority so as to exclude appeals as of right in respect of contraventions of the Declaration of Rights[6] to the Judicial Committee— is in any event incompetent as they have overlooked the fact that Section 71 is specially entrenched and its amendment requires in addition either reservation or

---

[1] At pp. 943–4.

[2] Southern Rhodesia Royal Instructions 1962, Clause 4.

[3] Jennings, op. cit., p. 147.

[4] *In re the Initiative and Referendum Act*, *supra* at 944. See also *Collins* v. *Minister of the Interior*, *supra* at 575 and the remarks of Beadle C.J. in *Minister of Justice, Law and Order* v. *Musururwa and Nkomo*, *supra* at 18.

[5] See H. W. R. Wade, *The Basis of Legal Sovereignty* (1955) C.J.L. at 191 and also at 188, et seq.

[6] Appeals as of right only lie in such circumstances.

approval by majorities in each of four separate racial referenda.[1] Even if amendment by either of these methods was procured this would only have the effect of abolishing appeals as of right in terms of Section 71(5) of the Constitution relative to alleged infringements of the Declaration of Rights. It would not on the basis of the arguments outlined above affect appeals granted by special leave in terms of the Judicial Committee Acts 1833 and 1844.[2]

Accordingly it is submitted that the proposals by the Faculty would not effectively abolish the remaining controls exercisable by the United Kingdom in respect of legislative, executive and judicial power in Southern Rhodesia nor would it result in Southern Rhodesia securing independence.[3]

---

[1] Third Schedule to the Constitution read with Section 107(1). Incidentally the Faculty also makes an error in assuming that the Constitutional Council could strike at any of this legislation if it were *ultra vires* (p. 3 of its proposals). The Council is only empowered to report adversely on measures which are in conflict with the Declaration of Rights: Section 84(2) read with Section 83 definition of 'adverse report'.

[2] *Nadan* v. *The King*, supra as interpreted in *British Coal Corporation* v. *The King*, supra.

[3] In fairness to the Faculty it must be said that it ends its proposals on a note of doubt suggesting that 'assuming (these amendments) are found to be in order' the Southern Rhodesian Government would be able to secure independence. I am indebted to Professor W. A. Joubert for an explanation of the general principles on which the Faculty's views were based and also for pointing to certain reservations which he had.

SELECT BIBLIOGRAPHY

1. OFFICIAL PUBLICATIONS AND COLLECTIONS OF MANUSCRIPTS AND DOCUMENTS IN PUBLIC ARCHIVES

(a) *Public Records Office, London*

MANUSCRIPTS
African, South: British South Africa Company. C.O. 417 series (1884–1912)
African, South: C.O. 806 series.

(b) *Foreign Office Library, London*

PUBLISHED MATERIAL
Foreign Office Confidential Print
Law Officers' Reports 1877–1901

(c) *National Archives, Southern Rhodesia*

MANUSCRIPTS
Coghlan Papers
Downie Papers
Jameson Papers
Leggate Papers
Milton Papers
Moffat Papers
Newton Papers
Rodwell Papers
Smit Papers

OFFICIAL CORRESPONDENCE
High Commissioner for South Africa to Administrator 1898–1923
Administrator to High Commissioner 1898–1923
Resident Commissioners Files 1898–1923
Executive Council Minutes
Cape Town Office Correspondence British South African Company
London Office Correspondence British South African Company
Native Affairs Department Files 1923–34

PUBLISHED MATERIAL
A Guide to the Public Records of Southern Rhodesia 1890–1923. Central African Archives 1956.
African, South. Confidential Print. *Further correspondence respecting the affairs of Bechuanaland and adjacent territories. 1886–1923.*

(d) *University College of Rhodesia and Nyasaland Library*
Foreign Office Confidential Print. *Further Correspondence re Affairs North of the Zambesi. 1891–1899.*

(e) *Official Publications*
    (i) *United Kingdom Government*
        House of Commons Debates 1888–

House of Lords Debates 1888–
Statutory Rules and Orders
Command Papers from 1890 to 1964 relevant to Southern Rhodesia
House of Commons Parliamentary Papers.

(ii) *Federal Government*

Federal Parliamentary Debates 1954–63
Federal Statutes 1954–63
Federal Subsidiary Legislation 1954–63
Federal Assembly Select Committee Reports 1954–63
Federal Command Papers 1954–63

(iii) *Southern Rhodesian Government*

PUBLISHED

Southern Rhodesian Command Papers 1923–
Southern Rhodesian Legislative Assembly Debates 1923–
Southern Rhodesian Legislative Assembly Votes and Proceedings 1923–
Southern Rhodesian Legislative Assembly Select Committee Reports 1923–
The Statute Law of Southern Rhodesia Annual Volumes 1923–
Revised Edition of the Statute Law of Southern Rhodesia 1939
Revised Edition of the Statute Law of Southern Rhodesia 1963
Southern Rhodesian Government Gazettes and Government Notices 1923–
Southern Rhodesian Information Department Press Statements 1963–
Central Statistical Office Publications
Constitutional Council Reports 1963–

UNPUBLISHED

Confidential Survey of Native Policy 1950

(iv) *British South Africa Company*

British South Africa Company Reports of the Directors, 1889–1923.
Statute Law of Southern Rhodesia from the Charter to December 1898 (ed.) M. O. Evans. Salisbury, 1899.
Statute Law of Southern Rhodesia from the Charter to 31 December 1910 (ed.) A. Speight. Salisbury, 1912.
Statute Law of Southern Rhodesia from 1 January 1911 to 31 December 1922 (ed.) A. Speight. Salisbury, 1923.
The Statute Law of Southern Rhodesia Annual Volumes 1899–1923.
Minutes of the Proceedings of the Legislative Council 1899–1923.
Debates in the Legislative Council 1899–1923. (Reprint from the Reports of the *Rhodesia Herald*).
Rhodesia High Commissioner's and Administrator's Proclamations, B.S.A. Company's and Government Notices 1891–1894. (Reprinted from the *Mashonaland Herald and Zambezi Times*.)

2. OTHER WORKS

(a) *Bibliographies*

Carnell, F., *The Politics of the New States*, Oxford, 1961.
Livingston, W. F. (ed.), *Federalism in the Commonwealth*, Cassell, 1963.

(b) *Newspapers and Periodicals*
The African Daily News
The Central African Examiner
The Chronicle
Federal Outlook
The Fortnightly Review
Keesing's Contemporary Archives
The Mashonaland Herald and Zambesi Times
The Rhodesia Herald
The Spectator
The Sunday Mail
The Times
Truth

(c) *Published Collections of Documents*
Headlam, C. K., *The Milner Papers 1897–1905*, Cassell, 1931, 1933, 2 vols.
Mansergh, N. (ed.), *Documents and Speeches on British Commonwealth Affairs 1931–1952*, Oxford, 2 vols., 1953.
Mansergh, N. (ed.), *Documents and Speeches on Commonwealth Affairs 1952–1962*, Oxford, 1963.
Williams, B., *The Selborne Memorandum*, Oxford, 1925.

(d) *Periodical Publications, Pamphlets, and Articles in Journals*
Adam, M. A., 'Trial by Jury in Southern Rhodesia', (1962), *R.N.L.J.*, Vol. 2, 38.
Annual Survey of South African Law, 1947–, published for the Faculty of Law, University of the Witwatersrand, by Juta and Co.
Armour, L. A. J., and Hasson, R. A., 'The Reservation of Separate Amenities: the Southern African Experience', (1963), *Public Law*, 275.
Baxter, G. H., and Hodgens, P. W., 'The Constitutional Status of the Federation of Rhodesia and Nyasaland', (1957), International Affairs, Vol. 33, 442.
Beinart, B., 'The Legal Relationship between the Government and its Employees', (1955), *Butterworth's South African Law Review*.
Beinart, B., (1952), *T.H.R.–H.R.*, Vol. 15.
Beloff, Max, 'The "Federal Solution" in its Application to Europe, Asia and Africa', *Political Studies*, June 1953, 114.
Carbutt, C. L., 'The Racial Problem in Southern Rhodesia', (1934), *N.A.D.A.* No. 12, p. 6.
Castles, A. C., 'Limitations on the Authority of the Australian States', (1962), *Public Law*, 175.
de Smith, S. A., 'Constitutional Monarchy in Buganda', (1955), *Political Quarterly*, Vol. XXVI, 4.
de Smith, S. A., 'Fundamental Rights in Commonwealth Constitutions', (1962), *Journal of the Parliaments of the Commonwealth*, Vol. XLIII, 10.
de Smith, S. A. 'Fundamental Rights in the New Commonwealth', (1961), 10 I.C.L.Q., 83, 215.
de Smith, S. A. 'Westminster's Export Models', (1961), *Journal of Commonwealth Political Studies*, Vol. 1, p. 1.
de Smith, S. A. 'The Independence of Ghana', (1957), 20 *M.L.R.*, 353.

Dvorin, E. P. 'Central Africa's First Federal Election. Background and Issues', (1954), *Western Political Quarterly*, Vol. 7.

Dworkin, G., 'Stare Decisis in the House of Lords', 24, (1962), *M.L.R.*, 163.

Fawcett, J. E. S. 'Treaty Relations of British Overseas Territories', (1949), *B.Y.I.L.*, 86.

Fieldhouse, D. K., 'Imperialism: An Historiographical Revision', *Economic History Review*, Vol. XIV.

Findlay, G., 'Application versus Trial', (1951), 68 *S.A.L.J.*, 20.

Fitzgerald, R., 'The Changing Commonwealth', (1957), *Current Legal Problems*, 229.

Fitzmaurice, Sir G., 'The Law and Practice of the International Court of Justice', (1953), XXX, *B.Y.I.L.*, 3.

Gallagher, J., and Robinson, R. E., 'The Imperialism of Free Trade', (1953), *Economic History Review*, Vol. VI, p. 1.

Gann, L. H., 'The Southern Rhodesian Land Apportionment Act 1930: An Essay in Trusteeship', National Archives. *Occasional Papers No. 1*, January 1963. Government Printer, Salisbury.

Ghai, Y. P., 'The Kenya Council of State and the African Affairs Board of the Central African Federation: An Experiment in the Protection of Minorities', (1963), *I.C.L.Q.*, Vol. 12, 1089.

Gray, Sir J., 'Early Treaties in Uganda', *Uganda Journal*, Vol. 12.

Grove, D. L., 'The Sentinels of Liberty: The Nigerian Judiciary and Fundamental Rights', (1963), *J.A.L.*, Vol. 7.

Gutteridge, W. F., 'The Debate on Central African Federation in Retrospect', *Parliamentary Affairs*, Vol. X, 210.

Hasson, R. A. and Armour, L. A. J., 'Comment', (1960), *Public Law*, 142.

Howman, R., 'Trial by Jury in Southern Rhodesia', (1949), *Rhodes-Livingstone Journal*, 41.

Huggins, G. M., 'Southern Rhodesia. Recent Progress and Development', Address 18 July 1934, Empire Parliamentary Association, London.

International Commission of Jurists, 'Southern Rhodesia: Human Rights and the Constitution', Bulletin No. 18, March 1964, 43.

Jearey, J. D., 'Trial by Jury and Trial with the Aid of Assessors in the Superior Courts of British African Territories', (1961), *J.A.L.*, Vol. 5, 36, 82.

Jennings, W. I., 'The Statute of Westminster and Appeals to the Privy Council', 52 *L.Q.R.*, 177.

Johnson, R. W. M., 'African Agricultural Development in Southern Rhodesia 1945–1960', Food Research Institute, Stanford, 1964.

Kahn, E., 'Crown Liability for Wrongful Act of Policemen', (1951), 68 *S.A.L.J.*

Kerr, A. J., 'The Reception and Codification of Systems of Law in Southern Africa', (1958), *J.A.L.*, Vol. 2, 82.

Kirkwood, K., 'The Proposed Federation of the Central African Territories', New Africa Pamphlet No. 21, S.A. Institute of Race Relations, Johannesburg, 1951.

Lauterpacht, E., 'The Contemporary Practice of the United Kingdom in the Field of International Law 1962, I and II', British Institute of Comparative and International Law.

Lauterpacht, Sir H., 'Allegiance, Diplomatic Protection and Criminal Jurisdiction over Aliens', (1947), *C.L.J.*, 330.

Leys, C., 'The Case Against Federation in Central Africa', (1960), *Public Law*, 18.

Lyall, Sir A. 'Imperial Frontiers and Protectorates', *Nineteenth Century*, Vol. XXX.

McNair, Sir A. D., 'Aspects of State Sovereignty', (1949), XXVI, *B.Y.I.L.*, 6.

Neethling, K., 'The Legal Position of the State in Relation to Payment of Interest a Temporae Morae', (1956), 73 *S.A.L.J.*, 409.

Normanbrook, Lord, 'Meetings of Commonwealth Prime Ministers', (1964), *Journal of the Parliaments of the Commonwealth*, Vol. XLV, 248.

O'Connell, D. P., 'Doctrine of Extra-Territorial Legislative Incompetence', (1959), 75 *L.Q.R.*, 318.

O'Connell, D. P., 'Independence and Succession to Treaties', (1962), *B.Y.I.L.*, Vol. 38.

O'Connell, D. P., 'State Succession and the Effect upon Treaties of Entry into a Composite Relationship', (1963), *B.Y.I.L.* Vol. 39.

Palley, C., 'Stare Decisis and the Federal Supreme Court', (1962), *R.N.L.J.*, Vol. 2, 126.

Phillips, O. Hood, 'Reports of Committees', (1947), 10 *M.L.R.*, 420.

Polack, K., 'The Defence of Act of State in Relation to Protectorates', (1963), 26 *M.L.R.*, 138.

Pont, D., 'Die Wetafskaffende Krag van die Gewoonte', (1937), 1 *T.H.R.–H.R.*, 49.

Rotberg, R. I., 'African Nationalism in East and Central Africa', (1960), *International Affairs*, 36, 464.

Rotberg, R. I., 'The Federation Movement in British East and Central Africa, 1889–1953', (1964), *Journal of Commonwealth Studies*, Vol. 2, 141.

Rutherford, G. W., 'Spheres of Influence: An Aspect of Semi-suzerainty', (1926), 20 *A.J.I.L.*

Salmond, Sir J., 'Citizenship and Allegiance', (1902), 18 *L.Q.R.*, 49.

Thomas, H. M., 'More Early Treaties in Uganda', (1949), *Uganda Journal*, Vol. 13.

University College of Rhodesia and Nyasaland, 'The Requirements and Supply of High Level Manpower in Southern Rhodesia 1961–1970', *Occasional Paper No. 3*, Department of Economics, Salisbury, 1964.

University of South Africa. 'Faculty of Law. Southern Rhodesia: Declaration of Independence: Brief Survey of the Legal Aspects', Mimeographed, 1964.

Verloren, Van Themaat J.P., (1953), 16 *T.H.R.–H.R.*, 69.

Made, E. C. S., 'Act of State in English Law', (1934), XV, *B.Y.I.L.*, 98.

Wade, H. W. R., 'The Basis of Legal Sovereignty', (1955), *C.L.J.*

Williams, Glanville, 'The Correlation of Allegiance and Protection', (1948), 10 *C.L.J.*, 54.

(e) *Biographies and Autobiographies*

Alport, Lord C. *Sudden Assignment*, Hodder and Stoughton, 1965.

Brett, M. V., *Journals and Letters of Reginald Viscount Esher 1870–1913*, Nicholson and Watson, 1934, 2 vols.

Cecil, Lady G., *Life of Robert, Marquis of Salisbury*, Vol. IV, Hodder and Stoughton, 1932.

Chandos, Viscount (O. Lyttleton), *The Memoirs of Lord Chandos*, Bodley Head, 1962.

Colquhoun, A. R., *From Dan to Beer Sheba*, Heinemann, 1908.

Colvin, I. D., *The Life of Jameson*, Arnold, 1922, 2 vols.

Dundas, C., *African Crossroads*, Macmillan, 1955.

Fitzmaurice, E. G. (Baron), *The Life of Granville*, Longmans, 3rd edition, 1905–6, 2 vols.

Flint, J., *Sir George Goldie and the Making of Nigeria*, Oxford, 1960.

Foot, H., *A Start in Freedom*, Hodder and Stoughton, 1964.

Gann, L. H., and Gelfand, M., *Huggins of Rhodesia*, Allen and Unwin, 1964.

Gardiner, A. G., *The Life of Sir William Harcourt*, Constable, 1923, 2 vols.

Garvin, J. L., *The Life of Joseph Chamberlain*, Vol. III, Macmillan, 1934.

Gross, F., *Rhodes of Africa*, Cassell, 1956.

Hensman, H., *Cecil Rhodes*, William Blackwood, 1901.

Imperialist, *Cecil Rhodes*, London, 1914.

James, J. R., *Rosebery*, Weidenfeld and Nicolson, 1963.

Johnson, F., *Great Days*, Bell, 1940.

Kennedy, A. L., *Salisbury, 1830–1903*, John Murray, 1953.

Le Sueur, G., *Rhodes*, London, 1914.

Lockhart, J. G., and Woodhouse, C. M., *Rhodes*, Hodder and Stoughton, 1963.

Long, B. K., *Drummond Chaplin*, Oxford, 1941.

Mackenzie, W. D., *John MacKenzie, South African Missionary and Statesman*, Hodder and Stoughton, 1902.

Metcalfe, G. E., *Maclean of the Gold Coast*, Oxford, 1962.

Michell, Sir Lewis, *Life of the Rt. Hon, C. J. Rhodes*, Edward Arnold, 1910, 2 vols.

Millin, S. G., *Rhodes*, Chatto and Windus, 1952.

Selous, F. C., *Sunshine and Storm in Rhodesia*, Ward, London, 1896.

Taylor, Don, *The Rhodesian*, Museum Press, 1955.

Wallis, J. P. R., *One Man's Hand: The Story of Sir Charles Coghlan and the Liberation of Southern Rhodesia*, Longmans, 1950.

Welensky, Sir R., *Welensky's 4,000 Days*, Collins, 1964.

Wolf, Lucien, *Life of Lord Ripon*, John Murray, 1921, 2 vols.

(f) *Historical Works*

Buell, R. L., *The Native Problem in Africa*, Macmillan, 1929, 2 vols.

Cambridge History of the British Empire, Vol. I, *The Old Empire*, Cambridge, 1959; Vol. II, *The New Empire*, Cambridge, 1940; Vol. III, *The Empire-Commonwealth*, Cambridge, 1959; Vol. VIII, *South Africa*, Cambridge, 1963, 2nd edition.

Dilke, C. W., *Problems of Greater Britain*, Macmillan, 1890.

Egerton, H. E., *A Short History of British Colonial Policy*, Methuen, 12th edition, 1950.

Fyfe, C., *A History of Sierra Leone*, Oxford, 1962.

Gann, L. H., *A History of Northern Rhodesia*, Chatto and Windus, 1964.

Gray, R., *Two Nations*, Oxford, 1960.

Grenville, J. A. S., *Lord Salisbury and Foreign Policy*, London, 1964.

Hanna, A. J., *The Beginnings of Nyasaland and North Eastern Rhodesia*, Oxford, 1956.

Hargreaves, J. D., *Prelude to the Partition of West Africa*, Macmillan, 1963.

Harris, J. H., *The Chartered Millions*, Swarthmore Press, 1920.

Henderson, W. O., *Studies in German Colonial History*, Cass, 1962.

Hobson, J. A., *Imperialism. A Study* (1902), Macmillan, 3rd edition, 1933.

Hobson, J. A., *The Evolution of Modern Capitalism*, Allen and Unwin, 1949.

Hole, H. M., *The Making of Rhodesia*, Macmillan, 1926.

Hole, H. M., *Old Rhodesian Days*, Macmillan, 1928.

Jollie, E. T., *The Real Rhodesia*, Hutchinson, 1924.

Kimble, D., *A Political History of Ghana*, Oxford, 1963.

Knorr, K. E., *British Colonial Theories 1570–1850*, Frank Cass, 1963.

Koebner, R., and Schmidt, H. D., *The Story and Significance of Imperialism*. Cambridge, 1964.

Langer, W. L., *The Diplomacy of Imperialism*, A. A. Knopf, 1956.

Lenin, V. I., *Imperialism: The Highest Stage of Capitalism*, Vanguard, 1926.

Low, D. A., and Pratt, R. C., *Buganda and British Overrule*, Oxford, 1960.

Lucas, C. P., *The Partition and Colonisation of Africa*, Oxford, 1922.

Lugard, F. D., *Rise of our East African Empire*, Blackwood, 1893.

Macdonald, J. F., *The War History of Southern Rhodesia*, Salisbury, Government Printer, 1947–50, 2 vols.

Mason, P., *The Birth of a Dilemma*, Oxford, 1958.

Moon, P. T., *Imperialism and World Politics*, Macmillan, 1928.

Oliver, R., *Sir Harry Johnston and the Scramble for Africa*, Chatto and Windus, 1957.

Pakenham, E. (Lady), *Jameson's Raid*, Weidenfeld and Nicolson, 1960.

Perham, M., *The Lugard Diaries*, Faber, 1959.

Perham, M., *Lugard: The Years of Adventure*, Collins, 1956.

Robinson, R. E., Gallagher, J., and Denny, A., *Africa and the Victorians*, Longmans.

Scott, Keltie J., *The Partition of Africa*, Stamford, 1895.

Seeley, J. R., *Expansion of England*, Macmillan, 1883.

Shaw, F., *A Tropical Dependency*, Nisbet, 1905.

Thompson, L. M., *The Unification of South Africa 1902–1910*, Oxford, 1960.

Thornton, A. P., *The Imperial Idea and its Enemies*, Macmillan, 1959.

Van der Poel, J. *The Jameson Raid*, Oxford, 1951.

Walker, E. A., *A History of South Africa*, Longmans, 1957, 3rd edition.

Warhurst, P. R., *Anglo-Portuguese Relations in South Central Africa 1890–1900*, Longmans, 1962.

(g) *Writing on Contemporary Events in Central Africa*

Brelsford, W. V. (ed.), *A Handbook of the Federation of Rhodesia and Nyasaland*, Cassell, 1960.

Carter, G. M., and Brown, W. O. (eds.), *Transition in Africa. Studies in Political Adaptation*, Boston, 1958.

Clegg, E. M., *Race and Politics. Partnership in the Federation of Rhodesia and Nyasaland*, Oxford, 1960.

Creighton, T. R. M., *The Anatomy of Partnership*, Faber, 1960.

Franck, T., *Race and Nationalism*, Fordham, 1960.

Franklin, H., *Unholy Wedlock*, Allen and Unwin, 1963.

Hazlewood, A., and Henderson, P. D., *Nyasaland: The Economics of Federation*, Blackwell, 1960.

Hirsch, M., *Focus on Southern Rhodesia*, Stuart Manning, Bulawayo, 1964.

Jones, G., *Britain and Nyasaland*, Allen and Unwin, 1964.

Mason, P., *Year of Decision: Rhodesia and Nyasaland in 1960*, Oxford, 1960.

Pratt, R. C., and Leys, C., *A New Deal in Central Africa*, Heinemann, 1960.

Sanger, C., *Central African Emergency*, Heinemann, 1960.

Yudelman, M., *Africans on the Land*, Oxford, 1964.

(h) *Constitutional, Government and Legal Texts*

Amery, L. S., *Thoughts on the Constitution*, Oxford, 1947.

Anderson, J. N. D. (ed.), *Changing Law in Developing Countries*, Allen and Unwin, 1963.

Anson, W. R., *Law and Custom of the Constitution*, Oxford, 1908 ed.; 4th edition (Keith), 1935.

Apthorp, R. (ed.), *From Tribal Rule to Modern Government*, Rhodes-Livingstone Institute, 1959.

Bamford, B. R., *The Law of Partnership and Voluntary Associations in South Africa*, Juta, 1958.

Birch, A. H., *Federalism, Finance and Social Legislation in Canada, Australia and the United States*, Oxford, 1955.

Broom, H., *Broom's Legal Maxims*, 9th edition, Sweet and Maxwell, 1924.

Cowen, D. V., *The Foundations of Freedom*, Oxford, 1961.

Craies, —., *On Statute Law*, 5th edition, Sweet and Maxwell, 1952.

Cross, R., *Precedent in English Law*, Oxford, 1961.

Davidson, J. W., *The Northern Rhodesian Legislative Council*, Faber, 1948.

de Smith, S. A., *Judicial Review of Administrative Action*, Stevens, 1959.

de Smith, S. A., *The New Commonwealth and its Constitutions*, Stevens, 1964.

Dicey, A. V., *Law of the Constitution*, 9th edition, Macmillan, 1939.

Engelhardt, E., *Les Protectorats anciens et modernes*, Paris, 1896.

Evatt, H. V., *The King and His Dominion Governors*, Oxford, 1936.

Fawcett, J. E. S., *The British Commonwealth and International Law*, Stevens, 1963.

Forsyth, W., *Cases and Opinions on Constitutional Law*, Stevens and Haynes, 1896.

Gane, P., *The Selective Vote, being the Commentary on the Pandects*, Butterworths, 1955.

Gardiner and Lansdown, *South African Criminal Law and Procedure*, 6th edition, Juta, 1957.

Gledhill, A., *Pakistan: The Development of its Laws and Constitution*, Stevens, 1957.

Glotz, G., *The Greek City and its Institutions*, Routledge and Kegan Paul, 1929.

Griffith, W. Brandford, *A Note on the History of the British Courts in the Gold Coast Colony with a Brief Account of Changes in the Constitutional History of the Colony*, Government Printer, Accra, 1936.

Guest, A. C. (ed.), *Oxford Essays in Jurisprudence*, Oxford, 1961.

Hahlo, H. R., *The South African Law of Husband and Wife*, 2nd edition, Juta, 1963.

Hahlo, H. R., and Kahn, E., *The Union of South Africa: Development of its Laws and Constitution*, Stevens, 1960.

Hailey, M. (Baron), *An African Survey*, Revsd. Ed., Oxford, 1957.

Hailey, M. (Baron), *Native Administration in the British African Territories*, London, 1953, 5 vols.

Halleck, *International Law*, 3rd edition, Kegan Paul, 1893.

Hall, W. E., *Treatise on the Foreign Powers and Jurisdiction of the British Crown*, Oxford, 1894.

Hall, W. E., *International Law*, 3rd edition, Oxford, 1889; 5th edition 1904.

Halsbury, *Laws of England*, 2nd edition, Vol. 6; 3rd edition, Vols. 5, 7, 33, and 36.

Hanbury, H., *Modern Equity*, 8th edition, Stevens, 1962.

Hancock, W. K., *Survey of British Commonwealth Affairs*, Oxford, 1937–42, 4 vols.

Hannay, D., *The Great Chartered Companies*, Williams and Norgate, 1926.

Harvey, H. J., *Consultation and Co-operation in the Commonwealth*, Oxford, 1952.

Herbstein, J., and van Winsen, L. de V., *Civil Procedure in the Superior Courts in South Africa*, Juta, 1954.

Hertslet, Sir E., *The Map of Africa by Treaty*, H.M.S.O., 1894, 2 vols.

Heuston, R. F. V., *Essays in Constitutional Law*, Stevens, 1961.

Hicks, U. K., *Development from Below: Local Government and Finance in Developing Countries in the Commonwealth*, Oxford, 1961.

Hicks, U. K. (ed.), *Federalism and Economic Growth in Undeveloped Countries*, Allen and Unwin, 1961.

Hodges, F. E., *Consular Jurisdiction in Her Majesty's Protectorate of the Niger Coast*, Stevens, 1895.

Holleman, J. H., *Shona Customary Law*, Oxford, 1952.

Howman, R., *African Local Government in British East and Central Africa*, University of Pretoria, 1963, Mimeographed.

Ilbert, C. P., *The Government of India*, 3rd edition, Oxford, 1915.

Jackson, R. H., *The Supreme Court in the American System of Government*, Harvard University Press, 1955.

Jenkyns, Sir H., *British Rule and Jurisdiction Beyond the Seas*, Oxford, 1902.

Jennings, R. Y., *The Acquisition of Territory in International Law*, Manchester University Press, 1963.

Jennings, W. I., *Cabinet Government*, Cambridge, 1947.

Jennings, W. I., *Constitutional Problems in Pakistan*, Cambridge, 1957.

Jennings, W. I., *The Law and The Constitution*, 5th edition, London.

Jennings, W. I., *Constitutional Laws of the Commonwealth*, Vol. I, 'The Monarchies', 3rd edition, Oxford, 1957; 2nd edition (with C. M. Young), 1952.

Keir, D. L., and Lawson, F. H., *Cases in Constitutional Law*, 4th edition, Oxford, 1953.

Keith, A. B., *The Belgian Congo and the Berlin Act*, Oxford, 1919.

Keith, A. B., *The Constitution, Administration and Laws of the Empire*, Collins, 1924.

Keith, A. B., *Imperial Unity and the Dominions*, Oxford, 1928.

Keith, A. B., *Responsible Government in the Dominions*, Oxford, 1928.

Keith, A. B., *The Sovereignty of the Dominions*, Macmillan, 1929.

Keith, A. B., *The Constitutional Law of the British Dominions*, Macmillan, 1933.

Keith, A. B., *The Governments of the British Empire*, Macmillan, 1935.

Keith, A. B., *Letters on Imperial Relations 1916–1935*, Oxford, 1935.

Keith, A. B., *The King and the Imperial Crown*, Longmans, 1936.

Keith, A. B., *The Dominions as Sovereign States*, Macmillan, 1938.

Keith, A. B., *The Constitution of England from Victoria to George VI*, Macmillan, 1940.

Lansdown, A. V., *Outlines of South African Criminal Law and Procedure*, Juta, 1960.

Latham, J. G., *Australia and the British Commonwealth*, Macmillan, 1928.

Latham, R. T. E., *The Law and the Commonwealth in Survey of British Commonwealth Affairs*, Vol. I, Oxford, 1937.

Leys, C., *European Politics in Southern Rhodesia*, Oxford, 1959.

Lindley, M. F., *The Acquisition and Government of Backward Territory in International Law*, Longmans, 1926.

Livingston, W. S., *Federalism and Constitutional Change*, Oxford, 1956.

Lugard, Sir F. D., *The Dual Mandate in British Tropical Africa*, 3rd edition, Blackwood, 1926.

Macmahon, A. W. (ed.), *Federalism: Mature and Emergent*, Doubleday, 1955.

Maine, H. S., *International Law*, London, 1888.

Mansergh, N., *Survey of British Commonwealth Affairs*, Oxford, 1952.

Marshall, G., *Parliamentary Sovereignty and the Commonwealth*, Oxford, 1957.

Maxwell, *On the Interpretation of Statutes*, 11th edition, Sweet and Maxwell, 1962.

May, Erskine, *Treatise on Law, Privileges, Proceedings and Usage of Parliament*, 16th edition, Butterworths, 1957.

Mitchell, J. D. B., *The Contracts of Public Authorities*, George Bell, 1954.

Mulford, D. C., *The Northern Rhodesian General Election 1962*, Oxford, 1964.

Newton, A. P., *Federal and Unified Constitutions*, Longmans, 1923.

Noel Baker, P. J., *The Present Juridical Status of the British Dominions in International Law*, Longmans, 1929.

O'Connell, D. P., *The Law of State Succession*, Cambridge, 1956.

Oppenheim, *International Law*, Ed. Lauterpacht, 7th edition, Vol. I, Longmans, 1948.

Parry, C., *Nationality and Citizenship Laws of the British Commonwealth and the Republic of Ireland*, Stevens, 1957, 1960, 2 vols.

Phear, H. H., *The Mineral Rights*, Salisbury, 1929.

Phillips, O. Hood, *Constitutional Law*, 3rd edition, Sweet and Maxwell, 1962, 2nd edition, 1957.

Piggott, F. T., *Exterritoriality*, Clowes, 1892; 2nd ed., Butterworths, 1907.

Ridges, *Constitutional Law*, Ed. A. B. Keith, 7th edition, Stevens, 1939.

Rolin, H., *Les Lois et l'administration de la Rhodesia*, Brussels, 1913.

Rose Innes, L. A., *Judicial Review of Administrative Tribunals in South Africa*, Juta, 1963.

Schwartz, B., *American Constitutional Law*, Cambridge, 1956.

Steyn, L. C., *Die Uitleg can Wette*, 2nd edition, Juta, 1952.

Tarring, C. J., *British Consular Jurisdiction in the East*, Stevens and Haynes, 1887.

Todd, Alpheus, *Parliamentary Government in the British Colonies*, 2nd edition, London, 1894.

Verloren van Themaat, J. P., *Staatsreg*, Butterworths, 1956.

Wade, E. C. S., and Phillips, G., *Constitutional Law*, 6th edition, Longmans, 1960.

Weis, P., *Nationality and Statelessness in International Law*, Stevens, 1956.

Weinberg, S., *An Outline of the Constitutional Law of the Federation of Rhodesia and Nyasaland*. For the Use of the Department of the Controller and Auditor-General, published for Private Circulation, Government Printer, Salisbury.

Wessels, J. W., *History of the Roman Dutch Law*, African Book Co., Grahamstown, 1908.

Wheare, K. C., *The Statute of Westminster and Dominion Status*, Oxford, 1938, 5th edition, 1953.

Wheare, K. C., *Federal Government*, 3rd edition, Oxford.

Wheare, K. C., *Constitutional Structure of the Commonwealth*, Oxford, 1960.

Wheare, K. C., *Modern Constitutions*, Oxford, H.U.L., 1962.

Wheaton, H., *International Law* (Ed. Keith), Stevens.

Wight, M., *British Colonial Constitutions, 1947*, Oxford, 1952.

Wight, M., *Development of the Legislative Council*, Faber, 1946.

Willson, F. M. G. (ed.), *Sourcebook of Parliamentary Elections in Southern Rhodesia*, U.C.R.N., Salisbury, 1963.

Wilson-Fox, F., *Memorandum on the Position, Policy and Prospects of the B.S.A. Co.*, B.S.A. Co., London, 1907.

Wilson-Fox, H., *Memorandum on Constitutional, Political, Financial and Other Questions concerning Rhodesia*, B.S.A. Co., London, 1912.

Wilson-Fox, H., *Notes Concerning the Cases Submitted to the Judicial Committee of the Privy Council with relation to the Unalienated Land of Southern Rhodesia*, B.S.A. Co., London, 1915.

Woolsey, T. D., *Introduction to the Study of International Law*, Sampson Low, 1888.

Wynes, W. A., *Legislative Executive and Judicial Power in Australia*, 3rd edition, Law Book Co. of Australasia, 1962.

(i) *Unpublished Material*

Fage, J. D., 'The Achievement of Self Government in Southern Rhodesia 1898–1923.' Unpublished Ph.D. Thesis, Cambridge, 1959. Copy in Southern Rhodesian Legislative Assembly Library.

Howman, R., 'Report on Native Courts for Southern Rhodesia.' Mimeographed, 1953. Copy in Southern Rhodesian Legislative Assembly Library.

Hyam, F., 'The Frontiers of Imperial Control in Self-governing Colonies and Liberal Experience in South Africa 1905–1908.' Institute of Commonwealth Studies Seminar Paper.

Passmore, G., 'Local Government Legislation in Southern Rhodesia.' Manuscript.

Ranger, T. O., 'The Organisation of the Rebellions of 1896 and 1897.' Paper read at the Central Africa Peoples Conference, Lusaka, 1963. Mimeographed.

Ranger, T. O., 'State and Church in Southern Rhodesia 1919–1939.' Historical Association of Southern Rhodesia Local Series No. 4. Mimeographed.

Wightwick, H. D., 'Alternative Proposals for the Franchise.' 1957. Mimeographed. Copy Southern Rhodesian Legislative Assembly Library.

3. PERSONAL COMMUNICATIONS

The Hon. Mr. Justice Davies

Lord Howick of Glendale G.C.M.G., K.C.V.O.

Major General Sir John Kennedy G.C.M.C., K.C.V.O., K.B.E., C.B., M.C.

Rt. Hon. Lord Malvern P.C., C.H.

The Hon. Mr. R. S. G. Todd

Rt. Hon. Sir Robert Tredgold P.C., K.C.M.G.

The Hon. Sir Edgar Whitehead K.C.M.G.

The Hon. Mr. W. A. E. Winterton

TABLE OF STATUTES

UNITED KINGDOM

ORDERS IN COUNCIL

CHARTERS

HIGH COMMISSIONER'S PROCLAMATIONS

LETTERS PATENT

BRITISH SOUTH AFRICA COMPANY ADMINISTRATOR'S REGULATIONS

BRITISH SOUTH AFRICA COMPANY AND LEGISLATIVE COUNCIL ORDINANCES

SOUTHERN RHODESIAN ACTS

FEDERAL ACTS

TABLE OF CASES

INDEX

56*